WEBSTER'S
NEW COMPACT DICTIONARY
and
ROGET'S THESAURUS

THOMAS NELSON PUBLISHERS
Nashville • Camden • Kansas City

Copyright © 1986 by Thomas Nelson, Publishers

Published in Nashville, Tennessee by Thomas Nelson, Publishers
and distributed in Canada by Lawson Falle, Ltd., Cambridge, On-
tario.

Library of Congress Cataloging-in-Publication Data

Webster's new compact dictionary.   And Roget's
    thesaurus.

    Includes index.
    1. English language—Dictionaries.   2. English
language—Synonyms and antonyms.   I. Roget's thesaurus.
1986.
PE1628.W55685   1986   423   86-5133
ISBN 0-8407-4924-4 (pbk.)

5 6 7 8 9 10 - 97 96 95 94 93 92 91 90 89 88

Table of Contents

Webster's New Compact Dictionary 1

Frequently Misspelled Words 257

Roget's Thesaurus 275

  How to Use Roget's Thesaurus 277

  Thesaurus 279

  Index 375

For Gift Giving 502

Weights and Measures 503

Metric Equivalents 504

States and Capitals 505

WEBSTER'S
NEW COMPACT DICTIONARY

A

A, a, *n.* 1. first letter of the English alphabet. 2. best grade.

a, *indef. art.* 1. one. 2. any single.

ab'a·cus, *n.* calculating device using sliding beads.

a·baft', *adj., adv., Nautical.* nearer the stern.

a·ban'don, *v.t.* 1. leave permanently. 2. give up. —*n.* 3. freedom from self-restraint. —**a·ban'don·ment,** *n.*

a·ban'doned, *adj.* 1. left or given up permanently. 2. without self-restraint; shameless.

a·base', *v.t.,* **abased, abasing.** degrade, humble. —**a·base'ment,** *n.*

a·bash', *v.t.* embarrass; shame. —**a·bashed',** *adj.* —**a·bash'ed·ly,** *adv.*

a·bate', *v.t., v.i.,* **abated, abating.** lessen, diminish. —**a·bate'ment,** *n.*

ab·at·toir (ab'ət twahr), *n.* slaughterhouse.

ab·bé (ab bā'), *n. French.* abbot; priest.

ab'bess, *n.* nun directing a convent.

ab'bey, *n., pl.* **ab'beys.** monastery or convent.

ab'bot, *n.* monk directing a monastery.

ab·bre'vi·ate'', *v.t.,* **-ated, -ating.** shorten to essentials. —**ab·bre'vi·a'tion,** *n.*

ab'di·cate'', *v.t.,* **-cated, -cating.** give up, as office or power. —**ab''di·ca'tion,** *n.*

ab'do·men, *n.* 1. part of the human body between the chest and hip. 2. part of an animal body in a similar location. —**ab·dom'in·al,** *adj.*

ab·duct', *v.t.* carry away, esp. by force. —**ab·duc'tion,** *n.* —**ab·duc'tor,** *n.*

a·beam', *adv., adj.,* across a ship or boat.

a·bed', *adv.* in bed.

ab''er·ra'tion, *n.* deviation from what is considered normal.

a·bet', *v.t.,* **abetted, abetting.** aid or encourage. —**a·bet'tor, a·bet'ter,** *n.*

a·bey'ance, *n.* suspension of activity.

ab·hor', *v.t.,* **abhorred, abhorring.** regard with horror or disgust. —**ab·hor'rence,** *n.* —**ab·hor'rent,** *adj.*

a·bide', *v.,* **abode** or **abided, abiding.** *v.i.* 1. remain. 2. dwell. —*v.t.* 3. wait for. 4. *Informal.* tolerate.

a·bid'ing, *adj.* enduring; steadfast.

a·bil'i·ty, *n., pl.* **-ties.** 1. power. 2. talent; aptitude.

ab'ject, *adj.* 1. downcast. 2. contemptible. —**ab·ject'ly,** *adv.*

ab·jec'tion, *n.* abject state.

ab·jure', *v.t.* **-jured, -juring.** renounce formally. —**ab''ju·ra'tion,** *n.*

ab'la·tive, *n.* grammatical case of origin, means, location, etc. —**ab'la·tive,** *adj.*

a·blaze', *adv., adj.* afire.

a'ble, *adj.,* **abler, ablest.** 1. with the power to do a certain thing. 2. competent. —**a'bly,** *adv.*

ab·lu'tion, *n.* washing; cleansing.

ab'ne·gate, *v.t.,* **-gated, -gating.** deny or renounce for oneself. —**ab''ne·ga'tion,** *n.*

ab·nor'mal, *adj.* not normal. —**ab''nor·mal'i·ty,** *n.*

a·board', *adv.* 1. onto a ship, train, etc. —*prep.* 2. on a ship, train, etc.; on board.

a·bode', *n.* 1. home; dwelling. 2. brief term of residence.

a·bol'ish, *v.t.* do away with. —**ab''o·li'tion,** *n.*

ab''o·li'tion·ist, *n.* favorer of the abolition of something.

A bomb, *n.* atomic bomb.

a·bom'in·a·ble, *adj.* disgusting; loathsome. —**a·bom'in·a·bly,** *adj.*

a·bom'in·ate'', *v.t.,* **-nated, -nating.** hate or loathe. —**a·bom''in·a'tion,** *n.*

ab''o·rig'i·nal, *adj.* 1. primitive; original. —*n.* 2. aborigine.

a''bo·rig'in·e, *n.* original inhabitant, esp. a savage.

a·bor'tion, *n.* 1. termination of pregnancy before full development of a fetus. 2. wretched piece of work. —**a·bor'tion·ist,** *n.*

a·bor'tive, *adj.* (of a hope or attempt) frustrated at an early stage.

a·bound', *v.i.* to have or offer something in abundance.

a·bout', *prep.* 1. concerning; regarding. 2. around. 3. near by. 4. on the point of. —*adv.* 5. nearly; approximately. 6. in all directions. 7. in the opposite direction.

a·bove', *prep.* 1. higher than. 2. greater than. —*adv., adj.* 3. to or in a higher place. 4. in a previous part of a text.

a·bove'board'', *adj., adv.* without deception or disguise.

a·brade', *v.t.,* **-braded, -brading.** scrape or rub. —**a·bra'sion,** *n.* —**a·bra'sive,** *adj., n.*

a·breast', *adv., adj.* 1. alongside. 2. side by side.

a·bridge', *v.t.,* **-bridged, -bridging.** shorten; abbreviate. —**a·bridg'ment,** *n.*

a·broad', *adv., adj.* 1. outside one's own country. 2. outdoors. 3. over a broad area.

ab'ro·gate'', *v.t.,* **-gated, -gating.** end or revoke, as a law. —**ab''ro·ga'tion,** *n.*

ab·rupt', *adj.* 1. sudden. 2. steep. —**ab·rupt'ly,** *adv.* —**ab·rupt'ness,** *n.*

ab'scess, *n.* area filled with pus.

abscond

ab·scond', *v.i.* leave secretly and hurriedly.

ab·sent, *adj.* (ab'sənt) not present. —*v.t.* (ab sent') remove. —**ab'sence**, *n.* —**ab'sent·ly**, *adv.*

ab"sen·tee', *n.* absent person. —**ab"sen·tee'ism**, *n.*

ab'sent-mind'ed, *adj.* 1. not paying attention. 2. forgetful.

ab'so·lute, *adj.* 1. perfect. 2. pure; unqualified. 3. unrestricted. —*n.* 4. that which is perfect, pure, or unmodified. —**ab"so·lute'ly**, *adv.*

ab·solve', *v.t.*, **-solved, -solving.** free from blame or guilt. —**ab"so·lu'tion**, *n.*

ab·sorb', *v.t.* 1. take in, as a fluid. 2. get the attention of; fascinate. —**ab·sorb'ent**, *adj.*, *n.* —**ab·sorp'tive**, *adj.* —**ab·sorp'tion**, *n.*

ab·stain', *v.i.* refrain. —**ab·sten'tion**, **ab'sti·nence**, *n.* —**ab'sti·nent**, *adj.*

ab·ste'mi·ous, *adj.* abstaining from excess.

ab·stract', *adj.* (ab'strakt) 1. reduced to essentials. 2. non-material; non-specific. —*n.* 3. summary; abridgment. —*v.t.* (ab strakt') 4. remove, esp. in a theft. 5. summarize; abridge. 6. cause attention to wander. —**ab·strac'tion**, *n.*

ab·struse', *adj.* hard to understand.

ab·surd', *adj.* nonsensical. —**ab·surd'ly**, *adv.* —**ab·surd'i·ty**, **ab·surd'ness**, *n.*

a·bun'dance, *n.* great supply. —**a·bun'dant**, *adj.* —**a·bun'dant·ly**, *adv.*

a·buse', *v.t.*, **-bused, -busing**, *n.* *v.t.* (ə byōoz') 1. use or treat wrongly. —*n.* (ə byōos') 2. wrong use or treatment. 3. insult. —**a·bus'ive**, *adj.*

a·but', *v.i.*, **-butted, -butting.** meet at an edge or end; border.

a·but'ment, *n.* construction touching or helping to support another construction.

a·bys'mal, *adj.* measureless in depth; bottomless.

a·byss', *n.* 1. great depth; chasm. 2. hell.

a·ca'cia, *n.* tropical plant with white or yellow flowers.

ac"a·dem'ic, *adj.* 1. pertaining to scholarship. 2. unconnected with actuality; theoretical.

a·cad'e·my, *n.* 1. school. 2. cultural organization. —**a·ca"de·mi'cian**, *n.*

ac·cede', *v.i.*, **-ceded, -ceding.** consent.

ac·cel'er·ate", *v.*, **-ated, -ating**. *v.t.*, *v.i.* increase in speed. —**ac·cel"er·a'tion**, *n.*

ac·cel'er·a"tor, *n.* vehicle speed control.

ac·cent, *n.* (ak'sent) 1. emphasis. 2. national or regional manner of pronouncing. —*v.t.* (ak sent') 3. emphasize; stress.

ac·cen'tu·ate", *v.t.*, **-ated, -ating.** emphasize; stress. —**ac·centu·a'tion**, *n.*

ac·cept', *v.t.* 1. receive or take willingly. 2. agree to. —**ac·cept'a·ble**, *adj.* —**ac·cept'a·bly**, *adv.* —**ac·cept"a·bil'i·ty**, *n.* —**ac·cept'ance**, *n.*

ac'cess, *n.* 1. means or way of approach. 2. right of approach. 3. outburst; attack.

ac·ces'si·ble, *adj.* readily approached or reached. —**ac·ces"si·bil'i·ty**, *n.*

ac·ces'sion, *n.* 1. increase or addition. 2. assumption of office or position.

ac·ces'so·ry, *n.*, *pl.* **-ries.** 1. additional working part, decorative object, etc. 2. companion in a crime.

ac'ci·dent, *n.* unexpected event, usually undesirable. —**ac"ci·den'tal**, *adj.* —**ac"ci·den'tal·ly**, *adv.*

ac·claim', *v.t.* 1. applaud; cheer. —*n.* 2. applause. —**ac"cla·ma'tion**, *n.*

ac'cli·mate", *v.t.*, **-ated, -ating.** accustom to a new environment. Also, **ac·clim'a·tize".**

ac·cliv'i·ty, *n.*, *pl.* **-ties.** upward slope.

ac·com'mo·date", *v.t.*, **-dated, -dating.** 1. provide with food, lodging, etc. 2. adjust to existing conditions. 3. help with a loan, favor, etc. —**ac·com'mo·da"tion**, *n.* —**ac·com'mo·dat"ing**, *adj.*

ac·com"mo·da'tions, *n.*, *pl.* lodgings, esp. temporary ones.

ac·com'pa·ni·ment, *n.* 1. something used with another thing; accessory. 2. music used to supplement that of a singer, soloist, etc.

ac·com'pa·nist, *n.* player of a musical accompaniment.

ac·com'pa·ny, *v.t.*, **-nied, -nying.** 1. travel with. 2. provide a musical accompaniment for.

ac·com'plice, *n.* associate in crime.

ac·com'plish, *v.t.* succeed in doing. —**ac·com'plish·ment**, *n.*

ac·com'plished, *adj.* 1. completed. 2. highly skilled.

ac·cord', *v.t.* 1. grant, as a favor. 2. cause to be in agreement or harmony. —*v.i.* 3. be in agreement or harmony. —*n.* 4. agreement; harmony. 5. consent. —**ac·cord'ance**, *n.* —**ac·cord'ant**, *adj.*

ac·cord'ing, *adj.*, *adv.* 1. in accordance. 2. according to, **a.** in accordance with. **b.** as stated by.

ac·cord'ing·ly, *adv.* 1. as is indicated or prescribed. 2. therefore.

ac·cor'di·on, *n.* reed instrument with keyboard and bellows. —**ac·cor'di·on·ist**, *n.*

ac·cost', *v.t.* approach and catch the attention of.

ac·count', *v.t.* 1. regard as. —*v.i.* 2. account for, **a.** explain or interpret. **b.** justify. **c.** be condemned or punished for. —*n.* 3. story; narrative. 4. explanation. 5. justification. 6. importance. 7. set of business transactions involving

one client or customer. **8.** business record.

ac·count'a·ble, *adj.* answerable; responsible.

ac·count'ing, *n.* keeping or interpretation of business accounts. —**ac·count'ant,** *n.* —**ac·count'an·cy,** *n.*

ac cou'ter·ment, *n.* piece of clothing or equipment carried on the person.

ac·cred'it, *v.t.* **1.** certify as competent or valid. **2.** attribute. —**ac·cred''it·a'tion,** *n.*

ac·cre'tion, *n.* growth, esp. by accumulation.

ac·crue', *v.i.* be added, esp. in a regular way. —**ac·cru'al,** *n.*

ac·cu'mu·late'', *v.,* **-lated, -lating.** *v.t., v.i.* gather; collect. —**ac·cu''mu·la'tion,** *n.* —**ac·cu·mu·la''tive,** *adj.* —**ac·cu'mu·la''tor,** *n.*

ac'cu·rate, *adj.* correct; truthful —**ac'cu·ra·cy, ac'cu·rate·ness,** *n.*

ac·curs'ed, *adj.* **1.** under a curse. **2.** damnable.

ac·cu'sa·tive, *n.* grammatical case for direct object of verb. —**ac·cu'sa·tive,** *adj.*

ac·cuse', *v.t.,* **-cused, -cusing.** denounce; blame. —**ac·cus'er,** *n.* —**ac''cu·sa'tion,** *n.*

ac·cus'tom, *v.t.* cause to become used to something.

ac·cus'tomed, *adj.* usual; customary.

ace, *n.* **1.** playing card with one pip. **2.** leading expert.

a·cer'bi·ty, *n.* harshness of temper or speech.

ac'e·tate'', *n.* fibre or fabric derived from cellulose.

a·cet'y·lene, *n.* highly inflammable gas.

ache, *v.i.,* **ached, aching,** *v.i.* **1.** suffer dull pain. —*n.* **2.** dull pain.

a·chieve', *v.t.,* **-chieved, -chieving.** succeed in reaching, finishing, or fulfilling. —**a·chieve'ment,** *n.*

ac'id, *n.* **1.** chemical compound reacting with base to form salt. **2.** sour substance. —*adj.* **4.** pertaining to acids. **5.** sour. —**a·cid'i·ty,** *n.*

a·cid'u·lous, *adj.* containing or suggesting acid.

ac·knowl'edge, *v.t.,* **-edged, -edging. 1.** admit as true or valid. **2.** show appreciation or gratitude for. —**ac·knowl'edg·ment,** *n.*

ac'me, *n.* summit.

ac'ne, *n.* skin complaint.

ac'o·lyte, *n.* priest's assistant; altar boy.

a'corn, *n.* nut of an oak tree.

a·cous'tic, *adj.* pertaining to transmission or reception of sound through air, etc. Also **a·cous'ti·cal.** —**a·cous'ti·cal·ly,** *adv.*

a·cous'tics, *n.* **1.** *sing.* science of transmission of sound through air, etc. **2.** *pl.* acoustic properties.

ac·quaint', *v.t.* **1.** make known. **2.** make familiar. —**ac·quain'tance,** *n.*

ac''qui·esce', *v.i.,* **-esced, -escing.** consent or comply. —**ac''qui·es'cence,** *n.* —**ac''qui·es'cent,** *adj.*

ac·quire', *v.t.,* **-quired, -quiring.** obtain; get.

ac''qui·si'tion, *n.* **1.** act or instance of acquiring. **2.** something acquired.

ac·quis'i·tive, *adj.* **1.** pertaining to acquisition. **2.** greedy, grasping.

ac·quit', *v.t.,* **-quitted, -quitting. 1.** release from blame or detention. **2.** conduct; behave. —**ac·quit'tal,** *n.*

a'cre, *n.* land area equal to 43,560 square feet or 4,047 square meters. —**a'cre·age,** *n.*

ac'rid, *adj.* harsh and bitter.

ac'ri·mo''ny, *n.* harshness of manner or expression. —**ac''ri·mo'ni·ous,** *adj.*

ac'ro·bat'', *n.* gymnastic entertainer, esp. one performing high above the ground. —**ac'ro·bat'ic,** *adj.*

ac''ro·nym, *n.* word formed from the initial letters of a phrase or title, as *NASA.*

a·cross', *prep.* **1.** from one side to the other of. **2.** on the other side. —*adv.* **3.** from one side to the other.

act, *n.* **1.** something done. **2.** law. **3.** one of the main divisions of a play, etc. —*v.i.* **4.** do something. **5.** conduct oneself. **6.** have an effect on something. **7.** perform in a play or plays.

act'ing, *n.* **1.** the profession of one who performs in plays. —*adj.* **2.** performing a specified function for the time being.

ac'tion, *n.* **1.** state of being active. **2.** something done. **3.** *Informal.* interesting activity. **4.** combat. **5.** lawsuit.

ac'ti·vate'', *v.t.,* **-vated, -vating.** cause to be active. —**ac''ti·va'tion,** *n.*

ac'tive, *adj.* **1.** performing actions. **2.** having an effect. **3.** *Grammar.* pertaining to verbs whose subjects act rather than being acted on. —**ac'tive·ly,** *adv.*

ac·tiv'i·ty, *n., pl.* **-ties.** action, esp. one of a number performed in a sequence.

ac'tor, *n.* man performing in plays. Also *fem.,* **ac'tress.**

ac'tu·al, *adj.* **1.** really existing. **2.** presently existing. —**ac''tu·al'i·ty,** *n.*

ac'tu·al·ly, *adv.* **1.** really. **2.** presently. **3.** in fact; nevertheless.

ac'tu·ar'y, *n., pl.* **-aries.** mathematician for an insurance company. —**ac''tu·ar'i·al,** *adj.*

ac'tu·ate', *v.t.,* **-ated, -ating.** cause to act.

a·cu'men, *n.* sharpness of mind.

a·cute', *adj.* **1.** sharp. **2.** mentally keen. **3.** highly sensitive or perceptive. **4.** severely threatening or distressing. —**a·cute'ly,** *adv.* —**a·cute'ness,** *n.*

ad'age, *n.* old saying.

a·da'gio (ə dah'jō), *adj., Music.* slow.

ad'a·mant, *adj.* unyielding.

a·dapt', *v.t.* change to suit conditions. —**a·dapt'a·ble**, *adj.* —**a''dap·ta'tion**, *n.*

add, *v.t.* 1. joint to another or others. 2. compute as a total. —*v.i.* 3. constitute an addition. —**ad·di'tion**, *n.* —**ad·di'tion·al**, *adj.* —**ad·di'tion·al·ly**, *adv.*

ad·dict', *v.t.* (ə dikt') 1. make dependent on a drug, etc. —*n.* (a' dikt) 2. addicted person. —**ad·dic'tion**, *n.*

ad'dle, *v.t.*, **-dled, -dling.** confuse; muddle.

ad·dress' (ə dres', or, for 2, ad'res), *n.* 1. speech; oration. 2. location of a business, residence, etc. 3. skill. —*v.t.* 4. speak to formally. 5. direct as a message. 6. apply. —**ad''dres·see'**, *n.*

ad·duce', *v.t.*, **-duced, -ducing.** offer as a reason, proof, or example.

ad'e·noid'', *n.* normal growth in the throat behind the nose.

a·dept', *adj.* (ə dept') 1. skilled. —*n.* (a' dept) 2. skilled person; expert.

ad'e·quate, *adj.* suitable or sufficient. —**ad'e·quate·ly**, *adv.* —**ad'e·qua·cy**, *n.*

ad·here', *v.i.*, **-hered, -hering.** 1. cling. 2. be loyal or obedient. —**ad·her'ent**, *adj.* —**ad·her'ence, ad·he'sion**, *n.* —**ad·he'sive**, *adj., n.*

ad'-hoc'' *adj.* for one special purpose.

a·dieu' (ə dyoE', a dyōō'), *interj., n., pl.* **-dieux.** *French.* goodbye.

ad'i·pose'', *adj.* fatty.

ad·ja'cent, *adj.* near or adjoining.

ad'jec·tive, *n.* word qualifying a noun. —**ad''jec·tiv'al**, *adj.*

ad·join', *v.t.* be next to.

ad·journ', *v.t.* 1. suspend operations of (a meeting, court, etc.). —*v.i.* 2. suspend operations. —**ad·journ'ment**, *n.*

ad·judge', *v.t.*, **-judged, -judging.** 1. decide or declare formally. 2. award by legal process.

ad·jud'i·cate'', *v.t.*, **-cated, -cating.** pass judgment regarding. —**ad·jud''i·ca'tion**, *n.*

ad'junct, *n.* something added.

ad·jure', *v.t.*, **-jured, -juring.** 1. command formally. 2. request solemnly.

ad·just', *v.t.* 1. cause to fit or function properly. 2. settle. —*v.i.* 3. adapt oneself. —**ad·just'a·ble**, *adj.* —**ad·just'er, ad·just'or**, *n.* —**ad·just'ment**, *n.*

ad'ju·tant, *n.* assistant to military commander.

ad''-lib'', *v.*, **-libbed, -libbing.** *Informal.* improvise while talking.

ad·min'is·ter, *v.t.* 1. direct or manage. 2. give, esp. according to prescribed rules.

ad·min''is·tra'tion, *n.* 1. act or process of administering. 2. term of office. 3. officials directing or managing. —**ad·min''is·tra''tive**, *adj.* —**ad·min'is·tra''tor**, *n.*

ad'mi·ral, *n.* naval officer of the highest rank.

ad'mi·ral·ty, *n., pl.* **-ies.** naval administrative department.

ad·mire', *v.t.*, **-mired, -miring.** regard with great respect or pleasure. —**ad'mir·a·ble**, *adj.* —**ad''mi·ra'tion**, *n.* —**ad·mir'er**, *n.*

ad·mis'si·ble, *adj.* 1. proper for admission. 2. allowable.

ad·mis'sion, *n.* 1. act or instance of admitting. 2. confession. 3. permission for one to enter a theater, etc.

ad·mit', *v.t.*, **-mitted, -mitting.** 1. allow to enter. 2. confess or concede. —**ad·mit'tance**, *n.*

ad·mix'ture, *n.* something added to a mixture.

ad·mon'ish, *v.t.* 1. urge, esp. as a warning. 2. reproach. —**ad''mo·ni'tion**, *n.* —**ad·mon'i·to''ry**, *adj.*

a·do', *n.* fussy talk or action.

a·do'be, *n.* dried, unfired brick.

ad''o·les'cence, *n.* youth between puberty and physical maturity. —**ad''o·les'cent**, *adj., n.*

a·dopt', *v.t.* take as one's own. —**a·dop'tion**, *n.*

a·dore', *v.t.*, **-dored, -doring.** worship. —**a''do·ra'tion**, *n.* —**a·dor'a·ble**, *adj.*

a·dorn', *v.t.* decorate. —**a·dorn'ment**, *n.*

a·dren'a·lin, *n.* hormone promoting vigorous bodily action.

a·drift', *adj., adv.* drifting.

a·droit', *adj.* clever. —**a·droit'ly**, *adv.* —**a·droit'ness**, *n.*

ad''u·la'tion, *n.* excessive praise or respect.

a·dult', *n.* 1. physically mature person or animal. —*adj.* 2. physically mature. —**a·dult'hood**, *n.*

a·dul'ter·ate'', *v.t.*, **-ated, -ating.** add undesirable ingredients to. —**a·dul'ter·a'tion**, *n.*

a·dul'ter·er, *n.* committer of adultery. Also, *fem.*, **a·dul'ter·ess.**

a·dul'ter·y, *n., pl.* **-ies.** *n.* infidelity of a spouse. —**a·dul'ter·ous**, *adj.*

ad·vance', *v.*, **-vanced, -vancing**, *n., adj.* *v.t.* 1. move forward. 2. suggest for consideration. 3. pay before earned. —*v.i.* 4. move forward. —*n.* 5. motion forward. 6. act intended to secure favor or friendship. 7. improvement. 8. sum to be repaid in money or work. 9. promotion. —*adj.* 10. early. —**ad·vance'ment**, *n.*

ad·van'tage, *n.* 1. more favorable situation. 2. benefit. —**ad''van·ta'geous**, *adj.*

ad'vent, 1. arrival. 2. **Advent**, **a.** coming of Christ. **b.** period before Christmas.

ad''ven·ti'tious, *adj.* coming or happening by accident.

ad·ven'ture, *n., v.*, **-tured, -turing.** *n.* 1.

risky undertaking. **2.** thrilling or exciting experience. —*v.t.* undertake with risk. —*v.i.* **4.** seek adventures. —**ad·ven'tur·er,** *n.* —**ad·ven'tur·ous,** *adj.*

ad'verb, *n. Grammar.* word modifying a verb. —**ad·ver'bi·al,** *adj.*

ad'ver·sar''y, *n., pl.* **-saries.** opponent or enemy.

ad·verse', *adj.* opposing or unfavorable. —**ad·verse'ly,** *adv.*

ad·ver'si·ty, *n., pl.* **-ties.** difficulty or misfortune.

ad·vert', *v.i.* refer.

ad'ver·tise, *v.,* **-tised, -tising.** *v.t.* **1.** call attention to in order to elicit a public response. —*v.i.* **2.** request something publicly. —**ad'ver·tis''er,** *n.* —**ad''ver·tise'ment,** *n.* —**ad'ver·tis''ing,** *n.*

ad·vice', *n.* **1.** opinion urging choice or rejection of a course of action. **2.** piece of information.

ad·vis'a·ble, *adj.* to be advised; desirable. —**ad·vis''a·bil'i·ty,** *n.*

ad·vise', *v.t.,* **-vised, -vising. 1.** urge to choose or reject a course of action. **2.** recommend. **3.** give information. —**ad·vis'er, ad·vis'or,** *n.* —**ad·vi'so·ry,** *adj.*

ad·vise'ment, *n.* thought; consideration.

ad'vo·cate, *n.* (ad'və kət) **1.** person arguing one side of a dispute, esp. a lawyer. —*v.t.* (ad'vo kāt'') **2.** to argue in favor of. —**ad'vo·ca·cy,** *n.*

adz, *n.* long-handled tool for dressing wood. Also **adze.**

ae·gis, (ē'jis), *n.* sponsorship.

ae'on (ē'on), *n.* extremely long time.

aer'ate, *v.t.,* **-ated, -ating.** expose to air.

aer'i·al, *adj.* **1.** in or of the air. **2.** pertaining to aviation. —*n.* **3.** antenna for sending or receiving radio waves.

ae·ro''bics, *n.* exercises to strengthen circulation and respiration.

aer''o·dy·nam'ics, *n.* study of the dynamics of gases in motion. —**aer''o·dy·nam'ic,** *adj.*

aer''o·nau'tics, *n.* science of flying. —**aer''o·nau'ti·cal,** *adj.*

aer''o·sol, *n.* liquid applied by spraying from a pressurized container.

aer'o·space'', *n.* all space, including the earth's atmosphere.

aes·thete (es'thēt''), *n.* person sensitive to art or beauty.

aes·thet'ic (es thet'ik), *adj.* **1.** pertaining to beauty. **2.** sensitive to art or beauty. —*n.* **3. aesthetics,** study of art or beauty.

a·far', *adv.* at a great distance.

af·fa'ble, *adj.* cordial; pleasant. —**af''fa·bil'i·ty,** *n.*

af·fair', *n.* **1.** business matter. **2.** event. **3.** amorous relationship.

af·fect', *v.t.* **1.** have influence on. **2.** move emotionally. **3.** make an affectation of.

af''fec·ta'tion, *n.* pretentious mannerism.

af·fect'ed, *adj.* **1.** characterized by affectation. **2.** moved emotionally.

af·fect'ing, *adj.* emotionally moving.

af·fec'tion, *adj.* **1.** love. **2.** sickness.

af·fec'tion·ate, *adj.* loving.

af''fi·da'vit, *n.* sworn written statement.

af·fil·i·ate, *v.t.,* **-ated, -ating,** *n. v.t.* (ə fil'ē āt'') **1.** combine, as independent businesses for mutual benefit. —*n.* (ə fil'ē ət) **2.** affiliated business, etc. —**af·fil'i·a'tion,** *n.*

af·fin'i·ty, *n., pl.* **-ties. 1.** attraction. **2.** similarity.

af·firm', *v.t.* **1.** state emphatically. **2.** confirm; ratify. —**af''fir·ma'tion,** *n.* —**af·fir'ma·tive,** *adj.*

af·fix', *v.t.* attach.

af·flict', *v.t.* trouble. —**af·flic'tion,** *n.*

af'flu·ent, *adj.* prosperous. —**af'flu·ence,** *n.*

af·ford', *v.t.* **1.** have enough money or other resources. **2.** supply; provide.

af·fray', *n.* fight.

af·front', *v.t.* **1.** insult or challenge openly. —*n.* **2.** open insult or challenge.

a·fire', *adv., adj.* on fire. Also **a·flame'.**

a·float', *adv., adj.* floating.

a·foot', *adv., adj.* **1.** on foot. **2.** in action or in progress.

a·fore'said, *adj.* previously said.

a·fraid', *adj.* **1.** full of fear. **2.** unable because of fear. **3.** regretful, as because of inability.

a·fresh', *adv.* from the beginning again.

aft, *adv., adj. Nautical.* toward or at the stern.

af'ter, *prep.* **1.** behind. **2.** later than. **3.** lower in rank or importance. **4.** in search or pursuit of. **5.** in imitation of. —*adv.* **6.** behind. **7.** later.

af'ter·ef·fect'', *n.* later consequence.

af'ter·math'', *n.* consequence, usually unfavorable.

af''ter·noon', *n.* period after noon and before evening.

af'ter·thought'', *n.* belated thought.

af'ter·ward, *adv.* later. Also, **af'ter·wards.**

a·gain', *adv.* **1.** once more. **2.** besides.

a·gainst', *prep.* **1.** toward or into contact with. **2.** opposed or hostile to.

age, *n., v.,* **aged, aging.** *n.* **1.** remoteness in time of birth or origin. **2.** distinctive period of history, geology, etc. **3. of age,** legally mature. —*v.t.* **4.** bring or allow to come to ripeness or maturity. —*v.i.* **5.** become old.

a'ged, *adj.* **1.** of a specified age. **2. the aged,** old people.

age''is·m, *n.* discrimination against the elderly.

age'less, *adj.* unaffected by time or age.

a′gen·cy, *n., pl.* **-cies. 1.** office handling business for others. **2.** government office. **3.** active force. **4.** means.

a·gen′da (ə jen′də), *n., pl.* business matters to be dealt with.

a′gent, *n.* **1.** person handling business for others. **2.** government official. **3.** active force or substance.

ag·glom′er·ate, *v.*, **-ated, -ating.**, *n.*, *adj. v.t., v.i.* (a glom′ər āt) **1.** gather into a mass. —*n.* (a glom′ər ət) **2.** mass of miscellaneous things. —*adj.* **3.** gathered into a mass. —**ag·glom″er·a′tion**, *n.*

ag·gran′dize, *v.t.*, **-dized, -dizing.** increase in power, status, wealth, etc. —**ag·gran′dize·ment**, *n.*

ag′gra·vate″, *v.t.*, **-vated, -vating. 1.** make worse. **2.** annoy. —**ag″gra·va′tion**, *n.*

ag′gre·gate, *v.*, **-gated, -gating**, *adj.*, *n. v.t., v.i.* (ag′gre gāt) **1.** collect or gather. —*adj.* (ag′gre gət) **2.** total; collective. —*n.* **3.** sum; total. —**ag″gre·ga′tion**, *n.*

ag·gres′sion, *n.* hostile act or policy. —**ag·gres′sor**, *n.*

ag·gres′sive, *adj.* **1.** disposed to commit aggressions. **2.** forceful, as in business.

ag·grieve′, *v.t.*, **-grieved, -grieving.** wrong or offend seriously.

a·ghast′, *adj.* horrified.

a′gile, *adj.* nimble; deft. —**a·gil′i·ty**, *n.*

a′gi·tate″, *v.t.*, **-tated, -tating. 1.** shake violently. **2.** disturb emotionally. —**a″gi·ta′tion**, *n.*

a·glow′, *adj., adv.* glowing.

ag·nos′tic, *n.* person regarding the existence of God as unknowable.

a·go′, *adj., adv.* in the past.

a·gog′, *adj.* eager and excited.

ag′o·nize, *v.t.*, **-nized, -nizing.** put in agony.

ag′o·ny, *n., pl.* **-ies.** intense suffering.

a·grar′i·an, *adj.* pertaining to farming or the country.

a·gree′, *v.* agreed, agreeing. *v.i.* **1.** consent or promise. **2.** be of the same opinion. **3.** be harmonious or in accord. **4.** match exactly. —*v.t.* **5.** concede as true. —**a·gree′ment**, *n.*

a·gree′a·ble, *adj.* **1.** pleasant. **2.** reacting favorably. —**a·gree′a·bly**, *adv.*

ag′ri·cul″ture, *n.* science or occupation of farming. —**ag″ri·cul′tur·al**, *adj.*

a·ground′, *adj., adv.* (of a ship) in water too shallow for floating.

a·head′, *adv., adj.* **1.** in front. **2.** with an advantage over competitors.

a·hoy′, *interj., Nautical.* hey!

aid, *n., v.* help.

aide-de-camp, *n., pl.* **aides-de-camp.** assistant military officer.

ail, *v.t.* distress or sicken. —**ail′ment**, *n.*

ail′er·on, *n.* an airplane wing that controls rolling.

aim, *v.t.* **1.** point, as for shooting. **2.** intend. —*v.i.* **3.** point a gun, etc. —*n.* **4.** act of pointing a gun, etc. **5.** intention or goal.

aim′less, *adj.* without a goal or purpose.

ain′t, *v.i., Dialect.* am, is, or are not.

air, *n.* **1.** gas compound surrounding the earth. **2.** appearance as derived from action, facial expression, etc. **3.** song or melody. **4. airs**, affectations. —*v.t.* **5.** ventilate.

air′borne″, *adj.* flying.

air conditioning, treatment of air to control purity, temperature, and humidity. —**air conditioner**, *n.* —**air′con·di″tion**, *v.t.*

air′craft, *n., pl.* **-craft.** flying craft.

air′field″, *n.* field for taxiing, takeoff, and landing of airplanes.

air force, flying fighting force.

air′line, *n.* company operating regularly scheduled aircraft flights. —**air′lin″er**, *n.*

air′plane, *n.* heavier-than-air flying craft with wings.

air′port″, *n.* airfield with terminal, storage, and service buildings.

air′ship″, *n.* lighter-than-air flying craft.

air′tight″, *adj.* **1.** preventing passage of air. **2.** unable to be disproven, as an argument.

air′y, *adj.*, **airer, airiest. 1.** open to air or breeze. **2.** loftily situated. **3.** impermanent as air. **4.** flippant; thoughtless. —**air′i·ly**, *adv.* —**air′i·ness**, *n.*

aisle (īl), *n.* **1.** passageway, esp. among seats as in a theater. **2.** a division of a church, esp. between pillars.

a·jar′, *adj., adv.* partly open, as a door.

a·kim′bo, *adj., adv.* with hands on hips and elbows out.

a·kin′, *adj.* **1.** of the same family. **2.** of the same sort.

à la carte, with each dish ordered and paid for separately.

a·lac′ri·ty, *n.* willing readiness.

à la mode, **1.** in fashion. **2.** with ice cream.

a·larm′, *n.* **1.** emergency signal. **2.** occasion for fear. **3.** fear. —*v.t.* **4.** startle or frighten.

a·las′, *interj.* (exclamation of regret).

al·be′it, *conj.* even though.

al·bi′no, *n., pl.* **-nos.** person or animal without skin pigmentation.

al′bum, *n.* **1.** blank book for mounting photographs, stamps, etc. **2.** blank book for sketching. **3.** booklike container for phonograph records.

al·bu′men, *n.* egg white or similar substance.

al′che·my, *n.* pre-scientific chemistry. —**al′che·mist**, *n.*

al′co·hol″, *n.* colorless liquid used as fuel, intoxicant, etc.

al''co·hol'ic, *adj.* **1.** pertaining to alcohol. —*n.* **2.** person addicted to alcohol.

al'cove, *n.* place set back from a larger adjoining space.

al'der, *n.* small tree of the birch family.

al'der·man, *n.* city ward representative.

ale, *n.* strong beerlike drink.

a·lert', *adj.* **1.** watchful. —*v.t., n.* **2.** alarm. —**a·lert'ly,** *adv.* —**a·lert'ness,** *n.*

al''fal'fa, *n.* fodder plant.

al·gae (al'jē), *n. pl.; sing.* **al'ga.** one-celled water plants.

al'ge·bra, *n.* mathematical system based on symbols, not numbers. —**al''ge·bra'ic,** *adj.*

al'i·as, *adv.* **1.** otherwise known as. —*n.* **2.** assumed name.

al'i·bi, *n., pl.* **-bis.** legal plea of absence from the scene of a crime.

al'i·en, *adj.* **1.** from outside; foreign. —*n.* **2.** foreigner.

al'i·en·ate'', *v.t.,* **-ated, -ating. 1.** deprive someone of. **2.** act so as to lose the friendship of. —**al''i·en·a'tion,** *n.*

al'i·en·ist, *n.* specialist in mental illness.

a·light', *v.i.* **1.** descend, as from a vehicle or animal. —*adv., adj.* **2.** lighted. **3.** afire.

a·lign (ə līn'), *v.t.* line up. —**a·lign'ment,** *n.*

a·like', *adj.* **1.** of the same kind or form. —*adv.* **2.** in the same way.

al''i·men'ta·ry, *adj.* pertaining to food or nourishment.

al'i·mo''ny, *n.* allowance paid to a divorced wife by her former husband.

a·live', *adj.* **1.** living. **2.** vigorous or lively. **3.** teeming.

al'ka·li'', *n., pl.* **-lis.** acid-neutralizing chemical. —**al'ka·line'',** *adj.*

al'ka·loid'', *n.* bitter, alkali-containing chemical.

all, *adj.* **1.** every. **2.** the whole of. —*n., pron.* **3.** everything or everybody. —*adv.* **4.** entirely.

Al'lah, *n.* Muslim name for God.

al'lay', *v.t.* calm or soothe.

al·lege', *v.t.,* **-leged, -leging.** assert, esp. without proof. —**al''le·ga'tion,** *n.* —**al·leg'ed·ly,** *adv.*

al·le'giance, *n.* loyalty.

al'le·go''ry, *n., pl.* **-ies.** story or display using symbols. —**al''le·gor'i·cal,** *adj.*

al'ler·gy, *n., pl.* **-gies.** excessive sensitivity to some substance. —**al·ler'gic,** *adj.*

al·le'vi·ate, *v.t.,* **-ated, -ating.** relieve; mitigate. —**al·le'vi·a''tion,** *n.*

al'ley, *n., pl.* **-leys. 1.** narrow service street. **2.** garden walk.

al·li'ance, *n.* **1.** combination of independent nations, etc. **2.** treaty for such a combination. **3.** organization or club. **4.** marriage.

al·lied', *adj.* **1.** joined in an alliance. **2.** closely related.

al''li·ga'tor, *n.* broad-snouted reptile of the southeastern U.S.

al·lit''er·a'tion, *n.* use of the same sound to start several succeeding words.

al'lo·cate'', *v.t.,* **-cated, -cating.** assign or allot. —**al''lo·ca'tion,** *n.*

al·lot', *v.t.,* **-lotted, -lotting. 1.** distribute to sharing parties. **2.** assign. —**al·lot'ment,** *n.*

all'-out', *adj.* without reservation; total.

al·low', *v.t.* **1.** permit. **2.** give or grant. **3.** grant to be true. —**al·low'a·ble,** *adj.* —**al·low'ance,** *n.*

al'loy', *v.t.* (əl loi') **1.** mix. **2.** weaken; dilute. —*n.* (al'loi) **3.** metal or metals with admixtures.

all'spice'', *n.* spice made from a West Indian berry.

al·lude', *v.i.,* **-luded, -luding.** make reference to. —**al·lu'sion,** *n.* —**al·lu'sive,** *adj.*

al·lure', *v.t.,* **-lured, -luring,** *n. v.t.* **1.** attract temptingly. —*n.* **2.** quality of attraction or temptation. —**al·lure'ment,** *n.*

al·lu'vi·um, *n.* soil deposited by moving water. —**al·lu'vi·al,** *adj.*

al·ly', *v.,* **-lied, -lying,** *n., pl.* **-lies.** *v.t., v.i.* **1.** unite for a common purpose. —*n.* **2.** person, country, etc. joined in an alliance.

alma mater, one's college or secondary school.

al'ma·nac'', *n.* annual publication including a calendar and diverse useful information.

al·might'y, *adj.* **1.** totally powerful. —*n.* **2. the Almighty,** God.

al'mond, *n.* edible nut from a tree.

al'most, *adv.* nearly.

alms (ahms), *n., pl.* **alms.** charitable gift or money.

a·loft', *adv., adj.* up high.

a·lone', *adj. adv.* **1.** by oneself or itself. **2.** only.

a·long', *prep.* **1.** in the lengthwise direction of. —*adv.* **2.** together with another or others. **3.** steadily forward or into the future.

a·long'side'', *prep.* **1.** beside. —*adv.* **2.** to or at the side.

a·loof'', *adv.* **1.** at some distance. —*adj.* **2.** showing no interest or concern. —**a·loof'ness,** *n.*

a·loud', *adv.* **1.** in the normal volume of voice. **2.** loudly.

al'pha·bet'', *n.* all the letters of a language in a customary order. —**al''pha·bet'i·cal,** *adj.* —**al''pha·bet·ize'',** *v.t.*

al·read'y, *adv.* **1.** before a stated time. **2.** so soon.

al'so, *adv.* additionally.

al'tar, *n.* block or table used for religious ceremonies.

al'ter, *v.t., v.i.* change. —**al''ter·a'tion,** *n.*

al''ter·ca'tion, *n.* quarrel; dispute.

al·ter·nate, *v.*, -nated, -nating, *adj.*, *n.* *v.i.* (ahl'tər nāt'') 1. act, appear, etc. in turns. —*v.t.* 2. employ in turns. —*adj.* (ahl'tər nət) 3. acting, appearing, etc. in turns. —*n.* 4. someone or something that acts, appears, etc. in turns. —al''ter·na'tion, *n.*

al·ter'na·tive'', *n.* 1. other choice. —*adj.* 2. available as another choice.

al·though', *conj.* even though.

al·tim'e·ter, *n.* gauge for measuring altitude.

al'ti·tude, *n.* height, esp. when considerable.

al'to, *n.*, *pl.* -tos. 1. musical range between soprano and tenor. 2. singer, instrument or part with this range.

al''to·geth'er, *adv.* 1. completely. 2. in general.

al'tru·ism, *n.* concern for others, not oneself. —al''tru·is'tic, *adj.* —al'tru·ist, *n.*

al'um, *n.* astringent used in medicine.

a·lu'mi·num, *n.* lightweight metal.

a·lum'nus, *n.*, *pl.* -ni. school graduate. Also, *fem.*, **a·lum'na**, *pl.* -nae.

al'ways, *adv.* 1. all of one's life. 2. forever. 3. continually.

am, *v.*, first person present singular indicative of *be*.

a·mal'gam, *n.* a mixture.

a·mal'gam·ate'', *v.*, -ated, -ating. *v.t.*, *v.i.* form a combination or mixture. —a·mal''ga·ma'tion, *n.*

a·mass', *v.t.* gather.

am·a'teur, *n.* 1. non-professional participant. 2. lover of an art. —*adj.* 3. by or for non-professional participants.

am·a·teur''ish, *adj.* without professional competence.

am·a·to''ry, *adj.* pertaining to love or sex.

a·maze', *v.t.*, -mazed, -mazing. stun with surprise. —a·maz'ing, *adj.* —a·maze'ment, *n.*

am·bas'sa·dor, *n.* senior diplomat. —am·bas''sa·do'ri·al, *adj.* —am·bas'sa·dor·ship'', *n.*

am'ber, *n.* 1. fossil resin. —*adj.* 2. yellow-brown.

am'ber·gris, *n.* whale secretion used for perfume.

am''bi·dex'trous, *adj.* equally able with both hands. —am''bi·dex·ter'i·ty, *n.*

am'bi·ence, *n.* quality or mood of an environment. Also **am'bi·ance.** —am'bi·ent, *adj.*

am·big'u·ous, *adj.* having more than one possible meaning. —am''bi·gu'i·ty, *n.*

am·bi'tion, *n.* 1. strong desire for success. 2. thing whose attainment is strongly desired. —am·bi'tious, *adj.*

am'ble, *v.i.*, -bled, -bling, *n.* *v.i.* 1. move easily and slowly. —*n.* 2. easy, slow walk.

am·bro'sia, *n.* divine food.

am'bu·lance, *n.* vehicle for the sick.

am'bu·la·to''ry, *adj.* able to walk.

am'bush, *n.* 1. concealment for attackers. 2. attack from a concealed position. —*v.t.* 3. attack from a concealed position.

a·mel'io·rate'', *v.t.*, -rated, -rating. improve. —a·mel''io·ra'tion, *n.*

a·men', *interj.* so be it.

a·me'na·ble, *adj.* agreeable.

a·mend', *v.t.* 1. alter. 2. improve. —*n.* 3. amends, compensation for damage, injury, etc. —a·mend'ment, *n.*

a·men'i·ty, *n.*, *pl.* -ties. something agreeable or polite.

A·mer''i·ca'na, *n.*, *pl.* literature, artifacts, etc. having to do with U.S. history or culture.

A·mer'i·can·ism, *n.* 1. partiality to things identified with the U.S. 2. something characteristic of the U.S.

am'e·thyst, *n.* 1. violet quartz or corundum. 2. shade of violet.

a'mi·a·ble, *adj.* creating friendly feelings. —a''mi·a·bly, *adj.* —a''mi·a·bil'i·ty, *n.*

a'mi·ca·ble, *adj.* without hostility or resentment. —a'mi·ca·bly, *adv.*

a·mid', *prep.* among. Also, **a·midst'.**

a·miss', *adj.* 1. not right. —*adv.* 2. not in the right way.

am'i·ty, *n.* friendship.

am·mo'nia, *n.* pungent, water-soluble gas.

am''mu·ni'tion, *n.* projectiles, together with their charges of gunpowder, etc. fired esp. from guns.

am·ne'sia, *n.* loss of memory.

am'nes·ty, *n.*, *pl.* -ties. general pardon by a government, esp. for political crimes.

a·mok', *adv.* amuck.

a·mong', *prep.* 1. surrounded closely by. 2. in the company or society of. Also, **a·mongst'.**

a·mor'al, *adj.* without a sense of right or wrong.

am'or·ous, *adj.* expressing love, esp. sexual love.

a·mor'phous, *adj.* shapeless or formless.

a'mor·tize'', *v.t.*, -tized, -tizing. pay off gradually. —am''or·ti·za'tion, *n.*

a·mount', *n.* 1. total. 2. quantity. —*v.i.* 3. add up.

a·mour', *n.* love affair.

am'pere, *n.* unit for measuring electric current. —am'per·age, *n.*

am·phib'i·an, *n.* 1. animal able to live on land and water. —*adj.* 2. Also, **am·phib'i·ous.** able to live on land and water.

am'phi·the''a·ter, *n.* arena or stadium with tiers of seats surrounding the central area. Also, **am'phi·the''a·tre.**

am'ple, *adj.,* **ampler, amplest. 1.** copious. **2.** sufficient. —**am'ply,** *adv.*

am'pli·fy", *v.t.,* **-fied, -fying. 1.** increase in size. **2.** increase in strength, as an electronic signal. —**am'pli·fi"er,** *n.* —**am"pli·fi·ca'tion,** *n.*

am'pli·tude", *n.* **1.** breadth or extent. **2.** abundance.

am'pu·tate", *v.t.,* **-tated, -tating.** remove, as a limb of a body. —**am"pu·ta'tion,** *n.* —**am"pu·tee',** *n.*

a·muck', *adv.* in a condition of murderous insanity.

am'u·let, *n.* magical charm worn on the person.

a·muse', *v.t.,* **-mused, -musing. 1.** be funny to. **2.** entertain. —**a·muse'ment,** *n.*

an, *indef. art.* variant of *a,* used when the following word begins with a vowel.

a·nach'ron·ism, *n.* something outside its proper historical period. —**a·nach"ron·is'tic,** *adj.*

an'a·gram", *n.* word formed from the letters spelling another word.

a'nal, *adj.* pertaining to the anus.

an"a·log, *n.* represented by physical variables.

a·nal'o·gy, *n., pl.* **-gies.** *n.* comparison of an unfamiliar thing to a more familiar one. —**a·nal'o·gous,** *adj.*

a·nal'y·sis, *n., pl.* **-ses. 1.** separation into component parts. **2.** summary of such a separation. **3.** psychoanalysis. —**an'a·lyst,** *n.* —**an"a·lyt'ic,** **an"a·lyt'ic·al,** *adj.* —**an'a·lyze",** *v.t.*

an·ar'chy, *n.* **1.** society without rulers. **2.** political or organizational chaos. —**an'ar·chism",** *n.* —**an'ar·chist,** *n.*

a·nath'e·ma, *n.* **1.** solemn curse. **2.** something hated and despised.

a·nat'o·my, *n.* **1.** study of the composition of animals and plants. **2.** composition of an animal or plant. —**an"a·tom'i·cal,** *adj.*

an'ces·tor, *n.* forebear; one from whom a person descends. Also, *fem.* **an"ces·tress.** —**an"ces·try,** *n.*

an'chor, *n.* **1.** device for mooring a ship or boat. —*v.i.* **2.** to secure by anchor.

an·cho'vy, *n., pl.* **-vies.** tiny, salty, herringlike fish.

an'cient, *adj.* **1.** of the oldest period of human history. **2.** very old. —*n.* **3.** person, esp. an author or philosopher, of the ancient period. **4.** very old person.

and, *conj.* **1.** along with. **2.** *Informal.* used in place of the infinitive *to.*

and'i'ron, *n.* horizontal iron support for firewood, used in pairs.

an'ec·dote", *n.* true short story.

a·ne'mi·a, *n.* shortage of hemoglobin or red cells in the blood. —**a·ne'mic,** *adj.*

an"es·the'sia, *n.* lack of sensation induced by a gas or drug. —**an"es·thet'ic,** *adj., n.* —**an·es'the·tize",** *v.t.*

a·new', *adv.* once more.

an'gel, *n.* messenger or attendant of God. —**an·gel'ic,** *adj.*

an'ger, *n.* **1.** strong annoyance. —*v.t.* **2.** make angry.

an·gi'na pec'to·ris, painful heart condition.

an'gle, *n., v.i.,* **-gled, gling.** *n.* **1.** divergence of two lines or surfaces that meet. —*v.i.* **2.** fish. **3.** *Informal.* use stratagems for personal gain. —**an'gler,** *n.*

an'gle·worm", *n.* earthworm.

An'gli·can, *n.* **1.** member of the Church of England or churches in communion with it, e.g. the Episcopal Church. —*adj.* **2.** pertaining to the Church of England or churches in communion with it. —**An'gli·can·ism,** *n.*

An'glo-Sax'on, *n.* **1.** person descended from the Angles and Saxons in England. **2.** person of English ancestry. —*adj.* **3.** pertaining to or characteristic of the Anglo-Saxons.

an'gry, *adj.* **-grier, -griest. 1.** seriously annoyed. **2.** suggesting human anger by action, appearance, etc. —**an'gri·ly,** *adv.*

an'guish, *n.* intense suffering.

an'gu·lar, *adj.* **1.** having angles. **2.** conspicuous for angles. —**an"gu·lar'i·ty,** *n.*

an'i·line, *n.* benzene derivative used for dyes.

an"i·mad·vert', *v.i.* comment disapprovingly. —**an"i·mad·ver'sion,** *n.*

an'i·mal, *n.* **1.** living thing other than a plant or bacterium. **2.** any such thing other than a human being. —*adj.* **3.** pertaining to animals.

an·i·mate, *v.t.,* **-mated, -mating,** *adj. v.t.* (an'ə māt) **1.** give life to. **2.** make lively. —*adj.* (an'ə mət) **3.** having life. —**an"i·ma'tion,** *n.*

an"i·mos'i·ty, *n., pl.* **-ties.** hostility. Also, **an'i·mus.**

an'i·seed", *n.* aromatic seed of the anise plant.

an'kle, *n.* joint between the foot and the leg.

an'nals, *n., pl.* historical records.

an·nex', *v.t.* (ən neks') **1.** join to a larger existing part. —*n.* (an'neks) **2.** a part so joined. —**an"nex·a'tion,** *n.*

an·ni'hil·ate", *v.t.,* **-ated, -ating.** destroy utterly. —**an·ni"hil·a'tion,** *n.*

an"ni·ver'sar·y, *n., pl.* **-ries.** same day of the year as that on which something occurred.

an'no·tate", *v.t.,* **-tated, -tating.** explain or elaborate with notes. —**an"no·ta'tion,** *n.*

an·nounce', *v.t.,* **-nounced, -nouncing.** make known, esp. publicly. —**an·noun'cer,** *n.* —**an·nounce'ment,** *n.*

an·noy′, *v.t.* trouble, esp. so as to provoke dislike. —**an·noy′ance**, *n.*

an′nu·al, *adj.* **1.** yearly. **2.** living only one year, as a plant. —*n.* **3.** something published once a year. **4.** annual plant. —**an′nu·al·ly**, *adv.*

an·nu′i·ty, *n., pl.* **-ties.** annual income bought from an insurance company.

an·nul′, *v.t.,* **-nulled, -nulling.** make legally void. —**an·nul′ment**, *n.*

An·nun″ci·a′tion, *n.* announcement to the Virgin Mary or the impending birth of Christ; celebrated March 25.

an′o·dyne, *n.* pain reliever.

a·noint′, *v.t.* put oil, etc. on as part of a ceremony of consecration. —**a·noint′ment**, *n.*

a·nom′a·ly, *n., pl.* **-lies.** something inconsistent or abnormal. —**a·nom′a·lous**, *adj.*

a·non′, *adv.* soon.

a·non′y·mous, *adj.* written or spoken by someone whose name is unknown or unpublished. —**an″o·nym′i·ty**, *n.*

an·oth′er, *adj.* **1.** one more. **2.** different. —*n.* **3.** one more. **4.** a different one.

an′swer, *n.* **1.** reply to a question. **2.** solution to a problem. **3.** action provoked by something competing. —*v.t.* **4.** reply to. —*v.i.* **5.** give an answer. **6.** be matching or well-suited. **7.** be accountable or responsible.

an′swer·a·ble, *adj.* **1.** able to be answered. **2.** accountable; responsible.

ant, *n.* small social insect.

an·tag′o·nism, *n.* hostility. —**an·tag′o·nist**, *n.* —**an·tag″o·nis′tic**, *adj.* —**an·tag′o·nize″**, *v.t.*

Ant·arc′tic, *n.* **1.** southernmost zone of the earth. —*adj.* **2.** pertaining to this zone.

an″te·ce′dent, *adj.* **1.** coming before. —*n.* **2.** something coming before.

an′te·date″, *v.t.,* **-dated, -dating.** precede in time.

an″te·di·lu′vi·an, *adj.* **1.** before the Flood. **2.** from remotest antiquity.

an′te·lope″, *n.* deerlike animal.

an·ten′na, *n.,pl.* —**nae** (for one), —**nas** (for 2). **1.** feeler on the head of an insect. **2.** aerial; conductor for sending or receiving radio waves.

an·te′ri·or, *adj.* **1.** previous. **2.** at the front end.

an′te·room″, *n.* room preceding a major room.

an′them, *n.* hymnlike song.

an·thol′o·gy, *n.* book of literary selections.

an′thra·cite″, *n.* hard coal.

an′thro·poid″, *adj.* **1.** resembling humanity. —*n.* **2.** anthropoid animal.

an″thro·pol′o·gy, *n.* study of mankind. —**an″thro·pol′o·gist**, *n.*

an″ti·bi·ot′ic, *n.* substance for destroying or weakening microorganisms.

an″ti·bod′y, *n., pl.* **-ies.** blood ingredient that fights foreign substances, e.g. bacteria.

an′tic, *n.* ridiculous or peculiar action.

an·tic′i·pate″, *v.t.,* **-pated, -pating. 1.** look forward to, esp. with pleasure. **2.** use forethought to deal with. **3.** predict. —**an·tic″i·pa′tion**, *n.*

an″ti·cli′max, *n.* disappointment of increasing expectations. —**an″ti·cli·mac′tic**, *adj.*

an′ti·dote″, *n.* substance to counteract a poison.

an″ti·his′ta·mine, *n.* substance to counteract allergic reaction.

an·tip′a·thy, *n., pl.* **-thies.** dislike. —**an·tip″a·thet′ic**, *adj.*

an″ti·quar′i·an, *n.* student of antiquities.

an·ti·quar′y, *n., pl.* **-quaries.** *n.* collector or student of antiquities.

an″ti·quat″ed, *adj.* obsolete.

an·tique′, *n.* **1.** old manufactured object, esp. a valuable one. —*adj.* **2.** ancient.

an·tiq′ui·ty, *n., pl.* **-ties. 1.** ancient times. **2.** something antique.

an″ti·sep′tic, *n.* **1.** substance for destroying harmful bacteria. —*adj.* **2.** destroying harmful bacteria.

an″ti·so′cial, *adj.* **1.** hostile to society. **2.** shunning society.

an·tith′e·sis, *n., pl.* **-ses.** direct opposite. —**an″ti·thet′i·cal**, *adj.*

an″ti·tox′in, *n.* substance for counteracting plant, animal, or bacterial toxin.

ant′ler, *n.* horn of a deer, moose, etc.

an′to·nym″, *n.* word meaning the opposite.

a′nus, *n.* opening at lower end of alimentary canal.

an′vil, *n.* object on which iron, etc. is rested while being hammered.

anx·i·e′ty, *n., pl.* **-ies. 1.** fear of possible harm. **2.** eagerness to act. —**anx′ious**, *adj.* —**anx′ious·ly**, *adv.*

an′y, *adj.* **1.** someone, as readily as all others. **2.** every. —*n.* **3.** any person or persons.

an′y·bod″y, *pron.* some one person, as readily as all others. Also, **an′y·one″**.

an′y·how″, *adv.* **1.** in any way. **2.** whatever the situation is. Also, **an′y·way″**.

an′y·thing″, *pron.* **1.** some one thing, as readily as all others. —*n.* **2.** something, whatever or how much it may be.

an′y·where″, *adv.* in or into any place. Also, **an′y·place″**.

a·or′ta, *n., pl.* **-as, -ae.** blood vessel from the heart. —**a·or′tic**, *adj.*

a·part′, *adv.* **1.** to pieces. **2.** separately.

a·part·heid′, *n.* racial segregation, esp. in the Union of South Africa.

a·part′ment, *n.* series of rooms forming a separate dwelling in a building.

a·pa′thy, *n.* lack of feeling or emotion. —**a″pa·thet′ic**, *adj.* —**a″pa·thet′ic·al·ly**, *adv.*

ape, *n., v.t.* **aped, aping.** *n.* **1.** large animal of the monkey family. —*v.t.* **2.** imitate.

ap'er·ture, *n.* opening.

a'pex, *n.* peak.

aph'o·rism, *n.* brief statement of a truth. —**aph''o·ris'tic,** *adj.*

aph''ro·dis'i·ac, *n.* drug promoting sexual excitement.

a'pi·ar''y, *n., pl.* **-ries.** bee farm.

a·piece', *adv.* for each.

a·plomb', *n.* self-possession.

A·poc'a·lypse, *n.* revelation to St. John the Apostle. —**A·poc''a·lyp'tic,** *adj.*

A·poc'ry·pha, *n., pl.* Biblical books not accepted by Protestants and Jews.

a·poc'ry·phal, *adj.* highly dubious.

ap'o·gee'', *n.* furthest distance of a satellite from its planet.

a·pol''o·get'ic, *adj.* confessing oneself to be at fault.

a·pol'o·gize'', *v.i.,* **-gized, -gizing.** confess oneself to be at fault and seek forgiveness.

a·pol'o·gy, *n., pl.* **-gies. 1.** confession of a fault in search of forgiveness. **2.** statement defending one's actions, etc.

ap'o·plex''y, *n.* bursting of blood vessel with consequent loss of bodily function. —**ap''o·plec'tic,** *adj.*

a·pos'tate'', *n.* renouncer of one's professed faith, etc. —**a·pos'ta·sy,** *n.*

a·pos'tle, *n.* **1.** one of the twelve disciples of Christ sent to preach. **2.** preacher of a new faith. —**n''pos·tol'ic,** *adj.*

a·pos'tro·phe, *n.* **1.** a sign, ', used to indicate possessives, omitted letters, plurals involving numerals or initials, etc. **2.** remark made to or as if to some individual in the course of a speech, etc.

a·pos'tro·phize'', *v.t.* **1.** spell with an apostrophe. **2.** address in an apostrophe.

a·poth'e·car''y, *n., pl.* **-ies.** druggist.

ap·pall', *v.t.* put in a state of horror or fear. Also **ap·pal'.** —**ap·pall'ing,** *adj.*

ap''pa·ra'tus, *n.* **1.** instruments, etc. required for an experiment, job, etc. **2.** organizational structure.

ap·par'el, *n.* clothes. —*v.t.* **2.** clothe.

ap·par'ent, *adj.* **1.** clear; obvious. **2.** as judged from appearances. —**ap·par'ent·ly,** *adv.*

ap''pa·ri'tion, *n.* ghost or phantom.

ap·peal', *n.* **1.** request for help, mercy, etc. **2.** request for reconsideration. **3.** attractiveness. —*v.t.* **4.** request to have reconsidered. —*v.i.* **5.** make an appeal. **6.** have appeal.

ap·pear', *v.i.* **1.** come into sight. **2.** seem. —**ap·pear'ance,** *n.*

ap·pease', *v.t.,* **-peased, -peasing.** satisfy when hostile or demanding. —**ap·pease'ment,** *n.*

ap·pel'lant, *n.* person who appeals, esp. in law.

ap·pel'late, *adj.* handling appeals, as a court.

ap''pel·la'tion, *n.* name given to something or someone.

ap·pend', *v.t.* add; join. —**ap·pend'age,** *n.*

ap''pen·dec'to·my, *n., pl.* **-ies.** surgical removal of an appendix.

ap·pen''di·ci'tis, *n.* inflammation of the appendix.

ap·pen'dix, *n., pl.* **-dixes, -dices. 1.** supplementary portion at the end of a book, etc. **2.** blind branch of the intestine.

ap'per·tain'', *v.i.* belong.

ap·pe·tite'', *n.* desire, as for food. —**ap'pe·tiz''er,** *n.* —**ap'pe·tiz''ing,** *adj.*

ap·plaud', *v.t.* show approval of, as by applause.

ap·plause', *n.* **1.** indications of approval of a dramatic performance, etc. **2.** public recognition and approval.

ap''ple, *n.* common, crisp fruit, generally red or green.

ap·pli'ance, *n.* machine, etc., esp. for home use.

ap'pli·ca·ble, *adj.* able to be applied.

ap·ply', *v.,* **-plied, -plying.** *v.t.* **1.** place, as on an object or surface. **2.** put to use, as a theory or rule. **3.** devote to a task. —*v.i.* **4.** make a formal request. **5.** be relevant. —**ap''pli·ca'tion,** *n.* —**ap'pli·cant,** *n.*

ap·point', *v.t.* **1.** choose and designate. **2.** provide; furnish. —**ap·poin'tive,** *adj.* —**ap·point''ee',** *n.*

ap·point'ment, *n.* **1.** meeting at a stated time. **2.** selection, as for public office. **3.** provision or furnishing.

ap·por'tion, *v.t.* divide into shares. —**ap·por'tion·ment,** *n.*

ap'po·site, *adj.* appropriate.

ap·praise', *v.t.,* **-praised, -praising.** estimate the value of. —**ap·prais'er,** *n.* —**ap·prais'al,** *n.*

ap·pre'ci·a·ble, *adj.* **1.** sufficient to be noted. **2.** worthy of note; considerable.

ap·pre'ci·ate'', *v.,* **-ated, -ating.** *v.t.* **1.** be grateful for. **2.** value truly. —*v.i.* **3.** gain in value. —**ap·pre''ci·a'tion,** *n.* —**ap·pre'ci·a·tive,** *adj.*

ap''pre·hend', *v.t.* **1.** fear. **2.** understand. **3.** capture and arrest. —**ap''pre·hen'sion,** *n.*

ap''pre·hen'sive, *adj.* fearful.

ap·pren'tice, *n., v.t.* **-ticed, -ticing.** *n.* **1.** assistant learning a trade. —*v.t.* **2.** enroll as an apprentice. —**ap·pren'tice·ship'',** *n.*

ap·prise', *v.t.,* **-prised, -prising.** inform; notify. Also, **ap·prize'.**

ap·proach', *v.t.* **1.** come close to. **2.** propose business to. —*v.i.* **3.** come close. —*n.* **4.** act or instance of coming close. **5.** way of coming close. **6.** manner of taking action.

ap·proach′a·ble, *adj*. willing to be talked with.

ap″pro·ba′tion, *n*. approval.

ap·pro·pri·ate, *adj*., *v.t.* **-ated, -ating**. *adj*. (əp pro′pri ət) 1. useful or proper. —*v.t.* (ap pro′pri āt″) 2. reserve for a purpose, as money. 3. take for oneself. —**ap″pro′pri·a′tion**, *n*.

ap·prove′, *v*., **-proved, -proving**. *v.t.* 1. state to be good or suitable. 2. think favorably of. —*v.i.* 3. regard favorably. —**ap·prov′al**, *n*.

ap·prox·i·mate, *adj*., *v.t.* **-ated, -ating**. *adj*. (ap prox′i mət) 1. reasonably accurate but not precise. —*v.t.* (ap prox′i māt″) 2. amount to as an approximate figure, etc. —**ap·prox′i·mate·ly**, *adv*. —**ap·prox″i·ma′tion**, *n*.

ap·pur′te·nance, *n*. additional device or feature; accessory.

a′pri·cot″, *n*. orange-colored peachlike fruit.

A′pril, *n*. fourth month.

a′pron, *n*. covering worn over a dress or trouser front when working.

ap·ro·pos (ap″rə pō′), *adv*. 1. apropos of, with regard to. 2. at the right time. —*adj*. 3. to the point; relevant.

apt, *adj*. 1. displaying a tendency. 2. likely. 3. able; intelligent. —**apt′ly**, *adv*. —**apt′ness**, *n*.

ap′ti·tude″, *n*. talent or ability.

aq″ua·ma·rine′, *n*. pale bluish-green.

a·quar′i·um, *n*. tank, bowl, etc., usually with glass walls, used for displaying live fish, etc.

a·quat′ic, *adj*. of the water.

aq′ue·duct, *n*. engineering structure for conducting water.

a′que·ous, *adj*. like, of, or created by water.

aq′ui·line″, *adj*. pertaining to or suggesting eagles.

ar′a·ble, *adj*. good for producing crops.

ar′bit·er, *n*. judge of controversial matters.

ar′bi·trar″y, *adj*. 1. unreasonable or unjustified. 2. admitting no discussion or complaint. 3. chosen at random as a basis for discussion. —**ar″bi·trar′i·ly**, *adv*.

ar′bi·trate″, *v.t.* **-trated, -trating**. 1. adjudicate after hearing disputants. 2. submit for adjudication. —**ar″bi·tra′tion**, *n*. —**ar″bi·tra′tor**, *n*.

ar′bor, *n*. shaded walk or garden.

ar·bo′re·al, *adj*. of or inhabiting trees.

ar·bu′tus, *n*. 1. shrub with dark green leaves and red berries. 2. trailing plant with white or pink blossoms.

arc, *n*. 1. segment of a circle. 2. light formed by electricity jumping between electrodes.

ar·cade′, *n*. 1. row of arches. 2. covered walk, esp. one between shops.

arch, *n*. 1. curved structure resisting compressive forces. —*v.i.* 2. bend as an arch does. —*adj*. 3. chief. 4. cheerfully mischievous. —**arch′way″**, *n*.

ar·cha′ic, *adj*. 1. out of date. 2. ancient.

arch·an·gel (ark′an″jəl), *n*. chief angel.

arch′bi′shop, *n*. superior bishop.

arch·duke′, *n*. Austrian royal prince. Also fem., **arch′duch′ess**.

ar″che·ol′o·gy, *n*. study of acient cultures through their artifacts. —**ar″che·ol′o·gist**, *n*. —**ar″che·o·log′i·cal**, *adj*. Also **archaeology**.

arch′er, *n*. user of a bow and arrow. —**arch′er·y**, *n*.

ar″chi·pel′a·go, *n*., *pl*. **-gos, -goes**. 1. group of closely spaced islands. 2. area of water surrounding and within such a group.

ar′chi·tect″, *n*. designer of buildings.

ar′chi·tec″ture, *n*. art of designing buildings. —**ar″chi·tec′tur·al**, *adj*.

ar·chives, *n.*, *pl*. official records.

Arc′tic, *n*. 1. northernmost zone of the earth. —*adj*. 2. pertaining to this zone.

ar′dent, *adj*. eager. —**ar′dent·ly**, *adv*.

ar′dor, *n*. eagerness; zeal.

ar′du·ous, *adj*. difficult or tedious.

are, *v*. present indicative plural of *be*.

ar′e·a, *n*. 1. surface measure. 2. region.

area code, three-digit code used in telephoning outside one's own area.

a·re′na, *n*. large space for athletic contests and spectators.

ar′gon, *n*. chemical element, an inert gas.

ar′go·sy, *n.*, *pl*. **-sies**. *Poetic*. large merchant ship or merchant fleet.

ar′gue, *v.*, **-gued, -guing**. *v.i.* 1. express a difference or differences of opinion. 2. offer reasons for or against something. —*v.t.* 3. present as true or valid. 4. express differences of opinion over. —**ar′gu·ment**, *n*. —**ar″gu·men·ta′tion**, *n*.

ar″gu·men′ta·tive, *adj*. given to argument or quarreling.

a′ri·a, *n*. song, as in an opera.

a′rid, *adj*. dry. —**a·rid′i·ty**, *n*.

a·rise′, *v.i.*, **arose, arisen, arising**. 1. get up. 2. happen.

ar″is·toc′ra·cy, *n.*, *pl*. **-cies**. 1. government by a small hereditary or select class. 2. such a class. —**a·ris′to·crat**, *n*. —**a·ris″to·crat′ic**, *adj*.

a·rith′me·tic, *n*. calculation with numerals. —**ar″ith·met′i·cal**, *adj*.

ark, *n*. 1. vessel of Noah. 2. wooden chest.

arm, *n*. 1. upper human limb. 2. anything suggesting this by form, position, or function. 3. weapon. 4. **arms**, the military profession. —*v.t.* 5. equip with weapons.

ar·ma′da, *n*. fleet of fighting ships or airplanes.

Ar″ma·ged′don, *n.* major decisive battle.

arm″a·ment, *n.* weapons with which a ship, airplane, etc. is equipped.

arm′chair″, *n.* chair with arm supports.

arm′ful″, *n., pl.* **-fuls.** amount that can be held in one or both arms.

ar′mi·stice, *n.* suspension of hostilities; truce.

ar′mor, *n.* material, usually metal, protecting against weapons and missiles. —**ar′mored,** *adj.*

ar′mor·y, *n., pl.* **-ies. 1.** building for military activities and equipment storage. **2.** place for storing weapons.

arm′pit″, *n.* area beneath the arm at the shoulder.

ar′my, *n., pl.* **-mies. 1.** land military force. **2.** large number of persons.

a·ro′ma, *n.* scent; odor. —**ar″o·mat′ic,** *adj.*

a·round′, *prep.* **1.** on all sides of. **2.** in any or all areas of. —*adv.* **3.** on all sides. **4.** in any or all areas. **5.** *Informal.* **a.** nearby. **b.** idly or aimlessly.

a·rouse′, *v.t.,* **aroused, arousing. 1.** awaken. **2.** call into activity. —**a·rous′al,** *n.*

ar·raign′, *v.t.* **1.** bring to court as a defendant. **2.** accuse. —**ar·raign′ment,** *n.*

ar·range′, *v.,* **-ranged, -ranging.** *v.t.* **1.** put in order. —*v.t., v.i.* **2.** plan; prepare. —**ar·range′ment,** *n.*

ar′rant, *adj.* utter; downright.

ar·ray′, *v.t.* **1.** arrange. **2.** dress. —*n.* **3.** order or arrangement. **4.** clothing.

ar·rears′, *n., pl.* things overdue, esp. payments.

ar·rest′, *v.t.* **1.** seize because of the commission of a crime. **2.** stop. —*n.* **3.** act or instance of arresting. **4.** state of being arrested.

ar·rive′, *v.i.* **1.** come to a place. **2.** happen. —**ar·riv′al,** *n.*

ar′ro·gant, *adj.* proud and insolent. —**ar′ro·gant·ly,** *adv.* —**ar′ro·gance,** *n.*

ar′ro·gate″, *v.t.,* **-gated, -gating.** claim or seize unjustly. —**ar″ro·ga′tion,** *n.*

ar′row, *n.* missile shot from a bow.

ar·roy′o, *n., pl.* **-os.** *Southwest U.S.* gully.

ar′se·nal, *n.* place for making or storing weapons.

ar′se·nic, *n.* silvery-white poisonous chemical element.

ar′son, *n.* crime of burning buildings, etc. —**ar′son·ist,** *n.*

art, *n.* **1.** activity of creating things that arouse the emotions through one or more senses. **2.** things so created. **3.** skill or profession. **4.** cunning.

ar′ter·y, *n., pl.* **-ies. 1.** major blood vessel. **2.** main line of travel or communication. —**ar·te′ri·al,** *adj.*

artesian well, well whose opening is lower than the head of water supplying it.

art′ful, *adj.* cunning.

ar·thri′tis, *n.* inflammation of a joint of the body. —**ar·thrit′ic,** *adj.*

ar′ti·choke, *n.* edible flower head of thistlelike plant.

ar′ti·cle, *n.* **1.** object for use. **2.** writing on a factual subject. **3.** *Grammar.* **a, an,** or **the.**

ar·tic·u·late, *adj., v.,* **-lated, -lating.** *adj.* (ahr tik′yo̅o̅ lət) **1.** readily understood. **2.** able in speech. **3.** jointed. —*v.t.* (ahr tik′yo̅o̅ lāt″) **4.** express clearly. **5.** arrange in a clear and orderly manner. **6.** assemble with joints. —*v.i.* **7.** speak clearly. —**ar·tic″u·la′tion,** *n.*

ar′ti·fice, *n.* **1.** cunning. **2.** cunning action.

ar′tif·i·cer, *n.* craftsman.

ar″ti·fi′cial, *adj.* **1.** manufactured, esp. in imitation. **2.** contrived or affected. —**ar″ti·fi′cial·ly,** *adv.* —**ar″ti·fi·ci·al′i·ty,** *n.*

ar·til′ler·y, *n.* **1.** guns or other devices for shooting large missiles. **2.** army branch handling such devices.

ar′ti·san, *n.* craftsman.

art′ist, *n.* practitioner of an art. —**ar·tist′ic,** *adj.* —**ar′tist·ry,** *n.*

art′less, *adj.* unaffected; natural.

art″y, *adj.,* **-ier, -iest.** feigning artistic sensitivity.

as, *adv.* **1.** equally. **2.** for example. **3.** if and when. —*conj.* **4.** equally to. **5.** in the manner that. **6.** while. **7.** because; since. **8.** though. —*pron.* **9.** that. —*prep.* **10.** in the guise of.

as·bes′tos, *n.* fibrous mineral used in fireproofing.

as·cen′an·cy, *n.* domination. Also, **as·cen′den·cy.**

as·cend′, *v.t., v.i.* climb or rise. —**as·cent′,** *n.* —**as·cen′dent,** *adj.*

As·cen′sion, *n.* ascent of Christ into heaven, celebrated 40 days after Easter.

as·cer·tain, *v.t.* find out.

as·cet′ic, *adj.* **1.** without pleasure or self-indulgence. —*n.* **2.** one who lives an ascetic life. —**as·cet′i·cism,** *n.*

as·cribe′, *v.t.,* **-scribed, -scribing.** relate to a supposed cause. —**as·crip′tion,** *n.*

a·sep′sis, *n.* absence of disease producing germs. —**a·sep′tic,** *adj.*

ash, *n., pl.* **ashes. 1.** remainder of something not fully burnt. **2.** tree of the olive family. —**ash′tray″,** *n.*

a·shamed′, *adj.* feeling shame.

a·shore′, *adj., adv.* on or onto the shore.

a·side′, *adv.* **1.** at or to the side. **2.** apart. **3.** in reserve.

as′i·nine″, *adj.* silly. —**as″i·nin′ity,** *n.*

ask, *v.t.* **1.** seek to know. **2.** seek information of. **3.** seek, as a favor. **4.** invite. —*v.i.* **5.** seek a favor, information, etc.

a·skance', *adv.* with suspicion or disapproval.

a·skew', *adv., adj.* slanted or twisted out of position.

a·sleep', *adj., adv.* in or into a state of sleep.

as·par'a·gus, *n.* plant with edible shoots.

a''spar'tame, *n.* a synthetic sweetener.

as·pect', *n.* **1.** way of interpreting or understanding something. **2.** appearance or manner. **3.** face or side toward a certain direction.

as'pen, *n.* type of poplar tree.

as·per'i·ty, *n., pl.* **-ties.** roughness of manner or speech.

as·per'sion, *n.* hostile or accusing remark.

as'phalt, *n.* black tarlike material.

as·phyx'i·ate'', *v.t.*, **-ated, -ating.** harm through deprivation of oxygen. **—as·phyx''i·a'tion**, *n.*

as·pire', *v.i.*, **-pired, -piring.** have ambitious intentions. **—as''pi·ra'tion**, *n.* **—as·pir'ant**, *n.*

as'pi·rin, *n.* white crystalline drug used to relieve minor pain and fever.

ass, *n.* **1.** donkey. **2.** silly person.

as·sail', *v.t.* attack. **—as·sail'ant**, *n.*

as·sas'sin, *n.* murderer, esp. of a statesman. **—as·sas'sin·ate''**, *v.t.* **—as·sas''sin·a'tion**, *n.*

as·sault', *n., v.t.* attack.

as·say', *n.* **1.** chemical evaluation, as of an ore. **—v.t.** **2.** perform an assay upon.

as·sem'ble, *v.t., v.i.*, **-bled, -bling.** gather. **—as·sem'blage, as·sem'bly**, *n.*

as·sent', *v.i.* **1.** agree; consent. **—n.** **2.** agreement; consent.

as·sert', *v.t.* **1.** declare. **2.** claim. **3.** assert oneself, present one's claims, demands, etc. boldly. **—as·ser'tion**, *n.* **—as·ser'tive,** *adj.*

as·sess', *v.t.* evaluate. **—as·sess'ment, as·ses'sor**, *n.*

as'set, *n.* something contributing to a profit or advantage.

as·sid'u·ous, *adj.* devoted to a task. **—as·sid'u·ous·ly**, *adv.* **—as''si·du'i·ty**, *n.*

as·sign', *v.t.* **1.** give out as a task or responsibility. **2.** appoint. **3.** transfer possession or enjoyment of. **—n.** **4.** *Law.* person to whom possession or enjoyment of something is transferred. **—as·sign'ment**, *n.* **—as·sign'a·ble**, *adj.* **—as·sign·ee'**, *n.*

as·sim'i·late'', *v.t.*, **-ated, -ating. 1.** absorb. **2.** make like some larger entity. **—as·sim''i·la'tion**, *n.*

as·sist', *v.t.* help in a task or occupation. **—as·sist'ant**, *n.* **—as·sist'ance**, *n.*

as·so·ci·ate', *v.*, **-ated, -ating,** *adj., n. v.t., v.i.* (əs so'shē āt) **1.** join in a social or business relationship. **—v.t.** **2.** connect in one's mind. **—adj.** (əs so'shē ət)

3. joined in a social or business relationship. **—n.** **4.** someone or something so joined. **—as·so''ci·a'tion**, *n.*

as·sort', *v.t.* classify. **—as·sort'ment**, *n.*

as·sort'ed, *adj.* **1.** of various kinds. **2.** classified.

as·suage (əs swāj'), *v.t.*, **-suaged, -suaging.** relieve, as suffering.

as·sume', *v.t.*, **-sumed, -suming. 1.** suppose without knowing. **2.** take upon oneself. **3.** take or receive from another. **4.** begin to cultivate, as a role or affectation. **5.** feign.

as·sump'tion, *n.* **1.** act or instance of assuming. **2. the Assumption,** ascent of the Virgin Mary to heaven, celebrated August 15.

as·sure', *v.t.*, **-sured, -suring. 1.** state emphatically. **2.** convince. **3.** make certain or safe. **4.** reassure. **—as·sur'ance**, *n.* **—as·sured'**, *adj.*

as'ter, *n.* daisylike flower.

as'ter·isk, *n.* a sign, used for footnote references, etc. in print.

a·stern', *adv., Nautical.* backwards.

as'ter·oid'', *n.* small planetlike body between Mars and Jupiter.

asth'ma, *n.* respiratory disorder. **—asth·mat'ic,** *adj., n.*

a·stig'ma·tism, *n.* eye defect which causes imperfect focusing. **—a''stig·mat'ic,** *adj.*

a·stir', *adj., adv.* full of diverse action.

as·ton'ish, *v.t.* surprise greatly. **—as·ton'ish·ment**, *n.*

as·tound', *v.t.* surprise very greatly.

a·stray', *adv., adj.* away from guidance or control.

a·stride', *prep., adv., adj.* straddling.

a·strin''gent, *adj.* **1.** constrictive, styptic. **—n.** **2.** substance which causes contraction of body tissues.

as·trol'o·gy, *n.* study of stars and planets as influences on events. **—as''trolog'i·cal,** *adj.* **—as·trol'o·ger**, *n.*

as'tro·naut'', *n.* person exploring or traveling through outer space.

as''tro·nom'i·cal, *adj.* **1.** pertaining to astronomy. **2.** fantastic, as a number of quantity.

as·tron'o·my, *n.* study of planets, stars, etc. and space. **—as·tron'o·mer**, *n.*

as·tute', *adj.* shrewd. **—as·tute'ness**, *n.*

a·sun'der, *adv., adj.* in parts.

a·sy'lum, *n.* home for persons needing protection, e.g., the insane.

at, *prep.* in, on, or near (used to specify time, place, or rate.)

a'the·ism, *n.* belief that no god exists. **—a'the·ist,** *n.* **—a''the·is'tic,** *adj.*

ath'lete'', *n.* a person who engages in athletics.

ath·let'ics, *n., pl.* sports involving vigorous bodily exercise. **—ath·let'ic,** *adj.*

a·thwart', *adv., prep.* from side to side.

at'las, *n.* book of maps.

at′mos·phere″, *n.* **1.** air closest to the earth. **2.** prevailing mood. —**at″mos·pher′ic**, *adj.*

at′oll, *n.* ring of coral islands or reefs.

a′tom, *n.* smallest unit constituting a distinct chemical element. —**a·tom′ic**, *adj.*

atomic bomb, bomb acting through atomic energy created by fission. Also, **atom bomb.**

atomic energy, energy created through fission or fusion of the nuclei of certain atoms.

at′om·iz″er, *n.* device creating a fine spray.

a·tone′, *v.i.*, atoned, atoning. make right or show regret for a wrong one has done. —**a·tone′ment**, *n.*

a·top′, *prep., adv.* on top of.

a·tro′cious, *adj.* **1.** vicious; outrageous. **2.** wretchedly bad. —**a·troc′i·ty**, *n.*

a″tro·phy, *n.* **1.** a wasting away. —*v.i., v.t.* **2.** to waste away.

at·tach′, *v.t.* **1.** fasten to something. **2.** bind by ties of affection. **3.** assume legal possession of, as to settle a bad debt. —**at·tach′ment**, *n.*

at″ta·ché′, *n.* special member of an embassy staff.

at·tack′, *v.t.* **1.** act against with physical violence, harsh words, etc. **2.** commence to solve, work out, etc. with vigor. —*n.* **5.** act or manner of attacking.

at·tain′, *n.* arrive at. —**at·tain′a·ble**, *adj.* —**at·tain′ment**, *n.*

at·tar′, *n.* scent extracted from flowers.

at·tempt′, *v.t., n.* try.

at·tend′, *v.t.* **1.** be present at. **2.** accompany. **3.** care for. —*v.i.* **4.** be present at a meeting, etc. **5.** give heed. —**at·ten′dance**, *n.*

at·tend′ant, *n.* **1.** minor assistant. —*adj.* **2.** accompanying.

at·ten′tion, *n.* **1.** heed. **2.** care, esp. medical care.

at·ten′tive, *adj.* paying heed or care. —**at·ten′tive·ly**, *adv.*

at·ten′u·ate″, *v.t.*, -ated, -ating. **1.** thin. **2.** weaken or dilute. —**at·ten″u·a′tion**, *n.*

at·test′, *v.t.* bear witness; certify. —**at″tes·ta′tion**, *n.*

at″tic, *n.* unfinished floor space beneath the roof of a house.

at·tire′, *v.t.*, -tired, -tiring, *n. v.t.* **1.** dress, esp. showily. —*n.* **2.** clothes, esp. showy ones.

at′ti·tude″, *n.* **1.** opinion or feeling. **2.** posture.

at·tor′ney, *n., pl.* -eys. lawyer.

at·tract′, *v.t.* **1.** pull towards oneself. **2.** draw by evoking interest, allure, etc. in. —**at·trac′tive**, *adj.* —**at·trac′tive·ly**, *adv.* —**at·trac′tive·ness**, *n.* —**at·trac′tion**, *n.*

at·trib·ute, *v.t.*, -uted, -uting. *n. v.t.* (ət trib′yo͞ot) **1.** name something as the cause for. —*n.* (at′trib yo͞ot) **2.** distinguishing quality or feature. —**at″tri·bu′tion**, *n.*

at·tri′tion, *n.* wearing-down.

at·tune′, *v.t.* -tuned, -tuning. put in harmony.

au′burn, *n.* reddish-brown.

auc′tion, *n.* **1.** public sale to the highest bidder for each item. —*v.t.* **2.** sell at an auction. —**auc′tion·eer′**, *n.*

au·da′cious, *adj.* daring. —**au·da′ci·ty**, *n.*

au′di·ble, *adj.* able to be heard. —**au′di·bly**, *adv.* —**au″di·bil′i·ty**, *n.*

au′di·ence, *n.* **1.** group attending a play, concert, lecture, etc. **2.** persons reached by a book, etc. **3.** formal interview.

au′di·o″, *adj.* pertaining to electronic reproduction of sound.

au′dit, *v.t.* **1.** examine financial accounts. —*n.* **2.** examination of financial accounts. —**au′dit·or**, *n.*

au·di′tion, *n.* **1.** trial of ability for an actor, musician, etc. —*v.t.* **2.** give an audition to. —*v.i.* **3.** perform at an audition.

au″di·to′ri·um, *n.* room for an audience.

au′di·to″ry, *adj.* pertaining to hearing.

au′ger, *n.* drill.

aught, *n.* Archaic. **1.** anything. **2.** zero. —*adv.* **3.** in any way.

aug·ment′, *v.t.* add to. —**aug″men·ta′tion**, *n.*

au·gur (ah′gər), *v.t.* **1.** predict. —*n.* **2.** prophet. —**au′gu·ry** (ah′gyo͞o rē), *n.*

au·gust′, *adj.* **1.** (ə gust′) grand; majestic. —*n.* **2.** August (ah′gəst), eighth month.

aunt, *n.* sister of a father or mother, or wife of an uncle.

au′ra, *n.* quality emanating from a particular place or person.

au′ral, *adj.* pertaining to hearing.

au′re·ole″, *n.* halo.

au re·voir (ō″rə vwahr′), *French.* until I see you again; goodbye.

au′ri·cle, *n.* **1.** outer ear. **2.** upper chamber of the heart. —**au·ric′u·lar**, *adj.*

au·rif′er·ous, *adj.* gold-bearing.

aus′pice, *n., usually pl.* sponsorship.

aus·pi′cious, *adj.* favorable; promising.

aus·tere′, *adj.* **1.** severe in manner. **2.** characterized by abstention. —**aus·ter′i·ty**, *n.*

au·then′tic, *adj.* true or genuine. —**au″then·tic′i·ty**, *n.*

au·then″ti·cate″, *v.t.*, -ated, -ating. prove the authenticity of. —**au·then″ti·ca′tion**, *n.*

au″thor, *n.* creator, esp. of a written work. Also, *fem.*, au′thor·ess. —**au′thor·ship″**, *n.*

au·thor″i·tar′i·an, *adj.* characterized by excessive show or use of authority. —**au·thor″i·tar′i·an·ism**, *n.*

au·thor'i·ta"tive, *adj.* **1.** confirmed by competent authority. **2.** having authority.

au·thor'i·ty, *n., pl.* -ties. **1.** official power. **2.** person having such power. **3.** proof for a statement. **4.** expert. **5.** the authorities, persons with legal power.

au'thor·ize, *v.t.,* -ized, -izing. give official consent to. —au"thor·i·za'tion, *n.*

au'to, *n.* automobile.

au"to·bi·og'ra·phy, *n., pl.* -ies. story of one's own life. —au"to·bi·o·graph'i·cal, *adj.*

au·toc'ra·cy, *n., pl.* -cies. government by one absolute ruler. —au'to·crat, *n.* —au"to·crat'ic, *adj.*

au'to·graph", *n.* one's name in one's handwriting.

au'to·mat", *n.* restaurant with coin-operated serving machines.

au"to·mat'ic, *adj.* controlled by machinery, etc. rather than humans. —au"to·mat'ic·al·ly, *adv.*

au'to·ma"tion, *n.* replacement of human beings as controlling elements by automatic devices.

au·tom'a·ton", *n., pl.* -ta. manlike self-controlled machine; robot.

au'to·mo·bile", *n.* self-propelled passenger vehicle.

au"to·mo'tive, *adj.* pertaining to self-propelled road vehicles.

au·ton'o·my, *n.* self-government. —au·ton'o·mous, *adj.*

au'top"sy, *n., pl.* -sies. examination of a corpse to determine the cause of death.

au'tumn, *n.* season between summer and winter. —au·tum'nal, *adj.*

aux·il'ia·ry, *adj., n., pl.* -ries. *adj.* **1.** serving to assist. **2.** supplementary. —*n.* **3.** something that assists or supplements. **4.** verb used in connection with the principal verb of a sentence.

a·vail', *v.t.* **1.** avail oneself, take advantage. —*v.i.* **2.** be of help or use. —*n.* **3.** advantage or benefit.

a·vail'a·ble, *adj.* able to be used or acquired. —a·vail"a·bil'i·ty, *n.*

av'a·lanche", *n.* sudden descent down a slope of a mass of snow, rock, etc.

av'a·rice, *n.* greed. —av"a·ri'cious, *adj.*

a·vast', *interj. Nautical.* stop.

a·venge', *v.t.,* avenged, avenging. take revenge for. —a·veng'er, *n.*

av'e·nue", *n.* **1.** major street. **2.** approach road.

av'er·age, *n., adj., v.,* -aged, -aging. *n.* **1.** number representing the sum of a group of added figures divided by the number of figures. —*adj.* **2.** typical. **3.** revealed by an average. —*v.t.* **4.** find the average of. —*v.i.* **5.** form an average.

a·verse', *adj.* opposed; reluctant. —a·verse'ly, *adv.*

a·ver'sion, *n.* strong dislike.

a·vert', *v.t.* **1.** prevent. **2.** turn away, as the eyes.

a'vi·ar"y, *n., pl.* -ries. place for captive birds.

a"vi·a'tion, *n.* practice of flying aircraft.

a'vi·a"tor, *n.* person who mes aircratt. Also, *fem.* a"vi·a'trix.

a'vid, *aaj.* eager. —a·vid'i·ty, *n.*

a"vo·ca'do, *n., pl.* -dos. pear-shaped tropical fruit.

av"o·ca'tion, *n.* spare-time pursuit; hobby.

a·void', *v.t.* keep oneself away or safe from. —a·void'a·ble, *adj.* —a·void'ance, *n*

av"oir·du·pois', *n.* system of weights using a pound of 16 ounces.

a·vow', *v.t.* confess. —a·vow'al, *n.* —a·vowed', *adj.*

a·wait', *v.t.* wait for.

a·wake', *v.,* awoke or awaked, awaking, *adj. v.t., v.i.* **1.** Also, a·wak'en, wake. —*adj.* **2.** not asleep.

a·ward', *v.t.* **1.** bestow, as a prize, favor, etc. —*n.* **2.** something awarded.

a·ware', *adj.* conscious or perceptive. —a·ware'ness, *n.*

a·wash', *adj., adv.* just below water level; flooded.

a·way', *adv.* **1.** to or in another place or direction. **2.** from a place. **3.** out of one's possession. **4.** continuously. —*adj.* **5.** absent. **6.** at a specified distance.

awe, *n., v.t.,* awed, awing. *n.* **1.** overwhelming respect, reverence, etc. —*v.t.* **2.** fill with awe. —awe'some, *adj.*

aw'ful, *adj.* **1.** bad. **2.** awe-inspiring.

aw'ful·ly, *adv.* **1.** in an awful manner. **2.** *Informal.* very.

a·while', *adv.* for a while.

awk'ward, *adj.* **1.** clumsy. **2.** embarrassing. **3.** dangerous or difficult. —awk'ward·ly, *adv.* —awk'ward·ness, *n.*

awl, *n.* pointed tool.

awn'ing, *n.* device for shading windows, porches, etc. usually made of canvas.

a·wry', *adv., adj.* **1.** twisted. **2.** not right.

ax, *n., pl.* axes. broad-bladed chopping tool. Also, axe.

ax·i·om, *n.* statement accepted as a basic truth. —ax"i·o·mat'ic, *adj.*

ax'is, *n., pl.* axes. line on which something is centered or rotates. —ax'i·al, *adj.*

ax'le, *n.* shaft on which a wheel turns.

ay"a·tol'lah, *n.* Shi'ite Muslim religious leader.

aye (ī), *adv., n.* yes, esp. in voting.

a·zal'ea, *n.* flowering shrub.

az'ure, *n.* sky blue.

B

B, b, *n.* **1.** second letter of the English alphabet. **2.** second-best grade.

bab'ble, *v.,* -bled, -bling, *n. v.t., v.i.* **1.** speak unclearly or meaninglessly. —*n.* **2.** unclear or meaningless spoken words or sounds. —**bab'bler,** *n.*

babe, *n.* baby.

ba'boon, *n.* large monkey.

ba'by, *n., pl.* -bies, *v.t.,* -bied, -bving. *n.* **1.** very young child. **2.** infantile person. —*v.t.* **3.** treat with excessive care or indulgence. —**ba'by·ish,** *adj.* —**ba'by·hood,** *n.*

bac'ca·lau're·ate, *n.* bachelor's degree.

bach'e·lor, *n.* **1.** unmarried man. **2.** person holding the lowest academic degree. —**bach'e·lor·hood'',** *n.*

ba·cil'lus (bə sil'ləs), *n., pl.* **bacilli** (bə sil' ī). rod-shaped bacterium.

back, *n.* **1.** part of a person opposite the face. **2.** uppermost part of an animal. **3.** side of an object opposite that usually faced; rear. **4.** spine. —*adj.* **5.** at the rear. **6.** related to the past. —*adv.* **7.** toward the rear. **8.** into the past. **9.** in return. —*v.t.* **10.** sponsor; support. —*v.t., v.i.* **11.** move backwards. —**back'er,** *n.* —**back'ing,** *n.*

back'bite'', *v.t., v.i.* slander, esp. someone absent. —**back'bit''er,** *n.*

back'bone', *n.* **1.** spine. **2.** strength of character.

back'fire', *v.i.* **1.** fire prematurely, as an engine. **2.** have adverse results, as a plan. —*n.* **3.** premature firing of an engine.

back'ground', *n.* **1.** area at the rear of a scene. **2.** information generally useful in a given situation. **3.** origin, experience or environment.

back'lash, *n.* sudden or sharp reaction.

back'log'', *n.* accumulation.

back'slide'', *v.i.,* -slid, -slidden or -slid, -sliding. forget good resolutions. —**back'slid''er,** *n.*

back talk, *Informal.* insolent reply.

back'ward, *adv.* Also, **back'wards, 1.** toward the rear. **2.** back foremost. **3.** toward the past. —*adj.* **4.** toward the rear or the past. **5.** not sufficiently advanced. —**back'ward·ly,** *adv.* —**back'ward·ness,** *n.*

back'woods', *n., pl.* region of sparsely settled forest. —**back'woods'man,** *n.*

ba'con, *n.* cured meat from the back and sides of a hog.

bac·ter'i·a, *n., pl.* of **bacterium.** microscopic vegetable organism. —**bac·te'ri·al,** *adj.* —**bac·te'ri·al·ly,** *adv.*

bac·te''ri·ol'o·gy, *n.* study of bacteria. —**bac·te''ri·ol·og'i·cal,** *adj.* —**bac·te''ri·ol'o·gist,** *n.*

bad, *adj.,* worse, *n., v.t. adj.* **1.** unfavorable evil, or unacceptable. —*n.* **2.** condition or realm of that which is bad. —*v.t.* **3.** Also, **bade.** Past tense of **bid.** —**bad'ly,** *adv.* —**bad'ness,***n.*

badge, *n.* object worn as a symbol of authority or distinction.

bad'ger, *n.* **1.** burrowing animal. —*v.t.* **2.** torment.

bad·i·nage (bad''ə nahzh'), *n.* teasing conversation.

bad'min·ton, *n.* game played with rackets.

baf'fle, *v.t.,* -fled, -fling, *n. v.t.* **1.** confuse. —*n.* **2.** passage made to divert or stop sound, light, etc. —**baf'fling,** *adj.* —**baf'fling·ly,** *adv.*

bag, *n., v.,* bagged, bagging. *n.* **1.** flexible container open at one end. **2.** purse. **3.** suitcase. —*v.t.* **4.** put into bags. **5.** kill. esp. in sport. —*v.i.* **6.** bulge.

bag'gage, *n.* containers for things taken on a journey.

bag'gy, *adj.* irregularly bulging. —**bag'gi·ness,** *n.*

bag'pipe'', *n., often pl.* reed musical instrument played with air under pressure in a bag. —**bag'pip''er,** *n.*

bail, *n., v. n.* **1.** security for temporary release of a prisoner. **2.** suspension handle. —*v.t.* **3.** have released temporarily by putting up security. **4.** empty of water with a vessel. —*v.i.* **5.** bail out, escape by parachute. —**bail'a·ble,** *adj.*

bail'iff, *n.* **1.** deputy sheriff. **2.** officer keeping order in a court.

bail'i·wick, *n.* **1.** area of a bailiff's authority. **2.** any area of authority or competence.

bait, *n.* **1.** something used as an attraction in trapping or fishing. —*v.t.* **2.** supply with bait. **3.** harass, as with dogs.

bake, *v.,* ked, baking. *v.t., v.i.* cook or harden with dry heat. —**bak'er,** *n.*

bak'er·y, *n., pl.* -eries. **1.** place for baking food made with flour, etc. **2.** place where such food is sold.

bal'ance, *n., v.,* -anced, -ancing. *n.* **1.** state of rest due to equal leverage around a point or line. **2.** state of harmony, stability, etc. **3.** weighing device. **4.** remainder from a subtraction. —*v.t.* **5.** put in balance. **6.** compare or contrast. **7.** review, as accounts. —*v.i.* **8.** come into or be in balance.

bal'co·ny, *n., pl.* -nies. **1.** floor area projecting from a building. **2.** interior floor area overlooking a lower floor.

bald, *n.* **1.** without hair. **2.** without dis-

guise or mitigation. —**bald'ly**, *adv.* —**bald'ness**, *n.*

bale, *n.*, *v.t.* **baled**, **baling**. *n.* 1. large compressed or tied bundle. —*v.t.* 2. make into bales.

bale'ful, *adj.* hostile; evil. —**bale'ful·ly**, *adv.* —**bale'ful·ness**, *n.*

balk (bawk), *v.i.* 1. refuse to act. 2. be daunted. —*v.t.* 3. obstruct. —*n.* 4. obstruction. —**balk'y**, *adj.*

ball, *n.* 1. evenly rounded object; sphere. 2. game or games played with such a solid. 3. an entertainment of dancing. —*v.t.* 4. form into spheres.

bal'lad, *n.* 1. narrative song or poem. 2. sentimental song.

bal'last, *n.* 1. weighty material used for stability. —*v.t.* 2. supply with ballast.

ball bearing, machinery bearing rotating on steel balls.

bal''le·ri'na, *n.* leading female ballet dancer.

bal·let (bal lā'), *n.* entertainment by dancers, esp. one acting out a story.

bal·lis'tics, *n.* study of the motion and behavior of projectiles. —**bal·lis'tic**, *adj.*

bal·loon', *n.* 1. baglike lighter-than-air vehicle with no engine or steering mechanism. —*v.i.* 2. travel in balloons. —**bal·loon'ist**, *n.*

bal'lot, *n.* 1. paper for indicating a vote. 2. collective vote for a candidate, proposal, etc.

ball'room, *n.* room for social dancing.

bal'ly·hoo'', *n. Informal.* ostentatious publicity.

balm (bahm), *n.* 1. healing or soothing substance. 2. anything that heals or soothes.

balm'y, *adj.*, **balmier**, **balmiest.** soothing or refreshing. —**balm'i·ness**, *n.*

bal·sa (bawl'sə), *n.* lightweight wood of a tropical American tree, used for model-making, etc.

bal'sam, *n.* aromatic resin from certain trees. —**bal·sam'ic**, *adj.*

bal'us·ter, *n.* columnlike support for a railing.

bal'us·trade'', *n.* railing supported by balusters.

bam·boo', *n.* tall tropical grass with hollow woodlike stems.

bam·boo'zle, *v.t. Informal.* mystify or cheat.

ban, *v.t.*, **banned**, **banning**, *n.* *v.t.* 1. forbid. —*n.* 2. act or instance of forbidding.

ba'nal, *adj.* boringly ordinary. —**ba·nal'i·ty**, *n.*

ba·nan'a, *n.* 1. treelike tropical plant. 2. fruit from this plant.

band, *n.* 1. strip of binding material. 2. stripe. 3. group of wind and percussion musicians. 4. informal group, esp. of armed persons. —*v.t.* 5. mark with bands. —*v.i.* 6. gather or unite. —**band'mas''ter**, *n.* —**bands'man**, *n.* —**band'stand''**, *n.*

band'age, *n.*, *v.t.*, **-aged**, **-aging**, *n.* 1. strip of cloth, etc., esp. for covering a wound. —*v.t.* 2. tie with a bandage.

ban·dan'na, *n.* printed cloth for the head or neck. Also, **ban·dan'a.**

ban'dit, *n.* armed robber. —**ban'dit·ry**, *n.*

band'wag''on, *n.* 1. wagon for the musicians in a circus parade. 2. obviously winning side of a controversy.

ban'dy, *v.t.*, **-died**, **-dying**, *adj.* *v.t.* 1. exchange rapidly, as words. 2. send back and forth rapidly, as a tennis ball. —*adj.* 3. bowed, as legs.

bane, *n.* evil or destructive influence.

bane'ful, *adj.* destructive. —**bane'ful·ly**, *adv.* —**bane'ful·ness**, *n.*

bang, *n.* 1. loud noise, as from an explosion or collision. 2. Often, **bangs**, short hair across the forehead. —*v.i.* 3. make a loud noise. 4. strike.

ban'gle, *n.* decorative band for the wrist or ankle.

ban'ish, *v.t.* drive away; exile. —**ban'ish·ment**, *n.*

ban'ister, *n.* stair railing.

ban'jo, *n.* plucked stringed instrument with circular body. —**ban'jo·ist**, *n.*

bank, *n.* 1. shore of a river or lake. 2. slope. 3. long mound. 4. tilt, as a vehicle or its supporting surface at a turn. 5. organization for the saving and lending of money. —*v.t.* 6. heap up. 7. tilt while turning. 8. put into a bank. 9. cover partly, as a fire. —*v.i.* 10. have a bank account.

bank'er, *n.* proprietor or officer of a bank.

bank'ing, *n.* 1. operation of a bank or banks. —*adj.* 2. pertaining to the activities of banks.

bank'rupt'', *adj.* 1. unable to pay debts. 2. without resources. —*n.* 3. bankrupt person. —*v.t.* 4. make bankrupt. —**bank'rupt·cy**, *n.*

ban'ner, *n.* flag.

banns, *n.*, *pl.* notice of a marriage to be performed. Also, **bans.**

ban'quet, *n.*, *v.i.*, **-queted**, **-queting**. *n.* 1. formal dinner or luncheon. —*v.i.* 2. participate in a banquet. —**ban'quet·er**, *n.*

ban'tam, *n.* 1. small fowl. —*adj.* 2. miniature; tiny.

ban'ter, *n.* 1. teasing. —*v.i.* 2. exchange teasing remarks. —**ban'ter·er**, *n.*

bap'tism, *n.* rite of initiation, as into a church. —**bap·tis'mal**, *adj.*

Bap'tist, *n.* Protestant baptized by immersion in water.

bap'tize, *v.t.*, **-ized**, **-izing.** initiate into a

church, esp. by sprinkling with or immersion in water.

bar, *n., v.t.,* **barred, barring,** *prep. n.* **1.** long round object, used in an enclosure as a lever, etc. **2.** stripe. **3.** obstruction. **4.** drinking place. **5.** counter for serving drinks. **6.** division of a musical composition. **7.** legal profession. —*v.t.* **8.** secure with a bar. **9.** exclude. **10.** obstruct. —*prep.* **11.** except for.

barb, *n.* **1.** sharp projection. —*v.t.* **2.** furnish with barbs.

bar·bar·i·an (bahr ber'ē ən), *n.* uncivilized person; savage. —**bar·bar'i·an·ism,** *n.*

bar·bar·ic (bahr ber'ik), *adj.* typical of or suggesting barbarians. —**bar·bar'i·cal·ly,** *adv.*

bar'bar·ism, *n.* barbaric act or state.

bar·bar·i·ty (bahr ber'ə tē), *n., pl.* **-ities. 1.** cruelty. **2.** barbaric state.

bar·bar·ous (bahr'bə rəs), *adj.* **1.** cruel. **2.** uncivilized. —**bar'bar·ous·ly,** *adv.* —**bar'bar·ous·ness,** *n.*

barbed, *adj.* **1.** having sharp projections. **2.** harsh, as a remark; caustic.

bar·bi·tu·rate (bahr bi'tshə rət), *n.* sedative.

bard, *n.* **1.** Celtic poet. **2.** any minstrel or poet. —**bard'ic,** *adj.*

bare, *adj.,* **barer, barest,** *v.t.,* **bared baring.** *adj.* **1.** uncovered or unconcealed. **2.** unfurnished. **3.** mere. —*v.t.* **4.** strip of covering or concealment. —**bare'ness,** *n.*

bare'back", *adv., adj.* without a saddle.

bare'faced", *adj.* **1.** shameless. **2.** with an uncovered face.

bare'ly, *adv.* **1.** by the smallest possible amount. **2.** nakedly.

bar'gain, *n.* **1.** business agreement. **2.** advantageous purchase. —*v.i.* **3.** reach or attempt to reach a business agreement. —**bar'gain·er,** *n.*

barge, *n., v,* **barged, barging.** *n.* **1.** slow freight-carrying boat. **2.** ceremonial barge carrying royalty, etc. —*v.t.* **3.** carry by barge. —*v.i.* **4. barge in,** *Informal.* intrude. —**barge'man,** *n.*

bar'i·tone", *n.* **1.** musical range between tenor and bass. **2.** singer, instrument or part with this range.

bark, *n.* **1.** short utterance of a dog. **2.** covering of the stem of a tree or shrub. **3.** sailing vessel square-rigged on all but the last of three or more masts. —*v.t.* **4.** utter in a barklike tone. **5.** utter a bark. **6.** strip bark from. **7.** skin by accident.

bar'ley, *n.* grass with edible grain.

barn, *n.* building for crop storage, keeping of cows, etc. —**barn'yard",** *n.*

bar'na·cle, *n.* shellfish that clings to ship bottoms, etc.

ba·rom'e·ter, *n.* device for measuring atmospheric pressure and thus foretell-

ing weather changes. —**bar"o·met'ric, bar"o·met'ri·cal,** *adj.*

bar'on, *n.* low-ranking noble. Also, *fem.,* **bar'on·ess.** —**bar'on·age,** *n.* —**ba·ro'ni·al,** *adj.*

bar'on·et, *n.* titled British commoner. —**bar'on·et·cy,** *n.*

Ba·roque', *n.* florid style in architecture, etc. in the 17th century. Also, **ba·roque'.**

bar'rack, *n.* **1.** Usually, **barracks, dormitory for soldiers.** —*v.t.* **2.** house in barracks.

bar·ra·cu·da (bar"rə k͞o͞o'də), *n., pl.* **-da, —das.** pikelike tropical fish.

bar·rage (bar rahzh'), *n.* defensive barrier of artillery fire, captive balloons, etc.

bar'rel, *n., v.,* **-reled, -reling.** *n.* **1.** container, usually wood, with circular ends and bulging sides. **2.** measure of about 31 gallons. —*v.t.* **3.** put into barrels. —*v.i.* **4.** *Informal.* move at high speed.

bar'ren, *adj.* **1.** unable to support plant life. **2.** unable to bear children. **3.** profitless. —**bar'ren·ness,** *n.*

bar·ri·cade", *n., v.t.,* **-caded, -cading.** *n.* **1.** obstruction, as to military advance. —*v.t.* **2.** defend or shut off with a barricade.

bar'ri·er, *n.* obstruction.

bar'ring, *prep.* excepting; aside from.

bar'row, *n.* **1.** hand-held frame for carrying loads. **2.** wheelbarrow.

bar'ter, *n., v.t., v.i.* trade with goods or services alone.

ba·salt (bə sahlt', bā'sahlt), *n.* dark volcanic rock. —**ba·sal'tic,** *adj.*

base, *n., v.t.,* **based, basing,** *adj. n.* **1.** part on which a thing rests or stands. **2.** basis. **3.** principal ingredient. **4.** center of military operations. —*v.t.* **5.** give a basis or foundation to. —*adj.* **6.** contemptible. **7.** inferior, as a metal. —**base'ly,** *adv.* —**base'ness,** *n.*

base'ball", *n.* **1.** game played in a diamond-shaped field with a batted ball. **2.** ball used in this game.

base'less, *adj.* unfounded in fact.

base'ment, *n.* **1.** lowermost part of a building. **2.** cellar.

bash, *v.t. Informal.* hit, as with a club.

bash'ful, *adj.* shy. —**bash'ful·ly,** *adv.* —**bash'ful·ness,** *n.*

bas'ic, *adj.* **1.** most important or significant; essential. —*n.* **2. basics,** most important or significant features. —**bas'i·cal·ly,** *adv.*

bas·il (baz'əl), *n.* herb of the mint family.

ba'sin, *n.* **1.** shallow bowl for liquids. **2.** pool. **3.** area drained by a river.

ba'sis, *n., pl.* **-ses. 1.** something on which a thing depends. **2.** main ingredient.

bask, *v.i.* **1.** lie in warmth. **2.** enjoy favor, etc.

bas'ket, *n.* container of woven wood, wire, etc.

bas'ket·ball'', *n*. **1.** game in which a ball is tossed over a hoop into a suspended net. **2.** ball used in this game.

bass, *n*. **1.** (bās) lowermost musical range. **2.** singer, instrument, or part with this range. **3.** (bas), *pl*. **basses, bass.** spiny-finned edible fish.

bas''si·net', *n*. basketlike bed for a baby.

bas·soon', *n*. bass woodwind. —**bas·soon'ist,** *n*.

bas'tard, *n*. **1.** person born out of wedlock. **2.** *Informal.* harsh or malicious person. —*adj.* **3.** born out of wedlock. **4.** not authentic. —**bas'tard·y,** *n*.

baste, *v.t.,* **basted, basting. 1.** sew temporarily. **2.** cover with juices, etc. while cooking. —**bast'ing,** *n*.

bat, *n., v.,* **batted, batting.** *n.* **1.** club used for striking a ball, as in baseball or cricket. **2.** nocturnal flying mammal. —*v.t.* **3.** hit with a bat. —*v.i.* **4.** have a turn batting.

batch, *n*. quantity of material prepared or gathered at one time.

bath, *n., pl.* **baths. 1.** complete washing or immersion. **2.** liquid for immersion or washing. —**bath'room'',** *n.* —**bath'tub'',** *n*.

bathe, *n.,* **bathed, bathing.** *n.i.* **1.** take a bath. **2.** go swimming, esp. in an ocean or lake. —*v.t.* **3.** give a bath to. —**bath'er,** *n*.

ba'thos, *n*. **1.** ridiculous anticlimax. **2.** insincere sentimentality.

bath'robe', *n*. robe used before and after bathing.

ba·ton', *n*. staff used for directing musicians, as a badge of office, etc.

bat·tal'ion, *n*. subdivision of a military division.

bat'ten, *n*. **1.** thin strip of wood. —*v.t.* **2.** secure or cover with battens. —*v.i.* **3.** thrive.

bat'ter, *v.t.* **1.** hit or attack repeatedly. —*n.* **2.** person who bats. **3.** cake mixture.

bat'ter·y, *n., pl.* **-ies. 1.** device for storing electricity. **2.** group of cannon used together. **3.** group of any machines, etc. used together. **4.** *Law.* illegal beating.

bat'ting, *n*. fiber packed in sheets.

bat'tle, *n., v.,* **-tled, -tling.** *n.* **1.** major military encounter. **2.** warfare. —*v.t., v.i.* **3.** fight. —**bat'tle·field'',** *n*.

bat'tle·ment'', *n.* defensive wall with openings for shooting.

bat'tle·ship'', *n*. warship with heavy guns and armor.

bau'ble, *n*. trinket.

bawd'y, *adj.,* **-ier, -iest.** obscene. —**bawd'i·ness,** *n*.

bawl, *v.i.* **1.** yell. **2.** weep loudly.

bay, *n*. **1.** distinct area of a wall. **2.** broad inlet, esp. of a sea. **3. at bay, a.** unable to escape. **b.** unable to attack. —*v.i.* **4.** give prolonged howls.

bay'o·net'', *n., v.t.,* **-netted, -netting.** *n.* **1.** sharp thrusting weapon attached to a gun muzzle. —*v.t.* **2.** stab with a bayonet.

bay'ou, *n*. marshy area of a river or lake, esp. in Louisiana.

bay window, window jutting from a building, esp. a window with its own foundations.

ba·zaar', *n*. **1.** Near Eastern salesplace. **2.** temporary sale, esp. for charity.

be, *v.i.* **was** or **were, been, being. 1.** exist: often refers to an adjective describing the subject. **2.** occur. **3.** continue. **4.** (Used variously as an auxiliary verb).

beach, *n*. **1.** flat shore, esp. a sandy one. —*v.t.* **2.** haul onto a beach.

beach'comb''er, *n*. seaside scavenger.

bea'con, *n*. **1.** signal light. **2.** navigational radio station.

bead, *n*. **1.** small decorative ball. **2.** small drop. **3. draw a bead on,** take aim at.

bead'y, *adj.,* **-ier, -iest.** beadlike; small and shiny.

beak, *n*. **1.** pointed mouth, esp. of a bird. **2.** projection suggesting this.

beam, *n*. **1.** horizontal structural member. **2.** shaft of light. **3.** steady radio or radar signal. **4.** width of a ship. —*v.t.* **5.** send as a radio or radar beam. —*v.i.* **6.** shine. **7.** smile kindly.

bean, *n*. any of various edible seeds.

bear, *v.t.* **1.** carry. **2.** endure. **3.** suffer. **4.** give birth to. **5.** produce. —*v.i.* **6.** head or move in a stated direction. **7. bear with,** be patient with. —*n.* **8.** large shaggy mammal. **9.** speculator in the fall of stock prices. —**bear'er,** *n*. —**bear'a·ble,** *adj*.

beard, *n*. **1.** hair on the lower jaw, etc. —*v.t.* **2.** intrude upon and confront. —**beard'ed,** *adj*.

bear'ing, *n*. **1.** posture or attitude. **2.** support for a rotating part. **3. bearings,** orientation.

beast, *n*. **1.** large animal. **2.** cruel or uncouth person.

beast'ly, *adj.,* **-lier, -liest.** nasty. —**beast'li·ness,** *n*.

beat, *v.,* **beat, beaten, beating,** *n. v.t.* **1.** hit with force. **2.** win against. **3.** move vigorously back and forth, as arms or wings. —*v.i.* **4.** throb, as the heart. —*n.* **5.** marked rhythm. **6.** unit of such a rhythm. **7.** regular round, as that of a policeman.

be''a·tif'ic, *adj.* **1.** blissful. **2.** imparting blessings.

beat'ing, *n*. **1.** act or instance of hitting, esp. a person or animal. **2.** defeat.

beau, *n., pl.* **beaus, beaux.** suitor.

beau'ti·ful, *adj.* having beauty. Also, **beau'te·ous.** —**beau'ti·ful·ly,** *adv*.

beau'ti·fy'', *v.t.,* **-fied, -fying.** make beautiful. —**beau''ti·fi·ca'tion,** *n*.

beau'ty, *n., pl.* **-ties. 1.** quality sensed in

that which is in perfect harmony. **2.** beautiful woman.

bea′ver, *n.* broad-tailed, dam-building rodent.

be·calm′, *v.t.* halt from a lack of wind in sails.

be·cause′, *conj.* **1.** for the reason that. **2.** because of, as a result of.

beck′on, *v.i.* **1.** make a summoning gesture. —*v.t.* **2.** summon with a gesture.

be·come′, *v.,* **-came, -come, -coming.** *v.i.* **1.** come to be as specified. —*v.t.* **2.** be suitable to.

be·com′ing, *adj.* **1.** suitable; seemly. **2.** attractively appropriate, as clothing. —be·com′ing·ly, *adv.*

bed, *n., v.,* **bedded, bedding.** *n.* **1.** object to lie upon. **2. to bed,** to rest in a lying position. **3. into bed,** beneath the upper bedclothes of a bed. **4.** layer of rock, etc. **5.** layer of surface soil, as for flowers. **6.** foundation for machinery. **7.** bottom of a body of water. —*v.t.* **8.** put into a bed. —*v.i.* **9.** go to or into bed. —bed′cov″er, *n.* —bed′fel″low, *n.* —bed′room″, *n.* —bed′side″, *n., adj.* —bed′spread″, *n.* —bed′spring″, *n.* —bed′time″, *n.*

be·daz′zle, *v.t.,* **-zled, -zling.** dazzle; amaze.

bed′clothes″, *n., pl.* sheets, covers, etc. for a bed.

bed′ding, *n.* all movable objects used with a bed.

be·dev′il, *v.t.,* **-iled, -iling.** harass; torment. —be·dev′il·ment, *n.*

bed′lam, *n.* chaotic situation.

be″drag′gle, *v.t.,* **-gled, -gling.** soil as by dragging through mud.

bed′rid″den, *adj.* confined to bed by permanent illness or feebleness. Also, **bed′fast″.**

bed′rock″, *n.* uppermost layer of solid rock.

bed′stead″, *n.* framework for bedding.

bee, *n.* **1.** four-winged, pollen-gathering insect. **2.** social meeting for joint work or competition. —bee′hive″, *n.* —bee′keep″er, *n.* —bee′keep″ing, *n.* —bees′wax″, *n.*

beech, *n.* hardwood tree.

beef, *n., pl.* **beeves** or **beefs. 1.** meat from cows, steers, etc. **2.** any such animal. —beef′steak″, *n.*

beef′y, *adj.* **-ier, -iest.** muscular; brawny.

bee′line″, *n.* straight route.

beer, *n.* **1.** drink of fermented malt, hops, etc. **2.** any of various soft drinks made from plants.

beet, *n.* plant with an edible root.

beet′le, *n.* **1.** insect with hard wings. **2.** large mallet. —*adj.* **3.** Also, **beet′ling.** overhanging. —bee′tle-browed″, *adj.*

be·fall′, *v.i.,* **-fell, -fallen.** happen.

be·fit′, *v.t.,* **-fitted, -fitting.** be suitable to. —be·fit′ting, *adj.* —be·fit′ting·ly, *adv.*

be·fore′, *prep.* **1.** at an earlier time than. **2.** in front of. **3.** in preference to. —*adv.* **4.** at an earlier time. **5.** in front. —*conj.* **6.** earlier than the time that something happens. **7.** rather than.

be·fore′hand″, *adv.* **1.** in advance. —*adj.* **2.** ahead of time.

be·foul′, *v.t.* make foul.

be·friend′, *v.t.* act as a friend to.

beg, *v.,* **begged, begging.** *v.t., v.i.* ask as a favor.

beg′gar, *n.* **1.** person who asks strangers for his livelihood. —*v.t.* **2.** impoverish. **3.** render inadequate, esp. any description of a thing. —beg′gar·y, *n.*

beg′gar·ly, *adj.* miserably inadequate.

be·gin′, *v.,* **began, begun.** *v.t., v.i.* start commence. —be·gin′ning, *n.*

be·gin′ner, *n.* **1.** person who begins. **2.** completely inexperienced person.

be·grudge′, *v.t.,* **-grudged, -grudging.** resent another's having or receiving. —be·grudg′ing·ly, *adv.*

be·guile′, *v.t.,* **-guiled, -guiling. 1.** charm. **2.** while away pleasantly. —be·guile′ment, *n.*

be·half′, *n.* **in** or **on behalf of, a.** in the name of. **b.** in support of.

be·have′, *v.,* **-haved, -having.** *v.i.* **1.** conduct oneself properly —*v.t.* **2.** conduct in a specified way. **3.** conduct properly. —be·hav′ior, *n.*

be·hest′, *n.* command; urging.

be·hind′, *prep.* **1.** at the rear of. **2.** at or to the far side of. **3.** too late or slow for. **4.** in defense or support of. **5.** concealed by. —*adv.* **6.** at the rear. **7.** into a state of lateness or slowness.

be·hold′, *v.t.,* **-held, -held, -holding.** see; look at. —be·hold′er, *n.*

be·hold′en, *adj.* indebted.

be·hoove′, *v.t.,* **-hooved -hooving.** obligate.

be′ing, *n.* **1.** existence. **2.** essential nature. **3.** something alive.

be·la′bor, *v.t.* attack by or as if by beating.

be·lat′ed, *adj.* later than expected or desirable. —be·lat′ed·ly, *adv.*

belch, *v.i.* **1.** emit stomach gas through the mouth. —*v.t.* **2.** emit violently, as smoke. —*n.* **3.** act or instance of belching.

be·lea′guer, *v.t.* harass, as by a siege.

bel′fry (bel′frē), *n., pl.* **fries.** tower or turret for bells.

be·lie′, *v.t.,* **-lied, -lying. 1.** represent deceptively. **2.** prove as false.

be·lieve′, *v.,* **-lieved, -lieving.** *v.t.* **1.** accept as true or truthful. **2.** guess to be so. —*v.i.* **3.** have faith. **4.** accept the existence of something. —be·lief′, *n.* —be·liev′er, *n.* —be·liev′able, *adj.*

be·lit′tle, *v.t.,* **-tled, -tling.** treat as of minor importance. —be·lit′tle·ment, *n.*

bell, *n.* **1.** hollow instrument, usually metal, that sounds when struck. **2.** something having the characteristic flared shape of this. **3.** *Nautical.* half-hour unit of time.

belle, *n.* attractive woman.

belles''-let'tres, *n., pl.* literature as an art.

bel'li·cose'', *adj.* warlike. —**bel'li·cos''i·ty**, *n.*

bel·lig'er·ent, *adj.* **1.** eager to fight. **2.** at war. —*n.* **3.** nation, etc. at war. —**bel'lig'er·ence, bel'lig'er·en·cy**, *n.*

bel'low, *v.t., n.* **1.** shout or roar. *n.* **2.** bellows, device for pumping air to a hearth.

bel'ly, *n., pl.* **-lies**, *v.i.*, **-lied, lying.** *n.* **1.** stomach. **2.** human abdomen. **3.** animal's underside. —*v.i.* **4.** swell.

be·long', *v.i.* **1.** be property. **2.** be a member, citizen, etc. of something. **3.** be appropriate.

be·long'ings, *n., pl.* possessions.

be·lov'ed, *adj.* **1.** loved. —*n.* **2.** loved one.

be·low', *prep.* **1.** lower than; under. **2.** inferior in worth or amount to. —*adv., adj.* **3.** to or in some lower place. **4.** later, as in a book. **5.** *Nautical.* on or to a lower deck.

belt, *n.* **1.** strap worn around the waist, over the chest, etc. **2.** long, narrow region, road, etc. **3.** strap for driving machinery. **4.** *Informal.* violent blow. —*v.t.* **5.** *Informal.* **a.** hit violently. **b.** sing emphatically.

be·moan', *v.t.* lament.

be·muse', *v.t.*, **-mused, -musing.** put in a thoughtful or bewildered frame of mind.

bench, *n.* **1.** broad seat or stool. **2.** massive worktable. **3.** judge's seat. **4. the bench**, jurisprudence. —*v.t.* **5.** put on a bench.

bend, *v.*, **bent, bending,** *n. v.t.* **1.** form as a curved or angled shape, esp. by force. **2.** bow or stoop. **3.** submit oneself. —*n.* **4.** bent section. **5.** curve, as in a road or river.

be·neath', *prep.* **1.** under. **2.** unworthy of. —*adj., adv.* **3.** underneath.

ben''e·dic'tion, *n.* blessing.

ben''e·fac'tion, *n.* act or instance of charity.

ben'e·fac''tor, *n.* conferrer of benefactions. Also, *fem.,* **ben'e·fac''tress.**

be·nef'i·cent, *adj.* doing good. —**be·nef'i·cence**, *n.* —**be·nef'i·cent·ly**, *adv.*

ben''e·fi'cial, *adj.* useful; advantageous. —**be''ne·fi'cial·ly**, *adv.*

ben''e·fi'ci·ar·y, *n., pl.* **-aries.** enjoyer of a benefit.

ben'e·fit, *n., v.t.*, **-fitted, -fitting.** *n.* **1.** advantage. **2.** entertainment to raise funds for charity, etc. **3.** payment from insurance, etc. —*v.t.* **4.** be of advantage to.

be·nev'o·lent, *adj.* kindly; well-intentioned. —**be·nev'o·lent·ly**, *adv.* —**be·nev'o·lence**, *n.*

be·night'ed, *adj.* **1.** lacking enlightenment. **2.** hampered or surrounded by darkness.

be·nign', *adj.* **1.** friendly; well-intentioned. **2.** *Medicine.* not malignant. —**be·nign'ly**, *adv.* —**be·nig'ni·ty**, *n.*

be·nig'nant, *adj.* **1.** benevolent. **2.** beneficial.

be·queath', *v.t.* transfer to heirs. —**be·quest'**, *n.*

be·rate', *v.t.* **-rated, -rating.** scold.

be·reave', *v.t.*, **-reft, -reaving. 1.** leave sorrowful, esp. by dying. **2.** deprive; strip. —**be·reave'ment**, *n.*

be·ret' (bə rā'), *n.* soft, flat, visorless cloth cap.

berm, *n.* earth embankment. Also, **berme.**

ber'ry, *n., pl.* **-ries. 1.** juicy cover for a seed or seeds. **2.** dried seed of a coffee plant, etc.

ber·serk', *adv., adj.* in violent frenzy.

berth, *n.* **1.** shelflike bed. **2.** job. **3.** ship's mooring place.

ber'yl, *n.* class of hard stone: includes emeralds and aquamarines.

be·seech', *v.t.*, **-sought, or -seeched, seeching.** request earnestly. —**be·seech'ing·ly**, *adv.*

be·set', *v.t.*, **-set, -setting.** harass.

be·set'ting, *adj.* obsessive, as a sin.

be·side', *prep.* **1.** at the side of. **2.** compared with. **3.** added to. **4.** irrelevant to.

be·sides', *adv.* **1.** in addition; else. —*prep.* **2.** in addition to; other than.

be·siege', *v.t.*, **-sieged, -sieging. 1.** lay siege to. **2.** distract repeatedly.

be·smirch', *v.t.* mark or soil.

be·speak', *v.t.*, **-spoke, -spoken or -spoke, speaking. 1.** speak for ahead of time; reserve. **2.** be eloquent of; reveal.

best, *adj.* **1.** superlative of *good.* **2.** major; greater. —*adv.* **3.** superlative of *well.* **4.** that which is best. **5.** one's utmost.

bes'ti·al, *adj.* savage. —**bes'ti·al'i·ty**, *n.*

be·stir', *v.t.*, **-stirred, -stirring.** rouse to action.

best man, groom's ring bearer at a wedding.

be·stow', *v.t.* give or grant. —**be·stow'al**, *n.*

bet, *n., v.*, **betted, betting.** *n.* **1.** guess on the unpredictable outcome of an event, made to gain money, etc. **2.** money, etc. put up to back one's guess. **3.** possible guess or action regarding an unpredictable matter. —*v.t.* **4.** put up to

back one's bet. **5.** guess in betting. —*v.i.* **6.** make a bet.

be·tray′, *v.t.* **1.** be treacherous to. **2.** reveal, as a secret. **3.** seduce with a false promise of marriage. **4.** reveal involuntarily. —**be·tray′al**, *n.*

be·troth′al, *n.* engagement to marry.

be·trothed′, *n.* fiancé or fiancée.

bet′ter, *adj.* **1.** comparative of *good.* **2.** major; greater. —*adv.* **3.** comparative of *well.* —*n.* **4.** social superior. **5.** that which is better. **6.** Also, **bet′tor**, person who bets.

bet′ter·ment, *n.* improvement.

be·tween′, *prep.* **1.** with two specified persons or things, one on each side. **2.** involving or relating two persons or things. **3.** as a result of two specified causes. **4.** from either one of, in choosing. **5.** as a secret shared by two persons.

bev′el, *n.* **1.** outer edge formed as a diagonal. —*v.t.* **2.** form as such a diagonal.

bev′er·age, *n.* something to drink other than water.

be·ware′, *v.,* **-wared, -waring.** *v.i.* **1.** be cautious. —*v.t.* **2.** be cautious of.

be·wil′der, *v.t.* confuse, esp. with surprise. —**be·wil′der·ment**, *n.*

be·witch′, *v.t.* **1.** cast a spell on. **2.** charm with delight.

be·yond′, *prep.* **1.** on the far side of. **2.** too late or advanced for. **3.** outside the power or domain of. **4.** after; past. —*adv.* **5.** further away.

bi·an′nu·al, *adj.* twice a year. —**bi·an′nu·al·ly**, *adv.*

bib, *n.* apronlike cloth to catch dribbles.

bib″li·og′ra·phy, *n., pl.* **-phies.** list of books, articles, etc. used, recommended, or in existence. —**bib″li·og′ra·pher**, *n.* —**bib″li·o·graph′i·cal**, *adj.*

bib′u·lous, *adj.* fond of alcoholic beverages.

bi·cam′er·al, *adj.* composed of two legislative chambers.

bick′er, *v.i.* quarrel over trifles. —**bick′er·er**, *n.*

bi′cy·cle, *n.* two-wheeled vehicle for a balancing rider. —**bi′cy·clist, bi′cy·cler**, *n.*

bid, *n., v.,* **bid, bad** or (for 4 and 6) **bade, bid** or (for 4 and 6) **bidden, bidding.** *n.* **1.** offer for an auctioned item. **2.** offer to fulfill a contract for a stated sum. **3.** attempt to gain victory, favor, notice, etc. —*v.t.* **4.** command or ask. **5.** offer for an auctioned item. **6.** express, esp. a goodbye. —*v.i.* **7.** make a bid. —**bid′der**, *n.*

bier, *n.* support for a coffin.

bi·fo′cals, *n., pl.* spectacles whose lenses have two areas apiece, each with two focuses.

big, *adj.,* **bigger, biggest. 1.** great in size or amount. **2.** full-grown. **3.** elder. **4.** important. —**big′ness**, *n.*

big′a·my, *n.* marriage to two spouses in a single period. —**big′a·mous**, *adj.* —**big′a·mist**, *n.*

big′ot, *n.* person with strong, intolerant, unreasoning attitudes. —**big′ot·ry**, *n.* —**big′ot·ed**, *adj.*

bike, *n. Informal.* bicycle.

bi·lat′er·al, *adj.* **1.** involving two sides or factions. **2.** reciprocal; mutual. —**bi·lat′er·al·ly**, *adv.*

bi·lin′gual, *adj.* **1.** familiar with two languages. **2.** expressed in two languages.

bil′ious, *adj.* ill-tempered.

bilk, *v.t.* cheat.

bill, *n.* **1.** itemized list or statement. **2.** written request for payment. **3.** printed announcement. **4.** piece of paper currency. **5.** beak of a bird. —*v.t.* request payment from in writing.

bill′board″, *n.* large board for advertising posters.

bil′let, *n.* **1.** job; position. **2.** order to house a soldier. **3.** accommodation obtained with such an order. —*v.t.* **4.** house with such an order.

bil″let-doux′, *n., pl.* **billets-doux.** love letter.

bill′fold″, *n.* wallet.

bil′liards, *n.* game using hard balls propelled by a cue.

bil′ling, *n.* public listing of entertainers on a program.

bil′lion, *n.* **1.** *U.S.* thousand million. **2.** *Great Britain.* million million. —**bil′lionth**, *adj.*

bill of fare, menu.

bil′low, *n.* **1.** swelling mass, as of water or smoke. —*v.i.* **2.** appear in billows. —**bil′low·y**, *adj.*

bi·month′ly, *adj.* every two months.

bin, *n.* large container for loose storage or display.

bi″na·ry, *adj.* of or pertaining to the mathematical base 2.

bind, *v.,* **bound, binding.** *v.t.* **1.** tie or fasten together. **2.** obligate. **3.** reinforce, as with tape. —*v.i.* **4.** stick fast or together. —**bind′er**, *n.* —**bind′ing**, *n.*

bin′na·cle, *n.* housing for a ship's compass.

bin·oc′u·lar, *n.* **1.** binoculars, twin telescopelike glasses, one for each eye —*adj.* **2.** pertaining to both eyes.

bi″o·chem′is·try, *n.* study of life processes as an aspect of chemistry.

bi″o·de·grad′able, *adj.* readily decomposed by bacteria.

bi·og′ra·phy *n., pl.* **phies.** story of a person's life or career. —**bi″o·graph′i·cal**, *adj.* —**bi·og′ra·pher**, *n.*

bi·ol′o·gy, *n.* study of animals and

plants. —bi''o·log'i·cal, *adj.* —bi·ol'o·gist, *n.*

bi·o''nics, *n.* the study of living systems for application to mechanical or electronic systems.

bi''o·phys'ics, *n.* study of biological phenomena as related to physics. —bi''o·phys'i·cal, *adj.* —bi''o·phys'i·cist, *n.*

bi'ped, *n.* two-footed animal.

birch, *n.* hardwood tree with smooth bark.

bird, *n.* warm-blooded, feathered, flying animal.

bird's-eye, *adj.* taken from high above, as a view.

birth, *n.* 1. emergence from a womb, egg, etc. 2. heredity. 3. origin or beginning. —birth'mark'', *n.* —birth'place'', *n.* —birth'rate'', *n.* —birth'right'', *n.*

birth'day'', *n.* anniversary of one's birth.

bis'cuit, *n., pl.* -cuits, -cuit. 1. small, hard-baked cookie or cracker. 2. breadlike lump eaten esp. with gravy.

bi'sect, *v.t.* divide in two parts, esp. equal ones.

bish'op, *n.* 1. clergyman overseeing a number of local churches or parishes. 2. chessman moving diagonally an unlimited number of squares. —bish'op·ric, *n.*

bi'son, *n.* shaggy, large North American mammal.

bit, *n.* 1. small piece or amount. 2. boring tool. 3. metal mouthpiece for controlling a horse. 4. (computers) one binary digit or piece of data.

bitch, *n.* 1. female dog. 2. *Informal.* disagreeable woman. —bitch'y, *adj.*

bite, *v.,* bit, bitten, biting, *n. v.t.* 1. close one's jaws firmly upon. 2. cut or eat into. —*v.i.* 3. make a biting motion. —*n.* 4. wound from being bitten. 5. snack. 6. ability to wound or disturb one's feelings.

bit'ing, *adj.* wounding to the feelings. —bit'ing·ly, *adv.*

bit'ter, *adj.* 1. harsh-tasting. 2. causing much suffering. 3. extremely resentful. —bit'ter·ly, *adv.* —bit'ter·ness, *n.*

bit'ter·sweet'', *adj.* causing both sadness and pleasure.

bituminous coal, soft coal, yielding tar when burned.

bi'valve'', *n.* mollusk with two hinged shells.

biv'ou·ac, *n., v.i.,* -acked, -acking. *n.* 1. temporary encampment. —*v.i.* 2. camp in a bivouac.

bi·week'ly, *adj., adv.* every two weeks.

bi·zarre', *adj.* odd; grotesque.

blab, *v.,* blabbed, blabbing, *n. v.t., v.i.* 1. reveal, as a secret. —*v.i.,* *n.* 2. chatter.

black, *n.* 1. perfectly dark color, opposite to white in shading. 2. something that is black, e.g. clothes. 3. person of central African descent; negro. —*adj.* 4.

of the color black. 5. negro. 6. dejected or sullen. 7. evil. —black'ness, *n.*

black'ball'', *v.t.* exclude or prevent from being a member.

black belt, belt denoting highest skill in karate or judo.

black'ber''ry, *n., pl.* ries. dark berry of various types of bramble.

black'bird'', *n.* bird whose male has black plumage.

black'board'', *n.* board of slate or other material for writing on with chalk.

black'en, *v.t.* 1. make black. 2. defame. —*v.i.* 3. become black.

black eye, 1. discoloration around the eye from a blow. 2. something causing disrepute.

black'jack'', *n.* 1. small, flexible club. 2. card game.

black'list'', *n.* 1. list of persons out of favor. —*v.t.* 2. put on such a list.

black'mail'', *n.* 1. extortion by threats, esp. to reveal harmful information. —*v.t.* 2. practice blackmail on. —black'mail''er, *n.*

black mark, something unfavorable recorded against one.

black market, unlawful system for selling legally restricted goods. —black marketeer.

black'out'', *n.* 1. putting-out of lights, as in a play or during an air raid. 2. sudden loss of consciousness.

black sheep, disreputable member, esp. of a family.

black'smith'', *n.* person who forges iron by hand.

blad'der, *n.* 1. sac for collecting and discharging body fluids. 2. any of various bags for air or liquid.

blade, *n.* 1. metal part with a cutting edge or point. 2. leaf, esp. of grass.

blame, *v.t.,* blamed, blaming, *n. v.t.* 1. accuse for a fault. 2. put the responsibility for on someone. 3. fail to sympathize with or understand. —*n.* 4. responsibility. —blame'less, *adj.* —blame'less·ly, *adv.* —blame'less·ness, *n.* —blame'wor''thy, *adj.*

blanch, *v.t., v.i.* turn pale or white.

blan'dish, *v.t.* flatter or coax. —blan'dish·ment, *n.*

blank, *adj.* 1. free of marks, as paper. 2. without thought, expression, etc. 3. unmitigated. 4. blank piece of paper. 5. blank space. 6. cartridge without a missile. 7. lapse of awareness. —blank'ly, *adv.* —blank'ness, *n.*

blank'et, *n.* 1. warm bedcover. 2. broad or thick cover. —*v.t.* 3. cover or obscure, as if with a blanket. —*adv.* 4. covering all or many possibilities.

blare, *v.,* blared, blaring, *n. v.t., v.i.* 1. sound loudly and harshly. —*n.* 2. loud, harsh sound. 3. ostentation.

blar'ney, *n.* wheedling, flattering talk.

bla·sé', *adj.* bored from over-familiarity.

blas·pheme′, v.t., -phemed, -pheming. speak sacrilegiously of. —**blas·phem′ er,**n. —**blas′phem·y**, n. —**blas′phem· ous,** adj.

blast, v.t. 1. shatter, as with lightning or explosives. 2. criticize harshly. —v.i. 3. blow violently. —n. 4. explosion or explosive force. 5. violent rush of air. 6. loud sound, as on a trumpet.

blast furnace, furnace for smelting iron, using a blast of air for draft.

blast′off″, n. departure of a rocket.

bla′tant, adj. shamelessly obvious. —**bla′ tant·ly,** adv. —**bla′tan·cy,** n.

blaze, v., blazed, blazing, n. v.t. 1. indicate the route of, esp. by cutting the bark of trees. —v.i. 2. burn brightly. —n. 3. bright fire. 4. brilliant display. 5. cut made on tree bark in blazing a trail.

blaz′er, n. jacket in a solid color, often with the badge of a school, etc.

bleach, v.t., v.i. 1. make or become light in color. —n. 2. something used for bleaching.

bleach′ers, n., pl. tiers of benches for spectators.

bleak, adj. 1. barren and gloomy. 2. unpromising; without hope. —**bleak′ly,** adv. —**bleak′ness,** n.

blear′y, adj., -ier, -iest. blurred, as the eyes.

bleat, v.i. 1. utter a light cry, as a goat or calf. —n. 2. cry made by such an animal.

bleed, v., bled, bleeding, v.i. 1. lose blood. 2. feel sympathetic grief. —v.t. 3. cause to lose blood. 4. practice embezzlement or extortion upon.

blem′ish, n. 1. skin flaw. 2. flaw or defacement. —v.t. 3. make or form a blemish upon.

blench, v.i. 1. become pale. 2. flinch.

blend, v., blended, blending, n. v.t. 1. mix. 2. shade into each other. —v.i. 3. mix. 4. harmonize. —n. 5. mixture. —**blend′er,** n.

bless, v.t., blessed, blessing. 1. invoke divine favor for. 2. approve heartily. 3. confer happiness upon. —**bles′sed,** adj. —**bles′sed·ly,** adv. —**bles′sed·ness,** n.

bles′sing, n. 1. invocation of divine favor. 2. approval. 3. favorable event or circumstance.

blight, n. 1. plant disease. 2. deterioration. 3. source of deterioration. —v.t. 4. put a blight on.

blimp, n. lighter-than-air vehicle without a rigid frame.

blind, adj. 1. without eyesight. 2. without perception. 3. closed at the end or rear. 4. hidden. 5. beyond human reason or control. —n. 6. device for shutting out light or view. 7. deceptive ruse. —v.t. 8. make blind. —**blind′ly,** adv. —**blind′ness,** n.

blind′fold″, n. 1. device to prevent a person temporarily from seeing. —v.t. 2. put a blindfold on.

blink, v.i. 1. wink repeatedly. 2. go on and off repeatedly, as a light. —v.t. 3. cause to blink.

bliss, n. intense, tranquil happiness. —**bliss′ful,** adj.

blis′ter, n. 1. raised area of skin enclosing watery matter. 2. anything similar in form. 3. form blisters on. —v.i. 4. become blistered.

blithe, adj. cheerful. —**blithe′ly,** adv. —**blithe′ness,** n.

blitz, n. sudden, massive attack.

bliz′zard, n. heavy storm of snow and wind.

bloat, v.t. swell abnormally.

blob, n. small, round form.

bloc, n. group of organizations or persons united in a common interest.

block, n. 1. thick, short piece of material. 2. auctioneer's platform. 3. Also, **blockage,** obstruction. 4. urban area bounded by streets. —v.t. 5. obstruct.

block·ade′, n., v.t., -aded, -ading. n. 1. barrier to navigation, created by warships, etc. —v.t. 2. impose such a barrier on.

block′head″, n. stupid person.

block′house″, n. fortified retreat.

blond, adj. 1. having light hair and skin. —n. 2. blond person. Also, fem., **blonde.**

blood, n. 1. fluid in the arteries of animals. 2. lineage. 3. temperament. 4. kinship. 5. bloodshed. —**blood′less,** adj.

blood′curd″ling, adj. horrifying.

blood′hound″, n. large hound tracking by scent.

blood′shed″, n. killing.

blood′shot″, adj. reddened from broken veins, as the eyes.

blood′tairst″y, adj. eager to kill. —**blood′thirst″i·ness,** n.

blood′y, adj., -ier, -iest. 1. covered with blood. 2. involving much bloodshed.

bloom, v.i. 1. put forth flowers. 2. be full of health or youth. —n. 3. flower. 4. period or state of flowering.

blos′som, n. 1. flower, esp. of a fruit. —v.i. 2. put forth blossoms.

blot, n., v., blotted, blotting. n. 1. stain, as from ink. 2. something that mars or discredits. —v.t. 3. stain. 4. efface. 5. dry, as writing in ink. —v.i. 6. make blots.

blotch, n. 1. skin discoloration. —v.t. 2. mark with blotches. —**blotch′y,** adj.

blot′ter, n. 1. sheet for blotting up excess ink. 2. log of events, esp. in a police station.

blouse, n. loose shirt.

blow, v., blew, blown, blowing, n. v.i. 1. move, as wind. 2. exhale with force. 3. **blow over, a.** pass by, as a storm. **b.**

cease to be troublesome, as a scandal. —*v.t.* 4. drive with wind or breath. 5. cause to sound with the breath, as a horn. 6. **blow up**, **a.** inflate. **b.** explode. **c.** enlarge. —*n.* 7. stroke, as with a fist or club. 8. saddening shock. —**blow′er**, *n.*

blow′out″, *n.* break of an automobile tire.

blow′torch″, *n.* lamp for burning or melting.

blub′ber, *n.* 1. whale fat. —*v.i.* 2. weep noisily. —**blub′ber·y**, *adj.* —**blub′ber·er**, *n.*

blud′geon, *n.* 1. short club. —*v.t.* 2. beat with a bludgeon. 3. coerce.

blue, *n.* 1. primary color, that of a clear sky. 2. **blues**, **a.** jazz tune with a slow tempo, and words, and a certain harmonic pattern. **b.** mental depression. —*adj.* 3. of the color blue. 4. sad.

blue′ber″ry, *n.*, *pl.* **-ries.** shrub with blue-black berries.

blue′blood″, *n.* person of distinguished ancestry. —**blue′blood″ed**, *adj.*

blue′-col′lar, *adj.* pertaining to manual workers.

blue′jay″, *n.* blue North American bird.

blue law, law restricting commerce or recreation on a quasi-religious basis.

blue′print″, *n.* 1. photographic reproduction of a measured drawing, appearing as white on blue. 2. any plan or project. —*v.t.* 3. reproduce all present as a blueprint.

blue′stock″ing, *n.* female pedant.

bluff, *v.t.* 1. deceive with an air of frankness or assurance. —*adj.* 2. frank or abrupt in manner. 3. rising steeply. —*n.* 4. steep cliff or ridge. 5. act or instance of bluffing.

blun′der, *n.* 1. avoidable error. —*v.i.* 2. make such an error. 3. move unthinkingly or awkwardly. —**blun′der·er**, *n.*

blunt, *adj.* 1. with a dull edge. 2. plain-spoken. —*v.t.* 3. dull the edge of. —**blunt′ly**, *adv.* —**blunt′ness**, *n.*

blur, *v.*, **blurred**, **blurring**, *n. v.t.* 1. cause to lose sharpness or clarity. —*v.i.* 2. become indistinct. —*n.* 3. something that blurs; smear. 4. indistinct image or impression. —**blur′ry**, *adj.* —**blur′ri·ness**, *n.*

blurt, *v.t.* say impulsively.

blush, *v.i.* 1. become red in the face with embarrassment or anger. 2. be ashamed. —*n.* 3. redness in the face. 4. pink tone.

blus′ter, *v.i.* 1. roar, as the wind. 2. pretend rage, bravery, etc. —*n.* 3. pretense of rage, bravery, etc. —**blus′ter·er**, *n.*

boar, *n.* 1. ungelded male pig. 2. wild hog.

board, *n.* 1. long, flat piece of wood. 2. sheet of fibrous material. 3. meals as part of one's accommodations. 4. administrative group. 5. **on board**, on or onto a ship, airplane, train, etc. —*v.t.* 6. go on or onto, as a ship. 7. pay for the accommodations, with meals, of. —*v.i.* 8. live as a boarder. —**board′er**, *n.*

boarding house, house offering lodgings with board.

boast, *v.i.* 1. talk to excess about one's merits or accomplishments. —*n.* 2. boasting remark. 3. something boasted about. —**boast′er**, *n.* —**boast′ful**, *adj.* —**boast′ful·ly**, *adv.* —**boast′ful·ness**, *n.*

boat, *n.* 1. small vessel or craft. 2. loosely, any ship. 3. container with curved sides converging at the ends. —*v.i.* 4. travel in a boat, esp. for recreation. —**boat′man**, *n.*

boat·swain (bō′sən), *n.* petty officer in charge of a deck crew.

bob, *v.*, **bobbed**, **bobbing**, *n. v.t.* 1. cut in a short hairdo. —*v.i.* 2. sink, then rise again quickly. —*n.* 3. short hairdo. 4. quick sinking and rising movement. 5. weight hung from a line or pendulum.

bob′sled″, *n.*, *v.i.*, **sledded**, **sledding.** *n.* 1. long high-speed sled. —*v.i.* 2. ride in such a sled.

bock, *n.* dark beer.

bode, *v.t.*, **boded**, **boding.** **bode ill** or **well**; foretell bad or good events.

bod′i·ly, *adj.* 1. pertaining to the body. —*adv.* 2. physically.

bod′y, *n.*, *pl.* **-ies.** *n.* 1. physical part of a man or animal. 2. corpse. 3. part of a vehicle that encloses passengers or freight. 4. distinct area of water or land. 5. object in outer space. 6. group or organization. 7. richness or flavor.

bod′y·guard″, *n.* person or group protecting against attack.

bog, *n.*, *v.*, **bogged**, **bogging.** *n.* 1. marshy or spongy area. —*v.t.*, *v.i.* 2. sink into a bog. 3. slow or halt, as in accomplishing something. —**bog′gy**, *adj.*

bog′gle, *v.i.*, **-gled**, **-gling.** hesitate.

bo′gus, *adj.* false.

bo′gy·man″, *n.*, *pl.* **-men.** imaginary demon. Also **bo′gey·man″**.

boil, *v.t.* 1. heat in water that bubbles from being heated. 2. heat to bubbling. —*v.i.* 3. be heated in either of these ways. 4. seethe, as with rage. —*n.* 5. enough heat for boiling. 6. inflamed, pus-filled swelling.

boil′er, *n.* 1. container for boiling things. 2. container for making steam or heating water.

bois′ter·ous, *adj.* 1. rowdy. 2. stormy. —**bois′ter·ous·ly**, *adv.*

bold, *adj.* 1. daring. 2. presumptuous. 3. conspicuous. —**bold′ly**, *adv.* —**bold′ness**, *n.*

bo·lo′gna, *n.* smoked sausage.

bol'ster, *n.* **1.** long pillow. —*v.t.* **2.** prop up.

bolt, *n.* **1.** fastener with a thread; screw. **2.** sliding device for securing a door, etc. **3.** arrow for a crossbow. **4.** stroke of lightning. **5.** sudden dash. **6.** roll, as of cloth. —*v.t.* **7.** fasten or secure with a bolt. **8.** swallow hastily. —*v.i.* **9.** flee or start suddenly.

bomb, *n.* **1.** explosive or incendiary device. —*v.t.* **2.** destroy or attack with bombs.

bom·bard', *v.t.* **1.** attack with bombs or shells. **2.** direct atomic particles against the nuclei of. —**bom·bard'ment,** *n.*

bom''bar·dier', *n.* person who bombs from an airplane.

bom'bast, *n.* grandiose, empty language. —**bom·bas'tic,** *adj.*

bomb'er, *n.* **1.** military plane for dropping bombs. **2.** person who plants bombs.

bomb'shell'', *n.* **1.** bomb. **2.** someone or something sensational.

bona fide (bō'nə fīd'', bō'nə fē'dā), in good faith.

bo·nan'za, *n.* source of prosperity.

bon'bon'', *n.* piece of candy.

bond, *n.* **1.** something that binds. **2.** business obligation. **3.** certificate of money lent at interest to an organization. **4.** monetary guarantee from a bailed prisoner, employee, etc.

bond'age, *n.* servitude.

bone, *n.,* *v.t.,* **boned, boning.** *n.* **1.** part of a skeleton. —*v.t.* **2.** remove the bones from.

bon'fire'', *n.* large outdoor fire.

bon mot (bâw'' mō''), *pl.* **bons mots.** witty or pithy remark.

bon'net, *n.* woman's cloth hat with a chin strap.

bo'nus, *n.,* *pl.* **-nuses.** payment in addition to that customary.

bon voyage (bâw vwah yahj') good journey: said to someone departing.

bon'y, *adj.,* **-ier, -iest.** with bones much in evidence. —**bon'i·ness,** *n.*

boo, *interj.,* *n.,* *pl.* **boos,** *v.t.,* **booed, booing** *interj.* *n.* **1.** sound made to startle or show disapproval. —*v.t.* **2.** disapprove of with boos.

boo'by, *n.,* *pl.* **-bies.** fool. Also, **boob.**

book, *n.* **1.** long piece of writing, etc., published or kept as a distinct entity. **2.** major subdivision of such a piece. **3.** libretto. **4. books,** business accounts. **5.** something suggesting a bound book in form. —*v.t.* **6.** record. **7.** make a reservation for. —**book'bind''er,** *n.* —**book' bind''ing,** *n.* —**book'case'',** *n.* —**book' keep''er,** *n.* —**book·keep''ing,** *n.* —**book'let,** *n.* —**book'shelf'',** *n.* —**book'shop'', book'store'',** *n.*

book'end'', *n.* device for holding books upright on a shelf.

book'mak''er, *n.* person who takes bets. Also, *Informal,* **book'ie.**

book'worm'', *n.* person fond of reading.

boom, *n.* **1.** loud, deep, hollow sound. **2.** spar hinged at one end. **3.** flurry of business or industrial activity. —*v.i.* **4.** make a booming noise. **5.** enjoy a boom, as a town or industry.

boom'er·ang'', *n.* **1.** Australian throwing stick that returns to the thrower. —*v.i.* **2.** be harmful to the originator, as a plot.

boon, *n.* favor or blessing.

boon'dog''gle, *n.* piece of meaningless, contrived work.

boor, *n.* uncouth person. —**boor'ish,** *adj.*

boost, *v.t.* **1.** lift from below. **2.** add to the power of. **3.** speak in praise of. —*n.* **4.** act or instance of boosting.

boot, *n.* **1.** shoe with tall sides. —*n.,* *v.t.* **2.** kick. —*v.t.* **3.** (computers) to load operating system software.

booth, *n.* small shelter or enclosure.

boot'leg''', *v.,* **-legged, -legging,** *adj.* *v.t.* **1.** make or sell unlawfully, esp. liquor. —*v.i.* **2.** act as a bootlegger. —*adj.* **3.** made or sold by bootleggers. —**boot' leg''ger,** *n.*

boo'ty, *n.,* *pl.* **-ties.** plunder; spoils.

booze, *n.,* *v.i.,* **boozed, boozing.** *Informal* *n.* **1.** liquor. —*v.i.* **2.** drink liquor heavily.

bo'rax, *n.* **1.** crystalline salt. **2.** *Informal.* cheap, showy furniture.

bor'der, *n.* **1.** edge. **2.** special area along an edge. **3.** political boundary. —*v.t.* **4.** give a border to. **5.** adjoin the edge of. —*v.i.* **6.** border on, a. adjoin. b. nearly belong to. —**bor'der·land'',** *n.* —**bor'der·line'',** *n.*

bore, *v.,* **bored, boring,** *n.* *v.t.,* *v.i.* **1.** penetrate with a rotating movement. —*v.t.* **2.** dig by boring. **3.** weary by being uninteresting. **4.** cylindrical hollow, e.g. in the barrel of a cannon. **5.** uninteresting person or thing. **6.** petty annoyance. —**bore'dom,** *n.*

bor'ough, *n.* incorporated town.

bor'row, *v.t.* **1.** take and later return. **2.** take for use in one's own creative work. —**bor'row·er,** *n.*

bos'om, *n.* **1.** human breast, esp. as the seat of emotion. **2.** midst.

boss, *n.* **1.** employer or manager. **2.** rounded projection. —*v.t.* **3.** *Informal.* order or control firmly.

bos'sy, *adj.* *Informal.* domineering.

bo'sun, *n.* boatswain.

bot'a·ny, *n.* study of plants. —**bo·tan'i·cal, bo·tan'ic,** *adj.* —**bot'a·nist,** *n.*

botch, *v.t.* **1.** ruin, as work. —*n.* **2.** clumsy or ineffectual work.

both, *adj.,* *pron.* **1.** one and the other. —*conj.,* *adv.* **2.** equally.

both'er, *v.t.* **1.** annoy or worry. —*v.i.* **2.**

take the trouble to do something. —*n.*
3. source of annoyance or worry.
—**both′er·some,** *adj.*

bot′tle, *n., v.t.,* **-tled, -tling.** *n.* 1. container, usually glass and with a stoppable narrow outlet, for liquids and gases. 2. capacity of such a container, used as a measure. —*v.t.* 3. put into a bottle. —**bot′tler,** *n.*

bot′tle·neck″, *n.* obstruction to a flow of work.

bot′tom, *n.* 1. lowermost part. 2. ground under a body of water. 3. cause or meaning. —**bot′tom·less,** *adj.*

bou·doir′, *n.* woman's private sitting room.

bough, *n.* limb of a tree.

bouil·lon (bool′yon), *n.* clear broth.

boul′der, *n.* large, rounded stone.

boul′e·vard″, *n.* major city street, often tree-lined.

bounce, *v.,* **bounced, bouncing,** *n.* *v.i.* 1. jump in a new direction after striking a hard surface. —*v.t.* 2. cause to jump in this way. —*n.* 3. act or instance of bouncing. 4. ability to bounce.

bound, *v.i.* 1. jump. 2. run with jumping steps. 3. bounce. —*v.t.* 4. adjoin or determine the boundaries of. —*n.* 5. act or instance of jumping or bouncing. 6. **bounds,** limits. —*adj.* 7. tied or joined. 8. obligated. 9. certain. 10. headed for a specified goal. —**bound′less,** *adj.*

bound′a·ry, *n., pl.* **-ries.** border of an area of land.

bou·quet′, *n.* 1. bunch or arrangement of flowers. 2. aroma of wine.

bour·bon (bər′bən), *n.* American whiskey made from corn mash.

bour·geois·ie (bōōr′zhwah′), *n., pl.* **-geois,** *adj.* *n.* 1. member of the bourgeoisie. —*adj.* 2. concerned with money, possessions, social conventions, etc. 3. pertaining to the bourgeoisie.

bour·geoi·sie (bōōr′zhwah zē′), *n., sing.* or *pl.* social class of merchants, businessmen, professionals, clerks, etc.; middle class.

bout, *n.* 1. fight or contest. 2. period or spell.

bou·tique (bōō tēk′), *n.* small shop for fashionable goods.

bow (bō for 1-3, 6; bou for 4, 5, 7-9). *n.* 1. springy length of wood for shooting arrows. 2. length of wood for playing various stringed instruments. 3. Also, **bow knot,** knot with two loops. 4. front part of a ship, etc. 5. forward bend of the upper body as a mark of respect or acceptance. —*v.t.* 6. play with a bow. 7. cause to stoop, as beneath a burden. —*v.i.* 8. bend the upper body forward. 9. agree or submit.

bow′el, *n.* 1. intestine. 2. **bowels,** inner depths.

bowl, *n.* 1. deep, wide-topped container.

—*v.t.* 2. roll with an underhanded motion. —**bowl′er,** *n.*

bow′leg″ged, *adj.* with legs curved outward at the knees.

box, *n.* 1. container, usually rectangular and with a lid. 2. compartment suggesting this in form. 3. blow of the hand. —*v.t.* 4. put into a box. 5. have a fistfight with. —**box′er,** *n.*

boy, *n.* young male. —**boy′hood″,** *n.* —**boy′ish,** *adj.*

boy′cott, *n.* 1. refusal to deal or associate with a person or persons in order to coerce them. —*v.t.* 2. practice a boycott on.

brace, *v.t.,* **braced, bracing,** *n.* *v.t.* 1. stiffen. 2. prepare for an emotional shock. 3. stimulate. —*n.* 4. stiffening device. 5. pair. 6. hand tool for drilling with a bit.

brace′let, *n.* decorative armband.

brack′et, *n.* 1. brace for a corner. 2. horizontally projecting support. classification. —*v.t.* 4. support with brackets.

brad, *n.* thin, small-headed nail.

brag, *v.i.,* **bragged, bragging,** *n.* *v.i.* 1. boast. —*n.* 2. boasting talk. —**brag′ ger, brag′gart,** *n.*

braid, *n.* 1. interweaving of three strands of fiber. —*v.t.* 2. make into a braid.

brain, *n.* 1. organ of thought, control of actions, etc. 2. **brains, a.** intelligence. **b.** cleverness. —**brain′y,** *adj.*

brain′storm″, *n. Informal.* sudden idea or impulse.

brain′wash″, *v.t.* change the attitudes or beliefs of through psychological conditioning.

braise, *v.t.* **braised, braising.** brown. then simmer, esp. meat.

brake, *n., v.,* **braked, braking.** *n.* 1. device for slowing or stopping machinery. —*v.t.,* *v.i.* 2. slow down or stop with a brake.

brake′man, *n.* assistant to a railroad conductor.

bram′ble, *n.* prickly shrub.

bran, *n.* grain husks separated from flour in milling.

branch, *n.* 1. woodlike extension from the body of a tree, etc. 2. anything derived or extending from a main body, system, etc. —*v.i.* 3. put forth branches. 4. extend as a branch.

brand, *n.* 1. identifying mark or symbol of a company's merchandise. 2. merchandise so identified. 3. identifying mark burned into hide or skin. 4. piece of burning wood. —*v.t.* 5. put a brand on.

bran′dish, *v.t.* wave, as a sword or club.

brand-new, *adj.* wholly new.

bran′dy, *n., pl.* **-dies,** *v.t.,* **-died, -dying.** *n.* 1. distilled grape or other wine. —*v.t.* 2. preserve in brandy.

brash, *adj.* **1.** hot-headed. **2.** noisy and uncouth. —**brash'ness,** *n.*

brass, *n.* **1.** alloy of copper and zinc. **2. brasses,** wind instruments of brass. **3.** *Informal.* high military officers.

bras·siere', *n.* supporter for women's breasts.

brat, *n.* ill-behaved child.

bra·va'do, *n.* false courage or confidence.

brave, *adj., n., v.t.,* **braved, braving.** *adj.* **1.** courageous. **2.** fine-looking. —*n.* **3.** American Indian warrior. —*v.t.* **4.** encounter defiantly. —**brave'ly,** *adv.* —**brav'er·y, brave'ness,** *n.*

bra'vo, *interj.* well done!

bra·vu'ra, *n.* brilliance or daring.

brawl, *v.i.* **1.** fight noisily. —*n.* **2.** noisy fight. —**brawl'er,** *n.*

brawn, *n.* muscular strength. —**brawn'y,** *adj.*

bray, *n.* **1.** cry of a donkey. —*v.i.* **2.** make this or a similar sound.

bra'zen, *adj.* **1.** made of brass. **2.** shameless. **3.** strident. —**bra'zen·ly,** *adv.* —**bra'zen·ness,** *n.*

breach, *n.* **1.** opening broken through. **2.** violation. **3.** rift, as in a friendship. —*v.t.* **4.** make a breach in or through.

bread, *n.* **1.** food of baked flour, water, etc. **2.** livelihood. —*v.t.* **3.** coat before cooking with bread crumbs.

breadth, *n.* **1.** width. **2.** range, as of knowledge.

bread'win''ner, *n.* sole support of a family.

break, *v.,* **broke, broken, breaking,** *n.* *v.t.* **1.** force to divide into pieces. **2.** put out of repair. **3.** terminate. **4.** violate. **5.** end the effectiveness of. **6.** reduce in health, wealth, rank, etc. —*v.i.* **7.** force one's way. **8.** end a relationship. **9.** appear or begin suddenly. **10.** pause in activity. **11.** be broken. **12. break down, a.** fail in health or operation. **b.** abandon self-restraint. —*n.* **13.** act or instance of breaking. **14.** stroke of luck or mercy. **15.** pause in activity. **16.** change. —**break'age,** *n.* —**break'a·ble,** *adj.*

break''danc·ing, *n.* style of dancing characterized by acrobatic spins and robotic movement.

break'down'', *n.* **1.** failure of health or operation. **2.** detailed analysis.

break'er, *n.* **1.** wave that breaks on the shore. **2.** device or person that breaks.

break'fast, *n.* morning meal.

break'neck'', *adj.* reckless, as speed.

break'through'', *n.* **1.** act or instance of forcing a way against opposition. **2.** major accomplishment or discovery.

break'wa''ter, *n.* wall for breaking the force of waves.

breast, *n.* **1.** upper forward part of the body. **2.** this part regarded as the seat of the emotions. **3.** woman's milk-secreting gland. —*v.t.* **4.** oppose or head into forcefully. —**breast'bone'',** *n.* —**breast'-feed'',** *v.t.*

breath, *n.* **1.** air going into and out of the lungs. **2.** manner of breathing. **3.** ability to breathe readily. —**breath'less,** *adj.* —**breath'less·ly,** *adv.* —**breath'y,** *adj.*

breathe, *v.,* **breathed, breathing.** *v.i.* **1.** move air into and out of the lungs. —*v.t.* **2.** speak or sing, esp. quietly.

breath'tak''ing, *adj.* astonishing or exciting.

breech, *n.* **1.** buttocks. **2.** loaded end of a gun. **3. breeches,** trousers.

breed, *v.,* **bred, breeding,** *n.* *v.t.* **1.** give birth to. **2.** raise, as animals. **3.** be a source of. —*v.i.* **4.** give birth to offspring. **5.** emerge or proliferate. —*n.* **6.** strain, as of animals. **7.** type, esp. of person. —**breed'er,** *n.*

breed'ing, *n.* **1.** act of one who breeds. **2.** manners or character.

breeze, *n., v.i.,* **breezed, breezing.** *n.* **1.** light wind. —*v.i.* **2.** become a breeze. **3.** move briskly or jauntily. —**breez'y,** *adj.*

breth'ren, *n.* *Archaic.* **1.** brothers. **2.** monks.

brev'i·ty, *n.* briefness.

brew, *v.t.* **1.** make by fermenting malt and hops, as beer. **2.** make by any of various means, as beverages or other liquids. **3.** plot. —*v.i.* **4.** begin to appear or take shape. —*n.* **5.** something brewed. —**brew'er,** *n.*

brew'er·y, *n., pl.* **-ies.** place for brewing malt beverages.

briar, *n.* brier.

bribe, *v.t.,* **bribed, bribing,** *n.* *v.t.* **1.** pay to abuse a position of trust. —*n.* **2.** payment offered for this. —**brib'er·y,** *n.*

bric'-a-brac'', *n.* miscellaneous decorative objects.

brick, *n.* **1.** oblong object of baked or unbaked clay, etc., used in construction. **2.** oblong object of any material. —*v.t.* **3.** enclose or cover with brickwork. —**brick'lay''er,** *n.* —**brick'work'',** *n.*

bride, *n.* woman at the time of her wedding. —**brid'al,** *adj.* —**brides'maid'',** *n.*

bride'groom'', *n.* man at the time of his wedding.

bridge, *n., v.t.,* **bridged, bridging.** *n.* **1.** structure for crossing a stream, valley, etc. **2.** any of various connecting structures, etc. **3.** control post of a ship. **4.** card game for four players. —*v.t.* **5.** cross with or as with a bridge.

bridge'head'', *n.* fortified position of invaders.

bri'dle, *n., v.t.,* **-dled, -dling.** *n.* **1.** harness for a horse's head. **2.** means of restraint. —*v.t.* **3.** put a bridle on. **4.** restrain.

brief, *adj.* **1.** short or concise. –*n.* **2.** legal summary. –*v.t.* **3.** supply with useful information. —**brief′ly,** *adv.* —**brief′ness,** *n.* —**brief′ing,** *n.*

brief′case″, *n.* handle-held case for business papers.

bri′er, *n.* thorny bush.

brig, *n.* **1.** two-masted square-rigged ship. **2.** navy or marine prison.

bri·gade′, *n.* **1.** military unit formed of battalions. **2.** pseudo-military organization.

brig″a·dier general, military officer between a colonel and a major general. Also, **brig″a·dier′.**

bright, *adj.* **1.** shedding or reflecting much light. **2.** intelligent or mentally active. **3.** cheerful. **4.** promising. —**bright′ly,** *adv.* —**bright′ness,** *n.* —**bright′en,** *v.t., v.i.*

bril′liant, *adj.* very bright. —**bril′liant·ly,** *adv.* —**bril′liance, bril′lian·cy,** *n.*

brim, *n., v.i.,* **brimmed, brimming.** *n.* **1.** rim. –*v.i.* **2.** run or run over with liquid.

brin′dled, *adj.* gray or tawny with darker spots. Also **brin′dle.**

brine, *n.* salty water.

bring, *v.t.,* **brought, bringing. 1.** carry or escort to a place. **2.** cause as a consequence. **3. bring about,** cause. **4. bring out,** make apparent. **5. bring up,** raise, as children.

brink, *n.* edge or verge.

brisk, *adj.* **1.** lively or abrupt. **2.** forceful, as the wind. —**brisk′ly,** *adv.* —**brisk′ness,** *n.*

bris′ket, *n.* breast meat.

bris′tle, *n., v.i.,* **-tled, -tling.** *n.* **1.** stiff hair, as on a pig. **2.** fiber on the head of a brush. –*v.i.* **3.** stand up stiffly. **4.** be tense with annoyance, etc.

brit′tle, *adj.* easily shattered. —**brit′tle·ness,** *n.*

broach, *v.t.* bring forth as a subject of discussion.

broad, *adj.* **1.** wide. **2.** diverse. **3.** not strict. **4.** not detailed. —**broad′ly,** *adv.* —**broad′ness,** *n.* —**broad′en,** *v.t., v.i.*

broad′cast″, *v.t.,* **-cast,** or (for 1) **-casted, -casting.** *v.t.* **1.** send by radio or television. **2.** scatter widely. –*n.* **3.** radio or television program. —**broad′cast″er,** *n.*

broad′-mind″ed, *adj.* not strict or opinionated. —**broad″-mind′ed·ly,** *adv.* —**broad″-mind′ed·ness,** *n.*

bro·chure′, *n.* pamphlet.

brogue, *n.* Irish accent, esp. in speaking English.

broil, *v.t.* cook with direct heat from a fire, etc. —**broil′er,** *n.*

broke, *adj.* Informal. without money; bankrupt.

brok′en, *adj.* **1.** past participle of *break,* used adjectivally. **2.** deprived of spirit, health, etc. **3.** badly pronounced, as by a foreigner. **4.** discontinuous. —**brok′en·ly,** *adv.*

brok′er, *n.* agent for buying and selling. —**brok′er·age,** *n.*

bron′co, *n., pl.* **-cos.** wild or half-wild horse of the West. Also, **bron′cho.**

bronze, *n., v.t.* **bronzed, bronzing.** *n.* **1.** alloy of copper and tin. **2.** reddish-brown. –*v.t.* **3.** color like or coat with bronze.

brooch, *n.* large ornamental pin.

brood, *n.* **1.** group of children or baby chickens. –*v.i.* **2.** worry or sulk at length.

brook, *n.* **1.** small stream. –*v.t.* **2.** endure.

broom, *n.* bundle of straws, etc. attached to a stick and used for sweeping. —**broom′stick″,** *n.*

broth, *n.* soup from boiled meat.

broth′el, *n.* house of prostitution.

broth′er, *n.* **1.** son of one's father. **2.** fellow-human as an object of love, etc. **3.** fellow-member of a religious order, lodge, etc. —**broth′er·hood,** *n.* —**broth′er·ly,** *adj.*

broth′er-in-law″, *n., pl.* **broth′ers-in-law″. 1.** brother of a spouse. **2.** husband of a sister or sister-in-law.

brow, *n.* **1.** eyebrow. **2.** forehead. **3.** edge of a cliff.

brow′beat″, *v.t.,* **-beat, -beaten, -beating.** bully.

brown, *n.* **1.** color combining red, yellow, and black. –*v.t., v.i.* **2.** make or become brown.

brown study, spell of deep thought.

browse, *v.i.,* **browsed, browsing.** look idly through things for sale. —**brows′er,** *n.*

bruise, *v.,* **bruised, bruising,** *n. v.t.* **1.** injure the skin or surface of with a blow or pressure. **2.** hurt, as the feelings. –*v.i.* **3.** become bruised. –*n.* **4.** mark made by bruising.

brunch, *n.* Informal. meal part-breakfast, part-lunch.

bru·net′, *n.* person with dark hair, esp. when with dark eyes. Also, *fem.,* **bru·nette′.**

brunt, *n.* shock, as of an attack.

brush, *n.* **1.** device for cleaning, painting, etc. consisting of bristles on a handle. **2.** act or instance of brushing. **3.** something suggesting a brush in form. **4.** Also, **brush′wood″,** underbrush. –*v.t.* **5.** remove or apply with a brush. **6.** apply a brush to. **7.** graze lightly in passing.

brush′off″, *n.* Informal. tactless act of dismissing or ignoring someone.

brusque, *adj.* abrupt in manner. —**brusque′ly,** *adv.* —**brusque′ness,** *n.*

bru′tal, *adj.* extremely cruel or harsh. —**bru·tal′i·ty,** *n.*

bru′tal·ize, *v.t.,* **-ized, -izing. 1.** make brutal. **2.** treat brutally. —**bru″tal·i·za′tion,** *n.*

brute, *adj.* **1.** beastlike, esp. in force or lack of intelligence. —*n.* **2.** beast. **3.** brutal person. —**brut′ish,** *adj.*

bub′ble, *n., v.i.,* **-bled, -bling.** *n.* **1.** void or body of gas surrounded by a liquid. **2.** something bubblelike in roundness and thinness. **3.** something insubstantial. —**bub′bly,** *adj.* —*v.i.* **4.** give off bubbles.

buc″ca·neer′, *n.* pirate, esp. in the Caribbean Sea.

buck, *n.* **1.** grown male deer, goat, etc. **2.** act or instance of bucking. **3.** *Informal.* dollar. —*v.t.* **4.** oppose with force. —*v.i.* **5.** rear upward, as a horse.

buck′et, *n.* open watertight container.

buck′le, *n., v.,* **-led, -ling.** *n.* **1.** fastener for two ends of a belt, etc. —*v.t.* **2.** fasten with a buckle. **3.** cause to bulge or bend, as sheet metal. —*v.i.* **4.** bulge or bend.

buck′tooth″, *n.* projecting front tooth. —**buck′toothed′,** *adj.*

buck′wheat″, *n.* wheat with triangular seeds.

bu·col′ic, *adj.* pastoral; serene and countrylike.

bud, *n., v.i.,* **budded, budding.** *n.* **1.** swelling from which a flower, leaf, etc. grows. —*v.i.* **2.** put forth such swellings.

budge, *v.,* **budged, budging.** *v.t., v.i.* move by or because of force.

budg′et, *n.* **1.** allotment of money, time, etc. for various purposes. —*v.t.* **2.** submit to a budget. —**budg′et·ar″y,** *adj.*

buff, *n.* **1.** dull tan color. —*v.t.* **2.** polish with a soft surface.

buf′fa·lo″, *n., pl.* **-loes. 1.** any of various wild oxen. **2.** American bison.

buf′fer, *n.* something that prevents or lessens the shocks of collision.

buf·fet′ (bəf fā′), *n.* **1.** sideboard. **2.** meal for eaters helping themselves.

buf·foon′, *n.* clownish person. —**buf·foon′er·y,** *n.*

bug, *n., v.t.* **bugged, bug·ging.** *n.* **1.** insect. **2.** (computers) an error in programming. *v.t.* **3.** *Informal.* **a.** plant listening devices in. **b.** pester.

bug′gy, *n., pl.* **-gies. 1.** light one-horse carriage. **2.** baby carriage.

bu′gle, *n.* trumpetlike brass instrument. —**bu′gler,** *n.*

build, *v.,* **built, building.** *n. v.t.* **1.** assemble, as a structure. **2.** found or base. **3.** bring into being or develop. —*v.i.* **4.** establish or base something. **5.** accumulate. —*n.* **6.** frame of the body. —**build′er,** *n.*

build′ing, *n.* habitable construction.

built′-in′, *adj.* integral or inherent.

built′-up′, *adj.* made from a number of parts.

bulb, *n.* **1.** any of various underground plant stems, roots, or buds. **2.** something swelling toward the end. —**bulb′ous,** *adj.*

bulge, *n., v.i.,* **bulged, bulging.** *n.* **1.** swelling. —*v.i.* **2.** swell.

bulk, *n.* **1.** size or weight. **2.** greater or principal part. —*v.i.* **3.** be massive or important. —*adj.* **4.** shipped without containers. —**bulk′y,** *adj.*

bull, *n.* **1.** male ox, elephant, etc. **2.** speculator in the rise of stock prices. **3.** papal decree. —**bul′lish,** *adj.*

bull′dog″, *n.* small, heavy-built fighting dog.

bull′doze″, *v.t.,* **-dozed, -dozing. 1.** push or level earth. **2.** *Informal.* force with aggressiveness. —**bull′doz·er,** *n.*

bul′let, *n.* pointed projectile from a firearm. —**bul′let-proof″,** *adj.*

bul′le·tin, *n.* **1.** announcement, esp. of news. **2.** official publication.

bul′lion, *n.* ingots of precious metal.

bulls′eye″, *n.* **1.** center of a target. **2.** direct hit.

bul′ly, *n., pl.* **-lies,** *v.t.,* **-lied, -lying.** *n.* **1.** person who injures or threatens weaker persons. —*v.t.* **2.** act as a bully toward.

bul′wark, *n.* defensive wall or barrier.

bum, *n., v.,* **bummed, bumming.** *n.* **1.** poor person who refuses to work. —*v.i.* **2.** live as a bum. —*v.t.* **3.** obtain by begging.

bum′ble·bee″, *n.* yellow-and-black bee.

bump, *v.t.* **1.** collide with, esp. not violently. —*v.i.* **2.** move over a bumpy surface. **3. bump into, a.** collide with. **b.** *Informal.* meet by chance. —*n.* **4.** act or instance of bumping or of being bumped. **5.** surface unevenness or swelling. —**bump′y,** *adj.*

bump′er, *n.* device to receive the shock of collisions. —*adj.* **2.** especially abundant, as a crop.

bump′tious, *adj.* annoyingly self-assertive. —**bump′tious·ly,** *adv.*

bun, *n.* small baked roll.

bunch, *n.* **1.** small cluster. **2.** *Informal.* group of persons. —*v.t., v.i.* **3.** gather into a bunch.

bun′dle, *n., v.t.,* **-dled, -dling. 1.** group of things bound or wrapped together. —*v.t.* **2.** make into a bundle.

bun′ga·low″, *n.* one-storied cottage.

bun′gle, *v.,* **-gled, -gling,** *n. v.t., v.i.* **1.** do or act stupidly. —*n.* **2.** act or instance of bungling. —**bun′gler,** *n.*

bun′ion, *n.* inflamed swelling at the joint of the big toe.

bunk, *n.* **1.** flat frame serving as a bed, esp. in barracks, camps, or ships. **2.** *Informal.* false statements. —*v.i.* **3.** sleep in a bunk. —**bunk′house″,** *n.*

bunk′er, *n.* **1.** storage space for coal, etc.

2. underground shelter against bombs or shells.

bun'ny, *n., pl.* **-nies.** *Informal.* rabbit.

bun'ting, *n.* cloth for making flags or flaglike decorations.

buoy, *n.* **1.** floating signal or marker. **2.** life preserver. *v.t.* **3.** lift up, as the spirits. **4.** keep afloat.

buoy'ant, *adj.* cheerful or optimistic. —**buoy'an·cy,** *n.*

bur, *n.* **1.** seed capsule with sharp, clinging extensions. **2.** burr.

bur'den, *n.* **1.** heavy load. **2.** theme. **3.** chorus or refrain. —*v.t.* **4.** put a load upon. —**bur'den·some,** *adj.*

bu'reau, *n., pl.* **-reaus, -reaux. 1.** official agency or department. **2.** chest of drawers.

bu·reau·cra·cy, (byŏō rah'krə sē), *n., pl.* **-cies. 1.** government by officials. **2.** government departments as a source of political power, obstruction to progress, etc. —**bu'reau·crat",** *n.* —**bu'reau·crat'ic,** *adj.*

bur'glar, *n.* person who breaks into buildings, esp. to steal. —**bur'gla·ry,** *n.* —**bur'glar·ize",** *v.t.*

bur'i·al, *n.* burying of the dead.

bur'lap, *n.* coarse jute or hemp cloth.

bur·lesque", *n., v.t.,* **-lesqued, -lesquing.** *n.* **1.** sexually allusive vaudeville. **2.** satirical parody. —*v.t.* **3.** make the subject of a burlesque.

bur'ly, *adj.,* **-lier, -liest.** big and strong. —**bur'li·ness,** *n.*

burn, *v.,* **burned.** or **burnt, burning.** *v.t.* **1.** use as fuel. **2.** damage with heat. **3.** create or finish with fire or intense heat. **4.** damage with acids, etc. —*v.i.* **5.** be on fire. **6.** give out light or heat. **7.** be damaged by heat. **8.** be full of eagerness or passion. —*n.* **9.** burned place. —**burn'a·ble,** *adj.*

burn'er, *n.* device for applying intense heat.

bur'nish, *v.t.* rub to a polish.

burn"out, *n.* lethargy resulting from excess stress.

burp, *Informal. n., v.i.* **1.** belch. —*v.t.* **2.** cause to burp.

burr, *n.* **1.** rough edge on cut metal. **2.** rough trilling of the sound *r,* as by a Scot.

bur'row, *n.* **1.** hole of a digging animal. —*v.i.* **2.** dig deep holes. **3.** hide in or as if in a burrow.

burst, *v.,* **burst, bursting,** *n. v.i.* **1.** be torn apart, as from pressure. **2.** make a sudden and vehement beginning into song, tears, etc. —*v.t.* **3.** cause to be torn apart. —*n.* **4.** act or instance of bursting. **5.** sudden show of energy. **6.** volley of shots.

bury, *v.t.,* **-ied, -ying. 1.** put under earth or other material. **2.** entomb. **3.** put out of sight or notice. **4.** immerse, as in work.

bus, *n., pl.* **-es, -ses,** *v.t.* **-ed** or **-sed, -ing** or **-sing.** *n.* **1.** vehicle for many passengers. **2.** (computers) a circuit for connecting two components. —*v.t.* **3.** transport by bus.

bush, *n.* **1.** low, spreading woody plant. **2.** land overgrown with bushes. —**bush'y,** *adj.*

bush'el, *n.* dry measure of 4 pecks or 32 quarts.

bus'i·ly, *adv.* in a busy manner.

busi'ness, *n.* **1.** type of work or commerce. **2.** duty or task. **3.** rightful concern. **4.** commerce. **5.** event or affair. **6. mean business,** have earnest intentions. —**busi'ness·man,** *n.* —**busi'ness·wom"an,** *n.*

busi'ness·like", *adj.* efficient.

bust, *n.* **1.** head, neck, and upper part of the chest. **2.** sculpture of these parts. **3.** *Informal.* **a.** failure. **b.** bankruptcy. —*v.t., v.i.* **4.** *Informal.* break or burst.

bus'tle, *n., v.i.,* **-tled, -tling.** *n.* **1.** activity, as of a crowd. —*v.i.* **2.** move hurriedly.

bus'y, *adj.,* **-ier, -iest,** *v.t.,* **-ied, -ying.** *adj.* **1.** with much to do. **2.** in action or use. **3.** full of distracting elements, as a decoration. —*v.t.* **4.** cause to be busy. —**bus'y·ness,** *n.*

bus'y·bod"y, *n., pl.* **-ies.** gossipy or meddlesome person.

but, *prep.* **1.** except for. —*conj.* **2.** and yet. **3.** on the other hand. —*adv.* **.4.** only; merely. **5.** just; only.

butch'er, *n.* **1.** slaughterer or seller of meat. —*v.t.* **2.** slaughter. —**butch'er·y,** *n.*

but'ler, *n.* head male house servant.

butt, *n.* **1.** thick end. **2.** remnant of a smoked cigarette or cigar. **3.** target. **4.** act or instance of butting. —*v.t.* **5.** ram with the head. **6.** join without overlapping.

butte, *n.* steep hill isolated in flat land.

but'ter, *n.* **1.** solid product made from churned cream. —*v.t.* **2.** spread with butter. **3. butter up,** *Informal.* ingratiate oneself with. —**but'ter·fat",** *n.*

but'ter·fly", *n., pl.* **-flies.** slender-bodied four-winged insect.

but'ter·milk", *n.* liquid remaining after butter is made from cream.

but'ter·scotch", *n.* candy of brown sugar, butter, etc.

but'tocks, *n., pl.* part on which one sits.

but'ton, *n.* **1.** broad object passed through holes or loops in cloth as a fastener. **2.** object pushed to operate a control mechanism. **3.** large badge with a slogan, etc. —*v.t., v.i.* **4.** fasten with buttons. —**but'ton·hole",** *n.*

but'tress, *n.* **1.** heavy mass resisting a thrust, as that of an arch. —*v.t.* **2.** give stability or support to.

bux'om, *adj.* attractively plump.

buy, *v.t.*, bought, buying, *n. v.t.* **1.** get in return for money. **2.** *Informal.* accept as true or wise. —*n.* **3.** *Informal.* something cheap at the price. —**buy′er**, *n.*

buzz, *v.i.* **1.** make a deep, rough hum. —*n.* **2.** hum of this sort. —**buzz′er**, *n.*

buz′zard, *n.* **1.** type of slow hawk. **2.** type of vulture.

by, *prep.* **1.** close to. **2.** past. **3.** a multiplier or other dimension being. **4.** in measures or units of. **5.** after. **6.** during the time of day or night. **7.** not later than. **8.** through the agency of. **9.** according to. **10.** by way of, **a.** past or through. **b.** as a means or form of. **11.** in readiness. **12.** aside. **13.** past. —**by′stand″er**, *n.*

by′gone″, *adj.* in the past.

by′gones″, *n., pl.* past events.

by′law″, *n.* rule for an organization's internal affairs.

by′pass″, *n.* route, etc. serving as an alternate way between two points.

by′-prod″uct, *n.* product incidental to a main one. Also, **by′prod″uct.**

byte, *n.* (computers) a group of eight bits of data.

C

C, c, *n.* **1.** third letter of the English alphabet. **2.** third best grade. **3.** centigrade.

cab, *n.* **1.** chauffeured vehicle for hire. **2.** shelter for the operator of a locomotive, etc.

ca·bal′, *n.* **1.** group of intriguers. **2.** intrigue of such a group.

cab·a·ret (kab″ə rā′), *n.* restaurant with musical entertainment.

cab′bage, *n.* vegetable with a head of thick leaves.

cab′in, *n.* **1.** primitive house. **2.** passenger room on a ship. **3.** passenger space in an airplane.

cab′i·net, *n.* **1.** boxlike piece of furniture. **2.** body of officials reporting to a head of state. —**cab′i·net·mak″er**, *n.* —**cab′i·net·work″**, *n.*

ca′ble, *n., v.t.,* -bled, -bling. *n.* **1.** heavy rope. **2.** heavy electric wire. **3.** cablegram. —*v.t.* **4.** send a cablegram to.

ca′ble·gram″, *n.* transoceanic telegraph message.

ca·boose′, *n.* car for the conductor and brakemen of a freight train.

cache. (kash), *n., v.t.,* cached, caching. *n.* **1.** hiding place, esp. for food and supplies. **2.** goods hidden in such a place. —*v.t.* **3.** put in a cache.

cack′le, *v.i.,* -led, -ling, *n. v.i.* **1.** make henlike noises. —*n.* **2.** henlike noise. **3.** *Informal.* busy, meaningless talk.

ca·coph′o·ny, *n., pl.* -nies. harsh, disagreeable sound. —**ca·coph′o·nous**, *adj.*

cac′tus, *n., pl.* -tuses, -ti. prickly desert plant.

cad, *n.* violator of a gentlemanly code. —**cad′dish**, *adj.*

ca·dav′er, *n.* corpse. —**ca·dav′er·ous**, *adj.*

cad′die, *n.* person who carries a golfer's clubs. Also, **cad′dy.**

ca′dence, *n.* **1.** rise and fall of a speaking voice. **2.** marching rhythm. **3.** end of a musical phrase.

ca·det′, *n.* **1.** military student. **2.** trainee.

cadge, *v.,* cadged, cadging. *v.t., v.i.* **1.** beg. —*v.t.* **2.** get by begging. —**cadg′er**, *n.*

ca′dre, *n.* organizational nucleus, esp. of military officers.

ca·fe (ka fā′), *n.* small restaurant. Also, **ca·fé′.**

caf″e·te′ri·a, *n.* self-service restaurant.

caf·feine′, *n.* stimulant in coffee or tea. Also, **caf·fein′.**

cage, *n. v.t.,* caged, caging. *n.* **1.** open-work structure for confinement. **2.** openwork structure of any kind. —*v.t.* **3.** confine in a cage.

ca·hoots′, *Informal.* in cahoots with, in a conspiracy with.

cais′son, *n.* **1.** watertight chamber for work under water. **2.** ammunition wagon.

ca·jole′, *v.t.,* -joled, -joling. coax or wheedle. —**ca·jol′er·y**, *n.*

cake, *n., v.,* caked, caking. *n.* **1.** sweetened piece of baked dough. **2.** flat piece of food, fried or baked. **3.** piece of soap. —*v.t., v.i.* **4.** cover with or form a solid crust.

ca·lam′i·ty, *n., pl.* -ties. disaster. —**ca·lam′i·tous**, *adj.*

cal′cu·late″, *v.,* -lated, -lation. *v.t.* **1.** ascertain through rational means. **2.** plan methodically. —*v.i.* **3.** reckon. **4.** rely. —**cal′cu·la″tor**, *n.* —**cal″cu·la′tion**, *n.* —**cal′cu·la·ble**, *adj.*

cal′cu·lat″ed, *adj.* intended to produce the actual result.

cal′cu·lat″ing, *adj.* scheming.

cal′cu·lus, *n.* method used in higher mathematics.

cal′dron, *n.* large kettle.

cal′en·dar, *n.* **1.** printed object or device for determining the day of the month, etc. **2.** system for reckoning the years. **3.** schedule of agenda.

cal′en·der, *n.* **1.** machine for giving a smooth finish. —*v.t.* **2.** smooth in a calender.

calf, *n., pl.* calves. *n.* **1.** young cow or bull. **2.** fleshy part of the lower leg. —**calf′skin″**, *n.*

cal'i·ber, *n.* **1.** diameter of a bullet, gun bore, etc. **2.** quality of character. Also, **cal'i·bre.**

cal'i·brate'', *v.t.,* **-brated, -brating. 1.** establish the scale of measurements of. **2.** determine the caliber of. —**cal''i·bra'tion,** *n.*

cal'i·co'', *n., pl.* **-coes, -cos.** printed cotton.

cal'i·per, *n.* device for measuring outside or inside diameters. Also, **cal'i·pers.**

cal'is·then'ics, *n. pl.* athletic exercises.

calk, *v.t.* caulk.

call, *v.t.* **1.** utter loudly. **2.** summon. **3.** name or describe. **4.** telephone. **5.** awaken. —*v.i.* **6.** make an order or request. **7.** impose a demand. **8.** make a visit. **9.** cry, as an animal. **10.** shout. —*n.* **11.** act or instance of calling. **12.** urge or appeal. —**call'er,** *n.*

call'ing, *n.* vocation.

cal·li'o·pe'', *n.* organ of steam whistles.

cal'lous, *adj.* insensitive to the sufferings of others. —**cal'lous·ly,** *adv.* —**cal'lous·ness, cal·los'i·ty,** *n.*

cal'low, *adj.* immature or inexperienced. —**cal'low·ness,** *n.*

cal'lus, *n., pl.* **-luses.** hard thickening on the skin.

calm, *adj.* **1.** without strong emotion. **2.** undisturbed. —*n.* **3.** state of quiet. —*v.t.* **4.** make quiet or tranquil. —**calm'ly,** *adv.* —**calm'ness,** *n.*

cal'o·rie, *n.* unit of heat measurement.

ca·lum'ni·ate'', *v.t.,* **-ated, -ating.** slander. —**ca·lum''ni·a'tion,** *n.* —**cal·lum'ni·a''tor,** *n.*

cal'um·ny, *n., pl.* **-nies.** slander.

cam, *n.* rotating machine part producing reciprocating motion.

ca''ma·ra·de'rie, *n.* cheerful companionship.

cam'ber, *n.* shallow upward curve.

cam'bric, *n.* fine linen or cotton.

cam'el, *n.* desert animal storing water in one or two humps.

cam'e·o, *n., pl.* **-os.** gem of contrasting layers of stone.

cam'er·a, *n.* **1.** boxlike device for taking photographs, shooting movie film, etc. **2.** optical device for copying a view. —**cam'er·a·man,** *n.*

cam·ou·flage (kam'ə flahzh'') *n., v.t.* **-flaged, -flaging.** *n.* **1.** paintwork, etc. making something hard to see or interpret. —*v.t.* **2.** apply camouflage to.

camp, *n.* **1.** temporary residence in the open. **2.** recreation area in the country. —*v.i.* **3.** establish or live in a camp. —**camp'fire'',** *n.* —**camp'site'',** *n.* —**camp'er,** *n.*

cam·paign', *n.* **1.** series of operations to attain a planned goal. —*v.i.* **2.** act in a campaign. —**cam·paign'er,** *n.*

cam'phor, *n.* aromatic crystalline substance.

cam'pus, *n., pl.* **-puses. 1.** open area of lawn and trees, esp. the grounds of a school. **2.** academic community.

can, *v.i.,* past tense **could** for 1 and 2, **canned, canning** for 3, *n. v.i.* **1.** be able or know how to. **2.** have the right to. **3.** preserve in sealed cans or jars. —*n.* **4.** metal container sealed to preserve food, etc. **5.** cylindrical container, esp. of sheet metal. —**can'ner,** *n.*

ca·nal', *n.* artificial waterway.

ca·nard', *n.* rumour, esp. a malicious one.

ca·nar'y, *n., pl.* **-ies.** yellow songbird.

can'cel, *v.t.,* **-celed, -celing. 1.** cover with marks, esp. in order to invalidate. **2.** invalidate or terminate. **3.** *Math.* remove from both sides of an equation. —**can''cel·la'tion,** *n.*

can'cer, *n.* spreading malignant tumor. —**can'cer·ous,** *adj.*

can''de·la'brum, *n., pl.* **-bra.** branched candlestick.

can'did, *adj.* **1.** frank. **2.** unposed, as a snapshot. —**can'did·ly,** *adv.* —**can'dor, can'did·ness,** *n.*

can'di·date'', *n.* competitor for public office, an honor, etc. —**can'di·da·cy,** *n.*

can'dle, *n., v.t.,* **-dled, -dling.** *n.* **1.** cylinder of wax, etc. with a central wick for burning. —*v.t.* **2.** inspect against a light, as eggs.

can'dle·stick'', *n.* holder for candles.

can'dy, *n., pl.* **-dies,** *v.t.,* **-died, -dying.** *n.* **1.** flavored sweet. —*v.t.* **2.** cook in sugar. **3.** form into sugar crystals.

cane, *n., v.t.,* **caned, caning.** *n.* **1.** hollow, jointed plant stalk. **2.** stick held while walking. —*v.t.* **3.** stretch with split rattan, as a chair seat. **4.** beat with a cane.

ca'nine, *adj.* **1.** pertaining to dogs. **2.** pertaining to wolves or foxes. —*n.* **3.** dog, wolf, or fox. **4.** sharp human tooth.

can'is·ter, *n.* small storage can used in a kitchen.

can'ker, *n.* ulcerous sore.

can'ner·y, *n., pl.* **-ries.** plant for canning food.

can'ni·bal, *n.* person or animal that eats its own kind. —**can'ni·bal·ism,** *n.*

can'ni·bal·ize'', *v.t.,* **-ized, -izing.** strip in order to reuse parts.

can'non, *n., pl.* **-nons, -non.** heavy gun.

can''non·ade', *n.* continuous firing of cannon.

can·not', *v.i.* can not.

can'ny, *adj.,* **-nier, -niest.** shrewd. —**can'ni·ly,** *adv.* —**can'ni·ness,** *n.*

ca·noe (kə nōō'), *n., v.i.,* **-noed, -noing.** *n.* **1.** narrow paddled boat. —*v.i.* **2.** travel by canoe.

can'on, *n.* **1.** basic principle or law. **2.** church official. **3.** official list of writings. —**ca·non'i·cal,** *adj.*

can'on·ize'', *v.t.,* **-ized, -izing.** declare to be a saint. —**can''on·i·za'tion,** *n.*

can'o·py, *n., pl.* **-pies. 1.** light, rooflike covering supported by poles. **2.** rooflike projection, as over a window.

cant, *n.* **1.** hypocritical jargon. **2.** slang or jargon of a group. —*v.t., v.i.* **3.** slant.

can·tan'ker·ous, *adj.* ill-tempered.

can·ta'ta, *n.* setting of a narrative for chorus.

can·teen', *n.* **1.** portable container for water. **2.** recreation center, as for soldiers.

can'ter, *n.* easy gallop.

can'ti·le"ver, *n.* **1.** projecting structural member secured at one end. —*v.t.* **2.** support with or treat as a cantilever.

can'to, *n., pl.* **-tos.** division of a long poem.

can'tor, *n.* singer at a Jewish service.

can'vas, *n.* **1.** tightly woven heavy cloth of hemp, cotton, etc. **2.** painting on canvas.

can'vass, *v.t., v.i.* solicit for votes, opinions, sales orders, etc.

cap, *n., v.t.,* **capped, capping.** *n.* **1.** soft, close-fitting hat. **2.** anything for capping. —*v.t.* **3.** cover the upper end of.

ca'pa·ble, *adj.* **1.** competent. **2.** capable of, with the ability, personality, etc. for. —**ca"pa·bil'i·ty,** *n.* —**ca'pa·bly,** *adv.*

ca·pa'cious, *adj.* spacious.

ca·pac'i·ty, *n., pl.* **-ties. 1.** ability to contain a quantity of material, number of persons, etc. **2.** amount that can be produced. **3.** role or function. **4.** capability.

cape, *n.* **1.** cloak. **2.** projection of land seaward.

ca'per, *v.i.* **1.** leap about playfully. —*n.* **2.** playful leap.

cap'il·lar"y, *adj.* pertaining to the attraction of liquids in narrow tubes to above normal levels.

cap'i·tal, *n.* **1.** location of a national or state government. **2.** money for investing or lending. **3.** upper feature of a column or pier. **4.** letter of the form used to begin a sentence or proper name. —*adj.* **5.** excellent. **6.** large, as letters. **7.** pertaining to the death penalty.

cap'i·tal·ism, *n.* economic system based on investment or lending at interest of privately owned money. —**cap'i·tal·ist,** *n.* —**cap"i·tal·is'tic,** *adj.*

cap'i·tal·ize", *v.,* **-ized, -izing.** *v.t.* **1.** spell with an initial capital. **2.** use as or change into capital (2). **3.** furnish with capital (2). —*v.i.* **4.** capitalize on, exploit. —**cap"i·tal·i·za'tion,** *n.*

cap'i·tol, *n.* legislative building.

ca·pit'u·late, *v.i.,* **-lated, -lating.** cease to fight or resist. —**ca·pit"u·la'tion,** *n.*

ca·price', *n.* whim or whimsy. —**ca·pri'cious,** *adj.*

cap'size, *v.,* **-sized, -sizing.** *v.t., v.i.* overturn, as a boat.

cap'stan, *n.* upright drum for winding cables.

cap'sule, *n.* sealed container.

cap'tain, *n.* **1.** military or naval officer. **2.** master of a ship. **3.** leader. —**cap'tain·cy,** *n.*

cap'tion, *n.* title, explanation, etc. for a printed picture.

cap'tious, *adj.* argumentative or fault-finding. —**cap'tious·ly,** *adv.* —**cap'tious·ness,** *n.*

cap'ti·vate", *v.t.,* **-vated, -vating.** fascinate, as with charm. —**cap"ti·va'tion,** *n.*

cap'tive, *n.* captured person or animal. —**cap·tiv'i·ty,** *n.*

cap'tor, *n.* person who takes a captive.

cap'ture, *v.t.,* **-tured, -turing,** *n.* *v.t.* **1.** prevent from fleeing, fighting, etc. by force. **2.** express through art or speech. —*n.* **3.** act or instance of capturing.

car, *n.* **1.** automobile. **2.** wheeled vehicle of any kind. **3.** elevator compartment.

ca·rafe', *n.* bottle for serving beverages, usually water or wine.

car'a·mel, *n.* **1.** burnt sugar, used as a flavor or color. **2.** type of candy.

car'at, *n.* **1.** unit of 200 milligrams for weighing gems. **2.** karat.

car'a·van", *n.* group of travelers, beasts of burden, etc. in a desert.

car'bine, *n.* **1.** short-barreled rifle. **2.** light automatic military rifle.

car"bo·hy'drate, *n.* starch or sugar.

car'bon, *n.* nonmetallic element found in organic compounds.

car'bun·cle, *n.* **1.** subcutaneous inflammation. **2.** type of gem.

car'bu·ret'or, *n.* device for making explosive mixtures of air and gasoline.

car'cass, *n.* **1.** dead animal body. **2.** rough frame or shell, as of a building.

card, *n.* **1.** stiff paper bearing writing, etc. **2.** one of such papers used in games. **3.** postcard. **4. cards,** game played with cards.

card'board", *n.* thick, papery sheeting.

car'di·ac", *adj.* pertaining to the heart.

car'di·gan, *n.* sweater buttoning in front.

car'di·nal, *n.* **1.** Roman Catholic ecclesiastic second to the pope. **2.** red American songbird. **3.** cardinal number. —*adv.* **4.** primary.

cardinal number, basic number, as 1, 2, 3, etc.

car'di·o·gram", *n.* electrocardiogram. —**car'di·o·graph",** *n.*

car'di·ol'o·gy, *n.* branch of medicine concerned with the heart.

care, *n., v.,* **cared, caring.** *n.* **1.** responsibility. **2.** charge or protection. **3.** cautionary heed. **4.** worry. —*v.i.* **5.** have responsibility. **6.** feel liking or de-

sire. **7.** feel affection. **8.** feel concern. —*v.t.* **9.** have as a subject of concern.

care′ful, *adj.* **1.** cautious. **2.** with attention to accuracy.

care′less, *adj.* not properly careful.

ca·ress′, *v.t.* **1.** touch lightly and affectionately. —*n.* **2.** gesture or touch indicating affection.

car′go, *n., pl.* **-goes, -gos.** freight.

car′i·ca·ture″, *n., v.t.* **-tured, -turing.** *n.* **1.** exaggerated rendering of a person's peculiarities. —*v.t.* **2.** render in caricature. —**car′i·ca·tur″ist,** *n.*

car′ies, *n.* decay of teeth or bones.

car′il·lon, *n.* set of bells tuned to a scale. —**car′il·lon·neur′,** *n.*

car′mine, *n.* purplish red or crimson.

car′nage, *n.* slaughter.

car′nal, *adj.* pertaining to the body or its appetites.

car′ni·val, *n.* **1.** time of merrymaking before Lent. **2.** fair with entertainments.

car′ni·vore″, *n.* flesh-eating animal or plant. —**car·niv′o·rous,** *adj.*

car′ol, *n., v.,* **-oled, -oling.** *n.* **1.** song of praise, esp. at Christmas. —*v.i., v.t.* **2.** sing exuberantly. —**car′ol·er, car′ol·ler,** *n.*

ca·rouse′, *v.i.,* **-roused, -rousing.** *n. v.i.* **1.** drink together boisterously. —*n.* **2.** Also, **ca·rous′al,** period of carousing.

ca″rou·sel′, *n.* carrousel.

carp, *v.i., n., pl.* **carp** or **carps.** *v.i.* **1.** find fault unjustly. —*n.* **2.** edible fresh-water fish. —**carp′er,** *n.*

car′pen·ter, *n.* builder in wood. —**car′pen·try,** *n.*

car′pet, *n.* **1.** cloth floor covering. —*v.t.* **2.** cover with or as if with a carpet. —**car′pet·ing,** *n.*

car′port″, *n.* open-ended shelter for an automobile.

car′riage, *n.* **1.** large animal-drawn passenger vehicle. **2.** any of various moving and carrying devices. **3.** posture.

car′ri·er, *n.* **1.** thing or person that carries. **2.** aircraft carrier.

car′ri·on, *n.* dead, decaying flesh.

car′rot, *n.* vegetable with an edible orange root.

car′rou·sel, *n.* merry-go-round.

car′ry, *v.,* **-ried, -rying.** *v.t.* **1.** support or suspend. **2.** take the weight of and move. **3.** transmit. **4.** win or attain. **5.** prosecute or develop. —*v.i.* **6.** be transmitted.

cart, *n.* **1.** small wagon. —*v.t.* **2.** transport in a small wagon.

car·tel′, *n.* monopolistic association of businesses.

car′ti·lage, *n.* tough, elastic skeletal tissue.

car′ton, *n.* cardboard box.

car·toon′, *n.* **1.** amusing or satirical drawing. **2.** motion picture of such drawings. **3.** artist's design for a fresco, tapestry, etc. —**car·toon′ist,** *n.*

car′tridge, *n.* **1.** unit of ammunition for a handgun, rifle, etc. **2.** any unit loaded or fitted into a machine.

cart′wheel″, *n.* sidewise handspring.

carve, *v.t.,* **carved, carving. 1.** form by cutting parts from. **2.** cut into parts, as meat. —**carv′er,** *n.* —**carv′ing,** *n.*

cas·cade′, *n., v.i.,* **-caded, -cading.** *n.* **1.** chain of shallow waterfalls. —*v.i.* **2.** fallin or as if in a cascade.

case, *n., v.t.,* **cased, casing.** *n.* **1.** box. **2.** instance. **3.** predicament. **4.** rational argument. **5.** form of a noun, etc. that shows its role in a sentence. —*v.t.* **6.** put in a case.

case′ment, *n.* window hinged on one side.

cash, *n.* **1.** money as opposed to checks, etc. **2.** money or check given in payment. —*v.t.* **3.** exchange for money, as a check or coupon.

cash·ier′, *n.* **1.** person in charge of cash in a bank, etc. —*v.t.* **2.** dismiss, as from the military.

cas′ing, *n.* outer cover.

ca·si′no, *n., pl.* **-nos. 1.** place for dances, entertainments, etc. **2.** place for gambling.

cask, *n.* barrel for liquids.

cas′ket, *n.* **1.** box for jewels, etc. **2.** ornate coffin.

cas′se·role″, *n.* **1.** dish for baking. **2.** food baked in such a dish.

cas·sette′, *n.* a compact, ready-to-use case containing audio or video tape.

cas′sock, *n.* clergyman's long, loose garment.

cast, *v.t.,* **cast, casting,** *n, v.t.* **1.** throw. **2.** directs or project. **3.** form in a mold. —*n.* **4.** act or instance of casting. **5.** something formed in a mold. **6.** casing of a broken limb. **7.** group performing a play, etc. **8.** air or appearance.

cast′a·way″, *n.* shipwrecked person.

caste, *n.,* rigid social division, esp. in India.

cast′er, *n.* **1.** small wheel supporting a furniture leg, etc. **2.** table pitcher for vinegar, etc. Also, **cast′or.**

cas′ti·gate″, *v.t.,* **-gated, -gating.** rebuke severely. —**cas″ti·ga′tion,** *n.* —**cas′ti·ga″tor,** *n.*

cast′ing, *n.* something cast in a mold.

cas′tle, *n.* **1.** heavily fortified residence. **2.** chess rook.

cast′-off″, *adj.* discarded.

cas′trate″, *v.t.,* **-trated, -trating.** remove the testicles of. —**cas·tra′tion,** *n.*

cas′u·al, *adj.* **1.** occurring by chance. **2.** not regular. **3.** informal. **4.** relaxed. —**cas′u·al·ly,** *adv.* —**cas′u·al·ness,** *n.*

cas′u·al·ty, *n., pl.* **-ties. 1.** victim of an accident or military action. **2.** serious accident.

cas′u·ist·ry, *n., pl.* **-tries.** sophistry. —**cas′u·ist,** *n.*

cat, *n.* **1.** small, furry, four-footed animal. **2.** any feline.

cat′a·clysm, *n.* sudden, drastic change. —cat′′a·clys′mic, *adj.*

cat′a·comb′′, *n.* underground passage with burial places.

cat′a·log′, *n., v.t.,* -loged, -loging. *n.* 1. list of things acquired, to be sold, etc. —*v.t.* 2. list in a catalog. Also, **cat′a·logue′′.**

cat′a·lyst, *n.* something that affects the speed of a chemical reaction without being altered in the process. —cat′′a·lyt′ic, *adj.*

cat′′a·ma·ran′, *n.* boat with two parallel hulls.

cat′a·pult′′, *n.* 1. machine for hurling missiles, launching airplanes, etc. —*v.t.* 2. hurl or launch from or as if from a catapult.

cat′a·ract′′, *n.* 1. large waterfall. 2. opacity in the eye causing blindness.

ca·tarrh′, *n.* inflammation of mucous membranes in the nose or throat.

ca·tas′tro·phe, *n.* major disaster. —cat′′a·stroph′ic, *adj.*

cat′call′′, *n.* shrill noise expressing contempt.

catch, *v.,* caught, catching, *n. v.t.* 1. capture or seize. 2. discover or surprise. 3. be infected with. —*v.i.* 4. become caught or entangled. 5. take or retain hold. —*n.* 6. act or instance of catching. 7. number of things caught, esp. fish. 8. something for catching hold. 9. desirable spouse or acquaintance. 10. *Informal.* drawback. **catch′er**, *n.*

catch′all′′, *n.* place, category, etc. for miscellaneous things.

catch′ing, *adj.* 1. contagious. 2. attractive.

catch′up, *n.* ketchup.

catch′y, *adj.* -ier, -iest. memorable, as a tune.

cat·e·chism (kat′ə kism), *n.* set of questions and answers, esp. on religious doctrine.

cat′e·chize′′, *v.t.,* -chized, -chizing. question in detail. Also, **cat′e·chise′′.**

cat′′e·gor′i·cal, *adj.* 1. pertaining to categories. 2. specific, as a statement. —cat′′e·gor′i·cal·ly, *adv.*

cat′e·go·rize′′, *v.t.,* -rized, -rizing. put into categories.

cat′e·go′ry, *n., pl.* ries. classification.

ca′ter, *v.i.* 1. supply food, drink, tableware, etc. to parties for a fee. 2. be overly accommodating. —ca′ter·er, *n.*

cat′er·cor′′nered, *adj., adv.* on diagonally opposite corners. Also, **cat′er·cor′′ner.**

cat′er·pil′′lar, *n.* crawling larva of a butterfly, moth, etc.

cat′gut′′, *n.* tough string made from dried intestines of sheep, etc.

ca·thar′sis, *n.* purging, esp. of morbid emotions.

ca·thar′tic, *n.* 1. medicine for clearing the bowels. —*adj.* 2. pertaining to cathartics. 3. pertaining to a catharsis.

ca·the′dral, *n.* church in which a bishop normally officiates.

cath′o·lic, *adj.* 1. universal. 2. **Catholic**, pertaining to the Roman Catholic Church. —*n.* 3. **Catholic**, member of the Roman Catholic Church. —cath′′o·lic′i·ty, *n.* —Ca·thol′i·cism, *n.*

cat′nap′′, *n., v.i.,* -napped, -napping. *n.* 1. brief nap. —*v.i.* 2. take such a nap.

cat′s′-paw′′, *n.* person used by another as a tool.

cat′sup, *n.* ketchup.

cat′tle, *n., pl.* cows, bulls, etc. —cat′tle·man, *n.*

cat′walk′′, *n.* narrow elevated walk, esp. for industrial workers.

cau′cus, *n., v.i.,* -cused or -cussed, -cusing or -cussing. *n.* 1. business meeting of political leaders. —*v.i.* 2. meet in a caucus.

caul′dron, *n.* caldron.

cau′li·flow′er, *n.* edible white head of a vegetable of the cabbage family.

caulk, *v.t.* make watertight, esp. a seam.

cau′sal, *adj.* pertaining to or involving the relation of cause and effect. —cau·sal′i·ty, *n.*

cause, *n., v.t.,* caused, causing. *n.* 1. something to which a later event or condition is attributed. 2. reason or motivation. 3. goal or purpose, esp. political or religious. 4. case for advocacy. —*v.t.* 5. be the cause of. —caus′er, *n.* —caus′a·tive, *adj.*

cause′way′′, *n.* raised roadway.

caus′tic, *adj.* 1. burning. 2. bitterly sarcastic.

cau′ter·ize′′, *v.t.,* -ized, -izing. *Medicine.* burn or sear, as the flesh of a wound, to seal it. —cau′′ter·i·za′tion, *n.*

cau′tion, *n.* 1. care, as to avoid danger. 2. warning. —*v.t.* 3. warn. —cau′tion·ar′′y, *adj.*

cau′tious, *adj.* careful to avoid danger.

cav′al·cade′′, *n.* procession, esp. on horseback.

cav′′a·lier′, *n.* 1. horseman, esp. a knight. 2. gallant. —*adj.* 3. casual. 4. arrogant.

cav′al·ry, *n., pl.* -ries. *n.* 1. fighting force on horseback. 2. fighting force in motor vehicles. —cav′al·ry·man, *n.*

cave, *n., v.,* caved, caving. *n.* 1. covered opening in the earth. —*v.i., v.t.,* 2. cave in, collapse. —cave′-in′′, *n.*

cav′ern, *n.* spacious cave. —cav′ern·ous, *adj.*

cav′i·ar′′, *n.* roe, esp. that of sturgeon. Also, **cav′i·are′′.**

cav′il, *n., v.i.,* -iled, -iling. quibble. —cav′il·er, cav′il·ler, *n.*

cav′i·ty, *n., pl.* -ities. hollow place.

ca·vort′, *v.i.* frolic.

cay·enne', *n.* extremely hot red pepper.

cay·use', *n.* small cowboy horse.

cease, *v.*, ceased, ceasing. *v.i.*, *v.t.*, *n.* stop, —cease'less, *adj.*

ce'dar, *n.* type of fragrant pine.

cede, *v.t.*, ceded, ceding. yield possession of.

ceil'ing, *n.* 1. structure or surface forming the upper part of a room, etc. 2. upper limit.

cel'e·brate", *v.*, -brated, -brating. *v.t.* 1. perform ritually. 2. mark or commemorate with festivity. 3. do honor to. —v.i. 4. have festivities. —cel''e·bra'tion, *n.* —cel'e·brant, *n.* —cel'e·brat"ed, *adj.*

ce·leb'ri·ty, *n., pl.* -ties, 1. fame. 2. currently famous person.

ce·ler'i·ty, *n.* swiftness.

cel'er·y, *n.* plant with edible leaf stalks.

ce·les'tial, *adj.* pertaining to heaven or outer space.

cel'i·bate", *n.* 1. unmarried person. 2. sexually abstinent person. —adj. 3. pertaining to celibates or celibacy. —cel'i·ba·cy, *n.*

cell, *n.* 1. unit of protoplasm. 2. unit of space. 3. habitable space in a prison, monastery, etc. 4. electric battery. 5. local unit of an organization. —celled, *adj.* —cel'lu·lar, *adj.*

cel'lar, *n.* 1. basement. 2. storage space totally or partly underneath a building. 3. collection of wine.

cel·lo (tshel'lo), *n., pl.* -los. large bowed stringed instrument. —cel'list, *n.*

cel'lo·phane", *n.* transparent wrapping material.

Cel'lu·loid", *n. Trademark.* plastic made from nitrocellulose and camphor.

Cel'sius, *adj.* centigrade.

ce·ment', *n.* 1. mixture of burned lime and clay, used for building. 2. adhesive substance. —v.t. 3. join with cement. 4. cover with cement.

cem'e·ter"y, *n., pl.* -ies. area of land for burying the dead.

cen'sor, *n.* 1. person who eliminates unauthorized material from writings, etc. 2. official who criticizes the state of government, society, etc. —cen'sor·ship", *n.*

cen·so'ri·ous, *adj.* given to harsh criticism.

cen'sure, *n., v.t.*, -sured, -suring. rebuke or condemnation. —v.t. 2. rebuke or condemn.

cen'sus, *n.* counting and analysis of population, etc.

cent, *n.* hundredth part of a dollar.

cen'taur", *n. Greek Mythology.* creature with the body of a horse and the head and trunk of a man.

cen"te·nar'i·an, *n.* person 100 years old.

cen'te·nar"y, *adj., n., pl.* -ies. centennial.

cen·ten'ni·al, *adj.* 1. pertaining to or marking a period of 100 years. —n. 2. hundredth anniversary. 3. celebration of such an anniversary.

cen'ter, *n.* 1. point or area equidistant from all outer points. 2. place of concentration. 3. area of political moderation. —v.t. 4. put or concentrate at a center.

cen'ti·grade", *adj.* pertaining to a system of temperature measurement in which the range between the freezing and boiling points of water is 100 degrees; Celsius.

cen'ti·gram", *n.* hundredth part of a gram. Also, cen'ti·gramme".

cen'ti·me"ter, *n.* hundredth part of a meter. Also, cen'ti·me"tre.

cen'ti·pede", *n.* many-legged crawling insect.

cen'tral, *adj.* 1. located at the center. 2. accessible from all points. 3. fundamental; basic. —cen'tral·ly, *adv.*

cen'tral·ize", *v.t.*, -ized, -izing. 1. unite under or control from a single authority. 2. place at a center. —cen"tral·i·za'tion, *n.*

cen·trif'u·gal force, force tending to pull a mass away from a point around which it moves.

cen·trip'e·tal force, force tending to pull a mass toward a point around which it moves.

cen'tu·ry, *n., pl.* -ries. 1. period of 100 years. 2. such a period as a unit, reckoned from A.D. 1.

ce·ram'ic, *n.* 1. ceramics, making of objects from baked clay or similar materials. 2. object so made. —adj. 3. pertaining to ceramics. 4. made as a ceramic.

ce're·al, *n.* 1. grain used as food. 2. food manufactured from such grain. —adj. 3. pertaining to grain.

cer·e'bral, *adj.* reasoned rather than felt.

cer"e·mo'ni·al, *adj.* 1. formal. —n. 2. ceremony.

cer'e·mo"ny, *n., pl.* -nies. 1. ordered set of actions for a formal occasion. 2. formality. —cer"e·mo'ni·ous, *adj.*

cer'tain, *adj.* 1. without doubt. 2. without error. 3. inevitable. 4. unspecified. —cer'tain·ly, *adv.* —cer'tain·ty, *n.*

cer·tif'i·cate, *n.* document that certifies.

cer'ti·fy", *v.t.*, -fied, -fying. 1. declare formally to be competent, valid, true, etc. 2. issue a certificate to. —cer"ti·fi·ca'tion, *n.*

cer'ti·tude", *n.* inevitability.

ces·sa'tion, *n.* stop.

ces'sion, *n.* act or instance of ceding.

cess'pool", *n.* receptacle for plumbing wastes.

chafe, *v.*, chafed, chafing. *v.t.* 1. wear by rubbing. 2. warm by rubbing, as the skin. —v.i. 3. become restless and annoyed.

chaff, *n.* **1.** waste from threshed grain. **2.** worthless stuff. —*n. v.i.* **3.** banter.

chafing dish, metal dish with a heating lamp underneath.

cha·grin′, *n., v.t.,* **-grined, -grining.** *n.* **1.** embarrassment at failure or disappointment. —*v.t.* **2.** cause chagrin in.

chain, *n.* **1.** flexible length formed of connected pieces. **2.** related series of events, arguments, etc. **3. chains,** bondage. —*v.t.* **4.** fasten with a chain.

chain reaction, series of reactions each caused by one immediately previous.

chair, *n.* **1.** seat with a back. **2.** official post or position, esp. a chairmanship of professorship. **3.** chairman. —*v.t.* **4.** preside over as chairman.

chair′man, *n.* person who presides over a meeting. —**chair′man·ship″,** *n.* Also, **chair′per″son.**

chaise longue, *pl.* **chaise longues.** daybed with a chairlike back at one end. Also, **chaise lounge.**

cha·let (sha lā′), *n.* Swiss farmhouse with a low, jutting roof.

chal′ice, *n.* wine goblet used in religious communions.

chalk, *n.* **1.** soft white limestone. **2.** white or dyed stonelike material for writing on blackboards. —*v.t.* **3.** write or mark with chalk. —**chalk′y,** *adj.*

chal′lenge, *v.t.,* **-lenged, -lenging,** *n. v.t.* **1.** call upon to fight, compete, or act bravely. **2.** demand identification of. **3.** demand proof from or for. **4.** reject as a juror. —*n.* **5.** act or instance of challenging. **6.** demand for one's best effort. —**chal′leng·er,** *n.*

cham′ber, *n.* **1.** room, esp. a bedroom. **2.** enclosed space, as in a machine, gun, or part of the body. **3.** legislative or official body. **4. chambers,** judge's office. —**cham′bered,** *adj.* —**cham′ber·maid″,** *n.*

chamber music, music written for small groups and intended for home entertaining.

cha·me·le·on (kə mē′lē ən), *n.* lizard able to change the color of its skin.

cham·ois (sham′ē), *n.* **1.** small European mountain antelope. **2.** Also, **cham′my,** soft leather of a chamois or other animal, used for polishing.

champ, *v.t., v.i.* bite or chew noisily.

cham·pagne (sham pān′), *n.* sparkling white wine, originally from northern France.

cham′pi·on, *n.* **1.** person who fights in another's behalf. **2.** athlete winning or getting first place in a series of competitions. **3.** advocate of a cause. —*v.t.* **4.** defend or advocate. —**cham′pi·on·ship″,** *n.*

chance, *n., adj., v.,* **chanced, chancing.** *n.* **1.** possibility of becoming, doing, or getting something desired. **2.** the un-predictable. **3.** unpredictable event. **4.** risk. **5.** lottery ticket. —*adj.* **6.** accidental. —*v.t.* **7.** risk. —*v.i.* **8.** transpire or come by accident.

chan′cel, *n.* area of a church around the altar.

chan′cel·lor, *n.* high government or academic official. —**chan′cel·lor·ship″** *n.*

chanc′y, *adj.,* **-ier, -iest.** risky or uncertain.

chan″de·lier′, *n.* lighting fixture suspended from a ceiling.

chand′ler, *n.* supplier, esp. to ships. —**chand′ler·ry,** *n.*

change, *v.,* **changed, changing,** *n. v.t.* **1.** make into a different form. **2.** give up one for the other, as articles of clothing, vehicles, etc. **3.** give lower denominations of money in exchange for. —*v.i.* **4.** become different. **5.** leave one vehicle for another. —*n.* **6.** act or instance of changing. **7.** variety. **8.** money returned from that offered in payment. **9.** money in small denominations, esp. coins. —**change′less,** *adj.* —**change′a·ble,** *adj.*

chan′nel, *n., v.t.,* **-neled, -neling.** *n.* **1.** deeper part of a watercourse. **2.** body of water linking two larger ones. **3.** groove. **4.** *Television and radio.* frequency band. **5. channels,** offices in an official sequence for a given purpose. —*v.t.* **6.** send through or as through a channel. **7.** make grooves in.

chant, *n.* **1.** sung liturgical music. **2.** heavily rhythmical song or speech. —*v.t.* **3.** sing or utter in a chant.

chan′tey, *n., pl.* **-teys.** rhythmical work song of a sailor. Also, **chan′ty.**

cha·os (kā′os), *n.* utter disorder. —**cha·ot′ic,** *adj.*

chap, *v.,* **chapped** or **chapt, chapping.** *v.t., v.i.* roughen or crack, as the skin or lips.

chap′el, *n.* **1.** minor church. **2.** private church, as in a school or house.

chap·er·on (shap′ə rōn), *n., v.t.,* **-oned, -oning.** *n.* **1.** person who accompanies young unmarried persons to ensure propriety. —*v.t.* **2.** accompany as a chaperon. Also, **chap′er·one″.**

chap′lain, *n.* **1.** clergyman employed by an institution, military force, etc. **2.** clergyman attached to a chapel.

chaps, *n., pl.* leather legging worn by cowboys.

chap′ter, *n.* **1.** division of a book. **2.** local branch of an association. **3.** council of a religious community.

char, *v.,* **charred, charring.** *v.t., v.i.* **1.** burn on the surface. **2.** burn to charcoal.

char′ac·ter, *n.* **1.** personality. **2.** moral strength. **3.** person as judged by his ac-

tions. 4. eccentric or conspicuous person. 5. reputation. 6. person in a work of fiction. 7. any symbol used in forming writing.

char″ac·ter·is′tic, *adj.* 1. typical. —2. typical or distinguishing quality. —**char″ac·ter·is′tic·al·ly,** *adv.*

char′ac·ter·ize″, *v.t.,* -ized, -izing. 1. attribute or give characteristics to. 2. be characteristic of. —**char″ac·ter·i·za′tion,** *n.*

cha·rade′, *n.* pantomime offering clues to guessing a secret word.

char′coal″, *n.* wood partially burned in the absence of air.

charge, *v.,* charged, charging, *n. v.t.* 1. supply or load. 2. electrify. 3. accuse. 4. make responsible. 5. ask as a price or fee. 6. enter as a debt. 7. attack with swift movement. 8. require payment. 9. move swiftly in an attack. —*n.* 10. act or instance of charging. 11. that with which something is charged. 12. care or responsibility. 13. object of one's care or responsibility. —**charge′a·ble,** *adj.*

char′i·ot, *n.* two-wheeled horse-drawn vehicle. —**char″i·o·teer′,** *n.*

cha·ris·ma (kə riz′mə), *n.* quality of leadership derived from the personality. —**char″is·mat′ic,** *adj.*

char′i·ta·ble, *adj.* 1. kindly. 2. generous. 3. pertaining to charities.

char′i·ty, *n., pl.* -ties. 1. love for mankind. 2. generosity to the needy. 3. organization for helping the needy. 4. kindness in judging others.

char·la·tan (shahr′lə tən), *n.* perpetrator of frauds. —**char′la·tan·ism, char′la·tan·ry,** *n.*

charm, *n.* 1. attractive or delightful quality. 2. trinket. 3. magic spell. —*v.t.* 4. exercise charm or a charm upon. —**charm′er,** *n.* —**charm′ing,** *adj.*

chart, *n.* 1. map, esp. for navigation. 2. graph or table. —*v.t.* 3. make a chart of. 4. map or plan.

char′ter, *n.* 1. license or franchise. 2. statement of fundamental organizational principles. 3. hire of a vehicle. —*v.t.* 4. grant a charter to. 5. hire, as for a trip.

char′y, *adj.,* -ier, -iest. 1. cautious. 2. sparing.

chase, *v.,* chased, chasing, *n. v.t.* 1. go after to overtake or capture. 2. drive away. 3. hunt. 4. engrave, as metal. —*v.i.* 5. *Informal.* rush. —*n.* 6. pursuit. 7. hunting of game.

chasm (kas′m), *n.* abyss.

chas·sis (chas′ē, chas′ē), *n., pl.* -sis. frame and running gear of an automobile, not including the engine.

chaste, *adj.* 1. pure, esp. of sexual desire or activity. 2. tastefully restrained. —**chas′ti·ty,** *n.*

chas′ten, *v.t.* correct or subdue, esp. by punishment or scolding.

chas·tise′, *v.t.,* -tised, -tising. punish or scold.

chat, *n., v.i.,* chatted, chatting. *n.* 1. light, informal conversation. —*v.i.* 2. have such a conversation.

cha·teau′, *n., pl.* -teaux, -teaus. castle or country house in France. Also, **châ·teau′.**

chat′tel, *n.* piece of movable personal property.

chat′ter, *v.i.* 1. make rapid sounds with the voice. 2. talk foolishly. 3. make rapid clashing sounds, as the teeth of a chilled person. —*n.* 4. chattering noise. 5. foolish talk.

chauf·feur′, *n.* person hired to drive an automobile.

chau′vin·ism, *n.* fanatical devotion to one's country, etc. —**chau′vin·ist,** *n.* —**chau″vin·is′tic,** *adj.*

cheap, *adj.* 1. low in price. 2. low in worth. 3. despicable. 4. *Informal.* stingy. —*adv.* 5. at low cost. —**cheap′ly,** *adv.* —**cheap′ness,** *n.* —**cheap′en,** *v.t., v.i.*

cheat, *v.t.* 1. deceive, esp. for money. 2. evade. —*v.i.* 3. be deceptive. —*n.* 4. deception. 5. deceiver.

check, *n.* 1. precaution. 2. inspection. 3. halt or frustration. 4. identification slip. 5. document transferring money. 6. bill, as in a restaurant. 7. square in a checkered pattern. 8. *Chess.* danger to a king. —*v.t.* 9. halt or restrain. 10. verify or investigate. 11. place with another for shipment or storage. —**check′book″,** *n.* —**check′room″,** *n.*

check′er, *n.* 1. person or thing that checks. 2. checkers, **a.** pattern of squares in alternating colors. **b.** game played on a board with this pattern. 3. disk used in playing checkers. —**check′er·board″,** *n.*

check′mate″, *n.,* -mated, -mating *n.* 1. *Chess.* inevitable capture of a king. 2. total defeat or ruin. —*v.t.* 3. impose a checkmate on.

check′up″, *n.* medical examination.

ched′dar, *n.* hard cheese, often sharp.

cheek, *n.* 1. side of the face below the eye. 2. impudence.

cheer, *n.* 1. happiness. 2. shout of delight, encouragement, etc. 3. food and entertainment. —*v.i.* 4. shout cheers. 5. become less unhappy. —*v.t.* 6. encourage, etc. with cheers. 7. make less unhappy. —**cheer′ful,** *adj.* —**cheer′less,** *adj.*

cheese, *n.* food made from milk curds.

cheese′burg″er, *n.* hamburger cooked with cheese.

cheese′cake″, *n.* cake made with cheese.

cheese′cloth″, *n.* loosely woven cotton.

chef, *n.* cook, esp. a supervising cook.

chem'i·cal, *adj*. **1.** pertaining to, or produced or operated by, chemistry. —*n*. **2.** substance produced by or used in chemistry. —**chem'i·cal·ly**, *adv*.

che·mise', *n*. loose-fitting woman's dress or slip.

chem'is·try, *n*. study of substances and their production and conversion. —**chem'ist**, *n*.

che·nille', *n*. fabric woven from a soft, tufted yarn.

cher'ish, *v.t*. regard as dear or precious.

cher'ry, *n., pl*. **-ries.** tree bearing a small, red fruit.

cher'ub, *n., pl*. **-ubs, -ubim.** angel often shown as a chubby, winged child. —**che·ru'bic**, *adj*.

chess, *n*. game played on a checkerboard with 16 pieces on each of two sides. —**chess'board''**, *n*. —**chess'man**, *n*.

chest, *n*. **1.** any of various boxlike containers for storage. **2.** part of the body within the ribs.

chest'nut, *n*. tree of the beech family with an edible nut.

chev'ron, *n*. sign like a V or inverted V, used for military insignia, heraldry, etc.

chew, *v.t*. reduce with the teeth, as for swallowing. —**chew'y**, *adj*.

Chi·an·ti, (kē ahn'tē), *n*. dry red table wine.

chic, *n*. elegance; smartness.

chi·can'er·y, *n., pl*. **-ries.** trickery.

chi·ca''no, *n., fem.* **-a.** a person of Mexican descent.

chick, *n*. young bird, esp. a chicken.

chick'en, *n*. hen or rooster.

chick'en-heart''ed, *adj*. cowardly.

chicken pox, contagious virus disease of children.

chick'pea'', *n*. edible seed of a bushy plant.

chic'o·ry, *n*. plant with leaves used in salad and roots used as a coffee substitute.

chide, *v.*, **chided** or **chid, chided** or **chid** or **chidden, chiding.** *v.t., v.i.* scold; rebuke.

chief, *n*. **1.** principal person. —*adj*. **2.** main. —**chief'ly**, *adv*.

chief'tain, *n*. leader of a tribe or clan.

chif·fo·nier (shif''ə nēr'), *n*. chest of drawers. Also, **chif''fon·ier'**.

Chi·hua·hua (tshi wa'wa), *n*. small dog.

child, *n., pl*. **children. 1.** human before puberty. **2.** offspring. —**child'birth''**, *n.* —**child'hood''**, *n.* —**child'less**, *adj.* —**child'like''**, *adj*.

child'ish, *adj*. characteristic of children, esp. as regards behavior or judgment.

chil'i, *n*. dish of beef, red pepper, etc. Also, **chili con car'ne**.

chill, *n*. **1.** perceptible cold. **2.** shiver from cold. —*adj*. **3.** chilly. —*v.t*. **4.** cause to be cold. —*v.i*. **5.** become cold.

chill'y, *adj.*, **-ier, -iest.** cold.

chime, *n., v.*, **chimed, chiming.** *n*. **1.** bell, esp. in a clock. **2.** chimes, tuned bells. —*v.t., v.i.* **3.** sound with chimes.

chi·me'ra (kī mē'rə), *n*. fantastic, imaginary thing. —**chi·mer'i·cal**, *adj*.

chim'ney, *n., pl*. **-nies.** passage for smoke or heat.

chim''pan·zee', *n*. medium-sized ape.

chin, *n*. part of the face at the lower jaw.

chi'na, *n*. **1.** porcelain. **2.** vitrified earthenware. **3.** dishes, etc. Also, **chi'na·ware**.

chink, *n*. **1.** narrow crack. **2.** clinking sound.

chintz, *n*. printed cotton, usually glazed.

chip, *n., v.*, **-ped, -ping.** *n*. **1.** small cut or broken piece. **2.** token used in gambling, etc. **3.** (computers) the basic component of miniaturized electronic circuitry. —*v.t*. **4.** knock chips from. —*v.i*. **5.** break into chips.

chip'munk'', *n*. small North American squirrel.

chip'per, *adj*. lively in spirit.

chi·rop·o·dy (kī rop'ə dē), *n*. podiatry. —**chi·rop'o·dist**, *n*.

chi·ro·prac·tic (kī''rə prak'tik), *n*. treatment of illness through manipulation of the joints. —**chi'ro·prac'tor**, *n*.

chirp, *v.i*. make short, shrill, birdlike noises.

chis'el, *n., v.t.*, **-eled** or **-eling.** *n*. **1.** cutting tool driven at one end. —*v.t*. **2.** cut with a chisel. —*v.i*. **3.** *Informal.* cheat, esp. on small matters. —**chis'el·er**, *n*.

chit'chat'', *n*. light conversation or gossip.

chit'ter·lings, *n., pl*. small intestines of pigs as a food. Also, **chit'lins, chit'lings**.

chiv'al·ry, *n*. **1.** medieval institution of knighthood. **2.** courage, gallantry, etc. —**chiv·al'ric**, *adj*. —**chiv'al·rous**, *adj*.

chlo·rine (klō'rēn), *n*. greenish chemical used for disinfection. —**chlo'ri·nate''**, *v.t*.

chlo'ro·form'', *n*. **1.** volatile liquid anaesthetic. —*v.t*. **2.** kill or anaesthetize with chloroform.

chlo'ro·phyll, *n*. green substance in plants. Also, **chlo'ro·phyl**.

chock, *n*. **1.** wedge stopping wheels from rolling. —*v.t*. **2.** stop with chocks.

chock'-full', *adj*. absolutely full.

choc'o·late, *n*. **1.** dark-brown substance made from or flavored with cacao seeds. **2.** reddish brown.

choice, *n., adj.*, **choicer, choicest.** *n*. **1.** fact or instance of choosing. **2.** thing chosen. —*adj*. **3.** superior in quality.

choir (kwīr), *n*. **1.** chorus, esp. one sing-

choke

ing religious music. 2. part of a church for such a chorus.

choke, *v.,* **choked, chocking,** *n. v.t.* 1. cut off the breath of. 2. clog. —*v.i.* 3. suffer from the cutting-off of breath. —*n.* 4. act, instance, or sound of choking.

cho·les·ter·ol (kə les'tə rōl''), *n.* solid found in bile, etc.

choose, *v.,* **chose, chosen, choosing.** *v.t.* 1. decide upon as best to take, do, etc. —*v.i.* 2. make a choice.

choos'y, *adj.,* **-ier, -iest.** *Informal.* taking great care or trouble over purchases, etc. Also, **choos'ey.**

chop, *v.,* **chopped, chopping.** *n. v.t., v.i.* 1. cut with small blows. —*n.* 2. small cutting blow. 3. meat cut from the rib, shoulder, or loin. 4. small, distinct waves of water. 5. **chops,** mouth and lower cheeks. —**chop'per,** *n.* —**chop'py,** *adj.*

chop'sticks'', *n., pl.* twin sticks used in eating, esp. in the Far East.

chop su'ey, quasi-Chinese food of meat, bean sprouts, etc.

chor·al (kōr'əl), *adj.* pertaining to or for a chorus.

cho·rale', *n.* 1. hymn tune. 2. choral composition. 3. chorus or choir.

chord (kôrd), *n.* 1. combination of musical tones. 2. straight line intercepting an arc at two points.

chore, *n.* routine or hard task.

chor·e·og·ra·phy (kōr''ē ahg'rə fē), *n.* art of planning or executing ballets or dances. —**chor''e·o·graph'ic,** *adj.* —**chor'e·o·graph'',** *v.t.* —**chor''e·og'ra·pher,** *n.*

chor'tle, *v.,* **-tled, -tling.** *v.i., v.t.* speak with chuckles.

cho·rus (kō'rəs), *n.* 1. singing group. 2. composition for such a group. 3. repeated part of a song composed in stanzas. 4. unison. —*v.t.* 5. utter in chorus.

chow, *n.* 1. medium-sized dog. 2. *Informal.* food.

chow'der, *n.* soup of milk, clams, fish, etc.

chow mein, quasi-Chinese dish of fried noodles, meat, bean sprouts, etc.

chris'ten, *v.t.* 1. baptize. 2. name formally. —**chris'ten·ing,** *n.*

Chris'ten·dom, *n.* Christian part of the world or of humanity.

Chris'tian, *n.* 1. believer in Christ. —*adj.* 2. pertaining to believers in Christ or to their churches. 3. consistent with the teachings of Christ, esp. regarding charity or salvation. —**Chris''ti·an'i·ty,** *n.*

Christian name, name given to a person, as at baptism.

Christ'mas, *n.* celebration of the birth of Christ, usually December 25.

chro·mat'ic, *adj.* 1. pertaining to color.

2. *Music.* composed of semitones, as a scale.

chrome, *n., adj., v.t.,* **chromed, chroming.** *n.* 1. chromium or a chromium alloy. —*adj.* 2. made with chromium. —*n.* 3. plate with chrome.

chro'mi·um, *n.* corrosion-resistant metallic element.

chro'mo·some'', *n.* gene-bearing body.

chron'ic, *adj.* 1. long-lasting or recurrent. 2. suffering from a chronic ailment. —**chron'i·cal·ly,** *adv.*

chron'i·cle, *n., v.t.,* **-cled, -cling.** *n.* 1. chronological record. —*v.t.* 2. put into such a record. —**chron'i·cler,** *n.*

chro·nol'o·gy, *n., pl.* **-gies.** 1. measurement of time. 2. recording of events in order of occurrence. 3. dating of events. —**chron''o·log'i·cal,** *adj.*

chro·nom'e·ter, *n.* highly accurate timepiece.

chrys'a·lis, *n.* pupa or cocoon of a butterfly.

chrys·an'the·mum, *n.* showy late-blooming flower.

chub'by, *adj.,* **-bier, -biest.** plump.

chuck, *v.t.* 1. toss. 2. tap, esp. under the chin. —*n.* 3. neck and shoulder cut of beef. 4. act or instance of chucking.

chuck'le, *v.i.,* **-led, -ling,** *n. v.i.* 1. laugh softly. —*n.* 2. soft laugh.

chug, *n., v.i.,* **chugged, chugging.** *n.* 1. sound of an engine exhaust. —*v.i.* 2. move with chugs.

chum, *n. Informal.* friend. **chum'my,** *adj.*

chump, *n. Informal.* person with bad judgment.

chunk, *n.* thick fragment.

chunk'y, *adj.,* **-ier, -iest.** short and thick.

church, *n.* 1. religious organization. 2. religious building. 3. whole community of Christians. —**church'go''er,** *n.* —**church'ly,** *adj.* —**church'man,** *n.*

church'yard'', *n.* grounds of a church, esp. when used as a cemetery.

churl, *n.* surly, ill-mannered person. —**churl'ish,** *adj.*

churn, *n.* 1. device for shaking cream to form butter. —*v.t., v.i.* 2. stir or shake.

chute (shoot), *n.* slide for transferring materials, etc.

chut'ney, *n.* Indian relish.

chutz·pah (khoōtz'pah), *n. Yiddish.* impudence; audacity. Also, **chutz'pa.**

ci·ca·da (si kā'də), *n.* large insect making a shrill rasping sound; often called a locust.

ci'der, *n.* apple juice.

ci·gar', *n.* roll of tobacco leaves for smoking.

cig''a·rette', *n.* roll of tobacco in paper for smoking.

cinch, *n.* 1. *Informal.* something easy. 2. strap for securing a saddle.

cin'der, *n.* ash.

cin'e·ma, *n.* motion picture or pictures. —**cin''e·mat'ic**, *adj.*

cin'na·mon, *n.* East Indian spice.

ci'pher, *n.* 1. code. 2. zero.

cir'ca, *prep.* around; used in dating.

cir'cle, *n., v.t.,* -**cled**, -**cling**. *n.* 1. closed two-dimensional curve with one center. 2. something formed like such a curve. 3. group of friends, persons with common interests, etc. —*v.t.* 4. go around in a circle.

cir'cuit, *n.* 1. continuous path of movement. 2. regular round of professional visits. 3. path of an electric current.

cir·cu'i·tous, *adj.* roundabout.

cir'cuit·ry, *n.* components of an electrical circuit.

cir'cu·lar, *adj.* 1. shaped like a circle. —*n.* 2. pamphlet, etc. for general distribution.

cir'cu·lar·ize'', *v.t.,* -**ized**, -**izing**. 1. solicit from or notify by means of circulars. 2. make circular.

cir'cu·late'', *v.,* -**ated**, -**ating**. *v.i.* 1. move in a closed, continuous path. 2. move from person to person or place to place. —*v.t.* 3. cause to move in either of these ways. —**cir'cu·la·to''ry**, *adj.*

cir''cu·la'tion, *n.* 1. act or instance of circulating. 2. normal movement of blood. 3. readership of a periodical.

cir'cum·cise'', *v.t.,* -**cised**, -**cising**. cut away the foreskin of. —**cir''cum·ci'sion**, *n.*

cir''cum·fer·ence, *n.* dimension along the line of a circle. —**cir·cum'fer·en''tial**, *adj.*

cir''cum·lo·cu'tion, *n.* wordy, evasive speech.

cir''cum·nav'i·gate, *v.t.,* -**gated**, **gating**. sail or fly entirely around.

cir'cum·scribe'', *v.t.,* -**scribed**, -**scribing**. 1. draw a circle around. 2. confine.

cir'cum·spect'', *adj.* cautious. —**cir''cum·spec'tion**, *n.*

cir''cum·stance'', *n.* 1. accompanying condition. 2. chance. 3. **circumstances**, state of material welfare.

cir''cum·stan'tial, *adj.* 1. pertaining to circumstances or circumstance. 2. pertaining to legal evidence implying but not proving something. 3. detailed.

cir''cum·vent'', *v.t.* prevent or overcome with cunning. —**cir''cum·ven'tion**, *n.*

cir'cus, *n.* 1. traveling show of animals, acrobats, etc. 2. ancient show of human and animal combats, etc.

cir'rus, *n.* feathery cloud formation.

cis'tern, *n.* tank for water storage.

cit'a·del, *n.* fortress, esp. in a city.

cite, *v.t.,* **cited**, **citing**. 1. mention as a scholarly authority. 2. mention as an example. 3. mention officially as meritorious. 4. summon before a court. —**ci·ta'tion**, *n.*

cit'i·zen, *n.* member of a state or other political entity. —**cit'i·zen·ry**, *n.* —**cit'i·zen·ship''**, *n.*

cit'ron, *n.* lemonlike fruit whose rind is candied.

cit''ron·el'la, *n.* oil used to repel mosquitoes, etc.

citrus, *adj.* of or pertaining to lemons, oranges, limes, etc. —**cit'ric**, *adj.*

cit'y, *n., pl.* -**ies**. 1. large community. 2. government of such a community.

civ'ic, *adj.* pertaining to cities or their citizens.

civ'ics, *n., pl.* study of the relation of citizens to political entities.

civ'il, *adj.* 1. not military or religious. 2. polite. —**ci·vil'i·ty** *n.*

civil engineering, engineering of public works or the like. —**civil engineer**.

ci·vil'ian, *n.* person outside any military or police organization.

civ''i·li·za'tion, *n.* 1. lawful, orderly state of society. 2. society characterized by order. 3. civilized part of the world.

civ'i·lize'', *v.t.,* -**ized**, -**izing**. cause to adopt civilization.

civil service, non-military, non-police government service. —**civil servant**.

civil war, war between factions of the same nation.

clad, *adj.* dressed.

claim, *v.t.* 1. designate for oneself. 2. assert as true. 3. require. —*n.* 4. act or instance of claiming. 5. something claimed. —**claim'ant**, **claim'er**, *n.*

clair·voy'ance, *n.* sensitivity to things not usually seen, esp. the supernatural. —**clair·voy'ant**, *adj., n.*

clam, *n.* bivalve mollusk.

clam'ber, *v.i.* climb laboriously.

clam'my, *adj.,* -**mier**, -**miest**. cold and moist.

clam'or, *n.* 1. loud outcry. —*v.i.* 2. make such an outcry, as in demanding or complaining. —**clam'or·ous**, *adj.*

clamp, *n.* 1. mechanical device for holding things together. —*v.t.* 2. fasten with a clamp.

clan, *n.* group of families with a common ancestor. —**clans'man**, *n.*

clan·des'tine, *adj.* secret; stealthy.

clang, *n.* loud ringing noise.

clang'or, *n.* clanging, as of bells.

clank, *n.* dull metallic sound.

clan'nish, *adj.* sociable together but excluding others.

clap, *v.t.* 1. strike together, as the palms of the hands. —*v.i.* 2. clap the palms together. —*n.* 3. sound of clapping. 4. act or instance of clapping.

clap·board, (kləb′bərd), *n.* board used as a siding for buildings.

clap'per, *n.* object for striking a bell.

claque, *n.* group for the purpose of applauding a performer, esp. for pay.

clar′et, *n.* dry red table wine.

clar′i·fy″, *v.t.,* **-fied, -fying.** make clear. —**clar″i·fi·ca′tion,** *n.*

clar′i·net′, *n.* reed woodwind instrument. —**clar″i·net′ist,** *n.*

clar′i·ty, *n.* clearness, esp. to the understanding.

clash, *v.i.* **1.** strike together violently. **2.** be in violent disagreement. —*n.* **3.** act or instance of clashing.

clasp, *n.* **1.** folding fastener. **2.** embrace. **3.** grasp, as of the hand. —*v.t.* **4.** hold with or in a clasp.

class, *n.* **1.** category or grade. **2.** social or economic level. **3.** *Informal.* stylishness. **4.** group of students taught or graduating together. —*v.t.* **5.** classify. —**class′less,** *adj.* —**class′mate″,** *n.* —**class′room″,** *n.*

clas′sic, *adj.* **1.** excellent of its kind. **2.** completely typical. **3.** harmonious. **4.** pertaining to Greco-Roman antiquity or art. —*n.* **5.** something excellent of its kind. **6.** Greek or Roman author.

clas′si·cal, *adj.* **1.** pertaining to Greco-Roman antiquity or art. **2.** *Music.* serious and of permanent value. **3.** traditional.

clas′si·cism, *n.* adherence to forms or principles deemed classic. —**clas′si·cist,** *n.*

clas′si·fy″, *v.t.,* **-fied, -fying. 1.** put into meaningful categories. **2.** designate officially as secret. —**clas″si·fi·ca′tion,** *n.*

clat′ter, *n.* **1.** loud rattling noise. —*v.i.* **2.** make a clatter. —*v.t.* **3.** cause to clatter.

clause, *n.* **1.** unit of a sentence. **2.** unit of a document.

claus″tro·pho′bi·a, *n.* morbid fear of enclosure. —**claus″tro·pho′bic,** *adj.*

clav′i·chord″, *n.* pianolike keyboard instrument.

clav′i·cle, *n.* collarbone.

claw, *n.* **1.** hooked paw or foot. —*v.t., v.i.* **2.** scratch or grasp with or as with a claw.

clay, *n.* earth in a readily molded state.

clean, *adj.* **1.** free of dirt, germs, impurities, etc. **2.** keeping things clean. **3.** irreproachable. **4.** thorough. —*v.t.* **5.** make clean. —**clean′er,** *n.* —**clean′up″,** *n.*

clean·ly (klen′lē), *adj.,* **-lier, -liest.** free of or avoiding dirt, etc. —**clean′li·ness,** *n.*

cleanse, *v.t.,* **cleansed, cleansing.** make clean.

clear, *adj.* **1.** perfectly transparent. **2.** lucid. **3.** unambiguous. **4.** obvious. **5.** unobstructed. **6.** free of blame, danger, debt, etc. —*adv.* **7.** clearly. —*v.t.* **8.** make clear. **9.** pass without colliding with. **10.** net a profit of. —**clear′ly,** *adv.* —**clear′ness,** *n.*

clear′ance, *n.* **1.** space between two obstructions. **2.** official approval to proceed.

clear′ing, *n.* forest area free of trees.

cleat, *n.* object attached to a surface to improve traction, give reinforcement, etc.

cleave, *v.,* **cleaved** or (for 1) **cleft** or **clove, cleaved** or (for 1) **cleft** or **cloven, cleaving.** *v.t., v.i.* **1.** split. —*v.i.* **2.** adhere or be faithful. —**cleav′er,** *n.* —**cleav′age,** *n.*

clef, *n. Music.* symbol establishing pitch.

cleft, *n.* narrow opening; crack.

clem′ent, *n.* **1.** merciful. **2.** mild, as the weather. —**clem′en·cy,** *n.*

clench, *v.t.* press or bind firmly together.

cler′gy, *n., pl.* **-gies.** priests, ministers, and other religious leaders. —**cler′gy·man,** *n.*

cler′i·cal, *adj.* **1.** pertaining to clerks. **2.** pertaining to clergy.

clerk, *n.* **1.** record keeper. **2.** retail employee.

clev′er, *adj.* able in understanding, contriving, etc. —**clev′er·ly,** *adv.* —**clev′er·ness,** *n.*

cli·ché, *n.* trite metaphor or phrase.

click, *n.* **1.** sharp noise from striking, buckling, etc. —*v.t., v.i.* **2.** move with a click.

cli′ent, *n.* person who buys professional services.

cli″en·tele′, *n.* clients of a professional man, merchant, etc.

cliff, *n.* abrupt rise of land.

cli·mac′ter·ic, *n.* critical period of life, esp. in middle age.

cli′mate, *n.* characteristic weather. —**cli·mat′ic,** *adj.*

cli′max, *n.* point of greatest interest, emotion, tension, etc. —**cli·mac′tic,** *adj.*

climb, *v.t.* **1.** move upward upon or within. —*v.i.* **2.** climb something. **3.** grow or become higher. —*n.* **4.** act or instance of climbing. **5.** something climbed. —**climb′er,** *n.*

clinch, *v.t.* **1.** establish firmly. **2.** bend to secure firmly, as a driven nail. —*n.* **3.** act or instance of clinching.

cling, *v.i.,* **clung, clinging. 1.** hold firmly. **2.** stay close.

clin′ic, *n.* **1.** session of medical treatment as a form of instruction. **2.** association of medical specialists. **3.** place for treating outpatients.

clin′i·cal, *adj.* **1.** pertaining to clinics. **2.** pertaining to medical education and treatment involving actual cases. **3.** impersonally analytical.

clink, *n.* **1.** high, muted ringing. —*v.i.* **2.** make such a sound. —*v.t.* **3.** strike so as to make such a sound.

clink′er, *n.* lump of coal ash, etc.

clip, *v.,* **clipped, clipping.** *v.t.* **1.** cut, as with scissors. **2.** fasten. **3.** *Informal.* hit

sharply. —v.i. 4. move swiftly. —n. 5. fastener. 6. *Informal.* sharp blow.

clip'per, n. 1. fast sailing vessel. 2. **clippers,** device for cutting hair.

clip'ping, n. article cut from a periodical.

clique, n. exclusive social group. —**cliqu'ish,** adj.

cloak, n. 1. long, loose garment worn over the shoulders. —v.t. 2. cover with a cloak. 3. obscure.

clob'ber, v.t. *Informal.* beat.

clock, n. 1. machine for measuring time. 2. narrow sock ornament. —v.t. 3. time. —**clock'work",** n., adj.

clock'wise", adv., adj. as the hands of a clock move, i.e. from left to right through 12 o'clock.

clod, n. 1. lump of earth. 2. *Informal.* stupid person.

clog, v., **clogged, clogging,** n. v.t. 1. stop flow through; choke. —v.i. 2. become stopped up. —n. 3. act or instance of clogging. 4. thick-soled shoe.

clois'ter, n. 1. covered walk in a monastery, etc. 2. monastic institution.

clone, n., v. (biology) a genetic duplicate of an organism.

close, v., **closed, closing,** adj., **closer, closest,** n. v.t. (klōz) 1. block or fill, as with a door. 2. move so as to block or fill. 3. deny public access to. 4. conclude. —v.i. 5. become closed. —n. 6. conclusion. —adj. (klōs) 7. near; not far. .8. confined. 9. intimate. 10. stuffy. 11. careful. 12. secretive. —**close'ly,** adv. —**close'ness,** n. —**clo'sure,** n.

clos'et, n. 1. small storage room. —v.t. 2. put in a small room for privacy.

close'-up", n. photograph at close range.

clot, n., v.i., **clotted, clotting.** n. 1. lump, esp. of coagulated blood. —v.i. 2. form a clot.

cloth, n., pl. **cloths.** 1. material of interwoven fibers. 2. piece of such material. 3. **the cloth,** the clergy.

clothe, v.t., **clothed, clothing.** 1. put clothes on. 2. give clothes to.

clothes, n., pl. things to cover the human body. Also, **cloth'ing.**

cloud, n. 1. mass of vapor in the sky. 2. mass of airborne material. 3. something marring happiness, reputation, etc. —v.t. 4. make indistinct, as from vapor. 5. mar. —v.i. 6. become cloudy. —**cloud'less,** adj. —**cloud'y,** adj.

cloud'burst", n. sudden, violent rainstorm.

clout, n. 1. blow. —v.t. 2. hit.

clove, n. 1. tropical spice. 2. section of a head of garlic, etc.

clo'ven, adj. divided or split.

clo'ver, n. three-leafed herb.

clo'ver-leaf", n. system of curved ramps between roads crossing at different grades.

clown, n. 1. entertainer with funny antics. —v.i. 2. act like a clown.

cloy'ing, adj. repulsively sweet, sentimental, etc.

club, n., v. **clubbed, clubbing.** n. 1. stick, etc. for striking blows. 2. similar object used in exercises or sports. 3. social group. 4. suit of playing cards. —v.t. 5. strike with a club. —v.i. 6. unite for a purpose. —**club'foot",** n. —**club'house",** n.

cluck, n. 1. henlike sound. —v.i. 2. make such a sound.

clue, n. 1. indication of the solution to a puzzle.

clump, n. cluster, as of trees.

clum'sy, adj., **-sier, -siest.** without skill or care. —**clum'si·ly,** adv. —**clum'si·ness,** n.

clus'ter, n. 1. loose group. —v.t., v.i. 2. gather in a group.

clutch, v.t., v.i. 1. grasp violently. —n. 2. grasp. 3. **clutches,** unrightful possession or power. 4. device for engaging a machine with its mover.

clut'ter, v.t. 1. fill with unwanted things. —n. 2. disorderly accumulation.

coach, n. 1. enclosed horse-drawn carriage. 2. bus. 3. railroad passenger car. 4. trainer, as in sports or performing arts. —v.t. 5. train, rehearse, or prompt. —**coach'man,** n.

co·ag'u·late", v., **-ated, -ating.** v.i., v.t. turn from a liquid to a semi-solid. —**co·ag"u·la'tion,** n. —**co·ag'u·lant,** n.

coal, n. 1. combustible mineral. 2. ember. —v.t. 3. supply with coal.

co"a·lesce', v.i., **-lesced, lescing.** unite. —**co"a·les'cence,** n.

co"a·li'tion, n. act of uniting for a specific purpose.

coal oil, kerosene.

coarse, adj. 1. composed of large grains, fibers, etc. 2. roughly made. 3. unrefined, as manners or language. —**coarse'ly,** adv. —**coarse'ness,** n. —**coars'en,** v.t., v.i.

coast, n. 1. land by a sea, etc. —v.i. 2. move by gravity or momentum. 3. sail along a coast.' —**coast'al,** adj. —**coast'line",** n.

coast'er, n. 1. person or thing that coasts. 2. mat or stand for wet glasses. 3. ship on a coastal run.

coat, n. 1. cold-weather garment. 2. jacket. 3. Also, **coat'ing,** layer of material. —v.t. 4. cover with a coat.

coat of arms, *Heraldry.* arms of a person, state, etc.

coax, v.t., persuade with flattery or wheedling.

co·ax'i·al, adj. having a common axis.

cob, n. corncob.

cob'ble, v.t., **-bled, -bling,** n. 1. repair, as shoes. 2. assemble clumsily. —n. 3.

Also, **cob'ble·stone"**, large pebble used for paving.

cob'bler, *n.* 1. person who cobbles. 2. fruit-filled pastry.

co'bra, *n.* poisonous Asian and African snake.

cob'web", *n.* web of a spider.

co·caine', *n.* narcotic from a tropical plant.

cock, *n.* 1. rooster. 2. faucet. —*v.t.* 3. tilt. 4. make ready for firing, as a gun.

cock·ade', *n.* hat badge or ribbon.

cock'a·too", *n.* crested East Indian parrot.

cocker spaniel, small, droopy-eared spaniel.

cock'eyed", *adj. Informal.* awry; wrong.

cock'le, *n.* edible shellfish.

cock'ney, *n., pl.* **-nies.** 1. native of London's East End. 2. dialect of such a native.

cock'pit", *n.* 1. place for a cockfight. 2. space for an airplane crew.

cock'roach", *n.* crawling insect found in buildings.

cock'sure", *adj.* foolishly self-assured.

cock'tail", *n.* 1. mixed alcoholic drink. 2. mixed appetizer.

cock'y, *adj.*, **-ier, -iest.** *Informal.* showily self-assured.

co'coa, *n.* drink made from roasted cacao powder.

co'co·nut", *n.* fruit of a palm tree, whose flesh and juice are consumed. Also, **co'coa·nut.**

co·coon', *n.* case of certain insect pupas, made of a thread.

cod, *n., pl.* **cod, cods.** edible northern saltwater fish. Also, **cod'fish".**

cod'dle, *v.t.*, **-dled, -dling.** 1. cook in water just below boiling. 2. take excessive care of; pamper.

code, *n., v.t.*, **coded, coding.** *n.* 1. set of laws or principles. 2. formula for secret messages. 3. formula for transcription by telegraph, wigwag, etc. —*v.t.* put into code.

co'deine, *n.* pain reliever derived from opium. Also, **co'dein.**

cod'i·cil, *n.* appendix to a will.

cod'i·fy", *v.t.*, **-fied, -fying.** put into systematic form, esp. in writing. —**cod"i·fi·ca'tion**, *n.*

co'-ed", *n. Informal.* woman in a coeducational school. Also, **co'ed".**

co·ed"u·ca'tion, *n.* enrollment of men and women in the same school. —**co·ed"u·ca'tion·al**, *adj.*

co"ef·fi'cient, *n.* multiplier.

co·erce', *v.t.*, **-erced, -ercing.** compel by force or threats. —**co·er'cion**, *n.*

co·e'val, *adj.* at or of the same age.

co"ex·ist', *v.i.* 1. exist together. 2. live together without dispute. —**co"ex·ist'ence**, *n.*

cof'fee, *n.* drink made from the roasted seed of a tropical shrub.

cof'fer, *n.* chest for valuables.

cof'fin, *n.* burial chest.

cog, *n.* gear tooth.

co·gent, (kō'jənt), *adj.* forcefully convincing, as an argument. —**co'gen·cy**, *n.*

cog'i·tate", *v.*, **-tated, -tating.** *v.t., v.i.* ponder. —**cog"i·ta'tion**, *n.* —**cog'i·ta"tor**, *n.*

co·gnac (kon'yak), *n.* a French brandy.

cog'nate", *adj.* 1. related. —*n.* 2. someone or something related.

cog·ni'tion, *n.* knowledge or perception. —**cog'ni·tive**, *adj.*

cog'ni·zance, *n.* official notice. —**cog'ni·zant**, *adj.*

cog·no'men, *n.* nickname.

cog'wheel", *n.* gear wheel, esp. in a clock, toy, etc.

co·hab'it, *v.i.* live together, esp. out of wedlock. —**co·hab"i·ta'tion**, *n.*

co·here', *v.i.*, **-hered, -hering.** 1. stick together. 2. be rationally connected. —**co·her'ent**, *adj.* —**co·her'ence**, *n.*

co·he'sion, *n.* tendency of particles, etc to hold together. —**co·he'sive**, *adj.*

coif·fure', *n.* hair style.

coil, *n.* 1. spiral or helix. —*v.t., v.i.* wind into a coil.

coin, *n.* 1. piece of metal used as money. 2. metal money. —*v.t.* 3. stamp as money. 4. invent as a new expression. —**coin'age**, *n.*

co"in·cide', *v.i.*, **-cided, -ciding.** 1. happen at the same time. 2. be in the same space. 3. be in agreement. —**co·in'ci·dence**, *n.* —**co·in"ci·den'tal, co·in'ci·dent**, *adj.*

co·i'tus, *n.* sexual intercourse. Also, **co·i'tion**, *n.*

coke, *n.* fuel derived from coal.

col'an·der, *n.* large strainer.

cold, *adj.* 1. having a temperature lower than normal or working temperature. 2. having a relatively low temperature. 3. feeling a lack of warmth. 4. unemotional. 5. hostilely unexpressive. 6. *Informal.* **a.** unprepared. **b.** unconscious. **c.** fully memorized. —*n.* 7. cold conditions, weather, etc. 8. illness associated with cold weather. —**cold'ly**, *adv.* —**cold'ness**, *n.*

cold'blood"ed, *adj.* 1. having blood the temperature of the environment. 2. without emotion, conscience, etc.

cold war, prolonged hostile situation without fighting.

cole'slaw", *n.* salad of shredded raw cabbage.

col'ic, *n.* abdominal cramp.

col·lab'o·rate", *v.i.*, **-rated, -rating.** 1. work together, as on a project. 2. assist

the invaders of one's country. —col·lab''o·ra'tion, *n.* —col·lab'o·ra''tor, *n.* —col·lab''o·ra'tion·ist, *n.*

col·lapse', *v.,* -lapsed, -lapsing, *n. v.i.* 1. fall because of weakness. 2. fold when not in use. 3. fail suddenly in bodily or mental health. —*v.t.* 4. cause to collapse. —*n.* 5. act or instance of collapsing. —col·laps'i·ble, *adj.*

col'lar, *n.* 1. band worn around the neck. 2. band of material applied to a shaft, etc. —*v.t.* 3. seize by the neck. 4. put a collar on.

col'lar·bone'', *n.* bone between the breastbone and shoulder blade; clavicle.

col·lat'er·al, *n.* 1. security for a loan. —*adj.* 2. accompanying. 3. related through a remote ancestor.

col'league, *n.* professional associate.

col·lect', *v.t., v.i.* 1. gather together. —*v.t.* 2. acquire to enjoy permanently. 3. enforce payment of. —*adv., adj.* 4. with the receiver paying the charges. —col·lect'a·ble, col·lect'i·ble, *adj., n.* —col·lect'or, *n.* —col·lec'tion, *n.*

col·lect'ed, *adj.* with one's emotions under control.

col·lec'tive, *adj.* 1. involving cooperation. —*n.* 2. collective enterprise or workplace. —col·lec'tive·ly, *adv.*

col·lec'tiv·ism, *n.* adoption of collective working methods. —col·lec'tiv·ist, *n., adj.* —col·lec'tiv·ize'', *v.t.*

col'lege, *n.* 1. generalized institution of higher learning. 2. specialized school. 3. official organization. —col·le'giate, *adj.*

col·lide', *v.i.* -lided, -liding. strike against another or each other while moving. —col·li'sion, *n.*

col'lie, *n.* large, long-haired dog.

col·lo'qui·al, *adj.* pertaining to or used in informal conversation only. —col·lo'qui·al·ism, *n.*

col'lo·quy, *n., pl.* -quies. discussion.

col·lu'sion, *n.* unlawful conspiracy. —col·lu'sive, *adj.*

co·logne', *n.* perfumed toilet water.

co'lon, *n.* 1. part of the large intestine. 2. punctuation mark written thus:.

colo·nel (kər'nəl), *n.* military officer between a lieutenant colonel and a brigadier general. —colo'nel·cy, *n.*

col'o·nize, *v.,* -nized, -nizing. *v.t.* 1. establish colonies in. —*v.i.* 2. settle in or as a colony.

col''on·nade', *n.* row of columns, esp. before a porch.

col'o·ny, *n., pl.* -nies. 1. region in the possession of a foreign nation. 2. community of settlers. 3. group of social insects, etc. —co·lon'i·al, *adj., n.* —col'on·ist, *n.*

col'or, *n.* 1. property deriving from specific wavelengths of light. 2. pigment.

3. vividness. 4. colors, a. national flag. b. uniform, badge, etc. distinctively colored. —*v.t.* 5. give color to. —*v.i.* 6. blush. —col''or·a'tion, *n.* —col'or·ful, *adj.* —col'or·ing, *n.*

col''or·a·tu'ra, *n.* soprano capable of brilliant effects.

col'ored, *n.* Negro; black.

col'or·less, *adj.* not vivid.

co·los'sal, *adj.* gigantic; enormous.

co·los'sus, *n., pl.* -si -suses. something gigantic.

colt, *n.* young male horse.

col'umn, *n.* 1. narrow, upright structural support. 2. stack of printed or written lines read together. 3. regular series of articles by a journalist. 4. file of troops. —col'um·nist, *n.*

co'ma, *n.* pathological unconsciousness. —co'ma·tose'', *adj.*

comb, *n.* 1. pronged device for arranging the hair or other fibers. 2. crest of a rooster, etc. 3. honeycomb. —*v.t.* 4. use a comb on. 5. search exhaustively.

com'bat, *n., v.t.,* -bated, -bating. *n.* (kom'bat) 1. battle. —*v.t.* (kəm bat') 2. fight or oppose. —com·bat'ant, *n., adj.* —com·bat'ive, *adj.*

com''bi·na'tion, *n.* 1. act or instance of combining. 2. group of successive settings of a lock dial that open the lock.

com·bine', *v.t., v.i.* (kəm bīn') 1. join together. —*n.* (kom'bīn) 2. machine that harvests and threshes grain. 3. syndicate.

com'bo, *n., pl.* -bos. *Jazz.* small instrumental group.

com·bus'tion, *n.* act of burning. —com·bus'ti·ble, *adj.*

come, *v.i.,* came, come, coming, *interj. v.i.* 1. move to this place. 2. attend; be present. 3. occur; happen. —*interj.* 4. be truthful, reasonable, etc.

co·me'di·an, *n.* humorous performer. Also, *fem.,* co·me''di·enne'.

com'e·dy, *n., pl.* -dies. 1. drama with a happy ending. 2. amusing situation.

come'ly, *adj.,* -lier, -liest. physically attractive.

co·mes'ti·ble, *n., adj.* edible.

com'et, *n.* cloud of fine dust in orbit around the sun.

com'fort, *n.* 1. feeling of physical well-being. 2. consolation. —*v.t.* 3. console or reassure.

com'fort·a·ble, *adj.* 1. enjoying comfort. 2. promoting comfort. —com'fort·a·bly, *adv.*

com'fort·er, *n.* 1. source of comfort. 2. quilt.

com'ic, *adj.* 1. Also, com'i·cal, amusing. 2. pertaining to comedy. 3. comics, comic strip. —*n.* 4. comedian. —com'i·cal·ly, *adv.*

com'ing, *adj.* **1.** on the way. **2.** destined for preeminence. —*n.* **3.** approach or arrival.

com'ma, *n.* a mark, used especially to separate phrases or clauses in a sentence.

com·mand', *v.t.* **1.** order or direct. **2.** have authority over. **3.** have the use or enjoyment of. **4.** overlook. —*n.* **5.** order. **6.** authority or control.

com'man·dant'', *n.* commanding officer.

com''man·deer', *v.t.* take control of by authority or force.

com·man'der, *n.* naval officer between a lieutenant commander and a captain in rank.

commander in chief, *n., pl.* **commander in chief.** supreme military commander.

com·mand'ment, *n.* order, esp. a standing one from a deity.

com·man'do, *n., pl.* **-dos, -does.** member of a raiding force.

com·mem'o·rate'', *v.t.*, **-rated, -rating.** honor or preserve the memory of. —**com·mem''o·ra'tion**, *n.* —**com·mem'o·ra·tive**, *adj.*

com·mence', *v.*, **-menced, -mencing.** *v.t., v.i.* begin.

com·mence'ment, *n.* **1.** beginning. **2.** high-school graduation ceremony.

com·mend', *v.t.* **1.** praise. **2.** recommend. **3.** entrust. —**com·mend'a·ble,** *adj.* —**com''men·da'tion**, *n.* —**com·mend'a·to''ry**, *adj.*

com·men'su·a·ble, *adj.* able to be measured or evaluated in the same way.

com·men'su·rate, *adj.* equal or in proportion.

com'ment, *n.* **1.** remark or remarks on something observed. **2.** opinion or explanation regarding something. —*v.i.* **3.** make a comment.

com'men·tar''y, *n., pl.* **-ries.** set of explanatory notes.

com'men·ta''tor, *n.* person who comments on current events.

com'merce, *n.* purchasing and sale of merchandise.

com·mer'cial, *adj.* **1.** pertaining to commerce. —*n.* **2.** television or radio advertisement.

com·mer'cial·ism, *n.* emphasis on ready mass saleability rather than on quality, taste, etc.

com·mer'cial·ize'', *v.t.*, **-ized, -izing.** make, sell, etc. for maximum profit.

com·min'gle, *v.*, **-gled, -gling.** *v.t., v.i.* blend.

com·mis'er·ate'', *v.i.* **-ated, -ating.** feel sympathetic sorrow. —**com·mis''er·a'tion**, *n.*

com''mis·sar'i·at, *n.* military department in charge of food.

com'mis·sar''y, *n., pl.* **-ries.** *n.* **1.** military food shop. **2.** factory canteen.

com·mis'sion, *n.* **1.** entrusted task. **2.** formal authorization. **3.** military officership. **4.** committee. **5.** salesman's percentage of the amount of a sale. —*v.t.* **6.** entrust or authorize. **7.** put in service, as a ship.

com·mis'sion·er, *n.* head of a municipal department or commission.

com·mit', *v.t.*, **-mitted, -mitting. 1.** obligate. **2.** state the position of in a controversy. **3.** do, esp. a crime. **4.** send for confinement. —**com·mit'ment**, *n.* —**com·mit'al**, *n.*

com·mit'tee, *n.* chosen group of persons with specified responsibilities. —**com·mit'tee·man**, *n.* —**com·mit'tee·wom''an,** *n.*

com·mode', *n.* **1.** chest of drawers. **2.** water closet.

com·mo'di·ous, *adj.* roomy.

com·mod'i·ty, *n., pl.* **-ties.** *Commerce.* material or article, as opposed to a service.

com'mo·dore'', *n.* **1.** naval officer ranking between a captain and a rear admiral. **2.** head of a yacht squadron.

com'mon, *adj.* **1.** pertaining to many or to all. **2.** not unusual. **3.** low in rank or status. **4.** vulgar. —*n.* **5.** area of public land in a village. —**com'mon·ly**, *adv.*

com'mon·er, *n.* citizen not of the nobility.

common law, law based on custom and court decisions.

com'mon·place'', *adj.* **1.** completely or tritely familiar. —*n.* **2.** something commonplace.

common sense, ordinary good judgment. —**com'mon-sense''**, **com'mon·sen'si·cal,** *adj.*

com'mon·weal'', *n.* general good.

com'mon·wealth'', *n.* **1.** federation of states. **2.** state.

com·mo'tion, *n.* uproar.

com·mu'nal, *adj.* pertaining to or shared by a community or group.

com·mune', *v.i.*, **-muned, -muning.** *n.* *v.i.* (kə myoon') **1.** be in intimate communication or sympathy. —*n.* (kom' yoon) **2.** community sharing goods, responsibilities, etc.

com·mu'ni·ca·ble, *adj.* **1.** able to be communicated. **2.** able to be transferred, as an illness.

com·mu'ni·cant, *n.* partaker of the Eucharist.

com·mu'ni·cate, *v.*, **-cated, -cating.** *v.t.* **1.** make understood to others. —*v.i.* **2.** exchange messages. **3.** be in communion. **4.** be connected, as rooms. —**com·mun''i·ca'tion**, *n.*

com·mu'ni·ca·tive, *adj.* talkative or confiding.

com·mun'ion, *n.* **1.** state of intimacy. **2.** *Christianity.* sharing of bread and wine

in remembrance of Christ. **3.** religious denomination.

com·mun′i·qué, *n.* official message or news release.

com′mu·nism, *n.* **1.** political theory demanding public ownership of economic resources. **2. Communism.** socialism derived from the theories of **Karl Marx.** —**com′mu·nis′tic**, *adj.* —**com′ mu·nist**, *n., adj.*

com·mun′i·ty, *n., pl.* **-ties. 1.** town, etc. **2.** group with common interests, etc. **3.** sharing in common.

com·mute′, *v.,* **-muted, -muting.** *v.t.* **1.** alter, as a prison sentence. —*v.i.* **2.** travel regularly, as between home and work. —**com·mut′er**, *n.* —**com′′mu· ta′tion**, *n.*

com·pact′, *adj.* (kəm pakt′) **1.** occupying a minimal space. **2.** succinct. —*n.* (kom′pakt) **3.** small cosmetic case. **4.** small-bodied car. **5.** mutual agreement. —**com·pact′ly**, *adv.* —**com·pact′ness**, *n.*

com·pan′ion, *n.* **1.** person who keeps one company. **2.** one of a pair or set. —**com·pan′ion·ship′′**, *n.*

com·pan′ion·a·ble, *adj.* willing to keep one company.

com·pan′ion·way′′, *n.* stair in a ship.

com′pa·ny, *n., pl.* **-nies. 1.** fellowship; companionship. **2.** group of persons. **3.** group of persons assembled for social purposes. **4.** guests. **5.** business organization or association. **6.** military unit.

com′pa·ra·ble, *adj.* allowing comparison.

com·par′a·tive, *adj.* **1.** involving comparison. **2.** in comparison to other cases. —**com·par′a·tive·ly**, *adv.*

com·pare′, *v.,* **-pared, -paring.** *n.* *v.t.* **1.** examine for similarities and differences. **2.** regard or describe as similar. —*v.i.* **3.** be similar to, esp. in worth. —*n.* **4. beyond compare,** without equal.

com·par′i·son, *n.* **1.** act or instance of comparing. **2.** similarity.

com·part′ment, *n.* division of a larger space.

com′pass, *n.* **1.** instrument for establishing or indicating direction. **2.** scope. **3. compasses,** instrument for drawing circles.

com·pas′sion, *n.* sympathy, esp. with suffering or weakness. —**com·pas′ sion·ate**, *adj.*

com·pat′i·ble, *adj.* **1.** content together. **2.** logically consistent. —**com·pat′′i· bil′i·ty**, *n.*

com·pa′tri·ot, *n.* fellow national.

com·pel′, *v.t.,* **-pelled, -pelling.** force.

com·pen′di·um, *n., pl.* **-ums, -a.** detailed summary. —**com·pen′di·ous**, *adj.*

com′pen·sate′′, *v.,* **-sated, -sating.** *v.t.* **1.** pay, as for work or damage. —*v.i.* **2.** serve to offset or make up for something else. —**com′′pen·sa′tion**, *n.* —**com·pen′sa·to′′ry**, *adj.*

com·pete′, *v.i.,* **-peted, -peting.** act in rivalry. —**com′′pe·ti′tion**, *n.* —**com·pet′ i·tive**, *adj.* —**com·pet′i·tor**, *n.*

com′pe·tent, *adj.* **1.** normal in mental ability. **2.** able to work, etc. adequately. **3.** adequately done. **4.** legally authorized. —**com′pe·tent·ly**, *adv.* —**com′pe·tence, com′pe·ten·cy**, *n.*

com·pile′, *v.t.,* **piled, piling.** gather or publish together, as documents. —**com·pil′er**, *n.* —**com′′pi·la′tion**, *n.*

com·pla′cen·cy, *n.* satisfaction, esp. with oneself. —**com·pla′cent**, *adj.*

com·plain′, *v.i.* **1.** discuss one's grievance with others. —*v.t.* **2.** state as a grievance. —**com·plain′er**, *n.*

com·plaint′, *n.* **1.** act or instance of complaining. **2.** wording in which one complains. **3.** distressing illness.

com·plai′sant, *adj.* willing or eager to please. —**com·plai′sance,** *n.*

com′ple·ment, *n.* (com′plə ment) **1.** something that completes. **2.** wholeness. —*v.t.* (com′plə ment′′) **3.** complete. —**com′′ple·men′ta·ry**, *adj.*

com·plete′, *adj., v.t.,* **-pleted, -pleting.** *adj.* **1.** entire; with nothing missing. **2.** accomplished. **3.** utter. —*v.t.* **4.** perfect. **5.** finish. —**com·plete′ly**, *adv.* —**com·plete′ness**, *n.* —**com·ple′tion,** *n.*

com·plex′, *adj.* (kəm pleks′) **1.** not readily analyzed or understood. —*n.* (kom′ pleks) **2.** something complex. **3.** *Psychology.* **a.** group of impulses controlling behavior. **b.** obsessive attitude. —**com·plex′i·ty**, *n.*

com·plex′ion, *n.* color and texture of the skin.

com′pli·cate′′, *v.t.,* **-cated, -cating. 1.** make difficult to do or understand. **2.** make unnecessarily complex. —**com′′ pli·ca′tion**, *n.*

com·plic′i·ty, *n., pl.* **-ties.** association, esp. in crime.

com·pli·ment, *n.* (kom′plə mənt) **1.** expression of praise. —*v.t.* (kom′plə ment′′) **2.** pay a compliment to.

com′′pli·men′tar·y, *adj.* **1.** serving as a compliment. **2.** granted free of charge.

com·ply′, *v.i.,* **-plied, -plying.** act as ordered or urged. —**com·pli′ance,** *n.* —**com·pli′ant,** *adj.*

com·po′nent, *n.* **1.** part of a whole. —*adj.* **2.** serving as a component.

com·port′, *v.t.* conduct or behave. —**com·port′ment**, *n.*

com·pose′, *v.t.,* **-posed, -posing. 1.** create or organize artistically. **2.** constitute. **3.** put in order. **4.** make calm.

com·posed′, *adj.* apparently calm.

com·pos'ite, *adj.* made of many constituents.

com''po·si'tion, *n.* **1.** something composed. **2.** method of composing. **3.** nature, as of constituents or traits.

com'post, *n.* decayed matter for use as fertilizer.

com·po'sure, *n.* apparent calm.

com'pote'', *n.* dish of stewed fruits.

com·pound, *adj.* (kom'pownd) **1.** not simple; complex. —*n.* **2.** substance of mixed elements. **3.** building enclosure. —*v.t.* (kəm pownd') **4.** mix or make by mixing. **5.** permit unlawfully.

com''pre·hend', *v.t.* **1.** have a conception or understanding of. **2.** include. —**com''pre·hen'sion,** *n.* —**com''pre·hen'si·ble,** *adj.*

com''pre·hen'sive, *adj.* including all or most elements. —**com''pre·hen'sive·ly,** *adv.* —**com''pre·hen'sive·ness,** *n.*

com·press, *v.t.* (kəm pres') **1.** press to lessen volume. **2.** put under pressure. —*n.* (kahm'pres) **3.** pad of cloth applied as an aid to medicine. —**com·pres'sion,** *n.* —**com·pres'sor,** *n.*

com·prise', *v.t.,* **-prised, -prising. 1.** include. **2.** consist of.

com'pro·mise', *n., v.,* **-mised, -mising.** *n.* **1.** expedient but not fully satisfactory agreement. **2.** something with disparate elements. —*v.i.* **3.** make a compromise. —*v.t.* **4.** endanger in reputation, etc.

comp·trol'ler, *n.* financial manager.

com·pul'sion, *n.* act or instance of compelling. —**com·pul'sive,** *adj.* —**com·pul'so·ry,** *adj.*

com·punc'tion, *n.* uneasy, guilty feeling.

com·pute', *v.t.,* **-puted, -puting.** determine by calculation. —**com''pu·ta'tion,** *n.*

com·put'er, *n.* electronic device for rapid calculation or data comparison. —**com·put'er·ize,** *v.t.* —**com·put''er·i·za'tion,** *n.*

com'rade'', *n.* **1.** close friend. **2.** associate. —**com'rade'ship'',** *n.*

comsat, *n.* artificial communications satellite.

con, *v.t.,* **conned, conning,** *adj., n. v.t.* **1.** survey carefully. —*n.* **2.** person or argument opposed. **3.** *Nautical.* responsibility, as for guiding a ship.

con·cave', *adj.* curving inward. —**con·cav'i·ty,** *n.*

con·ceal', *v.t.* hide or keep secret. —**con·ceal'ment,** *n.*

con·cede', *v.t.,* **-ceded, -ceding. 1.** admit as true. **2.** acknowledge defeat in. **3.** grant.

con·ceit', *n.* **1.** excessive pride. **2.** fanciful idea or expression.

con·ceit'ed, *adj.* full of conceit.

con·ceive', *v.,* **-ceived, -ceiving.** *v.i.* **1.** form an idea. **2.** become pregnant.

—*v.t.* **3.** imagine as possible or true. **4.** become pregnant with. —**con·ceiv'a·ble,** *adj.* —**con·ceiv'a·bly,** *adv.*

con'cen·trate'', *v.,* **-trated, -trating,** *n. v.t.* **1.** focus. **2.** increase in strength. —*v.i.* **3.** focus attention or effort. —*n.* **4.** something concentrated. —**con''cen·tra'tion,** *n.*

con·cen'tric, *adj.* having a common or identical center.

con'cept, *n.* idea of something possible. —**con·cep'tu·al,** *adj.*

con·cep'tion, *n.* act or instance of conceiving.

con·cern', *v.t.* **1.** be the business of. **2.** cause care or anxiety in. **3.** have as a subject. —*n.* **4.** business or affair. **5.** care or anxiety. **6.** business organization. **7.** importance.

con·cerned', *adj.* **1.** anxious. **2.** interested. **3.** engaged in political or social problems.

con·cern'ing, *prep.* on the subject of.

con'cert, *n.* **1.** series of musical compositions performed at one time. **2.** harmony.

con·cert'ed, *adj.* performed in an agreed manner.

con''cer·ti'na, *n.* small accordion.

con·cer'to, *n.* (kən cher'tō), *n., pl.* **-tos, -ti.** orchestral composition, usually with soloists.

con·ces'sion, *n.* **1.** act or instance of conceding. **2.** something conceded.

con·ces'sion·aire'', *n.* person allowed to engage in trade on another's property.

con·cil'i·ate'', *v.t.,* **-ated, -ating.** pacify or appease. —**con·cil'i·a''tor,** *n.* —**con·cil'i·a·to''ry,** *adj.* —**con·cil'i·a'tion,** *n.*

con·cise', *adj.* confined to essentials, as a piece of writing. —**con·cise'ly,** *adv.* —**con·cise'ness,** *n.*

con'clave, *n.* private meeting.

con·clude', *v.,* **-cluded, -cluding.** *v.t.* **1.** end. **2.** reach an opinion or decision. —*v.i.* **3.** bring a meeting, etc. to an end. —**con·clu'sion,** *n.*

con·clu'sive, *adj.* compelling a certain opinion or decision.

con·coct', *v.t.* **1.** make of varied ingredients. **2.** devise. —**con·coc'tion,** *n.*

con·com'i·tant, *adj.* **1.** accompanying. —*n.* **2.** something concomitant. —**con·com'i·tant·ly,** *adv.*

con'cord, *n.* harmonious agreement.

con·cord'ance, *n.* list of occurrences in a book of certain words, etc.

con'course, *n.* **1.** crowd. **2.** space or hall for accommodating crowds.

con·crete', *adj.* (kon krēt') **1.** real; material. **2.** specific. —*n.* (kon'krēt) **3.** material of cement and stone, etc. —*v.t., v.i.* **4.** solidify. —**con·cre'tion,** *n.*

con'cu·bine'', *n.* wife of less than full status.

con''cu·pis'cence, *n.* lust. —con''cu·pis'cent, *adj.*

con·cur', *v.i.,* -curred, -curring. 1. agree. 2. cooperate. 3. coincide. —con·cur'rent, *adj.* —con·cur'rence, *n.*

con·cus'sion, *n.* 1. shock, as from a blow. 2. malfunctioning of the mind or body from a blow.

con·demn', *v.t.* 1. disapprove of strongly. 2. reject as unfit. 3. acquire by legal authority. 4. sentence, as to prison. —con''dem·na'tion, *n.*

con·dense', *v.,* -densed, -densing. *v.t., v.i.* 1. turn from a gas to a liquid. —*v.t.* 2. put in succinct form. —con''den·sa'tion, *n.* —con·dens'er, *n.*

con''de·scend', *v.i.* 1. show kindness or affability to an inferior. —*v.t.* 2. do with a good grace despite superior status. —con''de·scen'sion, *n.*

con'di·ment, *n.* flavor or seasoning.

con·di'tion, *n.* 1. state of health, repair, etc. 2. good state of health, etc. 3. something necessary or required. —*v.t.* 4. put in condition. 5. accustom.

con·di'tion·al, *adj.* subject to certain conditions.

con·dole', *v.i.,* -doled, -doling. express sorrowful sympathy. —con·dol'ence, *n.*

con''do·min'i·um, *n.* 1. multi-unit group of privately owned dwellings. 2. territory under a joint rule.

con·done', *v.t.,* -doned, -doning. fail to forbid or disapprove of.

con·duce', *v.i.,* -duced, -ducing. tend or lead. —con·duc'ive, *adj.*

con·duct', *v.t.* (kən dukt') 1. lead or direct. 2. transmit. 3. behave. —*n.* (kahn' dukt) 4. behavior.

con·duc'tor, *n.* 1. leader of a band or orchestra. 2. person in charge of a train, etc. 3. thing that transmits electricity, heat, etc.

con·duit (kahn'dit), *n.* channel for wiring or fluids.

cone, *n.* 1. solid generated by rotating an isosceles triangle around its centerline. 2. fruit of an evergreen.

con·fec'tion, *n.* food made with sugar. —con·fec'tion·er, *n.* —con·fec'tion·er·y, *n.*

con·fed'er·a·cy, *n., pl.* -cies. alliance.

con·fed'er·ate, *n., adj., v.,* -ated, -ating. *n.* (kən fed'ər ət) 1. ally or accomplice. —*adj.* 2. allied. —*v.t., v.t.* (kən fed'ər āt'') 3. ally. —con·fed''er·a'tion, *n.*

con·fer', *v.,* -ferred, -ferring. *v.t.* 1. bestow. —*v.i.* 2. consult or discuss. —con·fer'ment, *n.* —con'fer·ence, *n.*

con·fess', *v.t.* 1. admit as true. 2. profess belief in. 3. hear the confession of.

con·fes'sion, *n.* 1. act or instance of confessing. 2. admission of sins by a penitent. 3. creed or sect.

con·fes'sion·al, *n.* place where a priest hears confessions.

con·fes'sor, *n.* priest who hears confessions.

con·fet'ti, *n.* finely chopped colored paper thrown about in celebration.

con·fi·dant'', *n.* person in whom one confides. Also, *fem.,* con''fi·dante''.

con·fide', *v.,* -fided, -fiding. *v.i.* 1. place trust, esp. by relating secrets. —*v.t.* 2. entrust to someone's care or hearing.

con'fi·dence, *n.* 1. trust. 2. self-assurance. —con''fi·dent, *adj.* —con'fi·dent·ly, *adv.*

con''fi·den'tial, *adj.* 1. to be kept a secret. 2. entrusted with secrets. —con''fi·den'tial·ly, *adv.*

con·fig''u·ra'tion, *n.* outline or contour.

con·fine', *v.t.,* -fined, -fining. *n.* *v.t.* (kənfin') 1. keep within limits or boundaries. 2. keep as if a prisoner. —*n.* 3. confines (khan'fīnz), boundaries. —con·fine'ment, *n.*

con·firm', *v.t.* 1. certify as true. 2. approve formally. 3. admit fully to a church. —con''fir·ma'tion, *n.*

con'fis·cate, *v.t.,* -cated, -cating. seize by authority. —con''fis·ca'tion, *n.*

con''fla·gra'tion, *n.* fire causing major damage.

con·flict', *n.* (kahn'flikt) 1. fight. 2. disagreement. 3. emotional malaise or quandary. —*v.i.* (kən flikt') 4. be hostile or in disagreement.

con'flu·ence, *n.* place where two rivers, etc. meet.

con·form', *v.i.* 1. form one's appearance, manners, etc. according to prevailing standards. 2. act or be in accordance with a law, rule, etc. 3. be similar. —*v.t.* 4. cause to conform. —con·form'i·ty, *n.*

con·form'ist, *n.* person who conforms unquestioningly.

con·found', *v.t.* confuse.

con·front', *v.t.* 1. approach or face hostilely. 2. force to face. —con''fron·ta'tion, *n.*

con·fuse', *v.t.,* -fused, -fusing. 1. hamper in the powers of perception, analysis, decision, etc. 2. embarrass. 3. mistake for another. —con·fu'sion, *n.*

con·fute', *v.t.,* -futed, -futing. show as wrong. —con''fu·ta'tion, *n.*

con·geal', *v.t., v.i.* thicken or freeze. —con·geal'ment, *n.*

con·gen'i·al, *adj.* agreeable. —con·gen''i·al'i·ty, *n.*

con·gen'i·tal, *adj.* from the time of birth. —con·gen'i·tal·ly, *adv.*

con·gest', *v.t.* fill to excess. —con·ges'tion, *n.*

con·glom·er·ate, *v.,* -ated, -ating, *adj., n. v.t., v.i.* (kən glahm'ə rāt'') 1. form into a mass. —*adj.* (kən glahm'ə rət) 2.

formed as a mass. —*n.* **3.** mass of small elements. **4.** corporation composed of diverse subsidiaries. —**con·glom″er·a′tion,** *n.*

con·grat′u·late″, *v.t.,* **-lated, -lating.** show sympathetic pleasure, as for success or good luck. —**con·grat″u·la′tion,** *n.* —**con·grat′u·la·to″ry,** *adj.*

con′gre·gate″, *v.,* **-gated, -gating.** *v.t., v.i.* gather into a group or assembly. —**con″gre·ga′tion,** *n.* —**con″gre·ga′tion·al,** *adj.*

con′gress, *n.* **1.** legislative body. **2.** former gathering. —**con·gres′sion·al,** *adj.*

Con′gress·man, *n.* member of the U.S. Congress, esp. the House of Representatives.

con′gru·ent, *adj.* in correspondence or harmony. —**con′gru·ence,** *n.*

con′gru·ous, *adj.* **1.** congruent. **2.** appropriate. —**con·gru′i·ty,** *n.*

con′ic, *adj.* **1.** Also, **con′i·cal,** cone-shaped. **2.** derived from a cone.

con′i·fer, *n.* tree or shrub bearing cones. —**co·nif′er·ous,** *adj.*

con·jec′ture, *n., v.* **-tured, -turing.** *n., v.t., v.i.,* guess. —**con·jec′tur·al,** *adj.*

con·join′, *v.t., v.i.* join together.

con′ju·gal, *adj.* marital.

con′ju·gate″, *v.t.,* **-gated, -gating.** give the inflections of a verb. —**con″ju·ga′tion,** *n.*

con·junc′tion, *n.* **1.** union or combination. **2.** coincidence. **3.** word linking others in a sentence. —**con·junc′tive,** *adj.*

con·junc′ture, *n.* combination of events.

con·jure′, *v.t.,* **-jured, -juring.** cause to appear as by magic. —**con′jur·er, con′jur·or,** *n.*

con·nect′, *v.t.* **1.** join. —*v.i.* **2.** adjoin. —**con·nec′tor, con·nec′ter,** *n.* —**con·nec′tive,** *adj.* —**con·nec′tion,** *n.*

con·nive′, *v.i.,* **-nived, -niving. 1.** conspire. **2.** permit crime, etc. to occur by ignoring it. —**con·niv′er,** *n.* —**con·niv′ance,** *n.*

con″nois·seur′, *n.* person with refined knowledge.

con·note′, *v.t.,* **-noted, -noting.** imply through wording, etc. —**con″no·ta′tion,** *n.*

con·nu′bi·al, *adj.* marital.

con′quer, *v.t.* overcome, as in war. —**con′quer·or,** *n.*

con′quest, *n.* **1.** act or instance of conquering. **2.** something conquered.

con″san·guin′i·ty, *adj.* blood relationship.

con′science, *n.* inner prompting to do good or repent evil. —**con″sci·en′tious,** *adj.*

con′scious, *adj.* **1.** aware of the surrounding world. **2.** aware of some specific thing. **3.** deliberate. —**con′scious·ness,** *n.*

con·script′, *v.t.* (kən skript′) **1.** enroll forcibly in an army, labor force, etc. —*n.* (kahn′skript) **2.** conscripted person. —**con·scrip′tion,** *n.*

con′se·crate″, *v.t.,* **-crated, -crating.** dedicate, as to deity. —**con″se·cra′tion,** *n.*

con·sec′u·tive, *adj.* one after the other. —**con·sec′u·tive′ly,** *adv.*

con·sen′sus, *n.* general agreement on a question.

con·sent′, *n.* **1.** permission. **2.** agreement. —*v.i.* **3.** give permission.

con′se·quence″, *n.* **1.** result. **2.** importance.

con′se·quent, *adj.* resulting.

con″se·quen′tial, *adj.* **1.** important. **2.** consequent.

con·serv′a·tive, *n.* **1.** person skeptical of change. **2.** pertaining to conservatives. **3.** avoiding excesses. —**con·serv′a·tive·ly,** *adv.* —**con·serv′a·tism,** *n.*

con·serv′a·to″ry, *n., pl.* **-ries. 1.** greenhouse. **2.** art or music school.

con·serve′, *v.t.,* **-served, -serving.** keep from decaying, being squandered, etc. —**con″ser·va′tion,** *n.* —**con″ser·va′tion·ist,** *n.*

con·sid′er, *v.t.* **1.** think of the importance, implications, etc. of. **2.** regard; believe. **3.** be considerate of.

con·sid′er·a·ble, *adj.* rather important.

con·sid′er·ate, *adj.* respectful of the feelings of others.

con·sid″er·a′tion, *n.* **1.** state of being considerate. **2.** act of considering. **3.** something to be considered. **4.** fee.

con·sign′, *n.* **1.** deliver. **2.** entrust. —**con·sign′ment,** *n.*

con·sist′, *v.i.* **1.** be composed. **2.** have essential nature.

con·sis′ten·cy, *n.* **1.** agreement with something already done, stated, or implied. **2.** ability to hold together, as of a liquid. —**con·sis′tent,** *adj.* —**con·sis′tent·ly,** *adv.*

con·sole′, *v.t.,* **-soled, -soling.** *n. v.t.* (kən sōl′) **1.** soothe or cheer in grief or annoyance. —*n.* (kahn′sōl) **2.** television set, etc. standing on the floor. **3.** instrument panel. —**con″so·la′tion,** *n.*

con·sol′i·date″, *v.,* **-dated, -dating.** *v.t., v.i.* unite into a solid; whole. —**con·sol″i·da′tion,** *n.*

con″som·mé″, *n.* soup based on a clear meat broth.

con′so·nant, *adj.* **1.** in harmony. —*n.* **2.** speech sound other than a vowel. —**con′so·nance,** *n.*

con·sort′, *v.i.* (kən sort′) **1.** be in company or association. —*n.* (kahn′sort) **2.** spouse of a sovereign.

con·sor′ti·um, *n., pl.* **-tia.** international business alliance.

con·spic′u·ous, *adj.* **1.** readily observed. **2.** compelling observation. —**con·spic′**

u·ous′ly, *adv.* —con·spic′u·ous·ness, *n.*

con·spire′, *v.t.*, -spired, -spiring. plan secretly as a group. —con·spir′a·cy, *n.* —con·spir′a·tor, *n.*

con′sta·ble, *n.* policeman. —con·stab′u·lar″y, *n.*

con′stant, *adj.* 1. continual. 2. faithful. —*n.* 3. unvarying element. —con′stant·ly, *adv.* —con′stan·cy, *n.*

con″stel·la′tion, *n.* pattern of stars.

con″ster·na′tion, *n.* horrified shock.

con′sti·pate″, *v.t.*, -pated, -pating. impair the movement of the bowels. —con″sti·pa′tion, *n.*

con·stit′u·ent, *adj.* 1. forming an essential part. 2. electing. —*n.* 3. voter. 4. constituent thing. —con·stit′u·en·cy, *n.*

con′sti·tute″, *v.t.*, -tuted, -tuting. 1. combine to form. 2. be tantamount to.

con″sti·tu′tion, *n.* 1. act or instance of constituting. 2. fundamental law. 3. body, esp. as regards health.

con″sti·tu′tion·al, *adj.* 1. pertaining to a constitution. 2. permitted by a constitution. 3. pertaining to health. —*n.* 4. health-promoting walk.

con·strain′, *v.t.* 1. compel. 2. restrain. —con·straint′, *n.*

con·strict′, *v.t.* force to be narrow. —con·stric′tion, *n.*

con·struct′, *v.t.* build. —con·struc′tor, *n.* —con·struc′tion, *n.*

con·struc′tive, *adj.* useful or helpful.

con·strue′, *v.t.*, -strued, -struing. interpret.

con′sul, *n.* government agent in a foreign city who assists his nationals there. —con′sul·ar, *adj.* —con′sul·ate, *n.*

con·sult′, *v.t.* 1. seek advice or information from. —*v.i.* 2. discuss business matters. —con″sul·ta′tion, *n.*

con·sult′ant, *n.* 1. person who is consulted. 2. person who seeks advice.

con·sume′, *v.t.*, -sumed, -suming. 1. use up in the process of living, etc. 2. destroy, as by fire.

con·sum′er, *n.* person who uses goods or services for himself rather than in business.

con·sum′mate, *adj., v.t.* -mated, -mating. (kən sum′ət) 1. perfect. —*v.t.* (kahn səm ǎt′) 2. complete, esp. the state of marriage by sexual intercourse. —con″sum·ma′tion, *n.*

con·sump′tion, *n.* 1. act or instance of consuming. 2. tuberculosis of the lungs. —con·sump′tive, *adj.*

con′tact, *n.* 1. touch. 2. communication. 3. connection.

con·ta′gious, *adj.* distributed by personal contact, as disease. —con·ta′gion, *n.*

con·tain′, *n.* 1. enclose; include. 2. restrain. —con·tain′er, *n.*

con·tam′in·ate″, *v.t.*, -ated, -ating. spoil. the purity of. —con·tam″in·a′tion, *n.* —con·tam′in·ant, *n.*

con′tem·plate″, *v.t.*, -plated, -plating. 1. regard or think of intently. 2. anticipate. —con″tem·pla′tion, *n.* —con·tem′pla·tive, *adj.*

con·tem′po·rar″y, *adj., n., pl.* -ries, *adj.* 1. Also, con·tem″po·ra′ne·ous, of the same time. 2. modern. —*n.* 3. person or thing of the same age.

con·tempt′, *n.* 1. disapproval involving a feeling of one's own superiority. 2. defiance, as of a court order. —con·tempt′i·ble, *adj.*

con·tend′, *v.t.* 1. assert forcibly. —*v.i.* 2. fight or be in opposition. —con·tend′er, *n.*

con·tent′, *n.* (kahn′tent) 1. something contained. 2. meaning or message. (kəntent′) 3. contentment. —*adj.* 4. satisfied. 5. willing. —*v.t.* 6. satisfy. —con·tent′ed, *adj.* —con·tent′ed·ly, *adv.* —con·tent′ed·ness, *n.*

con·ten′tious, *adj.* quarrelsome.

con·tent′ment, *n.* contented state.

con′test, *n.* (kahn′test) 1. competition or fight. —*v.i.* (kən test′) 2. dispute. 3. fight to gain or hold. —con·test′ant, *n.*

con′text, *n.* circumstances giving exact meaning. —con·tex′tu·al, *adj.*

con·tig′u·ous, *adj.* 1. in touch. 2. adjacent. —con″ti·gu′i·ty, *n.*

con′ti·nent, *n.* 1. major land mass. 2. the Continent, European mainland. —*adj.* 3. sexually abstemious. —con″ti·nen′tal, *adj.* —con′ti·nence, *n.*

con·tin′gen·cy, *n., pl.* -cies. chance occurrence.

con·tin′gent, *adj.* 1. depending on chance. —*n.* 2. chance occurrence. 3. group of recruits.

con·tin′u·al, *adj.* 1. repeated without pause. 2. continuous. —con·tin′u·al·ly, *adv.*

con·tin′ue, *v.*, -ued, -uing. *v.t., v.i.* 1. not stop. 2. recommence. 3. extend. —*v.i.* 4. remain. —con·tin″u·a′tion, con·tin′u·ance, *n.*

con·tin′u·ous, *adj.* uninterrupted. —con·tin′u·ous·ly, *adv.* —con″tin·u′i·ty, *n.*

con·tort′, *v.t.* twist out of shape. —con·tor′tion, *n.*

con′tour, *n.* outline of a form.

con′tra·band″, *n.* 1. goods unlawful to import or export. —*adj.* 2. constituting such goods.

con″tra·cep′tion, *n.* prevention of pregnancy. —con″tra·cep′tive, *adj., n.*

con·tract′, *n.* (kahn′trakt) 1. formal business agreement. —*v.t.* (kən trakt′) 2. undertake or establish by contract. 3. be afflicted with. 4. make smaller. —*v.i.* 5. make a contract. 6. become smaller. —con·trac′tion, *n.*

con'trac·tor, *n.* **1.** person who undertakes work by contract. **2.** builder.

con"tra·dict', *v.t.* **1.** declare to be falsely stated. **2.** declare to have not spoken the truth. **3.** be inconsistent with. —con"tra·dic'tion, *n.* —con"tra·dic'to·ry, *adj.*

con·tral'to, *n., pl.* -tos. lowest female singing voice.

con·trap'tion, *n. Informal.* gadget.

con·tra·ry, *n., pl.* -ries, *adj. n.* **1.** (kahn' trer ē) something opposite. —*adj.* **2.** opposite. **3.** (kən trer'ē) stubborn; perverse. —con·trar'i·ly, *adv.*

con·trast, *v.t.* (kən trast') **1.** show the differences of from another or others. —*v.i.* **2.** reveal differences from another or others. —*n.* (kahn'trast) **3.** act or instance or contrasting. **4.** something notably different.

con'tra·vene", *v.t.,* -vened, -vening. act in violation of. —con"tra·ven'tion, *n.*

con·trib·ute, *v.,* -uted, -uting. *v.t., v.i.* give toward a desired total. —con·trib' u·tor, *n.* —con"tri·bu'tion, *n.* —con· trib'u·to"ry, *adj.*

con·trite', *adj.* repentant. —con·trite' ness, con·tri'tion, *n.*

con·trive', *v.t.,* -trived, -triving. **1.** devise or invent. **2.** bring about. —con·triv' ance, *n.*

con·trol', *v.t.,* -trolled, -trolling. *n. v.t.* **1.** govern or direct. **2.** restrain. —*n.* **3.** ability to control. **4.** Often, **controls**, means of controlling. —con·trol'la· ble, *adj.*

con·trol'ler, *n.* financial manager.

con'tro·ver"sy, *n., pl.* -sies. earnest debate. —con"tro·ver'sial, *adj.*

con'tro·vert", *v.t.* **1.** dispute. **2.** debate.

con·tu"me·ly, *n., pl.* -lies. scornful abuse.

con·tu'sion, *n.* bruise.

co·nun'drum, *n.* riddle answered with a pun.

con"ur·ba'tion, *n.* area of urban density resulting from unchecked growth.

con'va·lesce", *v.i.,* -lesced, -lescing. become better after illness. —con"va·les' cent, *n., adj.* —con"va·les'cence, *n.*

con·vec'tion, *n.* movement of heated or cooled gases or liquids.

con·vene', *v.,* -vened, -vening. *v.i., v.t.* assemble in a meeting.

con·ven'ience, *n.* **1.** ease or handiness. **2.** something promoting this. —con·ven' ient, *adj.*

con'vent, *n.* community of nuns.

con·ven'tion, *n.* **1.** assembly of a political party, professional association, etc. **2.** something customary.

con·ven'tion·al, *adj.* **1.** ordinary. **2.** customary.

con·verge', *v.,* -verged, -verging. *v.t., or assertion.*

con·verge', *v.,* -verged, -verging. *v.t., v.i.* join by oblique movement. —con· ver'gence, *n.* —con·ver'gent, *adj.*

con·ver'sant, *adj.* familiar; skilled.

con"ver·sa'tion, *n.* **1.** informal talk. **2.** ability to carry on such talk. —con" ver·sa'tion·al, *adj.* —con"ver·sa'tion· al·ist, *n.*

con·verse, *v.i.,* -versed, -versing, *adj., n. v.i.* (kən vərs') **1.** carry on a conversation. —*adj.* (kahn'vərs) **2.** in reverse order or position. —*n.* **3.** something converse. —con·verse'ly, *adv.*

con·vert, *v.t.* (kən vərt') **1.** change from one thing or state to another. **2.** acquire a new religion. —*v.i.* **3.** be converted. —*n.* (kahn'vərt) **4.** person with a new religion. —con·vert'er, con· vert'or, *n.* —con·vert'i·ble, *adj.*

con·vex', *adj.* curving outward. —con· vex'i·ty, *n.*

con·vey', *v.t.* **1.** transport. **2.** transmit. **3.** succeed in expressing. —con·vey'er, con·vey'or *n.* —con·vey'ance, *n.*

con·vict, *v.t.* (kən vikt') **1.** find guilty. —*n.* (kahn'vikt) **2.** person found guilty.

con·vic'tion, *n.* **1.** act or instance of convicting or being convicted. **2.** strongly held belief.

con·vince', *v.t.,* -vinced, -vincing. cause to believe.

con·viv'i·al, *adj.* **1.** fond of company. **2.** festive.

con·voke', *v.t.,* -voked, -voking. call to an assembly. —con"vo·ca"tion, *n.*

con"vo·lu'tion, *n.* **1.** twist, fold, etc. **2.** formation of these.

con·voy, *n.* (kahn'voi) **1.** ships, etc. with a protective escort. **2.** protective escort. —*v.t.* (kən voi') **3.** escort protectively.

con·vulse', *v.t.,* -vulsed, -vulsing. **1.** agitate. **2.** rack with laughter or anger. —con·vul'sion, *n.* —con·vul'sive, *adj.*

coo, *v.i.,* cooed, cooing. **1.** make a dovelike sound. —*n.* **2.** dovelike sound.

cook, *v.t.* **1.** prepare (food) by heating. —*v.i.* **2.** act as a cook. **3.** become cooked or heated. —*n.* **4.** person who cooks. —cook'er·y, *n.* —cook'book", *n.*

cook'ie, *n.* small baked sweet biscuit.

cool, *adj.* **1.** slightly cold; not warm. **2.** not adding to body heat. **3.** showing no emotion. **4.** unenthusiastic. —*n.* **5.** cool condition. —*v.t.* **6.** make cool. —*v.i.* **7.** become cool. —cool'er, *n.* —cool'ly, *adv.* —cool'ness, *n.*

cool'ie, *n.* Far Eastern unskilled laborer.

coon, *n.* racoon. —coon'skin", *n.*

coop, *n.* **1.** shelter for chickens, etc. —*v.t.* **2.** confine.

coop'er, *n.* barrel maker.

co"op'er·ate", *v.i.,* -ated, -ating. act in harmony or together with others. Also, co"-op'er·ate". —co"op'er·a'tion, *n.*

co″op′er·a·tive, *adj.* **1.** willing to cooperate. **2.** jointly owned by the users. —*n.* **3.** cooperative store, apartment house, etc. Also, **co″-op′er·a·tive.**

co·or·di·nate, *adj., n., v.t.,* **-nated, -nating.** *adj.* (ko″or′də nət) **1.** equal in importance. **2.** pertaining to coordination. —*n.* **3.** something coordinate. *v.t.* (ko″or′də nāt″) **4.** put in proper interaction. **5.** make coordinate.

co″or′di·na′tion, *n.* **1.** act or instance of coordinating. **2.** proper interaction, esp. of the limbs or muscles.

cop, *n., v.t.,* **copped, copping.** *Informal. n.* **1.** policeman. **2.** arrest. —*v.t.* **3.** seize.

cope, *v.i.,* **coped, coping.** attack and overcome a problem or emergency.

cop′ing, *n.* uppermost course of an unroofed masonry wall.

co′pi·ous, *adj.* abundant.

cop′per, *n.* reddish metallic element.

cop′per·head″, *n.* poisonous North American snake.

copse, *n.* thicket. Also, **cop′pice.**

cop′u·late″, *v.i.,* **-lated, -lating.** have sexual intercourse. —**cop″u·la′tion,** *n.*

cop′y, *n., pl.* **-ies,** *v.t.,* **-ied, -ying.** *n.* **1.** imitation of an original. **2.** individual published book. **3.** words to be printed. —*v.t.* **4.** make or be a copy of. —**cop′y·ist,** *n.*

cop′y·right″, *n.* **1.** exclusive right to publish a book or license its publication. —*v.t.* **2.** obtain a copyright for.

co·quette′, *n.* flirtatious woman.

cor′al, *n.* **1.** hardened skeletons of a marine animal. **2.** yellowish red.

cord, *n.* **1.** strong string. **2.** electric wire. **3.** 128 cubic feet of chopped wood.

cor′dial, *adj.* **1.** warmly friendly. —*n.* **2.** liqueur. —**cor′dial·ly,** *adv.* —**cor″di·al′i·ty,** *n.*

cor′don, *n.* **1.** circle of guards. —*v.t.* **2.** put a cordon around.

cor′do·van, *n.* soft, dark leather.

cor′du·roy″, *n.* **1.** ribbed cotton. **2.** felled tree trunks used as a paving.

core, *n., v.t.,* **cored, coring.** *n.* **1.** central part or element. —*v.t.* **2.** remove the core from.

cork, *n.* **1.** bark of an oak tree. **2.** stopper made of this bark. —*v.t.* **3.** stop with a cork.

cork′screw″, *n.* augerlike device for pulling corks.

corn, *n.* **1.** American plant with kernels on a cob. **2.** small hard seed of a cereal plant. **3.** *Informal.* trite or sentimental art. **4.** painful growth on the foot. —*v.t.* **5.** pickle in brine. —**corn′starch″,** *n.*

cor′ne·a, *n.* outer coating of the eyeball.

cor′ner, *n.* **1.** angular junction. **2.** intersection of two streets. **3.** monopoly of a commodity or stock. —*v.t.* **4.** trap in a corner. **5.** get a monopoly on.

cor′ner·stone″, *n.* stone at the corner of a building with its date, etc.

cor′net′, *n.* trumpetlike musical instrument.

cor′nice, *n.* major horizontal molding on or at the top of a wall.

cor′nu·co′pi·a, *n.* hornlike container with fruits, flowers, etc. spilling from it.

cor′ol·lar″y, *n., pl.* **-ies.** statement deduced from one already proven.

cor′o·nar″y, *adj., n., pl.* **-ies.** *adj.* **1.** pertaining to the arteries supplying the heart. —*n.* **2.** coronary thrombosis.

cor″o·na′tion, *n.* installation of a monarch.

cor′o·ner, *n.* official who investigates suspicious deaths.

cor′o·net, *n.* crown of a noble.

cor′po·ral, *adj.* **1.** bodily. —*n.* **2.** lowest noncommissioned military officer.

cor′po·rate, *adj.* pertaining to organizations.

cor″po·ra′tion, *n.* **1.** business organization existing as an entity apart from its members. **2.** municipal government.

cor·po′re·al, *adj.* physical.

corps (kor), *n., pl.* **corps** (korz). military branch.

corpse, *n.* dead body.

cor′pu·lence, *n.* fatness. —**cor′pu·lent,** *adj.*

cor·pus·cle (kor′pus əl), *n.* blood or lymph cell.

cor·ral′, *n., v.t.,* **-ralled, -ralling.** *n.* **1.** enclosure for cattle, horses, etc. —*v.t.* **2.** enclose in a corral.

cor·rect′, *adj.* **1.** accurate. **2.** according to rules. —*v.t.* **3.** make correct. **4.** punish. —**cor·rect′ly,** *adv.* —**cor·rect′ness,** *n.* —**cor·rec′tion,** *n.* —**cor·rec′tive,** *adj.*

cor″re·late″, *v.,* **-lated, -lating.** *v.t.* **1.** put into a mutual relationship. —*v.i.* **2.** have a mutual relationship. —**cor″re·la′tion,** *n.* —**cor·rel′a·tive,** *adj.*

cor″re·spond″, *v.i.* **1.** write or exchange letters, news, etc. **2.** match. —**cor″re·spond′ence,** *n.* —**cor″re·spond′ent,** *n.*

cor′ri·dor, *n.* narrow passageway.

cor·rob′o·rate″, *v.t.,* **-rated, -rating.** support or confirm with evidence, etc. —**cor·rob″o·ra′tion,** *n.* —**cor·rob′o·ra·tive,** *adj.*

cor·rode′, *v.,* **-roded, -roding.** *v.t., v.i.* decay, esp. by chemical action. —**cor·ro′sion,** *n.* —**cor·ro′sive,** *adj., n.*

cor′ru·gate″, *v.,* **-gated, -gating.** *v.t., v.i.* bend into parallel ridges and furrows. —**cor″ru·ga′tion,** *n.*

cor·rupt′, *adj.* **1.** impure. **2.** depraved. —*v.t.* **3.** make corrupt. —*v.i.* **4.** become corrupt. —**cor·rupt′ly,** *adv.* —**cor·rupt′i·ble,** *adj.* —**cor·rup′tion,** *n.*

cor·sage (kor sahzh′), *n.* small bouquet for a party dress.

cor′set, *n.* garment for shaping the torso.

cor·tege′, *n.* ceremonial procession. Also, **cor·tège′.**

cor′us·cate″, *v.i.,* **-cated, -cating.** glitter. —**cor″us·ca′tion,** *n.*

cos·met′ic, *n.* **1.** preparation applied to the body to improve its appearance. —*adj.* **2.** improving outer appearance.

cos′mic, *adj.* pertaining to the cosmos.

cos′mo·naut″, *n.* astronaut.

cos″mo·pol′i·tan, *n.* **1.** Also, **cos·mop′o·lite″,** person regarding the entire world as his home. —*adj.* **2.** characteristic of such persons.

cos′mos, *n.* the entire universe.

cost, *v.t.,* **cost, costing,** *n. v.t.* **1.** require or exact as specified. —*n.* **2.** something given up in exchange. **3.** loss; grief.

cost′ly, *adj.,* **-lier, -liest.** costing much.

cos′tume, *n., v.t.,* **-tumed, -tuming.** *n.* **1.** dress, esp. of a special or unusual kind. —*v.t.* **2.** supply with such dress.

cot, *n.* narrow folding bed.

co·te′rie, *n.* small, exclusive group of friends.

cot′tage, *n.* small house. —**cot′tag·er,** *n.*

cot′ter pin″, split fastener passed through the things to be attached, then bent open.

cot′ton, *n.* fiber from a plant of the mallow family. —**cot′ton·y,** *adj.* —**cot′ton·seed,** *n.*

cot′ton·mouth″, *n.* water moccasin.

cot′ton·tail″, *n.* white-tailed American rabbit.

cot′ton·wood″, *n.* poplar with hairy seeds.

couch, *n.* **1.** bedlike article of furniture. —*v.t.* **2.** put into words.

cou′gar, *n.* tawny American wildcat.

cough, *n.* **1.** loud expulsion of breath from the lungs, as to clear the throat. —*v.i.* **2.** emit a cough. —*v.t.* **3.** expel with a cough.

coun′cil, *n.* body of legislators, advisors, etc. —**coun′cil·man, coun′cil·or, coun′cil·lor,** *n.*

coun′sel, *v.t.,* **-seled, seling.** *n. v.t.* **1.** advise. —*n.* **2.** legal representative. **3.** advice. —**coun′se·lor, coun′sel·lor,** *n.*

count, *v.t.* **1.** note one by one to get a total. **2.** include in a total or group. **3.** consider as being. —*v.i.* **4.** count numbers or items. **5.** be important. **6.** depend. —*n.* **7.** act or instance of counting. **8.** total. **9.** legal accusation. **10.** continental European nobleman equal to an earl.

count′down″, *n.* count of seconds in reverse order before an action.

coun′te·nance, *n., v.t.,* **-nanced, -nancing.** *n.* **1.** face, esp. with regard to expression. **2.** approval. —*v.t.* **3.** approve.

count′er, *n.* **1.** person or thing that counts. **2.** tablelike surface for serving, displaying goods, etc. **3.** token used in games.

coun′ter, *v.i.* **1.** act in retaliation. —*v.t.* **2.** oppose. —*adj.* **3.** opposed. —*adv.* **4.** in opposition. —**coun″ter·act′,** *v.t.* —**coun′ter·at·tack″,** *v.t., v.i., n.* —**coun′ter·bal″ance,** *v.t., n.* —**coun″ter·clock″wise,** *adj., adv.* —**coun″ter·rev″o·lu′tion,** *n.* —**coun′ter·rev′o·lu′tion·ar″y,** *adj., n.* —**coun′ter·weight″,** *n., v.t.*

coun′ter·feit″, *v.t.* **1.** imitate closely, esp. money. **2.** pretend. —*adj.* **3.** having been counterfeited. —*n.* **4.** something counterfeit. —**coun′ter·feit″er,** *n.*

coun′ter·mand″, *v.t.* cancel with a contrary order.

coun′ter·part″, *n.* **1.** similar person or thing. **2.** duplicate.

coun′ter·point″, *n. Music.* interaction of melodies.

coun′ter·sign″, *n.* **1.** reply to a password establishing identity. **2.** secret sign. **3.** confirming signature. —*v.t.* **4.** sign as a confirmation.

coun′ter·sink″, *v.t.,* **-sunk, -sinking. 1.** drive or set flush with or below a surface. **2.** cut to receive the head of a countersunk part.

count′ess, *n.* wife of a count or earl.

count′less, *adj.* innumerable.

coun′try, *n., pl.* **-tries. 1.** rural area. **2.** land of which one is a citizen. **3.** region. —**coun′try·man,** *n.*

coun′try·side″, *n.* rural terrain.

coun′ty, *n.* **1.** political division of a U.S. state. **2.** political division of a European country.

coup (kōō), *n., pl.* **coups** (kōōz). bold, adroit, successful act.

coup de grace (kōō′de grahs′), something putting an end to a miserable existence.

coupe (kōō pā′), *n.* two-door hard-top car.

cou′ple, *n., v.,* **-pled, -pling.** *n.* pair. —*v.t., v.i.* **2.** join one to another. —**coup′ling,** *n.*

coup′let, *n.* pair of verses that rhyme.

cou′pon, *n.* valuable certificate to be cut or detached from a bond, advertisement, etc.

cour′age, *n.* bravery or fortitude. —**cou·ra′geous,** *adj.*

cou′ri·er, *n.* messenger.

course, *n., v.i.,* **coursed, coursing.** *n.* **1.** path or direction of a moving thing. **2.** natural progress or outcome. **3.** way of acting. **4.** phase of a meal. **5.** program of instruction in one subject. **6.** layer of stones, shingles, etc. in a building. —*v.i.* **7.** run or race.

court, *n.* **1.** Also, **court′yard″,** area surrounded by buildings. **2.** agency for trying civil or criminal cases. **3.** group

immediately attached to a sovereign. **4.** act of wooing. **5.** place to play ball games. —*v.t.* **6.** woo. **7.** ingratiate oneself with. **8.** seek to obtain. —*v.i.* **9.** engage in courtship. —**court'house''**, *n.* —**court'room''**, *n.*

cour'te·ous, *adj.* polite.

cour'te·san, *n.* prostitute.

cour'te·sy, *n., pl.* -**sies.** politeness.

cour'ti·er, *n.* member of a royal court.

court'ly, *adj.,* -**lier, -liest.** worthy of a royal court, esp. in manner.

court'-mar''tial, *n., pl.* **courts-martial,** *v.t.,* -**tialed, -tialing.** *n.* **1.** military court or trial. —*v.t.* **2.** try before such a court.

court'ship'', *n.* wooing.

cous'in, *n.* offspring of an uncle or aunt.

cove, *n.* small inlet or bay.

cov'e·nant, *n.* agreement.

cov'er, *v.t.* **1.** put a lid, shelter, etc. over. **2.** conceal. **3.** protect or shield. **4.** clothe. **5.** hold at bay with a gun, etc. **6.** investigate or watch. —*n.* **7.** something that covers. **9.** means of concealing actions, identity, etc. —**cov'er·age**, *n.* —**cov'er·ing**, *n.*

cov'er·let, *n.* bedspread.

cov'ert, *adj.* concealed. —**cov'ert·ly**, *adv.*

cov'er-up'', *n.* plot to conceal guilt or guilty actions.

cov'et, *v.t.* desire enviously. —**cov'et·ous**, *adj.*

cov'ey, *n., pl.* -**ies.** flock of quail or partridge.

cow, *n.* **1.** four-footed milk-giving bovine animal. **2.** female elephant, whale, etc. —*v.t.* **3.** intimidate. —**cow'hide''**, *n.*

cow'ard, *n.* person without courage. —**cow'ard·ly**, *adj., adv.* —**cow'ard·ice**, *n.*

cow'boy'', *n.* ranch worker. Also, **cow'hand''.**

cow'er, *v.i.* cringe.

cowl, *n.* hood or hooded cloak.

co'work''er, *n.* fellow worker.

cox·swain (kok'sən), *n.* steerer of a boat.

coy, *adj.* affectedly shy.

coy·o'te, *n.* small North American wolf.

co'zy, *adj.,* -**zier, -ziest.** snug and comfortable. —**coz'i·ly**, *adv.* —**coz'i·ness**, *n.*

crab, *n.* four-legged crustacean.

crab'ap'ple, *n.* small, sour apple

crab'bed, *n.* **1.** Also, **crab'by**, ill-tempered. **2.** hard to read.

crab'grass', *n.* grass regarded as a weed.

crack, *v.i., v.t.* **1.** break across abruptly. —*n.* **2.** act or instance of cracking. **3.** narrow break or opening.

crack'er, *n.* **1.** crisp wafer. **2.** firecracker.

crack'le, *v.i.,* -**led, -ling,** *n.* **1.** make rapid snapping sounds in bending. —*n.* **2.** irregular cracked pattern.

crack'pot'', *n.* *Informal.* person with delusions.

cra'dle, *n., v.t.,* -**dled, -dling.** *n.* **1.** rocking, high-sided bed for a baby. **2.** concave support, as for a boat. —*v.t.* **3.** place or rock in a cradle. **4.** support in or as in a cradle.

craft, *n., pl.* **crafts** (for 1 and 2), **craft** (for 3). *n.* **1.** cunning. **2.** skilled trade. **3.** vehicle for movement through water or air.

crafts'man, *n.* **1.** skilled handworker. **2.** skilled, conscientious worker of any kind. —**crafts'man·ship''**, *n.*

craft'y, *adj.,* -**ier, -iest.** cunning. —**craft'i·ly**, *adv.*

crag, *n.* abruptly rising rock formation. —**crag'gy**, *adj.*

cram, *v.,* **crammed, cramming.** *v.t.* **1.** pack tightly or excessively. —*v.i.* **2.** *Informal.* study in a hasty, superficial way.

cramp, *n.* **1.** painful muscular contraction. **2.** Often, **cramps**, abdominal spasms. —*v.t.* **3.** afflict with cramp. **4.** hamper or confine.

cran'ber''ry, *n., pl.* -**ries.** sour red berry from an evergreen.

crane, *n., v.t.,* **craned, craning.** *n.* **1.** long-legged, long-billed water bird. **2.** hoisting machine. —*v.t.* **3.** stretch and bend, as the neck.

cra'ni·um, *n., pl.* -**niums, -nia. 1.** bone covering the brain. **2.** skull. —**cra'ni·al**, *adj.*

crank, *n.* **1.** rotating device incorporating a lever. **2.** *Informal.* person with an ill temper or delusion. —*v.t.* **3.** move with a crank. —**crank'case''**, *n.* —**crank'shaft''**, *n.*

crank'y, *adj.,* -**ier, -iest.** ill-tempered. —**crank'i·ly**, *adv.*

cran'ny, *n., pl.* -**nies.** crevice.

craps, *n.* dice game. —**crap'shoot''er**, *n.*

crash, *n.* **1.** destructive collision, fall, etc. **2.** noise of this. **3.** business failure. **4.** coarse linen. —*v.i.* **5.** suffer a crash. —*v.t.* **6.** cause to have or produce a crash. **7.** batter one's way through.

crass, *adj.* stupid and coarse.

crate, *n., v.t.,* **crated, crating.** *n.* **1.** wooden shipping case. —*v.t.* **2.** pack in a crate.

cra'ter, *n.* pit in the ground made by volcanic eruption, meteors, bombs, etc.

cra·vat', *n.* necktie.

crave, *v.t.,* **craved, craving.** desire or request eagerly. —**crav'ing**, *n.*

cra'ven, *n.* **1.** coward. —*adj.* **2.** cowardly.

craw, *n.* **1.** sac in a bird's gullet. **2.** stomach.

crawl, *v.i.* **1.** move on several legs with the body horizontal. **2.** move slowly. **3.** feel as if crawled on. —*n.* **4.** crawling movement. **5.** swimming stroke.

cray'fish'', *n.* small lobsterlike crustcean. Also, **craw'fish''**.

cray'on, *n.* stick of pigmented material for making lines or tones.

craze, *v.*, **crazed, crazing**, *n.* *v.t.* 1. make insane. 2. cause to crack in random patterns. —*v.i.* 3. become crazed. —*n.* 4. fad.

cra'zy, *adj.*, **-zier, -ziest.** 1. insane. 2. rickety. —**cra'zi·ly**, *adv.*

creak, *v.t.* 1. make a squeak or groan from bending or rubbing. —*n.* 2. sound from such a cause. —**creak'y**, *adj.*

cream, *n.* 1. richer part of milk. 2. substance with a creamlike or salvelike consistency. 3. yellowish white. 4. finest part or element. —*v.t.* 5. make with cream. 6. beat to a creamlike consistency. —**cream'y**, *adj.*

cream'er, *n.* cream pitcher.

cream'er·y, *n.*, *pl.* **-ies.** place for processing or selling dairy products.

crease, *n.*, *v.t.*, **creased, creasing.** *n.* 1. ridge made by pressing. 2. furrow. —*v.t.* 3. make a crease or creases in.

cre·ate', *v.t.* **-hated, -hating.** 1. bring into existence. 2. bring about. —**cre·a'tion**, *n.*

cre·a'tive, *adj.* 1. pertaining to creation. 2. of an original mind; inventive. —**cre''a·tiv'i·ty**, *n.*

cre·a'tor, *n.* 1. person who creates. 2. the **Creator**, God.

cre'dence, *n.* belief, as in the truth of a statement.

cre·den'tials, *n.* documentation proving authority, identity, etc.

cred'i·ble, *adj.* able to be believed. —**cred'i·bil'i·ty**, *n.*

cred'it, *n.* 1. deference of payment. 2. money paid or owed to one. 3. praise or good reputation. 4. source of this. 5. acknowledgment for participation. 6. unit of academic accomplishment. —*v.t.* 7. believe. 8. give a credit or credits to.

cred'it·a·ble, *adj.* deserving of credit.

cred'i·tor, *n.* person to whom a debt is owed.

cre'do, *n.*, *pl.* **-dos.** creed.

cred'u·lous, *adj.* too ready to believe things. —**cre·du'li·ty**, *n.*

creed, *n.* formally stated belief.

creek, *n.* small stream.

creep, *v.i.*, **crept, creeping.** 1. crawl. 2. move stealthily. 3. grow along the ground.

cre'mate'', *v.t.*, **-mated, -mating.** burn at a funeral. —**cre·ma'tion**, *n.* —**cre'ma·to''ry, cre''ma·to'ri·um**, *n.*

Cre'ole, *n.* descendant of the original settlers of Louisiana.

cre'o·sote'', *n.* wood preservative distilled from coal or coal tar.

crepe, *n.* 1. thin, crinkled cloth. 2. rolled, filled pancake. Also, **crêpe.**

cre·scen'do, *adj.*, *n.*, *pl.* **-dos.** *adj.*, *adv.* 1. increasing in loudness. —*n.* 2. increase in loudness.

cres'cent, *n.* shape like that of a new moon.

crest, *n.* 1. uppermost edge or feature. 2. feature surmounting a heraldic escutcheon.

crest'fal''len, *adj.* abashed.

cre'tin, *n.* idiot suffering from a thyroid deficiency.

cre'tonne, *n.* heavy, printed upholstery or curtain material.

cre·vasse', *n.* crevice, esp. in a glacier.

crev'ice, *n.* deep, narrow gap.

crew, *n.* labor force, esp. on a ship. —**crew'man**, *n.*

crib, *n.*, *v.t.*, **cribbed, cribbing.** *n.* 1. small child's bed with high slatted sides. 2. receptacle for corn, animal fodder, etc. 3. stall for cattle. 4. *Informal.* aid to cheating in school. —*v.t.* 5. confine as in a crib. 6. *Informal.* copy dishonestly.

crib'bage, *n.* card game.

crick, *n.* cramp in the neck or back.

crick'et, *n.* 1. grasshopperlike insect. 2. game played with wide bats, esp. in England.

cri'er, *n.* maker of vocal announcements.

crime, *n.* violation of the law.

crim'in·al, *adj.* 1. pertaining to or guilty of crime. —*n.* 2. committer of crimes.

crim''in·ol'o·gy, *n.* study of crime. —**crim''in·ol'o·gist**, *n.*

crimp, *n.*, *v.t.* pleat.

crim'son, *n.* deep red.

cringe, *v.i.*, **cringed, cringing.** 1. crouch or draw back from fear. 2. behave servilely.

crin'kle, *v.* **-kled, -kling.** *v.t.*, *v.i.* 1. wrinkle. 2. rustle, as crisp paper. —**crin'kly**, *adj.*

crip'ple, *v.t.*, **-pled, -pling.** *n.* *v.t.* 1. deprive of the use of arms or legs. 2. render ineffective. —*n.* 3. crippled person.

cri'sis, *n.*, *pl.* **-ses.** point that determines a good or bad outcome.

crisp, *n.* 1. brittle. 2. clear; fresh. 3. briskly abrupt in manner.

criss'cross'', *n.* 1. pattern of crossed lines. —*adj.*, *adv.* 2. in this pattern. —*v.t.* 3. mark with this pattern. —*v.i.* 4. move in or bear this pattern.

cri·te'ri·on, *n.*, *pl.* **-ions, -ia.** basis for judgment.

crit'ic, *n.* person who evaluates good and bad qualities.

crit'i·cal, *adj.* 1. pertaining to critics. 2. pertaining to crises. 3. fault-finding. —**crit'i·cal·ly**, *adv.*

crit'i·cize'', *v.t.*, **-cized**, **-cizing**. 1. evaluate. 2. find fault with. —**crit'i·cism**, *n.*

cri·tique', *n.* evaluation by a critic.

croak, *v.i.* 1. make a deep froglike noise. —*n.* 2. croaking sound.

cro·chet (krō shā'), *v.t.*, **-cheted**, **-cheting**. make with a hooked needle and thread.

crock, *n.* earthenware vessel. —**crock'er·y**, *n.*

croc'o·dile'', *n.* large tropical river reptile.

cro'cus, *n.*, *pl.* **-cuses**. early-blooming flower of the iris family.

crone, *n.* shriveled old woman.

cro'ny, *n.*, *pl.* **-nies**. close friend.

crook, *n.*, *v.*, **crooked**, **crooking**. *n.* 1. hooked staff. 2. curve. 3. *Informal.* thief. —*v.i.*, *v.t.*, 4. bend.

crook'ed, *adj.* 1. full of bends. 2. dishonest.

croon, *v.i.*, *v.t.* sing or hum in low, sweet sounds. —**croon'er**, *n.*

crop, *n.*, *v.t.*, **cropped**, **cropping**. *n.* 1. yield at a harvest. 2. whip. 3. craw of a bird. —*v.t.* 4. cut short.

cro·quet (krō kā'), *n.* lawn game with balls driven by mallets.

cro·quette', *n.* deep-fried piece of ground meat, etc.

cross, *n.* 1. upright with a side-to-side beam used in Roman crucifixions. 2. this form as a symbol of Christianity. 3. modification of this symbolizing Christian saints, sects, etc. 4. source of trouble or unhappiness. 5. mixture of breeds. —*v.t.* 6. go across. 7. thwart. 8. mix with another breed. —*adj.* 9. ill-tempered. —**cross'road''**, *n.* —**cross' roads''**, *n.*, *sing.* —**cross'wise''**, **cross' ways''**, *adv.* —**cross'ly**, *adv.*

cross'bow'', *n.* weapon with a short bow mounted on a guide for a type of arrow.

cross''-ex·am'ine, *v.t. Law.* examine after examination by an opposing attorney. Also, **cross''-ques'tion**. —**cross'' -ex·am'i·na'tion**, *n.*

cross'-eyed'', *adj.* with eyes not properly aligned.

cross'-ref'er·ence, *n.* reference to another part of a book. —**cross'-re·fer'**, *v.i.*, *v.t.*

crotch, *n.* 1. place where a tree limb branches from a larger one. 2. place where the legs meet.

crotch'et, *n.* eccentric whim or attitude. —**crotch'et·y**, *adj.*

crouch, *v.i.*, *v.t.* stoop or squat.

croup, *n.* inflammation of respiratory passages.

crow, *v.i.*, **crowed**. or (for 1) **crew**, **crowed crowing**, *n.* *v.i.* 1. cry like a rooster. 2. boast or exult. —*n.* 3. crowing sound. 4. shiny dark bird.

crow'bar'', *n.* heavy metal lever.

crowd, *n.* 1. large, random group. —*v.t.* 2. fill with a crowd. 3. force into a retricted space. —*v.i.* 4. push one's way. 5. gather in a crowd.

crown, *n.* 1. symbol of sovereignty. 2. royalty as the head of state. 3. upper part. —*v.t.* 4. give a crown to. 5. reward or fulfill.

cru'cial, *adj.* 1. decisive. 2. trying. —**cru' cial·ly**, *adv.*

cru'ci·ble, *n.* melting pot.

cru'ci·fix'', *n.* image of the Christian cross.

cru'ci·fy'', *v.t.*, **-fied**, **-fying**. 1. nail to a cross as punishment. 2. ruin the reputation, happiness, etc. of. —**cru''ci·fix' ion**, *n.*

crude, *adj.* 1. unrefined or unfinished. 2. boorish. —**crude'ly**, *adv.* —**crud'i·ty**, **crude'ness**, *n.*

cru'el, *adj.* 1. causing suffering. 2. desiring to cause suffering. —**cruel'ly**, *adv* —**cru'el·ty**, *n.*

cru'et, *n.* small bottle for oil, vinegar, etc.

cruise, *v.*, **cruised**, **cruising**, *n.* *v.i.* 1. travel slowly, as for recreation or inspection. 2. move at normal speed, as a ship. —*v.t.* 3. cruise in or over. —*n.* 4. act or instance of cruising.

cruis'er, *n.* large, lightly armored warship

crul'ler, *n.* piece of twisted deep-fried dough.

crumb, *n.* small fragment, esp. from dough.

crum'ble, *v.*, **-bled**, **-bling**. *v.t.*, *v.i.* break or drop in pieces.

crum'ple, *v.*, **-pled**, **-pling**. *v.i.*, *v.t.* collapse into wrinkles.

crunch, *v.t.* 1. crush, chew, grind, etc. with a brittle sound. —*v.i.* 2. emit such a sound.

cru·sade', *n.*, *v.i.*, **-saded**, **-sading**. *n.* 1. Christian campaign to recover the tomb of Christ from the Muslims. 2. idealistic campaign. —*v.i.* 3. engage in a crusade. —**cru·sad'er**, *n.*

crush, *v.t.* 1. break or squeeze with pressure. 2. reduce to helplessness or despair through an attack. —*v.i.* 3. become crushed. —*n.* 4. crowd. 5. *Informal.* infatuation. —**crush'er**, *n.*

crust, *n.* 1. hardened outer surface. —*v.t.* 2. cover with a crust. —**crust'y**, *adj.*

crus·ta'cean, *n.* sea animal with jointed feet and a hard outer shell.

crutch, *n.* prop for a lame person.

crux, *n.*, *pl.* **cruxes**, **cruces**. decisive feature or aspect.

cry, *v.*, **cried**, **crying**, *n.*, *pl.* **cries**. *v.i.* 1. weep loudly. 2. utter a call. 3. ask for something loudly. —*v.t.* 4. announce in a shout. —*n.* 5. act or instance of crying.

crypt, *n.* underground church vault, esp. for burial.

cryp'tic, *adj.* defying interpretation.

cryp'to·gram", *n.* code message.

cryp·tog'ra·phy, *n.* encoding and decoding of messages, etc. —**cryp·tog'ra·pher,** *n.*

crys'tal, *n.* **1.** clear quartz. **2.** geometrically formed fused mineral, sugar, etc. **3.** brilliant glass or glassware. **4.** window of a watch dial. —**crys'tal·line,** *adj.* —**crys'ta·lize",** *v.t., v.i.*

cub, *n.* young animal.

cub'by·hole", *n.* small enclosure.

cube, *n., v.t.,* **cubed, cubing.** *n.* **1.** solid with six square sides. **2.** *Math.* third power of a number. —*v.t.* **3.** divide into cubes. **4.** *Math.* multiply to the third power. —**cu'bic,** *adj.* —**cu'bic·al,** *adj.*

cu'bi·cle, *n.* small alcove.

cu'bit, *n.* measure of about 18 inches.

cuck'old, *n.* **1.** husband of an unfaithful wife. —*v.t.* **2.** make a cuckold of. —**cuck'old·ry,** *n.*

cuck'oo", *n.* **1.** bird with a two-note call. —*adj.* **2.** *Informal.* crazy.

cu'cum·ber, *n.* long, green fruit used in salads or as pickles.

cud, *n.* food chewed by cows, etc. after regurgitation.

cud'dle, *v.,* **-dled, -dling.** *v.t.* **1.** hold and caress. —*v.i.* **2.** lie or curl up snugly.

cudg'el, *n., v.t.,* **-eled, -eling.** *n.* **1.** short club. —*v.t.* **2.** beat with a cudgel.

cue, *n., v.t.,* **cued, cuing** or **cueing.** *n.* **1.** signal for speech or action. **2.** stick used in billiards or pool. —*v.t.* **3.** give a cue to.

cuff, *n.* **1.** feature terminating a sleeve or trouser leg. **2.** slap. —*v.t.* **3.** slap.

cui·sine", *n.* manner of cooking.

cul'-de-sac", *n.* blind street with a turning circle at the end.

cu'li·nar"y, *adj.* pertaining to cooking.

cull, *v.t.* select.

cul'mi·nate", *v.i.,* **-nated, -nating.** reach a final development. —**cul"mi·na'tion,** *n.*

cul'pa·ble, *adj.* at fault. —**cul"pa·bil'i·ty,** *n.*

cul'prit, *n.* **1.** accused person. **2.** guilty person.

cult, *n.* **1.** religious sect. **2.** religious practice or devotion. —**cult'ist,** *n.*

cul'ti·vate", *v.t.,* **-vated, -vating.** **1.** work on to grow crops. **2.** develop, as personal qualities. **3.** seek to make a friend or associate. —**cul'ti·va"tor,** *n.*

cul"ti·va'tion, *n.* **1.** development of culture, manners, etc. **2.** act or instance of cultivating.

cul'ture, *n.* **1.** familiarity with the arts, etc. **2.** society, esp. with regard to its art or technology. **3.** development through special care. —**cul'tur·al,** *adj.*

cul'vert, *n.* drain under an embankment.

cum'ber·some, *adj.* heavy; burdensome.

cu'mu·la"tive, *adj.* increasing from additions.

cu'mu·lus, *n., pl.* **-li.** dense cloud with domelike upper parts.

cun'ning, *adj.* **1.** crafty; sly. **2.** clever; skillful. —*n.* **3.** craftiness; slyness. **4.** skill.

cup, *n., v.t.,* **cupped, cupping,** *n.* **1.** small bowlike drinking utensil. **2.** contents of a cup. —*v.t.* **3.** form into a cuplike shape.

cup'board, *n.* storage cabinet, esp. for dishes or food.

cup'cake", *n.* small cup-shaped cake.

Cu'pid, *n.* mythological god of love, represented as a naked boy with a bow and arrow.

cu·pid'i·ty, *n.* greed; avarice.

cu·po·la (kyōō'pə lə), *n.* windowed structure on top of a roof.

cur, *n.* mongrel dog.

cu·rate (kōōr'it), *n.* clergyman with a parish. —**cu'ra·cy,** *n.*

cu·ra'tor, *n.* custodian or director of a museum department.

curb, *n.* **1.** Also, **curb'ing,** edge of a sidewalk. **2.** wall at the top of a well. **3.** border or framework. **4.** something that restrains. —*v.t.* **5.** check or restrain.

curd, *n.* coagulate milk substance, used esp. to make cheese.

cur'dle, *v.,* **-dled, dling.** *v.t., v.i.* form into curds.

cure, *n.* **1.** method of remedial treatment, esp. for disease. **2.** recovery from disease. —*v.t.* **3.** restore to health; heal. **4.** preserve, as food.

cur'few, *n.* ban on being out late.

cu·ri·o (kyōōr'ē ō"), *n.* small beautiful or rare object.

cu·ri·ous (kyōōr'ē əs), *adj.* **1.** inquisitive. **2.** odd. —**cu'ri·ous·ly,** *adv.* —**cu"ri·os'i·ty,** *n.*

curl, *v.t., v.i.* **1.** form into spiral shapes; coil. —*v.i.* **2.** become curved, spiraled or undulated. **3.** move in a curving direction. —*n.* **4.** something with a curved or twisted form. —**curl'y,** *adj.*

cur'lew, *n., pl.* **-lews** or **-lew.** shore bird with a downcurved beak.

curl'i·cue", *n.* fancifully curved ornamental figure.

cur'rant, *n.* **1.** small seedless raisin. **2.** acid edible berry of a wild shrub.

cur'ren·cy, *n.* **1.** money. **2.** general acceptance or use.

cur'rent, *adj.* **1.** happening in the present. **2.** practiced or accepted. —*n.* **3.** continuous movement of a fluid. **4.** flow of electricity. —**cur'rent·ly,** *adv.*

cur·ric'u·lum, *n., pl.* **-lums, -la.** program of studies. —**cur·ric'u·lar,** *adj.*

cur'ry, *n., pl.* **-ries,** *v.t.,* **-ried, -rying.** *n.*

1. spicy condiment. 2. food made with this. —*v.t.* 3. brush, as a horse. 4. make with curry.

curse, *n., v.t.,* **cursed,** or **curst, cursing.** *n.* 1. prayer, etc. invoking harm to another. 2. blasphemy, etc. 3. source of constant trouble. —*v.t.* 4. make the object of a curse. —**curs'ed,** *adj.*

cur''sor, *n.* indicator on a computer monitor showing where the next input will appear.

cur'so·ry, *adj.* hasty or superficial.

curt, *adj.* rude; abrupt. —**curt'ly,** *adv.*

cur'tail', *v.t.* cut short. —**cur·tail'ment,** *n.*

cur'tain, *n.* cloth hanging before a window, theater stage, etc.

curt'sy, *n., pl.* **-sies,** *v.i.,* **-sied, sying.** 1. woman's bow in which the knees are bent. —*v.i.* 2. make such a bow. Also, **curt'sey.**

cur'va·ture, *n.* 1. curve. 2. degree of curving. 3. abnormal curve, as of the spine.

curve, *n., v.,* **curved, curving.** *n.* 1. continuous line continually changing direction. 2. anything formed along such a line. —*v.t., v.i.* 3. bend along a curve.

cush'ion, *n.* 1. soft pad for support. —*v.t.* 2. preserve from a shock, as from impact.

cusp, *n.* pointed projection.

cus'pid, *n.* single pointed tooth; canine tooth.

cus'pi·dor'', *n.* spittoon.

cus'tard, *n.* sweet milk and egg mixture that sets after cooking.

cus'to·dy, *n., pl.* **-dies.** 1. guardianship; care. 2. legal restraint; imprisonment. —**cus·to'di·an,** *n.* —**cus·to'di·al,** *adj.*

cus'tom, *n.* 1. habitual practice or manner of thinking. 2. customs, revenue on foreign goods. —*adj.* 3. made to personal order. —**cus'tom·ar''y,** *adj.* —**cus''tom·ar'i·ly,** *adv.*

cus'to·mer, *n.* buyer; purchaser.

cut, *v.,* **cut, cutting,** *n. v.t.* 1. divide or penetrate with something sharp. 2. form with sharp tools. 3. terminate abruptly. 4. *Informal.* **a.** shun ostentatiously. **b.** be absent from. —*v.i.* 5. become cut. 6. swerve. —*n.* 7. wound from cutting. 8. act or instance of cutting. 9. wounding or snubbing remark. 10. illustration for printing.

cu·ta'ne·ous, *adj.* pertaining to the skin.

cute, *adj.,* **-ter, -test,** 1. attractive; pretty. 2. clever; shrewd.

cu'ti·cle, *n.* outer layer of skin.

cut'lass, *n.* short, heavy edged sword.

cut'ler·y, *n.* cutting tools, esp. for food.

cut'let, *n.* slice or patty food for frying or broiling.

cut'ter, *n.* 1. person or implement for cutting. 2. ship's boat with oars. 3. Coast Guard ship.

cy'a·nide'', *n.* potassium- or sodium-based poisonous substance.

cy''ber·net'ics, *n.* study of human control systems and functions and of mechanical systems that can be used to replace them. —**cy''ber·net'ic,** *adj.*

cy'cla·mate'', *n.* artificial sweetening agent.

cy'cle, *n., v.i.,* **-cled, -cling.** *n.* 1. repeated series. 2. repeated period of time. 3. two-wheeled vehicle. —*v.i.* 4. ride a cycle. —**cy'clic, cy'cli·cal,** *adj.* —**cy'clist,** *n.*

cy'clone, *n.* storm with rotating winds.

cy''clo·pe'di·a, *n.* encyclopedia. Also, **cy''clo·pae'di·a.**

cy'clo·tron'', *n.* machine for giving acceleration to charged particles by electric and magnetic forces.

cyl'in·der, *n.* 1. solid generated by a rectangle turned on its centerline. 2. expansion chamber in an engine. —**cy·lin'dri·cal,** *adj.*

cym·bal (sim'bal), *n.* one of a pair of concave brass or bronze plates struck together.

cyn'ic, *n.* person who sees all actions as selfishly motivated. —**cyn'i·cal,** *adj.* —**cyn·i·cism** (sin'ə siz''əm), *n.*

cy'no·sure'', *n.* center of attraction.

cy'press, *n.* scaly-leaved evergreen tree.

cyst, *n.* abnormal sac or growth, usually filled with fluid.

czar (zar), *n.* Slavic emperor. Also, fem., **cza·ri'na.**

D

D, d, *n.* 1. fourth letter of the English alphabet. 2. fourth-best grade.

dab, *v.,* **dabbed, dabbing,** *n. v.t.* 1. touch or apply lightly. —*n.* 2. small moist lump.

dab'ble, *v.i.,* **-bled, -bling.** 1. play in water. 2. be superficially active. —**dab'bler,** *n.*

daft, *adj.* 1. insane. 2. silly.

dag'ger, *n.* short pointed weapon.

dahl'ia, *n.* showy perennial flowering plant.

dai'ly, *adj., n., pl.* **-lies.** *adj.* 1. happening each day. —*n.* 2. daily periodical.

dain'ty, *adj.,* **-tier, -tiest,** *n., pl.* **-ties.** *adj.* 1. delicate; fine. —*n.* 2. delicacy. —**dain'ti·ly,** *adv.* —**dain'ti·ness,** *n.*

dair'y, *n. pl.* **-ies.** place where milk and milk products are produced. —**dair'y·man,** *n.*

da·is (dā'is), *n., pl.* **-ises.** raised platform.

dai'sy, *n., pl.* **-sies.** flower with a yellow diskshaped centre and white petals.

dale, *n.* valley.

dal′ly, *v.i.*, **-lied, -lying. 1.** play in a loving way. **2.** delay; waste time. —**dal′li·ance**, *n.*

dam, *n.*, *v.t.*, **dammed, damming.** *n.* **1.** barrier to hold back water. **2.** female parent, esp. of quadrupeds. —*v.t.* **3.** obstruct, as with a dam.

dam′age, *n.*, *v.t.*, **-aged, -aging.** *n.* **1.** injury. **2. damages,** compensation for injury. —*v.t.* **3.** injure; harm. —**dam′age·a·ble**, *adj.*

dam′ask, *n.* **1.** fabric woven in patterns. —*adj.* **2.** pink.

damn, *v.t.* condemn. —**dam′na·ble**, *adj.* —**dam·na′tion**, *n.*

damp, *adj.* **1.** moist. —*n.* **2.** moisture. —*v.t.* **3.** make moist. **4.** deaden, as a shock. —**damp′ness**, *n.*

damp′en, *v.t.* **1.** make damp. **2.** deaden or depress, as the spirits. —*v.i.* **3.** become damp.

damp′er, *n.* **1.** something that deadens or depresses. **2.** valve in a flue to regulate draft.

dam′sel, *n. Archaic.* girl.

dance, *v.*, **danced, dancing,** *n.* *v.i.* **1.** move one's body and feet in rhythm, esp. to music. —*v.t.* **2.** execute as a dance. **3.** cause to dance. —*n.* **4.** social gathering for dancing. —**dancer**, *n.*

dan′de·li′on, *n.* weedy plant with yellow flowers.

dan′druff, *n.* scales that form on the scalp and fall off.

dan′dy, *n. pl.*, **-dies,** *adj.*, **-dier, -diest.** *n.* **1.** man overly particular about his appearance. —*adj.* **2.** *Informal.* very good.

dan′ger, *n.* exposure to harm; risk. —**dan′ger·ous**, *adj.*

dan′gle, **-gled, -gling.** *v.i.*, *v.t.* hang loosely.

dank, *adj.* unpleasantly moist.

dap′per, *adj.* **1.** neat. **2.** small and active.

dap′ple, *adj.*, *n.*, *v.*, **-pled, -pling.** *adj.* **1.** Also, **dap′pled,** spotted. —*n.* **2.** spot or marking. —*v.t.* **3.** mark with spots.

dare, *v.*, **dared, daring,** *n.* *v.i.* **1.** have the necessary courage or audacity. —*v.t.*, *n.* **2.** challenge. —**dar′ling**, *adj.*, *n.*

dark, *adj.* **1.** having little or no light. **2.** tending in color toward black. **3.** gloomy. **4.** ignorant. —*n.* **5.** absence of light. —**dark′en**, *v.t.*, *v.i.* —**dark′ness**, *n.*

dar′ling, *n.* **1.** person dear to another. —*adj.* **2.** very dear; cherished.

darn, *v.t.* mend by weaving rows of stitches.

dart, *n.* **1.** small pointed missile usually thrown by hand. **2.** sudden motion. —*v.t.*, *v.i.* **3.** move suddenly and swiftly.

dash, *v.t.* **1.** hurl violently. **2.** smash. **3.** frustrate. —*v.i.* **4.** rush; sprint. —*n.* **5.** small amount shaken from a bottle, etc. **6.** short race. **7.** punctuation mark (—) indicating a break.

dash′board″, *n.* instrument panel.

dash′ing, *adj.* **1.** lively. **2.** showy; stylish. —**dash′ing·ly**, *adv.*

das′tard, *n.* coward; sneak. —**das′tard·ly**, *adj.*

da″ta, *n. pl.* **1.** facts; figures. **2.** (computers) information stored in a memory.

da″ta·base, *n.* (computers) a structured file facilitating data access and manipulation.

date, *n.*, *v.*, **dated, dating.** *n.* **1.** particular time. **2.** day of the month. **3.** appointment. **4.** sweet, fleshy fruit of a palm tree. —*v.t.* **5.** give a date to. —*v.i.* **6.** belong to a specific time.

dat′ed, *adj.* **1.** antiquated. **2.** showing a date.

daub, *v.t.* **1.** cover or smear with a soft, muddy substance. —*v.t.*, *v.i.* **2.** paint clumsily. —*n.* **3.** something daubed. —**daub′er**, *n.*

daugh′ter, *n.* female child. —**daugh′ter·ly**, *adj.*

daugh′ter-in-law″, *n. pl.*, **daughters-in-law.** son's wife.

daunt, *v.t.* frighten; dishearten. —**daunt′less**, *adj.*

dav′en·port″, *n.* large couch.

daw′dle, *v.i.*, **-dled, -dling.** waste time. —**daw′dler**, *n.*

dawn, *v.i.* **1.** begin to grow light in the morning. —*n.* **2.** break of day.

day, *n.* **1.** period between sunrise and sunset. **2.** period of earth's rotation on its axis. **3.** era; period of time.

day′dream″, *n.* **1.** period of pleasant, dreamy thought. —*v.t.* **2.** have daydreams.

day′light″, *n.* **1.** light of day. **2.** openness.

day′time″, *n.* period between sunrise and sunset.

daze, *v.t.*, **dazed, dazing,** *n.*, *v.t.* **1.** stun; bewilder. —*n.* **2.** stunned condition.

daz′zle, *v.t.*, **-zled, -zling. 1.** overwhelm with intense light. **2.** impress with brilliance.

dea′con, *n.* **1.** cleric just below a priest in rank. **2.** lay church officer. —**dea′con·ry**, *n.*

dead, *adj.* **1.** no longer alive. **2.** without life. **3.** obsolete. **4.** accurate; unerring. —*adj.*, *adv.* **5.** straight. —*n.* **6. the dead,** persons no longer living. —**dead′en**, *v.t.*

dead′line″, *n.* latest time by which something must be completed.

dead′lock″, *n.* **1.** frustrated standstill. —*v.t.*, *v.i.* **2.** bring or come to a deadlock.

dead′ly, *adj.* **-lier, -liest. 1.** likely to cause

death. **2.** typical of death. —**dead′li·
ness,** *n.*

deaf, *adj.* incapable of hearing. —**deaf′
ness,** *n.* —**deaf′en,** *v.t.*

deal, *v.,* dealt, dealing, *n. v.t.* **1.** portion
out. **2.** administer, as a blow. —*v.i.* **3.**
do or have business. **4.** portion out
cards, etc. —*n.* **5.** business transaction
or agreement. —**deal′er,** *n.*

dean, *n.* **1.** college official who supervises
students or faculty. **2.** presiding cleric
in a cathedral.

dear, *adj.* **1.** beloved. **2.** expensive. —*n.*
3. beloved person. —**dear′ly,** *adv.*

dearth (dərth), *n.* scarcity; lack.

death, *n.* **1.** act of dying. **2.** state of being
dead. —**death′less,** *adj.* —**death′like′′,**
adj. —**death′ly,** *adj., adv.*

de·ba′cle, *n.* ruinous collapse.

de·bar′, *v.t.,* -barred, -barring. exclude;
prohibit.

de·base′, *v.t.,* -based, -basing. lower in
value. —**de·base′ment,** *n.*

de·bate′, *v.* -bated, -bating. *n. v.t.* **1.** discuss; argue. **2.** consider. —*v.i.* **3.** take
part in discussion. —*n.* **4.** discussion of
opposing views. —**de·bat′a·ble,** *adj.*
—**de·bat′er,** *n.*

de·bauch′, *v.t.* **1.** corrupt; seduce. —*n.*
2. debauchery; seduction. —**de·bauch′
er·y,** *n.*

de·bil′i·tate, *v.t.,* -tated, -tating. weak-
en. —**de·bil′i·ta′tion,** *n.*

de·bil′i·ty, *n., pl.* -ties. weakness.

debt′it, *n.* **1.** recorded debt. —*v.t.* **2.**
charge with a debt.

deb′′o·nair′, *adj.* **1.** courteous; pleasantly mannered. **2.** carefree.

de·bris (də brē′), *n.* rubbish; remains.

debt, *n.* **1.** something owed. **2.** condition
of owing. —**debt′or,** *n.*

de·but (dā byōō′), *n.* **1.** first public appearance. **2.** formal introduction into
society.

deb′u·tante′′, *n.* girl making a society de-
but.

dec′ade, *n.* ten-year period.

dec′a·dence, *n.* decay; deterioration.
—**dec′a·dent,** *adj., n.*

dec′′a·he′dron, *n., pl.* -drons, -dra.
tensided solid.

de·cal′, *n.* transfer of a picture or design
from paper to glass, wood, etc. Also,
de·cal′′co·ma′ni·a.

Dec′a·logue′′, *n.* Ten Commandments.
Also, **Dec′a·log′′.**

de·camp′, *v.i.* **1.** break camp. **2.** depart
suddenly.

de·cant′, *v.t.* pour gently so as not to disturb sediment.

de·cant′er, *n.* ornamental bottle, esp. for
wine.

de·cap′i·tate′′, *v.t.,* -tated, -tating. behead. —**de·cap′′i·ta′tion,** *n.*

de·cath′lon, *n.* contest consisting of ten
track and field events.

de·cay′, *v.i., v.t.* **1.** deteriorate; rot. —*n.*
2. deterioration.

de·cease′, *n., v.i.* -ceased, -ceasing. *n.* **1.**
death. —*v.i.* **2.** die. —**de·ceased′,** *adj.,*
n.

de·ceit′, *n.* lying; fraud. —**de·ceit′ful,**
adj.

de·ceive′, *v.t.* -ceived, -ceiving. mislead.

De·cem′ber, *n.* twelfth and final month.

de′cent, *adj.* **1.** appropriate. **2.** not offensive to modesty. **3.** respectable. **4.** adequate. —**de′cent·ly,** *adv.* —**de′cen·cy,**
n.

de·cen′tral·ize′′, *v.t.,* -ized, -ising. free
from dependency on a central authori-
ty, source, etc. —**de·cen′′tral·i·za′
tion,** *n.*

de·cep′tion, *n.* **1.** act or instance of deceiving. **2.** fraud. —**de·cep′tive,** *adj.*

de·cide′, *v.,* -cided, -ciding. *v.t.* **1.** reach
a decision regarding. —*v.i.* **2.** make a
judgment or choice.

de·cid′ed, *adj.* **1.** clear-cut. **2.** determined. —**de·cid′ed·ly,** *adv.*

de·cid′u·ous, *adj.* shedding leaves at a
particular season, as a tree or shrub.

dec′i·mal, *adj.* **1.** based on the number
ten. **2.** pertaining to fractions whose
denominators are ten or some power of
ten. —*n.* **3.** decimal fraction.

dec′i·mate′′, *v.t.,* -mated, -mating. destroy a sizable number of.

de·ci′pher, *v.t.* determine the meaning
of.

de·ci′sion, *n.* **1.** choice or judgment. **2.**
emphasis; firmness.

de·ci′sive, *adj.* **1.** determining an outcome or conclusion. **2.** emphatic; firm.
—**de·ci′sive·ly,** *adv.* —**de·ci′sive·ness,**
n.

deck, *n.* **1.** floor of a ship, bridge, etc. **2.**
pack of playing cards. —*v.t.* **3.** adorn.

de·claim′, *v.i., v.t.,* speak or utter rhe-
torically. —**dec′′lam·a′tion,** *n.* —**de·
clam′a·to′′ry,** *adj.*

de·clare′, *v.t.* -clared, -claring. **1.** make
known. **2.** say emphatically. —**de·clar′
a·tive, de·clar′a·to′′ry,** *adj.* —**dec′′la·
ra′tion,** *n.*

de·clen′sion, *n.* **1.** grammatical inflection
of nouns, pronouns, or adjectives. **2.**
decline.

de·cline′, *v.,* -clined, -clining, *n. v.t., v.i.*
1. bend or slope downward. **2.** deteriorate. **3.** refuse. —*v.i.* **4.** give grammatical inflections. —*n.* **5.** deterioration. **6.**
downward slope.

de·cliv′i·ty, *n., pl.* -ties. downward
slope.

de·code′, *v.t.* -coded, -coding. decipher
from code.

de′′com·pose′, *v.,* -posed, -posing. *v.t.,*
v.i. **1.** break up into parts. **2.** decay.
—**de′′com·po·si′tion,** *n.*

de·cor′, *n.* style of decoration.

dec′o·rate″, *v.t.* -rated, -rating. 1. adorn. 2. give a medal to. —**dec′o·ra′tive**, *adj.* —**dec′o·ra″tor**, *n.* —**dec″o·ra′tion**, *n.*

dec′o·rous, *adj.* proper.

de·co′rum, *n.* propriety.

de·coy′, *n.* 1. artificial bird used as a lure in hunting. 2. lure. —*v.t.* 3. lure into a trap.

de·crease′, *v.*, -creased, -creasing. *n. v.t., v.i.* 1. gradually lessen. —*n.* 2. lessening.

de·cree′, *n.*, *v.*, -creed, -creeing. *n.* 1. edict. —*v.t.* 2. ordain by decree.

de·crep′it, *adj.* worn by old age or long use. —**de·crep′i·tude″**, *n.*

de·cry′, *v.t.*, -cried, -crying. denounce. —**de·cri′al**, *n.*

ded′i·cate″, *v.t.*, -cated, -cating. 1. set apart; devote. 2. inscribe. —**ded″i·ca′tion**, *n.*

de·duce′, *v.t.*, -duced, -ducing. infer; derive. —**de·duc′i·ble**, *adj.*

de·duct′, *v.t.* subtract; take away. —**de·duct′i·ble**, *adj.*

de·duc′tion, *n.* 1. act or result of reasoning from the general to the specific. 2. amount deducted. —**de·duc′tive**, *adj.*

deed, *n.* 1. something that is done; an act. 2. legal conveyance esp. of land. —*v.t.* 3. transfer by deed.

deem, *v.t., v.i.* believe; adjudge.

deep, *adj.* 1. extending far downward or inward. 2. difficult to understand. 3. profound; serious. 4. dark and rich, esp. a color. 5. low in pitch. —*n.* 6. deep place. —*adv.* 7. far down. —**deep′en**, *v.t., v.i.* —**deep′ly**, *adv.*

deer, *n.*, *pl.* **deer**, **deers**. ruminant animal, the male of which have antlers or horns.

de·face′, *v.t.*, -faced, -facing. mar; disfigure. —**de·face′ment**, *n.*

de fac′to, actually existing but not lawfully authorized.

de·fame′, *v.t.* -famed, -faming. attack the reputation of; slander. —**def″am·a′tion**, *n.* —**de·fam′a·to″ry**, *adj.*

de·fault′, *n.* 1. failure, esp. to pay a debt. —*v.i., v.i.* 2. fail, esp. to pay, when required.

de·feat′, *v.t.* 1. overthrow; conquer. —*n.* 2. act or instance of defeating.

de·feat′ist, *n.* person who accepts defeat. —**de·feat′ism**, *n.*

def′e·cate″, *v.i.*, -cated, -cating. *v.i.* excrete waste from the bowels. —**def″e·ca′tion**, *n.*

de·fect′, *n.* 1. (dē′fekt, dē fekt′) imperfection; fault. —*v.i.* (dē fekt′) 2. desert a cause, esp. to join another. —**de·fec′tive**, *adj.* —**de·fec′tion**, *n.* —**de·fec′tor**, *n.*

de·fend′, *v.t.* 1. protect; guard against attack. 2. support with one's words. —**de·fend′er**, *n.*

de·fend′ant, *n. Law.* accused person.

de·fense′, *n.* 1. protection against attack. 2. justification. 3. *Law.* reply to a charge. —**de·fense′·less**, *adj.* —**de·fen′si·ble**, *adj.*

de·fen′sive, *adj.* 1. pertaining to defense. 2. anxious to justify oneself. —*n.* 3. situation of a defender.

de·fer′, *v.*, -ferred, -ferring. *v.t., v.i.* 1. postpone. —*v.i.* 2. yield politely. —**de′fer′ment**, *n.* —**def′er·ence**, *n.* —**de″fer·en′tial**, *adj.*

de·fi′ance, *n.* open disregard of or bold resistance to authority. —**de·fi′ant**, *adj.*

de·fi′cien·cy, *n.*, *pl.* -cies. lack; inadequate amount. —**de·fi′cient**, *adj.*

def′i·cit, *n.* deficiency, esp. of assets.

de·file′, *v.*, -filed, -filing. *v.t.* 1. desecrate. 2. make filthy. —*v.i.* 3. march in file. —*n.* 4. narrow passage. —**de·file′ment**, *n.*

de·fine′, *v.t.*, -fined, -fining. 1. state the meaning of. 2. determine. —**def″i·ni′tion**, *n.* —**de·fin′a·ble**, *adj.*

def′i·nite, *adj.* 1. exact. 2. within precise limits. —**def′i·nite·ly**, *adv.*

de·fin′i·tive, *adj.* 1. conclusive. 2. defining.

de·flate′, *v.*, -flated, -flating. *v.t., v.i.* 1. collapse by releasing air. 2. increase in purchasing power. —**de·fla′tion**, *n.* —**de·fla′tion·ar″y**, *adj.*

de·flect′, *v.t., v.i.* turn from a course; swerve. —**de·flec′tion**, *n.*

de·form′, *v.t.* 1. mar the form of. 2. make ugly. —**de″for·ma′tion**, *n.* —**de·form′i·ty**, *n.*

de·fraud′, *v.t.* cheat; take rights or property of by fraud.

de·fray′, *v.t.* pay, as expenses.

de·frost′, *v.t., v.i.* free or be freed of ice.

deft, *adj.* skillful. —**deft′ly**, *adv.* —**deft′ness**, *n.*

de·funct′, *adj.* no longer alive or in existence.

de·fy′, *v.t.*, -fied, -fying. 1. openly resist. 2. challenge.

de·gen′er·ate″, *adj., n., v.,* -ated, -ating. *adj.* (dē jen′ər ət) 1. deteriorated. 2. depraved. *n.* 3. depraved person. —*v.i.* (dē jen′ər āt) 4. deteriorate. —**de·gen″er·a′tion**, *n.* —**de·gen′er·a·cy**, *n.* —**de·gen′er·a·tive**, *adj.*

de·grade′, *v.t.*, -graded, -grading. reduce in quality or rank. —**de″gra·da′tion**, *n.*

de·gree′, *n.* 1. stage or point, as in a process. 2. extent or intensity. 3. title conferred by a college. 4. unit of temperature. 5. 360th of a circle.

de·hu′man·ize″, *v.t.*, -ized, -izing. deny human qualities to.

de·hy′drate″, *v.*, -drated, -drating. *v.t. v.i.* remove or lose water. —**de″hy·dra′tion**, *n.*

de'i·fy'', v.t., -fied, -fying. make a god of. —de''i·fi·ca'tion, n.

deign, v.t., v.i. condescend.

de'ism, n. belief that a god created the world but has had no control over it. —de'ist, n.

de'i·ty, n., pl. -ties. god or goddess

de·ject', v.t. dishearten. —de·jec'tion, n.

de·lay', v.t. 1. postpone. 2. hinder; make late. —v.i. 3. linger; procrastinate. —n. 4. act or instance of delaying.

de·lec'ta·ble, adj. delightful; delicious. —de''lec·ta'tion, n.

del'e·gate, n., v.t., -gated, -gating. n. (del'ə gət) 1. representative. —v.t. (del' ə gāt) 2. send as arepresentative. 3. entrust to another, as authority. —del''e·ga'tion, n.

de·lete', v.t., -leted, -leting. remove from a text. —de·le'tion, n.

del''e·te'ri·ous, adj. injurious to health;

de·lib'er·ate, v., -ated, -ating, adj. v.t., v.i. (dē lib'ər āt) 1. ponder. —adj. (dēlib'ər ət) 2. intentional. 3. unhurried. —de·lib'er·ate·ly, adv. —de·lib''er·a'tion, n. —de·lib'er·a·tive, adj. —de·lib'er·a''tor, n.

del'i·ca·cy, n., pl. -cies. 1. fineness of quality. 2. choice food.

del'i·cate, adj. 1. fine in quality or texture. 2. easily damaged. 3. considerate; tactful. 4. functioning precisely. —del'i·cate·ly, adv.

del''i·ca·tes'sen, n. store selling food specialties.

de·li'cious, adj. 1. pleasing to taste. 2. delectable. —de·li'cious·ly, adv.

de·light', v.t., v.i. 1. give great pleasure. —n. 2. joy or great pleasure. —de·light'ed, adj. —de·light'ful, adj.

de·lin'e·ate'', v.t., -ated, -ating. trace the outline of. —de·lin''e·a'tion, n.

de·lin'quent, adj. 1. neglectful of duty or law. 2. late, as a debt. —n. 3. delinquent person. —de·lin'quen·cy, n.

de·lir'i·um, n. temporary excited mental disorder. —de·lir'i·ous, adj.

de·liv'er, v.t. 1. set free or save. 2. hand over. 3. assist at the birth of. 4. present to an audience. 5. distribute. —de·liv'er·ance, n. —de·liv'er·y, n.

del·phin'i·um, n. tall blue garden flower.

del'ta, n. deposit of soil formed at a divided river mouth.

de·lude', v.t., -luded, -luding. mislead.

del'uge (del'yoōj), n., v.t., -uged, -uging. n. 1. flood. 2. heavy rainfall. —v.t. 3. flood. 4. overwhelm.

de·lu'sion, n. false conception, esp. one persistent and opposed to reason. —de·lu'sive, adj.

de·luxe', adj. of specially fine quality.

delve, v.i., delved, delving. dig.

dem'a·gogue'', n. unscrupulous player on popular emotion. Also, dem'a·gog''. —dem'a·gog''y, dem'a·gogu''er·y, n.

de·mand', v.t. 1. ask for boldly; claim as a right. 2. require. v.i. 3. make a demand. —n. 4. act or instance of demanding. 5. thing demanded. —de·mand'ing, adj.

de·mean', v.t. 1. debase; humble. 2. behave; conduct.

de·mean'or, n. behavior or conduct.

de·ment'ed, adj. mentally deranged.

de·mer'it, n. 1. fault. 2. mark against a person for a fault.

dem'i·god, n. 1. mythological being who is divine and human. 2. godlike human.

de·mil'i·tar·ize'', v.t., -ized, -izing. free from military control. —de·mil''i·tar·i·za'tion, n.

de·mise', n., v.t., -mised, -mising. n. 1. death. —n., v.t. 2. transfer by lease.

de·mo'bi·lize'', v.t., -lized, -lizing. free from military service; disband. —de·mo''bi·li·za'tion, n.

de·moc'ra·cy, n. 1. government by the people. 2. country with such government. 3. social equality. —dem'o·crat'', n. —dem''o·crat'ic, adj. —de·moc'ra·tize'', v.t.

De·mo'crat, n. member of the Democratic party.

de·mol'ish, v.t. destroy. —dem''o·li'tion, n.

de'mon, n. 1. evil spirit; devil. 2. person regarded as evil. —de·mon'ic, de·mo'ni·ac'', de''mo·ni'a·cal, adj.

dem'on·strate'', v. -strated, -strating. v.t. 1. prove in detail. 2. explain by example. 3. reveal. —v.i. 4. call public attention to one's attitude. —dem''on·stra'tion, n. —dem'on·stra''tor, n. —de·mon'stra·ble, adj.

de·mon'stra·tive, adj. 1. self-expressive. 2. illustrative or explanatory. 3. conclusive.

de·mor'al·ize'', v.t., -ized, -izing. lower the morale of. —de·mor''al·i·za'tion, n.

de·mote', v.t., -moted, -moting. lower in rank. —de·mo'tion, n.

de·mur', v.i., -murred, -murring, n. v.i. 1. object. —n. 2. objection.

de·mure', adj. modest; coy. —de·mure'ly, adv.

den, n. 1. cave of a wild animal. 2. vile place. 3. small, private room for a man.

de·ni'al, n. 1. refusal of consent. 2. contradiction. 3. refusal to believe.

den'i·grate'', v.t., -grated, -grating. blacken or malign the character of. —den''i·gra'tion, n.

den'im, n. heavy twill cotton cloth.

den'i·zen, n. inhabitant.

de·nom'i·nate'', v.t., -nated, -nating. name.

de·nom''i·na'tion, *n.* 1. name. 2. act of naming. 3. religious sect. —**de·nom''i·na'tion·al,** *adj.*

de·nom'i·na'tor, *n. Math.* term below the line in a fraction; divisor.

de·note', *v.t.,* -noted, -noting. indicate; mean. —**de''no·ta'tion,** *n.*

de·noue·ment (dā nōō mähn'), *n. Literature.* resolution of a conflict.

de·nounce', *v.t.,* -nounced, -nouncing. 1. accuse openly. 2. inform against. —**de·nounce'ment,** *n.*

dense, *adj.* 1. thick. 2. stupid. —**dense'ly,** *adv.* —**dense'ness,** *n.* —**den'si·ty,** *n.*

dent, *n.* 1. hollow area made by a blow. —*v.t., v.i.* 2. make or receive a dent.

den'tal, *adj.* pertaining to teeth or dentistry.

den'ti·frice, *n.* preparation used in brushing the teeth.

den'tist, *n.* doctor specializing in teeth and gums. —**den'tist·ry,** *n.*

den'ture, *n.* set of false teeth.

de·nude', *v.t.,* -nuded, -nuding. strip. —**den''u·da'tion,** *n.*

de·nun''ci·a'tion, *n.* 1. condemnation. 2. accusation.

de·ny', *v.t.,* -nied, -nying. 1. reject as untrue. 2. refuse to give or allow. 3. refuse something to.

de·o'dor·ant, *n.* 1. preparation for destroying odors. —*adj.* 2. destroying odors.

de·part', *v.i.* 1. leave; go away. 2. die. —**de·par'ture,** *n.*

de·part'ment, *n.* 1. part or section. 2. field of activity. —**de·part''men'tal,** *adj.*

de·pend', *v.i.* 1. look outside oneself for support, help, etc. 2. be according to conditions. —**de·pend'a·ble,** *adj.* —**de·pend'a·bly,** *adv.* —**de·pend''a·bil'i·ty,** *n.* —**de·pend'ent,** *adj., n.* —**de·pend'ence, de·pend'en·cy,** *n.*

de·pict', *v.t.* 1. portray; delineate. 2. describe. —**de·pic'tion,** *n.*

de·plete', *v.t.,* -pleted, -pleting. exhaust or reduce in amount. —**de·ple'tion,** *n.*

de·plore', *v.t.,* -plored, -ploring. regret strongly. —**de·plor'a·ble,** *adj.*

de·pop'u·late', *v.t.,* -lated, -lating. remove remove the population of. —**de·pop''u·la'tion,** *n.*

de·port', *v.t.* expel from a country. —**de''por·ta'tion,** *n.*

de·port'ment *n.* conduct or behaviour.

de·pose', *v.t.,* -posed, -posing. 1. remove from office or power. 2. testify. —**dep''o·si'tion,** *n.*

de·pos'it, *v.t.* 1. put in a bank, etc. 2. give in partial payment. 3. drop or cause to settle. 4. something deposited. —**de·pos'i·tor,** *n.*

de·pot (dē'pō), *n.* 1. bus or railroad station. 2. storage place for military supplies.

de·prave', *v.t.* -praved, -praving. corrupt. —**de·prav'i·ty,** *n.*

dep're·cate'', *v.t.,* -cated, -cating. 1. express disapproval of. 2. belittle. —**dep''re·ca'tion,** *n.* —**dep're·ca·to''ry,** *adj.*

de·pre·ci·ate (dē prē'shē āt'), *v.,* -ated, -ating. *v.t., v.i.* 1. lessen in value or seeming importance. —*v.t.* 2. belittle. —**de·pre''ci·a'tion,** *n.*

dep''re·da'tion, *n.* robbery.

de·press', *v.t.* 1. deject; sadden. 2. push down. 3. weaken. —**de·pressed',** *adj.* —**de·press'ant,** *n.*

de·pres'sion, *n.* 1. act of depressing or being depressed. 2. depressed state. 3. period when business and employment decline. —**de·pres'sive,** *adj.*

de·prive', *v.t.,* -prived, -priving. withhold from. —**de''pri·va'tion,** *n.*

depth, *n.* 1. distance downward or inward. 2. quality of being deep. 3. intensity or profundity. 4. profundity. 5. **depths,** deepest part.

dep''u·ta'tion, *n.* delegation.

dep'u·ty, *n., pl.* -ties. person appointed to act as a substitute for another.

de·rail', *v.t., v.i.* run off the rails. —**de·rail'ment,** *n.*

de·range', *v.t.,* -ranged, -ranging. 1. disturb the arrangement of. 2. make insane. —**de·range'ment,** *n.*

der'by, *n.* stiff hat with a round crown.

der'e·lict'', *adj.* 1. abandoned by its owner. 2. negligent. —*n.* 3. something abandoned, esp. a ship. 4. destitute person.

der''e·lic'tion, *n.* 1. negligence of a duty. 2. forsakenness.

de·ride', *v.t.,* -rided, -riding. mock. —**de·ri'sion,** *n.* —**de·ri'sive,** *adj.*

de·rive', *v.* -rived, -riving. *v.t.* 1. obtain from a source. 2. trace to or from a source. 3. deduce; infer. —*v.i.* 4. originate or be derived. —**der''i·va'tion,** *n.* —**de·riv'a·tive,** *adj., n.*

der'o·gate', *v.,* -gated, -gating. *v.t., v.i.* detract. —**der''o·ga'tion,** *n.* —**de·rog'a·to''ry,** *adj.*

der'rick, *n.* 1. crane for lifting and moving heavy objects. 2. tall framework over an oil well.

des·cant, *n.* 1. (des'kant) melody. —*v.i.* (des kant') 2. sing. 3. discourse.

de·scend (di send') *v.t.* 1. move down, along or through. —*v.i.* 2. move downward. 3. slope downward. 4. make a sudden attack, etc. 5. be derived from specified ancestors. —**des·cent',** *n.* —**de·scen'dant,** *n.*

de·scribe', *v.t.,* -scribed, -scribing. 1. give a conception or account of. 2. trace by movement. —**de·scrib'a·ble,** *adj.* —**de·scrip'tion,** *n.* —**de·scrip'tive,** *adj.*

de·scry', *v.t.,* -scried, -scrying. perceive.

des''e·crate'', *v.t.*, -crated, -crating. profane. —des''e·cra'tion, *n.*

de·seg're·gate'', *v.*, -gated, -gating. *v.t.*, *v.i.* eliminate racial segregation in. —de·seg''re·ga'tion, *n.*

de·sert', *v.t.* (de zɜrt') 1. abandon. 2. abscond from permanently, as duty. —*n.* 3. Often, **deserts**, something deserved. 4. (dez'ɔrt) wasteland, esp. a sandy one. —*adj.* 5. desolate; barren. —de·sert'er, *n.* —de·ser'tion, *n.*

de·serve', *v.*, -served, -serving. *v.t.* have as a rightful outcome or reward. —*v.i.* 2. be worthy. —de·serv'ing, *adj.*

des'ic·cate'', *v.*, -cated, -cating. *v.t.*, *v.i.* dry completely. —des'ic·ca'tion, *n.*

de·sign', *v.t.* 1. plan the form and making of. 2. contrive. 3. intend. —*n.* 4. plan or pattern. 5. designing of artistic objects. 6. scheme or intention.

des'ig·nate'', *v.t.*, -nated, -nating. 1. specify; indicate. 2. name. 3. appoint. —des'ig·na'tion, *n.*

de·sign'er, *n.* 1. one who designs. —*adj.* 2. of or pertaining to clothing, etc. styled by a designer, as *designer jeans.*

de·sign'ing, *adj.* scheming.

de·sire', *v.*, -sired, -siring. *n. v.t.* 1. long for. 2. request. —*v.i.* 3. have a desire. —*n.* 4. craving. 5. request. 6. lust. 7. thing desired. —de·sir'a·ble, *adj.* —de·sir''a·bly, *adv.* —de·sir''a·bil'i·ty, *n.* —de·sir'ous, *adj.*

de·sist', *v.i.* stop; cease.

desk, *n.* table with drawers used for writing.

des'o·late, *adj.*, *v.* -lated, -lating. *adj.* (des'ə lit) 1. barren. 2. lonely. 3. uninhabited. —*v.t.* (des'ə lāt') 4. make barren. —des''o·la'tion, *n.*

de·spair', *v.i.* 1. lose hope. —*n.* 2. hopelessness.

des''per·a'do, *n.*, *pl.* -does, -dos. reckless criminal.

des'per·ate, *adj.* 1. reckless due to despair. 2. having an urgent need. 3. very serious. 4. extreme or drastic. —des''per·a'tion, *n.*

des'pi·ca·ble, *adj.* contemptible. —des'pi·ca·bly, *adv.*

de·spise', *v.t.*, -spised, -spising. scorn; loathe.

de·spite', *prep.* in spite of.

de·spoil', *v.t.* rob; pillage.

de·spond', *v.i.* lose hope or courage. —de·spond'en·cy, de·spond'ence, *n.* —de·spond'ent, *adj.*

des'pot, *n.* tyrant or absolute ruler. —des·pot'ic, *adj.* —des'pot·ism, *n.*

des·sert', *n.* sweet course ending a meal.

des''ti·na'tion, *n.* place to be reached.

des'tine, *v.t.*, -tined, -tining. 1. intend. 2. predetermine.

des'tin·y, *n.*, *pl.* -nies. 1. predetermined course of events. 2. rate.

des'ti·tute'', *adj.* 1. deprived. 2. without means of existence. —des''ti·tu'tion, *n.*

de·stroy', *n.* 1. damage so as to eliminate. 2. kill.

de·stroy'er, *n.* 1. light, fast warship. 2. person or thing that destroys.

de·struc'tion, *n.* 1. act or instance of destroying. 2. agency by which one is destroyed. —de·struct'i·ble, *adj.* —de·struc'tive, *adj.*

des'ul·to''ry, *adj.* 1. random. 2. disconnected. —des''ul·to'ri·ly, *adv.*

de·tach', *v.t.* separate; disconnect. —de·tach'a·ble, *adj.*

de·tached', *adj.* 1. separate; not connected. 2. disinterested.

de·tach'ment, *n.* 1. state of being detached. 2. military unit on a special mission.

de·tail', *n.* 1. subordinate part or feature. 2. soldiers for a specific duty. —*v.t.* 3. make, plan, or relate the details of. 4. assign to a duty.

de·tain', *v.t.* 1. keep from going on; delay. 2. keep in custody. —de·ten'tion, *n.*

de·tect', *v.t.* discover. —de·tec'tion, *n.* —de·tec'tor, *n.* —de·tect'a·ble, de·tect'i·ble, *adj.*

de·tec'tive, *n.* investigator seeking private or hidden information.

de·tente (dā tahnt'), *n.* lessening of tension, esp. internationally.

de·ter', *v.t.*, -terred, -terring. discourage or prevent. —de·ter'ment, *n.* —de·ter'rent, *n.*

de·ter'gent, *adj.* 1. cleansing. —*n.* 2. preparation used for cleaning.

de·te'ri·o·rate'', *v.*, -rated, -rating. *v.t.*, *v.i.* worsen. —de·te''ri·o·ra'tion, *n.*

de·ter''mi·na'tion, *n.* 1. act or instance of determining. 2. firmness of resolve. 3. firm intention.

de·ter'mine, *v.*, -mined, -mining. *v.t.* 1. settle. 2. ascertain. 3. direct; impel. 4. set limits to. —*v.i.* 5. decide. —de·ter'mi·na·ble, *adj.* —de·ter'mi·nate, *adj.*

de·ter'mined, *adj.* showing determination.

de·test', *v.t.* hate. —de·test'a·ble, *adj.* —de·test'a·bly, *adv.* —de''tes·ta'tion, *n.*

de·throne', *v.t.*, -throned, -throning. remove from sovereign power.

det'o·nate'', *v.*, -nated, -nating. *v.t.*, *v.i.* explode. —det''o·na'tion, *n.* —det''o·na'tor, *n.*

de'tour, *n.* 1. roundabout course. —*v.t.*, *v.i.* 2. go or route on a detour.

de·tract', *v.t.* 1. take away. —*v.i.* 2. take a desirable quality. —de·trac'tion, *n.*

det'ri·ment, *n.* 1. injury or loss. 2. something that causes injury or loss. —det''ri·men'tal, *adj.*

de·val'u·ate'', *v.t.*, -ated, ating. lessen in

value. Also, **de·val′ue.** —**de·val″u·a′ tion,** n.

dev′as·tate″, v.t., -tated, -tating. destroy everywhere. —**dev′as·ta′tion,** n.

de·vel′op, v.t. **1.** bring to maturity or completeness. **2.** elaborate. **3.** fall ill with. **4.** Photography. bring out the picture on. —v.i. **5.** be developed. —**de·vel′op·ment,** n. —**de·vel′op· men′tal,** adj.

de·vi·ate, v.i., -ated, ating, adj., n. v.i. (dē′vēāt″) **1.** turn aside; digress. —adj. (dē′vē it″) **2.** deviant. —n. **3.** deviant person. **4.** sexual pervert. —**de″vi·a′ tion,** n.

de·vice′, n. **1.** tool, etc. **2.** plan. **3.** symbol or representation.

dev′il, n., v.t., -iled or -illed, -iling or -illing. n. **1.** fiend of hell. **2.** the Devil, Satan. **3.** malicious or formidable person. —v.t. **4.** torment. —**dev′il·ish,** adj. —**dev′il·ry, dev′il·try,** n.

de·vi·ous, adj. **1.** indirect; circuitous. **2.** shifty; not straightforward. —**de′vi· ous·ly,** adv.

de·vise′, v.t., -vised, -vising, n. v.t. **1.** contrive. **2.** bequath. —n. **3.** bequest. —**de·vis′er,** n.

de·void′, adj. empty of something specified.

de·volve′, v., -volved, -volving. v.i., v.t. pass to another, as a duty.

de·vote′, v.t., -voted, -voting. dedicate. —**de·vot′ed,** adj.

de″vo·tee′, n. admirer or enthusiast.

de·vo′tion, n. **1.** dedication. **2.** devout act, esp. a prayer. —**de·vo′tion·al,** adj.

de·vour′, v.t. **1.** eat hungrily. **2.** consume or take in greedily.

de·vout′, adj. pious; very religious.

dew, n. moisture condensed at ground level. —**dew′drop″,** n. —**dew′y,** adj.

dex′ter·ous, adj. skillful; cunning. Also, **dex′trous.** —**dex·ter′i·ty,** n.

dex′trose, n. type or sugar found in plants and animals.

di″a·be′tes, n. disease characterized by the body's inability to use sugar properly. —**di″a·be′tic,** adj., n.

di″a·bol′ic, adj. devilish. Also, **di″a·bol′ i·cal.**

di·a·dem″, n. crown.

di′ag·nose″, v.t., -nosed, -nosing. **1.** make a diagnosis of. **2.** establish by diagnosis.

di″ag·no′sis, n., pl. -ses. determination of the nature of an illness or situation. —**di″ag·nos′tic,** adj.

di·ag′o·nal, adj. **1.** connecting two nonadjacent angles. **2.** oblique. —n. **3.** something that is diagonal.

di′a·gram″, n., v.t., -gramed, -graming. n. **1.** chart or plan that explains something simply. —v.t. **2.** make a diagram of. —**di″a·gram·mat′ic,** adj.

di′al, n., v.t., -aled or -aling. n. **1.** disk or strip with a calibrated edge, as on a clock or gauge. **2.** disk turned to get radio frequencies, make telephone calls, etc. —v.t. **3.** obtain or reach by turning a dial.

di′a·lect″, n. variety of a language peculiar to a region or class. —**di″a·lec′tal,** adj.

di′a·logue″, n. conversation between two or more people. Also, **di′a·log″.**

di·am′e·ter, n. **1.** straight line passing through the centre of a circle. **2.** length of such a line. —**di″a·met′ri·cal,** adj.

di′a·mond, n. **1.** hard, transparent crystallization of carbon. **2.** parallelogram. **3.** diamonds, suit of playing cards. **4.** baseball field.

dia′per, n. **1.** piece of absorbent material that forms a baby's undercloth. —v.t. **2.** put a diaper on.

di·a·phragm (dī′ə fram″), n. **1.** muscular wall, esp. between the chest and abdomen. **2.** vibrating disk in a microphone etc. **3.** contraceptive device for women.

di″ar·rhe′a, n. intestinal disorder characterized by too frequent and too loose bowel movements.

di′a·ry, n. daily record of experiences. —**di′a·rist,** n.

di·as′to·le, n. normal rhythmic expansion of the heart. —**di″a·stol′ic,** adj.

di′a·tribe″, n. bitter denunciation.

dice, n. pl., sing. **die,** v., diced, dicing. n. **1.** small cubes marked on each side with one to six spots, used in games. —v.i. **2.** play with dice. —v.t. **3.** cut into small cubes.

di·chot′o·my, n. division into two parts.

dick′er, v.i. bargain.

dic′tate″, v., -tated, -tating. v.t., v.i. **1.** speak for preservation in writing. **2.** impose on others, as terms. —**dic·ta′ tion,** n.

dic′ta·tor, n. de facto absolute ruler. —**dic″ta·tor·ship″,** n. —**dic″ta·to′ri· al,** adj.

dic′tion, n. **1.** choice of words. **2.** enunciation.

dic′tion·ar″y, n., pl. -ies. book explaining the meanings, etc. of alphabetically listed words.

dic′tum, n. authoritive statement; pronouncement.

di·dac′tic, adj. intended for instruction. —**di·dac′ti·cism,** n.

die, v.i., died, dying. n. v.i. **1.** cease to live. **2.** lose vigor or strength. —n. **3.** shaping device.

di·er′e·sis, n., pl. -ses. mark placed over a vowel to show that it is pronounced separately.

die′sel, n. internal-combustion engine in which fuel is ignited by air compression. Also, **diesel engine.**

di′et, n. **1.** food normally eaten. **2.** selec-

tion of food for purposes of health. 3. legislature. —*v.i.* 4. be on a diet. —**di′e·tar′y,** *adj.* —**di′′e·ti′tian, di′e·ti′cian,** *n.* —**di′′e·tet′ic,** *adj.*

dif′fer, *v.i.* 1. be different. 2. disagree.

dif′fer·ence, *n.* 1. unlikeness. 2. disagreement. 3. amount after subtraction. —**dif′fer·ent,** *adj.* —**dif′fer·ent·ly,** *adv.*

dif′′fer·en′tial, *adj.* 1. pertaining to difference. —*n.* 2. difference. 3. Also, **differential gear,** gear turning axles at individual speeds.

dif′′fer·en′ti·ate′′, *v.,* -ated, -ating. *v.t.* 1. make unlike. 2. distinguish between or from another. —*v.i.* 3. make a distinction.

dif′fi·cult, *adj.* 1. hard to do or understand. 2. hard to deal with or satisfy. —**dif′fi·cul′′ty,** *n.*

dif′fi·dent, *adj.* shy; self-conscious. —**dif′fi·dence,** *n.*

dif·frac′tion, *n.* breaking of light, sound, etc. into separate components.

dif·fuse, *v.* -fused, -fusing, *adj. v.t., v.i.* (dif fyōōz′) 1. disseminate; spread. —*adj.* (dif fyoos′) 2. not concentrated. 3. wordy. —**dif·fu′sion,** *n.*

dig, *v.,* dug, digging, *n.* *v.t.* 1. cut into or turn over. 2. form by digging. 3. discover or remove by or as if by digging. —*v.i.* 4. break up earth, etc. by digging. —*n.* 5. act or instance of digging. 6. taunting remark.

di·gest′, *v.t.* (də jest′) 1. transform food in the body so it is absorbable. 2. absorb mentally. —*n.* (dī′jest). 3. abridged and systematic collection of information; summary. —**di·gest′i·ble,** *adj.* —**di·ges′tion,** *n.* —**di·ges′tive,** *adj.*

dig′it, *n.* 1. finger or toe. 2. any Arabic figure: 0 to 9. —**dig′it·al,** *adj.*

dig′′i·tal, *adj.* represented by numerals.

dig′′i·tal′is, *n.* dried leaves or a plant, used as a heart stimulant.

dig′ni·fied′′, *adj.* showing dignity; stately.

dig′ni·fy′′, *v.t.,* -fied, -fying. honor; give dignity to.

dig′ni·tar′′y, *n., pl.* -ies. eminent person, esp. because of rank.

di·gress′, *v.i.* wander away from the main subject or purpose. —**di·gres′sion,** *n.* —**di·gres′sive,** *adj.*

dike, *n.* dam made to prevent flooding.

di·lap′i·dat′′ed, *adj.* ruined; broken down. —**di·lap′′i·da′tion,** *n.*

di·late′, *v.,* -lated, -lating. *v.t., v.i.* 1. widen; expand. 2. speak at length. —**di·la′tion, dil′′a·ta′tion,** *n.*

dil′a·to′′ry, *adj.* delaying.

di·lem′ma, *n.* predicament requiring a puzzling choice between two alternatives.

dil′′et·tante′, *n., pl.* -tantes, -tanti. amateur, superficial artist, thinker, etc.

dil′i·gent, *adj.* hard-working. —**dil′i·gence,** *n.*

dill, *n.* plant with aromatic leaves and seeds used for flavoring.

di·lute′, *v.t.,* -luted, -luting. water down; thin out. —**di·lu′tion,** *n.*

dim *adj.,* dimmer, dimmest, *v.,* dimmed, dimming. *adj.* 1. not bright; indistinct. 2. not clearly seeing or understanding. —*v.t., v.i.* 3. make or grow dim. —**dim′ly,** *adv.*

dime, *n.* ten-cent coin.

di·men′sion, *n.* 1. length, breadth, or height. 2. coordinate used in locating something in space and/or time. —**di·men′sion·al,** *adj.*

di·min′ish, *v.t., v.i.* lessen in size or importance. —**dim′′i·nu′tion,** *n.*

di·min′u·tive, *adj.* 1. very small. —*n.* 2. suffix or variant modifying a word to indicate smallness.

dim′i·ty, *n.* thin woven cloth.

dim′ple, *n., v.,* -pled, -pling. *n.* 1. small, natural hollow, esp. on the cheek or chin. —*v.t., v.i.* 2. form dimples.

din, *n., v.t.,* dinned, dinning. *n.* 1. confused or continuous noise. —*v.t.* 2. repeat insistently.

dine, *v.,* dined, dining. *v.i.* 1. eat dinner. —*v.t.* 2. provide dinner for.

di′ner, *n.* 1. person eating. 2. railroad dining car. 3. restaurant resembling such a car.

din′ghy, *n.* small boat belonging to a larger boat.

din·gy (din′jē), *adj.,* -gier, -giest. dark; grimy. —**din′gi·ness,** *n.*

din′ner, *n.* main meal of the day.

di′no·saur′′, *n.* large reptile of prehistoric times.

dint, *n.* 1. exertion. 2. dent.

di·o·cese (dī′ə sēs′′), *n.* district under a bishop. —**di·oc′e·san,** *adj., n.*

dip, *v.,* dipped, dipping. *n. v.t.* 1. lower briefly and raise. 2. remove with a scoop. —*v.i.* 3. be dipped. 4. plunge abruptly. —*n.* 5. short swim or bath. 6. abrupt plunge or slope.

diph·thong (dif′thong, dip′thong), *n.* sound containing two vowels.

di·plo′ma, *n.* certificate conferring a degree.

dip′lo·mat′′, *n.* 1. official representing a state. 2. person of tact. —**di·plo′ma·cy,** *n.* —**dip′′lo·mat′ic,** *adj.*

dip′per, *n.* 1. ladle. 2. **Dipper,** either of two constellations in the shape of a dipper.

dip′so·ma′ni·a, *n.* irresistible craving for alcohol. —**dip′′so·ma′ni·ac′′,** *n.*

dire, *adj.,* direr, direst. 1. Also, **dire′ful,** dreadful. 2. urgent.

di·rect′, *adj.* 1. straight. 2. straightforward. 3. unbroken; continuous. 4.

faithful to an original. —*v.t.* **5.** guide.
6. supervise or command. **7.** address.
—**di·rect'ly**, *adv.* —**di·rect'ness**, *n.*
—**di·rec'tor**, *n.*

di·rec'tion, *n.* **1.** line toward a place,
point of the compass, etc. **2.** instruction. **3.** act, instance, or responsibility
of directing. —**di·rec'tion·al**, *adj.*

di·rec'tive, *n.* general order.

di·rec'to·ry, *n., pl.* **-ries.** book with
names, addresses, etc.

dirge, *n.* funeral song.

dir'i·gi·ble, *n.* maneuverable airship.

dirk, *n.* dagger.

dirt, *n.* **1.** any unclean substance; filth. **2.**
soil.

dirt'y, *adj.,* **-ier, -iest,** *v.,* **-ied, -ying.** *adj.*
1. not clean; soiled. **2.** indecent. —*v.t.,*
v.i. **3.** make or become dirty. —**dirt'i·ness**, *n.* —**dirt'i·ly**, *adv.*

dis·a'ble, *v.t.,* **-bled, -bling.** make incapable or unfit. —**dis''a·bil'i·ty**, *n.*

dis'a·buse', *v.t.,* **-bused, -busing.** rid of
false ideas; set right.

dis''ad·van'tage, *n.* **1.** unfavorable circumstance. **2.** injury or detriment.
—**dis''ad·van'taged**, *adj.* —**dis·ad''van·ta'geous**, *adj.*

dis''af·fect', *v.t.* make unfriendly; antagonize. —**dis''af·fec'tion**, *n.*

dis''a·gree', *v.i.* **-greed, -greeing. 1.** fail
to agree. **2.** quarrel. —**dis''a·gree'ment**, *n.*

dis''a·gree'a·ble, *adj.* not agreeable; unpleasant —**dis''a·gree'a·bly**, *adv.*

dis''ap·pear', *v.i.* **1.** vanish. **2.** cease to
exist. —**dis''ap·pear'ance**, *n.*

dis''ap·point', *v.t.* thwart the expectations
or hopes of. —**dis''ap·point'ment**, *n.*

dis''ap·prove', *v.,* **-proved, -proving.**
v.t., v.i. not to approve. —**dis''ap·prov'al**, *n.*

dis·arm', *v.t.* **1.** take away or deprive of
weapons. **2.** make friendly. —*v.i.* **3.** reduce armed forces. —**dis·ar'ma·ment**, *n.*

dis''ar·range', *v.t.,* **-ranged, -ranging.**
put in disorder. —**dis''ar·range'ment**, *n.*

dis''ar·ray', *v.t.* **1.** throw into disorder.
—*n.* **2.** disorder; confusion.

dis·as'ter, *n.* cause of much damage.
—**dis·as'trous**, *adj.*

dis''a·vow', *v.t.* disclaim knowledge of
or responsibility for. —**dis''a·vow'al**, *n.*

dis·band', *v.t., v.i.* break up, as an organisation. —**dis·band'ment**, *n.*

dis·bar', *v.t.,* **-barred, -bar·ring.** expel
from the legal profession. —**dis·bar'ment**, *n.*

dis·be·lieve', *v.,* **-lieved, -lieving.** *v.t.,*
v.i. refuse to believe. —**dis''be·lief'**, *n.*

dis·burse', *v.t.,* **-bursed, -bursing. 1.** pay
out. **2.** scatter. —**dis·burse'ment**, *n.*

disc, *n.* disk.

dis·card, *v.t.* (dis kard') **1.** throw away.
—*n.* (dis'kard) **2.** state of being thrown
away. **3.** something thrown away.

dis·cern' (di sərn'), *v.t.* perceive; recognize; distinguish. —**dis·cern'i·ble**, *adj.*
—**dis·cern'ment**, *n.* —**dis·cern'ing**,
adj.

dis·charge', *v.,* **-charged, -charging,** *n.*
v.t. (dis charj') **1.** emit. **2.** shoot or
fire. **3.** unload. **4.** perform. **5.** release
or dismiss from service. —*v.i.* **6.** release a load, etc. —*n.* (dis'charj) **7.** act,
instance, or means of discharging. **8.**
something discharged.

dis·ci'ple, *n.* follower of a teacher or
teaching.

dis'ci·pline, *n., v.* **-plined, -plining.** *n.* **1.**
training that develops self-control. **2.**
punishment. **3.** set or system of rules
and regulations. **4.** branch of learning.
—*v.t.* **5.** train. **6.** punish. —**dis'ci·pli·na''ry**, *adj.* —**dis'ci·pli·nar''i·an**, *n.*

dis·claim', *v.t.* disown.

dis·claim'er, *n.* disavowal or renunciation.

dis·close', *v.t.,* **-closed, -closing.** reveal
or uncover. —**dis·clo'sure**, *n.*

dis'co, *n.* **1.** discotheque; a club featuring dancing to rock music. **2.** a style of
dance music with a pronounced beat.

dis·col'or, *v.t., v.i.* fade or stain. —**dis·col''or·a'tion**, *n.*

dis·com'fit, *v.t.* frustrate the plans of;
disconcert. —**dis·com'fi·ture**, *n.*

dis·com'fort, *n.* lack of comfort.

dis''con·cert', *v.t.* upset; disarrange; perturb.

dis''con·nect', *v.t.* finish the connection
of; separate. —**discon·nec'tion**, *n.*

dis·con'so·late, *adj.* unhappy; dejected.

dis''con·tent', *adj.* **1.** Also, **dis''con·tent'ed**, dissatisfied with something;
not content. —*n.* **2.** dissatisfaction;
lack of content.

dis''con·tin'ue, *v.,* **-ued, uing.** *v.t., v.i.*
stop. —**dis''con·tin'u·ance**, **dis''con·tin''u·a'tion**, *n.*

dis·cord', *n.* **1.** lack of harmony. **2.** disagreement. —**dis·cord'ance**, *n.* —**dis·cord'ant**, *adj.*

dis·co·thèque (dis''kō tek'), *n.* place
where people dance to recorded music.

dis'count', *n.* **1.** reduction in price. —*v.t.*
2. deduct from a bill. **3.** advance with
deduction or interest. **4.** sell at less
than the regular price. **5.** disregard.
—**dis·count'a·ble**, *adj.*

dis·cour'age, *v.t.,* **-aged, -aging.** hamper
or stop with predictions of failure, disapproval, etc. —**dis·cour'age·ment**,
n.

dis·course', *n., v.i.,* **-coursed, -coursing.**
n. (dis'kors) **1.** conversation. **2.** essay
or lecture. —*v.i.* (dis kors') **3.** converse.

dis·cour'te·sy, n., pl. -sies. lack of courtesy; rudeness. —dis·cour'te·ous, adj.

dis·cov'er, v.t. perceive for the first time. —dis·cov'er·er, n. —dis·cov'er·y, n. —dis·cov'er·a·ble, adj.

dis·cred'it, v.t. 1. cast doubt on. 2. injure the reputation of. —n. 4. state of being discredited.

dis·creet', adj. prudent. —dis·creet'ly, adv.

dis·crep'an·cy, n. inconsistency.

dis·crete', adj. separate; distinct.

dis·cre'tion, n. 1. prudence. 2. freedom of choice in actions. —dis·cre'tion·ary'', adj.

dis·crim·i·nate, v.i., -nated, -nating, adj. v.i. (dis krim ə nāt') 1. make careful distinctions. 2. show unjust favor or disfavor. —adj. (dis krim'ə nit) 3. making careful distinctions. —dis·crim'i·na'tion, n. —dis·crim'i·nat''ing, adj. —dis·crim'i·na·to''ry, adj.

dis·cur'sive, adj. rambling; wandering from topic to topic.

dis·cuss', v.t. talk or write about. —dis·cus'sion, n.

dis·dain', v.t. 1. scorn; despise. —n. 2. scorn. —dis·dain'ful, adj.

dis·ease', n. v.t., -eased, -easing. n. 1. ailment; sickness. —v.t. 2. affect with sickness.

dis''em·bark', v.i. leave a ship or aircraft. —dis''em·bar·ka'tion, dis''em·bark'ment, n.

dis''em·bod'y, v.t., -ied, -ying. free from the body. —dis''em·bod'i·ment, n.

dis''en·chant', v.t. destroy the enthusiasm of. —dis''en·chant'ment, n.

dis''en·gage', v., -gaged, -gaging. v.t., v.i. disconnect. —dis''en·gage'ment, n.

dis·fa'vor, n. 1. disapproval. —v.t. 2. treat with disfavour.

dis·fig'ure, v.t., -ured, -uring. mar. —dis·fig'ure·ment, n.

dis·fran'chise, v.t., -chised, -chising. deprive of a right or privilege, esp. voting. Also, dis''en·fran'chise.

dis·gorge', v., -gorged, -gorging. v.t., v.i. pour out.

dis·grace', n., v.t., -graced, -gracing. n. 1. state or cause of shame. —v.t. 2. bring shame upon. —dis·grace'ful, adj.

dis·grun'tle, v.t., -tled, -tling. make discontent or sulky.

dis·guise', v.t., -guised, -guising. n. v.t. 1. render temporarily unrecognizable. 2. misrepresent. —n. 3. something that disguises. —dis·guise'ment, n.

dis·gust', v.t. 1. offend the good taste or senses of. —n. 2. sickening dislike.

dish, n. 1. shallow container for food. 2. food that is served.

dis·heart'en, v.t. discourage.

di·shev'el, v.t., -eled, -eling. cause disarray in.

dis·hon'est, adj. not honest. —dis·hon'est·ly, adv. —dis·hon'es·ty, n.

dis·hon'or, n. 1. lack of respect; disgrace. —v.t. 2. disgrace. —dis·hon'or·a·ble, adj.

dis''il·lu'sion, v.t. free from illusion. —dis''il·lu'sion·ment, n.

dis''in·cline', v.t., -clined, -clining. make unwilling or averse. —dis·in''cli·na'tion, n.

dis''in·fect', v.t. rid of infection. —dis''in·fect'ant, n., adj.

dis''in·gen'u·ous, adj. not frank.

dis''in·her'it, v.t. deprive of inheritance.

dis''in'te·grate'', v., -grated, -grating. v.t., v.i. separate v.t., v.i. separate into elements. —dis''in''te·gra'tion, n.

dis·in'ter·est, n. indifference.

dis·in'ter·est·ed, n. 1. impartial. 2. indifferent.

dis·joint'ed, adj. 1. separated at the joints. 2. incoherent.

disk, n. 1. thin, flat, round object. 2. phonograph record.

disk·ette'', n. (computers) a 5 1/4-inch flexible disk used for data storage.

dis·like', v.t., -liked, -liking, n. v.t. 1. regard with aversion or distaste. —n. 2. aversion; distaste.

dis''lo·cate'', v.t., -cated, -cating. put out of the proper or customary place. —dis''lo·ca'tion, n.

dis·lodge', v.t., -lodged, -lodging. force from a place. —dis·lodg'ment, n.

dis·loy'al, adj. not loyal; unfaithful. —dis·loy'al·ty, n.

dis'mal, adj. 1. gloomy; dreary. 2. causing dreariness or misery.

dis·man'tle, v.t., -tled, -tling. 1. deprive or strip of equipment. 2. take apart.

dis·may', v.t. 1. dishearten. —n. 2. disheartenment.

dis·mem'ber, v.t. deprive of limbs. —dis·mem'ber·ment, n.

dis·miss', v.t. 1. direct or allow to leave. 2. discharge from employment. 3. put out of consideration. —dis·mis'sal, n.

dis·mount', v.i. 1. alight from a horse, bicycle, etc. —v.t. 2. take from a mounting. 3. dismantle.

dis''o·be'di·ent, adj. not obedient. —dis''o·be'di·ence, n. —dis''o·bey', v.t.

dis·or'der, n. 1. confusion. 2. ailment. 3. riot. —v.t. 4. create disorder in. —dis·or'der·ly, adj.

dis·or'gan·ize'', v.t., -ized, -izing. throw into confusion. —dis·or''gan·i·za'tion, n.

dis·own', v.t. repudiate.

dis·par'age, v.t., -aged, -aging. belittle. —dis·par'age·ment, n.

dis·pa·rate, *adj.* distinct in kind. —**dis·par'i·ty**, *n.*

dis·pas'sion·ate, *adj.* impartial. —**dis·pas'sion·ate·ly**, *adv.*

dis·patch', *v.t.* 1. send off. 2. kill. 3. transact quickly.—*n.* 4. sending-off. 5. killing. 6. promptness. 7. message. —**dis·patch'er**, *n.*

dis·pel', *v.t.*, **-pelled**, **-pelling**. scatter; drive off.

dis·pen'sa·ry, *n.*, *pl.* **-ries**. place where medical aid is given.

dis"pen·sa'tion, *n.* 1. act or instance of dispensing. 2. something dispensed. 3. release from obligation. 4. divine ordering of events.

dis·pense', *v.*, **-pensed**, **-pensing**. *v.t.* 1. distribute. 2. prepare and give out as medicine. —*v.i.* 3. **dispense with**, **a**. forgo **b**. get rid of. —**dis·pen'sa·ble**, *adj.*

dis·perse', *v.*, **-persed**, **-persing**. *v.t.*, *v.i.* scatter. —**dis·per'sal**, **dis·per'sion**, *n.*

dis·place', *v.t.*, **-placed**, **-placing**. 1. put out of place. 2. take the place of. —**dis·place'ment**, *n.*

dis·play', *v.t.*, *n.* exhibit.

dis·please', *v.t.*, **-pleased**, **-pleasing**. offend. —**dis·pleas'ure**, *n.*

dis·pose', *v.*, **-posed**, **-posing**. *v.t.* 1. arrange. 2. incline or make willing. —*v.i.* 3. rid oneself. —**dis·pos'a·ble**, *adj.* —**dis·pos'al**, *n.*

dis"po·si'tion, *n.* 1. temperament. 2. tendency. 3. arrangement. 4. settlement. 5. disposal.

dis"pos·sess', *v.t.* deprive of possession. —**dis"pos·ses'sion**, *n.*

dis"pro·por'tion, *n.* lack of proportion. —**dis"pro·por'tion·ate**, *adj.*

dis·prove', *v.t.*, **-proved**, **-proving**. prove false. —**dis·proof'**, *n.*

dis·pute', *v.*, **-puted**, **-puting**, *n.* *v.i.*, *v.t.* 1. argue. —*v.t.* 2. express doubt regarding. 3. oppose or fight. —*n.* 4. act or instance of disputing. 5. state of being disputed. —**dis·pu'tant**, *n.*, *adj.* —**dis·put'a·ble**, *adj.* —**dis"pu·ta'tion**, *n.* —**dis"pu·ta'tious**, *adj.*

dis·qual'i·fy", *v.t.*, **-fied**, **-fying**. make or declare unqualified. —**dis·qual"i·fi·ca'tion**, *n.*

dis·qui'et, *v.t.* 1. disturb; make uneasy. —*n.* 2. Also, **dis·qui'e·tude**, restlessness.

dis"qui·si'tion, *n.* formal discourse.

dis"re·gard', *v.t.* 1. ignore. 2. treat with little or no respect. —*n.* 3. neglect. 4. lack of respect.

dis"re·pair', *n.* impaired condition.

dis"re·pute', *n.* bad reputation. —**dis"rep'u·ta·ble**, *adj.*

dis"re·spect', *n.* lack of respect. —**dis"re·spect'ful**, *adj.*

dis·robe', *v.*, **-robed**, **-robing**. *v.t.*, *v.i.* undress.

dis·rupt', *v.t.*, *v.i.* 1. break up. 2. disturb. —**dis·rup'tion**, *n.* —**dis·rup'tive**, *adj.*

dis·sat'is·fy", *v.t.*, **-fied**, **-fying**. fail to satisfy; displease. —**dis·sat"is·fac'tion**, *n.*

dis·sect', *v.t.* 1. cut apart. 2. examine closely. —**dis·sec'tion**, *n.*

dis·sem'ble, *v.*, **-bled**, **-bling**. *v.t.*, *v.i.* disguise. —**dis·sem'blance**, *n.* —**dis·sem'bler**, *n.*

dis·sem'i·nate", *v.t.*, **-nated**, **-nating**. distribute widely. —**dis·sem"i·na'tion**, *n.*

dis·sen'sion, *n.* disagreement or quarreling.

dis·sent', *v.i.* 1. disagree. —*n.* 2. disagreement. —**dis·sent'er**, *n.*

dis"ser·ta'tion, *n.* formal essay; thesis.

dis·sim'i·lar, *adj.* not similar. —**dis·sim"i·lar'i·ty**, *n.*

dis·sim'u·late", *v.*, **-lated**, **-lating**. *v.t.*, *v.i.* dissemble. —**dis·sim"u·la'tion**, *n.*

dis·si'pate, *v.*, **-pated**, **-pating**. *v.t.* 1. scatter. 2. squander. —*v.i.* 3. live in extravagance or vice. —**dis"si·pa'tion**, *n.*

dis'si·pat"ed, *adj.* living in extravagance or vice.

dis·so'ci·ate", *v.t.*, **-ated**, **-ating**. break the connection between.

dis'so·lute", *adj.* dissipated. —**dis'so·lute"ly**, *adv.* —**dis'so·lu'tion**, *n.*

dis·solve', *v.*, **-solved**, **-solving**. *v.t.*, *v.i.* 1. melt; combine with a liquid. 2. terminate. 3. destroy. —**dis"so·lu·tion**, *n.*

dis'so·nance, *n.* musical discord. —**dis'so·nant**, *adj.*

dis·suade', *v.t.*, **-suaded**, **-suading**. deter by persuasion. —**dis·sua'sion**, *n.*

dis'tance, *n.* 1. interval of space or time. 2. remoteness. 3. reserve; aloofness. —**dis'tant**, *adj.*

dis·taste', *n.* dislike. —**dis·taste'ful**, *adj.*

dis·tem'per, *n.* infectious disease of dogs.

dis·tend', *v.t.*, *v.i.* expand. —**dis·ten'tion**, *n.*

dis·till', *v.t.* 1. make or purify by evaporation and condensation. —*v.t.* 2. become distilled. —**dis·till'er**, *n.* —**dis·till'er·y**, *n.* —**dis"til·la'tion**, *n.*

dis·tinct', *adj.* 1. individual. 2. clearly noticeable or understandable. —**dis·tinct'ly**, *adv.*

dis·tinc'tion, *n.* 1. act or instance of distinguishing. 2. difference. 3. eminence. 4. something that gives or betokens eminence.

dis·tinc'tive, *adj.* characteristic.

dis·tin'guish, *v.t.* 1. characterize as individual. 2. perceive. 3. make eminent or excellent. —**dis·tin'guish·a·ble**, *adj.* —**dis·tin'guished**, *adj.*

dis·tort', *v.t.* 1. alter from a normal

shape. **2.** corrupt the true meaning of. —**dis·tor'tion,** *n.*

dis·tract', *v.t.* **1.** prevent from concentrating. **2.** bewilder. —**dis·trac'tion,** *n.*

dis·tract'ed, *adj.* frantic. Also, **dis·traught'.**

dis·tress', *n.* **1.** pain or need. **2.** source of this. **3.** danger. —*v.t.* **4.** cause distress in.

dis·trib'ute, *v.t.,* **-uted, -uting. 1.** give out in portions. **2.** disperse. —**dis''tri·bu'tion,** *n.* —**dis·trib'u·tor,** *n.*

dis'trict, *n.* distinct geographical area.

dis·trust', *n.* **1.** lack of trust. —*v.t.* **2.** place no trust in. —**dis·trust'ful,** *adj.*

dis·turb', *v.t.* **1.** end the quiet state of. **2.** upset or trouble. **3.** interrupt. —**dis·turb'ance,** *n.*

dis·use', *n.* absence of use.

ditch, *n.* channel dug in the ground.

dit'to, *n., pl.* **-tos. 1.** the same as before. **2.** Also, **ditto mark,** a mark, '', used to indicate that the word or line above is repeated.

dit'ty, *n., pl.* **-ties.** simple tune.

di·ur'nal, *adj.* **1.** daily. **2.** pertaining to the day.

di·van', *n.* long, low couch.

dive, *v.i.,* **dived** or **dove, dived, diving,** *n. v.i.* **1.** fall intentionally. **2.** descend below the water. **3.** lose altitude quickly. —*n.* **4.** act, instance, or form of diving. —**div'er,** *n.*

di·verge', *v.i.,* **-verged, -verging. 1.** part in two or more directions. **2.** become of unlike opinion, etc. —**di·ver'gent,** *adj.* —**di·ver'gence,** *n.*

di'vers, *adj. Archaic.* various.

di·verse', *adj.* **1.** different. **2.** various. —**di·verse'ly,** *adv.* —**di·vers'i·ty,** *n.*

di·ver'si·fy'', *v.t.,* **-fied, -fying.** vary. —**di·ver''si·fi·ca'tion,** *n.*

di·vert', *v.t.* **1.** turn aside from a path or course. **2.** entertain; amuse. —**di·ver'sion,** *n.*

di·vest', *v.t.* **1.** deprive or strip. **2.** rid.

di·vide', *v.,* **-vided, -viding.** *v.t.* **1.** separate into parts or classes. **2.** prevent from uniting. —*v.i.* **3.** separate. —*n.* **4.** line separating two drainage areas. —**di·vid'er,** *n.*

div'i·dend'', *n.* **1.** number to be divided. **2.** sum allotted to a stockholder.

di·vine', *adj., v.t.,* **-vined, -vining.** *adj.* **1.** godly or godlike. **2.** religious. —*v.t.* **3.** prophesy. **4.** perceive intuitively. —**div''i·na'tion,** *n.*

di·vin'i·ty, *n., pl.* **-ties. 1.** deity. **2.** theology.

di·vis'i·ble, *adj.* able to be divided, esp. evenly.

di·vi'sion, *n.* **1.** act or instance of dividing. **2.** element or component. **3.** *Math.* process of determining the ratio of one number to another. **4.** military unit.

di·vi'sive, *adj.* causing disunity.

di·vi'sor, *n. Math.* number used to divide another.

di·vorce', *n., v.t.,* **-vorced, -vorcing.** *n.* **1.** legal dissolution of a marriage. **2.** conceptual separation. —*v.t.* **3.** separate oneself from by a divorce. **4.** separate by a divorce. **5.** separate conceptually. —**di·vorce'ment,** *n.*

di·vor''cee', *n.* divorced woman.

di·vulge', *v.t.,* **-vulged, -vulging.** reveal. —**di·vulg'ence,** *n.*

Dix'ie, *n.* southern part of the U.S.

diz'zy, *adj.,* **-zier, -ziest. 1.** unsteady. **2.** causing unsteadiness, as a height.

do, *v.,* **did, done, doing.** *v.t.* **1.** be at work upon or occupied with. **2.** complete. **3.** cause. —*v.i.* **4.** act. **5.** succeed in or accomplish something. **6.** suffice. **7.** happen.

doc'ile, *adj.* readily disciplined. —**do·cil'i·ty,** *n.*

dock, *n.* **1.** place for ships between voyages. **2.** pier or wharf. **3.** fleshy part of an animal's tail. —*v.t.* **4.** put into a dock. **5.** deduct from the wages of. —*v.i.* **6.** enter a dock.

dock'et, *n.* **1.** list of agenda, esp. of a court. —*v.t.* **2.** put on a docket.

doc'tor, *n.* **1.** person who practices medicine, etc. **2.** person with a high academic degree. —*v.t.* **3.** *Informal.* heal or fix. —**doc'tor·al,** *adj.* —**doc·tor·ate,** *n.*

doc''tri·naire', *adj.* rigidly adhering to or following doctrine.

doc'trine, *n.* body of teaching, esp. in religion or politics. —**doc'trin·al,** *adj.*

doc'u·ment, *n.* **1.** writing, etc. used as a proof. —*v.t.* **2.** prove or support with documents. —**doc''u·men·ta'tion,** *n.*

doc''u·men'ta·ry, *adj. n., pl.* **-ries.** *adj.* **1.** pertaining to documents. **2.** serving as a record of events. —*n.* **3.** film, etc. serving as a record of events.

dodge, *v.,* **dodged, dodging,** *n. v.t.* **1.** avoid by moving quickly. **2.** evade by a trick. —*v.i.* **3.** dodge something. —*n.* **4.** act or instance of dodging. **5.** trick.

doe, *n.* female or certain animals, as deer or rabbits.

doff, *v.t. Archaic.* remove, as a hat.

dog, *n., v.t.,* **dogged, dogging.** *n.* **1.** four-legged domestic animal. —*v.t.* **2.** track; follow.

dog'ged, *adj.* stubborn in difficulty.

dog'ger·el, *n.* bad verse.

dog'ma, *n.* doctrine, esp. in religion, regarded as unquestionable.

dog·mat'ic, *adj.* **1.** pertaining to or published as dogma. **2.** offering personal opinions as dogma. —**dog'ma·tism,** *n.*

dog'wood'', *n.* tree with white or pink blossoms.

doi'ly, *n.*, *pl.* **-lies.** small table mat, often of lace.

dol'drums, *n.*, *pl.* **1.** equatorial region with little wind. **2.** period of depression or inactivity.

dole, *n.*, *v.t.*, **doled, doling.** *n.* **1.** money, food, etc. given to the unemployed. —*v.t.* **2.** portion out sparingly.

dole'ful, *adj.* sad.

doll, *n.* toy shaped like a baby or other human being.

dol'lar, *n.* currency unit of the U.S., Canada, etc.

do'lor·ous, *adj.* sorrowful or painful.

dol'phin, *n.* aquatic mammal.

dolt, *n.* oaf. —**dolt'ish**, *adj.*

do·main', *n.* **1.** territory of a ruler. **2.** area of influence or power.

dome, *n.* structure like an upcurved segment of a sphere.

do·mes'tic, *adj.* **1.** pertaining to the home. **2.** belonging to or originating in one's own country. **3.** tamed. —**do''mes·ti'ci·ty**, *n.*

do·mes'ti·cate'', *v.t.*, **-cated, -cating.** adapt to domestic conditions. —**do·mes''ti·ca'tion**, *n.*

dom'i·cile'', *n.*, *v.t.*, **-ciled, -ciling.** *n.* **1.** residence. —*v.t.* **2.** house.

dom'i·nant, *adj.* prevailing. —**dom'i·nance**, *n.*

dom'i·nate'', *v.t.*, **-nated, -nating.** **1.** master. **2.** be most conspicuous in. —**dom''i·na'tion**, *n.*

dom''i·neer', *v.t.*, *v.i.* tyrannize.

do·min'ion, *n.* **1.** sovereign power. **2.** territory reigned over or ruled by a sovereign.

dom'i·no, *n.*, *pl.* **-noes. 1.** small plaque marked with spots. **2.** dominoes, a game played with these plaques. **3.** mask.

don, *n.*, *v.t.*, **donned, donning.** *n.* **1.** title of respect for a Spanish gentleman. —*v.t.* **2.** *Archaic* put on, as clothes.

do'nate'', *v.*, **-nated, -nating.** *v.t.*, *v.i.* give, esp. in charity or friendship. —**do·na'tion**, *n.* —**do'nor**, *n.*

don'key, *n.*, *pl.* **-keys.** domesticated ass.

doo'dle, *v.i.*, **-dled, -dling.** *n. v.i.* **1.** scribble or draw absentmindedly. —*n.* **2.** product of doodling.

doom, *n.* **1.** death or annihilation. **2.** fate. —*v.t.* **3.** predestine or sentence to death, damnation, etc.

door, *n.* **1.** movable partition for barring access. **2.** Also, **door'way''**, entrance. **3.** out of doors, outdoors.

dope, *n.*, *v.t.*, **doped, doping.** *n.* **1.** *Informal.* **a.** habit-forming drug. **b.** fool. **c.** information. **2.** thick liquid used for industrial purposes. —*v.t.* **3.** *Informal.* drug.

dor'mant, *adj.* **1.** asleep or at rest. **2.** not active. —**dor'man·cy**, *n.*

dor'mer, *n.* window structure in a roof.

dor'mi·to''ry, *n.*, *pl.* **-ries.** place for residents of an institution to sleep.

do'ry, *n.*, *pl.* **-ries.** flat-bottomed rowboat used for fishing, etc.

dose, *n.*, *v.t.*, **dosed, dosing.** *n.* **1.** amount of medicine taken at one time. —*v.t.* **2.** give medicine to. —**dos'age**, *n.*

dos·si·er (dos''sē a'), *n.* file of documents on one subject.

dot, *n.*, *v.t.*, **dotted, dotting.** *n.* **1.** tiny round mark. —*v.t.* **2.** mark or make with dots.

dote, *v.i.*, **doted, doting. 1.** show excessive fondness. **2.** be senile. —**dot'ing**, *adj.* —**dot'age**, *n.*

dou'ble, *adj.*, *adv.*, *n.*, *v.*, **-bled, -bling.** *adj.* **1.** twice as many or large as usual. **2.** intended for two. **3.** having two aspects. —*adv.* **4.** twice. —*n.* **5.** duplicate. —*v.t.* **6.** fold over. **7.** make twice as much or as many of. —*v.i.* **8.** fold in two. **9.** reverse one's direction. —**doub'ly**, *adv.*

dou'ble-cross', *v.t.* *Informal.* cheat or betray.

doubt, *v.t.* **1.** be unsure or skeptical of. —*n.* **2.** uncertainty or distrust. **3.** something unsettled or uncertain. —**doubt'ful**, *adj.* —**doubt'less**, *adv.*

dough, *n.* pastry mixture of flour and water for baking. —**dough'y**, *adj.*

dough'nut'', *n.* deep-fried ring-shaped cake.

dour, *adj.* gloomily severe.

douse, *v.t.*, **doused, dousing.** plunge into or drench with liquid.

dove, *n.* cooing pigeonlike bird.

dove'tail'', *n.* **1.** interlocking carpentry joint. —*v.t.* **2.** join with dovetails.

dow'a·ger, *n.* widow endowed with a title or property.

dow'dy, *adj.*, **-dier, -diest.** plainly or untidily dressed, made up, etc.

dow'el, *n.*, *v.t.*, **-eled, -eling.** *n.* **1.** round length of wood, used as a fastening between two joined pieces. —*v.t.* **2.** fasten with dowels.

down, *adv.*, *adj.* **1.** to or at a lower place. **2.** to or in a lower condition, amount, etc. **3.** in writing. **4.** in advance. **5.** out of operation. —*adv.* **7.** dejected. **8.** completed. —*prep.* **9.** descending along, through, etc. **10.** soft feathers or hair. —*v.t.* **11.** put down. —**down'stairs'**, *adv.*, *adj.*, *n.* —**down'ward**, **down'wards**, *adv.* —**down'y**, *adj.*

down'fall'', *n.* **1.** fall, as of snow. **2.** fall, as from power or eminence.

down'grade'', *v.t.*, **-graded, -grading.** *adv.*, *adj.*, *n. v.t.* **1.** demote. —*adv.*, *adj.* **2.** downward. —*n.* **3.** downward slope.

down'heart'ed, *adj.* discouraged. —**down'heart'ed·ly**, *adv.*

down'hill', adv., adj. downward.

down'pour'', n. heavy rainstorm.

down'right'', adj. **1.** utter. —adv. **2.** utterly.

down'stairs'', adv. to or at a lower level.

down'-to-earth', adj. realistic.

down'town', adv., adj. toward or in the business district of a town.

down'trod''den. adj. oppressed.

dow'ry, n., pl. **-ries.** property bestowed on a bride by her family.

dox·ol'o·gy, n., pl. **-gies.** hymn of praise.

doze, v.i., **dozed, dozing**, n. v.i. **1.** sleep lightly. —n. **2.** light sleep.

doz'en, n., pl. **-ens** or (after a number) **-en.** group of twelve. —**doz'enth**, adj.

drab, n, adj., **drabber, drabbest.** n. **1.** yellow-brown. —adj. **2.** dreary. —**drab'ly**, adv. —**drab'ness**, n.

draft, n. **1.** act or amount of drawing. **2.** swallowing or inhalation. **3.** current of air. **4.** tentative version of writing. **5.** order to pay. **6.** selection for conscription. —v.t. **7.** make a draft of. **8.** conscript. —**draft'ee**, n. —**draft'y**, adj.

drafts'man, n. person who makes working drawings or sketches.

drag, v., **dragged, dragging.** v.t. **1.** pull with effort. **2.** search with a dragnet. —v.t. **3.** move slowly or with effort. —n. **4.** act or instance of dragging. **5.** *Informal.* something or someone dreary or obstructive.

drag'net'', n. **1.** net for fishing up submerged objects. **2.** methodical police search.

drag'on, n. mythical large reptile.

drag'on·fly'', n. large, stiff-winged insect.

drain, n. **1.** channel for carrying away liquids. **2.** steady depletion. —v.t. **3.** remove through a channel. **4.** deplete steadily. —v.i. **5.** be drained. —**drain'age,** n.

dram, n. **1.** eighth part of an apothecary's ounce or fluid ounce. **2.** small drink.

dra'ma, n. **1.** play. **2.** theater as an art. **3.** sensational event. **4.** emotionalism. —**dram'a·tist,** n. —**dram'a·tize''**, v.t. —**dra·mat'ic,** adj.

drape, n., v., **draped, draping.** n. **1.** cloth hanging or curtain. —v.t., v.i. **2.** hang loosely or in folds. —**drap'er·y,** n.

dras'tic, adj. severe or extreme.

draught, n., v.i., adj. draft.

draw, v., **drew, drawn, drawing**, n. v.t. **1.** pull, attract, or take in. **2.** elicit or provoke. **3.** receive. **4.** sketch with a pencil, pen, etc. **5.** *Nautical.* need a depth of. —v.i. **6.** exert a pulling force. **7.** move. **8.** pass smoke, etc. readily. **9.** make demands. **10.** lessen in size. —n. **11.** act or instance of drawing. **12.** even final score. —**draw'ing,** n.

draw'back'', n. lessening of advantage.

draw'bridge'', n. bridge that can be lifted or pulled.

draw·er, n. (drah'ər) **1.** person or thing that draws. (drôr) **2.** sliding compartment in a piece of furniture. **3. drawers.** underpants.

drawl, n. **1.** slow speech. —v.t., v.i. **2.** speak in a drawl.

drawn, adj. haggard.

dray, n. heavy freight wagon.

dread, n. **1.** fearful anticipation. **2.** awe. —adj. **3.** awesome. —v.t. **4.** anticipate fearfully.

dread'ful, adj. **1.** very bad. **2.** inspiring dread.

dream, n., v., **dreamed** or **dreamt, dreaming.** n. **1.** succession of images appearing in sleep or reverie. **2.** vision of something possible or desirable. —v.t. **3.** imagine in a dream. —v.i. **4.** have a dream. **dream'er,** n. —**dream'less,** adj. —**dream'like''**, adj. —**dream'y,** adj.

drear'y, adj., **-ier, -iest.** causing sadness or boredom.

dredge, v., **dredged, dredging**, n. v.t. **1.** dig, esp. under water. **2.** coat with flour. —n. **3.** digging device.

dregs, n., pl. sediment, as of wine.

drench, v.t. soak with falling liquid.

dress, v.t. **1.** put clothing on. **2.** prepare or finish. —v.i. **3.** put on clothing. **4.** wear formal clothing. —n. **5.** clothing. **6.** skirt. —**dress'mak''er,** n.

dres'ser, n. **1.** person who dresses. **2.** chest of drawers with a mirror.

dres'sing, n. **1.** material applied to wounds, bruises, etc. **2.** sauce for salad. **3.** stuffing for fowl.

drib'ble, v., **-bled, -bling**, n. v.t. **1.** let drip untidily. —n. **2.** act or instance of dribbling.

dri'er, n. thing or substance for drying.

drift, v.i. **1.** be carried by a current. **2.** move or live aimlessly or passively. —n. **3.** drifting motion. **4.** force or gist, as of an argument. **5.** pile of wind-driven snow.

drift'wood'', n. wood weathered and driven ashore by the sea.

drill, n. **1.** boring tool. **2.** system of exercises. **3.** seed-planting machine. **4.** coarse fabric. —v.t. **5.** bore with a drill. **6.** train or exercise with a drill.

dri'ly, adv. in a dry manner.

drink, n., v., ⟍nk, **drunk, drinking.** n. **1.** liquid for swallowing. **2.** alcoholic liquor. —v.t. **3.** swallow as a drink. —v.i. **4.** swallow liquid. **5.** take alcoholic liquor. —**drink'er,** n.

drip, v., **dripped, dripping**, n. v.i. **1.** fall in drops —v.t. **2.** let liquid fall in drops. **3.** let fall in drops. —n. **4.** act, instance, or sound of dripping.

drive, v., **drove, driven, driving**, n. **1.** force along. **2.** compel to move. **3.** control, as a vehicle. **4.** transport in a road vehicle.

—*v.i.* 5. operate a road vehicle. 6. advance forcefully. —*n.* 7. forceful campaign. 8. energy. 9. motivation. 10. pleasure trip in an automobile. 11. road for pleasure driving. —**driv′er,** *n.* —**drive′way,** *n.* —**drive′-in″,** *adj., n.*

driv′el, *n., v.i.,* **-eled, -eling.** *n.* 1. stupid, nonsensical utterance. —*v.i.* 2. write or talk drivel.

driz′zle, *n., v.,* **-zled, -zling.** *n.* 1. fine rain. —*v.i., v.t.* 2. rain in fine drops.

droll, *adj.* 1. oddly amusing. —*n.* 2. oddly amusing person. —**drol′ly,** *adv.* —**droll′ness, drol′ler·y,** *n.*

drom·e·dar′′y, *n., pl.* **-ies.** single-humped camel.

drone, *n., v.i.,* **droned, droning.** *n.* 1. low hum. 2. nonworking male bee. 3. idler. —*v.i.* 4. emit a drone.

drool, *v.i.* 1. drip saliva. —*n.* 2. saliva that drips.

droop, *v.i.* 1. hang loosely. 2. lose energy or hope. —*n.* 3. act or instance of drooping. —**droop′y,** *adj.*

drop, *v.t.,* **dropped, dropping,** *n. v.t.* 1. allow to fall. 2. abandon. 3. put down. —*v.i.* 4. fall. —*n.* 5. globule of liquid that falls or is about to fall. 6. descent. 7. small drink. —**drop′per,** *n.*

drop′sy, *n.* edema.

dross, *n.* 1. waste on top of molten metal. 2. waste matter.

drought, *n.* long dry spell. Also, **drouth.**

drove, *n.* group of driven cattle. —**drov′er,** *n.*

drown, *v.i., v.t.* 1. suffocate in water. —*v.t.* 2. flood.

drowse, *v.i.,* **drowsed, drowsing,** *n. v.i.* 1. be close to sleep. —*n.* 2. sleepy state. —**drows′y,** *adj.*

drub, *v.t.,* **drubbed, drubbing.** beat. —**drub′bing,** *n.*

drudge, *v.i.,* **drudged, drudging,** *n. v.i.* 1. do dull, hard work. —*n.* 2. a person who drudges. —**drudg′er·y,** *n.*

drug, *n., v.t.,* **drugged, drugging.** *n.* 1. medicinal substance. 2. narcotic, hallucinogen, etc. —*v.t.* 3. stupefy with a drug. —**drug′gist,** *n.* —**drug′store″,** *n.*

drum, *n., v.* **drummed, drumming.** *n.* 1. percussion musical instrument. 2. eardrum. 3. cylindrical object. —*v.i.* 4. beat rhythmically. —*v.t.* 5. play on a drum. —**drum′mer,** *n.* —**drum′stick″,** *n.*

drunk, *adj.* 1. overcome by alcohol. —*n.* 2. *Informal.* **a.** drunken person. **b.** alcoholic.

drunk′ard, *n.* alcoholic.

drunk′en, *adj.* drunk.

dry, *adj.,* **drier, driest,** *v.,* **dried, drying.** *adj.* 1. free of moisture. 2. thirsty. 3. not sweet. 4. not emotional or expressive. —*v.t.* 5. free of moisture. —*v.i.*

6. become dry. —**dry′ly,** *adv.* —**dry′ness,** *n.*

dry′-clean″, *v.t.* clean with chemicals rather than water. —**dry cleaner,** *n.*

dry goods, cloth or things made of cloth.

du′al, *adj.* 1. pertaining to two. 2. twofold. —**du·al′i·ty,** *n.*

dub, *v.t.,* **dubbed, dubbing.** 1. make a knight of. 2. give a name to.

du′bi·ous, *adj.* doubtful.

du′cal, *adj.* pertaining to dukes.

duch′ess, *n.* woman equal in rank to a duke.

duch′y, *n., pl.* **-ies.** area ruled by a duke or duchess.

duck, *n.* 1. flat-billed waterfowl. 2. canvaslike cloth. —*v.i.* 3. stoop or crouch to avoid a blow. —*v.t., v.i.* 4. plunge into water briefly. —**duck′ling,** *n.*

duct, *n.* passage for fluids. —**duct′less,** *adj.*

duc′tile, *adj.* able to be stretched. —**duc·til′i·ty,** *n.*

dude, *n. Informal.* 1. fancy dresser. 2. man from the city.

due, *adj.* 1. owed. 2. proper. 3. adequate. 4. expected to arrive. —*adv.* 5. directly. —*n.* 7. something due.

du′el, *n., v.,* **-eled, -eling.** *n.* 1. formal mortal combat between two persons. —*v.t., v.i.* 2. fight in a duel. —**du′elist, duel′er,** *n.*

du·et′, *n.* 1. musical composition for two. 2. pair of musicians.

duke, *n.* nobleman next in rank to a prince. —**duke′dom,** *n.*

dull, *adj.* 1. not vivid. 2. not interesting. 3. not intelligent. 4. not sharp. —*v.t., v.i.* 5. make or become dull. —**dul′ly,** *adv.* —**dull′ness, dul′ness,** *n.*

du′ly, *adv.* in a due manner.

dumb, *adj.* 1. unable to speak or make sound. 2. silent. 3. *Informal.* stupid.

dumb′bell″, *n.* weight for exercising the arms.

dumb′found″, *v.t.* render speechless with astonishment. Also, **dum′found″.**

dumb″wait′er, *n.* 1. hoist for food. 2. small serving table.

dum′my, *n., pl.* **-ies,** *adj.* 1. lifesized object in human form. 2. imitation or mockup. —*adj.* 3. serving as an imitation.

dump, *v.t.* 1. throw or pour down and abandon. 2. unload in a heap. —*n.* 3. place for refuse. 4. military storage place.

dump′ling, *n.* rounded piece of baked dough, sometimes with a fruit filling.

dump″ster, *n.* a large, metal bin for holding garbage until pick-up.

dump′y, *adj.,* **-ier, -iest** squat.

dun, *n., v.t.,* **dunned, dunning.** *n.* 1. dull gray-brown. —*v.t.* 2. attempt to recover a debt from.

dunce, *n.* poor learner.

dune, *n.* mound of wind-driven sand.

dung, *n.* manure. —**dung'heap",** **dung'hill,** *n.*

dun"ga·rees', *n., pl.* blue cotton work pants or overalls.

dun'geon, *n.* dark prison, as in a castle.

dunk, *v.t.* dip into a drink.

du'o, *n., pl.* -os. duet.

dupe, *v.t.,* duped, duping, *n. v.t.* **1.** cheat. —*n.* **2.** person who is cheated. —**dup'er,** *n.*

du'plex, *adj.* **1.** double. —*n.* **2.** two-floored apartment. **3.** two-family house.

du·pli·cate, *v.t.,* -cated, -cating, *adj., n. v.t.* (dōō'pli kāt") **1.** imitate exactly. —*n.* (dōō pli kət) **2.** exact imitation. —*adj.* **3.** serving as a duplicate. —**du"pli·ca'tion,** *n.* —**du'pli·ca"tor,** *n.*

du·plic'i·ty, *n., pl.* -ties. deceit.

du'ra·ble, *adj.* long-lasting; sturdy. —**du'ra·bly,** *adv.* —**dura·bil'i·ty,** *n.*

du·ra'tion, *n.* period of existence.

du·ress', *n.* coercion.

dur'ing, *prep.* in or throughout the period of.

dusk, *n.* **1.** darker part of twilight. **2.** gloom. —**dusk'y,** *adj.*

dust, *n.* **1.** powder, esp. of earth. **2.** disintegrated human remains. —*v.t.* **3.** remove dust from. **4.** put powder on. —*v.i.* **5.** remove dust from furniture, etc. —**dust'y,** *adj.*

du'te·ous, *adj.* dutiful.

du'ti·a·ble, *adj.* subject to customs duty.

du'ti·ful, *adj.* faithful to duty. —**du'ti·ful·ly,** *adv.*

du'ty, *n., pl.* -ties. **1.** moral requirement. **2.** requirement by authority. **3.** action, conduct, etc. required by morality or authority. **4.** tax or import.

dwarf, *n., pl.* dwarfs, dwarves. *v.t.* **1.** abnormally small living thing. —*v.t.* **2.** make abnormally small. **3.** make seem small.

dwell, *v.i.,* dwelled or dwelt, dwelling. **1.** have one's habitation. **2.** linger, as in speech or thought. —**dwel'ler,** *n.* —**dwel'ling,** *n.*

dwin'dle, *v.i.,* -dled, -dling. diminish.

dye, *n., v.t.,* dyed, dying. *n.* **1.** stain for cloth, etc. —*v.t.* **2.** stain with dye. —**dy'er,** *n.* —**dye'stuff,** *n.*

dy·nam'ic, *adj.* **1.** pertaining to motion. **2.** vigorous, as a person. —**dy·nam'i·cal·ly,** *adv.* —**dy'na·mism,** *n.*

dy'na·mo", *n., pl.* -mos. electrical generator.

dy'nas·ty, *n., pl.* -ties. succession of rulers in one family. —**dy·nas'tic,** *adj.*

dys'en·ter"y, *n.* intestinal inflammation.

dys·pep'si·a, *n.* indigestion. —**dys·pep'tic,** *adj., n.*

E

E, e, *n.* **1.** fifth letter of the English alphabet. **2.** fifth-best grade.

each, *adj.* **1.** every one individually. —*adv.* **2.** apiece.

ea'ger, *adj.* full of desire. —**ea'ger·ly,** *adv.* —**ea'ger·ness,** *n.*

ea'gle, *n.* large bird of prey.

ear, *n.* **1.** part of the body for hearing. **2.** grain-bearing part of a plant. —**ear'drum",** *n.* —**ear'muffs",** *n., pl.*

earl, *n.* British nobleman equal to a count. —**earl'dom,** *n.*

ear'ly, *adj., adv.,* -lier, -liest. **1.** before the expected time. **2.** in good time. **3.** toward the beginning.

ear'mark", *v.t.* note for the future.

earn, *v.t.* work or deserve to acquire. —**earn'ings,** *n., pl.*

ear'nest, *adj.* **1.** sincere; serious. —*n.* **2.** pledge. —**ear'nest·ly,** *adv.*

ear'ring", *n.* ornament hung from an ear lobe.

ear'shot", *n.* hearing distance.

earth, *n.* **1.** this planet. **2.** ground level. **3.** regions below ground level. **4.** soil. —**earth'en,** *adj.* —**earth'en·ware",** *n.* —**earth'ly,** *adj.* —**earth'quake",** *n.*

earth'ly, *adj.* pertaining to this world.

earth'worm", *n.* worm living in soil.

earth'y, *adj.,* -ier, -iest. matter-of-fact.

ease, *n., v.t.,* eased, easing. *n.* **1.** freedom from toil, pain, etc. —*v.t.* **2.** make easy.

ea'sel, *n.* stand for a painting, etc.

east, *n.* **1.** direction to the right of north. **2.** eastern area. —*adj., adv.* **3.** toward, in, or from the east. —**east'er·ly,** *adj.* —**east'ern,** *adj.* —**east'ern·er,** *n.* —**east'ward,** *adv., adj.* —**east'wards,** *adv.*

East'er, *n.* celebration of the resurrection of Christ.

eas'y, *adj.,* -ier, -iest. **1.** not difficult. **2.** free of pain, etc. —**eas'i·ly,** *adv.* —**eas'i·ness,** *n.*

eat, *v.t.,* ate, eaten, eating. **1.** consume as food. **2.** dissolve, erode, etc.

eaves, *n., pl.* projecting edge of a roof.

eaves'drop", *v.i.,* -dropped, -dropping. overhear conversation, esp. intentionally.

ebb, *n.* **1.** going-out of a tide. **2.** decline or lessening. —*v.i.* **3.** go out, as the tide. **4.** decline or lessen.

eb'o·ny, *n.* **1.** hard, dark wood. **2.** very deep brown or black.

e·bul'lient, *adj.* 1. exuberant. 2. bubbling. —e·bul'lience, *n.*

ec·cen'tric, *adj.* 1. peculiar in manner. 2. off center. —*n.* 3. eccentric person. 4. eccentric machine part. —ec''cen·tric'i·ty, *n.*

ec·cle''si·as'tic, *adj.* 1. Also, ec·cle''si·as'ti·cal. pertaining to churches. —*n.* 2. clergyman.

ech·e·lon (esh'ə lon''), *n.* 1. formation of troops, etc., each line being to the right or left of that preceding it. 2. level of responsibility.

ech'o, *n., pl.* -oes, *v.t.,* -oed, -oing. *n.* 1. reflected sound. —*v.t.* 2. reflect as an echo.

e·clair', *n.* custard-filled pastry.

e·clec'tic, *adj.* using those thought best, regardless of source.

e·clipse', *n., v.t.,* -clipsed, -clipsing. *n.* 1. obscuring of the sun or moon. —*v.t.* 2. obscure.

e·clip'tic, *n.* apparent annual path of the sun.

e·col'o·gy, *n., pl.* -gies. 1. study of the relation of living things to their environment. 2. system permitting living things to exist. —e'co·log'i·cal, *adj.* —e·col'o·gist, *n.*

e''co·nom'i·cal, *adj.* thrifty.

e''co·nom'ics, *n.* 1. *sing.* study of wealth. 2. *pl.* resources and demands on wealth. —e''co·nom'ic, *adj.* —e·con'o·mist, *n.*

e·con'o·my, *n., pl.* -mies. 1. thrift. 2. system of producing and dividing wealth. —e·con'o·mize, *v.i.*

ec·sta·sy, *n., pl.* -sies. state of overwhelming emotion. —ec·stat'ic, *adj., n.*

ec''u·men'i·cal, *adj.* 1. universal. 2. promoting universal accord, esp. in religion.

ec'ze·ma, *n.* scaly skin disease.

ed'dy, *n., pl.* -dies, *v.i.,* -died, -dying. *n.* 1. turbulence of water or wind. —*v.i* 2. move in an eddy.

edge, *n., v.,* edged, edging. *n.* 1. outer limit. 2. sharp intersection. —*v.t.* 3. border. —*v.i.* 4. sidle. —edge'wise', edge'ways', *adv.* —edg'ing, *n.*

ed'i·ble, *adj.* suitable for eating. —ed''i·bil'i·ty, *n.*

e'dict, *n.* decree.

ed'i·fice, *n.* building.

ed'i·fy'', *v.t.,* -fied, -fying. educate or improve the mind of. —ed''i·fi·ca'tion, *n.*

ed'it, *v.t.* prepare for publication or presentation. —ed'i·tor, *n.* —ed''i·tor'ial *n., adj.*

e·di'tion, *n.* printing of a book.

ed''i·tor'i·al, *n.* 1. periodical's commentary on public issues. —*adj.* 2. pertaining to editing.

ed·u·cate'', *v.t.* -cated, -cating. develop the mind, knowledge or skill of. —ed''

u·ca'tion, *n.* —ed''u·ca'tion·al, *adj.* —ed'u·ca'tor, *n.*

eel, *n.* long, snakelike fish.

ee'rie, *adj.,* -rier, -riest. wierd; uncanny.

ef·face', *v.t.,* -faced, -facing. eliminate all trace of. —ef·face'ment, *n.*

ef·fect', *n.* 1. result. 2. influence. 3. effects, personal property. —*v.t.* 4. cause. —ef·fec'tive, *adj.* —ef·fec'tu·al, *adj.*

ef·fem'i·nate, *adj.* unmanly. —ef·fem'i·na·cy, *n.*

ef''fer·vesce', *v.i.,* -vesced, -vescing. bubble. —ef''fer·ves'cent, *adj.* —ef''fer·ves'cence, *n.*

ef·fete', *adj.* decadent.

ef''fi·ca'cious, *adj.* producing the desired result. —ef'fi·ca·cy, *n.*

ef·fi'cient, *adj.* efficacious without waste. —ef·fi'cient·ly, *adv.* —ef·fi'cien·cy, *n.*

ef'fi·gy, *n., pl.* -gies. copy or image, esp. in three dimensions.

ef'fort, *n.* 1. expenditure of strength, thought, etc. 2. attempt.

ef·front'er·y, *n., pl.* -ies. impudence.

ef·fu'sion, *n.* outpouring of enthusiasm. —ef·fu'sive, *adj.*

egg'head', *n. Informal.* intellectual.

egg'plant'', *n.* purple-skinned vegetable.

e'go, *n.* self. —e''go·cen'tric, *adj., n.*

e'go·ism, *n.* selfishness. —e'go·ist, *n.* —e''go·is'tic, e'go·is'ti·cal, *adj.*

e'go·tism, *n.* self-conceit; vanity. —e'go·tist'', *n.* —e''go·tis'tic, e'go·tis'ti·cal, *adj.*

e·gre'gious, *adj.* conspicuous in a bad way.

eight, *n.* seven plus one. —eighth, *adj.*

eight·een', *n.* seventeen plus one.

eight'y, *n.* eight times ten. —eight'i·eth, *adj.*

ei·ther (ē'thər, ī'thər), *adj.* 1. one or the other but not both. 2. each. —*pron.* 3. one or the other. —*conj.* 4. (used to emphasize choice). —*adj.* 5. as well.

e·jac'u·late'', *v.t., v.i.,* -lated, -lating. exclaim —e·jac''u·la'tion, *n.*

e·ject', *v.t.* hurl or force out. —e·jec'tion, *n.*

eke, *v.t.,* eked, eking. eke out, gain with difficulty.

e·lab'o·rate, *adj., v.t.,* -rated, -rating. *adj.* (ē lab'ə rət) 1. having many parts or aspects. —*v.t.* (ē lab'ə rāt') 2. plan in detail. —e·lab''o·ra'tion, *n.*

e·lapse', *v.i.,* -lapsed, -lapsing. pass, as time.

e·las'tic, *adj.* able to recover from stretching or bending. —*n.* elastic material or object. —e·las''tic'i·ty, *n.*

e·late', *v.t.,* -lated, -lating. raise in spirits. —e·la'tion, *n.*

el'bow, *n.* joint halfway up the arm. —*v.t., v.i.* push with the elbows.

el'der, *adj.* 1. senior. —*n.* 2. senior. 3.

shrub with red or purple berries. —**eld′ est**, *adj.* —**eld′er·ly**, *adj.*

e·lect′, *v.t.* 1. choose, esp. by a vote. —*adj.* 2. chosen. 3. elected to but not yet in public office. —**e·lec′tion**, *n.* —**e·lec′tor**, *n.* —**e·lec′tor·al**, *adj.* —**e·lec′tor·ate**, *n.* —**e·lec′tive**, *adj.*

e·lec″tric′i·ty, *n.* 1. property of motion in certain particles composing matter. 2. current created by such motion. —**e·lec′tric**, **e·lec′tri·cal**, *adj.* —**e·lec′tri·fy″**, *v.t.*

e·lec′tro·cute″, *v.t.*, **-cuted**, **-cuting**. injure or kill with electricity. —**e·lec″ tro·cu′tion**, *n.*

e·lec′trode, *n.* object conducting electricity into or out of a battery, etc.

e·lec·trol′y·sis, *n.* decomposition of a material by the passage of electricity. —**e·lec″tro·lyt′ic**, *adj.*

e·lec″tro·mag′net, *n.* magnet operating through an electric current. —**e·lec″ tro·mag·net′ic**, *adj.*

e·lec′tron, *n.* negatively charged particle of an atom.

e·lec·tron′ics, *n.*, *sing.* study of the action of electrons and its application to technology. —**e·lec″tron′ic**, *adj.*

el′e·gant, *adj.* tasteful and dignified. —**el′e·gance**, *n.*

el′e·gy, *n.*, *pl.* **-gies**. poem of lament, esp. for the dead. —**el″e·gi′ac**, **el″e·gi′a·cal**, *adj.*

el′e·ment, *n.* 1. major or basic component. 2. natural environment. 3. elements, natural forces, esp. of weather. —**el″e·men′tal**, *adj.*

el″e·men′ta·ry, *n.* fundamental; rudimentary.

el′e·phant, *n.* large four-legged animal with a long prehensile nose.

el′e·vate″, *v.t.*, **-vated**, **-vating**. 1. raise to a greater height. 2. raise in rank, spirits, etc.

el″e·va′tion, *n.* 1. height. 2. drawing of one side of a building, etc., in its true dimensions.

el′e·va″tor, *n.* 1. cabinet or platform for raising or lowering persons or goods. 2. storage place for grain.

e·lev′en, *n.* ten plus one.

elf, *n.*, *pl.* **elves**. small fairy. —**elf′in**, **elf′ ish**, *adj.*

e·lic′it, *v.t.* draw forth, as a reaction or comment.

el′i·gi·ble, *adj.* suitable for choice. —**el″ i·gi·bil′i·ty**, *n.*

e·lim′i·nate″, *v.t.*, **-nated**, **-nating**. get rid of. —**e·lim″i·na′tion**, *n.*

e·lite′ (i lēt′), *n.* choice element. —**e·lit′ ism**, *n.*

e·lix′ir, *n.* medicine in a solution of alcohol.

elk, *n.*, *pl.* **elks**, **elk**. large mooselike deer.

el·lipse′, *n.* oval symmetrical about two axes. —**el·lip′ti·cal**, *adj.*

elm, *n.* tall deciduous tree.

el′o·cu′tion, *n.* public speaking.

e·lon′gate″, *v.t.*, *v.i.*, **-gated**, **-gating**. lengthen. —**e″lon·ga′tion**, *n.*

e·lope′, *v.i.*, **-loped**, **-loping**. flee, esp. in order to marry. —**e·lope′ment**, *n.*

e′lo·quent, *adj.* convincing in speech. —**e′lo·quence**, *n.*

else, *adj.* 1. other. 2. more. —*adv.* 3. otherwise.

else′where″, *adv.* somewhere else.

e·lu′ci·date″, *v.t.*, **-dated**, **-dating**. clarify; explain. —**e·lu″ci·da′tion**, *n.*

e·lude′, *v.t.*, **-luded**, **-luding**. escape or evade. —**e·lu′sive**, *adv.*

e·ma′ci·ate″, *v.t.*, **-ated**, **-ating**. make abnormally thin. —**e·ma″ci·a′tion**, *n.*

em′a·nate″, *v.i.*, **-nated**, **-nating**. come forth; issue. —**em″a·na′tion**, *n.*

e·man′ci·pate″, *v.t.*, **-pated**, **-pating**. free, as from bondage. —**e·man″ci· pa′tion**, *n.* —**e·man′ci·pa″tor**, *n.*

e·mas′cu·late″, *v.t.*, **-lated**, **-lating**. castrate.

em·balm′, *v.t.* preserve against decay after death.

em·bank′, *v.t.* support, strengthen, etc. with piled earth, etc. —**em·bank′ment**, *n.*

em·bar′go, *n.*, *pl.* **-goes**. *n.* ban on shipping or commerce.

em·bark′, *v.i.* 1. set forth, esp. on a ship. —*v.t.*, *v.i.* 2. board, esp. a ship. —**em″ bar·ka′tion**, *n.*

em·bar′rass, *v.t.* 1. make ashamed or self-conscious. 2. put at a loss for money. —**em·bar′rass·ment**, *n.*

em′bas·sy, *n.*, *pl.* **-sies**. permanent mission to a foreign government.

em·bed′, *v.t.*, **-bedded**, **-bedding**. sink and fix firmly.

em·bel′lish, *n.* decorate. —**em·bel′lish· ment**, *n.*

em′ber, *n.* red-hot piece of fuel.

em·bez′zle, *v.t.*, **-zled**, **-zling**. steal from an employer, client, etc. —**em·bez′ zler**, *n.* —**em·bez′zle·ment**, *n.*

em·bit′ter, *v.t.* make bitter.

em′blem, *n.* symbolic design. —**em″ blem·at′ic**, *adj.*

em·bod′y, *v.t.*, **-died**, **-dying**. 1. realize in bodily form. 2. incorporate. —**em· bod′i·ment**, *n.*

em·boss′, mark with raised designs or lettering.

em·brace′, *v.*, **-braced**, **-bracing**. *n.* *v.t.* 1. put the arms around. 2. accept readily. —*v.i.* 3. embrace each other. —*n.* 4. act or instance of embracing.

em·broi′der, *v.t.* decorate with applied colored yarns. —**em·broi′der·y**, *n.*

em′bry·o″, *n.*, *pl.* **-os**. animal or plant in the first stage of development. —**em″bry·on′ic**, *adj.*

e·mend′, *v.t.* correct; edit. —**e″men·da′tion**, *n.*

em′er·ald, *n.* vivid green gem.

e·merge′, *v.i.*, **-merged**, **-merging.** appear into notice. —**e·mer′gence**, *n.*

e·mer′gen·cy, *n.*, *pl.* **-cies.** mishap demanding prompt action.

e·met′ic, *adj.* 1. causing vomiting. —*n.* 2. emetic substance.

em′i·grate″, *v.i.*, **-grated**, **-grating.** leave one's country to settle elsewhere. —**em″i·gra′tion**, *n.* —**em″i·grant**, *n.*, *adj.*

em′i·nent, *adj.* high in standing or rank. —**em′i·nence**, *n.* —**em′i·nent·ly**, *adv.*

em′is·sar″y, *n.*, *pl.* **-ies.** person sent on a mission.

e·mit′, *v.t.*, **-mitted**, **-mitting.** send out or forth; discharge. —**e·mis′sion**, *n.*

e·mo′tion, *n.* 1. natural feelings and reactions. 2. specific feeling or reaction. —**e·mo′tion·al**, *adj.*

em′per·or, *n.* ruler of an empire.

em′pha·sis, *n.*, *pl.* **-ses.** force or stress. —**em·phat′ic**, *adj.* —**em′pha·size″**, *v.t.*

em′pire, *n.* number of countries or regions under one monarch.

em·pir′i·cal, *adj.* derived from experience.

em·ploy′, *v.t.* 1. hire or use. —*n.* 2. hire. —**em·ploy′er**, *n.* —**em·ploy′ee**, *n.* —**em·ploy′ment**, *n.*

em·po′ri·um, *n.*, *pl.* **-ums**, **-a.** store with varied merchandise.

em·pow′er, *v.t.* give official power to.

em′press, *n.* woman married to or with the rank of an emperor.

emp′ty, *adj.*, **-tier**, **-tiest**, *v.*, **-tied**, **-tying.** *adj.* 1. lacking contents. —*v.t.* 2. make empty. —*v.i.* 3. become empty. —**emp′ti·ness**, *n.*

em′u·late″, *v.t.*, **-lated**, **-lating.** imitate, esp. in excellence. —**em″u·la′tion**, *n.* —**em′u·lous**, *adj.*

e·mul′sion, *n.* mixture of two liquids made possible by addition of a third. —**e·mul′si·fy″**, *v.t.*, *v.i.*

en·a′ble, *v.t.*, **-bled**, **-bling.** make able.

en·act′, *v.t.* 1. make into law. 2. represent in a play. —**en·act′ment**, *n.*

en·am′el, *n.*, *v.t.*, **-eled** or **-elled**, **-eling** or **-elling.** *n.* 1. glassy, fused coating. 2. hard, glossy paint. 3. exterior material of teeth. —*v.t.* 4. cover with enamel.

en·am′ored, *adj.* full of love.

en·camp′, *v.i.*, *v.t.* camp. —**en·camp′ment**, *n.*

en·case′, *v.t.*, **-cased**, **-casing.** enclose.

en·chant′, *v.t.* 1. charm. 2. put a magic spell on. —**en·chant′ment**, *n.*

en·cir′cle, *v.t.*, **-cled**, **-cling.** surround.

en·close′, *v.t.*, **-closed**, **-closing.** 1. surround. 2. put into a container, envelope, etc. —**en·clo′sure**, *n.*

en·com′pass, *v.t.* 1. surround. 2. include.

en·core′ (ahn′kōr), *interj.* 1. again: request to a musician. —*n.* 2. repetition of a musical performance.

en·coun′ter, *v.t.* 1. happen to meet. 2. meet in combat. —*n.* 3. act or instance of encountering.

en·cour′age, *v.t.*, **-aged**, **-aging.** give courage or resolution to. —**en·cour′age·ment**, *n.*

en·croach′, *v.i.* trespass. —**en·croach′ment**, *n.*

en·cum′ber, *v.t.* burden or hinder. —**en·cum′brance**, *n.*

en·cy″clo·pe′di·a, *n.* reference work dealing at length with all areas of knowledge. Also, **en·cy″clo·pae′di·a.** —**en·cy″clo·pe′dic**, *adj.*

end, *n.* 1. far or final part. 2. result. 3. purpose. —*v.t.* 4. put an end to. —*v.i.* 5. come to an end. —**end′less**, *adj.*

en·dan′ger, *v.t.* put in danger.

en·dear′, *v.t.* make dear. —**en·dear′ing**, *adj.* —**en·dear′ment**, *n.*

en·deav′or, *v.t.*, *n.* attempt.

end′ing, *n.* conclusion.

end′most″, *adj.* farthest.

en·dorse′, *v.t.*, **-dorsed**, **-dorsing.** 1. write on the back of, esp. a signature. 2. approve. —**en·dors′er**, *n.* —**en·dorse′ment**, *n.*

en·dow′, *v.t.* 1. provide with personal resources or qualities. 2. give money for. —**en·dow′ment**, *n.*

en·dure′, *v.*, **-dured**, **-during** *v.t.* 1. tolerate. 2. suffer. —*v.i.* 3. survive. —**en·dur′able**, *adj.* —**en·dur′ance**, *n.*

en′e·my, *n.*, *pl.* **-mies.** 1. person who wishes one harm. 2. hostile nation or military force.

en′er·gy, *n.*, *pl.* **-gies.** 1. force able to produce motion, heat, light, etc. 2. vigor. —**en″er·get′ic**, *adj.*

en′er·vate″, *v.t.*, **-vated**, **-vating.** deprive of vitality. —**en″er·va′tion**, *n.*

en·fee′ble, *v.t.*, **-bled**, **-bling.** make feeble.

en·fold′, *v.t.* wrap.

en·force′, *v.t.*, **-forced**, **-forcing.** administer forcefully, as a law. —**en·force′ment**, *n.*

en·gage′, *v.t.*, **-gaged**, **-gaging.** 1. commit. 2. commit to marriage. 3. hire. 4. hold or connect with. 5. meet and fight. —**en·gage′ment**, *n.*

en·gag′ing, *adj.* charming. —**en·gag′ing·ly**, *adv.*

en·gen′der, *v.t.* bring into being.

en′gine, *n.* 1. machine producing mechanical force, esp. by means of heat energy. 2. locomotive.

en″gi·neer′, *n.* 1. person who designs systems or structures applying static or dynamic forces or various sources of

en·er·gy. 2. skilled operator of machines, etc. —en'gi·neer'ing, *n.*

en·grave', *v.t.*, -graved, -graving. form designs or letters with shallow cuts on wood, steel, etc. —en·grav'er, *n.* —en·grav'ing, *n.*

en·gross', *v.t.* capture the attention of.

en·gulf', *v.t.* swallow up; submerge.

en·hance', *v.t.*, -hanced, -hancing. increase or improve.

e·nig·ma, *n.*, *pl.* -mas. puzzle. —e"nig·mat'ic, *adj.*

en·join', *v.t.* forbid.

en·joy', *v.t.* 1. get pleasure from. 2. have the benefit of. —en·joy'a·ble, *adj.* —en·joy'ment, *n.*

en·large', *v.*, -larged, -larging. *v.t.* 1. make larger. —*v.i.* 2. become larger. —en·large'ment, *n.*

en·light'en, *v.t.* free of ignorance or wrong attitudes. —en·light'en·ment, *n.*

en·list', *v.t.*, *v.i.* enroll. —en·list'ment, *n.*

en·liv'en, *v.t.* make lively.

en·mi·ty, *n.*, *pl.* -ties. hostility.

en·nui', *n.* boredom.

e·nor'mi·ty, *n.*, *pl.* -ties. 1. wickedness. 2. outrage.

e·nor'mous, *adj.* beyond normal size or extent. —e·nor'mous·ly, *adv.*

e·nough', *n.*, *adj.*, *adv.* *n.* 1. as much as is wanted; sufficiency. —*adj.* 2. adequate; sufficient. —*adv.* 3. sufficiently.

en·quire', *v.t.*, *v.i.*, -quired, -quiring. inquire. —en·quir'y, *n.*

en·rage', *v.t.*, -raged, -raging. put in a rage.

en·rich', *v.t.* make rich or richer. —en·rich'ment, *n.*

en·roll', *v.t.* name on a list or record. —en·roll'ment, *n.*

en route, on the way.

en·sconce', *v.t.* put in a snug or secure place.

en·sem'ble, *n.* related group.

en·shrine', *v.t.*, -shrined, -shrining. put in or as if in a shrine.

en·sign, *n.* 1. flag, as on a ship. 2. lowest commissioned naval officer.

en·slave', *v.t.*, -slaved, -slaving. make a slave of. —en·slave'ment, *n.*

en·sue', *v.i.*, -sued, -suing. follow, esp. as a consequence.

en·sure', *v.t.*, -sured, -suring. make sure.

en·tail', *v.t.* necessitate.

en·tan'gle, *v.t.*, -gled, -gling. trap or impede. —en·tan'gle·ment, *n.*

en'ter, *v.t.* 1. go into. 2. have enrolled in or admitted to something. 3. list or record.

en"ter·prise", *n.* 1. project with some risk. 2. willingness to undertake such projects. —en'ter·pris''ing, *adj.*

en"ter·tain', *v.t.* 1. have as a guest. 2. amuse. 3. consider. —en"ter·tain'er, *n.* —en"ter·tain'ment, *n.*

en·thu'si·asm, *n.* intense approval, or favor. —en·thu'si·ast, *n.* —en·thu"si·as'tic, *adj.*

en·tice', *v.t.*, -ticed, -ticing. tempt, esp. deceitfully. —en·tice'ment, *n.*

en·tire', *adj.* complete. —en·tire'ly, *adv.* —en·tire'ty, *n.*

en·ti'tle, *v.t.*, -tled, -tling. give a right or claim.

en'ti·ty, *n.*, *pl.* -ties. one that exists.

en"to·mol'o·gy, *n.* study of insects. —en"to·mol'o·gist, *n.*

en·tou·rage (ahn"tŏŏ rahzh'), *n.* followers of an important person.

en'trails, *n.*, *pl.* internal organs, esp. viscera.

en·trance, *n.*, *v.t.*, -tranced, -trancing. *n.* (in'trəns) 1. way of entering. 2. right to enter. 3. act of entering. —*v.t.* (entrans') 4. fill with wonder.

en·trap', *v.t.* catch, as if in a trap. —en·trap'ment, *n.*

en·treat', *v.t.*, *v.i.* ask earnestly. —en·treat'y, *n.*

en·tree (ahn trā'), *n.* main dinner course.

en·trench', *v.t.* secure the position of.

en·tre·pre·neur (ahn"trə prə nər'), *n.* undertaker of business ventures.

en·trust', *v.t.* 1. give to someone in trust. 2. trust with something.

en'try, *n.*, *pl.* -tries. 1. entrance. 2. something noted. 3. competitor.

e·nu'mer·ate", *v.t.*, -ated, -ating. 1. cite one by one. 2. count. —e·nu"mer·a'tion, *n.*

e·nun'ci·ate", *v.*, -ated, -ating. *v.t.*, *v.i.* speak distinctly. —e·nun"ci·a'tion, *n.*

en·vel'op, *v.i.* wrap up.

en've·lope", *n.* 1. paper cover for letters, papers, etc. 2. outer covering.

en·vi'ron·ment, *n.* 1. surroundings. 2. conditions. —en·vi"ron·men'tal, *adj.*

en·vi'rons, *n.*, *pl.* surrounding area.

en·vis'age, *v.t.*, -aged, -aging. visualize; contemplate.

en·vi'sion, *v.t.* contemplate as likely.

en'voy, *n.* diplomatic representative.

en'vy, *n.*, *v.t.*, -vied, -vying. *n.* 1. resentment over another's good luck. —*v.t.* 2. feel envy toward. —en'vi·a·ble, *adj.* —en'vi·ous, *adj.*

e'on, *n.* very long period.

e·phem'er·al, *n.* short-lived.

ep'ic, *adj.* 1. heroic. —*n.* 2. poem about heroism.

ep'i·cure", *n.* person with refined tastes, esp. for food and drink. —ep"i·cu·re'an, *adj.*, *n.*

ep"i·dem'ic, *adj.* 1. spreading through a community. —*n.* 2. epidemic disease.

ep"i·der'mis, *n.* outer layer of skin. —**ep"i·der'mal, ep"i·der'mic,** *adj.*

ep'i·gram", *n.* witty observation. —**ep"i·gram·mat'ic,** *adj.*

ep'i·lep'sy, *n.* nervous disease with convulsions and unconsciousness. —**ep"i·lep·tic,** *adj., n.*

ep'i·logue", *n.* final statement of a play, etc.

E·piph'a·ny, *n.* revelation of Jesus as the Christ, celebrated January 6.

e·pis'co·pal, *adj.* pertaining to or governed by a bishop.

ep'i·sode", *n.* occurrence. —**ep"i·sod'ic,** *adj.*

e·pis'tle, *n.* letter; written message.

ep'i·taph", *n.* inscription on a tomb.

ep'i·thet", *n.* characterizing name.

e·pit'o·me", *n., pl.* **-mes. 1.** summary. **2.** typical example. —**e·pit'o·mize",** *v.t.*

ep'och, *n.* distinct historical or geological period. —**ep'och·al,** *adj.*

eq'ua·ble, *adj.* emotionally steady.

e'qual, *adj., n., v.t.,* **-qualed, -qualing.** *adj.* **1.** of the same amount, rank, etc. **2.** competent; adequate. —*n.* **3.** equal person or thing. —*v.t.* **4.** be equal to. —**e·qual'i·ty,** *n.* —**e'qual·ize",** *v.t.*

e"qua·nim'i·ty, *n.* calm.

e·quate', *v.t.,* **-quated, -quating.** regard as equal. —**e·qua'tion,** *n.*

e·qua'tor, *n.* imaginary line bisecting the earth. —**e"qua·to'ri·al,** *adj.*

e"qui·dis'tant, *adj.* equally far.

e"qui·lat'er·al, *adj.* with equal sides.

e"qui·lib'ri·um, *n.* balance.

e'qui·nox", *n.* time of equal day and night periods, marking the beginning of spring or autumn. —**e"qui·noc'ti·al,** *adj.*

e·quip', *v.t.,* **-quipped, -quipping.** furnish with what is necessary. —**e·quip'ment,** *n.*

e'qui·ta·ble, *adj.* just; fair. —**e'qui·ta·bly,** *adv.*

e'qui·ty, *n.* **1.** fairness. **2.** value of something in excess of money owed for it.

e·quiv'a·lent, *adj., n.* equal. —**e·quiv'a·lence,** *n.*

e·quiv'o·cal, *adj.* of doubtful meaning or nature.

e·quiv'o·cate, *v.i.,* **-cated, -cating.** speak equivocally. —**e·quiv"o·ca'tion,** *n.*

er'a, *n.* distinctive historical period.

e·rad'i·cate", *v.t.,* **-cated, -cating.** eliminate by destroying. —**e·rad"i·ca'tion,** *n.*

e·rase', *v.t.,* **-rased, -rasing.** obliterate. —**e·ras'er,** *n.* —**e·ra'sure,** *n.*

e·rect', *adj.* **1.** upright. —*v.t.* **2.** build. —**e·rec'tion,** *n.*

er'mine, *n.* weasel with white winter fur.

e·rode', *v.,* **-roded, -roding.** *v.t., v.i.* wash away or out. —**e·ro'sion,** *n.*

e·rot'ic, *adj.* pertaining to or arousing

sexual desire. —**e·rot'i·cism,** *n.*

err, *v.i.* be in error.

er'rand, *n.* journey for some purpose.

er'rant, *adj.* wandering.

er·rat'ic, *adj.* unreliable.

er·rat'um, *n., pl.* **-a.** printing or writing error.

er·ro'ne·ous, *adj.* in error.

er'ror, *n.* mistaken belief or action.

erst'while", *adj.* former.

er'u·dite", *adj.* informed; scholarly. —**er"u·di'tion,** *n.*

e·rupt', *v.i.* break forth. —**e·rup'tion,** *n.*

es·ca·late", *v.i.,* **-lated, -lating. 1.** rise on an escalator. **2.** increase rapidly, as in intensity.

es·ca·la'tor, *n.* endless moving stair.

es·ca·pade", *n.* reckless adventure.

es·cape', *v.,* **-caped, -caping.** *n. v.t., v.i.* **1.** flee. —*v.t.* **2.** evade the notice of. —*n.* **3.** act or instance of escaping.

es·cap'ism, *n.* tendency to attempt to escape reality. —**es·cap'ist,** *n., adj.*

es·chew', *v.t.* shun; do without.

es·cort', *v.t.* (i skort') **1.** take charge of and accompany. —*n.* (es'kort) **2.** person or thing that escorts.

es'crow, *n. Law.* state of property that is temporarily held in trust for another.

es·cutch'eon, *n.* symbolic shield holding a coat of arms.

es"o·ter'ic, *adj.* reserved for an understanding few.

es·pe'cial, *adj.* special. —**es·pe'cial·ly,** *adv.*

es'pi·o·nage", *n.* practice of spying.

es·pouse', *v.t.,* **-poused, -pousing. 1.** marry. **2.** devote oneself to. —**es·pous'al,** *n.*

es·prit de corps (es prē'də kor'), morale of an organization.

es·py', *v.t.,* **-pied, -pying.** discern.

es·say', *n.* (es'sā) **1.** writing on some theme. —*v.t.* (es sā') **2.** attempt. —**es'say·ist,** *n.*

es'sence, *n.* **1.** basic nature. **2.** concentrated substance.

es·sen'tial, *adj.* **1.** indispensable. —*n.* **2.** something indispensable. —**es·sen'tial·ly,** *adv.*

es·tab'lish, *v.t.* **1.** bring into being. **2.** prove. —**es·tab'lish·ment,** *n.*

es·tate', *n.* **1.** personal property. **2.** grounds belonging to a house.

es·teem', *n.* **1.** evaluation. —*v.t.* **2.** deem. —**es'tim·a·ble,** *adj.*

es'thete", *n.* aesthete.

es·thet'ics, *n.* aesthetics.

es'ti·mate, *n., v.t.,* **-mated, -mating.** *n.* (es'tə mət) **1.** rough calculation or appraisal. —*v.t.* (es'tə māt") **2.** make an estimate of. —**esti·ma'tion,** *n.*

es·trange', *v.t.,* **-tranged, -tranging.** lose the affection of.

es'tu·ar·y, *n., pl.* **-ies.** tidal river mouth.

et cetera, and other persons or things. Abbreviated etc.

etch, *v.t.* make or mark by the corrosion of acid. —etch'ing, *n.*

e·ter'nal, *adj.* lasting or valid forever. —e·ter'nal·ly, *adv.* —e·ter'ni·ty, *n.*

e'ther, *n.* 1. upper part of the atmosphere. 2. volatile, flammable anaesthetic or solvent.

e·the're·al, *adj.* 1. delicate. 2. unearthly.

eth'ics, *n.* 1. study of right and wrong in actions. 2. *pl.* **a.** Also, **eth'ic**, personal standards of right and wrong action. **b.** standards of conduct adopted by professionals. —eth'i·cal, *adj.*

eth'nic, *adj.* 1. pertaining to distinct nations or tribes. —*n.* 2. member of a minority national group. —eth·nic'i·ty, *n.*

et'i·quette, *n.* code of acceptable conduct.

e"ty·mol'o·gy, *n.* study of word origins.

Eu'cha·rist, *n.* 1. Holy Communion. 2. bread and wine used at Holy Communion. —Eu'cha·ris'tic, *adj.*

Eu·clid'e·an, *adj.* pertaining to traditional geometry. Also, Eu·clid'i·an.

eu·gen'ics, *n.* attempt to improve humanity by controlled mating. —eu·gen'ic, *adj.*

eu'lo·gy, *n.*, *pl.* -gies. praise in speech or writing. —eu'lo·gize', *v.t.*

eu'nuch, *n.* castrated man.

eu'phe·mism, *n.* expression substituted for a less agreeable one. —euphe·mis'tic, *adj.*

eu·pho'ni·ous, *adj.* pleasant-sounding. —eu'pho·ny, *n.*

eu·pho'ri·a, *n.* sensation of well-being. —eu·phor'ic, *adj.*

eu·re'ka, *interj.* I have found it!

eu"tha·na'si·a, *n.* killing to prevent or end suffering.

e·vac'u·ate", *v.t.*, -ated, -ating. 1. empty. 2. send to a place of security. —e·vac"u·a'tion, *n.* —e·vac"u·ee', *n.*

e·vade', *v.t.*, -vaded, -vading. avoid or escape from. —e·va'sion, *n.* —e·va'sive, *adj.*

e·val'u·ate", *v.t.*, -ated, -ating. estimate the worth of. —e·val"u·a'tion, *n.*

e"van·gel'i·cal, *adj.* 1. pertaining to the New Testament. 2. emphasizing salvation through Jesus.

e·van'gel·ist, *n.* 1. author of a Gospel. 2. itinerant preacher. —e·van'gel·ism, *n.*

e·vap'o·rate", *v.t.*, *v.i.*, -rated, -rating. turn into vapor. —e·vap"o·ra'tion, *n.*

eve, *n.* time just before.

e'ven, *adj.* 1. level or smooth. 2. unvarying. 3. equal. 4. divisible by two. 5. with nothing owed. —*adv.* 6. although improbable. 7. yet; still. —*v.t.* 8. make even. —e'ven·ness, *n.*

eve'ning, *n.* time between afternoon and night.

e·vent', *n.* something that happens. —e·vent'ful, *adj.*

e·ven'tu·al, *adj.* at some future time. —e·ven'tu·al·ly, *adv.*

e·ven"tu·al'i·ty, *n.*, *pl.* -ties. possible occurrence.

ev'er, *adv.* at any time.

ev'er·green", *adj.* 1. with green leaves all the year round. —*n.* 2. evergreen tree or plant.

ev"er·last'ing, *adj.* eternal or lifelong.

ev'er·y, *adj.* 1. each individual. 2. any possible. —ev'er·y·one", *pron.* —ev'er·y·thing", *n.*

ev'er·y·bod"y, *n.* every person.

ev'er·y·where", *adv.* at or to every place.

e·vict', *v.t.* drive out, as from rented lodgings. —e·vic'tion, *n.*

ev'i·dence, *n.*, *v.t.*, -denced, -dencing. *n.* 1. matter supporting an argument. —*v.t.* 2. make evident.

ev'i·dent, *adj.* obvious. —ev'i·dent·ly, *adv.*

e'vil, *adj.* 1. wrong or wicked. 2. injurious. —e'vil·ly, *adv.*

e·vince', *v.t.*, -vinced, -vincing. make obvious.

e·voke', *v.t.*, -voked, -voking. call forth. —e·voc'a·tive, *adj.* —ev"o·ca'tion, *n.*

e·volve', *v.*, -volved, -volving. *v.t.*, *v.i.* develop gradually. —ev"o·lu'tion, *n.*

ex·ac'er·bate (eks as'ər băt), *v.t.*, -bated, -bating. aggravate.

ex·act', *adj.* 1. accurate. 2. precise. —*v.t.* 3. extort or demand. —ex·act'ly, *n.* —ex·act'ing, *adj.* —ex·ac'tion, *n.*

ex·ag'ger·ate", *v.t.*, -ated, -ating. overstate the importance of. —ex·ag"ger·a'tion, *n.*

ex·alt', *v.t.* 1. raise in status. 2. praise. —ex"al·ta'tion, *n.*

ex·am'ine, *v.t.*, -ined, -ining. 1. inspect. 2. test for knowledge. —ex·am"i·na'tion, *n.* —ex·am'in·er, *n.*

ex·am'ple, *n.* 1. sample. 2. illustrative instance.

ex·as'per·ate", *v.t.*, -ated, -ating. anger or annoy seriously. —ex·as"per·a'tion, *n.*

ex'ca·vate", *v.t.*, -vated, -vating. dig, as in or from earth. —ex"ca·va'tion, *n.*

ex·ceed', *v.t.* 1. be in excess of. 2. surpass.

ex·ceed'ing·ly, *adv.* extremely.

ex·cel', *v.*, -celled, -celling. *v.t.*, *v.i.* surpass.

ex'cel·lent, *adj.* among the finest of its kind. —ex'cel·lent·ly, *adv.* —ex'cel·lence, *n.*

ex·cept', *prep.* 1. Also, **ex·cept'ing**, aside from. —*v.t.* 2. exclude or disregard. —ex·cep'tion, *n.*

ex·cep'tion·a·ble, *adj.* objectionable.

ex·cep'tion·al, *adj.* highly unusual. —**ex·cep'tion·al·ly,** *adv.*

ex'cerpt, *n.* quotation, esp. printed.

ex·cess, *n.* (ik ses', ek'ses') **1.** lack of self-restraint or moderation. **2.** surplus. —*adj.* (ek'ses') **3.** surplus. —**ex·ces'sive,** *adj.*

ex·change', *v.t.,* -changed, -changing, *n. v.t.* **1.** give in return for something else. —*n.* **2.** act or instance of exchanging.

ex·cise', *n., v.t.,* -cised, -cising. *n.* (ek'sīz) **1.** tax on merchandise. —*v.t.* (ik sīz') **2.** cut out. —**ex·ci'sion,** *n.*

ex·cite', *v.t.,* -cited, -citing. **1.** stimulate. **2.** rouse emotionally. —**ex·cit'a·ble,** *adj.* —**ex·cite'ment,** *n.* —**ex·cit'ed·ly,** *adv.* —**ex·cit'ing,** *adj.*

ex·claim', *v.i., v.t.* shout or speak loudly and emotionally. —**ex''cla·ma'tion,** *n.*

ex·clude', *v.t.,* -cluded, -cluding. leave or keep out. —**ex·clu'sion,** *n.* —**ex·clu'sive,** *adj.*

ex·co'ri·ate'', *v.t.,* -ated, -ating. denounce bitterly. —**ex·co'ri·a'tion,** *n.*

ex'cre·ment, *n.* excreted matter.

ex·cres'cence, *n.* abnormal outgrowth.

ex·crete', *v.t.,* -creted, -creting. eliminate as waste from the body. —**ex·cre'tion,** *n.* —**ex'cre·to''ry,** *adj.*

ex·cru'ci·at''ing, *adj.* racking.

ex'cul·pate'', *v.t.,* -pated, -pating. prove guiltless. —**ex''cul·pa'tion,** *n.*

ex·cur'sion, *n.* short pleasure journey. —**ex·cur'sion·ist,** *n.*

ex·cuse', *v.t.,* -cused, -cusing, *n. v.t.* (iks kyōoz') **1.** remove or mitigate the blame of or for. **2.** forgive. **3.** permit to leave. —*n.* (eks kyōos') **4.** something that excuses. —**ex·cus'a·ble,** *adj.* —**ex·cus'a·bly,** *adv.*

ex'e·crate'', *v.t.,* -crated, -crating. **1.** denounce. **2.** detest. —**ex'e·cra·ble,** *adj.*

ex'e·cute'', *v.t.,* -cuted, -cuting. **1.** perform. **2.** kill after condemnation. —**ex''e·cu'tion,** *n.* —**ex''e·cu'tion·er,** *n.*

ex·ec'u·tive, *adj.* **1.** concerned with administration of laws, policies, etc. —*n.* **2.** person in an executive capacity.

ex·ec'u·tor, *n.* person who administers a will. Also, *fem.,* **ex·ec'u·trix.**

ex·em'pla·ry, *adj.* serving as a good example.

ex·em'pli·fy'', *v.t.,* -fied, -fying. be an example of. —**ex·em''pli·fi·ca'tion,** *n.*

ex·empt', *v.t., adj.* free from an obligation. —**ex·emp'tion,** *n.*

ex'er·cise'', *n., v.,* -cised, -cising. *n.* **1.** activity developing skill, knowledge, strength, etc. **2.** performance. **3.** exercises, ceremony. —*v.t.* **4.** cause to do exercises. **5.** put into effect.

ex·ert', *v.t.* put into action. —**ex·er'tion,** *n.*

ex·hale', *v.,* -haled, -haling. *v.t., v.i.* breathe out. —**ex''ha·la'tion,** *n.*

ex·haust', *v.t.* **1.** empty; deplete. **2.** tire thoroughly. —*n.* **3.** waste gas, etc. from machinery. —**ex·haus'tion,** *n.*

ex·haus'tive, *adj.* omitting nothing.

ex·hib'it, *v.t., n.* display. —**ex''hi·bi'tion,** *n.* —**ex·hib'i·tor,** *n.*

ex''hi·bi'tion·ism, *n.* ostentation; self-display. —**ex''hi·bi'tion·ist,** *n.*

ex·hil'a·rate'', *v.t.,* -rated, -rating. **1.** fill with delight. **2.** stimulate. —**ex·hil'a·ra'tion,** *n.*

ex·hort', *v.t.* urge strongly. —**ex''hor·ta'tion,** *n.*

ex·hume', *v.t.,* -humed, -huming. dig up after burial. —**ex''hu·ma'tion,** *n.*

ex'i·gen·cy, *n., pl.* -cies. urgency. —**ex'i·gent,** *adj.*

ex'ile, *v.t.,* -iled, -iling. *n. v.t.* **1.** banish from a country. —*n.* **2.** state of banishment. **3.** exiled person.

ex·ist', *v.i.* **1.** have being. **2.** be alive. —**ex·ist'ence,** *n.* —**ex·ist'ent,** *adj.*

ex'it, *n.* **1.** departure. **2.** means of departure.

ex of·fi·ci·o (eks ''ə fish'ē ō), by virtue of his or her office.

ex·on'er·ate'', *v.t.,* -ated, -ating. declare guiltless. —**ex·on''er·a'tion,** *n.*

ex·or'bi·tant, *adj.* beyond reason or moderation. —**ex·or'bi·tance,** *n.*

ex'or·cize'', *v.t.,* -cized, -cizing. expel with incantations. —**ex'or·cism,** *n.*

ex·ot'ic, *adj.* markedly foreign.

ex·pand', *v.t., v.i.* widen. —**ex·pan'sion,** *n.* —**ex·pan'sive,** *adj.*

ex·panse', *n.* broad, unbroken area.

ex·pa'ti·ate'', *v.i.,* -ated, -ating. talk or write at length.

ex·pa'tri·ate, *n.* person living outside his country.

ex·pect', *v.t.* **1.** regard as going to happen. **2.** regard as obligatory. —**ex''pec·ta'tion, ex·pect'an·cy,** *n.* —**ex·pec'tant,** *adj.*

ex·pec'to·rate'', *v.t., v.i.,* -rated, -rating. spit.

ex·pe'di·ent, *adj.* **1.** useful on a given occasion. **2.** determined by self-interest alone. —*n.* **3.** something expedient. —**ex·pe'di·en·cy,** *n.*

ex'pe·dite'', *v.t.,* -dited, -diting. **1.** make faster or easier. **2.** do quickly.

ex''pe·di'tion, *n.* journey for exploration or invasion. —**ex''pe·di'tion·ar''y,** *adj.*

ex''pe·di'tious, *adj.* prompt.

ex·pel', *v.t.,* -pelled, -pelling. **1.** oust. **2.** emit.

ex·pend', *v.t.* **1.** spend. **2.** use up. —**ex·pend'i·ture,** *n.*

ex·pend'a·ble, *adj.* able or intended to be sacrificed, as in war.

ex·pense', *n.* **1.** act or instance of spending. **2.** cost.

ex·pen'sive, *adj.* high in price.

ex·per'i·ence, *n., v.t.,* -enced, -encing. *n* 1. something lived through. 2. knowledge from life, work, etc. —*v.t.* 3. have experience of.

ex·per'i·ment, *n.* 1. test establishing facts. —*v.i.* 2. engage in experiments. —ex·per''i·men·ta'tion, *n.* —ex·per''i·men'tal, *adj.*

ex'pert, *n.* 1. person with specialized knowledge or skill. —*adj.* 2. pertaining to such persons. —ex'pert·ly, *adv.* —ex''per·tise', ex'pert·ness, *n.*

ex'pi·ate'', *v.t.,* -ated, -ating. atone for. —ex''pi·a'tion, *n.* —ex'pi·a·to''ry, *adj.*

ex·pire', *v.i.,* -pired, -piring. 1. die. 2. cease to be in effect. 3. breathe out. —ex''pi·ra'tion, *n.*

ex·plain', *v.t.* 1. make understandable or meaningful. 2. account for. —ex''pla·na'tion, *n.* —ex·plan'a·to''ry, *adj.*

ex'ple·tive, *n.* exclamation.

ex'pli·ca·ble, *adj.* able to be explained.

ex·plic'it, *adj.* 1. clear. 2. outspoken.

ex·plode', *v.,* -ploded, -ploding. *v.t., v.i.* burst from internal pressure. —ex·plo'sive, *adj.; n.* —ex·plo'sion, *n.*

ex·ploit, *n.* (eks'ploit) 1. daring deed. —*v.t.* (iks ploit') 2. take advantage of. —ex''ploi·ta'tion, *n.* —ex·ploit'a·tive, *adj.*

ex·plore', *v.,* -plored, -ploring. *v.t., v.i.* investigate thoroughly. —ex·plor'er, *n.* —ex''plo·ra'tion, *n.* —ex·plor'a·to''ry, *adj.*

ex·po'nent, *n.* 1. expounder of a principle. 2. *Math.* number indicating how many times a quantity is to be multiplied by itself.

ex·port, *v.t.* (ik sport', eks·port') 1. ship out of the country. —*n.* (eks·port') 2. something exported.

ex·pose', *v.t.,* -posed, -posing. 1. reveal. 2. make vulnerable. —ex·po'sure, *n.*

ex''po·si'tion, *n.* 1. event presenting manufactures, processes, etc. to the public. 2. explanation.

ex post facto, retroactive; retroactively.

ex·pos'tu·late'', *v.i.,* -lated, -lating. argue in objection. —ex·pos''tu·la'tion, *n.*

ex·pound', *v.t.* state or explain.

ex·press', *v.t.* 1. communicate adequately. 2. squeeze. —*adj.* 3. precise; definite. —*n.* 4. vehicle on a fast, direct schedule. 5. agency for sending things. —ex·press'ive, *adj.*

ex·pres'sion, *n.* 1. means of expressing. 2. facial attitude. 3. revelation of feeling.

ex·pro'pri·ate'', *v.t.,* -ated, -ating. seize for public use.

ex·pul'sion, *n.* act or instance of being expelled.

ex·punge', *v.t.,* -punged, -punging. erase.

ex'pur·gate'', *v.t.,* -gated, -gating. censor.

ex'qui·site, *adj.* of extreme refinement.

ex·tant', *adj.* alive; present.

ex·tem''po·ra'ne·ous, *adj.* without prior preparation.

ex·tend', *v.t.* 1. stretch or expand. 2. offer. —*v.i.* 3. be extended. —ex·ten'sion, *n.*

ex·ten'sive, *adj.* large in extent or scope.

ex·tent', *n.* amount or degree of extending.

ex·ten'u·ate'', *v.t.,* -ated, -ating. prompt leniency for.

ex·te'ri·or, *adj.* 1. outer or outward. —*n.* 2. outside.

ex·ter''mi·nate'', *v.t.,* -nated, -nating. destroy wholly. —ex·ter''mi·na'tion, *n.* —ex·ter''mi·na''tor, *n.*

ex·ter'nal, *adj.* exterior; outward.

ex·tinct', *adj.* no longer in existence.

ex·tinc'tion, *n.* dying-out or destruction.

ex·tin'guish, *v.t.* put out of existence, as a flame.

ex'tir·pate'', *v.t.,* -pated, -pating. uproot; exterminate.

ex·tol', *v.t.,* -tolled, -tolling. praise highly.

ex·tort', *v.t.* obtain by threats or force. —ex·tor'tion, *n.* —ex·tor'tion·ist, *n.* —ex·tor'tion·ate, *adj.*

ex'tra, *adj.* additional.

ex·tract, *v.t.* (ik strakt') 1. draw out. —*n.* (ek'strakt) 2. something extracted. —ex·trac'tion, *n.*

ex'tra·dite'', *v.t.,* -dited, -diting. surrender for prosecution to a foreign country. —ex'tra·di''tion, *n.*

ex·tra'ne·ous, *adj.* 1. from outside. 2. irrelevant.

ex·tra·or'di·nar''y, *adj.* 1. remarkable. 2. out of the ordinary.

ex·trav'a·gant, *adj.* beyond economy, reason, etc. —ex·trav'a·gance, *n.*

ex·treme', *adj.* 1. farthest. 2. ultimate. 3. immoderate. —*n.* 4. farthest point, position, etc. —ex·treme'ly, *adv.*

ex·trem'i·ty, *n., pl.* -ties. *n.* 1. something extreme. 2. end. 3. extremities, hands and feet.

ex'tri·cate'', *v.t.,* -cated, -cating. free.

ex'tro·vert'', *n.* person oriented toward the outside world. —ex''tro·ver'sion, *n*

ex·u'ber·ant, *adj.* full of health and spirits. —ex·u'ber·ance, *n.*

ex·ude', *v.,* -uded, -uding. *v.t., v.i.* 1. pass through the pores. 2. seem to radiate. —exu·da'tion, *n.*

ex·ult', *v.i.* rejoice. —ex''ul·ta'tion, *n.*

eye, *n.* 1. organ of sight. 2. eyelike opening. 3. visual sensitivity. —eye'brow'',

n. —eye′ball″, *n.* —eye′lid″, *n.* —eye′sight″, *n.*

eye′lash″, *n.* row of stiff hairs over the eye.

eye′sore″, *n.* unpleasant sight.

F

F, f., *n.* **1.** sixth letter of the English alphabet. **2.** sixth-best grade.

fa′ble, *n.* **1.** moralizing story. **2.** legend.

fab′ric, *n.* cloth.

fab′ri·cate″, *v.t.,* **-cated, -cating. 1.** assemble. **2.** invent for deception. —**fab″ri·ca′tion,** *n.*

fab′u·lous, *adj.* wonderful.

fa·cade′, (fə sahd′), *n.* decorative building front. Also, **fa·çade′.**

face, *n., v.,* **faced, facing. n. 1.** front of the human head. **2.** main surface. **3.** outer appearance. —*v.t.* **4.** confront. —*v.i.* **5.** look or be turned toward. —**fa′cial,** *adj.*

fac′et, *n.* **1.** plane surface of a gem, etc. **2.** aspect.

fa·ce′tious, *adj.* joking; impish; frivolous.

fac′ile, *adj.* revealing no effort.

fa·cil′i·tate″, *v.t.,* **-tated, -tating.** make easy.

fa·cil′i·ty, *n., pl.* **-ties. 1.** ease. **2.** skill. **3.** facilities, equipment, staff, etc.

fac·sim′i·le, *n.* copy; reproduction.

fact, *n.* objective truth. —**fac′tu·al,** *adj.*

fac′tion, *n.* group promoting its own interests. —**fac′tion·al,** *adj.*

fac′tor, *n.* **1.** influential thing. **2.** quantity multiplied by another.

fac′to·ry, *n., pl.* **-ries.** place of manufacture.

fac·to′tum, *n.* person who does odd jobs.

fac′ul·ty, *n., pl.* **-ties. 1.** aptitude or ability. **2.** teaching staff.

fad, *n.* brief fashion or whim.

fade, *v.,* **faded, fading.** *v.i.* **1.** lose color or freshness. **2.** disappear slowly.

fag, *v.t.,* **fagged, fagging.** tire.

Fahr′en·heit″, *adj.* pertaining to a temperature scale with the freezing point of water at 32 degrees and the boiling point at 212 degrees.

fail, *v.t.* **1.** attempt without success. **2.** not to do. **3.** disappoint. —*v.i.* **4.** have no success. **5.** die away. —**fail′ing,** *n.* —**fail′ure,** *n.*

faint, *adj.* **1.** weak. —*n.* **2.** temporary loss of consciousness. —*v.i.* **3.** go into a faint. —**faint′ly,** *adv.* —**faint′ness,** *n.*

fair, *adj.* **1.** honest; just. **2.** beautiful or handsome. **3.** light. **4.** mediocre. **5.** sunny. **6.** gathering for sales or display. —**fair′ly,** *adv.*

fair′y, *n., pl.* **-ies.** creature with magic powers.

faith, *n.* **1.** belief; confidence. **2.** loyalty. **3.** religion. —**faith′ful,** *adj.* —**faith′less,** *adj.*

fake, *adj., n., v.t.,* **faked, faking.** *adj.* **1.** false. —*n.* **2.** something false. —*v.t.* **3.** give a false appearance of. —**fak′er,** *n.*

fal′con, *n.* small hawk.

fall, *v.i.,* **fell, fallen, falling,** *n.* *v.i.* **1.** descend without support. —*n.* **2.** act or instance of falling. **3.** autumn.

fal′la·cy, *n., pl.* **-cies.** instance of false reasoning. —**fal·la′cious,** *adj.*

fal′li·ble, *adj.* capable of mistakes. —**fal″li·bil′i·ty,** *n.*

fal′low, *adj.* unplanted.

false, *adj.,* **falser, falsest. 1.** not true. **2.** untruthful or unfaithful. —**false′ly,** *adv.* —**false′hood″,** *n.* —**fal′si·fy″,** *v.t.* —**fal′si·ty,** *n.*

fal·set′to, *n., pl.* **-tos.** artificially high voice.

fal′ter, *v.i.* act, speak, etc. hesitantly or unsteadily.

fame, *n.* widespread reputation. —**fa′mous, famed,** *adj.*

fa·mil′iar, *adj.* **1.** well known. **2.** well acquainted. —**fa·mil′iar·ly,** *adv.* —**fa·mil″i·ar′i·ty,** *n.* —**fa·mil′iar·ize″,** *v.t.*

fam′i·ly, *n., pl.* **-lies. 1.** group of relatives. **2.** group of related things. —**fa·mil′ial,** *adj.*

fam′ine, *n.* severe food shortage.

fam′ish, *v.t.* starve.

fan, *n., v.t.,* **fanned, fanning. 1.** device for moving air. **2.** *Informal.* devotee. —*v.t.* **3.** cool or move with a fan.

fa·nat′ic, *n.* irrational enthusiast or hater. —**fa·nat′i·cal,** *adj.* —**fa·nat′i·cism,** *n.*

fan′ci·er, *n.* breeder of animals or plants.

fan′cy, *adj.,* **-cier, -ciest,** *n., v.t.,* **-cied, -cying.** *adj.* **1.** elaborate. —*n.* **2.** imagination. **3.** liking. —*v.t.* **6.** take a liking to. —**fan′ci·ful,** *adj.* —**fan′ci·ly,** *adv.*

fan′fare′, *n.* **1.** introductory call of trumpets, etc. **2.** publicity.

fang, *n.* long, pointed tooth.

fan·tas′tic, *adj.* odd and extravagant.

fan′ta·sy, *n., pl.* **-sies. 1.** imagination. **2.** something imagined.

far, *adj., adv.,* **farther, farthest.** at or to a great distance.

farce, *n.* ridiculous comedy. —**far′ci·cal,** *adj.*

fare, *n., v.i.,* **fared, faring.** *n.* **1.** money paid to travel. **2.** food. —*v.i.* **3.** prosper or succeed.

fare′well′, *interj., n., adj.* goodbye.

far′-fetched′, *adj.* implausible.

farm, *n.* **1.** place for raising plants or animals. —*v.t.* **2.** cultivate. —**farm′er**, *n.* —**farm′hand″**, *n.* —**farm′house″**, *n.* —**farm′yard″**, *n.*

far′-off′, *adj.* remote.

far′-reach′ing, *adj.* with extensive effects.

far′sight″ed, *adj.* **1.** provident. **2.** seeing distant objects better than close ones.

fas′ci·nate″, *v.t.,* **-nated, -nating.** hold the entire attention of. —**fas″ci·na′tion**, *n.*

Fas′cism, *n.* authoritarian, militaristic system of government. —**Fas′cist**, *n., adj.* —**Fas·cis′tic**, *adj.*

fash′ion, *n.* **1.** manner of acting. **2.** prevailing style. —*v.t.* **2.** make. —**fash′ion·a·ble**, *adj.*

fast, *adj.* **1.** speedy. **2.** firm; fixed. —*adv.* **3.** firmly. —*v.i.* **4.** abstain from food or drink. —*n.* **5.** act or instance of fasting.

fast′en, *v.t.* attach; make secure. —**fas′ten·er**, *n.* —**fast′en·ing**, *n.*

fas·tid′i·ous, *adj.* not readily pleased. —**fas·tid′i·ous·ly**, *adv.*

fat, *adj.,* **fatter, fattest,** *n. adj.* **1.** having much fat. —*n.* **2.** greasy material. —**fat′ness**, *n.* —**fat′ty**, *adj.*

fa′tal, *adj.* causing death or destruction. —**fa′tal·ly**, *adv.*

fa′tal·ism, *n.* **1.** belief in fate. **2.** resignation. —**fa′tal·ist**, *n.* —**fa″tal·is′tic**, *adj.* —**fa″tal·is′ti·cal·ly**, *adv.*

fa·tal′i·ty, *n., pl.* **-ties. 1.** deadliness. **2.** death by accident.

fate, *n.* **1.** power determining events. **2.** death.

fa′ther, *n.* **1.** male parent. **2.** founder or originator. **3.** Christian priest. —**fa′ther·hood″**, *n.* —**fa′ther·ly**, *adj.*

fa′ther-in-law″, *n., pl.* **fathers-in-law.** father of a spouse.

fath′om, *n.* **1.** *Nautical.* unit of 6 linear feet. —*v.t.* **2.** probe to understand.

fa·tigue′, *n., v.t.,* **-tigued, -tiguing.** *n.* **1.** weariness. **2.** fatigues, military work clothes. —*v.t.* **3.** tire thoroughly.

fat′ten, *v.t.* **1.** make fat. —*v.i.* **2.** become fat.

fat′ty, *adj.* containing fat.

fat′u·ous, *adj.* foolishly self-satisfied. —**fa·tu′i·ty**, *n.*

fau′cet, *n.* valve for running water; tap.

fault, *n.* defect. —**fault′y**, *adj.*

fau′na, *n., pl.* animals.

faux pas (fō′pah′), *pl.* **faux pas.** social mistake.

fa′vor, *n.* **1.** act of kindness. **2.** approval. —*v.t.* **3.** do a favor for. **4.** treat as a favorite. **5.** advocate or support. —**fa′vor·a·ble**, *adj.* —**fa′vor·ite**, *adj., n.*

fa′vor·it·ism, *n.* preferential treatment for favorites.

fawn, *v.i.* **1.** show servility. —*n.* **2.** young deer.

faze, *v.t.,* **fazed, fazing.** daunt.

fear, *n.* **1.** desire to escape danger. **2.** awe. —*v.t.* **3.** have fear of. **4.** believe with regret. —**fear′ful**, *adj.* —**fear′less**, *adj.*

fea′si·ble, *adj.* able to be done; practical. —**fea″si·bil′i·ty**, *n.*

feast, *n.* **1.** religious festival. **2.** lavish meal. —*v.i.* **3.** have a feast.

feat, *n.* act of skill or daring.

feath′er, *n.* part of a bird's covering. —**feath′er·y**, *adj.*

fea′ture, *n., v.t.,* **-tured, turing.** *n.* **1.** distinct aspect. **2.** features, face. —*v.t.* **4.** present as a feature.

Feb′ru·ar″y, *n.* second month.

fe′ces, *n., pl.* solid excrement. —**fe′cal**, *adj.*

feck′less, *adj.* **1.** ineffectual. **2.** irresponsible.

fe′cund, *adj.* fertile. —**fe·cun′di·ty**, *n.*

fed′er·al, *adj.* **1.** composed of federated states. **2.** pertaining to a federation.

fed″er·a′tion, *n.* union of states or organizations under a central government or authority.

fee, *n.* charge for services.

fee′ble, *adj.,* **-bler, -blest.** without energy or force. —**fee′bly**, *adv.* —**fee′ble·ness**, *n.*

feed, *v.,* **fed, feeding,** *n. v.t.* **1.** nourish with food. —*v.i.* **2.** eat. —*n.* **3.** animal food.

feed″back, *n.* **1.** noise caused by a microphone picking up its own amplified signal. **2.** reactions to an idea or course of action.

feel, *v.,* **felt, feeling,** *n. v.t.* **1.** sense by touch. **2.** be aware of. **3.** believe. —*v.i.* **4.** be sensed as specified. —*n.* **5.** feeling; sensation. —**feel′ing**, *n.*

feign, *v.t.* pretend.

feint, *n.* **1.** false attack made as a diversion. —*v.i.* **2.** make a feint.

fe·lic′i·tate″, *v.t.,* **-tated, -tating.** congratulate. —**fe·lic″i·ta′tion**, *n.*

fe·lic′i·tous, *adj.* appropriate. —**fe·lic′i·tous·ly**, *adv.*

fe·lic′i·ty, *n., pl.* **-ties.** happiness.

fe′line, *adj.* pertaining to the cat family.

fell, *v.t.* cause to fall.

fel′low, *n.* **1.** man. **2.** companion. —**fel′low·ship″**, *n.*

fel′on, *n.* committer of a major crime. —**fel′on·y**, *n.* —**fe·lo′ni·ous**, *adj.*

felt, *n.* fabric of compacted wool, etc.

fe′male, *adj.* **1.** pertaining to the sex bearing offspring. —*n.* **2.** someone or something female.

fem′i·nine, *adj.* characteristic of girls and women. —**fem″i·nin′i·ty**, *n.*

fence, *n., v.,* **fenced, fencing.** *n.* **1.** light barrier. —*v.i.* **2.** fight with thrusting swords.

fend, *v.t.* drive or ward.

fend′er, *n.* cover for a wheel on a vehicle.

fer·ment, *v.t.* (fər ment′) **1.** break down, as through bacterial action. —*v.i.* **2.** be broken down, as an organic substance. —*n.* (fər′ment) **3.** anticipatory excitement. —**fer′′men·ta′tion**, *n.*

fern, *n.* fronded plant reproduced by spores.

fe·ro′cious, *adj.* savage. —**fe·ro′cious·ly**, *adv.* —**fe·roc′i·ty**, *n.*

fer′ret, *n.* **1.** weasellike animal. —*v.i.* **2.** hunt; search.

fer′rous, *adj.* pertaining to iron. Also, **fer′ric.**

fer′ry, *n.*, *pl.* **-ries**, *v.t.*, **-ried**, **-rying**. *n.* **1.** Also, **fer′ry·boat′′**, boat on a shuttle service. **2.** service running such a boat. —*v.t.* **3.** transport by or as by a ferry.

fer′tile, *adj.* yielding offspring, crops, etc. —**fer·til′i·ty**, *n.* —**fer′til·ize′′**, *v.t.*

fer′vent, *adj.* passionate. Also, **fer′vid.** —**fer′vent·ly**, *adv.* —**fer′ven·cy**, **fer′vor**, *n.*

fes′ti·val, *n.* occasion of celebration or merrymaking. —**fes′tive**, *adj.* —**fes·tiv′i·ty**, *n.*

fes·toon′, *n.* **1.** decorative hanging suspended between two supports. —*v.t.* **2.** drape.

fetch, *v.t.* **1.** get. **2.** summon.

fete (fāt), *n.*, *v.t.*, **feted**, **feting**. *n.* **1.** festive entertainment. —*v.t.* **2.** honor with a fete. Also, **fête.**

fet′id, *adj.* evil-smelling.

fet′ish, *n.* subject of obsessive concern.

fet′ter, *n.*, *v.t.* shackle or chain.

fet′tle, *n.* **in fine fettle**, in excellent state.

fe′tus, *n.*, *pl.* **-tuses.** unborn young in its later state. —**fe′tal**, *adj.*

feud, *n.* murderous rivalry between families.

feu′dal·ism, *n.* system of serfs and overlords. —**feu′dal**, *adj.*

fe′ver, *n.* excess of body temperature. —**fe′ver·ish**, *adj.*

few, *adj.*, *pron.*, *n.* some but not many.

fi·an·cé (fē′′ahn sā′), *n.* man engaged to be married. Also, *fem.*, **fi′′an·cée′.**

fi·as′co, *n.*, *pl.* **-coes**, **-cos.** ridiculous failure.

fi′at, *n.* decree.

fib, *n.*, *v.i.*, **fibbed**, **fibbing**. *n.* **1.** minor

fi′ber, *n.* long, thin piece of material. Also, **fi′bre.**

fick′le, *adj.* capricious and untrustworthy.

fic′tion, *n.* **1.** not factually true. **2.** novels, etc. —**fic′tion·al**, *adj.*

fic·ti′tious, *adj.* not factually true.

fid′dle, *n.*, *v.i.*, **-dled**, **-dling**. *n.* **1.** violin. —*v.i.* **2.** play a fiddle. **3.** fumble. —**fid′dler**, *n.*

fi·del′i·ty, *n.* faithfulness.

fid′get, *v.i.* move or fumble nervously. —*n.* **2.** nervous state. —**fid′get′y**, *adj.*

fi·du′ci·ar′′y, *adj.*, *n.*, *pl.* **-ies.** *adj.* **1.** pertaining to a trust. —*n.* **2.** trustee.

field, *n.* **1.** area of open land. **2.** area of work or knowledge.

fiend, *n.* **1.** evil spirit. **2.** vicious person. —**fiend′ish**, *adj.*

fierce, *adj.*, **fiercer**, **fiercest**. **1.** savage. **2.** violent. —**fierce′ly**, *adv.*

fier′y, *adj.*, **-ier**, **-iest**. **1.** covered or filled with fire. **2.** passionate.

fi·es′ta, *n.* festival in a Spanish-speaking region.

fife, *n.* small flute.

fif·teen′, *n.* ten plus five. —**fif′teenth′**, *adj.*

fifth, *adj.* **1.** following the fourth. —*n.* **2.** fifth thing, person, or part.

fif′ty, *n.*, *adj.* five times ten. —**fif′ti·eth**, *adj.*

fig, *n.* small, sweet tree fruit.

fight, *n.*, *v.*, **fought**, **fighting**. *n.* **1.** dispute or competition with violence. **2.** angry argument. —*v.t.* **3.** make a fight against. —*v.i.* **4.** engage in a fight.

fig′ment, *n.* something merely imaginary.

fig′u·ra·tive, *adj.* using or forming a figure of speech.

fig′ure, *n.*, *v.t.*, **-ured**, **-uring**. *n.* **1.** shape. **2.** numeral. **3.** sum. —*v.t.*, *v.i.* **4.** calculate.

figure of speech, word or idiom not to be taken literally or in the usual way.

fil′a·ment, *n.* narrow thread or wire.

fil′bert, *n.* hazelnut.

filch, *v.t.* steal.

file, *n.*, *v.t.*, **-filed**, **-filing**. *n.* **1.** group of documents. **2.** tool for rubbing. **3.** front-to-rear row. —*v.t.* **4.** preserve in a file. **5.** rub with a file.

fil′i·al, *adj.* pertaining to or appropriate in a son or daughter.

fil′i·bus′′ter, *n.* meaningless speech hindering legislation.

fil′i·gree′′, *n.* lace-like gold or silver wirework.

fill, *v.t.* **1.** cause to be completely occupied. **2.** satisfy the requirements of. —*v.i.* **3.** become full. —*n.* **4.** enough to fill.

fil·let (fil′ā), *n.* boneless lean cut of meat or fish.

fil′lip, *n.* stimulus.

film, *n.* **1.** thin coating. **2.** strip or sheet for registering photographic images. —*v.t.* **3.** make a motion picture or photograph of.

fil′ter, *n.* **1.** something screening out unwanted things. —*v.i.* **2.** pass through a filter. —*v.t.* **3.** exclude with a filter.

filth, *n.* foul matter. —**filth′y**, *adj.*

fin, *n.* bladelike extension.

fi′nal, *adj.* at the end. —**fi′nal·ly**, *adv.* —**fi·nal′i·ty**, *n.*

fi·na·le (fi nä′lē), *n.* concluding feature.

fi'nal·ist, *n.* competitor in a final contest.

fi·nance (fi nans', fī'nans), *n., v.t.* **-nanced, -nancing.** *n.* **1.** management of money. **2. finances,** resources of money. —*v.t.* **3.** lend or obtain money for. —**fi·nan'cial,** *adj.* —**fi''nan·cier',** *n.*

find, *v.t.,* **found, finding,** *n. v.t.* **1.** come upon by chance. **2.** succeed in a search for. —*n.* **3.** valuable discovery. —**find'er,** *n.* —**find'ing,** *n.*

fine, *adj.,* **finer, finest,** *n., v.t.,* **fined, fining.** *adj.* **1.** in tiny pieces. **2.** excellent. —*n.* **3.** money penalty. —*v.t.* **4.** impose a fine on. —**fine'ly,** *adv.* —**fine'ness,** *n.*

fin'er·y, *n.* fine costume.

fi·nesse', *n.* skill, esp. in human relations.

fine''-tune'', *v.* to make minor adjustments.

fin'ger, *n.* extension of the hand.

fin'ick·y, *adj.* too particular or demanding. Also, **fin'i·cal, fin'ick·ing.**

fi'nis, *n., pl.* **-nises.** end; finish.

fin'ish, *v.t.* **1.** bring to an end. **2.** give a desired surface to. —*v.i.* **3.** end an activity.

fi·nite (fī'nīt), *adj.* not endless.

fir, *n.* cone-bearing evergreen tree.

fire, *n., v.* **fired, firing.** *n.* **1.** burning. **2.** deep feeling. **3.** discharge of guns. —*v.t.* **4.** set fire to. **5.** discharge, as of a gun. —**fire'proof',** *adj.*

fire'arm'', *n.* weapon operated by explosives.

fire'crack''er, *n.* a firework.

fire'man, *n.* **1.** person who extinguishes fires. **2.** person who tends fires.

fire'trap'', *n.* building dangerous in fires.

fire'works'', *n., pl.* explosive and burning devices used in celebrations.

firm, *adj.* **1.** unyielding. **2.** steady. —*n.* **3.** business organization. —**firm'ly,** *adv.* —**firm'ness,** *n.*

fir'ma·ment, *n.* heavens.

first, *adj., adv.* **1.** at the very front or beginning. **2.** before all others. —*n.* **3.** first person or thing.

first'-hand', *adj., adv.* without intermediaries.

fis'cal, *adj.* pertaining to income and expense; financial.

fish, *n., pl.* **fish,** *v.i. n.* **1.** cold-blooded water animal, breathing with gills. —*v.i.* **2.** attempt to catch fish. —**fish'er·man,** *n.*

fis'sion, *n.* splitting; cleaving. —**fis'sion·a·ble.** *adj.*

fis'sure, *n.* crack.

fist, *n.* ball of the hand and fingers for striking.

fit, *v.,* **fitted, fitting,** *adj.,* **fitter, fittest,** *n. v.i.* **1.** be suitable, esp. in size. —*v.t.* **2.** be suitable for. **3.** cause to be suitable. —*adj.* **4.** suitable. **5.** healthy. —*n.* **6.** manner of fitting. **7.** bodily seizure.

fit'ful, *adj.* intermittent; spasmodic. —**fit'ful·ly,** *adv.* —**fit'ful·ness,** *n.*

fit'ting, *adj.* suitable.

five, *adj., n.* four plus one.

fix, *v.t.,* **fixed, fixing. 1.** repair oradjust. **2.** prepare. **3.** establish firmly. —**fix'i·ty,** *n.*

fix·a'tion, *n.* psychological obsession.

fix'ture, *n.* attached piece of equipment.

fizz, *v.i.,* **fizzed, fizzing,** *n. v.i.* **1.** emit a buzzing bubbling sound. —*n.* **2.** such a sound.

fiz'zle, *v.i.,* **-zled, -zling,** *n. v.i.* **1.** fail. —*n.* **2.** failure.

flab'by, *adj.,* **-bier, -biest.** fat, soft, and weak.

flac·cid (flak'sid) *adj.* flabby.

flag, *n., v.,* **flagged, flagging.** *n.* **1.** emblem-bearing cloth. **2.** Also, **flag'stone'',** flat paving stone. —*v.t.* **3.** signal with a flag.

fla'grant, *adj.* outrageously evident. —**fla'grant·ly,** *adv.* —**fla'gran·cy,** *n.*

flail, *n.* **1.** hand-held threshing device. —*v.t.* **2.** beat or move in a flaillike manner.

flair, *n.* shrewd perceptiveness or talent.

flake, *n., v.,* **flaked, flaking.** *n.* **1.** thin piece. —*v.i.* **2.** fall off in flakes.

flam·boy'ant, *adj.* brashly ostentatious. —**flam·boy'ance,** *n.*

flame, *n., v.,* **flamed, flaming.** *n.* burning gas. —*v.i.* **2.** be burned with flames.

fla·min'go, *n., pl.* **-gos.** pink tropical wading bird.

flam'ma·ble, *adj.* burnable.

flange, *n.* perpendicular edge.

flank, *n.* **1.** side. —*v.t.* **2.** be beside. **3.** attack or get around the flank of.

flan'nel, *n.* loosely woven wool or cotton.

flap, *n., v.,* **flapped, flapping.** *n.* **1.** hinged panel. **2.** sound of flapping. —*v.t., v.i.* **3.** move to and fro.

flare, *v.i.,* **flared, flaring,** *n. v.i.* **1.** blaze. **2.** curve outward. —*n.* **3.** torchlike signal.

flash, *n.* **1.** momentary bright light. **2.** moment. —*v.i.* **3.** emit a flash. —*v.t.* **4.** cause to flash.

flash'light'', *n.* hand-held battery-operated light.

flash'y, *adj.,* **-ier, -iest.** showy. —**flash'i·ness,** *n.*

flask, *n.* bottle, often flat.

flat, *adj.,* **flatter, flattest** *n., adj.* **1.** without rises or hollows. **2.** absolute. **3.** featureless. **4.** *Music.* slightly low in pitch. —*n.* **5.** apartment. **6.** something flat. —**flat'ly,** *adv.* —**flat'ten,** *v.t., v.i.*

flat'ter, *v.t.* compliment, as in order to wheedle. —**flat'ter·y,** *n.*

flaunt, *v.t.* display proudly.

fla'vor, *n.* **1.** taste. **2.** Also, **fla'vor·ing,**

something giving a certain taste. —*v.t.* 3. add a flavor to.

flaw, *n.* shortcoming; fault. —**flaw′less**, *adj.*

flax, *n.* threadlike plant fiber for linen.

flay, *v.t.* skin.

flea, *n.* bloodsucking, wingless jumping insect.

fleck, *n.* spot or flake.

fledg′ling, *n.* beginner at a profession, etc.

flee, *v.*, **fled, fleeing.** *v.t.*, *v.i.* escape; run.

fleece, *v.i.* **1.** covering of a sheep, etc. —*v.t.* **2.** cheat. —**fleec′y**, *adj.*

fleet, *n.* **1.** ships under one command. —*adj.* **2.** swift.

fleet′ing *adj.* passing quickly.

flesh, *n.* **1.** muscle tissue. **2.** soft part of a plant. **3.** animal meat. —**flesh′y**, *adj.*

flesh′ly, *adj.* bodily; sensual.

flex, *v.t.*, *v.i.* bend. —**flex′i·ble**, *adj.*

flex″time, flex″i·time, *n.* system in which work hours are flexible.

flick, *n.* **1.** quick, light motion. —*v.t.* **2.** throw, etc. with such a motion.

flick′er, *v.i.* have a wavering light or appearance.

fli′er, *n.* **1.** aviator. **2.** advertising paper.

flight, *n.* **1.** act or instance of flying or fleeing. **2.** stair between floors.

flight′y, *adj.*, **-ier, -iest.** overly emotional or whimsical. —**flight′i·ness**, *n.*

flim′sy, *adj.*, **-ier, -iest.** readily torn or broken. —**flim′si·ly**, *adv.*

flinch, *v.i.* hold back or retreat, as from a blow.

fling, *v.t.*, **flung, flinging.** *n.* *v.t.* **1.** hurl. —*n.* **2.** act or instance of flinging. **3.** brief indulgence.

flint, *n.* spark-producing gray siliceous rock. —**flint′y**, *adj.*

flip, *v.t.*, **flipped, flipping.** *n.* *v.t.* **1.** toss jerkily. —*n.* **2.** act or instance of flipping.

flip′pant, *adj.* cheerfully disrespectful. —**flip′pan·cy**, *n.*

flip′per, *n.* flat limb for paddling.

flirt, *v.i.* **1.** make mild erotic advances. **2.** consider something unseriously. —**flir·ta′tion**, *n.* —**flir·ta′tious**, *adj.*

flit, *v.i.*, **flitted, flitting.** move quickly and lightly.

float, *v.i.* **1.** be carried on water, etc. —*n.* **2.** something that floats.

flock, *n.* **1.** group of sheep, etc. —*v.i.* **2.** join in a flock.

flog, *v.t.*, **flogged, flogging.** whip.

flood, *n.* **1.** overflow, as of a river. —*v.t.*, *v.i.* **2.** fill to excess.

flood′light″, *n.* lamp casting a directed light.

floor, *n.* **1.** supporting interior surface. **2.** bottom surface. **3.** right to speak. —*v.t.* **4.** supply with a floor. —**floor′ing**, *n.*

flop, *v.*, **flopped, flopping.** *n.* *v.t.*, *v.i.* **1.** overturn heavily. —*v.i.* **2.** move clumsily. **3.** *Informal.* fail. —*n.* **4.** act or instance of flopping.

flo′ra, *n.*, *pl.* plants.

flo′ral, *adj.* pertaining to flowers.

flor′id, *adj.* **1.** ruddy. **2.** gaudy.

flo′rist, *n.* flower merchant.

floss, *n.* soft down or twisted thread. —**flos′sy**, *adj.*

flo·til′la, *n.* small fleet.

flounce, *v.i.*, **flounced, flouncing.** *n.* *v.i.* **1.** move quickly and jerkily. —*n.* **2.** act or instance of flouncing.

floun′der, *n.* **1.** edible flat fish. —*v.i.* **2.** struggle.

flour, *n.* powdered grain, etc.

flour′ish, *v.i.* **1.** thrive. —*v.t.* **2.** wave.

flout, *v.t.* show scorn for.

flow, *v.i.* **1.** move steadily, as a liquid. —*n.* **2.** act or instance of flowing.

flow′er, *n.* **1.** petaled seed-producing part of a plant; blossom. —*v.i.* **2.** produce blossoms. —**flow′er·y**, *adj.*

flu, *n.* influenza.

fluc′tu·ate″, *v.i.*, **-ated, -ating.** change rate or quantity irregularly. —**fluc″tu·a′tion**, *n.*

flue, *n.* passage for smoke, etc.

flu′ent, *adj.* speaking or writing readily. —**flu′en·cy**, *n.*

fluff, *n.* soft fibrous material. —**fluf′fy**, *adj.*

flu′id, *adj.* **1.** flowing. —*n.* **2.** liquid or gas.

fluke, *n.* **1.** barb. **2.** stroke of luck.

flume, *n.* chute carrying water.

flunk, *v.t.*, *v.i. Informal.* fail at school.

flur′ry, *n.*, *pl.* **-ries.** brief spells of activity, weather, etc.

flush, *v.t.* **1.** wash out. **2.** frighten from cover. —*v.i.* **3.** be flushed. **4.** blush. —*n.* **5.** act or instance of flushing. —*adj.* **6.** even. **7.** wealthy.

flus′ter, *v.t.* confuse.

flute, *n.* **1.** high-pitched wind instrument. **2.** Also **flut′ing**, longitudinal concavity, —**flut′ist**, *n.*

flut′ter, *v.t.*, *v.i.* **1.** oscillate rapidly. —*n.* **2.** excited state. —**flut′ter·y**, *adj.*

flux, *n.* **1.** fluid state. **2.** substance aiding metal fusion.

fly, *v.*, **flew, flown, flying**, *n.*, *pl.* **flies**, *v.i.* **1.** move in the air. **2.** go quickly. —*v.t.* **3.** cause to move in the air. **4.** flee from. —*n.* **5.** two-winged insect.

flying colors, great success.

fly′wheel″, *n.* heavy wheel regulating a machine by inertia.

foam, *n.* **1.** fine bubbles. —*v.i.* **2.** emit or break into foam. —**foam′y**, *adj.*

fo′cus, *n.*, *pl.* **-cuses, -ci**, *v.*, **-cused, -cusing.** *n.* **1.** point of concentration. **2.** state of sharpness or clarity. —*v.t.* **3.** bring into focus.

fod'der, *n.* food for horses, cows, etc.

foe, *n.* enemy.

foe'tus, *n.* fetus.

fog, *n., v.,* fogged, fogging. *n.* 1. water vapor obscuring vision. —*v.t., v.i.* 2. obscure with fog. —**fog'gy,** *adj.*

fo'gy, *n., pl.* **-gies.** reactionary. Also, **fo'gey.**

foi'ble, *n.* weakness.

foil, *v.t.* 1. frustrate. —*n.* 2. thin metal sheeting. 3. pointed sword. 4. contrasting feature.

foist, *v.t.* get accepted by trickery.

fold, *v.t., v.i.* 1. double over. 2. wrap. —*n.* 3. folded place.

fold'er, *n.* 1. bent sheet for holding papers. 2. folded, unbound pamphlet.

fol'i·age, *n.* leaves.

folk, *n.* 1. folks, **a.** people. **b.** relatives. —*adj.* 2. pertaining to ethnic groups. —**folk'lore'',** *n.*

folk'sy, *adj.,* **-sier, -siest.** *Informal.* characteristic of ordinary people.

fol'low, *v.t.* 1. go after or along. 2. happen after. 3. conform to. 4. learn from or understand. —*v.i.* 5. go or happen after. 6. be logically deducible.

fol'low·er, *n.* disciple or adherent.

fol'low·ing, *adj.* 1. happening afterwards. —*prep.* 2. after. —*n.* 3. group of followers.

fol'ly, *n., pl.* **-lies.** mad or foolish thing or disposition.

fo·ment', *v.t.* incite, as trouble.

fond, *adj.* full of affection. —**fond'ly,** *adv.* —**fond'ness,** *n.*

fon'dle, *v.t.,* **-dled, -dling.** handle fondly.

font, *n.* baptismal basin.

food, *n.* material that nourishes. —**food'stuff'',** *n.*

fool, *n.* 1. person of bad judgment. —*v.t.* 2. deceive. —*v.i.* 3. act like a fool. —**fool'ish,** *adj.*

fool'hard''y, *adj.,* **-dier, -diest.** unwisely audacious.

fool'proof'', *adj.* proof against failure.

foot, *n.* 1. extremity of a leg. 2. lower-most feature; bottom; pedestal. 3. unit of 12 inches. —**foot'hold'',** *n.* —**foot'step'',** *n.*

foot'ball'', *n.* 1. game with a kicked ball. 2. ball used.

foot'ing, *n.* 1. support for a foot. 2. basis.

foot''print, *n.* 1. mark left by a foot. 2. area required for an office machine.

fop, *n.* dressy, affected person. —**fop'pish,** *adj.*

for, *prep.* 1. in favor of. 2. in place of. 3. in order to reach, etc. 4. to be used, etc. by. 5. during. 6. obtaining in exchange. 7. considering the nature of. —*conj.* 8. because.

for'age, *v.i.,* **-aged, -aging,** *n.* search, as for food.

for'ay, *n.* plundering expedition.

for·bear', *v.,* **-bore, -borne, -bearing.** *v.t.* 1. refrain. —*v.i.* 2. control oneself. —**for·bear'ance,** *n.*

for·bid', *v.t.,* **-bade** or **-bad, -bidden, -bidding.** 1. give an order against. 2. prevent.

for·bid'ding, *adj.* formidable or unapproachable.

force, *n., v.t.,* forced, forcing. *n.* 1. agency influencing events. 2. power. 3. compulsion. 4. organization or group. —*v.t.* 5. compel. —**force'ful,** *adj.* —**for'ci·ble,** *adj.*

ford, *n.* 1. wadeable part of a stream. —*v.t.* 2. wade across.

fore, *adj., adv.* 1. forward. —*n.* 2. front.

fore·arm, *n.* (for'ahrm) 1. arm between the elbow and wrist. —*v.t.* (for arm') 2. arm in advance.

fore'bear'', *n.* ancestor.

fore·bod'ing, *n.* premonition.

fore'cast'', *v.t.,* **-cast** or **-casted, -casting,** *n. v.t.* 1. predict. —*n.* 2. prediction.

fore·cas·tle (fōk'səl) *n.* upper forward part of a ship.

fore·close', *v.t.,* **-closed, -closing.** deprive a mortgagor of the right of redeeming. —**fore·clos'ure,** *n.*

fore'fath''er, *n.* ancestor.

fore'fin''ger, *n.* finger nearest the thumb.

fore'front'', *n.* extreme forward position.

fore·gath'er, *v.i.* come together.

fore·go''ing, *adj.* preceding.

fore·gone', *adj.* 1. determined in advance. 2. previous.

fore'ground'', *n.* area nearest the viewer.

fore'head, *n.* front of the head between the eyebrows and hair.

for'eign, *adj.* 1. belonging to an area outside the country. 2. not belonging where found. —**for'eign·er,** *n.*

fore'man, *n.* supervising worker.

fore'most', *adj., adv.* first.

fore'noon', *n.* morning after sunrise.

fo·ren'sic, *adj.* pertaining to legal proceedings or public debate.

fore''or·dain', *v.t.* predestine. —**fore·or''di·na'tion,** *n.*

fore'run'ner, *n.* predecessor.

fore·see', *v.t.,* **-saw, -seen, -seeing.** anticipate. —**fore·see'a·ble,** *adj.* —**fore'sight'',** *n.*

fore·shad'ow, *v.t.* hint at in advance.

for'est, *n.* area of trees. —**for''es·ta'tion,** *n.* —**for'est·ry,** *n.*

fore·stall', *v.t.* prevent by early action.

fore·tell', *v.t.,* **-told, -telling.** predict.

fore'thought'', *n.* planning, etc. in advance.

for·ev'er, *adv.* 1. eternally. 2. ceaselessly.

fore·warn', *v.t.* warn beforehand.

fore'word'', *n.* book introduction.

for'feit, *v.t.* 1. have taken away because of a misdeed, etc. —*n.* 2. something

forfeited. —*adj.* **3.** forfeited. —**for'fei·ture,** *n.*

forge, *n., v.,* **forged, forging.** *n.* **1.** place for hammering hot metal. —*v.t.* **2.** shape or assemble by hammering. **3.** counterfeit. —*v.i.* **4.** move against obstacles. —**forg'er,** *n.* —**forg'er·y,** *n.*

for·get', *v.t.,* **-got, -gotten, -getting. 1.** lose the memory of. **2.** ignore. —**for·get'ful,** *adj.*

for·give', *v.t.,* **-gave, -given, -giving.** regard without ill will despite an offense. —**for·giv'a·ble,** *adj.* —**for·giv'ing·ly,** *adv.*

for·go', *v.t.,* **-went, -gone, -going.** do without.

fork, *n.* **1.** pronged lifting instrument. **2.** division into two branches from one. —*v.i.* **3.** divide into two branches.

for·lorn', *adj.* forsaken. —**for·lorn'ly,** *adv.*

form, *n.* **1.** outline or contour. **2.** basic organizing principle. **3.** information blank. —*v.t.* **4.** give form to. **5.** develop. —**for·ma'tion,** *n.* —**form'a·tive,** *adj.*

for'mal, *adj.* **1.** emphasizing rules or customs. **2.** explicit. **3.** correct in manner. —**for'mal·ly,** *adv.* —**for·mal'i·ty,** *n.*

for'mat, *n.* basic design or plan.

for'mer, *adj.* **1.** past. **2.** being the first of two mentioned. —**for'mer·ly,** *adv.*

for·mi·da·ble, *adj.* **1.** awe-inspiring. **2.** difficult.

for'mu·la, *n., pl.* **-las, -lae. 1.** rule to be followed. **2.** words to be uttered. **3.** ingredients to be used. —**for'mu·late",** *v.t.*

for'ni·cate", *v.i.,* **-cated, -cating.** have illicit sexual intercourse. —**for"ni·ca'tion,** *n.* —**for"ni·ca"tor,** *n.*

for·sake', *v.t.,* **-sook, -saken, -saking. 1.** desert. **2.** give up.

fort, *n.* **1.** strongly fortified place. **2.** army post.

for·te, *adj., adv. Music.* loud; loudly.

forte (fort), *n.* special ability.

forth, *adv.* **1.** forward. **2.** outward.

forth'com"ing, *adj.* soon to appear.

forth'right", *adj.* frank.

forth"with', *adv.* without delay.

for'ti·fy", *v.t.,* **-fied, -fying. 1.** make resistant to attack. **2.** strengthen. —**for"ti·fi·ca'tion,** *n.*

for·tis'si·mo", *adj., adv. Music.* with extreme loudness.

for'ti·tude", *n.* persistent courage.

fort'night", *n.* two-week period. —**fort'night"ly,** *adj., adv.*

for'tress, *n.* large fort.

for·tu'i·tous, *adj.* happening by chance.

for'tu·nate, *adj.* lucky. —**for'tu·nate·ly,** *adv.*

for'tune, *n.* **1.** luck. **2.** riches.

for'ty, *adj., n.* four times ten. —**for'ti·eth,** *adj.*

fo'rum, *n.* place for or occasion of public discussion.

for'ward, *adv.* **1.** Also, **for'wards,** to the front. —*adj.* **2.** at the front. **3.** presumptuous.

fos'sil, *n.* hardened or petrified plant or animal. —**fos'sil·ize",** *v.t.*

fos'ter, *v.t.* **1.** raise, as young. **2.** promote. —*adj.* **3.** in a family relationship of adoption rather than blood.

foul, *adj.* **1.** dirty. **2.** disgusting. **3.** unethical. —*v.t.* **4.** make foul. **5.** obstruct or tangle. —*n.* **6.** illicit act. —**foul'ly,** *adv.* —**foul'ness,** *n.*

found, *v.t.* establish.

found'er, *v.i.* **1.** sink. **2.** break down. —*n.* **3.** person who founds.

found'ling, *n.* child abandoned by unknown parents.

foun'dry, *n., pl.* **-dries.** place for casting metal.

foun'tain, *n.* source of flowing water.

four, *adj., n.* three plus one. —**fourth,** *adj., n.*

four·teen', *adj., n.* ten plus four.

fowl, *n., pl.* **fowl. 1.** any bird. **2.** domestic bird eaten as food.

fox, *n.* **1.** small canine predatory animal. —*v.t.* **2.** cheat; trick.

fox'y, *adj.* cunning.

foy'er, *n.* lobby, esp. of a theater.

fra'cas, *n.* brawl.

frac'tion, *n.* portion. —**frac'tion·al,** *adj.*

frac'tious, *adj.* rebellious.

frac'ture, *n., v.t., v.i.,* **-tured, -turing.** break.

frag'ile, *adj.* readily broken. —**fra·gil'i·ty,** *n.*

frag'ment, *n.* **1.** broken or torn-away piece. —*v.t., v.i.* **2.** break into pieces. —**frag'men·tar'y,** *adj.*

fra'grant, *adj.* sweet-smelling. —**fra'grance,** *n.*

frail, *adj.* **1.** fragile. **2.** weak, physically or morally. —**frail'ty,** *n.*

frame, *n., v.t.,* **framed, framing.** *n.* **1.** open structure. **2.** border. —*v.t.* **3.** make a frame for. **4.** put into words or concepts. —**frame'work",** *n.*

franc, *n.* currency unit in French-speaking countries.

fran'chise, *n.* **1.** right to vote. **2.** right to do business.

frank, *adj.* **1.** not deceitful or evasive. —*n.* **2.** right to mail without postage. —**frank'ly,** *adv.* —**frank'ness,** *n.*

frank'furt·er, *n.* wiener.

fran'tic, *adj.* wild with emotion. —**fran'ti·cal·ly,** *adv.*

fra·ter'nal, *adj.* brotherly.

fra·ter'ni·ty, *n., pl.* **-ties.** male social organization.

frat'er·nize", *v.i.,* **-ized, -izing.** be in friendly association.

fraud, *n.* **1.** deceit for gain. **2.** impostor.

—fraud'u·lent, *adj.* —fraud'u·lent·ly, *adv.* —fraud'u·lence, *n.*

fraught, *adj.* filled, as with some quality.

fray, *v.t., v.i.* 1. wear thin. —*n.* 2. fight.

fraz'zle, *v.t., v.i.,* -zled, -zling, *n. Informal.* fatigue.

freak, *n.* oddity, esp. of nature.

freck'le, *n.* brownish skin spot.

free, *adj.,* freer, freest, *adv., v.t.,* freed, freeing. *adj.* 1. not bound or controlled. 2. without charge. 3. without obstructions. —*adv.* 4. without charge. —*v.t.* 5. make free. —free'ly, *adv.* —free'dom, *n.*

free'hand'', *adj., adv.* without rulers, compasses, etc.

free'lance'', *n., v.i.,* -lanced. *n.* 1. person paid by the assignment. —*v.i.* 2. work as a freelance.

free'think''er, *n.* person without standard religious beliefs.

freeze, *v.,* froze, frozen, freezing, *n. v.t., v.i.* 1. harden from cold. —*v.i.* 2. suspend all visible motion. —*n.* 3. suspension of change.

freight, *n.* 1. merchandise, etc. in transit. —*v.t.* 2. load with freight.

freight'er, *n.* freight ship.

French horn, coiled wind instrument with a flaring bell.

fre·net'ic, *adj.* frantic.

fren'zy, *n., pl.* -zies. wild excitement. —fren'zied, *adj.*

fre'quen·cy, *n., pl.* -cies. number of occurrences in a given period.

fre·quent, *adj.* (frē'kwənt) 1. occurring often. —*v.t.* (frē kwent') 2. be often present at. —fre'quent·ly, *adv.*

fresh, *adj.* 1. in good, new condition. 2. rested and energetic. 3. inexperienced. —fresh'ly, *adv.* —fresh'ness, *n.* —fresh'en, *v.t., v.i.*

fresh'et, *n.* flooded stream.

fresh'man, *n.* person in his first year, esp. in school or Congress.

fret, *v.,* fretted, fretting, *n. v.i.* 1. be anxious. —*v.t.* 2. fray or gnaw. —*n.* 3. state of anxiety. —*n.* 4. repeated geometrical design. —fret'ful, *adj.* —fret'work'', *n.*

Freud'i·an, *adj.* 1. pertaining to the theories of Sigmund Freud. —*n.* 2. follower of Freud.

fri'a·ble, *adj.* readily crumbled.

fri'ar, *n.* monk.

fric'as·see'', *n., v.t.,* -seed, -seeing. *n.* 1. cut and stewed meat. —*v.t.* 2. make a fricassee of.

fric'tion, *n.* 1. rubbing. 2. resistance to sliding. 3. conflict; antagonism. —fric'tion·al, *adj.*

Fri'day, *n.* sixth day.

friend, *n.* 1. person who likes or is helpful to one. 2. supporter or sympathizer. —friend'less, *adj.* —friend'ly, *adj.* —friend'ship, *n.*

frieze, *n.* horizontal decorative band.

frig'ate, *n.* 1. sailing warship with one gun deck. 2. medium-sized modern warship.

fright, *n.* sudden fear. —fright'en, *v.t.* —fright'ful, *adj.*

frig'id, *adj.* 1. cold. 2. sexually unresponsive. —fri·gid'i·ty, *n.*

frill, *n.* 1. minor ornament. 2. something unnecessary. —fril'ly, *adj.*

fringe, *n., v.t.,* fringed, fringing. *n.* 1. border. 2. edging or parallel loose strands. —*v.t.* 3. supply or constitute a fringe for.

frisk, *v.i.* 1. gambol; frolic. —frisk'y, *adj.*

frit'ter, *v.t.* 1. waste gradually. —*n.* 2. fried cake.

friv'o·lous, *adj.* without proper seriousness. —friv'o·lous·ly, *adv.* —fri·vol'i·ty, *n.*

fro, *adv.* to and fro, away and back again.

frock, *n.* robe; dress.

frog, *n.* leaping amphibian.

fro'lic, *v.i.,* -icked, -icking, *n. v.i.* 1. romp. 2. make merry. —*n.* 3. occasion of frolicking. —frol'ick·er, *n.* —frol'ic·some, *adj.*

from, *prep.* 1. beginning or originating at. 2. with no opportunity or use of. 3. as unlike. 4. because of.

frond, *n.* branchlike leaf.

front, *n.* 1. foremost part or surface. 2. vertical side. 3. pretense; mask. 4. forward battle area. —*v.i.* 5. face. —front'age, *n.* —front'al, *adj.*

fron·tier', *n.* outer limit. —fron'tiers'man, *n.*

fron'tis·piece'', *n.* illustration beginning a book.

frost, *n.* 1. frozen vapor. 2. freezing temperature. —*v.t.* 3. cover with frost. 4. cover with frosting. —frost'y, *adj.*

frost'bite'', *n.* injury to the body from freezing.

frost'ing, *n.* sweetened coating for a cake; icing.

froth, *n., v.i.* foam. —froth'y, *adj.*

fro'ward, *adj.* willful.

frown, *n.* 1. expression of displeasure. —*v.i.* 2. assume such an expression. 3. look with disapproval.

fru'gal, *adj.* 1. thrifty. 2. meager. —fru'gal·ly, *adv.* —fru·gal'i·ty, *n.*

fruit, *n.* 1. juicy, seedbearing growth. 2. reward of endeavor. —fruit'ful, *adj.* —fru·i'tion, *n.* —fruit'less, *adj.*

frump, *n.* dowdy woman. —frump'ish, frump'y, *adj.*

frus'trate'', *v.t.,* -trated, -trating. prevent from succeeding. —frus·tra'tion, *n.*

frus'tum, *n.* lower part of a severed cone.

fry, *v.t.* cook in a grease, directly over direct heat. —fry'er, *n.*

fuch·sia (fyoo'shə), *n.* shrub with pink-to-purple flowers.

fud'dle, *v.t.,* -dled, -dling. stupefy, as with liquor.

fudge, *n.* 1. soft candy made of butter, milk, sugar and flavouring. —*v.i.* 2. cheat.

fu'el, *n., v.,* -eled or -elled, -eling or -elling. *n.* 1. substance for burning. —*v.t.* 2. supply with fuel. —*v.i.* 3. take on fuel.

fu'gi·tive, *n.* 1. person who flees. —*adj.* 2. fleeing. 3. transitory.

ful'crum, *n.* support for a lever.

ful·fill', *v.t.,* -filled, -filling. 1. satisfy. 2. accomplish. —**ful·fill'ment, ful·fil'ment,** *n.*

full, *adj.* 1. completely occupied. 2. complete. 3. broad or ample. —*adv.* 4. completely. 5. directly. —**ful'ly,** *adv.* —**full'ness, ful'ness,** *n.*

full'-scale', *adj.* unreduced.

ful'some, *adj.* annoyingly excessive.

fum'ble, *v.,* -bled, -bling, *n. v.i.* 1. grope. —*v.t.* 2. handle clumsily. —*n.* 3. act or instance of fumbling.

fume, *n., v.,* fumed, fuming. *n.* 1. odor, smoke, etc. —*v.t.* 2. treat with fumes. —*v.i.* 3. show petulance. 4. give off fumes.

fum'i·gate", *v.t.,* -gated, -gating. expose to fumes, as to kill vermin. —**fum"i·ga'tion,** *n.*

fun, *n.* 1. enjoyment. 2. source of enjoyment.

func'tion, *n.* 1. purpose. 2. ceremony. —*v.i.* 3. operate; work. —**func'tion·al,** *adj.*

func"tion·ar"y, *n., pl.* -ries. official.

fund, *n.* 1. money for a purpose 2. funds, ready money.

fun"da·men'tal, *adj.* 1. basic; essential. —*n.* 2. something fundamental. —**fun"da·men'tal·ly,** *adv.*

fun"da·men'tal·ism, *n.* literal belief in a sacred text. Also, **Fun"da·men'tal·ism.** —**fun"da·men'tal·ist,** *n., adj.*

fu'ner·al, *n.* ceremony of farewell to the dead.

fu·ne're·al, *adj.* mournful; solemn.

fun'gus, *n., pl.* -gi or -guses. spore-reproduced plant without chlorophyll. —**fun'gous,** *adj.*

fun'nel, *n.* 1. tapered channel used to help pouring. 2. smokestack.

fun'ny, *adj.,* -nier, -niest. 1. comical. 2. peculiar.

fur, *n.* thick animal hair with its hide. —**fur'ry,** *adj.*

fu'ri·ous, *adj.* 1. wildly angry. 2. wild. —**fu'ri·ous·ly,** *adv.*

furl, *v.t.* bundle up.

fur'long, *n.* eighth of a mile.

fur'lough, *n.* 1. military leave of absence. —*v.t.* 2. grant a furlough to.

fur'nace, *n.* heating chamber.

fur'nish, *v.t.* 1. supply. 2. put furniture in.

fur'nish·ings, *n. pl.* 1. furniture and decorative objects. 2. minor clothing, etc.

fur'ni·ture, *n.* tables, chairs, etc.

fu'ror, *n.* frenzied excitement.

fur'ri·er, *n.* dealer in furs.

fur'row, *n.* 1. groove or wrinkle. —*v.t.* 2. make furrows in.

fur'ther, *adv.* 1. to a greater distance or extent. 2. in addition. —*adj.* 3. additional. 4. farther. —*v.t.* 5. promote. —**fur'ther·ance,** *n.*

fur'ther·more", *adv.* in addition.

fur'thest, *adj.* 1. most distant. —*adv.* 2. to the greatest distance or extent.

fur'tive, *adj.* sneaking. —**fur'tive·ly,** *adv.*

fu'ry, *n., pl.* -ries. 1. extreme rage. 2. violence.

fuse, *n., v.t.,* fused, fusing. *n.* 1. Also, **fuze,** detonating device. 2. device of fusible metal for preventing electrical overloads. —*v.t., v.i.* 3. melt. —**fu'si·ble,** *adj.* —**fu'sion,** *n.*

fu'sil·lade", *n.* discharge of massed guns.

fuss, *n.* 1. unreasonable show of concern. —*v.i.* 2. make a fuss. —**fus'sy,** *adj.*

fu'tile, *adj.* vain; useless. —**fu·til'i·ty,** *n.*

fu'ture, *n.* 1. time to come. 2. what will happen. 3. promise of success.

fuzz, *n.* fine hair or fibres. —**fuz'zy,** *adj.*

G

G, g, *n.* seventh letter of the English alphabet.

gab, *v.i.,* gabbed, gabbing, *n.* chatter.

gab'ble, *v.,* -bled, -bling, *v.i., v.t. n.* babble.

ga'ble, *n.* wall area perpendicular to a roof ridge.

gadg'et, *n.* mechanical contrivance. —**gadg'et·ry,** *n.*

gaff, *n.* 1. spar for the head of a fore-and-aft sail. 2. hook for landing fish.

gaffe, *n.* social blunder.

gag, *n., v.,* gagged, gagging. *n.* 1. device to prevent speech by stopping the mouth. 2. joke. —*v.t.* 3. silence with a gag. —*v.i.* 4. retch.

gai'e·ty, *n., pl.* -ties. 1. quality of being gay. 2. merrymaking.

gai'ly, *adv.* in a gay manner.

gain, *v.t.* 1. acquire. 2. reach. —*v.i.* 3. profit. —*n.* 4. profit. —**gain'ful,** *adj.*

gain"say', *v.t.,* -said, -saying. 1. deny. 2. contract.

gait, *n.* manner of walking or running.

ga'la, *adj.* 1. festive. —*n.* 2. celebration.

ga·lax·y, *n., pl.* -ies. vast cluster of stars. —**ga·lac'tic,** *adj.*

gale, *n.* high wind.

gall, *n.* 1. liquid secreted by the liver. 2. *Informal.* impudence.

gal'lant, *adj.* 1. brave; high-spirited. 2. polite to women. —**gal'lant·ry,** *n.*

gal'lery, *n., pl.* -ies. 1. covered passage. 2. uppermost theater balcony. 3. place for the display of art.

gal'ley, *n., pl.* -leys, 1. rowed ship. 2. ship's kitchen.

gal'lon, *n.* liquid measure of 4 quarts or 128 fluid ounces.

gal'lop, *n.* 1. fastest gait of a horse. —*v.i.* 2. move at a gallop.

gal'lows, *n., pl.* -lowses, -lows. frame for hanging condemned persons.

gall'stone", *n.* stony mass in the gall bladder.

ga·lore', *adv.* in abundance.

ga·losh', *n.* rubber or rubberized boot.

gal·van'ic, *adj.* pertaining to electric currents, esp. from batteries.

gal'va·nize", *v.t.,* -nized, -nizing. 1. apply electricity to. 2. plate with zinc. 3. stimulate.

gam'bit, *n.* opening in chess involving a sacrifice.

gam'ble, *v.,* -bled, -bling, *n. v.i.* 1. stake money on the outcome of a game, race, etc. —*v.t.* 2. stake by gambling. —*n.* 3. risky undertaking. —**gam'bler,** *n.*

gam'bol, *v.i.,* -boled or -bolled, -boling or -bolling, *n.* romp.

game, *n., adj., v.i.,* gamed, gaming. *n.* 1. contest decided by skill or chance. 2. hunted animals or birds. —*adj.* 3. *Informal.* willing to meet a challenge.

game'cock", *n.* rooster used in cockfights.

gam'ut, *n.* 1. musical scale. 2. complete range.

gan'der, *n.* male goose.

gang, *n.* group of workers, criminals, etc. acting or associating together.

gan'gling, *adj.* awkwardly tall. Also, **gan'gly.**

gan'gli·on, *n., pl.* -a, -ons. mass of nerve cells.

gan'grene, *n.* decay of body tissue deprived of blood. —**gan'gre·nous,** *adj.*

gang'ster, *n.* member of a criminal gang.

gang'way", *n.* 1. entrance to a ship. —*interj.* 2. clear the way!

gap, *n.* opening; hiatus.

gape, *v.i.,* gaped, gaping. 1. open the mouth wide. 2. stare with stupefied astonishment. 3. open wide.

ga·rage', *n.* place for keeping automobiles.

garb, *n.* clothing.

gar'bage, *n.* food refuse.

gar'ble, *v.t.,* -bled, -bling. confuse.

gar'den, *n.* 1. area for growing plants. —*v.i.* 2. work in a garden. —**gar'den·er,** *n.*

gar·de'ni·a, *n.* white fragrant flower.

gar·gan'tu·an, *adj.* gigantic.

gar'gle, *v.i.,* -gled, -gling. rinse the throat with liquid and air bubbles.

gar'goyle, *n.* fantastic waterspout.

gar'ish, *adj.* vulgarly showy.

gar'land, *n.* wreath.

gar'lic, *n.* strong-flavored material from a plant bulb.

gar'ment, *n.* article of clothing.

gar'net, *n.* deep-red gemstone.

gar'nish, *v.t.* 1. decorate. —*n.* 2. decoration.

gar"nish·ee', *v.t.,* -eed, -eeing. *Law.* attach (money or property) to settle a bad debt.

gar'ret, *n.* attic.

gar'ri·son, *n.* 1. resident body of troops. —*v.t.* 2. station as a defensive force.

gar·rote', *n., v.t.,* -roted, -roting. *n.* 1. device for strangling. —*v.t.* 2. kill with a garrote.

gar'ru·lous, *adj.* talkative. —**gar·ru'li·ty,** *n.*

gar'ter, *n.* band for holding up a stocking.

gas, *n., v.t.,* gassed, gassing. *n.* 1. expansive fluid. 2. *Informal.* gasoline. —*v.t.* 3. injure or kill with a gas. —**gas'e·ous,** *adj.* —**gas'sy,** *adj.*

gash, *n.* 1. long, deep cut. —*v.t.* 2. make a gash in.

gas'ket, *n.* seal against leakage.

gas'o·hol, *n.* a mixture of gasoline and alcohol.

gas'o·line", *n.* engine fuel derived from petroleum. Also, **gas'o·lene".**

gasp, *v.i.* 1. sudden, short breath. —*n.* 2. act or instance of gasping.

gas'tric, *adj.* pertaining to the stomach.

gas·tron'o·my, *n.* cooking as an art. —**gas"tro·nom'ic, gas"tro·nom'i·cal,** *adj.*

gate, *n.* 1. open-air door. 2. Also **gate'way",** structure holding such a door.

gath'er, *v.t.* 1. bring together. 2. infer. —*v.i.* 1. come together. 4. increase. —**gath'er·ing,** *n.*

gauche (gōsh), *adj.* socially awkward.

gaud'y, *adj.,* -ier, -iest. bright and showy. —**gaud'i·ly,** *adv.*

gauge (gāj), *n., v.t.,* gauged, gauging. *n.* 1. measuring instrument. 2. standard measure. —*v.t.* 3. measure. 4. estimate the amount of. Also, **gage.**

gaunt, *adj.* lean; bony.

gaunt'let, *n.* 1. glove with a flaring cuff. 2. hazardous route.

gauze, *n.* loosely woven cloth. —**gauz'y,** *adj.*

gav′el, *n.* hammerlike noisemaker.

gawk, *v.i.* stare stupidly.

gawk′y, *adj.,* **-ier, -iest.** ungainly.

gay, *adj.* **1.** cheerful. —*n., adj.* **2.** homosexual. —**gay″e·ty, gai″e·ty,** *n.* —**gay′ly,** *adv.*

gaze, *v.i.,* **gazed, gazing.** look steadily.

ga·zette′, *n.* published official record.

gaz″et·teer′, *n.* geographical reference work.

gear, *n.* **1.** Also, **gear′wheel″,** toothed machine wheel. **2.** mechanical assembly. **3.** equipment. —*v.t.* **4.** furnish with gears or a gear.

gee (jē), *interj.* (exclamation of surprise).

gel′a·tin, *n.* jellylike substance from bones or various vegetable substance. Also, **gel′a·tine.** —**ge·lat′i·nous,** *adj.*

geld, *v.t.,* **gelded, gelding.** castrate.

gel′id, *adj.* icy.

gem, *n.* jewel. Also, **gem′stone″.**

gen′der, *n.* classification into masculine, feminine, and neuter.

gene, *n.* entity by which hereditary characteristics are transmitted.

ge″ne·al′o·gy, *n., pl.* **-gies.** study of ancestry. —**ge″ne·a·log′i·cal,** *adj.* —**ge″ne·al′o·gist,** *n.*

gen′er·al, *adj.* **1.** pertaining to a whole group. **2.** unspecific. **3.** common. —*n.* **4.** military officer ranking above a colonel. —**gen′er·al·ly,** *adv.*

gen″er·al′i·ty, *n., pl.* **-ties.** statement supposed to be generally true.

gen′er·al·ize′, *v.i.,* **-ized, -izing.** infer or speak in generalities. —**gen″er·al·i·za′tion,** *n.*

gen′er·ate′, *v.t.,* **-ated, -ating.** bring into being. —**gen′er·a·tive,** *adj.*

gen″er·a′tion, *n.* **1.** group of persons of about the same age. **2.** period of about 30 years. **3.** production, esp. of electricity.

gen′er·a″tor, *n.* machine for producing electricity.

ge·ner′ic, *adj.* pertaining to a group. —**ge·ner′i·cal·ly,** *adv.*

gen′er·ous, *adj.* **1.** giving freely. **2.** ample. —**gen′er·ous·ly,** *adv.* —**gen″er·os′i·ty,** *n.*

ge·net′ics, *n.* study of heredity. —**ge·net′i·cal·ly,** *adv.* —**ge·net′ic,** *adj.* —**ge·net′i·cist,** *n.*

ge′ni·al, *adj.* warmly outgoing. —**ge″ni·al′i·ty,** *n.*

gen′i·tals, *n., pl.* sexual organs. Also, **gen″i·ta′li·a.** —**gen′i·tal,** *adj.*

gen′ius, *n.* **1.** presiding spirit. **2.** great mental power. **3.** person with such powers.

gen′o·cide″, *n.* willful killing of a whole race or nation.

gen·teel′, *adj.* overrefined. —**gen·til′i·ty** *n.*

gen′tile, *n.* **1.** non-Jew. —*adj.* **2.** non-Jewish.

gen′tle, *adj.* mild in manner or effect. —**gen′tly,** *adv.*

gen′tle·man, *n.* **1.** Also, *fem.,* **gen′tle·wom″an,** man of the upper class. **2.** well-mannered man.

gen′try, *n.* persons of the upper class.

gen′u·flect″, *v.i.* bend the knee in homage. —**gen″u·flec′tion,** *n.*

gen′u·ine, *adj.* **1.** true; real. **2.** sincere. —**gen′u·ine·ly,** *adv.* —**gen′u·ine·ness,** *n.*

ge′nus, *n., pl.* **genera, genuses. 1.** type. **2.** *Biology.* distinctive group of plant or animal species.

ge·og′ra·phy, *n., pl.* **-phies. 1.** study of the earth or its features. **2.** terrain. —**ge″o·graph′i·cal, ge″o·graph′ic,** *adj.* —**ge·og′ra·pher,** *n.*

ge·ol′o·gy, *n.* study of the earth's crust. —**ge″o·log′ic, ge″o·log′i·cal,** *adj.*

ge·om′e·try, *n., pl.* **-tries.** study of points, lines, planes, and solids. —**ge″o·met′ric, ge″o·met′ri·cal,** *adj.*

ge″o·phys′ics, *n.* study of the effects of climate, etc. on the earth.

ger′i·at′rics, *n.* branch of medicine dealing with old age. —**ger″i·at′ric,** *adj.*

germ, *n.* **1.** disease-causing organism. **2.** origin.

ger·mane′, *adj.* relevant.

ger′mi·cide″, *n.* destroyer of germs. —**ger″mi·ci′dal,** *adj.*

ger′mi·nate″, *v.,* **-nated, -nating.** *v.i., v.t.* sprout. —**ger″mi·na′tion** *n.*

ges′tate, *v.t.,* **-tated, -tating.** bear in the uterus. —**ges·ta′tion,** *n.*

ges·tic′u·late″, *v.i.,* **-lated, -lating.** make gestures. —**ges·tic·u·la′tion,** *n.*

ges′ture, *v.i.,* **-tured, -turing,** *n. v.i.* **1.** move the hands, arms, etc. as a signal. —*n.* **2.** act or instance of gesturing. **3.** act intended to impress others.

get, *v.,* **got, gotten, getting.** *v.t.* **1.** take or receive. **2.** cause to be or do. —*v.i.* **3.** become. **4.** go or arrive.

gey′ser, *n.* natural eruption of water or steam.

ghast′ly, *adj.,* **-lier, -liest. 1.** horrible. **2.** ghostlike. —**ghast′li·ness,** *n.*

gher′kin, *n.* small pickle.

ghet′to, *n., pl.* **-tos, -toes.** neighborhood populated by particular minority ethnic group.

ghost, *n.* spirit from the dead. —**ghost′ly,** *adj.*

ghoul, *n.* **1.** robber of the dead. **2.** person morbidly fascinated by disasters. —**ghoul′ish,** *adj.*

GI, *n., pl.* **GI′s, GIs,** *adj. n.* enlisted man. —*adj.* **2.** government issue.

gi′ant, *n.* **1.** greatly oversized creature or thing. —*adj.* **2.** gigantic. Also, *fem.,* **gi′ant·ess.**

gib′ber (jib′ər), *v.i.* make incoherent utterances. —**gib′ber·ish,** *n.*

gibe. (jīb), *v.i.,* **gibed, gibing,** *n.* jeer.

gib·let (jib'lit), *n.* internal organ of fowl.

gid'dy, *adj.*, **-dier, -diest. 1.** dizzy. **2.** frivolous.

gift, *n.* **1.** something given. **2.** natural ability.

gift'ed, *adj.* intelligent or talented.

gi·gan'tic, *adj.* huge.

gig'gle, *v.i.*, **-gled, -gling**, *n.* *v.i.* **1.** laugh in a quick, high-pitched way. —*n.* **2.** act or instance of giggling.

gild, *v.t.*, **gilded** or **gilt, gilding.** cover with gold leaf. —**gilt**, *adj.*

gill, *n.* **1.** (jil) quarter of a pint; 4 fluid ounces. **2.** (gill) breathing apparatus of a fish, etc.

gim·crack (jim'krak''), *adj.* showy and cheap.

gim'let, *n.* small boring tool.

gim'mick, *n. Informal.* gadget.

gin, *n.*, *v.t.*, **ginned, ginning.** *n.* **1.** distilled grain liquor. **2.** cotton seed remover. —*v.t.* **3.** process with a cotton gin.

gin'ger, *n.* tropical spice. —**gin'ger·y**, *adj.*

gin'ger·ly, *adj.* **1.** cautious. —*adv.* **2.** cautiously.

ging'ham, *n.* checked or striped cotton.

gi·raffe', *n.* long-necked, long-legged African animal.

gird, *v.t.*, **girded** or **girt, girding.** surround, as with a belt.

gird'er, *n.* major structural beam.

gir'dle, *n.*, *v.t.*, **-dled, -dling**. *n.* **1.** woman's undergarment. **2.** belt. —*v.t.* **3.** encircle.

girl, *n.* young female. —**girl'hood''**, *n.* —**girl'ish**, *adj.*

girth, *n.* circumference.

gist (jist), *n.* basic meaning or content.

give, *v.*, **gave, given, giving**, *n.* *v.t.* **1.** transfer. **2.** make a present of. **3.** supply or afford. **4.** concede. —*v.i.* **5.** yield, as to force. —*n.* **6.** compressibility. —**giv'er**, *n.*

giv'en, *adj.* **1.** specified. **2.** granted. **3.** habituated.

gla'cial, *adj.* icy.

gla'cier, *n.* broad, moving mass of ice.

glad, *adj.*, **gladder, gladdest. 1.** happy. **2.** quite willing. —**glad'ly**, *adv.* —**glad'ness**, *n.* —**glad'den**, *v.t.*, *v.i.*

glade, *n.* open space in a forest.

glad'i·a''tor, *n.* swordsman in ancient Roman contests.

glad''i·o'lus, *n.*, *pl.* **-luses, -li.** flower with spikes of funnel-shaped blossoms. Also, **glad''i·o'la.**

glam'or, *n.* mysterious charm. Also, **glam'our.** —**glam'or·ous**, *adj.* —**glam'or·ize**, *v.t.*

glance, *v.t.*, **glanced, glancing**, *n.*, *v.i.* **1.** look briefly. **2.** ricochet. —*n.* **3.** act or instance of glancing.

gland, *n.* bodily organ that extracts and

processes elements in the blood. —**glan'du·lar**, *adj.*

glare, *n.*, *v.i.*, **glared, glaring**. *n.* **1.** dazzling brightness. **2.** furious look. —*v.i.* **3.** cast a glare.

glar'ing, *adj.* **1.** dazzlingly bright. **2.** ostentatious; loud. **3.** flagrant.

glass, *n.* **1.** substance of fused silicates. **2.** object of this substance. **3.** object with a lens or lenses. **4. glasses,** lenses in a frame, used to aid vision. —**glass'ful**, *n.* —**glas'sy**, *adj.*

glaze, *v.t.*, **glazed, glazing**, *n.* *v.t.* **1.** fit with glass, as a window. **2.** put a glassy coating on. —*v.i.* **3.** become glassy. —*n.* **4.** glassy coating.

gla'zier, *n.* person who glazes windows.

gleam, *n.* **1.** beam of light. —*v.i.* **2.** emit a gleam.

glean, *adj.* gather.

glee, *n.* joy. —**glee'ful**, *adj.*

glen, *n.* isolated, small valley.

glib, *adj.*, **glibber, glibbest.** unconvincingly ready with explanations. —**glib'ly**, *adv.* —**glib'ness**, *n.*

glide, *v.*, **glided, gliding**, *n.* *v.i.*, *v.t.* **1.** slider —*n.* **2.** act or instance of gliding.

glid'er, *n.* unpowered aircraft.

glim'mer, *n.*, *v.i.* gleam.

glimpse, *v.t.*, **glimpsed, glimpsing**, *n.* *v.t.* **1.** see briefly or in part. —*n.* **2.** act or instance of glimpsing.

glint, *v.i.*, *n.* gleam or glitter.

glis'ten, *v.i.* reflect with a dull shine.

glitch, *n.* (computers) a problem or error in a program.

glit'ter, *v.i.* **1.** shine or reflect brightly. —*n.* **2.** act or instance of glittering.

gloam'ing, *n.* evening twilight.

gloat, *v.i.* experience proud or malicious pleasure.

globe, *n.* **1.** the earth. **2.** model of the earth. **3.** spherical object. —**glob'al**, *adj.*

glob'ule, *n.* tiny ball or drop. —**glob'u·lar**, *adj.*

gloom, *n.* **1.** darkness. **2.** sadness or dreariness. —**gloom'y**, *adj.*

glo''ri·fy', *v.t.*, **-fied, -fying. 1.** give glory to. **2.** exaggerate the importance or worth of. —**glo''ri·fi·ca'tion**, *n.*

glo'ry, *n.*, *pl.* **-ries**, *v.i.*, **-ried, -rying**. *n.* **1.** high honor. **2.** splendor or splendid feature. —*v.i.* **3.** take pride. —**glo'ri·ous**, *adj.*

gloss, *n.* **1.** sheen. **2.** explanation. —**glos'sy**, *adj.*

glos'sa·ry, *n.*, *pl.* **-ries.** list of terms with definitions.

glove, *n.* garment for the hand.

glow, *v.i.* **1.** give off soft light or color. —*n.* **2.** act or instance of glowing.

glow'er, *v.i.* stare threateningly.

glu'cose, *n.* sugar in fruit and honey.

glue, *n. v.t.*, **glued, gluing**. *n.* **1.** adhesive

substance. —*v.t.* 2. fasten with glue.

glum, *adj.*, **glummer, glummest.** gloomy; moody. —**glum'ly**, *adv.*

glut, *v.*, **glutted, glutting**, *n.*, *v.i.* 1. eat to excess. —*v.t.* 2. satiate. 3. oversupply. —*n.* 4. act or instance of glutting.

glu'ti·nous, *adj.* sticky.

glut'ton, *n.* person who overeats. —**glut'ton·ous**, *adj.* —**glut'ton·y**, *n.*

gly'cer·in, *n.* liquid derived from fats and oils. Also, **gly'cer·ine.**

gnarled, *adj.* twisted or knotted, like a tree trunk.

gnash, *v.t.* grind together, as the teeth, with anger or frustration.

gnat, *n.* small, stinging insect.

gnaw, *v.t.*, *v.i.* bite away gradually.

gnome, *n.* dwarf who guards treasure. —**gnom'ish**, *adj.*

go, *v.i.*, **went, going**, *n.*, *pl.* **goes.** *v.i.* 1. leave. 2. operate. 3. belong. 4. become.

goad, *n.*, *v.t.* prod.

goal, *n.* 1. object to be reached or attained. 2. *Sports.* area to be defended.

goat, *n.* horned, cud-chewing mammal.

goat·ee', *n.* small, pointed beard.

gob'ble, *v.*, **-bled, -bling**, *n.* *v.t.* 1. eat greedily. —*v.i.* 2. make turkeylike sounds. —*n.* 3. sound of a turkey.

gob'ble·dy·gook'', *n. Informal.* jargon.

go'-be·tween'', *n.* arranger of bargains between others.

gob'let, *n.* stemmed, deep-bowled drinking vessel.

gob'lin, *n.* evil supernatural being.

god, *n.* 1. one of the supreme beings. 2. **God**, the Supreme Being. Also, *fem.*, **god'dess.** —**god'hood''**, *n.* —**god'less**, *adj.*

god'child'', *n.* child sponsored in religion by a godparent.

god'head'', *n.* 1. godhood. 2. **the Godhead**, God.

god'ly, *adj.*, **-lier, -liest.** devout. —**god'li·ness**, *n.*

god'par''ent, *n.* sponsor of a godchild. Also, *masc.*, **god'fa''ther**, *fem.*, **god'mother.**

god'send'', *n.* piece of good luck.

gog'gle, *v.i.*, **-gled, -gling**, *n.* *v.i.* 1. stare with eyes bulging. —*n.* 2. **goggles**, protective glasses.

go'ing, *adj.* 1. current. 2. operative. —*n.* 3. departure. 4. conditions.

goi'ter, *n.* enlargement of the thyroid gland. Also, **goi'tre.**

gold, *n.* soft, yellow, precious metallic element. —**gold'en**, *adj.*

gold'en·rod'', *n.* plant with tiny yellow flowers.

golden rule, do unto others as you would have others do unto you.

gold'fish'', *n.* small yellow-orange fish.

golf, *n.* outdoor game played with balls

knocked from ground level with clubs. —**golf'er**, *n.*

go'nad, *n.* animal reproductive organ.

gon'do·la, *n.* 1. one-oared Venetian boat. 2. low-sided railroad freight car. 3. airship cabin. —**gon''do·lier'**, *n.*

gong, *n.* thin brass disk beaten to produce sound.

gon''or·rhe'a, *n.* a venereal disease.

good, *adj.*, **better, best**, *n.* *adj.* 1. right; proper. 2. kind. 3. beneficial. —*n.* 5. good purpose or result. 6. **goods**, valuable objects or material.

good''bye', *interj.* 1. (departing salutation). —*n.* 2. saying of goodbye. Also, **good''by'.**

Good Friday, Friday before Easter.

good'ly, *adj.*, **-lier, -liest.** 1. considerable in amount. 2. good. 3. good-looking.

goof, *Informal.* *n.* 1. blunderer. 2. blunder. —**goof'y**, *adj.*

goose, *n.*, *pl.* **geese.** web-footed duck-like bird.

go'pher, *n.* 1. burrowing rodent. 2. prairie squirrel.

gore, *n.*, *v.t.*, **gored, goring**. *n.* 1. blood. 2. triangular segment. —*v.t.* 3. pierce, as with a horn. —**gor'y**, *adj.*

gorge, *n.*, *v.*, **gorged, gorging**. *n.* 1. narrow canyon. 2. gullet. —*v.t.* 3. glut. —*v.i.* 4. eat greedily.

gor'geous, *adj.* dazzlingly attractive.

go·ril'la, *n.* powerful manlike African ape.

Gos'pel, *n.* 1. teachings of Jesus and the Apostles.

gos'sa·mer, *adj.* 1. light and frail. —*n.* 2. cobweb.

gos'sip, *n.* 1. rumors and conjectures about others. 2. person who originates or spreads these. —*v.i.* 3. engage in gossip. —**gos'sip·y**, *adj.*

gouge, *n.*, *v.t.*, **gouged, gouging**. *n.* 1. chisel for cutting grooves. —*v.t.* 2. cut out with a scooping motion.

gou'lash, *n.* stew seasoned with paprika.

gourd, *n.* decorative fruit of the squash or melon family.

gour·mand (gŏor'mənd), *n.* heavy eater and drinker.

gour·met (gŏor·mā') *n.* connoisseur of food and drink.

gout, *n.* illness causing pain in the joints. —**gout'y**, *adj.*

gov'ern, *v.t.* 1. have authority over. 2. guide. 3. determine.

gov'ern·ment, *n.* 1. system for running a country. 2. group in political control. —**gov''ern·men'tal**, *adj.*

gov'er·nor, *n.* 1. supreme local official. 2. device for controlling machinery speed. —**gov'er·nor·ship**, *n.*

gown, *n.* long outer garment.

grab, *v.t.*, *v.i.*, **grabbed, grabbing**, *n.* snatch.

grace, *n., v.t.,* **graced, gracing.** *n.* **1.** beauty of form, movement or manner. **2.** kindness or favor. **3.** prayer before a meal. —*v.t.* **4.** add grace to, as by being present. —**grace′ful,** *adj.* —**grace′less,** *adj.*

gra′cious, *adj.* **1.** charming in manner **2.** kind. **3.** discriminatingly luxurious.

grack′le, *n.* crowlike blackbird.

gra·da′tion, *n.* succession of increasing or decreasing amounts, etc.

grade, *n., v.t.,* **graded, grading.** *n.* **1.** step in a progressive series. **2.** Also, **gra′di·ent,** slope. —*v.t.* **3.** assign a grade to. **4.** give a level to, as a road.

grad′u·al, *adj.* in small amounts. —**grad′u·al·ly,** *adv.*

grad·u·ate, *v.,* **-ated, -ating,** *n., adj. v.t.* (grad′yōō āt″) **1.** leave after satisfying academic requirements. **2.** certify as having satisfied requirements. **3.** divide into grades. —*n.* (grad′yōō ət) **4.** person who has graduated. —*adj.* **5.** post-baccalaureate. —**grad″u·a′tion,** *n.*

graf·fi·to (grafe′tō), *n., pl.* **-ti.** writing or drawing by a passer-by.

graft, *n.* **1.** transplant of organic material. **2.** dishonest use of public funds. —*v.t.* **3.** transplant. **4.** obtain by graft.

grain, *n.* **1.** hard seed, as of wheat. **2.** hard particle. **3.** pattern of fiber, as in wood.

gram, *n.* metric unit of weight, about 1/28 of an ounce. Also, **gramme.**

gram′mar, *n.* forms and arrangement of words. —**gram·mat′i·cal,** *adj.*

gran′a·ry, *n., pl.* **-ries.** place for storing grain.

grand, *adj.* **1.** impressive. **2.** illustrious. —**grand′ly,** *adv.* —**gran′deur,** *n.*

grand′child″, *n.* child of a son or daughter. Also, *masc.,* **grand′son″,** *fem.,* **grand′daugh″ter.**

gran·dil′o·quent, *adj.* pretentious in speech. —**gran·dil′o·quence,** *n.*

gran′di·ose″, *adj.* **1.** full of grandeur. **2.** pompous.

grand′par″ent, *n.* parent of a parent. Also, *masc.,* **grand′fa″ther,** *fem.,* **grand′moth″er.**

grand′stand″, *n.* stand for spectators at sporting events.

gran′ite, *n.* grainy igneous rock.

grant, *v.t.* **1.** give. **2.** admit. —*n.* **3.** something granted.

gran′u·late″, *v.t.,* **-lated, -lating.** form as or in granules.

gran′ule, *n.* small particle —**gran′u·lar,** *adj.*

grape, *n.* small juicy fruit.

grape′fruit″, *n.* large, sharp-tasting citrus fruit.

graph, *n.* two-dimensional visual representation of interrelated data.

graph′ic, *adj.* **1.** pertaining to two-dimensional visual art. **2.** vividly realistic.

graph′ite, *n.* soft carbon used as a writing material or lubricant.

grap′ple, *v.,* **-pled, -pling.** *v.i.* **1.** wrestle; struggle. —*v.t.* **2.** grasp and hold.

grasp, *v.t.* **1.** take hold of with the hand; clutch. **2.** comprehend. —*v.i.* **3.** make clutching motions. —*n.* **4.** act or instance of grasping. **5.** ability to grasp.

grasp′ing, *adj.* avaricious.

grass, *n.* **1.** narrow-leafed green plant with seedlike fruit. —**grass′sy,** *adj.*

grass′hop″per, *n.* jumping, plant-eating insect.

grate, *v.,* **grated, grating,** *n. v.t.* **1.** scrape into particles. **2.** grind. —*v.i.* **3.** grind or rasp. **4.** be irritating. —*n.* **5.** Also, **grat′ing,** framework of metal, etc. bars. —**grat′er,** *n.*

grate′ful, *adj.* **1.** appreciative of favors. **2.** welcome.

grat′i·fy″, *v.t.,* **-fied, -fying.** be pleasing to. —**grat″i·fi·ca′tion,** *n.*

gra′tis, *adj.* free of charge.

grat′i·tude″, *n.* appreciation for favors.

gra·tu′i·tous, *adj.* **1.** gratis. **2.** uncalled-for.

gra·tu′i·ty, *n., pl.* **-ties.** gift, esp. a tip.

grave, *adj.* **1.** solemn. **2.** important; serious. —*n.* **2.** place of burial.

grav′el, *n.* mixture of stone fragments. —**grav′el·ly,** *adj.*

grav′i·tate″, *v.i.,* **-tated, -tating. 1.** move by gravity. **2.** move or tend naturally. —**grav″i·ta′tion,** *n.* —**grav″i·ta′tion·al,** *adj.*

grav′i·ty, *n.* **1.** seriousness. **2.** pull toward the center of the earth.

gra′vy, *n., pl.* **-ies.** meat juice, or a sauce from this.

gray, *adj.* **1.** mixed black and white. **2.** dreary.

gray matter, **1.** brain tissue. **2.** *Informal.* intelligence.

graze, *v.,* **grazed, grazing.** *v.t. v.i.* **1.** scrape in passing. —*v.i.* **2.** feed on grasses.

grease, *n., v.t.,* **greased, greasing.** *n.* (grēs) **1.** thick, fatty or oily substance. —*v.t.* (grēz) **2.** coat or lubricate with grease. —**greas′y,** *adj.*

great, *adj.* **1.** large. **2.** eminent. —**great′ly,** *adv.*

greed, *n.* excessive passion for money, food, etc. —**greed′y,** *adj.*

green, *n.* **1.** color of leaves and plants. **2.** **greens,** leafy vegetables. —*adj.* **3.** of the color green. **4.** unripened or unprocessed.

green′er·y, *n.* plant life.

green′house″, *n.* glazed building for growing plants.

greet, *v.t.* **1.** acknowledge meeting. **2.** receive in a specified way. —**greet′ing,** *n.*

gre·gar'i·ous, *adj.* associating with others of one's kind.

gre·nade', *n.* small hand bomb.

gren'a·dine'', *n.* pomegranate syrup.

grey, *adj.* gray.

grey'hound'', *n.* fast, slender hound.

grid, *n.* system of crisscrossed elements.

grid'dle, *n.* pan for cooking pancakes, etc.

grid'iron'', *n.* **1.** broiling frame. **2.** football field.

grid'lock, *n.* severe, urban traffic jam.

grief, *n.* **1.** great unhappiness. **2.** ruin; failure.

griev'ance, *n.* **1.** cause for complaint. **2.** complaint.

grieve, *v.,* **grieved, grieving.** *v.i.* **1.** suffer grief. —*v.t.* **2.** cause grief to.

griev'ous, *adj.* **1.** seriously injurious. **2.** being in grief.

grill, *n.* **1.** gridiron. **2.** broiled dish. —*v.t.* **3.** broil. **4.** *Informal.* question severely.

grille, *n.* open screen; grating. —**grille'work'',** *n.*

grim, *adj.,* **grimmer, grimmest. 1.** harsh. **2.** menacing. —**grim'ly** *adv.*

gri'mace, *n., v.i.,* **-maced, -macing.** *n.* **1.** smirk, esp. of displeasure. —*v.i.* **2.** give such a smirk.

grime, *n.* clinging dirt. —**grim'y** *adj.*

grin, *n., v.i.,* **grinned, grinning.** *n.* **1.** broad, toothy smile. —*v.i.* **2.** give such a smile.

grind, *v.t.,* **ground, grinding. 1.** wear down with pressure or friction. **2.** turn the crank of. —**grind'er,** *n.*

grip, *v.t.,* **gripped, gripping,** *n.* *v.t.* **1.** grasp firmly. —*n.* **2.** firm grasp. **3.** handle. **4.** small piece of luggage.

gripe, *v.,* **griped, griping,** *n.* *v.t.* **1.** produce pain in the bowels. —*v.i.* **2.** *Informal.* complain. —*n.* **3.** pain in the bowels. **4.** *Informal.* complaint.

gris'ly, *adj.,* **-lier, -liest.** horrible.

grist, *n.* grain for grinding. —**grist'mill'',** *n.*

gris'tle, *n.* cartilage. —**gris'tly,** *adv.*

grit, *n., v.t.,* **gritted, gritting.** *n.* **1.** rough, hard particles. **2.** fortitude. —*v.t.* **3.** grind together, as the teeth. —**grit'ty,** *adj.*

grits, *n. pl.* coarsely ground grain.

griz'zled, *adj.* with gray hair.

griz'zly, *adj.,* **-zlier, -zliest,** *n. adj.* **1.** grayish. —*n.* **2.** Also, **grizzly bear,** large, ferocious American bear.

groan, *n.* **1.** deep utterance, as of pain. —*v.i.* **2.** give such an utterance.

gro'cer, *n.* food merchant. —**gro'cer·y,** *n.*

grog'gy, *adj.,* **-gier, -giest.** befuddled.

groin, *n.* junction of the abdomen and thighs.

grom'met, *n.* eyelet.

groom, *n.* **1.** man at his wedding. **2.** tender of horses. —*v.t.* **3.** comb, etc. to make tidy.

groove, *n., v.t.,* **grooved, grooving.** *n.* **1.** long, shallow depression. —*v.t.* **2.** make a groove in.

grope, *v.i.,* **groped, groping.** feel for something blindly.

gross, *adj.* **1.** coarse. **2.** flagrant. **3.** before deductions. —*n.* **4.** *pl.* **gross,** quantity of 144.

gro·tesque', *adj.* fantastically distorted.

grot'to, *n., pl.* **-tos, -toes.** cave.

grouch, *v.i.* **1.** sulk. —*n.* **2.** sulky mood. **3.** person who sulks. —**grouch'y,** *adj.*

ground, *n.* **1.** solid surface of the earth. **2.** earth. **3.** grounds, **a.** basis **b.** land of an estate or institution. **c.** dregs of coffee, etc. —*v.t.* **4.** instruct in rudiments.

ground'hog'', *n.* woodchuck.

ground'less, *adj.* without reason.

ground'work'', *n.* basic or preparatory work.

group, *n.* **1.** number of persons or things considered together. *v.t., v.i.* **2.** form into a group or groups.

grouse, *n., pl.* **grouse,** *v.i.,* **groused, grousing.** *n.* **1.** plump game bird. —*v.i.* **2.** complain.

grove, *n.* cluster of trees.

grov'el, *v.i.,* **-eled, -eling. 1.** crouch low or crawl. **2.** behave servilely.

grow, *v.,* **grew, grown, growing.** *v.i.* **1.** become. **2.** develop. **3.** cause to live, as plants. —**grow'er,** *n.* —**growth,** *n.*

growl, *n.* **1.** low, rumbling vocal noise. —*v.i.* **2.** make such a noise.

grown'-up', *adj., n.* adult.

grub, *v.,* **grubbed, grubbing,** *n. v.i., v.t.* **1.** dig. —*n.* **2.** beetle larva. **3.** drudge. **4.** *Informal.* food.

grub'by, *adj.,* **-bier, -biest.** nastily dirty.

grudge, *n., v.t.,* **grudged, grudging.** *n.* **1.** long-held resentment. —*v.t.* **2.** begrudge. —**grudg'ing·ly,** *adv.*

gru'el·ing, *adj.* exhausting; very tiring.

grue'some, *adj.* horrifying or loathsome.

gruff, *adj.* curt.

grum'ble, *v.i.,* **-bled, -bling,** complain in a suppressed manner.

grum'py, *adj.,* **-pier, -piest.** surly.

grunt, *n.* **1.** throaty sound caused by exertion, etc. —*v.i.* **2.** utter such a sound.

guar''an·tee', *n., v.t.,* **-teed, -teeing.** *n.* **1.** firm assurance. **2.** promise to make good if necessary. —*v.t.* **3.** assure with a guarantee. Also, **guar'an·ty.** —**guar'an·tor''.**

guard, *v.t., v.i.* **1.** watch, esp. in order to protect or confine. —*n.* **2.** person or group that guards. **3.** protection. **4.** protective device.

guard'ed, *adj.* cautious.

guard'i·an, *n.* **1.** person who guards. **2.**

person responsible for a minor or incompetent. —**guard'ian·ship''**, n.

gu''ber·na·to'ri·al, adj. pertaining to governors.

guer·ril'la, n. irregular soldier using surprise tactics.

guess, v.t. 1. form an opinion about without knowing. —n. 2. act or instance of guessing. —**guess'work''**, n.

guest, n. 1. enjoyer of hospitality. 2. customer of a hotel, etc.

guf·faw', n. 1. raucous laugh. —v.i. 2. emit such a laugh.

guide, v.t., guided, guiding, n. v.t. 1. tell how to proceed. —n. 2. person or thing that guides. —**guid'ance**, n.

guile, n. unscrupulous cunning.

guilt, n. 1. responsibility for a wrong action. 2. shame. —**guilt'y**, adj.

guin'ea pig, 1. small, fat rodent. 2. subject of an experiment.

guise, n. semblance.

gui·tar', n. six-stringed plucked instrument. —**gui·tar'ist**, n.

gulch, n. deep narrow ravine.

gulf, n. 1. ocean area partly surrounded by land. 2. wide deep void.

gull, n. light-colored soaring water bird.

gul'let, n. throat.

gul'li·ble, adj. credulous. —**gul''li·bil'i·ty**, n.

gul'ly, n., pl. -lies. narrow ravine.

gulp, v.t., v.i. 1. swallow hastily. —n. 2. act or instance of gulping.

gum, n., v.t., gummed, gumming. n. 1. sticky, semisolid substance. 2. area of flesh surrounding teeth. —v.t. 3. stick with gum.

gump'tion, n. enterprise.

gun, n., v., gunned, gunning. n. 1. weapon shooting a missile by means of an explosive charge. —v.t., v.i. 2. hunt with a gun. —**gun'ner·y**, n.

gunk, n. Informal. viscous substance.

gun'ny, n. coarse cloth of jute or hemp.

gun'pow''der, n. explosive used in guns.

gun·wale (gun'l), n. upper edge of a ship's side.

gur'gle, v.i., -gled, -gling, n. v.i. 1. emit a bubbling sound in flowing. —n. 2. such a sound.

gu'ru, n. Hindu spiritual teacher.

gush, v.i. 1. flow out abundantly. 2. express oneself effusively. —n. 3. act or instance of gushing. —**gush'y**, adj.

gus'set, n. triangular reinforcement.

gust, n. 1. strong puff of air. 2. sudden outburst. —**gus'ty**, adj.

gus'ta·to''ry, adj. pertaining to the sense of taste.

gus'to, n. great enjoyment or vigor.

gut, n., v.t., gutted, gutting. n. 1. intestine. 2. guts, Informal. courage. —v.t. 3. destroy the inside of.

gut'ter, n. 1. channel for rain water. 2.

realm of sordidness. —v.t. 3. splutter before being extinguished, as a candle.

gut'tur·al, adj. pertaining to or produced in the throat.

guy, n. 1. Informal. male person. 2. Also, guy'wire'', steadying wire.

guz'zle, v.i., v.t., -zled, -zling. drink greedily.

gym·na'si·um, n., pl. -ums, -a. place for physical exercise. Also, Informal, gym.

gym·nas'tics, n. pl. physical exercises. —**gym'nast**, n. —**gym·nas'tic**, adj.

gy''ne·col'o·gy, n. branch of medicine concerned with women's diseases. —**gy''ne·col'o·gist**, n.

gyp, n., v.t., gypped, gypping. Informal. swindle.

gyp'sum, n. sulfate of calcium, used to make plaster of Paris.

gy·rate', v.i., -rated, -rating. whirl. —**gy·ra'tion** n.

gy'ro·scope'', n. object maintaining its position by the inertia of a rapidly turned wheel. —**gy''ro·scop'ic**, adj.

H

H, h, n. eighth letter of the English alphabet.

hab'it, n. 1. custom, esp. one hard to depart from. 2. distinctive costume. —**ha·bit'u·al**, adj. —**ha·bit'u·ate''**, v.t.

hab'it·a·ble, adj. able to be lived in.

hab'i·tat'', n. usual area of habitation.

hab''i·ta'tion, n. home.

hack, v.i. v.t. 1. chop roughly. —v.i. 2. cough hoarsely. —n. 3. artistic drudge.

hack''er, n. a computer enthusiast.

hack'saw'', n. frame-mounted metal-cutting saw.

had'dock, n., pl. -dock, -docks. Atlantic codlike fish.

Ha'des, n. hell. Also, ha'des.

haft, n. knife or ax handle.

hag, n. ugly old woman.

hag'gard, adj. weary-looking.

hag'gle, v.i., -gled, -gling. dispute over a price.

hail, v.t. 1. greet loudly. 2. shout to. 3. welcome as desirable. 4. shower heavily. —n. 5. frozen rain in small balls. —**hail'stone''**, n.

hair, n. 1. slender growth from the skin. 2. these growths collectively. —**hair'y**, adj. —**hair'i·ness**, n.

hair'rais''ing, adj. terrifying.

hair'split''ting, *n.* making of trivial distinctions.

hal'cy''on, *adj.* idyllic.

hale, *adj., v.t.,* **haled, haling.** *adj.* **1.** full of health and vigor. —*v.t.* **2.** summon forcibly.

half, *n., pl.* **halves,** *adj., adv. n.* **1.** one of two equal divisions. —*adj.* **2.** being a half. —*adv.* **3.** as far as a half.

half'-breed'', *n.* child of parents from different races.

half'-heart'ed, *adj.* without enthusiasm or determination. —**half'-heart'ed·ly,** *adv.*

half'way', *adj., adv.* **1.** at or to a midpoint. **2.** to a partial extent.

half'wit'', *n.* person of subnormal intelligence. —**half'-wit'ted,** *adj.*

hal'i·but, *n., pl.* **-but, -buts.** northern saltwater flatfish.

hal''i·to'sis, *n.* bad breath.

hall, *n.* **1.** large room, as for meetings. **2.** Also, **hall'way'',** corridor or vestibule.

hal''le·lu'jah, *interj.* praise the Lord! Also, **hal''le·lu'iah.**

hal'low, *v.t.* sanctify.

Hal''low·een', *n.* eve of All Saints' Day, celebrated October 31. Also, **Hal''low·e'en'.**

hal·lu''ci·na'tion, *n.* deluded perceptions of a nonexistent sight, sound, etc. —**hal·lu'ci·nate'',** *v.i.* —**hal·lu'ci·na·to''ry,** *adj.*

ha'lo, *n., pl.* **-los, -loes.** ring of light, as around the portrayed head of a holy person.

halt, *v.t., v.i., n.* stop.

hal'ter, *n.* line for securing an animal.

halve, *v.t.,* **halved, halving. 1.** divide into halves. **2.** reduce by half.

ham, *n.* upper part of a hog's hind leg.

ham'bur''ger, *n.* sandwich of ground beef in a bun. Also, **ham'burg.**

ham'let, *n.* small village.

ham'mer, *n.* **1.** device for beating or driving with blows. —*v.t., v.i.* **2.** strike with repeated blows.

ham'mock, *n.* flexible bed suspended at the ends.

ham'per, *v.t.* **1.** encumber. —*n.* **2.** covered basket.

hand, *n.* **1.** extremity of the arm. **2.** active part. **3.** hired worker. **4.** handwriting. **5.** side or direction. —*v.t.* **6.** give with the hand. —**hand'ful,** *n.*

hand'ball'', *n.* game with a thrown rubber ball.

hand'book'', *n.* manual.

hand'clasp'', *n.* handshake.

hand'gun'', *n.* pistol.

hand'i·cap'', *n., v.t.,* **-capped, -capping.** *n.* **1.** hindrance. —*v.t.* **2.** hinder.

hand'i·work'', *n.* **1.** work done by hand. **2.** work done personally.

hand'ker·chief'', *n.* small wiping cloth.

han'dle, *n., v.t.,* **-dled, -dling.** *n.* **1.** something to be grasped. —*v.t.* **2.** grasp, as in order to wield. **3.** manage or dominate. **4.** sell.

hand'out'', *n.* **1.** charitable gift. **2.** news release.

hand'-pick'', *v.t.* **1.** pick by hand. **2.** choose carefully and individually.

hand'shake'', *n.* friendly gripping and shaking of another's hand.

hand'some'', *adj.* **1.** good-looking. **2.** generous.

hands''-on'', *adj.* practical; making actual use of, as *hands-on training.*

hand'writ'ing, *n.* freehand writing. —**hand'writ''ten,** *adj.*

hand'y, *adj.,* **-ier, -iest.** convenient. —**hand'i·ly,** *adv.* —**hand'i·ness,** *n.*

hand'y·man, *n.* man who does odd jobs.

hang, *v.,* **hung** or (for 2) **hanged, hanged,** *n. v.t.* **1.** hold up from above. **2.** kill by suspending from a rope around the neck. —*v.i.* **3.** be hung or hanged. —**hang'man,** *n.*

hang'ar, *n.* aircraft shelter.

hang'dog'', *adj.* abject.

han'ker, *v.i.* yearn.

Ha'nu·ka'', *n. Judaism.* festival of the rededication of the Temple at Jerusalem. Also, **Ha'nuk·kah''.**

hap'haz'ard, *adj.* **1.** random. —*adv.* **2.** by chance.

hap'less, *adj.* unlucky.

hap'pen, *v.i.* come about by chance. —**hap'pen·ing,** *n.*

hap'py, *adj.,* **-pier, -piest. 1.** feeling pleased. **2.** fortunate. —**hap'pi·ly,** *adv.* —**hap'pi·ness,** *n.*

ha·rangue', *n., v.t.,* **-rangued, -ranguing.** *n.* **1.** long vehement speech. —*v.t.* **2.** deliver a harangue to.

ha·rass', *v.t.* trouble persistently. —**ha·rass'ment,** *n.*

har'bin·ger, *n.* forerunner.

har'bor, *n.* **1.** sheltered place for shipping. —*v.t.* **2.** shelter.

hard, *adj.* **1.** unyielding. **2.** difficult. —*adv.* **3.** energetically. —**hard'en,** *v.t., v.i.*

hard'-heart'ed, *adj.* callous.

hard'ly, *adv.* barely; scarcely.

hard'ship'', *n.* something hard to endure.

hard''ware, *n.* **1.** tools, fasteners, etc. **2.** (computers) equipment, as microchips, disk drives, printers, etc.

har'dy, *adj.* **-dier, -diest.** *n.* **1.** of much endurance. **2.** vigorous. —**har'di·ly,** *adv.*

hare, *n.* rabbitlike mammal.

ha'rem, *n.* **1.** women's quarters of a Muslim house. **2.** its inhabitants.

hark, *v.i.* listen.

hark'en, *v.i.* hearken.

har'lot, *n.* prostitute.

harm, *n.* **1.** injury. —*v.t.* **2.** injure.

—harm'ful, *adj.* —harm'ful·ly, *adv.*
—harm'less, *adj.* —harm'less·ly, *adv.*

har·mon'i·ca, *n.* mouth organ.

har'mo·ny, *n.* **1.** pleasant combination. **2.** agreement; accord. —har·mo'ni·ous, *adj.* —har'mo·nize", *v.t., v.i.*

har'ness, *n.* **1.** straps, etc. on an animal that pulls or carries. —*v.t.* **2.** put a harness on. **3.** control the energy of.

harp, *n.* **1.** large plucked stringed instrument. —*v.i.* **2.** speak tediously. —harp'ist, *n.*

har·poon', *n.* **1.** spear for whales, etc. —*v.t.* **2.** spear with a harpoon.

har'row, *n.* **1.** device for breaking and leveling plowed ground. —*v.t.* **2.** work on with a harrow. **3.** cause anxiety to.

har'ry, *v.t.,* -ried, -rying. harass.

harsh, *adj.* **1.** unpleasantly rough. **2.** severe. —harsh'ly, *adv.* —harsh'ness, *n.*

har'vest, *n.* **1.** occasion of gathering crops. **2.** crop gathered. —*v.t.* **3.** gather as a harvest. —har'vest·er, *n.*

hash, *v.t.* **1.** chop finely for cooking. —*n.* **2.** chopped mixture of meat and vegetables.

hasp, *n.* bolted fastening fitted over a shackle.

has'sle, *n., v.i.,* -sled, -sling. *Informal.* squabble.

has'sock, *n.* cushionlike seat.

haste, *n.* speed, esp. when excessive. —hast'y, *adj.* —hast'i·ly, *adv.*

has'ten, *v.t., v.i.* hurry.

hat, *n.* head garment, esp. a formal one.

hatch, *v.t.* **1.** bring forth from eggs. —*v.i.* **2.** open to release young. —*n.* **3.** Also, hatch'way", opening serving as a door or window.

hatch'et, *n.* short-handled chopping tool.

hate, *v.t.,* hated, hating, *n. v.t.* **1.** dislike violently. *n.* **2.** Also, hat'red, feeling of hating.

hate'ful, *adj.* to be hated.

haugh'ty, *adj.,* -tier, -tiest. arrogant. —haugh'ti·ness, *n.* —haugh'ti·ly, *adv.*

haul, *v.t., v.i.* **1.** pull. —*n.* **2.** act or instance of hauling.

haunch, *n.* area from upper thigh to buttock.

haunt, *v.t.* **1.** be often present at. —*n.* **2.** favorite place or resort.

have, *v.t.,* had, having. **1.** own or possess. **2.** acquire. **3.** experience or engage in. **4.** cause. **5.** be obliged.

ha'ven, *n.* place of shelter.

hav'oc, *n.* vast destruction.

hawk, *n.* **1.** bird of prey. —*v.t.* **2.** peddle.

haw'ser, *n.* mooring or towing rope.

hay, *n.* grass, etc. dried as fodder.

hay fever, allergy to pollen.

hay'wire", *adv. Informal.* awry.

haz'ard, *n., v.t.* risk. —haz'ard·ous, *adj.*

haze, *n, v.t.,* hazed, hazing. *n.* **1.** light mist or vapor. —*v.t.* **2.** harass or humiliate, as in an initiation. —haz'y, *adj.* —haz'i·ly, *adv.*

haz'el, *n.* tree of the birch family. —haz'el·nut", *n.*

he, *pron., pl.* they, *n., pl.* he's. *pron.* **1.** male person or animal mentioned. —*n.* **2.** male person or animal.

head, *n.* **1.** part of the body for thinking, eating, seeing, etc. **2.** director. **3.** uppermost or working feature. —*adj.* **4.** at or against the head. —*v.t.* **5.** direct. —*v.i.* **6.** direct oneself. —head'ache", *n.*

head'ing, *n.* title or subtitle.

head'line", *n.* title of a newspaper article.

head'long", *adv., adj.* **1.** with the head first. **2.** at reckless speed.

head'-on", *adj., adv.* with the front end or ends foremost.

head'quar"ters, *n., pl.* main center of command.

head'strong", *adj.* willful and impulsive.

head'way", *n.* forward motion.

head'y, *adj.,* -ier, -iest. intoxicating.

heal, *v.t.* **1.** return to health. **2.** make whole again.

health, *n.* **1.** well-being. **2.** condition of the body or mind. —health'ful, *adj.* —health'y, *adj.*

heap, *n.* **1.** loose pile. —*v.t.* **2.** pile up.

hear, *v.,* heard, hearing. *v.t.* **1.** perceive through the ears. **2.** understand from others. **3.** listen to. —hear'ing, *n.*

heark'en, *v.i.* listen carefully.

hear'say", *n.* rumor.

hearse, *n.* funeral car.

heart, *n.* **1.** organ that pumps blood. **2.** compassion or sensitivity. **3.** courage. **4.** enthusiasm. **5.** center. **6.** essence. —heart'less, *adj.*

heart'break", *n.* great sorrow. —heart'bro"ken, *adj.*

heart'en, *v.t.* encourage.

heart'felt", *adj.* deeply sincere.

hearth, *n.* floor of a fireplace, furnace.

heart'y, *adj.,* -ier, -iest. enthusiastic. —heart'i·ly, *adv.* —heart'i·ness, *n.*

heat, *n.* **1.** warmth. **2.** strong feeling. —*v.t., v.i.* **3.** warm. —heat'er, *n.*

hea'then, *n., pl.* -thens, -then, *adj. n.* **1.** person not Christian, Jewish, or Muslim. —*adj.* **2.** pertaining to such persons.

heave, *v.,* heaved or hove, heaving. *n. v.t.* **1.** lift, or lift and throw, with effort. —*v.i.* **2.** rise and fall in rhythm. —*n.* **3.** act or instance of heaving.

heav'en, *n.* **1.** heavens, sky. **2.** Heaven, dwelling of God, the angels, and the blessed. —heav'en·ly, *adj.*

heav'y, *adj.,* -ier, -iest. **1.** with much weight. **2.** with much difficulty. —heav'i·ly, *adv.*

heav'y-hand'ed, *adj.* **1.** clumsy. **2.** tyrannical.

heck'le, *v.t.,* **-led, -ling.** harass verbally.

hec'tare, *n.* area of 10,000 square meters.

hec'tic, *adj.* 1. feverish. 2. hasty and confused.

hedge, *n., v.,* **hedged, hedging.** *n.* 1. barrier of close-growing shrubs. —*v.t.* 2. partition off with a hedge. —*v.i.* 3. refuse to commit oneself.

hedge'hog'', *n.* American porcupine.

he'don·ism, *n.* doctrine that pleasure is the highest good. —**he'don·ist,** *n.* —**he''do·nis'tic,** *adj.*

heed, *v.t.* 1. pay attention to. —*n.* 2. attention. —**heed'ful,** *adj.* —**heed'less,** *adj.*

heel, *n.* 1. rear of the foot. 2. something similar in form or location. —*v.i., v.t.* 3. lean; list.

heft, *v.t.* pick up in order to weigh.

heft'y, *adj.,* **-ier, -iest.** 1. heavy. 2. large.

heif'er, *n.* young cow.

height, *n.* 1. dimension from bottom to top. 2. raised area. 3. highest point.

height'en, *v.t.* 1. make higher. —*v.i.* 2. increase.

hei'nous, *adj.* outrageously wicked.

heir, *n.* a person who inherits. Also, *fem.,* **heir'ess.**

heir'loom'', *n.* family possession.

hel'i·cop''ter, *n.* aircraft flying by means of a propellerlike rotor.

he'li·um, *n.* light gaseous chemical element.

he'lix, *n., pl.* **-lixes, -lices.** rising curve. —**hel'i·cal,** *adj.*

hell, *n.* Also **Hell,** place of confinement for those not redeemed. —**hel'lish,** *adj.*

hel·lo', *interj.* (exclamation of greeting).

helm, *n.* means of steering a ship. —**helms'man,** *n.*

hel'met, *n.* protective head covering.

help, *v.t.* 1. assist. 2. rescue. 3. prevent or mitigate. —*v.i.* 4. be useful. —*n.* 5. assistance. 6. rescue. —**help'ful,** *adj.*

help'ing, *n.* portion of food.

help'less, *adj.* unable to act. —**help'less·ly,** *adv.* —**help'less·ness,** *n.*

help'mate'', *n.* helpful companion. Also, **help'meet''.**

hem, *n., v.t.,* **hemmed, hemming.** *n.* 1. edge formed on a cloth. —*v.t.* 2. make a hem on.

hem'i·sphere'', *n.* 1. half a sphere. 2. half of the earth. —**hem''i·spher'i·cal,** *adj.*

hem'lock'', *n.* 1. pinelike evergreen. 2. poisonous plant related to parsley.

hem'or·rhage, *n.* massive loss of blood.

hemp, *n.* Asiatic plant used for rope and hashish.

hen, *n.* female bird, esp. a chicken.

hence, *adv.* 1. away. 2. from this time. 3. therefore.

hence'forth', *adv.* from now on.

hench'man, *n.* assistant villain.

her, *pron.* 1. objective of *she.* —*adj.* 2. pertaining to a female previously mentioned.

her'ald, *n.* 1. officer who announces. 2. signifier of what is to come. —*v.t.* 3. signify in advance.

her'ald·ry, *n.* study of coats of arms, etc. —**he·ral'dic,** *adj.*

herb, (ərb), *n.* annual seed plant used in cookery or medicine. —**her·ba'cious,** *adj.* —**herb'age,** *n.* —**herb'al,** *adj.*

her''cu·le'an, *adj.* with immense effort.

herd, *n.* 1. group of cows, sheep, etc. 2. person who tends such a group. —*v.i., v.t.* 3. gather or move as a herd.

here, *adv.* 1. in or to this place. 2. now.

here·af'ter, *adv.* 1. after this. —*n.* 2. next world.

here'by', *adv.* by this means.

he·red'i·tar''y, *adj.* so by inheritance or heredity.

here·in', *adv.* in this.

here·of', *adv.* of or concerning this.

her'e·sy, *n., pl.* **-sies.** contradiction of a dogma. —**her'e·tic,** *n.* —**he·ret'i·cal,** *adj.*

here·to·fore', *adv.* until now.

here·with', *adv.* 1. with this. 2. by this means.

her'it·age, *n.* traditions, etc. from predecessors.

her·met'ic, *adj.* airtight. Also, **her·met'i·cal.** —**her·met'i·cal·ly,** *adv.*

her'mit, *n.* person willingly living alone. —**her'mit·age** *n.*

her'ni·a, *n.* abdominal rupture.

he'ro, *n., pl.* **-roes.** 1. person of courage and accomplishment. 2. protagonist. Also, *fem.,* **he'ro·ine.** —**he·ro'ic,** *adj.* —**he'ro·ism,** *n.*

he'ro·in, *n.* morphine-based narcotic.

her'on, *n.* wading bird.

her''pes, *n.* a viral infection causing sores.

her'ring, *n.* North Atlantic fish.

hers, *pron.* something belonging or pertaining to *her.*

her·self', *pron.* 1. intensive and reflexive of *she.* 2. her true self.

hertz, *n. Physics.* one cycle per second.

hes'i·tate'', *v.i.,* **-tated, -tating.** 1. be unresolved. 2. pause briefly. 3. be reluctant. —**hes''i·ta'tion,** *n.* —**hes'i·tant,** *adj.*

het'er·o·dox'', *adj.* unorthodox. —**het'er·o·dox''y,** *n.*

het''er·o·ge'ne'ous, *adj.* 1. dissimilar. 2. of dissimilar components. —**het''er·o·ge·ne'i·ty,** *n.*

het''er·o·sex'u·al, *adj.* 1. attracted solely to the opposite sex. —*n.* 2. heterosexual person. —**het''er·o·sex'u·al'i·ty,** *n.*

hew, *v.t.,* **hewed, hewed** or **hewn, hewing.** chop.

hex, *v.t.* 1. put an evil spell on. —*n.* 2. evil spell.

hex'a·gon'', *n.* six-sided plane figure. —**hex'ag'o·nal**, *adj.*

hi·a'tus, *n., pl.* **-tuses, -tus.** gap.

hi'ber·nate'', *v.i.,* **-nated, -nating.** be dormant through winter. —**hi''ber·na'tion**, *n.*

hic'cup, *n., v.i.,* **-cuped, -cuping.** *n.* 1. sharp sound due to involuntary contraction of the diaphragm. —*v.i.* 2. emit such a sound. Also, **hic'cough.**

hick'o·ry, *n., pl.* **-ries.** tree of the walnut family.

hide, *v.,* **hid, hidden, hiding,** *n. v.t.* 1. keep from being seen. —*v.i.* 2. conceal oneself. —*n.* 3. animal skin.

hid'e·ous, *adj.* horribly ugly.

hi'er·ar''chy, *n., pl.* **-ies.** organization of higher officials.

hi''er·o·glyph'ic, *n.* picture representing a word or sound.

high, *adj.* 1. being or reaching far up. 2. of a specified height. 3. superior. 4. notably large in amount. —*adv.* 5. in or to a high place or situation. —**high'ly**, *adv.*

high'-flown'', *adj.* pretentious, as speech.

high'-hand'ed, *adj.* overbearing. —**high'-hand'ed·ly**, *adv.* —**high'-hand'ed·ness**, *n.*

high'land, *n.* hilly or mountainous region.

high'light'', *n.* 1. brilliant reflection. 2. salient fact. —*v.t.* 3. emphasize.

high'ness, *n.* 1. height. 2. Highness, title of respect for royalty.

high'-rise', *n.* multistoried building. Also, **high'rise''.**

high'-strung', *adj.* nervous.

high'way'', *n.* major road.

hi'jack'', *v.t. Informal.* take in transit by robbery. —**hi'jack''er**, *n.*

hike, *v.i.,* **hiked, hiking,** *n. v.i.* 1. go for a long walk. —*n.* 2. long walk.

hi·lar'i·ous, *adj.* 1. merry. 2. very funny. —**hi·lar'i·ty**, *n.*

hill, *n.* distinctive area of rising ground. —**hill'y**, *adj.*

hil'lock, *n.* small hill.

hilt, *n.* handle of a sword, etc.

him, *pron.* objective of **he.**

him·self', *pron.* 1. intensive or reflexive of **him.** 2. his true self.

hind, *adj.,* **hinder, hindmost** or **hindermost.** *adj.* behind.

hin'der, *v.t.* 1. stop or slow down. —*adj.* 2. rear. —**hin'drance**, *n.*

hind'sight'', *n.* belated perception.

hinge, *n., v.i.,* **hinged, hinging.** *n.* 1. support allowing the supported part to turn. —*v.i.* 2. depend.

hint, *n.* 1. something that allows an inference to be made. —*v.t.* 2. imply. —*v.i.* 3. make a hint.

hip, *n.* area around the upper leg joints.

hip'pie, *n., pl.* **-pies.** *Informal.* person alienated from conventional society.

hip'po·pot'a·mus, *n., pl.* **-muses, -mi.** large river-loving African mammal.

hire, *v.t.,* **hired, hiring,** *n. v.t.* 1. employ or use for wages or a fee. —*n.* 2. amount paid in hiring.

hire'ling, *n.* unscrupulous mercenary.

hir'sute, *adj.* hairy.

his, *pron.* 1. something belonging or pertaining to him. —*adj.* 2. pertaining to him.

hiss, *n.* 1. prolonged s-like sound. —*v.i.* 2. emit a hiss. —*v.t.* 3. hiss at to show disapproval.

his'to·ry, *n., pl.* **-ries.** 1. study of the past. 2. account of the past. 3. known or recorded past. 4. determining forces as inferred from past events. —**his·to'ri·an**, *n.* —**his·tor'ic, his·tor'i·cal**, *adj.*

hit, *v.,* **hit, hitting,** *n. v.t.* 1. come against or send something against with force. —*v.i.* 2. come by chance. 3. strike a blow. —*n.* 4. accurate discharge of a missile. 5. successful song, etc.

hitch, *v.t.* 1. tie or harness. —*n.* 2. simple knot. 3. obstacle or drawback.

hitch'hike'', *v.i.,* **-hiked, -hiking.** solicit a free automobile ride.

hith'er, *adv.* 1. to this place. —*adj.* 2. nearer.

hith'er·to'', *adv.* until now.

hive, *n.* 1. beehive. 2. **hives**, itchy skin condition.

hoard, *n.* 1. precious hidden accumulation. —*v.t.* 2. accumulate and secrete.

hoarse, *adj.* emitting or having a harsh, grating sound.

hoar'y, *adj.,* **-ier, -iest.** 1. gray-haired from age. 2. very old.

hoax, *n.* 1. fraud. —*v.t.* 2. perpetrate a hoax on.

hob'ble, *v.,* **-bled, -bling.** *v.i.* 1. limp. —*v.t.* 2. hamper.

hob'by, *n., pl.* **-bies.** spare-time activity. —**hob'by·ist**, *n.*

hob'nob'', *v.i.,* **-nobbed, -nobbing.** be on social terms.

ho'bo, *n., pl.* **-bos, -boes.** migrant worker.

hock'ey, *n.* game played on ice with long, clublike sticks and a puck.

ho'cus-po'cus, *n.* 1. meaningless jargon. 2. trickery.

hod, *n.* 1. trough for bricks or mortar. 2. coal scuttle.

hodge'podge'', *n.* random mixture.

hoe, *n., v.t.,* **hoed, hoeing.** *n.* 1. long-handled tool for loosening earth. —*v.t.* 2. dig with a hoe.

hog, *n.* 1. pig raised for meat. 2. *Informal.* greedy person.

hogs'head'', *n.* 1. large cask. 2. measure of 63 liquid gallons.

hoi'pol·loi', the common people.

hoist, *v.t.* 1. lift, as by a crane. —*n.* 2. hoisting device.

hold, *v.*, **held, holding,** *n.* *v.t.* 1. have in the hand. 2. keep from moving or changing. 3. embrace. 4. contain. 5. possess. 6. carry on. 7. consider. —*v.i.* 8. remain firm or fixed. —*n.* 9. act or instance of holding. 10. means of holding. 11. cargo space. —**hold′er**, *n.* —**hold′ing**, *n.*

hole, *n.* opening, esp. a deep one.

hol′i·day″, *n.* 1. day specially celebrated. 2. day of no work.

hol′i·ness, *n.* 1. quality of being holy. 2. **Holiness,** title of respect for a pope.

hol′low, *adj.* 1. empty inside. 2. worthless; vain. 3. booming. —*v.t.* 4. make hollow.

hol′ly, *n.*, *pl.* **-lies.** evergreen shrub with red berries.

hol′ly·hock″, *n.* tall plant with showy flowers.

ho′lo·caust″, *n.* widely destructive fire.

hol′ster, *n.* pistol holder.

ho′ly, *adj.*, **-lier, -liest.** 1. dedicated to religion. 2. spiritually pure.

Holy Communion, Christian ritual of bread and wine.

Holy Spirit, spirit of God. Also, **Holy Ghost.**

hom′age, *n.* reverent respect.

home, *n.* 1. place of residence. 2. one's own place. —*adv.* 3. to one's home. 4. into the proper place. —**home′land″**, *n.* —**home′ward**, *adv.*

home′ly, *adj.*, **-lier, -liest.** 1. commonplace. 2. not handsome or beautiful.

home′sick″, *adj.* sad at being away from home.

home′work, *n.* schoolwork done at home.

home′y, *adj.*, **-ier, -iest.** cozy.

hom′i·cide″, *n.* killing of one person by another. —**hom″i·cid′al**, *adj.*

hom′i·ly, *n.*, *pl.* **-lies.** sermon or moral lecture.

ho″mo·ge′ne·ous, *adj.* of uniform composition or content. —**ho·mo″ge·ne′i·ty**, *n.*

ho·mog′e·nize″, *v.t.*, **-nized, -nizing.** make homogeneous.

hom′o·nym, *n.* word like another in pronunciation but not in other ways.

Ho′mo sa′pi·ens″, man.

ho″mo·sex′u·al, *adj.* 1. sexually attracted to one's own sex. —*n.* 2. homosexual person. —**ho″mo·sex″u·al′i·ty**, *n.*

hone, *v.t.*, **honed, hone.** bring to a fine, sharp edge.

hon′est, *adj.* 1. without desire to steal, lie, etc. 2. genuine. 3. frank. —**hon′est·ly**, *adv.* —**hon′es·ty**, *n.*

hon′ey, *n.*, *pl.* **-neys.** syrup made by bees from flowers.

hon′ey·comb″, *n.* 1. structure with hexagonal cells made by bees to store honey. 2. openwork geometrical pattern.

hon′ey·dew″ melon, *n.* sweet, green melon.

hon′ey·moon″, *n.* vacation of newly-weds. —**hon′ey·moon″er**, *n.*

hon′ey·suck″le, *n.* climbing plant with small, sweet blossoms.

hon′or, *n.* 1. high respect. 2. good reputation. 3. integrity. 4. chastity. 5. conferred distinction. —*v.t.* 6. hold in honor. 7. confer distinction or praise on. 8. accept as valid. —**hon′or·a·ble**, *adj.* —**hon′or·ar″y**, *adj.*

hon″or·if′ic, *adj.* conferring honor.

hood, *n.* 1. cloth covering for the head and nape. 2. engine cover of an automobile, etc.

hood′lum, *n.* violent criminal.

hood′wink″, *v.t.* cheat.

hoof, *n.*, *pl.* **hoofs, hooves.** hard foot covering of a horse, etc.

hook, *n.* 1. curved object for hanging or attaching things. —*v.t.* 2. attach with a hook. —*v.i.* 3. curve as a hook does.

hoop, *n.* circular band.

hoot, *n.* 1. loud, shrill sound. —*v.i.* 2. utter a hoot. —*v.t.* 3. show scorn for by hooting.

hop, *v.i.*, **hopped, hopping,** *n.* *v.i.* 1. jump on one foot or with both feet together. —*n.* 2. act or instance of hopping.

hope, *n.*, *v.*, **hoped, hoping.** *n.* 1. belief that something good may happen. 2. source or cause of such a belief. —*v.t.*, *v.i.* 3. entertain hopes. —**hope′ful**, *adj.*, *n.* —**hope′less**, *adj.*

hop′per, *n.* funnel-like chute.

horde, *n.*, *v.i.*, **horded, hording.** *n.* 1. swarm; multitude. —*v.i.* 2. gather in a horde.

ho·ri′zon, *n.* apparent edge of a scene.

ho′ri·zon′tal, *adj.* running across, like a featureless horizon. —**ho″ri·zon′tal·ly**, *adv.*

hor′mone″, *n.* substance influencing one part of the body but made in another. —**hor·mo′nal**, *adj.*

horn, *n.* 1. hard, pointed protuberance from an animal head. 2. substance of this. 3. pointed projection. 4. wind instrument. —**horn′y**, *adj.*

hor′net, *n.* yellow and black wasp.

hor′o·scope″, *n.* chart of zodiacal signs.

hor·ren′dous, *adj.* horrible.

hor′ri·ble, *adj.* 1. causing horror. 2. *Informal.* very bad. —**hor′ri·bly**, *adv.*

hor′rid, *adj.* 1. causing horror. 2. very unpleasant.

hor′ri·fy″, *v.t.*, **-fied, -fying.** fill with horror.

hor′ror, *n.* strong fear and disgust.

hors de com·bat (or″də kom ba′), out of action.

hors d'oeuvre (or **derv'**), *n., pl.* **hors d'oeuvres**, appetizer.

horse, *n.* 1. four-footed grass eating animal. 2. supporting frame. —**horse'back''**, *adv., n.* —**horse'man, horse'wom''an,** *n.*

horse chestnut, large-leaved flowering tree.

horse'laugh'', *n.* loud, open laugh.

horse'play'', *n.* rough play.

horse'pow''er, *n.* unit of power equalling 33,000 foot-pounds/minute or 746 watts.

horse'rad''ish, *n.* plant with a pungent root used as a relish.

horse'shoe'', *n.* iron reinforcement for a hoof in the form of an open loop.

hor'ti·cul''ture, *n.* gardening. —**hor''ti·cul'tur·al**, *adj.* —**hor''ti·cul'tur·ist**, *n.*

ho·san'na, *interj.* (exclamation of praise to God).

hose, *n., pl.* (for 1) **hoses,** (for 2) **hose.** 1. flexible tube for water, etc. 2. long stocking.

ho'sier·y, *n.* stockings.

hos''pice, *n.* facility for terminally ill persons.

hos'pi·ta·ble, *adj.* readily offering hospitality.

hos'pi·tal, *n.* place for healing. —**hos'pi·tal·ize''**, *v.t.*

hos''pi·tal'i·ty, *n.* generosity and friendship toward visitors.

host, *n.* 1. Also, *fem.*, **hos'tess**, person who entertains guests. 2. organism supporting parasites. 3. multitude. 4. wafer eaten in Holy Communion.

hos'tage, *n.* prisoner kept to enforce demands.

hos'tel, *n.* institution providing lodgings.

hos'tile, *adj.* in a state of enmity. —**hos·til'i·ty**, *n.*

hot, *adj.*, **hotter**, **hottest**. 1. very warm. 2. very spicy. 3. intense, as in emotion. —**hot'ly**, *adv.*

hot'bed'', *n.* 1. miniature greenhouse. 2. prolific source.

hot'-blood'ed, *adj.* impetuous.

ho·tel', *n.* place renting rooms and often serving food.

hot'-head'ed, *adj.* quick-tempered. —**hot'head''**, *n.*

hot rod, standard automobile with a supercharged engine. —**hot rod'der.**

hound, *n.* 1. hunting dog. —*v.t.* 2. persecute.

hour, *n.* twenty-fourth of a day. —**hour'ly**, *adv., adj.*

house, *n., pl.* **houses**, *v.t.*, **housed**, **housing**. *n.* (hows) 1. building to live in. 2. family. 3. business firm. 4. legislative body. —*v.t.* (howz) 5. provide lodgings or shelter for.

house'fly'', *n.* ordinary fly.

house'hold'', *n.* inhabitants of a house.

house'hold''er, *n.* 1. head of a household. 2. owner of a house.

house'keep''er, *n.* person responsible for keeping a house in order.

house'wife'', *n.* wife who runs a home.

hous·ing (howz'ing), *n.* 1. complex of dwellings. 2. provision of dwellings.

hov'er, *v.i.* 1. remain poised in the air. 2. linger near by. 3. waver.

how, *adv.* 1. in what way. 2. in what state. 3. for what reason. 4. to what extent.

how·ev'er, *adv.* 1. regardless of how. —*conj.* 2. nevertheless.

how'itz·er, *n.* short-barreled, high-trajectory cannon.

howl, *v.i.* 1. raise a loud, animal-like cry. 2. laugh uproariously. 3. complain bitterly. —*n.* 4. act or instance of howling.

hub, *n.* center of a wheel.

hub'bub, *n.* confusion; disorder.

huck'le·ber''ry, *n., pl.* **-ries**. dark blue shrub berry.

huck'ster, *n.* vegetable peddler.

hud'dle, *n., v.*, **-dled**, **-dling**, *n.* 1. close, irregular group. —*v.t., v.i.* 2. gather in a huddle.

hue, *n.* 1. color. 2. tint.

huff, *n.* mood of silent resentment. —**huf'fy**, *adj.*

hug, *v.*, **hugged**, **hugging**, *n. v.t., v.i.* 1. embrace. —*v.t.* 2. keep close to. —*n.* 3. embrace.

huge, *adj.* very large. —**huge'ness**, *n.* —**huge'ly**, *adv.*

hulk, *n.* hull of a ship deprived of masts, etc.

hulk'ing, *adj.* large and bulky.

hull, *n.* 1. shell of a seed, etc. 2. body of a ship. —*v.t.* 3. remove the hulls from.

hul'la·ba·loo'', *n.* clamor.

hum, *v.*, **hummed**, **humming**, *n. v.i.* 1. make an inarticulate sound between closed lips. —*v.t.* 2. render by humming. —*n.* 3. low, continuous murmur.

hu'man, *adj.* 1. being a man, woman, or child. 2. characteristic of man. —**hu'man·ly**, *adv.* —**hu'man·kind''**, *n.*

hu·mane', *adj.* 1. merciful. 2. civilizing.

hu'man·ism, *n.* intellectual movement centered around man. —**hu'man·ist**, *n.* —**hu''man·is'tic**, *adj.*

hu·man''i·tar'i·an, *n.* 1. philanthropist. —*adj.* 2. philanthropic. —**hu·man''i·tar'i·an·ism**, *n.*

hu·man'i·ty, *n.* 1. human beings collectively. 2. quality of being humane.

hum'ble, *adj.*, **-bler**, **-blest**, *v.t.*, **-bled**, **-bling**. *adj.* 1. unpretentious; unconceited. 2. low in rank. —*v.t.* 3. make humble. —**hum'bly**, *adv.*

hum'drum'', *adj.* drearily ordinary.

hu'mid, *adj.* moist. —**hu·mid'i·fy"**, *v.t.* —**hu·mid'i·ty**, *n.*

hu·mil'i·ate", *v.t.*, **-ated, -ating.** cause to feel shame. —**hu·mil'i·a'tion**, *n.*

hu·mil'i·ty, *n.* humble quality.

hum'ming·bird, *n.* tiny bird with fast-moving wings.

hu'mor, *n.* **1.** mood. **2.** comical quality. **3.** bodily fluid. —**hu'mor·ist**, *n.* —**hu'mor·ous**, *adj.*

hump, *n.* high lump on a back of a camel.

hu'mus, *n.* soil with decayed leaf matter, etc.

hunch, *n.* **1.** *Informal.* intuitive feeling. **2.** hump.

hunch'back", *n.* person with a hump on the back. Also, **hump'back".**

hun'dred, *adj.*, *n.* ten times ten. —**hun'dredth**, *adj.*

hun'dred·weight", *n. U.S.* 100 pounds.

hun'ger, *n.* **1.** desire to eat. **2.** deprivation of food. **3.** strong desire. —*v.i.* **4.** be hungry. —**hun'gry**, *adj.* —**hun'gri·ly**, *adv.*

hunk, *n. Informal.* large piece.

hunt, *v.t.* **1.** pursue to kill or harass. —*v.i.* **2.** hunt game. **3.** search. —*n.* **4.** act or instance of hunting. —**hunt'er**, **hunts'man**, *fem.* **hunt'ress**, *n.*

hur'dle, *n.*, *v.t.*, **-dled, -dling.** *n.* **1.** barrier to be leapt. —*v.t.* **2.** leap over.

hurl, *n.* throw with force.

hur'ly-bur'ly, *n.*, *pl.* **-lies.** turmoil.

hur·rah', *interj.*, *n.* (shout of approval). Also **hur·ray'.**

hur'ri·cane", *n.* tropical cyclone.

hur'ry, *v.*, **-ried, -rying,** *v.i.* **1.** move or act quickly. —*v.t.* **2.** cause to hurry. —*n.* **3.** reason for hurrying. **4.** eagerness to hurry. —**hur'ried·ly**, *adv.*

hurt, *v.*, **hurt, hurting,** *v.t.* **1.** damage; injure. **2.** pain the feelings of. —*v.i.* **3.** cause pain. **4.** do harm. —*n.* **5.** damage; injury. —**hurt'ful**, *adj.*

hur'tle, *v.i.*, **-tled, -tling.** move at high speed.

hus'band, *n.* **1.** woman's spouse. —*v.t.* **2.** manage economically.

hus'band·ry, *n.* **1.** farming. **2.** management.

hush, *n.*, *v.t.* silence.

husk, *n.* **1.** outer covering. —*v.t.* **2.** remove the husk from.

hus'ky, *adj.* **1.** hoarse. **2.** robust.

hus'tle, *v.*, **-tled, -tling,** *n.* *v.t.* **1.** jostle. **2.** force roughly. —*v.i.* **3.** move or act energetically. —*n.* **4.** act or instance of hustling. **5.** *Informal.* enterprise.

hut, *n.* small, crude dwelling.

hutch, *n.* **1.** cupboard. **2.** coop for rabbits, etc.

hy'a·cinth", *n.* bell-shaped flower of the lily family.

hy'brid, *n.* **1.** offspring or product of mixed species or varieties. —**hy'brid·ize"**, *v.t.*

hy·dran'ge·a, *n.* shrub with clusters of white, blue, or pink flowers.

hy'drant, *n.* valved pipe from a water main.

hy·drau'lic, *adj.* **1.** operated by liquid pressure. —*n.* **2. hydraulics,** study of the mechanical properties of liquids. —**hy·drau'li·cal·ly**, *adv.*

hy'dro·car'bon, *n.* compound of hydrogen and carbon.

hy"dro·e·lec'tric, *adj.* pertaining to electricity produced by water power.

hy'dro·gen, *n.* flammable gaseous element.

hy"dro·pho'bi·a, *n.* rabies.

hy'dro·plane", *n.* **1.** seaplane. **2.** motorboat with hydrofoils or a planing hull.

hy"dro·pon'ics, *n.* growing of plants in liquids.

hy·e'na, *n.* wolflike African or Asian animal.

hy'giene, *n.* **1.** system of health preservation. **2.** cleanliness. —**hy"gi·en'ic**, *adj.* —**hy"gi·en'i·cal·ly**, *adv.*

hymn, *n.* poem or song of praise, as to God. —**hymn'book"**, **hym'nal**, *n.*

hype, *n.* exaggerated publicity.

hy·per'bo·le", *n.* exaggeration for rhetorical effect. —**hy"per·bol'ic**, *adj.*

hy"per·crit'i·cal, *adj.* over-critical.

hy"per·sen'si·tive, *adj.* too sensitive.

hy"per·ten'sion, *n.* excessive blood pressure.

hy'phen, *n.* dash, -, used to join words or syllables. —**hy'phen·ate"**, *v.t.* —**hy"phen·a'tion**, *n.*

hyp·no'sis, *n.*, *pl.* **-ses.** sleeplike, obedient condition induced by suggestion from another. —**hyp·not'ic**, *adj.* —**hyp'no·tism**, *n.* —**hyp'no·tist**, *n.* —**hyp'no·tize"**, *v.t.*

hy"po·chon'dri·a, *n.* fear of imaginary illness. —**hy"po·chon'dri·ac"**, *n.*, *adj.*

hy·poc'ri·sy, *n.*, *pl.* **-sies.** false pretension to virtue, affection, etc. —**hyp'o·crite**, *n.* —**hyp"po·crit'i·cal**, *adj.*

hy"po·der'mic, *adj.* **1.** under the skin. —*n.* **2.** hypodermic injection or injecting device. —**hy"po·der'mi·cal·ly**, *adv.*

hy·pot'e·nuse", *n.* side of a right triangle opposite the right angle.

hy·poth'e·sis, *n.*, *pl.* **-ses.** unproved theory. —**hy"po·thet'i·cal**, *adj.*

hys·te'ri·a, *n.* **1.** pathologically excitable condition. **2.** Also, **hys·ter'ics,** outbreak of uncontrolled emotion. —**hys·ter'i·cal**, *adj.*

I

I, i, *n.* **1.** ninth letter of the English alphabet. —*pron.* **2. I** (first person singular as a subject).

ibid., in the same place: used in scholarly notes.

ice, *n., v.,* **iced, icing.** *n.* **1.** water frozen solid. **2.** frozen dessert. —*v.t.* **3.** put ice over or around. **4.** put icing over. —*v.i.* **5.** freeze or form ice. —**ice′box″,** *n.* —**ice′skate″,** *n.* —**ic′y,** *adj.*

ice′berg″, *n.* floating fragment from a polar icecap.

ice′cap″, *n.* polar mass of ice.

ich″thy·ol′o·gy, *n.* study of fish. —**ich″thy·ol′o·gist,** *n.*

i′ci·cle, *n.* conical hanging mass of frozen water.

ic′ing, *n.* sweet cover for a cake.

i′con, *n.* religious image, esp. in an eastern church.

i·con′o·clast″, *n.* destroyer of long-held values. —**i·con″o·clas′tic,** *adj.*

i·de′a, *n.* image in the mind; conception.

i·de′al, *adj.* **1.** perfect. **2.** imaginary. —*n.* **3.** something perfect. —**i·de′al·ly,** *adv.* —**i·de′al·ize″,** *v.t.*

i·de′al·ism, *n.* conformity to or belief in ideals. —**i·de′al·ist,** *n.* —**i″de·al·is′tic,** *adj.*

i·den′ti·cal, *adj.* exactly alike or the same. —**i·den′ti·cal·ly,** *adv.*

i·den′ti·fy″, *v.t.,* **-fied, -fying. 1.** establish the identity of. **2.** associate with another person or thing. —**i·den″ti·fi·ca′tion,** *n.*

i·den′ti·ty, *n., pl.* **-ties. 1.** state of being identical. **2.** individuality.

i″de·ol′o·gy, *n., pl.* **-gies.** political or social doctrine. —**i″de·o·log′i·cal,** *adj.*

id′i·om, *n.* **1.** dialect. **2.** combination of words with a nonliteral meaning. —**id″i·o·mat′ic,** *adj.*

id″i·o·syn′cra·sy, *n., pl.* **-sies.** personal trait.

id′i·ot, *n.* feeble-minded person. —**id″i·ot′ic,** *adj.* —**id′i·o·cy,** *n.*

i′dle, *adj.,* **idler, idlest,** *v.i.,* **idled, idling.** *adj.* **1.** not at work or in use. **2.** lazy. **3.** frivolous. —*v.i.* **4.** be idle. —**id′ly,** *adv.* —**id′ler,** *n.*

i′dol, *n.* **1.** statue of a god. **2.** idealized person. —**i′dol·ize″,** *v.t.*

i·dol′a·try, *n., pl.* **-tries.** worship of idols. —**i·dol′a·ter,** *n.* —**i·dol′a·trous,** *adj.*

i′dyll, *n.* **1.** poem of pastoral life. **2.** beautiful episode. Also, **i′dyl.** —**i·dyl′ic,** *adj.*

i.e., that is.

if, *conj.* **1.** on condition that. **2.** supposing that. **3.** whether.

ig′loo, *n., pl.* **-loos.** domed Eskimo snow house.

ig·ne·ous, *adj.* resulting from intense heat.

ig·nite′, *v.,* **-nited, -niting.** *v.t.,* **1.** set on or catch fire. —*v.i.* **2.** catch fire. —**ig·ni′tion,** *n.*

ig·no′ble, *adj.* base; mean.

ig·no·min″y, *n.* shame. —**ig″no·min′i·ous,** *adj.*

ig″no·ra′mus, *n., pl.* **-muses.** ignorant person.

ig′no·rant, *adj.* **1.** uneducated. **2.** unaware. —**ig′no·rance,** *n.* —**ig′no·rant·ly,** *adv.*

ig·nore′, *v.t.,* **-nored, -noring.** take no heed of.

ill, *adj.,* **worse,** (for 1) **worst,** *adv.,* **worse, worst,** *n. adj.* **1.** bad. **2.** sick. —*adv.* **3.** badly. **4.** scarcely. —*n.* **5.** harm.

ill′-ad·vised′, *adj.* showing bad judgment.

il·le′gal, *adj.* unlawful. —**il·le′gal·ly,** *adv.* —**il″le·gal′i·ty,** *n.*

il·leg′i·ble, *adj.* unable to be read. —**il·leg″i·bil′i·ty,** *n.*

il·le·git′i·mate, *adj.* **1.** not legitimate. **2.** born out of wedlock. —**il″le·git′i·ma·cy,** *n.*

il·lic′it, *adj.* not allowed. —**il·lic′it·ly,** *adv.*

il·lit′er·ate, *adj.* **1.** unable to read. —*n.* **2.** illiterate person. —**il·lit′er·a·cy,** *n.*

ill′ness, *n.* sickness.

il·log′i·cal, *adj.* opposed to logic.

il·lu′mi·nate″, *v.t.,* **-nated, nating. 1.** Also, **il·lu′mine,** light up. **2.** elucidate. **3.** decorate with gold and color. —**il·lu″mi·na′tion,** *n.*

ill′-use′, *v.t.,* **-used, using.** abuse. —**ill′use′, ill′-us′age,** *n.*

il·lu′sion, *n.* **1.** deceptive impression. **2.** false conception. —**il·lu′sive,** —**il·lu′so·ry,** *adj.*

il′lus·trate″, *v.t.,* **-trated, -trating. 1.** explain with examples. **2.** add pictures to, as a narrative. —**il″lus·tra′tion,** *n.* —**il′lus·tra″tor,** *n.* —**il·lus′tra·tive,** *adj.*

il·lus′tri·ous, *adj.* distinguished; famous.

ill will, hostility.

im′age, *n.* **1.** picture. **2.** popular conception. —**im′age·ry,** *n.*

i·mag′ine, *v.t.,* **-ined, -ining. 1.** create in the mind. **2.** suppose to exist. **3.** believe wrongly to exist. —**i·mag′in·a·ble,** *adj.* —**i·mag′in·a·bly,** *adv.* —**i·mag′in·a″ry,** *adj.* —**i·mag″i·na′tion,** *n.* —**i·mag′i·na·tive,** *adj.*

im·bal'ance, *n.* lack of balance.

im'be·cile, *n.* idiot. —im''be·cil'ic, *adj.* —im''be·cil'i·ty, *n.*

im·bibe', *v.,* -bibed, -bibing. *v.t., v.i.* drink.

im·bro·gli·o (im·brōl'yō), *n., pl.* -os. confused situation.

im·bue', *v.t.,* -bued, -buing. permeate.

im'i·tate'', *v.t.,* -tated, -tating. have the same characteristics as. —im''i·ta'tion, *n.* —im'i·ta'tor, *n.* —im'i·ta''tive, *adj.*

im·mac'u·late, *adj.* without dirt or sin. —im·mac'u·late·ly, *adv.*

im'ma·nent, *adj.* inherent. —im'ma·nent·ly, *adv.* —im'ma·nence, *n.*

im''ma·te'ri·al, *adj.* 1. irrelevant. 2. not composed of matter.

im''ma·ture, *n.* with an undeveloped character. —im''ma·tu'ri·ty, *n.*

im·meas'ur·a·ble, *adj.* not to be measured. —im·meas'ur·a·bly, *adv.*

im·me'di·ate, *adj.* 1. unseparated by anything else. 2. direct. —im·me'di·a·cy, *n.* —im·me'di·ate·ly, *adv.*

im''me·mo'ri·al, *adj.* from before memory.

im·mense', *adj.* huge. —im·men'si·ty, *n.* —im·mense'ly, *adv.*

im·merse', *v.t.,* -mersed, -mersing. bury completely, as in a liquid. —im·mer'sion, *n.*

im'mi·grate'', *v.i.,* -grated, -grating. enter a country to settle. —im'mi·grant, *n., adj.* —im''mi·gra'tion, *n.*

im'mi·nent, *adj.* soon to happen. —im'mi·nence, im'mi·nen·cy, *n.*

im·mo'bile, *adj.* fixed in place. —im''mo·bil'i·ty, *n.* —im·mo'bi·lize'', *v.t.*

im·mod'e·rate, *adj.* lacking moderation. —im·mod'e·rate·ly, *adv.*

im·mod'est, *adj.* lacking modesty. —im·mod'es·ty, *n.*

im'mo·late'', *v.t.,* -lated, -lating. kill as a sacrifice. —im''mo·la'tion, *n.*

im·mor'al, *adj.* not moral. —im''mo·ral'i·ty, *n.*

im·mor'tal, *adj.* 1. never to die. 2. never to be forgotten. —*n.* 3. immortal being. —im·mor·tal'i·ty, *n.* —im·mor'tal·ize'', *v.t.*

im·mov'a·ble, *adj.* fixed in place.

im·mune', *adj.* proof against disease, etc. —im·mun'i·ty, *n.* —im'mu·nize'', *v.t.* —im''mu·ni·za'tion, *n.*

im·mu'ta·ble, *adj.* unchangeable. —im·mu''ta·bil'i·ty. *n.*

imp, *n.* small demon. —imp'ish, *adj.*

im·pact, *n.* (im'pakt) 1. violent shock. —*v.t.* (im·pakt') 2. force against something else.

im·pair', *v.t.* put out of order. —im·pair'ment, *n.*

im·pale', *v.t.,* -paled, -paling. pierce and support with a sharpened pole, etc.

im·pal'pa·ble, *adj.* 1. imperceptible to the touch. 2. subtle.

im·pan'el, *v.t.,* -eled, -eling. enroll for or as a jury.

im·part', *v.t.* reveal, as news.

im·par'tial, *adj.* unbiased. —im·par'tial·ly, *adv.* —im·par''ti·al'i·ty, *n.*

im·pas'sa·ble, *adj.* impossible to pass along or over.

im'passe, *n.* deadlock.

im·pas'sioned, *adj.* passionate.

im·pas'sive, *adj.* revealing no emotion. —im''pas·siv'i·ty, *n.*

im·pa'tient, *adj.* without patience. —im·pa'tience, *n.*

im·peach', *n.* try for wrongdoing in office. —im·peach'ment, *n.*

im·pec'ca·ble, *adj.* flawless.

im''pe·cu'ni·ous, *adj.* penniless.

im·pede', *v.t.,* -peded, -peding. hinder. —im·ped'ance, im·ped'i·ment, *n.*

im·ped''i·men'ta, *n., pl.* things to be carried along.

im·pel', *v.t.,* -pelled, -pelling. 1. drive forward. 2. urge.

im·pend', *v.i.* be about to happen.

im·pen'e·tra·ble, *adj.* impossible to penetrate.

im·pen'i·tent, *adj.* not repentant.

im·per'a·tive, *adj.* 1. vitally necessary. 2. pertaining to command.

im''per·cep'ti·ble, *adj.* impossible or difficult to perceive. —im''per·cep'ti·bly, *adv.*

im·per'fect, *adj.* 1. flawed; deficient. 2. pertaining to uncompleted or continuing action. —im·per'fect·ly, *adv.* —im''per·fec'tion, *n.*

im·pe'ri·al, *adj.* pertaining to empires or emperors.

im·pe'ri·al·ism, *n.* policy of creating or holding an empire. —im·pe'ri·al·ist, *n., adj.* —im·pe''ri·al·is'tic, *adj.*

im·per'il, *v.t.,* -iled, -iling. endanger.

im·pe'ri·ous, *adj.* imposing one's will on others. —im·pe'ri·ous·ly, *adv.*

im·per'ish·a·ble, *adj.* not perishable.

im·per'ma·nent, *adj.* not permanent.

im·per'me·a·ble, *adj.* impossible to seep through.

im·per'son·al, *adj.* pertaining to no individuals. —im·per'son·al·ly, *adv.*

im·per'son·ate'', *v.t.,* -ated, -ating. pretend to be, as in acting. —im·per''son·a'tion, *n.* —im·per'son·a''tor, *n.*

im·per'ti·nent, *adj.* insolent. —im·per'ti·nence, *n.*

im''per·turb'a·ble, *adj.* impossible to disturb visibly. —im''per·turb'a·bly, *adv.*

im·per'vi·ous, *adj.* impenetrable, esp. by moisture.

im·pet'u·ous, *adj.* hasty; rash. —im·pet''u·os'i·ty, *n.*

im·pe·tus, *n.* 1. force in motion. 2. motivation.

im·pi·e·ty, *n.* disrespect, esp. for God. —im'pi·ous, *adj.*

im·pinge', *v.i.*, -pinged, -pinging. 2. encroach. —im·pinge'ment, *n.*

im·plac'a·ble, *adj.* impossible to appease. —im·plac'a·bly, *adv.*

im·plant', *v.t.* fix or plant firmly.

im·plaus'i·ble, *adj.* not plausible.

im'ple·ment, *n.* 1. piece of equipment. —*v.t.* 2. put in effect. —im''ple·men·ta'tion, *n.*

im'pli·cate'', *v.t.*, -cated, -cating. reveal as party to a crime.

im''pli·ca'tion, *n.* act or instance of implying or implicating.

im·plic'it, *adj.* 1. implied. 2. absolute, as trust. —im·plic'it·ly, *adv.*

im·plore', *v.t.*, -plored, -ploring. plead earnestly with or for. —im·plor'ing·ly, *adv.*

im·ply', *v.t.*, -plied, -plying. suggest as existing or being so.

im''po·lite', *adj.* rude.

im·pol'i·tic, *adj.* unwise as giving offense.

im·pon'der·a·ble, *adj.* 1. immeasurable. —*n.* 2. something imponderable.

im·port, *v.t.* (im port') 1. bring into a country, esp. for sale. 2. signify. —*n.* (im'port) 3. something imported. 4. significance. —im·port'er, *n.* —im''por·ta'tion, *n.*

im·port'ant, *adj.* 1. of great significance. 2. of great power. —im·por'tance, *n.*

im''por·tune'', *v.t.*, -tuned, -tuning. urge insistently. —im''por·tun'i·ty, *n.* —im·por'tu·nate, *adj.*

im·pose', *v.*, -posed, posing. *v.t.* 1. force to accept. —*v.i.* 2. take advantage. —im''po·si'tion, *n.*

im·pos'ing, *adj.* impressive. —im·pos'ing·ly, *adv.*

im·pos'si·ble, *adj.* 1. not possible. 2. totally unsuitable or disagreeable. —im·pos''si·bil'i·ty, *n.*

im'post, *n.* tax on imports.

im·pos'tor, *n.* person pretending to an identity, competence, etc. he does not have. —im·pos'ture, *n.*

im·po'tent, *adj.* 1. helpless. 2. without strength. 3. incapable of sexual intercourse. —im'po·tence, im'po·ten·cy, *n.*

im·pound', *v.t.* 1. seize and hold legally. 2. dam.

im·pov'er·ish, *v.t.* make poor. —im·pov'er·ish·ment, *n.*

im·prac·ti·ca·ble, (im prak'ti kə bl), *adj.* impossible to do.

im''prac'ti·cal, *adj.* not practical.

im''pre·ca'tion, *n.* curse.

im''pre·cise', *n.* not precise; vague. —im''pre·ci'sion, *n.*

im·preg'na·ble, *adj.* proof against attack.

im·preg'nate'', *v.t.*, -nated, -nating. 1. saturate. 2. make pregnant. —im''preg·na'tion, *n.*

im·press', *v.t.* 1. command respectful attention. 2. print. 3. force into military service.

im·pres'sion, *n.* 1. mental effect. 2. vague idea. 3. pressed mark.

im·pres'sion·a·ble, *adj.* easily influenced.

im·pres'sive, *adj.* commanding respect. —im·pres'sive·ly, *adv.*

im·print, *v.t.* (im print') 1. affix or print as a mark. —*n.* (im'print) 2. imprinted mark. 3. effect.

im·pris'on, *v.t.* confine in prison. —im·pris'on·ment, *n.*

im·prob'a·ble, *adj.* unlikely. —im·prob''a·bil'i·ty, *n.*

im·promp'tu, *adj.*, *adv.* without preparation.

im·prop'er, *adj.* not proper. —im''pro·pri'e·ty, *n.*

im·prove', *v.*, -proved, -proving. make or become better. —im·prove'ment, *n.*

im·prov'i·dent, *adj.* not thrifty. —im·prov'i·dence, *n.*

im'pro·vise'', *v.*, -vised, -vising. *v.t.* 1. create at short notice or with what is available. —*v.i.* 2. perform extemporaneously. —im·prov''i·sa'tion, *n.*

im·prud'ent, *adj.* not prudent. —im·prud'ence, *n.*

im·pugn', *v.t.* oppose as false.

im'pulse, *n.* 1. surge of force. 2. sudden decision to act. —im·pul'sive, *adj.*

im·pu'ni·ty, *n.* freedom from punishment.

im·pure', *adj.* 1. adulterated. 2. immoral. —im·pur'i·ty, *n.*

im·pute', *v.t.*, -puted, -puting. attribute. —im''pu·ta'tion *n.*

in, *prep.* 1. surrounded or contained by. 2. during. 3. into. 4. subjected to. —*adv.* 5. to the inside.

in-, prefix meaning "not" or "lack of." inaccurate, inadequate, inapplicable, inappropriate, inarticulate, incertitude, inclement, incoherent, incompetent, incongruous, inconsequential, inconsistent, inconspicuous, incontinent, incredible, incredulous, incurable, indecent, indecision, indefinite, indelicate, indigestible, indiscreet, indispensable, indistinct, indivisible, inedible, ineligible, inequitable, inexact, infallible, infertile, informal, infrequent, inhumane, inhumanity, inoffensive, insane, insatiable, insecure, insincere, insufficient, intemperate, intolerable, intransitive, invisible, involuntary, invulnerable.

in ab·sen'ti·a in his, her, or their absence.

in''ad·vert'ent, *adj.* 1. unobservant. 2.

due to unawareness or oversight. —**in″ ad·vert′ent·ly**, *adv.* —**in″ad·vert′ence**, *n.*

in·al′i·en·a·ble, *adj.* not to be taken away.

in·ane′, *adj.* pointless; silly. —**in·an′i·ty**, *n.*

in″as·much′as 1. considering that. 2. to the extent that.

'in·au′gu·rate″, *v.t.*, **-rated, -rating.** begin formally in a term of office, service, etc. —**in″aug″u·ra′tion**, *n.* —**in·aug′u·ral**, *adj.*, *n.*

in′board″, *adj.*, *adv.* within a ship or aircraft.

in′born″, *adj.* present at birth; innate.

in′bred′, *adj.* 1. inborn. 2. resulting from inbreeding.

in′breed′, *v.*, **-bred, -breeding.** *v.t.*, *v.i.* breed from closely related stocks.

in″can·des′cent, *adj.* glowing from heat. —**in″can·des′cence**, *n.*

in″can·ta′tion, *n.* formula producing a magic spell.

in″ca·pac′i·tate″, *v.t.*, **-tated, -tating.** make unable or incompetent. —**in″ca·pac′i·ty**, *n.*

in·car′cer·ate″, *v.t.*, **-ated, -ating.** imprison.

in·car′nate, *adj.*, *v.t.*, **-nated, -nating.** *adj.* (in kahr′nət) 1. in fleshly, mortal form. —*v.t.* (in kahr′nāt) 2. create in incarnate form. —**in″car·na′tion**, *n.*

in·cen′di·ar″y, *adj.*, *n.*, *pl.* **-ies.** *adj.* 1. causing fires. —*n.* 2. incendiary bomb. 3. deliberate setter of fires.

in·cense′, *n.*, *v.t.*, **-censed, -censing.** *n.* (in′sens) 1. gum or resin giving off perfumed smoke. —*v.t.* (in sens′) 2. enrage.

in·cen′tive, *n.* motive.

in·cep′tion, *n.* beginning.

in·ces′sant, *adj.* never ceasing. —**in·ces′sant·ly**, *adv.*

in′cest, *n.* sexual relations between very close relatives. —**in·ces′tu·ous**, *adj.*

inch, *n.* 1. twelfth part of a foot, as a linear measure. —*v.i.*, *v.t.* 2. move very slowly.

in·cho′ate (in kō′it), *adj.* new and formless.

in′ci·dence, *n.* frequency of occurrence.

in′ci·dent, *n.* 1. something that happens. 2. minor fight, etc. —*adj.* 3. probably consequent.

in″ci·den′tal, *adj.* 1. happening in connection with something important. —*n.* 2. something incidental. 3. miscellaneous item.

in″ci·den′tal·ly, *adv.* 1. while we are on the subject. 2. in an incidental manner.

in·cin′er·ate″, *v.*, **-ated, -ating.** *v.t.*, *v.i.* burn to ashes. —**in·cin′er·at″or**, *n.*

in·cip′i·ent, *adj.* beginning to develop. —**in·cip′i·ence**, *n.*

in·cise′, *v.t.*, **-cised, -cising.** cut into. —**in·ci′sion**, *n.*

in·ci′sive, *adj.* penetrating in perception.

in·ci′sor, *n.* human front tooth.

in·cite′, *v.t.*, **-cited, -citing.** urge to act. —**in·cite′ment**, *n.*

in·cline′, *v.*, **-clined, -clining.** *v.i.* (inklīn′) 1. slope or slant. 2. have a tendency or liking. 3. cause to incline. —*n.* (in′klīn) 4. slope. —**in·cli·na′tion**, *n.*

in·close′, *v.t.*, **-closed, -closing.** enclose.

in·clude′, *v.t.*, **-cluded, -cluding.** have or consider among other things. —**in·clu′sion**, *n.*

in·clu′sive, *adj.* 1. including the limiting items mentioned. 2. considering everything.

in·cog·ni′to, *adj.* under an assumed name.

in′come, *n.* money received.

in″com·mu′ni·ca′do, *adj.* without being allowed to communicate.

in·com′par·a·ble, *adj.* not to be compared to others, esp. as an equal. —**im·com′par·a·bly**, *adv.*

in·cor′po·rate″, *v.*, **-rated, -rating.** *v.t.*, *v.i.* 1. form into a corporation. —*v.t.* 2. embody. —**in·cor″po·ra′tion**, *n.*

in·cor′ri·gi·ble, *adj.* incapable of correction.

in·crease′, *v.*, **-creased, -creasing,** *n.* *v.t.* (in krēs′) 1. add to. —*v.i.* 2. become larger or more numerous. —*n.* (in′ krēs) 3. act, instance, or amount of increasing. —**in·creas′ing·ly**, *adv.*

in′cre·ment, *n.* increase.

in·crim′i·nate″, *v.t.*, **-nated, -nating.** 1. accuse of crime. 2. subject to such accusation.

in·crust′, *v.t.* cover thickly. —**in″crus·ta′tion**, *n.*

in′cu·bate″, *v.t.*, **-bated, -bating.** 1. hatch. 2. encourage the development of. —**in″cu·ba′tion**, *n.* —**in′cu·ba″tor**, *n.*

in′cu·bus, *n.* annoying burden.

in·cul′cate, *v.t.*, **-cated, -cating.** impress on the mind.

in·cul′pate, *v.t.*, **-pated, -pating.** incriminate.

in·cum′bent, *adj.* 1. obligatory. 2. in office. —*n.* 3. present office holder. —**in·cum′ben·cy**, *n.*

in·cur′, *v.t.*, **-curred, -curring.** bring on oneself.

in·cur′sion, *n.* invasion.

in·debt′ed, *adj.* owing a debt of money or gratitude. —**in·debt′ed·ness**, *n.*

in·deed′, *adv.* 1. truly. —*interj.* 2. (exclamation of surprise).

in″de·fat′i·ga·ble, *adj.* tireless.

in·def′i·nite·ly, *adj.* 1. in an indefinite way. 2. with no known termination.

in·del′i·ble, *adj.* impossible to erase.

in·dem'ni·fy", v.t., -fied, -fying. compensate for. —in·dem'ni·ty, n.

in·dent', v.t. 1. notch. 2. begin to the right of the normal margin. —in·den'tion, in"den·ta'tion, n.

in·den'ture, n., v.t., -tured, -turing. n. 1. contract, esp. for work. —v.t. 2. bind with an indenture.

in"de·pen'dent, adj. free of or needing no outside control. —in"de·pen'dent·ly, adv. —in"de·pen'dence, n.

in'dex, n., pl. -dexes, -dices, v.t. n. 1. orderly list of subjects. 2. something that indicates. 3. forefinger. —v.t. 4. make an index for.

in'di·cate", v.t., -cated, -cating. 1. call attention to. 2. imply. —in"di·ca'tion, n. —in·dic'a·tive, adj. —in'di·ca"tor, n.

in·dict' (in dīt'), v.t. charge formally with crime. —in·dict'ment, n.

in·dif'fer·ent, adj. 1. not caring. 2. mediocre. 3. neutral. —in·dif'fer·ence, n.

in·dig'en·ous, adj. native.

in'di·gent, adj. needy. —in'di·gence, n.

in·dig'nant, adj. righteously angry. —in·dig'nant·ly, adv. —in"dig·na'tion, n.

in·dig'ni·ty, n., pl. -ties. offense to dignity.

in'di·go", n. deep blue dye. in'dip·posed, adj. 1. disinclined. 2. slightly ill.—in·dis"po·si'tion, n.

in"dis·posed', adj. 1. disinclined. 2. slightly ill.—in·dis"po·si'tion, n.

in"di·vid'u·al, adj. 1. separate or distinct. 2. pertaining to one person or thing. —n. 3. single or unique person or thing. —in"di·vid'u·al·ly, adv. —in"di·vid"u·al'i·ty, n.

in"di·vid'u·al·ism, n. use of personal judgment alone. —in"di·vid'u·al·ist, n.

in·doc'tri·nate", v.t., -nated, -nating. instill doctrine into. —in·doc"tri·na'tion, n.

in'do·lent, adj. making little effort. —in'do·lence, n.

in·dom'i·ta·ble, adj. impossible to defeat or dishearten.

in'door", adj. for use, etc. inside.

in'doors', adv. within a building.

in·du'bi·ta·ble, adj. impossible to doubt. —in·du'bi·ta·bly, adv.

in·duce', v.t., -duced, -ducing. 1. persuade. 2. cause. 3. infer. —in·duce'ment, n.

in·duct', v.t. enter formally, as in a military organization. —in·duc·tee', n.

in·duc'tion, n. 1. act or instance of inducing or inducting. 2. reasoning from the particular to the general. —in·duc'tive, adj.

in·dulge', v., -dulged, -dulging. satisfy.

in·dul'gence, n. 1. act or instance of indulging. 2. indulgent manner.

in·dul'gent, adj. leniently kind.

in·dus'try, n., pl. -tries. 1. manufacture and commerce. 2. type of manufacture or commerce. 3. diligent work. —in·dus'tri·al, adj. —in·dus'tri·al·ist, n. —in·dus'tri·al·ize", v.t. —in·dus'tri·ous, adj.

in·e·bri·ate, v.t., -ated, -ating, n. v.t. (inē'brē āt") 1. make drunk. —n. (in ē' brēət) 2. drunkard. —in·e"bri·a'tion, n.

in·ef'fa·ble, adj. indescribable in words

in"e·luc'ta·ble, adj. inescapable.

in·ept', adj. 1. unsuitable. 2. foolish or awkward. —in·ept'i·tude", in·ept'ness, n.

in·ert', adj. 1. powerless to move. 2. without active properties. —in·er'tia, n. —in·er'tial, adj.

in·ev'i·ta·ble, adj. impossible to avoid. —in·ev'i·ta·bly, adv. —in·ev'i·ta·bil'i·ty, n.

in·ex'o·ra·ble, adj. 1. impossible to persuade. 2. impossible to halt or change. —in·ex'o·ra·bly, adv.

in·ex'pli·ca·ble, adj. impossible to explain.

in ex·tre'mis, at the point of death.

in'fa·mous, adj. of evil reputation.

in'fa·my, n., pl. -mies. infamous state or act.

in'fant, n. very young child. —in'fan·cy, n. —in'fan·tile", adj.

in'fan·try, n., pl. -tries. corps of foot soldiers. —in'fan·try·man, n.

in·fat'u·ate", v.t., -ated, -ating. make foolish with love. —in·fat"u·a'tion, n.

in·fect', v.t. 1. afflict with germs or a virus. 2. influence with feelings. —in·fec'tion, n. —in·fec'tious, adj.

in·fer', v.t., -ferred, -ferring. conclude from evidence. —in'fer·ence, n. —in"fer·en'tial, adj.

in·fe'ri·or, adj. 1. of lesser worth. 2. inadequate. 3. of lesser rank. —n. 4. inferior person. —in·fe"ri·or'i·ty, n.

in·fer'nal, adj. hellish.

in·fer'no, n. hell, esp. as a fiery place.

in·fest', v.t. penetrate harmfully in large numbers. —in"fes·ta'tion, n.

in'fi·del, n. unbeliever.

in'fight"ing, n. combat at close range.

in'fil·trate", v.t., -trated, -trating. penetrate in many places. —in"fil·tra'tion, n.

in'fi·nite, adj. without bounds or end. —in'fin·ite·ly, adv. —in·fin'i·tude", n. —in·fin'i·ty, n.

in"fin·i·tes'i·mal, adj. extremely small.

in·fin'i·tive, n. form of a verb without person, number, or tense.

in·firm', adj. not in good health. —in·firm'i·ty, n.

in·fir'ma·ry, n., pl. -ries. place for treating the sick.

inflame 114

in·flame', *v.t.*, **-flamed, -flaming. 1.** cause to become red, sore, swollen, etc. **2.** rouse to anger, etc. —**in''flam·ma'tion,** *n.* —**in·flam'ma·to''ry,** *adj.*

in·flam'ma·ble, *adj.* **1.** readily burned. **2.** readily aroused to anger, etc.

in·flate', *v.*, **-flated, -flating.** *v.t.* **1.** cause inflation in or to. —*v.i.* **2.** be filled with air or gas. —**in·flat'a·ble,** *adv.*

in·fla'tion, *n.* **1.** filling with air or gas. **2.** fall in the value of money. —**in·fla'tion·ar''y,** *adj.*

in·flect', *v.t.* vary in tone, form, etc. —**in·flec'tion,** *n.* —**in·flec'tion·al,** *adj.*

in·flict', *v.t.* harm or punish someone with. —**in·flic'tion,** *n.*

in'flu·ence, *n., v.t.,* **-enced, -encing.** *n.* **1.** ability to determine events or decisions. **2.** person or thing that influences. —*v.t.* **3.** use influence on.

in''flu·en'tial, *adj.* having much influence.

in''flu·en'za. *n.* contagious virus infection.

in'flux'', *n.* inward flow.

in·form', *v.t.* give knowledge to. —**in·form'ant,** *in·form'er,* *n.* —**in''for·ma'tion,** *n.* —**in·form'a·tive,** *adj.*

in·formed', *adj.* **1.** in possession of essential facts. **2.** learned; erudite.

in·frac'tion, *n.* violation, as of a law.

in''fra·red', *adj.* pertaining to invisible rays beyond the red end of the spectrum.

in·fringe', *v.*, **-fringed, -fringing.** *v.t.* **1.** violate. —*v.i.* **2.** encroach. —**in·fringe'ment,** *n.*

in·fu'ri·ate'', *v.t.*, **-ated, -ating.** make furious.

in·fuse', *v.t.*, **-fused, -fusing. 1.** instill. **2.** steep. —**in''fu'sion,** *n.*

in·gen'ious, *adj.* clever. —**in·gen'ious·ly,** *adv.* —**in''gen·u'i·ty,** *n.*

in·gen'u·ous, *adj.* **1.** naive. **2.** candid. —**in·gen'u·ous·ness,** *n.*

in·gest', *v.t.* eat. —**in·ges'tion,** *n.*

in'got, *n.* cast piece of metal.

in·grained', *adj.* deeply imbedded.

in'grate, *n.* ungrateful person.

in·gra'ti·ate'', *v.t.*, **-ated, -ating.** make favored by another. —**in·gra''ti·a'tion,** *n.*

in·gre'di·ent, *n.* component.

in'gress, *n.* entry.

in'grown'', *adj.* grown into the flesh.

in·hab'it, *v.t.* live in. —**in·hab'it·ant,** *n.*

in·hale', *v.t., v.i.,* **-haled, -haling.** breathe in. —**in''ha'la'tion,** *n.*

in·here', *v.i.*, **-hered, -hering.** be naturally part of something. —**in·her'ent,** *adj.*

in·her'it, *v.t.* be an heir to. —**in·her'i·tance,** *n.*

in·hib'it, *v.t.* check; restrain. —**in''hi·bi'tion,** *n.*

in·hu'man, *adj.* emotionally cold; callous. —**in''hu·man'i·ty,** *n.*

in·im'i·cal, *adj.* hostile.

in·iq'ui·ty, *n., pl.* **-ties.** wickedness or wicked act. —**in·iq'ui·tous,** *adj.*

in·i'tial, *adj., n., v.t.,* **-tialed, -tialing.** *adj.* **1.** beginning. —*n.* **2.** beginning letter of a word. —*v.t.* **3.** mark with initials. —**in·i'tial·ly,** *adv.*

in·i'ti·ate'', *v.t.*, **-ated, ating. 1.** begin. **2.** acquaint with basics. **3.** accept as a member with ceremony. —**in·i'ti·a'tion,** *n.*

in·i'ti·a·tive, *n.* **1.** readiness to initiate actions. **2.** personal decision to act.

in·ject', *v.t.* force beneath the skin. —**in·jec'tion,** *n.*

in·junc'tion, *n.* order, as from a court.

in'jure, *v.t.*, **-injured, -juring.** harm. —**in''ju'ri·ous,** *adj.* —**in'ju·ry,** *n.*

ink, *n.* **1.** pigmented liquid for printing, writing, or drawing. —*v.t.* **2.** apply ink to. —**ink'y,** *adj.*

ink'ling, *n.* vague perception.

in'land'', *adj., adv.* **1.** away from the shore, etc. —*n.* **2.** inland region.

in'-law'', *n.* relative by marriage.

in'lay'', *v.t.,* **-laid, -laying.** *n. v.t.* **1.** set into another piece. —*n.* **2.** something inlaid.

in'let, *n.* small extension of a body of water.

in'mate'', *n.* person under confinement.

inn, *n.* small hotel or restaurant.

in·nate'', *adj.* present from birth. —**in·nate'ly,** *adv.*

in'ner, *adj.* farther inside. —**in'ner·most'',** *adj.*

in'ning, *adj.* turn at bat.

in'no·cent, *adj.* **1.** free of guilt. **2.** unsophisticated. —*n.* **3.** innocent person. —**in'no·cent·ly,** *adv.* —**in'no·cence,** *n.*

in·noc'u·ous, *adj.* harmless.

in''no·va'tion, *n.* new discovery or development. —**in''no·vat''or,** *n.* —**in'no·vat''ive,** *adj.*

in''nu·en'do, *n., pl.* **-does, -dos.** sly implication.

in·nu'mer·a·ble, *adj.* too many to count.

in·oc'u·late'', *v.t.*, **-lated, -lating.** immunize with an injection. —**in·noc''u·la'tion,** *n.*

in·or'di·nate, *adj.* excessive. —**in·or'di·nate·ly,** *adv.*

in''put'', *n.* **1.** something supplied. **2.** (computers) data entered into a computer.

in'quest'', *n.* coroner's investigation.

in·quire', *v.i.,* **-quired, -quiring. 1.** ask. **2.** investigate. —**in'quir'y,** *n.*

in·quis'i·tive, *adj.* desiring to know many things.

in'road'', *n.* encroachment.

in·scribe′, *v.t.*, -scribed, -scribing. write or letter. —**in·scrip′tion**, *n.*

in·scru′ta·ble, *adj.* hard to understand. —**in·scru′ta·bly**, *adv.*

in′sect, *n.* six-legged invertebrate.

in·sec′ti·cide″, *n.* insect-killing preparation.

in·sem′i·nate″, *v.t.*, -nated, -nating. inject semen into. —**in·sem′i·na′tion**, *n.*

in·sen′sate, *adj.* insensitive.

in·sen′si·ble, *adj.* 1. unconscious. 2. impossible to sense. —**in·sen′si·bil′i·ty**, *n.*

in·sert′, *v.t.* (in surt′) 1. place into something. —*n.* (in′sərt) 2. something inserted. —**in·ser′tion**, *n.*

in′side′, *adv.*, *prep.* 1. within. —*adj.* 2. inner. —*n.* 3. inner part. —**in·sid′er**, *n.*

in·sid′i·ous, *adj.* slyly dangerous.

in′sight″, *n.* deep understanding.

in·sig′ni·a, *n.*, *pl.* distinguishing badges, etc.

in·sin′u·ate″, *v.t.*, -ated, -ating. 1. imply slyly. 2. introduce imperceptibly. —**in·sin″u·a′tion**, *n.*

in·sip′id, *adj.* flavorless; dull. —**in″si·pid′i·ty**, *n.*

in·sist′, *v.t.* make repeated demands or assertions. —**in·sis′tent**, *adj.* —**in·sis′tence**, *n.*

in″so·far′, *adv.* to such an extent.

in′so·lent, *adj.* disrespectful. —**in′so·lence**, *n.*

in·som′ni·a, *n.* inability to sleep. —**in·som′ni·ac″**, *n.*

in·spect″, *v.t.* examine carefully. —**in·spec′tion**, *n.* —**in·spec′tor**, *n.*

in·spire′, *v.*, -spired, -spiring. *v.t.*, *v.i.* 1. breathe in. —*v.t.* 2. stimulate to mental activity. 3. arouse in someone. —**in″spi·ra′tor**, *n.* —**in″spi·ra′tion·al**, *adj.*

in·stall′, *v.t.* -stalled, -stalling. put in place. —**in″stal·la′tion**, *n.*

in·stall′ment, *n.* item in a series.

in′stance, *n.*, *v.t.*, -stanced, -stancing. *n.* 1. example. 2. occasion. —*v.t.* 3. cite.

in′stant, *n.* 1. moment. —*adj.* 2. happening or ready quickly. 3. imminent. —**in″stan·ta′ne·ous**, *adj.* —**in′stant·ly**, *adv.*

in·stead′, *adv.* in the place.

in′sti·gate″, *v.t.*, -gated, -gating. urge, as to action. —**in″sti·ga′tion**, *n.* —**in′sti·ga″tor**, *n.*

in·still′, *v.t.*, -stilled, -stilling. implant. Also, **in·stil′**.

in′stinct, *n.* inborn prompting or reaction. —**in·stinc′tive**, *adj.* —**in·stinc′tu·al**, *adj.*

in′sti·tute″, *n.*, *v.t.*, -tuted, -tuting. *n.* 1. professional organization or school. —*v.t.* 2. establish. 3. start.

in″sti·tu′tion, *n.* 1. act or instance of instituting. 2. institute. 3. established law or custom. —**in″sti·tu′tion·al**, *adj.*

in·struct′, *v.t.*, 1. inform or advise. 2. command. —**in·struc′tion**, *n.* —**in·struc′tive**, *adj.* —**in·struc′tor**, *n.*

in′stru·ment, *n.* 1. tool, etc. 2. means. 3. measuring device. 4. musical device. 5. legal document.

in″stru·men′tal, *adj.* 1. pertaining to music by instruments. 2. useful. —**in″stru·men′tal·ist**, *n.* —**in″stru·men·tal′i·ty**, *n.*

in′su·lar, *adj.* 1. pertaining to islands. 2. narrow-minded; parochial.

in′su·late″, *v.t.*, -lated, -lating. isolate, esp. from heat, sound, or electricity. —**in″su·la′tion**, *n.* —**in′su·la″tor**, *n.*

in′su·lin, *n.* hormone secreted by the pancreas.

in·sult′, *v.t.* (in sult′) 1. treat so as to hurt the feelings. —*n.* (in′sult) 2. epithet, etc. that insults. —**in·sult′ing**, *adj.*

in·su′per·a·ble, *adj.* impossible to overcome.

in″sup·port′a·ble, *adj.* 1. intolerable. 2. impossible to prove.

in·sure′, *v.t.*, -sured, -suring. 1. guarantee against loss with money. 2. make sure. —**in·sur′ance**, *n.*

in·sur′gent, *n*, *adj.* revolutionary. —**in·sur′gence**, *n.*

in″sur·rec′tion, *n.* revolution.

in·tact′, *adj.* undamaged.

in′take″, *n.* 1. amount received, absorbed, etc. 2. opening for receiving air, etc.

in·tan′gi·ble, *adj.* 1. non-material. 2. non-monetary. 3. indefinable.

in·te·ger, (in′tə jər), *n.* whole number.

in′te·gral, *adj.* 1. forming an essential part. 2. complete.

in′te·grate″, *v.t.*, -grated, -grating. 1. make complete. 2. bring together into a whole. 3. end racial segregation in or among. —**in″te·gra′tion**, *n.*

in·teg′ri·ty, *n.* 1. intactness. 2. firmness of character, honesty, etc.

in·teg′u·ment, *n.* covering, e.g. skin.

in′tel·lect, *n.* ability to comprehend or reason. —**in″tel·lec′tu·al**, *adj.*, *n.*

in·tel′li·gence, *n.* 1. ability to comprehend, reason, and think creatively. 2. news. —**in·tel′li·gent**, *adj.*

in·tel′li·gent′si·a, *n.*, *pl.* intellectuals as a group.

in·tel′li·gi·ble, *adj.* able to be understood.

in·tend′, *v.t.* have as a purpose.

in·tend′ed, *n.* fiancé or fiancée.

in·tense′, *adj.* 1. very strong. 2. with much emotion. —**in·ten′si·ty**, *n.* —**in·ten′si·fy**, *v.t.*, *v.i.*

in·ten′sive, *adj.* 1. thorough. 2. *Grammar.* giving emphasis.

in·tent′, *adj.* 1. earnest. 2. firmly intending. —*n.* 3. purpose. —**in·tent′ly**, *adv.*

in·ten'tion, *n.* purpose. —**in·ten'tion·al,** *adj.*

in·ter', *v.t.,* **-terred, -terring.** bury.

in''ter·cede', *v.i.,* **-ceded, -ceding.** mediate. —**in''ter·ces'sion,** *n.*

in''ter·cept', *v.t.* halt or attack along the way. —**in''ter·cep'tion,** *n.*

in·ter·change, *v.,* **-changed, -changing,** *n. v.i., v.t.* (in''tər chānj'), **1.** exchange. **2.** alternate. —*n.* (in'tər chānj') **3.** access to an express highway. —**in''ter·change'a·ble,** *adj.*

in''ter·con·nect', *v.i.* connect with one another. —**in''ter·con·nec'tion,** *n.*

in''ter·course'', *n.* **1.** communication. **2.** copulation.

in''ter·de·pen'dent, *adj.* dependent on one another. —**in''ter·de·pen'dence,** *n.*

in·ter·dict, *v.t.* (in''tər dikt') **1.** prohibit. —*n.* (in'tər dikt') **2.** prohibition. —**in'' ter·dic'tion,** *n.*

in''ter·dis·ci·pli·nar''y, *adj.* involving varied disciplines.

in'ter·est, *n.* **1.** willing attention. **2.** share in a business. **3.** profit on a loan. —*v.t.* **4.** obtain willing attention from.

in''ter·fere', *v.i.,* **-fered, -fering. 1.** meddle. **2.** intervene. —**in''ter·fer'ence,** *n.*

in'ter·im, *n.* intervening time.

in·te'ri·or, *n.* **1.** inside. **2.** room. —*adj.* **3.** inside. **4.** personal.

in''ter·ject', *v.t.* insert as an interruption or addition.

in''ter·jec'tion, *n.* **1.** exclamation. **2.** act or instance of interjecting.

in''ter·lace'', *v.i.* be entwined or woven together.

in''ter·lard'', *v.t.* scatter throughout.

in''ter·lock'', *v.i.* be connected or act together.

in''ter·lop''er, *n.* person who interferes.

in''ter·lude'', *n.* episode, musical piece, etc. between major events.

in''ter·mar'ry, *v.i.,* **-ried, -rying. 1.** become associated my marriage. **2.** marry a close relation. —**in''ter·mar'riage,** *n.*

in''ter·me'di·ar''y, *adj., n., pl.* **-ies.** *adj.* **1.** coming between. —*n.* **2.** go-between.

in''ter·me'di·ate, *adj.* coming between.

in·ter'ment, *n.* burial.

in·ter'min·a·ble, *adj.* seemingly endless. —**in·ter'min·a·bly,** *adv.*

in''ter·min·gle, *v.i.,* **-gled, -gling.** be blended.

in''ter·mis'sion, *n.* pause, as between acts of a play.

in''ter·mit'tent, *adj.* occurring at intervals. —**in''ter·mit'tent·ly,** *adv.*

in·tern, *n.* (in'tərn) **1.** Also, **in'terne.** assistant resident doctor. —*v.t.* (intərn') **2.** detain and confine. —**in·tern'ment,** *n.*

in·ter'nal, *adj.* **1.** interior. **2.** non-foreign. —**in·ter'nal·ly,** *adv.*

in''ter·na'tion·al, *adj.* **1.** among nations. **2.** regardless of nation.

in''ter·ne'cine, *adj.* deadly to both sides.

in'ter·nist, *n.* doctor using non-surgical treatment.

in''ter·play'', *n.* mutual influence.

in·ter'po·late'', *v.t.,* **-lated, -lating.** alter with new material. —**in·ter''po·la' tion,** *n.*

in''ter·pose'', *v.t.,* **-posed, -posing.** place between or among. —**in''ter·po·si' tion,** *n.*

in·ter'pret, *v.t.,* **1.** clarify. **2.** understand. **3.** translate. —**in·ter'pret·er,** *n.* —**in· ter''pre·ta'tion,** *n.* —**in·ter'pre·tive,** *adj.*

in''ter·ra'cial, *adj.* among races.

in''ter·re·late'', *v.t.,* **-lated, -lating.** relate one to the other. —**in''ter·re·la'tion,** *n.*

in·ter'ro·gate'', *v.t.,* **-gated, -gating.** question. —**in·ter''ro·ga'tion,** *n.* —**in· ter'ro·ga''tor,** *n.* —**inter·rog'a·tive,** **in''ter·rog'a·to·ry,** *adv.*

in''ter·rupt', *v.t.,* **1.** halt with an action, remark etc. **2.** break the uniformity of. —**in''ter·rup'tion,** *n.*

in''ter·sect', *v.t., v.i.* cross. —**in''ter·sec' tion,** *n.*

in''ter·sperse'', *v.t.,* **-spersed, -spersing. 1.** scatter. **2.** vary with scattered things.

in'ter·state'', *adj., adv.* from state to state.

in·ter'stice, *n.* gap.

in''ter·ur'ban, *adj.* from city to city.

in'ter·val, *n.* intervening period or space.

in''ter·vene', *v.i.,* **-vened, -vening. 1.** come or occur between. **2.** mediate. —**in''ter·ven'tion,** *n.*

in'ter·view'', *n.* **1.** person-to-person meeting. —*v.t.* **2.** question at an interview. —**in'ter·view''er,** *n.* —**in''ter· view''ee'',** *n.*

in·tes'tate'', *adj.* without having made a will.

in·tes'tine, *n.* either of two organs for converting food. Also, **in·tes'tines.** —**in·tes'tin·al,** *adj.*

in·ti·mate, *adj., n., v.t.,* **-mated, -mating.** *adj.* (in'tə mət) **1.** emotionally close. **2.** personal. **3.** thorough. —*n.* **4.** intimate friend. —*v.t.* (in'tə māt') **5.** hint. —**in'ti·mate·ly,** *adv.* —**in'ti·ma· cy,** *n.* —**in''ti·ma'tion,** *n.*

in·tim'i·date'', *v.t.,* **-dated, -dating.** command through fear. —**in·tim''i·da' tion,** *n.*

in'to, *prep.* **1.** to the interior or depths of. **2.** up against. **3.** to some material, number of parts, etc.

in·tone', *v.t.,* **-toned, -toning. 1.** utter in a songlike tone. **2.** utter with a con-

trolled or varied pitch. —in″to·na′ tion, n.

in to′to, as a whole.

in·tox′i·cate″, v.t., -cated, -cating. make drunk. —in·tox″i·ca′tion, n. —in·tox′i·cant, n.

in·trac′ta·ble, adj. unruly.

in″tra·mu′ral, adj. within an institution.

in·tran′si·gent, adj. uncompromising. —in·tran′si·gence, n.

in″tra·ve′nous, adj. into a vein from outside the body.

in·trep′id, adj. fearless. —in″tre·pid′i·ty, n.

in′tri·cate, adj. complicated; complex. —in″tri·cate·ly, adv. —in′tri·ca·cy, n.

in·trigue′, v., -trigued, -triguing. v.i. 1. plot in stealth. —v.t. 2. make curious. —n. 3. stealthy plot or plotting.

in·trin′sic, adj. essential; inherent. —in·trin′si·cal·ly, adv.

in″tro·duce′, v.t., -duced, -ducing. 1. present for the first time. 2. bring into use. 3. insert. —in″tro·duc′tion, n. —in″tro·duc′to·ry, adj.

in″tro·spec′tion, n. self-examination. —in″tro·spec′tive, adj.

in′tro·vert″, n. withdrawn person. —in″tro·ver′sion, n.

in·trude′, v., -truded, -truding. v.i. 1. come as an interruption or surprise. —v.t. 2. force upon others. —in·trud′er, n. —in·tru′sion, n. —in·tru′sive, adj.

in″tu·i′tion, n. non-logical insight. —in·tu′i·tive, adj.

in·un′date′, v.t., -dated, -dating. flood. —in″un·da′tion, n.

in·ure′, v.t., -ured, -uring. harden; accustom.

in·vade′, v.t., -vaded, -vading. enter with force. —in·vad′er, n. —in·va′sion, n.

in·val′id, n. (in′və lid) 1. sick person. —adj. (in val′id) 2. not valid. —in·val′i·date″,¹ v.t.

in·val′u·a·ble, adj. valuable beyond reckoning.

in·vec′tive, n. verbal attack.

in·veigh′, v.i. make a verbal attack.

in·vei′gle, v.t., -gled, -gling. trick into an action.

in·vent′, v.t. discover, as a product or process. —in·ven′tion, n. —in·ven′tive, adj. —in·ven′tor, n.

in′ven·to″ry, n., pl. -ries, v.t., -ried, -rying. n. 1. precise list. 2. stock of goods. —v.t. 3. make an inventory of.

in·verse′, adj. 1. opposite in kind. —n. 2. something inverse. —in·verse′ly, adv.

in·vert′, v.t. 1. turn upside down. 2. reverse in order or position. —in·ver′sion, n.

in·ver′te·brate, adj. 1. having no backbone. —n. 2. invertebrate animal.

in·vest′, v.t. 1. put into something in the hope of profit. 2. give authority or office to. —v.i. 3. invest money. —in·vest′or, n. —in·vest′ment, n. —in·vest′i·ture″, n.

in·ves′ti·gate″, v.t., -gated, -gating. examine or explore. —in·ves″ti·ga′tor, n. —in·ves″ti·ga′tion, n.

in·vet′er·ate, adj. habitual. —in·vet′er·a·cy, n.

in·vid′i·ous, adj. causing ill will.

in·vig′or·ate″, v.t., -ated, -ating. make vigorous. —in·vig″or·a′tion, n.

in·vin′ci·ble, adj. impossible to conquer. —in·vinc″i·bil′i·ty, n.

in·vi′o·la·ble, adj. not to be violated. —in·vi″o·la·bil′i·ty, n.

in·vi′o·late, adj. unviolated.

in·vite′, v.t., -vited, -viting. 1. ask to be present. 2. give a pretext for. —in″vi·ta′tion, n.

in·vit′ing, adj. enticing.

in″vo·ca′tion, n. prayerlike speech.

in′voice, n. list of goods supplied.

in·voke′, v.t., -voked, -voking. 1. call upon, as a god. 2. cite as a justification.

in″vo·lu′tion, n. intricacy. —in′vo·lut″ed, adj.

in·volve′, v.t., -volved, -volving. 1. include as relevant. 2. affect or trouble. 3. occupy. 4. complicate. —in·volve′ment, n.

in′ward, adj. 1. inside, 2. toward the inside. 3. mental. —adv. 4. Also, in′wards, towards the inside. —in·ward′ly, adv.

i′o·dine″, n. nonmetallic chemical element. —i′o·dize″, v.t.

i′on, n. electrically charged atom or group of these.

i·o′ta, n. minute quantity.

ip′so fac′to, by the very fact.

IQ, intelligence quotient (measure of intelligence). Also I.Q.

ir-, prefix meaning "not" or "lack of." irrational, irreconcilable, irredeemable, irregular, irrelevant, irreligious, irremediable, irreparable, irreplaceable, irresponsible, irreverent, irreversible, irrevocable.

i·ras·ci·ble (i ras′ə bl), adj. easily angered.

ire, n. wrath. —i·rate′, adj.

ir″i·des′cent, adj. with a play of rainbow-like colors. —ir″i·des′cence, n.

i′ris, n., pl. irises. n. 1. pigmented part surrounding the eye pupil. 2. plant with sword-shaped leaves.

irk, v.t. annoy. —irk′some, adj.

i′ron, n. 1. metallic element attracting magnets. 2. device made of iron. 3. irons,shackles. —v.t. 4. smooth with an iron.

Iron Curtain, barrier to travel, information, etc. around the communist countries.

i′ro·ny, n., pl. **-nies.** figure of speech conveying meaning through words of opposite meaning. —**i·ron′i·cal, i·ron′ic,** adj.

ir·ra′di·ate″, v.t., **-ated, ating.** expose to rays.

ir″re·gard′less, adj., adv. regardless.

ir″re·sist′i·ble, adj. 1. impossible to resist. 2. overwhelmingly tempting.

ir′ri·gate″, v.t., **-gated, -gating.** introduce water to, to raise crops. —**ir″ri·ga′tion,** n.

ir′ri·ta·ble, adj. readily irritated. —**ir′ri·ta·bly,** adv. —**ir″ri·ta·bil′i·ty,** n.

ir′ri·tate″, v.t., **-tated, -tating.** 1. annoy. 2. make sore. —**ir″ri·ta′tion,** n. —**ir′ri·tant,** adj., n.

ir·rupt′, v.i. 1. burst forth; expand. —**ir·rup′tion,** n.

i′sin·glass″, n. 1. gelatin from fish bladders. 2. mica.

Is′lam, n. religion of Muhammad.

is′land (ī′land) n. 1. body of land surrounded by water. 2. isolated platform, etc.

is·let (ī′lət), n. small island.

i′so·late″, v.t., **-lated, -lating.** keep apart. —**i″so·la′tion,** n.

i″so·la′tion·ist, n. believer in no alliances with other countries. —**i″so·la′tion·ism,** n.

i″so·met′ric, adj. 1. with all dimensions represented to the same scale. 2. pertaining to isometrics. —n. 3. isometrics, type of muscular exercise.

i·sos′cel·es″, adj. pertaining to triangles with two equal sides.

i′so·tope″, n. form of an element coinciding in atomic number but not in atomic weight with another.

is′sue, v., **-sued, -suing.** v.t. 1. give out. 2. publish. —v.i. 3. emerge. —n. 4. something that issues. 5. periodical of one date. 6. thing in dispute. 7. offspring. 8. result. —**is′su·ance,** n.

isth′mus, n., pl. **-muses.** narrow neck of connecting land between bodies of water.

it, pron., pl. **they** 1. thing referred to. 2. (subject of various impersonal verbs).

i·tal′ic, adj. 1. pertaining to letters printed thus: Italics. —n. 2. italics, italic letters. —**i·tal′i·cize″,** v.t.

itch, v.i. 1. feel a mild irritation tempting one to scratch. 2. desire restlessly. —n. 3. act or instance of itching. —**itch′y,** adj.

i′tem, n. 1. listed thing. 2. piece of news. —**i′tem·ize″,** v.t. —**i″tem·i·za′tion,** n.

it·er·ate″, v.t., **-ated, -ating.** repeat. —**it″er·a′tion,** n.

i·tin′er·ant, adj. 1. traveling; migratory. —n. 2. itinerant person.

i·tin′er·ar″y, n., pl. **-ies.** plan of travel.

its, pron. belonging or pertaining to it.

it′s, pron. contraction of it is.

it·self′, pron. 1. (intensive or reflexive of it). 2. its true self.

i′vo·ry, n. creamy-white substance of tusks.

i′vy, n., pl. **ivies.** climbing evergreen vine. —**i′vied,** adj.

J

J, j, n. tenth letter of the English alphabet.

jab, v., **jabbed, jabbing.** v.t., v.i. n. poke

jab′ber, n. 1. fast, incoherent talk. —v.i. 2. talk in a jabber.

jack, n. 1. lifting machine. 2. playing card; knave. 3. flag at a ship's stern. 4. point of connection; place where something is plugged in. —v.t. 5. to raise something with a jack.

jack′al, n. wild African and Asian dog.

jack′ass″, n. 1. male donkey. 2. fool.

jack′et, n. 1. short coat. 2. covering.

jack′knife″, n., v.i., **-knifed, -knifing.** n. 1. folding knife. 2. type of swimmer's dive. —v.i. 3. fold accidentally at a joint.

jack′pot″, n. accumulated stakes that are won.

jack′rab″bit, n. large North American hare.

jade, n., v.t., **jaded, jading.** n. 1. ornamental stone, usually green. —v.t. 2. satiate.

jag, n. 1. sharp point. 2. Informal. orgy.

jag′ged, adj. with a rough, sharp edge or surface.

jag′uar, n. large cat of Latin America and the U.S. Southwest.

jail, n. 1. prison for short confinements. —v.t. 2. put in jail. —**jail′er, jail′or,** n.

ja·lop′y, n., pl. **-ies.** old, ill-kept car.

jal′ou·sie, n. louvered blind.

jam, v., **jammed, jamming.** n. v.t., v.i. 1. crowd. 2. stick tight. —n. 3. act or instance of jamming. 4. fruit boiled with sugar. 5. Informal. adverse situation.

jamb, n. upright of a doorway or window.

jam″bo·ree′, n. Informal. noisy celebration.

jam′packed′, adj. crowded to capacity.

jan′gle, v. **-gled, -gling.** v.i. 1. jingle harshly. —v.t. 2. irritate, as the nerves.

jan′i·tor, *n.* person who takes care of a building.

Jan′u·ar″y, *n.* first month.

jar, *n., v.,* **jarred, jarring.** *n.* 1. cylindrical container. 2. jolt. —*v.t.* 3. jolt. —*v.i.* 4. clash. 5. have an irritating effect.

jar′gon, *n.* abstruse technical language.

jas′mine, *n.* fragrant-flowered plant.

jas′per, *n.* opaque, colored quartz.

jaun′dice, *n., v.t.,* **-diced, -dicing.** *n.* 1. disease characterized by yellowing due to bile in the blood. —*v.t.* 2. predispose against.

jaunt, *n.* 1. pleasure excursion. —*v.i.* 2. go on a jaunt.

jaun′ty, *adj.,* **-tier, -tiest.** cheerful. —**jaun′ti·ly,** *adv.*

jav′e·lin, *n.* throwing spear.

jaw, *n.* 1. bony framing member of the mouth. 2. gripping part of a vise, etc.

jay, *n.* 1. crowlike bird. 2. bluejay.

jay′walk″, *v.i.* cross a street heedlessly. —**jay′walk″er,** *n.*

jazz, *n.* syncopated, rythmic modern music.

jeal′ous, *adj.* 1. feeling jealousy. 2. watchful.

jeans, *n., pl.* trousers of strong cloth.

jeep, *n.* rugged, military-style car.

jeer, *v.i.* make scornful utterances. —*n.* 2. such an utterance.

je·june′, *adj.* 1. unfulfilling. 2. childish.

jell, *v.i.* 1. harden, as gelatin. 2. come to fulfillment.

jel′ly, *n., pl.* **-lies,** *v.t.* **-lied, -lying.** *n.* 1. gelatinous food. —*v.t.* 2. make into jelly.

jeo′pard·ize″, *v.t.,* **-ized, -izing.** put in danger. —**jeo′pard·y,** *n.*

jer′e·mi·ad′, *n.* tale of lamentation or anger.

jerk, *n.* 1. sharp pull. —*v.t.* 2. pull sharply. —*v.i.* 3. twitch. —**jerk′y,** *adj.*

jer′ry-built, *adj.* cheaply and flimsily built.

jer′sey, *n., pl.* **-sies.** closefitting knitted shirt.

jest, *n.* joke.

jet, *n., v.i.* **jetted, jetting.** *n.* 1. forced stream. 2. jet-propelled airplane. 3. coal-like mineral used in jewelry. —*v.i.* 4. emerge in a jet. 5. travel by jet.

jet propulsion, propulsion by the reactive thrust of a jet. —**jet′pro·pelled′,** *adj.*

jet′sam, *n.* material thrown overboard.

jet′ti·son, *v.t.* throw away or overboard.

jet′ty, *n., pl.* **-ties.** pier or wall into the water.

jew′el, *n.* precious stone. —**jew′el·er, jew′el·ler,** *n.* —**jew′el·ry,** *n.*

jib, *n.* triangular sail at the bow.

jibe, *v.i.,* **jibed, jibing,** *n.* gibe.

jif′fy, *n., pl.* **-fies.** *Informal.* short period.

jig, *n., v.i.,* **jigged, jigging.** *n.* 1. fast dance. 2. tool guide. —*v.i.* 3. dance a jig.

jig′ger, *n.* one-and-a-half ounce glass.

jig′gle, *v.,* **-gled, gling.** *n. v.i., v.t.* 1. move in rapid jerks. —*n.* 2. act or instance of jiggling.

jig′saw″, *n.* narrow-bladed saw.

jilt, *v.t.* reject.

jin′gle, *v.,* **-gled, -gling,** *n. v.i., v.t.* 1. ring lightly and rapidly. —*n.* 2. act or instance of jingling. 3. simple verse.

jinx, *n.* 1. bringer of ill-luck. —*v.t.* 2. bring ill-luck to.

jit′ney, *n., pl.* **-nies.** bus.

jit′ters, *n. Informal.* nervousness. —**jit′ter·y,** *adj.*

job, *n., v.t.,* **jobbed, jobbing.** *n.* 1. task. 2. occupation. 3. duty —*v.t., v.i.* 4. buy in quantity for resale to dealers. —**job′less,** *adj.* —**job′ber,** *n.*

jock′ey, *n., pl.* **-eys,** *v.i.,* **-eyed, -eying.** *n.* 1. rider of race horses. —*v.i.* 2. maneuver for advantage.

jo·cose′, *adj.* playful. Also, **joc′und.** —**jo·cos′i·ty,** *n.*

joc′u·lar, *adj.* joking; playful.

jog, *v.,* **jogged, jogging,** *n. v.t.* 1. nudge. —*v.i.* 2. run steadily. —*n.* 3. act or instance of jogging. 4. abrupt change of direction.

join, *v.t.* 1. put together. 2. become a member of. —*v.i.* 3. come or act together.

join′er, *n.* 1. woodworker. 2. *Informal.* person who likes to join groups. —**join′er·y,** *n.*

joint, *n.* 1. connection. —*adj.* 2. shared 3. sharing with others. —*v.t.* 4. assemble with joints. —**joint′ly,** *adv.*

joist, *n.* floor beam.

joke, *n., v.i.* **joked, joking.** *n.* 1. laugh-provoking story or remark. 2. playful act. —*v.i.* 3. make a joke.

jol′ly, *adj.* **-lier, -liest,** *v.t.,* **-lied, -lying.** *adj.* 1. full of high spirits. —*v.t.* 2. *Informal.* **a.** cajole. **b.** tease. —**jol′li·ly,** *adv.* —**jol′lity,** *n.*

jolt, *v.t.* 1. shake or bump. —*v.i.* 2. move bumpily. —*n.* 3. act or instance of jolting.

josh, *v.t.* banter.

jos′tle, *v.,* **-tled, -tling.** *v.t., v.i.* shove, as in a crowd.

jot, *n., v.t.,* **jotted, jotting.** *n.* 1. minimal amount. —*v.t.* 2. make a note of.

jounce, *v.i.,* **jounced, jouncing.** jolt and bounce. —**jounc′y,** *adj.*

jour′nal, *n.* 1. periodical. 2. diary. 3. section of an axle in a bearing.

jour′nal·ism, *n.* work for a periodical. —**jour′nal·ist,** *n.* —**jour″nal·is′tic,** *adj.*

jour′ney, *n., pl.* **-neys,** *v.i.,* **-neyed, -neying,** *n.* 1. long trip. —*v.i.* 2. go on a journey.

jour′ney·man, *n.* skilled worker.

jo'vi·al, *adj.* merry. —**jo''vi·al'i·ty,** *n.*

jowl, *n.* lower cheek.

joy, *n.* **1.** intense happiness. **2.** source of this. —**joy'ful, joy'ous,** *adj.*

joy''stick, *n.* (computers) grippable device for data manipulation, used mostly for graphics and games.

ju'bi·lant, *adj.* rejoicing. —**ju''bi·la'tion,** *n.*

ju'bi·lee'', *n.* **1.** major anniversary. **2.** time of rejoicing.

Ju'da·ism, *n.* Jewish religion. —**Ju·da'ic,** *adj.*

judge, *n., v.t.,* **judged, judging.** *n.* **1.** presider over a trial, contest, etc. **2.** qualified evaluator. —*v.t.* **3.** evaluate. —**judg'ment, judge'ment,** *n.* —**judge'ship'',** *n.*

ju·di'cial, *adj.* **1.** pertaining to judges or courts. **2.** impartial.

ju·di'ci·ar''y, *adj., n., pl.* **-ies.** *adj.* **1.** judicial. —*n.* **2.** judges.

ju·di'cious, *adj.* with sound judgment. —**ju·di'cious·ly,** *adv.*

ju'do, *n.* Japanese system of wrestling.

jug, *n.* broad vessel with a narrow neck.

jug'ger·naut'', *n.* crushing force.

jug'gle, *v.* **-gled, -gling.** *v.t.* toss, balance with skill. —*v.i.* **2.** perform such activities for a living. —**jug'gler,** *n.*

jug'u·lar, *adj.* **1.** pertaining to the neck. —*n.* **2.** neck vein.

juice, *n., v.t.,* **juiced, juicing.** *n.* **1.** liquid from a fruit, etc. —*v.t.* **2.** extract juice from. —**juic'y,** *adj.*

ju·jit'su, *n.* Japanese system of wrestling. Also, **ju·jut'su.**

juke'box'', *n.* coin-operated record player.

Ju'ly, *n.* seventh month.

jum'ble, *v.t.,* **-bled, -bling.** *n. v.t.* **1.** mix in disorder. —*n.* **2.** disorderly mixture.

jum'bo, *adj.* very large.

jump, *v.i.* **1.** leave the ground with a muscular effort. **2.** move abruptly. —*v.t.* **3.** jump over. —*n.* **4.** act or instance of jumping.

jump'er, *n.* sleeveless dress.

jum'py, *adj.,* **-pier, -piest.** very nervous.

junc'tion, *n.* place of joining.

junc'ture, *n.* **1.** junction. **2.** moment. **3.** crisis.

June, *n.* sixth month.

jun'gle, *n.* densely grown tropical area.

jun'ior, *adj.* **1.** being the son of a father with the same name. **2.** lesser in rank, size, etc. —*n.* **3.** junior person. **4.** third-year student.

ju'ni·per, *n.* evergreen with berry-like cones.

junk, *n.* **1.** rejected or worthless material. **2.** Chinese sailing boat. —*v.t.* **3.** scrap.

junk'et, *n.* **1.** curdled milk dish. **2.** excursion. —*v.i.* **3.** go on a junket.

junk'ie, *n. Informal.* narcotics addict. Also, **junk'y.**

jun·ta (hŏŏn tə), *n.* military in power after a coup d'etat.

ju''ris·dic'tion, *n.* **1.** administration of justice. **2.** area of authority. —**ju''ris·dic'tion·al,** *adj.*

ju''ris·pru'dence, *n.* philosophy of law.

ju'rist, *n.* expert in law.

ju'ry, *n., pl.* **-ries.** group deciding the outcome of a trial, hearing, or contest. —**ju'ry·man, ju'ror,** *n.*

just, *adj.* **1.** fair. **2.** righteous. **3.** accurate. —*adv.* **4.** exactly. **5.** only. **6.** by a short margin. —**just'ly,** *adv.* —**just'ness,** *n.*

jus'tice, *n.* **1.** fairness. **2.** righteousness. **3.** administration of law. **4.** judge.

jus'ti·fy'', *v.t.,* **-fied, -fying.** give valid reasons for. —**jus''ti·fi'a·ble,** *adj.* —**jus''ti·fi·ca'tion,** *n.*

jut, *v.i.,* **jutted, jutting.** project

jute, *n.* coarse plant fiber.

ju'ven·ile, *adj.* **1.** pertaining to children. **2.** childish. —*n.* **3.** child.

jux'ta·pose'', *v.t.,* **-posed, -posing.** place close or in contrast. —**jux''ta·po·si'tion,** *n.*

K

K, k, *n.* eleventh letter of the English alphabet.

kai'ser, *n.* Germanic emperor.

kale, *n.* type of cabbage. Also, **kail.**

ka·lei'do·scope'', *n.* device creating symmetrical patterns for viewing. —**ka·lei'do·scop'ic,** *adj.*

kan''ga·roo', *n.* leaping Australian marsupial.

ka·put', *adj.* destroyed or out of order.

kar'at, *n.* twenty-fourth part pure gold.

ka·ra'te, *n.* Japanese technique of fighting with hands and feet.

kar'ma, *n.* one's acts as a determinant of one's fate.

ka'ty·did'', *n.* shrill, green insect.

kay'ak, *n.* Eskimo canoe.

keel, *n.* central structural member of a ship.

keen, *adj.* **1.** sharp. **2.** eager. **3.** shrewd.

keep, *v.,* **kept, keeping,** *n. v.t.* **1.** retain. **2.** look after. **3.** protect or support. **4.** be observant of. —*v.i.* **5.** be preserved. **6.** abstain. **7.** remain or continue. —*n.* **8.** support; custody.

keep'ing, **1.** care; custody. **2.** conformity.

keep'sake'', *n.* souvenir.

keg, *n.* small barrel.

ken, *n.* range of awareness or knowledge.

ken'nel, *n.*, *v.t.*, **-neled**, **-neling.** *n.* doghouse. —*v.t.* **2.** put in a kennel.

ker'chief, *n.* cloth for covering the head.

ker'nel, *n.* **1.** seed. **2.** inner nut.

ker'o·sene'', *n.* petroleum derivative.

ketch'up, *n.* sauce, often made with tomatoes.

ket'tle, *n.* pot for boiling water.

ket'tle-drum'', *n.* large, potlike drum.

key, *n.*, *adj.*, *v.t.* **keyed**, **keying.** *n.* **1.** metal instrument operating a lock. **2.** device on a piano, etc. pressed in operating it. **3.** thing that explains. **4.** system of musical tones. —*adj.* **5.** decisive. —*v.t.* **6.** *Music.* put into a key. —**key'hole''**, *n.*

key''board, *n.* (computers) **1.** device resembling a typewriter keyboard used for data input. —*v.* **2.** to input data with a keyboard.

key'note'', *n.* **1.** lowest note of a scale. **2.** basic theme.

key'stone'', *n.* top stone of an arch.

kha'ki, *n.*, *pl.* **-kis. 1.** dull yellowish brown. **2.** khakis, clothing made of cloth this color.

kib'bitz, *v.t.* give unwanted advice.

kib·butz', *n.*, *pl.* **-butzim.** Israeli collective settlement.

kick, *v.t.*, *v.i.* **1.** strike with the foot. —*v.i.* **2.** recoil. **3.** *Informal.* complain. —*n.* **4.** act or instance of kicking. **5.** *Informal.* **a.** grievance. **b.** thrill.

kick'back'', *n.* *Informal.* rebate, usually illicit.

kid, *n.*, *v.*, **kidded**, **kidding.** *n.* **1.** young goat. **2.** *Informal.* child. —*v.t.* **3.** *Informal.* tease. —*v.i.* **4.** *Informal.* joke.

kid'nap'', *v.t.*, **-napped** or **-naped**, **-napping** or **-naping.** abduct and hold prisoner. —**kid'nap''er**, *n.*

kid'ney, *n.* **1.** organ that forms urine. **2.** sort or kind.

kill, *v.t.* **1.** cause to die. **2.** end abruptly. —*n.* **3.** act or instance of killing. **4.** game killed. —**kill'er**, *n.*

kiln (kil, kiln), *n.* furnace for processing materials.

ki'lo, *n.*, *pl.* **-los. 1.** kilogram. **2.** kilometer.

ki'lo·gram'', *n.* one thousand grams or 2.2046 pounds.

ki'lo·hertz'', *n.* one thousand hertz. Also, **ki'lo·cy''cle.**

ki'lo·me''ter, *n.* one thousand meters or 3,281 feet.

kil'o·watt'', *n.* one thousand watts.

kilt, *n.* knee-length Scottish skirt for men.

kil'ter, *n.* *Informal.* good condition.

ki·mo'no, *n.*, *pl.* **-nos.** *n.* full-length Japanese dress.

kin, *n.* relatives.

kind, *n.* **1.** sort. —*adj.* **2.** benevolent; compassionate. —**kind'ness**, *n.*

kin'der·gar''ten, *n.* pre-elementary school.

kin'dle, *v.*, **-dled**, **-dling.** *v.t.* **1.** set on fire. **2.** arouse. —*v.i.* **3.** be kindled. —**kind'ling**, *n.*

kind'ly, *adj.* **1.** kind. —*adv.* **2.** in a kind way. **3.** graciously; favorably. —**kind'li·ness**, *n.*

kin'dred, *n.*, *pl.* **1.** relatives. —*adj.* **2.** of the same kind.

ki·net'ic, *adj.* pertaining to motion.

kin'folk'', *n.*, *pl.* relatives. Also, **kin'folks''.**

king, *n.* **1.** male national ruler. **2.** playing card. —**king'ly**, *adj.*

king'dom, *n.* **1.** state ruled by a king. **2.** major category.

king'fish''er, *n.* diving bird that eats fish.

king'-size'', *adj.* *Informal.* extra-large.

kink, *n.* short loop or coil. —**kink'y**, *adj.*

kin'ship'', *n.* family relationship.

kins'man, *n.* male relative. Also, *fem.*, **kins'wom''an.**

ki'osk, *n.* small open shelter.

kip'per, *n.* salted, smoked herring.

kiss, *n.* **1.** touching with the lips as a sign of affection, etc. —*v.t.* **2.** give a kiss to. —*v.i.* **3.** exchange kisses.

kit, *n.* set of equipment.

kitch'en, *n.* place for preparing meals.

kite, *n.* flying toy on a string.

kith and kin, friends and relatives.

kitsch, *n.* vulgar, affected art. —**kitsch'y**, *adj.*

kit'ten, *n.* young cat. —**kit'ten·ish**, *adj.*

kit'ty, *n.*, *pl.* **-ties.** *n.* *Informal.* **1.** cat. **2.** accumulated stakes.

klep''to·ma'ni·a, *n.* compulsion to steal. —**klep''to·ma'ni·ac**, *n.*

knack, *n.* talent.

knap'sack'', *n.* sack worn on the back.

knave, *n.* **1.** *Archaic.* deceitful person. **2.** playing card; jack. —**knav'ish**, *adj.* —**knav'er·y**, *n.*

knead, *v.t.* press and work with the fingers.

knee, *n.* joint of the leg.

kneel, *v.i.*, **knelt** or **kneeled**, **kneeling.** be upright on the knees.

knell, *n.* slow tolling of a bell.

knick'ers, *n.*, *pl.* trousers ending at the knees. Also **knick'er·bock''ers.**

knick'knack'', *n.* small decorative object.

knife, *n.*, *pl.* **knives**, *v.t.*, **knifed**, **knifing.** *n.* **1.** small cutting tool. —*v.t.* **2.** stab with a knife.

knight, *n.* **1.** possessor of an honorable rank, formerly military. **2.** chesspiece. —*v.t.* **3.** declare to be a knight. —**knight'hood**, *n.* —**knight'ly**, *adj.*

knight'-er'rant, *n.*, *pl.* **knights-errant.** knight seeking adventure.

knish (kə nish'), *n.* filled, baked dish of thin dough.

knit, *v.*, **knitted** or **knit**, **kitting.** *v.t.* **1.** assemble from yarn with two needles. **2.**

draw together in wrinkles, as the brows. —*v.i.* 3. join again after a fracture.

knob, *n.* rounded projection or handle. —**knob′by,** *adj.*

knock, *v.t.* 1. hit, as with the fist. 2. *Informal.* disparage. —*v.i.* 3. strike blows. —*n.* 4. act or instance of knocking. 5. adverse happening. —**knock′er,** *n.*

knock′out″, *n.* victory in boxing, esp. by knocking an opponent unconscious.

knoll, *n.* small, round hill.

knot, *n., v.t.,* **knotted, knotting.** *n.* 1. fastening of intertwined cord. 2. small cluster. 3. hard lump in wood. 4. one nautical mile per hour. —*v.t.* 5. make into a knot. —**knot′ty,** *adj.*

know, *v.t.,* **knew, known, knowing.** 1. have full evidence. 2. be fully informed or skilled. 3. have as an acquaintance. 4. recognize. —**know′ing·ly,** *adv.*

know′-how″, *n.* technical ability.

know′ing, *n.* 1. ability to know. —*adj.* 2. shrewd.

know′-it-all″, *n.* pretender to omniscience.

know′ledge, *n.* 1. state of knowing. 2. what is known.

know′ledge·a·ble, *adj.* well-informed.

knuck′le, *n.* central finger joint.

Ko·ran′, *n.* Muslim holy scriptures.

ko′sher, *adj. Judaism.* fit to eat under religious law.

kow′tow′, *v.t.* show servility or deference.

ku′dos, *n. Informal.* praise; fame.

kum′quat″, *n.* small, tart citrus fruit.

L

L, l, *n.* twelfth letter of the English alphabet.

la′bel, *n., v.t.,* **-beled, -beling.** *n.* 1. attached paper with information. —*v.t.* 2. designate with a label.

la′bi·al, *adj.* pertaining to lips.

la′bor, *n.* 1. hard work. 2. workers collectively. 3. process of giving birth. —*v.i.* 4. work hard. —**la′bor·er,** *n.*

lab′o·ra·to″ry, *n., pl.* **ries.** place for scientific research.

la·bo′ri·ous, *adj.* difficult; tedious.

lab′y·rinth″, *n.* 1. maze. 2. intricate problem. —**lab′y·rin′thine,** *adj.*

lace, *n., v.t.,* **laced, lacing.** *n.* 1. binding string, as on a shoe. 2. openwork cloth. —*v.t.* 3. fasten or furnish with a lace. —**lace′work″,** *n.*

lac′er·ate″, *v.t.,* **-ated, -ating.** tear jaggedly. —**lac″er·a′tion,** *n.*

lach′ry·mose″, *adj.* tearful.

lack, *n.* 1. absence or shortage. —*v.t.* 2. be without. —*v.i.* 3. be deficient.

lack″a·dai′si·cal, *adj.* without spirit or drive.

lack′lus″ter, *adj.* dull.

la·con′ic, *adj.* short-spoken; terse. —**la·con′i·cal·ly,** *adv.*

lac′quer, *n.* 1. transparent varnish-like coating. —*v.t.* 2. coat with lacquer.

la·crosse′, *n.* game with netlike racquets.

la·cu′na, *n., pl.* **-nas, -nae.** gap.

lac′y, *adj.,* **-ier, -iest.** open and intricate.

lad, *n.* boy.

lad′der, *n.* steep set of steps.

la′den, *adj.* burdened; loaded.

lad′ing, *n.* freight.

la′dle, *n., v.t.,* **-dled, -dling.** *n.* 1. long-handled bowl for dipping. —*v.t.* 2. dip with a ladle.

la′dy, *n.,* **-dies.** 1. respectable woman. 2. title of certain British women. —**la′dy·like′,** *adj.* —**la′dy·ship′,** *n.*

la′dy·bug″, *n.* small, spotted red beetle. Also, **la′dy·bird″.**

lag, *v.i.,* **lagged, lagging,** *n. v.i.* 1. fall behind. —*n.* 2. act or instance of lagging. —**lag′gard,** *n., adj.*

la′ger, *n.* type of beer.

la·goon′, *n.* enclosed body of water near a larger one.

laid″back′, *adj.* relaxed; serene.

lair, *n.* den, as of an animal.

lais″sez faire′, noninterference, esp. in economic activity.

la′i·ty, *n., pl.* **-ties.** laymen collectively.

lake, *n.* inland body of water.

la′ma, *n.* Tibetan Buddhist monk. —**la′ma·ser″y,** *n.*

lamb, *n.* young sheep.

lam·baste′, *v.t.,* **-basted, -basting.** *Informal.* punish with blows or words.

lam′bent, *adj.* gently glowing. —**lam′ben·cy,** *n.*

lame, *adj., v.t.,* **lamed, laming.** *adj.* 1. unable to walk properly. 2. ineffectual. —*v.t.* 3. make lame. —**lame′ly,** *adv.*

la·ment′, *v.t., v.i.* 1. mourn. —*n.* 2. speech, poem, or song of mourning. —**la″men·ta′tion,** *n.* —**lam·en′ta·ble,** *adj.*

lam′i·nate″, *v.t.,* **-nated, -nating.** 1. build up in layers. 2. cover with a layer of material. —**lam″i·na′tion,** *n.*

lamp, *n.* device for emitting rays of light, etc. —**lamp′post″,** *n.*

lamp'black'', *n.* pigment of fine soot.

lam·poon', *n.* 1. satirical writing. —*v.t.* 2. satirize in a lampoon.

la·nai', *n.* Hawaiian open-air living area.

lance, *n.*, *v.t.*, **lanced, lancing.** *n.* 1. spear carried by a horseman. —*v.t.* 2. prick, as to discharge pus.

land, *n.* 1. earth's surface above water. 2. nation; country. 3. real estate. —*v.t.* 4. bring to shore or earth. 5. secure; obtain. —*v.i.* 6. come to shore or earth. 7. fall.

land'ed, *adj.* land-owning.

land'fall'', *n.* 1. land sighted from a ship. 2. sighting of such land.

land'ing, *n.* 1. act of coming to shore or earth. 2. place to land. 3. unstepped area on a stair.

land'locked'', *adj.* with little or no access to the sea.

land'lord'', *n.* 1. man from whom one rents. 2. innkeeper. Also, *fem.,* **land' la''dy.**

land'lub''ber, *n. Informal.* non-sailor.

land'mark'', *n.* visible aid to finding one's way.

land'mass'', *n.* major land area.

land'scape'', *n.*, *v.t.*, **-scaped, scaping** *n.* 1. large visible area of land. —*v.t.* 2. create a landscape from.

land'slide'', *n.* fall of earth down a slope.

lane, *n.* 1. path or narrow road. 2. path of highway travel.

lan'guage, *n.* system of communication.

lan'guid, *adj.* without energy. —**lan' guid·ly,** *adv.*

lan'guish, *v.i.* 1. long wistfully. 2. weaken.

lan'guor, *n.* lack of vitality. —**lan'guor ous,** *adj.*

lank, *adj.* 1. lean. 2. long and straight, as hair.

lan'ky, *adj.*, **-ier, iest.** awkwardly tall and lean.

lan'tern, *n.* 1. transparent lamp casing. 2. cupola.

lan'yard, *n.* short cord fastening.

lap, *n.*, *v.*, **lapped, lapping.** *n.* 1. arfa between waist and knees when seated. 2. overlap. 3. once around a racetrack. —*v.t.* 4. wrap. 5. overlap. —*v.i.* 6. drink by licking. 7. splash gently. —**lap'dog''.**

la·pel', *n.* continuation of a coat collar folded back.

lap'i·dar''y, *n.*, *pl.* **-ies,** *adj.* *n.* 1. worker in gems. —*adj.* 2. fine; meticulous.

lapse, *v.i.*, **lapsed, lapsing.** *n.* *v.i.* 1. go passively. 2. elapse. 3. become void. —*n.* 4. act or instance of lapsing. 5. minor error.

lar'ce·ny, *n.*, *pl.* **-nies.** theft. —**lar'ce nous** *adj.*

lard, *n.* rendered animal fat.

lard'er, *n.* place for storing food.

large, *adj.*, *adv.*, **larger, largest,** *n. adj.* 1. big. 2. large-scale. —*adv.* 3. in a large way. —*n.* 4. **at large, unconfined.** —**large'ly,** *adv.*

lar·gess', *n.* 1. generous gift. 2. generosity. Also, **lar·gesse'.**

lar'go, *adj.*, *adv. Music.* slow.

lar'i·at, *n.* tether or lasso.

lark, *n.* 1. songbird. 2. frolic. —*v.i.* 3. frolic.

lar·va, *n.*, *pl.* **-vae.** early form of an animal. —**lar'val,** *adj.*

lar''yn·gi'tis, *n.* inflammation of the larynx.

lar'ynx, *n.*, *pl.* **-ynxes, -ynges.** container of the vocal cords.

las·civ'i·ous, *adj.* lustful.

la'ser, *n.* device for amplifying and concentrating light waves.

lash, *v.t.* 1. tie. 2. whip. —*v.i.* 3. strike. —*n.* 4. whip. 5. blow from a whip. 6. eyelash.

lass, *Dialect.* young woman.

las'si·tude'', *n.* lack of vigor.

las'so, *n.*, *pl.* **-sos, -soes,** *v.t.*, **-soed, -soing.** *n.* 1. rope for capturing cattle, etc. —*v.t.* 2. capture with a lasso.

last, *adj.*, *adv.* 1. after all others. —*n.* 2. last one. —*v.i.* 3. remain. —*v.t.* 4. be enough for. —**last'ly,** *adv.*

latch, *n.* 1. device to hold a door, etc. shut. —*v.t.* 2. fasten with a latch.

late, *adj.*, *adv.*, **later** or (for adj.) **latter, latest,** or **last.** *adj.*, *adv.* 1. after the right time. 2. near the end. 3. in recent times. —*adj.* 4. recently alive.

late'ly, *adv.* recently.

la'tent, *n.* unmanifested or undeveloped. —**la'ten·cy,** *n.*

lat'er·al, *adj.* pertaining to a side. —**la' ter·al·ly,** *adv.*

lath, *n.*, *pl.* **laths.** 1. wood strip for holding plaster. 2. any material for this.

lathe, *n.* machine for cutting a rotating object.

lath'er, *n.* 1. foam. —*v.t.* 2. cover with foam.

lat'i·tude'', *n.* 1. north-south measurement. 2. scope.

la·trine', *n.* military bathroom.

lat'ter, *adj.* 1. more recently mentioned. 2. more recent. —**lat'ter·ly,** *adv.*

lat'tice, *n.* screen of crisscrossed strips. —**lat'tice·work''**, *n.*

laud, *v.t.* praise. —**laud'a·ble**, *adj.* —**laud'a·to''ry,** *adj.*

lau'dan·um, *n.* opium-alcohol solution.

laugh, *n.* 1. rhythmic sound indicating amusement, scorn, etc. —*v.i.* 2. make such a sound. —**laugh'a·ble**, *adj.* —**laugh'ter,** *n.*

launch, *v.t.* 1. send from land. 2. put into effect, use, etc. —*n.* 3. open boat.

laun′der, *v.t.* wash, as clothes. —**laun′-der·er,** *fem.,* **laun′dress,** *n.*

laun′dry, *n., pl.* **-dries.** place for laundering. —**laun′dry·man,** *n.*

lau′rel, *n.* **1.** shrub with glossy leaves. **2.** laurels, honors.

la′va, *n.* molten volcanic rock.

lav′a·to′ry, *n., pl.* **-ries.** washing place.

lav′en·der, *n.* **1.** pale purple. **2.** European mint with pale purple flowers.

lav′ish, *adj.* **1.** very ample. **2.** generous. —*v.t.* **3.** give generously. —**lav′ish·ly,** *adv.* —**lav′ish·ness,** *n.*

law, *n.* **1.** rule established by government. **2.** legal profession. **3.** police. **4.** rule of natural phenomena. —**law′-a·bid′ing,** *adj.* —**law′break′′er,** *n. adj.* —**law′giv′′-er,** *n.* —**law′less,** *adj.* —**law′mak′′er,** *n.* —**law′suit′′,** *n.*

lawn, *n.* **1.** expanse of grass. **2.** sheer cotton or linen.

law′yer, *n.* professional legal adviser and representative.

lax, *adj.* negligent. —**lax′i·ty,** *n.*

lax′a·tive, *adj.* **1.** easing constipation. —*n.* **2.** laxative medicine.

lay, *v.t.,* **laid, laying,** *n., adj. v.t.* **1.** set down gently. **2.** set in place. **3.** place, as emphasis or a claim. —*n.* **4.** situation. **5.** ballad. —*adj.* **6.** not professional or clerical. —**lay′man,** *n.*

lay′er, *n.* level or thickness of material.

lay′off′′, *n.* dismissal due to lack of work.

la′zy, *adj.,* **-zier, -ziest.** unwilling to work. —**la′zi·ly,** *adv.* —**la′zi·ness,** *n.*

leach, *v.t., v.i.* dissolve with a filtering liquid.

lead (lēd for 1 to 6; led for 7), *v.,* **led, leading,** *n. v.t.* **1.** direct or guide. **2.** be ahead of. **3.** conduct. —*v.i.* **4.** tend or result. —*n.* **5.** leading role or place. **6.** guidance. **7.** heavy metallic chemical element. —**lead·er** (lē′dər), *n.* —**lead′er·ship′′,** *n.* —**lead·en** (led′n), *adj.*

leaf, *n., pl.* **leaves,** *v.i. n.* **1.** flat thin termination of a plant stem. **2.** thin sheet. —*v.i.* **3.** turn over pages. —**leaf′y,** *adj.*

leaf′let, *n.* small printed sheet.

league, *n., v.,* **leaguing.** *n.* **1.** alliance. **2.** unit of about 3 miles. —*v.t., v.i.* **3.** form into a league.

leak, *n.* **1.** accidental release or admission. —*v.i.* **2.** have or pass through a leak. —*v.t.* **3.** pass through a leak. —**leak′-age,** *n.* —**leak′y,** *adj.*

lean, *v.,* **leaned** or **leant, leaning,** *adj. v.t., v.i.* **1.** stand against something supporting the upper end. —*v.i.* **2.** bend; incline. **3.** be predisposed. **4.** rely. —*adj.* **5.** with little fat.

leap, *v.,* **leaped** or **leapt, leaping,** *n.* jump.

leap year, year with 29 days in February.

learn, *v.,* **learned** or **learnt, learning.** *v.t.* **1.** come to know or know how. —*v.i.*

2. get information. —**learn′er,** *n.* —**learn′ing,** *n.* —**learn′ed,** *adj.*

lease, *n., v.t.,* **leased, leasing.** *n.* **1.** rental contract. —*v.t.* **2.** rent by lease.

leash, *n.* tether, as for a dog.

least, *adj.* **1.** smallest in size, importance, etc. —*adv.* **2.** to the smallest extent.

leath′er, *n.* tanned hide.

leave, *v.,* **left, leaving,** *n. v.i.* **1.** go away. —*v.t.* **2.** go away from. **3.** abandon. **4.** have remain behind one. **5.** bequeath. —*n.* **6.** departure. **7.** permission. —**leave′tak′′ing,** *n.*

leav·en (lev′n), *n.* **1.** substance making dough rise. —*v.t.* **2.** cause to rise.

leav′ings, *n., pl.* leftovers.

lech′er, *n.* lustful person. —**lech′er·ous,** *adj.* —**lech′er·y,** *n.*

lec′ture, *n., v.,* **-tured, -turing.** *n.* **1.** informative speech. —*v.t.* **2.** give a lecture to. —*v.i.* **3.** give a lecture.

ledge, *n.* narrow shelf or platform.

led′ger, *n.* accountant's book.

lee, *adj.* **1.** away from the wind. —*n.* **2.** lee side, etc. **3.** lees, dregs.

leech, *n.* blood-sucking worm.

leek, *n.* onionlike vegetable.

leer, *n.* **1.** sly, malicious or lustful look. —*v.i.* **2.** give a leer.

lee′way′′, *n.* **1.** *Informal.* scope for action. **2.** *Nautical.* leeward drift.

left, *n.* **1.** west when facing north. **2.** liberal or socialistic position. —*adv.* **3.** toward the left. **4.** at or in the left. —**left′-ist,** *n., adj.* —**left′-hand′,** *adj.*

left′o′′ver, *n.* remnant for later use.

left wing, political left. —**left′-wing′,** *adj.* —**left′-wing′er,** *n.*

leg, *n.* **1.** supporting and walking limb. **2.** vertical support.

leg′a·cy, *n., pl.* **-cies.** something left to posterity.

le′gal, *adj.* **1.** permitted by law. **2.** pertaining to law. —**le′gal·ly,** *adv.* —**le·gal′i·ty,** *n.* —**le′gal·ize′′,** *v.t.*

leg′ate, *n.* papal envoy.

leg′′a·tee′, *n.* recipient of a legacy.

le·ga′tion, *n.* office of a diplomat.

le·ga′to, *adj. Music.* smooth and even.

leg′end, *n.* **1.** folk tale. **2.** inscription. —**leg′end·ar′′y,** *adj.*

leg′′er·de·main′, *n.* cunning of the hand.

leg′ging, *n.* outer leg covering.

leg′i·ble, *adj.* possible to read. —**leg′′i·bil′i·ty,** *n.*

le′gion, *n.* large band, esp. of soldiers. —**le′gion·ar′′y,** *adj., n.* —**le′′gion·naire′,** *n.*

leg′is·late′′, *v.,* **-lated, -lating.** *v.t.* **1.** determine by law. —*v.i.* **2.** enact laws. —**leg′′is·la′tion,** *n.* —**leg′is·la′′tive,** *adj.* —**leg′is·la′′tor,** *n.*

leg′is·la′′ture, *n.* lawmaking body.

le·git′i·mate, *adj.* **1.** right; proper. **2.** of

married parents. —le·git'i·ma·cy, *n.*
—le·git'i·mize", *v.t.*

leg'ume, *n.* vegetable with seed pods.
—le·gu'mi·nous, *adj.*

lei (lā), *n., pl.* **leis.** Hawaiian flower garland.

lei'sure, *n.* **1.** time for rest or recreation. **2. at one's leisure,** when convenient.

lei'sure·ly, *adj. adv.* without haste or hurry.

lem'on, *n.* yellow citrus fruit. —lem"on·ade', *n.*

lend, *v.t.*, **lent, lending. 1.** give for later return. **2.** impart.

length, *n.* **1.** end-to-end extent. **2.** piece measured by length. —length'en, *v.t., v.i.* —length'wise", *adj.,* adv. —length'y, *adj.*

le'ni·ent, *adj.* not strict or harsh. —le'ni·en·cy, le'ni·ence, *n.*

lens, *n., pl.* **lenses.** transparent object concentrating or dispersing rays of light.

Lent, *n.* Christian time of penance from Ash Wednesday to Easter. —Lent'en, *adj.*

len'til, *n.* small legume seed used as food.

le'o·nine, *adj.* lion-like.

leop'ard, *n.* spotted cat of the panther family.

lep'er, *n.* person with leprosy.

le'pre·chaun", *n.* Irish fairy.

lep'ro·sy, *n.* deforming chronic disease. —lep'rous, *adj.*

les'bi·an, *n.* **1.** homosexual woman. —*adj.* **2.** pertaining to such women. —les'bi·an·ism, *n.*

le·sion, *n.* bodily injury resulting in impairment of function.

less, *adj.* **1.** smaller or fewer. —*adv.* **2.** to a smaller extent. —*prep.* **3.** minus. —les'sen, *v.t., v.i.*

les·see', *n.* tenant on a lease.

les'ser, *adj.* smaller; less important.

les'son, *n.* something learned at one time.

les'sor, *n.* landlord on a lease.

lest, *conj.* for fear that.

let, *v.t.*, **let, letting.** *n. v.t.* **1.** allow. **2.** rent. **3.** allow to issue. —*n.* **4.** obstacle.

let'down", *n.* **1.** disappointment. **2.** slackening.

le'thal, *adj.* deadly.

leth'ar·gy, *n., pl.* **-gies.** sluggishness. —le·thar'gic, *adj.*

let'ter, *n.* **1.** alphabetic character. **2.** message in an envelope. **3.** literal meaning. **4. letters,** literature. —*v.t.* **5.** write letter by letter. —let'ter·ing, *n.*

let'tered, *adj.* educated.

let'tuce, *n.* green, leafy vegetable.

leu·ke'mi·a, *n.* blood disease.

lev'ee, *n.* embankment against rising water.

lev'el, *n., v.t.,* **-eled, -eling.** *n.* **1.** point or plane between top and bottom. **2.** de-

vice for finding horizontals or verticals. **3.** point on a scale of values. —*adj.* **4.** flat. **5.** horizontal. **6.** even. —*v.t.* **7.** make level.

lev'el-head'ed, *adj.* of calm, sound judgment.

lev'er, *n.* pivoted raising device lifted at one end. —lev'er·age, *n.*

le·vi'a·than, *n.* sea monster.

lev"i·ta'tion, *n.* raising or rising without physical support.

lev'i·ty, *n.* mirth, often unseemly.

lev·y (lev'ē), *v.t.,* **-ied, -ying,** *n., pl.* **-ies.** *v.t.* **1.** impose for payment. **2.** enlist. —*n.* **3.** something levied.

lewd, *adj.* obscene. —lewd'ly, *adv.* —lewd'ness, *n.*

lex'i·con, *n.* dictionary.

li'a·bil'i·ty, *n., pl.* **-ties. 1.** loss or payment of money. **2.** state of being liable. **3.** disadvantage.

li'a·ble, *adj.* **1.** responsible. **2.** subject to something. **3.** likely.

li'ai·son", *n.* **1.** connection, as for communication. **2.** love affair.

li'ar, *n.* teller of lies.

li·ba'tion, *n.* outpouring of liquid.

li'bel, *n., v.t.,* **-beled, -beling.** *n.* **1.** defamation in writing or print. —*v.t.* **2.** defame by this means. —li'bel·ous, li'bel·lous, *adj.*

lib'er·al, *adj.* **1.** generous. **2.** not literal. **3.** favoring more civil liberty. —*n.* **4.** person favoring more civil liberty. —lib"er·al'i·ty, *n.* —lib'er·al·ism, *n.* —lib'er·al·ize", *v.t.*

lib'er·ate", *v.t.,* **-ated, -ating.** free. —lib"er·a'tion, *n.* —lib'er·a"tor, *n.*

lib"er·tar'i·an, *n.* believer in personal liberties.

lib'er·tine", *n.* licentious person.

lib'er·ty, *n., pl.* **-ties. 1.** freedom. **2.** privilege. **3.** liberties, impertinences.

li·bi'do, *n.* **1.** sexual urge. **2.** psychic energy.

li'brar"y, *n., pl.* **-ies. 1.** collection of books. **2.** place for books. —li·brar'i·an, *n.*

li·bret'to, *n., pl.* **-tos, -ti.** text of an opera, etc. —li·bret'tist, *n.*

li'cense, *n., v.t.,* **-censed, -censing.** *n.* **1.** privilege of doing. **2.** abuse of liberty. —*v.t.* **3.** grant a license to. —li"cen·see', *n.* —li·cen'tious, *adj.*

li·chen (lī'kən), *n.* mosslike growth.

lic'it, *adj.* permitted.

lick, *v.t.* **1.** rub with the tongue. **2.** *Informal.* **a.** defeat. **b.** beat. —*v.i.* **3.** lap. —*n.* **4.** act or instance of licking.

lic'o·rice, *n.* European root used for flavoring.

lid, *n.* cover.

lie, *v.i.,* **lay** (for 1, 2) or **lied** (for 3), **lain** (for 1, 2), **lying,** *n. v.i.* **1.** rest on something horizontal. **2.** be situated. **3.** make statements intended to deceive. —*n.* **4.** situation. **5.** lying statement.

lief, *adv. Archaic.* willingly.

lien, *n.* legal claim on property.

lieu, *n.* in lieu of, in place of.

lieu·ten'ant, *n.* commissioned military or naval officer below a captain or lieutenant commander. —**lieu·ten'an·cy,** *n.*

life, *n., pl.* **lives. 1.** period of existence. **2.** living things collectively. **3.** human experience. **4.** way of living. **5.** animation. **6.** biography. —**life'less,** *adj.* —**life'long'',** *adj.* —**life'time'',** *adj.*

life'boat'', *n.* emergency boat.

life'guard'', *n.* one employed to protect bathers, esp. from drowning, etc.

life'like'', *adj.* resembling a living being.

life'-size'', *adj.* as large as the living model. Also, **life'-sized''.**

lift, *v.t.* **1.** raise. —*v.i.* **2.** attempt to raise something. **3.** rise. —*n.* **4.** act or instance of lifting. **5.** hoist.

lig'a·ment, *n.* body connective tissue.

lig'a·ture, *n.* tie.

light, *n., adj., v.,* **lighted** or **lit, lighting.** *n.* **1.** visible radiant energy. **2.** lamp. **3.** flame. **4.** truth. **5.** public awareness. —*adj.* **6.** not dark or serious. **7.** not heavy. **8.** not serious. —*v.t.* **9.** set fire to. **10.** cause to give off light. **11.** show in light. —*v.i.* **12.** be lighted. **13.** alight. **14.** happen; venture. —**light'en,** *v.t., v.i.* —**light'weight'',** *adj.*

light'er, *n.* **1.** lighting device. **2.** freight barge.

light'-head'ed, *adj.* dizzy.

light'-heart'ed, *adj.* cheerful.

light'house'', *n.* tower with a navigational beacon.

light'ning, *n.* flash of electricity in the sky.

light'-year'', *n.* distance light travels in a year, about 6 trillion miles.

lig'nite, *n.* soft brown coal.

like, *prep., adj., n., v.t.,* **liked, liking** *prep.* **1.** similar or similarly to. **2.** characteristic or suggestive of. **3.** inclined to. —*adj.* **4.** similar. —*n.* **5.** similar person or thing. **6.** preference. —*v.t.* **7.** be pleased with. **8.** wish. —**like'a·ble,** **lik'a·ble,** *adj.* —**like'ness,** *n.*

like'ly, *adj.,* **-lier, -liest,** *adv. adj.* **1.** probable. **2.** suitable. —*adv.* **3.** probably.

lik'en, *v.t.* compare.

like'wise'', *adv.* similarly, also.

li'lac, *n.* pale purple flower.

lilt, *n.* light, bouncy rhythm.

lil'y, *n., pl.* **-ies.** flower with trumpet-shaped blossoms.

li'ma bean, broad, pale green bean.

limb, *n.* **1.** large tree branch. **2.** arm or leg.

lim'ber, *adj.* **1.** flexible. —*v.t.* **2.** make limber. —*v.i.* **3.** become limber.

lim'bo, *n.* **1.** abode of the unbaptized, innocent dead. **2.** oblivion.

lime, *n., v.t.,* **limed, liming.** *n.* **1.** calcium oxide. **2.** tart green citrus fruit. —*v.t.* **3.** treat with lime. —**lime'ade',** *n.*

lime'light'', *n.* state of much publicity.

lim'er·ick, *n.* amusing five-lined verse.

lime'stone'', *n.* stone containing much calcium carbonate.

lim'it, *n.* **1.** edge or boundary. **2.** permissible extent. —*v.t.* **3.** set a limit to. —**lim''i·ta'tion,** *n.* —**lim'it·ed,** *adj.* —**lim'it·less,** *adj.*

lim'ou·sine'', *n.* long, chauffeured automobile.

limp, *v.i.* **1.** walk lamely. —*n.* **2.** lame gait. —*adj.* **3.** not rigid or firm.

lim'pid, *adj.* perfectly clear. —**lim·pid'i·ty,** *n.*

lin'den, *n.* tree with heart-shaped leaves.

line, *n., v.,* **lined, lining.** *n.* **1.** long, narrow mark. **2.** row. **3.** boundary. **4.** course. **5.** transit system. **6.** rope, pipe, etc. **7.** occupation. —*v.t.* **8.** put a lining in. **9.** mark with lines. —*v.i.* **10.** assemble in a line.

lin'e·age, *n.* ancestry.

lin'e·al, *adj.* **1.** pertaining to direct ancestry. **2.** linear.

lin'e·a·ments, *n., pl.* features of the face.

lin'e·ar, *adj.* pertaining to lines or length.

lin'en, *n.* **1.** cloth made of flax. **2.** linens, bedsheets, etc.

lin'er, *n.* **1.** ship or airplane on scheduled service. **2.** something that lines.

line'up'', *n.* arrangement or muster in a row.

lin'ger, *v.i.* remain; stay.

lin·ge·rie (lan''ʒə rā'), *n.* women's underwear.

lin'go, *n., pl.* **-goes.** *Informal.* strange language.

lin'guist, *n.* **1.** speaker of many languages. **2.** student of languages. —**lin·guis'tics,** *n.* —**lin·guis'tic,** *adj.*

lin'i·ment, *n.* soothing liquid for external use.

lin'ing, *n.* material applied to an interior.

link, *n.* **1.** unit of a chain or series. **2.** connection. —*v.t., v.i.* **3.** connect. —**link'age,** *n.*

links, *n., pl.* golf course.

li·no'le·um, *n.* smooth sheeting for floors.

lin'seed'', *n.* flax seed.

lint, *n.* fibrous waste.

lin'tel, *n.* beam over a doorway, etc.

li'on, *n.* **1.** large catlike animal of Africa and southwest Asia. **2.** celebrity. Also, *fem.,* **li'on·ess.**

li'on·ize'', *v.t.,* **-ized, -izing.** treat as a celebrity.

lip, *n.* **1.** feature at top and bottom of the mouth. **2.** surface for pouring.

lip'stick'', *n.* coloring for the lips.

liq'ue·fy'', *v.*, **-fied**, **-fying**. *v.t.*, *v.i.* change to liquid. —**liq''ue·fac'tion**, *n.*

li'queur, *n.* sweet strong alcoholic drink.

liq'uid, *n.* **1.** fluid incapable of indefinite expansion. —*adj.* **2.** in the form of a liquid. **3.** readily turned into cash. —**li·quid'i·ty**, *n.*

liq'ui·date'', *v.t.*, **-dated**, **-dating**. **1.** terminate, as a business. **2.** convert into cash. **3.** kill. —**liq''ui·da'tion**, *n.*

liq'uor, *n.* alcoholic liquid.

lisle (līl), *n.* fine cotton.

lisp, *n.* **1.** mispronunciation of *s* and *z.* —*v.i.* **2.** make such mispronunciations.

lis'some, *adj.* agile and supple.

list, *n.* **1.** series of related items. **2.** tilt, as of a ship. —*v.t.* **3.** put on a list. —*v.i.* **4.** tilt.

lis'ten, *v.i.* **1.** hear attentively. **2.** pay heed. —**lis'ten·er**, *n.*

list'less, *adj.* indifferent from fatigue, etc. —**list'less·ly**, *adv.* —**list'less·ness**, *n.*

lit'a·ny, *n.*, *pl.* **-nies**. uttered prayer with responses.

li'ter, *n.* metric unit equal to 1.0567 liquid quarts or 0.908 dry quart. Also, **li'tre**.

lit'er·al, *adj.* according to the exact wording. —**lit'er·al·ly**, *adv.*

lit'er·ar''y, *adj.* pertaining to literature.

lit'er·ate, *adj.* **1.** able to read. **2.** well-read. —**lit'er·a·cy**, *n.*

lit''e·ra'ti, *n.*, *pl.* well-read persons.

lit'er·a·ture, *n.* fiction, poetry, etc. of lasting value.

lithe, *adj.* supple.

lith'o·graph'', *n.* print from a flat surface with special ink. —**lith''o·graph'ic**, *adj.* —**li·thog'ra·phy**, *n.* —**li·thog'ra·pher**, *n.*

lit'i·gate'', *v.*, **-gated**, **-gating**. *v.t.*, *v.i.* contest in a lawsuit. —**lit''i·ga'tion**, *n.* —**lit'i·gant**, **lit''i·ga'tor**, *n.*

lit'ter, *n.* **1.** trash. **2.** newly-born animals. **3.** animal bedding. **4.** frame for carrying a person. —*v.t.* **5.** scatter carelessly.

lit'tle, *adj.* littler or less or lesser, littlest or least, *adv.*, less, least, *n. adj.* **1.** small. **2.** petty. —*adv.* **3.** not much. —*n.* **4.** short while. **5.** small amount.

lit'ur·gy, *n.*, *pl.* **-gies**. ritual of worship. —**li·tur'gi·cal**, *adj.*

liv'a·ble, *adj.* pleasant to inhabit. Also, **live'a·ble**.

live'li·hood'', *n.* means of sustenance.

live (liv for 1-5; līv for 6-8). *v.i.* **1.** be alive. **2.** dwell. **3.** spend one's life. **4.** depend for existence. —*v.t.* **5.** experience or spend. —*adj.* **6.** alive. **7.** vital. **8.** electrically charged.

live'ly, *adj.*, **-lier**, **-liest**, *adv. adj.* **1.** full of vitality. —*adv.* **2.** in a lively way. —**live'li·ness**, *n.*

liv'en, *v.t.* **1.** make lively. —*v.i.* **2.** become lively.

liv'er, *n.* organ secreting bile.

liv'er·wurst'', *n.* sausage made with ground liver.

live'stock'', *n.* cattle, sheep, etc.

liv'id, *adj.* **1.** discolored, as flesh. **2.** enraged.

liv'ing, *adj.* **1.** alive. **2.** pertaining to being alive. —*n.* **3.** livelihood.

liz'ard, *n.* scaly, four-legged reptile.

lla'ma, *n.* South American beast of burden.

load, *n.* **1.** something carried. —*v.t.* **2.** put a load on or in. **3.** supply in large amounts. **4.** make ready for firing. —*v.i.* **5.** take on a load.

loaf, *n.*, *pl.* **loaves**, *v.i.*, *n.* **1.** regularly shaped piece of bread. —*v.i.* **2.** be idle. —**loaf'er**, *n.*

loam, *n.* rich soil. —**loam'y**, *adj.*

loan, *n.* **1.** act or instance of lending. **2.** something lent. —*v.t.*, *v.i.* **3.** lend.

loath, *adj.* reluctant.

loathe, *v.t.*, **loathed**, **loathing**. dislike intensely. —**loath'some**, *adj.*

lob, *v.t.*, **lobbed**, **lobbing**. hurl with a high curve.

lob'by, *n.*, *pl.* **-bies**. *v.i.*, **-bied**, **-bying**. *n.* **1.** entrance room. **2.** group seeking favorable legislation. —*v.i.* **3.** seek favorable legislation. —**lob'by·ist**, *n.*

lobe, *n.* rounded projection. —**lo'bar**, **lo'bate**, *adj.*

lob'ster, *n.* sea crustacean with pincers.

lo'cal, *adj.* **1.** pertaining or limited to a place. **2.** making most or all stops. —*n.* **3.** local train or bus. **4.** local branch of a labor union. —**lo'cal·ly**, *adv.*

lo·cale', *n.* scene of an event.

lo·cal'i·ty, *n.*, *pl.* **-ties**. **1.** location. **2.** district.

lo'cal·ize'', *v.t.*, **-ized**, **-izing**. trace or confine to one place. —**lo''cal·i·za'tion**, *n.*

lo'cate, *v.t.*, **-cated**, **-cating**. establish the place of. —**lo·ca'tion**, *n.*

lock, *n.* **1.** device for securing doors, etc. **2.** canal chamber between levels. **3.** firing mechanism. **4.** curl of hair. —*v.t.* **5.** fasten with a lock. **6.** shut in or out. —*v.i.* **7.** be jammed. —**lock'smith''**, *n.*

lock'er, *n.* compartment that can be locked.

lock'et, *n.* round case worn as a pendant to a necklace.

lock'jaw'', *n.* form of tetanus.

lock'out'', *n.* exclusion of workers from a workplace.

lo'co, *adj.* *Informal.* crazy.

lo''co·mo'tion, *n.* movement from place to place.

lo''co·mo'tive, *n.* **1.** railroad traction engine. —*adj.* **2.** pertaining to locomotion.

lo'cust, *n.* **1.** crop-eating insect. **2.** flowering tree.

lo·cu'tion, *n.* spoken expression.

lode, *n.* deposit of metallic ore.

lode'stone", *n.* magnetic iron ore.

lodge, *n., v.,* **lodged, lodging.** *n.* **1.** forest house. **2.** fraternity chapter. —*v.t.* **3.** house. **4.** push into a fixed position. —*v.i.* **5.** become fixed. **6.** dwell.

lodg'ing, *n.* **1.** temporary home. **2. lodgings,** rented rooms.

loft, *n.* open upper floor.

loft'y, *adj.,* **-ier, -iest.** very high. —**loft'i·ly,** *adv.*

log, *n., v.t.,* **logged, logging.** *n.* **1.** cut tree trunk or limb. **2.** record of events. —*v.t.* **3.** take logs from. **4.** record in a log.

lo'gan·ber"ry, *n.* hybrid of blackberry and red raspberry.

log'a·rithm, *n. Math.* power of one number if multiplied to equal another. —**log"a·rith'mic,** *adj.*

loge, *n.* theater mezannine.

log'ger·head", *n.* **at loggerheads,** in sharp dispute.

log'ic, *n.* **1.** correct reasoning. **2.** predictable sequence. —**log'i·cal,** *adj.* —**log'i·cal·ly,** *adv.* —**lo·gi'cian,** *n.*

lo·gis'tics, *n.* science of military housing, supply, etc. —**lo·gis'tic, lo·gis'ti·cal,** *adj.*

lo"go, *n.* symbol or trademark of an enterprise.

lo'gy, *adj.,* **-gier, -giest.** sluggish.

loin, *n.* **1.** Also, **loins,** lower human back. **2.** front hindquarter as a cut of meat.

loi'ter, *n.* linger in one place. —**loi'ter·er,** *n.*

loll, *v.i.* **1.** remain idle. **2.** hang loosely.

lol'li·pop", *n.* candy on a stick for sucking.

lone, *adj.* single; solitary.

lone'ly, *adj.,* **-lier, -liest. 1.** sad because alone. **2.** isolated. Also, **lone'some.** —**lone'li·ness,** *n.*

long, *adj., adv.,* **longer, longest,** *v.i. adj.* **1.** of great distance between ends. **2.** in length. **3.** occupying much time. —*adv.* **4.** for a long time. **5.** from start to finish. **6.** at a long time. —*v.i.* **7.** wish passionately. —**long'ing,** *n., adj.*

lon·gev'i·ty, *n.* long life.

long'hand", *n.* ordinary handwriting.

lon'gi·tude", *n.* east-west measurement.

lon"gi·tu'di·nal, *adj.* pertaining to length or longitude.

long'shore"man, *n.* loader and unloader of ships.

long'-stand'ing, *adj.* long-continued.

long'-suf'fer·ing, *adj.* patient.

long ton, ton of 2,240 pounds.

look, *v.i.* **1.** direct one's gaze. **2.** search. **3.** appear to be. —*v.t.* **4.** stare at. —*n.* **5.** act or instance of looking. **6.** appearance. —*interj.* **7.** pay heed!

look'out", *n.* **1.** vigilance. **2.** spy or sentinel. **3.** Informal. personal problem.

loom, *n.* **1.** weaving frame. —*v.i.* **2.** appear indistinctly as huge.

loon, *n.* diving bird.

loon'y, *adj.,* **-ier, -iest.** Informal. crazy.

loop, *n.* **1.** closed curve of rope, etc. —*v.t.* **2.** make into a loop. —*v.i.* **3.** form a loop.

loop'hole", *n.* **1.** slit for shooting. **2.** means of evasion.

loose, *adj.,* **looser, loosest,** *v.t.,* **loosed, loosing.** *adj.* **1.** not tight. **2.** not confined. **3.** not strict or precise. **4.** immoral. —*v.t.* **5.** make loose. —**loose'ly,** *adv.* —**loos'en,** *v.t., v.i.*

loot, *n.* **1.** things stolen. —*v.t.* **2.** steal the contents of.

lop, *v.t.,* **lopped, lopping.** chop.

lop'sid"ed, *adj.* out of balance.

lo·qua'cious, *adj.* talkative. —**lo·quac'i·ty,** *n.*

lord, *n.* **1.** landed noble. **2. the Lord, a.** God. **b.** Christ. —**lord'ly,** *adj., adv.* —**lord'ship',** *n.*

lore, *n.* traditional learning.

lose, *v.,* **lost, losing.** *v.t.* **1.** fail to keep. **2.** misplace. **3.** fail to win. —*v.i.* **4.** have a loss. —**los'er,** *n.* —**lost,** *adj.*

loss, *n.* **1.** act or instance of losing. **2.** something lost.

lot, *n.* **1.** chance. **2.** personal fate. **3.** area of ground. **4.** Also, **lots.** Informal. many or much.

lo'tion, *n.* skin preparation.

lot'ter·y, *n., pl.* **-ies.** choice by chance, esp. of a winner.

lo'tus, *n.* **1.** tropical waterlily. **2.** legendary plant causing forgetfulness.

loud, *adj.* **1.** with much noise. **2.** Informal. flashy. —*adv.* **3.** loudly. —**loud'ly,** *adv.* —**loud'ness,** *n.*

lounge, *v.i.,* **lounged, lounging.** *n. v.i.* **1.** be idle or relaxed. —*n.* **2.** couch. **3.** place for lounging.

louse, *n., pl.* **lice.** parasitic insect.

lous'y, *adj.,* **-ier, -iest.** Informal. bad.

lout, *n.* stupid, offensive person. —**lout'ish,** *adj.*

lou'ver, *n.* opening screened with inclined slats.

love, *n., v.t.,* **loved, loving.** *n.* **1.** powerful attraction to another. **2.** warm concern. **3.** loved person. —*v.t.* **4.** feel love for. —**lov'a·ble, love'a·ble,** *adj.* —**love'less,** *adj.* —**lov'er,** *n.* —**lov'ing,** *adj.* —**lov'ing·ly,** *adv.*

love'lorn", *adj.* pining with love.

love'ly, *adj.,* **-lier, -liest.** beautiful.

low, *adj.* **1.** of less than average height. **2.** of less than average quantity, etc. **3.**

depressed. **4.** vulgar. **5.** meanly wicked.
—*adv.* **6.** in a low way. —*n.* **7.** something low. —*v.i.* **8.** moo.

low'brow'', *n., adj.* non-intellectual.

low·er, *adj.* (lō'ər) **1.** more low. —*v.t.* **2.** cause to be low or lower. —*v.i.* **3.** become low or lower. **4.** (lou'ər) frown.

low'ly, *adj.*, **-lier, -liest.** humble.

loy'al, *adj.* faithful. —**loy'al·ly**, *adv.* —**loy'al·ty**, *n.*

loz'enge, *n.* cough drop, etc.

lu·au', *n.* Hawaiian feast.

lub'ber, *n.* clumsy person. —**lub'ber·ly**, *adj.*

lu'bri·cate'', *v.t.*, **-cated, -cating. 1.** make slippery. **2.** cause the wearing parts of to slide easily. —**lu'bri·ca'tion**, *n.* —**lu'bri·cant**, *n.*

lu'cid, *adj.* **1.** clear, as to understand. **2.** mentally competent. —**lu'cid·ly**, *adv.* —**lu·cid'i·ty**, *n.*

luck, *n.* **1.** chance. **2.** favorable chance. —**luck'less**, *adj.*

luck'y, *adj.*, **-ier, -iest.** having or marked by good luck. —**luck'i·ly**, *adv.*

luc'ra·tive, *adj.* profitable.

lu'cre, *n.* riches.

lu'di·crous, *adj.* laughable.

lug, *v.t.*, **lugged, lugging**, *n. v.t.* **1.** haul with effort. —*n.* **2.** projection for lifting, etc.

lug'gage, *n.* baggage.

lu·gu'bri·ous, *adj.* foolishly mournful.

luke'warm'', *adj.* **1.** slightly warm. **2.** unenthusiastic.

lull, *v.t., v.i., n.* calm.

lull'a·by'', *n., pl.* **-bies.** soothing song for children.

lum·ba'go, *n.* pain in the lower back.

lum'bar, *adj.* pertaining to the loins.

lum'ber, *n.* **1.** building wood. —*v.i.* **2.** move ponderously. —**lum'ber·man**, *n.*

lum'ber·jack'', *n.* feller of trees.

lu'mi·nar''y, *n., pl.* **-ies. 1.** light source. **2.** brilliant person.

lu''mi·nes'cence, *n.* light without heat. —**lu''min·nes'cent**, *adj.*

lu'mi·nous, *adj.* light-giving. —**lu''mi·nos'i·ty**, *n.*

lump, *n.* **1.** shapeless mass. **2.** swelling. —*adj.* **3.** collective. —*v.t.* **4.** assemble or treat in a lump. **5.** tolerate despite oneself. —*v.i.* **6.** form in lumps. —**lump'y**, *adj.*

lu'nar, *adj.* pertaining to the moon.

lu'na·tic, *n.* **1.** insane person. —*adj.* **2.** insane. —**lu'na·cy**, *n.*

lunch, *n.* **1.** midday meal. —*v.i.* **2.** eat lunch.

lunch'eon, *n.* formal lunch.

lung, *n.* breathing organ.

lunge, *n., v.*, **lunged, lunging**. *n.* **1.** sudden move forward. —*v.t., v.i.* **2.** move with a lunge.

lurch, *n.* **1.** sudden sideways movement. **2. leave in the lurch,** desert in time of need. —*v.i.* **3.** make a lurch.

lure, *v.t.*, **lured, luring**, *n. v.t.* **1.** entice —*n.* **2.** enticement; bait.

lur'id, *adj.* **1.** glowing through haze. **2.** violently sensational.

lurk, *v.i.* be in hiding.

lus'cious, *adj.* appealing to the senses.

lush, *adj.* **1.** rich; abundant. —*n.* **2.** *Informal.* alcoholic.

lust, *n.* **1.** strong appetite. **2.** strong sexual appetite. —*v.i.* **3.** feel lust. —**lust'ful**, *adj.*

lus'ter, *n.* **1.** sheen. **2.** brightness. —**lus'trous**, *adj.*

lust'y, *adj.*, **-ier, -iest.** vigorous. —**lust'i·ly**, *adv.*

lux·u'ri·ant, *adj.* lavishly growing. —**lux·u'ri·ance**, *n.*

lux·u'ri·ate'', *v.i.*, **-ated, -ating.** live luxuriously.

lux'u·ry, *n., pl.* **-ries. 1.** great comfort or pleasure. **2.** something superfluous. —**lux·u'ri·ous**, *adj.*

ly·ce'um, *n.* institute for lectures.

lye, *n.* strong alkaline substance.

ly'ing-in', *n.* confinement in childbirth.

lymph, *n.* clear, watery body liquid. —**lym·phat'ic**, *adj.*

lynch, *v.t.* kill as a mob.

lynx, *n., pl.* **lynxes, lynx.** wildcat of the northern hemisphere.

lyr'ic, *adj.* **1.** pertaining to emotion expressed in poetry. —*n.* **2.** lyric poem. **3.** Usually **lyrics,** words to music. —**lyr'i·cal**, *adj.* —**lyr'i·cist**, *n.*

M

M, m, *n.* thirteenth letter of the English alphabet.

mach·i·na·tion (mak''ə nā'shən), *n.* plot, scheme.

ma·chine', *n., v.t.*, **-chined, -chining**. *n.* **1.** device for doing work. **2.** political organization. —*v.t.* **3.** shape by machine. —**ma·chin'er·y**, *n.*

ma·chin'ist, *n.* worker with machine-operated tools.

ma·chis'mo, *n.* assertion of masculinity.

mack'er·el, *n., pl.* **-el, -els.** North Atlantic fish.

mack′i·naw″, *n.* heavy jacketlike coat.

mack′in·tosh″, *n.* rubberized cloth coat.

mac′ra·me″, *n.* lace or string tied in patterns.

mac″ro·bi·ot′ics, *n.* art of lengthening life. —**mac″ro·bi·ot′ic**, *adj.*

mac′ro·cosm, *n.* 1. universe. 2. complex of microcosms.

mad, *adj.*, **madder, maddest**. 1. insane. 2. infatuated. 3. angry. —**mad′ly**, *adv.* —**mad′ness**, *n.* —**mad′den**, *v.t.* —**mad′house″**, *n.* —**mad′man″**, **mad′wom″an**, *n.*

mad′am, *n.* 1. polite form of address to a woman. 2. woman running a brothel.

mad′ame, *n.*, *pl.* **mesdames**. *French.* madam or Mrs.

mad′cap″, *adj.* 1. reckless. —*n.* 2. reckless person.

ma″de·moi·selle′, *n.*, *pl.* **mesdemoiselles**. *French.* Miss.

Ma·don′na, *n.* Virgin Mary.

mad′ri·gal, *n.* unaccompanied part song.

mael′strom, *n.* whirlpool.

mag′a·zine″, *n.* 1. periodical with covers. 2. storage chamber, esp. for ammunition.

ma·gen′ta, *n.* purplish red.

mag′got, *n.* wormlike larva. —**mag′got·y**, *adj.*

mag′ic, *n.* 1. use of supernatural methods. 2. illusions using sleight of hand. —*adj.* 3. existing or operated by magic. —**mag′i·cal**, *adj.* —**ma·gi′cian**, *n.*

mag′is·te′ri·al, *adj.* authoritative.

mag′is·trate, *n.* minor judge. —**mag′is·tra·cy**, *n.*

mag·nan′i·mous, *adj.* above pettiness. —**mag·nan′i·mous·ly**, *adv.* —**mag″na·nim′i·ty**, *n.*

mag′nate, *n.* man of wealth or power.

mag·ne′sium, *n.* light metallic element.

mag′net, *n.* object attracting ferrous metal. —**mag·net′ic**, *adj.* —**mag′net·ism**, *n.* —**mag′net·ize″**, *v.t.*

mag·ne′to, *n.*, *pl.* **-toes**. generator with permanent magnets.

mag·nif′i·cent, *adj.* splendid in form, accomplishments, etc. —**mag·nif′i·cence**, *n.* —**mag·nif′i·cent·ly**, *adv.*

mag′ni·fy″, *v.t.*, **-fied, -fying**. increase the apparent or real size of. —**mag″ni·fi·ca′tion**, *n.* —**mag′ni·fi″er**, *n.*

mag′ni·tude″, *n.* size.

mag·no′li·a, *n.* flowering tree.

mag′pie″, *n.* black-and-white bird.

ma″ha·ra′jah, *n.* major Indian ruler. Also, **ma″ha·ra′ja**, *fem.*, **ma″ha·ra′ni**, **ma″ha·ra′nee**.

ma·hog′a·ny, *n.* reddish-brown tropical wood.

maid, *n.* 1. Also, **maid′ser″vant**, woman servant. 2. *Archaic.* young woman.

maid′en, *n.* 1. *Archaic.* young woman. —*adj.* 2. very first. —**maid′en·hood″**, *n.* —**maid′en·ly**, *adj.*

maid′en·head″, *n.* hymen.

mail, *n.* 1. material shipped by post offices. 2. flexible armor. —*v.t.* 3. give to a post office for shipping. —**mail′box″**, *n.* —**mail′man″**, *n.*

ma″il·gram, *n.* message teletyped between post offices and finally delivered by mail.

maim, *v.t.* mutilate.

main, *adj.* 1. principal. —*n.* 2. major utility line. 3. *Archaic.* sea. —**main′ly**, *adv.* —**main′spring″**, *n.*

main″frame, *n.*, *adj.* (computers) large-scale, high-speed computing system.

main′land″, *n.* continental land, as opposed to islands.

main′stay″, *n.* main support.

main′stream″, *n.* main way of thinking, acting, etc.

main·tain′, *v.t.* 1. keep in good order. 2. house, feed, etc. 3. assert persistently. —**main′ten·ance**, *n.*

mâi·tre d′ho·tel (me′trə dô tel′) *n.* headwaiter. Also, *Informal.*, **mai·tre d′** (mät′ər dē′).

maj′es·ty, *n.*, *pl.* **-ies**. 1. **Majesty**, title of respect for a sovereign. 2. grandeur. —**ma·jes′tic**, *adj.*

ma·jol′i·ca, *n.* glazed pottery.

ma′jor, *adj.* 1. greater. 2. *Music.* in a scale a half tone above the minor. —*v.i.* 3. *Education.* specialize. —*n.* 4. army officer. 5. specialty in school.

ma·jor′i·ty, *n.*, *pl.* **-ties**. 1. greater number. 2. legal adulthood.

make, *v.t.*, **made, making**. 1. cause to be or occur. 2. force. 3. constitute. 4. earn. 5. interpret.

make′-be·lieve″, *n.* 1. pretense to oneself. —*adj.* 2. imaginary.

make′shift″, *adj.* improvised; temporary.

make′up″, *n.* 1. constitution; contents. 2. cosmetics, etc.

mal″ad·just′ed, *adj.* badly adjusted, esp. to life. —**mal″ad·just′ment**, *n.*

mal″a·droit′, *adj.* clumsy.

mal′a·dy, *n.*, *pl.* **-dies**. illness.

ma·laise′, *n.* uneasiness.

ma·lar′i·a, *n.* mosquito-transmitted disease. —**ma·lar′i·al**, *adj.*

mal′con·tent″, *n.* person discontented, esp. with society.

male, *adj.* 1. of the sex that inseminates. —*n.* 2. male being.

mal″e·dic′tion, *n.* curse.

mal′e·fac″tor, *n.* doer of evil.

ma·lev′o·lent, *adj.* wishing harm. —**ma·lev′o·lence**, *n.*

mal·fea′sance, *n.* wrongdoing in office.

mal″for·ma′tion, *n.* bad formation, esp. of a body part. —**mal·formed′**, *adj.*

mal′ice, *n.* ill will. —**ma·li′cious**, *adj.*

ma·lign', *adj.* **1.** intending or doing harm. —*v.t.* **2.** slander.

ma·lig'nant, *adj.* harmful or dangerous. —**ma·lig'nan·cy,** *n.*

ma·lin'ger, *v.i.* pretend sickness or weakness.

mall, *n.* **1.** tree-lined walk or lawn. **2.** shopping area.

mal'lard, *n.* wild duck.

mal'le·a·ble, *adj.* readily shaped by hammering. —**mal''le·a·bil'i·ty,** *n.*

mal'let, *n.* short, heavy hammer.

mal''nu·tri'tion, *n.* inadequate nutrition. —**mal·nour'shed,** *adj.*

mal·o'dor·ous, *adj.* bad-smelling.

mal·prac'tice, *n.* improper professional practice.

malt, *n.* soaked and dried grain.

mal'treat'', *v.t.* treat badly. —**mal·treat'ment,** *n.*

mam''bo, *n.* dance of Latin American origin.

mam'ma, *n.* mother. Also, **ma'ma.**

mam'mal, *n.* **1.** animal giving milk. —*adj.* **2.** being such an animal. —**mam·mal'i·an,** *adj., n.*

mam'ma·ry, *adj.* pertaining to breasts.

Mam'mon, *n.* riches or their pursuit, personified.

mam'moth, *adj.* **1.** very large. —*n.* **2.** extinct, long-tusked elephant.

man, *n., pl.* **men,** *v.t.,* **manned, manning. 1.** human being. **2.** adult male human. **3.** humanity. —*v.t.* **4.** furnish with persons.

man'a·cles, *n., pl.* shackles.

man'age, *v.,* **-aged, -aging.** *v.t.* **1.** supervise. **2.** control. —*v.i.* **4.** contrive to succeed. —**man'age·a·ble,** *adj.* —**man'age·ment,** *n.* —**man'ag·er,** *n.* —**man''a·ge'ri·al,** *adj.*

ma·ña'na, *adv. Spanish.* tomorrow; some time later.

man'da·rin, *n.* imperial Chinese official.

man'date, *n.* command.

man'da·to''ry, *adj.* required.

man''di·ble, *n.* lower jaw bone.

man'do·lin, *n.* plucked musical instrument.

man'drel, *n.* support for work being shaped. Also, **man'dril.**

mane, *n.* long hair on an animal's neck.

ma·neu'ver, *n.* **1.** military exercise. **2.** controlled movement. —*v.t., v.i.* **3.** move under control.

man'ful, *adj.* courageous.

man'ga·nese'', *n.* grayish chemical element.

mange, *n.* animal skin disease. —**man'gy,** *adj.*

man'ger, *n.* feeding trough.

man'gle, *v.t.,* **-gled, -gling,** *n. v.t.* **1.** crush out of shape. —*n.* **2.** ironing machine.

man'go, *n., pl.* **-goes.** fruit-bearing tropical tree.

man'grove, *n.* tropical tree.

man'han''dle, *v.t.,* **-dled, -dling.** handle roughly.

man'hole'', *n.* small access hole.

man'hood'', *n.* **1.** virility. **2.** majority.

ma'ni·a, *n.* **1.** violent insanity. **2.** excitement.

ma'ni·ac'', *n.* violently insane person. —**ma·ni'a·cal,** *adj.*

man'ic, *adj.* displaying unstable, frenzied behavior.

man'i·cure, *n.* care of the hands. —**man'i·cur''ist,** *n.*

man'i·fest'', *v.t.* **1.** make apparent. —*adj.* **2.** obvious. —*n.* **3.** list of cargo or passengers.

man'i·fes'to, *n., pl.* **-toes.** public declaration.

man'i·fold'', *adj.* in many forms.

man'i·kin, *n.* professional model. Also, **man'ne·quin.**

man·il''a, *n.* a strong, light brown paper.

ma·nip'u·late'', *v.t.,* **-lated, -lating.** handle cunningly. —**ma·nip'u·la''tor,** *n.*

man'kind'', *n.* humanity.

man'ly, *adj.* **-lier, -liest.** virile; brave. —**man'li·ness,** *n.*

man·na, *n.* miraculous food.

man'ner, *n.* **1.** way of doing. **2.** sort. **3.** manners, personal conduct.

man'ner·ism, *n.* personal peculiarity.

man'ner·ly, *adj.* well-mannered.

man'nish, *adj.* man-like.

ma·noeu'vre, *n., v.,* **-vred, -vring.** *n., v.t., v.i.* maneuver.

man'-of-war'', *n.* warship.

man'or, *n.* large estate. —**ma·no'ri·al,** *adj.*

man'pow''er, *n.* available labor force.

man'sard, *n.* hip roof with two pitches.

manse, *n.* home of a clergyman.

man'sion, *n.* impressive house.

man'slaugh''ter, *n.* unintentional homicide.

man'tel, *n.* fireplace surround. Also, **man'tel·piece''.**

man·til'la, *n.* lace shawl.

man'tle, *n., v.t.,* **-tled, -tling.** cloak.

man'u·al, *adj.* **1.** pertaining to or operated by hands. —*n.* **2.** handbook. —**man'u·al·ly,** *adv.*

man''u·fac'ture, *v.t.,* **-tured, -turing,** *n. v.t.* **1.** make industrially. —*n.* **2.** act or instance of manufacturing. —**man''u·fac'tur·er,** *n.*

ma·nure', *n., v.t.,* **-nured, -nuring.** *n.* **1.** animal feces. —*v.t.* **2.** spread with manure as fertilizer.

man'u·script, *n.* **1.** unprinted writing. —*adj.* **2.** written or typed.

man'y, *adj.,* **more, most.** in a large number.

map, *n., v.t.,* **mapped, mapping.** *n.* **1.**

measured representation of an area of land, etc. —v.t. 2. measure for a map. 3. plan.

ma'ple, n. broad-leafed deciduous tree.

mar, v.t., **marred, marring.** make imperfect.

mar'a·thon", n. 1. foot race of 26 miles, 385 yards. 2. endurance contest.

ma·raud'er, n. raider and plunderer.

mar'ble, n. 1. hard, fine-grained limestone. 2. colored glass ball. 3. **marbles,** game played with such balls.

march, v.i. 1. walk with measured steps to a cadence. —v.t. 2. cause to march. —n. 3. marching walk or journey. 4. piece of music accompanying such a walk. 5. **March,** third month.

mar'chion·ess, n. wife of a marquess, or woman equal to one in rank.

mare, n. female horse.

mar'ga·rine, butter-like vegetable oil compound.

mar'gin, n. 1. border or border area. 2. difference in amounts. —**mar'gin·al,** adj.

mar'i·gold", n. orange-flowered plant.

ma"ri·jua'na, n. dried hemp leaves and blossoms, sometimes smoked. Also, **ma"ri·hua'na.**

ma·rim'ba, n. xylophone with tubelike resonators.

ma·ri'na, n. yacht landing.

ma"ri·nade', n. pickling solution.

mar'i·nate", v.t., **-nated, -nating.** steep in a marinade.

ma·rine', adj. 1. pertaining to the sea. —n. 2. soldier performing sea duty.

mar'i·ner, n. sailor.

mar"i·o·nette', n. puppet hung from strings.

mar'i·tal, adj. pertaining to marriage. —**mar'i·tal·ly,** adv.

mar'i·time", adj. pertaining to shipping.

mar'jo·ram, n. fragrant herb.

mark, n. 1. something visible on a surface. 2. target. —v.t. 3. make a mark on. 4. indicate. 5. note. 6. review and grade. —**mark'er,** n. —**mark'ing,** n.

marked, adj. noticeable; emphatic. —**mark'ed·ly,** adv.

mark'et, n. 1. place for selling. —v.t. 2. offer for sale. —v.i. 3. shop. —**mark'et·a·ble,** adj.

marks'man, n. shooter at targets. —**marks'man·ship",** n.

mar'lin, n., pl. **-lins, -lin.** large deep-sea fish.

mar'ma·lade", n. fruit preserve.

ma·roon', v.t. 1. abandon on a deserted island. —n. 2. dark brownish red.

mar·quee', n. open projecting shelter.

mar'quess, n. nobleman superior to an earl or count. Also, **mar'quis,** fem., **mar·quise'.**

mar'row, n. inner bone tissue.

mar'ry, v., **-ried, -rying.** v.t. 1. take as spouse. 2. unite as spouses. —v.i. 3. be married. —**mar'riage,** n. —**mar'riage·a·ble,** adj.

marsh, n. swamp. —**marsh'y,** adj.

mar'shal, n., v.t., **-shaled, -shaling.** n. 1. sheriff-like U.S. officer. —v.t. 2. put in order. 3. guide; escort.

marsh'mal"low, n. sweet, spongy confection.

mar·su'pi·al, n. animal carrying its young in a pouch.

mart, n. salesplace.

mar'ten, n. soft-furred weasel-like animal.

mar'tial, adj. pertaining to war or the military.

mar'tin, n. bird of the swallow family.

mar"ti·net', n. rigid disciplinarian.

mar·ti'ni, n. cocktail of gin or vodka and dry vermouth.

mar'tyr, n. 1. person who dies or suffers for beliefs. —v.t. 2. kill as a martyr. —**mar'tyr·dom,** n.

mar'vel, n., v.i., **-veled, -veling.** wonder. —**mar'vel·ous,** adj.

mas·ca'ra, n. cosmetic for eyelashes and eyebrows.

mas'cot, n. 1. thing kept for luck. 2. group pet.

mas'cu·line, adv. pertaining to or characteristic of males. —**mas"cu·lin'i·ty,** n.

mash, v.t. 1. crush to pulp. —n. 2. pulped and watered grain.

mask, n. 1. face covering. 2. concealment. —v.t. 3. cover with a mask.

mas'och·ism, n. abnormal pleasure obtained from suffering pain. —**mas'och·ist,** n. —**mas"och·is'tic,** adj.

ma'son, n. 1. builder with stones, bricks, etc. 2. **Mason,** Freemason. —**Ma·son'ic,** adj. —**ma'son·ry,** n.

mas'quer·ade", n., v.i., **-aded, -ading.** n. 1. ball of masked and costumed persons. 2. something falsified. —v.i. 3. appear falsely.

mass, n. 1. large, shapeless quantity. 2. Physics. matter as related to inertia. 3. Often **Mass,** Eucharistic service. —v.t., v.i. 4. gather in a mass.

mas'sa·cre, n., v.t., **-cred, -cring.** n. 1. killing of many. —v.t. 2. kill in a massacre.

mas·sage (mə sahzh'), n., v.t., **-saged, -saging.** n. 1. manipulation of muscles, as to stimulate circulation. —v.t. 2. give a massage to. —**mas·seur',** fem., **mas·seuse',** n.

mas'sive, adj. in a large mass.

mast, n. tall spar used as a support.

mas'ter, n. 1. person in control. 2. accomplished craftsman. —adj. 3. principal; controlling. —v.t. 4. make submissive. 5. become expert in. —**mas'ter·y,** n.

mas'ter·ful, *adj.* imposing one's will.

mas'ter·ly, *adj.* accomplished.

mas'ter·piece'', *n.* **1.** greatest accomplishment. **2.** proof of masterly skill. Also, **mas'ter·work''**.

master sergeant, army sergeant of high rank.

mas'ti·cate'', *v.t.*, **-cated**, **-cating**. chew.

mas'tiff, *n.* large, strong-jawed dog.

mas'to·don'', *n.* extinct elephant-like animal.

mas'tur·bate'', *v.i.*, **-bated**, **-bating**. manipulate one's genitals.

mat, *n.*, *v.t.*, **matted**, **matting**, *adj. n.* **1.** thick, flat, flexible object. **2.** tangled mass. —*v.t.* **3.** cover with mats. **4.** make into a mat. —*adj.* **5.** without gloss.

mat'a·dor'', *n.* bullfighter who kills.

match, *n.* **1.** fire-making friction device. **2.** equal or counterpart. **3.** marriage. **4.** game. —*v.t.* **5.** compare. **6.** equal. —*v.i.* **7.** be a match or matches. —**match'mak''er**, *n.*

match'less, *adj.* incomparable.

mate, *n.*, *v.*, **mated**, **mating**, *n.* **1.** spouse. **2.** companion. **3.** co-worker. **4.** one of a pair. **5.** ship's officer. —*v.t.*, *v.i.* **6.** join as mates.

ma·te'ri·al, *n.* **1.** that which an object is made of. —*adj.* **2.** composed of material. **3.** non-spiritual. **4.** relevant.

ma·te'ri·al·ism, *n.* **1.** doctrine that all is matter. **2.** concern with wealth, goods, etc. —**ma·te'ri·al·ist**, *n.*, *adj.* —**ma·te''ri·al·is'tic**, *adj.*

ma·te''ri·el', *n.* military supplies.

ma·ter'nal, *adj.* **1.** pertaining to mothers. **2.** mother-like. —**ma·ter'ni·ty**, *n.*

math''e·mat'ics, *n.* study of the relations of quantities or forms. Also, *Informal*, **math**. —**math''e·mat'i·cal**, *adj.* —**math''e·ma·ti'cian**, *n.*

mat'i·nee', *n.* afternoon performance.

mat'ins, *n.* morning prayer service.

ma'tri·arch'', *n.* woman acting as master or ruler. —**ma''tri·ar'chal**, *adj.* —**ma'tri·ar''chy**, *n.*

ma·tric'u·late'', *v.*, **-lated**, **-lating**. *v.i.*, *v.t.* enroll as a student.

mat'ri·mo''ny, *n.*, *pl.* **-nies**. marriage. —**mat''ri·mo'ni·al**, *adj.*

ma'trix, *n.* environment in which one comes to be.

ma'tron, *n.* **1.** mature woman. **2.** woman supervisor or guard. —**ma'tron·ly**, *adj.*

matte, *n.* not glossy; flat.

mat'ter, *n.* **1.** solid, liquid, or gas. **2.** affair. **3.** importance. —*v.i.* **4.** be important.

mat'tock, *n.* digging tool.

mat'tress, *n.* pad for a bed.

ma·ture', *adj.*, *v.*, **-tured**, **-turing**. *adj.* **1.** fully ripe or grown. **2.** due for payment. —*v.t.* **3.** make mature. —*v.i.* **4.** become mature. —**mat''u·ri'tion**, *n.* —**ma·tu'ri·ty**, *n.*

mat'zo, *n.*, *pl.* **-zos**, **-zot**, **-zoth**. unleavened wafer.

maud'lin, *adj.* foolishly sentimental.

maul, *v.t.* handle or beat severely.

mau''so·le'um, *n.*, *pl.* **-leums**, **-lea**. large and magnificent tomb.

mauve, *n.* light bluish purple.

mav'er·ick, *n.* nonconformist.

maw, *n.* mouth and throat.

mawk'ish, *adj.* weakly sentimental.

max'im, *n.* rule of conduct.

max'i·mum, *n.*, *pl.* **-mums**, **-ma**, *adj. n.* **1.** greatest amount. —*adj.* **2.** Also, **max'i·mal**, greatest.

may, *v.t.* **1.** am, are, or is permitted to. **2.** will possibly. **3.** can. —*n.* **4. May**, fifth month.

may'be, *adv.* possibly.

may''day, *n.* distress call used by aircraft and ships.

may'hem'', *n.* criminal maiming.

may'on·naise'', *n.* salad dressing made with egg yolks.

may'or, *n.* chief city official. —**may'or·al·ty**, *n.*

maze, *n.* intricate system of corridors, lines, etc.

ma·zur'ka, *n.* fast Polish dance.

mead'ow, *n.* area of grassy land.

mea'ger, *adj.* scanty; inadequate. Also, **mea'gre**. —**mea'ger·ly**, *adv.* —**mea'ger·ness**, *n.*

meal, *n.* **1.** food at one sitting. **2.** coarsely ground grain. —**meal'y**, *adj.*

meal'y-mouthed'', *adj.* not frank.

mean, *v.t.*, **meant**, **meaning**, *adj.*, *n.* *v.t.* **1.** intend. **2.** wish to say. **3.** signify. —*adj.* **4.** ill-tempered. **5.** shabby. **6.** average. —*n.* **7.** part between extremes. **8. means**, **a.** something serving a purpose. **b.** personal resources. —**mean'ly**, *adv.* —**mean'ness**, *n.*

me·an'der, *v.i.* wander aimlessly.

mean'ing, *n.* **1.** intended message. —*adj.* **2.** intended as expressive. —**mean'ing·ful**, *adj.* —**mean'ing·less**, *adj.*

mean'time'', *n.* **1.** time in between. —*adv.* **2.** during the meantime. **3.** at the same time. Also, **mean'while''**.

mea'sles, *n.* virus disease producing a rash.

meas'ly, *adj.*, **-lier**, **liest**. *Informal*. contemptibly small.

meas'ure, *v.*, **-ured**, **-uring**, *n.*, *v.t.* **1.** find the size or amount of. —*v.i.* **2.** amount to. —*n.* **3.** measurement. **4.** means of measuring. **5.** course of action. —**meas'ur·a·ble**, *adj.* —**meas'ure·less**, *adj.* —**meas'ure·ment**, *n.*

meas'ured, *adj.* deliberate.

meat, *n.* **1.** animal flesh. **2.** edible part of a nut. **3.** essential part. —**meat'y**, *adj.*

me·chan'ic, *n.* **1.** worker with machinery. **2. mechanics**, study of the action of forces.

me·chan'i·cal, *adj.* **1.** working by machinery. **2.** unthinkingly automatic.

mech'a·nism, *n.* piece of machinery.

mech'a·nize", *v.t.*, **-nized, -nizing.** equip with machinery.

med'al, *n.* metal disk indicating distinction, religious affiliation, etc.

me·dal'lion, *n.* round design.

med'al·ist, *n.* winner of a medal.

med'dle, *v.i.*, **-dled, -dling.** interfere mischievously. **—med'dler**, *n.* **—med'dle·some**, *adj.*

me'di·an, *n.* **1.** *Math.* central in a series of numbers. **—adj. 2.** *Math.* pertaining to a median. **3.** middle.

me'di·ate", *v.*, **-ated, -ating.** *v.i.* **1.** act as an intermediary. **—v.t. 2.** resolve as an intermediary. **—me'di·a'tor**, *n.*

med'i·cal, *adj.* pertaining to medicine.

med'i·cate", *v.t.*, **-cated, -cating. 1.** treat with medicine. **2.** put medicine in. **—med"i·ca'tion**, *n.*

me·dic'i·nal, *adj.* serving as medicine.

med'i·cine, *n.* **1.** science of healing. **2.** healing substance.

me"di·e'val, *adj.* pertaining to the Middle Ages.

me"di·o'cre, *adj.* of indifferent value. **—me"di·oc'ri·ty**, *n.*

med'i·tate", *v.i.*, **-tated, -tating.** think deeply. **—med"i·ta'tion**, *n.* **—med'i·ta'tive**, *adj.*

me'di·um, *n.*, *pl.* **-ums, -a**, *adj.* *n.* **1.** something in the middle. **2.** means. **3.** *pl,* **media**, means of communication. **4.** *pl,* **mediums**, communicator with the dead. **—adj. 5.** intermediate.

med'ley, *n.*, *pl.* **-leys.** mixture of tunes.

meek, *adj.* mild; submissive. **—meek'ly**, *adv.* **—meek'ness**, *n.*

meer'schaum, *n.* white, claylike mineral.

meet, *v.*, **met, meeting**, *n.*, *adj.* *v.t.* **1.** come into contact with. **2.** be introduced to. **—v.i. 3.** be mutually met. **—n. 4.** sports meeting. **—adj. 5.** *Archaic.* suitable. **—meet'ing**, *n.*

meg'a·hertz", *n.*, *pl.* **-hertz.** one million hertz.

meg"a·lo·ma'ni·a, *n.* delusions of or appetite for grandeur.

meg"a·lop'o·lis, *n.* huge urban area.

meg'a·phone", *n.* horn magnifying the voice.

meg'a·ton", *n.* explosive force equal to one million tons of TNT.

mel"an·cho'li·a, *n.* pathological melancholy.

mel'an·chol'y, *n.* **1.** sadness. **—adj. 2.** sad.

me'lee, *n.* confused combat.

mel·li'flu·ous, *n.* smooth and sweet-sounding. Also, **mel·lif'flu·ent.**

mel'low, *adj.* **1.** rich-flavored. **2.** gentle. **—v.t. 3.** make mellow. **—v.i. 4.** become mellow.

me·lo'di·ous, *adj.* tuneful.

mel'o·dra"ma, *n.* drama of suspense and extravagant emotion. **—mel"o·dra·mat'ic**, *adj.* **—mel"o·dra·mat'ics**, *n.*, *pl.*

mel'o·dy, *n.*, *pl.* **-dies.** tune. **—me·lod'ic**, *adj.*

mel'on, *n.* large, juicy fruit.

melt, *v.*, **melted, melted** or **molten, melting.** *v.t.*, *v.i.* liquefy by applying heat.

mem'ber, *n.* **1.** person in an organization. **2.** component part. **—mem'ber·ship"**, *n.*

mem'brane, *n.* thin organic tissue.

me·men'to, *n.*, *pl.* **-tos, -toes.** souvenir.

mem'oirs, *n.*, *pl.* written personal recollections.

mem'o·ra·ble, *adj.* compelling remembrance. **—mem'o·ra·bly**, *adv.*

mem"o·ran'dum, *n.*, *pl.* **-dums, -da.** note of something to be remembered. Also, *Informal,* **mem'o.**

me·mo'ri·al, *adj.* **1.** in remembrance. **—n. 2.** something made or done in remembrance.

Memorial Day, legal holiday in May, in memory of dead servicemen.

mem'o·rize", *v.t.*, **-rized, -rizing.** act so as to remember. **—mem"o·ri·za'tion**, *n.*

mem"o·ry, *n.*, *pl.* **-ries. 1.** ability to recall past experience. **2.** something remembered. **3.** thing of the past. **4.** (computers) electronic data storage through circuitry or a recording medium.

men'ace, *n.*, *v.t.*, **-aced, -acing.** *n.* **1.** visible threat. **—v.t. 2.** threaten. **—men'ac·ing·ly**, *adv.*

me·nag'er·ie, *n.* collection of captive wild animals.

mend, *v.t.* **1.** repair. **—v.i. 2.** improve in condition. **—n. 3.** mended place.

men·da'cious, *adj.* lying. **—men·dac'i·ty**, *n.*

men'di·cant, *adj.* **1.** begging. **—n. 2.** mendicant person.

me'ni·al, *adj.* **1.** servile. **—n. 2.** menial person.

men'o·pause", *n.* permanent end of menstruation.

men·o'rah, *n.* *Judaism.* branched candlestick.

men'ses, *n.*, *pl.* periodic discharge of blood from the uterus.

men'stru·ate", *v.i.*, **-ated, -ating.** experience menses. **—men'stru·al**, *adj.* **—men"stru·a'tion**, *n.*

men"su·ra'tion, *n.* measurement.

men'tal, *adj.* pertaining to the mind. **—men'tal·ly**, *adv.*

men·tal'i·ty, *n.*, *pl.* **-ties.** mental power.

men'thol, *n.* alcohol from oil of peppermint. —men'tho·lat"ed, *adj.*

men'tion, *n.* 1. brief allusion. —*v.t.* 2. make a mention of.

men'tor, *n.* teacher or advisor.

men'u, *n.* list of dishes offered.

me·ow', *n.* sound of a cat.

mer'can·tile, *adj.* pertaining to trade.

mer'ce·nar"y, *adj., n., pl.* -ies. *adj.* 1. devoted to money-making. 2. done for pay. —*n.* 3. hired soldier.

mer'cer·ize", *v.t.,* -ized, -izing. impart gloss and strength to, chemically.

mer·chan·dise, *n., v.t.,* -dised, -dising. *n.* (mər'chən dīs") 1. goods for sale. —*v.t.* (mər'chən dīz") 2. Also, **mer'**chan·dize", promote the sale of.

mer'chant, *n.* seller of goods.

merchant marine, commercial ships of a country.

mer·cu'ri·al, *adj.* quick to change, esp. in emotion.

mer'cu·ry, *n.* heavy metallic chemical element.

mer'cy, *n., pl.* -cies. 1. kindness toward the helpless. 2. lucky thing. —mer'ci·ful, *adj.* —mer'ci·less, *adj.*

mere, *adj.* no more than. —mere'ly, *adv.*

mer"e·tri'cious, *adj.* showy and specious.

merge, *v.* merged, merging. *v.t., v.i.* combine

merg'er, *n.* unification of business organizations.

me·rid'i·an, *n.* north-south line.

me·ringue', *n.* stiff-beaten egg white.

mer'it, *n.* 1. worth. 2. merits, aspects right or wrong. —*v.t.* 3. deserve. —mer"i·to'ri·ous, *adj.*

mer'maid", *n.* legendary sea creature, half-woman, half-fish. Also, *masc.,* mer'man".

mer'ry, *adj.,* -rier, -riest. cheerful. —mer'ri·ly, *adv.* —mer'ri·ment, *n.*

mer'ry-go-round", *n.* rotating structure giving a pleasure ride.

mer'ry·mak"ing, *n.* festivity. —mer'ry·mak"er, *n.*

me'sa, *n.* high, steep-sided plateau.

mesh, *n.* 1. open space in a net. 2. net-like material. 3. engagement of gears. —*v.t., v.i.* 4. entangle. —*v.i.* 5. become engaged.

mes'mer·ize", *v.t.,* -ized, -izing. hypnotize. —mes'mer·ism, *n.* —mes'mer·ist, *n.*

mes·quite (mes kēt), *n.* southwestern U.S. tree.

mess, *n.* 1. disorder or disorderly scene. 2. difficult situation. 3. military meal. —*v.t.* 4. make untidy. 5. do badly. —*v.i.* 6. eat mess. —mes'sy, *adj.* —mes'si·ly, *adv.* —mes'si·ness, *n.*

mes'sage, *n.* 1. communication. 2. idea, etc. to communicate.

mes'sen·ger, *n.* carrier of messages.

Mes·si'ah, *n.* deliverer of mankind.

mes·ti'zo (mes tē'zō) *n., pl.* -zos, -zoes. Hispano-Indian.

me·tab'o·lism, *n.* breakdown of an organism's nourishment into protoplasm, energy, and waste. —met"a·bol'ic, *adj.*

met'al, *n.* iron, gold, brass, etc. —me·tal'lic, *adj.*

met'al·lur"gy, *n.* separation and refining of metals. —met"al·lur'gi·cal, *adj.* —met'al·lur"gist, *n.*

met"a·mor'pho·sis, *n.* transformation. —met"a·mor'phic, *adj.* —met"a·mor'phose, *v.t., v.i.*

met'a·phor", *n.* use of an analogous idea. —met"a·phor'i·cal, *adj.*

met"a·phys'ics, *n.* study of the nature of being and reality. —met"a·phys'i·cal, *adj.* —met"a·phy·si'cian, *n.*

met"em·psy·cho'sis, *n., pl.* -ses. transfer of souls from body to body.

me'te·or, *n.* meteoroid in the earth's atmosphere.

me"te·or'ic, *adj.* temporarily brilliant.

me'te·or·ite", *n.* meteoroid surviving a fall to earth.

me'te·or·oid", *n.* solid body traveling through outer space.

me"te·or·ol'o·gy, *n.* study of climate and weather. —me"te·or·o·log'i·cal, *adj.* —me"te·or·ol'o·gist, *n.*

me'ter, *n.* 1. unit of 100 centimeters or 39.37 inches. 2. rhythmic pattern. 3. measuring device for fluids, etc. —*v.t.* 4. measure with a meter.

meth'od, *n.* process or system of doing.

me·thod'i·cal, *adj.* orderly; deliberate. —me·thod'i·cal·ly, *adv.*

meth"od·ol'o·gy, *n., pl.* -gies. system of methods.

me·tic'u·lous, *adj.* attentive to details.

met'ric, *adj.* 1. pertaining to the metric system. 2. metrical. —met'ri·cal·ly, *adv.*

met'ri·cal, *adj.* 1. pertaining to poetic meter. 2. pertaining to measurement.

met'ri·cize", *v.t.,* -cized, -cizing. express in the metric system.

metric system, decimal system of measurement based on the meter, gram, and liter.

met'ro·nome", *n.* time-beating machine.

me·trop'o·lis, *n.* 1. principal or major city. 2. city and surrounding built-up area. —met"ro·pol'i·tan, *adj.*

met'tle, *n.* spirit; courage. —met'tle·some, *adj.*

mez'za·nine", *n.* balcony-like floor.

mez'zo·so·pra'no, *n., pl.* -nos, -ni. singer with a range between soprano and contralto.

mi·as'ma, *n.* marsh vapor.

mica

mi'ca, *n.* crystallized transparent laminated mineral.

mi'crobe, *n.* microorganism, esp. harmful.

mic"ro·com·pu'ter, *n.* a complete computing system of compact size, sometimes portable.

mi'cro·cosm, *n.* little world.

mi'cro·fiche", *n.* card of microfilm images.

mi'cro·film", *n.* **1.** film with images at greatly reduced size. —*v.t.* **2.** record on microfilm.

mi·crom'e·ter, *n.* instrument for fine measurements.

mi'cro·or'gan·ism, *n.* organism visible only through a microscope.

mi'cro·phone", *n.* instrument transforming sound into electrical impulses.

mi'cro·scope", *n.* instrument for very high magnification. —**mi"cro·scop'ic**, *adj.*

mic"ro·wave, *n.* electromagnetic radiation of extremely high frequency.

mid'air', *n.* area away from the ground.

mid'day", *n.* noon.

mid'dle, *n.* **1.** place with ends equally far away. —*adj.* **2.** intermediate.

mid'dle-aged', *adj.* neither young nor old.

mid'dle·man", *n.* intermediary between producer and consumer.

mid'dling, *adj.* **1.** intermediate. —*adv.* **2.** *Informal.* moderately.

midge, *n.* small insect.

mid'land, *n.* middle region.

mid'night", *n.* twelve o'clock at night.

mid'point", *n.* center point.

mid'riff, *n.* middle part of the torso.

mid'ship"man, *n.* naval cadet.

midst, *n.* middle part.

mid'way", *n.* **1.** thoroughfare of sideshows. —*adj., adv.* **2.** halfway.

mid'wife", *n.* woman deliverer of babies. —**mid'wife"ry**, *n.*

mid'year", *n.* middle of the year.

mien, *n.* manner; bearing.

miff, *v.t.* offend.

might, *n.* **1.** strength. —*v.* **2.** (past tense of *may*). **3.** will possibly. —**might'y**, *adj.* —**might'i·ly**, *adv.*

mi'graine, *n.* intense headache.

mi'grate, *v.i.,* -grated, -grating. move in a group. —**mi·gra'tion**, *n.* —**mi'grant**, *adj., n.* —**mi'gra·to"ry**, *adj.*

milch, *adj.* for milking.

mild, *adj.* not severe or harsh. —**mild'ly**, *adv.* —**mild'ness**, *n.*

mil'dew", *n.* fungus of damp cloth, etc.

mile, *n.* unit equal to 5,280 feet on land, 6,076 feet on water.

mile'age, *n.* **1.** rate per mile. **2.** number of miles per unit.

mi·lieu', *n.* social or working environment.

mil'i·tant, *adj.* **1.** fighting for a cause. —*n.* **2.** militant person. —**mil'i·tan·cy**, *n.*

mil'i·tar·ism, *n.* emphasis on military affairs. —**mil'i·tar·ist**, *n.* —**mil"i·ta·ris'tic**, *adj.*

mil'i·tar·ize", *v.t.,* -ized, -izing. invest or equip with military force.

mil'i·tar"y, *adj.* **1.** pertaining to armed forces. —*n.* **2. the military,** armed forces.

mil'i·tate", *v.i.,* -tated, -tating. be an influence.

mi·li'tia, *n.* emergency citizen army. —**mi·li'tia·man**, *n.*

milk, *n.* **1.** white fluid secreted by female mammals for nourishing their young. —*v.t.* **2.** get milk from. —**milk'maid"**, *n.* —**milk'man"**, *n.* —**milk'y**, *adj.*

milk'shake", *n.* shaken drink of milk, ice cream, and flavoring.

mill, *n.* **1.** place for processing or manufacturing; factory. **2.** tenth of a cent. —*v.t.* **3.** process in a mill. —*v.i.* **4.** move about confusedly. —**mill'er**, *n.*

mil·len'i·um, *n., pl.* -ums, -a. **1.** period of a thousand years. **2.** time of perfection.

mil'li·gram", *n.* thousandth of a gram.

mil'li·me"ter, *n.* thousandth of a meter.

mil'li·ner, *n.* dealer in women's hats. —**mil'lin·er·y**, *n.*

mil'lion, *n.* a thousand thousand. —**mil'lionth**, *adj.*

mil'lion·aire', *n.* owner of at least a million dollars.

mill'stone", *n.* stone for grinding flour.

mime, *n., v.t.,* mimed, miming. *n.* **1.** acting without words. —*v.t.* **2.** imitate in mime. —**mi·met'ic**, *adj.*

mim'ic, *n., v.t.,* -icked, -icking. *n.* **1.** person who imitates mannerisms of others. —*v.t.* **2.** imitate as a mimic. —**mim'ic·ry**, *n.*

mi·mo'sa, *n.* flowering plant of warm regions.

min"a·ret', *Islam.* tower for summoning to prayer.

mince, *v.,* minced, mincing. *v.t.* **1.** chop finely. **2.** mitigate the meaning of. —*v.i.* **3.** be affectedly dainty. —**minc'ing**, *adj.*

mince'meat", *n.* finely chopped fruit, etc.

mind, *n.* **1.** that which thinks. **2.** personality. **3.** sanity. —*v.t.* **4.** heed. **5.** be troubled or annoyed by.

mind'ful, *adj.* heedful.

mind'less, *adj.* **1.** heedless. **2.** stupid.

mine, *pron., n., v.,* mined, mining. *pron.* **1.** my own. —*n.* **2.** excavation for coal or minerals. **3.** buried or floated bomb.

—*v.t.* **4.** dig from a mine. **5.** put mines in. —*v.i.* **6.** work a mine. —**min′er,** *n.*

min′er·al, *n.* **1.** something neither vegetable nor animal. **2.** inorganic earth material.

min″er·al′o·gy, *n.* study of minerals. —**min″er·al·og′i·cal,** *adj.* —**min″er·al′o·gist,** *n.*

min′gle, *v.,* -**gled,** -**gling.** *v.t., v.i.* mix together.

min′i·a·ture″, *n.* **1.** small copy. **2.** small painting. —*adj.* **3.** smaller than standard. —**min′i·a·tur·ize″,** *v.t.*

mi″ni·com·pu′ter, *n.* a computing system that is larger than a microcomputer but smaller than a mainframe computer.

min′im, *n.* **1.** *Pharmacy.* liquid measure equalling a drop. **2.** *Music.* half note.

min′i·mize″, *v.t.,* -**mized,** -**mizing. 1.** reduce to a minimum. **2.** treat as of minimum importance.

min′i·mum, *n., pl.* -**mums,** -**ma,** *adj., n.* **1.** least amount. —*adj.* **2.** Also, **min′i·mal,** least.

min′ion, *n.* minor official.

min′is·ter, *n.* **1.** clergyman. **2.** diplomat. **3.** cabinet member. —*v.i.* **4.** give help. —**min′′is·te′ri·al,** *adj.* —**min′′is·tra′tion,** *n.* —**min′is·trant,** *n., adj.*

min′is·try, *n., pl.* -**tries. 1.** profession of a minister. **2.** government department. **3.** act of ministering.

mink, *n.* weasel-like mammal.

min′now, *n.* tiny fresh-water fish.

mi′nor, *adj.* **1.** lesser in size or importance. **2.** *Music.* in a scale a half tone below the major. —*n.* **3.** person not of age.

mi·nor′i·ty, *n., pl.* -**ities. 1.** lesser part. **2.** social group too small to have control. **3.** state of being a minor.

min′strel, *n.* **1.** medieval strolling singer. **2.** blackface singer.

mint, *n.* **1.** place for coining money. **2.** plant with aromatic leaves. —*adj.* **3.** absolutely fresh. —*v.t.* **4.** coin.

min′u·end″, *n. Math.* number subtracted from.

min′u·et, *n.* slow dance.

mi′nus, *prep.* **1.** from which is subtracted. **2.** without.

mi·nus′cule, *adj.* tiny.

min·ute, *n.* (min′ət) **1.** one sixtieth of an hour. **2.** one sixtieth of a degree of arc. **3.** minutes, record of a meeting. —*adj.* (mī nyōōt′) **4.** tiny. **5.** precise.

min′ute·man″, *n.* volunteer soldier of the American Revolution.

mi·nu′ti·ae, *n., pl.* minor details.

mir′a·cle, *n.* supernatural event. —**mi·rac′u·lous,** *adj.*

mi·rage′, *n.* optical illusion caused by the atmosphere.

mire, *n., v.t.,* **mired, miring.** *n.* **1.** sticky mud.—*v.t.* **2.** stick fast, as with mud. —**mir′y,** *adj.*

mir′ror, *n.* **1.** reflecting object.—*v.t.* **2.** reflect.

mirth, *n.* gaiety. —**mirth′ful,** *adj.* —**mirth′less,** *adj.*

mis- prefix meaning "wrong" or "wrongly." **misapply, misbehave, miscalculate, misconceive, misconduct, misconstrue, miscount, misdeed, misdirect, misdoing, misgovern, misguide, mishandle, misinform, misinterpret, misjudge, mismanage, mismatch, misprint, mispronounce, misquote, misread, misrule, misshapen, misspell, misspend, misstate, mistime, mistreat, misunderstand.**

mis′′ad·ven′ture, *n.* bad luck.

mis′an·thrope″, *n.* hater of mankind. Also **mis·an′thro·pist.** —**mis″an·throp′ic,** *adj.* —**mis·an′thro·py,** *n.*

mis·ap″pre·hend′, *v.t.* understand wrongly. —**mis·ap″pre·hen′sion,** *n.*

mis″ap·pro′pri·ate″, *v.t.,* -**ated,** -**ating.** take and use wrongly.

mis′′be·got′ten, *adj.* begotten wrongly; illegitimate.

mis·car′ry, *v.i.,* -**ried,** -**rying. 1.** give birth to a fetus that cannot live. **2.** go wrong. —**mis·car′riage,** *n.*

mis″ce″ge·na′tion, *n.* interbreeding of races.

mis″cel·la′ne·ous, *adj.* various. —**mis′cel·la·ny,** *n.*

mis·chance′, *n.* bad luck.

mis′chief, *n.* **1.** damage. **2.** malice. **3.** gentle malice. —**mis′chie·vous,** *adj.*

mis″con·struc′tion, *n.* wrong interpretation.

mis′cre·ant, *n.* villain.

mis″de·mea′nor, *n.* offence less serious than a felony.

mi′ser, *n.* morbid saver of money. —**mi′ser·ly,** *adj.*

mis′er·a·ble, *adj.* **1.** very unhappy. **2.** causing misery. **3.** contemptibly meager or poor. —**mis′er·a·bly,** *adv.*

mis′er·y, *n., pl.* -**ies. 1.** suffering. **2.** source of suffering.

mis·fire′, *v.i.,* -**fired,** -**firing. 1.** fail to fire. **2.** fail to be effective.

mis′fit′, *n., v.i.,* -**fitted,** -**fitting.** *n.* **1.** person unhappy in society. —*v.t., v.i.* **2.** fit badly.

mis·for′tune, *n.* **1.** bad luck. **2.** piece of bad luck.

mis·giv′ing, *n.* apprehension; doubt.

mis′hap′, *n.* unfortunate incident.

mis·lay′, *v.t.,* -**laid,** -**laying.** put somewhere later forgotten.

mis·lead′, *v.t.,* -**led,** -**leading. 1.** advise or urge wrongly. **2.** deceive.

mis·no′mer, *n.* wrong name.

mi·sog'y·ny, *n.* hatred of women. —**mi·sog'y·nist,** *n.*

mis·place', *v.t.,* **-placed, -placing. 1.** mislay. **2.** put in a wrong place.

mis·pri'sion, *n.* deviation from duty.

mis''rep·re·sent', *v.t.* give a wrong idea of. —**mis''rep·re·sen·ta'tion,** *n.*

miss, *v.t., n., pl.* **misses.** *v.t.* **1.** fail to hit, seize, meet, etc. **2.** be lonely without. —*n.* **3.** act or instance of missing. **4. Miss,** title for an unmarried woman.

mis'sal, *n.* book of prayers for Mass.

mis'sile, *n.* something thrown or shot to hit a target.

mis'sing, *adj.* lost or absent.

mis'sion, *n.* **1.** commanded or requested journey. **2.** group of missionaries. **3.** group sent to a place. **4.** duty or purpose.

mis'sion·ar''y, *n., pl.* **-ies.** person sent to make religious conversions.

mis'sive, *n.* written message.

mis·step', *n.* **1.** wrong step. **2.** wrong act.

mist, *n.* **1.** thin fog. —*v.t.* **2.** fog. —*v.i.* **3.** become misty. —**mist'y,** *adj.*

mis·take', *n., v.t.,* **-took, -taken, -taking.** *n.* **1.** wrong act or opinion. —*v.t.* **2.** understand wrongly. —**mis·tak'a·ble,** *adj.*

mis'tle·toe'', *n.* parasitic evergreen.

mis'tress, *n.* **1.** female master. **2.** unmarried female sexual partner.

mis·tri'al, *n.* trial invalidated for technical reasons.

mis·trust', *v.t.* **1.** have no trust in. —*n.* **2.** lack of trust. —**mis·trust'ful,** *adj.*

mis·use, *v.t.,* **-used, -using,** *n., v.t* (mis yōoz') **1.** use wrongly. **2.** mistreat. —*n.* (mis yōos') **3.** wrong use or treatment.

mite, *n.* **1.** tiny arachnid. **2.** tiny sum of money.

mi'ter, *n.* **1.** bishop's headpiece. **2.** diagonal joint. —*v.t.* **3.** join in a miter.

mit'i·gate'', *v.,* **-gated, -gating.** *v.t., v.i.* lessen in severity. —**mit''i·ga'tion,** *n.*

mitt, *n.* padded glove.

mit'ten, *n.* glove with only the thumb separate.

mix, *v.,* **mixed, mixing,** *n., v.t.* **1.** assemble and make uniform. **2.** have together. —*v.i.* **3.** be on social terms. —*n.* **4.** mixture. —**mix'ture,** *n.*

mixed, *adj.* **1.** blended. **2.** imperfect or impure.

mix'up'', *n.* confusion.

mne·mon'ic, *adj.* helping memory.

moan, *n.* **1.** low, sad sound. —*v.i.* **2.** make such a sound.

moat, *n.* defensive, water-filled ditch.

mob, *n., v.t.,* **mobbed, mobbing.** *n.* **1.** disorderly or hostile crowd. —*v.t.* **2.** attack in a mob.

mo'bile, *adj.* movable. —**mo·bil'i·ty,** *n.*

mo'bi·lize'', *v.,* **-lized, -lizing.** *v.t., v.i.* make ready for war.

moc'ca·sin, *n.* soft heelless slipper.

mo'cha, *n.* **1.** type of coffee. —*adj.* **2.** coffee-flavored.

mock, *n.* **1.** ridicule. **2.** imitate; mimic. —*adj.* **3.** imitation. —**mock'er·y,** *n.*

mock'ing·bird'', *n.* bird imitating calls of other birds.

mock'up'', *n.* full-scale model.

mode, *n.* **1.** manner of doing. **2.** fashion. —**mod'ish,** *adj.*

mod'el, *n.* **1.** small-scale three-dimensional copy. **2.** something to imitate. **3.** poser for pictures. —*adj.* **4.** exemplary. —*v.t.* **5.** copy in three dimensions. **6.** mold as in making a model. **7.** make as a copy.

mo''dem, *n.* (computers) device for linking computers via telephone lines.

mod·er·ate, *adj., n., v.,* **-ated, -ating.** *adj.* (mod'ər ət) **1.** avoiding extremes. —*n.* **2.** moderate person. —*v.t.* (mod' ər āt) **3.** make moderate. **4.** preside over. —*v.i.* **5.** become moderate. —**mod'er·ate·ly,** *adv.* —**mod'er·a''tor,** *n.*

mod'ern, *adj.* **1.** pertaining to the present. **2.** reflecting advance taste, thought, technology, etc. —*n.* **3.** modern person. —**mo·dern'i·ty,** *n.* —**mod'ern·ize'',** *v.t., v.i.*

mod'ern·ism, *n.* advocacy of something deemed modern.

mod''ern·is'tic, *adj.* self-consciously modern in style.

mod'est, *adj.* **1.** disliking praise, publicity, etc. **2.** avoiding self-exposure. **3.** not outstanding. —**mod'est·ly,** *adv.* —**mod·es'ty,** *n.*

mod'i·cum, *n.* small amount.

mod'i·fy'', *v.,* **-fied, -fying.** *v.t., v.i.* **1.** alter in nature. —*v.t.* **2.** limit slightly. —**mod''i·fi·ca'tion,** *n.* —**mod'i·fi''er,** *n.*

mod'u·late'', *v.t.,* **-lated, -lating.** vary or adjust. —**mod''u·la'tion,** *n.*

mod'ule, *n.* **1.** unit of measurement. **2.** part scaled to the dimensions of such a unit.

mo'hair, *n.* fabric of Angora goat hair.

Mo·ham'med·an, *n., adj.* Muslim. —**Mo·ham'med·an·ism,** *n.*

moist, *adj.* slightly wet. —**moist'en,** *v.t., v.i.* —**mois'ture,** *n.*

mo'lar, *n.* grinding tooth.

mo·las'ses, *n.* syrup from sugar refining.

mold, *n.* **1.** device for forming a casting. **2.** model. **3.** destructive fungus. —*v.t.* **4.** model. **5.** cast in a mold. —*v.i.* **6.** become moldy. —**mold'y,** *adj.*

mold'er, *v.i.* crumble to dust.

mold'ing, *n.* shaped strip or band.

mole, *n.* **1.** spot on the skin. **2.** burrowing animal. **3.** breakwater. —**mole'hill'',** *n.* —**mole'skin'',** *n.*

mol'e·cule'', *n.* smallest characteristic

particle of an element or compound.
—mo·lec'u·lar, *adj.*

mo·lest', *v.t.* trouble or interfere with.
—mo"les·ta'tion, *n.*

mol'li·fy", *v.t.,* -fied, -fying. 1. appease.
2. mitigate.

mol'lusk, *n.* soft-bodied invertebrate, often in a shell. Also, **mol'lusc.**

molt, *v.i.* shed hair, feathers, etc. for replacement.

mol'ten, *adj.* melted.

mo'ment, *n.* 1. very brief period. 2. present time. 3. importance. —mo'men·tar"y, *adj.* —mo'men·tar'i·ly, *adv.*

mo·men'tous, *adj.* of great importance.

mo·men'tum, *n., pl.* -tums, -ta. force of a moving object.

mom'my, *n., pl.* -mies. mother: child's word.

mon'arch, *n.* king, queen, etc. —mon'arch·y, *n.* —mo·nar'chi·cal, *adj.*

mon'arch·ist, *n.* person in favor of a monarchy. —mon'ar·chism", *n.*

mon'as·ter"y, *n., pl.* -ies. *n.* home of monks or nuns.

mo·nas'tic, *adj.* pertaining to monks and nuns. Also, mo·nas'ti·cal, *adj.*

mon·au'ral, *adj.* reproducing sound on one channel.

Mon'day, *n.* second day.

mon'ey, *n., pl.* -eys, -ies. paper or metal accepted everywhere in payment of debts. —mon'eyed, *adj.* —mon'e·tar"y, *adj.*

mon'grel, *adj.* 1. of mixed breed. —*n.* 2. mongrel animal.

mon'i·tor, *n.* 1. device for checking or supervising. —*v.t.* 2. check or supervise.

monk, *n.* member of a religious order.

mon'key, *n., pl.* -keys. 1. primate other than a human or lemur. 2. small, long-tailed primate.

mon'o·chrome", *n.* color with shading varied but not hue.

mon'o·cle, *n.* corrective lens for one eye.

mo·nog'a·my, *n.* marriage to one spouse at a time. —mo·nog'a·mous, *n.*

mon'o·graph", *n.* scholarly work on one subject.

mon'o·lith", *n.* object made from one stone. —mon"o·lith'ic, *adj.*

mon'o·logue", *n.* uninterrupted speech of one person. Also, **mon'o·log".** —mon'o·log"ist, *n.*

mon"o·ma'ni·a, *n.* obsession with one thing. —mon"o·ma'ni·ac", *n.*

mo·nop'o·ly, *n., pl.* -lies. exclusive use, control, or possession. —mo·nop'o·list, *n.* —mo·nop"o·lis'tic, *adj.* —mo·nop'o·lize", *v.t.*

mon'o·rail", *n.* one-rail railway.

mon'o·syl'la·ble, *n.* one-syllable word. —mon"o·syl·lab'ic, *adj.*

mon"o·the'ism, *n.* belief in one god. —mon"o·the·ist, *n.* —mon"o·the·is'tic, *adj.*

mon'o·tone", *n.* sound with unvarying pitch.

mo·not'o·nous, *adj.* tediously unvaried. —mo·not'o·ny, *n.*

mon·sieur' (mə syur'), *n., pl.* messieurs. *French.* 1. gentleman. 2. Monsieur. a. Sir. b. Mister.

Mon·si·gnor (mon sēn'yər), *n., pl.* -gnors, -gnori. high-ranking Roman Catholic priest.

mon·soon', *n.* season of wind and rain in south Asia.

mon'ster, *n.* 1. frightening legendary creature. 2. grotesque or disgusting person. —mon'strous, *adj.* —mon·stros'i·ty, *n.*

mon·tage (mahn tahzh'), *n.* composite photograph, etc.

month, *n.* one of the twelve divisions of the year. —month'ly, *adj., adv., n.*

mon'u·ment, *n.* 1. something built or put up in remembrance. 2. formal, impressive construction. —mon"u·men'tal, *adj.*

moo, *n., v.i.,* mooed, mooing. *n.* 1. sound of a cow. —*v.i.* 2. make this sound.

mooch, *Informal. v.i.* 1. beg; cadge. —*v.t.* 2. obtain by begging.

mood, *n.* state of mind.

mood'y, *adj.,* -ier, -iest. 1. gloomy. 2. changing mood quickly. —mood'i·ly, *adv.* —mood'i·ness, *n.*

moon, *n.* 1. satellite of the earth. 2. lighted portion of this satellite as seen from the earth. —*v.i.* 3. be abstracted or sentimental. —moon'beam", *n.* —moon'light", *n.* —moon'lit", *adj.* —moon'scape", *n.*

moon'light"ing, *n.* holding of a second job.

moon'shine", *n.* 1. illicit whiskey. 2. moonlight. —moon'shin"er, *n.*

moon'shot", *n.* start of a trip to the moon.

moon'struck", *adj.* 1. crazy. 2. dreamy.

moon'walk", *n.* walk on the moon.

moor, *v.t.* tie or anchor.

moor'ings, *n., pl.* 1. tackle for mooring. 2. place to moor.

moose, *n., pl.* moose. large animal of the deer family.

moot, *adj.* 1. hypothetical. 2. open to question.

mop, *n., v.t.,* mopped, mopping. *n.* 1. long-handled device for washing or dusting. —*v.t.* 2. clean with a mop.

mope, *v.i.,* moped, moping. brood. —mop'ey, mop'y, *adj.*

mo·raine', *n.* mass of rock, etc. left by a glacier.

mor'al, *adj.* 1. pertaining to morality. 2.

in accord with morality. **3.** pertaining to morale. —*n.* **4.** lesson of an experience. **5. morals,** moral principles. —**mor'al·ist,** *n.* —**mo·ral'i·ty,** *n.*

mo·rale', *n.* confidence in oneself, a situation, etc.

mor''al·is'tic, *adj.* **1.** pertaining to morals. **2.** overconcerned with morals.

mor'al·ize'', *v.i.,* **-ized, -izing.** discuss morality.

mo·rass', *n.* swamp.

mor''a·to'ri·um, *n., pl.* **-ums, -a.** authorized delay.

mor'bid, *adj.* **1.** pertaining to disease. **2.** mentally unhealthy. —**mor·bid'i·ty,** *n.* —**mor'bid·ly,** *adv.*

mor'dant, *adj.* biting. —**mor'dan·cy,** *n.*

more, *adj.* **1.** greater in number, amount, etc. **2.** additional. —*adv.* **3.** additionally. —*n.* **4.** greater number, amount, etc. **5.** something additional.

more·o'ver, *adv.* besides.

mo'res, *n., pl.* prevailing social customs.

morgue, *n.* place for keeping the unidentified dead.

mor'i·bund, *adj.* about to die.

morn'ing, *n.* early part of the day.

morning glory, vine with trumpet-shaped flowers.

mo·roc'co, *n.* goat leather.

mo'ron, *n.* feeble-minded person. —**mo·ron'ic,** *adj.*

mo·rose', *adj.* downhearted or surly. —**mo·rose'ly,** *adv.* —**mo·rose'ness,** *n.*

mor'phine, *n.* analgesic opiate.

morse, *n.* code of dots and dashes. Also, **Morse.**

mor'sel, *n.* small portion of food.

mor'tal, *adj.* **1.** having eventually to die. **2.** human. **3.** fatal. **4.** threatening the soul. —*n.* **5.** human being. —**mor'tal·ly,** *adv.* —**mor·tal'i·ty,** *n.*

mor'tar, *n.* **1.** adhesive for masonry. **2.** bowl for grinding. **3.** short cannon.

mor'tar·board'', *n.* academic cap.

mort'gage, *n., v.t.,* **-gaged, -gaging.** *n.* **1.** pledge or property as security for a loan. —*v.t.* **2.** pledge in this way. —**mort''ga·gee',** *n.* —**mort'ga·gor,** *n.*

mor·ti'cian, *n.* undertaker.

mor'ti·fy'', *v.t.,* **-fied, -fying. 1.** humiliate. **2.** suppress with austerities. —**mor''ti·fi·ca'tion,** *n.*

mor'tise, *n., v.t.* **-tised, -tising.** *n.* **1.** socket forming part of a joint. —*v.t.* **2.** join with a mortise.

mor'tu·ar''y, *adj., n., pl.* **-ies.** *adj.* **1.** pertaining to death or funerals. —*n.* **2.** place for receiving the dead.

mo·sa'ic, *n.* picture of inlaid pieces.

mo'sey, *v.i. Informal.* amble.

Mos'lem, *n.* Muslim.

mosque, *n.* Muslim house of prayer.

mos·qui'to, *n., pl.* **-toes, -tos.** small blood-sucking insect.

moss, *n.* green, velvety plant. —**mos'sy,** *adj.*

most, *adj.* **1.** greatest in number, amount, etc. **2.** in the majority. —*adv.* **3.** to the greatest extent. —*n.* **4.** greatest number, extent, etc.

most'ly, *adv.* in most cases.

mo·tel', *n.* hotel for motorists.

moth, *n., pl.* **moths.** nocturnal flying insect.

moth'ball'', *n.* ball of moth repellent.

moth'er, *n.* **1.** female parent. —*v.t.* **2.** act as a mother to. —**moth'er·hood'',** *n.* —**moth'er·less,** *adj.* —**moth'er·ly,** *adj.*

moth'er-in-law'', *n., pl.* **mothers-in-law.** mother of a spouse.

moth'er-of-pearl', *n.* inner shell of the pearl oyster.

mo·tif', *n.* basic theme or subject.

mo'tion, *n.* **1.** movement. **2.** formal proposal. —*v.i.* **3.** gesture. —*v.t.* **4.** direct with a gesture. —**mo'tion·less,** *n.*

motion picture, series of photographs projected at high speed.

mo'ti·vate'', *v.t.,* **-vated, -vating.** give desire or incentive. —**mo''ti·va'tion,** *n.*

mo'tive, *n.* **1.** desire for action. **2.** motif. —*adj.* **3.** pertaining to motion.

mot'ley, *adj.* of many colors or kinds.

mo'tor, *n.* **1.** machine providing motive force. —*adj.* **2.** causing motion. —**mo'tor·bike'',** *n.* —**mo'tor·boat'',** *n.* —**mo'tor·car'',** *n.* —**mo'tor·ize'',** *v.t.*

mo'tor·cade'', *n.* procession of automobiles.

mo'tor·cy''cle, *n.* two-wheeled motorized vehicle.

mo'tor·ist, *n.* automobile driver.

mo'tor·man, *n.* driver of a streetcar.

mot'tle, *v.t.,* **-tled, -tling.** mark with spots, etc.

mot'to, *n., pl.* **-toes, -tos.** formal statement of aims or ideals.

mould, *n., v.t.* mold.

mound, *n., v.t.* heap.

mount, *v.t.* **1.** climb onto or up. **2.** set in place. —*v.i.* **3.** climb. —*n.* **4.** steed. **5.** setting or support. —**mount'ing,** *n.*

moun'tain, *n.* very high feature of the earth. —**moun'tain·ous,** *adj.*

moun''tain·eer', *n.* **1.** mountain dweller. **2.** mountain climber. —**moun''tain·eer'ing,** *n.*

moun'te·bank'', *n.* charlatan.

mourn, *v.t., v.i.* lament. —**mourn'ful,** *adj.* —**mourn'ing,** *n.*

mouse, *n., pl.* **mice. 1.** small, timid rodent. **2.** (computers) compact device for convenient data manipulation on a monitor.

mous·tache', *n.* mustache.

mous'y, *adj.,* **-ier, -iest.** mouse-like, esp. in timidity.

mouth, *n.* **1.** orifice for eating and

breathing. **2.** opening of a river, etc. —**mouth'ful,** n.

mouth'piece", n. **1.** part of a horn, etc. blown through. **2.** spokesman or apologist.

move, v., **moved, moving,** n. v.t. **1.** change the place of. **2.** inspire or motivate. **3.** propose formally. —v.i. **4.** change place. **5.** change residence or workplace. **6.** become in motion. —n. **7.** act or instance of moving. **8.** purposeful action. —**mov'a·ble, move'a·ble,** adj.

move'ment, n. **1.** motion. **2.** action in a cause. **3.** assembly of clockwork. **4.** division of a musical composition.

mov'ie, n. motion picture. Also, **moving picture.**

mow, v.t., **mowed, mowed** or **mown, mowing. 1.** cut down, as grass. **2.** cut down the plants on.

Mr. (mis'tər), title for a man. Also, **Mis'ter.**

Mrs. (mis'iz), title for a married woman.

Ms. (miz, em'es'), n. title for a woman disregarding marital status.

much, adj., adv., n. adj. **1.** in great quantity. —adv. **2.** to a great extent. **3.** about. —n. **4.** something considerable. **5.** a great amount.

mu'ci·lage, n. liquid glue.

muck, n. sticky filth. —**muck'y,** adj.

muck'rak''ing, n. searching for scandalous information. —**muck'rak''er,** n.

mu'cous, adj. **1.** having mucus. **2.** slimy.

mu'cus, n. slimy body secretion, esp. from the nose.

mud, n. sticky earth. —**mud'dy,** adj., v.t.

mud'dle, v.t., **-dled, -dling,** n. v.t. **1.** bungle or confuse. —n. **2.** act or instance of muddling. —**mud'dle·head'ed,** adj.

mud'sling''ing, n. defamation, esp. of a political opponent. —**mud'sling''er,** n

mu·ez'zin, n. Muslim caller to prayer.

muff, n. **1.** cylinder made esp. of fur for keeping the hands warm. —v.t. **2.** bungle.

muf'fin, n. small round bread or cake.

muf'fle, v.t., **-fled, -fling. 1.** wrap closely. **2.** deaden, as sound.

muf'fler, n. **1.** heavy scarf. **2.** sound deadener.

muf'ti, n. dress other than a uniform.

mug, n., v.t., **mugged, mugging.** n. **1.** cylindrical cup. —v.t. **2.** attack from behind, esp. in order to rob.

mug'gy, adj., **-gier, -giest.** hot and humid.

Mu·ham'ma·dan, n., adj. Muslim.

mu·lat'to, n., pl. **-toes.** person of mixed white and colored blood.

mul'ber''ry, n., pl. **-ries.** tree with purplish-red fruit.

mulch, n. plant matter spread to keep the ground from freezing.

mulct, v.t. **1.** fine. **2.** obtain by fraud.

mule, n. **1.** offspring of a donkey and a mare. **2.** heelless slipper. —**mu·le·teer',** n.

mul'ish, adj. stubborn.

mull, v.t. **1.** warm and spice, as wine. —v.i. **2.** Informal. ponder.

mul''ti·far'i·ous, adj. with many components.

mul''ti·mil''lion·aire', n. one who has many millions of dollars.

mul'ti·ple, adj. **1.** in a large number. —n. **2.** number evenly divisible by another.

mul''ti·pli·cand', n. Math. number to be multiplied.

mul''ti·plic'i·ty, n. large number or variety.

mul'ti·ply'', v., **-plied, -plying.** v.t. **1.** repeat a specified number of times for a final sum. —v.i. **2.** increase in size or number. —**mul''ti·pli'er,** n. —**mul''ti·pli·ca'tion,** n.

mul''ti·stage'', adj. in many stages.

mul'ti·tude'', n. large number. —**mul''ti·tu'di·nous,** adj.

mum, adj. unspeaking.

mum'ble, v.i., **-bled, -bling,** n. v.i. **1.** say something quietly and indistinctly. —n. **2.** mumbling speech or remark.

mum'bo jum'bo, pretentious or meaningless ceremony.

mum'mer, n. wearer of a mask or costume. —**mum'mer·y,** n.

mum'my, n., pl. **-mies.** preserved dead body. —**mum'mi·fy'',** v.t., v.i.

mumps, n. communicable disease.

munch, v.t., v.i. chew crunchingly.

mun·dane', adj. **1.** wordly. **2.** common-place.

mu·nic'i·pal, adj. pertaining to city government.

mu·nic''i·pal'i·ty, n., pl. **-ties.** incorporated community.

mu·nif'i·cent, adj. lavish; generous. —**mu·nif'i·cence,** n.

mu·ni'tions, n., pl. military supplies, esp. guns and ammunition.

mu'ral, n. wall painting. —**mu'ral·ist,** n.

mur'der, n. **1.** willful unlawful killing. —v.t. **2.** commit murder against. —**mur'der·er,** fem., **mur'der·ess,** n. —**mur'der·ous,** adj.

murk, n. gloom; darkness. —**murk'y,** adj.

mur'mur, n. **1.** low, indistinct speech or sound. —v.i. **2.** make a murmur.

mus''ca·tel', n. sweet wine.

mus'cle, n. body tissue which contracts to cause movement. —**mus'cu·lar,** adj. —**mus'cu·la·ture,** n.

muse, *v.i.* **1.** be meditative. —*n.* **2. Muse**, goddess presiding over an art.

mu·se′um, *n.* public institution for displaying things of interest.

mush, *n.* **1.** porridge of boiled meal. **2.** *Informal.* foolish sentiment. —**mush′y**, *adj.*

mush′room″, *n.* **1.** edible fungus. —*v.i.* **2.** grow rapidly.

mu′sic, *n.* art of composing series of tones, etc. —**mu·si′cian**, *n.* —**mu″si·col′o·gy**, *n.*

mu′si·cal, *adj.* **1.** pertaining to music. **2.** sweet-sounding. —*n.* **3.** Also, **musical comedy**, play with frequent musical numbers.

mu″si·cale′, *n.* party with music.

musk, *n.* animal secretion used in perfumes. —**musk′y**, *adj.*

mus′ket, *n.* antique smooth-bored gun. —**mus″ket·eer′**, *n.*

musk′mel″on, *n.* type of sweet melon.

Mus′lim, *n.* **1.** follower of the teachings of Muhammad. —*adj.* **2.** pertaining to Islam or the Muslims.

mus′lin, *n.* cotton cloth.

muss, *n.* **1.** disorderly state. —*v.t.* **2.** put in a muss. —**mus′sy**, *adj.*

mus′sel, *n.* type of bivalve.

must, *v.* **1.** have or has to. **2.** am, is, or are very probably being or doing as stated.

mus·tache′, *n.* hair on the upper lip.

mus′tang, *n.* wild horse of the Southwest.

mus′tard, *n.* condiment made from ground yellow seeds.

mus′ter, *v.t.* **1.** summon; rally. **2.** enlist or discharge from military service. —*n.* **3.** gathering, as for inspection.

mus′ty, *adj.*, **-ier, -iest.** moldy in smell or taste.

mu′ta·ble, *adj.* changeable. —**mu″ta·bil′i·ty**, *n.*

mu·ta′tion, *n.* **1.** living thing with characteristics not inherited; sport. **2.** change. —**mu′tate**, *v.i.*, *v.t.* —**mu′tant**, *adj.*, *n.*

mute, *adj.*, *n.*, *v.t.*, **muted, muting.** *adj.* **1.** unable to speak. **2.** not speaking. —*n.* **3.** mute person. —*v.t.* **4.** soften the effect of. —**mute′ly**, *adv.* —**mute′ness**, *n.*

mu′ti·late″, *v.t.*, **-lated, -lating.** injure severely and conspicuously. —**mu″ti·la′tion**, *n.*

mu·ti·ny, *n.*, *pl.* **-nies,** *v.i.*, **-nied, -nying.** revolt against superiors. —**mu″ti·neer′**, *n.* —**mu′ti·nous**, *adj.*

mut′ter, *v.i.* **1.** speak in a low, indistinct voice. —*n.* **2.** muttering voice.

mut′ton, *n.* sheep meat.

mu′tu·al, *adj.* affecting one another. —**mu′tu·al·ly**, *adj.*

muz′zle, *n.*, *v.t.*, **-zled, -zling.** *n.* **1.** nose and jaws of an animal. **2.** device to prevent biting. **3.** end of a gun facing the target. —*v.t.* **4.** put a muzzle on. **5.** keep from talking.

my, *pron.* pertaining or belonging to me.

my·o′pi·a, *n.* nearsightedness. —**my·op′ic**, *adj.*

myr′i·ad, *adj.* **1.** very many. —*n.* **2.** great number.

myr′mi·don, *n.* follower.

myrrh, *n.* fragrant resin.

myr′tle, *n.* flowering evergreen shrub.

my·self′, *pron.*, *pl.* **ourselves. 1.** (intensive and reflexive of *me*). **2.** my true self.

mys′ter·y, *n.*, *pl.* **-ies. 1.** something not readily explained. **2.** secrecy. **3.** story based on the solution of a criminal case. —**mys·te′ri·ous**, *adj.*

mys′tic, *adj.* **1.** pertaining to secret rites and teachings. **2.** Also, **mys′ti·cal**, of spiritual significance. —*n.* **3.** person having deep spiritual experiences. —**mys′ti·cism**, *n.*

mys′ti·fy″, *v.t.*, **-fied, -fying.** puzzle. —**mys″ti·fi·ca′tion**, *n.*

mys·tique′, *n.* air of mysticism surrounding a person, profession, etc.

myth, *n.* **1.** religious legend. **2.** false belief. —**myth′i·cal**, *adj.* —**my·thol′o·gy**, *n.* —**myth″o·log′i·cal**, *adj.* —**my·thol′o·gist**, *n.*

N

N, n, *n.* fourteenth letter of the English alphabet.

nab, *v.t.*, **nabbed, nabbing.** *Informal.* seize

na′dir, *n.* lowest point.

nag, *v.t.*, **nagged, nagging,** *n.* *v.t.* **1.** pester. —*n.* **2.** poor horse.

nail, *n.* **1.** pointed, driven fastening. **2.** horny growth on fingers or toes. —*v.t.* **3.** fasten with nails.

na·ive (nah ēv′), *adj.* simple; unsophisticated. —**na·ive·té′**, *n.*

na′ked, *adj.* **1.** unclothed; unconcealed. **2.** unassisted by lenses.

nam′by-pam′by, *adj.* insipid; characterless.

name, *n.*, *v.t.*, **named, naming.** *n.* **1.** word or words by which a person or thing is recognized. **2.** reputation. **3.** insulting epithet. —*v.t.* **4.** give a name to. **5.** appoint. —**name′less**, *adj.*

name'ly, *adv.* that is to say.

name'sake'', *n.* person or thing having the same name as another.

nap, *n., v.i.,* **napped, napping.** *n.* 1. brief sleep. 2. fuzzy surface. —*v.i.* 3. have a brief sleep.

nape, *n.* back of the neck.

naph'tha, *n.* inflammable fluid.

nap'kin, *n.* cloth covering the lap at meals.

nar·cis·sism, *n.* love of oneself. —**nar'cis·sist,** *n.* —**nar''cis·sis'tic,** *adj.*

nar·cis'sus, *n.* flowering bulb plant.

nar·co'sis, *n.* unconsciousness from a narcotic.

nar·cot'ic, *n.* 1. pain-relieving drug, often addictive. —*adj.* 2. pertaining to narcotics.

nar'rate, *v.t.,* **-rated, -rating.** tell the story of. —**nar'ra·tor,** *n.*

nar'ra·tive, *adj.* 1. story-telling. —*n.* 2. story; account.

nar'row, *n.* 1. not wide. 2. not ample 3. illiberal. —*v.t.* 4. make narrow. —*v.i.* 5. become narrow.

nar'row-mind'ed, *adj.* lacking a broad, liberal outlook.

nar'whal, *n.* small, tusked whale.

nar'y, *adj. Dialect.* not any.

na'sal, *adj.* spoken through the nose.

nas'cent, *adj.* coming into being.

nas·tur'tium, *n.* pungent-smelling flower.

nas'ty, *adj.,* **-tier, -tiest.** 1. revolting as from filth. 2. unpleasant.

na'tal, *adj.* pertaining to birth.

na'tion, *n.* 1. group with common ancestral and traditional associations. 2. politically independent state. —**na'tion·al,** *adj.* —**na'tion·wide'',** *adj., adv.*

na'tion·al·ism, *n.* assertion of the rights, cultural values, etc. of a nation. —**na'tion·al·ist,** *n., adj.* —**na''tion·al·is'tic,** *adj.*

na'tion·al·ize'', *v.t.,* **-ized, -izing.** put under government ownership. —**na''tion·al·i·za'tion,** *n.*

na'tive, *adj.* 1. born in or characteristic of a certain place. 2. inborn. —*n.* 3. native person.

na·tiv'i·ty, *n., pl.* **-ties.** 1. birth. 2. **the Nativity,** birth of Jesus.

nat'ty, *adj.,* **-tier, -tiest.** neat and stylish.

nat'u·ral, *adj.* 1. pertaining to nature. 2. inborn. 3. unaffected; easy. 4. to be expected. 5. *Music.* not sharped or flatted.

nat'u·ral·ist, *n.* student of nature.

nat'u·ral·ize'', *v.t.,* **-ized, -izing.** admit to citizenship.

nat'u·ral·ly, *adv.* 1. by nature. 2. of course. 3. in a natural way.

na'ture, *n.* 1. everything not man-made. 2. essential quality or composition.

naught, *n.* 1. nothing. 2. zero.

naugh'ty, *adj.,* **-tier, -tiest.** ill-behaved. —**naugh'ti·ly,** *adv.*

nau'se·a, *n.* sickness at the stomach. —**nau'se·ate'',** *v.t.* —**nau'se·ous,** *adj.*

nau'ti·cal, *adj.* pertaining to ships and navigation.

nau'ti·lus, *n.* mollusk with a spiral shell.

na'val, *adj.* 1. pertaining to navies. 2. pertaining to ships.

na'vel, *n.* mark where the umbilical cord was attached.

nav'i·ga·ble, *adj.* able to be sailed over.

nav'i·gate', *v.,* **-gated, -gating.** *v.t.* 1. cross or pass through in a ship or aircraft. 2. determine the position and course of. —*v.i.* 3. direct a ship or aircraft. —**nav'i·ga''tor,** *n.*

na'vy, *n., pl.* **-ies.** seagoing fighting force.

nay, *n.* vote of no.

neap tide, lowest of high tides.

near, *adj.* 1. short in distance. 2. closely related. —*adv.* 3. at a short distance. —*prep.* 4. close to. —*v.t.* 5. approach.

near'by', *adj., adv.* near.

near'ly, *adv.* almost.

near'sight'ed, *adj.* seeing distant objects poorly.

neat, *adj.* 1. free of dirt and clutter. 2. finely done.

neb'u·la, *n., pl.* **-lae, -las.** cloudlike cluster of stars, etc. —**neb'u·lar,** *adj.*

neb'u·lous, *adj.* vague.

nec'es·sar''y, *adj.* 1. not to be dispensed with. 2. inevitable. —**nec''es·sar'i·ly,** *adv.*

ne·ces'si·tate'', *v.t.,* **-tated, -tating.** require.

ne·ces'si·tous, *adj.* needy.

ne·ces'si·ty, *n., pl.* **-ties.** 1. state of needing. 2. something needed.

neck, *n.* 1. part of the body which supports the head. 2. narrow feature. —**neck'wear',** *n.*

neck'er·chief, *n.* broad covering for the neck.

neck'lace, *n.* ornamental chain, string of beads, etc. worn around the neck.

neck'tie'', *n.* decorative band of cloth tied around the neck.

ne·crol'o·gy, *n., pl.* **-gies.** list of the dead.

nec'ro·man''cy, *n.* 1. divination by communication with the dead. 2. sorcery. —**nec'ro·man''cer,** *n.*

nec'tar, *n.* 1. drink of the classical gods. 2. sweetish liquid of flowers.

nec''tar·ine'', *n.* small, smooth peach.

nee, *adj.* born as: said of the maiden name of a married woman. Also, **née.**

need, *v.t.* 1. be obliged to have or do. —*n.* 2. state of needing. 3. thing needed. 4. poverty or trouble. —**need'ful,** *adj.* —**need·less,** *adj.*

nee′dle, *n.*, *v.t.*, **-dled**, **-dling**. *n*. **1**. sharp object used for passing thread through cloth. **2**. any of various sharp or pointed objects. —*v.t.* **3**. *Informal.* goad; annoy. —**nee′dle·work″**, *n*.

nee′dle·point″, *n*. **1**. embroidery on canvas. **2**. lace made on a paper pattern.

needs, *adv.* of necessity.

need′y, *adj.*, **-ier**, **-iest**. in need. —**need′i·ness**, *n*.

ne′er-do-well′, *n*. shiftless person.

ne·far′i·ous, *adj.* wicked.

ne·gate′, *v.t.*, **-gated**, **-gating**. **1**. deny. **2**. render ineffective.

neg′a·tive, *adj.* **1**. saying or meaning no. **2**. opposite to positive. **3**. less than zero. —*n.* **4**. negative statement or attitude. **5**. photographic film, etc. that reverses light and shade. —**neg′a·tive·ly**, *adv.*

neg·lect′, *v.t.* **1**. deny proper care to. **2**. disregard. —*n.* **3**. state of being neglected. **4**. state of neglecting. —**neg′lect′ful**, *adj.*

neg′li·gee (neg″lə zhā′), *n*. loosely fitting woman's gown.

neg′li·gent, *adj.* neglecting responsibilities. —**neg′li·gence**, *n*.

neg′li·gi·ble, *adj.* too unimportant to matter.

ne·go′ti·a·ble, *adj.* transferable.

ne·go′ti·ate′, *v.*, **-ated**, **-ating**. *v.i.* **1**. bargain. —*v.t.* **2**. establish by bargaining. **3**. succeed in passing through or across. —**ne·go′ti·a″tor**, *n*.

Ne′gro, *n.*, *pl.* **-groes**. dark-skinned person of African origin. —**Neg′roid**, *adj*.

neigh, *n*. **1**. sound of a horse. —*v.i.* **2**. emit such a sound.

neigh′bor, *n.* **1**. person living near by. **2**. fellow human. —*v.i.* **3**. be situated near by. —**neigh′bor·ing**, *adj.* —**neigh′bor·ly**, *adj.*

neigh′bor·hood″, *n.* **1**. area within a town. **2**. approximate area or range.

neither, *adj.*, *pron.*, *conj.* not either.

nem′e·sis, *n.*, *pl.* **-ses**. **1**. just fate or vengeance. **2**. bringer of this.

Ne″o·lith′ic, *adj.* pertaining to the later Stone Age.

ne·ol′o·gism, *n.* newly invented word or expression.

ne′on, *n.* rare gaseous element used in lighting tubes.

ne′ophyte″, *n.* beginner.

neph′ew, *n.* son of a brother, sister, brother-in-law, or sister-in-law.

nep′o·tism, *n.* favoritism toward relatives in giving employment.

nerve, *n.* **1**. fiber carrying signals through the body. **2**. courage. **3**. insolent boldness. **4**. **nerves**, nervousness.

nerve′less, *adj.* **1**. without strength. **2**. not nervous.

nerve′-rack″ing, *adj.* emotionally upsetting. Also, **nerve′wrack″ing**.

nerv′ous, *adj.* **1**. full of apprehension or restlessness. **2**. pertaining to nerves.

nerv′y, *adj.*, **-ier**, **-iest**. *Informal.* impudent.

nest, *n.* **1**. place for bearing and sheltering young. —*v.i.* **2**. settle in a nest.

n′est-ce pas? (nes pah′), *French.* isn't it so?

nes′tle, *v.i.*, **-tled**, **-tling**. settle down.

net, *n.*, *adj.*, *v.t.*, **netted**, **netting**. *n.* **1**. open cloth for capturing or supporting. **2**. amount after deductions. —*adj.* **3**. after deductions. —*v.t.* **4**. capture, as in a net.

neth′er, *adj.* lower. —**neth′er·most″**, *adj.*

net′tle, *n.*, *v.t.*, **-tled**, **-tling**. *n.* **1**. prickly weed. —*v.t.* **2**. irritate; annoy.

net′work″, *n.* **1**. net-like arrangement. **2**. system of isolated entities working in coordination.

neu′ral, *adj.* pertaining to nerves.

neu·ral′gia, *n.* pain along a nerve.

neu″ras·the′ni·a, *n.* neurosis with lassitude, anxiety, etc. —**neu″ras·the′nic**, *adj.*, *n*.

neu·ri′tis, *n.* inflammation of a nerve.

neu·rol′o·gy, *n.* study of nerves. —**neu″ro·log′i·cal**, *adj.* —**neu·rol′o·gist**, *n*.

neu·ro′sis, *n.*, *pl.* **-ses**. compulsive mental disorder. —**neu·rot′ic**, *adj.*, *n*.

neu′ter, *adj.* **1**. without sex. **2**. without gender. —*v.t.* **3**. remove the sex organs of.

neu′tral, *adj.* **1**. taking no sides. **2**. having no pronounced character. —*n.* **3**. neutral person or country. —**neu′tral·ism**, *n.* —**neu·tral′i·ty**, *n.* —**neu′tra·lize**, *v.t.*

neu′tron, *n.* uncharged atomic particle.

nev′er, *adv.* at no time.

nev″er·more′, *adv.* never again.

never-never land, purely imaginary place.

nev″er·the·less′, *adv.* despite this.

new, *adj.* **1**. never existing before. **2**. unfamiliar. **3**. fresh. **4**. additional. —**new′born″**, *adj.* —**new′com″er**, *n*.

new′el, *n.* support for a winding stair.

news, *n.*, *sing.* **1**. information of public interest, esp. as published. **2**. recent information. —**news′boy″**, *n.* —**news′deal″er**, *n.* —**news′let″ter**, *n.* —**news′man″**, *n.* —**news′pa″per**, *n.* —**news′stand″**, *n.* —**news′wor″thy**, *adj.*

news′cast″, *n.* broadcast of news.

newt, *n.* amphibious salamander.

next, *adj.* **1**. directly alongside another. —*adv.* **2**. directly afterward.

next′-door′, *adj.* in the next building.

nib, *n.* **1**. bird's beak. **2**. pen point.

nib′ble, *v.*, **-bled**, **-bling**, *n.* *v.t.*, *v.i.* **1**. eat with small bites. —*n.* **2**. small bite.

nice, *adj.,* **nicer, nicest. 1.** agreeable. **2.** delicate; subtle.

ni'ce·ty, *n., pl.* **-ties. 1.** precision. **2.** fine detail or distinction.

niche, *n.* recessed area in a wall, as for a statue.

nick, *n.* **1.** small notch. —*v.t.* **2.** cut with such a notch.

nick'el, *n.* **1.** white metallic element. **2.** five-cent piece.

nick"el·o'de·on, *n.* coin-operated automatic piano.

nick'name", *n, v.t.,* **-named, -naming.** *n.* **1.** informal name. —*v.t.* **2.** give a nickname to.

nic'o·tine", *n.* poisonous extract from tobacco leaves.

niece, *n.* daughter of a brother, sister, brother-in-law, or sister-in-law.

nif'ty, *adj.,* **-tier, -tiest.** *Informal.* smart; handsome.

nig'gard·ly, *adj.* stingy.

nigh, *adj., adv. Archaic.* near.

night, *n.* period when the sun is absent. —**night'clothes",** *n., pl.* —**night' dress",** *n.* —**night'fall",** *n.* —**night' gown",** *n.* —**night'ly,** *adv., adj.* —**night'time",** *n.* —**night'wear",** *n.*

night'cap", *n.* **1.** cap for sleeping in. **2.** *Informal.* drink just before bed.

night'mare", *n.* bad dream. —**night' mar"ish,** *adj.*

night'shade", *n.* plant related to potatoes, tomatoes, etc.

ni'hil·ism, *n.* rejection of all social institutions. —**ni'hil·ist,** *n.* —**ni"hil·is'tic,** *adj.*

nim'ble, *adj.,* **-bler, -blest.** quick and deft.

nim'bus, *n., pl.* **-bi, -buses.** halo.

nin'com·poop", *n.* fool.

nine, *n.* eight plus one. —**ninth,** *adj.*

nine·teen', *n.* ten plus nine. —**nine' teenth',** *adj.*

nine'ty, *adj., n.* nine times ten. —**nine'ti· eth,** *adj.*

nip, *v.t.,* **nipped, nipping,** *n. v.t.* **1.** bite or pinch lightly. **2.** freeze injuriously. —*n.* **3.** act or instance of nipping. **4.** sharp chill. **5.** tiny drink. —**nip'per,** *n.* —**nip'pers,** *n.*

nip'ple, *n.* **1.** small projection from the breast from which milk is sucked. **2.** anything resembling this.

nir·va'na, *Buddhism.* loss of self in ultimate bliss.

nit'-pick"ing, *n.* quibbling. —**nit'-pick" er,** *n.*

ni'tro·gen, *n.* gaseous element. —**ni· trog'e·nous,** *adj.*

ni'tro·glyc'er·in, *n.* explosive oil used in dynamite.

nit'ty-grit'ty, *n. Informal.* fundamentals.

nit'wit", *n.* stupid person.

nix, *adv. Informal.* no.

no, *adv., adj., n., pl.* **noes.** *adv.* **1.** it is not so. **2.** I will not. **3.** do not. **4.** not at all. —*adj.* **5.** not any. —*n.* **6.** vote of no.

no'ble, *adj.,* **-bler, -blest.** *adj.* **1.** of high and titled rank. **2.** having or revealing a fine character. **3.** of high quality. —*n.* **4.** person of noble rank. —**no'bly,** *adv.* —**no·bil'i·ty,** *n.* —**no'ble·man,** *n.*

no'bod·y, *pron., n., pl.* **-ies.** *pron.* **1.** no person. —*n.* **2.** unimportant person.

noc·tur'nal, *adj.* pertaining to night.

noc'turne, *n.* musical composition to be heard at night.

nod, *v.i.,* **nodded, nodding,** *n. v.i.* **1.** give a quick forward motion of the head. —*n.* **2.** act or instance of nodding.

node, *n.* **1.** swelling. **2.** focal point. —**nod'al,** *adj.*

nog'gin, *n.* small cup.

noise, *n.* loud sound. —**noise'less,** *adj.* —**nois'y,** *adj.* —**nois'i·ly,** *adv.*

noi'some, *adj.* smelly.

no'mad, *n.* wanderer. —**no·mad'ic,** *adj.*

nom de plume, author's assumed name.

no'men·cla"ture, *n.* system of names.

nom'in·al, *adj.* **1.** in name only. **2.** trifling in amount.

nom'i·nate", *v.t.,* **-nated, -nating. 1.** appoint. **2.** propose for election. —**nom" i·nee',** *n.*

nom'i·na·tive, *n. Grammar.* case of a verb subject.

non-, prefix meaning "not." nonalcoholic, nonassignable, nonattendance, nonbeliever, nonbreakable, nonburnable, noncombatant, noncombustible, noncommunicable, noncompetitive, noncompliance, nonconducting, nonconductor, nonconforming, nonconformist, nonconformity, nondeductible, nonessential, nonexclusive, nonexempt, nonexistence, nonexistent, nonfactual, nonfiction, nonflammable, nonhazardous, nonhereditary, nonhuman, noninclusive, noninterference, nonintervention, nonintoxicating, nonirritating, nonliterary, nonmilitary, nonobjective, nonobligatory, nonobservance, nonpartisan, nonpayment, nonperishable, nonpolitical, nonproductive, nonprofessional, nonracial, nonreciprocal, nonreligious, nonresident, nonresidential, nonresistant, nonreturnable, nonscientific, nonseasonal, nonsectarian, nonsmoker, nonspiritual, nonstandard, nonstop, nonstructural, nonsupport, nontaxable, nontoxic, nontransferable, nonuser, nonviolent, nonvoter, nonvoting.

non'age, *n.* minority; non-adulthood.

non"a·ge·nar'i·an, *n.* person in his or her nineties.

nonce, *n.* time being.

non''cha·lant', *adj.* casual in manner. —**non''cha·lance',** *n.*

non''com·mis'sioned officer, military or naval officer with no commission, e.g. a sergeant or petty officer.

non''com·mit'tal, *adj.* not committing oneself.

non' com'pos men'tis, of unsound mind.

non''de·script', *adj.* not to be described precisely.

none, *pron.* 1. not one or any. —*n.* 2. not any amount. —*adv.* 3. by no means.

none''the·less', *adv.* nevertheless.

non'plus', *v.t.,* **-plused, -plusing.** baffle into inaction.

non·prof'it, *adj.* not established for profit.

non'sense, *n.* meaningless talk or action. —**non·sen'si·cal,** *adj.*

non·se'qui·tur, illogical continuation of something previously said.

noo'dle, *n.* strip of dough.

nook, *n.* semi-enclosed place.

noon, *n.* twelve o'clock in the daytime.

no one, nobody.

noose, *n.* loop made with a knot.

nor, *conj.* and not; and yet not.

norm, *n.* something generally expected.

nor'mal, *adj.* 1. conforming to a norm. 2. average. —**nor·mal'i·ty,** *n.* —**nor'mal·ize'',** *v.t.*

norm'a·tive, *adj.* establishing a norm.

north, *n.* 1. direction of the north pole. 2. region lying northward. —*adv.* 3. toward or in the north. —**north'ern,** *adj.* —**north'ern·er,** *n.* —**north'er·ly,** *adj.* —**north'ward,** *adj., adv.* —**north'wards,** *adv.*

north''east', *n.* 1. direction halfway between north and east. 2. region lying northeastward. —*adj., adv.* 3. toward or in the northeast. —**north''east'ern,** *adj.* —**north''east·ern·er,** *n.*

north''west', *n.* 1. direction halfway between north and west. 2. region lying northwestward. —*adj.* 3. toward or in the northwest. —**north''west'ern,** *adj.* —**north''west'ern·er,** *n.*

nose, *n., v.,* **nosed, nosing.** *n.* 1. part of the head with nostrils. 2. noselike features. —*v.t.* 3. nuzzle. —*v.i.* 4. sniff. 5. advance. —**nose'bleed'',** *n.*

nose dive, headlong plunge. —**nose'dive'',** *v.i.*

nose'gay'', *n.* small bouquet.

nos·tal'gia, *n.* sentiment over the bygone or remote. —**nos·tal'gic,** *adj.*

nos'tril, *n.* one of the openings in the nose for breathing.

nos'trum, proprietary medicine.

nos'y, *adj.,* **-ier, -iest.** *Informal.* inquisitive. Also, **nos'ey.**

not, *adv.* in no way.

no'ta·ble, *adj.* remarkable.

no'ta·ry, *n., pl.* **-ries.** official who certifies documents. Also, **notary public.** —**no'ta·rize'',** *v.t.*

no·ta'tion, *n.* 1. symbol or system of symbols. 2. brief note.

notch, *n.* 1. shallow knife cut. —*v.t.* 2. make such cuts in.

note, *n., v.t.,* **noted, noting.** *n.* 1. short message. 2. reminder of something. 3. sound. 4. notice. 5. distinction. 6. feeling; air. —*v.t.* 7. observe. 8. make a note of. —**note'book'',** *n.* —**note'wor''thy,** *adj.*

not'ed, *adj.* well-known.

noth'ing, *n.* 1. not any thing. 2. something non-existent. 3. something insignificant. —*adv.* 4. in no way. —**noth'ing·ness,** *n.*

no'tice, *v.t.,* **-ticed, -ticing,** *n., v.t.* 1. be aware of. —*n.* 2. awareness. 3. announcement or warning. —**no'tice·a·ble,** *adj.*

no'ti·fy'', *v.t.,* **-fied, -fying.** give notice to.

no'tion, *n.* 1. idea, 2. vague opinion. 3. whim. 4. **notions,** minor but useful merchandise. —**no'tion·al,** *adj.*

no·to'ri·ous, *adj.* unfavorably well-known. —**no''to·ri'e·ty,** *n.*

not''with·stand'ing, *adv.* 1. nevertheless. —*prep.* 2. in spite of. —*conj.* 3. although.

nou'gat, *n.,* soft candy with nuts.

nought, *n.* 1. nothing. 2. zero.

noun, *n.* name of a person, place, or thing.

nour'ish, *v.t.* feed. —**nour'ish·ment,** *n.*

nov'el, *adj.* 1. new; unprecedented. —*n.* 2. long written story. —**nov'el·ty,** *n.* —**nov''el·ette',** *n.* —**nov'el·ist,** *n.*

No·vem'ber, *n.* eleventh month.

nov'ice, *n.* 1. monk or nun in a religious house who has not yet taken the vow. 2. beginner. —**no·vi'ti·ate,***n.*

now, *adj.* 1. at present. 2. at some past or future moment. 3. as matters are. —*conj.* 4. inasmuch. —*n.* 5. present moment.

now'a·days'', *adv.* at present.

no'where'', *adv.* not in any place.

nox'ious, *adj.* harmful.

noz'zle, *n.* pouring end of a pipe, etc.

nth, *adj.* concluding an unspecified number or amount.

nu'ance, *n.* slight variation in meaning, etc.

nu'bile, *adj.* mature enough to take a husband.

nu'cle·ar, *adj.* 1. forming a nucleus. 2. pertaining to atomic nuclei.

nu'cle·us, *n., pl.* **-clei, -cleuses.** 1. core.

2. center of growth or development. 3. center of an atom.

nude, *adj.* 1. naked. —*n.* 2. state of nakedness. —**nu'di·ty,** *n.*

nudge, *v.t.,* nudged, nudging, *n. v.t.* 1. jab with the elbow. 2. hint to sharply. —*n.* 3. act or instance of nudging.

nud'ism, *n.* practice of nudity. —**nud'ist,** *n., adj.*

nu'ga·to''ry, *adj.* 1. worthless. 2. invalid.

nug'get, *n.* lump of natural gold.

nui'sance, *n.* source of annoyance.

null, *adj.* null and void, invalid; without force.

nul'li·fy'', *v.t.,* -fied, -fying. invalidate.

numb, *adj.* 1. without feeling. —*v.t.* 2. make numb.

num'ber, *n.* 1. expression of quantity or order. 2. quantity or order. 3. item on a program of entertainment. —*v.t.* 4. establish the number of. 5. include in a group. —**num'ber·less,** *adj.*

numb'skull'', *n. Informal.* stupid person. Also, **num'skull''.**

nu'mer·al, *n.* symbol for a number.

nu'mer·a''tor, *n.* expression of the number of parts in a fraction.

nu·mer'i·cal, *adj.* pertaining to or expressed in numbers.

nu''mer·ol'o·gy, *n.* study of occult meanings in numbers.

nu'mer·ous, *adj.* in large numbers.

nu''mis·mat'ics, *n.* study of money and medals. —**nu·mis'ma·tist,** *n.*

nun, *n.* female member of a religious order. —**nun'ner·y,** *n.*

nup'tial, *adj.* 1. pertaining to marriage. —*n.* 2. nuptials, wedding.

nurse, *n., v.t.,* nursed, nursing. *n.* 1. attendant of the sick. 2. attendant of children. —*v.t.* 3. suckle. 4. tend in illness. 5. conserve or foster.

nurse'maid'', *n.* children's nurse.

nurs'er·y, *n., pl.* -ies. 1. day room for children. 2. place for the care of children. 3. place for raising plants. —**nurs'er·y·man,** *n.*

nur'ture, *v.t.,* -tured, -turing, *n. v.t.* 1. nourish. 2. raise, as a child. —*n.* 3. food. 4. upbringing.

nut, *n.* 1. dry seed in a woody husk. 2. threaded block used with a bolt. 3. *Informal.* insane person. —*adj.* 4. nuts, *Informal.* crazy. —*interj.* 5. nuts, bah! —**nut'crack''er,** *n.* —**nut'meat'',** *n.* —**nut'shell'',** *n.* —**nut'ty,** *adj.*

nut'meg'', *n.* East Indian spice.

nu'tri·ent, *adj.* 1. nourishing. —*n.* 2. Also, **nu'tri·ment,** nourishment.

nu·tri'tion, *n.* 1. assimilation of food. 2. food. —**nu·tri'tion·al,** *adj.* —**nu'tri·tive,** *adj.* —**nu·tri'tious,** *adj.*

nuz'zle, *v.,* -zled, -zling. *v.t., v.i.* rub with the nose.

ny'lon, *n.* synthetic material.

nymph, *n.* classical nature goddess.

nym''pho·ma'ni·a, *n.* uncontrollable sexual desire in women. —**nym''pho·ma'ni·ac'',** *n., adj.*

O

O, o, *n.* fifteenth letter of the English alphabet.

oaf, *n.* clumsy person. —**oaf'ish,** *adj.*

oak, *n.* acorn-bearing hardwood tree. —**oak'en,** *adj.*

oar, *n.* bladed lever for rowing. —**oars'man,** *n.* —**oar'lock'',** *n.*

o·a'sis, *n., pl.* -ses. place in the desert with water.

oat, *n.* cereal grass. —**oat'meal',** *n.*

oath, *n., pl.* oaths. 1. vow in the name of a god. 2. blasphemous remark.

ob'du·rate, *adj.* stubborn. —**ob'du·ra·cy,** *n.*

o·bei'sance, *n.* bow.

ob'e·lisk, *n.* tapered monument.

o·bese', *adj.* very fat. —**o·bes'i·ty,** *n.*

o·bey', *v.i.* 1. do as told. —*v.t.* 2. perform as told. 3. perform the orders of. —**o·be'di·ent,** *adj.* —**o·be'di·ence,** *n.*

ob'fus·cate'', *v.t.,* -cated, -cating. obscure or confuse.

o·bit'u·ar''y, *n., pl.* -ies. death notice.

ob·ject, *n.* (ob'jekt) 1. something tangible. 2. something acted toward or aimed for. 3. matter for consideration. —*v.i.* (ob ject') 4. protest. —**ob·jec'tion,** *n.* —**ob·jec'tion·a·ble,** *adj.* —**ob·jec'tion·a·bly,** *adv.* —**ob·jec'tor,** *n.*

ob·jec'tive, *adj.* 1. in the world outside the mind. 2. concerned with reality, rather than thought or emotion. —**ob''jec·tiv'i·ty,** *n.*

ob'jur·gate'', *v.t.,* -gated, -gating. rebuke. —**ob''jur·ga'to''ry,** *adj.*

ob'li·gate'', *v.t.,* -gated, -gating. bind with a duty. —**ob'li·ga'to''ry,** *adj.*

o·blige', *v.t.,* -bliged, -bliging. 1. force. 2. put in one's debt.

o·blig'ing, *adj.* ready to do favors. —**o·blig'ing·ly,** *adv.*

ob·lique', *adj.* 1. slanting. 2. indirect. —**ob·liq'ui·ty, ob·lique'ness,** *n.*

ob·lit'er·ate'', *v.t.,* -ated, -ating. efface.

ob·liv'i·on, *n.* 1. forgetfulness. 2. unremembered past. —**ob·liv'i·ous,** *adj.*

ob'long, *adj.* 1. longer than broad. —*n.* 2. oblong figure, esp. a rectangle.

ob'lo·quy, *n., pl.* -quies. 1. censure. 2. infamy.

ob·nox'ious, *adj.* offensive.

o'boe, *n.* low-pitched musical reed instrument. —**o'bo·ist,** *n.*

ob·scene', *adj.* offensive to decency. —**ob·scen'i·ty,** *n.*

ob·scure', *adj., v.t.,* **-scured, -scuring.** *adj.* **1.** indefinite. **2.** dark. **3.** little-known. —*v.t.* **4.** make obscure. —**ob·scur'i·ty,** *n.* —**ob''scu·ra'tion,** *n.*

ob·se·quies, *n., pl.* funeral ceremonies.

ob·se'qui·ous, *adj.* fawningly servile.

ob·serv'a·to''ry, *n., pl.* **-ries.** place for observing heavenly bodies.

ob·serve', *v.t.,* **-served, -serving. 1.** study with the eye. **2.** notice. **3.** remark. **4.** obey or respect. —**ob·serv'ance,** *n.* —**ob·serv'ant,** *adj.* —**ob''ser·va'tion,** *n.* —**ob·serv'er,** *n.*

ob·sess', *v.t.* preoccupy constantly. —**ob·ses'sive,** *adj.* —**ob·ses'sion,** *n.*

ob''so·les'cent, *adj.* going out of date. —**ob''so·les'cence,** *n.* —**obso·lesce',** *v.i.*

ob''so·lete', *adj.* out of date.

ob'sta·cle, *n.* something hindering advance.

ob·stet'rics, *n.* branch of medicine for pregnancy and childbirth. —**ob·stet'ric, ob·stet'ri·cal,** *adj.* —**ob''ste·tri'cian,** *n.*

ob'sti·nate, *adj.* stubborn. —**ob'sti·na·cy,** *n.*

ob·strep'er·ous, *adj.* rowdy.

ob·struct', *v.t.* **1.** hinder; thwart. **2.** block. —**ob·struc'tion,** *n.* —**ob·struc'tion·ism,** *n.* —**ob·struc'tion·ist,** *n., adj.* —**ob·struc'tive,** *adj.*

ob·tain', *v.t.* **1.** get. —*v.i.* **2.** be in effect. —**ob·tain'ment,** *n.*

ob·trude', *v.,* **-truded, -truding.** *v.t.* **1.** force on others. —*v.i.* **2.** obtrude oneself. —**ob·tru'sion,** *n.* —**ob·tru'sive,** *adj.*

ob·tuse', *adj.* **1.** blunt, as an angle. **2.** slow to understand.

ob·verse', *adj.* **1.** toward an observer. **2.** being a counterpart. —*n.* **3.** counterpart.

ob'vi·ate'', *v.t.,* **-ated, -ating.** avoid by alternatives.

ob'vi·ous, *adj.* perceived or understood without effort.

oc·ca'sion, *n.* **1.** specific time or event. **2.** opportunity. **3.** reason; pretext. —*v.t.* **4.** bring about.

oc·ca'sion·al, *adj.* occurring now and then.

Oc'ci·dent, *n.* Europe and the Americas. —**Oc''ci·den'tal,** *adj.*

oc·cult', *adj.* **1.** hidden from ordinary persons. **2.** mystical. —**oc·cult'ism,** *n.*

oc''cu·pa'tion, *n.* **1.** type of work. **2.** act or instance of occupying.

oc·cu·py'', *v.t.,* **-pied, -pying. 1.** be in. **2.** be engaged in or concerned with. **3.** take possession of, as by capture. —**oc'cu·pan·cy,** *n.* —**oc'cu·pant,** *n.*

oc·cur', *v.i.,* **-curred, -curring. 1.** happen. **2.** come to mind. —**oc·cur'rence,** *n.*

o'cean, *n.* vast body of salt water. —**o·ce·an'ic,** *adj.*

o''cean·og'ra·phy, *n.* study of the ocean.

o'ce·lot'', *n.* American wildcat.

o'cher, *n.* yellow or reddish-brown clay used as pigment. Also, **o'chre.**

o'clock', *adv.* by the clock.

oc'ta·gon, *n.* eight-sided plane figure. —**oc·tag'o·nal,** *adj.*

oc''ta·he'dron, *n.* eight-sided solid.

oc'tave, *n.* **1.** *Music.* group including eight full tones. **2.** *Poetry.* unit of eight lines.

oc·tet', *n.* group of eight musicians. Also, **oc·tette'.**

Oc·to'ber, *n.* tenth month.

oc''to·ge·nar'i·an, *n.* person in his or her eighties.

oc'to·pus, *n., pl.* **-puses, -pi.** soft mollusk with eight arms.

oc'u·lar, *adj.* pertaining to the eyes.

oc'u·list, *n.* ophthalmologist.

odd, *adj.* **1.** not evenly divisible by two. **2.** peculiar. **3.** occasional. **4.** remaining. —*n.* **5.** odds, factors for or against. —**odd'i·ty,** *n.*

odds and ends, miscellaneous things.

ode, *n.* poem of praise.

o'di·ous, *adj.* hateful.

o'di·um, *n.* hatred or disgrace.

o'dor, *n.* smell. —**o'dor·ous,** *adj.* —**o'dor·less,** *adj.*

o''dor·if'er·ous, *adj.* giving off an odor.

of, *prep.* **1.** coming from or produced by. **2.** belonging to. **3.** owning. **4.** regarding. **5.** specified as.

off, *prep.* **1.** away or up from. **2.** with sustenance from. —*adv.* **3.** away or up. **4.** so as not to work or be in effect. —*adj.* **5.** not working or in effect. **6.** on one's way. **7.** not right.

of'fal, *n.* garbage.

off'-col''or, *adj.* risqué.

of·fend', *v.i.* **1.** commit an offense. —*v.t.* **2.** annoy or wound. **3.** displease.

of·fense', *n.* **1.** unlawful act. **2.** resentment or hurt. **3.** cause of this. **4.** attack. Also, **of·fence'.**

of·fen'sive, *adj.* **1.** tending to offend. **2.** attacking. —*n.* **3.** attacker's status.

of'fer, *v.t.* **1.** present, as for acceptance or consideration. **2.** shown signs of. —*v.i.* **3.** present itself. —*n.* **4.** act or instance of offering. —**of'fer·ing,** *n.*

off'hand', *adv.* **1.** unprepared. —*adj.* **2.** Also, **off'hand'ed,** casual.

of'fice, *n.* **1.** position of authority. **2.** Often, **offices,** endeavor for another. **3.**

place for commercial or government work.

of·fi·cer, *n.* **1.** holder of a position of authority. **2.** policeman.

of·fi′cial, *adj.* **1.** pertaining to or coming from supreme authority. —*n.* **2.** person in public office. —**of·fi′cial·dom,** *n.*

of·fi′ci·ate″, *v.i.,* **-ated, -ating.** perform official or ceremonial duties.

of·fi′cious, *adj.* giving unwanted help or orders.

off′ing, *n.* distance.

off′-lim′its, *adj. Military.* not to be entered.

off″-line″, *n.* not connected to a network or system.

off″-road″, *adj.* designed to be used in rough terrain, as an *off-road vehicle.*

off′set″, *v.t.,* **-set, -setting.** compensate for.

off′shoot″, *n.* thing derived from a major source.

off′shore′, *adj., adv.* away from the shore.

off′spring″, *n., pl.* **-spring. -springs.** young of a human or animal.

off′-white′, *n.* white tinted with grey or yellow.

of′ten, *adv.* many times.

o′gre, *n.* man-eating giant. Also, *fem.* **o′gress.** —**o′gre·ish,** *adj.*

oh, *n.* (exclamation of surprise, etc.).

ohm, *n. Electricity.* unit of resistance.

o·ho′, *n.* (exclamation of surprise or triumph).

oil, *n.* **1.** any of various combustible liquids. **2.** paint with an oil vehicle. —*v.t.* **3.** lubricate with oil. —**oil′y,** *adj.* —**oil′i·ness,** *n.*

oil′cloth″, *n.* cloth treated to be waterproof.

oint′ment, *n.* fatty salve.

O.K., *interj., adj., adv., v.t.,* **O.K.′d, O.K.′ing.** *interj., adj., adv.* **1.** all right. —*v.t.* **2.** approve.

o′kra, *n.* plant with edible pods.

old, *adj.,* **older** or **elder, oldest** or **eldest. 1.** long in existence. **2.** experienced. **3.** longer in existence than another. **4.** former.

old′-fash′ioned, *adj.* **1.** obsolete. **2.** favoring older manners, etc. —*n.* **3.** whiskey cocktail.

old maid, mature, virginal woman.

old school, conservatives collectively. —**old′-school′,** *adj.*

old′-tim′er, *n. Informal.* **1.** old man. **2.** long-time incumbent.

Old World, Europe, Asia, and Africa. —**Old′-World′, old′-world′,** *adj.*

o″le·o·mar′ga·rine, *n.* margarine. Also, **o″le·o·mar′ga·rin.**

ol·fac′to·ry, *adj.* pertaining to smell.

ol′i·garch″y, *n., pl.* **-ies.** government by a few. —**ol′i·garch′ic,** *adj.* —**oli·garch,** *n.*

ol′ive, *n.* fruit of a Mediterranean tree.

om·buds′man, *n., pl.* **-men.** investigator of citizen's complaints.

om′e·let, *n.* fried pancake of beaten eggs. Also, **om′e·lette.**

o′men, *n.* sign of the future.

om′i·nous, *adj.* threatening.

o·mit′, *v.t.,* **-mitted, -mitting. 1.** leave out. **2.** forget; neglect. —**o·mis′sion,** *n.*

om′ni·bus, *n.* **1.** bus. **2.** complete anthology.

om·nip′o·tent, *adj.* all-powerful. —**om·nip′o·tence,** *n.*

om″ni·pres′ent, *adj.* present everywhere at once. —**om″ni·pres′ence,** *n.*

om·nis′cient, *adj.* knowing everything. —**om·nis′cience,** *n.*

om·niv′o·rous, *adj.* consuming anything.

on, *prep.* **1.** supported by. **2.** down against. **3.** regarding. **4.** with the help or sustenance of. **5.** at the time of. **6.** engaged in. **7.** being part of. —*adv.* **8.** onto oneself or something else. **9.** further; forward. **10.** into operation. —*adj.* **11.** in operation or effect.

once, *adv.* **1.** one time. **2.** formerly. **3.** at any time. —*conj.* **4.** when.

on′com″ing, *adj.* approaching.

one, *n.* **1.** lowest whole cardinal number. **2.** person. —*adj.* **3.** being one in number. **4.** identical. **5.** united. —*pron.* **6.** one person or thing.

on′er·ous, *adj.* burdensome.

one·self′, *pron.* **1.** person's own self. **2.** person's true self. Also, **one's self.**

one′-sid′ed, *adj.* **1.** involving only one side. **2.** with all advantages on one side. **3.** prejudiced.

on′go″ing, *adj.* in progress.

on′ion, *n.* edible bulb of the lily family.

on″-line″, *n.* connected to a network or system.

on′look″er, *n.* spectator.

on′ly, *adj.* **1.** single; sole. —*adv.* **2.** solely. **3.** at last, however. **4.** as lately as.

on·o·mat·o·poe′ia (ahn″ə mat″ə pē′ə), *n.* coining of a word imitating a sound.

on′set″, *n.* attack.

on′slaught″, *n.* vigorous attack.

on′to, *prep.* into a position on.

o′nus, *n.* **1.** burden. **2.** blame.

on′ward, *adv.* **1.** Also, **on′wards, forward.** —*adj.* **2.** forward.

on′yx, *n.* striped agate.

oo′dles, *n., pl. Informal.* vast amounts.

ooze, *v.* **oozed, oozing,** *n. v.i.* **1.** flow slowly. —*v.t.* **2.** emit slowly. —*n.* **3.** slime. —**ooz′y,** *adj.*

o'pal, *n.* gem of multicolored silica. —**o''pal·es'cent**, *adj.*

o·paque', *adj.* **1.** passing no light. **2.** obscure. —**o·paque'ness**, **o·pac'i·ty**, *n.*

o'pen, *adj.* **1.** able to be entered, seen through, etc. **2.** with the inside revealed. **3.** available or accessible. **4.** candid. —*v.t.* **5.** make open. —*v.i.* **6.** become open. —*v.t.*, *v.i.* **7.** start. —*n.* **8.** open or unconcealed place or state.

o'pen-air', *adj.* outdoor.

o'pen-end'ed, *adj.* unrestricted.

o'pen-hand'ed, *adj.* generous.

o'pen·ing, *n.* **1.** perforation. **2.** beginning. **3.** opportunity.

op'er·a, *n.* musical drama. —**op''er·at'ic**, *adj.*

op'er·a·ble, *adj.* **1.** treatable by surgery. **2.** able to be operated.

op'er·ate'', *v.*, **-ated, -ating.** *v.t.* **1.** cause to function. **2.** control; manage. —*v.i.* **3.** function; act. **4.** perform surgery. —**op''er·a'tion**, *n.* —**op''er·a'tion·al**, *adj.* —**op'er·a''tor** *n.*

op'er·a·tive, *adj.* **1.** pertaining to operations. **2.** able to operate. —*n.* **3.** detective.

op'er·a''tor, *n.* **1.** person who operates something, as telephone equipment. **2.** *Informal.* person living on his wits.

op''er·et'ta, *n.* light opera.

ophth''al·mol'o·gy, *n.* branch of medicine concerning the eye. —**opth''al·mo·log'i·cal**, *adj.* —**opth''al·mol·o·gist**, *n.*

o'pi·ate, *n.* opium-based drug.

o·pin'ion, *n.* **1.** personal belief. **2.** personal evaluation.

o·pin'ion·at''ed, *adj.* stubborn in one's opinions.

o'pi·um, *n.* drug derived from poppies.

o·pos'sum, *n.* small tree-dwelling marsupial,

op·po'nent, *n.* adversary.

op''por·tune', *adj.* occuring when useful.

op''por·tun'ism, *n.* unprincipled advantage-taking.

op''por·tun'i·ty, *n., pl.* **-ties.** favorable occasion.

op·pose', *v.t.*, **-posed, -posing.** **1.** resist; fight. **2.** be in contrast with. —**op''po·si'tion**, *n.*

op'po·site, *adj.* **1.** in the other direction from somewhere between. **2.** totally different in nature. —*n.* **3.** something opposite.

op·press', *v.t.* **1.** bully or exploit. **2.** worry or make uncomfortable. —**op·pres'sion**, *n.* —**op·pres'sor**, *n.* —**op·pres'sive**, *adj.*

op·pro'bri·um, *n.* scorn; shame. —**op·pro'bri·ous**, *adj.*

opt, *v.i.* make a choice.

op'tic, *adj.* pertaining to sight.

op'ti·cal, *adj.* **1.** visual. **2.** pertaining to optics.

op·ti'cian, *n.* dealer in aids to eyesight.

op'tics, *n.* study of light and vision.

op'ti·mism, *n.* readiness to see or predict the best. —**op'ti·mist**, *n.* —**op''ti·mis'tic**, *adj.*

op'ti·mum, *adj.* **1.** best, esp. in amount, etc. —*n.* **2.** optimum amount, etc.

op'tion, *n.* **1.** choice. **2.** right to buy or not buy something. —**op'tion·al**, *adj.*

op·tom'e·try, *n.* profession of testing and prescribing for eye conditions. —**op·tom'e·trist**, *n.*

op'u·lent, *adj.* **1.** rich. **2.** lavish. —**op'u·lence**, *n.*

o'pus, *n., pl.* **-pera, -puses.** work of an artist, musician, etc., esp. when numbered.

or, *conj.* **1.** (indicating alternatives). **2.** (indicating synonyms).

or'a·cle, *n.* **1.** medium for consulting a god. **2.** great authority. —**o·rac'u·lar**, *adj.*

o'ral, *adj.* **1.** pertaining to the mouth. **2.** spoken.

or'ange, *n.* **1.** mixture of red and yellow. **2.** fruit of this color. —**or'ange·ade'**, *n.*

o·rang'u·tan'', *n.* manlike ape of Indonesia. Also, **o·rang'u·tang''.**

o·ra'tion, *n.* formal speech. —**o·rate'**, *v.i.* —**o'ra'tor**, *n.*

or''a·to'ri·o'', *n., pl.* **-os.** play sung but not acted.

or''a·to'ry, *n., pl.* **-ies.** **1.** public speaking. **2.** small chapel. —**or''a·tor'i·cal**, *adj.*

orb, *n.* heavenly body.

or'bit, *n.* **1.** path of a heavenly body. —*v.i.* **2.** be in orbit. —**or'bit·al**, *adj.*

or'chard, *n.* grove of fruit trees.

or'ches·tra, *n.* **1.** large, varied musical group. **2.** main floor in an auditorium. —**or·ches'tral**, *adj.*

or'ches·trate'', *v.t.*, **-trated, -trating.** arrange for orchestra.

or'chid, *n.* tropical flowering plant.

or·dain', *v.t.* **1.** decree; establish. **2.** grant the office of clergyman to. —**or·dain'ment**, **or''di·na'tion**, *n.*

or·deal', *n.* severe trial.

or'der, *n.* **1.** proper or meaningful condition. **2.** command. **3.** request to purchase. **4.** group of monks, etc. —*v.t.* **5.** make an order for. **6.** put in order.

or'der·ly, *adj., n., pl.* **-lies.** *adj.* **1.** in order. **2.** quiet in behavior. —*n.* **3.** attendant.

or'di·nal, *adj.* **1.** pertaining to a meaningful series. —*n.* **2.** ordinal number.

or'di·nance, *n.* law.

or'di·nar''y, *adj.* **1.** usual, customary. —*n.* **2.** customary experience.

ord'nance, *n.* military weapons.

ore, *n.* metal-bearing mineral.

o·reg′a·no, *n.* fragrant-leafed plant.

or′gan, *n.* 1. body part performing a specific function. 2. keyboard wind or electronic instrument. 3. institutional periodical. —**or′gan·ist,** *n.*

or·gan′ic, *adj.* 1. pertaining to or suggesting organisms. 2. pertaining to bodily organs. 3. containing carbon.

or′gan·ism, *n.* living thing.

or′gan·ize″, *v.,* -**ized,** -**izing.** *v.t., v.i.* 1. join in a coordinated group. —*v.t.* 2. coordinate the functioning of. 3. arrange for. 4. cause to join a group. —**or″gan·i·za′tion,** *n.* —**or″gan·i·za′tion·al,** *adj.*

or′gasm, *n.* climax of a sex act.

or·gy (or′jē), *n., pl.* -**gies.** wild revelry.

o′ri·ent, *v.i.* 1. establish one's location or course. —*v.t.* 2. establish the location or course of. 3. initiate in fundamentals. 4. face in a certain direction. —*n.* 4. the Orient, Asia. —**o″ri·en·ta′tion,** *n.* —**O″ri·en′tal,** *adj., n.*

or′i·fice, *n.* opening.

or′i·gin, *n.* 1. commencement. 2. source.

o·rig′i·nal, *adj.* 1. earliest. 2. copied to make others. 3. never before seen. 4. creative. —*n.* 5. original thing. —**o·rig′i·nal′i·ty,** *n.* —**o·rig′i·nate″,** *v.t., v.i.* —**o·rig′i·na″tor,** *n.*

o′ri·ole″, *n.* black and orange bird.

or′na·ment, *n.* (or′nə ment) 1. decoration. —*v.t.* (or′nə ment″) 2. decorate. —**or″na·men′tal,** *adj.* —**or″na·men·ta′tion,** *n.*

or·nate′, *adj.* greatly ornamented.

or′ner·y, *adj. Dialect.* mean or stubborn. —**or′ner·i·ness,** *n.*

or″ni·thol′o·gy, *n.* study of birds. —**or″ni·thol′o·gist,** *n.* —**or″ni·tho·log′i·cal,** *adj.*

o′ro·tund″, *adj.* with resonant, often pompous, speech.

or′phan, *n.* 1. child of dead parents. —*v.t.* 2. kill the parents of.

or′phan·age, *n.* home for orphans.

or″tho·don′tics, *n.* branch of dentistry that corrects irregular teeth. —**or″tho·don′tist,** *n.*

or′tho·dox″, *adj.* 1. conforming to standard doctrine. 2. **Orthodox,** pertaining to an east European or Near Eastern church. —**or′tho·dox″y,** *n.*

or·thog′ra·phy, *n., pl.* -**phies.** spelling. —**or″tho·graph′ic,** *adj.*

or″tho·pe′dics, *n.* surgery of bones and joints. —**or″tho·pe′dic,** *adj.* —**or″tho·pe′dist,** *n.*

os′cil·late″, *v.* -**lated,** -**lating.** *v.t., v.i.* swing back and forth.

os′cu·late″, *v.,* -**lated,** -**lating.** *v.i., v.t.* kiss.

os·mo′sis, *n.* passage of fluids through membranes. —**os·mot′ic,** *adj.*

os′se·ous, *adj.* bony.

os′si·fy″, *v.,* -**fied,** -**fying.** *v.t., v.i.* 1. turn to bone. 2. turn inadaptable, as a custom.

os·ten′si·ble, *adj.* seeming.

os″ten·ta′tion, *n.* great and deliberate display. —**os″ten·ta′tious,** *adj.*

os″te·op′a·thy, *n.* school of medicine emphasizing bones and muscles. —**os″te·o·path′ic,** *adj.* —**os′te·o·path″,** *n.*

os′tra·cize″, *v.t.,* -**cized,** -**cizing.** expel; exclude. —**os′tra·cism,** *n.*

os′trich, *n.* running bird of Africa and the Near East.

oth′er, *adj.* 1. not yet mentioned. 2. additional; remaining. —*pron.* 3. other one. —*adv.* 4. otherwise.

oth′er·wise″, *adv.* 1. in a different way. 2. in other respects. 3. under other conditions.

o′ti·ose″, *adj.* idle; useless.

ot′ter, *n.* furred swimming mammal.

ot′to·man, *n.* upholstered footstool.

ouch, *interj.* (exclamation of pain).

ought, *aux. v.* 1. am, is, or are obligated. 2. will very probably.

oui, *adv. French.* yes.

ounce, *n.* 1. sixteenth of an avoirdupois pound or twelfth of a troy pound. 2. thirty-second of a liquid quart.

our, *adj.* pertaining to us.

ours, *pron.* our own.

our·selves′, *pron.* 1. (intensive or reflexive of *we*). 2. our true selves.

oust, *v.t.* expel.

oust′er, *n.* act or instance of ousting.

out, *adv.* 1. away from inside. 2. away from existence, action, etc. 3. away from a group. 4. away from consciousness. —*adj.* 5. away from one's usual place. 6. out of existence, action, etc. 7. inaccurate. 8. unconscious. 9. **out of,** with no supply of. —*n.* 10. *Informal.* means of evasion.

out′-and-out″, *adj.* utter.

out′board″, *adj., adv.* outside the hull of a boat.

out′break″, *n.* sudden manifestation.

out′build″ing, *n.* separate, subsidiary building.

out′burst″, *n.* vigorous outbreak.

out′cast″, *adj.* 1. rejected by all. —*n.* 2. outcast person.

out′come″, *n.* result.

out′crop″, *n.* rock rising above the soil.

out′cry″, *n., pl.* -**cries.** strong protest.

out′dat′ed, *adj.* obsolete.

out′dis′tance, *v.t.,* -**tanced,** -**tancing.** get ahead of in a race or pursuit.

out′do′, *v.t.,* -**did,** -**done,** -**doing.** act more effectively than.

out′door′, *adj.* pertaining to the outdoors.

out′doors′, *adv.* 1. away from the insides of buildings. —*n.* 2. nature.

out'er, *adj.* further out. —**out'er·most'**, *adj.*

out'fit', *n., v.t.,* -**fitted**, -**fitting**. *n.* 1. equipment. 2. ensemble of clothes. —*v.t.* 3. supply with an outfit.

out''fox', *v.t.* outwit.

out·go''ing, *adj.* 1. departing. 2. affable.

out'grow'', *v.t.,* -**grew**, -**grown**, -**growing**. become too large or mature for.

out'growth'', *n.* 1. something that grows out. 2. development; consequence.

out'guess'', *v.t.* guess better than.

out'ing, *n.* pleasure trip.

out'land'ish, *adj.* strange.

out'last'', *v.t.* last longer than.

out'law', *n.* 1. criminal. —*v.t.* 2. forbid by law.

out'lay', *n.* expenditure.

out'let'', *n.* 1. means of emergence. 2. sales market.

out'line'', *n., v.t.,* -**lined**, -**lining**. *n.* 1. outer edge; silhouette. 2. summary of essentials. —*v.t.* 3. make an outline of.

out''live', *v.t.,* -**lived**, -**living**. live longer than.

out'look'', *n.* 1. view. 2. viewing place. 3. prospect.

out'ly''ing, *adj.* situated at a distance.

out·mod'ed, *adj.* no longer in use.

out''num'ber, *v.t.* be more than.

out'-of-date', *adj.* obsolete.

out'-of-the-way', *adj.* not often encountered.

out'pa'tient, *n.* non-resident hospital patient.

out'post'', *n.* remote fort, settlement, etc.

out''put', *n.* 1. production. 2. (computers) data sent from a computer after processing.

out'rage', *n., v.t.,* -**raged**, -**raging**. *n.* 1. indignation. 2. act causing indignation. —*v.t.* 3. make indignant. —**out·ra'geous**, *adj.*

out'rig'ger, *n.* 1. floating spar giving a narrow boat stability. 2. boat with such a spar.

out'right'', *adj.* 1. pure and unambiguous. —*adv.* 2. entirely. 3. candidly.

out'set', *n.* beginning.

out'side', *n.* 1. exterior. —*adj.* 2. pertaining to an exterior. 3. extreme. 4. remotely possible. —*adv.* 5. to the exterior. —*prep.* 6. away from the interior of.

out''sid'er, *n.* non-member.

out''size', *adj.* over normal size.

out'skirts', *n., pl.* border areas.

out''smart', *v.t.* be more cunning than.

out''spo'ken, *adj.* frank.

out'spread', *adj.* extended.

out'stand'ing, *adj.* 1. prominent. 2. unpaid.

out''stretch', *v.t.* extend.

out''strip', *v.t.,* -**stripped**, -**stripping**. 1. go faster than. 2. surpass.

out'ward, *adj.* 1. outer; exterior. —*adv.* 2. Also, **out'wards**, towards the outside.

out''weigh', *v.t.* 1. matter more than. 2. be heavier than.

out''wit', *v.t.,* -**witted**, -**witting**. outsmart.

o'val, *n.* 1. closed curve with a longer and a shorter axis. —*adj.* 2. shaped like such a curve.

o'va·ry, *n., pl.* -**ries**. female reproductive gland. —**o·var'i·an**, *adj.*

o·va'tion, *n.* act of enthusiastic applause.

ov'en, *n.* heating chamber.

o'ver, *prep.* 1. above or on. 2. to or on the far side of. 3. superior to. 4. more than. 5. concerning. —*adv.* 6. above. 7. across. 8. more. 9. again. 10. upside down. 11. to a new attitude or belief. 12. to completion. —*adj.* 13. upper. 14. finished.

o'ver-, prefix indicating "to excess." **overabundant**, **overactive**, **overanxious**, **overburden**, **overcautious**, **overcharge**, **overconfident**, **overcrowd**, **overdo**, **overdose**, **overeat**, **overemphasize**, **overestimate**, **overexert**, **overexpose**, **overheat**, **overindulge**, **overload**, **overmuch**, **overpopulate**, **overprice**, **overproduce**, **overreact**, **overripe**, **oversexed**, **overspend**, **overstock**, **overstrict**, **oversupply**, **overwork**.

o''ver·all'', *adj., adv.* 1. end-to-end. —*adj.* 2. total. —*n.* 3. **overalls**, protective covering for other clothes.

o''ver·awe'', *v.t.,* -**awed**, -**awing**. subdue with awe.

o''ver·bear'ing, *adj.* domineering.

o'ver·board'', *adv.* into the water from a vessel.

o'ver·cast'', *adj.* cloudy, as the sky.

o'ver·coat'', *n.* heavy outer coat.

o''ver·come'', *v.t.,* -**came**, -**come**, -**coming**. get the better of.

o''ver·dose'', *v.* to ingest, with harmful effect, too much of a drug.

o''ver·draw'', *v.t.,* -**drew**, -**drawn**, -**drawing**. draw on in excess of one's balance. —**o'ver·draft''**, *n.*

o''ver·due', *adj.* past the time when due.

o''ver·es'ti·mate'', *v.t.,* -**mated**, -**mating**. esteem too highly or as too much. —**o''ver·es'ti·mate**, **o''ver·es'ti·ma'tion**, *n.*

o·ver·flow, *v.t.* (o''vər flō') 1. spill over the rim of. —*v.i.* 2. be filled beyond capacity. —*n.* (o'vər flō') 3. act or instance of overflowing. 4. amount that overflows.

o''ver·grow'', *v.t.* -**grew**, -**grown**, -**growing**. cover with growth.

o'ver·hand'', *adv., adj.* with the hand raised.

o''ver·haul'', *v.t.* 1. inspect thoroughly. 2. repair. —*n.* 3. act or instance of overhauling.

o'ver·head'', *adj.*, *adv.* **1.** above one's head. —*n.* **2.** continuing business costs.

o''ver·hear', *v.t.*, **-heard**, **-hearing**. hear without being spoken to.

o''ver·joyed', *adj.* filled with joy.

o''ver·land'', *adj.*, *adv.* across the land.

o·ver·lap', *v.*, **-lapped**, **-lapping**, *n. v.t.* (ō′vər lap′) **1.** extend within the edge of. —*v.i.* **2.** extend within each other's edges. —*n.* (ō′vər lap′′) **3.** act or instance of overlapping.

o''ver·lay', *v.t.*, **-laid**, **-laying**. cover or lay over.

o''ver·look', *v.t.* **1.** omit by mistake. **2.** look out over.

o'ver·ly, *adv.* excessively.

o·ver·night, *adv.* (ō′vər nīt′) **1.** during the night. —*adj.* (ō′vər nīt′′) **2.** from beginning to end of one night. **3.** for one night.

o''ver·pass'', *n.* roadway passing over another, etc.

o''ver·pow'er, *v.t.* reduce to helplessness.

o''ver·rate', *v.t.*, **-rated**, **-rating**. rate too highly.

o''ver·reach', *v.t.* reach beyond.

o''ver·ride', *v.t.*, **-rode**, **-ridden**, **-riding**. prevail against or nullify.

o''ver·rule', *v.t.*, **-ruled**, **-ruling**. nullify with superior authority.

o''ver·run', *v.t.*, **-ran**, **-run**, **-running**. **1.** overflow. **2.** infest.

o'ver·seas', *adv.*, *adj.* **1.** beyond the sea. —*adj.* Also, **o'ver·sea''**. **2.** foreign.

o''ver·see', *v.t.*, **-saw**, **-seen**, **-seeing**. supervise.

o'ver·shoe'', *n.* waterproof shoe covering.

o'ver·sight'', *n.* mistaken omission.

o''ver·sim'pli·fy'', *v.t.*, **-fied**, **-fying**. distort by simplification.

o''ver·size', *adj.* **1.** too large. **2.** larger than usual. Also, **o'ver·sized''**.

o''ver·sleep', *v.i.*, **-slept**, **-sleeping**. sleep too long.

o''ver·state', *v.t.*, **-stated**, **-stating**. exaggerate.

o''ver·step', *v.t.*, **-stepped**, **-stepping**. exceed.

o''ver·stuff', *v.t.* **1.** upholster with stuffing all over. **2.** stuff to excess.

o·vert', *adj.* **1.** unhidden. **2.** open and deliberate.

o''ver·take', *v.t.*, **-took**, **-taken**, **-taking**. catch up with.

o''ver-the-coun''ter, *adj.* (drugs) available without a prescription.

o·ver·throw', *v.t.*, **-threw**, **-thrown**, **-throwing**, *n. v.t.* (ō′vər thrō′) **1.** cause to fall over. **2.** banish from power. —*n.* (ō′vər thrō′′) **3.** act or instance of overthrowing.

o'ver·time'', *adj.*, *adv.* **1.** beyond regular hours. —*n.* **2.** time beyond regular hours. **3.** overtime pay.

o'ver·tone'', *n.* **1.** tone modifying a pure tone. **2.** subtle implication.

o'ver·ture'', *n.* **1.** musical composition beginning an opera, etc. **2.** friendly advance.

o''ver·turn', *v.t.*, *v.i.* upset.

o''ver·ween'ing, *adj.* arrogant.

o'ver·weight'', *adj.* too heavy.

o''ver·whelm', *v.t.* render powerless.

o''ver·wrought'', *adj.* very nervous.

o'void, *adj.* egg-shaped.

o'vum, *n.*, *pl.* **-va**. female germ cell.

owe, *v.t.*, **owed**, **owing**. **1.** be obligated to give or pay. **2.** be obligated to. **3.** have someone to thank for.

owl, *n.* nocturnal bird of prey.

own, *v.t.* **1.** be the rightful possessor of. —*v.t.*, *v.i.* **2.** admit or confess. —*adj.* **3.** personally or individually possessed. —**own'er·ship**, *n.*

ox, *n.*, *pl.* **oxen**. castrated bull.

ox'ide, *n.* compound containing oxygen.

ox'i·dize'', *v.*, **-dized**, **-dizing**. *v.i.* unite with oxygen. —**ox'i·dant**, *n.* —**ox''i·da'tion**, *n.*

ox'y·gen, *n.* gaseous element needed for breathing and burning.

oys'ter, *n.* edible mollusk.

o'zone, *n.* a form of oxygen created by electric spark.

P

P, p, *n.* sixteenth letter of the English alphabet.

pab'u·lum. *n.* soft food, esp. for babies.

pace, *n.*, *v.*, **paced**, **pacing**. *n.* **1.** rate of movement, esp. in walking or running. **2.** linear measure roughly equivalent to a footstep. **3.** an individual step. —*v.t.* **4.** establish the pace for, esp. in a race. **5.** measure by pacing off. —*v.i.* **6.** take slow, measured steps.

pace''mak·er, *n.* artificial device to regulate the heartbeat.

pach·y·derm (pak′i·derm), *n.* thick-skinned mammal, e.g., an elephant.

pa·cif'ic, *adj.* **1.** peaceful; calm. **2.** peace-making; conciliatory.

pac'i·fism, *n.* opposition to violence and war. —**pac'i·fist**, *n.* —**pac''i·fis'tic**, *adj.*

pac'i·fy'', *v.t.*, **-fied**, **-fying**. **1.** quiet or calm. **2.** appease. —**pac'i·fi·ca'tion**, *n.* —**pac'i·fi''er**, *n.*

pack, *n.* **1.** bundle or package. **2.** group of people, animals, or things. **3.** complete set of. —*v.t.* **4.** make into a bundle. **5.** fill, as with things for a journey. **6.** cram. **7.** carry, as a gun.

pack'age, *n., v.t.,* **-aged, -aging.** *n.* **1.** bundle; parcel. **2.** container. —*v.t.* **3.** enclose or wrap in a package.

pack'et, *n.* **1.** small package or bundle. **2.** passenger boat on a regular schedule.

pact, *n.* agreement; treaty.

pad, *n., v.t.,* **padded, padding.** *n.* **1.** soft cushion **2.** tablet of writing paper. **3.** cushioned part of an animal foot. —*v.t.* **4.** furnish with pads. **5.** lengthen or falsify with extraneous matter.

pad'dle, *n., v.,* **-dled, -dling.** *n.* **1.** oarlike implement, esp. for a canoe. **2.** ping pong racket. —*v.t.* **3.** move with paddles. **4.** spank. —*v.i.* **5.** move in water using the hands.

pad'dock, *n.* enclosed area for horses.

pad'lock, *n.* **1.** portable lock with a shackle. —*v.t.* **2.** fasten with a padlock.

pae·an (pē'ən), *n.* song of praise, joy, or thanksgiving.

pa'gan, *n.* **1.** heathen. —*adj.* **2.** heathen: barbaric. —**pa'gan·ism,** *n.*

page, *n., v.t.* **paged, paging.** *n.* **1.** single side of a leaf, as in a book. **2.** young servant. —*v.t.* **3.** number the pages of. **4.** hail by naming loudly.

pag'eant, *n.* elaborate spectacle. —**pag'eant·ry,** *n.*

pag''er, *n.* electronic device for remote alerting and communication with a person.

pa·go'da, *n.* tall Oriental building, usually in a Buddhist temple.

pail, *n.* bucket.

pain, *n.* **1.** physical or mental suffering. **2.** effort; struggle. **3.** punishment. —*v.t.* **4.** hurt; distress. —**pain'ful,** *adj.* —**pain'less,** *adj.*

pains'tak''ing, *adj.* careful.

paint, *n.* **1.** pigmented liquid used to coat surfaces. —*v.i.* **2.** engage in the art of painting. —*v.t.* **3.** cover with paint. —**paint'er,** *n.*

pair, *n., pl.* **pairs, pair,** *v.i.n.* **1.** set of two, esp. when matching. —*v.t.* **2.** arrange in pairs. —*v.i.* **3.** **pair off,** separate in couples.

pais'ley, *n.* soft fabric with colorful, intricate design.

pa·ja'mas, *n., pl.* loose, two-piece sleeping clothes.

pal, *n. Informal.* friend or acquaintance.

pal'ace, *n.* official residence of a sovereign, etc. —**pa·la'tial,** *adj.*

pal'at·a·ble, *adj.* tasty.

pal'ate, *n.* roof of the mouth. —**pal'a·tal,** *adj.*

pa·lav'er, *n.* long parley.

pale, *adj.,* **paler, palest,** *v.* **paled, paling.**

n. adj. **1.** lacking intensity of color; whitish. **2.** lacking vividness. —*v.i.* **3.** become pale. —*n.* **4.** stake. **5.** limits, bounds. **6.** enclosed area.

pa''le·o·lith'ic, *adj.* pertaining to the Old Stone Age.

pal'ette, *n.* board on which a painter spreads colors.

pal'id, *adj.* pale, drawn. —**pal'lor,** *n.*

pal'ing, *n.* board or picket.

pal'i·sade'', *n.* **1.** high fence of palings. **2.** line of high cliffs.

pall (pol), *n.* **1.** cloth draped over a coffin. —*v.i.* **2.** become tiresome or distasteful.

pall'bear''er, *n.* person who attends or carries the coffin at a funeral.

pal'let, *n.* **1.** straw mattress. **2.** platform used to support freight.

pal'li·ate'', *v.t.* **1.** ease without curing. **2.** mitigate with excuses. —**pal'li·a''tive,** *adj.*

palm, *n.* **1.** soft inner surface of the hand. **2.** tall unbranched tropical tree or shrub topped with large leaves. —*v.t.* **3.** conceal in the hand.

palm'is·try, *n.* fortune-telling from the lines on a person's palm.

pal·o·mi·no (pal''ō mē'nō), *n., pl.* **-nos.** *n.* light tan horse.

pal'pa·ble, *adj.* **1.** tangible. **2.** obvious, clear. —**pal'pa·bly,** *adv.*

pal'pi·tate'', *v.i.,* **-tated, -tating.** pulsate with unnatural rapidity. —**pal''pi·ta'tion,** *n.*

pal·sy (pahl'zē), *n., pl.* **-sies,** *v.t.,* **-sied, -sying.** *n.* **1.** paralysis. **2.** condition characterized by tremors. —*v.t.* **3.** paralyze.

pal'try, *adj.,* **-trier, -triest.** *adj.* trifling, trivial.

pam'per, *v.t.* treat with excessive indulgence; coddle.

pam·phlet, *n.* unbound booklet with a paper cover.

pan, *n., v.* **panned, panning.** *n.* **1.** broad, shallow metal container. —*v.t.* **2.** separate from sand by washing. **3.** *Informal.* criticize severely, in a review.

pan·a·ce·a (pan''a sē'a), *n.* cure-all.

pan'cake'', *n.* flat batter cake fried on both sides.

pan'cre·as, *n.* gland that secretes digestive fluid. —**pan''cre·at'ic,** *adj.*

pan'da, *n.* bear-like, black and white Asiatic mammal.

pan''de·mo'ni·um, *n.* wild uproar, chaos.

pan'der, *n.* **1.** pimp. —*v.i.* **2.** cater to another's passions or weaknesses. —**pan'der·er,** *n.*

pane, *n.* sheet of glass, esp. for doors and windows.

pan·e·gyr·ic (pan''ə jir'ik), *n.* eulogy.

pan'el, *n.* **1.** list of persons called for a special task, e.g. jury duty. **2.** wood

filling for a wall or door. **3.** mounting for controls or instruments. —**pan'el·ing,** *n.* —**pan'el·ist,** *n.*

pang, *n.* sudden feeling of distress or guilt.

pan'han'dle, *v.i.* -dled, -dling. *Informal.* beg for money on the street. —**pan'han'dler,** *n.*

pan'ic, *n.* **1.** sudden, overpowering fear. —*v.i.* **2.** be affected by panic. —**pan'ick·y,** *adj.* —**pan'ic-strick''en,** *adj.*

pan'o·ply, *n., pl.* -plies. *n.* **1.** impressive array. **2.** suit of armor.

pan''o·ram'a, *n.* **1.** wide view of a large area. **2.** continuously changing scene or unfolding of events. —**pan''o·ram'ic,** *adj.*

pan'sy, *n.* colorful outdoor flower related to the violet.

pant, *v.i.* **1.** breathe hard and quickly, as after exercise. **2.** long or yearn for.

pan'the''ism, *n.* doctrine that equates God with nature and natural forces.

pan'ther, *n.* large wild cat, e.g. leopard, cougar, puma.

pan'to·mime'', *n., v.t.,* -mimed, miming. *n.* **1.** expression through movement and gesture only. **2.** drama using movement and no speech. —*v.t.* **3.** express in pantomime; mime.

pan'try, *n., pl.* -tries. small supply room or closet off a kitchen.

pants, *n., pl.* trousers.

pap, *n.* soft food for babies or the infirm.

pa'pa, *n.* father.

pa'pa·cy, *n.* office of the pope. —**pa'pal,** *adj.*

pa·pa·ya (pa pah'yə), *n.* tropical tree with yellow-black edible fruit.

pa'per, *n.* **1.** fibrous compound made in sheets to receive writing, etc. **2.** scholarly essay. **3.** newspaper. **4.** **papers,** documents. —*v.t.* **5.** decorate with wallpaper.

pa'per·back'', *n.* inexpensive book with paper cover.

pa·pier-ma·che (pa''per mə shā'), *n.* molding material made of wet paper pulp and glue.

pa·pil'la, *n., pl.* -pillae (pə pil'lē), *n.* small protuberance concerned with the senses, e.g. taste buds.

pa'pist, *n. Disparaging.* Roman Catholic. —**pa'pism,** *n.* —**pa·pis'ti·cai, pa·pis'tic,** *adj.*

pa·poose', *n.* North American Indian baby.

pap·ri'ka, *n.* red spice made from sweet peppers.

pa·py'rus, *n.* plant from the Nile from which the Egyptians prepared paperlike material.

par, *n.* **1.** equality in level or value. **2.** accepted standard; average.

par'a·ble, *n.* story conveying a moral.

par'a·chute'', *n., v., -chuted, -chuting, n.* **1.** umbrellalike device used for descents from aircraft. —*v.i.* **2.** jump with a parachute. —*v.t.* **3.** send by parachute.

pa·rade', *n., v.,* -raded, -rading. *n.* **1.** ostentatious display. **2.** ceremonial procession or march. —*v.t.* **3.** display ostentatiously. —*v.i.* **4.** march in a parade.

par·a·digm (par'ə dîm), *n.* ideal; model.

par'a·dise'', *n.* **1.** heaven. **2.** Garden of Eden.

par'a·dox'', *n.* true statement that seems to contradict itself. —**par''a·dox'i·cal,** *adj.*

par'af·fin, *n.* waxy substance used in candles and to seal jars.

par'a·gon'', *n.* model of perfection.

par'a·graph'', *n.* **1.** subdivision of a writing that contains one or more sentences. —*v.t.* **2.** divide into paragraphs.

par'a·keet'', *n.* any of numerous slender, small parrots.

par'al·lax'', *n.* apparent displacement of an object seen from different positions.

par'al·lel'', *adj., n., v.t.* -leled, -leling. *adj.* **1.** lying or moving in the same direction but equidistant at all points. **2.** essentially similar or comparable. —*n.* **3.** anything parallel. **4.** counterpart. **5.** similarity. —*v.t.* **6.** compare. **7.** be parallel to.

par''al·lel'o·gram'', *n.* quadrilateral with parallel opposite sides.

pa·ral'y·sis, *n., pl.* -ses, loss of voluntary muscular control. —**par''a·lyt'ic,** *n., adj.* —**par'a·lyze'',** *v.t.*

par'a·mount'', *adj.* superior; predominant.

par'a·mour'', *n.* extra-marital lover.

par''a·noi'a, *n.* mental disorder characterized by delusions. —**par''a·noid'',** *n., adj.* —**par''a·noi'ac,** *n., adj.*

par'a·pet'', *n.* protecting wall or railing.

par''a·pher·nal'ia, *n., pl.,* **1.** personal belongings. **2.** equipment.

par'a·phrase'', *v.t.,* -phrased, -phrasing, *n. v.t.* **1.** restate in other words. —*n.* **2.** restatement in different words.

par·a·ple·gi·a (par''ə plē'gēa), *n.* paralysis of the lower half of the body. —**par''a·pleg'ic,** *n.*

par'a·site'', *n.* **1.** organism which lives in or on another. **2.** person who depends on or exploits another. —**par''a·sit'ic,** *adj.*

par'a·sol'', *n.* sun umbrella.

par'a·troops'', *n., pl.* soldiers who parachute from planes. —**par'a·trooper,** *n.*

par'boil'', *v.t.* boil partly.

par'cel, *n., v.t.,* -celed, -celing. *n.* **1.** wrapped package, esp. for mailing. **2.** lot, esp. for sale. **3.** tract of land. —*v.t.* **4.** divide.

parch, *v.t.* **1.** dry by heat. —*v.i.* **2.** suffer from heat or thirst.

parch'ment, *n.* skin of sheep or goat prepared for writing on.

par'don, *n.* **1.** official release from penalty or punishment. **2.** indulgence, forgiveness. —*v.t.* **3.** grant pardon to. —**par'don·a·ble,** *adj.*

pare, *v.t.* pared, paring. **1.** trim off the outside part or skin of. **2.** reduce.

par''e·gor'ic, *n.* soothing medicine, esp. to control diarrhea.

par'ent, *n.* mother or father. —**pa·ren'tal,** *adj.* —**par'ent·hood''.** *n.*

par'ent·age, *n.* descent, origin or lineage.

pa·ren'the·sis, *n., pl.* -ses, **1.** punctuation marks, (or), used to enclose parenthetic material. **2.** matter interpolated in writing to modify or explain the idea. —**par''en·thet'ic, par''en·thet'i·cal,** *adj.*

par·fait (pahr fā') *n.* frozen, layered dessert.

pa·ri·ah (pa rī'ah), *n.* outcast.

par''i·mu'tu·el, *n.* system of betting in which winners share the winnings and the management takes a percentage.

par'ish, *n.* **1.** ecclesiastical district under one pastor. **2.** local church community. —**pa·rish'ion·er,** *n.*

par'i·ty, *n.* equality; equivalence.

park, *n.* **1.** land set aside as a recreation area or game preserve. **2.** site for athletic events. —*v.t., v.i.* **3.** halt for an extended period.

par'ka, *n.* hooded, cold-weather coat.

park'way'', *n.* highway with landscaped median strip.

par'lance, *n.* manner of speaking; idiom.

par'lay, *n.* **1.** bet of previous winnings along with the original sum betted. —*v.t.* **2.** bet as a parlay.

par'ley, *n., pl.* -leys, *v.i.,* -leyed, -leying. *n.* **1.** informal conference, esp. to settle differences. —*v.i.* **2.** hold a parley.

par'lia·ment, *n.* national legislative body. —**par''lia·men·tar'i·an,** *n.* —**par''lia·men'ta·ry,** *adj.*

par'lor, *n.* room for entertaining.

pa·ro·chi·al (pa rō'kē al), *adj.* **1.** pertaining to a parish. **2.** narrow or limited in scope. —**pa·ro'chi·al·ism,** *n.*

par'o·dy, *n., pl.* -dies, *v.t.,* -died, -dying. *n.* **1.** satiric or humorous imitation. —*v.t.* **2.** ridicule, travesty. —**par'o·dist,** *n.* —**pa·rod'ic,** *adj.*

pa·role', *n., v.t.,* -roled, -roling. *n.* **1.** conditional early release from prison. —*v.t.* **2.** put on parole.

par·ox·ysm (par'ok siz''im), *n.* sudden, sharp attack; convulsion, fit.

par·quet (par ka'), *n.* floor with an inlaid design, esp. in wood.

par'ri·cide, *n.* killing of a parent or close relative.

par'rot, *n.* **1.** hook-billed tropical bird capable of talking. —*v.t.* **2.** repeat or imitate unthinkingly.

par'ry, *v.t.,* -ried, rying, *n., pl.* -ries. —*v.t.* **1.** evade, avoid. —*n.* **2.** act or instance of parrying.

par'si·mo''ny, *n.* extreme frugality or cheapness. —**par''si·mo'ni·ous,** *adj.*

pars'ley, *n.* garden herb used as garnish or seasoning.

pars'nip, *n.* plant with long, white edible root.

par'son, *n.* clergyman, esp. Protestant.

par'son·age, *n.* house for a parson.

part, *n.* **1.** portion or division. **2.** spare or replacement piece for a machine. **3.** function, duty, job. **4.** role in drama, etc. —*v.t.* **5.** divide. —*v.i.* **6.** dissolve a relationship.

par·take', *v.i.,* -took -taken, -taking. *v.i.* **1.** participate. **2.** receive or take a portion.

par·tial (par'shal), *adj.* **1.** favoring one over another; biased. **2.** especially fond. **3.** affecting a part only. —**par·tial'i·ty,** *n.* —**par'tial·ly,** *adv.*

par·tic'i·pate'', *v.i.,* -pated, -pating. take part; share. —**par·tic'i·pant,** *n.* —**par·tic''i·pa'tion,** *n.*

par·ti·ci·ple, *n.* adjective based on a verb. —**par''ti·cip'i·al,** *adj.*

par'ti·cle, *n.* **1.** very small piece or amount. **2.** small, functional word, e.g. a preposition, etc.

par·tic'u·lar, *adj.* **1.** pertaining to a specific person or thing. **2.** distinctive, special. **3.** attentive to details; fastidious. —*n.* **4.** detail. —**par·tic'u·lar·ly,** *adv.*

part'ing, *n.* **1.** separation, division. **2.** departure. —*adj.* **3.** done, etc. in farewell.

par'ti·san, *n.* **1.** person who takes a side in a controversy. **2.** guerrilla.

par·ti'tion, *n.* **1.** division into parts. **2.** divider. —*v.t.* **3.** divide into parts.

part'ly, *adv.* in some measure; not fully.

part'ner, *n.* **1.** associate, colleague. **2.** spouse. **3.** joint owner. —**part'ner·ship'',** *n.*

par'tridge, *n.* any of various game birds.

par'ty, *n., pl.* -ties. *n.* **1.** social gathering. **2.** group of people with common political interests and opinions. **3.** person or group concerned in a specific action; participant. **4.** group engaged in a special task.

pass, *v.t.* **1.** go past. **2.** hand over; serve. **3.** spend, as time. **4.** approve or ratify. **5.** succeed at, as a test. —*v.i.* **6.** go past. **7.** come to an end. **8.** go from place to place. **9.** be approved or ratified. —*n.* **10.** situation. **11.** paper granting admission, leave, etc. **12.** route, as between mountains. **13.** motion of the hands.

pass'a·ble, *adj.* **1.** able to be passed or

crossed. **2.** good enough; tolerable —**pass′ab·ly**, *adv.*

pas′sage, *n.* **1.** right or freedom to pass. **2.** means of passing. **3.** transportation, esp. ship passage. **4.** act or instance of passing. **5.** enactment. —**pas′sage·way″**, *n.*

pass′book″, *n.* bankbook, esp. for a savings account.

pas′sen·ger, *n.* traveler, esp. on a vehicle.

pas·sé (pa sā′), *adj.* out of date; old fashioned.

pas′sing, *adj.* **1.** transitory; fleeting. —*n.* **2.** act of a person who passes, esp. in death.

pas′sion, *n.* **1.** strong feeling or emotion. **2.** love, esp. sexual desire. **3.** anger, rage. **4.** the Passion, sufferings of Christ. —**pas′sion·ate, pas′sion·less**, *adj.* —**pas′sion·ate·ly**, *adv.*

pas′sive, *n.* **1.** inactive; not in action. **2.** acted upon. **3.** submissive, meek; patient. —**pas·siv′i·ty, pas′sive·ness**, *n.* —**pas′sive·ly**, *adv.*

Pass′o″ver, *n.* Jewish holiday celebrating the Hebrews' liberation from slavery in Egypt.

pass′port″, *n.* official document carried by a foreign traveler.

past, *adj.* **1.** gone by or elapsed. **2.** pertaining to an earlier time or age. **3.** *Grammar.* pertaining to a verb tense expressing time gone by. —*n.* **4.** time gone by. **5.** past tense. **6.** secret past life. —*prep. adv.* **7.** beyond.

pas′ta, *n.* food, Italian in origin, prepared from flour and egg dough.

paste, *n., v.t.,* **pasted, pasting**, *n.* **1.** soft mixture, esp. for sticking things together. **2.** shiny glass used in imitation gems. —*v.t.* **3.** fasten with paste. —**pas′ty**, *adj.*

paste′board″, *n.* board made of sheets of paper pasted together.

pas·tel′, *n.* **1.** light or pale color. **2.** drawing or painting in pastel.

pas′tern, *n.* part of horse's foot between the fetlock and the hoof joint.

pas′teur·ize″, *v.t.,* **-ized, -izing**. heat to destroy harmful bacteria. —**pas′teur·i·za′tion**, *n.*

pas·tiche (pas tēsh′), *n.* artistic composition composed of selections or motifs from other works.

pas′time″, *n.* diversion; hobby.

pas′tor, *n.* clergyman serving a local parish or church.

pas′to·ral, *adj.* **1.** pertaining to shepherds or the rural life. **2.** pertaining to a golden age. **3.** pertaining to pastors.

pas′try, *n.* sweet baked goods.

pas′ture, *n., v.t.,* **-tured, -turing**, *n.* **1.** grassy land used for grazing animals. —*v.t.* **2.** feed by allowing to graze.

pat, *n., adj., v.i.,* **patted, patting**. *n.* **1.** light stroke with the flat of the hand. **2.** flat piece of butter, etc.—*adj.* **3.** glib. **4.** perfectly learned.—*v.i.* **5.** place the flat of the hand on lightly.

patch, *n.* **1.** piece used to cover or repair a worn spot. **2.** a small area distinct from that around it. —*v.t.* **3.** mend or cover with a patch. **5.** repair hastily. —**patch′work″**, *n., adj.* —**patch′y**, *adj.*

pate, *n.* head, esp. the crown.

pa·tel′la, *n., pl.* **-tellae**. kneecap.

pat′en, *n.* plate, esp. one used in the Eucharist.

pat′ent, *n.* **1.** certificate of exclusive rights to an invention. —*v.t.* **2.** secure a patent on. —*adj.* **3.** something protected by a patent. **4.** evident; obvious.

pa·ter′nal, *adj.* **1.** fatherly. **2.** related through or derived from a father.

pa·ter′nal·ism, *n.* benevolent or fatherly administration. —**pa·ter″nal·is′tic**, *adj.*

pa·ter′ni·ty, *n.* fatherhood.

path, *n.* **1.** narrow road. **2.** course of action. —**path′way″**, *n.*

pa·thet′ic, *adj.* **1.** evoking pity. **2.** miserably inadequate. —**pa·thet′i·cal·ly**, *adv.*

pa·thol′o·gy, *n.* **1.** study of the nature of disease. **2.** characteristics of a disease. —**path″o·log′i·cal**, *adj.* —**pa·thol′o·gist**, *n.*

pa′thos, *n.* element evoking pity or compassion.

pa′tient, *n.* **1.** person under the care of a doctor. —*adj.* **2.** enduring without complaint. —**pa′tience**, *n.* —**pa′tient·ly**, *adv.*

pa·ti′na, *n.* green film formed on copper and bronze.

pa′ti·o″, *n., pl.* **patios**, open courtyard

pa′tri·arch″, *n.* **1.** father or founder, e.g. of a tribe or institution. **2.** venerable old man; father. **3.** ecclesiastical dignitary. —**pa′tri·ar″chal**, *adj.* —**pa′tri·ar″chy**, *n.*

pa·tri′cian, *adj.* **1.** aristocratic; of high birth. —*n.* **2.** aristocrat.

pat′ri·mo″ny, *n.* inherited estate.

pa′tri·ot, *n.* person who loves and supports his country. —**pa″tri·ot′ic**, *adj.* —**pa′tri·ot″ism**, *n.*

pa·trol′, *n., v.t.,* **-trolled, -trolling**. *n.* **1.** guard making a round. —*v.t.* **2.** guard with a patrol. **3.** pass along regularly. —**pa·trol′man**, *n.*

pa′tron, *n.* **1.** influential or wealthy supporter. **2.** customer or client.

pa′tron·age, *n.* **1.** support by a patron. **2.** support of a business by customers. **3.** personal control of appointments to government jobs.

pa′tron·ize″, *v.t.,* **-ized, -izing**. **1.** be a customer of. **2.** treat with condescension.

pat'ter, *v.i.* 1. make a succession of light tapping sounds. 2. talk glibly or nonsensically. 3. walk quickly and lightly. —*n.* 4. glib, rapid speech. 5. quick pattering sound.

pat'tern, *n.* 1. decorative design. 2. ideal model. 3. model for making or copying. —*v.t.* 4. make after a pattern.

pat'ty, *n., pl.* **-ties.** 1. little pie. 2. flat, round cake of chopped food, e.g. hamburger.

pau'ci·ty, *n.* scarcity.

paunch, *n.* belly, esp. when large. —**paunch'y,** *adj.*

pau'per, *n.* poor person.

pause, *n.* 1. temporary stop. —*v.i.* 2. stop temporarily.

pave, *v.t.,* **paved, paving.** cover with hard material, as a road. —**pave'ment,** *n.*

pa·vil'ion, *n.* 1. light, open structure for entertainment or shelter. 2. large tent.

paw, *n.* 1. animal foot with nails or claws. —*v.t., v.i.* 2. scrape or strike with or as with paws.

pawn, *v.t.* 1. pledge or stake. 2. deposit as security for a loan. 3. state of being pawned. 4. chess piece of the lowest value.

pawn'bro'ker, *n.* person who lends money on pledged goods.

pay, *v.,* **paid, paying,** *n. v.t.* 1. give money to in return for goods or services. 2. satisfy, as a debt. —*v.i.* 3. give money in exchange. 4. yield a profit. 5. undergo punishment. —*n.* 6. wages or salary. 7. paid employment. 8. profit. —**pay·ee',** *n.* —**pay'er,** *n.* —**pay'ment,** *n.*

pay'a·ble, *adj.* 1. to be paid. 2. able to be paid.

pay'-off, *n.* 1. final payment. 2. final consequence.

pea, *n.* round, edible vegetable seed.

peace, *n.* 1. calm and quiet. 2. state of accord. 3. freedom from troubling emotions or thoughts. —**peace'a·ble, peace'ful,** *adj.* —**peace'time",** *n.*

peach, *n.* sweet juicy fruit.

pea'cock", *n.* male peafowl with long, brilliant tail feathers.

pea'fowl", *n.* large, domesticated Asiatic pheasant.

pea'hen", *n.* female peafowl.

peak, *n.* 1. pointed top. 2. top of a mountain or hill.

peaked, *adj.* 1. pointed. 2. (pē'kid) pale, sickly.

peal, *n.* 1. loud, prolonged ringing of bells. 2. set of tuned bells. 3. any loud, prolonged series of sounds. —*v.i.* 4. sound in a peal.

pea'nut", *n.* pod or edible seed of an annual herb.

pear, *n.* fleshy fruit related to the apple.

pearl, *n.* hard, lustrous gem formed within the shell of an oyster. —**pearl'y,** *adj.*

peas'ant, *n.* poor farm worker.

peat, *n.* highly organic soil dried for use as fuel.

peb'ble, *n.* small stone. —**peb'bly,** *adj.*

pe·can (pē kahn'), *n.* smooth-shelled nut from the hickory tree.

pec"ca·dil'lo, *n., pl.* **-loes, -los,** slight or minor offense.

pec'ca·ry, *n.* small pig-like animal.

peck, *v.t., v.i.* 1. jab repeatedly with a beak. —*v.t.* 2. dig with such jabs. —*n.* 3. dry measure of eight quarts.

pec'tin, *n.* plant substance used to thicken jellies, etc.

pec'u·late", *v.t.,* **-lated, -lating,** embezzle. —**pec"u·la'tion,** *n.*

pe·cu'liar, *adj.* 1. strange, odd. 2. unique. 3. distinctive, characteristic. —**pe·cu"li·ar'i·ty,** *n.* —**pe·cul'iar·ly,** *adv.*

pe·cu'ni·ar"y, *adj.* pertaining to money; monetary.

ped'a·gogue", *n.* teacher; scholar. Also, **ped'a·gog",** —**ped'a·go"gy,** *n.* —**ped" a·gog'ic, ped"a·gog'i·cal,** *adj.*

ped'al, *n.* 1. lever worked by the foot. —*v.t., v.i.* 2. move by means of pedals.

ped'ant, *n.* 1. person who makes a display of his learning. 2. unimaginative adherent to the letter of a doctrine. —**pe·dan'tic,** *adj.* —**ped'an·try,** *n.*

ped'dle, *v.t., v.i.,* **-dled, -dling.** sell on the street or road. —**ped'dler,** *n.*

ped'es·tal, *n.* base for a statue, etc.

pe·des'tri·an, *n.* 1. walker. —*adj.* 2. prosaic; commonplace.

pe"di·at'rics, *n.* study of care and diseases of children. —**pe"di·a·tri"cian,** *n.* —**pe"di·at'ric,** *adj.*

ped'i·gree", *n.* 1. certificate of ancestry. 2. ancestry, esp. when distinguished. —**ped'i·greed",** *adj.*

ped'i·ment, *n.* decorative triangular gable.

peek, *v.i.* 1. glance furtively. —*n.* 2. brief or furtive glance.

peel, *v.t.* 1. strip or remove. —*n.* 2. skin of fruit or vegetable. —**peel'ing,** *n.*

peen, *n.* wedge or ball-shaped end of a hammer.

peep, *v.i.* 1. peek. 2. utter a faint, shrill cry. —*n.* 3. quick look or glance. 4. faint sound.

peer, *v.i.* 1. look intently or searchingly. —*n.* 2. equal in rank or abilities. 3. nobleman. —**peer'age,** *n.*

peer'less, *adj.* without equal, supreme.

peeve, *n., v.t.,* **peeved, peeving,** *v.t.* 1. annoy, irritate. —*n.* 2. source of annoyance. 3. complaint. —**peev'ish,** *adj.*

peg, *n., v.t.,* **pegged, pegging.** *n.* 1. small hook, pin or fastener, esp. one fitting into a hole. —*v.t.* 2. fasten with pegs.

pe·jo'ra·tive, *adj.* disparaging, negative.

pe·koe (pē'kō), *n.* black Oriental tea.

pelf, *n.* money; riches.

pel'i·can, *n.* large bird with a pouched lower bill.

pel·la'gra, *n.* chronic disease caused by inadequate diet.

pel'let, *n.* small ball.

pell'-mell', *adv.* in a disorderly or hasty manner.

pel·lu·cid (pe lōō'sid), *adj.* clear or limpid; transparent.

pelt, *n.* 1. animal hide, esp. with fur. —*v.t.* 2. attack with blows or missiles. —*v.i.* 3. beat relentlessly, as rain.

pel'vis, *n.* basinlike bone in the lower part of the trunk. —pel'vic, *adj.*

pen, *n., v.t.,* penned, penning. *n.* 1. instrument for writing with ink. 2. small enclosure for animals or storage. —*v.t.* 3. write. 4. enclose.

pe'nal, *adj.* pertaining to punishment. —pe'nal·ize'', *v.t.*

pen·al'ty, *n., pl.* -ties. 1. punishment. 2. disadvantage, hardship.

pen'ance, *n.* 1. self-imposed punishment for sin. 2. sacrament of confession of sin.

pen'chant, *n.* strong inclination; liking.

pen'cil, *n.* 1. cylindrical implement containing graphite for writing, etc. —*v.t.* 2. paint, draw or write.

pend'ant, *n.* 1. hanging ornament, e.g. an earring. 2. duplicate or balancing feature.

pend'ent, *adj.* hanging; overhanging.

pend'ing, *adj.* 1. undecided; imminent. —*prep.* 2. while awaiting; until.

pen'du·lum, *n.* freely swinging suspended weight.

pen'e·trate'', *v.t.* -trated, -trating. 1. enter. 2. permeate. 3. understand. 4. affect deeply. —pen'e·tra·ble, *adj.* —pen''e·tra'tion, *n.*

pen'guin, *n.* short-legged, flightless aquatic bird.

pen''i·cil'lin, *n.* antibiotic produced by certain molds.

pen·in'su·la, *n.* land body surrounded by water on three sides.

pe'nis, *n.* male organ of copulation and urination.

pen'i·tent, *adj.* 1. feeling repentance. —*n.* 2. repentant person. —pen'i·tence, *n.* —pen''i·ten'tial, *adj.*

pen''i·ten'tia·ry, *n.* prison.

pen'knife'', *n.* small pocketknife; jackknife.

pen'man, *n., pl.* -men. person skilled in using a pen. —pen'man·ship'', *n.*

pen'nant, *n.* 1. small flag for signaling. 2. flag of championship.

pen'ny, *n., pl.* -nies. smallest denomination of currency. —pen'ni·less, *adj.*

pe·nol'o·gy, *n.* study of criminal punishment. —pe·nol'o·gist, *n.* —pe''no·log'i·cal, *adj.*

pen'sion, *n.* 1. fixed, periodic payment to a retiree. —*v.t.* 2. give a pension to. —pen'sion·er, *n.*

pen'sive, *adj.* sadly or dreamily thoughtful;quiet.

pent, *adj.* confined; shut up.

pen'ta·gon'', *n.* polygon of five sides.

pen·tam'e·ter, *n.* verse line of five metrical feet.

Pen·ta·teuch (pen'ta tōōk''), *n.* first five books of the Old Testament.

pent'house'', *n.* habitable structure on the roof of a building.

pent'-up', *adj.* confined, as emotions.

pen·ul'ti·mate, *adj.* next to the last.

pe·num'bra, *n.* partial shadow. —pe·num'bral, *adj.*

pe·nu'ri·ous, *adj.* 1. miserly; stingy. 2. impoverished. —pen'u·ry, *n.*

pe'on, *n.* unskilled worker, esp. one in bondage. —pe'on·age, *n.*

pe'o·ny, *n., pl.* -nies, perennial garden plant with large colorful flowers.

peo'ple, *n., v.t.,* -pled, -pling. *n.* 1. humanity generally. 2. random group of persons. 3. peoples, national, cultural, or racial group. —*v.t.* 4. populate.

pep, *Informal. n.* 1. energy, vigor. —*v.t.* 2. pep up, make lively; energize. —pep'py, *adj. adj.*

pep'per, *n.* 1. pungent condiment from an East Indian plant. 2. hot or mild fruit used as a condiment vegetable. —*v.t.* 3. season with pepper. 4. pelt with missiles. 5. sprinkle as with pepper. —pep'per·y, *adj.*

pep'per·mint'', *n.* aromatic herb used as a flavoring.

pep'sin, *n.* stomach enzyme which digests proteins.

pep'tic, *adj.* pertaining to digestion; digestive.

per, *prep.* through; by means of; according to.

per·am'bu·late'', *v.i.* -ated, -ating, walk about; stroll. —per·am''bu·la'tion, *n.*

per·cale', *n.* smooth, closely woven cotton.

per·ceive', *v.t.* 1. become aware of. 2. apprehend or understand. —per·ceiv'a·ble, per·cep'ti·ble, *adj.* —per·cep'tion, *n.*

per·cent', *n.* part in a hundred.

per·cent'age, *n.* 1. proportion per hundred. 2. allowance, commission, or rate of interest.

per·cep'tive, *adj.* 1. pertaining to perception. 2. understanding; discerning.

perch, *n.* 1. roost for birds. 2. high spot. 3. freshwater food fish. —*v.t., v.i.* 4. set or rest as on a perch.

per·chance', *adv.* perhaps.

per′co·late″, v.t., v.i. -lated, -lating. filter. —**per″co·la′tion**, n.

per·cus′sion, n. 1. hard, sharp impact. 2. musical instruments plucked or struck. —**per·cus′sive**, adj.

per·di·em, (pər dē′əm), by the day.

per·di′tion, n. damnation.

per″e·gri·na′tion, n. travel from one place to another. —**per′e·gri·nate″**, v.i.

per·emp′to·ry, adj. 1. giving no opportunity to refuse or deny. 2. imperative. —**per·emp′to·ri·ly**, adv.

per·en′ni·al, adj. 1. enduring. 2. lasting more than two years. —n. 3. plant growing every year. —**per·en·ni′al·ly**, adv.

per·fect, adj. (pər′fəkt) 1. flawless and complete. 2. unmodified. 3. *Grammar.* denoting completed action. —v.t. (pərfekt′) 4. make perfect. —**per′fect·ly**, adj. —**per·fec′tion**, n.

per·fec′tion·ist, n. person who demands perfection.

per′fi·dy, n., pl. -dies, treachery; faithlessness. —**per·fid′i·ous**, adj.

per′fo·rate″, v.t., -rated, -rating. pierce through.

per·force′, adv. necessarily.

per·form′, v.t. 1. carry out; execute. 2. enact, play, etc. for an audience. —v.i. 3. appear in a play, concert, etc. —**per·form′ance**, n. —**per·form′er**, n.

per·fume, n., v.t., -fumed, -fuming, n. (pər′fyōōm) 1. sweet odor; fragrance. 2. sweet-smelling liquid for scenting. —v.t. (pər fyōōm′) 3. scent.

per·func′to·ry, adj. routine and unenthusiastic. —**per·func′to·ri·ly**, adv. —**per·func′tori·ness**, n.

per·haps′, adv. maybe, possibly.

per·i·gee (per′i jē″), n. nearest point of an orbit to the earth.

per″i·he′li·on, n. nearest point of an orbit to the sun.

per′il, n. 1. danger. 2. source of danger. —**per′il·ous**, adj.

pe·rim′e·ter, n. outer boundary.

pe′ri·od, n. 1. division or extent of time. 2. end; stop. 3. punctuation point at the end of a declarative sentence.

pe″ri·od′ic, adj. intermittently or regularly recurring.

pe″ri·od′i·cal, adj. 1. periodic. 2. publication appearing at regular intervals. —**pe″ri·od′i·cal·ly**, adv.

pe·riph′er·y, n., pl. -eries, 1. boundary of a rounded figure. 2. outer limits; border. —**pe·riph′er·al**, adj.

per′i·scope, n. optical instrument for viewing around an obstruction with prisms or mirrors.

per′ish, v.i. 1. die, esp. from privation or violence. 2. decay. —**per′ish·a·ble**, adj.

per·i·to·ni·tis (per″i to ni′tis), n. inflammation of the abdominal lining.

per′i·win′kle, n. 1. edible snail. 2. trailing evergreen plant.

per′jure, v.t., -jured, -juring. make guilty of perjury. —**per′jur·er**, n. —**per′jured**, adj.

per′ju·ry, n., pl. -ries. 1. lying under oath. 2. lie so uttered. —**per·ju′ri·ous**, adj.

perk, v.i. 1. become lively or vigorous. —v.t. 2. raise jauntily, as the head. —**perk′y**, adj.

per′ma·nent, adj. existing always. —**per′ma·nence**, **per′ma·nen·cy**, n. —**per′ma·nent·ly**, adj.

per′me·ate″, v.t., -ated, -ating, v.t. 1. penetrate. 2. be diffused through. —v.i. 3. become diffused. —**per″me·a′tion**, n. —**per′me·a·ble**, adj.

per·mis′sive, adj. 1. granting permission. 2. indulgent; lenient.

per·mit, v.t.c., -mitted, -mitting, n. v.t. (pərmit′) 1. allow. 2. tolerate. 3. give opportunity for. —n. (pər′mit) 4. written permission; license. —**per·mis′sion**, n. —**per·mis′si·ble**, adj.

per″mu·ta′tion, n. change, alteration.

per·ni′cious, adj. injurious, hurtful.

per″o·ra′tion, n. concluding part of a speech.

per·ox′ide, n. 1. oxide containing a large amount of oxygen. —v.t. 2. bleach with a peroxide, esp. the hair.

per″pen·dic′u·lar, adj. 1. vertical. 2. meeting another line at a right angle. —n. 3. perpendicular plane or line.

per′pe·trate″, v.t., -trated, -trating, commit; be guilty of. —**per″pe·tra′tion**, n. —**per′pe·tra″tor**, n.

per·pet′u·al, adj. 1. permanent. 2. unceasing; constant. —**per·pet′u·al·ly**, adv. —**per·pet′u·ate″** v.t. —**per·pet″u·a′tion**, n.

per″pe·tu′i·ty, n. endless duration.

per·plex′, v.t. bewilder. —**per·plex′i·ty**, n.

per′quis·ite, n. benefit added to regular salary.

per se (pər sā′), by, of, or in itself.

per′se·cute″, v.t., -cuted, -cuting, continually harass or oppress. —**per″se·cu′tion**, n. —**per′se·cu″tor**, n.

per″se·vere′, v.t., -vered, -vering, persist in spite of obstacles. —**per″se·ver′ance**, n.

per·sim′mon, n. astringent, edible North American fruit.

per·sist′, v.i. 1. continue resolutely. 2. last; endure. —**per·sist′ence**, n. —**per·sist′ent**, adj. —**per·sist′ent·ly**, adv.

per′son, n. 1. human being; individual. 2. personality. 3. one's body.

per′son·a·ble, adj. 1. pleasing in appearance. 2. sociable.

per'son·age, *n.* person of distinction or note.

per'son·al, *adj.* 1. pertaining to one individual. 2. pertaining to the body and its care, clothing, etc. —**per'son·al·ly,** *adv.* —**per'son·al·ize",** *v.t.*

per"son·al'i·ty, *n., pl.* **-ties.** 1. distinctive personal character. 2. personally disparaging remark. 3. notable person.

per·so·na non gra·ta (per sō'nə non grat'ə), unwelcome or unacceptable person.

per·son'i·fy, *v.t.,* **-fied, -fying.** 1. attribute personal character to. 2. embody; typify. —**per·son"i·fi·ca'tion,** *n.*

per"son·nel', *n.* employees of an organization.

per·spec'tive, *n.* 1. technique of three-dimensional representation. 2. extended view. 3. basis for interpretation.

per"spi·ca'cious, *adj.* acutely perceptive; discerning. —**per"spi·cac'i·ty,** *n.*

per·spire', *v.i.* sweat. —**per"spi·ra'tion,** *n.*

per·suade', *v.t.,* **-suaded, -suading,** 1. prevail on by argument. 2. induce belief in; convince. —**per·sua'sive,** *adj.*

per·sua'sion, *n.* 1. process or act of persuading. 2. conviction or belief, opinion.

pert, *adj.* 1. bold; saucy, impudent. 2. lively, sprightly.

per·tain', *v.i.* have reference to; relate.

per"ti·na'cious, *adj.* holding firmly to an opinion or purpose. —**perti·nac'i·ty,** *n.*

per'ti·nent, *adj.* relevant; applicable. —**per'ti·nence, per'ti·nen·cy,** *n.*

per·turb', *v.t.* greatly disturb in mind; upset. —**per·tur·ba'tion,** *n.*

pe·ruse', *v.t.* read or survey, esp. with thoroughness. —**pe·ru'sal,** *n.*

per·vade', *v.t.,* **-vaded, -vading.** extend or spread throughout; permeate. —**per·va'sive,** *adj.*

per·verse', *adj.* 1. abnormal; corrupt. 2. stubbornly contrary; obstinate. —**per·verse'ly,** *adv.* —**per·ver'si·ty,** *n.*

per·vert', *n.* 1. perverted person, esp. sexually. —*v.t.* 2. deviate from the proper or right course of action. 3. misapply; misconstrue; distort. —**per·ver'sion,** *n.*

pe'so, *n.* monetary unit of Mexico, etc.

pes'si·mism", *n.* disposition toward the least favorable interpretation or expectation. —**pes'si·mist,** *n.* —**pessi·mis'tic,** *adj.*

pest, *n.* troublesome person or thing; nuisance.

pes'ter, *v.t.* annoy.

pes'ti·cide", *n.* insecticide.

pes'ti·lence, *n.* deadly epidemic or disease; plague. —**pes'ti·lent,** *adj.*

pes'tle, *n.* implement for grinding or crushing (with a mortar).

pet, *n., adj., v.t.,* **petted, petting.** *n.* 1. tamed animal kept for pleasure. 2. darling; favorite. —*v.t.* 3. indulge; pamper. 4. stroke or fondle affectionately. —*adj.* 5. treated lovingly.

pet'al, *n.* colored leaf of a flower.

pe·tite (pə tēt'), *adj.* small or tiny: used in reference to women.

pe·ti'tion *n.* 1. request or entreaty, esp. when written. —*v.i.* 2. present a petition; ask for. —**pe·ti'tion·er,** *n.*

pet'rel, *n.* small sea bird.

pet'ri·fy", *v.,* **-fied, -fying.** *v.t.* 1. turn into stone; stiffen. 2. paralyze or stupefy with horror, wonder, etc. —*v.i.* 3. become petrified.

pet"ro·chem'i·cal, *n.* chemical derived from petroleum.

pe·tro·le'um, *n.* natural oily liquid found underground.

pe·trol'o·gy, *n.* study of rocks.

pet'ti·coat", *n.* skirt worn under a dress.

pet'tish, *adj.* peevish; petulant.

pet'ty, *adj.,* **-tier, -tiest.** 1. of little importance; trivial. 2. narrow-minded; mean. —**pet'ti·ness,** *n.*

pet'u·lant, *adj.* marked by impatient irritation; irritable, peevish.

pe·tu'nia, *n.* annual garden plant with bright funnelshaped flowers.

pew, *n.* enclosed church bench.

pe'wee, *n.* any of various small birds.

pew'ter, *n.* alloy composed primarily of tin.

pey·o·te, (pā ō'tē), *n.* hallucinogenic drug derived from the mescal cactus.

pha'lanx, *n., pl.* **planxes, phalanges,** 1. body or group in formation, e.g. troops. 2. any of the bones of the fingers or toes of mammals.

phal'lus, *n., pl.* **phalli,** 1. penis. 2. symbolic representation of the phallus. —**phal'lic,** *adj.*

phan'tasm, *n.* apparition; illusion.

phan·tas"ma·go'ria, *n.* succession of imagined things.

phan'tom, *n.* insubstantial image; dreamlike apparition.

Phar·aoh, (fa'ro), *n.* ancient Egyptian ruler.

phar'i·see", *n.* self-righteous person.

phar"ma·ceu'ti·cal, *adj.* of or pertaining to pharmacy. Also, **phar"ma·ceu'tic.**

phar"ma·col'o·gy, *n.* study of drugs, esp. for medical use. —**phar"ma·col'o·gist,** *n.*

phar'ma·cy, *n., pl.* **-cies.** 1. practice of preparing medicines. 2. drug store. —**phar'ma·cist,** *n.*

phar'ynx, *n., pl.* **pharynges, pharynxes.** cavity that connects mouth and nasal passages with the esophagus. —**pha·ryn'ge·al,** *adj.*

phase, *n.* **1.** stage of a process. **2.** aspect. —*v.t.* **3.** introduce or withdraw in stages.

pheas'ant, *n.* large, long-tailed, brightly colored game bird.

phe''no·bar'bi·tol, *n.* white powder used as sedative and hypnotic.

phe·nom'e·nal, *n.* **1.** amazing. **2.** pertaining to phenomena.

phe·nom'e·non, *n.*, *pl.* **-na, -nons. 1.** apparent occurrence, circumstance, or fact. **2.** extraordinary person or thing.

phi'al, *n.* vial.

phi·lan'der, *v.i.* (of a man) make love with no serious intentions, —**phi·lan'der·er**, *n.*

phi·lan'thro·py, *n.*, *pl.* **-pies. 1.** love of mankind. **2.** charitable act, work, or organization. —**phil''an·throp'ic, phil''an·throp'i·cal**, *adj.* —**phi·lan'thro·pist**, *n.*

phi·lat'e·ly, *n.* collection and study of postage stamps. —**phi·lat'e·list**, *n.*

phil'har·mon'ic, *adj.* music-loving.

phi·lis'tine, *n.* person indifferent to cultural matters.

phi·lol'o·gy, *n.* linguistics. —**phi·lol'o·gist**, *n.*

phi·los'o·pher, *n.* **1.** reflective thinker; **2.** scholar trained in philosophy. **3.** person who meets difficulties calmly.

phi·los'o·phy, *n.*, *pl.* **-phies. 1.** study of the fundamental truths of life and the universe. **2.** system of philosophical concepts. —**phil''o·soph'i·cal, phil''o·soph'ic**, *adj.* —**phi·los'o·phize''**, *v.i.*

phlegm, (flem), *n.* thick mucus secreted in the nose and throat.

phleg·ma'tic, *adj.* stolid, impassive; apathetic.

phlox, *n.* garden plant with colorful flowers.

pho'bi·a, *n.* persistent and irrational morbid fear.

phoe·be (fē'bē), *n.* small eastern American bird.

phoe·nix (phē'nicks), *n.* mythical bird said to rise from its own ashes.

phone, *n.*, *v.t.*, **phoned, phoning. 1.** telephone. —*v.t.* **2.** make a phone call to.

pho·net'ics, *n.* study of speech sounds. —**pho·net'ic**, *adj.*

pho'no·graph'', *n.* machine for playing records.

pho'ny, *n.*, *adj.*, **-nier, -niest**, *Informal.* *n.* **1.** fake person or thing.—*adj.* **2.** fake; counterfeit.

phos'phate, *n.* chemical salt often used in fertilizers,

phos''pho·res'cence, *n.* luminescence without sensible heat. —**phos''pho·res'cent**, *adj.*

phos'pho·rus, *n.* solid nonmetallic element found in bones, nerves, etc. —**phos·phor'ic, phos'pho·rous**, *adj.*

pho'to, *n.*, *pl.* **-tos**, photograph.

pho''to·e'lec·tric, *adj.* pertaining to electric effects resulting from light.

pho'to·en·grav''ing, *n.* process of producing an etched printing plate from a photograph or drawing. —**pho'to·en·grave''**, *v.t.*

pho''to·gen'ic, *adj.* suitable for being photographed.

pho'to·graph'', *n.* **1.** picture taken by photography. —*v.i.* **2.** take a photograph. —**pho·tog'ra·pher**, *n.*

pho·tog'ra·phy, *n.* process of producing images on treated surfaces by the action of light. —**pho''to·graph'ic**, *adj.*

pho''to·sen'si·tive, *adj.* sensitive or sensitized to light.

pho''to·syn'the·sis, *n.* process by which chlorophyll-containing plants exposed to sunlight produce carbohydrates.

phrase, *n.*, *v.t.*, **phrased, phrasing. 1.** sequence of words conveying a thought. **2.** brief expression or remark. **3.** unit of musical composition. —*v.t.* **4.** express in a certain way.

phra''se·ol'o·gy, *n.* **1.** manner of speaking. **2.** collective expressions or phrases.

phre·net'ic, *adj.* delirious.

phre·nol'o·gy, *n.* study that infers personal characteristics from the shape of the skull. —**phre·nol'o·gist**, *n.*

phy'lum, *n.*, *pl.* **-la.** major division of plant and animal classes.

phys'ic, *n.* medicine, esp. a purgative.

phys'i·cal, *adj.* **1.** pertaining to the body. **2.** pertaining to matter or the material world. **3.** pertaining to physics. —*n.* **4.** medical examination. —**phys'i·cal·ly**, *adv.*

phy·si'cian, *n.* medical doctor.

phys'ics, *n.* science dealing with motion, matter, energy, and force. —**phys'i·cist**, *n.*

phys''i·og'no·my, *n.*, *pl.* **-mies.** facial appearance.

phys''i·og'ra·phy, *n.* science of the earth's surface.

phys''i·ol'o·gy, *n.* science of the functioning of living matter and beings. —**phys''i·o·log'i·cal**, *adj.* —**phys''i·ol'o·gist**, *n.*

phys''i·o·ther'a·py, *n.* treatment of disease by physical means, e.g. exercise, massage, etc.

phy·sique (fə zēk'), *n.* physical constitution of the body; build.

pi, (pī), *n.* Greek letter π, symbol for the value 3.1416, ratio of circumference to diameter.

pi''a·nis'si·mo, *adj* or *adv. Music.* very soft.

pi·an'o, *n.*, *pl.* **-anos**, *adj.*, *adv. n.* **1.** Also, **pi·an''o·for'te**, percussive, musical keyboard instrument with steel strings struck by hammers! —*adj.* **2.** soft. —*adv.* **3.** softly. —**pi·an'ist**, *n.*

pi·az′za, *n.* veranda or porch.

pi′ca, *n.* measure of printing type equal to about a sixth of an inch.

pic′′a·yune′, *adj.* insignificant; trivial; petty.

pic′ca·lil′li, *n.* spicy vegetable relish.

pic′co·lo′′, *n., pl.* -**los**, small shrill flute.

pick, *v.t.* **1.** choose or select. **2.** gather, e.g. flowers. **3.** separate or pull apart. **4.** pierce with a pointed instrument. **5.** provoke, e.g. pick a fight. —*n.* **6.** choice; selection. **7.** Also, **pick′ax**, **pick′axe**, sharp tool for breaking rock. —**pick′er**, *n.*

pick′er·el, *n.* small pike.

pick′et, *n.* **1.** protestor stationed by a striking labor union. **2.** body or group of soldiers on lookout. **3.** pointed fence with pickets. —*v.i.* **4.** serve as a picket.

pick′ings, *n.* **1.** gleanings. **2.** rewards; spoils.

pick′le, *n., v.t.,* -**led**, -**ling**, *n.* **1.** cucumber cured in spiced vinegar. **2.** any food preserved in a pickling solution. **3.** *Informal.* difficult predicament; bind. —*v.t.* **4.** preserve in brine or vinegar.

pick′pock′′et, *n.* thief who steals from pockets.

pick′up, *n.* **1.** acceleration; energy. **2.** revival of action. **3.** small open-body truck for hauling.

pick′y, *adj.* fussy, finicky.

pic′nic, *n., v.i.,* -**nicked**, -**nicking**, *n.* **1.** outing with an outdoor meal. —*v.t.* go on a picnic. —**pic′nick·er**, *n.*

pic′ture, *n., v.t.,* -**tured**, -**turing**, *n.* **1.** painting, drawing, photograph, etc. **2.** motion picture. —*v.t.* **3.** represent in a picture. **4.** conceive; visualize. —**pic·tor′i·al**, *adj.*

pic′′tur·esque′, *adj.* **1.** charming; quaint. **2.** striking; vivid.

pie, *n.* baked dish of pastry crust and filling, e.g. meat, fruit, etc.

pie′bald′′, *adj.* marked by patches of different colors.

piece, *n., v.t.,* -**pieced**, **piecing**, *n.* **1.** part or single portion. **2.** artistic creation. **3.** firearm. —*v.t.* **4.** join or repair from pieces.

piece′meal′′, *adv.* **1.** piece by piece. **2.** into fragments.

pied (pīd), *adj.* many-colored; variegated.

pier, *n.* **1.** massive support. **2.** structure loading and unloading vessels.

pierce, *v.t.,* **pierced**, **piercing**, **1.** penetrate into or through. **2.** make a hole into.

pi′e·ty, *n.* religious dutifulness; devoutness.

pig, *n.* **1.** swine, esp. young. **2.** oblong metal casting.

pi′geon, *n.* short-legged, stout-bodied bird.

pi′geon·hole′′, *n., v.t.,* -**holed**, -**holing**, *n.* **1.** small compartment, e.g. in a

desk. —*v.t.* **2.** place in a pigeonhole; classify.

pig′ment, *n.* coloring matter. —**pig′′men·ta′tion**, *n.*

pig′tail, *n.* tight braid of back hair.

pike, *n.* **1.** large, slender freshwater fish. **2.** long wooden spear. **3.** highway.

pik′er, *n. Informal.* person who does things in a small or cheap way.

pi·laf (pē′laf′′), *n.* seasoned rice dish.

pi·las′ter, *n.* column that projects slightly from a wall.

pile, *n., v.t.,* **piled**, **piling**. *n.* **1.** heap. **2.** support driven into the ground. **3.** short standing fibers, as in a rug. **4.** nuclear reactor. **5. piles**, hemorrhoids —*v.t.* **6.** put in a pile. —*v.t., v.i.* **7.** accumulate.

pil′fer, *v.i., v.t.* steal.

pil′grim, *n.* traveler in foreign lands, esp. to a holy place. —**pil′grim·age**, *n.*

pill, *n.* medicine in tablet or capsule form.

pil′lage, *v.t.,* -**laged**, -**laging**. loot; plunder.

pil′lar, *n.* masonry column.

pill′box′′, *n.* **1.** low shelter against gunfire. **2.** small container for pills.

pil′lory, *n., pl.* -**ries**. wooden frame with head and arm holes for public punishment.

pil′low, *n.* cushion filled with feathers, etc. for support, esp. of the head. —**pil′low·case′′**, *n.*

pi′lot, *n.* **1.** person who guides a ship or airplane. —*v.t.* **2.** steer; guide. —*adj.* **3.** experimental.

pi·men′to, *n., pl.* -**tos**. **1.** dried fruit of a tropical tree; allspice. **2.** pimiento.

pi·mien′to, *n., pl.* -**tos**. sweet, red, garden pepper.

pimp, *n.* person who finds clients for a prostitute.

pim′ple, *n.* small, inflamed swelling on the skin. —**pim′ply**, *adj.*

pin, *n., v.t.,* **pinned**, **pinning**, *n.* **1.** slender, pointed fastener. **2.** piece of jewelry fastened to a garment. **3.** wooden target piece in bowling. —*v.t.* **4.** fasten with a pin. **5.** hold tight, bind.

pin′a·fore′′, *n.* sleeveless dress or apron, esp. for a child.

pince·nez (pans′nā′′), *n.* eyeglasses held on the nose by a pinching spring.

pin′cers, *n.* gripping tool with two handles.

pinch, *v.t.* **1.** squeeze, e.g. with the thumb and forefinger. **2.** economize. **3.** steal. **4.** arrest. —*n.* **5.** act or instance of pinching. **6.** tiny amount.

pinch′hit′′, *v.i.,* -**hit**, -**hitting**, substitute for someone else. —**pinch′hit′ter**, *n.*

pine, *n., v.i.,* **pined**, **pining**, *v.i.* **1.** yearn, esp. painfully. **2.** gradually fail in health from grief. —*n.* **3.** cone-bearing evergreen tree with needle-like leaves.

pine'ap''ple, *n.* tropical plant with a juicy, edible fruit.

pin'feath''er, *n.* feather just beginning to develop.

pin·ion (pin'yən), *n.* **1.** end of a bird's wing. **2.** small gear wheel. —*v.t.* **3.** restrain; bind.

pink, *n.* **1.** light red. **2.** colorful, showy garden flower. **3.** highest condition of health. —*adj.* **4.** of the color pink.

pin'na·cle, *n.* highest part or position.

pi·noch·le, (pē'nuk il''), *n.* game played with forty-eight cards.

pint, *n.* **1.** unit of liquid measure equal to 16 fluid ounces or half a quart. **2.** unit of dry measure equal to half a quart.

pin'to, *n., pl.* **-tos.** horse with white and brown patches.

pin'up'', *n.* picture of a beautiful man or woman, esp. unclothed.

pin'wheel'', *n.* toy with a wheel that spins on the end of a stick.

pi''o·neer', *n.* **1.** early settler or adventurer. **2.** first person to do something. —*v.i.* **3.** prepare a way for others.

pi'ous, *adj.* **1.** devout. **2.** sacred. —*pi'ous·ly,* *adv.* —*pi'ous·ness, n.*

pipe, *n., v.t.,* **piped, piping,** *n.* **1.** tube for carrying gas, water, etc. **2.** tube with a bowl at one end for smoking tobacco. **3.** tube used in a musical instrument. —*v.t.* **4.** carry by pipe. —*pi'per, n.* —*pipe'line'', n.*

pip'ing, *n.* **1.** pipes; plumbing. **2.** music of pipes. **3.** material to trim edges.

pip'pin, *n.* kind of yellowish apple.

pi·quant (pē'kənt), *adj.* **1.** pleasantly sharp; pungent. **2.** provocative; charming. —*pi'quan·cy, n.*

pique, *n., v.t.,* **piqued, piquing,** *n.* **1.** irritation; resentment. —*v.t.* **2.** arouse resentment in, esp. by wounding pride. **3.** provoke or incite.

pi'ra·cy, *n., pl.* **-cies.** **1.** robbery at sea or in the air. **2.** unauthorized use of copyrighted or patented material. —*pi'rate, n., v.t.*

pir''ou·ette', *v.i.,* **-etted, -etting.** *n. v.i.* **1.** whirl about on one foot or on the toes, esp. in ballet. —*n.* **2.** such a movement.

pis·ca·to·ri·al (pis''kə to'bi al), *adj.* pertaining to fishing.

pis·ta'chi·o'', *n., pl.* **-os.** nut with an edible greenish seed.

pis'til, *n.* seed-bearing organ in a flower.

pis'tol, *n.* small hand-carried firearm.

pis'ton, *n.* reciprocating disk moved by the pressure of steam, combustion gas, etc. in a cylinder.

pit *n., v.t.,* **pitted, pitting,** *n.* **1.** hole in the ground. **2.** cavity or hollow in the body. **3.** front part of the main floor in a theater. **4.** stone or seed of a fruit.

—*v.t.* **5.** set against another. **6.** remove the pit from.

pitch, *v.t.* **1.** set up, as a tent. **2.** throw or toss. **3.** set at a certain level or point. —*v.i.* **4.** fall or plunge. —*n.* **5.** height. **6.** slope. **7.** musical tone. **8.** sticky substance from coal tar or pine bark. **9.** act or instance of pitching.

pitch'blende'', *n.* mineral that is the principal source of radium and uranium.

pitch'er, *n.* **1.** spouted container for liquids. **2.** one who pitches.

pitch'fork'', *n.* large, sharp-pointed fork for pitching hay.

pit'e·ous, *adj.* pitiful; pathetic.

pit'fall'', *n.* snare; hidden difficulty.

pith, *n.* **1.** loose spongy tissue. **2.** essence; gist. —*pith'y, adj.*

pit'i·a·ble, *adj.* **1.** deserving pity. **2.** contemptible. —*pit'i·a·bly, adv.*

pit'i·ful, *adj.* deserving pity. **2.** feeling pity. —*pit'i·ful·ly, adv.* —*pit'i·ful·ness, n.*

pit'tance, *n.* small portion or amount.

pi·tu'i·tar''y, *n.* pertaining to a gland at the base of the brain.

pity, *n., pl.* **pities,** *v.t.,* **pitied, pitying,** *n.* **1.** sympathy for wretchedness. **2.** cause for regret. —*v.t.* **3.** feel pity for. —*pit'i·less, adj.* —*pit'i·less·ly, adv.*

piv'ot, *n.* **1.** point or object for turning. —*v.i.* **2.** turn around a point.

pix'y, *n., pl.* **pixies.** fairy; mischievous sprite. Also, **pix'ie.**

piz'za, *n.* flat pie covered with a spiced mixture of tomato sauce, cheese, etc.

plac'ard, *n.* posted public notice.

pla'cate, *v.t.,* **-cated, -cating.** appease; pacify. —*pla'ca·ble, adj.* —*pla·ca'tion, n.*

place, *n., v.t.,* **placed, placing,** *n.* **1.** particular point in space. **2.** function. **3.** social position. **4.** stead; lieu. —*v.t.* **5.** put in a place. **6.** identify; recognize. —*place'ment, n.*

pla·cen'ta, *n.* uterine organ which nourishes the fetus.

plac'er, *n.* gravel containing gold particles.

plac'id, *adj.* serene; peaceful. —*plac'id·ly, adv.* —*pla·cid'i·ty, n.*

plack'et, *n.* slit in a garment.

pla'gi·a·rize'', *v.t.,* **-rized, -rizing.** appropriate wrongfully, as another's writings. —*pla'gi·a·rism'', n.* —*pla'gi·a·rist, n.*

plague, *n., v.t.,* **plagued, plaguing,** *n.* **1.** pestilence. **2.** affliction, vexation; irritation. —*v.t.* **3.** trouble; annoy.

plaid, *n.* **1.** woolen garment with a pattern of multi-colored crossbars. —*adj.* **2.** such a pattern.

plain, *adj.* **1.** evident; obvious. **2.** candid. **3.** unpretentious. **4.** simple, uncomplicated. **5.** homely. —*n.* **6.** flat, open

area or space of ground. —**plain′ly**, *adv.*

plain′tiff, *n.* complaining party in a civil case.

plain′tive, *adj.* melancholy, sad.

plait, *n., v.t.* 1. braid. 2. pleat.

plan, *n., v.t.*, **planned, planning**. *n.* 1. drawing or diagram. 2. intended scheme or method. —*v.t.* 3. make a plan of. —**plan′ner**, *n.*

plane, *n., adj., v.*, **planed, planing**. *n.* 1. flat surface. 2. level, e.g. of experience, attainment, etc. 3. airplane. 4. bladed tool for smoothing wood. —*adj.* 5. flat, level. —*v.t.* 6. smooth or shape with a plane. —*v.i.* 7. glide.

plan′et, *n.* solid celestial body that revolves around the sun. —**plan′e·tar″y**, *n.*

plan″e·tar′i·um, *n.* optical device which projects images of celestial bodies on a dome.

plank, *n.* long slab of lumber.

plant, *n.* 1. any of the vegetable group of organisms. 2. buildings and equipment of a business. —*v.t.* 3. put in the ground to grow. 4. put plants in. —**plant′er**, *n.*

plan·ta′tion, *n.* estate esp. for farming, etc.

plaque, *n.* decorative or commemorative tablet.

plas′ma, *n.* liquid element of blood or lymph.

plas′ter, *n.* 1. composition applied to walls, etc. 2. medicinal dressing. —*v.t.* 3. treat or cover with plaster.

plas′tic, *n.* 1. molded synthetic material.—*adj.* 2. capable of being molded. 3. characterized or produced by molding. —**plas·tic′i·ty,** *n.*

plate, *n., v.t.*, **plated, plating**. *n.* 1. thin, flat piece of material. 2. shallow dish from which food is served and eaten. 3. silver or gold ware. 4. denture. —*v.t.* 5. coat with metal.

pla·teau′, *n.* large, raised plain.

plat′form, *n.* 1. raised floor area. 2. declaration of political principles.

plat′i·num, *n.* valuable, silver-white metallic element.

plat′i·tude″, *n.* trite, pompous, or self-righteous remark. —**plat″i·tu′di·nous,** *adj.*

pla·ton′ic, *adj.* 1. spiritual; idealistic. 2. pertaining to close, non-sexual love.

pla·toon′, *n.* small military unit.

plat′ter, *n.* large, shallow serving dish.

plat′y·pus, *n.* small Australian aquatic mammal.

plau′dit, *n.* burst of applause.

plau′si·ble, *adj.* seemingly true or believable. —**plau″si·bil′i·ty,** *n.* **plau′si·bly**, *adv.*

play, *n.* 1. dramatic composition. 2. recreational activity. 3. fun; pleasure. 4. maneuver, as in sports. 5. free motion. —*v.t.* 6. participate in a play or game. 7. perform on a musical instrument. —*v.i.* 8. amuse onself. 9. move freely. —**play′er**, *n.* —**play′ful**, *adj.*

play′pen, *n.* portable enclosed play area for a baby.

play′thing, *n.* toy.

play′wright, *n.* writer of plays.

pla′za, *n.* 1. public square. 2. shopping center.

plea, *n.* 1. appeal. 2. acknowledgment of denial of guilt.

plead, *v.*, **pleaded** or **plead, pleading**, *v.i.* 1. appeal earnestly. 2. make allegations in court. 3. argue a case in court. —*v.t.* 4. allege in excuse or justification.

pleas′ant, *adj.* agreeable; pleasing. —**pleas′ant·ly,** *adv.*

pleas′an·try, *n., pl.* **-tries,** humorous or agreeable remark.

please, *v.*, **pleased, pleasing**, *v.t.* 1. give satisfaction or pleasure to. —*v.i.* 2. give pleasure. —*interj.* 3. will you kindly? —**pleas′ing·ly,** *adv.*

pleas′ure, *n.* 1. enjoyment. 3. will or desire. —**pleas′ur·a·ble,** *adj.*

pleat, *n.* 1. double fold in cloth. —*v.t.* 2. fold in pleats.

ple·be′ian (ple bē′ən), *adj.* 1. of or pertaining to the common people. 2. common; vulgar. —*n.* 3. plebeian person.

pleb″i·scite″, *n.* direct vote by the people.

plec′trum, *n.* pick for a guitar, etc.

pledge, *n., v.*, **pledged, pledging**, *n.* 1. solemn promise or oath. 2. property given in security for a loan. —*v.t.* 3. bind or vow by a pledge. 4. stake.

ple′na·ry, *adj.* full; complete.

plen″i·po·ten′ti·ar″y, *n., pl.* **-aries,** diplomat having full authority.

plen′i·tude″, *n.* fullness.

plen′ty, *n.* abundant supply. —**plen′te·ous, plen′ti·ful,** *adj.*

pleth′o·ra, *n.* profuseness.

pleu′ri·sy, *n.* inflammation of chest and lung membranes.

plex′us, *n.* 1. network of nerves or blood vessels. 2. intricate network of component parts.

pli′a·ble, *adj.* 1. flexible or easily bent. 2. easily influenced; adaptable. —**pli″a·bil′i·ty,** *n.*

pli′ant, *adj.* pliable. —**pli′an·cy,** *n.*

pli′ers, *n., pl.* small pincers for grabbing, bending, etc.

plight, *n.* 1. predicament. —*v.t.* 2. promise in marriage.

plod, *v.i.*, **plodded, plodding,** 1. walk slowly or heavily. 2. work laboriously; drudge. —**plod′der,** *n.*

plot, *v.*, **plotted, plotting**, *n.* 1. secret scheme. 2. outline of a novel, etc. 3. piece of land. —*v.t.* 4. plan secretly. 5.

mark on a map, esp. position or course. —*v.i.* 6. make secret plans; conspire. —**plot'ter,** *n.*

plov'er, *n.* shore bird related to the sandpiper.

plow, *n.* 1. implement for dividing soil. 2. scraping implement for removing snow. —*v.t.* 3. turn or furrow with or as with a plow. —*v.i.* 4. move slowly or forcefully. Also, **plough.** —**plow' man,** *n.*

plow'share", *n.* blade of a plow.

ploy, *n.* trick intended to trap or embarrass; tactic.

pluck, *v.t.* 1. pull things from. 2. pull suddenly or forcefully. —*n.* 3. courage.

plug, *n., v.,* **plugged, plugging.** *n.* 1. object for stopping a hole. 2. device on an electrical cord which makes the connection in the socket. 3. *Informal.* endorsement or advertisement. —*v.t.* 4. stop or close with a plug; insert.

plum, *n.* sweet, juicy fruit.

plum'age, *n.* feathers of a bird; finery, esp. in dress.

plumb, *n.* 1. heavy weight on a measuring line. —*adv.* 2. vertically. 3. fully. —*adj.* 4. vertical. —*v.t.* 5. measure the depth of.

plumb'ing, *n.* system of water pipes. —**plumb'er,** *n.*

plume, *n.* 1. feather, esp. a large, conspicuous one. 2. ornamental tuft.

plum'met, *n.* 1. plumb on a line. —*v.i.* 2. plunge.

plump, *adj.* 1. fat; chubby. —*v.i.* 2. drop or fall heavily. 3. favor something strongly.

plun'der, *v.t.* 1. rob or pillage. —*n.* 2. act or instance of plundering. 3. loot; spoils.

plunge, *v.,* **plunged, plunging** *v.,* *v.t.* 1. thrust, as into liquid. 2. thrust into a condition or predicament. —*v.i.* 3. rush; dash. 4. pitch forward. —*n.* 5. dive or fall.

plu'ral, *adj.* denoting more than one.

plu·ral'i·ty, *n.* 1. majority. 2. number of votes for a leading candidate over the number for a rival.

plus, *prep.* 1. increased by. —*n.* 2. mathematical sign for addition or for a positive number. 3. something additional. —*adj.* 4. pertaining to addition. 5. positive.

plush, *n.* 1. long-piled fabric. —*adj.* 2. fancy. —**plush'y,** *adj.*

plu·toc'ra·cy, *n., pl.* **-cies,** 1. rule by or power of the wealthy. 2. controlling wealthy group. —**plu'to·crat",** *n.*

plu·to'ni·um, *n.* radioactive element.

ply, *v.,* **plied, plying,** *n., pl.* **plies.** *v.t.* 1. work at or with. 2. attempt to persuade. —*v.t., v.i.* 3. travel regularly. —*n.* 4. thickness or layer.

ply'wood, *n.* sheeting of thin plies of wood glued together.

pneu·mat'ic (noo mat'ik), *adj.* pertaining to, or using air or wind.

pneu·mo·nia (noo mō'nyə), *n.* inflamed lung disease.

poach, *v.i.* 1. trespass to hunt or fish illegally. —*v.t.* 2. cook in hot but not boiling water. —**poach'er,** *n.*

pock, *n.* mark on the skin; scar, esp. from smallpox.

pock'et, *n.* 1. pouch in a garment. 2. cavity. 3. isolated group or area. —*v.t.* 4. put in one's pocket. 6. take possession of.

pock'et·book", *n.* purse; handbag.

pod, *n.* vegetable seed covering.

po·di'a·try, *n.* medical treatment of the foot. —**po·di'a·trist,** *n.*

po'di·um, *n.* small platform.

po'em, *n.* composition in verse.

po'et·ry, *n.* rhythmical, verse composition. —**po'et,** *fem.,* **po'et·ess,** *n.* —**po·et'ic, po·et'i·cal,** *adj.*

po'grom, *n.* organized massacre.

poign·ant (poin'yənt), *adj.* deeply moving. —**poign'an·cy,** *n.*

poin·set'ti·a, *n.* tropical plant with scarlet flowers.

point, *n.* 1. sharp end. 2. dot. 3. specific time or position. 4. individual detail or idea. 5. reason or meaning. —*v.i.* 6. indicate a direction. —*v.t.* 7. direct or turn. —**point'less,** *adj.*

point'-blank', *adj.* 1. direct; plain. —*adv.* 2. directly.

point'er, *n.* 1. something that points or indicates. 2. breed of hunting dog.

poise, *n., v.,* **poised, poising.** *n.* 1. balance; composure. —*v.i.* 2. be balanced. 3. hover, e.g. a bird in the air. —*v.t.* 4. balance.

poi'son, *n.* 1. substance that kills or harms. —*v.t.* 2. administer poison to. 3. corrupt. —**poi'son·ous,** *adj.*

poke, *v.,* **poked, poking** *n., v.i., v.t., n.* thrust.

pok'er, *n.* 1. metal rod for poking fires. 2. card game.

po'lar, *adj.* pertaining to a pole of the earth, a magnet, etc.

pole, *n.* 1. long, slender, round object. 2. end of an axis. 3. terminal of a battery. 4. areas where magnetism is concentrated.

pole'cat", *n.* skunk.

po·lem'ics, *n.* art of argument. —**po·lem'ic,** *adj.*

po·lice', *n., v.t.,* **-liced, -licing.** *n.* 1. governmental organization for enforcing the law. —*v.t.* 2. control or regulate. —**po·lice'man,** *fem.,* **po·lice'wom"an,** *n.*

pol'i·cy, *n., pl.* **-cies,** 1. course of principle action. 2. insurance contract.

pol″i·o·my″e·li′tis *n.* infantile spinal paralysis. Also, **po′li·o.**

pol′ish, *v.t.* 1. make smooth and glossy. 2. refine in behavior. 3. bring to a perfected state. —*n.* 4. polishing material. 5. gloss. 6. refinement.

po·lit′bu″ro, *n.* primary governing body of a Communist country.

po·lite′, *adj.* 1. marked by good manners. 2. cultivated. —**po·lite′ly,** *adv.* —**po·lite′ness,** *n.*

pol′i·tic, *adj.* 1. expedient. 2. political.

pol′i·tics, *n.* 1. theory and conduct of government. 2. political affairs and methods. —**po·lit′i·cal,** *adj.* —**pol″i·ti′cian,** *n.*

pol′ka, *n.* lively dance.

poll, *n.* 1. casting of votes. 2. total of votes. 3. place of voting. 4. solicitation of opinion. —*v.t.* 5. receive votes. 6. question regarding opinions.

pol′len, *n.* spores of a seed plant. —**pol′li·nate″,** *v.t.* —**pol″li·na′tion,** *n.*

pol·lute′, *v.t.,* **-luted, -luting.** make impure; contaminate. —**pol·lu′tion,** *n.*

po′lo, *n.* ball game played on horseback.

pol″o·naise′, *n.* slow dance from Poland.

po·lo′ni·um, *n.* radioactive metallic element.

pol′ter·geist″, *n.* mischievous ghost or spirit.

pol·troon′, *n.* coward.

pol′y·an″dry, *n.* marriage to more than one husband at a time.

po·lyg′a·my, *n.* marriage to more than one spouse at a time. —**po·lyg′a·mist,** *n.* —**po·lyg′a·mous,** *adj.*

pol′y·glot″, *adj.* 1. knowing a number of languages. 2. made up of several languages.

pol′y·gon″, *n.* closed plane figures with three or more sides. —**po·lyg′o·nal,** *adj.*

pol″y·graph, *n.* a lie detector.

pol″y·he′dron, *n., pl.* **-drons, -dra,** closed solid figure.

pol′y·mer, *n.* chemical compound of large molecules formed by smaller but similar molecules.

pol′yp, *n.* 1. projecting growth from a mucous membrane surface. 2. small aquatic organism.

po·ly′pho·ny, *n.* musical composition with independent melodic lines. —**pol″y·phon′ic,** *adj.*

pol″y·syl·lab′ic, *adj.* having many syllables.

pol′y·the′ism, *n.* belief in more than one god. —**pol′y·the′ist,** *n.* —**pol″y·the′is·tic,** *adj.*

pome′gran″ate, *n.* tropical, red fruit with edible seeds.

pom·mel (pum′əl), *n., v.t.,* **-eled, -eling.** *n.* 1. knob, e.g. on a sword hilt. —*v.t.* 2. beat or strike repeatedly.

pomp, *n.* stately display.

pom′pa·dour″, *n.* hair style with hair brushed high over the forehead.

pom′pon, *n.* ornamental ball or tuft.

pomp′ous, *adj.* 1. pretentiously self-important; ostentatious. 2. excessively dignified. —**pom·pos′i·ty,** *n.* —**pomp′ous·ly,** *adv.*

pon′cho, *n., pl.* **-chos,** *n.* blanket-like cloak with an opening for the head.

pond, *n.* small body of water.

pon′der, *v.i., v.t.* consider deeply.

pon′der·ous, *adj.* 1. heavy. 2. lacking grace.

pone, *n.* oval-shaped cornmeal biscuit.

pon′iard, *n.* dagger.

pon′tiff, *n.* bishop or head priest, esp. a pope. —**pon·tif′i·cal,** *adj.*

pon·tif′i·cate, *v.i.,* **-cated, -cating.** speak dogmatically.

pon·toon′, *n.* flat-bottomed boat used esp. in construction.

po′ny, *n., pl.* **-nies.** young horse.

poo′dle, *n.* curly-haired breed of dog.

pool, *n.* 1. small, still body of fresh water. 2. group of available workers, automobiles, etc. 3. game similar to billiards. —*v.t.* 4. put into a common fund or effort.

poop, *n.* upper deck at the stern of a ship.

poor, *adj.* 1. having little money. 2. lacking. 3. inferior. —*n.* 4. poor people. —**poor′ly,** *adv.*

pop, *v.,* **popped, popping,** *n., v.i., v.t.* 1. burst with a quick, explosive sound. —*v.i.* 2. bulge, as the eyes. —*n.* 3. sound of popping. 4. carbonated soft drink.

pop′corn″, *n.* Indian corn whose kernels open into a soft, starchy mass when heated.

pope, *n. Often cap.* head of the Roman Catholic Church.

pop′lar, *n.* any of various quick-growing trees.

pop′lin, *n.* ribbed, plain-woven fabric.

pop′o′ver, *n.* very light biscuit.

pop′py, *n., pl.* **-pies,** herb with a showy flower, one type of which yields opium.

pop′u·lace, *n.* people; general public.

pop′u·lar, *adj.* 1. pertaining to the general public. 2. widely liked or approved. —**pop′u·lar·ly,** *adv.* —**pop″u·lar′i·ty,** *n.* —**pop′u·lar·ize,** *v.t.*

pop′u·late″, *v.t.,* **-lated, -lating.** 1. inhabit. 2. furnish with inhabitants.

pop″u·la′tion, *n.* 1. number of people. 2. body of inhabitants.

pop′u·lous, *adj.* having many people.

por′ce·lain, *n.* shiny ceramic ware.

porch, *n.* open, often roofed, appendage to a building; veranda.

por·cine (por' sīn), *adj.* of or suggesting swine.

por'cu·pine'', *n.* rodent covered with stiff, sharp quills.

pore, *v.i.*, pored, poring, *n.*, *v.i.* 1. meditate or read attentively. —*n.* 2. minute opening in the skin.

por'gy, *n.* salt-water food fish.

pork, *n.* flesh of swine used as food.

por·nog'ra·phy, *n.* erotic writing or art intended for sexual excitement. —**por'' no·graph'ic**, *adj.*

po'rous, *adj.* permeable to liquids and air.

por'poise, *n.* any of several aquatic mammals including the common dolphin.

por'ridge, *n.* cereal boiled in milk or water.

por'rin·ger, *n.* low dish, often with a handle.

port, *n.* 1. loading and unloading place for ships and aircraft. 2. when facing the bow, the left side of a ship. 3. a sweet, red wine. 4. (computers) point at which peripheral components can be connected.

port'a·ble, *adj.* easily carried; small. —**port''a·bil'i·ty**, *n.*

por'tage, *n.* carrying cf goods and boats overland.

por'tal, *n.* gate or door.

por·tend', *v.t.* 1. indicate in advance. 2. indicate; signify.

por'tent, *n.* 1. omen. 2. ominous significance. —**por·ten'tous**, *adj.*

por'ter, *n.* 1. doorman. 2. baggage carrier.

por'ter·house'', *n.* choice cut of beefsteak with a large tenderloin.

port'fo''li·o'', *n.* 1. portable case for documents. 2. office and duties of a government minister. 3. securities and stocks held by an investor.

port'hole'', *n.* window, esp. round, in the side of a plane or ship.

por'ti·co'', *n.*, *pl.* **-coes** or **-cos.** roof supported by a colonnade; porch.

por'tion, *n.* 1. part or share. 2. personal fate. —*v.t.* 3. divide into portions.

port'ly, *adj.* fat; chubby.

por'trait, *n.* picture or description of a person. —**por'trai·ture**, *n.*

por·tray', *v.t.* 1. depict or represent in a portrait. 2. represent dramatically. —**por·tray'al**, *n.*

por·tu·lac'a, *n.* tropical herb with showy flowers.

pose, *v.*, posed, posing, *n.*, *v.i.* 1. hold a position. 2. assume a character or attitude. —*v.t.* 3. propound or state. —*n.* 4. fixed position. 5. assumed character. —**pos'er**, *n.*

po·si'tion, *n.* 1. location. 2. posture. 3. opinion on an issue. 4. job. —*v.t.* 5. place.

pos'i·tive, *adj.* 1. affirmative. 2. certain. 3. with light and shade as in the original. 4. numerically greater than zero. 5. electrical charge with more protons than electrons. 6. showing the presence of something tested for. —*n.* 7. something positive. —**pos'i·tive·ly**, *adv.* —**pos'i·tive·ness**, *n.*

pos'se, *n.* group of persons assisting a law enforcement officer.

pos·sess', *v.t.* 1. have or own. 2. dominate. —**pos·ses'sive**, *adj.* —**pos·ses'sion**, *n.* —**pos·ses'sor**, *n.*

pos'si·ble, *adj.* capable of existing or happening. —**pos'sibly**, *adv.* —**pos''si·bil'i·ty**, *n.*

pos'sum, *n.* opossum.

post, *n.* 1. upright column or pole. 2. appointed job, station or task. 3. permanent military station. —*v.t.* 4. put up, as a public announcement. 5. assign to a place. 6. enter in a ledger. 7. mail.

post'age, *n.* 1. charge for mailing. 2. stamps, etc. for mailing.

post'al, *adj.* pertaining to mail.

post'card, *n.* message card mailed without an envelope.

post'er, *n.* public advertisement.

pos·te'ri·or, *adj.* 1. situated behind. 2. later in time. —*n.* 3. buttocks, rump.

pos'ter''i·ty, *n.* 1. descendants. 2. succeeding or future generations.

pos'tern, *n.* 1. back door or gate. 2. private entrance.

post'haste', *adv.* as quickly as possible.

post'hu·mous, *adj.* 1. published after the death of the author. 2. born after the death of the father. —**post'hu·mous·ly** *adv.*

post'man, *n.* mailman.

post'mark'', *n.* 1. postal mark indicating a time and place of reception by a post office. —*v.t.* 2. put a postmark on.

post'mas''ter, *n.* manager of a post office.

post-mor'tem, *adj.* 1. following death. —*n.* 2. examination of a corpse.

post'of''fice, *n.* government agency that handles mail.

post·op'er·a·tive, *adj.* following a surgical operation.

post'paid', *adj.*, *adv.* with postage prepaid.

post·pone', *v.t.*, -poned, -poning, delay, as action. —**post·pone'ment**, *n.*

post'script'', *n.* note added to a finished letter.

pos·tu·late, *v.t.*, -lated, -lating, *n.*, *v.t.* (pos'tyŏŏ lāt) 1. assume as true. —*n.* (pos'tyŏŏ lət) 2. postulated proposition.

pos'ture, *n.*, *v.*, -tured, -turing, *n.* 1. position of the body. 2. attitude on a given subject. —*v.i.* 3. affect an attitude. —*v.t.* 4. place in a specific position.

post'war', *adj.* after a war.

po'sy, *n., pl.* **-sies**, small bouquet.

pot, *n., v.t.*, **potted**, **potting**. *n.* 1. deep, round container. —*v.t.* 2. put or plant in a pot.

po'ta·ble, *adj.* drinkable.

pot'ash'', *n.* potassium carbonate, esp. from wood ashes.

po·tas'si·um, *n.* silver, metallic, chemical element used in glass, fertilizer, etc.

po·ta'tion, *n.* drink, esp. alcoholic.

po·ta'to, *n., pl.* **-toes**. edible tuber of a common vegetable plant.

po'tent, *adj.* 1. powerful. 2. sexually capable. —**po'tence, po'ten·cy,** *n.*

po'ten·tate'', *n.* sovereign; ruler.

po·ten'tial, *adj.* 1. possible; capable of being realized. —*n.* 2. possible ability. —**po·ten''ti·al'i·ty,** *n.* —**po·ten'tial·ly,** *adv.*

po'tion, *n.* drink, esp. a medicinal one.

pot·pour'ri (pŏ′ pə rē′), *n.* miscellaneous collection.

pot'ter, *n.* maker of earthenware.

pot'ter·y, *n.* 1. dishes, pots, mugs, etc. made of baked clay. 2. place where earthenware is made.

pouch, *n.* 1. sack or bag. 2. baglike part of a marsupial.

por·l'try, *n.* domestic fowl, e.g. chicken.

pounce, *v.i.*, **pounced**, **pouncing**. swoop down suddenly.

pound, *n.* 1. unit of avoirdupois weight equal to 16 ounces or troy weight equal to 12 ounces. 2. British monetary unit. 3. enclosure for stray dogs, etc. —*v.t.* 4. strike forcefully and repeatedly. 5. crush or compact by pounding. —*v.i.* 6. throb or beat violently, as the heart.

pound'cake'', *n.* rich, sweet cake.

pour, *v.t.* 1. cause to flow. —*v.i.* 2. rain heavily. —*n.* 3. act or instance of pouring.

pout, *v.i.* 1. look sullen; act hurt. —*n.* 2. sullen mood, look or behavior.

pov'er·ty, *n.* 1. lack of money. 2. deficiency.

pow'der, *n.* 1. dry substance of very fine particles. —*v.t.* 2. reduce to powder. 3. apply powder to. —**pow'der·y,** *adj.*

pow'er, *n.* 1. ability to act. 2. personal ability. 3. authority. 4. influential person, nation, etc. 5. physical force. 6. magnifying capacity of a lens. —**pow'er·ful,** *adj.* —**pow'er·ful·ly,** *adv.* —**pow'er·less,** *adj.*

pow'wow'', *n.* American Indian conference.

pox, *n.* any disease marked by skin pustules.

prac'ti·ca·ble, *adj.* feasible.

prac'ti·cal, *adj.* 1. pertaining to practice. 2. useful. 3. aware of realities. 4. virtual. —**prac''ti·cal'i·ty,** *n.* —**prac'ti·cal·ly,** *adv.*

prac'tice, *n., v.,* **-ticed**, **-ticing**. *n.* 1. cus-

tom. 2. actual performance. 3. repeated exercise. 4. professional activity. —*v.i., v.t.* 5. Also, **prac'tise**, perform habitually or repeatedly. —**prac'ticed,** *adj.*

prac'ti·tion·er, *n.* person who practices a profession.

prag·ma'tic, *adj.* concerned with practical values and consequences. —**prag'ma·tist,** *n.* —**prag'ma·tism,** *n.*

prai'rie, *n.* flat, treeless, rolling grassland.

praise, *n., v.t.*, **praised**, **praising**. *n.* 1. expressed approval. 2. homage. —*v.t.* 3. express approval of. 4. worship. —**praise'wor''thy,** *adj.*

prance, *v.i.*, **pranced**, **prancing**. 1. spring on the hind legs. 2. swagger.

prank, *n.* mischievous trick. —**prank'ster,** *n.*

prate, *v.*, **prated**, **prating**, *v.i., v.t.* talk excessively and foolishly.

prat'tle, *v.i.*, **-tled**, **-tling**, *n., v.i.* 1. chatter childishly or foolishly. —*n.* 2. chatter. —**prat'tler,** *n.*

prawn, *n.* large, edible, shrimplike shellfish.

pray, *v.i.* 1. petition or worship a divinity. —*v.t.* 2. implore. 3. ask earnestly for.

prayer, *n.* 1. act of addressing a divinity. 2. earnest request. —**prayer'ful,** *adj.*

preach, *v.t.* 1. advocate. —*v.i.* 2. give a sermon. —**preach'er,** *n.*

pre'am''ble, *n.* introductory section.

pre·car'i·ous, *adj.* risky. —**pre·car'i·ous·ly,** *adv.*

pre·cau'tion, *n.* caution beforehand. —**pre·cau'tion·ar''y,** *adj.*

pre·cede', *v.*, **-ceded**, **-ceding**, *v.i., v.t.* go before. —**pre·ced'ence,** *n.*

prec'e·dent, *n.* past occurrence or principle used as an example or justification.

pre'cept, *n.* principle or rule of conduct.

pre·cep'tor, *n.* teacher or tutor.

pre'cinct, *n.* administrative district.

pre'cious, *adj.* 1. valuable. 2. cherished. 3. overly refined. —**pre'cious·ly,** *adv.*

prec'i·pice, *n.* steep cliff.

pre·cip'i·tate', *v.t.*, **-tated**, **-tating**, *adj., n., v.t.* 1. throw down violently. 2. hasten in occurring. 3. separate from a solution. 4. condense. —*adj.* 5. hasty; rash; headlong. —*n.* 6. condensed moisture. —**pre·cip''i·ta'tion,** *n.*

pre·cip'i·tous, *adj.* 1. steep. 2. precipitate.

pré·cis' (prā sē), *n.* concise summary.

pre·cise', *adj.* 1. specific. 2. scrupulous; strict. —**pre·ci'sion, pre·cise'ness,** *n.* —**pre·cise'ly,** *adv.*

pre·clude', *v.t.*, **-cluded**, **-cluding**. exclude the possibility of. —**pre·clu'sion,** *n.* —**pre·clu'sive,** *adj.*

pre·co'cious, *adj.* advanced in development, esp. of the mind. —**pre·coc'i·ty,** *n.*

pre‴con·ceive, *v.t.* form an idea or opinion of in advance. —**pre‴con·cep′tion**, *n.*

pre·cur′sor, *n.* 1. forerunner. 2. harbinger.

pred‴e·ces′sor, *n.* person or thing that precedes another.

pre·des‴ti·na′tion, *n.* determination in advance of actions and consequences; fate. —**pre·des′tine**, *v.t.*

pre·dic′a·ment, *n.* difficult or dangerous situation.

pred·i·cate, *v.t.*, **-cated**, **-cating**, *n.*, *v.t.* (pred′ə kāt″) 1. declare; assume. 2. base on an assumption. —*n.* (pred′ək ət) 3. *Grammar.* part of a sentence or clause expressing what is said of its subject. —**pred‴i·ca′tion**, *n.*

pre·dict′, *v.t.*, tell in advance. —**pre·dic′tion**, *n.* —**pre·dict′a·ble**, *adj.*

pre‴di·lec′tion, *n.* preference; inclination.

pre·dom′i·nate″, *v.*, **-nated**, **-nating**, *v.i.* 1. be stronger or more numerous. —*v.t.* 2. master. —**pre·dom′i·nance**, *n.* —**pre·dom′i·nant**, *adj.* —**pre·dom′i·nant·ly**, *adv.*

pre·em′i·nent, *adj.* outstanding; superior. —**pre·em′i·nent·ly**, *adv.* —**pre·em′i·nence**, *n.*

pre‴empt′, *v.t.* 1. acquire before others do. 2. settle on to establish the right of purchase.

preen, *v.t.* 1. trim with the beak, as a bird. —*v.i.* 2. fuss over one's appearance.

pre·fab′ri·cate″, *v.t.*, **-cated**, **-cating**, assemble from large, previously finished, components.

pre′face, *n.*, *v.t.*, **-aced**, **-acing**, *n.* 1. introductory text. —*v.t.* 2. serve as a preface to. —**pref′a·to″ry**, *adj.*

pre′fect, *n.* magistrate; high official.

pre·fer′, *v.t.*, **-ferred**, **-ferring**. 1. like better or favor more than others. 2. present, as an accusation. —**pref′er·a·ble**, *adj.* —**pref′er·a·bly**, *adv.* —**pref′er·ence**, *n.* —**pref‴er·en′tial**, *adj.*

pre·fer′ment, *n.* promotion; advancement.

pre′fix, *n.* 1. qualifying beginning of a word. —*v.t.* 2. put before.

preg′nant, *adj.* 1. being with child. 2. significant; meaningful. —**preg′nan·cy**, *n.*

pre·hen′sile, *adj.* able to grasp.

pre‴his·tor′ic, *adj.* pertaining to the time before recorded history.

prej′u·dice, *n.*, *v.t.*, **-diced**, **-dicing**, *n.* 1. opinion without adequate basis. 2. disadvantage or injury. —*v.t.* 3. influence or affect with prejudice. —**prej‴u·di′cial**, *adj.*

prel′ate, *n.* high church official.

pre·lim′i·nar″y, *adj., pl.* **-naries**, *adj.* 1. —

introductory. —*n.* 2. introductory feature.

prel′ude, *n.* preliminary to a larger work.

pre‴ma·ture″, *adj.* 1. born or happening too early. 2. overly hasty. —**pre‴ma·ture′ly**, *adv.* —**pre‴ma·tur′i·ty**, *n.*

pre·med′i·tate″, *v.*, **-tated**, **-tating**. *v.i.*, *v.t.* plan or consider beforehand. —**pre‴med·i·ta′tion**, *n.*

pre·mier (pre mir′), *n.* 1. chief officer, esp. a prime minister. —*adj.* 2. first in rank.

pre·miere (pre mir′), *n.* first public performance.

prem′ise, *n.* 1. basis of an argument or conclusion. 2. **premises**, building and grounds; property.

pre′mi·um, *n.* 1. prize. 2. high evaluation. 3. bonus. 4. cost of an insurance policy.

pre‴mo·ni′tion, *n.* foreboding; presentiment. —**pre·mon′i·to″ry**, *adv.*

pre·na′tal, *adj.* prior to birth.

pre·oc′cu·pied″, *adj.* completely engrossed. —**pre·oc′cu·py″**, *v.t.* —**pre·oc′cu·pa′tion**, *n.*

pre·pare′, *v.*, **-pared**, **paring**, *v.t.* 1. put in readiness. 2. manufacture. —*v.i.* 3. get or put oneself in readiness. —**prep′a·ra′tion**, *n.* —**pre·par′a·to″ry**, *adj.* —**pre·par′ed·ness**, *n.*

pre·pon′der·ant, *adj.* superior in numbers, strength, etc. —**pre·pon′der·ance**, *n.*

prep‴o·si′tion, *n.* word or words placed before a noun or adjective to form a modifying phrase. —**prep‴o·si′tion·al**, *adj.*

pre‴pos·sess′ing, *adj.* impressing favorably.

pre·pos′ter·ous, *adj.* absurd.

pre·req′ui·site, *n.* something required beforehand; condition.

pre·rog′a·tive, *n.* special power, right, or privilege.

pres′age, *v.t.*, **-aged**, **-aging**. 1. foreshadow. 2. predict.

pres‴by·te′ri·an, *adj.* 1. of or pertaining to the principle of church government by a presbytery. 2. pertaining to a Protestant church with this form of government. —*n.* 3. member of a Presbyterian church.

pres′by·ter″y, *n., pl.* **-teries**, group of church elders and ministers.

pre·sci·ence (pre′shē əns, presh′əns), *n.* foreknowledge; foresight. —**pre′sci·ent**, *adj.*

pre·scribe′, *v.t.*, **-scribed**, **-scribing**, order for use, or adoption. —**pre·scrip′tion**, *n.* —**pre·scrip′tive**, *adj.*

pres′ence, *n.* 1. state of being present. 2. vicinity or view. 3. figure or bearing of a person.

pres′ent, *adj.* (prez′ənt) 1. being or hap-

pening now. **2.** being in a specific place. **3.** *Grammar.* denoting state or action now taking place. —*n.* **4.** present time. **5.** present tense. **6.** gift. —*v.t.* (pri zent′) **7.** give, bring, or offer. **8.** furnish or allow. **9.** introduce or make public. —**pres″en·ta′tion**, *n.*

pre·sent′a·ble, *adj.* suitable in appearance, manners, etc. —**pre·sent′ab·ly**, *adv.*

pre·sen′ti·ment, *n.* premonition.

pres′ent·ly, *adv.* **1.** soon. **2.** at present; now.

pre·serve′, *v.t.*, **-served**, **-serving**, *n.*, *v.t.* **1.** keep safe. **2.** keep in good condition. **3.** prepare for storage, as food. —*n.* **4.** **preserves**, preserved fruit. **5.** sanctuary for game animals. —**pres″er·va′tion**, *n.* —**pre·serv′a·tive**, *n.*, *adj.*

pre·side′, *v.i.*, **-sided**, **-siding.** act as chairman; be at the head of.

pres′i·dent, *n.* **1.** chief officer of a corporation. **2.** highest elected official. —**pres′i·den·cy**, *n.* —**pres″i·den′tial**, *adj.*

pre·sid′i·um, *n.* major administrative committee of a communist state.

press, *v.t.* **1.** act against with weight or force. **2.** urge forcefully. **3.** oppress. **4.** iron, as clothing. —*v.i.* **5.** move or push forcefully. —*n.* **6.** journalism. **7.** machine for printing. **8.** urgency.

press′ing, *adj.* urgent.

pres′sure, *n.* **1.** exertion of force. **2.** compulsion toward a certain action or decision. **3.** urgency.

pres″ti·dig″i·ta′tion, *n.* sleight of hand. —**pres″ti·dig′i·ta′tor**, *n.*

pres·tige (pres tēzh′) *n.* respected standing or reputation. —**pres·tig′ious**, *adj.*

pres′to, *adv.* quickly.

pre·sume′, *v.*, **-sumed**, **-suming**, *v.t.* **1.** take for granted. —*v.i.* **2.** act with unwarranted boldness. —**pre·sum′a·ble**, *adj.* —**pre·sum′a·bly**, *adv.*

pre·sump′tion, *n.* **1.** assumption. **2.** unwarranted boldness. —**pre·sump′tive**, *adj.* —**pre·sump′tu·ous**, *adj.*

pre″sup·pose′, *v.t.*, **-posed**, **-posing.** **1.** suppose beforehand. **2.** require beforehand as a condition.

pre·tend′, *v.t.* **1.** imagine as a fantasy. **2.** profess or appear falsely. —*v.i.* **3.** make believe. **4.** make a claim. —**pre·ten′der**, *n.* —**pre·tense′**, *n.*

pre·ten′sion, *n.* **1.** ostentation; self-importance. **2.** act or instance of alleging or pretending. —**pre·ten′tious**, *adj.* —**pre·ten′tious·ly**, *adv.*

pre″ter·nat′u·ral, *adj.* **1.** supernatural. **2.** abnormal or exceptional.

pre′text, *n.* ostensible or false reason; excuse.

pret′ty, *adj.*, **-tier**, **-tiest**, *adv. adj.* **1.** pleasingly attractive. —*adv.* **2.** moderately. —**pret′ti·fy″**, *v.t.* —**pret′ti·ly**, *adv.* —**pret′ti·ness**, *n.*

pret′zel, *n.* brittle, salted cracker, usually twisted.

pre·vail′, *v.i.* **1.** be widespread. **2.** prove superior in force, etc. **3.** succeed in persuasion. —**prev′a·lent**, *adj.* —**prev′a·lence**, *n.*

pre·var′i·cate″, *v.i.*, **-cated**, **-cating**, speak falsely; lie. —**pre·var″i·ca′tion**, *n.*

pre·vent′, *v.t.* stop; hinder. —**pre·vent′a·ble**, **pre·vent′i·ble.** *adj.* —**pre·ven′tion**, *n.* —**pre·ven′tive**, **pre·vent′a·tive**, *adj.*

pre′view″, *n.* **1.** advance showing, as of a motion picture. —*v.t.* **2.** show or view in advance.

pre′vi·ous, *adj.* happening or going earlier. —**pre′vi·ous·ly**, *adv.*

prey, *n.* **1.** animal hunted for food. **2.** victim. —*v.i.* **3.** search for prey. **4.** have an oppressive effect.

price, *n.*, *v.t.* **-priced**, **pricing**, *n.* **1.** amount for which something is sold. **2.** value. —*v.t.* **3.** set a price on. **4.** check or ask the price of.

price′less, *adj.* invaluable; beyond any price.

prick, *n.* **1.** puncture or cut from a thorn, needle, etc. —*v.t.* **2.** pierce or stab lightly.

prick′ly, *adj.* sharp; scratchy.

pride, *n.*, *v.t.*, **prided**, **priding**. *n.* **1.** high opinion of one's worth. **2.** self-respect. **3.** person or object one is proud of. —*v.t.* **4.** give pride to.

priest, *n.* **1.** clergyman; person authorized to perform religious ceremonies. Also, *fem.*, **priest′ess**, one who performs religious rites. —**priest′hood**, *n.* —**priest′ly**, *adj.*

prig, *n.* self-righteous person. —**prig′gish**, *adj.*

prim, *adj.* rigidly proper. —**prim′ly**, *adv.*

pri′ma don′na, *n.* **1.** principal female opera singer. **2.** *Informal.* temperamental or vain person.

pri′mal, *adj.* **1.** primitive; original. **2.** most important; basic.

pri′ma′ry, *adj.*, *n.*, *pl.* **-ries.** *adj.* **1.** first in rank or importance. **2.** first in time. —*n.* **3.** preliminary election. —**pri·mar′i·ly**, *adv.*

pri′mate, *n.* **1.** any of the order of mammals that includes man. **2.** high church official.

prime, *adj.*, *n.*, *v.t.*, **primed**, **priming**, *adj.* **1.** first in rank, value, etc. **2.** original. —*n.* **3.** best part or period. —*v.t.* **4.** prepare.

prim′er, *n.* (prim′ər) **1.** elementary or basic book. **2.** (prī′mər) material for preparing a surface.

pri·me′val, *adj.* pertaining to the earliest ages.

prim′i·tive, *adj.* **1.** earliest. **2.** simple; crude. —*n.* **3.** naive work of art.

—**prim′i·tive·ly**, *adv.* —**prim′i·tive·ness**, *n.*

primp, *v.t., v.i.* dress or adorn oneself fastidiously.

prim′rose″, *n.* colorful perennial garden flower.

prince, *n.* 1. son of royalty. 2. ruler. Also, *fem.*, **prin′cess**.

prince′ly, *adj.* lavish.

prin′ci·pal, *adj.* 1. most important. —*n.* 2. leader. 3. head of a school. 4. capital sum. —**prin′ci·pal·ly**, *adv.*

prin″ci·pal′i·ty, *n., pl.* **-ties**. state governed by a prince.

prin′ci·ple, *n.* 1. rule of action, conduct, or belief. 2. adherence to rules of conduct. 3. scientific law.

print, *v.t.* 1. reproduce from inked type. 2. produce a photographic positive from. —*v.i.* 3. draw letters or characters. —*n.* 4. state of being printed. 5. printed lettering. 6. printed picture. —**print′er**, *n.*

print″er, *n.* 1. one who prints. 2. (computers) device for transcribing data to paper.

print″out, *n.,v.* (computers) data transcribed onto paper.

pri′or, *adj.* 1. earlier. —*adv.* 2. previously. —*n.* 3. Also, *fem.*, **pri′or·ess**, head of a religious house. —**pri′o·ry**, *n.*

pri·or′i·ty, *n., pl.* **-ties**. 1. state of being earlier in time. 2. precedence in order, privilege, etc.

prism, *n.* three-sided glass object that breaks light into its spectrum. —**pris·ma′tic**, *adj.*

pris′on, *n.* jail; building for confining criminals. —**pris′on·er**, *n.*

pris′tine, *adj.* unspoiled; pure.

pri′vate, *adj.* 1. belonging to a specific person or group. 2. confidential. —*n.* 3. lowest soldier. —**pri′vate·ly**, *adv.* —**pri′va·cy**, *n.*

pri″va·teer′, *n.* private ship commissioned for warfare.

pri·va′tion, *n.* 1. deprivation. 2. lack; want; need.

priv′i·lege, *n.* special advantage. —**priv′i·leged**, *adj.*

priv′y, *adj., n., pl.* **privies**. *adj.* 1. admitted to a secret. 2. private; personal. —*n.* 3. outhouse; outdoor toilet.

prize, *n., v.t.,* **prized, prizing**. *n.* 1. reward for victory. 2. something desirable. —*v.t.* 3. value or esteem highly.

pro, *n., pl.* **pros**, *adv., adj. n.* 1. *Informal.* professional. —*adv., adj.* 2. in favor.

prob′a·ble, *adj.* 1. likely to happen, etc. 2. giving ground for belief. —**prob′a·bly**, *adv.* —**prob″a·bil′i·ty**, *n.*

pro′bate, *n., adj., v.t.,* **-bated, -bating**, *n.* 1. certification of a will. —*adj.* 2. of or pertaining to probate. —*v.t.* 3. establish the validity of.

pro·ba′tion, *n.* act or instance of testing. —**pro·ba′tion·ar″y**, *adj.*

probe, *v.t.,* **probed, probing**, *n., v.t.* 1. search into thoroughly. —*n.* 2. surgical instrument for examining wounds, etc.

pro′bi·ty, *n.* honesty; uprightness.

prob′lem, *n.* question or situation involving difficulty. —**prob″lem·at′i·cal**, *adj.*

pro·bos·cis (prō bos′is), *n., pl.* **-ces**. flexible snout, e.g. an elephant's trunk.

pro·ceed′, *v.i.* 1. go onward. 2. continue an action. 3. issue forth. —*n.* 4. **proceeds**, revenue from selling. —**pro·ce′dure**, *n.* —**pro·ce′du·ral**, *adj.*

pro·ceed′ing, *n.* 1. action or conduct. 2. **proceedings**, **a.** records of a meeting, etc. **b.** legal action.

pro′cess, *n.* 1. series of actions ending in a result. 2. continuous action. 3. legal summons. —*v.t.* 4. treat or prepare by a specific process.

pro·ces′sion, *n.* parade.

pro·ces′sion·al, *n.* 1. hymn for a procession. 2. hymnbook.

pro·claim′, *v.t.* 1. announce publicly. 2. reveal conspicuously. —**proc″la·ma′tion**, *n.*

pro·cliv′i·ty, *n., pl.* **-ties**. natural tendency or inclination.

pro·cras′ti·nate″, *v.,* **-nated, -nating**. *v.i., v.t.* put off to another time. —**pro·cras″ti·na′tion**, *n.* —**pro·cras′ti·na″tor**, *n.*

pro·cure′, *v.t.,* **-cured, -curing**. 1. obtain. 2. bring about. —**pro·cure′ment**, *n.*

prod, *v.t.,* **prodded, prodding**, *n., v.t.* 1. poke; jab. 2. goad; incite. —*n.* 3. poke. 4. pointed instrument.

prod′i·gal, *adj.* 1. recklessly extravagant. 2. lavish. —**prod″i·gal′i·ty**, *n.*

pro·di′gious, *adj.* 1. wonderful. 2. huge. —**pro·di′gious·ly**, *adv.*

prod′i·gy, *n., pl.* **-gies**. very talented person.

pro·duce′, *v.,* **-duced, -ducing**. *v.t.* (prə′dyŏŏs) 1. bring into existence. 2. give birth to or bear. 3. exhibit. —*n.* (prō′dŏŏs) 4. product. 5. fresh fruit and vegetables. —**pro·duc′er**, *n.* —**pro·duc′tion**, *n.* —**pro·duc′tive**, *adj.* —**pro″duc·tiv′i·ty**, *n.* —**pro·duc′tive·ness**, *adj.* —**pro″duc·tiv′i·ty**, *n.* —**pro·duc′tive·ness**, *n.*

prod′uct, *n.* something produced.

pro·fane′, *adj., v.t.,* **-faned, -faning**, *adj.* 1. secular. 2. impure; foul. 3. irreverent; disrespectful. —*v.t.* 4. treat with irreverence.

pro·fan′i·ty, *n.* 1. sacrilege. 2. cursing.

pro·fess′, *v.t.* 1. claim of oneself. 2. affirm allegiance to or faith in.

pro·fes′sion, *n.* 1. learned occupation. 2. act or instance of professing.

pro·fes′sion·al, *adj.* 1. persuing a pro-

fession. 2. pertaining to a profession. 3. meeting the standards of a profession. —*n*. 4. professional person. —pro·fes'sion·al·ly, *adv.* —pro·fes'sion·al''ism, *n.*

pro·fes'sor, *n.* college teacher of the highest rank. —pro''fes·sor'i·al, *adj.*

prof'fer, *v.t., n.,* offer.

pro·fi'cient, *adj.* skillful; learned. —pro·fi'cient·ly, *adv.* —pro·fi'cien·cy, *n.*

pro'file, *n.* 1. side view. 2. succinct sketch of a person. —*v.t.* 3. do a biographical profile of.

prof'it, *n.* 1. gain from a business deal. 2. net gain from business. 3. benefit. —*v.i.* 4. gain a profit. 5. take advantage. —prof'it·a·ble, *adj.* —prof'it·a·bly, *adv.*

prof''it·eer', *n.* 1. person who takes an unreasonably large profit. —*v.i.* 2. act as a profiteer.

prof'li·gate, *adj.* 1. licentious. 2. extravagant. —*n.* 3. profligate person. —prof'li·ga·cy, *n.*

pro·found', *adj.* 1. characterized by deep thought. 2. deeply felt. 3. deep. —pro·found'ly, *adv.* —pro·fun'di·ty, *n.*

pro·fuse', *adj.* 1. plentiful. 2. lavish. —pro·fuse'ly, *adv.* —pro·fu'sion, pro·fuse'ness, *n.*

pro·gen'i·tor, *n.* forefather; precursor.

prog'e·ny, *n., pl.* -nies. children; descendants.

prog·no'sis, *n., pl.* -noses, forecast of the course of a disease.

prog·nos'ti·cate'', *v.,* -cated, -cating, *v.t.* 1. predict; presage. —*v.i.* 2. prophesy. —prog·nos''ti·ca'tion, *n.*

pro''gram, *n.* 1. plan, method. 2. list of subjects or events. 3. (computers) a set of instructions to perform specific operations to data. —*v.* 4. create a computer program. —pro''gram·ming, *n.*

prog·ress, *n.* (prog'res) 1). advancement. 2. improvement. —*v.i.* (pro gres') 3. advance. 4. improve. —pro·gres'sion, *n.* —pro·gres'sive, *adj.* —pro·gres'sive·ly, *adv.*

pro·hib'it, *v.t.* 1. forbid. 2. prevent. —pro·hib'i·tive, *adj.* —pro''hi·bi'tion, *n.* —pro''hi·bi'tion·ist, *n.*

proj·ect, *n.* (proj'ekt) 1. plan; scheme. —*v.t.* (prō jekt') 2. plan or intend. 3. throw or impel forward. 4. cast on a surface, as an image. —*v.i.* 5. protrude. —pro·jec'tion, *n.* —pro·jec'tor, *n.*

pro·jec'tile, *n.* missile from a gun.

pro''le·tar'i·at, *n.* working class. —pro''le·tar'i·an, *n., adj.*

pro·lif'er·ate'', *v.,* -ated, ·ating, *v.i., v.t.* 1. grow rapidly by multiplication. 2. spread rapidly. —pro·lif''er·a'tion, *n.*

pro·lif'ic, *adj.* productive.

pro'logue, *n.* introduction to a play, novel, etc. Also, pro'log.

pro·long', *v.t.* lengthen, esp. in duration.

prom''e·nade', *n., v.,* -naded, -nading. *n.* 1. leisurely walk. 2. place for strolling. —*v.i.* 3. take a promenade. —*v.t.* 4. promenade on or through.

prom'i·nent, *adj.* 1. conspicuous. 2. distinguished. —prom'i·nence, *n* —prom'i·nent·ly, *adv.*

pro·mis'cu·ous, *adj.* indiscriminate —prom''is·cu'i·ty, *n.* —pro·mis'cu·ous·ly, *adv.*

prom'ise, *n., v.t.,* -ised, -ising. *n.* 1. assurance to do or not to do something 2. indication of future improvement or success. —*v.t.* 3. make a promise. —*v.i.* 4. give grounds for hope —prom'is·ing, *adj.*

prom''is·so''ry, *adj.* containing a promise.

prom'on·to''ry, *n., pl.* -ries, high land mass jutting into the sea.

pro·mote', *v.t.* 1. advance in rank or position. 2. further the growth or progress of. —pro·mo'ter, *n.* —pro·mo'tion, *n.*

prompt, *adj.* 1. ready to act. 2. quick or punctual. —*v.t.* 3. induce to action. —prompt'ly, *adv.*

pro·mul'gate, *v.t.,* -gated, -gating. proclaim publicly. —pro''mul·ga'tion, *n.*

prone, *adj.* 1. inclined; liable. 2. lying face downward.

prong, *n.* pointed projection.

pro'noun'', *n.* word used as a substitute for a noun.

pro·nounce', *v.,* -nounced, -nouncing. *v.t.* 1. utter; deliver. 2. declare to be. —*v.i.* 3. articulate words or phrases. —pro·nounce'ment, *n.*

pro·nounced', *adj.* strongly marked or apparent.

pro·nun''ci·a'tion, *n.* act or manner of speaking.

proof, *n.* 1. evidence demonstrating a fact. 2. standardized strength for liquor. 3. preliminary printing, for inspection. —*adj.* 4. impervious; invulnerable.

proof'read'', *v.t.,* -read, -reading. read to check for errors. —proof'read''er, *n.*

prop, *n., v.t.,* propped, propping, *n.* 1. rigid support. 2. emotional support. 3. any object used in a stage play. —*v.t.* 4. support; strengthen.

prop''a·gan'da, *n.* assertions, etc. intended to help or oppose a cause. —prop''a·gan'dist, *n.* —prop''a·gan·dis'tic, *adj.* —prop''a·gan'dize, *v.t., v.i.*

prop''a·gate'', *v.,* -gated, -gating. *v.t., v.i.* 1. reproduce; breed. —*v.t.* 2. transmit, as ideas. —prop''a·ga'tion, *n.*

pro·pel'ler, *n.* screwlike propelling device.

pro·pen'si·ty, *n.* inclination; tendency.

prop'er, *adj.* 1. suitable. 2. correct. 3. *Grammar.* indicating a specific person, place, or thing. —prop'er·ly, *adv.*

prop'er·ty, *n., pl.* -ties. 1. possessions. 2. attribute.

proph·e·sy (prŏf'ə sī), *v.,* -sied, -sying. *v.t.* 1. foretell; predict. —*v.i.* 2. speak by divine inspiration. —proph'e·cy, *n.*

proph'et, *n.* 1. utterer of divine revelations. 2. person who prophesies the future. Also, *fem.,* proph'et·ess. —proph'et'ic, *adj.* —pro·phet'i·cal·ly, *adv.*

pro''phy·lax'is, *n.* prevention of or protection from disease. —pro''phy·lac'tic, *adj.*

pro·pin'qui·ty, *n.* kinship; nearness.

pro·pi'ti·ate'', *v.t.,* -ated, -ating. make favorable; appease.

pro·pi'tious, *adj.* favorable; auspicious. —pro·pi'tious·ly, *adv.*

pro·po'nent, *n.* advocate; backer.

pro·por'tion, *n.* 1. quantitative relation. 2. due relationship. 3. proportions, dimensions. —*v.t.* 4. put in due proportion. —pro·por'tion·al, pro·por'tion·ate, *adj.*

pro·pose', *v.,* -posed, -posing. *v.t.* 1. suggest or offer. 2. intend. —*v.i.* 3. suggest marriage. —prop''o·si'tion, *n.* —pro·pos'al, *n.*

pro·pound', *v.t.* offer for consideration.

pro·pri'e·tor, *n.* manager or owner. —pro·pri'e·tor·ship'', *n.* —pro·pri'e·tar''y, *adj.*

pro·pri'e·ty, *n., pl.* -ties. 1. respectability. 2. suitability.

pro·pul'sion, *n.* propelling force.

pro·rate', *v.,* -rated, -rating. *v.i., v.t.* distribute or divide proportionally.

pro·sa'ic, *adj.* commonplace; dull.

prose, *n.* ordinary language of speech and writing.

pros'e·cute'', *v.t.,* -cuted, -cuting. 1. begin legal proceedings against. 2. continue to completion. —pros''e·cu'tion, *n.* —pros''e·cu'tor, *n.*

pros'e·lyte'', *n.* convert.

pros'pect, *n.* 1. likelihood, esp. of success. 2. view. 3. potential customer or buyer. —*v.i.* 4. search or explore, e.g. for gold. —pros·pec'tive, *adj.* —pros'pec·tor, *n.*

pro·spec'tus, *n.* description of a new venture, etc. for prospective buyers.

pros'per, *v.i.* be successful. —pros·per'i·ty, *n.* —pros'per·ous, *adj.* —pros'per·ous·ly, *adv.*

pros'tate, *n.* gland at the base of the male bladder.

pros'ti·tute'', *n., v.t.,* -tuted, -tuting. *n.* 1. person who engages in sexual intercourse for pay. —*v.t.* 2. misuse, as talent. —pros''ti·tu'tion, *n.*

pros'trate, *v.t.,* -trated, -trating, *adj. v.t.* 1. lay flat. 2. exhaust of strength. —*adj.* 3. lying. 4. without strength. —pros·tra'tion, *n.*

pros'y, *adj.,* prosier, prosiest. dull; uninteresting.

pro·tect', *v.t.* defend or preserve. —pro·tec'tion, *n.* —pro·tec'tive, *adj.* —pro·tec'tive·ly, *adv.* —pro·tec'tor, *n.*

pro·tec'tor·ate, *n.* protection and partial control of one state by another.

pro·té·gé (prō'tə zhā''), *n.* person under patronage. Also, *fem.,* pro'té·gée''.

pro'te·in, *n.* nitrogenous compound essential for life processes present in living matter.

pro'test, *n.* 1. objection. —*v.i., v.t.* 2. make an objection. —*v.t.* 3. declare solemnly. —prot''es·ta'tion, *n.* —pro·tes'ter, *n.*

Prot'es·tant, *n.* western Christian not belonging to the Roman Catholic Church. —Prot'es·tant·ism'', *n.*

pro'to·col, *n.* code of etiquette, esp. diplomatic.

pro'ton, *n.* elementary atomic particle carrying a positive charge.

pro'to·plasm'', *n.* basic protein substance of living matter.

pro'to·type'', *n.* model; first specimen.

pro·tract', *v.t.* lengthen; prolong. —pro·trac'tion, *n.*

pro·trac'tor, *n.* instrument for measuring angles.

pro·trude', *v.i.,* -truded, truding. project. —pro·tru'sion, *n.* —pro·tru'sive, *adj.*

pro·tu'ber·ant, *adj.* bulging out. —pro·tu'ber·ance, *n.*

proud, *adj.* 1. having self-respect. 2. feeling honored. 3. arrogant. 4. glorious. —proud'ly, *adv.*

prove, *v.,* proved, proving. *v.t.* 1. establish the truth of. 2. test. —*v.i.* 3. turn out. —prov'a·ble, *adj.*

prov'en·der, *n.* food.

prov'erb, *n.* wise popular saying. —pro·ver'bi·al, *adj.*

pro·vide', *v.,* -vided, -viding. *v.t.* 1. supply; equip. 2. yield. —*v.i.* 3. prepare beforehand. —pro·vi'der, *n.*

pro·vi'ded, *conj.* if; on condition that.

prov'i·dence, *n.* 1. divine care or guidance. 2. economy. —prov'i·den''tial, *adj.* —prov'i·dent, *adj.*

prov'ince, *n.* 1. administrative district. 2. personal area of operations or expertise.

pro·vin'cial, *adj.* 1. of a province. 2. narrow-mindedly local.

pro·vi'sion, *n.* 1. stipulation. 2. act or instance of providing. 3. prearrangement. 4. provisions, food supply; goods. —*v.t.* 5. supply with provisions.

pro·vi'sion·al, *adj.* temporary; conditional.

pro·vi'so, *n., pl.* **-sos, -soes.** stipulation.

pro·voke', *v.t.,* **-voked, -voking. 1.** exasperate. **2.** call into being or effect. **—prov''o·ca'tion,** *n.* **—pro·voc'a·tive,** *adj.* **—pro·voc'a·tive·ly,** *adv.*

pro·vost (prō'vōst) *n.* high official, esp. of a university.

prow, *n.* bow of a ship or airplane.

prow'ess, *n.* **1.** bravery; strength, esp. military. **2.** extraordinary ability.

prowl, *v.i.* roam about or search stealthily. **—prowl'er,** *n.*

prox·im'i·ty, *n.* nearness.

prox'y, *n., pl.* **proxies. 1.** agent. **2.** authority to act or vote for another.

prude, *n.* extremely modest person. **—prud'ish,** *adj.*

pru'dence, *n.* **1.** caution. **2.** practical wisdom. **—pru'dent,** *adj.*

prune, *v.t.,* **pruned, pruning,** *n., v.t.* **1.** cut off; trim. **—***n.* **2.** dried plum.

pru'ri·ent, *adj.* having lewd thoughts. **—pru'ri·ence,** *n.*

pry, *v.,* **pried, prying,** *n., v.i.* **1.** inquire unjustifiably into another's affairs. **—***v.t.* **2.** move by leverage. **—***n.* **3.** act or instance of prying. **4.** lever.

psalm (sahm), *n.* sacred song or poem.

pseu·do (soo'dō), *adj.* false; spurious.

pseu'do·nym, *n.* assumed name.

psy·che (si'kē), *n.* human self or soul.

psy·che·del·ic (si''kə del'ik), *adj.* **1.** pertaining to intense hallucinatory effects. **—***n.* **2.** hallucination-producing drug.

psy·chi'a·try, *n.* science of healing mental disorders. **—psy·chi'a·trist,** *n.* **—psy''chi·at'ric,** *adj.*

psy'chic, *n., adj. n.* **1.** medium or clairvoyant. **—***adj.* Also, **psy'chi·cal. 2.** pertaining to the psyche. **3.** supernatural.

psy''cho·a·nal'y·sis, *n.* detailed study and treatment of neuroses. **—psy''cho·an'a·lyst,** *n.* **—psy''cho·an'a·lyze,** *v.t.* **—psy''cho·an''a·lyt'ic,** *adj.*

psy·chol'o·gy, *n.* **1.** study of the mind and behavior. **2.** mental and behavioral constitution. **—psy''cho·log'i·cal,** *adj.* **—psy·chol'o·gist,** *n.*

psy''cho·neu·ro'sis, *n., pl.* **-ses,** *n.* emotional disorder or disease. **—psy''cho·neu·rot'ic,** *adj.*

psy'cho·path'', *n.* mentally ill person. **—psy''cho·path'ic,** *adj.* **—psy·chop'a·thy,** *n.*

psy·cho'sis, *n., pl.* **-ses,** mental disease marked by loss of contact with reality. **—psy·chot'ic,** *n., adj.*

psy''cho·so·mat'ic, *adj.* pertaining to physical effects caused by mental states.

psy''cho·ther'a·py, *n.* treatment of mental and emotional disorders. **—psy''cho·ther'a·pist,** *n.*

pto·maine (tō'mān), *n.* substance produced by bacteria in decaying matter.

pub, *n. British.* bar; tavern.

pu'ber·ty (pyoo'bər tē), *n.* sexual maturity.

pub'lic, *adj.* **1.** of or for all people. **2.** known by or knowable to all. **—***n.* **3.** people generally. **—pub'lic·ly,** *adv.*

pub''li·ca'tion, *n.* **1.** act or instance of publishing. **2.** published work.

pub·lic'i·ty, *n.* **1.** public attention or notice. **2.** material claiming public attention.

pub'li·cize', *v.t.,* **-cized, -cizing,** bring to public attention or notice.

pub'lish, *v.t.* **1.** print or issue for distribution. **2.** announce publicly. **—pub'lish·er,** *n.*

puck'er, *v.t., v.i., n.* curl; wrinkle.

pud'ding, *n.* soft, sweet dessert.

pud'dle, *n.* small pool of water.

pudg'y, *adj.,* **pudgier, pudgiest.** *adj.* short and fat; chubby. **—pudg'i·ness,** *n.*

pueb·lo (pweb'lō), *n.* **1.** adobe Indian village of U.S. Southwest. **2. Pueblo,** Southwestern U.S. Indian people.

pu·er·ile (poo'ər il), *adj.* silly; childish. **—pu''er·il'i·ty,** *n.*

pu·er·per·al (poo ur'pər əl), *adj.* pertaining to childbirth.

puff, *n.* **1.** short quick gust, e.g. of wind. **2.** anything soft and light. **3.** light piece of pastry. **—***v.i.* **4.** blow or breathe in puffs. **5.** become inflated or swollen. **—***v.t.* **6.** blow or puff on.

puf'fin, *n.* sea bird.

pug, *n.* small short-haired dog.

pu'gil·ism'', *n.* boxing. **—pu'gil·ist,** *n.*

pug·na'cious, *adj.* fond of fighting; belligerent. **—pug·nac'i·ty,** *n.*

puke, *v.,* **puked, puking.** *v.i., v.t.* vomit.

pul'chri·tude'', *n.* beauty.

pull, *v.t.* **1.** move toward or after one. **2.** strain by pulling. **3.** select from a group. **—***v.i.* **4.** attempt to move toward one. **5.** move oneself. **—***n.* **6.** act or instance of pulling. **7.** something to pull on. **8.** *Informal.* influence.

pul'let, *n.* young hen.

pul'ley, *n., pl.* **-leys.** wheel with a rim grooved for a rope.

pul'mo·nar''y, *adj.* of the lungs.

pulp, *n.* **1.** soft, fleshy material. **—***v.t.* **2.** crush or grind to pulp. **—***v.i.* **3.** become pulp. **—pulp'y,** *adj.*

pul'pit, *n.* raised platform or lectern used by a clergyman.

pul'sate, *v.i.,* **-sated, -sating.** throb; quiver. **—pul·sa'tion,** *n.*

pulse, *n.* **1.** regular throb of the arteries

produced by the heart. —*v.i.* **2.** throb regularly.

pul′ver·ize″, *v.*, **-ized, -izing.** *v.t.* **1.** reduce to powder or dust. **2.** completely crush. —*v.i.* **3.** become reduced to dust. —**pul″ver·i·za′tion,** *n.*

pu′ma, *n.* cougar.

pum′ice, *n.* porous volcanic glass.

pum′mel, *v.t.* beat; thrash.

pump, *n.* **1.** device for applying force to liquids and gases. **2.** low shoe. —*v.t.* **3.** move with a pump. **4.** inflate. **5.** attempt to wheedle information from.

pum″per·nick′el, *n.* hard rye bread.

pump′kin, *n.* large orange fruit that grows on a vine.

pun, *n.*, *v.i.*, **punned, punning,** *n.* **1.** play with similar-sounding words with different meanings. —*v.i.* **2.** make a pun.

punch, *n.* **1.** quick blow, esp. with the fist. **2.** piercing or sinking implement. **3.** sweet mixed beverage. —*v.t.* **4.** hit. **5.** perforate. —**punch′er,** *n.*

punc·til′i·ous, *adj.* adhering to correct procedure.

punc′tu·al, *adj.* on time; prompt. —**punc″tu·al′i·ty,** *n.* —**punc′tu·al·ly,** *adv.*

punc′tu·ate″, *v.t.*, **-ated, -ating.** **1.** mark with commas, periods, etc. **2.** mark or interrupt periodically. **3.** give emphasis to. —**punc″tu·a′tion,** *n.*

punc′ture, *v.t.*, **-tured, -turing,** *n. v.t.* **1.** pierce with a pointed object. —*n.* **2.** act or instance of puncturing.

pun′dit, *n.* expert.

pun′gent, *adj.* **1.** sharp of taste. **2.** biting. —**pun′gen·cy,** *n.* —**pun′gent·ly,** *adv.*

pun′ish, *v.t.* **1.** subject to a penalty or revenge. **2.** inflict a penalty for. —**pun′ish·a·ble,** *adj.* —**pun′ish·ment,** *n.*

pu′ni·tive, *adj.* punishing.

punt, *n.* **1.** flat-bottomed shallow boat. **2.** kick in football. —*v.i.* **3.** kick in mid-air.

pu′ny, *adj.*, **-nier, -niest.** small; slight; weak.

pup, *n.* young dog. Also, **pup′py.**

pu′pa, *n.*, *pl.* **-pae, -pas.** insect halfway between larva and adult.

pu′pil, *n.* **1.** student. **2.** dark opening in the iris of the eye.

pup′pet, *n.* **1.** small figure moved by hand or by wires. **2.** supposedly autonomous party obeying another. —**pup″pe·teer′,** *n.*

pur′chase, *v.t.*, **-chased, -chasing,** *n.* **1.** buy. —*n.* **2.** act or instance of purchasing. **3.** thing purchased. **4.** leverage. —**pur′chas·er,** *n.*

pure, *adj.*, **purer, purest. 1.** unmixed or unpolluted. **2.** absolute. **3.** abstract. —**pure′ly,** *adv.*

pu·ree (pyŏŏ rā′), *n.* cooked and sieved food.

pur′ga·to″ry, *n.*, *pl.* **-ries, 1.** temporary punishment. **2.** place for purification from sin after death.

purge, *v.t.*, **purged, purging, 1.** cleanse; purify. **2.** rid; remove. **3.** eliminate or kill for political reasons. —*n.* **4.** act or instance of purging. —**pur′ga′tion,** *n.* —**pur′ga·tive,** *adj.*, *n.*

pu′ri·fy, *v.*, **-fied, -fying.** *v.t.* **1.** make pure. **2.** free from sin or guilt. —*v.i.* **3.** become pure. —**pu″ri·fi·ca′tion,** *n.*

pu′ri·tan, *n.* **1.** member of a strict religious group. **2.** adherent to an unusually strict moral code. —**puri·tan′i·cal,** *adj.*

pu′ri·ty, *n.* quality or condition of being pure.

purl, *v.t.*, *v.i.* knit with an inverted stitch.

pur′lieu (par′lōō), *n.* bordering or outlying district.

pur·loin′, *v.t.* steal.

pur′ple, *n.* **1.** bluish-red color. —*adj.* **2.** of the color purple.

pur·port, *v.t.* (par″port′) **1.** claim or profess. **2.** express; imply. —*n.* **3.** (par′port) significance.

pur′pose, *n.*, *v.t.*, **-posed, -posing.** *n.* **1.** intention; object. —*v.t.* **2.** intend. —**pur′pose·ful,** *adj.* —**pur′pose·less,** *adj.*

pur′pose·ly, *adv.* intentionally.

purr, *n.* **1.** soft continuous sound made by a cat. —*v.i.* **2.** make this sound.

purse, *n.*, *v.t.*, **pursed, pursing.** *n.* **1.** small bag for money. **2.** sum of money offered as a prize. —*v.t.* **3.** pucker.

purs′er, *n.* financial officer of a ship.

pur·su′ant, *adv.* according.

pur·sue′, *v.t.*, **-sued, -suing. 1.** chase. **2.** proceed with. —**pur·su′ance,** *n.* —**pur·su′er,** *n.*

pur·suit′, *n.* **1.** act or instance of pursuing. **2.** occupation; calling.

pu·ru·lent (pyŏŏr′ə lənt), *adj.* containing pus. —**pu·ru′lence,** *n.*

pur·vey, *v.t.* furnish; supply. —**pur·vey′ance,** *n.* —**pur·vey′or,** *n.*

pus, *n.* yellowish fluid found in sores.

push, *v.t.* **1.** press against to move. **2.** urge; press. —*v.i.* **3.** move with force. —*n.* **4.** act or instance of pushing. —**push′er,** *n.*

push′y, *adj.*, **-ier, -iest.** aggressive.

pu·sil·lan″i·mous, *adj.* cowardly.

puss′y, *n.*, *pl.* **-sies.** cat. Also, **puss.**

puss′y·foot, *v.i.* tread stealthily.

pussy willow, *n.* small American willow tree.

pus′tule, *n.* pus-filled pimple.

put, *v.*, **put, putting.** *v.t.* **1.** carry to a specified place. **2.** cause to be in a specified condition. **3.** present for consideration. **4.** hurl overhand. **5.** put off, postpone. **6.** put out, **a.** extinguish. **b.** trouble. —*v.i.* **7.** put up with, tolerate.

pu′ta·tive, *adj.* reputed; supposed.

pu'tre·fy", v., -fied, -fying. v.i., v.t. decay; rot. —**pu"tre·fac'tion**, n.

pu'trid, adj. **1.** rotten; decayed. **2.** corrupt; vile.

putt, v.t. Golf. **1.** hit gently. —n. **2.** act or instance of putting.

put'ter, v.i. **1.** be active without effect. —n. **2.** golf club for putting.

put'ty, n., v.t., -tied, -tying. n. **1.** cement of linseed oil and whiting. —v.t. **2.** secure with putty.

puz'zle, n., v., -zled, -zling, n. **1.** device or problem posing difficulties. —v.t. **2.** mystify; perplex. —v.i. **3.** attempt to study or figure out a problem.

pyg'my, n., pl. -mies. dwarf.

py'lon, n. thin tower.

py"or·rhe'a, n. disease of the gums.

pyr'a·mid, n. **1.** structure or form with triangular sides. —v.t. **2.** increase gradually. —**py·ram'i·dal**, adj.

pyre, n. heap of material for burning a corpse.

py'rite, n. yellow sulfur and iron.

py"ro·ma'ni·a, n. mania for starting fires. —**py"ro·ma'ni·ac"**, n.

py"ro·tech'nics, n. **1.** fireworks **2.** display of virtuosity. —**pyro·tech'nic**, adj.

py'thon, n. large constricting snake.

Q

Q, q, n. seventeenth letter of the English alphabet.

quack, n. **1.** fraudulent doctor. **2.** sound of a duck. —v.i. **3.** utter a quack. —**quack'er·y**, n.

quad'ran"gle, n. **1.** closed figure with four angles. **2.** enclosed four-sided yard. —**quad·ran'gu·lar**, adj.

quad'rant, n. **1.** arc of 90°. **2.** instrument for measuring altitudes.

quad"ri·lat'er·al, adj. **1.** four-sided. —n. **2.** plane figure with four sides.

qua·drille (kwə·dril'), n. square dance of five parts for four couples.

qua·droon', n. a person of one-quarter black ancestry.

quad'ru·ped", n. animal with four feet.

quad'ru·ple, adj., v., -pled, -pling. adj. **1.** fourfold. **2.** having four parts. —v.t., v.i. **3.** multiply by four.

quad'ru·plet, n. one of four children born together.

quad·ru'pli·cate, n. any of four copies.

quaff (kwof), v.t. drink with gusto.

quag'mire", n. boggy area.

qua·hog (quo'hog), n. edible American clam.

quail, n., pl. quails, quail, v.i., n. **1.** game bird. —v.i. **2.** lose heart or courage.

quaint, adj. pleasingly odd or old-fashioned. —**quaint'ness**, n. —**quaint'ly**, adv.

quake, v.i., quaked, quaking, n. v.i. **1.** tremble or shake. —n. **2.** earthquake.

Quak'er, n. member of the Society of Friends.

qual'i·fy", v., -fied, -fying. v.t. **1.** make eligible or capable. **2.** modify. —v.i. **3.** be qualified. —**qual"i·fi·ca'tion**, n. —**qual'i·fied"**, adj.

qual'i·ty, n., pl. -ties. **1.** essential characteristic. **2.** degree of merit. **3.** excellence. —**qual'i·ta"tive**, adj.

qualm (kwahm), n. **1.** misgiving. **2.** sick feeling.

quan'da·ry, n., pl. -ries. perplexed state.

quan'ti·ty, n., pl. -ties. **1.** amount or number. **2.** large or considerable amount. —**quan'ti·ta"tive**, adj.

quar'an·tine", n., v.t., -tined, -tining. n. **1.** isolation of suspected disease bearers. —v.t. **2.** put in quarantine.

quar'rel, n. **1.** angry argument; fight. —v.i. **2.** have a quarrel. —**quar'rel·some**, adj.

quar'ry, n., pl. -ries, v.t., -ried, -rying. **1.** place from which stone is extracted. **2.** object of pursuit; prey. —v.t. **3.** get or take from a quarry.

quart, n. unit of measure equal to one fourth of a gallon.

quar'ter, n. **1.** fourth part. **2.** coin with the value of 25 cents. **3.** quarters, lodgings. **4.** mercy. —v.t. **5.** divide into quarters. **6.** lodge. —adj. **7.** being a quarter.

quar'ter·back", n. position in football.

quar'ter·ly, adj., n., pl. -lies. adj. **1.** occurring every three months. —n. **2.** periodical published four times a year.

quar'ter·mas"ter, n. **1.** army officer who oversees supplies, etc. **2.** petty officer in charge of a ship's signals, steering, etc.

quar·tet', n. **1.** group of four, esp. musicians. **2.** composition for four instruments. Also, **quar·tette'**.

quar'to, n. book printed on sheets folded into quarters.

quartz, n. common shiny crystalline mineral.

quash, v.t. **1.** put down completely. **2.** invalidate.

qua·si (kwah'sī), adj. **1.** resembling. —adv. **2.** seemingly.

quat'rain, n. four-line verse unit.

qua'ver, v.i. **1.** tremble. **2.** speak or sing tremulously. —n. **3.** quavering tone.

quay (kē), n. pier; wharf.

quea'sy, adj., -sier, -siest. **1.** nauseous. **2.** uneasy.

queen, n. **1.** female sovereign. **2.** spouse of a king. **3.** fertile female of bees.

queer, *adj.* peculiar. —**queer'ly,** *adv.*
—**queer'ness,** *n.*

quell, *v.t.* 1. subdue. 2. pacify.

quench, *v.t.* 1. slake, as thirst. 2. extinguish. 3. cool by immersion.

quer'u·lous, *adj.* peevish.

que'ry, *n., pl.* -ries, *v.t.,* -ried, -rying. *n.*
1. question; inquiry. —*v.t.* 2. inquire regarding.

quest, *n., v.i.* search.

ques'tion, *n.* 1. interrogative sentence. 2. problem or issue. —*v.t.* 3. ask questions of. 4. challenge; doubt. —**ques'tion·a·ble,** *adj.* —**ques'tion·er,** *n.*

ques"tion·naire', *n.* set or list of questions.

queue (kyōō), *n., v.,* queued, queuing. *n.* 1. line of waiting persons. 2. braid of hair at the back of the head. —*v.t., v.i.* 3. form in a line.

quib'ble, *v.i.,* -bled, -bling, *n. v.i.* 1. speak evasively. 2. cavil; carp. —*n.* 3. act or instance of quibbling.

quiche (kēsh), *n.* French tart filled with egg, cheese, etc.

quick, *adj.* 1. prompt. 2. intelligent. 3. speedy. —*n.* 4. living persons. 5. vital part. —**quick'ly,** *adv.* —**quick'ness,** *n.*

quick'en, *v.t.* 1. hasten. —*v.i.* 2. become alive or sensitive.

quick'sand", *n.* watery, soft mass of sand that yields under weight.

quick'sil"ver, *n.* mercury.

quid, *n.* cut of something chewable, esp. tobacco.

qui·es'cent (kwē·es'ǝnt), *adj.* inactive. —**qui·es'cence,** *n.*

qui'et, *adj.* 1. at rest. 2. silent. 3. restrained. —*v.t.* 4. make quiet. —*v.i.* 5. become quiet. —*n.* 6. silence; tranquillity. —**qui'et·ly,** *adv.* —**qui'et·ness,** *n.* —**qui'e·tude",** *n.*

qui·e·tus (kwī·ēt'ǝs), *n.* 1. final settlement. 2. death.

quill, *n.* 1. large stiff feather. 2. bristle or spine.

quilt, *n.* lined and padded bedspread.

quince, *n.* hard yellowish fruit.

qui'nine, *n.* bitter saltlike substance used medically.

quin·tes'sence, *n.* 1. purest essence. 2. completely typical example. —**quin"tes·sen'tial,** *adj.*

quin·tet', *n.* 1. group of five, esp. musicians. 2. composition for five instruments. Also **quin·tette'.**

quin·tu'ple, *adj., v.,* -pled, -pling. *adj.* 1. fivefold. 2. having five parts. —*v.t., v.i.* 3. multiply by five.

quin'tu·plet, *n.* 1. one of five children born together. 2. group of five.

quip, *n., v.i.,* quipped, quipping. *n.* 1. sarcastic or clever remark. —*v.i.* 2. make a quip.

quire, *n.* set of 24 sheets of paper.

quirk, *n.* peculiarity.

quis'ling, *n.* traitor.

quit, *v.,* quitted, quitting. *v.t., v.i.* 1. discontinue. —*v.t.* 2. leave. 3. abandon. —**quit'ter,** *n.*

quite, *adv.* 1. completely. 2. positively.

quits, *adj.* on equal terms.

quit'tance, *n.* 1. recompense. 2. discharge from obligation or debt.

quiv'er, *v.t., v.i.* 1. tremble; shake. —*n.* 2. case for arrows.

quix·ot'ic, *adj.* foolishly idealistic.

quiz, *v.t.,* quizzed, quizzing, *n., v.t.* 1. give a brief test to. 2. question closely. —*n.* 3. test or questioning.

quiz'zi·cal, *adj.* 1. comically odd. 2. questioning. 3. chaffing. —**quiz'zi·cal·ly,** *adv.*

quoit, *n.* flat ring used in throwing games.

quon'dam, *adj.* former.

quo'rum, *n.* sufficient number of attending members.

quo'ta, *n.* assigned share or number.

quo·ta'tion, *n.* 1. word-for-word citation. 2. specified price.

quo·ta'tion marks, *n.* pair of punctuation marks, " ", used to mark the beginning and end of a direct quotation.

quote, *v.t.,* quoted, quoting, *n. v.t.* 1. repeat verbatim. 2. cite as evidence. 3. state, as a price. —*n.* 4. quotation. —**quot'a·ble,** *adj.*

quoth, *v.t. Archaic.* said.

quo'tient, *n. Math.* number of times one number contains another.

R

R, r, *n.* eighteenth letter of the English alphabet.

rab'bet, *n., v.t.,* -beted, -beting. *n.* 1. L-shaped notch on an edge of timber, etc. —*v.t.* 2. cut a rabbet on. 3. join with rabbets.

rab'bi, *n., pl.* -bis. Jewish preacher. —**rab·bin'ic, rab·bin'i·cal,** *adj.*

rab'bit, *n.* small long-eared mammal.

rab'ble, *n.* mob.

rab'id, *adj.* 1. irrationally extreme. 2. having rabies.

ra'bies, *n.* infectious disease transmitted by animal bites.

rac·coon', *n.* small nocturnal mammal.

race, *n., v.,* raced, racing. *n.* 1. contest of speed. 2. group of persons with a common origin. —*v.i.* 3. participate in a race. 4. move quickly. —*v.t.* 5. cause to move quickly.

ra'cial, *adj.* concerning race (2), or the

differences between races. —**rac'ism,** *n.*

rack, *n.* **1.** framework for storage. **2.** bar-like gear engaging a pinion. —*v.t.* **3.** torture. **4.** strain.

rack'et, *n.* **1.** noise; commotion. **2.** dishonest or illegal activity. **3.** cross-stringed light bat, used esp. in tennis.

rack"e·teer', *n.* gangster.

rac·on·teur (rak"on·tər') *n.* story-teller.

rac'y, *adj.,* **-ier, -iest. 1.** lively. **2.** risqué.

ra'dar, *n.* device using radio waves to locate objects.

ra·di·al, *adj.* pertaining to rays or a radius.

ra'di·ant, *adj.* **1.** bright; shiny. **2.** emitting light. —**ra'di·ance,** *n.*

ra'di·ate", *v.,* **-ated, -ating.** *v.i.* **1.** move or spread like rays from a center. —*v.t.* **2.** emit, as rays.

ra'di·a"tor, *n.* convection heater.

rad'i·cal, *adj.* **1.** fundamental. **2.** favoring drastic or extreme change. —*n.* **3.** person with radical ideas. —**rad'i·cal·ism",** *n.*

ra'di·o", *n.* **1.** wireless transmission of sound by electromagnetic waves. **2.** device for receiving radio transmissions.

ra"di·o·ac'tive, *adj.* emitting nuclear radiation.

rad'ish, *n.* edible root of a garden plant.

ra'di·um, *n.* radioactive metallic element.

ra'di·us, *n., pl.* **-dii, -diuses. 1.** straight line to an arc from its center. **2.** forearm bone.

raf'fle, *n., v.t.,* **-fled, -fling.** *n.* **1.** lottery for which chances are sold. —*v.t.* **2.** dispose of by raffle.

raft, *n.* floating platform.

raf'ter, *n.* roof beam.

rag, *n.* torn or waste piece of cloth. —**rag'ged,** *adj.*

rag'a·muf"fin, *n.* scruffy child.

rage, *n., v.i.,* **raged, raging.** *n.* **1.** violent anger. **2.** popular vogue. —*v.i.* **3.** be violently angry. **4.** proceed or prevail with violence.

rag'lan, *n.* loose overcoat with shoulders continuing from the sleeves.

ra·gout (ra gōō'), *n.* stew.

rag'time", *n.* syncopated American popular music.

rag'weed", *n.* weed whose pollen causes hay fever.

raid, *n.* **1.** sudden attack. —*v.t.* **2.** attack suddenly.

rail, *n.* **1.** horizontal bar or beam. **2.** guide for a wheel of a railroad car. **3.** railroad. **4.** wading bird. —*v.i.* **5.** complain bitterly.

rail'ing, *n.* barrier of uprights and rails.

rail'ler·y, *n.* banter; ridicule.

rail'road", *n.* **1.** road of rails on which trains run. —*v.t.* **2.** transport by rail-road. **3.** *Informal.* convict wrongly an innocent person.

rain, *n.* **1.** condensed water falling in drops from the clouds. **2.** rainstorm. —*v.i.* **3.** fall as rain. —*v.t.* **4.** give abundantly; shower. —**rain'y,** *adj.* —**rain'fall",** *n.*

rain'bow", *n.* colored arc of sunlight refracted through raindrops.

rain'coat", *n.* water-repellent overcoat.

raise, *v.t.,* **raised, raising,** *n., v.t.* **1.** lift. **2.** set upright. **3.** solicit and collect. **4.** grow. **5.** bring up. **6.** call to attention. —*n.* **7.** increase in salary.

rai'sin, *n.* sweet dried grape.

ra'jah, *n.* oriental prince or king. Also **ra'ja.**

rake, *n., v.t.,* **raked, raking.** *n.* **1.** pronged implement for collecting leaves, etc. **2.** libertine. **3.** slope. —*v.t.* **4.** smooth, collect, etc. with a rake.

rak'ish, *adj.* jaunty.

ral'ly, *v.,* **-lied, -lying,** *n., pl.* **-lies.** *v.t., v.i.* **1.** gather. —*v.t.* **2.** reorganize. **3.** tease. —*v.i.* **4.** recover strength. —*n.* **5.** gathering. **6.** recovery of strength.

ram, *n., v.t.,* **rammed, ramming.** *n.* **1.** male sheep. **2.** device for battering, crushing, etc. —*v.t.* **3.** run into forcibly.

ram'ble, *v.i.,* **-bled, -bling,** *n. v.i.* **1.** wander leisurely. **2.** talk discursively. —*n.* **3.** leisurely stroll.

ram'i·fy", *v.,* **-fied, -fying.** *v.t., v.i.* branch out.

ramp, *n.* sloping road or walk.

ram'page, *n., v.i.,* **-paged, -paging.** *n.* **1.** violent behavior. —*v.i.* **2.** rush about furiously.

ramp'ant, *adj.* **1.** unchecked; raging. **2.** standing on the hind legs.

ram'part, *n.* mound of earth erected as a defense; parapet.

ram'shack"le, *adj.* shaky; rickety.

ranch, *n.* large stock farm.

ran·cid (ran'sid), *adj.* stale; spoiled. —**ran·cid'i·ty,** *n.*

ran'cor, *n.* resentment. —**ran'cor·ous,** *adj.*

ran'dom, *adj.* without pattern or aim.

range, *n., v.* **ranged, ranging.** *n.* **1.** extent. **2.** row. **3.** mountain chain. **4.** grazing area. **5.** distance of gunfire, reach, etc. **6.** shooting ground. **7.** stove. —*v.t.* **8.** put in a row. **9.** pass over. —*v.i.* **10.** have a range.

rang'er, *n.* warden or trooper policing a rural area.

rank, *n.* **1.** group, class, or standing. **2.** high position. **3.** row. **4. ranks,** ordinary troops. —*v.t.* **5.** arrange in formation. —*v.i.* **6.** have a specified standing. —*adj.* **7.** excessively grown. **8.** offensively strong in taste or smell. **9.** utter.

ran'kle, *v.* **-kled, -kling.** *v.t.* **1.** cause

long-lasting resentment in. —*v.i.* **2.** cause long-lasting resentment.

ran′sack, *v.t.* **1.** search thoroughly. **2.** plunder; pillage.

ran′som, *n.* **1.** price demanded for return of a prisoner. —*v.t.* **2.** redeem for money.

rant, *v.i.* **1.** speak violently or wildly. —*n.* **2.** violent or extravagant speech.

rap, *v.t.*, **rapped, rapping**, *n.*, *v.t.* **1.** strike sharply. —*n.* **2.** quick, sharp blow. **3.** *Informal.* blame; responsibility.

ra·pa′cious, *adj.* predatory.

rape, *n.*, *v.t.*, **raped, raping.** *n.* **1.** forced sexual violation of a woman. —*v.t.* **2.** commit rape on. **3.** seize and carry off by force. —**ra′pist**, *n.*

rap′id, *adj.* **1.** speedy. —*n.* **2.** rapids, fast-moving sections of a river. —**ra·pid′i·ty**, *n.*

ra·pi·er (rā′pē ər), *n.* small narrow sword.

rap·ine (rap′in), *n.* plunder.

rapt, *adj.* engrossed.

rap′ture, *n.* ecstatic or beatific joy. —**rap′tur·ous**, *adj.*

rare, *adj.* **rarer, rarest. 1.** unusual. **2.** thin. **3.** not completely cooked. —**rar′i·ty**, *n.*

rar·e·fy′′, *v.*, **-fied, -fying.** *v.t.*, *v.i.* thin. —**rar′′e·fac′tion**, *n.*

ras′cal, *n.* unscrupulous person. —**ras·cal′i·ty**, *n.*

rash, *adj.* **1.** unreasonably hasty. —*n.* **2.** skin irritation.

rash′er, *n.* thin slice of ham or bacon.

rasp, *v.t.* **1.** scrape or grate. **2.** talk with a grating sound. —*n.* **3.** rasping sound. **4.** coarse file.

rasp′ber′′ry, *n.*, *pl.* **-ries.** juicy small red or black fruit.

rat, *n.* long-tailed rodent larger than a mouse.

ratch′et, *n.* gear controlled by a pawl.

rate, *n.*, *v.*, **rated, rating.** *n.* **1.** fixed relation between variables. —*v.t.* **2.** establish a rate for. **3.** judge to be as specified. —*v.i.* **4.** have a specified value.

rath′er, *adv.* **1.** to a certain extent. **2.** on the contrary. **3.** in preference.

rat′i·fy′′, *v.t.*, **-fied, -fying.** approve formally.

ra′tion, *n.* **1.** limited allotment. —*v.t.* **2.** put on a ration.

ra′tion·al, *adj.* **1.** reasonable. **2.** sane. —**ra′′tion·al′i·ty**, *n.*

ra·tion·ale, *n.* rational basis.

ra′tion·al·ize′′, *v.t.*, **-ized, -izing. 1.** attempt to justify with reasons. **2.** make methodical. —**ra′′tion·al·i·za′tion**, *n.*

ra·tio, (rā′shō) *n.* relation of quantities.

rat·tan′, *n.* hollow stem of a climbing palm.

rat′tle, *v.*, **-tled, -tling**, *n.*, *v.i.* **1.** make

successive short sharp noises. **2.** chatter. —*v.t.* **3.** confuse; disconcert. —*n.* **4.** rattling sounds. **5.** child's toy that rattles.

rat′tle·snake′, *n.* poisonous American snake.

rau·cous, *adj.* harsh; hoarse.

rav′age, *n.*, *v.t.*, *v.i.*, **-aged, -aging.** ruin; pillage.

rave, *v.i.*, **raved, raving**, *n.*, *v.i.* **1.** talk wildly. —*n.* **2.** *Informal,* unequivocally favorable review.

rav′el, *v.t.* **1.** disengage the threads of. **2.** solve; make clear. —*v.i.* **3.** fray. **4.** become tangled.

ra′ven, *n.* large glossy black bird.

rav′en·ous, *adj.* exceedingly hungry.

ra·vine′, *n.* narrow valley.

rav′ish, *v.t.* **1.** transport or fill with joy. **2.** rape.

raw, *adj.* **1.** in a natural state; naked. **2.** uncooked. **3.** untrained; young.

raw′hide′′, *n.* untanned hide.

ray, *n.* **1.** narrow beam of light. **2.** glimpse. **3.** radiating line. **4.** flat ocean fish.

ray′on, *n.* synthetic silk-like fabric.

raze, *v.t.*, **razed, razing.** demolish.

ra′zor, *n.* sharp instrument for shaving.

re (rē), *prep.* in the affair of.

re-, prefix meaning "again." reaccustom, reacquaint, reacquire, readapt, reaffirm, realign, reappear, reapply, reappoint, reappraisal, rearrange, reassemble, reassert, reassess, reassign, rebind, rebutton, recheck, recommence, reconnect, reconquer, recopy, rededicate, redefine, redevelop, rediscover, redo, reelect, reemerge, reemphasize, reerect, reestablish, reevaluate, reexperience, refill, reformulate, refurnish, regrow, reheat, reignite, reinsert, reinterpret, rekindle, remarry, rename, renumber, reoccur, reorient, replant, replay, reread, resell, resupply, retake, retell, retest, retrain, retransmit, retype, reusable, reuse, reunion, reunite, reverify, rewarm, rewin, rework, rewrap.

reach, *v.t.* **1.** arrive at. **2.** extend. **3.** be able to touch. **4.** communicate with. —*v.i.* **5.** extend the hand. —*n.* **6.** act, instance, or extent of reaching.

re·act′, *v.i.* **1.** act in response. **2.** interact.

re·ac′tion, *n.* **1.** action in response. **2.** extreme political conservatism. —**re·ac′tion·ar′′y**, *adj.*, *n.*

read′ing, *n.* interpretation of a play or musical composition.

read′y, *adj.*, *v.t.*, **readied, readying**, *n.*, *adj.* **1.** prepared. **2.** willing. **3.** imminent. —*v.t.* **4.** make ready. —*n.* **5.** state of readiness. —**read′i·ly**, *adv.* —**read′i·ness**, *n.*

re′al, *adj.* **1.** not false; genuine. **2.** not imaginary or ideal. —**re·al′i·ty**, *n.* —**re′al·ly**, *adv.*

real estate, *n.* property, esp. land with buildings. Also, **re′al·ty.**

re′al·ism, *n.* **1.** close imitation of reality. **2.** acceptance of actual conditions. —**re′al·ist,** *n.* —**re″al·is′tic,** *adj.*

re′al·ize″, *v.t.* **1.** understand completely. **2.** bring into actuality. **3.** obtain as a profit. —**re″al·i·za′tion,** *n.*

realm (relm), *n.* **1.** special field of expertise. **2.** kingdom.

re′al·tor, *n.* agent selling real estate.

ream, *n.* **1.** twenty quires of paper. —*v.t.* **2.** make or enlarge by a rotary tool.

reap, *v.t.* **1.** harvest. **2.** get as a reward. —**reap′er,** *n.*

rear, *n.* **1.** back part. **2.** backside. —*adj.* **3.** pertaining to the rear. —*v.t.* **4.** raise; erect. **5.** bring up to maturity. —*v.i.* **6.** rise on the rear legs.

rea′son, *n.* **1.** cause or justification. **2.** objectivity; logic. **3.** sanity. —*v.i.* **4.** think or argue logically. —*v.t.* **5.** infer or conclude. —**rea′son·a·ble,** *adj.* —**rea′son·a·bly,** *adv.*

re″as·sure′, *v.t.*, **-sured, -suring.** restore the confidence of. —**re″as·sur′ance,** *n.*

re′bate, *v.t.*, **-bated, -bating,** *n.*, *v.t.* **1.** refund after payment. —*n.* **2.** amount rebated.

re·bel′, *v.i.*, **-belled, -belling,** *n.*, *v.i.* (rĕbel′) **1.** arise against authority. —*n.* (reb′əl) **2.** person who rebels. —**re·bel′lion,** *n.* —**re·bel′lious,** *adj.*

re·bound′, *v.i.* (rē bownd′) **1.** bounce back after impact. —*n.* (rē′bownd) **2.** act or instance of rebounding.

re·buff′, *n.* **1.** blunt rejection or refusal. —*v.t.* **2.** reject curtly.

re·buke′, *v.t.*, **-buked, -buking,** *n.* reprimand.

re′bus, *n.* combination of pictures whose names combine to form a word.

re·but′, *v.t.*, **-butted, -butting.** refute. —**re·but′tal,** *n.*

re·cal·ci·trant (rē kal′sə trənt) *adj.* stubborn; refractory. —**re·cal′ci·trance,** *n.*

re·call′, *v.t.* **1.** remember. **2.** withdraw. **3.** call or summon back. —*n.* **4.** act or instance of recalling. **5.** memory.

re·cant′, *v.t.*, *v.i.* retract; renounce. —**re″can·ta′tion,** *n.*

re·ca·pit·u·late, *v.* **-lated, -lating.** *v.t.*, *v.i.* restate briefly; sum up. —**re″ca·pit″u·la′tion,** *n.*

re·cede′, *v.i.*, **-ceded, -ceding. 1.** move back. **2.** diminish.

re·ceipt′, *n.* **1.** act or instance of receiving. **2.** document acknowledging payment or delivery. **3.** receipts, income.

re·ceive′, *v.t.*, **-ceived, -ceiving. 1.** take when offered or sent. **2.** sustain; experience. **3.** welcome. —**re·ceiv′a·ble,** *adj.*

re·ceiv′er, *n.* **1.** person or thing that receives. **2.** apparatus receiving radio sig-

nals. **3.** administrator of property in litigation. —**re·ceiv′er·ship,** *n.*

re′cent, *adj.* not long past. —**re′cen·cy,** *n.*

re·cep′ta·cle, *n.* container.

re·cep′tion, *n.* **1.** act or instance of receiving. **2.** formal social function. **3.** quality of radio signals, etc. as received.

re·cep′tive, *adj.* **1.** ready to consider new ideas. **2.** amenable.

re·cess′, *n.* **1.** pause in work. **2.** hollowed-out space. **3.** recesses, inner areas. —*v.i.* **4.** pause in work.

re·ces′sion, *n.* **1.** withdrawal. **2.** economic decline.

re·ces′sion·al, *n.* hymn sung during the withdrawal of clergy.

rec′i·pe″, *n.* method or formula, esp. in cooking.

re·cip′i·ent, *n.* receiver.

re·cip′ro·cal, *adj.* **1.** mutual. —*n.* **2.** counterpart.

re·cip′ro·cate″, *v.*, **-cated, -cating.** *v.t.*, *v.i.* **1.** give, receive, etc. in return. **2.** move back and forth. —**rec″i·proc′i·ty,** *n.*

re·ci′tal, *n.* **1.** account or narration. **2.** performance of music.

re·cite′, *v.t.*, **-cited, -citing. 1.** repeat from memory. **2.** narrate; read aloud. —**rec″i·ta′tion,** *n.*

reck′less, *adj.* foolhardy, careless.

reck′on, *v.t.* **1.** calculate. **2.** esteem. **3.** *Dialect.* believe; suppose. —*v.i.* **4.** deal; cope.

reck′on·ing, *n.* **1.** computation. **2.** settling of accounts. **3.** accounting.

re·claim′, *v.t.* **1.** make usable. **2.** make reusable. **3.** redeem from vice, etc. —**re″cla·ma′tion,** *n.*

re·cline′, *v.*, **-clined, -clining.** *v.i.*, *v.t.* lie or lay back.

rec′luse, *n.* person who lives in seclusion. —**re·clu′sive,** *adj.*

re·cog′ni·zance, *n.* formal pledge of action.

rec′og·nize″, *v.t.*, **-nized, -nizing. 1.** identify from memory. **2.** be aware of. **3.** acknowledge formally. —**rec″og·ni′tion,** *n.*

re·coil′, *v.i.* **1.** draw or shrink back. **2.** spring back. —*n.* **3.** act or instance of recoiling.

re″col·lect′, *v.t.*, *v.i.* remember. —**rec″ol·lec′tion,** *n.*

rec″om·mend′, *v.t.* **1.** speak favorably of. **2.** advise. —**rec″om·men·da′tion,** *n.*

rec′om·pense″, *v.t.*, **-pensed, -pensing,** *n.* *v.t.* **1.** reward or compensate. —*n.* **2.** reward or compensation.

rec′on·cile″, *v.t.*, **-ciled, -ciling. 1.** return to harmony. **2.** make compatible. **3.** settle amicably. **4.** make acquiescent. —**rec″on·cil′a·ble,** *adj.* —**rec″on·cil′i·a′tion,** *n.*

re′′con·noi′ter, v.t., v.i. search or scout. —**re·con′nais·sance,** n.

re·cord, v.t. (rē kord′) **1.** make a written account of. **2.** put in reproducible form. —n. (rek′ərd) **3.** written account. **4.** disk for sound reproduction. **5.** best performance. —adj. **6.** being the best to date.

re·count, v.t. (re kownt′) **1.** narrate. **2.** count again. —n. **3.** (rē′kownt). second count.

re·coup (ri kōōp′), v.t. recover; make up.

re′course, n. **1.** appeal for help. **2.** possible source of help.

re·cov′er, v.t. **1.** get back. **2.** salvage. —v.i. **3.** regain health. **4.** regain composure. —**re·cov′er·a·ble,** adj. —**re·cov′er·y,** n.

rec′′re·a′tion, n. refreshing occupation. —**rec′′re·a′tion·al,** adj.

re·crim′i·nate′′, v.i., -nated, -nating. make an accusation in return.

re·cruit′, n. **1.** newly enlisted person. —v.t. **2.** enlist. —**re·cruit′ment,** n.

rec′tan·gle, n. parallelogram with four right angles. —**rec′tan′gu·lar,** adj.

rec′ti·fy′′, v.t., -fied, -fying. correct. —**rec′′ti·fi′a·ble,** adj. —**rec′′ti·fi·ca′ tion,** n.

rec′′ti·lin′e·ar, adj. **1.** forming a straight line. **2.** bounded by straight lines.

rec′ti·tude′′, n. moral uprightness.

rec′tor, n. **1.** clergyman in charge of a parish. **2.** head of certain universities and colleges.

rec′to·ry, n. parsonage.

rec′tum, n. terminal part of the large intestine. —**rec′tal,** adj.

re·cum′bent, adj. lying down. —**re·cum′ ben·cy,** n.

re·cu′per·ate′′, v.i., -ated, -ating. regain health. —**re·cu′per·a·tive,** adj.

re·cur′, v.i., -curred, -curring. **1.** occur again or repeatedly. **2.** return to one's thoughts. —**re·cur′rence,** n. —**re·cur′ rent,** adj. —**re·cur′rent·ly,** adv.

re·cy′cle, v.t. convert into reusable material.

red, n., adj., redder, reddest. n. **1.** color of blood. **2. Red,** Informal. Communist. —adj. **3.** of or pertaining to red. —**red′den,** v.t., v.i.

re·deem′, v.t. **1.** recover. **2.** pay off. **3.** exchange for premiums. **4.** deliver from sin. **5.** fulfill, as a promise. —**re·demp′ tion,** n.

Re·deem′er, n. Jesus Christ.

red′-let′ter, adj. memorable.

red′o·lent, adj. **1.** odorous. **2.** suggestive. —**red′o·lence,** n.

re·doubt′a·ble, adj. formidable.

re·dound′, v.i. occur as a consequence.

re·dress, v.t. (re dres′) **1.** right, as a wrong. —n. (rē′dres) **2.** act or instance of redressing.

red tape, bureaucratic procedures.

re·duce′, v., -duced, -ducing. v.t. **1.** lessen. **2.** alter. **3.** lower in rank, etc. **4.** subdue. —v.i. **5.** act so as to lose weight. —**re·duc′i·ble,** adj. —**re·duc′ tion,** n.

re·dun′dant, adj. **1.** excess; surplus. **2.** repetitive. —**re·dun′dance, re·dun′ dan·cy,** n.

red′wood′′, n. huge California evergreen tree.

reed, n. **1.** tall marsh grass. **2.** vibrating part of the mouthpiece on certain wind instruments. —**reed′y,** adj.

reef, n. **1.** ridge near the surface of a body of water. **2.** part of a sail. —v.t. **3.** shorten, as a sail.

reef′er, n. **1.** short jacket or coat. **2.** Informal. marijuana cigarette.

reek, v.i. **1.** smell strongly. —n. **2.** strong or foul smell.

reel, n. **1.** revolving drum for winding. **2.** lively dance. —v.t. **3.** wind on a reel. —v.i. **4.** stagger or sway. **5.** whirl.

re·fec′to·ry, n. dining hall.

re·fer′, v., referred, referring. v.i. **1.** allude. **2.** look for information. —v.t. **3.** direct for help or information. **4.** submit for arbitration. —**ref′er·a·ble,** adj. —**re·fer′ral,** n.

ref·er·ee′, n. **1.** arbiter. v.t., v.i. **2.** arbitrate.

ref′er·ence, n. **1.** act or instance of referring. **2.** something referred to. **3.** recommendation. **4.** person giving a recommendation.

ref′′er·en′dum, n. submission of a proposed law for citizen approval.

re·fine′, v.t., -fined, -fining. **1.** free from impurities. **2.** make cultured. —**re·fine′ment,** n.

re·fin′er·y, n., pl. -eries. factory for refining, esp. petroleum.

re·flect′, v.t. **1.** return, as images, light, etc. **2.** period of rule. Also, **ré·gime′.** carefully. —**re·flec′tion,** n. —**re·flec′ tive,** adj. —**re·flec′tor,** n.

re′flex, adj. **1.** denoting involuntary reaction. —n. **2.** involuntary reaction.

re·flex′ive, adj. **1.** having the same subject and object as a verb. **2.** used as the object of a reflexive verb, as a pronoun.

re·form′, n. **1.** correction of wrongs. —v.t. **2.** correct the wrongs of. —v.i. **3.** correct one's wrongdoing. —**ref′′or· ma′tion,** n.

re·form′a·to′′ry, n., pl. -ries. penal institution for minors.

re·frac′tion, n. bending of light or heat rays in passing from one medium to another. —**re·fract′,** v.t. —**re·frac′ tive,** adj. —**re·frac′tor,** n.

re·frain′, v.i. **1.** hold back; forbear. —n. **2.** recurring passage in a song or poem.

re·fresh′, v.t. **1.** revive after stress. **2.**

quicken; stimulate. —re·fresh'ment, n.

re·frig'er·ate", v.t., -ated, -ating. keep or make cold. —re·frig'er·ant, n. —re·frig'er·a"tor, n.

ref'uge, n. shelter from danger.

ref"u·gee', n. seeker of refuge.

re·fund', v.t. (re fund') 1. repay. —n. 2. (rē'fund). repayment.

re·fur'bish, v.t. renovate.

re·fuse', v.t., -fused, -fusing, n. v.t. (rē fyōōz') 1. decline. 2. decline to accept. 3. deny, as a request. —n. (ref'yōōz). 4. rubbish. —re·fus'al, n.

re·fute', v.t., -futed, -futing. prove wrong or false. —ref'u·ta·ble, adj. —ref"u·ta'tion, n.

re·gain', v.t. 1. get again. 2. return to again.

re'gal, adj. royal.

re·gale', v.t., -galed, -galing. entertain lavishly.

re·ga'li·a, n. pl. royal or official insignia.

re·gard', v.t. 1. look on. 2. consider. 3. concern; relate to. 4. hold in respect. —n. 5. look; gaze. 6. relation. 7. affection and respect. 8. particular point. 9. regards, good wishes.

re·gard'less, adj. 1. careless. —adv. 2. anyway.

re·gat'ta, n. boat race.

re·gen'er·ate", v.t., adj., -ated, -ating. v.t. 1. produce anew. 2. reform. 3. Biol. regrow. —adj. 4. renewed; reformed. —re·gen"er·a'tive, adj.

re'gent, n. 1. appointed substitute for a monarch. 2. member of a governing board. —re'gen·cy, n.

re·gime', n. 1. system of government, etc. 2. period of rule. Also, ré·gime'.

reg'i·men, n. 1. government; rule. 2. Medicine. system of diet, etc.

reg·i·ment, n. (rej'ə mənt) 1. army unit of two or more battalions. —v.t. (rej'ə ment") 2. subject to strict discipline. —reg"i·men'tal, adj. —reg"i·men'ta·tion, n.

re'gion, n. part of the earth's surface. —re'gion·al, adj.

re'gion·al·ism, n. 1. sponsorship of or adherence to regional culture. 2. regional peculiarity.

reg'is·ter, n. 1. written record, list, etc. 2. cash register. 3. device for regulating the passage of air. 4. Music. range. —v.t., v.i. 5. enroll. —v.t. 6. show, as on the face. —v.i. 7. make an impression. —reg'is·trant, n. —reg"is·tra'tion, n. —reg'is·try, n.

reg'is·trar", n. official record keeper.

re·gress', v.i. 1. go back. 2. revert. —n. 3. going back. —re·gres'sion, n. —re·gres'sive, adj.

re·gret', v.t., -gretted, -gretting, n. v.t. 1. feel sorry about. —n. 2. sorrow or re-

morse. —re·gret'ful, adj. —re·gret'ta·ble, adj.

reg'u·lar, adj. 1. customary. 2. consistent. 3. symmetrical. 4. permanent, as an army. 5. Informal. a. complete. b. likeable. —n. 6. someone regularly seen. 7. regular soldier. —reg"u·lar'i·ty, n. —reg'u·lar·ize", v.t.

reg'u·late", v.t., -lated, -lating. 1. control by rule. 2. make regular. —reg'u·la"tor, n. —reg"u·la·to'ry, adj. —reg'u·la"tive, adj.

re·gur'gi·tate", v., -tated, -tating. v.i., v.t. belch or vomit.

re"ha·bil'i·tate", v.t., -tated, -tating. restore to a former good condition. —re"ha·bil'i·ta"tive, adj.

re·hash', v.t. 1. work over again. —n. 2. rehashing.

re·hearse', v., -hearsed, -hearsing. v.t., v.i. practice for a performance. —re·hears'al, n.

reign (rān), n. 1. royal power. 2. period of rule. —v.i. 3. rule as a monarch. 4. prevail.

re"im·burse', v.t., -bursed, -bursing. pay back. —re"im·burse'ment, n.

rein (rān), strap for controlling a horse.

re"in·car·na'tion, n. rebirth in a new body.

rein'deer", n., pl. -deer. large northern deer.

re"in·force', v.t., -forced, -forcing. strengthen. —re"in·force'ment, n.

re"in·state', v.t., -stated, -stating. restore to a former state. —re"in·state'ment, n.

re·it'er·ate", v.t., -ated, -ating. say or do again. —re·it'er·a"tive, adj.

re·ject', v.t. (ri'jekt') 1. refuse to accept. 2. discard. —n. (rē jekt) 3. rejected person or thing. —re·jec'tion, n.

re·joice', v., -joiced, -joicing. v.t. 1. gladden. —v.i. 2. feel joy. —re·joic'ing, n.

re·join', v.t., v.i. 1. join again. 2. answer.

re·join'der, n. 1. reply. 2. Law. defendant's response.

re·ju've·nate", v.t., -nated, -nating. make young again.

re·lapse', v.i., -lapsed, -lapsing, n. v.i. 1. fall into a former state. —n. 2. act or instance of relapsing.

re·late', v., -lated, -lating. v.t. 1. tell; narrate. 2. connect; associate. —v.i. 3. have a relation.

re·la'tion, n. 1. narrative. 2. connection; association. 3. connection by blood or marriage. —re·la'tion·ship", n.

rel'a·tive, adj. 1. comparative. 2. related to each other. —n. 3. person related by blood or marriage.

rel"a·tiv'i·ty, n. 1. interdependence. 2. Physics. theory of the relative character of position, motion, etc. and the interdependence of time and space.

re·lax', *v.t., v.i.* rest, as from work or tension. —**re''lax·a'tion**, *n.*

re·lay *n.* (rē'lā) 1. relief crew or team. 2. race in which team members run individual portions. —*v.t.* (rē' lā; also ri lā') 3. send by relay or relays. 4. lay again.

re·lease', *v.t.*, **-leased, -leasing**, *n. v.t.* 1. free. 2. let go of. 3. license for publication. —*n.* 4. act or instance of releasing. 5. communication, etc. 6. *Law.* surrender, as of a claim.

rel'e·gate'', *v.t.*, **-gated, -gating.** 1. consign to a lesser place or position. 2. refer for decision.

re·lent', *v.i.* become less severe, cruel, etc. —**re·lent'less**, *adj.*

rel'e·vant, *adj.* relating to the matter at hand. —**rel'e·vance, rel'e·van·cy**, *n.*

re·li'a·ble, *adj.* dependable. —**re·li''a·bil'i·ty**, *n.*

re·li'ance, *n.* 1. trust; confidence. 2. something relied on. —**re·li'ant**, *adj.*

rel'ic, *n.* 1. survival from the past. 2. souvenir.

re·lief', *n.* 1. release from pain, discomfort, etc. 2. means of such relief. 3. sculptured surface. 4. projection from a background.

re·lieve', *v.t.*, **-lieved, -lieving.** 1. ease, as from pain or discomfort. 2. vary. 3. release from duty.

re·li'gion, *n.* 1. belief in a divine being or beings. 2. specific form of belief and practice. —**re·li'gious**, *adj.*

re·lin'quish, *v.t.* 1. give up. 2. renounce, as a right. —**re·lin'quish·ment**, *n.*

rel'ish, *n.* 1. zest. 2. condiment. 3. appetizing flavor. —*v.t.* 4. take pleasure in.

re·live', *v.t.*, **-lived, -living.** experience again in the imagination.

re·lo'cate, *v.*, **-cated, -cating.** *v.t., v.i.* settle in a new location.

re·luc'tant, *adj.* unwilling. —**re·luc'tance**, *n.*

re·ly', *v.i.*, **-lied, -lying.** depend; trust.

re·main', *v.i.* 1. stay behind. 2. endure; persist. 3. continue as before. —*n.* 4. remains, **a.** remainder. **b.** corpse. —**re·main'der**, *n.*

re·mand', *v.t.* send back or consign again.

re·mark', *v.t., v.i., n.* 1. comment. —*v.t., n.* 2. notice.

re·mark'a·ble, *adj.* worthy of notice or comment.

rem'e·dy, *n., v.t.*, **-died, -dying.** *n.* 1. medicine or treatment. 2. something that corrects wrong. —*v.t.* 3. cure; correct. —**re·me'di·al**, *adj.*

re·mem'ber, *v.t.* 1. recall to mind. 2. not forget. 3. carry greetings from. —**re·mem'brance**, *n.*

re·mind', *v.t.* cause to remember. —**re·mind'er**, *n.*

rem''i·nisce', *v.i.*, **-nisced, -niscing.** discuss or think of the past. —**rem''i·nis'cence**, *n.* —**rem''i·nis'cent**, *adj.*

re·miss', *adj.* careless; slack.

re·mis'sion, *n.* 1. forgiveness. 2. diminution, as of disease.

re·mit', *v.t.*, **-mitted, -mitting.** 1. forgive. 2. refrain from imposing. 3. relax; abate. 4. send in payment. —**re·mit'tance**, *n.*

rem'nant, *n.* something left over.

re·mod'el, *v.t.*, **-eled, -eling.** make over; rebuild.

re·mon'strate, *v.*, **-strated, -strating.** *v.t., v.i.* protest; object. —**re·mon'strance**, *n.*

re·morse', *n.* mental anguish from guilt. —**re·morse'ful**, *adj.* —**re·morse'less**, *adj.*

re·mote', *adj.*, **-moter, -motest.** 1. distant. 2. slight.

re·move', *v.*, **-moved, -moving**, *n. v.t.* 1. move from a place. 2. dismiss, as from office. —*v.i.* 3. change residence. —*n.* 4. interval; step. —**re·mov'a·ble**, *adj.* —**re·mov'al**, *n.*

re·mu'ner·ate'', *v.t.*, **-ated, -ating.** pay; recompense. —**re·mu'ner·a''tive**, *adj.*

ren''ais·sance'', *n.* 1. rebirth. 2. Renaissance, revival of classical learning in Europe.

re'nal, *adj.* pertaining to the kidneys.

re·nas'cence, *n.* rebirth; revival.

rend', *v.*, **rent, rending.** *v.t., v.i.* split apart by force.

ren'der, *v.t.* 1. give in return. 2. submit. 3. state, as a decision. 4. furnish. 5. express or interpret. 6. translate.

ren·dez·vous (rän'dā voo''), *n., pl.* **-vous.** 1. meeting place. 2. appointment to meet.

ren·di'tion, *n.* rendering; performance.

ren'e·gade'', *n.* deserter of a cause.

re·nege', *v.i.*, **-neged, -neging.** *Informal.* go back on one's word.

re·new', *v.t.* 1. make new. 2. revive. —**re·new'al**, *n.*

re·nounce', *v.t.*, **-nounced, -nouncing.** give up formally. —**re·nun''ci·a'tion, re·nounce'ment**, *n.*

ren'o·vate'', *v.t.* **-vated, -vating.** make as if new.

re·nown', *n.* great reputation. —**re·nowned'**, *adj.*

rent, *n.* 1. Also **rent'al**, payment for temporary use. 2. tear; rip. —*v.t.* 3. use by paying. 4. grant temporarily for payment.

re·pair', *v.t.* 1. return to good condition. 2. set right. —*v.i.* 3. go. —*n.* 4. act or instance of repairing. 5. good condition. —**rep'a·ra·ble, re·pair'a·ble**, *adj.*

rep''a·ra'tion, *n.* 1. amends for injury. 2. reparations, compensation for war damage.

rep''ar·tee', *n.* clever, quick-witted talk.

re·past', *n.* meal.

re·pa'tri·ate'', *v.*, **-ated, -ating.** *v.t.*, *v.i.* return to one's country.

re·pay', *v.t.*, **-paid, -paying.** pay back. —**re·pay'ment**, *n.*

re·peal', *v.t.* 1. revoke. —*n.* 2. revocation.

re·peat', *v.t.*, *v.i.* 1. say or do again. —*n.* 2. act or instance of repeating. —**rep''e·ti'tion**, *n.* —**rep''e·ti'tious**, *adj.*

re·pel', *v.t.*, **-pelled, -pelling.** 1. drive back. 2. disgust. —**re·pel'lent**, *adj.*, *n.*

re·pent', *v.t.*, *v.i.* regret as wrong or mistaken. —**re·pent'ance**, *n.* —**re·pent'ant**, *adj.*

re''per·cus'sion, *n.* 1. indirect result. 2. reverberation. —**re''per·cus'sive**, *adj.*

rep·er·toire'', *n.* stock of songs, plays, etc. performed. Also **rep'er·to''ry**, *n.*

re·place', *v.t.*, **-placed, -placing.** 1. put back in place. 2. substitute for. —**re·place'a·ble**, *adj.* —**re·place'ment**, *n.*

re·plen'ish, *v.t.* make full again. —**re·plen'ish·ment**, *n.*

re·plete', *adj.* plentifully filled. —**re·ple'tion**, *n.*

rep'li·ca, *n.* copy.

re·ply', *v.*, **-plied, -plying,** *n.*, *pl.* **-plies.** *v.t.*, *v.i.*, *n.* answer.

re·port', *n.* 1. statement. 2. rumor. 3. explosive noise. —*v.t.* 4. give an account of. 5. inform against. —*v.i.* 6. make a report. 7. present oneself.

re·pose', *v.t.*, **-posed, -posing,** *n.* *v.t.* 1. rest or sleep. 2. place. 3. depend. —*n.* 4. rest or sleep. 5. tranquillity.

re·pos'i·tor''y, *n.*, *pl.* **-tories.** place of storage.

rep''re·hend', *v.t.* rebuke. —**rep''re·hen'si·ble**, *adj.* —**rep''re·hen'sion**, *n.*

rep''re·sent', *v.t.* 1. exemplify. 2. portray. 3. act or speak for. —**rep''re·sen·ta'tion**, *n.*

rep''re·sen'ta·tive, *adj.* 1. serving as an example. 2. acting or speaking for others. —*n.* 3. person who represents. 4. elected legislator.

re·press', *v.t.* restrain; check. —**re·pres'sive**, *adj.* —**re·pres'sion**, *n.*

re·prieve', *v.t.*, **-prieved, -prieving,** *n.* *v.t.* 1. relieve temporarily. —*n.* 2. temporary delay; respite.

rep'ri·mand'', *n.* 1. severe or formal rebuke. —*v.t.* 2. rebuke; censure.

re·pris'al, *n.* retaliation.

re·proach', *v.t.* 1. scold for a fault; blame. —*n.* 2. discredit. —**re·proach'ful**, *adj.*

rep'ro·bate'', *n.*, *adj.*, *v.t.*, **-bated, -bating.** *n.* 1. depraved person. —*adj.* 2. depraved. —*v.t.* 3. condemn.

re''pro·duce', *v.t.*, **-duced, -ducing.** 1. copy; duplicate. 2. produce by propagation. —**re''pro·duc'tion**, *n.* —**re''pro·duc'tive**, *adj.*

re·proof', *n.* rebuke; censure.

re·prove', *v.t.*, **-proved, -proving.** rebuke; censure. —**re·prov'al**, *n.*

rep'tile, *n.* cold-blooded vertebrate. —**rep·til'i·an**, *adj.*

re·pub'lic, *n.* state governed by elected legislators.

re·pub'li·can, *adj.* 1. pertaining to or favoring a republic. —*n.* 2. **Republican,** member of the Republican party. 3. partisan of a republican form of government. —**re·pub'li·can·ism**, *n.*

re·pu'di·ate'', *v.t.*, **-ated, -ating.** disown; disavow.

re·pug'nant, *adj.* distasteful. —**re·pug'nance**, *n.*

re·pulse', *v.t.*, **-pulsed, -pulsing,** *n.* *v.t.* 1. drive back, as an attack. 2. reject; rebuff. —*n.* 3. act or instance of repulsing. —**re·pul'sion**, *n.*

re·pul'sive, *adj.* disgusting.

rep'u·ta·ble, *adj.* of good reputation.

rep''u·ta'tion, *n.* 1. estimation of a person or thing. 2. fame.

re·pute', *n.*, *v.t.*, **-puted, -puting.** *n.* 1. reputation. —*v.t.* 2. consider or regard.

re·quest', *v.t.* 1. ask for. —*n.* 2. act or instance of requesting. 3. something requested.

re'qui·em, *n.* service for the dead.

re·quire', *v.t.*, **-quired, -quiring.** 1. need. 2. demand. —**re·quire'ment**, *n.*

req'ui·site, *n.* 1. something necessary. —*adj.* 2. required; necessary.

req''ui·si'tion, *n.* 1. act or instance of requiring. 2. formal order for goods, etc. —*v.t.* 3. take by authority.

re·quite', *v.t.*, **-quited, -quiting.** repay; return. —**re·quit'al**, *n.*

re·scind', *v.t.* revoke; annul.

res'cue, *v.t.*, **-cued, -cuing,** *n.* *v.t.* 1. free or save. —*n.* 2. act or instance of rescuing.

re·search', *n.* 1. careful investigation. —*v.t.* 2. do research on or in.

re·sem'ble, *v.t.*, **-bled, -bling.** be like or similar to. —**re·sem'blance**, *n.*

re·sent', *v.t.* feel indignant at. —**re·sent'ful**, *adj.* —**re·sent'ment**, *n.*

res''er·va'tion, *n.* 1. act or instance of reserving. 2. advance request for accommodation. 3. public land for Indians.

re·serve', *v.t.*, **-served, -serving,** *n.* *v.t.* 1. keep back; set aside. —*n.* 2. something reserved. 3. reticence, as about feelings. 4. inactive troops subject to call. 5. reserved district.

re·serv'ist, *n.* member of a military reserve.

res'er·voir'', *n.* storage place for water.

re·side', *v.i.*, **-sided, -siding.** 1. dwell. 2. be present.

res'i·dence, *n.* 1. dwelling place. 2. act or

residue 186

instance of residing. —**res'i·dent**, *n.*,
adj. —**res'i·den'tial**, *adj.*

res'i·due'', *n.* remainder. —**re·sid'u·al**,
adj.

re·sign', *v.i.* **1.** give up a job or duty.
—*v.t.* **2.** give up. **3.** yield or submit.

res''ig·na'tion, *n.* **1.** act or instance of re-
signing. **2.** submission, as to the inevitable.

re·signed', *adj.* reluctantly submissive.

re·sil'i·ent, *adj.* elastic; buoyant. —**re·
sil'i·ence**, *n.*

res'in, *n.* substance exuded by certain
plants. —**res'in·ous**, *adj.*

re·sist', *v.t.*, *v.i.* withstand; oppose.
—**re·sist'ance**, *n.*

res'o·lute'', *adj.* firm in purpose; determined.

res''o·lu'tion, *n.* **1.** formal expression of
opinion. **2.** decision. **3.** firmness of
purpose.

re·solve', *v.*, **-solved**, **-solving**, *n.* *v.t.*,
v.i. **1.** decide; determine. —*v.t.* **2.** analyze. **3.** solve. **4.** dispel, as fear. —*n.* **5.**
determination.

res'o·nant, *adj.* **1.** resounding. **2.** vi-
brant; sonorous. —**res'o·nance**, *n.*
—**res'o·nate''**, *v.t.*, *v.i.* —**res'o·na''
tor**, *n.*

re·sort', *v.i.* **1.** have recourse. —*n.* **2.**
public place, as for recreation. **3.** recourse.

re·sound', *v.i.* reverberate; ring out.
—**re·sound'ing**, *adj.*

re·source', *n.* **1.** source of help or support. **2.** **resources**, money; means.

re·source'ful, *adj.* clever; able.

re·spect', *n.* **1.** esteem; honor. **2.** consideration. **3.** detail. **4.** deference; regard.
—*v.t.* **5.** show consideration for. **6.**
hold in honor. —**re·spect'a·ble**, *adj.*
—**re·spect'ful**, *adj.*

re·spect'ing, *prep.* concerning.

re·spec'tive, *adj.* relating to each of several.

res'pi·ra''tor, *n.* apparatus for artificial
breathing.

re·spire', *v.*, **-spired**, **-spiring**. *v.t.*, *v.i.*
breathe. —**res''pi·ra'tion**, *n.* —**re·spir'
a·to''ry**, *adj.*

res'pite, *n.* temporary relief.

re·splend'ent, *adj.* shining brightly.
—**re·splend'ence**, *n.*

re·spond', *v.i.* **1.** answer. **2.** react.

re·spond'ent, *n. Law.* defendant.

re·sponse', *n.* reply. —**re·spon'sive**, *adj.*

re·spon''si·bil'i·ty, *n.*, *pl.* **-ties. 1.** state
of being responsible. **2.** obligation.

re·spon'si·ble, *adj.* **1.** accountable. **2.** reliable. **3.** distinguishing between right
and wrong. —**re·spon'si·bly**, *adv.*

rest, *n.* **1.** sleep; repose. **2.** inactivity after
work. **3.** support; base. **4.** *Music.* silent
interval. —*v.i.* **5.** be at rest. **6.** lay. **7.**

lie. —*v.t.* **8.** cause to rest. **9.** base.
—**rest'ful**, *adj.* —**rest'less**, *adj.*

res'tau·rant, *n.* public eating place.

res''tau·ra·teur', *n.* proprietor of a restaurant.

res''ti·tu'tion, *n.* **1.** return of something
taken away. **2.** reparation.

res'tive, *adj.* **1.** balky; stubborn. **2.** restless.

re·store', *v.t.*, **-stored**, **-storing**. **1.** return
to a former state. **2.** give back. —**res'
to·ra'tion**, *n.* —**re·stor'a·tive**, *adj.*

re·strain', *v.t.* **1.** hold back; check. **2.**
confine.

re·straint', *n.* **1.** control of emotions, etc.
2. confinement. **3.** something that restrains.

re·strict', *v.t.* limit; confine. —**re·stric'
tion**, *n.* —**re·stric'tive**, *adj.* —**re·strict'
ed**, *adj.*

re·sult', *n.* **1.** consequence; outcome.
—*v.i.* **2.** follow as a consequence.
—**re·sult'ant**, *adj.*, *n.*

re·sume', *v.t.*, **-sumed**, **-suming**. **1.** continue. **2.** take again. —**re·sump'tion**,
n.

ré·su·mé', *n.* summary, as of work experience.

re·sur'gent, *adj.* tending to rise again.
—**re·sur'gence**, *n.*

res''ur·rect', *v.t.* raise from the dead.
—**res''ur·rec'tion**, *n.*

re·sus'ci·tate'', *v.*, **-tated**, **-tating**. *v.t.*,
v.i. revive from unconsciousness. —**re·
sus''ci·ta'tion**, *n.* —**re·sus'ci·ta''tor**, *n.*

re'tail, *n.* **1.** sale of consumer goods.
—*v.t.*, *v.i.* **2.** sell at retail.

re·tain', *v.t.* **1.** keep; hold. **2.** hire by a
retainer.

re·tain'er, *n.* **1.** fee for continuing services. **2.** servant.

re·tal'i·ate'', *v.i.*, **-ated**, **-ating**. give like
for like, esp. in revenge. —**re·tal'i·a·
to''ry**, *adj.*

re·tard', *v.t.* hinder; slow. —**re·tar·da'
tion**, *n.* —**re·tard'ant**, *n.*

re·tard'ed, *adj.* limited or slow in mental
development.

retch (rech), *v.i.* try to vomit.

re·ten'tion, *n.* **1.** act or instance of retaining. **2.** power of remembering.
—**re·ten'tive**, *adj.*

ret'i·cent, *adj.* disposed to silence; taciturn. —**ret'i·cence**, *n.*

ret'i·na, *n.* coating of the posterior interi-
or of the eyeball.

ret'i·nue'', *n.* group of attendants.

re·tire', *v.*, **-tired**, **-tiring**. *v.i.*, *v.t.* **1.**
withdraw. **2.** withdraw from working
life. —*v.i.* **3.** go to bed. —*v.t.* **4.** pay
off, as bonds. —**re·tir''ee'**, *n.* —**re·
tire'ment**, *n.*

re·tir'ing, *adj.* shy; reserved.

re·tort', *v.t.*, *v.i.* **1.** answer smartly or
wittily. —*n.* **2.** quick, witty answer.

re·touch', *v.t.* touch up or improve, as a photograph.

re·tract', *v.t., v.i.* withdraw. —**re·tract'a·ble**, *adj.* —**re·trac'tion**, *n.*

re·treat', *n.* 1. withdrawal, as from danger. 2. secluded place. —*v.i.* 3. withdraw.

re·trench', *v.t., v.i.* cut down as an economy. —**re·trench'ment**, *n.*

ret'ri·bu'tion, *n.* retaliation; punishment. —**re·trib'u·tive**, *adj.*

re·trieve', *v.t.,* -trieved, -trieving. 1. regain. 2. recover. 3. make good, as a mistake. —**re·triev'al**, *n.*

ret'ro·ac'tive, *adj.* valid for some past period.

ret'ro·grade'', *adj., v.i.,* -graded, -grading. *adj.* 1. directed backward; reversed. —*v.i.* 2. go backward. 3. degenerate. —**ret''ro·gres'sion**, *n.* —**ret''ro·gres'sive**, *adj.*

ret'ro·spect'', *n.* look to the past. —**ret''ro·spec'tive**, *adj.* —**ret''ro·spec'tion**, *n.*

re·turn', *v.i.* 1. go back. 2. reply. —*v.t.* 3. put back. 4. repay. 5. elect or re-elect. 6. yield, as a profit. —*n.* 7. act or instance of returning. 8. recurrence. 9. repayment; yield. 9. report; response. —**re·turn'a·ble**, *adj.*

rev, *v.t.,* revved, revving. *n. Informal.* *v.t.* 1. increase the speed of, as a motor. —*n.* 2. revolution, as of a machine.

re·vamp', *v.t.* redo; revise.

re·veal', *v.t.* 1. disclose. 2. manifest.

rev·eil·le (rev'ə lē), *n. Military.* signal for awakening.

rev·el, *v.i.,* -eled, -eling, *n. v.i.* 1. take great delight. 2. make merry. —*n.* 3. merrymaking. —**rev'el·ry**, *n.*

rev''e·la'tion, *n.* 1. act or instance of revealing. 2. Revelation, last book of the New Testament.

re·venge', *n., v.t.,* -venged, -venging. *n.* 1. retaliation. 2. vindictiveness. —*v.t.* 3. take revenge for. —**re·venge'ful**, *adj.*

rev'e·nue'', *n.* income, as from taxes.

re·ver'ber·ate'', *v.,* -ated, -ating. *v.t., v.i.* reecho; resound.

re·vere', *v.t.,* -vered, -vering. regard with deep respect, love, etc.

rev'er·ence, *n., v.t.,* -enced, -encing. *n.* 1. deep respect. —*v.t.* 2. revere; honor. —**rev'er·ent**, **rev''er·en'tial**, *adj.*

rev'er·end, *adj.* 1. worthy of reverence. 2. Reverend, title of respect for a clergyman.

rev'er·ie, *n., pl.* -ies. daydreaming; deep musings. Also **rev'er·y**.

re·verse', *adj., n., v.,* -versed, -versing. *adj.* 1. turned backward. 2. making an opposite motion. —*n.* 3. opposite; contrary. 4. misfortune. —*v.t.* 5. turn back or in an opposite direction. 6. ex-change; transpose. —*v.i.* 7. move in an opposite direction. —**re·vers'i·ble**, *adj.*

re·vert', *v.i.* return as to a former way or state, etc. —**re·ver'sion**, *n.*

re·view', *n.* 1. reexamination. 2. general survey or report. 3. critical writing. —*v.t.* 4. reexamine. 5. look back on. 6. write a review of. 7. inspect formally.

re·vile', *v.t.,* -viled, -viling. speak abusively. —**re·vile'ment**, *n.*

re·vise', *v.t.,* -vised, -vising. amend. —**re·vi'sion**, *n.*

re·viv'al, *n.* 1. return to life, use, etc. 2. emotional religious meeting. —**re·viv'al·ist**, *n.*

re·vive', *v.,* -vived, -viving. *v.i., v.t.* return to consciousness or effectiveness.

re·voke', *v.t.,* -voked, -voking. repeal or nullify. —**rev'o·ca·ble**, *adj.* —**rev''o·ca'tion**, *n.*

re·volt', *n.* 1. uprising; rebellion. —*v.i.* 2. rebel. —*v.t.* 3. disgust.

rev''o·lu'tion, *n.* 1. war against one's government. 2. complete change 3. rotation. —**rev''o·lu'tion·ar''y**, *adj., n.* —**rev''o·lu'tion·ist**, *n.*

rev''o·lu'tion·ize'', *v.t.,* -ized, -izing. change completely or radically.

re·volve', *v.,* -volved, -volving. *v.t.* 1. cause to rotate. —*v.i.* 2. rotate.

re·volv'er, *n.* pistol with a revolving magazine.

re·vue', *n.* light musical show.

re·vul'sion, *n.* 1. violent change of feeling. 2. disgust.

re·ward', *n.* 1. grateful gift or payment. —*v.t.* 2. give a reward to.

rhap'so·dy, *n., pl.* -dies. free, irregular musical composition. —**rhap·sod'ic**, *adj.*

rhe'o·stat'', *n.* device for varying an electric current.

rhe'sus, *n.* monkey of India.

rhet'o·ric, *n.* 1. art of using language effectively. 2. exaggerated speech. —**rhe·tor'i·cal**, *adj.*

rheu·ma·tism'', *n.* painful condition of the muscles and joints. —**rheu·mat'ic**, *adj.*

rhine'stone'', *n.* imitation diamond.

rhi·noc'er·os, *n.* massive, thick-skinned mammal with a horned snout.

rho''do·den'dron, *n.* evergreen shrub with pink, white, or purple flowers.

rhom'bus, *n., pl.* -buses, -bi. equilateral parallelogram with oblique angles.

rhu'barb, *n.* edible plant with long, thick stalks.

rhyme, *n., v.* rhymed, rhyming. *n.* 1. similarity of sound at verse ends. 2. poetry with such similarity. —*v.i., v.t.* 3. compose in rhyme.

rhythm, *n.* regular recurrence of stress, as in poetry or music. —**rhyth'mic**, *adj.*

rib, *n.*, *v.t.*, **ribbed, ribbing.** *n.* **1.** one of the curved bones around the chest cavity. **2.** rib-like structure. —*v.t.* **3.** reinforce with ribs. **4.** *Informal.* tease.

rib'ald, *adj.* indecent or vulgar in language. —**rib'ald·ry,** *n.*

rib'bon, *n.* narrow strip of fabric.

ri·bo·fla''vin, *n.* component of the vitamin B complex found in milk, eggs, meat, etc.

rice, *n.* edible cereal of warm climates.

rich, *adj.* **1.** having much wealth. **2.** abundant; abounding. **3.** full of desirable qualities or resources. **4.** appetizing but hard to digest. **5.** mellow. —*n.* **6. the rich,** people of wealth. **7. riches,** wealth. —**rich'ly,** *adv.* —**rich'ness,** *n.*

rick, *n.* stack of hay, straw, etc.

rick'ets, *n.* nutritional deficiency disease of childhood characterized by bone deformities.

rick'et·y, *adj.* shaky; feeble.

rick'shaw, *n.* carriage pulled by a man. Also **rick'sha.**

ric·o·chet (rik'ə sha''), *n.*, *v.i.*, **-cheted, -cheting.** *n.* **1.** rebound of an object from a hard surface. —*v.i.* **2.** rebound.

rid, *v.t.* rid or ridded, ridding. free; clear. —**rid'dance,** *n.*

rid'dle, *n.*, *v.*, **-dled, -dling.** *n.* **1.** puzzle; enigma. **2.** coarse sieve. —*v.t.* **3.** pierce with holes. **4.** sift through a riddle. **5.** permeate.

ride, *v.*, **rode, ridden, riding,** *n.*, *v.t.* **1.** be carried on or within. **2.** be carried over or through. —*v.i.* **3.** be carried. **4.** depend (on). **5.** be at anchor. —*n.* **6.** act or instance of riding.

rid'er, *n.* **1.** person who rides. **2.** addition to a document.

ridge, *n.*, *v.*, **ridged, ridging.** *n.* **1.** narrow, raised edge. **2.** sharp crest or elevation of land. —*v.t.*, *v.i.* **3.** form into a ridge.

rid'i·cule'', *n.*, *v.t.*, **-culed, -culing.** *n.* **1.** derision. —*v.t.* **2.** make fun of; mock. —**ri·dic'u·lous,** *adj.*

rife, *adj.* **1.** widespread. **2.** abundant.

riff'raff'', *n.*, *pl.* worthless people.

ri'fle, *n.*, *v.t.*, **-fled, -fling.** *n.* **1.** shoulder gun with a rifled barrel. —*v.t.* **2.** ransack and rob. **3.** cut spiral grooves in, as a gun barrel. —**ri'fle·man,** *n.*

rift, *n.*, *v.t.*, *v.i.* split.

rig, *v.t.*, **rigged, rigging,** *n.*, *v.t.* **1.** equip, as for sailing. **2.** manipulate. —*n.* **3.** arrangement of the sails, etc. on a ship. **4.** equipment. **5.** tractor-trailer.

rig'a·ma·role'', *n.* complicated, often meaningless, procedure or talk. Also, **rig'ma·role''.**

rig'ging, *n.* ropes and other tackle for a ship, crane, etc.

right, *adj.* **1.** good; virtuous. **2.** correct. **3.** suitable. **4.** opposite to left. **5.** straight. —*n.* **6.** what is right, just, etc. **7.** lawful power or privilege. **8.** *Politics.* conservative. —*adv.* **9.** properly. —*v.t.* **10.** correct; put in order. **11.** set upright.

right angle, 90-degree angle.

right'eous, *adj.* **1.** virtuous; blameless. **2.** just; worthy.

right'ful, *adj.* just; legitimate.

right'ist, *n.*, *adj.* conservative in politics.

right-wing, *adj.* politically conservative.

rig'id, *adj.* **1.** stiff; unyielding. **2.** strict. —**rig'id·ness, ri·gid'i·ty,** *n.*

rig'or, *n.* **1.** strictness. **2.** hardship. —**rig'or·ous,** *adj.*

ri'gor mor'tis, stiffening of the muscles after death.

rile, *v.t.*, **riled, riling.** *Informal.* anger; irritate.

rill, *n.* small stream.

rim, *n.*, *v.t.*, **rimmed, rimming.** *n.* **1.** edge; border; margin. —*v.t.* **2.** furnish with a rim.

rime, *n.*, *v.*, **rimed, riming.** *n.* **1.** rhyme. **2.** hoarfrost —*v.t.*, *v.i.* **3.** form a rhyme.

rind, *n.* hard outer coating, as of cheese or fruit.

ring, *n.*, *v.*, **rang, rung, ringing.** *n.* **1.** sound of a bell. **2.** finger band. **3.** circular object or area. **4.** group of conspirators. **5.** telephone call. —*v.t.* **6.** sound, as a bell. **7.** call by telephone. **8.** encircle. —*v.i.* **9.** resound. **10.** sound clearly. **11.** seem to be true or false.

ring'er, *n.* **1.** person who rings bells. **2.** *Informal.* **a.** fraudulent substitute. **b.** identical-seeming person or thing.

ring'lead'er, *n.* person who leads others in mischief.

ring'let, *n.* **1.** little ring. **2.** curl of hair.

ring'worm'', *n.* contagious fungous skin disease.

rink, *n.* area for skating.

rinse, *v.*, **rinsed, rinsing,** *n.* *v.t.* **1.** wash lightly, as to remove soap. —*n.* **2.** act or instance of rinsing. **3.** solution for rinsing.

ri'ot, *n.* **1.** act of mob violence. —*v.i.* **2.** take part in a riot. —**ri'ot·ous,** *adj.*

rip, *v.t.*, *v.i.*, **ripped, ripping,** *n.* tear.

ripe, *adj.*, **riper, ripest.** fully aged or developed. —**rip'en,** *v.i.*, *v.t.*

rip'ple, *v.*, **-pled, -ling,** *n.* *v.i.*, *v.t.* **1.** form in little waves. —*n.* **2.** little wave.

rip'-roar'ing, *adj.* *Informal.* lively and boisterous.

rip'saw'', *n.* saw for cutting wood along the grain.

rise, *v.i.*, **rose, risen, rising,** *n.* *v.i.* **1.** get up. **2.** rebel. **3.** ascend. **4.** begin. **5.** increase in amount, degree, etc. **6.** originate. —*n.* **7.** act or instance of rising. **8.** small hill. **9.** increase. **10.** advance in rank, power, etc.

ris''i·bil'i·ty, *n.*, *pl.* **-ties.** ability to laugh.

ris′i·ble, *adj.* causing laughter; ridiculous.

risk, *n.* **1.** chance of defeat, injury, loss, etc. —*v.t.* **2.** expose to risk. **3.** incur the risk of. —**risk′y,** *adj.*

ris·qué′, *adj.* suggestive of indency.

rite, *n.* ceremonial act.

rit′u·al, *n.* **1.** set form for rites. —*adj.* **2.** according to a ritual. —**rit′u·al·ism″,** *n.* —**rit′u·al·ist,** *n.* —**rit″u·al·is′tic,** *adj.*

ri′val, *n., adj., v.t.* **-valed, -valing.** *n.* **1.** competitor. **2.** equal. —*adj.* **3.** competing. —*v.t.* **4.** compete with. **5.** equal. —**ri′val·ry,** *n.*

rive (rīv), *v.t., v.i.,* **rived, rived** or **riven, riving. 1.** tear apart. **2.** split.

riv′er, *n.* large natural stream of water.

riv′et, *n.* **1.** metal bolt forged tight after insertion. —*v.t.* **2.** fasten with rivets.

riv′u·let, *n.* small brook.

roach, *n.* cockroach.

road, *n.* way for travel. —**road′side″,** *n., adj.* —**road′way″,** *n.*

roam, *v.i.* wander.

roan, *n.* horse with white or gray spots.

roar, *v.i.* **1.** emit a bellow. —*n.* **2.** act or instance of roaring.

roast, *v.t.* **1.** cook with dry heat. —*n.* **2.** roasted piece of meat.

rob, *v.t.,* **robbed, robbing.** take from without right. —**rob′ber·y,** *n.*

robe, *n., v.t.,* **robed, robing.** *n.* **1.** long, loose piece of clothing. —*v.t.* **2.** clothe in a robe.

rob′in, *n.* bird with a red breast.

ro′bot, *n.* man-like machine.

ro·bust′, *adj.* vigorous.

rock, *n.* **1.** piece of stone. —*v.i., v.t.* **2.** swing back and forth. —**rock′y,** *adj.*

rock′er, *n.* curved base for rocking objects.

rock′et, *n.* object propelled by reactive thrust. —**rock′et·ry,** *n.*

rock′ n′ roll, *n., adj.* a form of popular music originating in the U.S. and characterized by a distinct beat. Also, **rock.**

ro·co′co, *n.* **1.** light 18th-century style —*adj.* **2.** in this style.

rod, *n.* **1.** round, slender object. **2.** five-and-a-half linear yards.

ro′dent, *n.* gnawing mammal.

ro′de·o″, *n., pl.* **-os.** cowboy show.

roe, *n.* fish eggs.

rogue, *n.* rascal. —**ro′guish,** *adj.* —**ro′guer·y,** *n.*

roil, *v.t.* soil. —**roil′y,** *adj.*

rois′ter, *v.i.* carouse.

role, *n.* character assumed. Also, **rôle.**

roll, *v.i.* **1.** move like a ball, or as if on wheels. **2.** revolve; turn over and over. **3.** move like waves; billow. —*v.t.* **4.** cause to roll. **5.** move on wheels. **6.** shape into a round or cylindrical form.

7. smooth or flatten with a cylinder, as metal. —*n.* **8.** act or instance of rolling. **9.** a cylinder, as of paper, wire, etc. **10.** list of names. **11.** small loaf of bread.

rol′lick·ing, *adj.* jolly; boisterous.

ro·maine′, *n.* type of lettuce.

ro·mance′, *n.* **1.** love affair. **2.** fanciful story. **3.** realm of fantasy. —**ro·man′tic,** *adj.* —**ro·man′ti·cal·ly,** *adv.*

Roman numerals, I for 1, V for 5, X for 10, L for 50, C for 100, D for 500, M for 1,000.

ro·man′ti·cism, *n.* romantic artistic movement. —**ro·man′ti·cist,** *n., adj.*

romp, *v.i.* **1.** play boisterously. —*n.* **2.** act or instance of romping.

romp′ers, *n., pl.* loose overall for a child.

roof, *n., pl.* **roofs,** *v.t., n.* **1.** covering for a building. —*v.t.* **2.** furnish with a roof. —**roof′ing,** *n.* —**roof′less,** *adj.* —**roof′top″,** *n.*

rook, *n.* **1.** castle-like chesspiece. —*v.t.* **2.** *Informal.* cheat.

rook′ie, *n. Informal.* raw recruit.

room, *n.* **1.** space. **2.** fully enclosed space in a building. —*v.i.* **3.** lodge. —**room′ful″,** *n.* —**room′mate″,** *n.* —**room′y,** *adj.*

roost, *n., v.i.* perch.

roost′er, *n.* male chicken.

root, *n.* **1.** buried part of a plant. **2.** similar part of a tooth, hair, etc. **3.** basic cause. —*v.t.* **4.** plant. **5.** dig. —*v.i.* **6.** grow roots. **7.** cheer.

rope, *n., v.t.,* **roped, roping.** *n.* **1.** length composed of strands used for pulling or binding. —*v.t.* **2.** tie with rope.

ro′sa·ry, *n., pl.* **-ries. 1.** chain of beads used by Roman Catholics to count prayers said. **2.** series of prayers.

rose, *n.* pink or yellow scented flower. —**rose′bud″,** *n.* —**rose′bush″,** *n.*

ro·sé′, *n.* pink light wine.

ro′se·ate, *adj.* **1.** rose-colored. **2.** brightly promising.

rose′mar″y, *n.* leaves of an evergreen shrub, used in cooking.

ro·sette′, *n.* round ornament.

rose′wood″, *n.* reddish wood used in cabinetmaking.

ros′in, *n.* solid substance remaining after distilling turpentine, used esp. for treating bows of violins, etc.

ros′ter, *n.* list.

ros′trum, *n., pl.* **-trums, -tra.** speaker's platform.

ros′y, *adj.* **-ier, -iest. 1.** pink. **2.** optimistic; promising. —**ros′i·ly,** *adv.*

rot, *v.,* **rotted, rotting,** *n., v.t., v.i.* decay. —**rot′ten,** *adj.*

ro′ta·ry, *adj.* rotating as a whole or in part.

ro′tate″, *v.,* **-tated, -tating.** *v.t., v.i.* **1.** turn around a point. —*v.t.* **2.** assign regular turns to. —**ro′ta·to″ry,** *adj.*

rote, *n.* memorization.

ro′tor, *n.* rotating part of a machine.

ro·tund′, *adj.* plump. **—ro·tun′di·ty,** *n.*

ro·tun′da, *n.* round hall.

rou·é′, *n.* dissipated man.

rouge, *n.* red cosmetic or polishing powder.

rough, *adj.* 1. unfinished. 2. violent. 3. *Informal.* troublesome. **—rough′en,** *v.t., v.i.*

rough′age, *n.* coarse food.

rough′house″, *n. Informal.* violent amusement or fight.

rough′neck″, *n. Informal.* boisterous or violent person.

rou·lette′, *n.* gambling wheel.

round, *adj.* 1. curved, or with a curved exterior. 2. approximate. **—n.** 3. repeated series. 4. single shot. **—adv., prep.** 5. around. **—v.t.** 6. make round. 7. go around.

round′a·bout″, *adj.* indirect.

round′ly, *adv.* 1. in a round way. 2. thoroughly.

round′up″, *n.* 1. gathering of cattle. 2. summary.

rouse, *v., roused, rousing. v.t., v.i.* 1. awaken. **—v.t.** 2. excite.

rout, *v.t.* 1. put to flight. 2. gouge. **—n.** 3. disorderly flight.

route, *n., v.t., routed, routing. n.* 1. course of travel. **—v.t.** 2. assign a route to.

rou·tine′, *n.* 1. standard course of action. **—adj.** 2. ordinary; customary.

rove, *v.i., roved, roving.* wander.

row, *v., rowed, rowing. n. v.t., v.i.* (rō) 1. move with oars. **—n.** 2. group in a line. 3. (row) fight; quarrel. **—row′boat″,** *n.*

row′dy, *adj., -dier, -diest, n., pl. -dies. adj.* 1. boisterous or violent. **—n.** 2. rowdy person.

roy′al, *adj.* 1. pertaining to kings or queens. **—n.** 2. sail above a top gallant. **—roy′al·ist,** *n.*

roy′al·ty, *n., pl. -ties.* 1. kings and queens. 2. fee to an author, patentee, etc.

R.S.V.P., Abbr. for (*French*) *répondez s'il vous plaît:* please send an answer.

rub, *v., rubbed, rubbing. n. v.t.* 1. apply friction to. 2. apply with friction. **—v.i.** 3. apply friction. **—n.** 4. act or instance of rubbing. 5. source of difficulty.

rub′ber, *n.* 1. resilient substance. 2. decisive game. **—rub′ber·ize″,** *v.t.* **—rub′ber·y,** *adj.*

rub′bish, *n.* 1. cast-off material. 2. worthless speech, etc.

rub′ble, *n.* broken stone or masonry.

rub′i·cund, *adj.* ruddy.

rub′ric, *n.* note to a text.

ru′by, *n., pl. -bies.* deep red precious stone.

ruck′us, *n. Informal.* disturbance.

rud′der, *n.* steering device.

rud′dy, *adj., -dier, -diest.* reddish. **—rud′di·ness,** *n.*

rude, *adj.* ruder, rudest. 1. offensive in manner. 2. rough; rugged.

ru′di·ment, *n.* basic principle, etc. **—ru″di·men′ta·ry,** *adj.*

rue, *v.t., rued, ruing, n., v.t.* 1. feel remorse or regret for. **—n.** 2. remorse or regret. **—rue′ful,** *adj.*

ruf′fi·an, *n.* hoodlum.

ruf′fle, *v.t., -fled, fling.* 1. disturb the surface of. 2. disturb the calm of.

rug, *n.* floor cloth.

rug′ged, *adj.* 1. rough in surface or outline. 2. harsh.

ruin, *n.* 1. Also, **ruins,** remains of something destroyed or injured. 2. downfall. 3. source of one's downfall. **—v.t.** 4. bring to ruin. **—ru″in·a′tion,** *n.* **—ru′in·ous,** *adj.*

rule, *n., v., ruled, ruling. n.* 1. principle or law. 2. government; dominion. 3. measuring stick. **—v.t., v.i.** 4. govern. **—v.t.** 5. make a formal authoritative decision. **—rul′ing,** *n., adj.*

rul′er, *n.* 1. sovereign. 2. measuring stick.

rum, *n.* alcoholic liquor made from sugar.

rum′ba, *n.* Cuban dance.

rum′ble, *v.i., -bled, -bling, n., v.i.* 1. dull continuous noise. **—n.** 2. act or instance of rumbling.

ru′mi·nate″, *v.i., -nated, -nating.* 1. chew the cud. 2. muse; meditate. **—ru′mi·nant,** *adj., n.*

rum′mage, *v., -maged, -maging. v.t., v.i.* search thoroughly.

ru′mor, *n.* 1. unconfirmed popular report. **—v.t.** 2. tell in a rumor.

rump, *n.* hindquarters.

rum′ple, *v.t., -pled, -pling.* muss.

rum′pus, *n.* disorderly or noisy activity.

run, *v., ran, run, running, n., v.i.* 1. move quickly on the feet. 2. be in motion; operate. 3. flow. **—v.t.** 4. operate or manage. 5. drive. **—n.** 6. act or instance of running. 7. route or journey. 8. series. 9. brook.

run′a·round″, *n. Informal.* evasive treatment.

run′a·way″, *n., adj.* fugitive.

run′-down″, *adj.* 1. without energy. 2. out of repair. 3. (of a clock, etc.) needing to be wound up.

run′down″, *n.* summary.

rung, *n.* rodlike crosspiece.

run′let, *n.* small stream. Also, **run′nel.**

run′ner, *n.* 1. person who runs. 2. long foot or slide, as on a sled, etc. 3. long rug.

run′ner-up″, *n., pl. -ners-up.* second-best racer or performer.

run′ning, *n.* 1. competitive condition.

—*adj.* **2.** operating. **3.** (of measurement) linear. **4.** continuous.

run'-of-the-mill', *adj.* not special.

runt, *n.* stunted creature. —**runt'y**, *adj.*

run'way'', *n.* strip, pavement, etc. for running, esp. by airplanes landing or taking-off.

rup'ture, *n., v.,* **-tured, -turing.** *n.* **1.** hernia. **2.** break. —*v.t.* **3.** cause a rupture. —*v.i.* **4.** undergo a rupture.

rur'al, *adj.* pertaining to the country.

ruse, *n.* trick.

rush, *v.t., v.i., n.* **1.** hurry. —*v.t.* **2.** charge; attack with speed. —*n.* **3.** hurry. **4.** grasslike marsh plant.

rus'set, *n.* reddish brown.

rust, *n.* **1.** coating of oxydized iron or steel. **2.** plant fungus disease. —*v.i.* **3.** have rust. —*v.t.* **4.** cause to rust. —**rust'y**, *adj.*

rus'tic, *adj.* **1.** rural. —*n.* **2.** rural person.

rus'tle, *v.,* **-tled, -tling,** *n., v.i.* **1.** make a soft, whispering sound. —*v.t.* **2.** steal, as cattle. —*n.* **3.** rustling sound.

rut, *n., v.t.,* **rutted, rutting.** *n.* **1.** worn track. **2.** fixed routine. —*v.t.* **3.** make ruts in. —**rut'ty**, *adj.*

ru''ta·ba·ga, *n.* type of turnip.

ruth'less, *adj.* without compunction or compassion.

rye, *n.* **1.** edible grain. **2.** whiskey distilled from this.

S

S, s, *n.* nineteenth letter of the English alphabet.

Sab'bath, *n.* day of worship and rest.

sa'ber, *n.* single-edged curved sword. Also, **sa'bre.**

sa'ble, *n.* weasel-like mammal with dark-brown fur.

sab'o·tage'', *n., v.t.* **-taged, -taging.** *n.* **1.** intentional damage to equipment. —*v.t.* **2.** damage intentionally. —**sab'o·teur''.**

sac, *n.* baglike part of the body.

sac'cha·rin (sak'kə rin), *n.* sugar substitute.

sac·cha·rine, *adj.* **1.** too sweet, as in manner. —*n.* **2.** saccharin.

sac·er·do·tal (sas''ər dō'təl, sak''ər dō'təl), *adj.* pertaining to or suggesting priests.

sa·chet (sa chā'), *n.* bag of scented powder.

sack, *n.* **1.** bag, esp. a large, strong one. **2.** plunder. —*v.t.* **3.** put into a sack or sacks. **4.** plunder.

sack'cloth, *n.* coarse cloth worn by penitents.

sac'ra·ment, *n.* **1.** ceremony or act regarded as sacred. **2.** Sacrament, Eucharist. —**sac''ra·men'tal**, *adj.*

sa'cred, *adj.* **1.** holy. **2.** safe from attack, ridicule, etc. **3.** binding, as a promise. —**sa'cred·ly**, *adv.* —**sa'cred·ness**, *n.*

sac'ri·fice, *n., v.,* **-ficed, -ficing.** *n.* **1.** offer of something valuable to a deity. **2.** intentional loss of one thing to gain another. —*v.t.* **3.** offer or lose in a sacrifice. —*v.i.* **4.** make a sacrifice. —**sac''ri·fi'cial**, *adj.*

sac'ri·lege, *n.* violation or mockery of something sacred. —**sac''ri·le'gious**, *adj.*

sac'ris·tan, *n.* person in charge of a sacristy.

sac'ris·ty, *n., pl.* **-ties.** place for keeping the sacred vessels, etc. of a church.

sac'ro·sanct, *adj.* sacred.

sad, *adj.,* **sadder, saddest.** low in spirits; melancholy. —**sad'ly**, *adv.* —**sad'ness**, *n.* —**sad'den**, *v.t., v.i.*

sad'dle, *n., v.t.,* **-dled, -dling.** *n.* **1.** seat for the rider of a horse, bicycle, etc. —*v.t.* **2.** put a saddle on. **3.** impose a burden on. —**sad'dle·bag**, *n.*

sad'ism, *n.* practice of cruelty for pleasure. —**sad'ist**, *n.* —**sa·dis'tic**, *adj.*

sa·fa·ri (sə fah'rē), *n.* journey, esp. in central Africa, for hunting or exploration.

safe, *adj.,* **safer, safest**, *n., adj.* **1.** free from danger or risk. —*n.* **2.** container protecting against theft, fire, etc. —**safe'ly**, *adv.* —**safe'ty**, *n.*

safe'guard, *v.t.* **1.** protect from danger. —*n.* **2.** something protective.

sag, *v.i.,* **sagged, sagging,** *n., v.i.* **1.** bend or hang downwards where not supported; droop. —*n.* **2.** distortion caused by sagging.

sa'ga, *n.* Nordic heroic legend.

sa·ga'ci·ty, *n.* wisdom. —**sa·ga'cious**, *adj.* —**sa·ga'cious·ly**, *adv.*

sage, *n., adj.,* **sager, sagest.** *n.* **1.** wise and learned person. **2.** seasoning herb. —*adj.* **3.** wise. —**sage'ly**, *adv.* —**sage'ness**, *n.*

sa·hib (sah'ēb), *n.* respectful term for a European, used in the Indian subcontinent.

said, *adj.* previously mentioned.

sail, *n.* **1.** area of cloth used to drive a ship or boat by the force of moving air. **2.** excursion in a ship or boat so driven. —*v.i.* **3.** make such an excursion or excursions. **4.** depart in a ship.

sail'boat'', *n.* boat moved by sails.

sail'fish, *n.* large fish with sail-like back fin.

sail'or, *n.* **1.** member of a ship's crew. **2.** enlisted man in a navy.

saint, *n.* **1.** person officially venerated by a church. **2.** person leading a religious or upright life. —**saint'hood**, *n.* —**saint'ly**, *adj.*

sake, *n.* **1.** (sāk) benefit. **2.** purpose. **3.** (sak'ē) Japanese rice wine.

sal'a·ble, *adj.* able to be sold. Also, **sale'a·ble.**

sa·la·cious, *adj.* obscene; lewd.

sal'ad, *n.* dish mainly of raw vegetables or fruits.

sal'a·man''der, *n.* small, tailed amphibian.

sa·la·mi, *n.* spiced sausage.

sal'a·ry, *n., pl.* **-ries.** regular payment for a permanent employee. —**sal'a·ried,** *adj.*

sale, *n.* **1.** act or occasion of selling. **2.** demand for something sold. **3.** offer of goods at reduced prices. —**sales'clerk'',** *n.* —**sale'room'',** **sales'room'',** *n.*

sales'man, *n.* man who sells merchandise, etc. Also, *fem.,* **sales'wom''an,** **sales' la''dy,** **sales'girl''.**

sa'lient, *adj.* **1.** outstanding. **2.** projecting. —*n.* **3.** area that projects. —**sa'li·ent·ly,** *adv.* —**sa'li·ence,** *n.*

sa·line (sā'līn), *adj.* salty. —**sa·lin'i·ty,** *n.*

sa·li'va, *n.* fluid secreted in mouth by glands to aid digestion. —**sal'i·va''ry,** *adj.*

sal'low, *adj.* with a sickly, yellowish complexion.

sal'ly, *n., pl.* **-lies,** *v.i.,* **-lied, -lying.** *n.* **1.** counterattack from a fortified position. **2.** witticism. —*v.i.* **3.** emerge briskly.

sal'mon, *n.* edible fish with pink flesh.

sa·lon', *n.* **1.** room for conversation. **2.** art gallery.

sa·loon', *n.* **1.** place where liquor is served and drunk. **2.** public room, esp. on a ship.

salt, *n.* **1.** sodium chloride. **2.** *Chemistry.* compound derived from an acid. **3.** wit; piquancy. —*v.t.* **4.** treat with salt. —**salt'y,** *adj.* —**salt'shak''er,** *n.*

salt·ine', *n.* salted cracker.

salt''pe'ter, *n.* potassium nitrate. Also, **salt'pe'tre.**

sa·lu'bri·ous, *adj.* promoting health. —**sa·lu'bri·ous·ly,** *adv.*

sal'u·tar''y, *adj.* beneficial.

sal''u·ta'tion, *n.* **1.** greeting. **2.** opening phrase of a letter, naming the addressee.

sa·lute', *n., v.* **-luted, -luting.** *n.* **1.** act expressing respect or attention in military etiquette. **2.** greeting. **3.** firing of cannons, etc. as a sign of welcome. —*v.t.* **4.** recognize with a salute. —*v.i.* **5.** perform a salute.

sal'vage, *v.t.,* **-vaged, -vaging,** *n., v.t.* **1.** rescue from loss, as a ship. **2.** gather for reuse, as discarded material. —*n.* **3.** salvaged material.

sal·va'tion, *n.* act of saving or state of being saved, as from damnation or destruction.

salve (sav), *n., v.t.,* **salved, salving.** *n.* **1.** soothing or healing ointment. —*v.t.* **2.** cover with salve.

sal'vo, *n., pl.* **salvos, salvoes.** discharge of many guns, etc. in rapid succession.

same, *adj.* **1.** identical. **2.** without change. **3.** previously mentioned. —*n.* **4.** same thing or person. —**same'ness,** *n.*

sam'o·var, *n.* metal tea urn.

sam'pan, *n.* sculled Chinese or Japanese boat.

sam'ple, *n., adj., v.t.,* **-pled, -pling.** *n.* **1.** something representing more or others of its kind. —*adj.* **2.** serving as a sample. —*v.t.* **3.** take a sample of.

sam'pler, *n.* piece of needlework demonstrating skill.

san''a·to'ri·um, *n.* sanitarium.

sanc'ti·fy, *v.t.,* **-fied, -fying. 1.** make sacred. **2.** free of sin. —**sanc''ti·fi·ca'tion,** *n.*

sanc''ti·mo''ny, *n.* showy or false piety. —**sanc''ti·mo·ni'ous,** *adj.*

sanc'tion, *n.* **1.** permission or support. **2.** non-belligerent measure against a nation by other nations. —*v.t.* **3.** authorize.

sanc'ti·ty, *n.* holiness or sacredness.

sanc'tu·ar''y, *n., pl.* **-aries. 1.** consecrated place. **2.** place of refuge.

sanc'tum, *n.* consecrated place.

sand, *n.* **1.** fine pieces of rock. **2.** **sands,** sandy area. —*v.t.* **3.** rub with sandpaper. —**sand'er,** *n.* —**sand'storm'',** *n.*

san'dal, *n.* open shoe secured by straps.

san'dal·wood, *n.* aromatic Asiatic wood.

sand'bar'', *n.* low island of sand.

sand'pa''per, *n.* **1.** sand-coated paper for smoothing or reducing surfaces. —*v.t.* **2.** rub with sandpaper.

sand'pip''er, *n.* small shore bird.

sand'stone, *n.* stone made of sand naturally cemented together.

sand'wich, *n.* **1.** bread, roll, etc. in two slices with meat, etc. between them. —*v.t.* **2.** insert.

sand'y, *adj.,* **-ier, -iest. 1.** abounding in sand. **2.** colored like sand.

sane, *adj.,* **saner, sanest.** mentally sound. —**sane'ly,** *adv.*

sang-froid (sāh''frwah'), *n.* control of one's emotions.

san'gui·nar''y, *adj.* **1.** bloody. **2.** bloodthirsty.

san'guine, *adj.* optimistic.

san''i·tar'i·um, *n.* place for the recovery of health.

san'i·tar''y, *adj.* **1.** free of harmful bacteria, etc. **2.** pertaining to health.

san''i·ta'tion, *n.* provisions against disease.

san'i·ty, *n.* mental soundness.

sap, *n., v.t.,* **sapped, sapping.** *n.* **1.** juice of a tree, etc. **2.** *Informal.* fool. —*v.t.* **3.** weaken.

sa'pi·ent, *adj.* wise; knowing. —**sa'pi·ence,** *n.*

sap'ling, *n.* young tree.

sap'phire, *n.* blue gemstone.

sap'suck''er, *n.* variety of woodpecker.

sar'casm, *n.* **1.** making of agreeably worded but harshly intended remarks. **2.** such a remark. —**sar·cas'tic,** *adj.* —**sar·cas'ti·cal·ly,** *adv.*

sar·coph'a·gus, *n.,* *pl.* -gi. stone coffin.

sar·dine', *n.* trade name for a small canned ocean fish.

sar·don'ic, *adj.* bitterly sarcastic. —**sar·don'i·cal·ly,** *adv.*

sar·sa·pa·ril'la (sas''pə ril'ə, sahrs''pəril'ə), *n.* tropical vine with fragrant roots.

sar·to'ri·al, *adj.* pertaining to tailors or tailoring.

sash, *n.* **1.** cloth band worn over the upper part of the body or around the waist. **2.** frame for window glass.

sas'sa·fras, *n.* American tree with aromatic bark at the roots.

Sa'tan, *n.* the Devil. —**sa·tan'ic,** *adj.*

satch'el, *n.* small cloth suitcase or bag.

sate, *v.t.,* sated, sating. satisfy fully or to excess, as an appetite.

sa·teen', *n.* satinlike cotton fabric.

sat'el·lite, *n.* **1.** heavenly body moving around a planet. **2.** organization, etc. dominated or controlled by another.

sa·ti·ate (sā'shē āt), *v.t.,* -ated, -ating. glut. —**sa''ti·a'tion,** sa'ti·e'ty, *n.*

sat'in, *n.* glossy fabric or silk or a silk substitute. —**sa'tin·y,** *adj.*

sat'ire, *n.* **1.** sarcasm or ridicule in the exposure of wrongful actions or attitudes. **2.** story, etc. using these means. —**sa·tir'i·cal,** sa·tir'ic, *adj.* —**sa·tir'i·cal·ly,** *adv.* —**sa'tir·ist,** *n.*

sat'ir·ize, *v.t.,* -ized, -izing. portray satirically.

sat'is·fy, *v.t.,* -fied, -fying. **1.** fulfill the wishes or needs of. **2.** convince. **3.** pay, as a debt. —**sat''is·fac'tion,** *n.* —**sat''is·fac'to·ry,** *adj.*

sat'u·rate, *v.t.,* -rated, -rating. cause complete absorption by. —**sat''u·ra'tion,** *n.*

Sat'ur·day, *n.* seventh day of the week.

Sat'urn, *n.* second-largest planet in the solar system.

sat·ur·nine (sat'ər nīn''), *adj.* gloomy.

sa'tyr, *n.* **1.** classical forest deity. **2.** lecherous man.

sauce, *n.* **1.** liquid for flavoring or cooking. **2.** semiliquid stewed fruit.

sauce'pan'', *n.* small, handled cooking pot.

sau'cer, *n.* small dish.

sau'cy, *adj.,* -cier, -ciest. impudent. —**sau'ci·ness,** *n.* —**sau'ci·ly,** *adv.*

sauer'kraut'', *n.* chopped fermented cabbage.

sau'na, *n.* Finnish hot-air bath.

saun'ter, *v.i.,* *n.* stroll.

sau'sage, *n.* minced and seasoned meat, often in a casing.

sau·té (sō tā'), *v.t.,* -téed, -téeing. fry quickly in a little fat.

sau·terne (sō tərn'), *n.* sweet white wine.

sav'age, *adj.* **1.** uncivilized. **2.** fierce or harsh. —*n.* **3.** uncivilized person. —**sav'age·ly,** *adv.* —**sav'age·ry,** *n.*

sa·vant (sa vahnt'), *n.* learned person.

save, *v.t.,* saved, saving, *prep., conj., v.t.* **1.** keep from harm. **2.** keep for future use. **3.** keep from being wasted. **4.** keep from sin or its consequences. —*prep., conj.* except.

sav'ing, *adj.* **1.** redeeming. **2.** thrifty. —*n.* **3.** economy. **4.** savings, money saved. —*prep.* **5.** with the exception of.

sav'ior, **1.** rescuer. **2.** the Savior, Christ. Also, **sav'iour.**

sa·voir-faire (sav''wahr fār'), *n.* skill in human relations.

sa'vor, *n.,* *v.t.* taste or smell. Also, **sa'vour.**

sa'vor·y, *adj.* pleasant-tasting or smelling.

saw, *n.,* *v.t.,* sawed, sawing. *n.* **1.** cutting tool with a row of teeth. **2.** saying or proverb. —*v.t.* **3.** cut with a saw. —**saw'mill'',** *n.* —**saw'yer,** *n.*

sax'o·phone, *n.* keyed metal reed instrument. —**sax'o·phon''ist,** *n.*

say, *v.t.,* said, saying, *n.,* *v.t.* **1.** speak. **2.** declare to be true. —*n.* **3.** chance to speak.

say'ing, *n.* proverb.

scab, *n.,* *v.i.,* scabbed, scabbing. *n.* **1.** crust over a healing wound or sore. **2.** worker who replaces a striking worker. —*v.i.* **3.** form a scab. —**scab'by,** *adj.*

scab'bard, *n.* sword sheath.

sca'bies, *n.* itching skin disease.

scaf'fold, *n.* **1.** Also, **scaf'fold·ing,** temporary platform. **2.** platform for execution of condemned persons.

scal'a·wag'', *n.* scoundrel.

scald, *v.t.* **1.** burn with hot fluid. **2.** heat almost to boiling. —*n.* **3.** burn made by hot fluid.

scale, *n.,* *v.t.,* scaled, scaling. *n.* **1.** platelike portion of the covering of a fish, snake, etc. **2.** flake or layer of material. **3.** Also, **scales,** weighing device. **4.** range of musical tones. **5.** system of relations, as of actual size to represented size or of different degrees of a thing. —*v.t.* **6.** remove scales from. **7.** climb. **8.** determine the relative size of. —**scal'y,** *adj.*

scal'lion, *n.* any of several varieties of small onion.

scal·lop (skol'ləp), *n.* **1.** bivalve mollusk.

2. any of the curves forming part of a decorative border. —*v.t.* **3.** decorate with scallops.

scalp, *n.* **1.** hair and skin covering the top of the head. —*v.t.* **2.** take a scalp from, esp. as a trophy.

scal′pel, *n.* surgical knife.

scam, *n.* con game; deception practiced to defraud.

scamp, *n.* rascal; imp.

scam′per, *v.i.* **1.** run quickly. —*n.* **2.** fast run.

scan, *v.t.,* **scanned, scanning. 1.** examine in detail. **2.** examine quickly. **3.** analyze the rhythmic pattern of.

scan′dal, *n.* **1.** malicious gossip. **2.** disgraceful occurrence or situation. —**scan′dal·ous,** *adj.*

scan′dal·ize, *v.t.,* **-ized, -izing.** shock with a scandal.

scant, *adj.* scarcely sufficient. Also, **scant′y.** —**scant′i·ly,** *adv.* —**scant′i·ness,** *n.*

scape′goat, *n.* person blamed for the misdeeds of others.

scape′grace, *n.* rascal.

scap′u·la, *n., pl.* **-lae, -las.** shoulder blade. —**scap′u·lar,** *adj.*

scar, *n., v.t.,* **scarred, scarring.** *n.* **1.** mark left by a cut. —*v.t.* **2.** cut so as to make a scar.

scar′ab, *n.* carved image of a beetle.

scarce, *adj.,* **scarcer, scarcest.** not plentiful or common. —**scarc′i·ty, scarce′ness,** *n.*

scarce′ly, *adv.* **1.** only just; barely. **2.** hardly.

scare, *n., v.t.,* **scared, scaring,** *v.t.* **1.** frighten. —*v.i.* **2.** become frightened. —*n.* **3.** frightening occurrence.

scare′crow″, *n.* device to frighten birds from a planted field.

scarf, *n., pl.* **scarfs, scarves.** length of cloth for warming the neck and chest.

scar′i·fy, *v.t.,* **-fied, -fying.** scratch.

scar′let, *adj., n.* bright red.

scarlet fever, contagious disease marked by fever and a scarlet rash.

scat, *v.i.,* **scatted, scatting.** *Informal.* run away.

scath′ing, *adj.* bitterly harsh, as something said or written. —**scath′ing·ly,** *adv.*

scat′ter, *v.t.* **1.** throw in all directions. —*v.i.* **2.** move away rapidly in all directions.

scav′enge, *v.,* **-enged, -enging.** *v.t.* **1.** clean out. —*v.i.* **2.** search for refuse that can be eaten or reused. —**scav′en·ger,** *n.*

sce·nar′i·o, *n.* story outline, esp. in motion pictures.

scene, *n.* **1.** what is seen from a certain place. **2.** location of an action. **3.** sub-division of a dramatic act. **4.** emotional display in public. —**scen′ic,** *adj.*

scen′er·y, *n.* **1.** pleasant outdoor scene. **2.** painted canvases, etc. representing the scene of a dramatic action.

scent, *n.* **1.** distinctive smell. **2.** trail left by something with such a smell. **3.** perfume. **4.** sense of smell. —*v.t.* **5.** smell. **6.** perfume.

scep′ter (sep′tər), *n.* short staff symbolizing royal power. Also, **scep′tre.**

scep′tic, *n.* skeptic.

sched′ule, *n., v.t.,* **-uled, -uling.** *n.* **1.** list of the times of planned actions or events. **2.** any orderly list. —*v.t.* **3.** put on a schedule.

scheme, *n., v.i.,* **schemed, scheming.** *n.* **1.** plan or design. **2.** plot; intrigue. —*v.i.* **3.** plot to do or attain something. —**schem′er,** *n.*

sche·miel′, *n. Yiddish.* a person who is a habitual failure.

schism (siz′əm), *n.* division, as between factions in an organization. —**schis·mat′ic,** *adj., n.*

schist (shist), *n.* layered crystalline rock.

schiz·o·phre·ni·a (skit″zə frē′nē ə), *n.* mental disorder. —**schiz″o·phre′nic, schiz′oid,** *adj.*

schlock, *Yiddish. n.* **1.** inferior goods or materials. —*adj.* **2.** inferior in material or workmanship.

schmaltz, *n. Informal.* sentimental art.

schol′ar, *n.* **1.** person who studies to acquire knowledge. **2.** school pupil.

schol′ar·ly, *adj.* pertaining to or in the manner of scholars.

schol′ar·ship, *n.* **1.** activities and accomplishments of scholars. **2.** grant of money to make school attendance possible.

scho·las′tic, *adj.* pertaining to education.

school, *n.* **1.** place or institution for education or training. **2.** educational activity. **3.** group with a common set of beliefs or practices. **4.** group of fish, etc. —*v.t.* **5.** educate or train. —**school′book,** *n.* —**school′boy,** *n.* —**school′girl,** *n.* —**school′mate,** *n.* —**school′house,** *n.* —**school′room,** *n.* —**school′teacher,** *n.*

schoon′er, *n.* fore-and-aft rigged sailing vessel with two or more masts, including a foremast.

schwa (shwah), *n.* unstressed vowel sound, e.g. the *o* in *factor,* represented by the symbol ə.

sci·at′i·ca (sī at′ik ə), *n.* neuralgia of the hip and thigh. —**sci·at′ic,** *adj.*

sci′ence, *n.* **1.** systematic acquisition of knowledge, esp. knowledge that can be measured precisely. **2.** precise method or skill. —**sci″en·tif′ic,** *adj.* —**sci″en·tif′i·cal·ly,** *adv.* —**sci′en·tist,** *n.*

scin·til·la (sin til′ə), *n.* glimmering; trace.

scin·til·late (sin'təl lāt), *v.i.* **-lated, -lating.** sparkle. —**scin''til·la'tion,** *n.*

sci·on (sī'ən), *n.* **1.** descendant. **2.** plant shoot or bud, esp. for grafting.

scis'sors, *n.* instrument for cutting by means of two moving blades.

scle·ro'sis, *n.* hardening of body tissue. —**scle·rot'ic,** *adj.*

scoff, *n., v.i.,* jeer. —**scof'fer,** *n.*

scold, *v.t.* **1.** reproach at length. —*n.* **2.** person who scolds.

sconce, *n.* wall bracket for lights.

scone, *n.* flat biscuit.

scoop, *n.* **1.** device for digging deeply. **2.** act or instance of scooping. **3.** amount held by a scoop. **4.** *Informal.* prior publication of news. —*v.t.* **5.** remove or empty with a scoop. **6.** *Informal.* get the better of by publishing news first.

scoot, *v.i.* go quickly.

scoot'er, *n.* small, low-built two-wheeled vehicle.

scope, *n.* range of responsibility or possibility for action.

scorch, *v.t.* **1.** burn on the surface. —*n.* **2.** surface burn.

score, *n., v., scored, scoring.* *n.* **1.** total, as of points in a game. **2.** *Informal.* **know the score,** know the actual situation. **3.** long, shallow cut. **4.** group of twenty. **5.** musical arrangement. —*v.t.* **6.** add, as points in a game. **7.** mark with a long, shallow cut. —*v.i.* **8.** gain points, as in a game.

scorn, *n.* **1.** contempt. **2.** derision. —*v.t.* **3.** treat with scorn. —**scorn'ful,** *adj.* —**scorn'ful·ly,** *adv.*

scor'pi·on, *n.* poisonous, long-tailed eight-legged animal.

Scotch, *n.* malted-barley whisky made in Scotland.

scotch, *v.t.* make ineffective.

scoun'drel, *n.* rascal.

scour, *v.t.* **1.** clean with a steady rubbing action. **2.** go over repeatedly, as during a search.

scourge (skərj), *n., v.t., scourged, scourging.* *n.* **1.** whip. **2.** major affliction. —*v.t.* **3.** beat with a whip. **4.** punish or harass severely.

scout, *n.* **1.** person sent to explore or search. —*v.t.* **2.** reject as absurd. —*v.i.* **3.** act as a scout.

scow, *n.* flat-bottomed barge or boat.

scowl, *v.t.* **1.** frown angrily. —*n.* **2.** angry frown.

scrab'ble, *v.i., -bled, -bling.* **1.** scratch or scrape with the hands. **2.** struggle without dignity.

scrag'gly, *adj., -glier, -gliest.* ragged.

scraggy, *adj., -gier, -giest.* scrawny.

scram'ble, *v., -bled, -bling, n., v.t.* **1.** mix up; confuse. —*v.i.* **2.** move in short, rapid steps. —*n.* **3.** scrambling motion or gait. **4.** undignified struggle, as for something of value.

scrap, *n., adj., v.t.,* **scrapped, scrapping.** *n.* **1.** small piece. **2.** refuse material, esp. when reclaimable. **3.** *Informal.* fight. —*adj.* **4.** in the form of scrap. —*v.t.* **5.** make into scrap. **6.** discard. —**scrap'heap,** *n.*

scrap'book, *n.* album for printed and written material, etc.

scrape, *v., scraped, scraping, n., v.t.* **1.** rub against roughly. **2.** remove by rough rubbing. **3.** get by tedious labor. —*v.i.* **4.** rub roughly against something. —*n.* **5.** act of scraping. **6.** area scraped. **7.** dangerous situation. —**scrap'er,** *n.*

scrap'ple, *n.* fried dish of meal and meat scraps.

scratch, *v.t.* **1.** make a long, shallow cut in. **2.** cross out; eliminate. —*n.* **3.** long, shallow cut. **4.** **from scratch,** from the beginning. **5.** **up to scratch,** up to standard.

scratch'y, *adj., -ier, -iest.* suggesting scratching, esp. in sound.

scrawl, *v.t., v.i.* **1.** write with a bad hand. —*n.* **2.** writing in a bad hand.

scrawn'y, *adj., -nier, -niest.* disagreeably thin.

scream, *n.* **1.** loud, high-pitched cry. —*v.i.* **2.** utter such a cry.

screech, *n.* **1.** harsh screamlike sound. —*v.i.* **2.** utter such sounds.

screen, *n.* **1.** flat object or surface for division, protection, or concealment. **2.** surface on which motion pictures, television programs, etc. are projected. **3.** **the screen,** motion-picture industry. —*v.t.* **4.** enclose or protect with or as if with a screen. **5.** sift through a screen. **6.** investigate for suitability.

screw, *n.* **1.** simple machine for fastening, moving, etc., in the form of an inclined plane wound around an axis. **2.** propeller. —*v.t.* **3.** fasten with screws. **4.** turn as one does a screw. —**screw'driv''er,** *n.*

scrib'ble, *v., -bled, -bling, n., v.t., v.i.* **1.** write hastily and carelessly. —*n.* **2.** hasty or careless writing.

scribe, *n. Archaic.* writer or clerk.

scrim'mage, *n., v.i.* **-maged, -maging.** *n.* **1.** play in football. —*v.i.* **2.** take part in a scrimmage.

scrimp, *v.i.* save; economize.

scrip, *n.* certificate used in place of money.

script, *n.* **1.** handwriting. **2.** manuscript, esp. of a play.

Scrip'ture, *n.* **1.** portion or portions of the Bible. **2.** **the Scriptures,** the Bible. —**scrip'tur·al,** *adj.*

scrof'u·la, *n.* tuberculosis of the lymph glands.

scroll, *n.* **1.** roll of paper, etc. bearing writing or print. **2.** spiral ornamental motif. —*v.* **3.** (computers) to move the

display on a monitor so that other data can be read.

scro′tum, *n.* baglike skin enclosure for testicles.

scrounge, *v.,* **scrounged, scrounging.** *v.t.* **1.** *Informal.* beg or steal in a minor way. —*v.i.* **2.** *Informal.* look for something desired.

scrub, *v.t.,* **scrubbed, scrubbing,** *n., adj., v.t.* **1.** wash with a vigorous rubbing action. **2.** *Informal.* eliminate; cross off. —*n.* **3.** stunted trees or shrubbery. —*adj.* **4.** inferior.

scruff, *n.* nape of the neck.

scru′ple, *n.* prompting of the conscience.

scru′pu·lous, *adj.* **1.** conscientious. **2.** careful. —**scru′pu·lous·ly** *adv.*

scru′ti·nize, *v.t.,* **-nized, -nizing.** examine carefully. —**scru′ti·ny,** *n.*

scud, *v.i.,* **scudded, scudding.** move rapidly.

scuff, *v.t.* **1.** wear by rubbing or scraping. —*v.t., v.i.* **2.** shuffle, as the feet.

scuf′fle, *v.i.,* **-fled, -fling,** *n., v.i.* **1.** flight confusedly at close quarters. —*n.* **2.** confused fight at close quarters.

scull, *n.* **1.** oar used at a boat's stern. **2.** racing rowboat. —*v.t., v.i.* **3.** move with a scull.

scul′ler·y, *n.* room for cleaning dishes, kitchen utensils, etc.

sculp′ture, *n.* **1.** art of composing in three dimensions. **2.** example of this art. —**sculp′tur·al,** *adj.* —**sculp′tor,** *n., fem.,* **sculp′tress.**

scum, *n.* **1.** film on a liquid surface. **2.** rabble. —**scum′my,** *adj.*

scup′per, *n.* drainage opening in a deck or flat roof.

scurf, *n.* flecks of dead skin.

scur′ril·ous, *adj.* grossly insulting. —**scur′ril·ous·ly,** *adv.* —**scur·ril′i·ty, scur′ril·lous·ness,** *n.*

scur′ry, *v.i.,* **-ried, -rying,** *n., pl.* **-ries.** *v.i.* **1.** move hastily. —*n.* **2.** hasty movement.

scur′vy, *n.* disease due to vitamin deficiency.

scut′tle, *n., v.,* **-tled, -tling.** *n.* **1.** hatchlike opening in a deck or roof. **2.** coal bucket. —*v.t.* **3.** sink intentionally. —*v.i.* **4.** scurry.

scythe, *n.* mowing instrument with curved blade and long handle.

sea, *n.* **1.** part of an ocean, esp. one partly bounded by land. **2. the sea,** the oceans. **3.** large inland body of water. **4.** relative turbulence of ocean water at a given time. —**sea′board″, sea′coast″,** *n.*

sea′far″ing, *n.* activity of one who travels on or works at sea. —**sea′far″er,** *n.*

sea′go″ing, *adj.* pertaining to or suitable for travel on the sea.

sea horse, semitropical fish with head of horselike form.

seal, *n.* **1.** device for giving official character to or preventing tampering with a document, locked space, etc. **2.** stamp used to shape such a device. **3.** device to prevent passage of air, etc. **4.** four-flippered sea mammal. —*v.t.* **5.** put seal on. **6.** enclose with a seal.

sea′lion, large seal.

seam, *n.* **1.** line of junction. **2.** mineral stratum. —*v.t.* **3.** join at or with a seam. —**seam′less,** *adj.*

sea′man, *n., pl.* **-men.** sailor. —**sea′man·ship″,** *n.*

seam′stress, *n.* sewing woman.

seam′y, *adj.,* **seamier, seamiest. 1.** having seams. **2.** less attractive; sordid.

sé·ance (sā′ahns), *n.* meeting for communication with the dead.

sea′plane, *n.* airplane able to land on water.

sea′port″, *n.* port fronting on an ocean.

sear, *v.t.* **1.** burn the surface of. **2.** wither.

search, *n.* **1.** methodical attempt to find something. —*v.t.* **2.** examine in making a search. —*v.i.* **3.** hunt. —**search′er,** *n.*

search′ing, *adj.* deep and perceptive, as an investigation.

search′light, *n.* directed light for distinguishing objects in the dark.

sea′shell″, *n.* shell of a saltwater mollusk.

sea′shore″, *n.* shore of an ocean. Also, **sea′side″.**

sea′sick″, *adj.* sick from the motion of a ship. —**sea′sick″ness,** *n.*

sea′son, *n.* **1.** quarter of the year beginning at a solstice or equinox. **2.** appropriate time. —*v.t.* **3.** flavor with salt, spices, herbs, etc. **4.** prepare for use by aging or exposure to weather. —**sea′son·al,** *adj.*

sea′son·a·ble, *adj.* coming at the appropriate time.

sea′son·ing, *n.* flavoring of salt, spices, herbs, etc.

seat, *n.* **1.** place for sitting. **2.** place of governmental activities, residence, etc. **3.** location. **4.** place in a legislature, etc. —*v.t.* **5.** put onto a seat. **6.** install in a seat.

sea′way″, *n.* **1.** inland waterway to the sea. **2.** area of open sea.

sea′weed″, *n.* ocean plant.

sea′wor″thy, *adj.* suitable for navigation at sea.

se·ba·ceous (si bā′shəs), *adj.* fatty.

se·cede′, *v.i.,* **-ceded, -ceding.** withdraw from a political state, etc. —**se·ces′sion,** *n.*

se·clude′, *v.t.,* **-cluded, -cluding.** isolate, esp. from society or activity. —**se·clu′sion,** *n.*

sec′ond, *adj.* **1.** next after the first. —*n.* **2.** sixtieth of a minute. **3.** person serving as an assistant or witness. **4. seconds,** goods rejected for ordinary sale.

—*v.t.* **5.** approve. —*adv.* **6.** as a second point. —**sec′ond·ly,** *adv.*

sec′ond·ar·y, *adv.* **1.** forming a second stage or phase. **2.** of a second level of importance. —**sec′on·dar″i·ly,** *adv.*

sec′ond-hand′, *adj.* **1.** belonging or offered to a new owner. **2.** not original.

se′cret, *n.* **1.** something not to be known by everyone. **2.** hidden cause or reason. —*adj.* **3.** hidden or not to be known by everyone. —**se′cret·ly,** *adv.* —**se′cre·cy,** *n.*

sec″re·tar′i·at, *n.* group of administrative officials.

sec′re·tar″y, *n., pl.* **-taries. 1.** assistant to a businessman, official, etc. **2.** head of a government department. **3.** writing desk. —**sec″re·tar′i·al,** *adj.*

se·crete′, *v.t.,* **-creted, -creting. 1.** produce and release substances, as a gland. **2.** hide. —**se·cre′tion,** *n.* —**se′cre′to·ry,** *adj.*

se′cre·tive, *adj.* **1.** reluctant to reveal information. **2.** pertaining to secretion. —**se′cre·tive·ly,** *adv.* —**se′cre·tive·ness,** *n.*

sect, *n.* religious group.

sec·tar′i·an, *adj.* **1.** pertaining to separate sects. —*n.* **2.** member of a sect.

sec′tion, *n.* **1.** separate part. **2.** act or instance of dividing. **3.** view of a thing as if divided. —*v.t.* **4.** divide. —**sec′tion·al,** *adj.*

sec′tor, *n.* **1.** *Geometry.* plane figure formed of a segment of a circle and two of its radii. **2.** area, esp. of military operation.

sec′u·lar, *adj.* not religious. —**sec′u·lar·ize,** *v.t.*

se·cure′, *adj., v.t.,* **-cured, -curing.** *adj.* **1.** safe or certain. **2.** firmly in place. —*v.t.* **3.** make secure. **4.** obtain. —**se·cure′ly,** *adv.*

se·cur′i·ty, *n., pl.* **-ties. 1.** state of being secure. **2.** protection or precaution. **3.** pledge on a loan, etc. **4. securities,** bonds, stocks, etc.

se·dan′, *n.* closed automobile with front and rear seats.

se·date′, *n.* quiet in manner.

sed′a·tive, *n.* **1.** medicine to relieve pain or nervousness. —*adj.* **2.** relieving pain or nervousness. —**se·da′tion,** *n.*

sed′en·tar″y, *adj.* not physically active.

Se·der (sā′dər″), *n.* Jewish home ceremony at Passover.

sed′i·ment, *n.* matter falling to the bottom of a body of liquid.

se·di′tion, *n.* incitement to rebellion. —**se·di′tious,** *adj.*

se·duce′, *v.t.,* **-duced, -ducing. 1.** tempt or induce to commit a wrong. **2.** induce to perform a sexual act. —**se·duc′er,** *fem.,* **se·duc′tress,** *n.* —**se·duc′tion,** *n.*

se·duc′tive, *adj.* tempting; attractive.

sed′u·lous, *adj.* diligent.

see, *v.,* saw, seen, seeing, *n., v.t.* **1.** sense with the eyes. **2.** realize or understand. **3.** make sure. **4.** escort. —*v.i.* **5.** have use of the eyes. **6.** find out or understand. **7.** attend, as to a task. **8.** bishopric.

seed, *n., pl.* seeds, seed, *v.t., v.i.* **1.** thing from which a plant grows. **2.** offspring. —*v.t.* **3.** sow seed in. **4.** remove seeds from. —**seed′less,** *adj.*

seed′ling, *n.* new growth from a seed.

seed′y, *adj.* seedier, seediest. **1.** having seeds. **2.** shabby.

see′ing, *conj.* in view of the fact.

seek, *v.t.,* sought, seeking. **1.** look for. **2.** intend and attempt. —**seek′er,** *n.*

seem, *v.t., v.i.* give the effect of being or acting in some specified way.

seem′ing, *adj.* apparent. —**seem′ing·ly,** *adv.*

seem′ly, *adj.,* **-lier, -liest.** proper in appearance or effect. —**seem′li·ness,** *n.*

seep, *v.i.* ooze. —**seep′age,** *n.*

seer, *n.* person who professes to foresee the future. Also, *fem.,* **seer′ess.**

seer′suck″er, *n.* crinkled striped fabric.

see′saw″, *n.* recreation of swinging up and down on a balanced plank.

seethe, *v.,* seethed, seething. *v.t., v.i.* boil.

seg′ment, *n.* **1.** portion. —*v.t.* **2.** divide into portions. —**seg′men′tal,** *adj.* —**seg″men·ta′tion,** *n.*

seg′re·gate, *v.t.,* **-gated, -gating.** keep apart from others. —**seg″re·ga′tion,** *n.*

seine (sān), *n.* **1.** weighted fishing net. —*v.t., v.i.* **2.** fish with such a net.

seis·mic (sīz′mik), *adj.* pertaining to or affected by earth tremors.

seis′mo·graph, *n.* device for measuring earth tremors.

seize, *v.t.,* seized, seizing. **1.** take by authority or force. **2.** grasp, as an idea.

seiz′ure, *n.* **1.** taking by authority or force. **2.** attack of illness.

sel′dom, *adv.* rarely.

se·lect′, *v.t.* **1.** choose. —*adj.* **2.** selected; choice. —**se·lec′tion,** *n.*

se·lec′tive, *adj.* **1.** pertaining to selection. **2.** careful in selecting.

se·lect′man, *n.* New England town officer.

self, *n.* **1.** one's own person. **2.** one's own well-being. —*adj.* **3.** of the same kind.

self″-as·sur′ance, *n.* self-confidence. —**self″-as·sured′,** *adj.*

self′-cen′tered, *adj.* seeing all things in reference to one's self or self-interest.

self′-con·ceit′, *n.* excessively good opinion of oneself.

self″-con′fi·dence, *n.* confidence in one's own ability, rightness, etc —**self″-con′fi·dent,** *adj.*

self″-con′scious, *adj.* excessively aware of the impression one may be making.

self″-con·tained′, *adj.* **1.** complete in itself. **2.** reserved in manner.

self″-con·trol′, *n.* ability to restrain one's impulses or expressions of emotion.

self′-de·ni′al, *n.* readiness to forgo gratifications to further a cause, help another, etc. —**self″-de·ny′ing,** *adj.*

self′-es·teem′, *n.* good opinion of one's self.

self′-ev′ident, *adj.* evident without further proof or explanation.

self″-ex·plan′a·to″ry, *adj.* needing no explanation; obvious.

self″-im·por′tant, *adj.* seeming to have an excessive idea of one's own importance.

self″-in′ter·est, *n.* concern for one's own well-being.

self′ish, *adj.* acting for or thinking of one's own well-being alone. —**self′ish·ly,** *adv.* —**self′ish·ness,** *n.*

self′less, *n.* self-sacrificing.

self′-made′, *n.* prosperous, famous, or powerful through one's own efforts.

self″-pos·ses′sion, *n.* self-control. —**self″-pos·sessed′,** *adj.*

self″-re·li′ance, *n.* reliance on one's own resources. —**self″-re·li′ant,** *adj.*

self′-re·spect′, *n.* respect for one's own dignity, rights, etc. —**self′-re·spect′ing,** *adj.*

self″-right′eous, *adj.* conceitedly sure of one's righteousness.

self′same″, *adj.* identical.

self″-sat′is·fied, *adj.* satisfied with one's own personality, accomplishments, etc. —**self′-sat″is·fac′tion,** *n.*

self-seek′ing, *adj.* motivated by self-interest.

self′-styled′, *adj.* thus named by the one so named.

self″-suf·fi′cient, *adj.* able to depend on one's own resources. —**self″-suf·fi′cien·cy,** *n.*

sell, *v.t.,* **sold, selling. 1.** exchange for money. **2.** offer for sale. —*v.i.* **3.** attract the buying public. —**sel′ler,** *n.*

selt′zer, *n.* carbonated water.

sel′vage, *n.* woven edge on a length of cloth. Also, **sel′vedge.**

se·man′tics, *n.* study of word meanings. —**se·man′tic,** *adj.*

sem′a·phore″, *n.* signal using different positions of arms or flags.

sem′blance, *n.* **1.** seeming state. **2.** resemblance.

se′men, *n.* fluid containing sperm.

se·mes′ter, *n.* unit consisting of half a school year.

se″mi·cir′cle, *n.* half a circle. —**se″mi·cir′cu·lar,** *adj.*

sem′i·col″on, *n.* punctuation mark of the form; that is used to divide clauses of a sentence.

sem″i·con·duc′tor, *n.* a material used to modify electrical current, used in solid-state circuitry.

sem′i·nar″, *n.* academic class with a format of discussion or research.

sem′i·nar″y, *n., pl.* **-naries. 1.** school for divinity students. **2.** school for young women. —**sem″i·nar′i·an,** *n.*

sem″i·pre′cious, *adj.* not considered precious, as certain decorative stones used as gems.

sen′ate, *n.* **1.** senior legislative body. **2.** **the senate,** upper legislative house in the United States or Canada. —**sen′a·tor,** *n.* —**sen″a·tor′i·al,** *adj.*

send, *v.,* **sent, sending.** *v.t.* **1.** cause to go. —*v.i.* **2.** send for, cause to come. —**send′er,** *n.*

se·nile (sē′nīl), *adj.* decrepit, esp. mentally, in old age. —**se·nil′i·ty,** *n.*

sen′ior, *adj.* **1.** older. **2.** higher in authority. **3.** having more years of employment or service. **4.** in the last year of school. —*n.* **5.** senior person. —**sen·ior′i·ty,** *n.*

se·ñor (senyor′), *n., pl.* **-nores.** *Spanish.* Mr. or Sir.

se·ño·ra (se nyor′ah), *n., pl.* **-noras.** *Spanish.* Mrs. or Madam.

se·ño·ri·ta (se″nyō rē′tah), *n., pl.* **-ritas.** *Spanish.* Miss.

sen·sa′tion, *n.* **1.** use of the senses. **2.** experience obtained through the senses. **3.** intuition or feeling. **4.** something causing excited public interest.

sen·sa′tion·al, *adj.* causing or intended to cause excited public interest. —**sen·sa′tion·al·ly,** *adv.* —**sen·sa′tion·al·ism,** *n.*

sense, *n., v.t.,* **sensed, sensing.** *n.* **1.** sight, hearing, touch, taste, or smell. **2.** impression obtained through one of these. **3.** intuition regarding a situation. **4.** Often, **senses,** reason. **5.** meaning. —*v.t.* **6.** perceive by or as if by one of the senses.

sense′less, *adj.* **1.** unreasonable. **2.** unconscious.

sen″si·bil′i·ty, *n., pl.* **-ties. 1.** ability to sense or be aware of things. **2.** Often, **sensibilities,** emotional sensitivity.

sen′si·ble, *n.* **1.** reasonable. **2.** perceptible through the senses. **3.** aware. —**sen′si·bly,** *adv.*

sen′si·tive, *n.* **1.** able to sense or register objects, data, etc. in small amounts. **2.** easily disturbed. —**sen″si·tiv′i·ty,** *n.* —**sen′si·tize,** *v.t.,* **-tized, -tizing.** make sensitive.

sen′so·ry, *adj.* pertaining to the senses.

sen′su·al, *adj.* **1.** given to the pleasures of the senses. **2.** pertaining to such pleasure. —**sen′su·al·ism,** *n.* —**sen′su·al·ist,** *n.*

sen'su·ous, *n.* **1.** pertaining to the senses. **2.** pleasing to the senses or emotions. —**sen'su·ous·ly,** *adv.* —**sen'su·ous·ness,** *n.*

sen'tence, *n., v.t.,* **-tenced, -tencing.** *n.* **1.** unit of prose writing expressing one thought. **2.** legal decision, esp. regarding a punishment. **3.** punishment, esp. a term of imprisonment. —*v.t.* **4.** determine the punishment of.

sen''ten'tious, *adj.* tiresomely opinionated or voluble on matters of right and wrong.

sen'tient (sen'shǝnt), *adj.* having feeling or perception. —**sen'tience,** *n.*

sen'ti·ment, *n.* **1.** personal feeling. **2.** statement of such feeling. **3.** opinion.

sen''ti·men'tal, *adj.* characterized by love, pity, etc., esp. to an unreasonable extent. —**sen''ti·men''tal'i·ty,** *n.* —**sen''ti·men'tal·ism,** *n.* —**sen''ti·men'tal·ist,** *n.*

sen'ti·nel, *n.* guard.

sen'try, *n., pl.* **-tries.** soldier on guard duty.

sep'a·rate, *v.,* **-rated, -rating,** *adj. v.t., v.i.* (sep'ǝ rāt) **1.** part. —*adj.* (sep'ǝ rǝt) **2.** unconnected; individual. —**sep'a·rate·ly,** *adv.* —**sep''a·ra'tion,** *n.* —**sep'a·ra·ble,** *adj.* —**sep'a·ra''tor,** *n.*

se'pi·a, *n.* dark brown.

sep'sis, *n.* infection of the blood. —**sep'tic,** *adj.*

Sep·tem'ber, *n.* ninth month.

sep'tic, *adj.* **1.** pertaining to putrefaction. **2.** pertaining to sepsis.

sep·tu·a·ge·nar·i·an (sep''chōō ǝ jǝ ner'ēǝn), *n.* person in his or her seventies.

sep·ul·cher (sep'ǝl kǝr), *n.* tomb. Also, **sep'ul·chre.**

se·pul'chral, *adj.* **1.** lugubrious or gloomy. **2.** pertaining to sepulchers.

se'quel, *n.* **1.** event that follows. **2.** story continuing the subject of a previous one.

se'quence, *n.* **1.** succession or series. **2.** consequence. **3.** episode in a motion picture or television program.

se·ques'ter, *v.t.* **1.** set apart. **2.** seize or impound. —**se''ques·tra'tion,** *n.*

se'quin, *n.* small glittering disk sewn to a costume.

ser'aph, *n., pl.* **-aphs, -aphim.** angel of the highest order. —**se·raph'ic,** *adj.*

sere, *adj.* withered.

ser'e·nade'', *n., v.t.,* **-naded, -nading.** *n.* **1.** musical composition for outdoor evening performance. —*v.t.* **2.** perform a serenade for.

se·rene', *adj.* **1.** calm. **2.** fair, as the weather. —**se·ren'i·ty,** *n.* —**se·rene'ly,** *adv.*

serf, *n.* person in bondage to a landlord. —**serf'dom,** *n.*

serge, *n.* twilled fabric.

ser'geant, *n.* highest noncommissioned army officer.

se'ri·al, *adj.* **1.** forming part of a series. —*n.* **2.** story appearing in installments. —**se'ri·al·ly,** *adv.*

se'ries, *n., pl.* **-ries.** group of things coming one after the other.

se'ri·ous, *adj.* **1.** solemn. **2.** earnest, sincere. **3.** important. —**se'ri·ous·ly,** *adv.* —**se'ri·ous·ness,** *n.*

ser'mon, *n.* speech to a religious congregation.

ser'pent, *n.* any large snake.

ser·pen·tine (sǝr'pǝn tēn), *adj.* winding in snakelike loops.

ser'rat·ed, *adj.* resembling sawteeth in outline. —**ser·ra'tion,** *n.*

se'rum, *n.* liquid part of the blood, sometimes used in inoculation.

serv'ant, *n.* person hired to work in a household.

serve, *v.,* **served, serving.** *v.t.* **1.** act in the service of. **2.** be of use to. **3.** present for consumption, as food or drink. **4.** undergo, as a prison sentence. —*v.i.* **5.** act in the service of a person, organization, or cause. **6.** suffice.

serv'ice, *n., v.t.,* **-viced, -vicing.** *n.* **1.** activity in behalf of a person, organization, or cause. **2.** employment as a domestic worker. **3.** military organization or the military. **4.** favor. **5.** session of public worship. **6.** set of matched dishes, eating implements, etc. —*v.t.* **7.** supply, maintain, or repair.

serv'ice·a·ble, *adj.* useful.

serv'ice·man'', *n.* **1.** member of an armed force. **2.** person who maintains, repairs, or fuels machinery.

ser'vile (sǝr'vīl), *adj.* slavelike; obsequious. —**ser·vil'i·ty,** *n.*

ser'vi·tude, *n.* bondage.

ses'a·me, *n.* East Indian plant yielding oil and edible seeds.

ses''qui·cen·ten'ni·al, *n.* **1.** one hundred fiftieth anniversary. —*adj.* **2.** pertaining to such an anniversary.

ses'sion, *n.* **1.** occasion of the gathering of members of a group. **2. in session,** formally convened.

set, *v.,* **set, setting,** *n., adj. v.t.* **1.** place or put. **2.** put in proper or specified order or condition. **3.** place before others, as an example, problem, etc. —*v.i.* **4.** become fixed or firm. **5.** go below the horizon, as a star or planet. **6. set out** or **off,** begin to travel. —*n.* **7.** apparatus. **8.** complete group or collection. **9.** television or radio receiver. **10.** arrangement of theatrical scenery. —*adj.* **11.** firm or fixed. **12.** determined. **13.** prearranged.

set'back'', *n.* temporary defeat or hindrance.

set·tee', *n.* sofa or bench with a back.

set'ter, *n.* hunting dog.

set'ting, *n.* **1.** locale of a story. **2.** environment. **3.** music of a song.

set'tle, *v.*, **-tled, -tling.** *v.t.* **1.** resolve, as a dispute. **2.** free from disturbance. **3.** pay, as a debt. **4.** set in a position of rest. **5.** colonize. —*v.i.* **6.** fall gently into a position of rest. **7.** reach an agreement or compromise. **8.** take up residence. —**set'tler,** *n.* —**set'tle·ment,** *n.*

sev'en, *n., adj.* one more than six.

sev''en·teen', *n., adj.* seven more than ten. —**sev''en·teenth',** *adj.*

sev'en''ty, *n., adj.* seven times ten. —**sev' en·ti'eth,** *adj.*

sev'er, *v.t.* cut off or separate. —**sev'er· ance,** *n.*

sev'er·al, *adj.* **1.** a few. **2.** individual. **3.** respective. —**sev'er·al·ly,** *adv.*

se·vere', *adj.* **1.** sternly demanding. **2.** harsh or violent. **3.** seriously bad. **4.** austerely simple. —**se·vere'ly,** *adv.* —**se·ver'i·ty,** *n.*

sew, *v.t.*, **sewed, sewed** or **sewn, sewing.** join with thread. —**sew'er,** *n.*

sew'age, *n.* waste material in sewers. Also, **sew'er·age.**

sew'er, *n.* covered channel for waste.

sex, *n.* **1.** individual nature as determined by the reproductive system. **2.** either of two divisions of a species as so determined. **3.** activities, thoughts, etc. as influenced by the reproductive system. —**sex'u·al,** *adj.* —**sex'u·al·ly,** *adv.*

sex''is·m, *n.* discrimination on the basis of sex.

sex'tant, *n.* navigational instrument using the elevation of the sun.

sex·tet', *n.* **1.** group of six, esp. musicians. **2.** musical composition for six instruments. Also, **sex·tette'.**

sex'ton, *n.* caretaker of a church.

sex'tu·ple, *adj.* occurring six times.

shab'by, *adj.*, **-bier, -biest. 1.** worn and untidy-looking. **2.** mean. —**shab'bi· ness,** *n.* —**shab'bi·ly,** *adv.*

shack, *n.* shanty.

shack'le, *n.*, *v.t.*, **-led, -ling.** *n.* **1.** Usually, **shackles,** chains for binding prisoners. **2.** binding part of a padlock. —*v.t.* **3.** bind with or as with shackles.

shad, *n.*, *pl.* **shads, shad.** herringlike fish spawning in rivers.

shade, *n.*, *v.t.*, **shaded, shading.** *n.* **1.** area sheltered from direct light. **2.** device for cutting off direct light. **3.** variety of color or tone. **4.** slight degree. **5.** soul of a dead person. —*v.t.* **6.** shelter from direct light. **7.** vary, as a color or tone.

shad'ow, *n.* **1.** darkness of a shaded area. **2.** slight remnant or trace. —*v.t.* **3.** shade. **4.** follow secretly. —**shad'ow·y,** *adj.*

shad'y, *adj.* **1.** in the shade. **2.** *Informal.* to be suspected.

shaft, *n.* **1.** long, cylindrical object for support, rotation, etc. **2.** beam of light. **3.** narrow vertical space.

shag, *n.* long, rough hair, fur, or nap. —**shag'gy,** *adj.*

shah, *n.* ruler of Persia.

shake, *v.*, **shook, shaken, shaking,** *n. v.t.* **1.** cause to move rapidly back and forth. **2.** upset emotionally. —*v.i.* **3.** move rapidly back and forth. —*n.* **4.** act or instance of shaking. **5.** wood shingle.

shak'er, *n.* **1.** device for sprinkling seasoning. **2. Shaker,** member of an American celibate religious sect.

shak'y, *adj.*, **-kier, -kiest. 1.** unstable. **2.** tending to shake. **3.** of doubtful validity. —**shak'i·ly,** *adv.* —**shak'i·ness,** *n.*

shale, *n.* layered rock of hardened clay.

shall, *v.* am, is, or are going to.

shal'lot, *n.* onionlike plant used in cooking.

shal'low, *adj.* **1.** not deep. **2.** without depth of thought or feeling.

sham, *adj., n., v.*, **shammed, shamming.** *adj.* **1.** false; imitation. —*n.* **2.** something false or imitative. —*v.t.* **3.** pretend; feign.

sham'ble, *v.i.*, **-bled, -bling,** *n. v.i.* **1.** walk draggingly or awkwardly. —*n.* **2. shambles, a.** scene of disorder. **b.** slaughterhouse. **3.** shambling gait.

shame, *n., v.t.*, **shamed, shaming,** *n.* **1.** painful sense of guilt or inadequacy. **2.** disgrace. **3.** deplorable situation. —*v.t.* **4.** put to shame. —**shame'ful,** *adj.* —**shame'less,** *adj.*

shame'faced', *adj.* showing embarrassment. —**shame'fac'ed·ly,** *adv.*

sham·poo', *v.t.*, **-pooed, -pooing,** *n. v.t.* **1.** wash with soap, as the hair or a carpet. —*n.* **2.** soap, etc. used for shampooing.

sham'rock, *n.* cloverlike plant with a triple leaf: symbol of Ireland.

shang'hai', *v.t.*, **-haied, -haiing.** abduct for work on a ship.

shank, *n.* **1.** lower leg above the ankle. **2.** shaft of a hand tool between the handle and working end.

shan'tung, *n.* textured silk.

shan'ty, *n., pl.* **-ties.** roughly built wooden house.

shape, *n., v.t.*, **shaped, shaping,** *n.* **1.** form. **2.** *Informal.* condition. —*v.t.* **3.** give form to. —**shape'less,** *adj.*

shape'ly, *adj.* handsome in form. —**shape'li·ness,** *n.*

share, *n., v.t.* **shared, sharing,** *n.* **1.** rightful or predetermined portion. —*v.t.* **2.** divide into such portions. **3.** use or experience together.

shark, *n.* **1.** large predatory fish. **2.** person who preys on others.

sharp, *adj.* **1.** having or as if having a cutting point or edge. **2.** clearly defined. **3.** shrewd. **4.** alert. **5.** abrupt. **6.** *Music.* raised in pitch. —*adv.* **7.** punctually. —*n.* **8.** a semitone higher than a stated tone. —**sharp'en·er,** *n.* —**sharp'ly,** *adv.* —**sharp'ness,** *n.* —**sharp'en,** *v.t.*

sharp'er, *n.* swindler.

sharp'shoot''er, *n.* good marksman.

shat'ter, *v.t., v.i.* break in small pieces.

shave, *v.,* **shaved, shaved** or **shaven, shaving,** *n. v.t.* **1.** cut the hair off with a razor. **2.** remove with a razor. **3.** cut in thin layers with a tool. —*n.* **4.** act or instance of being shaved.

shav'ing, *n.* thin layer of material shaved from a larger piece.

shawl, *n.* cloth covering head and shoulders.

she, *pron.* woman or female previously mentioned.

sheaf, *n., pl.* **sheaves.** bundle.

shear, *v.t.,* **sheared, sheared** or **shorn, shearing,** *n. v.t.* **1.** divide as with the motion of one blade across another. —*n.* **2.** device for shearing.

shears, *n., pl.* large scissors.

sheath, *n., pl.* **sheaths.** closely fitting case or cover.

sheathe, *v.t.,* **sheathed, sheathing.** put into a sheath.

shed, *v.t.,* **shed, shedding,** *n. v.t.* leave or cast off. **2.** pour forth, as light. —*n.* **3.** rough shelter.

sheen, *n.* dull reflection.

sheep, *n., pl.* **sheep.** mammal yielding fleece and mutton.

sheep'ish, *adj.* bashful or embarrassed.

sheer, *adj.* **1.** absolute; utter. **2.** very steep or perpendicular. **3.** transparent, as a fabric. —*v.i.* **4.** swerve.

sheet, *n.* **1.** broad, thin piece of material. **2.** cloth used to cover a mattress or a sleeper. **3.** rope for controlling the position of a sail.

sheik, *n.* Arab chief.

shek'el, *n.* ancient Hebrew coin.

shelf, *n., pl.* **shelves. 1.** horizontal ledge or slab for supporting objects. **2.** ledge, as of rock.

shell, *n.* **1.** hard outer covering. **2.** shotgun cartridge. **3.** explosive artillery missile. **4.** racing rowboat. —*v.t.* **5.** separate from its shell. **6.** bombard with shells.

shel·lac', *n.* **1.** varnish containing a certain resin. **2.** the resin itself. —*v.t.* **3.** varnish with shellac.

shell'fish'', *n.* any aquatic animal with a shell.

shel'ter, *n.* **1.** something serving as a protection, as against the weather. —*v.t.* **2.** protect. —*v.i.* **3.** take shelter.

shelve, *v.,* **shelved, shelving. 1.** put on a shelf. **2.** postpone action or decision

on. **3.** provide with shelves. —*v.i.* **4.** slope.

shep'herd, *n.* **1.** Also, *fem.,* **shep'herdess,** person who leads and guards sheep. —*v.t.* **2.** escort with close vigilance.

sher'bet, *n.* frozen dessert of water, gelatin, flavoring, and sometimes milk.

sher'iff, *n.* county police officer.

sher'ry, *n., pl.* **-ries.** Spanish fortified wine.

shield, *n.* **1.** piece of armor worn on the arm. **2.** any defensive device. —*v.t.* **3.** protect or hide.

shift, *v.t., v.i.* **1.** move from place to place. **2.** change, as one's place. **3.** change, as the gears of a motor vehicle. —*n.* **4.** act or instance of shifting. **5.** lever for changing gears in a motor vehicle. **6.** daily period of labor.

shift'less, *n.* lazy or feeble.

shift'y, *adj.,* **shiftier, shiftiest.** tricky; unreliable. —**shift'i·ly,** *adv.* —**shift'i·ness,** *n.*

shil'ling, *n.* former British coin, one-twentieth of a pound.

shil'ly-shal'ly, *v.i.,* **-lied, -lying.** hesitate or quarrel over trifles. or quarrel over trifles.

shim, *n.* thin piece for raising an object or filling a gap.

shim'mer, *v.i.* **1.** glow or appear in a flickering, unsteady way. —*n.* **2.** effect given in so doing. —**shim'mer·y,** *adj.*

shin, *n.* front of the shank of the leg.

shine, *v.,* **shone** or, for *v.t.,* **shined, shining,** *n. v.i.* **1.** emit or reflect strong light. **2.** gain distinction. —*v.t.* **3.** polish to a high gloss. —*n.* **4.** shining light. —**shin'y,** *adj.*

shin'gle, *n.* **1.** thin plate of wood or other material used in courses as a roof covering or siding. **2.** shingles. virus disease with blisters as a symptom. —*v.t.* **3.** cover with shingles.

shin'ny, *n.* street hockey.

ship, *n., v.,* **shipped, shipping.** *n.* **1.** large ocean-going vessel. **2.** sailing vessel square-rigged on all of at least three masts. —*v.t.* **3.** send by a freight carrier. —*v.i.* **4.** engage to work on a voyage. —**ship'mate'',** *n.* —**ship'ment,** *n.* —**ship'per,** *n.*

ship'ping, *n.* vessels, esp. merchant ships.

ship'shape'', *adj., adv.* in good order.

ship'wreck'', *n.* destruction of a ship from running aground.

ship'yard'', *n.* place for building or repairing ships.

shire, *n.* British county.

shirk, *v.t.* **1.** evade, as an obligation. —*n.* **2.** person who shirks something. —**shirk'er,** *n.*

shirr, *v.t.* gather on parallel strands for decorative effect, as curtain material.

shirt, *n.* a long- or short-sleeved upper garment usually having a front opening, collar and cuffs, worn esp. by men.

shiv'er, *v.i.* 1. tremble. —*v.t.* 2. smash to pieces. —*n.* 3. trembling movement. 4. broken fragment. —**shiv'er·y,** *adj.*

shoal, *n.* 1. area of shallow water. 2. large number of fish.

shoat, *n.* young pig.

shock, *n.* 1. violent impact. 2. violent emotional disturbance. 3. bodily disturbance caused by loss of blood circulation, a current of electricity passing through the body, etc. 4. stack of sheaves of grain. 5. tangled mass, as of hair. —*v.t.* 6. disturb with a shock. —**shock'ing,** *adj.*

shod'dy, *adj.* poor in quality. —**shod'di·ness,** *n.*

shoe, *n., v.t.,* **shod, shoeing.** *n.* 1. protective covering for the foot. 2. something suggesting this. —*v.t.* 3. provide with shoes. —**shoe'lace'', shoe'string'',** *n.* —**shoe'mak'er,** *n.*

shoe'horn'', *n.* device to assist slipping the foot into a shoe.

shoot, *v.t.* 1. send a missile from. 2. hit with a missile. 3. emit rapidly, as a missile. —*v.i.* 4. use a gun, bow, etc. 5. grow or sprout. —*n.* 6. sporting event with shooting. 7. young plant growth. —**shoot'er,** *n.*

shop, *n., v.i.,* **shopped, shopping.** *n.* 1. store, esp. a small specialized one. 2. industrial workroom. —*v.i.* 3. look for or make purchases. —**shop'per,** *n.* —**shop'keep'er,** *n.*

shop'lift'er, *n.* person who steals from shops.

shore, *n., v.t.,* **shored, shoring.** *n.* 1. land bordering a body of water. 2. seacoast. 3. prop. —*v.t.* 4. prop.

short, *n.* 1. not tall or long. 2. abrupt in manner. 3. scanty, as a supply. 4. below the required amount. 5. flaky, as pastry. —*adv.* 6. abruptly. —*n.* 7. short circuit. 8. shorts, short-legged pants or underpants. —*v.t.* 9. create a short circuit in. —**short'ly,** *adv.* —**short'ness,** *n.* —**short'en,** *v.t.*

short'age, *n.* short supply.

short circuit, deviation of current in an electrical circuit rendering it useless.

short'com'ing, *n.* fault or inadequacy.

short'cut', *n.* shorter way than the usual.

short'en·ing, *n.* greasy substance for making pastry short.

short'hand'', *n.* system of writing for fast note-taking.

short-lived (shôrt'līvd''), *adj.* not living or existing long.

short'-sight'ed, *adj.* without foresight.

shot, *n., pl.* **shots** or (for 3) **shot.** 1. discharge of a missile. 2. range of a gun, bow, etc. 3. *Often pl.* missiles, esp.

shotgun pellets or cannonballs. 4. iron ball for hurling in athletic contests. 5. marksman.

shot'gun, *n.* gun firing shells filled with metal pellets.

should, *v.* 1. ought to. 2. were to. 3. past tense of *shall.*

shoul'der, *n.* 1. part of the human body between the upper arms and neck. 2. corresponding area in animals. 3. unpaved strip alongside a road. —*v.t.* 4. push with the shoulder. 5. take up and carry.

shout, *n.* 1. very loud call or voice. —*v.i.* 2. give such a call. —*v.t.* 3. utter in such a voice.

shove, *v.,* **shoved, shoving,** *n., v.t., v.i.* 1. push vigorously. —*n.* 2. vigorous push.

shov'el, *n.* 1. hand tool or machine for scooping up material. —*v.t.* 2. raise or move with a shovel. 3. clear with a shovel.

show, *v.,* **showed, shown** or **showed, showing,** *v.t.* 1. display. 2. guide. 3. prove or demonstrate. —*v.i.* 4. be visible or apparent. —*n.* 5. entertainment. 6. exhibit. 7. ostentation. —**show'boat'',** *n.* —**show'case'',** *n.* —**show'man,** *n.* —**show'piece'',** *n.* —**show'room,** *n.*

show'down'', *n.* 1. confrontation, as between enemies. 2. climactic moment.

show'er, *n.* 1. brief rainstorm. 2. bath in which water is sprayed from above. 3. large number of small objects dropped or hurled. —*v.t.* 4. bestow liberally. —*v.i.* 5. rain briefly.

show'off'', *n.* vain, ostentatious person.

show'y, *adj.,* **-ier, -iest.** attracting attention, esp. through gaudiness.

shrap'nel, *n.* small fragments hurled by the bursting of an artillery shell.

shred, *n., v.t.,* **shredded, shredding.** *n.* 1. torn strip. 2. bit, as of doubt or evidence. —*v.t.* 3. tear into shreds.

shrew, *n.* 1. small mouselike mammal. 2. quarrelsome woman. —**shrew'ish,** *adj.*

shrewd, *adj.* clever in dealing with or understanding others. —**shrewd'ly,** *adv.* —**shrewd'ness,** *n.*

shriek, *n.* 1. loud, shrill cry. —*v.i.* 2. utter such a cry.

shrike, *n.* bird of prey.

shrill, *adj.* high-pitched. —**shril'ly,** *adv.* —**shrill'ness,** *n.*

shrimp, *n.* small, long-tailed shellfish.

shrine, *n.* sacred place.

shrink, *v.,* **shrank** or **shrunk, shrunk** or **shrunken, shrinking** *v.i.* 1. become smaller. 2. draw back, as in fear. —*v.t.* 3. cause to shrink. —**shrink'age,** *n.*

shrivel, *v.i.* shrink and become wrinkled.

shroud, *n.* 1. wrapping for a corpse. 2. line steadying a ship's mast. —*v.t.* 3. wrap or conceal.

shrub, *n.* small, treelike plant. —**shrub′ber·y**, *n.*

shrug, *n., v.,* **shrugged, shrugging.** *n.* 1. movement of raising both shoulders. —*v.i.* 2. make such a movement. —*v.t.* 3. move in shrugging.

shuck, *n., v.t.* husk or shell.

shud′der, *v.i.* 1. tremble violently and briefly. —*n.* 2. act or instance of shuddering.

shuf′fle, *v.i.,* **-fled, -fling**, *n., v.i.* 1. walk with feet scraping the ground. 2. mix, as playing cards. —*n.* 3. shuffling gait.

shuf′fle·board″, *n.* game played by shoving wooden disks along a marked surface.

shun, *v.t.,* **shunned, shunning.** avoid.

shunt, *v.t.* 1. divert, 2. move, as cars in a railroad yard.

shut, *v.,* **shut, shutting,** *adj., v.t.* 1. close. 2. keep in or out. —*v.i.* 3. be closed. —*n.* 4. closed.

shut′ter, *n.* 1. cover for a window opening. 2. device for timed exposure of film in a camera.

shut′tle, *v.i.,* **-tled, -tling**, *n., v.i.* 1. go short distances back and forth. —*n.* 2. device on a loom for moving warp thread back and forth. 3. public transit vehicle that runs between two closely spaced terminals.

shy, *adj.,* **shier, shiest**, *v.,* **shied, shying,** *n., pl.* **shies.** *adj.* 1. timid in the presence of others. 2. lacking by a specified number. —*v.t.* 3. toss, esp. with a sideways motion. —*v.i.* 4. start with surprise, as a horse. —*n.* 5. act or instance of shying. —**shy′ly,** *adv.* —**shy′ness,** *n.*

sib′i·lant, *adj.* 1. hissing. —*n.* 2. hissing sound. —**sib′i·lance,** *n.*

sib′ling, *n.* brother or sister.

sic, *v.t.,* **sicked, sicking,** *adv. v.t.* 1. urge to an attack. —*adv.* 2. *Latin:* thus; (it is written).

sick, *adj.,* 1. not in health. 2. suffering nausea. 3. disgusted or upset. 4. *Informal.* mentally warped. —*n.* 5. sick people. —**sick′ness,** *n.* —**sick′en,** *v.t., v.i.*

sick′le, *n.* crescent-shaped tool for mowing.

sick′ly, *adj.,* **-lier, -liest.** not healthy or robust.

side, *n., adj., v.i.,* **sided, siding.** *n.* 1. area of someone or something to the right or left of the face or front. 2. direction or location to the right or left. 3. any direction or location from a central point. 4. line or surface defining a form. 5. aspect. 6. person or group in a dispute or conflict. 7. opinion or causeof such a person or group. —*adj.* 8. pertaining to a side direction or location. 9. of secondary importance. —*v.i.* 10. ally oneself.

side′board″, *n.* article of furniture for dishes, silver, and napkins.

side′burns″, *n., pl.* whiskers down the sides of the face.

side′line″, *n.* secondary source of income.

side′long″, *adj., adv.* to the side.

si·de′re·al, *adj.* pertaining to stars.

side′show″, *n.* minor entertainment at a circus.

side′step″, *v.t.,* **stepped, stepping.** evade by or as if by stepping sideways.

side′swipe″, *v.t.,* **swiped, swiping.** brush the side of in passing.

side′track″, *v.t.* divert or distract from accomplishing a purpose.

side′walk″, *n.* walk beside a roadway.

side′ways″, *adv., adj.* 1. with a side foremost. 2. to or from one side. Also, **side′wise″.**

sid′ing, *n.* short track for trains halted beside a through track.

sidle, *v.i.,* **-dled, -dling.** move sideways.

siege, *n.* prolonged attack on a fortified place.

sienna, *n.* reddish- or yellowish-brown.

si·es″ta, *n.* brief daytime nap.

sieve, *n., v.t.,* **sieved, sieving.** *n.* 1. strainer of wire mesh. —*v.t.* 2. run through or separate with a sieve.

sift, *v.t.* separate with a sieve. —**sift′er,** *n.*

sigh, *v.i.* 1. release pent-up breath in reaction to grief, annoyance, etc. —*n.* 2. such a release of breath.

sight, *n.* 1. sense perceived by the eyes. 2. something seen. 3. something remarkable to see. 4. range of distances one's eyes can see clearly. 5. aiming device for shooting or bombing. —*v.t.* 6. discover with the eye. 7. aim with a sight. —**sight′less,** *adj.*

sight′ly, *adj.,* **-lier, -liest.** pleasing to see.

sign, *n.* 1. indication. 2. written, printed, or hand-given symbol. 3. display surface containing such symbols or writing. —*v.t.* 4. put a signature on. —**sign′er,** *n.*

sig′nal, *n., adj., v.t.,* **-naled, -naling.** *n.* 1. device presenting a message in symbols. 2. message so presented. —*adj.* 3. acting as a signal. 4. marked. —*v.t.* 5. indicate through a signal. 6. communicate through a signal. —**sig′nal·er,** *n.* —**sig′nal·man,** *n.* —**sig′nal·ly,** *adv.*

sig′nal·ize″, *v.t.,* **-ized, -izing.** call attention to or make noteworthy.

sig′na·to″ry, *n., pl.* **-ries.** signer, esp. of a document.

sig′na·ture, *n.* 1. one's name in one's handwriting. 2. *Music.* sign indicating key and tempo.

sig′net, *n.* letter seal, often mounted on a ring.

sig·nif′i·cance, *n.* 1. meaning. 2. importance. —**sig·nif′i·cant,** *adj.*

sig′ni·fy″, *v.t.,* **-fied, -fying.** 1. mean. 2. indicate. —**sig″ni·fi·ca′tion,** *n.*

si′lence, *n., v.t.,* **-lenced, -lencing.** *n.* 1.

absence of noise, conversation, or sound. 2. absence of information or communication. —*v.t.* 3. make silent. 4. put out of action, as enemy guns. —si'lent, *adj.* —si'lent·ly, *adv.,*

sil·hou·ette (sil″ō̄ et′), *n., v.t.,* -etted, -etting *n.* 1. outline figure, usually filled in with black. —*v.t.* 2. cause to appear in outline against a lighter background.

sil'i·ca, *n.* hard, glassy substance appearing as sand, quartz, etc.

sil'i·con, *n.* nonmetallic element appearing in various compounds.

silk, *n.* cloth made of fiber spun by silkworms.

silk'en, *adj.* 1. made of silk. 2. suggesting silk in smoothness. Also, silk′y.

silk'worm″, *n.* moth caterpillar whose cocoons provide silk fiber.

sill, *n.* horizontal structural member, esp. below a wall or opening.

sil'ly, *adj.,* -lier, -liest. 1. foolish or stupid. 2. unreasonable. —sil'li·ness, *n.*

si'lo, *n.* airtight place for storing fodder.

silt, *n.* 1. fine earth, etc. deposited by running water. —*v.t.* 2. fill or clog with silt.

sil'ver, *n.* 1. white noble metallic element. 2. coins, utensils, etc. customarily made of silver. 3. lustrous whitish gray. —*adj.* 4. made of or colored silver. 5. pertaining to a twenty-fifth wedding anniversary. 6. eloquent, as the tongue. —sil'ver·y, *adj.* —sil'ver·smith″, *n.*

sil'ver·ware″, *n.* tableware traditionally made of silver.

sim'i·an, *adj.* 1. pertaining to or suggesting apes and monkeys. —*n.* 2. ape or monkey.

sim'i·lar, *adj.* of the same sort. —sim'i·lar·ly, *adv.* —sim″i·lar'i·ty, *n.*

sim'i·le″, *n.* expression comparing one thing to another.

si·mil'i·tude″, *n.* likeness.

sim'mer, *v.t., v.i.* almost boil.

sim″mul·ta'ne·ous, *adj.* at the very same time. —si″mul·ta'ne·ous·ly, *adv.*

si'mo·ny, *n.* profiting financially from religion.

sim'per, *v.i.* 1. smile foolishly or affectedly. —*n.* 2. foolish or affected smile.

sim'ple, *adj.,* -pler, -plest. 1. of the most basic kind. 2. readily understood or mastered. 3. low in intelligence. —sim'ply, *adv.* —sim·plic'i·ty, *n.*

sim'ple-mind'ed, *adj.* foolish; low in intelligence.

sim'ple·ton, *n.* foolish or naive person.

sim'pli·fy, *v.t.,* -fied, -fying. make easier to understand or master. —sim″pli·fi·ca'tion, *n.*

sim·plis'tic, *adj.* unrealistically oversimplified.

sim'u·late, *v.t.,* -lated, -lating. 1. pretend feign. 2. imitate closely. —sim″u·la'tion, *n.*

sin, *n., v.i.,* sinned, sinning. *n.* 1. violation of religious law. —*v.i.* 2. commit such a violation. —sin'ful, *adj.* —sin'ful·ly, *adv.* —sin'ful·ness, *n.*

since, *conj.* 1. during the time after. 2. because or inasmuch as. —*adv.* 3. from that time on. 4. at some time afterwards.

sin·cere', *adj.,* -cerer, -cerest. genuine; honest and unaffected. —sin·cere'ly, *adv.* —sin·cer'i·ty, *n.*

si·ne·cure' (si′ne kyoor″), *n.* salaried job requiring no serious work.

sin'ew, *n.* 1. tendon. 2. muscular strength. —sin'ew·y, *adj.*

sing, *v.,* sang or sung, sung, singing. *v.i.* 1. make musical sounds with the voice. —*v.t.* 2. render by singing. —sing'er, *n.*

singe, *v.t.,* singed, singeing. burn on the surface.

sin'gle, *adj., v.t.,* -gled, -gling, *n. adj.* 1. alone or unique. 2. unmarried. —*v.t.* 3. single out, select. —*n.* 4. something single. —sin'gly, *adv.*

sing'song″, *adj.* monotonously rhythmical.

sin'gu·lar, *adj.* 1. peculiar or extraordinary. 2. unique. 3. *Grammar.* pertaining to one person or thing. —*n.* 4. *Grammar.* singular number of a word. —sin'gu·lar·ly, *adv.* —sin″gu·lar'i·ty, *n.*

sin·is'ter, *adj.* evilly threatening.

sink, *v.,* sank or sunk, sunk or sunken, sinking *n. v.i.* 1. descend beneath a surface. 2. pass into a depressed state. —*v.t.* 3. cause to descend or penetrate beneath a surface. —*n.* 4. basin with a drain. —sink'er, *n.*

sin'ner, *n.* person who sins.

sin'u·ous, *adj.* meandering; serpentine.

si'nus, *n.* cavity, esp. one in the skull opening into the nasal passages.

sip, *v.,* sipped, sipping, *n. v.t.* 1. drink in tiny amounts. —*n.* 2. act or instance of sipping. 3. amount sipped at a time.

si'phon, *n.* 1. curved tube for sucking liquids automatically from place to place. —*v.t.* 2. pass through a siphon.

sir, *n.* 1. formal term used in addressing a man. 2. title given a British knight or baronet.

sire, *n., v.t.,* sired, siring. *n.* 1. male parent, esp. of an animal. 2. formal term used in addressing a king. —*v.t.* 3. beget.

si'ren, *n.* 1. mythical sea nymph luring sailors with singing to shipwreck. 2. horn with a wavering tone used on emergency vehicles.

sir'loin, *n.* cut of beef at the loin end by the rump.

sir'up, n. syrup.

si'sal, n. plant fiber used for ropes, etc.

sis'sy, n. *Informal.* timid or unmanly male.

sis'ter, n. 1. daughter of one's own parents. 2. nun. —sis'ter·ly, adj.

sis'ter·hood'', n. 1. organization of nuns. 2. condition of being a sister.

sis'ter-in-law'', n., pl. sisters-in-law. 1. sister of a spouse. 2. wife of a brother.

sit, v., sat, sitting. v.i. 1. rest on the behind. 2. be located. 3. pose, as for a portrait. 4. be in session, as a court. —v.t. 5. seat. —sit'ter, n.

site, n. location, as of a building.

sit'ting, n. session.

sit'u·ate'', v.t., -ated, -ating. place or locate.

sit''u·a'tion, n. 1. location. 2. condition or predicament. 3. job.

six, n., adj. one more than five. —sixth, adj.

six''teen', n., adj. six more than ten. —six·teenth', adj.

six'ty, n., adj. six times ten. —six'ti·eth, adj.

siz'a·ble, adj. fairly large. Also, size'a·ble.

size, n., v.t., sized, sizing. n. 1. area, volume, number, etc. by which something is measured or graded. 2. Also, siz'ing pasty substance used to coat or fill cloth, paper, etc. —v.t. 3. size up, measure or appraise intuitively. 4. treat with sizing.

siz'zle, v.i., -zled, -zling, n. v.i. 1. hiss or crackle, as from being fried. —n. 2. hissing or crackling, as from being fried.

skate, n., v.i., skated, skating. n. 1. piece of footwear for gliding across ice. 2. roller skate. 3. flat-bodied fish of the ray family. —v.i. 4. go on skates. —skat'er, n.

skein (skān), n. coil of yarn or thread.

skel'e·ton, n. 1. bone structure of an animal. 2. structural frame. —skel'e·tal, adj.

skep'tic, n. doubter. —skep'ti·cal, adj. —skep'ti·cal·ly, adv. —skep'ti·cism'', n.

sketch, n. 1. rough drawing. 2. brief outline. —v.t. 3. make a sketch of.

sketch'y, adj. vague or without detail. —sketch'i·ly, adv.

skew, v.t., v.i. 1. slant. —adj. 2. aslant.

skew'er, n. 1. needle for holding pieces of meat together. —v.t. 2. pierce with or as if with a skewer.

ski, n., pl. skis, v.i., skied, skiing. n. 1. long flat runner for gliding or walking on snow. —v.i. 2. glide on skis. —ski'er, n.

skid, v., skidded, skidding, n. v.i., v.t. 1. lide, by accident or intention. —n. 2. object or surface on which objects are skidded. 3. skidding motion.

skiff, n. rowboat.

skill, n. practised ability. —skilled, adj. —skill'ful, adj. —skill'ful·ly, adv.

skil'let, n. frying pan.

skim, v., skimmed, skimming. v.t. 1. remove from a liquid surface. —v.i. 2. move lightly across a surface.

skimp, v.i. economize; scrimp.

skimp'y, adj., skimpier, skimpiest. scant.

skin, n., v.t., skinned, skinning. n. 1. outer covering of an animal body. —v.t. 2. remove skin or hide from. —skin'ner, n. —skin'less, adj.

skin'flint'', n. miserly person.

skin'ny, adj. thin of body.

skip, v., skipped, skipping, n., v.i. 1. jump lightly. —v.t. 2. omit. —n. 3. light jump

skip'per, n. ship or boat captain.

skir'mish, n. 1. brief, minor battle. —v.i. 2. have a skirmish.

skirt, n. 1. open-bottomed garment fastened around the waist. 2. Often, skirts, portion of a coat, dress, etc. that falls below the waist. —v.t. 3. pass around the border of. 4. evade, as subject of controversy.

skit, n. brief comic play.

skit'tish, adj. readily excited or frightened.

skul''dug'ger·y, n. treacherous intrigue.

skulk, v.i. lurk.

skull, n. bony shell of a head.

skunk, n. small mammal defending itself with foul-smelling liquid.

sky, n., pl. skies. 1. part of the atmosphere visible from the earth. 2. condition of this at a certain place and time.

sky'light'', n. window in the surface of a roof or ceiling.

sky'line'', n. silhouette against the horizon.

sky'rock''et, n. 1. firework rising high before exploding. —v.i. 2. rise rapidly.

sky'scrap''er, n. very tall building, esp. one for offices.

slab, n. flat, fairly thick piece of material.

slack, adj. 1. loose. 2. inactive. 3. lazy or indifferent. —n. 4. slack part. 5. period of inactivity. —v.t., v.i. 6. slacken. —slack'ly, adv. —slack'ness, n.

slack'en, v.t., v.i. 1. make or become slack. 2. lessen in intensity or vigor.

slacks, n., pl. loosely fitting trousers.

slag, n. molten waste from smelting.

slake, v.t., slaked, slaking. 1. quench with a drink. 2. pour water on, as quicklime.

slam, v.t., slammed, slamming, n., v.t. 1. push violently and noisily into place. —n. 2. act of pushing thus.

slan'der, n. 1. maliciously untrue statement or statements about someone

—v.t. **2.** utter such statements about. —**slan'der·ous,** adj.

slang, n. highly informal speech. —**slang'y,** adj.

slant, v.t., v.i. **1.** move or head diagonally. —n. **2.** diagonal movement or heading. **3.** attitude or opinion.

slap, v.t., **slapped, slapping,** n., v.t. **1.** hit with a flat object, esp. the hand. **2.** put together, etc. in haste. —n. **3.** act or instance of slapping.

slash, v.t. **1.** cut deeply with a long, sweeping motion. —n. **2.** long, deep cut.

slat, n. thin board.

slate, n., v.t., **slated, slating.** n. **1.** stone that can be cleaved into thin pieces. **2.** list of candidates. —v.t. **3.** cover with slate. **4.** intend for nomination, promotion, dismissal, etc.

slat'tern, n. slovenly woman.

slaugh'ter, n. **1.** mass killing; massacre. **2.** killing of animals for meat. —v.t. **3.** submit to slaughter. —**slaugh'ter·house'',** n.

slave, n., v.i., **slaved, slaving.** n. **1.** person treated as the property of another. —v.i. **2.** drudge. —**slav'ery,** n.

slav·er (slăhv'ər), v.i. drool.

slav'ish, adj. in the manner of a slave, esp. in lacking originality or initiative.

slaw, n. coleslaw.

slay, v.t., **slew, slain, slaying.** skill. —**slay'er,** n.

slea'zy, adj., **-zier, -ziest.** shoddy.

sled, n., v.i., **sledded, sledding.** n. **1.** vehicle for gliding across snow or ice. —v.i. **2.** travel by sled.

sledge, n., v.t., **sledged, sledging.** n. **1.** sledlike vehicle. **2.** Also, **sledge'hammer,** heavy hammer. —v.t. **3.** transport by sledge.

sleek, adj. **1.** smooth or glossy. —v.t. **2.** make smooth. —**sleek'ly,** adv. —**sleek'ness,** n.

sleep, n., v.i., **slept, sleeping.** n. **1.** periodic state of unconscious rest. —v.i. **2.** be in such a state. —**sleep'y,** adj. —**sleep'less,** adj.

sleep'er, n. **1.** sleeping person. **2.** sill-like timber. **3.** railroad car with berths.

sleet, n. rain frozen in fine particles.

sleeve, n. part of a shirt or coat covering an arm.

sleigh, n. horse-drawn light sled.

sleight of hand (slīt), rapid, secret hand movements for creating illusions.

slen'der, adj. **1.** attractively thin. **2.** meager, as means of livelihood. —**slen'der·ness,** n.

sleuth, n. Informal. detective.

slice, n., v.t., **sliced, slicing.** n. **1.** thin piece cut from a larger one. —v.t. **2.** cut as a slice. **3.** cut slices from. —**slic'er,** n.

slick, adj. **1.** smooth or slippery. **2.** cunning. —n. **3.** area of floating oil. —v.t. **4.** make smooth.

slick'er, n. raincoat with a slick outer surface.

slide, v., **slid, slidding,** n. v.t., v.i. **1.** move with surface contact between the object moving and something else. —n. **2.** act or instance of sliding. **3.** object or surface used in sliding. **4.** fall of earth, rock, etc. down a slope. **5.** transparent plate used with a microscope, magic lantern, etc.

slight, adj. **1.** unimportantly little. **2.** slender. —v.t., n. **3.** snub. —**slight'ly,** adv. —**slight'ness,** n. —**slight'ing·ly,** adv.

sli'ly, adv. slyly.

slim, adj., **slimmer, slimmest. 1.** slender. **2.** small in amount or size. —**slim'ness,** n.

slime, n. semi-liquid, sticky matter.

slim'y, adj., **slimier, slimiest. 1.** of the nature of slime. **2.** disgustingly wheedling.

sling, n., v.t., **slung, slinging.** n. **1.** flexible device for hurling missiles. **2.** suspended cloth support. —v.t. **3.** hurl or shy. **4.** put in a sling.

slink, v.i., **slunk, slinking.** walk furtively

slip, v., **slipped, slipping.** v.t., v.i. **1.** slide smoothly. **2.** escape. —v.i. **3.** loose grip or footing. **4.** make a mistake. —n. **5.** act or instance of slipping. **6.** underskirt. **7.** space between piers for a ship.

slip'per, n. soft, unlaced shoe for household wear.

slip'per·y, adj., **-ier, -iest. 1.** allowing slipping. **2.** cunning and unreliable.

slip'shod'', adj. careless.

slit, n., v.t., **slitted, slitting.** n. **1.** long, deep opening. —v.t. **2.** cut with slits.

slith'er, v.i. slide with a side-to-side motion.

sliv'er, n., v.t. splinter.

slob, n. Informal. uncouth or clumsy person.

slob'ber, v.i., n. drool.

slog, v.i., **slogged, slogging.** advance heavily or with difficulty; plod.

slo'gan, n. motto.

sloop, n. one-masted sailing vessel.

slop, v., **slopped, slopping,** n., v.t., v.i. **1.** spill or toss carelessly, as a liquid. —n. **2.** something slopped. **3.** swill.

slope, n., v., **sloped, sloping.** n. **1.** angled rise or descent. —v.t. **2.** cause to rise or descend in a slope. —v.i. **3.** form a slope.

slop'py, adj. **1.** untidy. **2.** carelessly done. —**slop'pi·ly,** adv. —**slop'pi·ness,** n.

slosh, v.t. splash or slop.

slot, n. narrow opening.

sloth (sloth, slôth), n. **1.** South American aboreal mammal. **2.** laziness. —**sloth'ful,** adj.

slouch, *v.i.* **1.** have a drooping posture. —*n.* **2.** drooping posture. **3.** incompetent or lazy person. —**slouch′y,** *adj.*

slough, *n.* **1.** (sloo͞ or slō) muddy or marshy area. **2.** (sluf) dead, cast-off skin. —*v.t.* **3.** cast off. —*v.i.* **4.** be cast off, as dead skin.

slov·en (sluv′ən), *n.* untidy or careless person. —**slov′en·ly,** *adj.*

slow, *adj.* **1.** moving or acting without speed. **2.** not learning or understanding readily. **3.** behind the correct or appointed time. **4.** lacking in activity or vigor. —*adv.* **5.** slowly. —*v.t.* **6.** cause to move or act slowly. —*v.i.* **7.** move or act slowly. —**slow′ly,** *adv.* —**slow′ ness,** *n.*

sludge, *n.* semi-liquid sediment.

slue, *v.,* **slued, sluing.** *v.t., v.i.* turn or swerve.

slug, *v.t.,* **slugged, slugging,** *n., v.t.* **1.** hit, esp. with the fists. —*n.* **2.** crawling mollusk leaving a slimy trail. **3.** bullet. **4.** false coin.

slug′gard, *n.* lazy person.

slug′gish, *adj.* abnormally slow or lacking in vigor. —**slug′gish·ly,** *adv.* —**slug′ gish·ness,** *n.*

sluice, *n.* **1.** artificial channel controlled by a gate. **2.** Also, **sluice gate,** gate controlling this channel.

slum, *n.* squalid home or residential area.

slum′ber, *v.i.* **1.** sleep deeply. —*n.* **2.** deep sleep.

slump, *v.i.* **1.** drop or sag heavily. —*n.* **2.** act or instance of slumping.

slur, *v.t.,* **slurred, slurring,** *n., v.t.* **1.** say indistinctly. **2.** disparage. —*n.* **3.** indistinct speech. **4.** disparaging remark.

slush, *n.* melting snow. —**slush′y,** *adj.*

slut, *n.* immoral or slatternly woman.

sly, *adj.,* **slyer** or **slier, slyest** or **sliest. 1.** cunning; tricky. **2.** gently mischievous. —**sly′ly, sli′ly,** *adv.* —**sly′ness,** *n.*

smack, *v.t.* **1.** separate noisily, as the lips. **2.** slap. —*v.i.* **3.** have a taste or suggestion. —*n.* **4.** act or instance of smacking. **5.** taste or suggestion. **6.** fishing boat.

small, *adj.* **1.** little. **2.** of no great importance, value, etc. **3.** petty or mean. —*adv.* **4.** into small pieces. —*n.* **5.** narrow part, esp. of the back. —**small′ ness,** *n.*

small′pox″, *n.* contagious disease with fever and pustules as symptoms.

smart, *adj.* **1.** severe, as a blow. **2.** intelligent or clever. **3.** briskly efficient. **4.** in style. —*n.* **5.** sharp, stinging pain. —*v.i.* **6.** feel such a pain. —**smart′ly,** *adv.* —**smart′ness,** *n.* —**smart′en,** *v.t.*

smash, *v.t.* **1.** break into fragments. —*n.* **2.** act or instance of smashing. **3.** serious automobile accident.

smat′ter·ing, *n.* slight knowledge.

smear, *v.t.* **1.** rub with greasy clinging material. **2.** slander. —*n.* **3.** smeared area. **4.** slander.

smell, *n.* **1.** sense perceived by the nose and olfactory organs. **2.** odor. —*v.t.* **3.** sense with the nose and olfactory organs. —*v.i.* **4.** have an odor.

smelt, *n., pl.* **smelts, smelt,** *v.t., n.* **1.** small northern salt-water fish. —*v.t.* **2.** melt or fuse to as to extract metal. **3.** extract from ore by melting or fusing. —**smelt′er,** *n.*

smile, *v.i.,* **smiled, smiling,** *n., v.i.* **1.** assume a look of pleasure, etc., by upturning the corners of the mouth. **2.** look favorably. —*n.* **3.** smiling appearance.

smirch, *v.t.* **1.** stain or soil. —*n.* **2.** stain.

smirk, *v.i.* **1.** have an affected or self-satisfied smile. —*n.* **2.** such a smile.

smite, *v.t.,* **smote, smitten** or **smitting,** *Archaic.* **1.** hit; strike. **2.** overcome with charm.

smith, *n.* metalworker.

smith′y, *n., pl.* **smithies.** blacksmith's shop.

smock, *n.* loose garment covering the whole body.

smog, *n.* fog with smoke.

smoke, *n., v.,* **smoked, smoking.** *n.* **1.** unconsumed material emitted by a fire. —*v.i.* **2.** inhale and exhale smoke from smoldering tobacco, etc. —*v.t.* **3.** burn in order to inhale and exhale the smoke. **4.** treat with smoke. —**smok′y,** *adj.* —**smoke′stack″,** *n.*

smok′er, *n.* **1.** person who smokes. **2.** railroad car or compartment where smoking is permitted.

smol′der, *v.i.* **1.** burn flamelessly. **2.** exist partly suppressed. Also, **smoul′der.**

smooth, *adj.* **1.** without unevenness. **2.** without difficulty. **3.** without harsh or disturbing qualities. **4.** ingratiating. —*v.t.* **5.** make smooth. —**smooth′ly,** *adv.* —**smooth′ness,** *n.*

smoth′er, *v.t.* **1.** suffocate. **2.** cover completely.

smudge, *n., v.t.,* **smudged, smudging.** *n.* **1.** spot of smoke, dirt, ink, etc. —*v.t.* **2.** stain or treat with smoke, dirt, ink, etc.

smug, *adj.* excessively self-satisfied. —**smug′ly,** *adv.* —**smug′ness,** *n.*

smug′gle, *v.t.,* **-gled, -gling.** bring in or out secretly in violation of laws or regulations. —**smug′gler,** *n.*

smut, *n.* **1.** soot or smudge. **2.** obscenity. **3.** fungous plant disease. —**smut′ty,** *adj.*

snack, *n.* small meal.

snag, *n., v.,* **snagged, snagging.** *n.* **1.** projection that catches or tears. **2.** obstacle. —*v.t.* **3.** catch or damage, as with a snag.

snail, *n.* crawling mollusk with a shell.

snake, *n.*, *v.i.* **snaked, snaking**. *n.* **1.** scaly reptile without limbs. —*v.i.* **2.** move or lie sinuously.

snap, *v.*, **snapped, snapping**, *n.*, *adj.* *v.i.* **1.** make a sharp clicking sound. **2.** go into or out of a close-fitting socket. **3.** break abruptly. **4.** bite. **5.** speak crossly and abruptly. —*v.t.* **6.** cause to snap. **7.** photograph. —*n.* **8.** act or instance of snapping. **9.** fastener that snaps shut. —*adj.* **10.** hasty, as a judgement.

snap'drag''on, *n.* plant with flowers in spikes.

snap'pish, *adj.* short-tempered.

snap'py, *adj.* quick.

snap'shot'', *n.* uncomposed photograph from a small, hand-held camera.

snare, *n.*, *v.t.* **snared, snaring**. trap.

snarl, *v.i.* **1.** growl. —*v.t.* **2.** tangle.

snatch, *v.t.* **1.** grab. —*v.i.* **2.** reach suddenly or eagerly. —*n.* **3.** act or instance of snatching. **4.** fragment.

sneak, *v.i.* **1.** go furtively. —*v.t.* **2.** bring in or out furtively. —*n.* **3.** furtive, dishonest person. —**sneak'y**, *adj.*

sneak'er, *n.* low, soft-soled shoe.

sneer, *v.i.* **1.** express contempt. —*n.* **2.** expression of contempt.

sneeze, *v.i.*, **sneezed, sneezing**, *n.*, *v.i.* **1.** expel breath explosively and involuntarily. —*n.* **2.** act or instance of sneezing.

snick'er, *n.* **1.** contemptuous, high-pitched laugh. —*v.i.* **2.** give such a laugh. Also, **snig'ger**.

snide, *adj.* malicious, as a remark.

sniff, *v.i.* **1.** inhale quickly through the nose. **2.** exhale loudly through the nose. —*n.* **3.** act or instance of sniffing.

snif'fer, *v.i.* **1.** inhale through the nose. —*n.* **2.** **sniffles**, *Informal.* mild cold symptoms.

snip, *v.t.*, **snipped, snipping**, *n.*, *v.t.* **1.** cut as with scissors. —*n.* **2.** snipped-off fragment. **3.** **snips**, shears.

snipe, *n.*, *v.i.*, **sniped, sniping**. *n.* **1.** wading bird. —*v.i.* **2.** shoot from a hidden position. —**snip'er**, *n.*

snip'pet, *n.* small piece, as of information.

sniv'el, *v.i.* plead, complain, etc. in a whining tone.

snob, *n.* person with ostentatious likes and dislikes based on pretentious standards of excellence. —**snob'bish**, *adj.* —**snob'ber·y**, *n.*

snood, *n.* net covering the back of a woman's hair.

snoop, *Informal. v.i.* **1.** seek information furtively. —*n.* **2.** Also, **snoop'er**, person who snoops.

snooze, *v.i.*, **snoozed, snoozing**, *n.* nap.

snore, *v.i.*, **snored, snoring**, *n.*, *v.i.* **1.** breathe noisily while sleeping. —*n.* **2.** sound of such breathing.

snor'kel, *n.* ventilating tube for a submarine, etc. under water.

snort, *n.* **1.** loud exhalation through the nose. —*v.i.* **2.** give such an exhalation.

snot, *n.* *Informal.* mucus from the nose.

snout, *n.* protruding front of an animal head.

snow, *n.* **1.** precipitation frozen in crystalline flakes. —*v.i.* **2.** precipitate snow. —**snow'drift''**, *n.* —**snow'fall''**, *n.* —**snow'flake''**, *n.* —**snow'storm''**, *n.* —**snow'y**, *adj.*

snow'ball'', *n.* **1.** ball of compacted snow. —*v.i.* **2.** increase with gathering speed.

snow'shoe'', *n.* webbed flat frame for supporting the foot on snow.

snub, *v.t.*, **snubbed, snubbing**, *n.*, *adj.* *v.t.* **1.** refuse attention or respect to. —*n.* **2.** act or instance of snubbing. —*adj.* **3.** short and upturned, as a nose.

snuff, *v.t.* **1.** trim, as a burned wick. **2.** extinguish or eliminate. —*n.* **3.** powdered tobacco.

snuf'fle, *v.i.*, **-fled, -fling**. sniffle.

snug, *adj.*, **snugger, snuggest**. **1.** cozy. **2.** neat. **3.** tight in fit. —**snug'ly**, *adv.*

snug'gle, *v.i.* **-gled, -gling**. cuddle or nestle.

so, *adv.* **1.** as stated or indicated. **2.** to such an extent. **3.** *Informal.* very; very much. **4.** in this way. —*conj.* **5.** therefore. **6.** in order that. —*adj.* **7.** true.

soak, *v.t.* **1.** put into a cover with a liquid. **2.** absorb. —*v.i.* **3.** become absorbed. —*n.* **4.** act or instance of soaking.

soap, *n.* **1.** substance used in washing. —*v.t.* **2.** cover with soap. —**soap'y**, *adj.*

soar, *v.i.* **1.** rise into the air. **2.** glide or hover in the air.

sob, *v.i.*, **sobbed, sobbing**, *n.*, *v.i.* **1.** weep convulsively. —*n.* **2.** sound of sobbing.

so'ber, *adj.* **1.** not drunk. **2.** serious or quiet. —*v.t.* **3.** make sober. **4.** cause grave feelings in. —**so'ber·ly**, *adv.* —**so''bri'e·ty, so'ber·ness**, *n.*

so-called, *adj.* called thus; used esp. when so named without justification.

soc'cer, *n.* a variety of football played without using the hands and arms.

so'cia·ble, *adj.* friendly; gregarious. —**so'cia·bly**, *adv.* —**so''cia·bil'i·ty**, *n.*

so'cial, *adj.* **1.** pertaining to society. **2.** sociable. —**so'cial·ly**, *adv.*

so'cial·ism, *n.* theory advocating public ownership of means of production, with work and products shared. —**so'cial·ist**, *n.* —**so''cial·is'tic**, *adj.* —**so'cial·ize''**, *v.t.*

so'cial·ite'', *n.* person in fashionable society.

so·ci'e·ty, *n.*, *pl.* **-ties**. **1.** group sharing a common culture, location, etc. **2.** human beings, in their relations with one

another. **3.** world of the upper class. **4.** organization, esp. a professional or public-service one.

so''ci·ol'o·gy, *n.* study of society. —**so''ci·o·log'i·cal,** *adj.* —**so''ci·ol'o·gist,** *n.*

sock, *n.* **1.** short stocking. —*v.t.* **2.** *Informal.* hit.

sock'et, *n.* a hollow part in which something is inserted and held.

sod, *n.* earth with growing grass.

so'da, *n.* **1.** drink with soda water. **2.** mixture of soda water, ice cream, and flavoring. **3.** chemical containing sodium.

so·dal'i·ty, *n., pl.* **-ties.** Catholic religious or charitable society.

soda water, water charged with carbon dioxide.

sod'den, *n.* **1.** stupefied. **2.** soggy.

so'di·um, *n.* alkaline chemical element.

sod·o·my (sod'ə mē), *n.* abnormal sexual intercourse. —**sod'o·mite,** *n.*

so'fa, *n.* wide, upholstered seat with a back and arms.

soft, *adj.* **1.** yielding readily to pressure. **2.** gentle. **3.** quiet. **4.** weak. **5.** non-alcoholic. **6.** permitting lathering, as water. —**soft'ly,** *adv.* —**soft'ness,** *n.* —**soft'en,** *v.t., v.i.*

soft'ball'', *n.* baseball-like game using a softer ball.

soft''ware'', *n.* (computers) programming enabling a system to function.

sog'gy, *adj.* moist and heavy with absorbed liquid.

soil, *v.t.* **1.** dirty. —*n.* **2.** earth. **3.** sewage.

so'journ, *v.i.* **1.** stay briefly. —*n.* **2.** brief stay.

sol·ace (sol'əs), *n.* comfort in unhappiness.

so'lar, *adj.* pertaining to the sun.

sol·der (sod'ər), *n.* **1.** alloy with low melting point for joining or patching metal. —*v.t.* **2.** treat with solder.

sol'dier, *n.* **1.** member of an army. —*v.i.* **2.** live as a soldier. —**sol'dier·ly,** *adj.* —**sol'dier·y,** *n.*

sole, *n, v.t.,* **soled, soling.** *adj. n.* **1.** salt-water flatfish. **2.** wearing surface on the bottom of a shoe. —*v.t.* **3.** fit with soles. —*adj.* **4.** single; only. —**sole'ly,** *adv.*

sol'emn, *adj.* **1.** serious; earnest. **2.** formal. **3.** sacred. —**sol'emn·ly,** *adv.* —**so·lem'ni·ty,** *n.*

sol'em·nize, *v.t.,* **-nized, -nizing.** observe or put into effect with a ceremony. —**sol''em·ni·zation,** *n.*

so·lic'i·tor, *n.* **1.** person who solicits. **2.** English lawyer other than a barrister.

so·lic'it (sə lis'ət), *v.t.* **1.** request. **2.** canvass for. —**so·li''ci·ta'tion,** *n.*

so·lic'i·tous, *adj.* showing friendly concern. —**so·lic'i·tous·ly,** *adv.* —**so·lic'i·tude'',** *n.*

sol'id, *adj.* **1.** pertaining to or existing in three dimensions. **2.** firm; substantial. **3.** not hollow. **4.** dense. **5.** reliable. **6.** entire. —*n.* **7.** three-dimensional object. **8.** non-fluid material. —**sol'id·ly,** *adv,* —**so·lid'i·ty,** *n.* —**so·lid'i·fy'',** *v.i.*

sol''i·dar'i·ty, *n.* unity of purpose, resolve, etc.

sol''id-state', *adj.* designating electronic circuitry that uses solid semiconductors, as transistors, to control current.

so·lil'o·quy, *n., pl.* **-quies.** speech made to or as if to oneself. —**so·lil'o·quize,** *v.i.*

sol'i·taire'', *n.* **1.** card game for one. **2.** single gemstone in a setting.

sol'i·tar'y, *adj.* **1.** single. **2.** alone. **3.** isolated.

sol'i·tude, *n.* state of being alone or isolated.

so'lo, *n.* performance by one person, esp. in music or aviation. —**so'lo·ist,** *n.*

sol'stice, *n.* point when the sun is furthest from the equator; beginning of summer or winter.

sol'u·ble, *adj.* able to be dissolved. —**sol'u·bil'i·ty,** *n.*

so·lu'tion, *n.* **1.** means of solving a problem. **2.** dispersal of one material in another. **3.** material, usually a liquid, that results from this.

solve, *v.t.,* **solved, solving.** explain or find means to overcome, as a problem. —**solv'a·ble,** *adj.*

sol'vent, *n.* **1.** material that dissolves another. —*adj.* **2.** able to dissolve something. **3.** able to meet one's debts. —**sol'ven·cy,** *n.*

som'ber, *adj.* gloomy. Also, **som'bre.** —**som'ber·ly,** *adv.*

som·bre·ro (som brā'rō), *n.* broad-brimmed hat worn in Hispanic countries.

some, *adj.* **1.** indefinite amount or number of. **2.** certain unknown or unspecified. —*pron.* **3.** unknown or unspecified number.

some'body'', *pron.* unspecified person. Also, **some'one''.**

some'how'', *adv.* in some way. Also, **some'way''.**

som'er·sault'', *n.* **1.** overturn forward or backward of a crouched person. —*v.i.* **2.** execute a somersault.

some'thing, *n.* thing not specified.

some'time'', *adv.* **1.** at an indefinite time. —*adj.* **2.** *Archaic.* former.

some'times'', *adv.* now and then.

some'what'', *adv.* to some extent.

some'where'', *adv.* at or to an unspecified place.

som·nam'bu·lism, *n.* sleepwalking. —**som·nam'bu·list,** *n.*

som'no·lent, *adj.* drowsy. —**som'no·lence,** *n.*

son, *n.* male offspring.

so·na'ta, *n.* instrumental musical composition.

song, *n.* vocal musical composition.

son'ic, *adj.* pertaining to sound.

son'-in-law, *n., pl.* **sons-in-law.** husband of one's daughter.

son'net, *n.* poem with one eight-line and one six-line part.

so·no'rous, *adj.* deep or rich in sound. —**so·nor'ous·ly,** *adv.* —**so·nor'i·ty,** *n.*

soon, *adv.* after a short time.

soot, *n.* black particles in smoke. —**soot'y,** *adj.*

soothe, *v.t.,* **soothed, soothing. 1.** free of agitation or annoyance. **2.** relieve, as pain.

sooth'say''er, *n.* person who claims to know the future.

sop, *n.* **1.** morsel dipped in liquid. **2.** something that appeases. —*v.t., v.i.* **3.** soak. —*v.t.* **4.** absorb.

so·phis·ti·cate, *v.t.* **1.** (sǒ fis'tǝ kāt'') make sophisticated. —*n.* **2.** (sǒ fis'tǝ kǝt) sophisticated person.

so·phis'ti·cat''ed, *adj.* **1.** acquainted with the ways of society. **2.** technologically advanced. —**so·phis''ti·ca'tion,** *n.*

soph'is·try, *n.* specious, unsound reasoning. —**soph'ist,** *n.*

soph'o·more'', *n.* second-year secondary or college student.

soph''o·mor'ic, *adj.* intellectually immature.

so''po·rif'ic, *adj.* **1.** sleep-inducing. —*n.* **2.** soporific drug.

so·pran'o, *n.* singer in the highest vocal range.

sor'cer·er, *n.* magician. Also, *fem.,* **sor'cer·ess,** *n.*

sor'did, *adj.* **1.** disgustingly mean or ignoble. **2.** filthy.

sore, *adj.,* **sorer, sorest,** *n., adj.* **1.** aching or tender. **2.** grieving. **3.** causing trouble or annoyance. **4.** *Informal.* angry. —*n.* **5.** sore place on the body. —**sore'ly,** *adv.* —**sore'ness,** *n.*

sor·ghum (sor'gǝm), *n.* cereal grass made into syrup, etc.

so·ror'i·ty, *n., pl.* **-ties.** women's organization, esp. in a college.

sor'rel, *n.* **1.** reddish-brown. **2.** horse of this colour. **3.** plant with sour-tasting leaves.

sor'row, *n.* **1.** great unhappiness or regret. —*v.i.* **2.** feel sorrow. —**sor'row·ful,** *adj.* —**sor'row·ful·ly,** *adv.*

sor'ry, *adj.* **1.** feeling regret. **2.** feeling pity. **3.** miserable.

sort, *n.* **1.** type; classification. **2.** quality. —*v.t.* **3.** arrange by type.

sor'tie, *n.* **1.** swift counterattack, as from

a besieged place. **2.** aerial combat mission.

SOS, call for help.

so'-so', *adj.* **1.** not especially good or bad. —*adv.* **2.** not especially well or badly.

sot, *n.* drunkard.

souf·flé, *n.* light, puffy baked dish.

sough (sow, suf), *v.i.* rustle or sigh, as the wind.

soul, *n.* **1.** non-material aspect of a person. **2.** emotional or moral aspect of the personality. **3.** feeling or sensitivity. **4.** essence. **5.** human being. —**soul'ful,** *adj.* —**soul'less,** *adj.*

sound, *n.* **1.** air vibrations perceptible in part to the ear. **2.** tone or noise that is heard. **3.** inlet or channel of sea water. —*v.t.* **4.** cause to make a sound. **5.** measure the depth of. **6.** determine the attitude or opinion of. —*v.i.* **7.** make a sound. **8.** seem. **9. sound like,** imply. —*adj.* **10.** healthy. **11.** reasonable. **12.** reliable. —**sound'less,** *adj.* —**sound'proof'',** *adj.* —**sound'ly,** *adv.* —**sound'ness,** *n.*

soup, *n.* savoury, mainly liquid food.

sour, *adj.* **1.** acid-tasting. **2.** fermented beyond the normal state. **3.** ill-tempered. —*v.i.* **4.** become sour. —**sour'ly,** *adv.* —**sour'ness,** *n.*

source, *n.* origin.

souse, *v.t.,* **soused, sousing,** *n., v.t.* **1.** immerse or steep. **2.** pickle. —*n.* **3.** pickled food. **4.** act or instance of sousing.

south, *n.* **1.** direction of the South Pole. **2.** region located in this direction. —*adj., adv.* **3.** to or toward the south. **4.** from the south, as a wind. —**south'ward,** *adv., adj.* —**south'ern,** *adj.* —**south'ern·er,** *n.* —**south'er·ly,** *adj., adv.*

south''east', *n.* direction halfway between south and east. —**south''east',** *adj., adv.*

south''west', *n.* direction halfway between south and west. —**south''west',** *adj., adv.*

sou·ve·nir (sōō'vǝ nēr), *n.* thing to remember a place, event, etc. by.

sov·er·eign (sov'rǝn), *n.* **1.** monarch. **2.** former British gold coin. —*adj.* **3.** having supreme political power. **4.** politically independent. —**sov'er·eign·ty,** *n.*

so'vi·et, *adj.* **1. Soviet,** pertaining to the Soviet Union. —*n.* **2.** Russian governmental council.

sow, *v.t.* **1.** (sō) plant, as seed. —*n.* **2.** (sow) female hog. —**sow'er,** *n.*

soy'bean'', *n.* plant grown for its seeds.

spa, *n.* resort with mineral springs.

space, *n., v.t.,* **spaced, spacing,** *n.* **1.** limitless three-dimensional expanse. **2.** specific area within this. **3.** outer space. **4.** distance. —*v.t.* **5.** separate, esp. as regular intervals.

space′craft″, *n.* vehicle for exploration of outer space.

space′flight″, *n.* flight through outer space.

space′ship″, *n.* vehicle for travel in outer space.

space′walk″, *n.* personal movement away from a spacecraft in outer space.

spa′cious, *adj.* amply extensive.

spade, *n., v.t.,* **spaded, spading.** *n.* **1.** shovel with long shaftlike handle. **2. spades,** black suit of playing cards. —*v.t.* **3.** dig with a spade.

spa·ghet′ti, *n.* stringy pasta, usually served with a sauce.

span, *n., v.t.,* **spanned, spanning.** *n.* **1.** something between two supports. **2.** distance between the thumb and little finger, when extended. **3.** duration. **4.** pair of harnessed animals. —*v.t.* **5.** cross.

span′gle, *n., v.t.,* **-gled, -gling.** *n.* **1.** glittering decoration. —*v.t.* **2.** decorate with spangles.

span′iel, *n.* short-legged, long-eared dog.

spank, *v.t.* slap on the behind.

spank′ing, *adj.* brisk.

spar, *v.i.,* **sparred, sparring,** *n., v.i.* **1.** box with the fists. —*n.* **2.** pole. **3.** crystalline rock.

spare, *v.t.,* **spared, sparing,** *adj.,* **sparer, sparest.** *v.t.* **1.** use or spend with restraint. **2.** prevent from occurring, being known, etc., as something unpleasant. **3.** treat leniently. **4.** give without inconvenience. —*adj.* **5.** in reserve; extra. **6.** gaunt; lean.

spare′rib″, *n.* pork rib cut at the thin end.

spark, *n.* **1.** glowing, burning piece of matter from a fire. **2.** electric flash. **3.** trace, as of life.

spar′kle, *v.i.,* **-kled, -kling,** *n., v.i.* **1.** emit or reflect small flashes of light. **2.** effervesce, as wine. **3.** glitter, as eyes. —*n.* **4.** act or instance of sparkling.

spar′row, *n.* bird of the finch family.

sparse, *adj.,* **sparser, sparsest. 1.** scattered. **2.** scanty. —**sparse′ly,** *adv.* —**sparse′ness, spars′i·ty,** *n.*

Spar′tan, *adj.* austere; disciplined.

spasm, *n.* sudden and involuntary contraction of the muscles.

spas·mod′ic, *adj.* **1.** in spasms. **2.** at unpredictable intervals. —**spas·mod′i·cal·ly,** *adv.*

spas′tic, *adj.* characterized by spasms.

spat, *n. Informal.* quarrel about a small matter.

spa′tial, *adj.* pertaining to space.

spatter, *v.t.* splash, esp. in small amounts over a wide area.

spat·u·la (spach′ə lə), *n.* broad-bladed device for handling foods, etc.

spawn, *n.* **1.** eggs of some animals, esp. fish and mollusks. —*v.t.* **2.** originate in

abundance. —*v.i.* **3.** lay spawn.

speak, *v.,* **spoke, spoken, speaking.** *v.i.* **1.** communicate with the voice. **2.** give a speech or lecture. —*v.t.* **3.** present by means of the voice. **4.** use in speaking, as a language.

speak′er, *n.* **1.** person who speaks. **2.** president of a legislature. **3.** loudspeaker.

spear, *n.* **1.** long-handled, pointed weapon for hurling or thrusting. —*v.t.* **2.** wound with a spear. —**spear′head,** *n.*

spear′mint″, *n.* fragrant mint used as flavoring.

spe′cial, *adj.* **1.** distinct from all others. **2.** remarkable. —**spe′cial·ly,** *adv.*

spe′cial·ize, *v.i.,* **-ized, -izing.** study, work, or trade in a special area. —**spe′cial·ist,** *n.*

spe′cial·ty, *n., pl.* **-ties.** area of specialization.

spe·cie (spē′shē), *n.* coins.

spe′cies, *n.* group of fundamentally identical plants or animals.

spe·cif′ic, *adj.* **1.** detailed. **2.** exact. **3.** characteristic.

spe′ci·fy″, *v.t.,* **-fied, -fying.** state or demand specifically.

spec′i·men, *n.* typical example.

spe′cious, *adj.* falsely seeming good or valid. —**spe′cious·ly,** *adv.* —**spe′cious·ness,** *n.*

speck, *n.* **1.** small particle or spot. —*v.t.* **2.** mark with specks.

speck′le, *n., v.t.,* **-led, -ling.** *n.* **1.** small spot. —*v.t.* **2.** mark with speckles.

spec′ta·cle, *n.* **1.** marvelous event or sight. **2.** grandiose public entertainment. **3. spectacles,** eyeglasses.

spec·tac′u·lar, *adj.* marvelous or grandiose in appearance, etc.

spec′ta·tor, *n.* person who sees an event or view.

spec′ter, *n.* ghost; apparition. Also, **spec′tre.** —**spec′tral,** *adj.*

spec′tro·scope, *n.* instrument for producing and analyzing spectra. —**spec″tro·scop′ic,** *adj.*

spec′trum, *n., pl.* **-tra, -trums.** group of color bands produced when light is dispersed by a prism.

spec′u·late, *v.i.,* **-lated, -lating. 1.** think contemplatively. **2.** undertake a business risk in the hope of large profits. —**spec″u·la′tion,** *n.* —**spec′u·la·tive,** *adj.* —**spec″u·la′tor,** *n.*

speech, *n.* **1.** ability to speak. **2.** way of speaking. **3.** something spoken. **4.** talk to an audience. —**speech′less,** *adj.*

speed, *n., v.,* **sped** or **speeded, speeding.** *n.* **1.** swiftness of motion or action. **2.** rate of motion or action. —*v.t.* **3.** increase the speed of. —*v.i.* **4.** move swiftly. **5.** drive with excessive speed. —**speed′y,** *adj.* —**speed′i·ly,** *adv.* —**speed′er,** *n.*

speed·om'e·ter, *n.* speed-registering device.

spell, *v.,* **spelled** or **spelt, spelling,** *n.,* *v.t.* 1. name the letters of. 2. comprise the letters of. 3. take over from, as in a shared task. —*v.i.* 4. name the letters forming ordinary words. —*n.* 5. enchantment. 6. period of time.

spell'bound'', *adj.* entranced.

spend, *v.t.,* **spent, spending.** 1. pay. 2. pass, as a period of time. 3. use up or exhaust. —**spend'er,** *n.*

spend'thrift'', *n.* spender to excess.

spent, *adj.* 1. exhausted. 2. used up or worn out.

sperm, *n.* male germ cell carried by semen. —**sper·mat'ic,** *adj.*

spew, *v.t.,* *v.i.* vomit or pour with force.

sphere, *n.* 1. round solid with all radii equal; ball. 2. area of influence, activity, knowledge, etc. —**spher'i·cal,** *adj.*

spher'oid, *n.* approximately spherical solid.

sphinx, *n. Classical mythology.* creature with a human head and the body of a lion.

spice, *n.,* *v.t.,* **spiced, spicing.** *n.* 1. aromatic plant substance for seasoning, preservation, etc. —*v.t.* 2. season or treat with spice. —**spic'y,** *adj.*

spi'der, *n.* eight-legged predatory animal that captures insects in a web. —**spi'·der·y,** *adj.*

spig'ot, *n.* faucet.

spike, *n.,* *v.t.,* **spiked, spiking.** *n.* 1. large hammer-driven fastener. 2. pointed feature. 3. long stalk bearing grains or blossoms. —*v.t.* 4. fasten with spikes. 5. frustrate; thwart.

spill, *v.,* **spilled** or **spilt, spilling.** *v.t.* 1. lose, as from the tipping of a container. 2. shed, as blood. —*v.i.* 3. be lost, as over the rim of a container.

spill'way'', *n.* channel letting excess water escape.

spin, *v.,* **spun, spinning,** *n.,* *v.t.* 1. make from twisted yarn. 2. make into yarn or thread. 3. make from secretions, as a spider web. —*v.t.,* *v.i.* 4. whirl. —*n.* 5. whirling motion. 6. *Informal.* brief ride. —**spin'ner,** *n.*

spin'ach, *n.* plant with dark-green edible leaves.

spin'dle, *n.* 1. rod used in spinning thread. 2. any slender round rod.

spin'dling, *adj.* Also, **spin'dly.**

spin'drift'', *n.* spray from wave crests.

spine, *n.* 1. Also called **spinal column.** backbone; vertebrae. 2. thorn. —**spin'al,** *adj.* —**spin'y,** *adj.*

spine'less, *adj.* without courage.

spin'et, *n.* small upright piano.

spin'ster, *n.* unmarried woman past the normal marriageable age.

spi'ral, *n.* 1. flat curve with steadily increasing radius. —*adj.* 2. formed along such a curve. —*v.i.* 3. move in such a curve. —**spi'ral·ly,** *adj.*

spire, *n.* tall pyramidal structure forming the roof of a tower.

spir'it, *n.* 1. spiritual part of a person; soul. 2. ghost. 3. mood, sentiment, or intent. 4. vigor or courage. 5. **spirits, a.** state of mind. **b.** distilled alcoholic liquor. 6. Holy Ghost. —*v.t.* 7. smuggle. —**spir'it·ed,** *adj.* —**spir'it·less,** *adj.*

spir'it·u·al, *adj.* 1. pertaining to religion. 2. pertaining to the soul. 3. concerned with matters of the soul. —*n.* 4. Negro religious song. —**spir'it·u·al·ly,** *adv.* —**spir''it·u·al'i·ty,** *n.*

spir'it·u·al·ism'', *n.* belief that the living and the dead can communicate. —**spir''it·u·al·ist,** *n.* —**spir''it·u·al·is'tic,** *adj.*

spir'it·u·ous, *adj.* alcoholic and distilled.

spit, *v.,* **spat, spit,** or (for 2) **spitted, spitting,** *n.,* *v.t.* 1. eject from the mouth. 2. skewer. —*v.i.* 3. eject saliva from the mouth. —*n.* 4. saliva. 5. long skewer. 6. small peninsula.

spite, *n.,* *v.t.,* **spited, spiting.** *n.* 1. small-minded hostility or vengefulness. 2. **in spite of,** notwithstanding. —*v.t.* 3. offend or hurt out of spite. —**spite'ful,** *adj.* —**spite'ful·ly,** *adv.* —**spite'ful·ness,** *n.*

spit'tle, *n.* saliva.

spit·toon', *n.* receptacle for spit.

splash, *v.t.* 1. cause to fly in various directions, as a liquid. —*v.i.* 2. fly in various directions, as a liquid. —*n.* 3. act, instance, or sound of splashing.

splat'ter, *v.i.* be splashed.

splay, *v.t.,* *v.i.* 1. spread apart. —*adj.* 2. spreading apart.

spleen, *n.* 1. organ for modifying the blood structure. 2. anger or irritation. —**sple·net'ic,** *adj.*

splen'did, *adj.* 1. magnificent. 2. excellent. —**splen'did·ly,** *adv.* —**splen'dor,** *n.*

splice, *v.t.,* **spliced, splicing,** *n.,* *v.t.* 1. join into a single piece. —*n.* 2. joint created by splicing.

splint, *n.* 1. temporary reinforcement for a broken bone. 2. thin slip of wood forming part of a basket.

splin'ter, *n.* 1. sharp, broken fragment. —*v.t.,* *v.i.* 2. break into splinters.

split, *v.,* **split, splitting,** *n.,* *adj.,* *v.t.,* *v.i.* 1. break or pull in two. —*v.t.* 2. share or divide. —*n.* 3. act or instance of splitting. —*adj.* 4. having been split.

splotch, *n.,* *v.t.* spot or stain. —**splotch'y,** *adj.*

splurge, *v.i.,* **splurged, splurging,** *n.,* *v.i.* 1. spend money lavishly and showily. —*n.* 2. act or instance of splurging.

splut'ter, *v.i.* 1. babble, as with confusion or rage. —*n.* 2. spluttering speech.

spoil, v., spoiled or spoilt, spoiling, n., v.t. 1. ruin. 2. damage the character of with indulgence. —v.i. 3. become unfit to eat, drink, or use. —n. 4. spoils, loot. —spoil′er, n. —spoil′age, n.

spoke, n. shaft between the hub and rim of a wheel.

spokes′man, n. person who speaks for a group.

spo″li·a′tion, n. looting.

sponge, n., v., sponged, sponging. n. 1. marine animal. 2. skeleton of this animal or an imitation in plastic, used to absorb water. —v.t. 3. wipe with a sponge. —v.i. 4. Informal. live at the expense of others. —spong′y, adj.

sponger, n. Informal. one who lives at the expense of others.

spon′sor, n. 1. person who undertakes responsibility for another. 2. godparent. 3. advertiser who buys television or radio time. —v.t. 4. act as sponsor for.

spon·ta′ne·ous, adj. 1. occurring without an external cause. 2. lively and natural in manner. —spon·ta′ne·ous·ly, adv. —spon″ta·ne′i·ty, spon·ta′ne′ousness, n.

spook, n. Informal. ghost. —spook′y, adj.

spool, n. small drum on which thread, film, recording tape, etc. is wound.

spoon, n. 1. utensil for handling or stirring liquids or food. —v.t. 2. handle or serve with a spoon.

spoor (spŏŏr), n. trail of animal scent.

spo·rad′ic, adj. occasional. —spo·rad′i·cal·ly, adv.

spore, n. seedlike body from which fungi, mosses, etc. grow.

sport, n. 1. recreation involving bodily activity. 2. amusement. 3. plant or animal of abnormal form. —v.i. 4. play vigorously. —sports′man, n. —sports′man·ship″, n. —sports′man·ly, adj.

spor′tive, adj. playful. —spor′tive·ly, adv. —spor′tive·ness, n.

spot, n., v.t., spotted, spotting. n. 1. round mark. 2. place. —v.t. 3. mark with spots. 4. notice. —adj., 5. immediate. 6. random, as a survey. —spot′less, adj. —spot′ty, adj. —spot′ter, n.

spouse, n. husband or wife.

spout, n. 1. channel for discharging liquids, grain, etc. —v.t. 2. emit with force. 3. recite enthusiastically.

sprain, v.t. 1. injure by wrenching muscles or ligaments. —n. 2. injury so produced.

sprat, n. small fish of the herring family.

sprawl, v.i. 1. stretch out in an ungraceful way. —n. 2. act or instance of sprawling.

spray, n. 1. liquid driven in fine particles. 2. device for shooting such liquid. 3. small branch with flowers or leaves. —v.t. 4. drive as a spray. 5. apply spray to. —spray′er, n.

spread, v., spread, spreading, n., v.t., v.i. 1. extend. 2. scatter or disperse. —v.i. 3. cover or apply thinly. —n. 4. extent, 5. distribution. 6. cloth for covering a bed. 7. soft food eaten with breadstuffs. —spread′er, n.

spree, n. occasion of uninhibited activity.

sprig, n. twig or spray.

spright′ly, adj., -lier, -liest. lively. —spright′li·ness, n.

spring, n., v., sprang or sprung, sprung, springing, adj. n. 1. season between winter and summer, beginning at the vernal equinox. 2. stream emerging from the earth. 3. resilient elastic device, e.g. a wire coil. 4. jump. —v.i. 5. jump. 6. arise or emerge. —v.t. 7. cause to act suddenly. 8. disclose suddenly. —spring′time, n. —spring′y, adj.

sprin′kle, v., -kled, -kling, n. v.t. 1. scatter thinly. —v.i. 2. rain lightly. —n. 3. act or instance of sprinkling. 4. something sprinkled. —sprink′ler, n.

sprint, n. 1. short run. —v.i. 2. make a short run. —sprint′er, n.

sprite, n. elf or fairy.

sprock′et, n. gear tooth engaging with a chain.

sprout, v.i. 1. begin to grow or send forth shoots. —n. 2. shoot that has sprouted.

spruce, n., adj., sprucer, spruciest, v.t., n. 1. coniferous evergreen. —adj. 2. tidy; neat. —v.t. 3. make tidy.

spry, adj., sprier or spryer, spriest or spryest. active; lively. —spry′ly, adv. —spry′ness, n.

spud, n. 1. type of spade. 2. Informal. potato.

spume, n. foam.

spunk, n. Informal. courage. —spunk′y, adj.

spur, n., v.t., spurred, spurring. n. 1. sharp device for urging on a horse. 2. short extension. —v.t. 3. urge on.

spur·i·ous (spyŏŏr′ē əs), adj. false; fraudulent. —spur′i·ous·ly, adv. —spur′i·ous·ness, n.

spurn, v.t. reject with scorn.

spurt, v.t., v.i. 1. shoot forth, as a liquid. —v.i. 2. have a sudden, short increase of energy or activity. —n. 3. act or instance of spurting.

sput′nik, n. man-made satellite, esp. one from the U.S.S.R.

sput′ter, v.t. 1. eject in drops or particles. —v.i. 2. splutter. —n. 3. act, instance, or sound of sputtering.

spu·tum (spyŏŏ′təm), n. saliva, etc. ejected from the mouth.

spy, n., pl. spies, v. spied, spying. n. 1. person who attempts to obtain secret information. —v.t. 2. notice, esp. at a distance. —v.i. 3. act as a spy.

squab, *n.* young pigeon.

squab'ble, *n., v.i.,* **-bled, -bling.** quarrel over trifles.

squad, *n.* small group, as of soldiers.

squad'ron, *n.* military unit of airplanes, ships, or cavalry.

squal'id, *adj.* **1.** dirty or nasty. **2.** in miserable condition. —**squal'id·ly,** *adv.* —**squal'id·ness,** *n.* —**squal'or,** *n.*

squall, *n.* **1.** strong, brief storm or gust of wind. —*v.i.* **2.** weep loudly. —**squal'ly,** *adj.*

squan'der, *v.t.* spend or use up wastefully.

square, *n., adj.,* **squarer, squarest,** *v.t.,* **squared, squaring.** *n.* **1.** right-angled figure with four equal sides. **2.** paved public area. **3.** tool for laying out or checking angled lines. **4.** *Math.* product of a number multiplied by itself. —*adj.* **5.** formed like a square. **6.** of an area equal to linear measure squared. **7.** honest or substantial. —*adv.* **8.** fairly; straightforwardly. —*v.t.* **9.** make square. **10.** *Math.* multiply by itself. —*v.i.* **11.** be consistent. —**square'ly,** *adv.*

square'-rigged', *adj.* with sails rigged athwart the vessel. —**square'-rig'ger,** *n.*

squash, *v.t.* **1.** crush. —*n.* **2.** game played with rackets. **3.** gourdlike fruit.

squat, *v.i.,* **squatted** or **squat, squatting,** *n., adj., v.i.* **1.** crouch with the legs doubled under the body. **2.** settle without authority. —*n.* **3.** squatting position. —*adj.* **4.** Also, **squat'ty,** short and broad of figure. —**squat'ter,** *n.*

squaw, *n.* American Indian woman.

squawk, *n.* **1.** loud, harsh cry. —*v.i.* **2.** utter a squawk.

squeak, *n.* **1.** shrill noise. —*v.i.* **2.** make squeaks. —**squeak'y,** *adj.*

squeal, *n.* **1.** shrill cry. —*v.i.* **2.** make squeals.

squeam'ish, *adj.* **1.** easily disgusted. **2.** prudish. —**squeam'ish·ly,** *adv.* —**squeam'ish·ness,** *n.*

squee'gee, *n.* flat-bladed cleaner for plate glass.

squeeze, *v.t.,* **squeezed, squeezing,** *n., v.t.* **1.** press from both sides. **2.** cram. —*n.* **3.** act or instance of squeezing. **4.** hug.

squelch, *v.t.* **1.** silence with a crushing remark. —*n.* **2.** crushing remark.

squid, *n.* ten-armed sea mollusk.

squint, *v.i.* **1.** see through partly-closed eyes. **2.** be crosseyed. —*n.* **3.** act or instance of squinting.

squire, *n., v.t.,* **squired, squiring.** *n.* **1.** country gentleman. **2.** gentleman escorting a lady. —*v.t.* **3.** escort.

squirm, *v.i., n.* wriggle.

squir'rel, *n.* bushy-tailed rodent living in trees.

squirt, *v.t., v.i.* **1.** shoot, as a liquid. —*n.* **2.** jet of liquid. **3.** device for squirting.

stab, *v.t.,* **stabbed, stabbing,** *n., v.t.* **1.** wound with a knife, etc. —*n.* **2.** wound or thrust from such a weapon.

sta'bil·ize, *v.t.,* **-lized, -lizing.** cause to be or remain stable. —**sta'bi·liz''er,** *n.* —**sta''bi·li·za''tion,** *n.*

sta'ble, *n., v.t.,* **-bled, -bling,** *adj. n.* **1.** Also, **stables,** accommodation for animals, esp. horses. —*v.t.* **2.** put into a stable, as a horse. —*adj.* **3.** resistant to displacement or change. —**sta·bil'i·ty,** *n.*

stac·ca·to (stə kah'tō), *adj. Music.* separated by brief silences.

stack, *n.* **1.** orderly pile. **2.** Often, **stacks,** storage space for library books. **3.** chimney or funnel. —*v.t.* **4.** gather into stacks.

sta'di·um, *n., pl.* **-diums, -dia.** outdoor arena for spectator sports.

staff, *n., pl.* **staves** or **staffs** (for 1), **staffs** (for 1, 3), *v.t., n.* **1.** stick carried in the hand. **2.** group of employees, esp. in administrative jobs. **3.** *Music.* group of five horizontal lines used in musical notation. —*v.t.* **4.** provide or work as a staff for.

stag, *n.* **1.** adult male deer. —*adj.* **2.** for men only.

stage, *n., v.t.,* **staged, staging.** *n.* **1.** distinct phase of a process, journey, etc. **2.** performers' platform. **3.** theatrical profession. —*v.t.* **4.** present on a stage. **5.** divide into phases.

stage'coach'', *n.* horse-drawn coach for long-distance travel.

stag'ger, *v.i.* **1.** walk or stand unsteadily. —*v.t.* **2.** cause to stagger or falter. **3.** schedule over a range of times. —*n.* **4.** staggering gait.

stag'ing, *n.* scaffolding.

stag'nant, *adj.* **1.** not flowing, as a body of water. **2.** undesirably inactive. —**stag'nate,** *v.i.* —**stag''na'tion,** *n.*

staid, *adj.* sober and quiet; sedate. —**staid'ly,** *adv.* —**staid'ness,** *n.*

stain, *n.* **1.** discoloration. **2.** dye applied to wood or other materials. —*v.t.* **3.** discolor. **4.** apply dye to.

stair, *n.* tall flight of steps. Also, **stairs, stair'way''. —stair'well'',** *n.*

stair'case'', *n.* interior stair.

stake, *n., v.t.,* **staked, staking.** *n.* **1.** upright post. **2.** something wagered. **3.** **stakes,** something to be gained through risk. **4.** **at stake,** in danger of loss. —*v.t.* **5.** mark or secure with a stake. **6.** wager.

sta·lac'tite, *n.* icicle-like deposit of lime on a cave roof.

sta·lag'mite, *n.* conical deposit of lime on a cave floor.

stale, *adj., v.i., adj.* **staler, stalest,** *v.i., adj.* **1.** no

longer fresh. —*v.i.* **2.** become stale.
—**stale′ness,** *n.*

stale′mate″, *n.* **1.** *Chess.* situation making a move impossible. **2.** deadlock.
—*v.t.* **3.** halt through a stalemate.

stalk, *v.t.* **1.** pursue stealthily. —*v.i.* **2.** walk proudly or deliberately. —*n.* **3.** plant stem.

stall, *n.* **1.** compartment. **2.** stop because of malfunctioning. **3.** *Informal.* pretext for delay. —*v.t.* **4.** put or keep in a stall. **5.** *Informal.* delay or keep waiting. —*v.i.* **6.** stop because of malfunctioning.

stal′lion, *n.* ungelded male horse.

stal′wart, *adj.* **1.** reliable through bravery, vigor, or faithfulness. —*n.* **2.** stalwart person.

stam′i·na, *n.* enduring vigor.

stam′mer, *v.i.* **1.** speak with involuntary repetitions or pauses. —*n.* **2.** stammering way of speaking.

stamp, *v.t.* **1.** step on forcefully. **2.** form or print with a stamp. **3.** affix a stamp to. —*n.* **4.** act or instance of stamping. **5.** descending device for printing, embossing, cutting, etc. **6.** adhesive paper proving payment of postage, etc. **7.** type of personal character.

stam″pede′, *n., v.,* **-peded, -peding.** *n.* **1.** mass flight, as of frightened cattle. —*v.i.* **2.** flee in a stampede. —*v.t.* **3.** cause to stampede.

stance, *n.* **1.** position of a standing person. **2.** attitude or policy.

stanch, *adj.* **1.** (stonch) stalwart. —*v.t.* **2.** (stanch) stop from escaping, as blood. **3.** stop from bleeding. —**stanch′ly,** *adv.* —**stanch′ness,** *n.*

stan′chion, *n.* structural post.

stand, *v.,* **stood, standing,** *n., v.i.* **1.** be or become upright on the feet. **2.** be located, as a tall object. **3.** halt or refrain from moving. **4.** take a position, as in a controversy. **5.** have toleration. —*v.t.* **6.** cause to be upright. **7.** endure or tolerate. —*n.* **8.** small platform or table. **9.** small sales booth. **10.** position, as in a controversy. **11.** halt, **12.** area of trees.

stand′ard, *n.* **1.** basis for evaluation or measurement. **2.** upright support. **3.** military or personal flag. —*adj.* **4.** of the normal or typical sort.

stan′dard·ize, *v.,* **-ized, -izing.** *v.t., v.i.* conform to a standard. —**stan″dard·i·za′tion,** *n.*

stand′-by, *n., pl.* **-bys,** *adj., n.* **1.** possible substitute. —*adj.* **2.** for emergency use.

stand′ing, *n.* **1.** status. **2.** duration. —*adj.* **3.** upright. **4.** permanent. **5.** fixed in place. **6.** stagnant.

stand′point″, *n.* viewpoint.

stan′za, *n.* set of verses.

sta′ple, *n., v.t.,* **-pled, -pling,** *adj., n.* **1.**

fastener of bent wire or bar stock. **2.** main or standard commodity. **3.** textile fiber. —*v.t.* **4.** fasten with staples. —*adj.* **5.** main or standard. —**sta′pler,** *n.*

star, *n., adj., v.,* **starred, starring.** *n.* **1.** heavenly body of incandescent gas. **2.** figure with radiating points. **3.** prominent or leading performer or player. —*v.t.* **4.** have in a leading role. **5.** mark with a star. —*v.i.* **6.** have a leading role. —**star′ry,** *adj.*

star′board″, *Nautical. n.* **1.** right-hand side, facing forward. —*adj.* **2.** located on this side. —*adv.* **3.** toward this side.

starch, *n.* **1.** tasteless vegetable substance found in potatoes, flour, etc. and used for stiffening. —*v.t.* **2.** treat with starch. —**starch′y,** *adj.*

stare, *v.i.,* **stared, staring,** *n., v.i.* **1.** gaze with fixed, open eyes. —*n.* **2.** act or instance of staring.

star′fish″, *n.* star-shaped sea animal.

stark, *adj.* **1.** outright. **2.** bleak. **3.** stiff. —*adv.* **4.** utterly.

star′ling, *n.* small bird of European origin.

start, *v.t., v.i.* **1.** begin. —*v.t.* **2.** knock loose. —*v.i.* **3.** jump with surprise. **4.** move or arise suddenly. —*n.* **5.** beginning. **6.** sudden movement from surprise. **7.** lead in a race or pursuit. —**start′er,** *n.*

star′tle, *v.t.,* **-tled, -tling.** disturb with sudden surprise.

starve, *v.,* **starved, starving.** *v.t.* **1.** skill or trouble with hunger. —*v.i.* **2.** die or be troubled from hunger. —**star″va′tion,** *n.*

state, *n., adj., v.t.,* **stated, stating.** *n.* **1.** condition. **2.** politically autonomous or semi-autonomous region. **3.** civil government. **4.** pomp. —*adj.* **5.** formally conducted. —*v.t.* **7.** declare. —**state′hood″,** *n.*

state′house″, *n.* U.S. state capitol.

state′ly, *adj.,* **-lier, -liest.** dignified. —**state′li·ness,** *n.*

state′ment, *n.* **1.** declaration. **2.** financial account or bill.

state-of-the-art, *adj.* of or pertaining to the highest level of technological achievement to date.

state′room″, *n.* private cabin on a ship.

states′man, *n.* person wise in government. —**states′man·ship,** *n.*

stat′ic, *adj.* **1.** not moving. —*n.* **2.** unmoving electrical charges. **3.** radio interference caused by such charges.

sta′tion, *n.* **1.** building where a train, bus, etc. stops or originates. **2.** place for sending broadcasts. **3.** place of duty. **4.** place where one stops. **5.** position, as in society. —*v.t.* **5.** assign to a place.

sta′tion·ar″y, *adj.* **1.** not in motion. **2.** not moving to another place.

sta'tion·er, *n.* seller of paper and writing materials. —sta'tion·er''y, *n.*

sta·tis'tics, *n.* collection and analysis of numerical data. —sta·tis'ti·cal, *adj.* —sta·tis'ti·cal·ly, *adv.* —sta''tis·ti'cian, *n.*

stat'u·ar''y, *n.* statues collectively.

stat'ue, *n.* three-dimensional sculpture of a human or animal.

stat'u·esque', *adj.* like a statue, esp. in posture.

stat''u·ette', *n.* small statue.

stat'ure, *n.* 1. tallness. 2. eminence or achievement.

status quo, *Latin.* present condition.

sta·tus (stā'təs, stăt'əs), *n.* 1. position, as in society. 2. state or condition.

stat'ute, *n.* law; ordinance. —stat'u·to''ry, *adj.*

staunch, *n., adj.* stanch.

stave, *n., v.t.,* staved or (for 3) stove, staving. *n.* 1. curved board forming part of a barrel side. 2. *Music.* staff. —*v.t.* 3. break in or crush. 4. repel.

stay, *v.,* stayed, staying, *n., v.i.* 1. remain or continue. —*v.t.* 2. halt or delay. 3. support or prop. —*n.* 4. temporary residence. 5. halt or delay. 6. support or prop. 7. fore-and-aft line supporting a mast.

stead, *n.* 1. in one's stead, in place of one. 2. in good stead, advantageously.

stead'fast'', *adj.* 1. unchanging. 2. loyal or determined. —stead'fast''ly, *adv.* —stead'fast''ness, *n.*

stead'y, *adj.,* steadier, steadiest, *v.,* steadied, steadying. *adj.* 1. firm; unwavering. 2. regular; unvarying. 3. reliable. —*v.t., v.i.* 4. make or become steady. —stead'i·ly, *adv.*

steak, *n.* slice of meat or fish for broiling or frying.

steal, *v.,* stole, stolen, stealing. *v.t.* 1. take without right. —*v.i.* 2. move silently.

stealth, *n.* secret activity. —stealth'y, *adj.* —stealth'i·ly, *adv.*

steam, *n.* 1. gaseous or vaporized water. —*v.t.* 2. treat with steam. —*v.i.* 3. turn into or give off steam. —*adj.* 4. working by steam. 5. carrying steam. —steam'y, *adj.* —steam'boat'', *n.* —steam'ship'', *n.*

steam'er, *n.* 1. vehicle operated by steam, esp. a ship or automobile. 2. device for treating with steam.

steed, *n.* riding horse.

steel, *n.* 1. iron alloyed with carbon. —*adj.* 2. made of or resembling steel. —*v.t.* 3. make resolute or courageous. —steel'y, *adj.*

steel'yard'', *n.* scale with a weighted arm.

steep, *adj.* 1. far from horizontal. —*v.t.* 2. soak. 3. absorb. —steep'ly, *adv.* —steep'ness, *n.*

steep'le, *n.* 1. tall tower with a spire. 2. spire.

steep'le·chase'', *n.* horse race over obstacles.

steer, *v.t.* 1. direct or guide. —*n.* 2. castrated bull.

steer'age, *n.* cheap, cabinless passenger accommodations on a ship.

stein, *n.* beer mug, esp. one of earthenware.

stel'lar, *adj.* pertaining to or suggesting stars.

stem, *n., v.,* stemmed, stemming. *n.* 1. support of a plant, leaf, or fruit. 2. single support, as of a glass. 3. uninflected part of a word. 4. extreme forepart of a ship's bow. —*v.t.* 5. take the stem from. 6. check, as liquid. 7. make headway against. —*v.i.* 8. be derived or originate.

stench, *n.* stink.

sten'cil, *n., v.t.,* -ciled, -ciling. *n.* 1. pierced sheet allowing paint or ink to mark an underlying surface. —*v.t.* 2. paint or ink with a stencil.

ste·nog'ra·phy, *n.* shorthand writing. —sten''o·graph'ic, *adj.* —ste·nog'ra·pher, *n.*

sten·to'ri·an, *adj.* very loud of voice.

step, *n., v.i.* stepped, stepping. *n.* 1. movement of the walking foot. 2. gait. 3. raised surface on which one walks upwards. 4. stage of a process. —*v.i.* 5. walk. 6. press down with the foot.

step-, by the remarriage of a parent: a prefix.

step'lad''der, *n.* ladder with steps.

steppe, *n.* plain, esp. in southeast Europe or Asia.

ster''e·o, *n.* device for playing recorded or broadcast music in stereophonic sound.

ster''e·o·phon'ic, *adj.* pertaining to realistic sound reproduction through two or more loudspeakers.

ster'e·o·scope'', *n.* viewer using twin pictures and two eyepieces for a realistic effect.

ster'e·o·type'', *n., v.t.,* -typed, typing. *n.* 1. process for casting printing plates. 2. unimaginative or oversimplified conception. —*v.t.* 3. reproduce by the stereotype process. 4. conceive as a stereotype.

ster'ile, *adj.* 1. free of microbes. 2. barren. 3. uncreative or unimaginative. —ster·il'i·ty, *n.*

ster'i·lize'', *v.t.,* -lized, -lizing. make sterile. —ster'i·liz''er, *n.* —ster''i·li·za'tion, *n.*

ster'ling, *adj.* 1. composed of 92.5° silver. 2. in British money. 3. fine; noble.

stern, *adj.* 1. grimly strict. —*n.* 2. after end of a ship. —stern'ly, *adv.* —stern'ness, *n.*

ster'num, *n.* breastbone.

steth'o·scope", *n.* instrument for listening to body sounds.

ste've·dore", *n.* handler of ship's cargoes.

stew, *n.* 1. dish of simmered food. —*v.t.* 2. simmer to cook.

stew'ard, *n.* 1. business manager, esp. on an estate. 2. person in charge of food, supplies, and services. 3. attendant. Also, *fem.*, **stew'ard·ess.**

stick, *v.*, **stuck, sticking,** *n.*, *v.t.* 1. pierce. 2. thrust. 3. cause to adhere. —*v.i.* 4. fail to move properly. 5. adhere. 6. project. 7. remain. —*n.* 8. length of wood. 9. short length. 10. lever. 11. walking cane.

stick'er, *n.* 1. person or thing that sticks. 2. adhesive label.

stick'ler, *n.* person who insists on something.

stick'y, *adj.*, **stickier, stickiest.** 1. adhesive. 2. *Informal.* **a.** muggy. **b.** troublesome or difficult.

stiff, *adj.* 1. unbending. 2. not moving easily. 3. formal or distant in manner. —**stiff'ly**, *adv.* —**stiff'ness**, *n.* —**stif'fen**, *v.t.*, *v.i.*

sti'fle, *v.*, **-fled, -fling.** *v.t.* 1. smother. 2. suppress. —*v.i.* 3. suffer from lack of air.

stig'ma, *n.*, *pl.* **stigmata, stigmas.** mark or indication of disrepute. —**stig'ma·tize"**, *v.t.*

stile, *n.* 1. steps over a fence. 2. upright framing member.

sti·let'to, *n.* Italian dagger.

still, *adj.* 1. motionless or silent. 2. tranquil. 3. not sparkling, as wine. —*adv.* 4. up to an indicated time. 5. even more or even less. —*adv.*, *conj.* 6. nevertheless. —*v.t.*, *v.i.* 7. make or become still. —*n.* 8. distillation apparatus. —**still'ness**, *n.*

still'born", *adj.* 1. born dead. 2. abortive.

stilt, *n.* pole serving as an extention of the legs.

stilt'ed, *adj.* affectedly dignified.

stim'u·late, *v.t.*, **-lated, -lating.** 1. cause to be active or more active. 2. inspire. —**stim'u·la'tion**, *n.* —**stim'u·la·tive**, *adj.* —**stim'u·lant**, *n.*

stim'u·lus, *n.*, *pl.* **-li.** something stimulating.

sting, *v.t.*, **stung, -ing.** *n.*, *v.t.* 1. inflict a small, painful wound or blow. 2. annoy or goad severely. —*n.* 3. wound from stinging. 4. sharp part for stinging. 5. undercover operation run by a law enforcement agency to catch suspected criminals.

stin'gy, *adj.* characteristic of or suggesting miserliness. —**stin'gi·ly**, *adv.* —**stin'gi·ness**, *n.*

stink, **stank** or **stunk, stunk, stinking,** *n.*, *v.i.* 1. have a bad smell. —*n.* 2. bad smell.

stint, *v.t.* 1. limit. 2. limit oneself. —*n.* 3. limitation. 4. task or work period.

sti'pend, *n.* regular payment.

stip'ple, *v.t.*, **-pled, -pling,** *n.*, *v.t.* 1. paint in small dots. —*n.* 2. texture of small dots.

stip'u·late, *v.t.*, **-lated, -lating.** require as a condition. —**stip"u·la'tion**, *n.*

stir, *v.t.*, **stirred, stirring,** *n.*, *v.t.* 1. mix by moving. 2. move. 3. rouse. —*n.* 4. public excitement or commotion.

stir'ring, *adj.* 1. exciting. 2. active.

stir'rup, *n.* foothold hanging from a saddle.

stitch, *n.* 1. single repeated operation in sewing, knitting, etc. 2. sharp pain. —*v.t.* 3. sew.

stock, *n.* 1. goods, materials, etc. on hand. 2. cattle. 3. any of various parts of guns, implements, etc. 4. ancestry. 5. soup or stew base. 6. dividend-bearing shares. —*adj.* 7. standard; uniform. —*v.t.* 8. keep for sale or use. 9. supply with stock. 10. supply with live fish, as a pond. —**stock'brok"er**, *n.* —**stock'hold"er**, *n.* —**stock'pile"**, *n.* —**stock'yard"**, *n.*

stock·ade', *n.*, *v.t.*, **-aded, -ading.** *n.* 1. barrier of upright stakes. —*v.t.* 2. put a stockade around.

stock'ing, *n.* clothing for the foot and lower parts of the leg.

stock'y, *adj.* broad and short of figure.

stodg'y, *adj.*, **stodgier, stodgiest.** heavy and boring. —**stodg'i·ly**, *adv.* —**stodg'i·ness**, *n.*

sto'ic, *n.* 1. person who maintains indifference to pain or sorrow. —*adj.* 2. Also, **sto'i·cal**, characteristic of a stoic. —**sto'i·cal·ly**, *adv.* —**sto'i·cism**, *n.*

stoke, *v.t.*, **stoked, stoking.** keep burning by adding fuel. —**stok'er**, *n.*

stole, *n.* scarflike garment worn behind the neck and over the shoulders.

stol'id, *adj.* showing no liveliness. —**stol'id·ly**, *adv.* —**sto·lid'i·ty**, *n.*

stom'ach, *n.* 1. organ of digestion. 2. tolerance. —*v.t.* 3. take into the stomach. 4. tolerate. —**sto·mach'ic**, *adj.* —**stom'ach·ache"**, *n.*

stone, *n.*, *pl.* **stones,** *adj.*, *v.t.*, **stoned, stoning.** *n.* 1. hard mineral substance. 2. small piece of this. 3. gem. 4. pit of a fruit. 5. hard object formed in a digestive organ. —*adj.* 6. made of stone. —*v.t.* 7. attack with stones. 8. pit, as a fruit. —**ston'y**, *adj.*

stooge, *n. Informal.* 1. comedian's assistant. 2. underling or henchman.

stool, *n.* armless, backless seat.

stoop, *v.i.* 1. bend forward. 2. demean oneself. —*n.* 3. bent posture. 4. small porch.

stop, v., **stopped, stopping**, n., v.t. **1.** prevent from starting or going on. **2.** clog or plug. —v.i. **3.** act or move no further or not at all. **4.** stay briefly. —n. **5.** act, instance or place of stopping. **6.** device for controlling tone in a musical instrument. —**stop'page**, n.

stop'gap', n., adj. makeshift.

stop'ov·er, n. brief pause during a journey.

stop'per, n. **1.** plug, as for a bottle. —v.t. **2.** close with a stopper. Also, **stop'ple**.

stop'watch'', n. watch for measuring elapsed time.

stor'age, n. **1.** act or instance of storing. **2.** condition of being stored.

store, n., v.t., **stored, storing**. n. **1.** place for the sale of goods. **2.** place of storage. **3.** stores, supplies. **4.** in store, waiting in the future. —v.t. **5.** accumulate and save. **6.** put away for future use. —**store'front**, n. —**store'house''**, n. —**store'keeper''**, n. —**store'room,''** n.

stork, n. long-billed, long-legged wading bird.

storm, n. **1.** high wind, often with rain, snow, etc. **2.** sudden attack. —v.t. **3.** attack suddenly and violently. —v.i. **4.** blow as a storm. **5.** rage. —**storm'y**, adj. —**storm'i·ly**, adv.

stor'y, n., pl. **-ries. 1.** account of events, often fictitious. **2.** newspaper report. **3.** Informal. lie. **4.** level in a building.

stoup (stoōp), n. basin for holy water.

stout, adj. **1.** sturdy. **2.** courageous; resolute. **3.** heavy-set. —n. **4.** dark, sweet, beerlike drink. —**stout'ly**, adv. —**stout'ness**, n.

stove, n. device for heating or cooking.

stow, v.t. **1.** put in storage, as on a ship. —v.i. **2.** stow away, hide on a ship for a free passage. —**stow'age**, n. —**stow'a·way''**, n.

strad'dle, v.t., **-dled, -dling**, n., v.t. **1.** stand over or mount with a leg on each side. —n. **2.** straddling posture.

strafe, v.t., **strafed, strafing**. fire down upon from an aircraft.

strag'gle, v.i., **-gled, -gling**. stray or fall behind. —**strag'gler**, n.

straight, adj. **1.** from point to point in the shortest way; direct. **2.** unmodified or undiluted. **3.** in good order or condition. **4.** honest or unevasive. —adv. **5.** directly. **6.** without modification. **7.** honestly; without evasion. **8.** so as to be clearly understood. —**straight'ness**, n. —**straight'en**, v.t., v.i.

straight'a·way'', n. **1.** straight part of a racetrack, etc. —adv. **2.** Also, **straight'way''**, at once.

straight''for'ward, adj. unevasive; honest.

strain, v.t. **1.** tax the strength of. **2.** injure or distort through force. **3.** run

through a filter or sieve. —n. **4.** major effort or burden. **5.** injury from straining. **6.** trying experience. **7.** melody. **8.** chain of ancestors or descendants. **9.** heredity. —**strain'er**, n.

strait, n. **1.** narrow natural waterway. **2.** straits, difficulties.

strait'en, v.t. make narrow or meager.

strand, n. **1.** length of fiber for twisting into rope. **2.** length of hair. **3.** river or ocean shore. —v.t. **4.** run aground. **5.** put in a helpless position.

strange, adj., **stranger, strangest. 1.** strikingly unfamiliar; odd. **2.** not known to one. —**strange'ly**, adv. —**strange'ness**, n.

stran'ger, n. unfamiliar person.

stran'gle, v., **-gled, -gling**. v.t. **1.** kill by choking. —v.i. **2.** choke. —**stran'gler**, n. —**stran''gu·la'tion**, n.

strap, n., v.t., **strapped, strapping**. n. **1.** band for fastening. —v.t. **2.** fasten with a strap.

stra·ta·gem (strā'tə jəm), n. plot; trick.

stra·teg'ic, adj. **1.** pertaining to strategy. **2.** important in a strategy.

strat'e·gy, n., pl. **-gies. 1.** art of planning military operations. **2.** stratagem or series of stratagems. —**strat'e·gist**, n.

strat'i·fy, v., **-fied, -fying**. v.t., v.i. form in layers. —**strat''i·fi·ca'tion**, n.

strat'o·sphere'', n. atmospheric zone 6 to 15 miles above the earth. —**strat''o·spher'ic**, adj.

stra'tum, n., pl. **strata, stratums**. layers, as of rock.

straw, n. **1.** stalk of threshed grain. **2.** quantity of such stalks. **3.** tube for sucking liquids.

straw'ber''ry, n., pl. **-ries**. red fruit of a vinelike plant.

stray, v.i. **1.** wander aimlessly. **2.** wander away. —adj. **3.** passing or occurring by chance. —n. **4.** animal that strays.

streak, n. **1.** long mark. **2.** trait of character. **3.** brief period, as of luck. —v.t. **4.** mark with streaks. —v.i. **5.** move swiftly. **6.** run naked through a public place. —**ing**, n.

stream, n. **1.** body of running water. **2.** steady flow. —v.i. **3.** flow quickly and steadily. **4.** run with moisture.

stream'er, n. long, narrow flag or piece of bunting.

stream'line'', v.t. **1.** make with a form minimizing air or water resistance. **2.** purge of unnecessary elements.

street, n. road in an urban area.

street'car'', n. rail car for transportation along streets.

strength, n. **1.** power of the muscles. **2.** resistance to force. **3.** ability of the mind. **4.** purity.

strength'en, v.t., v.i. make or become stronger.

stren'u·ous, *adj.* **1.** involving great effort. **2.** vigorous.

stress, *n.* **1.** emphasis. **2.** difficulties. **3.** force causing a strain. —*v.t.* **4.** put a stress on.

stretch, *v.t., v.i.* **1.** extend or spread. **2.** strain, as a muscle. **3.** pull taut. —*n.* **4.** act or instance of stretching. **5.** unbroken extent.

stretch'er, *n.* **1.** device for carrying a sick person lying down. **2.** device for stretching.

strew, *v.t.,* **strewed, strewed** or **strewn, strewing.** scatter.

stri'at·ed, *adj.* with closely-spaced grooves or furrows. —**stri·a'tion,** *n.*

strict, *adj.* **1.** demanding exact conformity. **2.** conforming exactly. —**strict'ly,** *adv.* —**strict'ness,** *n.*

stric'ture, *n.* adverse criticism.

stride, *v.t.,* **strode, stridden, striding,** *n., v.i.* **1.** walk with long steps. —*n.* **2.** long step. **3.** distance covered by such a step.

stri'dent, *adj.* loud and harsh.

strife, *n.* conflict.

strike, *v.,* **struck, struck** or **stricken, striking,** *v.t., v.i.* **1.** hit. **2.** make an impression on. **3.** afflict. **4.** discover, as a mineral. **5.** ignite, as a match. —*v.i.* **6.** stop work to enforce demands. —*n.* **7.** act or instance of striking. **8.** *Baseball.* failure to bat. **9.** *Bowling.* perfect score with the first bowl. —**strik'er,** *n.*

strik'ing, *adj.* remarkable.

string, *n., v.t.,* **strung, stringing.** *n.* **1.** thin cord. **2.** cord on a musical instrument. **3. strings,** musical instruments using such cords. **4.** series or row. —*v.t.,* **5.** furnish with strings. **6.** hang from a cord. **7.** set in a series or row. —**stringed,** *adj.* —**string'y,** *adj.*

string bean, bean with edible pods.

strin'gent, *adj.* very strict. —**strin'gent·ly,** *adv.* —**strin'gen·cy,** *n.*

strip, *n., v.t.,* **stripped, stripping.** *n.* **1.** long narrow piece. —*v.t.* **2.** remove the clothing or covering from. **3.** remove from an underlying surface. **4.** steal or confiscate the possessions of.

stripe, *n.* **1.** long, broad mark. **2.** sort or kind. —*v.t.* **3.** mark with stripes.

strip'ling, *n.* boy.

strive, *v.i.,* **strove, striven, striving.** try hard; strain.

stroke, *v.t.,* **stroked, stroking,** *n., v.t.* **1.** rub or graze gently. —*n.* **2.** act or instance of stroking. **3.** blow. **4.** single movement that is repeated. **5.** sudden attack of illness, esp. apoplexy. **6.** sudden occasion, as of luck. **7.** line made by a pen or pencil. **8.** way of swimming.

stroll, *v.i.* **1.** walk idly. **2.** wander. —**strol'ler,** *n.*

strong, *adj.* having strength. —**strong'ly,** *adv.*

strong'hold", *n.* place secure against attack.

strop, *n., v.t.,* **stropped, stropping.** *n.* **1.** leather strap for sharpening. —*v.t.* **2.** sharpen with a strop.

struc'ture, *n.* **1.** part of a building giving strength. **2.** something built. **3.** basic form, as of a composition. —**struc'tur·al,** *adj.* —**struc'tur·al·ly,** *adv.*

strug'gle, *v.i.,* **-gled, -gling,** *n., v.i.* **1.** strive. **2.** fight. —*n.* **3.** strenuous effort. **4.** fight.

strum, *v.t.* **strummed, strumming.** play lightly or carelessly, as a piano or plucked string instrument.

strut, *v.i.,* **strutted, strutting,** *n., v.i.* **1.** walk affectedly. —*n.* **2.** act or instance of strutting. **3.** postlike brace.

strych·nine (strik'nin), *n.* poisonous alkaloid.

stub, *n., v.t.,* **stubbed, stubbing.** *n.* **1.** short remnant. **2.** stump. —*v.t.* **3.** ram against something, esp. a toe.

stub'ble, *n.* **1.** plant stalks mown short. **2.** short growth of beard.

stub'born, *adj.* refusing to obey, give up, etc. —**stub'born·ly,** *adv.* —**stub'born·ness,** *n.*

stuc'co, *n., pl.* **-coes, -cos,** *v.t.,* **-coed, -coing.** *n.* **1.** coarse exterior plaster. **2.** fine interior plaster. —*v.t.* **3.** cover with stucco.

stud, *n., v.t.,* **studded, studding.** *n.* **1.** projecting feature. **2.** upright wall-framing member. **3.** buttonlike fastener. **4.** collection of horses. **5.** male animal, esp. a horse, for breeding. —*v.t.* **6.** furnish or sprinkle with or as if with studs.

stu'dent, *n.* person who studies.

stud'ied, *adj.* intentional.

stu'di·o, *n.* **1.** artist's workplace. **2.** room for television or radio performers. **3.** place for television or radio performers. **4.** place for making motion pictures.

stu'di·ous, *adj.* studying diligently. —**stu'di·ous·ly,** *adv.*

study, *n., pl.* **studies,** *v.t.,* **studied, studying.** *n.* **1.** methodical acquisition of skill or knowledge. **2.** subject of such activity. **3.** room for reading or writing. **4.** deep thought. —*v.t.* **5.** make a subject of study.

stuff, *n.* **1.** material. **2.** assorted or worthless objects or materials. —*v.t.* **3.** fill under pressure.

stuf'fing, *n.* material stuffed into a hollow object.

stuff'y, *adj.,* **stuffier, stuffiest. 1.** dull and formal. **2.** lacking fresh air.

stul'ti·fy, *v.t.,* **-fied, -fying.** cause to seem foolish.

stum′ble, *v.i.,* **-bled, -bling.** trip and begin to fall.

stump, *n.* **1.** remnant of something cut off. —*v.t.* **2.** baffle. —*v.i.* **3.** walk ponderously. **4.** travel on a political campaign.

stun, *v.t.,* **stunned, stunning. 1.** shalt with amazement. **2.** knock unconscious.

stunt, *n.* **1.** act displaying skill. —*v.t.* **2.** hinder in growing.

stu′pe·fy, *v.t.,* **-fied, -fying. 1.** put in a stupor. **2.** amaze. —**stu″pe·fac′tion,** *n.*

stu·pen′dous, *adj.* astounding.

stu′pid, *adj.* **1.** low in intelligence. **2.** pointless. —**stu′pid·ly,** *adv.* —**stu·pid′i·ty,** *n.*

stu′por, *n.* unconscious or semi-conscious state.

stur′dy, *n.* **1.** strong. **2.** vigorous. —**stur′di·ly,** *adv.* —**stur′di·ness,** *n.*

stur′geon, *n.* large fish whose roe is caviar.

stut′ter, *v.i., n.* stammer.

sty, *n., pl.* **sties. 1.** pig shelter. **2.** swollen inflammation of the eyelid.

style, *n., v.t.,* **styled, styling. n. 1.** manner of artistic composition, writing, living, etc. **2.** kind or variety. **3.** elegance. **4.** formal name. —*v.t.* **5.** apply a style to. —**sty′lis′tic,** *adj.*

styl′ish, *adj.* in style; elegant.

styl′ist, *n.* artist as a possessor of a style.

sty′lus, *n.* **1.** pointed writing instrument. **2.** phonograph needle.

sty′mie, *v.t.,* **-mied, -mying.** hinder.

styp′tic, *adj.* stopping the flow of blood.

sua·sion (swa′zhən), *n.* persuasion. —**sua′sive,** *adj.*

suave (swahv), *adj.* smoothly polite. —**suave′ly,** *adv.* —**suav′i·ty, suave′ness,** *n.*

sub·com·mit′ee, *n.* committee reporting to a committee.

sub·con′scious, *n.* **1.** part of the mind beyond consciousness. —*adj.* **2.** pertaining to this part of the mind. —**sub·con′scious·ly,** *adv.*

sub·con′ti·nent, *n.* large land mass within a continent.

sub·di·vide″, *v.t.,* **-vided, -viding.** divide still further. —**sub′di·vi″sion,** *n.*

sub·due′, *v.t.,* **-dued, -duing. 1.** overcome. **2.** lower in intensity.

sub·ject, *n.* (sub′jekt) **1.** thing thought, written, etc. about. **2.** person or thing acted upon. **3.** person ruled by a government. **4.** *Grammar.* person or thing about which a sentence tells. —*adj.* **5.** being a subject. **6.** exposed to a specified treatment. —*v.t.* (sub jekt′) **7.** submit to a specified treatment. —**sub·jec′tion,** *n.*

sub·jec′tive, *adj.* existing or originating in one person's mind. —**sub·jec′tive·ly,** *adv.* —**sub″jec·tiv′i·ty,** *n.*

sub·join′, *v.t.* add at the end.

sub′ju·gate″, *v.t.,* **-gated, -gating.** conquer. —**sub″ju·ga′tion,** *n.*

sub·junc′tive, *Grammar. adj.* **1.** pertaining to a verbal mode of possibility, etc. —*n.* **2.** subjunctive mode.

sub·lease′, *n., v.t.,* **-leased, -leasing. n.** (sub′lēs) **1.** lease from a tenant. —*v.t.* (sub lēs′) **2.** rent with such a lease.

sub·let′, *v.t.,* **-letted, -letting.** sublease.

sub·li·mate′, *v.t.,* **-mated, -mating,** *n., v.t.* (sub lə māt′) **1.** divert into a more acceptable form. **2.** sublime. —*n.* (sub′lə mət) **3.** product of subliming. —**sub″li·ma′tion,** *n.*

sub·lime′, *adj., n., v.t.,* **-limed, -liming.** *adj.* **1.** noble and exalted. —*n.* **2.** realm of sublime things. —*v.t.* **3.** vaporize, then solidify. —**sub·lime′ly,** *adv.* —**sub·lim′i·ty,** *n.*

sub·ma·rine′, *n.* (sub′mə rēn) **1.** underwater vessel. —*adj.* (sub mə rēn′) **2.** undersea. **3.** pertaining to submarines.

sub·merge′, *v.,* **-merged, -merging.** *v.t., v.i.* sink into a liquid. —**sub·mer′gence,** *n.*

sub·merse′, *v.t.,* **-mersed, -mersing.** submerge. —**sub·mer′sion,** *n.* —**sub·mers′i·ble,** *adj.*

sub·mit′, *v.,* **-mitted, -mitting.** *v.t.* **1.** offer, as in surrender. **2.** offer for consideration. **3.** subject to a specified treatment. —*v.i.* **4.** surrender or yield oneself. —**sub·mis′sion,** *n.* —**sub·mis′sive,** *adj.*

sub·or·di·nate, *v.t.,* **-ated, -ating,** *adj., n., v.t.* (sub ôr′də nāt″) **1.** subject to the will of another. —*adj.* (sub ôr′də nət) **2.** lower in rank or importance. —*n.* **3.** someone or something subordinate. —**sub·or″di·na′tion,** *n.*

sub·orn′, *v.t.* induce to commit a wrong.

sub·poe·na (sə pē′nə), *n., v.t.,* **-naed, -naeing. n. 1.** summons to court. —*v.t.* **2.** serve with such a summons.

sub·scribe′, *v.,* **-scribed, -scribing.** *v.i.* **1.** pay for continued supply of a periodical, service, etc. **2.** promise to contribute money. **3.** agree. —*v.t.* **4.** sign. —**sub·scrib′er,** *n.* —**sub·scrip′tion,** *n.*

sub′se·quent, *adj.* occurring after. —**sub′se·quent·ly,** *adv.*

sub·ser′vi·ent, *adj.* **1.** servile. **2.** subordinate. —**sub·ser′vi·ence,** *n.* —**sub·ser′vi·ent·ly,** *adv.*

sub·side′, *v.i.,* **-sided, -siding. 1.** settle or sink. **2.** die down. —**sub·sid′ence,** *n.*

sub·sid′i·ar″y, *adj., n., pl.* **-ries.** *adj.* **1.** subordinate or auxiliary. —*n.* **2.** subsidiary entity.

sub′si·dy, *n., pl.* **-dies.** monetary aid, esp. from a government. —**sub′si·dize″,** *v.t.*

sub·sist′, *v.i.* **1.** exist. **2.** maintain one's existence. —**sub·sist′ence,** *n.*

sub′stance, *n.* **1.** material. **2.** essential part or aspect. **3.** basic meaning.

sub·stan'tial, *adj.* **1.** solid. **2.** considerable in amount. **3.** material. **4.** essential. **5.** important in the community. —**sub·stan'tial·ly,** *adv.*

sub·stan'ti·ate, *v.t.,* **-ated, -ating.** show to be true. —**sub·stan''ti·a'tion,** *n.*

sub'stan·tive, *n.* **1.** noun or word used as a noun. —*adj.* **2.** pertaining to essences. **3.** serving as a substantive.

sub'sti·tute, *v.,* **-tuted, -tuting,** *n., v.t., v.i.* **1.** put or act in another's place. —*n.* **2.** person or thing that substitutes. —**sub'sti·tu'tion,** *n.*

sub'ter·fuge'', *n.* evasive trick or trickery.

sub''ter·ra'ne·an, *adj.* underground.

sub·tle (sut'əl), *adj.* **1.** highly sensitive. **2.** scarcely perceived. **3.** cunning. —**sub'tly,** *adv.* —**sub'tle·ty,** *n.*

sub·tract', *v.t.* remove, as one quantity from another. —**sub·trac'tion,** *n.*

sub·trop'i·cal, *adj.* close to the tropics.

sub·urb, *n.* community adjoining or dependent on a city. —**sub·ur'ban,** *adj.*

sub·vert', *v.t.* undermine or corrupt. —**sub·ver'sion,** *n.* —**sub·ver'sive,** *adj., n.*

sub'way'', *n.* **1.** underground railroad. **2.** pedestrian underpass.

suc·ceed', *v.i.* **1.** obtain good results. **2.** attain success. —*v.t.* **3.** follow in an office, inheritance, etc.

suc·cess', *n.* **1.** favorable outcome of an attempt. **2.** commonly sought goals. **3.** person or thing that attains success. —**suc·cess'ful,** *adj.*

suc·ces'sion, *n.* **1.** sequential order of things. **2.** act of succeeding another. —**suc·ces'sive,** *adj.* —**suc·ces'sive·ly,** *adv.* —**suc·ces'sor,** *n.*

suc·cinct (suk sinkt'), *adj.* restricted to essential information. —**suc·cinct'ly,** *adv.* —**suc·cinct'ness,** *n.*

suc'cor, *n., v.t.* help in need.

suc'co·tash, *n.* cooked corn and lima beans.

suc'cu·lent, *adj.* juicy. —**suc'cu·lence,** *n.*

suc·cumb', *v.i.* **1.** yield. **2.** die.

such, *adj.* **1.** of the kind mentioned. **2.** so much of. —*adv.* **3.** so greatly. —*pron.* **4.** the kind mentioned. **5.** such a person or thing.

suck, *v.t.* **1.** draw by suction. **2.** absorb by capillarity. **3.** lick and absorb.

suck'er, *n.* **1.** person or thing that sucks. **2.** fresh-water fish. **3.** lollipop. **4.** *Informal.* person easily cheated.

suck'le, *v.t.,* **-led, -ling.** feed at the breast.

suck'ling, *n.* unweaned child or animal.

suc'tion, *n.* forcing of a fluid into a vacuum by atmospheric pressure.

sud'den, *adj.* quick and unexpected. —**sud'den·ly,** *adv.* —**sud'den·ness,** *n.*

suds, *n., pl.* **1.** fine soap bubbles. **2.** soapy water.

sue, *v.,* **sued, suing.** *v.t.* **1.** claim damages from in court. —*v.i.* **2.** make an appeal.

suede (swād), *n.* soft leather with a nap.

su'et, *n.* hard animal fat.

suf·fer, *v.t.* **1.** undergo. **2.** permit or tolerate. —**suf'fer·er,** *n.*

suf'fer·ance, *n.* **1.** tacit permission. **2.** endurance.

suf·fice', *v.i.,* **-ficing, -ficing.** be enough.

suf·fi'cient, *adj.* enough. —**suf·fi'cient·ly,** *adv.* —**suf·fi'cien·cy,** *n.*

suf'fix, *n. Grammar.* ending added to a word to give a new meaning.

suf'fo·cate, *v.,* **-cated, -cating.** *v.t., v.i.* cut off or be without air for breathing. —**suf''fo·ca'tion,** *n.*

suf'frage, *n.* right to vote.

suf·fuse', *v.t.* spread light, color, etc. over.

sug'ar, *n.* **1.** sweet carbohydrate. —*v.t.* **2.** add sugar to. —**sug'ar·y,** *adj.*

sug·gest', *v.t.* **1.** offer as advice. **2.** propose. **3.** imply. —**sug·ges'tion,** *n.*

sug·ges'tive, *adj.* full of implication, esp. of impropriety.

su'i·cide'', *n.* **1.** willful killing of oneself. **2.** person who kills himself willfully. —**su''i·cid'al,** *adj.*

suit, *n.* **1.** complete set of clothes. **2.** lawsuit. **3.** appeal. **4.** playing cards with a common symbol. —*v.t.* **5.** satisfy; please. **6.** adapt. **7.** clothe.

suit'a·ble, *adj.* right; appropriate. —**suit'a·bly,** *adv.*

suit'case'', *n.* travel case for clothes, etc.

suite (swēt), *n.* **1.** apartment of connected rooms. **2.** set of musical compositions.

suit'or, *n.* wooer.

sul'fate, *n.* salt of sulfuric acid.

sul·fur'ic, *adj.* pertaining to or containing sulfur. Also, **sul'fur·ous.**

sulk, *v.i.* **1.** be angry and aloof. —*n.* **2.** fit of sulking. —**sulk'y,** *adj.*

sul'len, *adj.* **1.** quietly resentful. **2.** gloomy. —**sul'len·ly,** *adv.* —**sul'len·ness,** *n.*

sul'ly, *v.t.,* **-lied, -lying. 1.** disgrace. **2.** soil or pollute.

sul'phur, *n.* sulfur.

sul'tan, *n.* Muslim ruler.

sul'try, *adj.,* **-trier, -triest. 1.** hot and humid. **2.** sexually inviting —**sul'tri·ness,** *n.*

sum, *n., v.t.,* **summed, summing.** *n.* **1.** number obtained by addition. **2. in sum,** as a summary. —*v.t.* **3.** add up. **4.** summarize.

su·mac (shoo'mak), *n.* small tree. Also, **su'mach.**

sum'ma·rize, *v.t.,* **-rized, -rizing.** present in a summary.

sum'ma·ry, *n., pl.* **-ries,** *adj., n.* **1.** presentation of essential information only. —*adj.* **2.** without formalities or preliminaries. —**sum·ma'ri·ly,** *adv.*

sum·ma'tion, *n.* concluding summary.

sum'mer, *n.* **1.** season between spring and autumn, beginning at the summer solstice. —*v.i.* **2.** spend the summer. —**sum'mer·y,** *adj.*

sum'mit, *n.* highest point.

sum'mon, *v.t.* order or ask to come.

sum'mons, *n.* **1.** order to appear in court. **2.** order or request to come.

sump, *n.* pit for collecting ground water.

sump'tu·ous, *adj.* costly and luxurious. —**sump'tu·ous·ly,** *adv.* —**sump'tu·ous·ness,** *n.*

sun, *n., v.t.,* **sunned, sunning.** *n.* **1.** star of the solar system. **2.** rays from this star. —*v.t.* **3.** expose to the sun. —**sun'ny,** *adj.* —**sun'beam'',** *n.* —**sun'light'',** *n.* —**sun'lit'',** *adj.*

sun'bathe'', *v.i.,* **-bathed, -bathing.** lie down to receive solar rays. —**sun'bath,** *n.*

sun'burn'', *n., v.t.,* **-burned, -burning.** burn from or with the rays of the sun.

sun'dae, *n.* ice cream topped with flavored syrup.

Sun'day, *n.* first day of the week.

sun'di''al, *n.* instrument telling time by the shadow of a pointer.

sun'down'', *n.* time of sunset.

sun·dry (sun'drē), *adj.* various.

sun'flow''er, *n.* tall plant with large, yellow-petaled blossoms.

sun'glas''ses, *n., pl.* spectacles tinted to weaken the sun's rays.

sun'lamp'', *n.* ultraviolet lamp.

sun'rise'', *n.* rise of the sun above the horizon.

sun'set'', *n.* descent of the sun below the horizon.

sun'shine, *n.* rays of the sun.

sun'stroke'', *n.* collapse from overexposure to the sun.

sun'tan'', *n.* darkening of the skin resulting from sunbathing.

sup, *v.i.,* **supped, supping.** have supper

su·perb', *adj.* admirably excellent. —**su·perb'ly,** *adv.*

su·per·cil·i·ous (sōō''pər sil'ē əs), *adj.* proudly contemptuous. —**su''per·cil'i·ous·ly,** *adv.* —**su''per·cil'i·ous·ness,** *n.*

su''per·fi'cial, *adj.* **1.** on the surface only. **2.** lacking depth of thought or feeling. —**su''per·fi'cial·ly,** *adv.* —**su''per·fi·ci·al'i·ty,** *n.*

su·per'flu·ous, *adj.* **1.** more than is useful. **2.** redundant; useless. —**su·per'flu·ous·ly,** *adv.* —**su''per·flu'i·ty,** *n.*

su''per·hu'man, *adj.* beyond ordinary human limitations.

su''per·im·pose'', *v.t.,* **-posed, -posing.** place over something else.

su''per·in·tend'', *v.t.* supervise. —**su''per·in·ten'dence,** *n.* —**su''per·in·ten'dent,** *n., adj.* —**su''per·in·ten'den·cy,** *n.*

su·pe'ri·or, *adj.* **1.** better. **2.** excellent. **3.** proud; haughty. **4.** higher in position. —*n.* **5.** superior person. **6.** head of a religious community. —**su·pe'ri·or'i·ty,** *n.*

su·per'la·tive, *adj.* **1.** of the highest excellence. **2.** *Grammar.* denoting the extreme in a comparison. —*n.* **3.** something superlative. —**su·per'la·tive·ly,** *adv.*

su''per·nat'u·ral, *adj.* **1.** outside the laws of nature. —*n.* **2.** realm of things outside such laws. —**su''per·nat'u·ral·ly,** *adv.*

su''per·nu'mer·ar·y, *adj., n., pl.* **-ries.** *adj.* **1.** extra; nonessential. —*n.* **2.** something supernumerary. **3.** non-speaking actor.

su''per·scribe'', *v.t.,* **-scribed, -scribing.** write over. —**su''per·scrip'tion,** *n.*

su''per·sede'', *v.t.,* **-seded, -seding.** replace, esp. in importance or function.

su''per·son'ic, *adj.* pertaining to speeds faster than that of sound.

su''per·sti'tion, *n.* unconfirmed belief, esp. in the supernatural. —**su''per·sti'tious,** *adj.* —**su''per·sti'tious·ly,** *adv.*

su''per·struc'ture, *n.* upper structure.

su''per·vene'', *v.i.,* **-vened, -vening.** **1.** arrive or occur in addition. **2.** occur afterward. —**super·ven'tion,** *n.*

su'per·vise'', *v.t.,* **-vised, -vising.** direct and inspect. —**su'per·vis'or,** *n.* —**su''per·vi'so·ry,** *adj.* —**su''per·vi'sion,** *n.*

su'pine, *adj.* **1.** lying on the back. **2.** wrongly passive. —**su'pine·ly,** *adv.*

sup'per, *n.* late dinner.

sup·plant', *v.t.* replace, as in favor or function.

sup'ple, *adj.,* **-pler, -plest.** flexible. —**sup'ple·ly,** *adv.* —**sup'ple·ness,** *n.*

sup·ple·ment, *n.* (sup'plə mənt) **1.** desirable addition. —*v.t.* (sup'pləment'') **2.** give a supplement to. —**sup''ple·men'tal, sup''ple·men'ta·ry,** *adj.*

sup'pli·cate'', *v.t.,* **-cated, -cating.** implore. —**sup''pli·ca'tion,** *n.* —**sup''pli·ant, sup'pli·cant,** *n.*

sup·ply', *v.t.,* **-plied, -plying,** *n., pl.* **-plies.** *v.t.* **1.** provide, as goods. **2.** fill, as a need. —*n.* **3.** act or instance of supplying. **4.** something supplied. **5.** stock, as of goods. —**sup·pli'er,** *n.*

sup·port', *v.t.* **1.** hold up. **2.** provide a livelihood for. **3.** endure. **4.** be loyal to. **5.** confirm. —*n.* **6.** someone or something that supports.

sup·pose', *v.t.,* **-posed, -posing.** **1.** assume as true. **2.** expect to act as stated. —**sup·pos'ed·ly,** *adv.* —**suppo·si'tion,** *n.*

sup·press', *v.t.* **1.** force into inaction. **2.** kept from being known or apparent. —**sup·pres'sion,** *n.*

sup·pu·rate (sup'yə rāt), *v.i.*, **-rated, -rating.** form pus. —**sup'pu·ra'tion,** *n.*

su·preme', *adj.* highest or greatest. —**su·preme'ly,** *adv.* —**su·prem'a·cy,** *n.*

sur·charge, *n., v.t.,* **-charged, -charging.** *n.* (sər'chärj) 1. added or excessive charge. —*v.t.* 2. (sər chärj') 2. impose a surcharge on.

sure (shŏŏr), *adj.,* **surer, surest.** 1. convinced; positive. 2. reliant. 3. reliable. 4. unerring. 5. *Informal.* yes indeed. —**sure'ly,** *adv.*

sure·ty (shŏŏr'ĭ tē, shŏŏr'tē), *n., pl.* **-ties.** 1. certainty. 2. security against risk. 3. guarantor.

surf, *n.* waves breaking against land, shoals, etc.

sur'face, *n., adj., v.,* **-faced, -facing.** *n.* 1. outer area. 2. upper area of a body of water. 3. outer appearance. —*adj.* 4. apparent; specious. —*v.t.* 5. finish or dress the surface of. —*v.i.* 6. come to the surface, as of a body of water.

sur·feit (sər'fĭt), *n.* 1. excess, as of eating or drinking. 2. revulsion from such excess. —*v.t.* 3. cause to feel such revulsion.

surge, *v.i.* **surged, surging,** *n., v.i.* 1. move in a sudden swell. 2. gather volume or force suddenly. —*n.* 3. act or instance of surging.

sur'geon, *n.* practitioner of surgery.

sur'ger·y, *n., pl.* **-ries** *n.* 1. treatment of illness by physical rather than chemical means. 2. place where such treatment is given. —**sur'gi·cal,** *adj.* —**sur'gi·cal·ly,** *adv.*

sur'ly, *adj.,* **-lier, -liest.** sullenly ill-tempered. —**sur'li·ness,** *n.*

sur·mise', *v.t.,* **-mised, -mising,** *n.* guess.

sur·mount', *v.t.* 1. get or be on top of. 2. overcome, as an obstacle. —**sur·mount'a·ble,** *adj.*

sur'name'', *n.* last name; family name.

sur·pass', *v.t.* 1. be superior to. 2. exceed.

sur·plice (sər'plĭs), *n.* loose-fitting robe.

sur'plus, *adj.* 1. beyond the needed amount. —*n.* 2. surplus amount.

sur·prise', *n., v.t.,* **-prised, -prising.** *n.* 1. emotion on encountering the unexpected. 2. unexpected occurrence. —*v.t.* 3. fill with surprise. 4. attack, etc. when not expected.

sur·ren'der, *v.t.* 1. give up. —*v.i.* 2. yield to superior force. —*n.* 3. act or instance of surrendering.

sur''rep·ti'tious, *adj.* stealthy. —**sur''rep·ti'tious·ly,** *adv.*

sur'ro·gate'', *n.* 1. substitute. 2. judge for legacies and estates.

sur·round', *v.t.* enclose or be close to on all sides. —**surrounding,** *adj.*

sur·round'ings, *n., pl.* things all around; environment.

sur'tax'', *n.* tax added to a tax.

sur·veil'lance, *n.* close observation.

sur·vey', *v.t., n., pl.* **-veys.** *v.t.* (sər vā') 1. measure or evaluate precisely. 2. view. —*n.* (sər'vā) 3. act or instance of surveying. 4. general summary. —**sur'vey·or,** *n.*

sur·vive', *v.,* **-vived, -viving.** *v.i.* 1. remain alive. 2. outlive. —**sur·viv'or,** *n.* —**sur·viv'al,** *n.*

sus·cep·ti·ble (sus sep'tə bəl), *adj.* easily affected. —**sus·cep''ti·bil'i·ty,** *n.*

sus·pect, *v.t.* (səs pekt') 1. regard without trust. 2. guess. —*n.* (sus'pekt) 3. suspected person. —*adj.* 4. to be regarded without trust.

sus·pend', *v.t.* 1. hang. 2. postpone. 3. dismiss or expel temporarily.

sus·pen'ders, *n., pl.* straps for holding up the trousers.

sus·pense', *n.* anxiety due to uncertainty.

sus·pen'sion, *n.* 1. act or instance of suspending. 2. postponement. 3. distribution of particles throughout a fluid.

sus·pi'cion, *n.* 1. feeling of one who suspects. 2. state of being suspected. 3. trace.

sus·pi'cious, *adj.* 1. having suspicions. 2. arousing suspicion. —**sus·pi'cious·ly,** *adv.*

sus·tain', *v.t.* 1. maintain; continue. 2. support. 3. endure. 4. suffer. —**sus·tain'er,** *n.*

sus'te·nance, *n.* 1. means of existence. 2. act or instance of sustaining.

su·ture (sōō'chər), *n., v.t.,* **-tured, -turing.** *n.* 1. line of junction. 2. means by which a wound is sewn. —*v.t.* 3. join with a suture.

svelte, *adj.* slender.

swab, *n., v.t.,* **swabbed, swabbing.** *n.* 1. absorbent wiping device. —*v.t.* 2. wipe with a swab.

swag'ger, *v.i.* 1. walk arrogantly. —*n.* 2. swaggering gait.

swale, *n.* 1. low, marshy area. 2. valley-like area between slopes.

swal'low, *v.t.* 1. take down the throat. 2. suppress, as an emotion. 3. *Informal.* accept foolishly as true. —*n.* 4. small, forked-tailed bird. 5. act or instance of swallowing.

swamp, *n.* 1. area of wet land and water vegetation. —*v.t.* 2. drench. 3. overload, as with work. —**swamp'y,** *adj.*

swan, *n.* large, long-necked water bird.

swap, *v.t.,* **swapped, swapping,** *n. Informal.* exchange.

swarm, *n.* 1. large, unorganized group. —*v.i.* 2. move in a swarm.

swarth'y, *adj.,* **-ier, -iest.** rather dark-skinned. —**swarth'i·ness,** *n.*

swash'buck'ling, *adj.* showily brave or belligerent.

swas'ti·ka, *n.* cross with end pieces form-

ing right angles: in one form the Nazi symbol.

swat, *v.t.*, **swatted, swatting**, *n. Informal*, *v.t.* 1. hit sharply. —*n.* 2. act or instance of swatting. —**swat'ter**, *n.*

swath (swoth), *n.* mown pathlike area.

sway, *v.i.* 1. move unsteadily from side to side. —*v.t.* 2. influence through argument. —*n.* 3. act or instance of swaying. 4. domination.

swear, *v.*, **swore, sworn, swearing**. *v.t.* 1. affirm with an oath. 2. bind with an oath. —*v.i.* 3. utter profanity.

sweat, *v.i.*, **sweat** or **sweated, sweating**, *n., v.i.* 1. pass moisture through the pores. 2. accumulate surface moisture. —*n.* 3. sweated body moisture. 4. sweating condition. —**sweat'y**, *adj.*

sweat'er, *n.* knitted garment covering the area from waist to neck.

sweep, *v.*, **swept, sweeping**. *v.t.* 1. free of loose dirt, etc., esp. with brushing motions. 2. free of enemies or rivals. —*v.i.* 3. move swiftly and continuously. —*n.* 4. act or instance of sweeping. 5. scope.

sweep'stakes'', *n.* race for a prize given by the competitors.

sweet, *adj.* 1. somewhat sugarlike in taste. 2. agreeable, esp. to the senses. 3. gentle. —*n.* 4. piece of candy, etc. —**sweet'ly**, *adv.* —**sweet'ness**, *n.* —**sweet'en**, *v.t., v.i.*

sweet'heart'', *n.* loved one.

sweet'pea'', *n.* fragrant, flowering climbing plant.

sweet potato, trailing plant with sweet, edible, orange root.

swell, *v.*, **swelled, swelled** or **swollen, swelling**, *n., adj., v.t., v.i.* 1. expand beyond natural size from pressure. —*n.* 2. act or instance of swelling. 3. large rounded ocean wave or waves. —*adj.* 4. *Informal.* excellent.

swel'ter, *v.i.* suffer from heat.

swerve, *v.*, **swerved, swerving**, *n., v.t., v.i.* 1. turn suddenly aside. —*n.* 2. act or instance of swerving.

swift, *adj.* 1. quick or prompt. 2. fast. —*n.* 3. fast, swallowlike bird. —**swift'ly**, *adv.* —**swift'ness**, *n.*

swig, *n., v.t.*, **swigged, swigging**. *Informal. n.* 1. swallow. —*v.t.* 2. drink in swallows.

swill, *v.t.* 1. drink greedily. —*n.* 2. liquified garbage used as pig food.

swim, *v.i.*, **swam, swum, swimming**, *n., v.i.* 1. move through water by actions of the body. 2. be drenched or immersed. 3. be confused or dizzy. —*n.* 4. occasion of swimming. —**swim'mer**, *n.*

swin'dle, *v.t.*, **-dled, -dling**, *n., v.t.* 1. cheat. 2. fraud. —**swin'dler**, *n.*

swine, *n., pl.* **swine**. pig or hog.

swing, *v.*, **swung, swinging**, *n., v.t., v.i.* 1. move back and forth through part of a circle. 2. move one way in a circular path. —*n.* 3. suspended seat for swinging. 4. swinging blow. 5. act, example, or magnitude of swinging.

swipe, *v.t.*, **swiped, swiping**. *n. Informal. v.t.* 1. steal. 2. hit with a swinging blow. —*n.* 3. act or instance of swiping.

swirl, *v.t., v.i., n.* whirl.

swish, *v.t., v.i.* 1. whirl through the air with a sound. —*n.* 2. sound of such whirling.

switch, *n.* 1. change. 2. device for controlling electric current. 3. device for directing train movements. 4. rodlike whip. 5. change or exchange. 6. control or direct with a switch. 7. beat with a switch. —**switch'board''**, *n.*

swiv'el, *n.* 1. rotating support. —*v.t., v.i.* 2. turn on or as if on a swivel.

swoon, *n., v.i.* faint.

swoop, *v.i.* 1. descend speedily, as a bird of prey. —*n.* 2. act or instance of swooping.

sword (sōrd), *n.* long, sharp-pointed or -bladed weapon. —**sword'play''**, *n.* —**swords'man**, *n.*

sword'fish'', *n.* large salt-water fish with swordlike upper jawbone.

syb'a·rite'', *n.* lover of luxury. —**syb''a·rit'ic**, *adj.*

syc'a·more'', *n. U.S.* plane tree.

syc·o·phant (sīk'ə fənt), *n.* flatterer and parasite. —**syc'o·phan·cy**, *n.*

syl'la·ble, *n.* individual sound that is part of a spoken word. —**syl·lab'ic**, *adj.*

syl'la·bus, *n., pl.* **-buses, -bi.** academic course outline.

sylph, *n.* graceful, slender woman.

syl'van, *adj.* 1. pertaining to forests. 2. forested.

sym'bol, *n.* 1. something representing another thing. 2. sign representing instructions or orders. —**sym·bol'ic, sym·bol'i·cal**, *adj.* —**sym·bol'i·cal·ly**, *adv.* —**sym'bol·ize''**, *v.t.*

sym'bol·ism, *n.* group of symbols.

sym'me·try, *n., pl.* **-tries.** 1. mirror-image uniformity on opposite sides. 2. harmony of arrangement. —**sym·met'ric, sym·met'ri·cal**, *adj.* —**sym·met'ri·cal·ly**, *adv.*

sym'pa·thize'', *v.i., v.i.*, **-thized, -thizing.** 1. be in sympathy. 2. express sympathy. —**sym''pa·thiz'er**, *n.*

sym'pa·thy, *n., pl.* **-thies.** 1. oneness of feeling or opinion. 2. regret for another's unhappiness. 3. loyalty. —**sym''pa·thet'ic**, *adj.* —**sym''pa·thet'i·cal·ly**, *adv.*

sym'pho·ny, *n., pl.* **-nies.** major orchestral composition. —**sym·phon'ic**, *adj.*

sym·po'si·um, *n., pl.* **-siums, -sia.** 1. formal discussion by experts. 2. collection of papers on a topic.

symp'tom, *n.* characteristic indication, esp. of an illness. —**symp''to·mat'ic,** *adj.*

syn'a·gogue'', *n.* congregation or house of Jewish worship.

syn'chro·nize'', *v.t.,* **-nized, -nizing. 1.** cause to occur at the same time or rate of speed. **2.** cause to register the same time. —**syn''chro·ni·za'tion,** *n.* —**syn'chro·nous,** *adj.*

syn'co·pate'', *v.t.,* **-pated, -pating.** *Music.* stress the normally unaccented beat. —**syn''co·pa'tion,** *n.*

syn·di·cate, *n., v.t.,* **-cated, -cating.** *n.* (sin'də kit) **1.** organization of independent organizations for a major effort. **2.** organization selling material to newspapers. —*v.t.* (sin'di kāt'') **3.** sell as a syndicate to newspapers. —**syn''di·ca'tion,** *n.*

syn'drome'', *n.* group of symptoms of a given illness.

syn''fuel'', *n.* synthetic fuel.

syn·od (sin'əd), *n.* ecclesiastical council.

syn'o·nym, *n.* different word of similar meaning. —**syn·on'y·mous,** *adj.* —**syn·on'y·mous·ly,** *adv.*

syn·op'sis, *n., pl.* **-ses.** summary; brief outline.

syn'tax, *n.* arrangement of words, as in a sentence.

syn'the·sis, *n., pl.* **-ses.** combination of different parts.

syn'the·size'', *v.t.,* **-sized, -sizing.** make into or as a synthesis.

syn·thet'ic, *adj.* **1.** imitating a natural material, esp. in composition. **2.** pertaining to synthesis. —**syn·thet'i·cal·ly,** *adv.*

syph'i·lis, *n.* a venereal disease. —**syph''i·lit'ic,** *adj., n.*

syr·inge', *n.* plunger-operated device for drawing up and ejecting fluids.

sy'rup, *n.* heavy, sweet liquid, esp. one of sugar and water. —**syr'up·y,** *adj.*

sys'tem, *n.* **1.** order or method. **2.** coordinated arrangement of working elements. —**sys''tem·at'ic,** *adj.* —**sys''tem·at'i·cal·ly,** *adv.*

sys'tem·a·tize'', *v.t.,* **-tized, -tizing.** arrange according to a system.

sys·to·le (sis'tə lē), *n.* rhythmic contraction of the heart. —**sys·tol'ic,** *adj.*

T

T, t, . twentieth letter of the English alphabet.

tab, *n.* **1.** extension for pulling. **2.** bill of charges.

tab'by, *n., pl.* **-bies.** house cat.

tab'er·nac''le, *n.* place of worship.

ta'ble, *n., v.t.,* **-bled, -bling.** *n.* **1.** piece of furniture with a broad horizontal surface. **2.** orderly arrangement of data. —*v.t.* **3.** postpone, as legislation. —**ta'ble·cloth'',** *n.* —**ta'ble·ware'',** *n.*

tab'leau, *n., pl.* **-leaux.** picture: scene

ta·ble d'hôte (tah''bəl dōt'), *n.* fixed-price meal.

ta'ble·land'', *n.* plateau.

ta'ble·spoon'', *n.* spoon of one half a fluid ounce. —**ta'ble·spoon''ful,** *n.*

tab'let, *n.* **1.** slab for writing or lettering. **2.** pill. **3.** pad of paper.

tab'loid, *n.* small-format newspaper.

ta·boo', *n., pl.* **-boos,** *adj., v.t.,* **-booed, -booing.** *n.* **1.** prohibition, as by society. —*adj.* **2.** prohibited. —*v.t.* **3.** prohibit. Also, **ta·bu'.**

tab'u·lar, *adj.* in table form.

tab'u·late'', *v.t.,* **-lated, -lating.** arrange in a table. —**tab''u·la'tion,** *n.* —**tab'u·la''tor,** *n.*

tac'it, *adj.* understood though not stated. —**tac'it·ly,** *adv.*

tac'i·turn'', *adj.* choosing to speak little. —**tac''i·turn'i·ty,** *n.*

tack, *n.* **1.** short, pointed fastener. **2.** change of course. —*v.t.* **3.** fasten with tacks. **4.** cause to change course. —*v.i.* **5.** change course.

tack'le, *n., v.t.,* **-led, -ling.** *n.* **1.** equipment. **2.** system of ropes and pulleys. **3.** felling, as in football, by grasping the legs. —*v.t.* **4.** undertake. **5.** fell with a tackle.

tack'y, *adj.,* **-ier, -iest. 1.** sticky. **2.** *Informal.* of poor quality.

ta'co, *n.* folded and filled fried tortilla.

tact, *n.* sense of how not to offend —**tact'ful,** *adj.* —**tact'less,** *adj.*

tac'tics, *n.* **1.** science of maneuvering armed forces. **2.** connivance; artifice. —**tac'ti·cal,** *adj.* —**tac·ti'cian,** *n.*

tac'tile, *adj.* pertaining to touch. —**tac·til'i·ty,** *n.*

tad'pole'', *n.* larva of a frog or toad.

taf'fe·ta, *n.* stiff silky fabric.

taf'fy, *n.* chewy candy.

tag, *n., v.,* **tagged, tagging.** *n.* **1.** label attached with a cord. **2.** chasing game. —*v.t.* **3.** apply a tag to. —*v.i.* **4.** follow closely.

tail, *n.* **1.** distinct hindmost extremity of an animal. **2.** feature similar in shape or location, as on a vehicle. —**tail'gate'',** *n.* —**tail'light'',** *n.* —**tail'less'',** *adj.*

tail'or, *n.* **1.** maker of clothes. —*v.t.* **2.** make as a tailor does.

tail'spin'', *n.* winding plunge of an airplane.

taint, *v.t.* **1.** pollute or poison. —*n.* **2.** trace of pollution.

take, *v.,* **took, taken, taking.** *v.t.* **1.** carry.

2. escort. 3. accept. 4. seize. 5. make use of. 6. select. 7. require. 8. react to. 9. assume. 10. engage in. —*v.i.* 11. be effective.

take'off", *n.* beginning of a flight.

take'o"ver, *n.* assumption of control.

tak'ing, *adj.* 1. attractive. —*n.* 2. takings, profits.

talc, *n.* soft mineral. Also, **tal'cum.**

tale, *n.* 1. narrative. 2. piece of gossip. 3. lie. —**tale'bear"er**, *n.*

tal'ent, *n.* 1. personal ability. 2. person or persons of talent. —**tal'ent·ed**, *adj.*

tales'man, *n.* person called for jury duty.

tal'is·man, *n.* object warding off evil.

talk, *v.i.* 1. speak words. 2. confer. 3. gossip. —*v.t.* 4. persuade. —*n.* 5. conversation. 6. speech 7. gossip or rumor.

talk'a·tive, *adj.* loving to talk.

talk'ing-to", *n. Informal.* scolding.

tall, *adj.* 1. very high. 2. of a specified height.

tal'low, *n.* solid animal fat.

tal'ly, *n., pl.* **-lies,** *v.,* **-lied, -lying.** *n.* 1. sum. 2. account; score. —*v.t.* 3. add up. —*v.i.* 4. correspond.

Tal'mud, *n.* compilation of Hebrew law. —**Tal·mud'ic**, *adj.*

tal'on, *n.* bird claw.

ta·ma'le, *n.* Mexican dish of meat, red peppers, and corn meal in corn husks.

tam'bou·rine", *n.* shallow drumlike instrument.

tame, *adj.,* **tamer, tamest,** *v.t.,* **tamed, taming.** *adj.* 1. obedient to a master. 2. without spirit. —*v.t.* 3. make tame. —**tame'ly,** *adv.* —**tame'ness,** *n.* —**tam'a·ble, tame'a·ble,** *adj.* —**tam'er,** *n.*

tamp, *v.t.* pack or drive with gentle blows.

tam'per, *v.i.* interfere wrongly.

tan, *n., adj.,* **tanner, tannest,** *v.t.,* **tanned, tanning.** *n.* 1. yellow-brown. 2. suntan. —*adj.* 3. yellow-brown. —*v.t.* 4. convert into leather.

tan'a·ger, *n.* small, colorful American songbird.

tan'dem, *adv., adj.* with one behind the other.

tang, *n.* penetrating flavor. —**tang'y,** *adj.*

tan'gent, *n.* line touching a curve. —**tan·gen'tial,** *adj.* —**tan'gen·cy,** *n.*

tan"ger·ine', *n.* type of orange.

tan'gi·ble, *adj.* 1. able to be touched. 2. able to be defined. —**tan"gi·bil'i·ty,** *n.*

tan'gle, *v.,* **-gled, -gling,** *n., v.t.* 1. intertwine in a disorderly way. —*n.* 2. tangled state.

tan'go, *n., pl.* **-gos.** South American dance.

tank, *n.* 1. container for fluids. 2. armored fighting vehicle. —**tank'ful,** *n.*

tank'ard, *n.* tall mug with a side handle.

tank'er, *n.* ship carrying liquids in bulk.

tan'ner, *n.* maker of leather. —**tan'ner·y,** *n.*

tan'ta·lize", *v.t.,* **-lized, -lizing.** torment with gratification withheld. —**tan"tal·i·za'tion,** *n.*

tan'ta·mount", *adj.* equivalent.

tan'trum, *n.* outburst of rage.

tap, *v.,* **tapped, tapping,** *n., v.t., v.i.* 1. strike lightly. —*v.t.* 2. draw off or upon. —*n.* 3. light blow. 4. valve or plug.

tap dance, dance with light taps of the foot. —**tap'-dance",** *v.i.*

tape, *n., v.t.,* **taped, taping.** *n.* 1. thin, flat, long strip. —*v.t.* 2. bind with tape. 3. record on tape.

ta'per, *n.* 1. convergence of sides or edges. —*v.t., v.i.* 2. decrease steadily in thickness.

tap'es·try, *n., pl.* **-tries.** *n.* woven decorative panel.

tape'worm", *n.* flat parasitic worm.

tap"i·o'ca, *n.* starchy substance from cassava roots.

tap'root", *n.* single, deep-going root.

taps, *n. Military.* bugle call signifying retirement for the night and also played after military funerals.

tar, *n., v.t.,* **tarred, tarring.** *n.* 1. thick black liquid distilled from wood, coal, etc. —*v.t.* 2. coat with tar.

ta·ran'tu·la, *n.* large, hairy spider.

tar'dy, *adj.,* **-dier, -diest.** behind the expected time. —**tar'di·ly,** *adv.* —**tar'di·ness,** *n.*

tare, *n.* container weight.

tar'get, *n.* something aimed at.

tar'iff, *n.* 1. tax on imports or exports. 2. price or charge.

tar'nish, *v.t.* 1. spoil the luster of. —*v.i.* 2. become tarnished. —*n.* 3. tarnished state.

ta·rot (ta'rō), *n.* set of fortune-telling cards.

tar·pau'lin, *n.* waterproof cloth cover.

tar'pon, *n.* large west Atlantic game fish.

tar'ra·gon, *n.* seasoning of fragrant leaves.

tar·ry, *v.i.,* **-ried, -rying,** *adj. v.i.* (tar'ē) 1. linger. —*adj.* (tahr'ē) 2. covered with or suggesting tar.

tart, *adj.* 1. acid, as to the taste. —*n.* 2. small pie.

tar'tan, *n.* cloth pattern of crisscrossed bands of color.

tar'tar, *n.* 1. potassium salt used as a condiment. 2. deposit on the teeth. —**tar·tar'ic,** *adj.*

task, *n.* 1. something to be done. —*v.t.* 2. burden.

task'mas"ter, *n.* person who exacts work of others.

tas'sel, *n.* ornamental gathering of hanging threads.

taste, *v.,* **tasted, tasting,** *n., v.t.* 1. sense

with the tongue. 2. experience. —*v.i.* 3. have a specific flavor. —*n.* 4. sense operating through the tongue. 5. flavor. 6. sense of what is appropriate or seemly. 7. liking. —**tast'er**, *n.* —**taste'less**, *adj.*

taste'ful, *adj.* in good taste.

tast'y, *adj.*, **-ier, -iest.** good-tasting. —**tast'i·ness**, *n.*

tat'ter, *n.* 1. ragged fragment. —*v.t.* 2. reduce to tatters. —**tat'tered**, *adj.*

tat'tle, *v.i.*, **-tled, -tling.** gossip.

tat'tle·tale, *n.* betrayer of secrets.

tat·too', *v.t.*, **-tooed, -tooing**, *n.*, *pl.* **-toos**. *v.t.* 1. mark with pigments under the skin. —*n.* 2. tattooed design. 3. military drum or bugle signal.

taunt, *v.t.* 1. mock. —*n.* 2. mocking remark.

taut, *adj.* tight or tense. —**taut'ly**, *adv.* —**taut'ness**, *n.*

tau·tol'o·gy, *n.*, *pl.* **-gies**. use of redundant words. —**tau''to·log'i·cal**, *adj.*

tav'ern, *n.* public drinking place.

taw'dry,· *adj.*, **-drier, -driest**. cheap and showy. —**taw'dri·ly**, *adv.* —**taw'dri·ness**, *n.*

taw'ny, *adj.*, **-nier, -niest.** tan.

tax, *n.* 1. money exacted by a government. 2. demand on resources. —*v.t.* 3. exact a tax on or from. 4. accuse. —**tax'a·ble**, *adj.* —**tax·a'tion**, *n.* —**tax'pay''er**, *n.*

tax'i, *n.*, *pl.* **-is**, *v.i.*, **-ied, -iing** or **-ying**. *n.* 1. Also, **tax'i·cab''**, hired vehicle with metered charges. —*v.i.* 2. travel by taxi. 3. move without flying, as an airplane.

tax'i·der''my, *n.* art of simulating animals using their skins. —**tax''i·der'mist**, *n.*

tea, *n.* 1. drink made from the dried leaves of a shrub grown in Asia. 2. drink made from other leaves and flowers. 3. meal, etc. at which tea is served. —**tea'cup''**, *n.* —**tea'ket''tle**, *n.* —**tea'pot''**, *n.*

teach, *v.*, **taught, teaching**. *v.t.* 1. inform on a subject. 2. inform students regarding. —*v.i.* 3. be a teacher. —**teach'a·ble**, *adj.* —**teach'er**, *n.*

teak, *n.* brown East Indian hardwood.

teal, *n.*, *pl.* **teals, teal**. freshwater duck.

team, *n.* 1. group of animals or persons acting together. —*v.i.* 2. join or act in a team. —**team'mate''**, *n.* —**team'work''**, *n.*

tear, *v.*, **tore, torn, tearing**, *n.*, *v.t.* (ter) 1. pull apart by force. 2. make by piercing or rending. 3. lacerate or harass. —*v.i.* 4. be torn. 5. hurry. —*n.* 6. torn place. 7. (tēr) liquid from the weeping eye. —**tear'drop''**, *n.* —**tear'ful**, *adj.*

tea'room'', *n.* restaurant serving tea predominantly.

tease, *v.t.*, **teased, teasing**. 1. bother with gentle malice. 2. comb.

tea'spoon'', *n.* spoon holding one and a third fluid drams. —**tea'spoon·ful''**, *n.*

teat, *n.* nipple.

tech'ni·cal, *adj.* 1. pertaining to technology. 2. pertaining to technique. 3. pertaining to specific details. —**tech'ni·cal·ly**, *adv.* —**tech''ni·cal'i·ty**, *n.* —**tech·ni'cian**, *n.*

tech·nique', *n.* 1. working method. 2. proficiency. Also, **tech'nic.**

tech·nol'o·gy, *n.*, *pl.* **-gies**. application of science, esp. to industry. —**tech''no·log'i·cal**, *adj.*

te'di·um, *n.* wearisome or boring quality or state. —**te'di·ous**, *adj.*

tee, *n.* stand for a golf ball being driven.

teem, *v.i.* swarm.

teen'-age', *adj.* pertaining to the teens as an age. Also **teen'age''.** —**teen'ag''er**, *n.*

teens, *n.*, *pl.* 1. years of life between 13 and 19. 2. numbers in a series between 10 and 19.

tee'ny, *adj.*, **-nier, -niest.** *Informal.* tiny.

teethe, *v.i.*, **teethed, teething**. grow teeth.

tee·to'tal·er, *n.* total abstainer from alcohol. Also, **tee·to'tal·ler.**

tel'e·cast'', *v.t.*, **-cast** or **-casted, -casting**, *n.* broadcast via television. —**tel'e·cast''er**, *n.*

tel'e·graph'', *n.* 1. apparatus sending messages in code by electrical impulses. —*v.t.* 2. reach by telegraph. 3. send by telegraph. —**tel''e·graph'ic**, *adj.* —**te·leg'ra·phy**, *n.* —**te·leg'ra·pher**, *n.* —**tel'e·gram''**, *n.*

te·lep'a·thy, *n.* extra-sensory communication. —**tel''e·path'ic**, *adj.* —**te·lep'a·thist**, *n.*

tel'e·phone'', *n.*, *v.t.*, **-phoned, -phoning**. *n.* 1. device for transmitting personal spoken messages. —*v.t.* 2. reach by telephone. 3. transmit by telephone. —**tel''e·phon'ic**, *adj.*

tel'e·scope'', *n.*, *v.*, **-scoped, scoping**. *n.* 1. device for magnifying distant images. —*v.t.*, *v.i.* 2. slide lengthwise into one another. —**tel''e·scop'ic**, *adj.*

tel''e·type'writ''er, *n.* telegraphic apparatus sending and receiving typed messages.

tel'e·vise'', *v.t.*, **-vised, -vising**. transmit by television.

tel'e·vi''sion, *n.* 1. method of transmitting images by radio waves and electrical impulses. 2. industry using this method. 3. television receiving set.

tell, *v.*, **told, telling**. *v.t.* 1. inform. 2. recount. 3. order. 4. distinguish; recognize. —*v.i.* 5. give a narrative. 6. have an effect. —**tel'ling**, *adj.* —**tel'ling·ly**, *adv.*

tel'ler, *n.* 1. narrator. 2. bank clerk.

tell'tale'', *adj.* secret-revealing.

te·mer'i·ty, *n.* audacity.

tem'per, *n.* 1. mood. 2. anger. 3. control of one's anger. 4. hardness and flexibility, as of steel. —*v.t.* 5. moderate. 6. give toughness to.

tem'per·a, *n.* paint with egg, glue, etc.

tem'per·a·ment, *n.* natural mental disposition. —**tem''per·a·men'tal,** *adj.*

tem'per·ance, *n.* moderation, esp. in drinking.

tem'per·ate, *adj.* 1. moderate. 2. **Temperate,** situated between a tropic and the Arctic or Antarctic Circle.

tem'per·a·ture, *n.* 1. relative heat. 2. condition of excessive body heat.

tem'pered, *adj.* 1. modified. 2. having a specified temperament.

tem'pest, *n.* violent storm. —**tem·pes'tu·ous,** *adj.*

tem'plate, *n.* pattern for forming.

tem'ple, *n.* 1. place of worship. 2. area to either side of the brow.

tem'po, *n., pl.* **-pos, -pi.** rate of speed, as for music.

tem'po·ral, *adj.* 1. worldly, not spiritual. 2. pertaining to time.

tem'po·rar''y, *adj.* for a limited time. —**tem''po·rar'i·ly,** *adv.*

tem'po·rize'', *v.i.,* **-rized, -rizing.** evade argument or time requirements. —**tem''po·ri·za'tion,** *n.*

tempt, *v.t.* create an appetite or inclination in. —**temp·ta'tion,** *n.* —**tempt'er,** *fem.,* **tempt'ress,** *n.*

ten, *n.* nine plus one.

ten'a·ble, *adj.* defensible, as an argument. —**ten''a·bil'i·ty,** *n.* —**ten'a·bly,** *adv.*

te·na'cious, *adj.* 1. holding firmly. 2. stubborn. —**te·na'cious·ly,** *adv.* —**te·nac'i·ty,** *n.*

ten'ant, *n.* renter of building space or land. —**ten'an·cy,** *n.*

tend, *v.i.* 1. have a tendency. —*v.t.* 2. manage or care for.

ten'den·cy, *n., pl.* **-cies.** mild predominance of a certain result, preference, etc.

ten·den'tious, *adj.* expressed with a bias. —**ten·den'tious·ly,** *adv.*

ten'der, *adj.* 1. soft. 2. warmly affectionate. 3. feeling pain readily. —*n.* 4. person who tends. 5. railroad car for fuel. 6. something offered in payment. —*v.t.* 7. offer. —**ten'der·ly,** *adv.* —**ten'der·ness,** *n.* —**ten'der·heart'ed,** *adj.* —**ten'der·ize'',** *v.t.*

ten'der·foot'', *n., pl.* **-foots, -feet.** newcomer to out-of-door pursuits.

ten'der·loin'', *n.* 1. tenderest cut of beef or pork loin. 2. graft-ridden city neighborhood.

ten'don, *n.* muscle attachment.

ten'dril, *n.* attachment on a climbing plant.

ten'e·ment, *n.* 1. shabby apartment building. 2. apartment in such a building.

ten'et, *n.* doctrine accepted as truth.

tennis, *n.* game played with rackets and a ball.

ten'on, *n.* end of a rail, etc., held in the mortise of another such piece.

ten'or, *n.* 1. highest male singing voice. 2. gist.

ten'pins'', *n.* bowling game.

tense, *adj.,* **tenser, tensest,** *v.,* **tensed, tensing,** *n., adj.* 1. taut. 2. nervous: strained. —*v.t.* 3. make tense. —*v.i.* 4. become tense. —*n.* 5. *Grammar.* expression of past, present, future, etc. —**tense'ly,** *adv.* —**ten'sion, tense'ness, ten'si·ty,** *n.*

ten'sile, *adj.* capable of being stretched.

tent, *n.* 1. fabric shelter spread over poles. —*v.i.* 2. lodge in a tent.

ten'ta·cle, *n.* grasping or feeling attachment of an invertebrate.

ten'ta·tive, *adj.* made or done as a trial. —**ten'ta·tive·ly,** *adv.*

ten'ter·hook'', *n.* **on tenterhooks,** in suspense.

tenth, *adj.* 1. following nine others. —*n.* 2. one of ten equal parts.

ten'u·ous, *adj.* 1. thin. 2. insubstantial. —**ten'u·ous·ly,** *adv.* —**ten·u'i·ty, ten'u·ous·ness,** *n.*

ten'ure, *n.* 1. right to continuing employment. 2. occupation, as of public office.

te'pee, *n.* conical tent of American Indians.

tep'id, *adj.* lukewarm. —**te·pid'ity, tep'id·ness,** *n.* —**tep'id·ly,** *adv.*

te·qui'la, *n.* Mexican distilled liquor.

term, *n.* 1. word with a specific meaning. 2. period of time. 3. **terms, a.** requirements of an agreement. **b.** basis of a relationship.

ter'min·al, *n.* 1. station at the end of a railroad, etc. 2. electrical connecting point. 3. (computers) work station for data processing. —*adj.* 4. coming at the end. 5. causing death. —**ter''min·al·ly,** *adv.*

ter'mi·nate'', *v.,* **-nated, -nating.** *v.t., v.i.* finish. —**ter'mi·na·ble,** *adj.* —**ter''mi·na'tion,** *n.*

ter''mi·nol'o·gy, *n., pl.* **-gies.** employment of terms.

ter'mi·nus, *n., pl.* **-ni, -nuses.** 1. end or limit. 2. station at the end of a railroad, etc.

ter'mite, *n.* wood-eating insect.

tern, *n.* gull-like bird.

ter'race, *n., v.t.,* **-raced, -racing.** *n.* 1. raised outdoor platform. —*v.t.* 2. form in terraces.

ter''ra cot'ta, earthenware material used in building and decoration.

ter·ra fir'ma, dry land.

ter·rain', *n.* land with its natural features.

ter'ra·pin, *n.* type of turtle.

ter·rar'i·um, *n., pl.* **-iums, -ia.** glass box for growing small plants and animals.

ter·res'tri·al, *adj.* pertaining to the earth.

ter'ri·ble, *adj.* 1. bad; poor. 2. awesome.

ter'ri·bly, *adv.* 1. in a terrible manner. 2. *Informal.* extremely.

ter'ri·er, *n.* small hunting dog.

ter·rif'ic, *adj.* 1. awesome in force. 2. *Informal.* very good.

ter'ri·fy", *v.t.,* **-fied, -fying.** fill with terror.

ter'ri·to"ry, *n., pl.* **-ries.** 1. region without full political status. 2. distinct area of land. —**ter"ri·to'ri·al,** *adj.*

ter'ror, *n.* 1. great fear. 2. cause of such fear.

ter'ror·ism, *n.* use of terror to enforce demands. —**ter'ror·ist,** *n., adj.* —**ter"ror·is'tic,** *adj.*

ter'ror·ize", *v.t.,* **-ized, -izing.** intimidate with terror. —**ter"ror·i·za'tion,** *n.*

terse, *adj.,* **terser, tersest.** short-spoken; concise. —**terse'ly,** *adv.* —**terse'ness,** *n.*

ter'ti·ar"y, *adj.* third in order.

test, *n.* 1. act or event that reveals qualities, accomplishments, illnesses, etc. —*v.t.* 2. subject to a test. —*v.i.* 3. perform a test. —**test'er,** *n.*

tes'ta·ment, *n.* 1. *Law.* will. 2. part of the Bible. —**tes"ta·men'ta·ry,** *adj.*

tes'ta·tor, *n.* maker of a will.

tes'ti·cle, *n.* male sex gland.

tes'ti·fy", *v.,* **-fied, -fying.** *v.t., v.i.* bear witness.

tes"ti·mo'ni·al, *adj.* 1. expressing gratitude. —*n.* 2. recommendation.

tes'ti·mo"ny, *n., pl.* **-nies.** declaration.

tes'ty, *adj.,* **-tier, -tiest.** irritable. —**tes'ti·ly,** *adv.* —**tes'ti·ness,** *n.*

tet'a·nus, *n.* acute spasmodic disease.

tête-a-tête (tet'ə tet'), *n.* intimate conversation.

teth'er, *n.* 1. long tying rope. —*v.t.* 2. fasten with a tether.

tet"ra·he'dron, *n., pl.* **-drons, -dra.** four-sided solid.

text, *n.* 1. written matter. 2. textbook. —**tex'tu·al,** *adj.*

text'book", *n.* school book.

tex'tile, *n.* cloth.

tex'ture, *n.* surface quality. —**tex'tur·al,** *adj.*

than, *conj.* (introduces a basis of comparison).

thank, *v.t.* express gratitude to. —**thank'ful,** *adj.* —**thank'ful·ly,** *adv.* —**thank'less,** *adj.* —**thank'less·ly,** *adv.*

thanks, *n.* 1. gratitude. —*interj.* 2. I thank you.

thanks'giv"ing, *n.* 1. expression of

thanks to God. 2. **Thanksgiving,** U.S. holiday.

that, *pron., adj., pl.* **those,** *conj., pron., adj.* 1. the one. 2. the other. —*pron.* 3. which. —*conj.* 4. (used to introduce noun and adverbial clauses). —*adv.* 5. to such an extent.

thatch, *n.* 1. roof surface of straw, reeds, etc. —*v.t.* 2. cover with such a surface.

thaw, *v.i.* 1. warm above freezing. —*n.* 2. state of thawing.

the, *def. article.* (refers to a particular person, thing, or type).

the'a·ter, *n.* 1. place for plays, etc. 2. theatrical profession. Also, **the'a·tre.** —**the·at'ri·cal,** *adj.* —**the·at'ri·cal·ly,** *adv.*

theft, *n.* stealing.

their, *adj.* pertaining to them.

theirs, *pron.* something pertaining to them.

them, *pron.* (objective of they).

theme, *n.* 1. subject. 2. basic melody. —**the·mat'ic,** *adj.*

them·selves', *pron.* 1. (intensive and reflexive of they). 2. their true selves.

then, *adv.* 1. at that time. 2. and after. 3. in that case. —*n.* 4. that time.

thence, *adv.* from there or then.

thence"forth', *adv.* from then on. Also, **thence"for'ward.**

the·oc'ra·cy, *n., pl.* **-cies.** rule by priests. —**the"o·crat'ic,** *adj.*

the·ol'o·gy, *n., pl.* **-gies.** study of religious doctrine. —**the"o·log'i·cal,** *adj.* —**the"o·lo'gian,** *n.*

the'o·rem, *n.* something to be proved.

the'o·ry, *n., pl.* **-ies.** 1. statement of a possible truth. 2. untried assumption. —**the"o·ret'i·cal,** *adj.* —**the"o·ret'i·cal·ly,** *adv.* —**the'o·rize",** *v.i.* —**the'o·rist,** *n.*

the·os'o·phy, *n.* mystical religion. —**the"o·soph'ic,** *adj.* —**the·os'o·phist,** *n.*

ther"a·peu'tic, *adj.* aiding health. —**ther"a·peu'tics,** *n.*

ther'a·py, *n., pl.* **-pies.** healing process. —**ther'a·pist,** *n.*

there, *adv.* 1. at or to that place. 2. in that respect. 3. (used to introduce expressions of existence or nonexistence).

there·af'ter, *adv.* from then on.

there·by', *adv.* in connection with that.

there'fore", *adj.* for this reason.

there·in', *adv.* in that.

there·of', *adv.* of that.

there·on', *adv.* 1. on that. 2. just afterward.

there·to', *adv.* to that place.

there·up·on', *adv.* 1. just afterward. 2. in consequence.

ther'mal, *adj.* pertaining to heat.

ther·mom'e·ter, *n.* heat-measuring device.

ther″mo·nu′cle·ar, adj. pertaining to atomic fusion at high heat.

ther′mos, n. heat-insulated bottle.

ther′mo·stat″, n. heating control.

the·sau′rus, n., pl. -ri, -ruses. n. book of synonyms and antonyms.

the′sis, n. pl. -ses. 1. belief to be defended. 2. research paper.

thes′pi·an, n. 1. actor or actress. —adj. 2. pertaining to the theater.

they, n. (plural of he, she, or it.)

thick, n. 1. deep from front to back. 2. dense. —thick′ly, adv. —thick′ness, n. —thick′en, v.t., v.i.

thick′et, n. thick clump of shrubbery.

thick′set′, adj. stout.

thick′-skinned′, adj. coarse; insensitive.

thief, n., pl. thieves. person who steals. —thiev′er·y, n. —thiev′ish, adj.

thigh, n. upper leg. —thigh′bone″, n.

thim′ble, n. fingertip protector.

thin, adj., thinner, thinnest, v.t., thinned, thinning. adj. 1. shallow from front to back. 2. not dense; meager. —v.t. 3. make thin. —thin′ly, adv. —thin′ness, n. —thin′ner, n.

thing, n. inanimate entity.

think, v., thought, thinking. v.t. 1. have in the mind. 2. believe. —v.i. 3. employ the mind. —think′er, n.

thin′-skinned″, adj. sensitive to insult.

third, adj. 1. being number three. —n. 2. one of three equal parts.

thirst, n. desire to absorb liquids. —thirst′y, adj. —thirst′i·ly, adv.

thir·teen′, adj., n. ten plus three. —thir·teenth″, adj.

thir′ty, adj., n. three times ten. —thir′ti·eth, adj., n.

this, pron., adj., pl. these, adv., pron., adj. 1. (designating something near at hand). —adv. 2. to this extent.

this′tle, n. prickly plant.

thith′er, adv. to that place.

thong, n. small flexible strap.

tho′rax, n., pl. -raxes, -races. center of the body. —tho·rac′ic, adj.

thorn, n. spike of a plant stalk. —thorn′y, adj.

thor′ough, adj. complete in every detail. —thor′ough·ly, adv. —thor′ough·ness, n.

thor′ough·bred″, adj. pedigreed.

thor′ough·fare″, n. way through.

thor′ough·go′ing, adj. thorough.

thou, pron. Archaic. you.

though, conj. 1. despite the fact that. —adv. 2. however.

thought, n. 1. thinking process. 2. something thought. 3. something to consider. —thought′ful, adj. —thought′ful·ly, adv. —thought′ful·ness, n. —thought′less, adj. —thought′less·ly, adv. —thought′less·ness, n.

thou′sand, adj., n. ten times one hundred. —thou′sandth, adj., n.

thrash, v.t. beat vigorously.

thread, n. 1. length of spun fiber. 2. ridge on a screw. —v.t. 3. put a thread through.

thread′bare″, adj. worn thin.

threat, n. warning of revenge or danger.

threat′en, v.t. make or constitute a threat against.

three, n. two plus one.

thresh, v.t. separate from husks. —thresher, n.

thresh′old, n. doorway pavement.

thrice, adv. three times.

thrift, n. saving of money, etc.

thrift′y, adj., -ier, -iest. characterized by thrift. —thrift′i·ly, adv.

thrill, v.t. 1. excite emotionally. —v.i. 2. be excited emotionally. —n. 3. act or instance of thrilling.

thrive, v.i., thrived or throve, thrived or thriven, thriving. be prosperous or healthy.

throat, n. interior of the neck.

throb, v.i., throbbed, throbbing, n., v.i. 1. beat, as the heart or pulse, with more than usual force. —n. 2. act or instance of throbbing.

throe, n. pang.

throm·bo′sis, n. clotting of blood.

throne, n. chair of state.

throng, n., v.i. crowd.

throt′tle, n., v.t., -tled, -tling. n. 1. valve. —v.t. 2. squeeze and choke.

through, prep. 1. from end to end of. 2. by means of. —adv. 3. from end to end. —adj. 4. from end to end. 5. finished.

through·out′, prep. 1. in every part of. —adv. 2. in every part.

throw, v.t., threw, thrown, n., v.t. 1. propel unsupported. 2. send forcefully. —n. 3. act or instance of throwing. 4. distance of throwing. —throw′er, n.

throw′back″, n. reversion.

thru, prep., adv., adj. through.

thrush, n. songbird.

thrust, v., thrust, thrusting, n., v.t., v.i., n. push.

thud, v.i., thudded, thudding, n. boom with a dull sound.

thug, n. hoodlum.

thumb, n. 1. innermost hand digit. —v.t. 2. move with the thumb.

thumb′tack″, n. broad-headed tack.

thump, n. 1. heavy blow. 2. sound produced by such a blow.

thun′der, n. 1. sound following lightning. —v.t. 2. say loudly or vehemently. —thun′der·ous, adj. —thun′der·bolt″, n. —thun′der·clap″, n. —thun′der·cloud″, n. —thun′der·show″er, n. —thun′der·storm″, n.

thun′der·struck″, adj. stupefied with

amazement. Also, **thun'der·strick"en.**

Thurs'day, *n.* fifth day of the week.

thus, *adv.* **1.** in this way. **2.** to this extent. **3.** therefore.

thwart, *v.t.* obstruct.

thy, *adj. Archaic.* your.

thyme (tīm), *n.* plant used for seasoning.

thy'roid gland, ductless gland regulating growth.

thy·self', *pron. Archaic.* yourself.

ti·ar'a, *n.* woman's decorative coronet.

tic, *n.* repeated muscular spasm.

tick, *n.* **1.** sound of a mechanical clock. **2.** bloodsucking insect. **3.** mattress cloth. —*v.i.* **4.** make a ticking sound. —**tick' er,** *n.*

tick'et, *n.* **1.** paper giving admission. **2.** list of candidates.

tick'le, *v.,* **-led, -ling.** *v.t.* **1.** cause to twitch by light stroking. **2.** amuse. —*v.i.* **3.** cause tickling.

tick'lish, *adj.* **1.** susceptible to tickling. **2.** needing caution.

tid'bit", *n.* small morsel.

tide, *n.* periodic fluctuation of sea level. —**tid'al,** *adj.* —**tide'wa"ter,** *n., adj.*

ti'dings, *n., pl.* news.

ti'dy, *adj.,* **-dier, -diest,** *v.t.,* **-died, -dying.** *adj.* **1.** orderly. —*v.t.* **2.** make orderly. —**ti'di·ness,** *n.* —**ti'di·ly,** *adv.*

tie, *v.t.,* **tied, tying,** *n., v.t.* **1.** fasten with ropes, etc. **2.** equal in scoring. —*n.* **3.** something that ties. **4.** something that prevents spreading. **5.** equal score. **6.** necktie.

tier, *n.* horizontal row.

tie'-up", *n.* stoppage.

tiff, *n.* slight quarrel.

ti'ger, *n.* large catlike African and south Asian animal. Also, *fem.,* **ti'gress.**

tight, *adj.* **1.** preventing movement. **2.** fully stretched. —*adv.* **3.** securely. —*n.* **4.** tights, tight-fitting trousers. —**tight' ly,** *adv.* —**tight'ness,** *n.* —**tight'en,** *v.t., v.i.* —**tight'-fit"ting,** *adj.*

tight"-fist'ed, *adj.* stingy.

tight'rope", *n.* taut rope for balancing acrobats.

tile, *n., v.t.,* **tiled, tiling.** *n.* **1.** thin piece of material, originally baked earth. —*v.t.* **2.** furnish with tiles. —**til'ing,** *n.*

till, *prep., conj.* **1.** until. —*v.t.* **2.** prepare for growing crops. —*n.* **3.** money drawer. —**till'age,** *n.*

til'ler, *n.* steering lever.

tilt, *v.t., v.i.* **1.** slant from an upright position. —*n.* **2.** act or instance of tilting.

tim'ber, *n.* **1.** cut wood. **2.** trees collectively. —**tim'bered,** *adj.*

tim·bre (tam'bər), *n.* distinctive quality of sound.

time, *n., v.t.,* **timed, timing.** *n.* **1.** past, present, and future. **2.** Often, **times,** period of occurrence. **3.** instance. —*prep.* **4. times,** multiplied by. —*v.t.*

5. determine the time or duration of. —**tim'er,** *n.*

time'-hon'ored, *adj.* honored after long duration.

time'less, *adj.* eternal.

time'ly, *adj.,* **-lier, -liest.** coming at the right time. —**time'li·ness,** *n.*

time'piece", *n.* clock or watch.

time'serv"er, *n.* exploiter of popular trends. —**time'serv"ing,** *n., adj.*

time'ta"ble, *n.* schedule of times.

time'worn", *adj.* worn or hackneyed by long use.

tim'id, *adj.* lacking self-confidence. —**tim'id·ly,** *adv.* —**ti·mid'i·ty,** *n.*

tim'ing, *n.* performance with regard to time.

tim'or·ous, *adj.* fearful. —**tim'or·ous· ly,** *adv.*

tim'o·thy, *n.* grass used for hay.

tim·pa·ni, *n., pl.* kettledrums. —**tim'pa· nist,** *n.*

tin, *n., v.t.,* **tinned, tinning.** *n.* **1.** white metallic element. —*v.t.* **2.** plate with tin. —**tin'foil",** *n.* —**tin'smith",** *n.*

tinc'ture, *n.* **1.** tinge. **2.** medicine in alcohol.

tin'der, *n.* dry flammable material. —**tin' der·box".**

tine, *n.* fork prong.

tinge, *n., v.t.,* **tinged, tingeing** or **tinging.** *n.* **1.** slight color or trace. —*v.t.* **2.** give a tinge to.

tin'gle, *v.i.,* **-gled, -gling.** feel a slight prickle.

tin'ker, *v.i.* work inexpertly.

tin'kle, *v.i.,* **-kled, -kling,** *n., v.i.* **1.** ring lightly. —*n.* **2.** light ringing sound.

tin'sel, *n.* metal foil.

tint, *n.* **1.** light color or shade. —*v.t.* **2.** give a tint to.

ti'ny, *adj.,* **-nier, -niest.** very small.

tip, *n., v.,* **tipped, tipping.** *n.* **1.** outermost point. **2.** reward for a service. —*v.t., v.i.* **3.** overturn. —*v.t.* **4.** give a tip to. —**tip'per,** *n.*

tip'sy, *adj.,* **-sier, -siest.** intoxicated. —**tip'si·ly,** *adv.*

tip'toe", *v.i.,* **-toed, -toing.** walk on the balls of the feet.

tip'top", *adj.* **1.** highest. **2.** best.

ti'rade, *n.* vehement speech.

tire, *v.,* **tired, tiring,** *n., v.t.* **1.** make tired. —*v.i.* **2.** become tired. —*n.* **3.** wearing surface of a wheel.

tired, *adj.* without strength because of exertion. —**tired'ly,** *adv.*

tire'less, *adj.* without becoming tired. —**tire'less·ly,** *adv.*

tire'some, *adj.* annoying; tedious. —**tire' some·ly,** *adv.* —**tire'some·ness,** *n.*

tis'sue, *n.* **1.** thin cloth or paper. **2.** organic matter.

ti'tan, *n.* giant. —**ti·tan'ic,** *adj.*

tit'il·late'', *v.t.*, **-lated**, **-lating**. excite pleasantly. —**tit''il·la'tion**, *n.*

ti'tle, *n.*, *v.t.*, **-tled**, **-tling**. *n.* **1.** formal name. **2.** right of ownership. —*v.t.* **3.** give a title to. —**ti'tled**, *adj.*

tit'ter, *v.i.*, *n.* giggle.

tit'tle, *n.* minute amount.

tit'u·lar, *adj.* **1.** having a title. **2.** in name only. —**tit'u·lar·ly**, *adv.*

tiz'zy, *n.*, *pl.* **-zies**. *Informal*. excited state.

to, *prep.* **1.** as far as. **2.** in the direction of. **3.** until; before. **4.** being supported or held by. **5.** along with. **6.** in comparison or equivalence with.

toad, *n.* froglike animal.

toad'stool'', *n.* poisonous mushroom.

toast, *n.* **1.** browned sliced bread. **2.** drink in honor of someone. —*v.t.* **3.** brown with heat. **4.** drink in honor of. —**toas'ter**, *n.* —**toast'mas''ter**, *n.*

to·bac'co, *n.*, *pl.* **-cos**. leaves prepared for smoking, chewing, etc. —**to·bac'co·nist**, *n.*

to·bog'gan, *n.* **1.** long, flat sled. —*v.i.* **2.** coast on such a sled.

to·day', *adv.* **1.** on the present day. —*n.* **2.** present day. **3.** modern times.

tod'dle, *n.*, *v.i.*, **-dled**, **-dling**. *n.* **1.** unsteady walk. —*v.i.* **2.** walk in a toddle.

tod'dy, *n.*, *pl.* **-dies**. hot alcoholic drink.

toe, *n.* foot digit. —**toed**, *adj.* —**toe'nail''**, *n.*

to·geth'er, *adv.* one with another.

toil, *n.*, *v.i.* labor. —**toil'er**, *n.* —**toil'some**, *adj.*

toi'let, *n.* **1.** dress and grooming. **2.** place or fixture for excretion.

toil'et·ry, *n.*, *pl.* **-ries**. aid to grooming.

toils, *n.*, *pl.* snare.

to'ken, *n.* **1.** souvenir. **2.** indication. **3.** metal disk used in payment. —*adj.* **4.** intended as a token.

tol'er·ance, *n.* **1.** patience or understanding. **2.** permissible deviation. **3.** resistance to poison, etc. —**tol'er·ant**, *adj.*

tol'er·ate'', *v.t.*, **-ated**, **-ating**. **1.** be patient with. **2.** endure. —**tol''er·a'tion**, *n.* —**tol'er·a·ble**, *adj.* —**tol'er·a·bly**, *adv.*

toll, *n.* **1.** tariff. —*v.t.*, *v.i.* **2.** ring solemnly. —**toll'gate''**, *n.*

tom, *adj.* male.

tom'a·hawk'', *n.* American Indian ax.

to·ma'to, *n.*, *pl.* **-toes**. juicy red or yellow vegetable.

tomb, *n.* burial place. —**tomb'stone,''** *n.*

tom'boy'', *n.* boyish girl.

to·mor'row, *n.*, *adv.* day after this.

tom'-tom'', *n.* hand drum.

ton, *n.* U.S. unit of 2,000 pounds.

tone, *n.* **1.** sound of a certain pitch. **2.** shade of color. **3.** air or appearance. —**ton'al**, *adj.* —**to·nal'i·ty**, *n.* —**tone'deaf''**, *adj.*

tongs, *n.*, *pl.* pincers.

tongue, *n.* **1.** flexible licking and tasting organ in the mouth. **2.** language. **3.** projection.

tongue'-lash''ing, *n.* severe scolding.

tongue'-tied'', *adj.* rendered speechless.

ton'ic, *n.* **1.** invigorating medicine. **2.** *Music.* keynote.

to·night', *n.*, *adv.* this night.

ton'nage, *n.* shipping, esp. in terms of cargo capacity.

ton'sil, *n.* oval growth at the back of the throat. —**ton''sil·li'tis**, *n.*

ton·so'ri·al, *adj.* pertaining to barbering.

too, *adv.* **1.** also. **2.** excessively.

tool, *n.* **1.** object for shaping, fastening, etc. **2.** something or someone used. —*v.t.* **3.** shape with a tool.

toot, *v.i.* **1.** give a shrill whistle. —*n.* **2.** shrill whistle.

tooth, *n.*, *pl.* **teeth**. **1.** hard white growth used for biting. **2.** similar object in a gear, etc. —**tooth'ache''**, *n.* —**tooth'brush''**, *n.* —**toothed**, *adj.* —**tooth'less**, *adj.* —**tooth'pick''**, *n.* —**tooth'y**, *adj.*

tooth'some, *adj.* tasty.

top, *n.*, *v.t.*, **topped**, **topping**. *n.* **1.** uppermost point or part. **2.** spinning toy. —*v.t.* **3.** put a top on. **4.** remove a top from. **5.** surpass.

to'paz, *n.* yellow gem.

top'coat'', *n.* light overcoat.

top'-draw'er, *Informal*. first-rate. Also, **top'-flight'**, **top'-notch'**.

top'-heav''y, *adj.* liable to tip.

top'ic, *n.* subject of discussion. —**top'i·cal**, *adj.*

top'most'', *adj.* at the very top.

to·pog'ra·phy, *n.*, *pl.* **-phies**. **1.** study of the earth's surface. **2.** terrain. —**top''o·graph'i·cal**, **top''o·graph'ic**, *adj.* —**to·pog'ra·pher**, *n.*

top'ping, *n.* something put on top.

top'ple, *v.*, **-pled**, **-pling**. *v.t.*, *v.i.* overturn.

top'sail'', *n.* *Nautical.* second sail up.

top'soil'', *n.* fertile surface soil.

top'sy-tur''vy, *adj.*, *adv.* in disorder.

To'rah, *n.* Hebrew scriptures.

torch, *n.* flame-bearing object. —**torch'light''**, *n.*, *adj.*

tor'e·a·dor'', *n.* bullfighter.

tor·ment, *v.t.* (tor ment') **1.** harass or torture. —*n.* (tor'ment) **2.** tormented state. **3.** something that torments. —**tor·men'tor**, **tor·men'ter**, *n.*

tor·na'do, *n.*, *pl.* **-does**, **-dos**. violent whirlwind.

tor·pe'do, *n.*, *pl.* **-does**, *v.t.*, **-does**, **-doing**. *n.* **1.** explosive water projectile. —*v.t.* **2.** hit with a torpedo.

tor′pid, *adj.* without energy. —**tor′pid·ly,** *adv.* —**tor′por, tor·pid′i·ty,** *n.*

torque, *n.* twisting force.

tor′rent, *n.* rush of fluid. —**tor·ren′tial,** *adj.*

tor′rid, *adj.* 1. hot. 2. **Torrid,** between the tropics on either side of the equator.

tor′sion, *n.* twisting. —**tor′sion·al,** *adj.*

tor′so, *n., pl.* **-sos.** trunk of the human body.

tort, *n. Law.* basis of a civil suit.

tor·til·la (tôr tē′ya), *n.* flat Mexican cake of corn meal.

tor′toise, *n.* land turtle.

tor′tu·ous, *adj.* winding; involved. —**tor′tu·ous·ly,** *adv.* —**tor′tu·ous·ness,** *n.*

tor′ture, *n., v.t.,* **-tured, -turing.** *n.* 1. application of severe pain, etc. —*v.t.* 2. subject to torture. —**tor′tur·er,** *n.*

toss, *v.t.* 1. throw lightly. 2. jerk upward. —*n.* 3. act or instance of tossing.

toss′up″, *n.* even chance.

tot, *n.* small child.

to′tal, *adj.* 1. being a sum. 2. complete. —*n.* 3. sum. —**to′tal·ly,** *adv.* —**to·tal′i·ty,** *n.*

to·tal′i·tar′i·an·ism, *n.* absolute control by one political group. —**to·tal″i·tar′i·an,** *n., adj.*

tote, *v.t.,* **toted, toting.** carry.

to′tem, *n.* natural object used as a clan symbol. —**to·tem′ic,** *adj.*

tot′ter, *v.i.* walk unsteadily.

touch, *v.t.* 1. tap, pat, or feel. 2. move emotionally. —*n.* 3. act or instance of touching. 4. distinctive manner. 5. slight amount. —**touch′ing,** *adj.* —**touch′ing·ly,** *adv.*

touch and go, precarious situation.

touch′down, *n.* football score.

touched, *adj.* 1. emotionally moved. 2. insane.

touch′stone″, *n.* test of genuineness or worth.

touch′y, *adj.,* **-ier, -iest.** readily hurt or annoyed. —**touch′i·ness,** *n.*

tough, *adj.* 1. resistant to injury. 2. enduring. 3. brutal. 4. difficult. —**tough′ness,** *n.* —**tough′en,** *v.t., v.i.*

tou·pee (tōō pā′), *n.* small wig worn esp. by men.

tour, *n.* 1. trip with many stops. —*v.t.* 2. make a tour through.

tour de force, *n., pl.* **tours de force.** example of high skill.

tour′ist, *n.* person on a pleasure tour. —**tour′ism,** *n.*

tour′na·ment, *n.* 1. knightly contest. 2. series of athletic contests.

tour′ni·quet, *n.* twisted device to stop bleeding.

tou′sle, *v.t.,* **-sled, -sling.** muss.

tout, *Informal. v.t.* 1. praise highly. 2. sell bets. —*n.* 3. person who touts.

tow, *v.t.* 1. pull with a line. —*n.* 2. act or instance of towing. —**tow′line″, tow′rope″,** *n.* —**tow′path″,** *n.*

to·ward′, *prep.* in the direction of. Also, **to·wards′.**

tow′el, *n.* drying cloth.

tow′er, *n.* 1. tall construction. —*v.i.* 2. stand high.

tow′er·ing, *adj.* 1. standing high. 2. violent.

town, *n.* 1. large community. 2. urban center. —**towns′man,** *n.* —**towns′-peo″ple,** *n., pl.*

town′ship″, *n.* unit of local government.

tox′ic, *adj.* poisonous. —**tox·ic′i·ty,** *n.*

tox″i·col′o·gy, *n.* study of poisons. —**tox″i·col′o·gist,** *n.*

tox′in, *n.* poison from organisms.

toy, *n.* 1. something to play with. —*v.i.* 2. play; trifle.

trace, *n., v.t.,* **traced, tracing.** *n.* 1. faint sign or trail. —*v.t.* 2. follow the trail of. 3. copy by following the lines of. —**trace′a·ble,** *adj.* —**trac′er,** *n.* —**trac′ing,** *n.*

trac′er·y, *n., pl.* **-ies.** decorative frame in a window.

track, *n.* 1. trail or trace. 2. pair of rails, etc. used as a guide. —*v.t.* 3. follow or trace. —**track′less,** *adj.*

tract, *n.* 1. expanse of land. 2. series of bodily organs. 3. religious leaflet.

trac′ta·ble, *adj.* readily managed. —**trac′ta·bly,** *adv.* —**trac″ta·bil′i·ty,** *n.*

trac′tion, *n.* 1. pulling effort. 2. friction between a foot or wheel and a surface.

trac′tor, *n.* pulling vehicle.

trade, *v.,* **traded, trading,** *n., v.t.* 1. exchange. —*v.i.* 2. have business dealings. 3. make an exchange. —*n.* 4. buying and selling. 5. skilled occupation. 6. swap. —**trad′er,** *n.*

trade′-in″, *n.* return of a used object in partial payment for a new one.

trade′mark″, *n.* symbol of a business or product.

trade′off″, *n.* sacrifice of one advantage for another.

trades′man, *n.* 1. skilled worker. 2. merchant.

trade wind, tropical wind blowing toward the equator.

tra·di′tion, *n.* long-accepted custom or belief. —**tra·di′tion·al,** *adj.* —**tra·di′tion·al·ly,** *adv.* —**tra·di′tion·al·ist,** *n., adj.*

tra·duce′, *v.t.,* **-duced, -ducing.** slander.

traf′fic, *n., v.i.,* **-ficked, -ficking.** *n.* 1. movement along roadways. 2. commerce. —*v.i.* 3. have dealings. —**traf′fick·er,** *n.*

trag′e·dy, *n., pl.* **-ies.** 1. drama ending unhappily. 2. disastrous event. —**tra·ge′di·an,** *n., fem.,* **tra·ge′di·enne″.** —**trag′ic, trag′i·cal,** *adj.* —**trag′i·cal·ly,** *adv.*

trail, *n.* **1.** mark left in passing. **2.** route, esp. in wild country. —*v.t.* **3.** trace. **4.** drag. —*v.i.* **5.** drag or grow along the ground.

trail'er, *n.* vehicle pulled by another.

train, *n.* **1.** string of railroad cars. **2.** trailing skirt or cape. **3.** connected series. **4.** procession. —*v.t.* **5.** educate for a purpose. **6.** exercise for sports. —**train · ee',** *n.* —**train'er,** *n.* —**train'ing,** *n.*

traipse, *v.i.* **traipsed, traipsing.** *Informal.* walk.

trait, *n.* distinctive quality.

trai'tor, *n.* betrayer of one's country. —**trai'tor · ous,** *adj.*

tra · jec'to · ry, *n., pl.* **-ries.** path of a missile.

tram, *n.* car on rails.

tram'mel, *n.* **1.** Usually **trammels,** hindrance or restraint. —*v.t.* **2.** hinder or restrain.

tramp, *v.i.* **1.** walk heavily. **2.** travel on foot. —*n.* **3.** vagrant. **4.** hike. **5.** unscheduled freighter.

tram'ple, *v.,* **-pled, -pling.** *v.i.* **1.** tread heavily. —*v.t.* **2.** crush under foot.

tram · po · line (tram'pə lēn''), *n.* stretched horizontal sheet used by tumblers.

trance, *n.* sleeplike or abstracted state.

tran'quil, *adj.* serene; relaxed. —**tran' quil · ly,** *adv.* —**tran · quil'i · ty,** *n.* —**tran'quil · ize'',** *v.t.* —**tran'quil · iz''er,** *n.*

trans · act', *v.t.* complete, as a business deal. —**trans · ac'tion,** *n.* —**trans · ac' tor,** *n.*

trans''at · lan'tic, *adj.* **1.** from across the Atlantic Ocean. **2.** across the Atlantic Ocean.

tran · scend', *v.t.* **1.** go outside the limits of. **2.** surpass. —**tran · scend'ent,** *adj.*

tran''scen · den'tal, *adj.* beyond the limits of the apparent world. —**tran''scen · den'tal · ism,** *n.* —**tran''scen · den'tal · ist,** *n., adj.*

trans''con · ti · nen'tal, *adj.* across a continent.

tran · scribe', *v.t.,* **-scribed, -scribing.** copy elsewhere or in another medium.

tran'script, *n.* copy of a document.

tran · scrip'tion, *n.* **1.** transcript. **2.** arrangement of a musical score. **3.** radio or television recording.

tran'sept, *n.* arm of a church crossing the nave.

trans · fer', *v.,* **-ferred, -ferring,** *n., v.t., v.i.* (trans fər') **1.** move to another place. —*n.* (trans'fər) **2.** act or instance of transferring. **3.** authorization for transferring. —**trans · fer'a · ble,** *adj.* —**trans · fer'ence,** *n.*

trans · fig'ure, *v.t.,* **-ured, -uring.** make glorious. —**trans · fig''u · ra'tion,** *n.*

trans · fix', *v.t.* **1.** pierce. **2.** halt in one's tracks.

trans · form', *v.t., v.i.* change in nature.

—**trans''for · ma'tion,** *n.* —**trans · form' er,** *n.*

trans · fuse', *v.t.,* **-fused, -fusing. 1.** instill. **2.** admit to a blood vessel. —**trans · fu'sion,** *n.*

trans · gress', *v.t.* **1.** sin against. **2.** go beyond. —**trans · gres'sion,** *n.* —**trans · gres'sor,** *n.*

tran'sient, *adj.* **1.** temporary. —*n.* **2.** temporary lodger. —**tran'sient · ly,** *adv.* —**tran'science, tran'scien · cy,** *n.*

tran · sis'tor, *n.* device controlling electrical current flow. —**tran · sis'tor · ize'',** *v.t.*

tran'sit, *n.* **1.** movement from place to place. **2.** public transportation.

tran · si'tion, *n.* gradual change of nature or condition. —**tran · si'tion · al,** *adj.*

tran'si · tive, *adj. Grammar.* taking a direct object.

tran'si · to''ry, *adj.* impermanent. —**tran' si · to''ri · ness,** *n.*

trans · late', *v.t.,* **-lated, -lating. 1.** alter in language. **2.** alter in condition. —**trans · la'tion,** *n.* —**trans · la'tor,** *n.* —**trans · lat'a · ble,** *adj.*

trans · lit'er · ate', *v.t.,* **-ated, -ating.** put into a different alphabet, etc. —**trans · lit''er · a'tion,** *n.*

trans · lu'cent, *adj.* passing light but not images. —**trans · lu'cence, trans · lu'cen · cy,** *n.*

trans · mi'grate, *v.i.,* **-grated, -grating.** enter a new body after death. —**trans'' mi · gra'tion,** *n.*

trans · mis'sion, *n.* **1.** act or instance of transmitting. **2.** something transmitted. **3.** gear assembly.

trans · mit', *v.t.,* **-mitted, -mitting. 1.** convey through a medium. **2.** send out in radio waves. **3.** hand down, as to a new generation. —**trans · mit'tal, trans · mit' tance,** *n.* —**trans · mit'ti · ble, trans · mit' ta · ble,** *adj.* —**trans · mit'ter,** *n.*

trans · mute', *v.t.,* **-muted, -muting.** alter in nature. —**trans''mu · ta'tion,** *n.* —**trans · mut'a · ble,** *adj.*

trans''o · ce · an'ic, *adj.* across the ocean.

tran'som, *n.* **1.** crosspiece. **2.** window over a door.

trans''pa · cif'ic, *adj.* **1.** from across the Pacific Ocean. **2.** across the Pacific Ocean.

trans · par'ent, *adj.* **1.** passing light and images. **2.** obvious. —**trans · par'ent · ly,** *adv.* —**trans · par'en · cy,** *n.*

tran · spire', *v.i.,* **-spired, -spiring. 1.** become known. **2.** *Informal.* occur. —**tran''spi · ra'tion,** *n.*

trans · plant', *v.t.* **1.** plant in a new place. **2.** graft surgically. —*n.* **3.** act or instance of transplanting. —**trans''plan · ta'tion,** *n.*

trans · port', *v.t.* (trans pōrt') **1.** carry. —*n.* (trans'pōrt) **2.** transportation. **3.**

state of rapture. **4.** carrier for troops. —**trans′por·ta′tion**, *n.*

trans·pose′, *v.*, **-posed, -posing.** *v.t., v.i.* change in order or position. —**trans′po·si′tion**, *n.*

trans·sex′u·al, *n.* person who identifies with the opposite sex.

trans·ship′, *v.t.*, **-shipped, -shipping.** put on a new conveyance. —**trans·ship′ment**, *n.*

trans·verse′, *adj.* crosswise. —**trans·verse′ly**, *adv.*

trans·ves′tite, *n.* dresser in clothes for the opposite sex.

trap, *n.*, *v.t.*, **trapped, trapping.** *n.* **1.** device for catching animals. **2.** trick for detection or capture. —*v.t.* **3.** catch. **4.** adorn. —**trap′per**, *n.* —**trap′pings**, *n., pl.*

trap′door′, *n.* horizontal door.

tra·peze′, *n.* swing with a bar.

trap′e·zoid′′, *n.* four-sided figure with two parallel sides. —**trap′′e·zoi′dal**, *adj.*

trash, *n.* discarded matter. —**trash′y**, *adj.*

trau′ma, *n.*, *pl.* **-mas, -mata.** bodily or emotional shock. —**trau·mat′ic**, *adj.* —**trau′ma·tize′′**, *v.t.*

tra·vail′, *n.* agony.

trav′el, *v.i.*, **-eled** or **-elled, -eling** or **-elling**, *n.* *v.i.* **1.** go on a journey. —*n.* **2.** traveling, esp. for pleasure. —**trav′el·er, trav′el·ler**, *n.*

trav·erse′, *v.t.*, **-ersed, -ersing.** pass across.

trav′es·ty, *n.*, *pl.* **-ties,** *v.t.*, **-tied, -tying.** *n.* **1.** mocking imitation. —*v.t.* **2.** make a travesty of.

trawl, *n.* **1.** dragged fish net. —*v.i.* **2.** use a trawl. —**trawl′er**, *n.*

tray, *n.* shallow, broad receptacle.

treach′er·y, *n.*, *pl.* **-ies.** betrayal of trust. —**treach′er·ous**, *adj.*

tread, *v.*, **trod, trodden, treading.** *v.i.* **1.** walk deliberately. —*v.t.* **2.** press, make, etc. by treading. —*n.* **3.** manner of treading. **4.** step. **5.** surface of a wheel, tire, etc. that touches the ground.

trea′dle, *n.* foot-operated lever.

trea′son, *n.* betrayal of one's country. —**trea′son·a·ble, trea′son·ous**, *adj.*

treas′ure, *n.*, *v.t.*, **-ured, -uring.** *n.* **1.** precious possession. —*v.t.* **2.** regard as a treasure.

treas′ur·er, *n.* handler of funds.

treas′ure-trove′′, *n.* discovered treasure.

treas′ur·y, *n.*, *pl.* **-ies.** department or place for storing money.

treat, *v.t.* **1.** act toward as specified. **2.** handle as specified. **3.** give medical care to. **4.** have as a guest. —*n.* **5.** something offered a guest. **6.** source of pleasure. —**treat′ment**, *n.*

trea′tise, *n.* paper on a subject.

trea′ty, *n.*, *pl.* **-ties.** agreement between nations.

tre′ble, *adj.*, *v.t.*, **-bled, -bling.** *adj.* **1.** triple. **2.** high-pitched. —*v.t.* **3.** multiply by three. —**treb′ly**, *adv.*

tree, *n.*, *v.t.*, **treed, treeing.** *n.* **1.** tall plant with a woody stem and branches. —*v.t.* **2.** chase up a tree —**tree′less**, *adj.*

trek, *v.i.*, **trekked, trekking,** *n.* *v.i.* **1.** travel with difficulty. —*n.* **2.** long, difficult journey.

trel′lis, *n.* frame for climbing plants.

trem′ble, *v.i.*, **-bled, -bling.** **1.** shiver. **2.** be in fear or awe.

tre·men′dous, *adj.* huge. —**tre·men′dous·ly**, *adv.*

trem′o·lo′′, *n.*, *pl.* **-os.** wavering of a musical tone.

trem′or, *n.* quiver.

trem′u·lous, *adj.* timid.

trench, *n.* deep, narrow ditch.

trench′ant, *adj.* incisive.

trend, *n.* current style or tendency.

trep′′i·da′tion, *n.* fear and doubt.

tres′pass, *v.i.* **1.** enter property without right. —*n.* **2.** sin. —**tres′pas·ser**, *n.*

tress, *n.* lock of hair.

tres′tle, *n.* **1.** transverse frame. **2.** viaduct on framed towers.

tri′ad, *n.* group of three.

tri′al, *n.* **1.** test, as for value. **2.** annoyance or source of annoyance. **3.** examination in a law court.

tri′an·gle, *n.* three-sided figure. —**tri·an′gu·lar**, *adj.*

tribe, *n.* group of related persons under one leader. —**trib′al**, *adj.* —**tribes′man**, *n.*

trib′′u·la′tion, *n.* distress.

tri·bu′nal, *n.* court of justice.

trib′une, *n.* speaking platform.

trib′u·tar′′y, *adj.*, *n.*, *pl.* **-ies.** *adj.* **1.** paying tribute. **2.** flowing into a larger stream. —*n.* **3.** tributary stream or river.

trib′ute, *n.* **1.** compulsory payment. **2.** expression of gratitude or honor.

trice, *n.* instant.

trick, *n.* **1.** cunning or treacherous act. —*v.t.* **2.** cheat. —**trick′er·y**, *n.* —**trick′ster**, *n.*

trick′le, *v.i.*, **-led, -ling.** flow in a thin, slow stream.

trick′y, *adj.*, **-ier, -iest.** **1.** treacherous; wily. **2.** challenging the skill or cunning.

tri′cy·cle, *n.* three-wheeled vehicle.

tri′dent, *n.* three-pronged spear.

tried, *adj.* proved, esp. as trustworthy.

tri′fle, *n.*, *v.i.*, **-fled, -fling.** *n.* **1.** something of little importance. —*v.i.* **2.** talk or act frivolously. —**tri′fler**, *n.*

tri′fling, *adj.* unimportant; insignificant.

tri'fo''cals, *n.* spectacles with three focuses.

trig'ger, *n.* **1.** lever for firing a gun. —*v.t.* **2.** precipitate; cause to happen.

trig''o·nom'e·try, *n.* mathematics based on the triangle. —**trig''o·no·met'ric,** *adj.*

trill, *n.* **1.** high, warbling sound. —*v.i.* **2.** emit a trill.

tril'lion, *n.* one thousand billion.

tril'o·gy, *n., pl.* **-gies.** trio of related novels, etc.

trim, *v.t.,* trimmed, trimming, *n., adj.,* trimmer, trimmest. *v.t.* **1.** make neat. **2.** decorate. **3.** balance. —*n.* **4.** good condition. —*adj.* **5.** neat. —**trim'ly,** *adv.* —**trim'mer,** *n.*

tri·mes'ter, *n.* third of an academic year.

trim'ming, *n.* something added, as a decoration.

trin'i·ty, *n., pl.* **-ties. 1.** set of three. **2.** the Trinity, God as Father, Son, and Holy Spirit.

trin'ket, *n.* small ornament.

tri·o (trē'ō), *n., pl.* **-os.** group of three.

trip, *v.,* tripped, tripping, *n. v.i.* **1.** stumble and lose balance. —*v.t.* **2.** cause to stumble. **3.** set in motion. —*n.* **4.** act or instance of tripping. **5.** journey.

tri·par'tite, *adj.* in three parts.

tripe, *n.* **1.** edible part of an animal stomach. **2.** *Informal.* drivel.

trip'ham''mer, *n.* heavy mechanical hammer.

tri'ple, *adj., v.,* **-pled, -pling.** *adj.* **1.** in three parts. **2.** three times normal size. —*v.t., v.i.* **3.** multiply three times. —**tri'ply,** *adv.*

tri'plet, *n.* one of three siblings born at the same time.

trip'li·cate, *n.* threefold form.

tri'pod, *n.* three-legged support.

tri·sect', *v.t.* divide in three. —**tri·sec'tion,** *n.*

trite, *adj.,* triter, tritest. overly familiar. —**trite'ly,** *adv.* —**trite'ness,** *n.*

tri'umph, *n.* **1.** victory. **2.** delight in victory. —*v.i.* **3.** be victorious. —**tri·um'phal,** *adj.* —**tri·um'phant,** *adj.*

tri·um'vi·rate, *n.* trio in power.

triv'et, *n.* stand for hot things.

triv'i·a, *n., pl.* trivial things.

triv'i·al, *adj.* petty and unimportant. —**triv''i·al'i·ty,** *n.* —**triv''i·al·ly,** *adv.*

troll, *n.* supernatural cave dweller.

trol'ley, *n., pl.* **-leys. 1.** raised structure for collecting electricity. **2.** streetcar with such a structure. **3.** wheeled container.

trom·bone', *n.* brass musical instrument. —**trom·bon'ist,** *n.*

troop, *n.* **1.** uniformed group. —*v.i.* **2.** move in a group. —**troop'er,** *n.*

tro'phy, *n., pl.* **-phies.** memento of victory.

trop'ic, *n.* **1.** boundary of the Torrid Zone. **2.** tropics, Torrid Zone or nearby areas. —*adj.* **3.** Also, **trop'i·cal,** pertaining to the Torrid Zone.

tro'pism, *n. Biology.* response, as in growth, to stimuli.

trot, *v.i.,* trotted, trotting, *n. v.i.* **1.** run at moderate speed. —*n.* **2.** trotting gait. —**trot'ter,** *n.*

trou'ba·dour'', *n.* medieval singer.

trou'ble, *n., v.,* **-bled, -bling.** *n.* **1.** worry or exertion. **2.** source of these. —*v.t.* **3.** cause trouble to. —*v.i.* **4.** go to trouble. —**trou'ble·some,** *adj.* —**trou'ble·mak''er,** *n.*

trough, *n.* long, open container.

trounce, *v.t.,* trounced, trouncing. beat.

troupe, *n.* group of performers. —**troup'er,** *n.*

trou'sers, *n., pl.* pants.

trous'seau, *n., pl.* **-seaux, -seaus.** bride's clothing, etc.

trout, *n., pl.* trout, trouts. edible freshwater fish.

trow'el, *n.* spreading or scooping hand tool.

troy, *adj.* pertaining to a jeweler's weight with a twelve-ounce pound.

tru'ant, *n.* unauthorized absentee from school. —**tru'an·cy,** *n.*

truce, *n.* temporary suspension of hostilities.

truck, *n.* **1.** freight motor vehicle. **2.** hand cart for loads. —*v.t.* **3.** carry by truck. —**truck'er,** *n.*

truck'le, *v.i.,* **-led, -ling.** be servilely submissive.

truc'u·lent, *adj.* fierce. —**truc'u·lent·ly,** *adv.* —**truc'u·lence,** *n.*

trudge, *v.i.,* trudged, trudging, *n. v.i.* **1.** walk laboriously. —*n.* **2.** laborious walk.

true, *adj.,* truer, truest. *adj.* **1.** according with truth. **2.** faithful. —**tru'ly,** *adv.* —**true'ness,** *n.*

tru'ism, *n.* tritely true statement.

trump, *n.* highest-ranking card.

trump'er·y, *n., pl.* **-ies.** worthlessly pretentious things.

trum'pet, *n.* brass musical wind instrument. —**trum'pet·er,** *n.*

trun'cate, *v.t.,* **-cated, -cating.** remove part of. —**trun·ca'tion,** *n.*

trun'cheon, *n.* club.

trun'dle, *v.t.,* **-dled, -dling.** roll out or along.

trunk, *n.* **1.** large piece of luggage. **2.** main stem of a tree. **3.** body apart from head and limbs.

truss, *n.* **1.** frame of triangular parts. **2.** support for the ruptured. —*v.t.* **3.** bind up. **4.** support with a truss.

trust, *n.* **1.** reliance; faith. **2.** custody. **3.** monopolistic combination. —*v.t.* **4.** have reliance or faith in. —**trust'ful, trust'ing,** *adj.* —**trust'worth''y, trust'y,** *adj.*

trus·tee', *n.* person to whom property is entrusted. —**trus·tee'ship,** *n.*

trust'y, *adj.,* **-ier, -iest.** trustworthy.

truth, *n.* **1.** that which is actually so. **2.** accuracy. —**truth'ful,** *adj.* —**truth'ful·ly,** *adv.* —**truth'ful·ness,** *n.*

try, *v.t.,* **tried, trying.** *n. v.t.* **1.** attempt. **2.** test. **3.** examine in a court of law. **4.** annoy or afflict. —*n.* **5.** attempt or test. —**try'ing,** *adj.*

try'out'', *n. Informal.* test operation.

tryst, *n.* lovers' appointment.

tsar, *n.* Slavic emperor.

tub, *n.* broad, deep vessel.

tu'ba, *n.* large brass wind musical instrument.

tub'by, *adj.,* **-bier, -biest.** chubby.

tube, *n.* hollow cylinder. —**tub'ing,** *n.* —**tub'u·lar,** *adj.*

tu'ber, *n.* swelling part of an underground plant stem. —**tu'ber·ous,** *adj.*

tu·ber'cu·lo'sis, *n.* illness with swelling lesions. —**tu·ber'cu·lar, tu·ber'cu·lous,** *adj.*

tuck, *v.t.* insert by pressing.

Tues'day, *n.* third day of the week.

tuft, *n.* cluster of fibers, threads, etc.

tug, *v.t.,* **tugged, tugging.** *n. v.t.* **1.** pull forcefully. —*n.* **2.** act or instance of tugging. —**tug'boat'',** *n.*

tu·i'tion, *n.* fee for teaching.

tu'lip, *n.* plant with a cup-shaped flower.

tum'ble, *v.i.,* **-bled, -bling. 1.** fall or roll helplessly. **2.** perform acrobatics on a flat surface.

tum'bler, *n.* **1.** drinking glass. **2.** acrobat who tumbles.

tu'mid, *adj.* swollen.

tum'my, *n., pl.* **-mies.** *Informal.* stomach

tu'mor, *n.* abnormal growth.

tu'mult, *n.* commotion. —**tu·mul'tu·ous,** *adj.*

tun, *n.* large cask.

tu'na, *n., pl.* **-na, -nas.** large ocean fish.

tun'dra, *n.* barren Arctic plain.

tune, *n., v.t.,* **tuned, tuning.** *n.* **1.** melody. **2.** harmony. —*v.t.* **3.** put in tune. —**tune'ful,** *adj.* —**tune'less,** *adj.*

tun'ic, *adj.* jacket, often belted.

tun'nel, *n., v.i.,* **-neled, -neling.** *n.* **1.** route cut underground. —*v.i.* **2.** dig a route.

tur'ban, *n.* headdress of wound cloth.

tur'bid, *adj.* cloudy or muddy. —**tur·bid'i·ty,** *n.*

tur'bine, *n.* rotary engine driven by the passing of a fluid.

tur'bo·jet'', *n.* jet engine using turbine-compressed air.

tur'bu·lent, *adj.* in disturbed motion. —**tur'bu·lence,** *n.*

tu·reen', *n.* covered soup container.

turf, *n.* earth held by grass roots. —**turf'y,** *adj.*

tur'gid, *adj.* pompously or excessively worded. —**tur'gid·ly,** *adv.* —**tur·gid'i·ty, tur·gid·ness,** *n.*

tur'key, *n.* large North American fowl.

tur'moil, *n.* confused activity.

turn, *v.t., v.i.* **1.** change in direction. **2.** change in nature. —*n.* **3.** curve. **4.** loop. **5.** place in a sequence. **6.** act toward another. —**turn'ing,** *n.*

turn'a·bout'', *n.* reversal of conditions

turn'coat'', *n.* renegade.

tur'nip, *n.* edible root.

turn'out'', *n.* attendance at a meeting.

turn'o''ver, *n.* **1.** rate of sale, replacement, etc. **2.** baked dish of crust folded over filling.

turn'pike'', *n.* toll road.

turn'stile'', *n.* rotating gate.

turn'ta''ble, *n.* rotating platform.

tur'pen·tine'', *n.* oil from coniferous trees.

tur'pi·tude'', *n.* vileness.

tur'quoise, *n.* greenish-blue stone.

tur'ret, *n.* **1.** small tower. **2.** housing for cannon.

tur'tle, *n.* shell-encased reptile.

tusk, *n.* long, projecting tooth.

tus'sle, *n., v.i.,* **-sled, -sling.** struggle.

tu'te·lage, *n.* **1.** guardianship. **2.** education. —**tu'te·lar, tu'te·lar''y,** *adj.*

tu'tor, *n.* **1.** private teacher. —*v.t.* **2.** teach privately. —**tu·to'ri·al,** *adj., n.*

tux·e'do, *n.* semiformal evening suit.

TV, television.

twang, *n.* **1.** sound of a plucked string. **2.** nasal accent.

tweak, *v.t., n.* pinch with a twist.

tweed, *n.* rough woolen cloth.

tweet, *n., v.i.* chirp.

tweez'ers, *n., pl.* small pincers.

twelve, *n., adj.* ten plus two. —**twelfth,** *adj., n.*

twen'ty, *adj., n.* two times ten. —**twen'ti·eth,** *adj.*

twice, *adv.* two times.

twid'dle, *v.t.,* **-dled, -dling.** play with absently.

twig, *n.* tiny plant branch.

twi'light'', *n.* half-light, as between day and night.

twill, *n.* cloth with a diagonal pattern.

twin, *n.* **1.** one of two siblings born at the same time. **2.** exact match. —*adj.* **3.** matching another or each other exactly.

twine, *n., v.,* **twined, twining.** *n.* **1.** string. —*v.t., v.i.* **2.** twist together.

twinge, *n.* stab of pain.

twin′kle, *v.i.,* **-kled, -kling,** *n. v.i.* **1.** gleam intermittently. **2.** show amusement. —*n.* **3.** act or instance of twinkling.

twin′kling, *n.* instant.

twirl, *v.t., v.i.* rotate rapidly.

twist, *v.t.* **1.** wind around, rotate, or bend into a helical form. **2.** distort the actuality of. —*v.i.* **3.** assume a twisted form. **4.** squirm. —*n.* **5.** act or instance of twisting.

twit, *v.t.,* **twitted, twitting.** address teasingly.

twitch, *v.i.* **1.** jerk spasmodically. **2.** pluck. —*n.* **3.** spasmodic jerk.

twit′ter, *v.i.* chirp rapidly.

two, *n., adj.* one plus one. —**two′fold″,** *adj., adv.* —**two′some,** *n.*

two′-edged″, *adj.* interpretable two ways.

ty·coon′, *n.* man of great wealth and power.

type, *n., v.t.,* **typed, typing.** *n.* **1.** variety; sort. **2.** reproducible characters used in printing. —*v.t.* **3.** classify. **4.** produce with a typewriter.

type′writ″er, *n.* machine for producing letters by mechanical means.

ty′phoid, *n.* acute infectious disease.

ty·phoon′, *n.* violent storm of the west Pacific Ocean.

ty′phus, *n.* acute infectious disease.

typ′i·cal, *n.* **1.** representative of a type. **2.** customary. —**typ′i·cal·ly,** *adv.*

typ′i·fy″, *v.t.,* **-fied, -fying.** be typical of.

typ′ist, *n.* user of typewriters.

ty·pog′ra·phy, *n.* art of composing and printing with type. —**ty″po·graph′ic,** *adj.* —**ty·pog′ra·pher,** *n.*

ty′rant, *n.* harsh, arbitrary ruler. —**tyr′an·ny,** *n.* —**ty·ran′ni·cal,** *adj.* —**tyr′an·nize″,** *v.i., v.t*

ty′ro, *n., pl.* **-ros.** beginner; novice.

U

U, u, *n.* twenty-first letter og the English alphabet.

u·biq′ui·ty, *n.* presence everywhere simultaneously. —**u·biq′ui·tous,** *adj.*

ud′der, *n.* mammary gland of a cow.

ug′ly, *adj.,* **-lier, -liest. 1.** unattractive. **2.** discomfiting: difficult. —**ug′li·ness,** *n.*

u·ke·le·le (yōō″kə lā′lē), *n.* small guitar.

ul′cer, *n.* open break in tissue. —**ul′cer·ous,** *adj.* —**ul′cer·ate″,** *v.i., v.t.*

ul′na, *n.* large bone of the forearm. —**ul′nar,** *adj.*

ul·te′ri·or, *adj.* **1.** further; beyond. **2.** concealed; disguised.

ul′ti·mate, *adj.* **1.** final; conclusive. **2.** fundamental; basic. —**ul′ti·mate·ly,** *adv.*

ul″ti·ma′tum, *n., pl.* **-matums** or **-mata,** final, decisive demand.

ul′ti·mo, *adj.* of or occurring in the preceding month.

ul′tra·light, *n.* miniature aircraft for solo, powered flight.

ul′tra·ma·rine′, *adj.* deep blue.

ul″tra·vi′o·let, *adj.* beyond the visible spectrum at its violet end.

um′bel, *n.* cluster of flower with the stalks having a common center.

um′ber, *n.* reddish brown.

um·bil′i·cus, *n.* navel. —**um·bil′i·cal,** *adj.*

um′brage, *n.* resentment; pique.

um·brel′la, *n.* collapsible device with a fabric-covered frame, carried for protection against the weather.

um′pire, *n., v.t.,* **-pired, -piring.** *n.* **1.** final authority; judge. —*v.t.* **2.** to serve as umpire for.

un-, prefix indicating "not." unable, unassuming, unavoidable, unaware, unbalanced, unbend, unborn, unbridled, uncertain, uncivil, unclean, unclothe, uncommon, unconcern, unconscious, uncork, undeniable, undeclared, undress, undue, unduly, uneasy, unequal, unerring, unexpected, unfailing, unfaithful, unfasten, unfit, unfold, unfortunate, unfriendly, ungodly, unhinge, unholy, unlike, unlock, unnatural, unpack, unroll, unscrew, unsettle, unshackle, unsightly, untangle, untouchable, untrue, untruth, untypical, unusual, unveil, unwell, unwind, unwise, unyoke.

u·nan′i·mous, *adj.* totally agreed. —**u·na·nim′i·ty,** *n.* —**u·nan′i·mous·ly,** *adv.*

un″a·wares′, *adv.* not aware.

un·bo′som, *v.t.* disclose; reveal.

un·called′-for″, *adj.* unwarranted; unneeded.

un·can′ny, *adj.* unnatural; eerie.

un′cle, *n.* brother of one's mother or father, or husband of one's aunt.

Uncle Sam, the United States.

un·con′scion·a·ble, *adj.* excessive; unreasonable. —**un·con′scion·a·bly,** *adv.*

un·couth′, *adj.* lacking grace; clumsy.

unc′tion, *n.* consecration with oil.

unc′tu·ous, *adj.* **1.** oily. **2.** unpleasantly suave.

un′der, *prep., adj., adv.* **1.** below; beneath. **2.** less than. —*adj.* **3.** lower.

un′der·brush″, *n.* low-growing forest shrubs and grass.

un′der·cov″er, *adj.* disguised; secret.

un′der·cut″, *v.t.,* **-cut, -cutting.** offer at a lower price than.

un′der·dog″, *n.* predicted loser.

un″der·es′ti·mate″, *v.t.*, **-ated**, **-ating**. value or estimate too low.

un″der·go′, *v.t.* **-went**, **-gone**, **-going**. endure; experience.

un·der·grad′u·ate, *n.* college student working toward a bachelor's degree.

un′der·ground″, *adj.* **1.** below the ground. **2.** secret; confidential. —*adv.* **3.** below the ground. —*n.* **4.** secret army of resistance.

un′der·hand″, *adj.* secret; sly. Also, **un′der·hand″ed**.

un·der·mine″, *v.t.* **-mind**, **-mining**. weaken; sabotage.

un·der·neath′, *prep.*, *adv.* beneath.

un·der·stand′, *v.t.*, *v.i.* **-stood**, **-standing**. **1.** comprehend; take the meaning of. —*v.i.* **2.** sympathize. —**un·der·stand′ing**, *n.*, *adj.*

un·der·stood′, *adj.* assumed; agreed upon.

un′der·stud″y, *n.*, *pl.* **-dies**. performer on call for emergencies.

un·der·take′, *v.t.*, **-took**, **taken**. **1.** set about; enter upon. **2.** accept as an obligation.

un′der·tak″er, *n.* director of funerals.

un′der·world″, *n.* world of criminals.

un′der·write″, *v.t.* **-wrote**, **-written**, **-writing**. accept, as an expense or liability. —**un′der·writ″er**, *n.*

un″do′, *v.t.* **-did**, **-done**, **-doing**. **1.** unfasten. **2.** nullify. **3.** ruin.

un′du·late″, *v.t.*, *v.i.*, **-lated**, **-lating**. **1.** move or form in waves. **2.** fluctuate in pitch and cadence. —**un″du·la′tion**, *n.*

un·earth′, *v.t.* discover; reveal.

un′guent, *n.* ointment; salve.

u·ni·corn, (yoo′ ni korn), *n.* mythical horselike animal with a single horn.

u′ni·form″, *adj.* **1.** alike; similar. —*n.* **2.** distinctive or stylized dress for a particular group. —*v.t.* **3.** clothe with a uniform. —**u·ni·form′i·ty**, *n.*

u′ni·fy″, *v.t.* **-fied**, **-fying**. make into a whole; unite. —**u″ni·fi·ca′tion**, *n.*

u·ni·lat′er·al, *adj.* one-sided.

un′ion, *n.* **1.** act or instance of uniting. **2.** labor group organized for mutual aid. —**un′ion·ize″**, *v.t.*, *v.i.*

Union Jack, British flag.

u″nique′, *adj.* **1.** single; only. **2.** rare; unusual. —**u·nique′ly**, *adv.*

u′ni·son″, *n.* agreement; harmony.

u′nit, *n.* single amount, item, etc.

u·nite′, *v.t.*, *v.i.*, **-nited**, **-niting**. join into one group or entity.

u′ni·ty, *n.* **1.** state of being united; oneness. **2.** agreement.

u″ni·ver′sal, *adj.* including all. —**u″ni·ver·sal′i·ty**, *n.*

u′ni·verse″, *n.* entirety of physical creation.

u″ni·ver′si·ty, *n.*, *pl.* **-ties**. large institution of higher learning.

un·kempt′, *adj.* untidy; shabby; messy.

un·less′, *conj.*, *prep.* if not; except.

un·rav′el, *v.t.* **1.** disentangle; undo. **2.** solve.

un·rest′, *n.* **1.** uneasy state. **2.** discontent.

un·ru′ly, *adj.* undisciplined; rebellious. —**un·rul′i·ness** *n.*

un·tie′, *v.t.*, **-tied**, **-tying**. loosen or undo.

un·til′, *conj.*, *prep.* **1.** up to the time when. **2.** before.

un′to, *prep. Archaic.* to.

un·told′, *adj.* vast; incalculable.

un·to·ward′, *adj.* **1.** improper. **2.** adverse.

un·wield′y, *adj.* awkward; bulky.

un·wit′ting, *adj.* unintentional; inadvertent. —**un·wit′ting·ly**, *adv.*

un·wont″ed, *adj.* not usual; uncharacteristic.

up, *adv.*, *adj.*, *prep.*, *v.t.*, **-ped**, **-ping**. *adv.* **1.** to a higher level or location. **2.** straight; erectly. **3.** at bat. **4.** awake; out of bed. **5.** (computers) operating. —*prep.* **6.** to a higher level or place in or on. —*v.t.* **7.** increase.

up·braid′, *v.t.* scold; chide.

up·heav′al, *n.* turmoil; unrest; agitation.

up·hold′, *v.t.* **-held**, **-holding**. support; advocate.

up·hol′ster, *v.t.* furnish with padding and fabric covering. —**up·hol′ster·er**, *n.*

up′keep″, *n.* maintenance; support.

up·lift′, *v.t.* (up lift′) **1.** elevate; exalt. —*n.* (up′lift) **2.** edification.

up·on′, *prep.* on; onto.

up′per, *adj.* higher. —**up′per·most″**, *adj.*

up′ris″ing, *n.* rebellion; revolt.

up′roar″, *n.* tumult; din.

up·root″, *v.t.* **1.** to pull up by the roots. **2.** displace from a home or homeland.

up·set′, *v.*, **-set**, **-setting**, *adj.*, *n. v.t.* (up set′) **1.** overturn. **2.** defeat. **3.** put in confusion or distress. —*v.i.* **4.** be overturned. —*adj.* **5.** distressed in mind. —*n.* (up′set″) **6.** act or instance of upsetting.

up′shot, *n.* final result.

up″stairs′, *adj.* **1.** situated on an upper floor. —*adv.* **2.** to or on an upper floor. —*n.* **3.** floor above a ground floor.

up′start″, *n.* person of recent power or wealth.

up′-to-date′, *adj.* latest; modern; current.

up′ward, *adv.* **1.** Also, **up′wards**, to a higher level or place. —*adj.* **2.** toward a higher level or place.

u·ra′ni·um, *n.* radioactive metallic element used as a source for atomic energy.

ur′ban, *adj.* pertaining to cities.

ur·bane', *adj.* sophisticated; polite. —**ur·ban'i·ty**, *n.*

ur'chin, *n.* unkempt child; ragamuffin.

urge, *v.t.*, **urged, urging**, *n. v.t.* **1.** advocate. **2.** implore. —*n.* **3.** impulse; desire; longing.

ur'gent, *adj.* pressing; vital; crucial. —**ur'gen·cy**, *n.* —**ur'gent·ly**, *adv.*

u'ri·nate', *v.i.* **-nated, -nating.** pass urine. —**u''ri·na'tion**, *n.*

u'rine, *n.* fluid waste from kidneys.

urn, *n.* vase.

us, *pron.* objective case of we.

us'age, *n.* **1.** custom. **2.** treatment; handling.

use, *v.t.*, **used, using**, *n. v.t.* (yo͞oz) **1.** employ or engage for a purpose. **2.** expend; consume. **3.** behave toward; treat. **4.** do regularly. **5.** accustom; habituate. —*n.* (yo͞os) **6.** application; employment. **7.** value; service. —**us'a·ble**, *adj.* —**use'ful**, *adj.* —**use'less**, *adj.*

us''er-friend''ly, *adj.* (computers) designed for ease of use.

ush'er, *n.*, *v.t.* escort; guide.

u'su·al, *adj.* **1.** habitual; customary. **2.** ordinary; common. —**u'su·al·ly**, *adv.*

u·surp', *v.t.* take or assume without right. —**u·surp'er**, *n.*

u'su·ry, *n.* lending of money at excessive interest. —**u'sur·er**, *n.*

u·ten'sil, *n.* implement or vessel useful esp. in the kitchen.

u'ter·us, *n.* female bodily organ in which fetuses develop.

u·til''i·tar'i·an, *adj.* practical; useful; functional.

u·til'i·ty, *n.*, *pl.* **-ties. 1.** usefulness; function. **2.** service provided for public use.

u'ti·lize, *v.t.*, **-lized, -lizing.** make use of. —**u''ti·li·za'tion**, *n.*

ut'most'', *adj.* **1.** furthest. **2.** greatest.

u·to'pi·an, *adj.* impossibly ideal.

ut'ter, *v.t.* **1.** say; speak; enunciate. —*adj.* **2.** total; complete. —**ut'ter·ance**, *n.* —**ut'ter·ly**, *adv.*

u·vu·la (yo͞o'vyə lə), *n.* fleshy pendant lobe of the soft palate.

ux·o·ri·ous (o͝ok sôr'ē əs), *adj.* excessively fond of one's wife.

V

V, v, *n.* twenty-second letter of the English alphabet.

va'can·cy, *n.*, *pl.* **-cies. 1.** state of being vacant. **2.** void. **3.** available rental space.

va'cant'', *adj.* **1.** empty; uninhabited. **2.** stupid; foolish. **3.** expressionless. —**va'cant''ly**, *adv.*

va'cate'', *v.* **-cated, -cating.** *v.t.* **1.** deprive of an occupant or incumbent. **2.** leave. **3.** void; annul. —*v.i.* **4.** vacate a tenancy, office, or post.

va·ca'tion, *n.* **1.** respite from duty or occupation. **2.** period of rest and relaxation. —*v.i.* **3.** take a vacation. —**va·ca'tion·er, va·ca'tion·ist**, *n.*

vac'ci·nate'', *v.t.*, **-nated, -nating.** inoculate with cowpox virus for immunity to smallpox. —**vac''ci·na'tion**, *n.*

vac·cine (vak sēn'), *n.* substance used for vaccinating. —**vac'ci·nal**, *adj.*

vac·il·late'' (vas'ə lāt''), *v.i.* **-lated, -lating. 1.** sway; oscillate; fluctuate. **2.** waver; hesitate. —**vac''il·la'tion**, *n.*

va·cu'i·ty, *n.*, *pl.* **-ties. 1.** emptiness. **2.** emptyheadedness. —**vac'u·ous**, *adj.* —**vac'u·ous·ly**, *adv.*

vac'u·um, *n.* **1.** space devoid of matter. —*v.t.* **2.** use a vacuum cleaner on.

vag'a·bond'', *adj.* **1.** wandering; rootless. —*n.* **2.** person leading a vagabond life.

va'gar·y, *n.*, *pl.* **-garies.** capricious action or notion.

va·gi·na (və jī'nə), *n.* canal in the female from the vulva to the uterus. —**vag'i·nal**, *adj.*

va'grant, *n.* **1.** wanderer, esp. without visible means of support. —*adj.* **2.** wandering; itinerant. **3.** random; wayward. —**va'gran·cy**, *n.*

vague, *adj.*, **vaguer, vaguest. 1.** not definite; imprecise. **2.** indistinct; blurred. —**vague'ly**, *adv.* —**vague'ness** *n.*

vain, *adj.* **1.** futile. **2.** conceited. —**vain'ly**, *adv.*

val·ance (val'əns), *n.* drapery or frame disguising the top of a window.

vale, *n.* valley.

val·e·dic'tion, *n.* act of bidding farewell. —**val''edic'to·ry**, *adj.*

va'lence, *n. Chemistry.* combining power of an element or radical.

val'en·tine, *n.* **1.** sentimental greeting on St. Valentine's Day. **2.** sweetheart chosen on St. Valentine's Day.

val·et, (val'it, val'ā), *n.* man's personal servant.

val'iant, *adj.* possessing valor; courageous. —**val·ian·tly**, *adv.*

va'lid, *adj.* **1.** reasonable. **2.** having legal force. —**va·lid'i·ty**, *n.* —**val'id·ly**, *adv.* —**val'i·date**, *v.t.*

va·lise (və lēs'), *n.* traveling bag; suitcase.

val'ley, *n.* long depression between mountains, plateaus, etc.

val'or, *n.* courage; bravery. —**val'o·rous**, *adj.* —**val'o·rous''ly**, *adv.*

val'u·a·ble, *adj.* **1.** having worth or use-

fulness. —*n.* 2. **valuables,** valuable possessions. —**val′u·a·bly,** *adv.*

val·u·a′tion, *n.* estimated value.

val′ue, *n., v.t.* -ued, -ing. *n.* 1. importance; worth. 2. relative worth. 3. basic principle. —*v.t.* 4. estimate the worth of. 5. prize; esteem. —**val′ue·less,** *n.*

valve, *n.* device for regulating the flow of a fluid. —**val′vu·lar,** *adj.*

vamp, *n.* 1. uppermost front part of a shoe, etc. 2. seductive woman. 3. repeated introductory musical passage. —*v.i.* 4. play a musical vamp.

vam′pire′, *n.* 1. corpse believed to rise and suck the blood of sleepers at night. 2. Also, **vampire bat,** South American bat subsisting on blood.

van, *n.* 1. foremost part; vanguard. 2. enclosed truck.

van′dal, *n.* person who willfully damages property. —**van′dal·ism,** *n.* —**van′dal·ize,** *v.t.*

Vandyke, *n.* short, pointed, trimmed beard.

vane, *n.* blade rotated by moving air, steam, etc.

van′guard″, *n.* 1. advance troops. 2. forefront of an action, movement, or cause.

va·nil′la, *n.* extract of a tropical American orchid used in cookery.

van′ish, *v.i.* disappear.

van′i·ty, *n., pl.* -ties. inflated pride; conceit.

van′quish, *v.t.* defeat; conquer.

van′tage, *n.* position giving strategic advantage.

va′pid, *adj.* dull; uninteresting; flat. —**vap′id·ly,** *adv.* —**va·pid′i·ty,** *n.*

va′por, *n.* gaseous substance, as steam or mist. —**va′por·ous,** *adj.*

va′por·ize″, *v.,* -ized, -izing. *v.t., v.i.* turn into vapor. —**va″por·i·za′tion,** *n.* —**va′por·i″zer,** *n.*

var′i·a·ble, *adj.* 1. changeable; fluctuating. 2. inconstant; fickle. —**var′i·a·bil′i·ty,** *n.* —**var′i·a·bly,** *adv.*

var′i·ance, *n.* 1. divergence. 2. disagreement.

var′i·ant, *adj.* 1. varying. 2. altered in form. —*n.* 3. variant form or structure.

var″i·a′tion, *n.* 1. change; alteration. 2. degree of change. 3. elaboration of a musical theme. —**var″i·a′tion·al,** *adj.* —**var″i·a′tion·al·ly,** *adv.*

var′i·e·gate″, *v.t.,* -gated, -gating. 1. add different colors to; dapple. 2. add variety to. —**var″i·e·gat′ed,** *adj.* —**var″i·e·ga′tion,** *n.*

va·ri′e·ty, *n., pl.* -ties. 1. diversity. 2. assortment. 3. category; kind; type. —**va·ri′e·tal,** *adj.*

va·ri′o·la, *n.* smallpox; cowpox.

var′i·ous, *adj.* 1. several. 2. diverse; different. —**var′i·ous·ly,** *adv.*

var′nish, *n.* 1. resinous liquid preparation drying to a hard, glossy surface. 2. outward appearance; gloss. —*v.t.* 3. apply varnish to. 4. gloss over; conceal.

var′y, *v.,* varied, varying. *v.t., v.i.* 1. change; fluctuate. 2. differ. —**var′i·ance,** *n.*

vase, *n.* ornamental vessel.

vas′sal, *n.* 1. landholder subservient to a feudal lord. 2. person under domination of another. —**vas′sal·age,** *n.*

vast, *adj.* enormous; huge; immense. —**vast′ly,** *adv.* —**vast′ness,** *n.*

vat, *n.* large vessel for holding fluids.

vaude′ville, *n.* stage entertainment with a series of acts. —**vaude·vil′lian,** *n.*

vault, *n.* 1. arched structure forming a ceiling. 2. space covered by such a structure. 3. burial chamber. 4. room or container for valuables. —*v.t.* 5. form or cover with a vault. 6. leap over. —*v.i.* 7. perform a leap; jump.

vaunt, *v.i.* 1. brag; boast. —*v.t.* 2. call attention to boastfully. —*n.* 3. boast.

veal, *n.* flesh of a young calf.

veep, *n. Informal.* vice-president.

veer, *v.i.* 1. change direction or course. —*n.* 2. act or instance of veering.

veg′e·ta·ble, *n.* 1. partly edible plant. —*adj.* Also, **veg′e·tal.** 2. being a vegetable. 3. pertaining to plants.

veg″e·tar′i·an, *n.* 1. abstainer from meat. —*adj.* 2. advocating the exclusion of meat in the diet. 3. consisting solely of vegetables. —**veg″e·tar′i·an·ism,** *n.*

veg′e·tate″, *v.i.,* -tated, -tating. 1. grow in the manner of a plant. 2. lead a passive life. —**veg′i·ta″tive,** *adj.*

ve′he·ment, *adj.* 1. passionate; emotional; fervid. 2. violent. —**ve′he·ment·ly,** *adv.* —**ve′he·mence,** *n.*

ve′hi·cle, *n.* 1. inert medium containing an active agent. 2. means of transporting or conveying. —**ve·hic′u·lar,** *adj.*

veil, *n.* 1. net-like cloth for covering the face. 2. outer covering of a nun's headdress. 3. screen; cover-up. —*v.t.* 4. cover with or as if with a veil.

vein, *n.* 1. tubular vessel conveying blood within the body. 2. tubular thickening in an insect wing or a leaf. 3. stratum of mineral, ore, or ice. 4. spirit; mood. —*v.t.* 5. pattern with or as if with veins.

vel′lum, *n.* parchment.

ve·loc′i·ty, *n., pl.* -ties. speed.

vel′vet, *n.* fabric with a thick, short, soft pile. —**vel′vet·y,** *adj.*

ve′nal, *adj.* open to bribery or corruption; mercenary. —**ve′nal·ly,** *adv.* —**ve·nal′i·ty,** *n.*

vend, *v.t.* sell; peddle. —**ven′dor,** *n.*

ve·neer′, *n.* 1. facing of fine material. 2. outer appearance. —*v.t.* 3. cover with or as with a veneer.

ven·er·a·ble, *adj.* worthy of or commanding reverence. —**ven·er·a·bil′i·ty,** *n.*

ven·er·ate″, *v.t.* -ated, -ating. respect deeply; worship; revere. —**ven″er·a′tion,** *n.*

ve·ne′re·al, *adj.* relating to or resulting from sexual activity.

venge′ance, *n.* retaliation; retribution.

venge′ful, *adj.* seeking revenge; vindictive. —**venge′ful·ly,** *adv.*

ve′ni·al, *adj.* pardonable; forgivable. —**ve′nial·ly,** *adv.*

ven′i·son, *n.* deer meat.

ven′om, *n.* **1.** poisonous secretion. **2.** malice; spite. —**ven′om·ous,** *adj.*

vent, *n.* **1.** means of outlet or escape. —*v.t.* **2.** provide or serve as a vent. **3.** give free expression to.

ven′ti·late, *v.t.,* -ated, -ating. **1.** provide with or expose to fresh air. **2.** express openly and freely. —**ven·ti·la′tion,** *n.*

ven·tril′o·quism, *n.* technique of projecting the voice so that it seems to emanate from a source other than the speaker. —**ven·tril′o·quist,** *n.*

ven′ture, *v.t.,* -tured, -turing, *n. v.t.* **1.** expose to hazard; risk. **2.** offer at risk of rejection. —*n.* **3.** challenging or risky undertaking. —**ven′ture·some, ven′tur·ous,** *adj.*

Ve′nus, *n.* **1.** goddess of love. **2.** second planet in distance from the sun.

ve·ra′cious, *adj.* openly honest; truthful. —**ve·ra′cious·ly,** *adj.* —**ve·rac′i·ty,** *n.*

ve·ran′da, *n.* an open portico attached to a building; porch. Also, **ve·ran′dah.**

verb, *n. Grammar.* part of speech indicating action, occurrence, being, etc.

ver′bal, *adj.* **1.** relating to or formed of words. **2.** oral; spoken. **3.** relating to or constituting a verb or form of a verb. —**ver′bal·ly,** *adv.*

ver′bal·ize″, *v.,* -ized, -izing. *v.t.* **1.** express in words. —*v.i.* **2.** speak in words. —**ver″bal·i·za′tion,** *n.*

ver·ba′tim, *adv.* word for word; literally.

ver′bi·age, *n.* excess of words.

ver·bose′, *adj.* wordy; loquacious. —**ver·bose′ness, ver·bos′i·ty,** *n.*

ver′dant, *adj.* green. —**ver′dant·ly,** *adj.* —**ver′dan·cy,** *n.*

ver′dict, *n.* decision.

ver′dure, *n.* **1.** greenery. **2.** greenness.

verge, *n., v.i.,* verged, verging. *n.* **1.** margin; edge. —*v.i.* **2.** border; surround. **3.** tend; incline.

ver′i·fy, *v.t.,* -fied, -fying. prove or ascertain the correctness of. —**ver·i·fi′a·ble,** *adj.* —**ver″i·fi·ca′tion,** *n.*

ver′i·ly, *adv.* truly.

ver″i·sim·il′i·tude, *n.* appearance of truth or reality.

ver′i·ta·ble, *adj.* true; genuine. —**ver′i·ta·bly,** *adj.*

ver′i·ty, *n., pl.* -ties. truth.

ver′min, *n., pl.* obnoxious animals or creatures collectively. —**ver′min·ous,** *adj.*

ver·nac′u·lar, *adj.* **1.** locally native. —*n.* **2.** language characteristic, esp. of a particular group or class.

ver′nal, *adj.* pertaining to spring.

ver′sa·tile, *adj.* changing tasks or activities easily. —**ver·sa·til′i·ty,** *n.*

verse, *n.* **1.** poetry. **2.** part of a poem, esp. when rhymed. **3.** passage from the Bible.

versed, *adj.* accomplished; skilled; knowledgeable.

ver·si·fy, *v.,* -fied, -fying. *v.t.* **1.** put into verse. —*v.i.* **2.** compose verse. —**ver″si·fi·ca′tion,** *n.* —**ver′si·fi″er,** *n.*

ver′sion, *n.* **1.** account. **2.** translation.

ver′te·bra, *n., pl.* -bras, -brae. segment of the spinal column. —**ver′te·bral,** *adj.*

ver′te·brate, *adj.* **1.** having vertebras. —*n.* **2.** creature having vertebras.

ver′ti·cal, *adj.* **1.** perpendicular to the horizon. —*n.* **2.** vertical plane, line, etc. —**ver′ti·cal·ly,** *adv.*

ver·ti·go″, *n., pl.* -gos. dizziness.

ver′y, *adv., adj.,* -ier, -iest. *adv.* **1.** to a great extent. —*adj.* **2.** identical; actual. **3.** absolute.

ves′pers, *n., sing.* evening religious service.

ves′sel, *n.* **1.** ship, boat, etc. **2.** container for fluid. **3.** channel for blood.

vest, *n.* **1.** sleeveless garment worn under a coat or jacket. —*v.t.* **2.** put in possession or control of. **3.** endow with authority.

ves′ti·bule, *n.* antichamber. —**ves·ti′bu·lar,** *adj.*

ves′tige, *n.* remnant; trace. —**ves·tig′i·al,** *adj.*

vest′ment, *n.* gown; robe.

vest-pocket, *adj.* small enough to fit a pocket.

ves′try, *n., pl.* -tries. **1.** auxiliary room of a church. **2.** church committee. —**ves′try·man,** *n.*

vet′er·an, *n.* **1.** person who has served, esp. in the military forces. —*adj.* **2.** greatly experienced.

vet′er·i·nar″y, *adj., n., pl.* -ies. *adj.* **1.** pertaining to the healing of animals. —*n.* **2.** Also, **vet″er·i·nar′i·an,** doctor for animals.

ve′to, *n., pl.* -toes, *v.t.,* -toes, -toing. *n.* **1.** power to reject, prohibit, or ignore. **2.** prohibition. —*v.t.* **3.** reject or prohibit by veto.

vex, *v.t.* **1.** irritate. **2.** trouble. —**vex″a′tious,** *adj.* —**vex′ed·ly,** *adj.*

vexed, *adj.* controversial.

vi·a (vī′ə, vē′ə), *prep.* by way of.

vi′a·ble, *adj.* capable of or fit for living. —**vi′a·bly,** *adv.*

vi′a·duct″, *n.* long road bridge.

vi′and, *n.* item of food, esp. when very choice or tasty.

vi′brant, *adj.* **1.** oscillating; fluctuating. **2.** vigorous; energetic. —**vi′brant·ly**, *adj.* —**vi′bran·cy**, *n.*

vi′brate, *v.*, **-brated, -brating.** *v.t.* **1.** move rapidly back and forth. —*v.i.* **2.** shiver. **3.** resound. —**vi·bra′tion**, *n.* —**vi′bra·to″ry**, *adj.* —**vi·bra·tor**, *n.*

vic′ar, *n.* **1.** parish priest. **2.** representative of the pope or of a bishop. **3.** Vicar of Christ, pope. —**vic′ar·ship″**, *n.*

vi·car′i·ous, *adj.* **1.** serving in the place of another. **2.** experienced in imagination only. —**vi·car″i·ous·ly**, *adv.* —**vi·car′i·ous·ness**, *n.*

vice, *n.* **1.** moral depravity. **2.** habitual personal shortcoming.

vice′-pres′i·dent, *n.* official next in rank below president. —**vice′-pres″i·den′tial**, *adj.* —**vice″-pres′i·den·cy**, *n.*

vice′roy, *n.* deputy sovereign; representative ruler. —**vice-re′gal**, *adj.*

vi′ce ver′sa, with the order changed; conversely.

vi·cin′i·ty, *n., pl.* **-ties.** local area; neighborhood.

vi′cious, *adj.* **1.** depraved; immoral. **2.** spiteful; malicious. **3.** evil. —**vi′cious·ly**, *adv.* —**vi′cious·ness**, *n.*

vi·cis·si·tude (və sis′ə tōōd″), *n.* unpredictable change.

vic′tim, *n.* **1.** sufferer from a force or action. **2.** dupe. —**vic″tim·ize″**, *v.t.*

vic′tor, *n.* winner; conqueror.

vic′to·ry, *n., pl.* **-ries.** success in a contest; triumph. —**vic·to′ri·ous**, *adj.* —**vic·to′ri·ous·ly**, *adv.*

vict·ual (vi′təl), *n.* **1.** victuals, food. —*v.t.* **2.** provision.

vid″e·o, *n., adj.* **1.** television. **2.** a short, visual performance featuring a rock music soundtrack.

vid″e·o·tape′, *n.* electromagnetic tape for recording visual images.

vie, *v.i.* **vied, vying.** contend; compete.

view, *n.* **1.** seeing; beholding. **2.** area or range of vision. **3.** landscape. **4.** purpose. **5.** opinion; attitude. —*v.* **6.** look at; regard. —**view′er**, *n.* —**view′less**, *adj.*

vig′il, *n.* act of keeping awake and alert.

vig′i·lant, *adj.* alert; keenly aware. —**vig′i·lant·ly**, *adv.* —**vig′i·lance**, *n.*

vig′or, *n.* robust health, energy, or strength. —**vig′or·ous**, *adj.* —**vig′or·ous·ly**, *adv.*

vile, *adj.*, **viler, vilest.** **1.** of little account; mean. **2.** nasty; contemptible. —**vile′ly**, *adv.* —**vile′ness**, *n.*

vil′i·fy″, *v.t.* **-fied, -fying.** denounce; defame. —**vil″i·fi·ca′tion**, *n.*

vil′la, *n.* country or suburban house.

vil′lage, *n.* small town; hamlet. —**vil′lager**, *n.*

vil′lain, *n.* wicked person; scoundrel. —**vil′lain·ous**, *adj.* —**vil′lain·y**, *n.*

vim, *n.* vigor; robustness.

vin′di·cate″, *v.t.* **-cated, -cating.** absolve from suspicion or doubt. —**vin″di·ca′tion**, *n.* —**vin′di·ca·ble**, *adj.*

vin·dic′tive, *adj.* holding a grudge. —**vin·dic′tive·ly**, *adv.* —**vin·dic′tive·ness**, *n.*

vine, *n.* slender, creeping or climbing plant.

vin′e·gar, *n.* sour fermented liquid. —**vin′e·gar·y**, *adj.*

vine·yard (vin′yərd), *n.* garden or plantation for the growth of vines.

vin′tage, *n.* **1.** wine extracted from a single harvest of grapes. **2.** harvest of grapes.

vi·o·la (vē ō′lə), *n.* stringed instrument with a pitch slightly below that of a violin.

vi′o·late″, *v.t.*, **-lated, -lating.** **1.** break; transgress. **2.** desecrate. **3.** rape. —**vi″o·la′tion**, *n.* —**vi′o·la″tor**, *n.*

vi′o·lent, *adj.* **1.** physically aggressive. **2.** severe; turbulent. —**vi′o·lent·ly**, *adv.* —**vi′o·lence**, *n.*

vi′o·let, *n.* **1.** low-growing herb bearing purplish or bluish blossoms. **2.** bluish purple.

vi·o·lin′, *n.* small, stringed musical instrument played with a bow. —**vi″o·lin′ist**, *n.*

vi″o·lon·cel′lo, *n., pl.* **-los.** cello. —**vi″o·lon·cel′list**, *n.*

vi′per, *n.* **1.** venomous snake. **2.** ill-tempered, malicious person. —**vi′per·ous**, *adj.*

vi·ra′go, *n., pl.* **-gos, -goes.** malicious woman; shrew; witch.

vir′gin, *n.* **1.** sexually inexperienced person. —*adj.* **2.** being a virgin. **3.** unexplored, unexploited, etc. —**vir′gin·al**, *adj.*

vir′ile, *adj.* **1.** capable of siring offspring. **2.** vigorous; manly; potent. —**vi·ril′i·ty**, *n.*

vir′tu·al, *adj.* so in effect. —**vir′tu·al·ly**, *adv.*

vir′tue, *n.* **1.** morality. **2.** chastity. **3.** merit. —**vir′tu·ous**, *adj.* —**vir′tu·ous·ly**, *adv.* —**vir′tu·ous·ness**, *n.*

vir″tu·o′so *n., pl.* **-sos, -si.** musician, etc., of outstanding skill. —**vir″tu·os′i·ty**, *n.*

vir′u·lent, *adj.* **1.** poisonous; deadly. **2.** hostile. —**vir′u·lence, vir′u·len·cy**, *n.* —**vir′u·lent·ly**, *adv.*

vi′rus, *adj.* infectious agency. —**vi′ral**, *adj.* —**vi′ral·ly**, *adv.*

vi·sa (vē′zə), *n.* endorsement to a passport.

vis′age, *n.* **1.** face. **2.** aspect; look.

vis·cer·a (vis'ər ə), *n.*, *pl.* internal bodily organs. —**vis'cer·al**, *adj.*

vis·cid (vis'id), *adj.* sticky to the touch; tacky. Also, **vis'cous.** —**vis·cos'i·ty**, *n.*

vise, *n.* holding tool attached to a work bench, etc.

vis'i·ble, *adj.* 1. capable of being seen. 2. perceptible. —**vis'i·bly**, *adv.* —**vis·i·bil'i·ty**, *n.*

vi'sion, *n.* 1. sense of sight. 2. supernatural apprehension. 3. foresight. —**vi'sion·al**, *adj.*

vi'sion·ar''y, *adj.* 1. fanciful. 2. apprehended by or as by supernatural means. 3. unreal; fancied. —*n.* 4. person seeing visions. 5. impractical person; dreamer.

vi'sit, *v.t.* 1. go to and stay briefly at. 2. afflict. —*n.* 3. brief stay, esp. as a guest. —**vis'i·tor**, *n.* —**vis'i·tant**, *adj.* —**vis''i·ta'tion**, *n.*

vi'sor, *n.* forward projecting part, as of a helmet or cap.

vis'ta, *n.* panoramic view.

vis'u·al, *adj.* pertaining to sight. —**vis'u·al·ly** *adj.*

vis'u·a·lize'', *v.t.*, -ized, -izing. obtain or create a picture or conception of. —**vis''u·al·i·za'tion**, *n.*

vi'tal, *adj.* 1. pertaining to life or existence. 2. extremely important. 3. full of exuberance, creativity, etc. —**vi'tal·ly**, *adv.* —**vi·tal'i·ty**, *n.*

vi'ta·min, *n.* organic substance vital in small quantities to proper nutrition. —**vi''ta·min'ic**, *adj.*

vi·ti·ate (vish'ē āt''), *v.t.*, -ated, -ating. 1. impair. 2. invalidate; negate. —**vi''ti·a'tion**, *n.*

vit're·ous, *adj.* glazed or glassy.

vit'ri·ol, *n.* sulfuric acid.

vit''ri·ol'ic, *adj.* 1. pertaining to vitriol. 2. caustic, as criticism.

vi·tu·per·ate (vī tōō' pər āt''), *v.t.*, -ated, -ating. 1. criticize harshly or abusively. 2. revile. —**vi·tu''per·a'tion**, *n.* —**vi·tu'per·a·tive**, *adj.*

vi·va'cious, *adj.* animated; lively. —**vi·va'cious·ly**, *adj.* —**vi·vac'i·ty**, **vi·va'cious·ness**, *n.*

viv'id, *adj.* 1. bright; brilliant. 2. intense. —**viv'id·ly**, *adj.* —**viv'id·ness**, *n.*

viv'i·sect'', *v.t.* dissect while alive. —**viv''i·sec'tion**, *n.* —**viv''i·sec'tion·ist**, *n.*

vix'en, *n.* 1. female fox. 2. mischievious girl or woman.

vo·cab'u·lar''y, *n.*, *pl.* -ies. 1. stock of words used by a person, people, or group. 2. collection of words in alphabetical order.

vo'cal, *adj.* 1. pertaining to the voice. 2. pertaining to singing. 3. articulate; outspoken. —**vo'cal·ly**, *adj.* —**vo'cal·ize**, *v.t.*, *v.i.* —**vo''cal·i·za'tion**, *n.*

vo·ca'tion, *n.* profession; occupation. —**vo·ca'tion·al**, *adj.*

voc'a·tive, *adj.* 1. relating to a grammatical case indicating person or thing addressed. —*n.* 2. vocative case.

vo·cif'er·ate (vō sif'ər āt''), *v.*, -ated, -ating. *v.i.*, *v.t.* shout. —**vo·cif''er·a'tion**, *n.* —**vo·cif''er·ous**, *adj.*

vogue, *n.* 1. fashion; trend. 2. popular favor or approval.

voice, *n.*, *v.t.* voiced, voicing. *n.* 1. sound uttered through the mouth. 2. singing or speaking voice. 3. expression. 4. choice. 5. right to express one's opinion. 6. *Grammar.* verbal inflection indicating whether subject is acting or acted upon. —*v.t.* 7. express; declare. —**voice'less**, *adj.*

void, *adj.* 1. without legal power. 2. useless; fruitless. 3. empty; hollow. —*n.* 4. empty or hollow space. —*v.t.* 5. cancel; invalidate. —**void'a·ble**, *adj.* —**void'ance**, *n.*

vol'a·tile, *adj.* 1. evaporating rapidly. 2. energetic; lively. 3. tending to erupt into violence. —**vol·a·til'i·ty**, *n.*

vol·ca'no, *n.*, *pl.* -noes, -nos. mountain that ejects molten lava, rock, and steam. —**vol·can'ic**, *adj.* —**vol·can'i·cal·ly**, *adv.*

vo·li'tion, *n.* 1. power of choosing or determining; will. 2. act of willing. —**vo·li'tion·al**, *adj.*

vol'ley, *n.*, *pl.* -leys, *v.t.* *n.* 1. simultaneous discharge of a number of missiles. —*v.t.* 2. fire in a volley.

volt, *n.* unit of electromotive force.

vol'u·ble, *adj.* fluent; talkative. —**vol'u·bly**, *adv.* —**vol·u·bil'i·ty**, *n.*

vol'ume, *n.* 1. size in three dimensions. 2. quantity; mass. 3. degree of loudness. 4. book.

vo·lu'mi·nous, *adj.* 1. great in size or degree. 2. consisting of or filling many books. —**vo·lu'min·ous·ly**, *adv.*

vol'un·tar''y, *adj.* 1. performed or acted on by choice. 2. controlled by the will. —**vol''un·tar'i·ly**, *adv.*

vol''un·teer', *v.t.* 1. offer freely or spontaneously. —*v.i.* 2. volunteer oneself. —*n.* 3. person who volunteers.

vo·lup'tu·ous, *adj.* sensuous; sensual; luxurious. —**vo·lup'tu·ous·ly**, *adv.* —**vo·lup'tu·ous·ness**, *n.*

vom'it, *v.i.* 1. disgorge the contents of the stomach through the mouth. —*v.t.* 2. eject with force. —*n.* 3. matter ejected by vomiting.

vo·ra'cious, *adj.* ravenous; greedy. —**vo·ra'cious·ly**, *adv.* —**vo·rac'i·ty**, **vo·ra'cious·ness**, *n.*

vor'tex, *n.*, *pl.* -tices, -texes. whirling mass drawing objects to a central cavity.

vote, *n.*, *v.*, voted, voting. *n.* 1. formal ex-

pression of opinion or choice, as by ballot. **2.** right to such opinion or choice. **3.** votes collectively. —*v.t.* **4.** express or endorse by vote. —*v.i.* **5.** cast one's vote. —**vot′er** *n.*

vouch, *v.i.* **1.** give a guarantee or surety. **2.** give personal assurance.

vouch′er, *n.* **1.** person who vouches. **2.** document certifying the occurrence of a transaction.

vouch·safe′, *v.t.,* **-safed, -safing.** permit; grant; allow.

vow, *n.* **1.** pledge; solemn promise. —*v.t.* **2.** promise solemnly; swear. —*v.i.* **3.** make a vow.

vow′el, *n.* **1.** speech sound made with the central part of the breath channel unblocked. **2.** letter representing a vowel: *a, e, i, o, u* and sometimes *y.*

voy′age, *n., v.,* **-aged, -aging.** *n.* **1.** an extended journey, esp. by sea. —*v.i.* **2.** make a journey; travel. —*v.t.* **3.** traverse; sail. —**voy′ag·er** *n.*

vul′can·ize″, *v.t.,* **-ized, -izing.** treat crude or synthetic rubber chemically to give it elasticity and strength. —**vul″can·i·za′tion,** *n.* —**vul′can·i″zer,** *n.*

vul′gar, *adj.* **1.** lacking taste or breeding; unrefined. **2.** ordinary; plebian. **3.** ostentatiously showy. **4.** indecent; obscene. **5.** vernacular. —**vul′gar·ly,** *adv.* —**vul·gar′i·ty, vul′gar·ness,** *n.*

vul′ner·a·ble, *adj.* **1.** capable of being physically or emotionally wounded. **2.** open to damage or attack. —**vul′ner·a·bly,** *adv.* —**vul″ner·a·bil′i·ty,** *n.*

vul′ture, *n.* **1.** large bird subsisting chiefly on carrion. **2.** predatory or rapacious person. —**vul′tur·ous,** *adj.*

vul′va, *n., pl.* **-vas, -vae.** external female genital organs. —**vul′val, vul′var,** *adj.*

vy′ing, *adj.* competing; competitive.

W

W, w, *n.* twenty-third letter of the English alphabet.

wack′y, *adj.* **-ier, -iest.** *Informal.* odd, erratic, crazy. —**wack′i·ly,** *adv.* —**wack′i·ness,** *n.*

wad′dle, *v.i.,* **-dled, -dling.** *n.* *v.i.* **1.** walk like a duck. —*n.* **2.** waddling gait.

wade, *v.,* **waded, wading.** *v.i.* **1.** walk through water. —*v.t.* **2.** cross by wading. —**wad′er,** *n.*

wa′fer, *n.* **1.** thin, crisp cracker or cookie.

2. thin disk of bread used in the Eucharist.

waf′fle, *n.* crisp batter cake baked in a double griddle.

waft, *v.t., v.i.* float through air or over water.

wag, *v.,* **wagged, wagging,** *n. v.t., v.i.* **1.** shake in an arc. —*n.* **2.** wit, joker. —**wag′ger·y,** *n.* —**wag′gish,** *adj.*

wage, *n., pl.* **wages,** *v.t.,* **waged, waging.** *n.* **1.** pay. —*v.t.* **2.** carry on, as war.

wa′ger, *n., v.t., v.i.* bet.

wag′gle, *v.,* **-gled, -gling,** *n. v.t., v.i.* **1.** shake. —*n.* **2.** shake.

wag′on, *n.* four-wheeled draft freight vehicle.

waif, *n.* homeless child or animal.

wail, *v.i., v.t.* **1.** cry mournfully. —*n.* **2.** mournful cry. —**wail′er,** *n.*

wain′scot, *n.* **1.** woodwork along an interior wall. —*v.t.* **2.** line with woodwork.

waist, *n.* part of the body between ribs and hips. —**waist′band″,** *n.* —**waist′ line″,** *n.*

wait, *v.i.* **1.** stop briefly; pause. **2.** be in expectation. **3.** be patient. **4.** remain undone. **5.** serve food, etc. —*n.* **6.** act, instance, or period of waiting. **7. in wait,** in ambush.

wait′er, *n.* **1.** person who waits. **2.** Also, *fem.,* **wait′ress,** server of diners.

waive, *v.t.,* **waived, waiving.** give up; relinquish.

waiv′er, *n.* document that relinquishes.

wake, *v.,* **waked,** or **woke, woked** or **woken, waking,** *n. v.i.* **1.** awake. **2.** be alert. —*v.t.* **3.** arouse. —*n.* **4.** vigil, as over a corpse. —**wake′ful,** *adj.* —**wake′ful·ly,** *adv.* —**wake′ful·ness,** *n.*

wale, *n., v.t.,* **waled, waling.** *n.* **1.** welt as from a whip. —*v.t.* **2.** mark with wales.

walk, *v.i.* **1.** go on foot. —*v.t.* **2.** cause to walk. **3.** accompany on foot. —*n.* **4.** act or instance of walking. **5.** place for walking. —**walk′er,** *n.*

walk′ie-talk′ie, *n.* portable two-way radio.

wall, *n.* **1.** upright enclosure. —*v.t.* **2.** enclose or separate.

wall′board″, *n.* light material for covering interior walls or ceilings.

wal′let, *n.* pocket case for money, cards, etc.

wall′flow″er, *n.* *Informal.* **1.** girl onlooker at a party. **2.** sweet-scented flowering plant that sometimes grows on walls.

wal′lop, *v.t.* **1.** beat or thrash. —*n.* **2.** powerful blow.

wal′low, *v.i.* **1.** roll about, as in mud. **2.** indulge oneself. —*n.* **3.** muddy area.

wall′pa″per, *n.* **1.** decorative paper for

interior walls. —v.t. **2.** put wallpaper on.

Wall Street, U.S. financial world.

wal'nut", n. edible nut from a northern tree.

wal'rus, n. large sea mammal with two tusks.

waltz, n. **1.** dance in three-quarter time. —v.i. **2.** dance a waltz. —v.t. **3.** Informal. lead briskly. —**waltz'er,** n.

wam'pum, n. shell beads used by North American Indians as money or ornaments.

wan, adj., **wanner, wannest.** pale or sick-looking. —**wan'ly,** adv.

wand, n. rod with supposed magical power.

wan'der, v.i. **1.** move about aimlessly. **2.** stray. —v.t. **3.** travel over. —**wan'der·er,** n.

wan'der·lust", n. desire to wander or travel.

wane, v.i., n., **wane, waning.** v.i. **1.** grow dim, as the moon's light. **2.** decline in strength or power. —n. **3.** decrease or decline.

wan'gle, v.t., **-gled, -gling.** Informal. get by scheming or persuasion.

want, v.t. **1.** wish for. **2.** desire, crave, demand. —v.i. **3.** be lacking or deficient. —n. **4.** something needed. **5.** deficiency or lack. —**want'ing,** adj., prep.

wan'ton, adj. **1.** gratuitous. **2.** sexually loose. n. **3.** lascivious woman. —v.t. **4.** squander. —**wan'ton·ly,** adv. —**wan'ton·ness,** n.

wap'i·ti, n., pl. **-tis, -ti.** elk with wide antlers.

war, n., v.i., **warred, warring.** n. **1.** armed conflict, as between nations. **2.** hostility or struggle. —v.i. **3.** be in conflict. —**war'fare",** n. —**war'like,** adj.

war'ble, v., **-bled, -bling,** n. v.t., v.i. **1.** sing with trills, as a bird. —n. **2.** warbling. —**war'bler,** n.

ward, n. **1.** administrative division of a city. **2.** division of a hospital. **3.** person under the care of a guardian. —v.t. **4.** repel or avert.

war'den, n. **1.** chief officer of a prison. **2.** person in charge of others or things, keeper.

ward'er, n. guard.

ward'robe", n. **1.** collection of clothes. **2.** closet for clothes.

ward'room", n. living and dining area for commissioned officers on a warship.

ware, n. goods for sale.

ware'house", n., v.t., **-housed, -housing.** n. **1.** storage building. —v.t. **2.** store in a warehouse.

war'head", n. explosive front part of a bomb, missile, or torpedo.

war'horse", n. **1.** veteran of many conflicts. **2.** overfamiliar concert number.

war'lock", n. male with magical power; sorcerer.

war'lord", n. military ruler.

warm, adj. **1.** having or giving moderate heat. **2.** friendly or affectionate. **3.** irritated or angry. —v.t., v.i. **4.** heat moderately. —**warm'ly,** adv. —**warmth, warm'ness,** n. —**warm'ish,** adj.

warm'heart'ed, adj. friendly; sympathetic.

war·mon·ger (wor'mun"gər), n. inciter of war.

warn, v.t. give notice of danger; caution. —**warn'ing,** n., adj.

warp, n. **1.** distortion. **2.** lengthwise threads in cloth. —v.t., v.i. **3.** distort.

war'rant, n. **1.** authorization, as by law. **2.** guarantee. —v.t. **3.** authorize. **4.** guarantee. —**war'rant·a·ble,** adj.

war'ran·ty, n., pl. **-ties.** guarantee on something sold.

war'ri·or, n. soldier.

wart, n. small hard protuberance on the skin. —**wart'y,** adj.

war'y, adj., **warier, wariest.** cautious; watchful. —**war'i·ly,** adv. —**war'i·ness,** n.

was, v. 1st and 3rd person singular, past indicative of be.

wash, v.t. **1.** clean with or in water or a solution. **2.** flow over. —v.i. **3.** wash oneself. **4.** undergo washing. —n. **5.** washing, as of clothes. **6.** current behind a moving ship or plane. —**wash'a·ble,** adj. —**wash'board',** n. —**wash'bowl',** n. —**wash'cloth',** n. —**wash'stand',** n.

wash'er, n. **1.** washing machine. **2.** pierced disk for tightening a joint to prevent leakage, etc.

wash'out", n. **1.** washing away of earth, soil, etc. **2.** Informal. failure.

WASP, n. white Anglo-Saxon Protestant. Also, **W.A.S.P., Wasp.**

wasp, n. stinging insect. —**wasp'ish,** adj.

was'sail (wos'əl), n. **1.** drinking or toasting a person's health, as with a spiced ale. **2.** drinking festivity. —v.i., v.t. **3.** toast.

waste, v., **wasted, wasting,** n., adj. v.t. **1.** use up needlessly. **2.** ruin. —v.i. **3.** be used up gradually. —n. **4.** needless consumption or expenditure. **5.** unused remains. **6.** neglect. **7.** ruin. —adj. **8.** unused. —**waste'bas'ket,** n. —**waste'ful,** adj. —**waste'pa'per,** n.

wast·rel (wās'trəl), n. wasteful person; spendthrift.

watch, v.i. **1.** observe; be on the alert. —v.t. **2.** observe. **3.** guard or tend. —n. **4.** period of watching; observation. **5.** small timepiece worn on the person —**watch'band,** n. —**watch'**

dog, *n.* —**watch′ful,** *adj.* —**watch′ man,** *n.* —**watch′tow′er,** *n.*

watch′word′′, *n.* **1.** password. **2.** motto; slogan.

wa′ter, *n.* **1.** colorless, odorless liquid forming rain, rivers, etc. —*v.t.* **2.** supply with water. —*v.i.* **3.** dischargewater or tears. —**wa′ter·y,** *adj.*

wa′ter·bed′′, *n.* heavy water-filled bag used as a bed.

water closet, toilet.

wa′ter·col′or, *n.* **1.** pigment mixed with water. **2.** painting with such pigments.

wa′ter·course′′, *n.* channel for water, as a river, canal, etc.

wa′ter·fall′′, *n.* steep fall of water, as over a precipice.

wa′ter·fowl′′, *n.* water bird.

water glass, drinking glass.

water lily, aquatic plant with floating leaves and flowers.

wa′ter-logged′′, *adj.* saturated with water.

wa′ter·mark′′, *n.* **1.** mark showing height of water, as of a river, etc. **2.** manufacturer's impression on paper. —*v.t.* **3.** mark with a watermark.

wa′ter·mel′′on, *n.* large fruit with juicy, red pulp.

wa′ter·proof′′, *adj.* **1.** impervious to water. —*v.t.* **2.** make waterproof.

wa′ter·shed′′, *n.* **1.** ridge between two drainage areas. **2.** drainage area.

wa′ter-ski′′, *v.,* **-skied, -skiing,** *n. v.i.* **1.** skim over water on ski-like boards drawn by a line attached to a speedboat. —*n.* **2.** short, broad board for water-skiing.

wa′ter·spout′′, *n.* **1.** pipe for discharging water. **2.** tubelike column of air and water occurring over water.

water table, *n.* level below which the ground is saturated.

wa′ter·wheel′′, *n.* mill wheel moved by water.

wa′ter·works′′, *n.* plant for supplying water.

watt, *n.* unit of electric power. —**watt′ age,** *n.*

wat′tle, *n.* **1.** stakes interwoven with twigs, as for fences, walls, etc. **2.** fleshy skin hanging from the throat or chin.

wave, *n., v.* **waved, waving.** *n.* **1.** ridge along the ocean's surface. **2.** undulation. **3.** movement back and forth, as of a hand or flag. —*v.i., v.t.,* **4.** move to and fro. —*v.i.* **5.** signal with the hand. —**wav′y,** *adj.*

wa′ver, *v.i.* **1.** hesitate. **2.** sway. —*n.* **3.** wavering.

WAVES, *n.* W(omen) A(ppointed for) V(oluntary) E(mergency) S(ervice); women in the U.S. Navy.

wax, *n.* **1.** readily melted, molded, and burned substance. —*v.t.* **2.** treat with wax. —*v.i.* **3.** increase, as the moon. **4.** *Archaic.* become. —**wax′en,** *adj.* —**wax′er,** *n.* —**wax′y,** *adj.*

wax′wing′′, *n.* crested bird with scarlet wings' ends.

way, *n.* **1.** manner, custom, or fashion. **2.** plan. **3.** direction or route. **4. ways,** tracks for launching a ship.

way′far′′er, *n.* traveler or rover.

way′′lay′, *v.t.,* **-laid, -laying.** lie in wait for; ambush.

way′ward, *adj.* **1.** willful. **2.** capricious —**way′ward·ness,** *n.*

we, *pron.* nominative plural of *I.*

weak, *adj.* **1.** not strong physically. **2.** lacking moral or mental strength. **3.** easily broken. —**weak′ly,** *adj., adv.* —**weak′en,** *v.t., v.i.* —**weak′ling,** *n.* —**weak′ness,** *n.*

wealth, *n.* **1.** abundance of money or property. **2.** large and valuable amount. —**wealth′y,** *adj.*

wean, *v.t.* **1.** accustom to food other than mother's milk. **2.** cure of a dependency or delusion.

weap′on, *n.* instrument for fighting. —**weap′on·ry,** *n.*

wear, *v.,* **wore, worn, wearing.** *v.t.* **1.** have on the body, as clothing. **2.** diminish by use. —*v.i.* **3.** deteriorate as through use. —*n.* **4.** diminution or impairment through use. **5.** clothing. —**wear′a·ble,** *adj.* —**wear′er,** *n.*

wea′ri·some, *adj.* tiresome.

wear′y, *adj.,* **-rier, -riest,** *v.t.,* **-rying, -ried.** *adj.* **1.** very tired. **2.** causing fatigue. —*v.t.* **3.** tire. —**wear′i·ly,** *adv.* —**wear′i·ness,** *n.*

wea′sel, *n.* small, flesh-eating mammal.

weath′er, *n.* **1.** condition of the sky. **2.** storms, rains, etc. —*v.t.* **3.** withstand. **4.** expose to the weather. —*adj.* **5.** toward the wind.

weath′er·beat′′en, *adj.* showing the effect of weather.

weave, *v.,* **wove, woven** or **weaved, weaving,** *n. v.t.* **1.** interlace threads, etc., as on a loom. **2.** construct, as in the mind. —*v.i.* **3.** become interlaced. —*n.* **4.** type of weaving. —**weav′er,** *n.*

web, *n., v.t.,* **webbed, webbing.** *n.* **1.** something woven. **2.** network spun by spiders. **3.** trap. —*v.t.* **4.** join or cover,as by or with a web. —**webbed,** *adj.* —**web′bing,** *n.*

web′foot′′, *n., pl.* **-feet.** foot with webbed toes. —**web′-foot′′ed, web′-toed′′,** *adj.*

wed, *v.,* **wedded, wedded** or **wed, wedding.** *v.t., v.i.* **1.** marry. **2.** join. —**wed′ ding,** *n.*

wedge, *n., v.,* **wedged, wedging.** *n.* **1.** object with two faces meeting at a sharp angle. —*v.t.* **2.** force or fix with a wedge. —*v.i.* **3.** become wedged.

wed′lock, *n.* state of marriage.

Wednes'day, *n.* fourth day of the week.

wee, *adj.* tiny.

weed, *n.* 1. useless plant. —*v.i.* 2. free from weeds. —**weed'er,** *n.* —**weed'y,** *adj.*

week, *n.* 1. period of seven days, esp. starting from Sunday. 2. working days of the week.

week'day", *n.* 1. any day except Saturday or Sunday. —*adj.* 2. pertaining to such days.

week'end", *n.* Saturday and Sunday.

week'ly, *adj., adv., n., pl.* **-lies.** *adj.* 1. appearing or occurring once a week. 2. lasting a week. —*adv.* 3. every week. —*n.* 4. weekly periodical.

weep, *v.i.,* **wept, weeping.** mourn or shed tears. —**weep'er,** *n.*

wee'vil, *n.* beetle destructive to grain, fruit, etc.

weigh, *v.t.* 1. measure the heaviness of. 2. consider carefully. —*v.i.* 3. have significance. 4. be a burden. —**weigh'er,** *n.*

weight, *n.* 1. heaviness or pressure. 2. burden, influence, or importance. —*v.t.* 3. burden. —**weight'y,** *adj.* —**weight'i·ness,** *n.*

weird, *adj.* strange, uncanny, or queer. —**weird'ly,** *adv.* —**weird'ness,** *n.*

wel'come, *n., v.t.,* **-comed, -coming,** *adj.* *n.* 1. friendly greeting. —*v.t.* 2. greet with pleasure. —*adj.* 3. happily or readily received. 4. freely permitted.

weld, *v.t.* 1. unite, as by heat or pressure. —*n.* 2. welded joint. —**weld'er,** *n.*

wel'fare", *n.* 1. well-being. 2. aid for the poor.

well, *adv.,* **better, best,** *adj., n., v.i., interj. adv.* 1. in a benevolent, good, or thorough manner. —*adj.* 2. in good health. 3. suitable. —*n.* 4. opening in the earth as a source of water, oil, etc. —*v.i.* 5. flow or gush. —*interj.* 6. (exclamation denoting surprise or introducing a sentence).

well- prefix meaning "in a good or thorough manner." **well-accomplished, well-adjusted, well-aimed, well-argued, well-armed, well-arranged, well-attended, well-aware, well-behaved, well-built, well-considered, well-contented, well-controlled, well-developed, well-disciplined, well-documented, well-earned, well-educated, well-equipped, well-governed, well-hidden, well-justified, well-kept, well-liked, well-loved, well-managed, well-planned, well-prepared, well-protected, well-qualified, well-regulated, well-remembered, well-respected, well-satisfied, well-secured, well-situated, well-spent, well-stated, well-suited, well-taught, well-trained, well-traveled, well-treated, well-understood, well-used.**

well'-be'ing, *n.* state of being well and happy.

well'-bred', *adj.* with good manners.

well'-es·tab'lished, *adj.* settled; firmly in place.

well'-found'ed, *adj.* based on good reason. Also, **well'-ground'ed,** *adj.*

well'head", *n.* fountainhead; source.

well'-man'nered, *adj.* polite; courteous.

well'-mean'ing, *adj.* having good intentions. —**well'-meant',** *adj.*

well'-nigh', *adv.* almost.

well'-off', *adj.* 1. in a good condition. 2. prosperous.

well'-pre·served', *adj.* 1. in good condition. 2. youthful for one's age.

well'-round'ed, *adj.* 1. having varied abilities. 2. well-diversified.

well'-spo'ken, *adj.* speaking well or pleasantly.

well'spring", *n.* source.

well'-to-do', *adj.* wealthy.

well'-wish"er, *n.* person who wishes well to another.

welt, *n.* 1. ridge or wale on the body from a blow. 2. leather strip on the seam of a shoe. —*v.t.* 3. beat soundly.

welt'er, *v.i.* 1. roll or heave, as waves. 2. wallow. —*n.* 3. jumble or muddle.

wen, *n.* skin cyst or tumor.

wench, *n.* 1. young woman. 2. strumpet. —*v.i.* 3. associate with promiscuous women.

went, *v.i.* past form of *go.*

were, *v.* past plural form of *be.*

were'wolf", *n., pl.* **-wolves.** person changed into a wolf.

west, *n.* 1. compass point to the left of north. 2. direction of such point. 3. Also, **West,** the Occident. —*adj., adv.* 4. toward or from the west. —**west'ern,** *adj.* —**west'ern·er,** *n.*

west'er·ly, *adj., adv.* 1. from the west, as wind. 2. toward the west.

west'ern·ize", *v.t.,* **-ized, -izing.** make Occidental in culture.

west'ward, *adj.* 1. toward the west. —*adv.* 2. Also, **west'wards,** toward the west. —*n.* 3. westward direction.

wet, *adj.,* **wetter, wettest,** *n., v. adj.* 1. covered with water or liquid. —*n.* 2. water or moisture. —*v.t.* 3. make wet. —*v.i.* 4. become wet. —**wet'ness,** *n.*

whack, *Informal. v.t., v.i.* 1. slap or strike. —*n.* 2. sharp blow.

whale, *n., v.i.,* **whaled, whaling.** *n.* 1. large sea mammal. —*v.i.* 2. hunt whales. —**whal'er,** *n.*

whale'bone", *n.* elastic material in the upper jaw of some whales.

wharf, *n., pl.* **wharves.** pier or quay.

what, *pron., pl.* **what,** *adj., adv., interj. pron.* 1. which one? 2. that which. —*adj.* 3. which kind of. —*adv.* 4. how? 5. partly. —*interj.* 6. (exclamation of surprise).

what·ev'er, *pron.* **1.** anything that. —*adj.* **2.** of any kind.

what'not", *n.* open cupboard, as for bric-a-brac.

wheal, *n.* small swelling, as from an insect bite.

wheat, *n.* cereal grass used in flour, etc.

whee'dle, *v.t.,* **-dled, -dling.** persuade by coaxing.

wheel, *n.* **1.** rotating disk that transmits power or facilitates movement. —*v.t., v.i.* **2.** move on wheels. **3.** revolve.

wheel'bar"row, *n.* one-wheeled container for moving loads.

wheel'base", *n.* distance between the front and rear wheel hubs of an automobile.

wheel'er-deal'er, *n. Informal.* person skillful in business deals.

wheeze, *v.i.,* **wheezed, wheezing.** *n. v.i.* **1.** breathe with a whistling sound. —*n.* **2.** a wheezing sound. —**wheez'y,** *adj.*

whelm, *v.t.* **1.** submerge. **2.** overwhelm.

whelp, *n.* **1.** young of a dog, bear, etc. —*v.t., v.i.* **2.** give birth to.

when, *adv.* **1.** at what time? —*conj.* **2.** at the time that. —*pron.* **3.** what or which time.

whence, *adv.* from what place, cause, etc.

when·ev'er, *adv.* **1.** when. —*conj.* **2.** at whatever time.

where, *adv.* **1.** at what place? **2.** in what way? —*conj.* **3.** at which place; wherever. —*pron.* **4.** the place at which.

where'a·bouts", *adv.* **1.** where. —*n.* **2.** location.

where·as', *conj.* **1.** considering that. **2.** on the contrary.

where'fore", *adv., conj.* for what.

where·in', *conj.* in which.

where'up·on', *conj.* upon which.

where'with·al", *n.* means.

wher'ry, *n., pl.* **-ries.** light rowboat.

whet, *v.t.,* **whetted, whetting. 1.** sharpen. **2.** stimulate, as the appetite. —**whet'stone",** *n.*

wheth'er, *conj.* **1.** if it is so that. **2.** if either.

whey, *n.* water part of curdled milk.

which, *pron.* **1.** what one? **2.** that. —*adj.* **3.** what one.

which·ev'er, *pron., adj.* **1.** any. **2.** regardless of which.

whiff, *n.* light odor or puff.

whif'fle·tree", *n.* crossbar to which harness traces are fastened.

while, *n., conj., v.t.,* **whiled, whiling.** *n.* **1.** time. —*conj.* **2.** during the time that. **3.** although. —*v.t.* **4.** spend pleasantly, as time.

whim, *n.* sudden fancy; caprice. —**whim'si·cal,** *adj.* —**whim'sy,** *n.*

whine, *v.i.,* **whined, whining. 1.** complain childishly. **2.** make a high-pitched, nasal sound. —**whin'ing·ly,** *adv.* —**whin'y,** *adj.*

whin'ny, *v.i.,* **-nied, -nying,** *n., pl.* **-nies.** neigh.

whip, *v.,* **whipped, whipping,** *n. v.t.* **1.** strike or lash. —*v.i.* **2.** move quickly. —*n.* **3.** instrument for whipping.

whip'cord", *n.* hard, braided cord.

whip'lash", *n.* neck injury from jerking of the head as in an automobile accident.

whip'per·snap"per, *n.* presumptuous person.

whip'pet, *n.* fast dog.

whip'poor·will", *n.* gray bird with nocturnal cry.

whir, *v.,* **whirred, whirring,** *n. v.i., v.t., n.* hum or buzz. Also, **whirr.**

whirl, *v.i., v.t.* **1.** move or revolve rapidly. —*n.* **2.** whirling movement. **3.** uproar or confusion.

whirl'pool", *n.* whirling current of water.

whirl'wind", *n.* whirling current of air.

whisk, *v.t., v.i.* **1.** brush with a quick motion. —*n.* **2.** act or instance of whisking. —**whisk'broom",** *n.*

whisk'er, *n.* **1.** a facial hair. **2.** long bristle, as on a cat.

whis'key, *n., pl.* **-keys, -kies.** liquor distilled from fermented grain. Also, **whis'ky.**

whis'per, *v.i., v.t.* **1.** speak softly. **2.** make a low rustling. —*n.* **3.** act or instance of whispering.

whist, *n.* card game.

whis'tle, *v., -tled, -tling, n. v.i.* **1.** make a high-pitched sound through pursed lips. —*n.* **2.** act or instance of whistling. **3.** noise-making device using steam or air.

whit, *n.* small bit.

white, *adj.* **1.** of the color of snow. **2.** pale. **3.** pure. —*n.* **4.** opposite to black. **5.** Caucasoid. —**white'ness,** *n.* —**whit'ish,** *adj.* —**whit'en,** *v.t., v.i.*

white elephant, 1. albino elephant. **2.** awkward, useless possession.

white'fish", *n.* edible lake fish.

White House, 1. residence of the U.S. president. **2.** executive branch of the U.S. government.

white lie, small, pardonable lie.

white slave, woman forced into prostitution. —**white slavery.**

white'wash", *n.* **1.** mixture for whitening walls. —*v.t.* **2.** apply whitewash to. **3.** *Informal.* conceal the guilt of.

white'y, *Informal.* white person or people. Also, **White'y, whit'y.**

whith'er, *adv., conj. Archaic.* to what place.

whit'ing, *n.* **1.** food fish. **2.** chalk for paints.

whit'low, *n.* inflammation of a finger or toe.

whit'tle, *v., -tled, -tling. v.t., v.i.* **1.** cut or

carve, as from wood. —*v.t.* **2.** reduce the amount of.

whiz, *v.i.,* **whizzed, whizzing.** *n. v.i.* **1.** make a buzzing sound in motion. —*n.* **2.** such a sound. **3.** *Informal.* expert. Also, **whizz.**

who, *pron.* **1.** which person? **2.** person that.

whoa, *interj.* stop!

who·ev'er, *pron.* anyone that.

whole, *adj.* **1.** entire. **2.** intact. **3.** *Math.* not a fraction. —*n.* **4.** all the amount. —**whole'ly,** *adv.* —**whole'ness,** *n.*

whole'heart'ed, *adj.* enthusiastic; dedicated. —**whole'heart'ed·ly,** *adv.*

whole'sale", *n., adj., v.,* **-saled, saling.** *n.* **1.** sale of goods in quantity, as to retailers. —*adj.* **2.** selling by wholesale. —*v.t., v.i.* **3.** sell wholesale. —**whole'sal'er,** *n.*

whole'some, *adj.* healthful, salutary. —**whole'some·ly,** *adv.* —**whole'some·ness,** *n.*

whom, *pron. Grammar.* objective case of who.

whoop, *n.* **1.** shout of joy. **2.** sound in whooping cough. —*v.t., v.i.* **3.** utter with whooping.

whop·per, *n. Informal.* **1.** something unusually large. **2.** outrageous lie. —**whop'ping,** *adj.*

whore, *n., v.i.,* **whored, whoring.** *n.* **1.** prostitute. —*v.i.* **2.** consort with whores. —**whor'ish,** *adj.*

whorl, *n.* spiral or circular arrangement.

whose, *pron. Grammar.* possessive case of who.

who'so·ev'er, *pron.* whoever.

why, *adv., n., pl.* **whys,** *interj. adv.* **1.** for what reason or cause. —*n.* **2.** reason, cause, or purpose. —*interj.* **3.** exclamation of surprise.

wick, *n.* length of fiber that absorbs fuel to burn.

wick'ed, *adj.* **1.** bad, evil. **2.** mischievous. —**wick'ed·ly,** *adv.* —**wick'ed·ness,** *n.*

wick'er, *n.* **1.** flexible twig. —*adj.* **2.** made of wicker. —**wick'er·work",** *n.*

wick'et, *n.* **1.** small gate. **2.** upright frame used in cricket or croquet.

wide, *adj., wider, widest. adj.* **1.** broad. —*adv.* **2.** far. —**wide'ly,** *adv.* —**wide'ness,** *n.* —**wid'en,** *v.t., v.i.* —**wide'spread',** *adj.*

wide'-a·wake', *adj.* alert.

widg'eon, *n.* fresh-water wild duck. Also, **wig'eon.**

wid'ow, *n.* **1.** unmarried woman whose husband has died. —*v.t.* **2.** make into a widow. Also, *masc.,* **wid'ow·er.** —**wid'ow·hood",** *n.*

width, *n.* breadth.

wield, *v.t.* **1.** handle or manage. **2.** exercise, as authority or power. —**wield'er,** *n.*

wie'ner, *n.* frankfurter. Also, *Informal,* **wee'nie** or **wie'nie.**

wife, *n., pl.* **wives.** married woman. —**wife'less,** *adj.* —**wife'ly,** *adj.*

wig, *n., v.,* **wigged, wigging.** *n.* **1.** artificial hair piece. —*v.t.* **2.** furnish with a wig.

wig'gle, *v.,* **-gled, -gling.** *n. v.i., v.t.* **1.** move with quick motions from side to side. —*n.* **2.** act or instance of wiggling. —**wig'gly,** *adj.*

wig'wag", *v.,* **-wagged, -wagging.** *n. v.t., v.i.* **1.** signal with swung flags. —*n.* **2.** act or instance of wigwagging.

wig'wam, *n.* American Indian hut.

wild, *adj.* **1.** uncivilized. **2.** uncontrollable. **3.** lacking restraint; dissolute. —*n.* **4.** desolate region. —**wild'ly,** *adv.* —**wild'ness,** *n.*

wild'cat", *n., v.,* **-catted, -catting.** *n.* **1.** large, fierce feline. **2.** savage person. **3.** exploratory oil or gas well. —*v.i., v.t.* **4.** search for oil or gas.

wil'der·ness, *n.* uninhabited region.

wild'-goose' chase, search for a nonexistent thing.

wile, *n., v.t.,* **wiled, wiling.** *n.* **1.** sly trick. —*v.t.* **2.** beguile. **3. wile away,** pass leisurely, as time.

will, *n., v.,* **willed, willing.** *n.* **1.** power of conscious choice or action. **2.** determination. **3.** disposition toward another. **4.** legal document of one's wishes after death. —*v.t., v.t.* **5.** desire, wish, or want. **6.** bequeath by a will. —*auxiliary v.* **7.** am, is, or are about to. **8.** am, is, or are willing to. **9.** am, is, or are expected to. —**will·a·ble,** *adj.*

will'ful, *adj.* **1.** intentional. **2.** stubborn. Also, **wil'ful.** —**will'ful·ly,** *adv.* —**will'ful·ness,** *n.*

will'ing, *adj.* **1.** favorably inclined. **2.** cheerfully done. —**will'ing·ly,** *adv.* —**will'ing·ness,** *n.*

will''-o'-the-wisp', *n.* **1.** elusive light. **2.** anything that deludes.

wil'low, *n.* slender tree with flexible limbs and narrow leaves. —**wil'low·y,** *adj.*

wil'ly-nil'ly, *adv., adj.* whether willingly or not.

wilt, *v.i.* **1.** become limp or weak; droop. —*v.t.* **2.** cause to wilt. —*n.* **3.** wilted state.

wil'y, *adj.,* **-lier, -liest.** sly. —**wi'li·ness,** *n.*

win, *n.,* **won, winning.** *n. v.i.* **1.** succeed. —*v.t.* **2.** gain, as a victory, favor, etc. **3.** influence. —*n.* **4.** victory.

wince, *v.i.,* **winced, wincing.** *n. v.i.* **1.** shrink, as from a blow or pain. —*n.* **2.** act or instance of wincing.

winch, *n.* **1.** crank. **2.** windlass. —*v.t.* **3.** hoist or haul by a winch.

wind *v.,* **wound, winding.** *n. v.t.* (wīnd) **1.** turn. —*v.i.* **2.** coil. **3.** make one's way,

as along a path. —*n.* (wind) **4.** air in motion, as a gale. **5.** breath. **6.** intestinal gas. —**wind'er**, *n.* —**wind'y**, *adj.*

wind'bag'', *n. Informal.* empty talker.

wind'break'', *n.* shield against the wind.

wind'burn'', *n.* inflammation of the skin from the wind. —**wind'burned''**, *adj.*

wind'ed, *adj.* out of breath.

wind'fall, *n.* **1.** unexpected good fortune. **2.** something blown down by the wind.

wind instrument, musical instrument sounded by the breath.

wind'jam''mer, *n.* large sailing ship.

wind'lass, *n.* winch.

wind'mill'', *n.* wind-driven machine.

win'dow, *n.* opening in a wall for light, air, etc. —**win'dow·pane''**, *n.* —**win'dow·sill''**, *n.* —**window shade.**

window dressing, 1. store display. **2.** specious display.

wind'pipe'', *n.* trachea.

wind'row'', *n.* row of leaves, hay, etc.

wind'shield'', *n.* glass above and across a car's dashboard.

wind'up'', *n.* **1.** conclusion or end. **2.** *Baseball.* pitcher's arm and body movements before throwing.

wind'ward, *n.* **1.** direction from which the wind blows. —*adj.* **2.** moving to windward. —*adv.* **3.** toward the wind.

wine, *n., v.,* **wined, wining.** *n.* **1.** fermented juice from grapes, other fruits, or plants. —*v.i.,* *v.t.* **2.** entertain with wine. —**win'y**, *adj.*

win'er·y, *n., pl.* **-ies.** wine-making place.

wing, *n.* **1.** organ for flight of birds, insects, bats, etc. **2.** supporting surface of an airplane. **3.** distinct section. —*v.t.* **4.** shoot in an arm or wing. —*v.i.* **5.** travel on wings. —**wing'ed**, *adj.* —**wing'less**, *adj.* —**wing'like**, *adj.* —**wing'tip''**, *n.*

wing'span'', *n.* distance between an airplane's wingtips.

wing'spread'', *n.* distance between the tips of extended wings.

wink, *v.i., v.t.* **1.** close and open quickly, as one eye. **2.** signal by winking. —*v.i.* **3.** shine or twinkle. —*n.* **4.** winking, as a signal. **5.** instant.

win'ner, *n.* person or thing that wins.

win'ning, *adj.* **1.** pleasing; charming. **2.** victorious. —*n.* **3.** Often **winnings,** something won, as money. —**win'ning·ly**, *adv.*

win'now, *v.t., v.i.* **1.** blow away from grain. **2.** separate.

win·o, *n., pl.* **-os.** *Informal.* alcoholic who drinks cheap wine.

win'some, *adj.* attractive. —**win'some·ly** *adv.* —**win'some·ness**, *n.*

win'ter, *n.* **1.** cold season between autumn and spring. **2.** time like winter, as of decline, cold, etc. —*v.i.* **3.** spend the winter. —**win'ter·time''**, *n.* —**win'try,** **win'ter·y**, *adj.*

win'ter·green'', *n.* small evergreen aromatic shrub with white flowers.

win'ter·ize'', *v.t.,* **-ized, -izing.** prepare for winter.

wipe, *v.t.,* **wiped, wiping,** *n., v.t.* **1.** clean or rub. —*n.* **2.** act or instance of wiping. —**wip'er**, *n.*

wire, *n., v.,* **wired, wiring.** *n.* **1.** stringlike piece of metal. **2.** *Informal.* telegram. —*v.t.* **3.** install or bind with wire. —*v.t., v.i.* **4.** telegraph.

wire'hair'', *n.* fox terrier.

wire'less, *adj. Archaic.* pertaining to radio.

wire'tap''ping, *n.* listening secretly to the telephone calls of others.

wir'y, *adj.,* **-ier, -iest.** lean and tough.

wis'dom, *n.* **1.** knowledge and good judgment. **2.** wise teachings.

wisdom tooth, back molar.

wise, *adj.,* **wiser, wisest. 1.** showing knowledge and judgment. **2.** erudite or informed. **3.** *Informal.* insolent. —**wise'ly**, *adv.*

wise'a·cre, *n.* person who affects to have wisdom. Also, *Informal,* **wise guy.**

wise'crack'', *Informal.* *n.* **1.** flippant remark. —*v.i.* **2.** make wisecracks.

wish, *v.t.* **1.** want or desire. —*v.i.* **2.** yearn. —*n.* **3.** desire; longing. —**wish' er**, *n.* —**wish'ful**, *adj.* —**wish'ful·ly**, *adv.* —**wish'ful·ness**, *n.*

wish'bone'', *n.* forked breastbone of a bird.

wish'y-wash'y, *adj.* weak and vacillating.

wisp, *n.* thin film or strand. —**wisp'y**, *adj.*

wis·te'ri·a, *n.* climbing shrub with showy flowers.

wist'ful, *adj.* longing or yearning. —**wist' ful·ly**, *adv.* —**wist'ful·ness**, *n.*

wit, *n.* **1.** intelligence. **2.** cleverness of expression. **3.** person clever with words. —**wit'less**, *adj.* —**wit'less·ly**, *adv.* —**wit'ty**, *adj.* —**wit'ti·ly**, *adv.*

witch, *n.* **1.** woman with supposed supernatural power. **2.** ugly woman. —**witch'craft''**, *n.* —**witch'er·y**, *n.*

witch doctor, man who uses magic to cure sickness.

witch hazel, 1. shrub with yellow leaves. **2.** liquid extracted from it.

with, *prep.* **1.** accompanied by. **2.** characterized by. **3.** against. **4.** in regard to.

with·draw'', *v.,* **-drew, -drawn, -drawing.** *v.t.* **1.** take back. **2.** retract, as a statement, etc. —*v.i.* **3.** remove oneself. —**with·draw'al,** *n.*

withe, *n.* willow twig.

with'er, *v.t., v.i.* **1.** shrivel. —*v.t.* **2.** confuse and humiliate. —**with'er·ing·ly**, *adv.*

with'ers, *n. pl.* lower nape of the neck of a sheep, horse, etc.

with·hold', *v.t.,* **-held, -holding. 1.** hold back. **2.** deduct, as taxes.

with·in', *adv.* **1.** inside; indoors. —*prep.* **2.** inside. **3.** in the area of.

with·out', *prep.* **1.** lacking; not with. **2.** outside. —*adv.* **3.** outside; externally.

with·stand', *v.t.,* **-stood, -standing.** resist or oppose.

wit'ness, *n.* **1.** person who sees. **2.** testimony. —*v.t.* **3.** see. **4.** attest.

wit'ti·cism", *n.* witty remark.

wit'ting, *adj.* knowing; intentional. —**wit'ting·ly,** *adv.*

wiz'ard, *n.* magician; sorcerer. —**wiz'ard·ry,** *n.*

wiz'ened, *adj.* withered.

wob'ble, *v.,* **-bled, -bling,** *n.* *v.i., v.t.* **1.** shake. —*n.* **2.** wobbling motion. —**wob'bly,** *adj.* —**wob'bli·ness,** *n.*

woe, *n.* **1.** grief. **2.** trouble. —*interj.* **3.** alas! —**woe'ful,** *adj.* —**woe'ful·ly,** *adv.* —**woe'ful·ness,** *n.*

woe'be·gone", *adj.* showing woe. —**woe'be·gone"ness,** *n.*

wolf, *n., pl.* **wolves. 1.** wild, doglike mammal. **2.** *Informal.* man who flirts with women. **3.** cruel person. —*v.t.* **4.** devour greedily. —**wolf'hound",** *n.* —**wolf'ish,** *adj.* —**wolf'like",** *adj.*

wol''ver·ine', *n.* stocky, carnivorous mammal.

wom'an, *n., pl.* **women.** female human being. —**wom'an·hood",** *n.* —**wom'an·ish,** *adj.* —**wom'an·like",** *adj.* —**wom'an·ly,** *adj.* —**wom'an·li·ness,** *n.*

wom'an·ize", *v.* **-ized, -izing.** *v.t.* **1.** make effeminate. —*v.i.* **2.** pursue women habitually. —**wom'an·iz"er,** *n.*

womb, *n.* **1.** uterus. **2.** source of being.

won'der, *n.* **1.** awe or amazement. **2.** source of such an emotion. —*v.i.* **3.** be curious. **4.** be filled with wonder. —**won'der·ful,** *adj.* —**won'der·ful·ly,** *adv.* —**won'der·ing·ly,** *adv.* —**won'der·ment,** *n.* —**won'drous,** *adj.* —**won'drous·ly,** *adv.*

wont, *adj.* **1.** Also, **wont'ed,** accustomed. —*n.* **2.** habit.

won't, *v.* contraction of *will not.*

woo, *v.i., v.t.* solicit for love or favor. —**woo'er,** *n.*

wood, *n.* **1.** hard substance beneath the bark of trees. **2.** Also, **woods,** forest. **3.** lumber. —*adj.* **4.** wooden; made of wood. —**wood'en,** *adj.* —**wood'en·ness,** *n.* —**wood'craft",** *n.* —**wood'cut"ter,** *n.* —**wood'ed,** *adj.* —**wood'pile",** *n.* —**wood'shed",** *n.* —**woods'man,** *n.* —**woods'y,** *adj.* —**wood'y,** *adj.*

wood'bine", *n.* honeysuckle or the Virginia creeper.

wood'chuck", *n.* burrowing and hibernating marmot.

wood'cock", *n.* snipelike game bird.

wood'cut", *n.* **1.** carved block of wood. **2.** print from this block.

wood'en, *adj.* **1.** made of wood. **2.** without natural feeling or expression. —**wood'en·ly,** *adv.*

wood'land", *n.* land covered with trees.

wood'peck"er, *n.* bird with a hard bill for pecking.

wood'wind", *n.* musical non-brass wind instrument.

wood'work", *n.* **1.** objects made of wood. **2.** wooden fittings of a house, as doors, moldings, etc. —**wood'work"er,** *n.* —**wood'work"ing,** *n.*

woof, *n.* cross-threads of a fabric.

wool, *n.* **1.** soft, curly hair, as from sheep, goats, etc. **2.** yarn or garments made from such. —**wool'en, wool'len,** *adj.* —**wool'ly, wool'y,** *adj.* —**wool'i·ness, wool'li·ness,** *n.*

wool'gath"er·ing, *n.* absentmindedness or daydreaming.

wooz'y, *adj.,* **-ier, -iest.** *Informal.* muddled or dizzy. —**wooz'i·ly,** *adv.* —**wooz'i·ness,** *n.*

word, *n.* **1.** spoken or written sounds with meaning as a unit of language. **2.** **words,** speech or talk. **3.** promise or assurance. **4.** news or information. **5.** (computers) several bits of data treated as a unit. —*v.t.* **6.** express in words —**word''age,** *n.* —**word''ing,** *n.* —**word''less,** *adj.* —**word''y,** *adj.* —**word''i·ness,** *n.*

work, *n., v.,* **worked** or **wrought, working,** *n.* **1.** labor or toil. **2.** occupation. **3.** something on which one is working. —*v.i.* **4.** do work. **5.** act or operate. —*v.t.* **6.** manage or manipulate. **7.** solve. **8.** cultivate, as the soil. **9.** provoke or excite. —**work'a·ble,** *adj.* —**work'bench",** *n.* —**work'book",** *n.* —**work'er,** *n.* —**work'day",** *n.* —**work'ing·man",** *n.* —**work'man,** *n.* —**work'shop",** *n.* —**work'week",** *n.*

work'a·day", *adj.* **1.** ordinary; humdrum. **2.** characteristic of a workday.

work'day", *n.* **1.** day on which work is done. **2.** part of the day one works.

work'man·like", *adj.* skillful.

work'man·ship", *n.* **1.** workman's art or skill. **2.** quality of work.

work'out", *n.* practice athletic session.

world, *n.* **1.** earth; universe. **2.** people; mankind. **3.** part of the earth. **4.** great quantity or extent. —**world'wide",** *adj.*

world'ly, *adj.,* **-lier, -liest. 1.** secular. **2.** Also, **world'ly-wise",** sophisticated. —**world'li·ness,** *n.*

worm, *n.* **1.** long, soft, legless, creeping animal. **2.** something like this creature. **3.** *Informal.* contemptible person. **4.**

worms, intestinal disease from parasitic worms. —*v.i.* 5. move or act stealthily. —*v.t.* 6. get by insidious efforts. 7. free from worms. —**worm′y,** *adj.* -ier, -iest. —**worm′i·ness,** *n.*

worm′wood″, *n.* 1. bitter, strong-smelling herb. 2. something bitter or unpleasant.

worn, *adj.* 1. used by wear, handling, etc. 2. exhausted; tired. —**worn′-out′,** *adj.*

wor′ry, *v.,* -ried, -rying, *n., pl.* -ies. *v.i.* 1. feel anxious. —*v.t.* 2. make anxious. —*n.* 3. anxiety. 4. cause of anxiety. —**wor′ri·er,** *n.* —**wor′ri·some,** *adj.*

worse, *adj.* 1. bad in a greater or higher degree. 2. in poorer health. —*n.* 3. that which is worse. —*adv.* 4. in a worse manner. —**wors′en,** *v.t., v.i.*

wor′ship, *n., v.,* -shiped, or -shipped, -shiping or -shipping. *n.* 1. reverence for a deity. 2. admiration or love. —*v.t., v.i.* 3. show religious reverence. —**wor′ship·er, wor′ship·per,** *n.* —**wor′ship·ful,** *adj.*

worst, *adj.* 1. bad in the highest degree. 2. least well. —*n.* 3. that which is worst. —*adv.* 4. in the worst manner. —*v.t.* 5. beat; defeat.

wor·sted (wōōs′tid), *n.* 1. firmly twisted wool yarn. 2. garment made of it. —*adj.* 3. consisting of worsted.

wort, *n.* infusion with malt before fermentation, as in making beer or mash.

worth, *n.* 1. material value, as in money. 2. importance; value. —*adj.* 3. worthy of; justifying. 4. having equal value. —**worth′less,** *adj.* —**worth′less·ness,** *n.*

worth′while′, *adj.* worthy of doing, etc.

worth′y, *adj.,* -ier, -iest. deserving. —**worth′i·ly,** *adv.* —**worth′i·ness,** *n.*

would, *auxiliary v.* (expressing condition, futurity, habitual action, or request).

would′-be″, *adj.* wishing or intending to be.

wound, *n.* 1. physical injury. 2. injury to feelings, sensibilities, etc. —*v.t.,* 3. injure. —**wound′ed,** *adj., n., pl.*

wrack, *n.* ruin or destruction.

wraith, *n.* ghost.

wran′gle, *v.t., v.i.,* -gled, -gling, *n.* dispute. dispute.

wrap, *v.,* wrapped or wrapt, wrapping, *v.t., v.i.* 1. wind or fold, as around something. —*v.t.* 2. enclose or envelop. —*n.* 3. outer garment wrapped around the body. —**wrap′ping,** *n.*

wrap′per, *n.* 1. person who wraps. 2. something wrapped around as a cover.

wrath, *n.* 1. anger; rage. 2. vengeance. —**wrath′ful,** *adj.* —**wrath′ful·ly,** *adv.*

wreak, *v.t.* inflict.

wreath, *n., pl.* wreaths. circular formation, as of flowers, etc.

wreathe, *v.t.,* wreathed, wreathing. 1. form into a wreath. 2. encircle.

wreck, *n.* 1. structure or object in ruins. 2. run-down person. —*v.t.* 3. tear down or destroy. —**wreck′age,** *n.* —**wreck′er,** *n.*

wren, *n.* small, active songbird.

wrench, *n.* 1. sudden twist or pull, as to the arms, back, etc. 2. sudden emotional strain. 3. tool for turning bolts, etc. —*v.t., v.i.* 4. turn suddenly. —*v.t.* 5. overstrain or injure.

wrest, *v.t.* 1. pull violently. 2. usurp. —*n.* 3. twist.

wres′tle, *v.,* -tled, -tling. *v.t.* 1. grapple and attempt to throw down. —*v.i.* 2. engage in wrestling. 3. struggle. —**wrest′ler,** *n.*

wretch, *n.* 1. unhappy person. 2. despicable person.

wretch′ed, *adj.* 1. pitiful. 2. contemptible. 3. worthless. —**wretch′ed·ly,** *adv.* —**wretch′ed·ness,** *n.*

wrig′gle, *v.i., n.,* -gled, -gling. *v.i.* 1. squirm; twist and turn. —*n.* 2. act or instance of wriggling. —**wrig′gly,** *adj.*

wright, *n.* constructor.

wring, *v.t.,* wrung, wringing, *n., v.t.* 1. twist; press; squeeze. —*n.* 2. act or instance of wringing. —**wring′er,** *n.*

wrin′kle, *n., v.,* -kled, -kling. *n.* 1. ridge or furrow on a surface. 2. ingenious trick or device. —*v.t., v.i.* 3. crease or furrow. —**wrin′kly,** *adj.*

wrist, *n.* joint between the hand and forearm. —**wrist′band″,** *n.* —**wrist′watch″,** *n.*

writ, *n.* 1. *Law.* formal legal order or document. 2. something written.

write, *v.* wrote, written, writing. *v.i.* 1. form letters, words, etc., as with a pen, pencil, etc. —*v.t.* 2. compose. 3. communicate with. —**writ′er,** *n.*

writhe, *v.,* writhed, writhing, *n. v.t., v.i.* 1. squirm, twist, or bend, as in pain. —*n.* 2. act or instance of writhing.

wrong, *adj.* 1. not right or good. 2. not truthful or factual. 3. inappropriate. —*n.* 4. injustice; evil. —*v.t.* 5. do wrong to. —**wrong′ly,** *adv.* —**wrong′ness,** *n.* —**wrong′do″er,** *n.* —**wrong′do″ing,** *n.* —**wrong′ful,** *adj.* —**wrong′ful·ly,** *adv.*

wrong′head″ed, *adj.* deeply erroneous.

wroth, *adj. Archaic.* angry.

wrought, *adj.* 1. worked. 2. shaped by beating.

wrought′-up′, *adj.* upset; excited.

wry, *adj.,* wrier, wriest. 1. distorted or lopsided. 2. misdirected or perverse. 3. bitterly ironic. —**wry′ly,** *adv.* —**wry′ness,** *n.*

wurst, *n.* sausage.

X

X, x, *n.* twenty-fourth letter of the English alphabet.

xe·non (zē'non), *n.* chemically inactive gaseous element.

xen·o·pho·bi·a (zen''ə fō'bē ə), *n.* irrational fear of that which is foreign or strange. —**xen''o·pho'bic**, *adj.*

Xmas, *n.* Christmas.

x'-ray, *n.* 1. electromagnetic radiation which penetrates solids. 2. picture made by x-rays. —*v.t.* 3. treat or photograph with x-rays.

xy·lem (zī'ləm), *n.* woody tissue of plants and trees.

xy'lo·phone'', *n.* musical instrument with wooden sounding bars struck by small hammers.

Y

Y, y, *n.* twenty-fifth letter of the English alphabet.

yacht, *n.* pleasure ship. —**yachts'man**, *n.*

ya·hoo', *n.* coarse or rowdy person.

Yah·weh (Yah'we), *n.* God of the Hebrews.

yak, *n.* long-haired Tibetan ox.

yam, *n.* edible potatolike root; sweet potato.

yam'mer, *v.i.,* -mered, -mering. 1. complain or whine. 2. talk persistently; chatter.

yank, *v.t.,* *v.i.* 1. pull strongly and abruptly. —*n.* 2. strong, abrupt pull.

Yan'kee, *n.* native or inhabitant of the U.S., the northeastern U.S., or New England.

yap, *v.i.,* **yapped, yapping**, *n. v.i.* 1. yelp; bark shrilly. —*n.* 2. shrill bark.

yard, *n.* 1. linear unit of measure equal to 3 feet. 2. open area. 3. long spar that supports a sail.

yard'age, *n.* amount in yards.

yard'stick'', *n.* one-yard measuring stick.

yarn, *n.* 1. multi-stranded thread for sweaters, etc. 2. story; tall tale.

yaw, *v.i.* 1. deviate from a course. —*n.* 2. deviation.

yawl, *n.* two-masted sailboat.

yawn, *v.i.* 1. involuntarily open the mouth wide as from drowsiness. —*n.* 2. act or instance of yawning.

yawp (yap), *v.i.,* *n. Informal.* yelp; squawk.

yea, *adv.,* *n.* yes.

year, *n.* 1. time period equal to 365 or 366 days. 2. years, age. —**year'ly**, *adv., adj.*

year'ling, *n.* year-old animal.

yearn, *v.i.* 1. desire earnestly or strongly. 2. feel affection or tenderness. —**yearn'ing**, *n., adj.*

yeast, *n.* fungous substance used to leaven bread, etc.

yell, *v.i.,* *n.* cry; shout.

yel'low, *n.* 1. bright color of butter, etc. —*adj.* 2. of the color yellow. 3. *Informal.* cowardly; chicken.

yel'low fe'ver, *n.* tropical disease.

yelp, *v.i.* 1. cry quickly or shrilly like a dog. —*n.* 2. quick, sharp bark.

yen, *n. Informal.* desire; urge.

yeo'man (yō'mən), *n.* 1. naval petty officer. 2. small independent farmer. —*adj.* 3. valiant.

yes, *adv., n.* (expression of assent, agreement or affirmation).

yes'ter·day, *adv., n.* day before today.

yet, *adv.* 1. up to now. 2. besides. 3. nevertheless. 4. eventually. —*conj.* 5. but; still.

yew, *n.* coniferous evergreen tree or bush.

yield, *v.t.,* *v.i.* 1. produce. 2. surrender. 3. concede. —*v.i.* 4. give way to force. —*n.* 5. amount produced.

yo·del (yōd'əl), *v.,* -deled, -deling, *n. v.t., v.i.* 1. shout or sing alternating falsetto with chest voice. —*n.* 2. act or instance of yodeling.

yo'ga, *n.* 1. Hindu philosophy teaching suppression of the body to free the soul. 2. system of exercises for total bodily control.

yo·gi (yōg'ē) *n.* adherent of yoga.

yo'gurt, *n.* fermented milk food.

yoke, *n.,* *v.,* **yoked, yoking**, *n.* 1. device for joining oxen. 2. pair, esp. of oxen. 3. something oppressive. —*v.t.* 4. put a yoke on.

yo'kel, *n.* rustic; bumpkin.

yolk, *n.* yellow part of the egg.

Yom Kip·pur (yom kē pŏŏr'), *n.* Jewish Day of Atonement.

yon'der, *adj., adv.* over there.

yore, *adv. adj. Archaic.* long ago.

you, *pron.* 1. person or persons addressed. 2. any person.

young, *adj.* 1. in the early stages of life, etc. 2. pertaining to youth. —*n.* 3. children; young people. —**young'ish**, *adj.*

young'ster, *n.* child; youth.

your, *adj.* pertaining to you.

yours, *pron.,* belonging to you.

your·self′, *pron., pl.* **-selves. 1.** form of you used reflexively or emphatically. **2.** your true self.

youth, *n.* **1.** young state. **2.** child; young person. **—youth′ful,** *adj.* **—youth′ful·ly,** *adv.* **—youth′ful·ness,** *n.*

yowl, *v.i., n.* howl.

yuc′ca, *n.* tropical American plant.

yule, *n.* Christmas.

yule′tide″, *n.* Christmas season.

Z

Z, z, *n.* twenty-sixth letter of the English alphabet.

za′ny, *n., pl.* **-nies,** *adj. n.* **1.** clown. **2.** silly person. **—adj. 3.** crazy; foolish.

zeal, *n.* intense or eager interest. **—zeal′ous,** *adj.* **—zeal′ous·ly,** *adv.* **—zeal′ous·ness,** *n.*

zeal·ot (zel′ot), *n.* enthusiast; fanatic. **—zeal′ot·ry,** *n.*

ze′bra, *n.* black and white striped horselike African mammal.

Zen, *n.* Buddhist sect.

ze′nith, *n.* **1.** celestial point directly overhead. **2.** highest point.

zeph′yr, *n.* mild or gentle breeze.

zep′pe·lin, *n.* large dirigible. Also, **Zep′pe·lin.**

ze′ro, *n.* **1.** numerical symbol, 0, denoting the absence of quantity. **2.** nothing.

zest, *n.* **1.** something enhancing enjoyment. **2.** enjoyment. **—zest′ful,** *adj.* **—zest′ful·ly,** *adv.*

zig′zag″, *n., adj., adv., v.i.,* **-zagged, -zagging.** *n.* **1.** short sharp alternations in a line. **—adj., adv. 2.** with or having sharp back and forth turns. **—v.i. 3.** proceed in a zigzag.

zinc, *n.* bluish metallic element.

zinc ox′ide, *n.* zinc and oxygen salve.

zing, *n.* **1.** sharp singing or whistling sound. **2.** vitality. **—v.i. 3.** move with or make a zinging sound.

zin′ni·a, *n.* colorful annual garden flower.

Zi′on·ism″, *n.* political movement for re-establishment of the Jewish Biblical homeland. **—Zi′on·ist,** *n.*

zip, *v.,* **zipped, zipping.** *n. v.i.* **1.** act or move speedily or energetically. **—v.t. 2.** fasten with a zipper. **—n. 3.** energy.

zip′per, *n.* slide fastener with interlocking teeth.

zith′er, *n.* stringed musical instrument.

zo′di·ac, *n.* imaginary heavenly region including the paths of all planets except Pluto, with divisions for the twelve constellations.

zom′bi, *n.* reanimated dead body. Also, **zom′bie.**

zone, *n., v.t.,* **zoned, zoning.** *n.* **1.** special area or region. **—v.t. 2.** mark off or arrange in zones.

zoo, *n.* park where animals are exhibited.

zo·ol′o·gy, *n.* study of animals. **—zo·o·log′i·cal,** *adj.* **—zo·ol′o·gist,** *n.*

zoom, *v.i.* **1.** move quickly with a humming sound. **2.** fly upward sharply and at great speed.

zuc·chi·ni (zoo kē′nē), *n.* green cylindrical summer squash.

Frequently Misspelled Words

Words shown with an asterisk below also have an alternate correct spelling. See any good dictionary for the alternate spelling.

A
abominable
abridgment
absence
abundance
abundant
academic
academically
academy
accelerating
accentuation
acceptable
acceptance
accepting
accessible
accessory*
accidental
accidentally
acclaim
accommodate
accompanied
accompanies
accompaniment
accompanying
accomplish
accountant
accuracy
accurate
accurately
accuser
accuses
accusing

accustom
achievement
achieving
acknowledgment*
acquaintance
acquire
across
actuality
actually
acutely
adequately
adhering
admirable
admissible*
admission
admittance
adolescence
adolescent
advancement
advantageous
adversaries
advertisement*
advertiser*
advertising*
advice
advise
aerial
aesthetic
affect
affiliate
afraid
against

ageless
aging
aggravate
aggressive
alibis
allegedly
allergies
alleviate
allotment
allotted
allowed
allows
all right*
all together
already
altar
alter
alternate
alternative
altogether
amateur
amenable
amiable
amicably
among
amount
amplified
amusing
analogies
analysis
analyze
anarchy

anecdote
angrily
annihilate
announcing
annually
anonymous
another
anticipated
antique
anxieties
apiece
apologetically
apologized
apology
apostrophe
appall*
apparatus
apparent
appearance
applies
applying
appraise
appreciate
appreciation
apprehend
approaches
appropriate
approval
approximate
apropos
aptly
aquarium
arbitrary
arduous
area
aren't
arguing
argument
arise
arising
armies
arouse

arousing
arrangement
arrears
arriving
artfully
article
artificial·
ascent
ascetic
asinine
asphalt
asphyxiation
aspiration
assassin
assemblies
assertiveness
assiduous
assignment
assimilate
assistance
associating
assortment
assuming
asthma
astonish
astronaut
astute
asylum
atheist
athlete
athletic
atrocious
atrocity
attachment
attack
attempts
attendance
attendant
attended
attirement
attitude
attractive

attribute
audacious
audacity
audience
augment
auspicious
authenticity
author
authoritarian
authoritative
authority
authorization
authorize
autumn
available
awareness
awesome
awfully

B

babbling
balancing
ballerina
balminess
bankruptcy
bare
barely
bargain
barrenness
barrier
barroom
bashfulness
basically
basis
battling
bawdiness
bazaar
bearable
beauteous
beautified
beautiful
beautifying

beauty
become
becoming
before
began
beggar
beginner
beginning
begrudging
beguile
behaving
behavior
belatedly
belief
believe
belittling
belligerence
beneath
benefactor
beneficent
beneficial
benefited*
benevolence
benign
biannual
bicycle
bicycling
bigamy
bigger
biggest
binoculars
biscuit
biting
bitten
blameless
bluing
blurred
blurry
boastfully
bohemian
boisterous
boloney

booby trap
boring
born
borne
bossiness
botanical
bottling
boulevard
bouncing
boundary
bounties
braggadocio
breath
breathe
breezier
brief
brilliance
brilliant
brimming
Britain
Britannica
brochure
bronchial
brutally
budget
bulging
bulletin
bumptious
buoy
buoyant
buried
bursar
bury
bushiness
business
busy

C
cabaret
cafeteria
caffeine

calamity
calculation
calendar
callous
callus
calves
camaraderie
canceled*
candescence
canniness
canning
canoeing
capably
capacity
capitalism
capital
capitol
capricious
captaincy
captivity
careen
career
careless
cargoes
caribou
caricature
caring
carnally
carousing
carpentry
carpeted
carried
carrier
carries
carrousel*
carrying
cascade
casserole
casually
cataclysmal
cataloged*

catalyst
catastrophe
category
caught
causally
causing
caustic
cautious
ceaseless
celibacy
celluloid
cemetery
centrifugal
centuries
ceramics
cerebellum
certainly
certificate
certified
cessation
chafe
chagrined
chalice
challenge
chancing
changeable
changing
chaotic
characteristic
characterized
charging
charlatan
chastise
chatty
chauffeur
chauvinism
cheerier
chief
children
chilliness
chiseling*
chivalry

choice
choose
choosing
chose
choreography*
Christianity
chronically
chronicle
cigarette
cinema
cipher
circling
circuit
circulating
circumstantial
cite
citizen
claimant
clairvoyance*
clamorous
clarify
classification
claustrophobia
cleanly
cleanness
cleanse
clemency
climactic
climatic
closely
clothes
cloudiest
coarse
cocoa
coerce
cognizance*
cohort
coincidence
collaborate
collectively
collegiate

collision
colloquial
colossal
combining
comfortable
coming
commentary
commercial
commiserate
commission
commitment
committee
commodities
commotion
communicate
companies
comparative
comparing
compassion
compatible
compel
compelled
competition
competitive
competitor
complacence
complement
completely
compliment
comprehendible
comprehensible
compromising
concede
conceit
conceive
conceivable
concentrate
concern
concession
condemn
condescend

conditionally
conferred
confidentially
confuse
confusion
congenial
conniving
connotation
connote
conquer
conscience
conscientious
conscious
consciousness
consequence
consequently
conservatively
considerably
considerately
consistency
consistent
conspicuous
constancy
consul
contagious
contemporary
contemptible
contemptuous
continuing
continuously
contrarily
contritely
contrivance
controlled
controlling
controversial
controversy
convalesce
convenience
convenient
conveyance

convincingly
coolly
cooperate
cooperative
coordinate
coordination
corporal
correlate
correspondent
corroborate
corruption
council
counsel
counselor*
countenance
countries
courtesy
cowardice
cozier
crazily
create
credibility
crescendo
crescent
crevice
criminally
cringing
criticism
criticize
crucially
crudely
cruelly
cruelty
crystal
cultivating
cultural
cunning
curing
curiosity
curious
curriculum

cycle
cynicism

D
dahlia
dallying
dauntless
dazedly
debatable*
deceased
deceitfully
deceive
decent
decided
decision
dedicating
deductible
defenseless
deferred
deficiency
define
definitely
definition
degeneracy
deliberating
delicately
delightfully
delinquency
demoralize
denied
denominational
denouncement
department
dependent*
deplorable
depreciate
depressant
depression
derangement
derisive
descend

261

describe
description
desert
deservedly
desirability
desire
desolately
despair
desperate
desperation
despising
despondency
desert
dessert
destitution
destruction
detach
deteriorate
determining
detriment
deuce
devastating
development*
deviation
device
devise
dexterity
diabolic
diagonally
dialogue
dictionary
difference
different
difficult
dilapidated
dilemma
diligence
diminutive
diner
dinghy
dining

dinner
dinosaur
diphthong
dipsomania
direness
disagreeable
disappear
disappoint
disapproval
disarray
disastrous
disbelief
discernible*
disciple
discipline
disconsolately
discourteous
discreditable
discrimination
discussion
disease
disguise
disgusted
dishevelment
disillusioned
disintegrate
dismally
dismissal
disparaging
disparity
dispersal
dispirited
dispossess
disprove
disqualified
disreputable
dissatisfied
dissension
dissoluteness
dissolve
dissuading
distraught

distressingly
disuse
diversely
divide
divine
divisible
docilely
doesn't
dolorous
dominant
dormitories
double
doubtfulness
drastically
dropped
drudgery
dually
during
duteous
dye
dyed
dyeing
dying

E
eager
easel
easily
eccentric
echelon
ecstasy*
eczema
edified
educating
eerily
effect
efficiency
efficient
effortlessly
egotistical
eighth

262

eightieth
either
elaborate
elapse
elegy
element
elementary
eligible
eliminate
emaciate
embarrass
embarrassment
embellish
embitter
emergencies
emerging
eminence
emperor
emphasize
employment
emptiness
emulate
enabling
enamel
enamored
encourage
encyclopedia
endeavor
energies
engaging
enjoy
enormous
enough
enrapture
enroute
ensconce
ensuing
enterprise
entertain
entertainment
enthusiastic

enthusiastically
enticement
entirely
entrance
enumerate
enunciate
envelop
envelope
enviable
environment
epitome
equable
equally
equipment
equipped
erratic
erroneous
escapade
escape
especially
essence
et cetera*
ethical
etiquette
eulogy
evacuate
evaporate
eventful
everything
evidently
exaggerate
exceed
excellence
excellent
except
excessive
excising
excitable
excruciating
excusing
exercise

existence
existent
expelled
expense
experience
experiment
explanation
expulsion
extensively
extenuate
extremely

F
fabricator
facetious
facility
facing
facsimile
factually
fallacy
falsely
falsified
familiar
families
fanatical
fancied
fantasies
fantasy
farewell
fascinate
fashions
fastidious
fatally
fatigue
favorable
favorite
feasible
ferocity
fertility
fetish
fiancé
fiancée

fickleness
fictitious
fidelity
field
fierce
fifteenth
figuring
finally
financially
financier
finesse
fitfully
flamboyant
flammable
flatterer
flexible
flimsiness
flippancy
flourish
fluidity
fluorescent
forbearance
forbidding
foreigners
forfeit
forgotten
formally
formerly
formidable
fortieth
fortitude
fortunately
forty
forward
fourth
freer
frequency
friendliness
frightfully
frivolous
fulfill

fundamentally
furrier
further

G
gaiety
galvanizing
gamble
gambol
garish
garnishee
garrulous
gaseous
gauche
gauging
gazette
generally
generating
generic
geniality
genius
gentlest
gesticulating
ghastliest
gladden
glamorous
glamour*
glorified
gluttony
government
governor
gradually
grammar
grammatically
grandeur
grandiloquence
grandiose
graphically
gratefully
gratification
gratuitous
greasing

grieving
grimacing
group
grudgingly
gruesome
guaranteed
guidance
guiding
guileless
guillotine
gullible
gutturally
gypped

H
habitable
hackneyed
hallucination
halving
hamster
handicapped
handled
handsomely
happen
happened
happiness
harangue
harassment
harmfully
harmonizing
hear
height
heinous
hemorrhage
hereditary
heresy
heretofore
heroes
heroic
heroine
hesitancy
heterogeneity

heuristic
hibernate
hierarchy
hilarity
hindrance
hirable
hoarsely
holocaust
homage
homely
homilies
homogeneous
hopeful
hopeless
hoping
horizontally
horrendous
horrified
hospitality
hospitalization
huge
human
humane
humanistic
humidified
humiliating
humorist
humorous
hundred
hundredth
hunger
hungrily
hungry
hydrophobia
hygiene
hygienic
hyphenation
hypnotizing
hypocrisy
hypocrite
hypothesis
hysterical

I

icicle
ideally
ideologies
idiocy
idiomatic
idiosyncrasy
ignoramus
ignorance
ignorant
illegible
illiteracy
illuminate
illusory
imagination
imagine
imbibing
imitating
immaculate
immanent
immediately
immense
immigrant
imminent
immobilized
impartially
impasse
impeccable
impeding
imperceptible
impersonally
impinging
implausible
imploring
impoliteness
importance
impresario
imagery
imaginary
impressionistic
improbability

improvement
inadequacy
inappeasable
inattentively
incalculable
incessantly
incidentally
incomparable
incomprehensible
inconceivable
inconsequential
inconstancy
incorrigible
increase
indefinite
independence
independent
indeterminate
indexes*
indispensable
individually
industries
inebriation
inefficiency
inevitable
inexcusable
inferred
infinitely
inflame
inflammation
inflammatory
influence
influential
informally
infringement
infuriating
ingenious
ingenuity
ingenuous
ingratiate
ingredient

inimitable
initiative
injurious
innervate
inoculate
inquiries
inscrutable
inseparable
insincere
insouciance
installment
instinctive
insuperable
insusceptible
intangible
intellect
intelligence
intelligent
interceding
interchanging
interest
interference
interim
interlining
intermediary
intermittent
internally
interpretation
interrogator
interrupt
intervening
intimately
intricately
intrigue
intuition
involve
invulnerability
irascible
ironical
irrationality
irrefutable

irrelevant
irreproachable
irresistible
irreverence
irreversible
irritable
irritating
irruptive
issuing
itinerary
its
it's

J
jauntily
jealousy
jeopardy
jettison
jocundity
jolliness
jovially
judgment*
judicially
juiciness
juvenile

K
kaleidoscope
keenness
khaki
kidnaped*
kindlier
kinescope
knowledge

L
laboratory
laborer
laboriously
labyrinth
laconic
laid
lamentable

languorous
largess*
laryngitis
lascivious
lassitude
lately
later
laureate
lazier
lead (v.)
lead (n.)
leafy
learnedly
legacy
legality
legibility
leisurely
lengthening
leniency
lenses
lesion
lethally
lethargy
letup
levying
libelous*
liberally
libidinous
license*
licentious
liege
likelihood
likely
likeness
limousine
linage
lineage
listener
literally
literary
literate

literature
litigation
liveliest
livelihood
liveliness
lives
lodging
loneliness
lonely
longitudinal
looniness
loose
lose
losing
loss
lugubrious
luminosity
lustfulness
luxury
lyricism

M
macabre*
macaroni
mademoiselle
magazine
magnanimity
magnificence
magnificent
maintenance
malefactor
malleable
manageability
management
maneuver
manful
manginess
maniacal
manifesto
manner
manning
manually

manufacturers
marauder
marionette
marriage
marveled
masquerade
massacre
massacring
material
maternally
mathematics
matriculating
matter
maturely
maturing
mausoleum
maybe
meant
measurement
mechanics
medallion
medical
medicine
medieval*
mediocrity
melancholia
melancholy
melee
meltable
memorability
memorizing
menacingly
mentally
merchandise
mere
merely
methods
microscopic
middling
mien
mightily

mileage
milieu
millennium
millionth
mimicker
mincingly
miniature
minority
minuscule
minutes
miraculous
mirrored
misalliance
misanthrope
miscalculation
miscellaneous
mischief
mischievous
misconstruing
mismanagement
misshapen
misspell
mistakable
moderately
moisturize
mollification
momentarily
monetary
monitor
monopolies
monosyllable
monotonous
monstrosity
moodily
moral
morale
morally
morbidity
morosely
mortally
mortifying
mosaic

mosquitoes
motif
mottoes*
mousiness
movable*
mucilage
multiplicity
multitudinous
mundanely
munificent
musing
mutuality
mysterious
musically

N
naïve*
naïveté*
namely
narcissus
narrative
natively
naturalistic
naturally
naughtily
nauseate
nearly
necessary
needlessly
nefarious
negativism
negligence
negligible
Negroes
neighbor
neither
neurotic
nevertheless
nicety
niggardly
nihilism
nimbly

nineteen
ninetieth
ninety
ninth
noble
noisily
nominally
noncombustible
normally
nostalgia
noticeable
noticing
notifying
notoriety
nourishment
nudity
nuisance
nullify
numerous
nuptial

O
obedience
objectively
obliging
obliquely
obliterate
obsequious
observance
obsess
obsolescent
obstacle
obstinately
obtuseness
occasion
occupancy
occupying
occur
occurred
occurrence
occurring
o'clock

oculist
oddly
odoriferous
odyssey
Oedipus
off
offense
offensively
officially
officiating
officious
omission
omit
omitted
oncoming
opaque
operate
opinion
opponent
opportunely
opportunity
oppose
opposite
oppression
optimism
optionally
oracular
orating
orderliness
ordinarily
ordinary
organization
original
ornamental
ornateness
orthodoxy
oscillate
ostentatious
ostracism
outrageous
outweigh

overdevelopment
overrun

P
pacified
pageant
paid
painstaking
palatable
palladium
palpitating
pamphlets
pancreas
panicky
pantomime
papier-mâché*
parable
parading
paradoxically
parallel
paralleled
paralyzed
parental
parentheses
parenthesis
parliament
paroxysm
parsimonious
partaking
partiality
participating
participial
participle
particular
passable
passed
passionately
passivity
past
pasteurize
pastime
pastoral

pastorale
pastries
pathetically
pathologist
patriarch
patriotically
patrolling
patronize
paunchy
pausing
peace
pealing
peculiar
pecuniary
pedagogue
pedagogy
pedantic
pedestrian
peeve
peignoir
penetrate
penicillin
penitent
penniless
penology
penury
perambulating
perceive
perceptible
percipience
peremptorily
perfidious
performance
perfunctory
perilous
periodic
permanent
permit
perpetually
persevering
persistent

personal
personally
personnel
perspicacity
persuade
pertain
perversely
pessimism
pestilence
petticoat
petulancy
pharmaceutical
phase
phenomenon
philosophy
phlegmatic
phobia
phonetically
phosphoric
photogenic
phraseology
phrasing
physical
physician
physique
pianos
picayune
piccolo
picnicked*
pictorially
piece
piecing
piling
pinnacle
piquancy
pirouette
piteous
pitifulness
placating
placidity
plagiary

269

plaintively
planetarium
planned
platitude
plausible
playwright
pleasant
pleasurable
plebeian
plenteous
pliability
poetically
poignant
politely
political
politician
polyethylene
pontifical
popularize
populous
pornographic
porosity
portable
portfolios
positively
possession
possibility
possible
postponement
potentiality
practicability
practical
practically
practice
precautionary
precede
precipice
precipitous
precisely
precursor
predecessor

predictable
predominant
preexistence
preferred
prejudice
prematurely
prepare
preposterous
presence
preservable
prestige
presumedly
pretension
prettily
prevalent
primitive
principal
principle
prisoners
privilege
probably
procedure
proceed
producible
profession
professor
proficient
prognosticating
progressively
prominent
promissory
pronounce
pronunciation
pronouncing
propaganda
propagate
prophecy*
prophesy*
psychoanalysis
psychology
psychopathic

psychosomatic
ptomaine
puerile
pugnacity
punctilious
purposeless
pursue

Q

quadruplicate
quantity
quarreled*
queasiness
querulous
questionnaire
queue
quiescent
quintessence
quipster
quixotic
quotable
quotient

R

rabies
raconteur
radiating
raising
ramification
rapidity
rarely
rarity
rationalize
readily
readmitted
reality
realize
really
reasonable
rebel
receive
receiving

270

receptacle
recipient
recognize
recollect
recommend
reconciling
recoup
recoverable
recreation
rectangular
rectified
recurrence
redoubling
reexamining
referring
refrigerate
regard
registrant
regretful
regulating
rehearsal
reimbursement
reissuing
reiterate
rejuvenate
relative
relevant
reliability
relieve
religion
remarkable
remember
reminisce
remotely
renaissance
repeatedly
repelled
repentance
repetition
replacement
reprehensible

represent
reprieve
reproachfully
reproducible
repudiating
repulsion
reputable
requisite
rescind
resembling
resignedly
resources
respectful
response
responsible
restaurant
resurrect
resuscitate
retaliating
retrieve
revealed
revenging
reverence
revering
reversible
revising
revocable
revolutionize
rhapsodies
rhinoceros
rhyming
rhythm
ricochet
ridicule
ridiculous
rigidity
risqué
ritualistic
rogue
rollicking
romantically

roommate
rottenness
rudely

S
sabbatical
sacrifice
sadistically
safety
salacious
salutary
sanatorium*
sanitarium*
sapphire
sarsaparilla
satellite
satiety
satisfied
satisfy
saturating
sauerkraut
saxophone
scandalous
scared
scarred
scene
schedule
schemer
scintillating
scissors
sclerosis
scoundrelly
scrupulous
scurrilous
scurrying
secretive
secureness
sedentary
seducible*
seemingly
seize
self-abasement

self-conscious
semantics
senatorial
sensitivity
sensuality
sentence
sentience*
sentimentality
separable
separate
separation
sergeant*
serviceable
seventieth
sexually
Shakespearean*
shamefacedly
shellacked*
shepherd
shining
short circuit
short-lived
shredded
shrinkage
shrubbery
shyly
sibilance
sickliness
sidesplitting
sideways
siege
significance
silhouette
similar
simile
sincerely
situating
skied
skyscraper
slatternly
sleepily

sleigh
sleight of hand
sliest
slipperiness
slurred
smoky*
smuggest
snobbery
snowcapped
sobriety
sociability
socialistic
sociology
solemnity
solicitude
solidity
solitaire
solvable
somnambulist
soothe
sophomore
soporific
sorcery
sorely
sorrier
source
souvenir
spaghetti
sparing
sparsely
speaking
spectrum
speech
speedometer
spirituality
spitefulness
sponsor
spontaneity
spurious
squalid
squarely

squaring
stabilization
starry
startling
stationary
stationery
statuary
stealthy
stepped
stiffen
stimulating
stodginess
stoically
stolidity
straight
strangely
strategy
strength
stretch
stretchable
stubborn
studying
stultify
stupefaction
stylistic
suavely
subjectivity
sublimity
submissiveness
submitted
subsidiary
subsistence
substantial
substituting
subterranean
subtle
succeed
succession
sufficient
suggestible
suitable

summary
summed
superannuate
superficially
superintendent
superlatively
supersede°
superstitious
suppress
supremacy
surcease
surfeited
surreptitious
surrounding
surveillance
susceptible
suspense
suspicious
sustenance
swimming
syllabication
syllable
symbol
sympathetic
symphonic
synonymous
synthesis
systematically

T
tableau
tabooed°
taciturn
tactically
talkativeness
tangible
tassel
tasteless
taught
taut
tawdriness

technique
tedious
telepathy
temperament
temporarily
tenacious
tendency
tentatively
tenuous
terminology
terrifically
terrifying
testicle
thankfully
thatched
themselves
theories
theory
therapeutic
therefore
thesaurus
theses
thesis
thieve
thinkable
thirstily
thirties
thorough
thought
thriving
through
ticklish
timidity
timing
tiresomely
titillate
to
tobaccos
together
tolerable
tomato
tomatoes

tomorrow
too
topography
tormentor
torpedoes
torrential
totally
tousled°
tragedy
tragically
tranquillity°
transcendental
transferred
translucence
transmitter
transparent
treachery
tremendous
trichinosis
tricycle
trivially
tropical
truculence
tubular
tumultuous
tuneful
turmeric°
turquoise
tying
typewriter
tyranny

U
ugliness
ukulele°
ultimately
umbrella
unaccountable
unanimous
unconcernedly
unctuous
undeniable

undoubtedly
unfortunately
uniformity
uniquely
unlikely
unnecessary
unoccupied
unprincipled
unruliness
unusually
urbanely
useful
useless
using
utterly

V

vacating
vacillate
vacuum
validity
valuable
vanquish
vaporous
variegated
varies
various
velocity
venerable
vengeance
ventriloquist
veracity

veritable
vernacular
versatility
vicarious
vicissitude
villain
vinegar
virtually
virulence
visibility
visitor
visualize
vitally
vivacity
vocalist
vociferous
voicing
voluminous
voluntarily
voluptuous
voracity
voucher
vulnerable

W

wakefully
wantonness
wariness
warrant
watery
weakened

wearisome
weather
weighty
weird
weren't
wheeze
where
whether
whistling
whole
wholly
whose
wieldy
wiliness
willfully*
winery
wintry
wireless
wishful
witticism
woeful
wonderfully
wondrous
workable
worrying
wrathfully
wrench
wretchedness
writhe
writhing
writing
wryly

ROGET'S THESAURUS

How to Use Roget's Thesaurus

PETER MARK ROGET (1779–1869) was a British lexicographer and physician. *Roget's Thesaurus*, a standard reference work for over a century, represents his highly personal view of how the English language reflects the structure of the universe. In some ways, that view is dated today; but the complex structure and breadth of the thesaurus still prove surprisingly helpful to the modern user.

For most users, the key to the synonyms in the body of the book lies in the alphabetical listing in the index. The uniqueness of Roget's original plan of classification provides the user with access to related words and requires nothing more than a near-synonym to help locate the word sought. *Roget's Thesaurus* is more than simply a synonym dictionary—both in the lists following individual headwords and in the grouping of headwords under the various sections, it is a diverse collection of associated and related words and phrases.

For example, suppose you are looking for a synonym for *lull:* a check in the index yields the reference number, 403; turning to that entry provides the synonyms *silence*, *stillness*, *quiet*, *hush*, *peace*.

But, suppose you are trying to find a verb meaning 'to feel very dissatisfied' and the synonyms listed under *discontent* are not "strong" enough for your purpose. A brief check of the related, contiguous headwords will lead you to the entry for *regret* which provides the synonyms *lament*, *deplore*, *bemoan*, *bewail*, *rue*.

This edition of *Roget's Thesaurus* has a number of other special features. Dictionaries of synonyms, unless they are of considerable size, rarely provide alphabetical listings of all the words in the book. In this edition, you will find every word listed in the index.

Larger books may provide more synonyms, but the user of a thesaurus is rarely looking for a rare or unusual word: he wants an equivalent word that is part of everyday language. This edition is the only abridged *Roget's Thesaurus* available. While retaining the original structure and all the 1,000 headwords, all antiquated words and phrases have been removed. In addition, the book has been modernized to include the most current usage and the newest developments in language.

In this abridgment, many duplications have been omitted to save space. For maximum usefulness, the user should look through other associated parts of speech for the word he is seeking, for adjectives and verbs can yield nouns and adverbs, and vice versa. For example, adverbs can be formed by adding *-ly* to some adjectives and nouns by adding *-ness* to some adjectives.

The Publisher

Caution: If the word selected is not completely familiar, check its meaning and usage in this volume's dictionary before risking its use in an incorrect or unidiomatic context.

Thesaurus

Class I

Words Expressing Abstract Relations

I. Existence

1 existence *n* being, entity, subsistence, reality, actuality, presence, fact, matter of fact, truth. science of existence: ontology.

v exist, be, subsist, live, breathe; occur, happen, take place; consist in, lie in; endure, remain, abide, survive, last, stay, continue.

adj existent, extant; prevalent, current, afloat; real, actual, true, positive, absolute; substantial, substantive; well founded, well grounded.

adv actually, in fact, in reality.

2 nonexistence *n* inexistence; insubstantiality, nonentity; blank, *tabula rasa*, void, emptiness, nothingness; potential, possibility; annihilation, extinction, obliteration, total destruction.

v not exist; pass away, perish, die, die out, disappear, dissolve; annihilate, destroy, obliterate, wipe off the face of the earth; nullify, void; take away, remove.

adj nonexistent, inexistent; blank, void, empty; unreal, baseless, unsubstantial, intangible, ineffable, spiritual, spectral; unborn, uncreated, unbegotten, unconceived; potential, possible; exhausted, gone, lost, departed, extinct, defunct; fabulous, visionary, imaginative, ideal, conceptual, abstract.

3 substantiality *n* materiality, corporality, tangibility, material existence, bodiliness, matter, stuff; creature, being, person, body, flesh and blood, substance; thing, object, article.

adj substantive, substantial, corporeal, material, bodily, physical, concrete, tangible, palpable, corporal, materialistic.

4 unsubstantiality *n* nothingness; nothing, naught, nil, nullity, zero; shadow, phantom, apparition, dream, illusion; fallacy, inanity, frivolity; hollowness, blank, void; flimsiness, thinness, slightness.

v vanish, evaporate, fade, dissolve, melt away, disappear.

adj unsubstantial, baseless, groundless, ungrounded, without foundation, fallacious, erroneous, untenable; insignificant, slight, thin, trifling, frivolous; imaginary, visionary, dreamy, shadowy, ethereal, airy, immaterial, spectral, illusory, incorporeal, intangible, bodiless, abstract; vacant, vacuous, empty, blank, hollow.

5 intrinsicality *n* ego, essence, quintessence, gist, pith, marrow, sap, lifeblood, backbone, heart, soul, core; principle, nature, constitution, construction, character, type, quality; habit, temper, temperament, personality, spirit, humor, grain, moods, features, peculiarities, aspects, idiosyncrasies, tendencies, bents; inbeing, inherence, essentiality.

v be intrinsic, be inherent.

adj intrinsic, inherent, implanted, innate, inborn, inbred, ingrained; essential, fundamental, basic, normal; inherited, congenital, hereditary, indigenous, in the blood, in the genes; instinctive, instinctual, internal, personal, subjective; characteristic, peculiar, idiosyncratic; fixed, set in one's ways, invariable, unchangeable, incurable, ineradicable.

adv intrinsically, at bottom, in effect, practically, virtually, substantially.

6 extrinsicality *n* extraneousness, externals.

adj extrinsic, extraneous, external, adventitious; collateral, accidental, incidental, objective.

adv extrinsically.

7 state *n* condition, case, circumstances, situation, status, surroundings, pass; plight, pickle; mood, temper, frame; constitution, structure, form, phase, frame, fabric, stamp, set, fit, mold; mode, style, fashion, light, complexion, character; tone, tenor, turn.

v be in a state.

8 circumstance *n* situation, phase, position, condition, posture, attitude, place, point; footing, standing, status; occasion, happening, event, juncture, conjunction; predicament, exigency,

emergency, crisis, pinch, plight, pass; climax, apex, turning point.

adj circumstantial, conditional, provisional; contingent, incidental, adventitious; critical, climactic.

adv under the circumstances, under the conditions; thus, in such wise; accordingly, that being the case, since, seeing that, as matters stand; conditionally, provided, if, in case; if so, if it so happen, in the event of, provisionally, unless.

II. Absolute Relation

9 relation *n* connection, concern, bearing, reference; correlation, analogy; similarity, affinity, homogeneity, alliance, association, nearness; approximation, relationship; comparison, ratio, proportion; link, tie, bond.

v relate to, refer to; bear upon, regard, concern, touch, affect, have to do with, pertain to, appertain to, belong to; bring into relation with, associate, connect, parallel; link, bind, tie.

adj relative, relative to, relating to, referable to, with reference to; belonging to; related, connected, associated, affiliated, allied; in the same category, relevant.

adv as regards, about, concerning, with relation to, with reference to, with regard to, with respect to, in connection with, under the head of, in the matter of.

10 [absence of relation] **non-relation** *n* irrelation, dissociation, lack of connection; disconnection, disjunction; inconsequence, irreconcilability, disagreement, heterogeneity; independence.

v have no relation to, have no bearing upon, have nothing to do with, have no connection with.

adj unrelated, irrespective, unallied, unconnected, disconnected, heterogeneous, independent; adrift, insular, isolated; extraneous, strange, alien, foreign, outlandish, exotic; irrelevant, inapplicable, not pertinent, beside the mark, off base; remote, farfetched, out-of-the-way, forced, detached, distanced; incidental, parenthetical.

adv parenthetically, by the way, by the by; incidentally.

11 [relations of kindred] **consanguinity** *n* relationship, kindred, blood; parentage, paternity, maternity, lineage, heritage; filiation, affiliation, connection, alliance, tie; family, blood relation, ties of blood, kinsman, kinfolk, kith and kin, relation, relative, one's own, one's own flesh and blood;

fraternity, sorority, brotherhood, sisterhood; race, stock, generation.

v be related to, claim relationship with.

adj related, akin, consanguineous, allied, affiliated, connected; kindred, familial.

12 [double or reciprocal relation] **correlation** *n* correspondence, reciprocity, reciprocation, interdependence, mutuality, interchange, exchange.

v reciprocate, alternate, interchange, interact, interdepend; interchange, exchange; correlate, correspond, relate.

adj reciprocal, mutual, correlative, corresponding, analogous, complementary; equivalent, interchangeable, alternate.

adv reciprocally.

13 identity *n* sameness, exactness, equality, correspondence, parallelism, unity, convertibility; resemblance, similarity; self, oneself, name, personality; facsimile, duplicate, replica, copy, reproduction.

v be identical, coincide, coalesce.

adj identical, self, the same, selfsame; coincident, coinciding, coalescent, indistinguishable; one, equal, equivalent.

adv identically.

14 contrariety *n* contrast, foil, antithesis, oppositeness, opposition, contradiction, antipathy, antagonism; the reverse, the inverse, the converse, inversion, subversion, reversal, the opposite, antipodes.

v be contrary, contrast with, differ from, oppose; invert, revert, turn upside down; contradict, contravene; antagonize.

adj contrary, opposite, counter, converse, reverse; opposed, antithetical, contrasted, antipodean, antagonistic, opposing; conflicting, inconsistent, contradictory; negative, hostile.

15 difference *n* discrepancy, disparity, dissimilarity, inconsistency, variance, variation, diversity, imbalance, disagreement, inequality, inequity, divergence, contrast, contrariety; discrimination, distinction, nice distinction, shade, nuance, subtlety.

v differ, vary, diversify, modify, change, alter; contrast, mismatch; discriminate, distinguish.

adj different, diverse, heterogeneous, unlike, divergent, altered, changed, deviant, deviating, variant, varied, modified; diversified, various, divers, miscellaneous, manifold; other, another, not the same, unequal, un-

matched, wide apart; distinctive, characteristic, discriminative.

16 uniformity *n* homogeneity, permanence, continuity, consistency, stability, accordance, standardization, conformity, agreement; regularity, constancy, evenness, sameness; monotony, routine, invariability.

v be uniform, accord with; conform to, assimilate; level, smooth, even.

adj uniform, homogeneous, of a piece, consistent; consistent, regular, constant, even, level; invariable, unchanging, unvarying, unvaried, unchanged, constant, regular; undiversified, solid, plain, dreary, monotonous, routine.

adv uniformly; always, invariably, without exception; ever, forever.

16a lack of uniformity *n* diversity, irregularity, unevenness, inconsistency, nonconformity, heterogeneity.

adj diversified, varied, irregular, inconsistent, motley, patchwork, uneven, rough; multifarious, of various kinds.

17 similarity *n* resemblance, likeness, similitude, semblance, affinity, approximation, parallelism; agreement, correspondence, analogy; brotherhood, family likeness; repetition, sameness, uniformity, identity; the like, fellow, match, pair, mate, twin, double, counterpart; alter ego, chip off the old block, birds of a feather, like two peas in a pod; simile, parallel, type, image, representation.

v be similar, resemble, look like, bear a resemblance, take after, approximate, parallel, match, rhyme with.

adj similar, resembling, like, alike; twin; analogous, parallel, of a piece; allied to, akin to, corresponding; approximate, much the same, near, close, something like; imitative, mock, pseudo, simulating, representing, representative; exact, true, lifelike, faithful, true to life, identical.

adv as if, so to speak; as it were, as if it were; quasi, just as.

18 dissimilarity *n* dissimilitude, unlikeness, difference; diversity, disparity, divergence; novelty, originality, uniqueness.

v be unlike, differ from, bear no resemblance; vary, diversify, differentiate.

adj dissimilar, unlike, different, disparate; unique, new, novel, unprecedented, unmatched, unequaled; diversified.

19 imitation *n* copying; copy, duplication, reproduction, replica; mocking, mimicry, aping; simulation, impersonation, representation, semblance, approximation, paraphrase, parody; plagiarism, forgery.

v imitate, copy, mirror, reflect, impersonate, duplicate, reproduce, simulate, counterfeit; mock, take off, mimic, ape, personate, parody, caricature, travesty; follow, emulate, pattern after, model oneself on, parallel, follow, take after.

adj imitative, modeled after, modeled on, based on; fake, phony, counterfeit, false, imitation, mock; duplicate, second hand.

adv literally, word for word, to the letter.

20 nonimitation *n* originality, uniqueness.

adj unimitated, uncopied; unmatched, unparalleled; inimitable, original, unique, special, one of a kind, rare, exceptional.

20a variation *n* alteration, change, modification; divergency, deviation, aberration, innovation.

v vary, change; deviate, diverge, alternate, modify.

adj varied, modified, diversified, altered, changed.

21 [result of imitation] **copy** *n* facsimile, counterpart, effigy, form, likeness, similitude, semblance, cast, mold, model, representation, image, portrait; reflexion, shadow, echo; transcript, transcription, reproduction, imitation, carbon, ditto, stencil, duplicate, reprint, transfer, replica; parody, caricature, burlesque, travesty, paraphrase; counterfeit, forgery, deception.

adj faithful, lifelike, exact, similar.

22 [thing copied] **prototype** *n* original, model, pattern, precedent, standard; type, archetype, exemplar, paradigm, module, example; text, copy, design; die, mold; matrix, mint, seal, punch, intaglio, negative, plate, stamp.

v be an example, set an example.

23 agreement *n* unanimity, harmony, accord, accordance, concord, union, unity, understanding, settlement, treaty, pact; uniformity, conformity, consistency, congruity, logic, correspondence, parallelism, apposition; consent, assent, concurrence, cooperation.

v agree, accord, harmonize; correspond, tally, (*informal*) jibe; meet, suit, fit, befit, square with, dovetail,

match; adapt, fit, accommodate, adjust.

adj agreeing, accordant, correspondent, congenial, harmonious; reconcilable, comfortable, compatible, congruous, consistent, logical, consonant, commensurate; in accordance with, in harmony with, in keeping with; apt, apposite, pat, pertinent; agreeable, happy, felicitous.

24 disagreement *n* discord, dissonance, dissidence, disunion, discrepancy, nonconformity, incongruity, dissension, conflict, opposition, antagonism, difference; disparity, disproportion, mismatch, variance, divergence, inequity, inequality.

v disagree, clash, jar, argue, quarrel, dispute.

adj disagreeing, discordant, dissonant, inharmonious; at variance, hostile, conflicting, antagonistic, clashing, disputing, factious, dissenting, irreconcilable, incompatible, inconsistent with; incongruous, disproportionate, disparate, divergent; disagreeable, uncongenial, mismatched; out of joint, out of step, out of tune.

III. Simple Quantity

25 [absolute quantity] **quantity** *n* size, mass, volume, amount, measure, measurement, substance, strength; mouthful, spoonful, handful; stock, batch, lot, dose.

adj quantitative, some, any, more or less.

26 [relative quantity] **degree** *n* grade, extent, measure, amount, ratio, standard, height, pitch; reach, range, scope, rate, caliber; gradation, shade, tint; tenor, tone, compass; sphere, station, rank, standing; point, mark, stage, level; intensity, strength.

adj comparative, gradual, shading off.

adv by degrees, gradually, step by step, bit by bit, little by little, inch by inch, drop by drop; in some degree, to some extent; up to a point.

27 [sameness of quantity or degree] **equality** *n* parity, symmetry, balance, counterbalance; evenness, monotony, level; equivalence, equipoise, equilibrium; par, even keel, quits; identity, similarity; tie, dead heat, draw, drawn game, neck and neck race; match, peer, equal, mate, fellow, brother; equivalent.

v equal, match, reach, keep pace with, run abreast; come up to; balance, even the score; equalize, level, trim, adjust; strike a balance; restore equilibrium.

adj equal, even, level, monotonous, coequal, symmetrical, balanced; on a par with, on a level with, on an equal footing with, up to the mark; equivalent, tantamount, synonymous, quits, even, much the same, all one, one and the same; drawn, half and half, six of one and half a dozen of another.

adv equally, to all intents and purposes.

28 [difference of quantity or degree] **inequality** *n* disparity, dissimilarity, difference, odds; unevenness, imbalance; inferiority, shortcoming, deficiency, imperfection, inadequacy; mediocrity; superiority.

v be unequal, have the advantage, turn the scale, turn the tide; topple, overmatch; not come up to, fall short of, not come up to snuff.

adj unequal, uneven, imbalanced; disparate, partial, inferior, insufficient, deficient, inadequate, mediocre, short.

29 mean *n* medium, average, balance, middle, mid-point, center, median, golden mean; compromise, neutrality.

v split the difference, take the average, move to the center.

adj mean, intermediate, middle, average, standard, normal, neutral; mediocre, middle class, bourgeois, commonplace, run of the mill, egalitarian.

adv on the average, in the long run.

30 compensation *n* equation; indemnification, requital; compromise, measure for measure, tit for tat, eye for an eye, retaliation, equalization; setoff, off-set, counterpoise, ballast; indemnity, equivalent, *quid pro quo*, amends, reparation.

v compensate, indemnify, recompense, remunerate; counterbalance, counterpoise, countervail, offset, counteract, balance, balance out, make up for, square, even out, equalize; cover, neutralize, nullify; redeem, atone, make amends.

adj compensatory, compensating, equivalent, equal.

adv but, however, yet, still, notwithstanding, nevertheless, although, though, nonetheless; howbeit, albeit; at all events, at any rate, be that as may, even so, on the other hand, at the same time.

31 greatness *n* magnitude, size, bulk, dimensions, vastness; multitude; enormousness, immensity, might, strength, intensity, fullness; importance, distinction, eminence, renown; quantity,

store, volume, mass, bulk, heap; abundance, sufficiency.

v be great, soar, tower, rise above, transcend; enlarge, increase, expand.

adj great, large, considerable, big, huge, mammoth, gigantic; ample, abundant, sufficient; full, intense, strong; widespread, extensive, wholesale; goodly, noble, precious, mighty; utter, uttermost, arch, profound, intense, consummate; extraordinary, important, unsurpassed, supreme; complete, total; vast, immense, enormous, extreme, inordinate, excessive, extravagant, exorbitant, outrageous, monstrous; towering, stupendous, prodigious, marvelous; unlimited, infinite; absolute, positive, stark, decided, unequivocal, essential, perfect; remarkable, notable, noteworthy.

adv [in a positive degree] truly; decidedly, unequivocally, absolutely, essentially, fundamentally, downright; [in a complete degree] entirely, completely, totally, wholly; abundantly, fully, amply, widely; [in a great or high degree] greatly, much, indeed, very, very much, most, pretty, pretty well, enough, in a great measure, to a large extent; richly, on a large scale, ever so much; mightily, powerfully; extremely, exceedingly, intensely, exquisitely, consummately, acutely, indefinitely, immeasurably, beyond compare, beyond measure, beyond all bounds, incalculably, infinitely; [in a supreme degree] pre-eminently, superlatively, supremely, incomparably; [in a too great degree] immoderately, inordinately, exorbitantly, excessively, enormously, preposterously, monstrously, out of all proportion, with a vengeance; [in a marked degree] particularly, remarkably, singularly, curiously, uncommonly, unusually, peculiarly, notably, signally, strikingly, pointedly, mainly, chiefly; famously, egregiously, prominently, glaringly, emphatically, strangely, wonderfully, amazingly, surprisingly, astonishingly, incredibly, marvelously, stupendously; [in a violent degree] violently, furiously, severely, desperately, tremendously, extravagantly; [in a painful degree] painfully, sadly, sorely, bitterly, piteously, grievously, miserably, cruelly, woefully, lamentably, shockingly, frightfully, fearfully, dreadfully, terribly, horribly.

32 smallness *n* littleness, tininess, diminutiveness; slenderness, thinness, paltriness, slightness; paucity, fewness, sparseness, scarcity; unimportance, triviality, inconsequentiality, pettiness, insignificance; meanness, sordidness, selfishness, narrow-mindedness; small quantity, modicum, atom, particle,

molecule, point, speck, dot, dab, mote, jot, iota; minutiae, details, soupçon, scintilla, granule; drop, droplet, drizzle, sprinkling, dash, smack, tinge; dole, scrap, shred, splinter; mite, bit, morsel, crumb, seed; snippet, snatch, slip; chip, sliver; nutshell, thimbleful, spoonful, handful, mouthful; fragment, fraction, drop in the ocean; trifle.

v be small.

adj small, little, tiny, diminutive, petite, miniature, minuscule, minute, microscopic, infinitesimal, fine; unimportant, trivial, minor, secondary, trifling, inconsequential, petty, paltry, insignificant; slender, thin, slight, scanty, scant, meager, insufficient; few, sparse, scarce; low, so-so, middling, tolerable, inconsiderable, inappreciable; mean, sordid, selfish, narrow, narrow-minded, illiberal, ungenerous; feeble, weak, faint.

adv [in a small degree] to a small extent; a wee bit; slightly, imperceptibly, faintly; miserably, wretchedly; insufficiently, imperfectly; passably, pretty well, well enough; [in a certain or limited degree] partially, in part, to a certain degree; some, rather, to some degree; simply, only, purely, merely, at the least; ever so little; almost, nearly, well nigh, short of, not quite, all but, near the mark; scarcely, hardly, barely, only just, no more than; [in an uncertain degree] about, thereabouts, somewhere about; [in no degree] noway, nowise, not at all, not in the least, not a bit, not a jot, not a whit, in no respect, by no means, on no account.

33 superiority *n* supremacy, pre-eminence, ascendancy, transcendence; excellence, greatness, nobility, eminence, worthiness, preponderance, predominance, prevalence, advantage; majority; quality, high caliber.

v be superior, exceed, excel, transcend, outdo, outweigh, outrival, outrank; pass, surpass; top, cap, outstrip, eclipse, predominate, prevail; take precedence, come first.

adj superior, greater, major, higher, exceeding; supreme, greatest, utmost, paramount, pre-eminent, foremost, crowning; first-rate, important, excellent, unrivaled, matchless, priceless, unparalleled, unequaled, unsurpassed, inimitable, incomparable, superlative, beyond compare, transcendent.

adv beyond, more, over, over and above, at its height; [in a superior or supreme degree] eminently, pre-eminently, prominently, surpassingly, superlatively, supremely, above all, to crown all, *par excellence*; principally, especially, particularly, peculiarly.

34 inferiority *n* low quality, deficiency, imperfection, shortcoming, inadequacy; mediocrity, commonalty, commonness, poorness, meanness; minority, subordination, subjection.

v be inferior, fall short of, come short of, not come up to, not pass muster; want, lack.

adj inferior, minor, less, lesser, deficient; poor, indifferent, mean, base, bad, shabby, paltry, humble, imperfect, mediocre, common, commonplace, second-rate; poorer; secondary, minor, subordinate, lower; diminished, reduced, unimportant.

adv less, subpar; short of, under.

35 increase *n* growth, augmentation, enlargement, extension, expansion, addition, increment, accretion, aggrandizement; development, rise, ascent.

v. increase, grow, dilate, enlarge, expand, multiply; augment, add to, enlarge, greaten; extend, spread out, prolong; advance, rise, sprout, ascend; raise, exalt, deepen, heighten, intensify, magnify, redouble; aggrandize.

adj increasing, growing; additional, incremental; developmental.

36 decrease *n* diminution, abatement, decline, reduction, wane, falling-off, contraction, dwindling, shrinking, lessening, ebb, ebbing; subtraction, abridgment, shortening; depreciation, deterioration.

v decrease, lessen, abate, fall off, decline, contract, shrink, dwindle, wane, ebb, subside; diminish, deteriorate, depreciate, languish, decay; abridge, shorten, subtract.

adj decreased, decreasing, on the wane.

37 addition *n* increment, increase, enlargement, aggrandizement, accession; supplement, adjunct, attachment, addendum; annexation, interposition, insertion; uniting, joining.

v add, annex, affix, subjoin, tack on, append, attach, join, supplement, increase, augment, make an addition to; accrue, accumulate, pile up; total, sum, add up; reinforce.

adj additional, supplemental, supplementary; extra, accessory, auxiliary.

adv in addition, more, plus; and, also, likewise, too, further, furthermore, besides, to boot, etc., and so on, and so forth; over and above, moreover; with, as well as, together with, along with, in conjunction with.

38 deduction *n* subtraction, retrenchment, withdrawal, removal; mutilation, amputation, curtailment; shortening, abbreviation; decrease, cutback.

v deduct, subtract, retrench, withdraw, remove; take from, take away; shorten, abbreviate, cut back, pare down, reduce, decrease, diminish, curtail, eliminate, deprive of; mutilate, amputate, cut off, cut away, excise; pare, thin, thin out, prune, scrape, file.

adj subtracted, subtracting; removable, reducible; deductible.

adv less, short of; minus, without, excepting, except, with the exception of, save, exclusive of.

39 [thing added] **adjunct** *n* addition, affix, suffix, appendage, annex, augmentation, increment, reinforcement, accessory, accompaniment, sequel; addendum, complement, supplement, appendix, attachment; rider, offshoot, episode, corollary.

adj additional.

40 [thing remaining] **remainder** *n* residue, remains, remnant, leftover, excess, superfluity, balance, surplus, rest, relic; leavings, odds and ends, residuum, dregs, refuse, crumbs, stubble, ruins, skeleton, stump.

v remain, survive, be left; be left over.

adj remaining, left, left over, residual; over, odd, spare, unused; superfluous; surviving.

40a [thing deducted] **decrement** *n* discount, defect, loss, deduction.

41 mixture *n* admixture, mix, combination, mingling, amalgamation, junction; infusion, suffusion, transfusion; infiltration, interlarding, interpolation; adulteration. thing mixed: tinge, tincture, touch, dash, sprinkling, spice, seasoning, infusion. compounds: alloy, amalgam, mélange, pastiche, miscellany, medley, patchwork, hotchpotch, gallimaufry, conglomeration, jumble, potpourri, farrago; cross, hybrid, mongrel.

v mix, join; combine, blend, mingle, commingle, confuse, jumble, unite, compound, amalgamate, adulterate; interlard, interlace, intertwine, interweave, interpolate; conjoin, associate, consort; instill, imbue, infuse, suffuse, transfuse, infiltrate, dash, tinge, tincture, season, blend, cross.

adj mixed, composite, half-and-half, hybrid, cross, mongrel, heterogeneous; motley, variegated, miscellaneous, promiscuous, indiscriminate.

adv among, amongst, amid, amidst, with; in the midst of.

42 [freedom from mixture] **simpleness** *n* purity, homogeneity; elimination, sifting, purification.

v simplify; sift, winnow, eliminate, strain, clean, purify; disentangle.

adj simple, uniform, homogeneous, single, pure, clear; unmixed, unadulterated, elemental, elementary, basic.

43 junction *n* joining, union; connection, conjunction, annexation, attachment; coupling, marriage, wedlock; confluence, communication, concatenation; meeting, assemblage, assembly, reunion; joint, joining, juncture, pivot, hinge, articulation; seam, stitch, linkage, link.

v join, unite, connect, link up, link; associate; put together, piece together, bind together; attach, fix, affix, fasten, bind, secure, clinch, twist, tie, string, strap, sew, lace, stitch, hem, knit, button, buckle, hitch, lash, splice, gird, tether, picket, moor, harness, leash; chain; fetter, lock, hook, couple, link, yoke, bracket; marry, wed, bridge over, span; pin, bolt, clasp, clamp, screw, rivet; solder, weld, fuse; entwine, interlace, intertwine, interweave; entangle.

adj joined, joint; corporate, compact; firm, fast, close, tight, taut, secure, set, inseparable, indissoluble.

adv jointly, in conjunction with; fast, firmly; intimately.

44 disjunction *n* disconnection, disunion, disengagement, dissociation, discontinuity; isolation, insularity, insulation, separateness; dispersion; separation, parting; detachment, segregation; divorce; division, subdivision, break, fracture, rupture; dismemberment, dislocation, severance; fissure, breach, rent, split, rift, crack, cut, slit, incision.

v disjoin, disconnect, disengage, disunite, dissociate, divorce, part, detach, separate, disentangle, cut off, rescind, discontinue; segregate, set apart, keep apart, isolate, insulate; cut adrift, loose, set free, liberate; divide, subdivide, sever, dissever, cut, saw, snip, chop, ax, cleave, rive, rend, slit, split, splinter, chip, crack, snap, break, tear, burst, rend; wrench, rupture, shatter; hack, hew, slash, slice, cut up, carve, dissect, tear to pieces; disband, disperse, dislocate, break up, apportion, divide; part, part company, separate, leave.

adj disjoined, discontinuous, disjunctive; isolated, insular; separate, apart, asunder, loose, adrift, free; unattached, unconnected.

adv separately, one by one, severally, apart, adrift, asunder.

45 link *n* connective, connection, vinculum, copula, tie, bond, bridge; junction, bracket.

v link, bond, join, connect, conjoin, fasten, pin, bind, tie; bridge, span.

46 coherence *n* cohesion, cohesiveness, adherence, adhesion, adhesiveness; connection, union, conglomeration, aggregation, consolidation; stickiness, inseparability.

v cohere, adhere, stick, cling, cleave, hold, take hold, clasp, hug; hang together, stay together; glue, cement, paste, solder, weld; consolidate, solidify, agglomerate.

adj cohesive, adhesive, adhering, sticky; tenacious, tough; united, unified, inseparable, inextricable, (*informal*) together, (*informal*) tight.

47 incoherence *n* looseness, laxity, relaxation, nonadhesion; loosening, disjunction, disconnection; disagreement, inconsistency, incongruity.

v loosen, make loose, slacken, relax; detach, disjoin.

adj nonadhesive, noncohesive, detached, loose, slack, lax, relaxed, segregated, unconsolidated; inconsistent, incongruous, illogical, absurd, rambling.

48 combination *n* mixture; junction; union, unification, synthesis, incorporation, amalgamation, coalescence fusion, blend, blending, mix, centralization; compound, alloy, amalgam, composition, composite.

v combine, unite, incorporate, amalgamate, absorb, blend, mix merge, fuse, marry, consolidate, coalesce, centralize, cement, harden, solidify.

adj combined, unified.

49 decomposition *n* analysis, dissection, dissolution, breaking down; disjunction; corruption, decay, rot, putrefaction.

v decompose, analyze, dissolve resolve into its elements, dissect, disperse, crumble; decay, rot, turn.

adj decomposed.

50 [principal part] **whole** *n* totality, entirety, total, sum, aggregate; unity, completeness, integrity, indivisibility; bulk, mass, lump; body, trunk.

v form a whole, integrate, embody, amass, aggregate, assemble; amount to, come to, add up to.

adj whole, total, full, entire, undiminished, undivided, integral, complete, unimpaired, unbroken, faultless, sound, intact; indivisible, indissoluble.

adv wholly, altogether; totally, completely, entirely, all, all in all, wholesale, in a body, collectively, in the main, on the whole.

51 part *n* division, portion, piece, fragment, fraction, lump, bit, component, constituent, ingredient, ele-

ment, section, segment, subdivision; member, limb, branch, bough, offshoot, ramification; compartment, department, class.

v part, divide, break, disjoin; partition, apportion, allot.

adj fractional, fragmentary, sectional; divided, split up.

adv partly, in part, partially; piecemeal, bit by bit, by installments, in dribs and drabs, in drips and snatches; in detail.

52 completeness *n* wholeness, entirety, totality, solidarity, fullness, intactness, unity, perfection; thoroughness.

v complete, accomplish, fulfill, finish; fill, charge, load, replenish; fill up, fill in; saturate.

adj complete, entire, whole, full, intact, undivided, one, perfect, fulfilled; full, good, absolute, thorough, solid; exhaustive, radical, sweeping, thoroughgoing; consummate, unmitigated, sheer, unqualified, unconditional; brimming, brimful, chock-full, saturated, crammed, replete, fraught.

adv completely, altogether, outright, wholly, totally, quite, utterly; fully, thoroughly, in all aspects, in every respect, out and out, to all intents and purposes; throughout, from first to last, from beginning to end, from top to bottom, from head to foot, every whit, every inch.

53 incompleteness *n* deficiency, shortcoming, insufficiency, imperfection; immaturity; noncompletion.

[part wanting] defect, deficit, omission, interval, break; discontinuity, missing link.

v be incomplete, fall short of; lack; neglect.

adj incomplete, imperfect, unfinished, uncompleted; defective, deficient, wanting, lacking, failing, short, short of; meager, lame, limp, perfunctory, sketchy, crude, immature; in progress, in preparation, going on, ongoing, proceeding.

adv incompletely.

54 composition *n* constitution, make-up, form; combination, compilation, incorporation, inclusion, synthesis.

v be composed of, be made up of, consist of; include, contain, hold, comprehend, take in, admit, embrace, embody; compose, constitute, form, make.

adj constituting.

55 exclusion *n* omission, exception, rejection, repudiation; exile, seclusion, segregation, separation, elimination, prohibition; restraint, keeping out.

v exclude, bar, leave out, shut out, keep out; reject, repudiate, blackball, throw out; lay aside, put aside, set aside; relegate, segregate, separate, seclude, banish, exile; pass over, omit, eliminate, weed out, winnow.

adj exclusive, not included in; inadmissible.

56 component *n* component part, integral part, element, constituent, ingredient; contents, feature, member part; personnel.

v enter into, be part of, form part of; merge in, share in, participate; belong to, appertain to; form, make, constitute.

adj inclusive, comprehensive.

57 extraneousness *n* extrinsicality, externality; superfluousness; foreign body, foreign substance; intrusion.

v be extraneous, be unnecessary.

adj extraneous, foreign, alien, extrinsic, external; not germane, nonessential, superfluous; excluded.

IV. Order

58 order *n* regularity, uniformity, arrangement, harmony, symmetry; course, routine, method, methodology; disposition, array, arrangement, system, economy, discipline, orderliness; gradation, progression, series, sequence, continuity; rank, place, grade, class, degree.

v order, regulate, manage, adjust, arrange, systematize, standardize, rank.

adj orderly, regular, systematic, methodical; in order, neat, tidy, wellregulated, well-organized, organized, uniform, symmetrical, businesslike, shipshape.

adv in order, methodically, in turn, in its turn; step by step, at regular intervals, systematically.

59 disorder *n* derangement, disarray, untidiness, irregularity, anomaly; anarchy, anarchism, disunion, discord; confusion, jumble, mess, muddle, hash, hodgepodge, chaos; perplexity, labyrinth, wilderness, jungle; raveling, entanglement, complication, convolution; turmoil, ferment, agitation, trouble, row, disturbance, convulsion, tumult, uproar, riot, rumpus, ruckus, scramble, fracas, melee, pandemonium.

v disorder, put out of order, derange, ruffle, rumble; confuse, jumble, mess up.

adj disorderly, out of order, out of place, irregular, desultory; anomalous, disorganized, straggling, unsystematic,

untidy, slovenly, messy; indiscriminate, chaotic, confused, deranged; anarchic, inverted, convoluted, topsyturvy; complex, complicated, perplexed, involved, raveled, entangled, knotted, tangled; troublesome, problematical; riotous, violent, turbulent, tumultuous.

adv irregularly, helter skelter; at cross purposes, (*informal*), after the flood.

60 [reduction to order] **arrangement** *n* plan, method, organization; preparation, groundwork, planning; sorting, disposal, disposition, distribution, assortment, allotment, apportionment, graduation, groupings; analysis, classification, division, ordering, systematization.

v arrange, dispose, place, form; set out, marshal, range, array, rank, group, parcel out, allot, apportion, assign, dole out, distribute; sort, sift, put into shape; plan, prepare, organize, lay the groundwork; classify, divide, file, register, catalog, record, tabulate, index, graduate, rank; regulate, systematize, coordinate, organize, settle, fix; unravel, disentangle, straighten out.

adj arranged, ordered; methodical, orderly, regular, systematic.

61 [subversion of order] **derangement** *n* disorder, mess, disarray, disorganization; discomposure, disturbance, dislocation, perturbation, interruption.

v derange, disarrange, discompose, displace, misplace; mislay, disorder, disorganize; embroil, disconcert, convulse, unsettle, disturb, confuse, trouble, perturb, jumble, muddle, fumble; unhinge, dislocate, throw out of gear, throw out of whack; invert, turn upside down, turn topsy-turvy; complicate, confound, tangle, entangle; litter, scatter, mix.

62 **precedence** *n* coming before, the lead, superiority; precursor, antecedence; importance, consequence; priority, preference.

v precede, come before, forerun, come first; head, lead the way, usher in, introduce; set the fashion, influence, establish; have precedence, take precedence; place before, prefix, preface.

adj preceding, precedent, antecedent, anterior, prior, before; former, foregoing; preliminary, prefatory, introductory; preparatory.

adv before; in advance.

63 **sequence** *n* coming after, following, succession, order, series; posteriority; continuation; order of succession; outcome, consequence, result, sequel.

v succeed, come after, follow, ensue; replace.

adj succeeding, following; consequent, subsequent; proximate, next; sequential, consecutive.

adv after, subsequently; behind.

64 **precursor** *n* antecedent, precedent, predecessor, forerunner, pioneer, leader, bellwether; herald, harbinger; prelude, preamble, preface, prolog, proem, prefix, foreword, introduction; heading, frontispiece, groundwork; preparation.

adj prefatory, introductory, preliminary, precursory.

65 **sequel** *n* continuation, extension, supplement, outgrowth, offshoot, result, consequence, inference, deduction; result, consequence, aftermath, outcome, effect; conclusion, end, culmination, dénouement, finale, finish; appendage, suffix, epilog, postscript, tag, train, trail, wake; afterthought, afterpiece, second thoughts.

66 **beginning** *n* commencement, opening outset, start, initiation, inauguration; introduction, prelude; outbreak, onset, brunt; initiative, first move; origin, cause, source, bud, germ, genesis, birth, nativity, cradle; starting point, first step, square one; title page, head, heading; rudiments, basics, elements.

v begin, commence, open, start, initiate, inaugurate; conceive; set out, embark, depart; usher in, lead the way, take the lead, take the initiative, head, stand at the head, launch, set in motion, get going, take the first step, break ground; burst forth, break out; begin at the beginning, start again, start over, make a fresh start; originate, conceive, think up.

adj initial, introductory, inaugural; incipient; embryonic, rudimental, primal, essential, natal, nascent; first, foremost, leading; maiden, virgin.

adv first, in the first place, first and foremost; in the bud, in its infancy; from the beginning.

67 **end** *n* close, termination, conclusion, finale, finish, last word; consummation, climax, apex, dénouement; goal, destination; expiration, death, finality; limit, extreme, extremity; breakup, last stage, final stage, turning point, death blow.

v end, close, finish, terminate, conclude; expire, die, come to a close, draw to a close, run its course, run out, pass away; bring to an end, put an end to, make an end of, wrap up; get

through, complete, consummate; stop, desist, call it quits.

adj final, terminal, concluding; conclusive, crowning, definitive, last, ultimate, consummate; ended, settled, decided, over, concluded, played out.

adv finally, at last, once and for all, over and done with.

68 middle *n* center, midpoint, midst; mean, midcourse, middle ground, compromise; core, kernel, heart, nucleus, nub; equidistance, bisection; equator, diaphragm, midriff.

adj middle, medial, mean, mid, median, midmost; intermediate, equidistant, central, halfway.

adv midway, halfway, in the middle.

69 [uninterrupted sequence] **continuity** *n* continuousness, consecutiveness, progression, constant flow, succession, train, series, chain, string, scale, gradation; round, suite; procession, column, retinue; pedigree, genealogy, lineage; rank, file, line, row, range, tier.

v follow in a line; arrange in a series, string together, file, thread, graduate, tabulate.

adj continuous, progressive, successive, serial, consecutive, unbroken, uninterrupted, gradual; linear, in a line; perennial, constant.

adv continuously, in succession, consecutively; gradually, step by step, in a column.

70 [interrupted sequence] **discontinuity** *n* disjunction, disconnectedness; interruption, break, fracture, fault, flaw, crack, cut; gap, interval, caesura, pause, *(informal)* breather, rest, intermission, parenthesis, episode.

v alternate; discontinue, break, interrupt, intervene; pause, rest, take a breather, stop; break in upon, interpose; disconnect.

adj discontinuous, disconnected, unconnected, broken, interrupted; fitful, spasmodic, desultory, intermittent, irregular; alternate, recurrent, periodic.

adv at intervals, in snatches, by fits and starts.

71 term *n* rank, station, stage, step, phase; scale, grade, degree, status, position, place, point, mark, period, limit; stand, standing, footing.

72 assemblage *n* collection, levee, gathering, ingathering, muster; concourse, conflux, congregation; meeting, reunion; assembly, congress, convention, conclave, council; miscellany, compilation, menagerie; crowd,

throng, mob, flood, rush, rash, deluge, press, crush, horde, body, tribe, crew, gang, squad, band, party, swarm, flock, bevy; company, troop, regiment, squadron, army; host, multitude, populace, clan, brotherhood, sisterhood, association; group, cluster, clump, batch, pack, assortment; accumulation, heap, lump, pile, mass, conglomeration, conglomerate, aggregation, aggregate; quantity.

v assemble, come together, collect, gather, muster; meet, unite, join, rejoin; cluster, flock, swarm, surge, stream, herd, crowd, throng, associate; congregate, concentrate, huddle; bring together, draw together, place together, lump together; convene, invoke; compile, group, assemble, unite; amass, accumulate, store.

adj assembled; closely packed, dense, crowded, teeming, swarming, populous.

73 dispersion *n* divergence, spreading, radiation, dissemination, diffusion, dissipation, distribution, apportionment, division.

v disperse, scatter, sow, disseminate, diffuse, shed, spread, dispense, disband, distribute, apportion, divide; break up, dispel, cast forth, strew, cast, sprinkle; issue, deal out, dole out.

adj dispersed, spread, scattered, strewn, diffuse, diffusive; sparse, widespread, broadcast; adrift, stray, disheveled.

74 [place of meeting] **focus** *n* center, gathering place, haunt, rendezvous, rallying point, headquarters, club, retreat.

v focus, bring to a point, bring to a focus; center on, bring out, clarify, elucidate.

75 class *n* division, subdivision, category, heading, order, section; department, province, domain; type, kind, sort, genus, species, variety, family, race, tribe, cast, clan, breed, sect.

76 inclusion *n* admission, acceptance into, incorporation, comprehension, reception.

v include, comprise, comprehend, contain, admit, embrace, receive, accept; inclose, circumscribe, encircle, encompass, embody, incorporate; number among, count among, fall under.

adj inclusive, comprehensive, extensive, all-embracing, compendious, sweeping; including, incorporating.

77 exclusion *n* (see 55).

78 generality *n* universality, catholicity, miscellany, miscellaneousness;

generalization, simplification, over-simplification; prevalence, common run.

v be general, be universal, prevail, be true for everyone; render general, generalize, universalize; make a generalization, abstract, simplify.

adj general, universal, catholic, common, ecumenical, egalitarian, worldwide; prevalent, prevailing, rife, current; generic, collective, all-encompassing, comprehensive, all-inclusive, broad, widespread.

79 specialty *n* speciality, skill, ability, talent; individuality, singularity, distinctive feature, particularity, personality, characteristic, mannerism, idiosyncrasy, nonconformity; particulars, details, items; special feature.

v specify, particularize, individualize, specialize; designate, determine, single out, isolate, differentiate; be specific, come to the point, detail, get down to particulars.

adj special, particular, especial, individual, specific, proper, personal, original, private, respective, definite, certain, endemic, peculiar, characteristic, marked, appropriate, exclusive, singular, exceptional, idiomatic, unique.

adv specially, especially, in particular; each, apiece, severally, respectively, each to each, each to his own; in detail.

80 regulation *n* regularity, uniformity, constancy, clockwork, precision, exactness; routine, custom, formula, rule, form, procedure; standard, model, precedent, prototype; conformity, convention; nature, law, principle; normal state, ordinary condition, normalcy; hard and fast law.

adj regular, uniform, constant, steady; customary, conventional, formal, formulaic, procedural.

81 multiformity *n* variety, diversity.

adj multifold, multifarious, manifold, many-sided; heterogeneous, motley, mosaic; indiscriminate, irregular, diversified, diverse; of every description, all manner of kinds.

82 conformity *n* observance, compliance, assent; conventionality, customariness, agreement; example, instance, specimen, sample, illustration, exemplification, case in point.

v conform to, accommodate oneself to, adapt to; be regular, conform, follow the rules, obey the rules, go by the rules, comply, assent, agree, yield, give in, accept, harmonize; illustrate, stand as an example, embody.

adj conformable to rule, adaptable,

agreeable, compliant, malleable; conventional, customary, standard, ordinary, common, habitual, usual, natural, normal, typical; formal, orthodox, strict, rigid, uncompromising; exemplary, illustrative.

adv by rule, in conformity with, in accordance with, in keeping with, consistent with; for the sake of conformity, as a matter of course, for form's sake; invariably, uniformly.

83 unconformity *n* nonconformity, unconventionality, nonobservance, informality; anomaly, variation, inconsistency, irregularity, incongruity, oddity, eccentricity, peculiarity, aberration, abnormality, exception; violation of custom, infraction, infringement; individuality, originality, mannerism, idiosyncrasy, quirk.

v be unconformable.

adj unconformable, unconventional; unnatural, odd, eccentric, peculiar, aberrant, abnormal, exceptional; anomalous, inconsistent, irregular, incongruous, arbitrary, whimsical, wanton; unusual, uncustomary, uncommon, rare, singular, unique, extraordinary; queer, quaint, strange; original, fantastic, newfangled, bizarre, outlandish, exotic, esoteric.

adv unless, except, save, beside.

V. Number

84 number *n* numeral, symbol, figure, cipher, digit, integer, round number, whole number, fraction; sum, total, product.

adj numeral; prime, fractional, decimal; positive, negative.

85 numeration *n* numbering; tallying, enumeration, reckoning, computation, calculation; arithmetic, calculus, algebra; statistics, poll, census, roll call; arithmetic operations.

v number, count, tell, tally, enumerate, add up, sum, reckon, compute, calculate, take account; muster, poll, recite; add, subtract, multiply, divide.

adj numeral, numerical; arithmetical, analytic, algebraic, statistical, numerable, computable, calculable.

86 list *n* catalog, index, listing, inventory, schedule, register, record, ledger, tally, file, table, calendar; directory gazette, atlas, dictionary, thesaurus, roll, checklist.

87 unity *n* oneness, singleness, singularity, individuality; unification, unison, uniformity.

v unite, join, combine; isolate, insulate, seclude.

adj one, sole, single, solitary, lone; individual, apart, alone; unaccom-

panied, unattended, singlehanded, solo; singular, odd, unique; isolated, insular.

adv singly.

88 accompaniment *n* association, partnership, company; accessory, adjunct, concomitant, attachment, complement, attendant, fellow, associate, coexistence.

v accompany, join, escort, convoy, wait on; coexist with, consort with; associate with, couple with.

adj accompanying, fellow, twin, joint; associated with, coupled with; accessory, concomitant, attendant.

adv with, together with, along with, in company with, hand in hand, side by side; therewith, herewith.

89 duality *n* dualism, doubleness, polarity, biformity, duplexity; two, deuce, couple, brace, pair, twins.

v pair, mate, couple, bracket, pair off, yoke.

adj two, twain; dual, twin, two-sided, binary, binomial, duplex; coupled, both.

90 duplication *n* doubling, reduplication; iteration, repetition; renewal.

duplicate, double, copy, carbon, facsimile.

v double; redouble, reduplicate; repeat, renew; duplicate.

adj double; doubled, duplicated; twin, duplicate, second.

adv twice, once more, over again.

91 bisection *n* halving, bifurcation, twofold division, forking, dichotomy, (*informal*) fifty-fifty split.

v bisect, divide in two, halve, divide, split, cut in two, cleave, fork, bifurcate; split down the middle, (*informal*) go halves.

adj bisected, cloven, cleft, halved; bipartite; bifurcated; semi-, demi-, hemi-.

92 triality *n* trinity; three, triad, triplet, trio.

adj three, threefold, triform, tertiary.

93 triplication *n* tripling; triplicity.

v triple, treble, cube.

adj triple, treble; threefold, triplicate; third.

adv three times, thrice; in the third place, thirdly; triply, trebly.

94 trisection *n* tripartition, threefold division, third, third part.

v trisect, divide into three parts.

95 quaternity *n* four, tetrad, quartet, quarter.

v square, reduce to a square.

adj four, fourfold, quadrilateral.

96 quadruplication *n* quadrupling, multiplying by four.

v multiply by four, quadruplicate.

adj four, fourfold, quadruple; fourth.

adv four times, in the fourth place, fourthly.

97 quadrisection *n* quartering, quadripartition, fourfold division; fourth part, quarter.

v quarter, divide into four parts.

adj quartered, quadripartite.

98 five, etc. *n* five; six, half a dozen; seven; eight; nine; ten, decade; eleven; twelve, dozen; thirteen, baker's dozen, long dozen; twenty, score; twenty-five, quarter of a hundred; fifty, half a hundred; hundred, century, centenary; thousand.

99 quinquesection *n* fivefold division.

adj quinquepartite.

100 [more than one] **plurality** *n* two or more, couple, few, several; majority, multitude.

adj plural, more than one, upwards of, some, several, many, numerous.

100a [less than one] **fraction** *n* fractional part, segment, subdivision, part, portion.

101 zero *n* nothing, naught, (*informal*) zip; none, shutout; nobody.

102 multitude *n* multitudinous, multiplicity, profusion, mass, quantity, volume, abundance, amplitude, enormity; numbers, array, scores, droves, host, throng, collection; mob, crowd, assemblage.

v be numerous, swarm with, teem with, crowd, swarm, outnumber, multiply; people, populate.

adj multitudinous, manifold, profuse, multiple, teeming, populous, crowded, thick; many, several, sundry, various, numerous; endless, infinite.

103 fewness *n* paucity, scarcity, sparseness, scantiness; small number, small quantity; infrequency.

diminution of number: reduction, weeding, elimination.

v render few, reduce, diminish, weed, thin, eliminate, eradicate.

adj few, not many, scanty, scarce, sparse, rare, few and far between, limited, meager; sporadic, occasional, infrequent; reduced, diminished, pared back.

104 repetition *n* iteration, reiterat-

ion, recapitulation, restatement; sameness, monotony, harping, recurrence, tautology; redundance; rhythm, beat, echo, reverberation; reappearance, reproduction, duplication.

v repeat, iterate, reiterate, recapitulate, restate, rehash, go over again, harp on, hammer; reproduce, duplicate, echo; recur, revert, return, reappear; resume, return to, go back to; rehearse, go over the same ground.

adj repeated, repetitious, recurrent, recurring, frequent, incessant, never-ending, unceasing; repetitive, redundant, tautological; rhythmic, reverberant, reverberating; monotonous, harping, iterative; habitual.

adv repeatedly, often, again, anew, afresh, over again, once more; over and over, again and again, year after year; ditto, encore.

105 infinity *n* infinitude, infiniteness, perpetuity, endlessness, boundlessness, inexhaustibility, immeasurability, limitlessness, vastness, expanse.

v be infinite, have no limits, know no bounds, go on forever.

adj infinite, countless, numberless, limitless, boundless, measureless, unlimited, interminable, inexhaustible, incalculable; immense, vast, endless, perpetual; incomprehensible; eternal, perfect, omnipotent, absolute.

adv infinitely, *ad infinitum.*

VI. Time

106 time *n* duration, extent; period, interval, spell, term, space, span, season, stage; course; interim, interlude; interregnum, intermission; respite, break, timeout; era, epoch, season, age, year, date.

v time, measure, pace; continue, last, endure, go on, remain, persist, stand; pass time, spend time, while away the time, waste time, kill time, fill up the time.

adj permanent, lasting, durable; timely.

adv while, whilst, during, in the course of, for the time being, in due time; meantime, meanwhile, in the meantime, in the interim; till, until, up to, yet; the whole time, all the time, throughout, for good, (*informal*) for keeps.

107 absence of time *n* no time; outside time.

adv never, at no time; on no occasion, nevermore.

108 [definite duration or period of time] **period** *n* interval, age, era, eon, epoch, term, time; year, decade,

century, millennium; lifetime, generation.

109 [indefinite duration] **course** *n* march of time, course of time, flux, passing time.

v elapse, lapse, flow, run, proceed, advance, pass, flit, fly, slip, slide, drag, creep, crawl; run its course; expire, go by, pass by.

adv in due time, in due course, in due season, in time.

110 [long duration] **durability** *n* permanence, persistence, continuance, lastingness, standing, stability; survival, longevity; protraction, prolongation.

v last, remain, stand, endure, abide, continue, persist; tarry, drag on, drag out, prolong, protract, eke out, draw out, lengthen; outlive, outlast, survive.

adj permanent, durable, lasting, longstanding, stable, immutable, invariable, constant; enduring, abiding, perpetual; lingering, protracted, prolonged, spun-out.

adv long, for a long time, ever so long; long ago; all day long, all the livelong day.

111 [short duration] **transience** *n* impermanence, evanescence, ephemerality, transitoriness, mortality; suddenness, swiftness, changeableness, vicissitude, uncertainty.

v be transient, flit, pass away, fly, gallop, vanish, fade, evaporate, melt.

adj transient, transitory, evanescent, ephemeral, fleeting, flitting, flying, passing; impermanent, temporal, temporary, provisional, short-lived; perishable, precarious, vulnerable, mortal; brief, quick, brisk; sudden, momentary, instantaneous.

adv temporarily, for the moment, for a time; awhile, soon; briefly.

112 [endless duration] **perpetuity** *n* eternity, timelessness, everlastingness, endlessness, infinity; constancy, endurance, durability, ceaselessness.

v last forever, endure, go on forever; perpetuate, immortalize, eternalize.

adj perpetual, eternal, timeless, everlasting, endless; unceasing, ceaseless, interminable, neverending, continuous, incessant, uninterrupted; unfading, imperishable, unvulnerable, immortal.

adv perpetually, always, ever, evermore, forever; constantly, continuously.

113 [point of time] **instantaneousness**

n suddenness, abruptness; moment, instant, second, twinkling, trice, flash, crack, burst.

v be instantaneous, twinkle, flash.

adj instantaneous, momentary, sudden, instant, abrupt.

adv instantaneously, in no time, (*informal*) in two shakes (of a lamb's tail), presto, suddenly, like a shot, in a moment, all of a sudden, in a jiffy; immediately, on the spur of the moment, on a moment's notice.

114 [estimation, measurement and record of time] **chronometry** *n* chronology, timetable; almanac, calendar, register, chronicle, log, annal(s), journal, diary; clock, watch, stopwatch, timepiece, chronometer.

v fix the time, mark the time; date, register, chronicle; measure time, mark time, beat time.

adj chronological.

115 [false estimate of time] **anachronism** *n* misdate, misplacement, chronological error; disregard of time.

v misdate, antedate, postdate, anticipate; take no note of time.

adj misdated; undated, overdue; anachronistic, out of place, misplaced.

116 antecedence *n* priority, anteriority, precedence, pre-existence; antecedent, predecessor, precursor, forerunner.

v precede, antedate, come before; go before, lead, forerun; dawn, presage, herald, break the ground.

adj antecedent, prior, previous, anterior, preceding, pre-existent; former, foregoing, aforementioned; precursory, introductory.

adv before, prior to; earlier, previously, ere, already, yet, beforehand.

117 posteriority *n* succession, sequence; subsequence, following, continuance; successor, sequel, follower; future, futurity.

v follow after, come after, go after, succeed, be subsequent to.

adj posterior, subsequent, following, after, later, succeeding, successive, ensuing, resulting; posthumous.

adv subsequently, after, afterwards, since, later; next, close upon, thereafter, thereupon; ultimately.

118 present time *n* the present juncture, the present day; the times, the time being, right now.

adj present, actual, instant, current, existing.

adv at this time, at this moment; at the present time, now, at present, nowadays.

119 different time *n* other time; another time.

adv at that time, at that instant; then, on that occasion; when, whenever, whensoever; at some other time, at a different time, at some time or other.

120 contemporaneousness *n* simultaneousness, synchronism, simultaneity, coincidence, concurrence, coexistence, concomitance.

v coexist, concur, accompany, go side by side, keep pace with; synchronize.

adj simultaneous, coincident, concurrent, concomitant, coexisting; contemporary, contemporaneous, coeval.

adv simultaneously, concurrently, together, at the same time.

121 the future *n* futurity, hereafter, time to come, tomorrow, morrow; millennium, doomsday, day of judgment, crack of doom, flood; advent, eventuality; destiny, fate; heritage, heirs, posterity; prospect, expectation, anticipation.

v look forward, anticipate, expect, foresee; approach, await, threaten, impend, come near, draw near, come on.

adj future, to come; coming, impending, near, close at hand, in prospect; eventual, ulterior.

adv prospectively, hereafter, in future, in course of time, tomorrow; eventually, ultimately, sooner or later; henceforth, from this time; soon, early, on the eve of, on the point of, on the brink of.

122 the past *n* past time, days of old, days of yore, days gone by, yesterday, yesteryear, former times, ancient times; retrospection, memory; antiquity, history, time immemorial, remote past; ancestry, lineage, forbears; heritage.

v run its course, pass away, pass, lapse, blow over.

adj past, gone, gone by, passed away, bygone, elapsed, lapsed, expired, extinct, forgotten, irrecoverable, obsolete, former, pristine, late; foregoing, last, latter, recent; looking back, retrospective; retroactive.

adv formerly, of old, of yore, ago, over; long ago, years ago, a long while back, some time ago; lately, of late; retrospectively, ere now, before now, hitherto, heretofore; already, yet, up to this time.

123 newness *n* novelty, recentness, freshness; immaturity, greenness, youth, juvenility; innovation, unique-

ness, originality; renovation, restoration; modernity, modernism, stylishness, fashionableness, newfangledness, fashion, faddishness, the latest thing, futurism, trendiness.

v renew, renovate, restore; modernize.

adj new, novel, recent, fresh; green, immature, unripe, young, youthful, untried, untested, virgin, virginal; modern, late, new, newfangled, stylish, fashionable, faddish, trendy, brand-new, up-to-date; renovated, restored, spick and span.

adv newly, afresh, anew, lately, just now, of late.

124 oldness *n* age, antiquity; maturity, ripeness; decline, decay, old age, senility, superannuation; archaism, antiquarianism, relic, thing of the past; tradition, custom, common law.

v be old, have had its day, have seen its day; become old, age, fade.

adj old, ancient, antique; timehonored, venerable, traditional, vintage, of long standing; elderly, aged, hoary, decayed, senile, decrepit; primeval, primitive, aboriginal, primordial, antediluvian, prehistoric, archaic; traditional, prescriptive, customary, immemorial, inveterate, rooted; antiquated, outdated, outmoded, of other times; out of date, obsolete, out-of-fashion, out-of-style, gone by, stale, old-fashioned; timeworn, crumbling, ramshackle, run-down, wasted.

125 morning. noon *n* morning, morn, dawn, daybreak, sunrise, sunup, forenoon, break of day, peep of day, prime of day, morningtide, matins, cockcrow, first blush, antemeridian, A.M.

noon, midday, noonday, noontide, meridian, prime, height, noontime.

spring, springtime; summer, summertime, midsummer.

126 evening. midnight *n* evening, eve, eventide, dusk, vespers, nightfall, sundown, sunset, twilight, curfew, bedtime; afternoon, post meridian, P.M.

midnight, end of the day, close of the day, witching hour, dead of night.

autumn, fall, harvest time; winter.

127 youth *n* juvenility, infancy childhood, boyhood, girlhood; minority, tender years, young years, formative years, next generation, tender age; cradle, nursery; puberty.

adj young, youthful, juvenile, green, callow, budding, immature, developing, underage, formative; younger, junior.

128 age *n* old age, advanced age, senility, years, gray hairs, declining years, golden years, mature years, decrepitude, anility, superannuation, longevity, ripe age, ripe old age; maturity, seniority, eldership.

adj aged, old, advanced, gray, elderly; senile, decline, failing, waning, ripe, overripe, mellow, venerable, wrinkled, wizened; older, elder, eldest.

129 infant *n* baby, babe, babe in arms, nursling, little one, tot, toddler, chick, kid, lamb, cherub; youth, youngster, child, minor; girl, lass, maiden, miss, schoolgirl; boy, lad, stripling, master, schoolboy.

adj infantile, infantlike, puerile, girlish, boyish, childish, babyish; newborn, young.

130 veteran *n* old man, old woman, patriarch, matriarch, grandmother, grandfather, grandsire, seer, graybeard, forefather, elder.

adj aged, old.

131 adolescence *n* majority, adulthood, manhood, womanhood, maturity, ripeness, fullness, puberty, pubescence; teenage years, prepubescence.

v come of age, grow up, attain majority.

adj adolescent, teenage, pubescent, of age, grown up, full grown, adult, womanly, manly, marriageable, nubile.

132 earliness *n* punctuality, promptitude, speediness, readiness, expedition, alacrity, quickness, haste; suddenness; prematurity, precocity, precipitation, anticipation.

v be early, be beforehand; anticipate, forestall, steal a march on, get a head start; bespeak, secure, engage, pre-engage; accelerate, expedite, quicken, hasten, make haste, make time, hurry.

adj early, timely, punctual, on time, prompt; premature, precipitate, precocious, anticipatory; sudden, instantaneous, immediate, expeditious; unexpected.

adv early, soon, anon, betimes, before long; punctually, to the minute, on time, on the dot; beforehand, prematurely, precipitately, too soon, hastily, in anticipation, unexpectedly; suddenly, instantaneously, at short notice, on the spur of the moment; at once, on the spot, on the instant, at sight, straight, offhand, straightway; forthwith, summarily, immediately, shortly, quickly, speedily; presently, by and by, directly.

133 lateness *n* tardiness, slowness,

sloth, tarrying, dilly-dallying, loitering; delay, procrastination, postponement, adjournment, retardation, protraction, prolongation; respite, reprieve, suspension, moratorium, stop, stay.

v be late, tarry, wait, stay, bide, take time, linger, loiter, dawdle, shilly-shally, dilly-dally; put off, defer, delay, lay over, suspend; retard, postpone, adjourn; procrastinate, prolong, protract, drag out, draw out, lengthen, table, shelve, stall.

adj late, tardy, slow, dilatory, backward, unpunctual; delayed, overdue, belated.

adv late; backward, at the eleventh hour, at length, at last; ultimately, behind time; too late; slowly, leisurely, deliberately, at one's leisure, on one's own time.

134 opportuneness *n* timeliness, opportunity, occasion, suitable time, proper time, suitability, high time; crisis, turn, juncture; turning point, given time; nick of time, golden opportunity; clear stage, open field.

v be opportune, be suitable; seize the opportunity, seize the time, seize the day, *carpe diem*, use the occasion; suit the occasion, be expeditious, strike while the iron is hot.

adj opportune, timely, well-timed, seasonable, suitable, appropriate; providential, lucky, fortunate, happy, favorable, fortuitous, propitious, auspicious.

adv opportunely, in due time, in the nick of time, just in time, now or never; by the way, by the by, speaking of, while on the subject; on the spot, on the spur of the moment, since the occasion presents itself.

135 inopportuneness *n* untimeliness, unseasonableness, improper time, unsuitable time; (*informal*) bad timing; intrusion; anachronism.

v be ill timed, mistime, intrude, break in upon, (*informal*) butt in; lose an opportunity, waste an occasion, (*informal*) blow one's chance, let the opportunity slip by; waste time.

adj inopportune, untimely, unpropitious, unseasonable, unsuitable, inauspicious, unfavorable, unfortunate, unsuited, untoward, unlucky; ill-timed, mistimed, poorly timed; unpunctual, premature.

136 frequency *n* repetition, recurrence, iteration, reiteration.

v recur, repeat, reiterate; keep on, continue; attend regularly, visit often, patronize.

adj frequent, oft-repeated, recur-

ring, incessant, constant, continual, perpetual; habitual, customary.

adv often, oft, oftentimes, frequently, repeatedly, day after day; daily, hourly, every day; perpetually, continually, constantly, incessantly, at all times; commonly, habitually, customarily; sometimes, occasionally, at times, now and then, every once in a while, from time to time.

137 infrequency *n* rarity, rare occurrence; long shot, surprise, (*informal*) mindblower.

v be rare, be infrequent.

adj infrequent, occasional, sporadic, rare, uncommon, unusual, unheard of, unprecedented; few, scant, scarce.

adv infrequently, rarely, seldom, scarcely, hardly; not often, hardly ever.

138 regularity [of recurrence] *n* periodicity, intermittence; beat, pulse, pulsation, rhythm; alternation, oscillation, vibration; bout, round, turn, revolution, rotation, rpm; cycle, period, routine; punctuality, regularity, steadiness.

v recur, revolve, return, come in its turn, come round again; beat, pulsate, alternate.

adj regular, periodic, periodical; serial, recurrent, cyclical, cyclic, recurring, rhythmical, rhythmic; intermittent, alternate, every other; regular, steady, punctual, continual, constant, regular as clockwork.

adv regularly, periodically, serially, cyclically; intermittently, alternately; by turns, in turn, in rotation, off and on, round and round.

139 irregularity [of recurrence] *n* uncertainty, unpredictability, haphazardness, fitfulness, capriciousness.

v be irregular, be haphazard.

adj irregular, uncertain, unpredictable, haphazard, fitful, capricious, flickering; spasmodic, sporadic.

adv irregularly, fitfully, capriciously, by fits and starts.

VII. Change

140 change *n* alteration, modulation, modification, variation, mutation, permutation, qualification, deviation, turn, shift, innovation; diversion; break; transformation, transfiguration, transmutation, metamorphosis; conversion, revolution, inversion, reversal; displacement, transference, transposition; changeableness.

v change, alter, vary, modulate, qualify, diversify, tamper with, play with, experiment with; turn, shift, veer,

tack, swerve, warp, deviate, turn aside; turn, take a turn, (*informal*) hang a turn; modify, revamp, transform, transfigure, transmute, metamorphose, convert; innovate, restructure, give a new turn to, recast, redesign, remodel.

adj changed, newfangled; changeable, variable, transformable; innovative.

141 permanence *n* stability, invariability, unalterability, immutability, constancy; endurance, durability, persistence; maintenance, preservation, conservation; obstinacy, immovability, inflexibility, immobility, rigidity.

v endure, bide, abide, stay, remain, last, persist, stand, stand fast; maintain, keep, keep up, preserve; subsist, live, outlive, survive.

adj permanent, lasting, unchanged, unchanging, fixed, stable, invariable, constant; enduring, durable, abiding, everlasting; intact, inviolate; persistent.

adv permanently, for good, for good and all.

142 cessation *n* discontinuation, discontinuance, halt, stoppage, termination, suspension, interruption, stopping; pause, rest, lull, respite, truce, break; interregnum, abeyance; completion, end, finish; stop, death.

v cease, discontinue, terminate, desist, stay; break off, leave off, hold, stop, pull up, stop short, halt, pause, rest; suspend, interrupt, delay, cut short, arrest, bring to a standstill; complete, end, finish, close up shop; wear away, go out, die out, pass away, die.

143 continuance [in action] *n* continuation, continuity, protraction, prolongation, maintenance, perpetuation; persistence, perseverance, repetition.

v continue, persist, go on, keep on, hold on; abide, keep, pursue, stick to; maintain course, carry on, keep up; sustain, uphold, hold up, keep going, maintain, preserve, perpetuate, prolong.

adj continuing, uninterrupted, unvarying; continuous, persistent, perpetual

144 conversion *n* transformation, transmutation, reduction, change, changeover, resolution, assimilation; passage, transit, transition, shifting, flux; growth, progress, development; chemistry, alchemy.

v be converted into, become, turn into, lapse, shift; pass into, grow into, ripen into, merge into; melt, grow, ripen, mature, mellow; convert into

resolve into; make, render; mold, form, model, remodel, remake, do over, reform, reorganize; assimilate, bring into, reduce to.

adj convertible, transmutable, changeable.

145 reversion *n* return, revulsion, reverting, returning; alternation, rotation; inversion; recoil, reaction, reflex, repercussion, rebound, boomerang, ricochet, backlash, repulse; retrospection, retrogression, retrogradation, falling back; restoration, going back; turning point, turn of the tide.

v revert, return, turn back, reverse; relapse, regress, fall back; recoil, rebound; retreat; restore; undo, unmake; turn the tide.

146 [sudden or violent change] **revolution** *n* revolt, rebellion, overthrow, overturn, coup, *coup d'état*, rising, uprising, mutiny, counterrevolution; breakup, destruction, subversion, clean sweep; spasm, convulsion, throe, revulsion.

v revolt, rebel, rise, rise up; revolutionize, remodel, recast, change.

adj revolutionary, rebellious; new

147 substitution *n* replacement, supplanting, commutation, exchange, change, shift.

substitute, expedient, makeshift, stopgap, equivalent, double, alternative, representative.

v substitute, put in the place of, change, exchange, interchange; replace, supplant, supersede, take the place of, stand for, represent, pinch hit, substitute for, sub; redeem commute, alternate.

adv instead, in place of, in lieu of.

148 [double or mutual change] **interchange** *n* exchange, commutation, permutation, transposition; reciprocation, reciprocity, intercourse; barter, swap, trade; interchangeability; retaliation, reprisal, requital, retort, crossfire.

v interchange, exchange, barter, trade, swap, bandy, transpose, commute, reciprocate; give and take, battle with words; retort, requite, retaliate.

adj interchangeable, all-purpose multi-purpose; reciprocal; mutual.

adv in exchange, vice versa, turn and turn about.

149 changeableness *n* mutability, inconstancy, volatility, instability; malleability, adaptability, versatility, mobility; vacillation, irresolution, indecision, capriciousness, oscillation, alternation, fluctuation, vicissitude;

restlessness, fidgetiness, disquiet, disquietude; unrest, agitation.

v fluctuate, oscillate, vary, waver, flounder, shuffle, hem and haw, vacillate, tremble, alternate.

adj changeable, mutable, variable, malleable, adaptable, adjustable, versatile, mobile, transformable, convertible; inconstant, unsteady, unstable, unreliable, vacillating, oscillating, fluctuating; volatile, fitful, fickle, capricious, mercurial, indecisive, irresolute, flighty, impulsive, fanciful, erratic, wayward, wanton; restless, fidgety, tremulous, agitated; unfixed, unsettled.

150 stability *n* immutability, unchangeableness, constancy; firmness, fixity, solidity, steadiness, soundness, balance, stabilization, equilibrium, quiescence; immobility, immovability, fixedness; steadfastness, reliability, resolution, determination, obstinacy, stubbornness, pertinacity, tenacity, doggedness, will, pluck, resoluteness; permanence, endurance, perseverance, durability; continuity, uniformity, changelessness.

v be firm, stick fast, stand firm; settle, establish, fix, set, stabilize; retain, keep hold; make sure, fasten, make solid.

adj stable, fixed, rigid, firm, steady, established, strong, sturdy, immovable, invariable, unvarying, permanent, unchangeable, unchanging, unalterable, immutable; enduring, constant, durable, lasting, abiding, secure, fast, perpetual; unwavering, steadfast, staunch, reliable, steady, solid, sound, balanced; resolute, obstinate, dogged, willful, stubborn, pertinacious, tenacious.

151 present events *n* event, occurrence, incident, affair, eventuality, happening, proceeding, transaction, fact; phenomenon; circumstance, situation, particular; adventure, episode, thrill; crisis, pass, emergency, contingency, impasse; things, doings, affairs, matters, issues; the world, life, the times.

v happen, occur, take place, come to pass, take place, come about, come round; fall out, turn out, befall, chance, prove, eventuate; turn up, crop up, arise, arrive, issue, ensue, start, hold; take its course, pass off; experience, meet with, meet up with, fall to, be one's lot, be one's fortune, find, encounter, undergo, go through, live through, endure, put up with.

adj happening, going on, doing, current; eventful, stirring, bustling, busy, full of incident.

adv eventually, finally; as things go, in the course of things, as it happens.

152 future events *n* destiny, luck, lot, chance, fortune, karma, doom, end; future, futurity, next world, hereafter; prospects, expectations, tomorrow.

v impend, hang over, hover, threaten, loom, await, come on, approach; foreordain, preordain; destine, predestine, doom, have in store for.

adj impending, destined; coming, in store, to come, at hand, near, close by, imminent, brewing, forthcoming; in the wind, in the cards, in prospect, looming, on the horizon.

adv in time, in the long run, in good time, in its own sweet time, eventually.

VIII. Causation

153 cause *n* origin, source, principle, element; prime mover, first cause; author, producer, creator; mainspring, agent, catalyst; groundwork, foundation, support; spring, fountain, well, fount, font; genesis, descent, remote cause, influence; pivot, hinge, axis, turning point; egg, germ, embryo, root, nucleus, seed; causality, causation, origination, production.

v cause, originate, give rise to, occasion, sow the seeds of, kindle, bring to pass, bring about; produce, create, set up, develop; found, broach, institute; induce, evoke, elicit, draw, provoke; determine, decide; conduce to, contribute, have a hand in, influence, effect.

adj causal, generative, productive, formative, creative; primal, primary, original, embryonic.

adv because.

154 effect *n* consequence, issue, derivation, upshot, outgrowth, development, fruit, crop, harvest, product, outcome, end, conclusion; offspring, offshoot; complications, concomitants, side effects.

v be the effect of, be due to, be owing to; originate in, originate from, rise from, spring from, proceed from, emanate from, come from, grow from, issue from, flow from, result from; depend upon, hinge upon.

adj owing to, resulting from, due to, derivable from, caused by; derived from, evolved from; derivative, hereditary.

adv consequently, as a consequence, necessarily.

155 [assignment of cause] **attribution** *n* theory, ascription, assignment, ra-

tionale, reference to, accounting for; imputation, derivation; explanation, interpretation, reason why.

v attribute to, ascribe to, impute to, refer to, point to, trace to, assign to; account for, derive from; theorize, speculate.

adj attributed, attributable, referable, due to, owing to.

adv hence, thence, therefore, *ergo*, for, since, on account of, because; why? wherefore? whence? how come? how so?

156 [absence of assignable cause] **chance** *n* fortune, fate, accident, hap, hazard, luck, fluke, (*informal*) freak; gamble, lottery, tossup, fifty-fifty chance, throw of the dice, heads or tails; probability, possibility, contingency, odds; speculation, gaming, gambling.

v chance, hap, turn up; fall to one's lot; stumble on, light on; take one's chances.

adj chancy, causal, fortuitous, accidental, (*informal*) iffy, adventitious, haphazard, random, indeterminate, flukey, (*informal*) freaky.

adv by chance, by accident; at random; perchance, as chance will have it.

157 power *n* potency, strength, puissance, might, force, energy, vigor; control, command, dominion, authority, rule, sway, ascendancy, sovereignty, omnipotence; ability, capability, capacity, facility, competence, competency, efficacy; validity, cogency.

v be powerful, control, command, rule; confer power, empower, invest, endow; arm, strengthen, authorize; compel, force.

adj powerful, potent, strong, mighty, energetic; able, capable, competent, efficacious, equal to, up to, effective, efficient, adequate; omnipotent, almighty; influential, forceful.

adv powerfully.

prep by virtue of, by dint of.

158 impotence *n* inability, incapability, incapacity, infirmity, debility, disability; inefficacy, inefficiency, incompetence, ineptitude, feebleness, weakness, frailty, powerlessness; helplessness, prostration, paralysis, collapse, exhaustion; decrepitude, senility; sexual failure, barrenness.

v be impotent; collapse, faint, swoon, drop; render powerless, disable, disarm, incapacitate, disqualify, invalidate; cramp, tie the hands, paralyze, muzzle, cripple, maim, laim, hamstring, throttle, strangle, tie up in knots; unman, unnerve, enervate; shatter, exhaust, weaken; emasculate.

adj impotent, powerless, incapable, unable, incompetent, ineffective, inefficient, ineffectual, inept, unfit, unfitted, unqualified; disabled, incapacitated, crippled, paralyzed, paralytic; decrepit, senile, exhausted, worn out, used up, limp, spent; weak, frail, infirm, feeble, helpless; harmless; sterile, barren, frigid; emasculated, inadequate, inoperative; futile, fruitless, bootless, vain.

159 strength *n* power, force, might, vigor, health, stoutness, hardiness, lustihood, stamina, energy, potency, capacity; spring, bounce, tone, elasticity, tension; virility, vitality, nerve, verve; strengthening, invigoration, refreshment.

v strengthen, invigorate, brace, nerve, fortify, sustain, harden, steel; vivify, revivify, refresh, reinforce, restore.

adj strong, mighty, vigorous, forceful, hard, stout, robust, sturdy, hardy, powerful, potent, puissant; irresistible, invincible, indomitable, unconquerable, impregnable, inextinguishable incontestable; able-bodied, athletic, muscular, sinewy, strapping, gigantic, Herculean.

adv strongly, by force.

160 weakness *n* debility, relaxation, languor, enervation; impotence, infirmity, fragility, flaccidity; frailty, delicacy, softness; senility, decrepitude.

v be weak, drop, crumble, give way, teeter, totter, tremble, shake, halt, limp, fade, languish, decline, flag, fail; weaken, enfeeble, cramp, debilitate, shake, enervate, unnerve; relax; dilute, water down.

adj weak, feeble, infirm, sickly; languid, faint, dull, slack, spent; limp, flaccid, powerless, impotent; relaxed, unstrung, unnerved; frail, fragile, delicate, flimsy; rickety, drooping, teetering, tottering, withered, shaky, shattered; palsied, decrepit, lame; decayed, rotten, worn, seedy, wasted, laid low.

161 production *n* creation, formation, fabrication, construction, manufacture; building, architecture, erection; organization, establishment; workmanship, craftsmanship, performance; achievement, product, end result; flowering, fructification, fruition, fulfillment; gestation, evolution, development, growth; genesis, generation, procreation; authorship, publication, works, *oeuvre*.

v produce, perform, operate, do, make, form, construct, fabricate, frame, contrive, manufacture; build,

raise, rear, erect, put up; set up, establish, constitute, compose, organize, institute; achieve, accomplish, fulfill; bud, flower, blossom, bloom, bear fruit, bring forth; propagate, beget, generate, procreate, engender; breed, hatch, develop, bring up; induce, cause.

adj productive, constructive, formative, creative; generative; prolific, blooming.

162 [nonproduction] **destruction** *n* waste, dissolution, breaking up, disruption; consumption; fall, downfall, ruin, perdition; breakdown, wreck, wrack, havoc, mess, chaos, cataclysm; desolation, extinction, annihilation; demolition; overthrow, subversion, suppression; dilapidation, devastation, road to ruin.

v perish, fall, tumble, topple, fall to pieces, break up, crumble, go to the dogs, go to wrack and ruin; destroy, do away with, demolish, tear up, overturn, overthrow, wipe out, (*informal*) waste; upset, subvert, undo; waste, squander, dissipate, dispel, dissolve; smash, squash, squelch, shatter, crumble, batter, crush, pull to pieces; fell, sink, scuttle, wreck, swamp, ruin, raze, level, expunge, erase, sweep away; lay waste, ravage, gut; disorganize, dismantle, take apart; devour, devastate, desolate, sap, exterminate, extinguish, stamp out, trample out, crush out, eradicate.

adj destructive, subversive, ruinous, incendiary, deadly, lethal, fatal; destroyed, wiped out, extinct.

163 **reproduction** *n* renovation, restoration, renewal, revival, regeneration, revivification, resuscitation, reanimation, resurrection; reappearance; generation, childbirth.

v reproduce, renovate, restore, renew, revive, regenerate, revivify, resuscitate, breathe new life into, reanimate, refashion, resurrect, bring back to life; give birth to, multiply, people the world.

adj reproductive; regenerative, restorative; renascent, reappearing, resurgent.

164 **producer** *n* originator, inventor, author, founder, generator, mover, creator, maker, architect; backer, angel.

165 **destroyer** *n* spoiler, waster, ravager, wrecker, killer, assassin, executioner; cankerworm, bane; iconoclast, rebel, pessimist, cynic, nihilist, misanthrope.

166 **parentage** *n* family, ancestry, lineage, genealogy; procreator, progenitor.

paternity: fatherhood, fathership; father, dad, pop, sire, papa, (*informal*) old man; grandfather, grandsire.

maternity: motherhood; mother, mom, ma, mamma, mummy, mum, (*informal*) old lady; grandmother.

adj parental, familial, ancestral, lineal, paternal, maternal; patriarchal, matriarchal.

167 **posterity** *n* progeny, breed, issue, offspring, brood, litter, family, children, grandchildren, heirs; child, son, daughter; descendant, heir, scion, (*informal*) chip off the old block; heredity.

adj filial.

168 **productiveness** *n* fecundity, fertility, fruitfulness, productivity; multiplication, propagation, procreation; creativity, inventiveness, originality.

v make productive, fructify, fulfill; procreate, generate, conceive, impregnate, fertilize; teem, multiply, produce, reproduce.

adj productive, prolific, fruitful, copious; teeming, fertile, fecund; procreative, generative, life-giving.

169 **unproductiveness** *n* infertility, sterility, barrenness, unfruitfulness, impotence; unprofitableness, wastefulness.

v be unproductive, do nothing, produce nothing, come to nothing.

adj unproductive, unfruitful, infertile, barren, sterile, arid; unprofitable, useless.

170 **agency** *n* operation, force, working, function, office, maintenance, exercise, work, play; causation, instigation, instrumentality, influence.

v operate, work, do; act, perform, play, support, sustain, maintain, take effect, quicken, strike; come into play, have free play; bring to bear upon, influence.

adj operative, efficient, efficacious, effectual, practical; at work, on foot, in operation, in force, in play, in action.

adv through the agency of, by means of.

171 **energy** *n* force, power, strength, intensity, vigor, zeal, dynamism, pep, fire, spirit, ebullience, life; activity, agitation, exertion, effervescence, ferment, fermentation, ebullition, bustle.

v give energy, energize, stimulate, kindle, excite, inflame, exert; strengthen, invigorate; sharpen, intensify.

adj energetic, strong, forcible, potent, forceful, active, powerful,

intense, vigorous, zealous, dynamic, ebullient, spirited, animated, keen, vivid, sharp, acute, incisive, trenchant, biting; invigorating, rousing, stimulating; energized.

172 inertness n inertia, inactivity, torpor, languor, dullness, immobility, passivity, passiveness, lifelessness; quiescence, latency; inexcitability, sloth, indolence, irresolution, indecisiveness, cowardice, spinelessness.

v be inert, be inactive.

adj inert, inactive, immobile, unmoving, motionless, lifeless, passive, dead; sluggish, dull, heavy, flat, slack, tame, slow, blunt, torpid, languid; latent, dormant, sleeping, smoldering, quiescent.

adv in suspense, in abeyance.

173 violence n vehemence, fury, ferocity, impetuosity, boisterousness, turbulence, ebullition, effervescence, intensity, severity, acuteness; energy, force, might; fit, paroxysm, orgasm, spasm, convulsion, throe; exacerbation, exasperation, hysterics, excitability, passion; outbreak, outburst, uproar, riot, explosion, blow-up, blast, eruption; turmoil, disorder, ferment, agitation, storm, tempest; destruction, brutality, fighting, combat, warfare, hostilities; injury, wrong, outrage, injustice.

v be violent, ferment, effervesce; romp, rampage, run wild, run riot, rush, tear, run headlong, run amuck, go wild, kick up a row, (informal) flip out, go beserk; bluster, rage, roar, riot, storm, boil, boil over, fume, foam; explode, go off, detonate, thunder, blow up, flare, burst; render violent, sharpen, stir up, quicken, excite, incite, urge, lash, whip up, stimulate; irritate, inflame, kindle, accelerate, aggravate, exasperate, exacerbate, convulse, infuriate, madden, fan the fire, whip into a frenzy.

adj violent, vehement, acute, sharp; rough, rude, bluff, boisterous, brusque, abrupt, wild, impetuous, rampant; disorderly, turbulent, blustering, raging, riotous, tumultuous, obstreperous; raving, frenzied, (informal) freaked, mad, unhinged, insane; desperate, furious, frantic, hysterical; savage, fierce, ferocious, physical, brutal, combative; uncontrollable, ungovernable, irrepressible, excited; spasmodic, convulsive, orgasmic; explosive, volcanic, stormy.

adv violently; by storm, by force.

174 moderation n temperateness, temperance, reasonableness, judiciousness, deliberateness, fairness; gentleness, mildness, calmness, peaceful-

ness; quiet, calm, composure; lenity, lenience; relaxation, assuagement, tranquilization, pacification, mitigation; measure, middle ground, middle of the road.

v moderate, ally, meliorate, calm, pacify, assuage, lull, smooth, compose, still, calm, quiet, hush, sober, mitigate, soften, mollify, temper, qualify, alleviate, appease, lessen, abate, diminish; slake, curb, tame; arbitrate, referee, umpire, regulate.

adj moderate, temperate, reasonable, judicious, deliberate, fair, gentle, mild, calm, cool, sober, measured, unruffled, quiet, tranquil, still, peaceful, pacific; unexciting, even, smooth, bland, palliative; lenient, relaxed, easy going.

adv moderately, in moderation, within reason.

175 influence n importance, weight, pressure, preponderance, prevalence, sway; predominance, ascendancy; dominance, reign, rule, authority, power, control, capability; input, (informal) say, persuasion, play, leverage, vantage ground; patronage, protection, auspices.

v be influential, have a say, have input, carry weight, affect, sway, impress, bias, direct, control; move, activate, incite, impel, rouse, arouse, induce, persuade; dominate, predominate, outweigh, override, prevail.

adj influential, important, weighty; prevalent, rife, rampant, dominant, predominant; potent, powerful, effective, authoritative.

175a absence of influence n impotence, powerlessness; unimportance, irrelevancy.

adj uninfluential, unpersuasive, weak, impotent, (informal) wishywashy.

176 tendency n aptness, aptitude, disposition, predisposition, proclivity, proneness, propensity, susceptibility, inclination, leaning, bias, drift, trend, bent, turn; quality, nature, temperament; idiosyncrasy, cast, vein, mood, humor.

v tend, contribute, conduce, lead, dispose, incline, verge, bend to, gravitate toward, lean, drift, tend, affect; promote, influence.

adj tending, leaning; conducive, working toward, in a fair way to; liable, likely; influential, instrumental, useful, subsidiary, subservient.

177 liability n susceptibility, penchant, vulnerability, predilection, propensity, tendency; drawback, hindrance, obstacle, difficulty, impedi-

ment; responsibility, obligation, debt, debit, indebtedness, pledge.

v be liable, incur, lay oneself open to, run the risk of, stand a chance, expose oneself to.

adj liable, subject, exposed, likely, open, in danger of; obliged, responsible, accountable, answerable; contingent, incidental, possible.

178 concurrence *n* accordance, accord, agreement, consent, assent; cooperation, collaboration, partnership, alliance, concert, union.

v concur, conduce, conspire, contribute; agree, unite, combine, hang together, pull together, cooperate, collaborate; keep pace with, run parallel, go hand in hand with.

adj concurrent, cooperative, collaborative, joint, allied with, of one mind, at one with, in concert with.

179 counteraction *n* opposition, antagonism, contrariety, polarity; clashing, collision, interference, resistance, friction; reaction, response, counterblast, counter maneuver; neutralization, check, curb, hindrance; repression, restraint.

v counteract, run counter to, clash, cross, interfere with, conflict with; jostle, run up against, oppose, antagonize, withstand, resist, hinder, impede, check, curb, repress, restrain; recoil, react; neutralize, nullify, cancel out, undercut, undermine, undo; counter poise, offset, balance out, compensate.

adj counteracting, antagonistic, conflicting, contrary, reactionary.

adv although.

prep in spite of, against.

Class II

Words Relating to Space

I. Space in General

180 [indefinite space] **space** *n* extension, extent, expanse, span, stretch, scope, range, latitude, spread, proportions, sweep, capacity, play, swing, expansion; elbowroom, room, breathing space, leeway; open space(s), free space, waste, desert, wild, wilderness; unlimited space, wide world, heavens, universe, solar system, outer space, abyss, the void, infinity.

adj spacious, roomy, extensive, expansive, capacious, ample; widespread, vast, worldwide, boundless, limitless, unlimited, infinite.

adv extensively, far and wide, right and left, from the four corners of the world, all over, from pole to pole, under the sun, on the face of the earth,

from all points of the compass, to the four winds.

180a inextension *n* nonextension, point, atom.

181 [definite space] **region** *n* sphere, ground, soil, area, realm, quarter, orb, hemisphere, circuit, circle; domain, tract, territory, country, county, province; clime, climate, zone, meridian, latitude.

adj regional, provincial, territorial.

182 [limited space] **place** *n* spot, point; niche, nook, hole, pigeonhole; locality; locale, situation.

adv somewhere, in some place, here and there, in various places.

183 situation *n* position, locality, locale, latitude and longitude, location; footing, standing, standpoint; aspect, attitude, posture, perspective, pose; place, site, station, post, predicament, whereabouts; bearings, direction; topography, geography; map, chart.

v be situated, be located, lie, have its seat in; situate, locate.

adj situated, located; local, topical, topographical.

adv here and there, hereabouts, thereabouts, in such and such a place.

184 location *n* place, situation; establishment, settlement, installation; anchorage, mooring, encampment.

v locate, place, situate, put, lay, set, make a place for, seat; station, lodge, quarter, house, post, install; establish, fix, settle, root; graft, plant; inhabit, domesticate, colonize, take root, establish roots, come to rest, settle down, take up quarters, locate oneself, relocate, squat, perch, bivouac, burrow, get a footing, encamp.

adj located, placed, ensconced, rooted, settled, moored.

185 displacement *n* dislocation, misplacement, derangement, transposition; ejection, expulsion, banishment, removal, exile.

v displace, dislodge, disestablish; misplace, disturb, disorder, unsettle, derange, confuse; transpose, set aside, transfer, remove, unload, empty, eject, expel, banish, exile; vacate, depart, leave.

adj displaced; unplaced, unhoused, unsettled, unestablished; homeless, out of place, misplaced, out of its element.

186 presence *n* attendance, company; occupancy, occupation; ubiquity, omnipresence, permeation, pervasion, pervasiveness, diffusion, dispersion;

nearness, vicinity, proximity, closeness.

v be present; look on, attend, stand by, remain, find oneself; occupy, inhabit, dwell, stay, sojourn, live, abide, lodge, nestle, roost, perch, tenant; fill, pervade, permeate, run through.

adj present, attending; occupying, inhabiting, resident, moored; ubiquitous, omnipresent, pervasive, diffused; near, close, in proximity.

adv here, there, and everywhere; in presence of.

187 absence *n* nonappearance, nonattendance, absenteeism, nonresidence; emptiness, void, vacuum, vacancy, vacuity.

v be absent; keep away, play truant, absent oneself, stay away.

adj absent, not present, away, out, not here, not in, not present, off; wanting, lacking, missing, nonexistent; vacant, empty, void, vacuous, devoid.

adv without, minus, nowhere, sans; elsewhere.

188 inhabitant *n* resident, dweller, occupant; tenant, inmate, boarder, lodger; native, townsman, villager, citizen; population, community, society, state, people, race, nation.

v inhabit, live, reside, dwell.

adj indigenous, native, domestic.

189 habitation *n* abode, residence, domicile, lodging, dwelling, address, habitation, housing, quarters; home, homestead, motherland, fatherland, country; nest, lair, den, cave, hole, hiding place, cell, hive, haunt, habitat, perch, roost, retreat, *(informal)* pad, *(informal)* crashpad.

v inhabit, take up one's abode.

190 [things contained] **contents** *n* stuffing, cargo, lading, freight, shipment, haul, load, bale, burden.

v load, lade, ship, haul, charge, fill, stuff.

191 receptacle *n* container, holder, repository, vessel, receiver, depository, reservoir; storage areas; bulk containers; liquid containers; wrapping.

II. Dimensions

192 size *n* proportions, dimensions, magnitude, bulk, volume; largeness, greatness; expanse, amplitude, mass; capacity, tonnage; corpulence, obesity, plumpness; hugeness, enormousness, immensity; monstrosity, enormity; giant, monster, mammoth, behemoth, leviathan, elephant; lump, bulk, block,

mass, clod, thumper, whopper, strapper, *(informal)* mother, mountain, mound, heap.

v be large; become large, expand.

adj sizable, large, big, great, considerable, bulky, voluminous, ample, massive, massy; capacious, comprehensive, spacious; mighty, towering, magnificent; corpulent; stout, fat, plump, obese, portly; full-grown, stalwart, brawny; hulky, unwieldy, bulky lumpish, whopping, thundering, thumping; overgrown; huge, immense, enormous, mighty, vast, amplitudinous, stupendous; monstrous, gigantic, colossal.

193 littleness *n* smallness, diminutiveness, tininess; epitome; microcosm; vanishing point.

v be little; become little, decrease.

adj little, small, minute, diminutive, microscopic, submicroscopic; tiny, puny, wee, miniature, pigmy, dwarf, undersized, underdeveloped, dwarfish, stunted, dumpy, squat; imperceptible, invisible, infinitesimal.

194 expansion *n* increase, enlargement, extension, growth, development; augmentation, aggrandizement, increment, amplification; spreading, swelling, distention, puffiness, dropsy.

v expand, widen, enlarge, extend, grow, increase, swell, fill out; dilate, stretch, spread; bud, sprout, shoot, germinate, open, burst forth; outgrow, overrun; spread, extend, aggrandize; distend, develop, amplify, spread out, magnify; inflate, puff up, blow up, stuff, pad, cram, fatten; exaggerate.

adj expanded, larger; swollen, expansive, widespread, overgrown, exaggerated, bloated, fat, turgid, tumid, dropsical; pot-bellied, chubby, corpulent, obese, heavy; full-blown, full-grown.

195 contraction *n* reduction, diminution; decrease, lessening, shrinking; collapse, emancipation, attenuation, atrophy; condensation, compression, compactness, compendium, squeezing.

v contract, become small, lessen, decrease, dwindle, shrink, narrow, shrivel, collapse, wither, wizen, fall away, waste, wane, ebb, decay, deteriorate; diminish, contract, draw in, constrict, condense, compress, squeeze, crush, crumple up, pinch, squash, cramp; pare, reduce, attenuate, scrape, file, grind, chip, shave, shear, cut down; circumscribe, limit, restrain, confine.

adj contracting, astringent; shrunk, shrunken, contracted; wizened, stunted, waning; compact.

196 distance *n* remoteness, farness,

background, offing, far cry to, horizon, elongation; interval, remove, gap, span, reach, range; outpost, outskirts, foreign parts.

v be distant; extend to, stretch to, reach to, spread to; range.

adj distant, far off, far away, remote, far, afar, outlying, removed, at a distance, away, yonder, yon; inaccessible, out of the way, unapproachable.

adv far off, far away, afar, away, a long way off.

197 nearness *n* closeness, propinquity, proximity, proximation; vicinity, neighborhood, contiguity; short distance, earshot, close quarters, stone's throw, gunshot, hair's breadth; approach, access.

v be near, adjoin, neighbor, border upon, touch, stand next to; approximate, come close to, resemble; converge, crowd.

adj near, nigh, close, neighboring, adjoining, adjacent, bordering; proximate, approximate; at hand, handy; intimate.

adv near, nigh, hard by, close to, close upon, within reach, at one's fingertips.

198 interval *n* separation, space, break, gap, caesura, interspace, interstice, distance, hiatus, skip, division, opening; pause, recess, interim, respite, interlude, interregnum, interruption, term, spell, period; cleft, crevice, chink, cranny, crack, slit, fissure, rift, flaw, breach, rent, gash, cut, leak; ditch, dike, gorge, ravine, abyss, gulf.

v gape, open; intervene, interrupt.

199 continuity *n* contact, contiguousness, proximity, apposition, juxtaposition, touching, abutment, meeting.

v be contiguous, join, adjoin, abut on, border, touch, meet, graze, adhere; coincide, coexist.

adj contiguous, touching, in contact, end to end; close, near.

200 length *n* distance, extent, longitude, span, reach, range; lengthiness, elongation, size; duration, continuance, term, period.

v be long, stretch out, sprawl; extend to, reach to, stretch to; lengthen, stretch, elongate, extend; prolong, protract, draw out, spin out.

adj long, lengthy, extended, outstretched; lengthened, interminable; linear, lineal, longitudinal; tall, stringy, protracted, lanky.

adv lengthwise, at length, longitudinally.

201 shortness *n* brevity, littleness; shortening, abridgment, abbreviation, conciseness, condensation; retrenchment, curtailment, reduction.

v be short; shorten, abridge, abbreviate, condense, compact, compress, epitomize; retrench, cut short, reduce, pare down, clip back, cut back, prune, shear, shave, crop, chop up, hack up, truncate.

adj short, brief, curt; compendious, compact, compressed, condensed; stubby, stunted, stumpy, squat, dumpy; concise, pointed; curtailed, cut back, reduced, shortened, abbreviated, abridged.

202 breadth. thickness *n* breadth, width, latitude, amplitude, extent, diameter.

thickness, density, denseness, heaviness, bulk, body.

v be broad; expand, widen. be thick; thicken.

adj broad, wide, ample, extended, expansive, large; outspread, outstretched.

thick, dense, heavy, bulky, solid, compact; dumpy, squat, thickset.

203 narrowness. thinness *n* narrowness, slenderness, exiguity, closeness, straitness, scantiness, slightness, slimness.

thinness, slenderness, slimness, leanness, lankness, meagerness, skinniness.

v be narrow; narrow, taper. be thin; thin, slenderize, slim; dilute, water down.

adj narrow, close, slender, thin, fine, threadlike, slim, delicate; restricted, confined, limited; thin, emaciated, lean, skinny, meager, gaunt, spindly, lanky, scrawny, haggard, pinched, skeletal, wasted; frail, unsound, fragile; weak, shrill, faint, feeble; watery, waterish, diluted, unsubstantial.

204 layer *n* stratum, substratum, bed, zone, floor, stage, story, tier, slab, tablet, board, sheet, platter; scale, coat, peel, membrane, film, leaf, slice.

v slice, shave, pare, peel; plate, coat, veneer; cover; layer.

adj layered, stratified, tiered; scaly, filmy, membranous, flaky.

205 filament *n* thread, fiber, strand, hair, cilia, tendril, gossamer, wire, strand, vein.

adj fibrous, threadlike, wiry, stringy, ropy; capillary.

206 height *n* altitude, stature, elevation, tallness; prominence, eminence, pre-eminence, loftiness, sublimity; top,

peak, pinnacle, acme, summit, zenith, culmination.

v tower, soar, hover, cap, command; mount, bestride, surmount, overhang; heighten, elevate, raise up, rise up.

adj high, tall, elevated, towering, skyscraping, gigantic, huge, colossal; distinguished, prominent, eminent, pre-eminent, exalted, lofty, sublime; overhanging, overlying.

207 lowness *n* depression, debasement, prostration; flatness, proneness; lowlands, flatlands.

v be low; lie low, lie flat, crouch, slouch, wallow, grovel; underlie; lower, depress.

adj low, flat, level, low-lying; crouched, squat, prone, supine, prostrate, depressed; groveling, abject, sordid, mean, base, lowly, degraded, debased, ignoble, vile.

adv under, beneath, underneath, below, down, downward; underfoot, underground; downstairs, belowstairs.

208 depth *n* deepness, profundity, obscurity; depression, bottom, unfathomable space; pit, hollow, shaft, well, crater, chasm, abyss, bottomless pit; central part, midst, middle, bosom, womb, base, heart, core; soundings, draft, submersion, dive.

v deepen, hollow, plunge, sink, dig, excavate; sound, have the lead, take soundings.

adj deep, deep-seated, profound, mysterious, obscure, unfathomable; sunk, buried, submerged; bottomless, soundless, fathomless, unfathomed, abysmal, yawning, gaping.

adv beyond one's depth, out of one's depth, over one's head.

209 shallowness *n* superficiality, banality, triviality, frivolity, flimsiness, emptiness, vacancy; shallow, shoal, sand bar.

adj shallow, superficial, slight, cursory, trivial, banal, trashy, flimsy, substanceless, empty, vacuous, vacant; skin-deep, ankle-deep, knee-deep.

210 summit *n* top, peak, apex, pinnacle, vertex, acme, culmination, zenith; height, pitch, maximum, climax; crowning point, turning point, watershed.

v culminate, climax, crown, top.

adj highest, top, topmost, uppermost, tiptop; capital, head, polar; supreme, supernal.

211 base *n* bottom, stand, rest, pedestal, dado, understructure, substructure, foot, basis, foundation, ground,

groundwork; principle, touchstone, fundamental part, element, ingredient; bottom, nadir, foot, sole, heel.

adj bottom, undermost, nethermost; fundamental, basic, elemental; based on, founded on, grounded on, built on; base, vile, venal.

212 verticality *n* perpendicularity, erectness; wall, precipice, cliff.

v be vertical, stand up straight, stand upright, stand erect, stand straight and tall.

adj vertical, upright, erect, perpendicular, straight, bolt upright, plumb.

adv vertically, on end, endwise.

213 horizontality *n* flatness; level, plane, stratum; horizon; recumbency, lying down, reclination, proneness, supination, prostration.

v be horizontal, lie, recline, lie down, lie flat, sprawl; render horizontal, flatten, level, prostrate, knock down, floor, fell.

adj horizontal, level, even, plane, flat, smooth; prone, supine, prostrate.

adv horizontally, on one's back.

214 suspension *n* hanging down, free swinging; pendant, tail, train, flap, pendulum.

v suspend, hang, swing, dangle; flap, trail, flow; depend.

adj suspended, pendent, hanging, swinging, dangling, pendulous; dependent.

215 support *n* foundation, base, basis, ground, footing, hold; supporter, prop, brace, stay, rib, truss, stalk, stilts, splint; bar, rod, boom, outrigger; staff, stick, crutch; bracket, ledge, shelf, trestle, buttress.

v support, bear, carry, hold, sustain, shoulder, bolster; shore up, hold up, prop up, brace; help, aid, maintain, sustain; base, found, ground.

adj supporting, supported; fundamental.

216 parallelism *n* coextension; comparison, affinity, correspondence, semblance, likeness, resemblance, analogy, equation.

v parallel, compare, relate, associate, connect, correspond to, equate.

adj parallel, coextensive, collateral, aligned, equal; like, similar, allied, corresponding, correlative, analogous, equivalent.

217 obliquity *n* incline, inclination, slope, slant, leaning, tilt, list, bend, curve; acclivity, rise, ascent, grade, rising ground, hill, bank; declivity, decline, downhill, dip, fall; steepness.

v be oblique, slope, slant, lean,

incline, stoop, decline, descend; bend, careen, slouch, sidle; render oblique, sway, bias, slant, warp, incline, bend, crook, tilt, distort.

adj oblique, inclined; sloping, tilted; askew, asquint, awry, crooked; uphill, rising, ascending; downhill, falling, descending; declining, declivitous; steep, abrupt, sharp, precipitous; diagonal, transverse.

adv obliquely, on one side; askew, askance, edgewise, at an angle; sidelong, sideways, slantwise.

218 inversion *n* subversion, reversion, contraposition, transposition, transposal, conversion; contrariety, contradiction, opposition, polarity, antithesis; reversal, overturn, somersault, turn of the tide, revulsion, revolution.

v be inverted, turn about, wheel about, go about, turn over, go over, tilt over; invert, subvert, reverse, overturn, upturn, upset, turn topsy-turvy; transpose.

adj inverted, inside out, wrong side out, upside down, topsy-turvy; inverse, reverse, obverse, opposite.

adv inversely.

219 crossing *n* intersection, grade crossing, crossroad, interchange; network, reticulation; net, netting, network, web, mesh, wicker, lace; mat, matting, plait, trellis, lattice, grating, grille, gridiron, tracery, fretwork, filigree; knot, entanglement.

v cross, intersect, interlace, intertwine, interweave, interlink, crisscross; twine, intwine, weave, twist, wreathe; dovetail, splice, link, link up; mat, plait, plat, braid; tangle, entangle, ravel; net, knot, twist.

adj crossing; crossed, matted, transverse; weaved, woven, intertwined, interlaced.

220 exteriority *n* outside, exterior; surface, superficies; covering, skin, face, appearance, façade, aspect, facet.

v be exterior, lie around, encircle.

adj exterior, external, outer, outside, outward, superficial; outlying, extraneous, foreign, extrinsic.

adv externally, out, over, outwards.

221 interiority *n* interior, inside, inner part, center, interspace; subsoil, substratum, contents, substance, pith, marrow, backbone, heart, bowels, belly, guts, lap, womb; recesses, innermost recesses, hollows, nook, niche, cave.

v be interior, be inside; inclose, circumscribe; intern; embed, insert.

adj interior, internal, inside, inner,

inward, inmost, innermost; deepseated, inlaid, embedded, ingrained, innate, inherent, intrinsic, inborn; private, secret, intimate, confidential; home, domestic.

adv internally; inward, within, indoors, withindoors.

222 centrality *n* center, middle, midst; core, kernel, nucleus, heart, pole, axis, pivot, navel, nub, hub; centralization; center of gravity.

v be central; centralize, concentrate; focus on, bring into focus, get to the heart of.

adj central, middle, pivotal, focal, concentric; middlemost.

adv centrally; middle, midst.

223 covering *n* cover; canopy, awning, tent, marquee; umbrella, parasol, sunshade; shade, screen, shield; roof, ceiling, thatch, shed; top, lid; bandage, wrappings; coverlet, blanket, sheet, quilt, tarpaulin; skin, fleece, fur, hide; clothing, mask; peel, crust, bark, rind; veneer, coating, facing, varnish.

v cover, superimpose, overlay, overspread; wrap, encase, face, case, veneer, paper; conceal, cover over.

adj covered, clothed, wrapped; protected.

224 lining *n* inner coating, coating; filling, stuffing, padding, wadding.

v line, stuff, wad, pad, fill; coat, incrust, face, cover.

adj lined.

225 dress *n* clothing, covering, raiment, drapery, costume, attire, garb, apparel, wardrobe, outfit, clothes; equipment, livery, gear, rigging, trappings, togs, accouterments; uniforms, regimentals, suit.

v dress, clothe, drape, robe, array, fit out, deck out, garb, rig out, apparel; equip, harness, outfit, uniform; cover, wrap, wrap up, sheathe, swathe, swaddle.

adj dressed, clothed, clad, invested.

226 undress *n* nudity, nakedness, bareness, dishabille.

v undress, uncover, divest, expose, disrobe, strip, bare, doff, peel, take off, put off, lay open.

adj undressed, nude, naked, bare, stark-naked, exposed, in the buff, *au naturel*, in the altogether, in one's birthday suit; undressed, unclad, undraped, disrobed.

227 environment *n* environs, surroundings, outskirts, suburbs, purlieus, precincts, neighborhood.

v environ, surround, encompass,

compass, inclose, enclose, circle, encircle, gird, twine round, hem in.

adj surrounding, circumjacent.

adv around, about; without; on
every side, on all sides, right and left,
every which way.

228 interspersion *n* interjacence,
interlocation, interpenetration, permeation; interjection, interpolation,
interlineation, intercalation; intervention, interference, interposition, intrusion; insinuation; insertion.

v intervene, come between, get
between, interpenetrate; intersperse,
permeate, introduce, throw in, work
in, interpose, interject, interpolate,
insert; interfere, intrude, obtrude.

adj intervening, interjacent; parenthetical, episodic; intrusive.

adv between, betwixt, among,
amid, amongst; in the thick of, betwixt
and between; parenthetically.

229 circumscription *n* limitation,
enclosure; confinement, restraint.

v circumscribe, limit, bound, confine, inclose; surround, hedge in, fence
in, wall in; imprison, restrain; enfold,
bury, incase.

adj circumscribed, confined, restrained, imprisoned; buried in, immersed in, embosomed, embedded.

230 outline *n* circumference, perimeter, periphery; circuit, lines, contour,
profile, silhouette.

v outline, draw, sketch, trace,
profile.

231 edge *n* frame, fringe, trimming,
trim, edging, skirting, hem; verge,
brink, brim, lip, margin, border, skirt,
rim, mouth; threshold, door, porch,
portal; coast, shore.

v edge, skirt, border; trim, hem.

232 enclosure *n* envelope, case, wrapper; girdle; pen, fence, fold, cote,
corral, stockyard, paddock, yard,
pound, compound; fence, pale, paling,
balustrade, rail, railing; hedge; wall,
barrier, barricade; gate, gateway, door,
doorway; boundary, border.

v enclose, circumscribe.

233 limit *n* boundary, bounds, extent,
confine, term, pale, verge; termination,
terminus; frontier, marches, outer
edges, unknown; boundary line, border, edge; turning point, flood gate.

v limit, restrain, restrict, confine,
check, hinder, bound, circumscribe,
define.

adj limited, definite; terminal.

adv thus far, only so far, thus far
and no further.

234 front *n* forefront, foreground,
lead; face, frontage, façade, frontispiece, proscenium; vanguard, front
rank, first rank, head of the column,
advanced guard.

v front, face, confront; be in front,
stand in front; come to the front.

adj fore, foremost; front, frontal,
anterior, forward.

adv before, in front, in advance;
ahead, right ahead, in the foreground;
in the lead.

235 rear *n* back, background, rearguard, rear rank; distance, hinterland;
rump, buttocks, posterior, rear, backside, hindquarters; wake, train; reverse, other side of the coin, (*informal*) flipside.

v be behind, bring up the rear;
rear, bring up, nurture, raise; elevate,
lift, loft, lift up, hold up; build, put up,
erect.

adj rear, back, hindmost; posterior.

adv behind, in the rear, in the
background, at the heels; after, aft,
rearward.

236 side *n* laterality, flank, quarter,
lee, hand; cheek, jowl, shoulder;
profile, lee side, broadside.

v be on the side; be side by side,
be cheek to cheek; flank, skirt,
outflank, sidle.

adj sidelong, lateral; flanking, skirting; flanked.

adv sideways, sidelong; broadside,
on one side, abreast, alongside, beside,
side by side, cheek by jowl; laterally.

237 opposition *n* opposite, contraposition, opposite side, opposite poles,
polarity, antithesis, reverse, inverse;
counterpart, companion piece, complement.

v be opposite; stand as opposites,
oppose.

adj opposite, reverse, inverse, converse; antipodal, antithetical, countering, opposing; fronting, facing, diametrically opposite; complementary.

adv over, over the way, over
against; poles apart; face to face.

238 right *n* right hand, right side,
offside, starboard.

adj right-handed, dextral.

239 left *n* left hand, left side; near
side, port.

adj left-handed, sinistral.

III. Form

240 form *n* shape, outline, mold,
appearance, cast, cut, configuration;
make, formation, frame, construction,

cut, set, build, trim; mold, model, pattern; posture, attitude, convention, rule, formality, formula, ceremony, conformity.

v form, shape, figure, fashion, carve, cut, chisel, hew, cast; shape, model, mold, fashion, cast, construct, build; stamp, cast, type.

adj formal, ceremonial, ceremonious, conventional; regular, set, fixed, stiff, rigid.

241 formlessness *n* shapelessness, amorphism, asymmetry; disorder, chaos; misproportion, deformity, disfigurement, defacement, mutilation, truncation.

v deface, disfigure, deform, mutilate, truncate.

adj formless, shapeless, amorphous, asymmetrical, unformed, unshaped, unfashioned, unshapely, misshapen, out of proportion, disordered, chaotic; rough, rude, coarse, barbarous, rugged.

242 [regularity of form] **symmetry** *n* shapeliness, finish, comeliness, gracefulness, grace, beauty; proportion, uniformity, parallelism; regularity, evenness, balance, order, harmony, agreement.

adj symmetrical, shapely, well set, finished; beautiful, lovely; classic, classical, formal, chaste, severe; regular, uniform, balanced, harmonious, ordered; even, parallel, equal.

243 [irregularity of form] **distortion** *n* contortion, warp, buckle, screw, twist; crookedness, obliquity; deformity, malformation, misproportion, disfigurement, monstrosity, ugliness; asymmetry.

v distort, contort, warp, buckle, screw, twist, wrest; writhe, grimace, make faces; deform, disfigure, misshape.

adj distorted, out of shape, irregular, unsymmetrical, awry, askew, crooked; not true, not straight, uneven; misshapen, ill-made, ill-fashioned, ill-proportioned, malformed, deformed.

244 angularity *n* bifurcation, bend, fork, crook, notch, angle; elbow, knee, knuckle, crotch; right angle, acute angle, obtuse angle; corner, nook, niche, recess.

v angle, tilt, bend, fork, bifurcate.

adj angular, bent, crooked, jagged, serrated; forked, bifurcate, cornered, V-shaped, hooked; akimbo.

245 curvature *n* curve, incurvature, bend; flexure, bending, crook, hook; deflection, turn, deviation, detour,

sweep, curl, winding; curve, arc, arch, arcade, vault, bow, crescent, half-moon, horse-shoe, loop; parabola, hyperbola.

v be curved, sweep, sag; deviate, turn; render curved, bend, curve, deflect, inflect, crook; turn, round, arch, arch over, bow, curl, coil, recurve.

adj curved, bowed, vaulted, hooked, arched, arced; circular, nonlinear, semi-circular, rounded, crescent, crescent-shaped, lunar, demi-lune.

246 straightness *n* directness; inflexibility, stiffness; straight line, direct line, bee line.

v be straight, go straight; render straight, straighten, rectify, correct, right; put right, put straight, unbend, unfold, uncurl, unravel.

adj straight, even, true, unbent, direct, rectilinear, linear, not curved, uncurved; square, erect, perpendicular, vertical, upright; candid, forthright, definite, reliable, plain, blunt, frank, sure, positive, irrefutable, certain, unequivocal, inescapable; honest, honorable, fair, just, equitable, impartial, aboveboard, reputable, scrupulous, worthy, lawful, licit, conscientious, decent, ethical; correct, sound, sane, accurate, true; sober, conventional, provincial, (*informal*) unhip, (*informal*) square, (*informal*) not with it.

247 [simple circularity] **circularity** *n* roundness, rotundity; circle, ring, hoop, areola; bracelet, armlet; eye, loop, wheel, cycle, orb, orbit; zone, belt, cord, band, sash, girdle, circuit; wreath, garland, crown, corona, coronet; necklace, collar; ellipse, oval.

v round; go around, encircle, circle.

adj round, rounded, circular, oval, elliptic, elliptical, egg-shaped.

248 [complex circularity] **convolution** *n* involution, winding, wave, undulation, sinuosity, meandering, twist, twirl; coil, roll, curl, buckle, spiral, corkscrew, worm, tendril; serpent, snake, eel; maze, labyrinth.

v wind, twine, entwine, twirl, wave, undulate, meander, turn; twist, coil, roll; wrinkle, curl, frizz, frizzle; wring, contort.

adj convoluted, winding, twisted; wavy, undulating, circling, snaky, serpentine; involved, intricate, complex, complicated, labyrinthine, tortuous, mazy; spiral, coiled.

adv in and out, round and round.

249 rotundity *n* roundness, cylindri-

cality, sphericity, globularity; cylinder, barrel, drum; roll, roller, rolling pin; sphere, globe, ball, spheroid, globule; bulb, pellet, pill, marble, pea, knob, pommel.

v sphere, form into a sphere, roll into a ball, round.

adj rotund, round, circular, ball-shaped; cylindrical, spherical, globular; egg-shaped, pear-shaped, ovoid.

250 convexity *n* prominence, projection, swelling, bulge, protuberance, protrusion; hump, hunch, bunch; knob, node, nodule, bump, clump; pimple, pustule, pock, growth, polyp, blister, boil; nipple, teat, pap, breast; nose, beak, snout, nozzle; peg, button, stud, ridge; cupola, dome, arch; relief, high relief, low relief; hill, mountain, cape, ness, promontory, headland; jetty, ledge, spur.

v project, bulge, protrude, jut out, stand out, stick out, stick up, start up, shoot up, swell up; raise; emboss.

adj convex, prominent, protuberant; bossed, nodular, bunchy, hummocky, bulbous, swollen, swelling, bloated, bowed, arched, bellied; salient, in relief, raised.

251 flatness *n* smoothness, evenness; plane, level; plate, platter, table, tablet, slab.

v flatten, level, even off.

adj flat, plane, even, smooth; level, smooth, horizontal; flat as a pancake.

252 concavity *n* depression, dip, hollow, indentation, dent, cavity, dint, dimple; excavation, pit, trough; cup, basin, crater; valley, vale, dale, dell, glade, grove, glen, cave, cavern.

v render concave, depress, hollow, scoop, scoop out, gouge; dig, delve, excavate, mine, stave in, tunnel.

adj concave, hollow, hollowed out; indented, dented, sunken, cupped; cavernous, rounded inward, incurved.

253 sharpness *n* acuteness, pointedness; point, spike, spine, needle, pin, prick, prickle, spur, barb, thorn; knife edge, cutting edge, razor edge.

v be sharp, taper to a point; sharpen, point, whet, barb, strop, grind, whittle.

adj sharp, keen, acute, trenchant; pointed, peaked, conical, spiked, spiky, tapering; studded, prickly, barbed, spiny, thorny, bristling, thistly; craggy, snaggy; cutting, sharp edged, razor sharp.

254 bluntness *n* dullness; obtuseness, roughness.

v be blunt; render blunt, dull, take off the point, round the edge.

adj blunt, dull, obtuse, dimwitted; rough, gruff; rounded, round, unsharpened, unpointed.

255 smoothness *n* polish, gloss; lubrication, lubricity.

v smooth, plane, file, scrape, shave, sand, sandpaper; level, press, flatten, roll; iron, steam press; polish, burnish, rub, wax, sleek, buff, glaze; lubricate, oil, grease.

adj smooth, polished, glossy, shiny, sleek, silken, silky; even, level, sanded; soft, downy, velvety; slippery, glassy, oily.

256 roughness *n* asperity, irregularity, corrugation, nodulation; grain texture, pile, nap.

v roughen, rough up, crinkle, ruffle, rumple, crumple.

adj rough, uneven, irregular, rugged, scabrous, knotted, craggy, gnarled; shaggy, coarse, hairy, bristly, hirsute; scraggly, prickly, bushy; unpolished, unsmooth, rough-hewn, textured; downy, velvety, fluffy, woolly.

adv against the grain.

257 notch *n* dent, nick, cut, scratch, indentation; saw, tooth, scallop.

v notch, nick, cut, scratch, indent, jag, scarify, scallop.

adj notched, toothed, serrated.

258 fold *n* plait, ply, crease, pleat, tuck; wrinkle, ripple, rimple, pucker, ruffle.

v fold, double, plait, crumple, crease, pleat, wrinkle, crinkle, ripple, curl, rumple, frizzle, rimple, ruffle, pucker, corrugate; tuck, hem, gather.

adj folded.

259 furrow *n* groove, rut, scratch, streak, cut, crack, score, incision, slit; channel, gutter, trench, gulley, ditch, dike, moat, trough; ravine, valley.

v furrow, dig, plow; channel, flute, groove, incise, cut, engrave, etch, seam, cleave, score; wrinkle, knit, pucker.

adj furrowed, ribbed, striated, fluted.

260 opening *n* hole, gap, aperture, orifice, perforation, pinhole, peephole, keyhole; slot, slit, rift, breach, cleft, chasm, fissure, rent; outlet, inlet, vent; portal, porch, gate, hatch, door, doorway, gateway; way, path, channel, passage.

v open, ope, gape, yawn; perforate, pierce, tap, bore, drill; mine, tunnel, dig to daylight; impale, spike, spear, gore, spit, stab, puncture, lance, stick, prick, riddle; uncover, unclose, lay

bare, expose, bare, reveal; lay open, cut open, rip open, throw open.

adj open, unclosed, uncovered, exposed; ajar, wide-open, gaping, yawning; perforated, porous, reticulated, permeable; accessible, available, public.

261 closure *n* blockade, shutting up, obstruction, stoppage, clogging, sealing, plugging; contraction; constipation; culmination; cessation, completion, termination, windup; lid, top, cap, stopper, plug, barrier.

v close, plug, block up, stop up, fill up, cork up, cork, button up, stuff up, shut up, dam up; blockade, obstruct, hinder; bar, bolt, stop, seal, choke, throttle, shut.

adj closed, shut, unopened; unpierced, impervious, impermeable; impenetrable, impassable, pathless; tight, snug, airtight, unventilated, watertight, hermetically sealed.

262 perforator *n* piercer, borer, auger, drill, awl, scoop, corkscrew, probe, lancet, scalpel, needle, pin, stiletto, puncher, hole puncher, gouge; knife, spear, bayonet.

263 stopper *n* lid, cap, cover; cork, spike, stopcock, pin, plug, tap, faucet, valve, spigot, rammer, ramrod; wadding, stuffing, padding, stopping, bandage, tourniquet.

IV. Motion

264 motion *n* movement, action, activity, move, going; progress, locomotion; mobilization, mobility, movableness, motive power; unrest, restlessness; stream, flow, flux, run, course, stir; rate, pace, step, tread, stride, gait; velocity, speed.

v move, go, hie, budge, stir, pass, flit; hover around, hover about; shift, slide, glide, roll, roll on, flow, drift, stream, run, sweep along; wander, meander, browse, stroll, walk, perambulate; dodge, keep on one's toes, keep moving, hit the road, (*informal*) truck; move, impel, propel; mobilize.

adj moving, in motion, traveling, on the road; transitional, shifting, mobile, movable; mercurial, restless, unquiet, nomadic, transient.

adv under way; on the move, on the go, on the march.

265 rest *n* quiescence, stillness, quietude, calm, calmness, tranquillity, repose, serenity, peace, silence; pause, lull, cessation; stagnation, immobility, fixity.

v rest, be still, stand still, lie still, stand immobile, keep quiet, repose;

remain, stay, pause, wait, mark time, hold, halt, stop short, cease, desist, discontinue, stop; stagnate, be inactive, immobilize; dwell, settle, settle down, establish roots; alight, arrive; stand fast, stand firm, stick fast; quell, becalm, hush, stay, lull, lull to sleep, tranquilize.

adj restful, quiescent, still, calm, tranquil, peaceful, undisturbed, unruffled, serene, silent; motionless, fixed, stationary; unmoved, stable, at rest, at a standstill, stock-still, sleeping, dormant, inactive, stagnant.

266 [locomotion by land] **journey** *n* traveling, travel, excursion, tour, trip, expedition, jaunt, pilgrimage; wayfaring, roving, gadding about, (*informal*) bumming around, nomadism, vagabondism; migration, immigration, moving; walk, promenade, constitutional, stroll, peregrination, perambulation, march, stroll, saunter, jaunt, outing, hike, airing; horsemanship, horseback riding; drive, driving, motoring, ride, spin; cycling, biking; procession, cavalcade, caravan, file, cortege, column.

v journey, travel, tour, take a trip; flit, take wing, (*informal*) hit the road, rove, ramble, roam, prowl, (*informal*) bum, (*informal*) bum around, range, traverse, scour the country, wander, meander, saunter, gad about; move, migrate, immigrate.

adj journeying, traveling, on the road; itinerant, peripatetic, rambling, roving, gadding, flitting, vagrant, nomadic, migratory, wayfaring.

267 [locomotion by water or air] **navigation** *n* voyage, sail, cruise, passage, boat ride; aquatics, boating, yachting, sailing, shipping.

flight, air travel, flying, gliding; aeronautics, aviation.

v navigate; sail, put to sea, embark, shove off, spread the sails, make sail, take oar; go boating, cruise, float, drift, coast; row, paddle, pull, scull, punt, steam; ride the waves.

fly, take off, take wing, take to the skies; aviate, soar, glide, fly over, plane, jet.

adj sailing, nautical, naval, maritime, seagoing, seafaring, ocean-going; afloat; navigable.

flying, jetting, aloft, in flight; aviational, aeronautical, aerial.

268 traveler *n* wayfarer, journeyer, rover, rambler, wanderer, free spirit, nomad, vagabond, bohemian, gypsy, itinerant, vagrant, tramp, hobo, straggler, waif; pilgrim, palmer, seeker, quester; voyager, passenger, tourist,

sightseer, excursionist, vacationer, globe-trotter, jet-setter; immigrant, emigrant, refugee, fugitive; pedestrian, walker, cyclist, biker, rider, horsewoman, horseman, equestrian, driver.

269 mariner, flier *n* mariner, sailor, seaman, seafaring man, sea dog; pilot, skipper, captain, commander, helmsman, steersman; crew, hands, mates; navigator, flier, airman, aviator, aviatrix, pilot, skipper; astronaut, cosmonaut, spaceman.

270 transference *n* transfer, move, shift, transit, transition, passage, transmission, transport, transplantation, transposition; removal, relegation, deportation, extradition.

v transfer, transmit, transport, convey, carry, bear, pass; move, shift, conduct, convey, bring, fetch, reach; send, delegate, consign, turn over, hand over, deliver; transpose, transplant, displace, remove, relegate, deport, extradite; shovel, ladle.

adj transferable, transmittable, transmissible, transportable, movable, portable.

271 carrier *n* porter, bearer, messenger, runner, courier; postman, letter carrier; conductor, conveyor, transporter; freighter, ship, barge; train, locomotive; truck, vehicle, carriage; beast of burden.

272 vehicle *n* conveyance, carriage, transportation, rig; car, motorcar, automobile, (*informal*) wheels, truck; wagon, cart, coach, chaise, buggy; bicycle, bike, motorcycle, motorscooter; train, sleeping car, cattle car, boxcar.

273 ship *n* vessel, boat, liner, freighter, steamer, schooner, sailboat, motorboat, merchant ship, barge, tugboat, tanker, trawler, yacht, cruiser, yawl, ketch, brig, brigantine, square-rigger, sloop, cutter, launch; navy, fleet.

airplane, plane, jet, jumbo jet, aircraft, glider, helicopter, dirigible, blimp, balloon, spaceship, capsule, module, space station.

274 velocity *n* rapidity, quickness, swiftness, celerity, speed, alacrity; acceleration, pickup; spurt, rush, dash, race, flying, flight.

v move quickly, speed, hie, hasten, post, scamper, run, race, shoot, tear, whisk, sweep, rush, dash, dash off; bolt, bound, spring, dart, flit; hurry, hasten, haste, accelerate, (*informal*) turn on the juice, quicken, speed up, take off like a shot.

adj fast, speedy, swift, rapid, quick, brisk, fleet; nimble, agile, expeditious,

light-footed, fast as a bullet, quick as lightning.

adv swiftly, apace, at full speed, at full gallop, posthaste.

275 slowness *n* languor, sluggishness, slackness, sloth, indolence; deliberateness, moderation, leisureliness; tardiness.

v move slowly, creep, crawl, lag, drawl, linger, loiter, saunter, trail, drag, dawdle; plod, trudge, lumber; grovel, sneak, steal, worm one's way, inch; waddle, wobble, shuffle, hobble, limp, shamble, amble, traipse, slouch, mince, mince steps, halt; flag, totter, teeter, stagger; retard, hinder, impede, obstruct; slacken, check, relax, moderate; brake, curb, slow, put on the brakes.

adj slow, slack, late, tardy; gentle, easy, unhurried, deliberate, gradual, moderate, leisurely; languid, sluggish, indolent, lazy; tedious, humdrum, dull, boring; dense, stupid.

adv slowly, leisurely; at half speed, at a snail's pace; gradually, little by little, step by step, inch by inch, bit by bit, one step at a time.

276 impulse *n* impetus, implosion, push, thrust, shove; propulsion; sudden impulse, yearning, craving; reaction, response, reflex; collision, clash, encounter, shock, bump, crash; impact; blow, stroke, knock, rap, tap, slap, smack, pat, dab; hit, whack, thwack, slam, punch, belt, kick, thump, cut, thrust, lunge.

v impel, push, urge, thrust, shove, heave, prod, shoulder, jostle, hustle, hurtle, jog, jolt; start, give a start to, set going, get going, drive; run against, bump against, butt against; collide with, run into, bang into, butt; strike, knock, bang, hit, thump, beat, slam, dash, punch, thwack, whack; batter, pelt, buffet, butt; hit, rap, slap, tap, pat, dab.

277 recoil *n* reflex, rebound, ricochet, boomerang, backfire, backlash; snap, elasticity; reverberation, resonance; reaction, response, rebuff, repulse, revulsion.

v recoil, rebound, ricochet, boomerang, snap back, spring back, fly back; react, respond; reverberate, echo, quiver.

adj reactionary; elastic, backfiring.

278 direction *n* bearing, course, set, drift, tenor, trend, tendency, inclination; tack, aim, determination, intention; points of the compass, cardinal points; line, path, road, range, line of march; alignment.

v direct, point, aim; tend toward,

point toward, conduct to, go to; bend, tend, verge, incline, determine; steer for, make for, aim at, level at, set one's sights on, take aim, hold a course for, be bound for.

adj direct, straight; bound for; undeviating, unswerving.

adv toward, on the road to; hither, thither, whither; directly, straight, straightforward, point-blank, on a line with.

279 deviation *n* diversion, digression, departure from, aberration; divergence, zigzag, detour, circuit; warp, refraction; swerving.

v deviate, alter one's course, turn, bend, curve, swerve, heel, bear off; divert, deflect, shift, shunt, draw aside, crook, warp; stray, straggle, digress, ramble, rove, drift, go astray, go adrift; wander, wind, twist, meander; veer, turn aside, change direction, steer clear of, dodge.

adj deviating, errant, aberrant; discursive, desultory, loose, rambling, digressive, stray, erratic, undirected; circuitous, indirect, zigzag, roundabout, crooked.

adv astray, roundabout, wide of the mark; circuitously.

280 [going before] **precedence** *n* priority; leading, heading, the lead, van, vanguard; precursor, coming beforehand.

v precede, go before, forerun; usher in, introduce, herald; head, take the lead, lead the way; take precedence, have priority, come first, come before.

adv in advance, before, ahead, in the vanguard, in front.

281 [going after] **sequence** *n* coming after, following, sequel; shadow, dangler, train.

v follow, come in sequence, go after; attend, be attendant on, follow in the steps of, follow in the wake of, trail, shadow; pursue; lag, fall behind.

adj following; sequential.

adv behind, after; in the rear.

282 [motion forward] **progression** *n* progress, improvement proceeding, advance, advancement, headway; growth, rise, increase, development.

v proceed, advance, progress, get on, get along, gain ground, press onward, forge ahead, make headway, make progress, make strides, stride forward; grow, develop, increase, improve.

adj advancing; progressive, advanced.

adv forward, onward; forth, on, ahead.

283 [motion backward] **regression** *n* retrogression, retreat, recession, retirement, withdrawal; reflux, backwater, return, recoil; backsliding; deterioration, decrease, fall.

v regress, recede, return, revert, retreat, back out, back down, turn back, fall back, drop out, retire, withdraw; lose ground, drop off, fall behind; ebb, shrink, shy.

adj retrograde, retrogressive; regressive, refluent, reflex.

adv backwards; aboutface.

284 propulsion *n* propulsive force, impulse, push, projection, thrust, drive, impulsion, impetus; throw, fling, toss, shot, discharge.

v propel, project, throw, fling, cast, pitch, chuck, toss, heave, hurl; drive, sling, push, shove; send off, fire off, discharge, shoot, launch, let fly; put in motion, set in motion, start, get going, impel; expel.

adj propulsive.

285 traction *n* drawing, hauling, pulling, towing, towage; yank, tug, drag, jerk.

v draw, pull, haul, lug, drag, tug, tow, trail, train, take in tow; wrench, jerk, yank.

adj tractile; in tow.

286 [motion towards] **approach** *n* access, advent, advance; nearness, approximation.

v approach, near, draw near, move towards, get close to; gain on, get closer to; pursue, trail.

adj approaching; approximate; impending, imminent.

287 [motion from] **recession** *n* retirement, withdrawal; flight, removal, retreat; regression, return, falling back, regress; reaction, reversal, recoil; departure, leave-taking.

v recede, move back, go back, move away from, retire, withdraw; drift, abate, fade, wane, ebb, subside, drift away, fall back, shrink; react, revert, relapse, recoil, regress; run away, fly, avoid.

288 attraction *n* attractiveness, inclination, affinity; pull, magnetism, gravity.

v attract, draw, drag, pull, magnetize, exert force; interest, invite, engage, fascinate, lure, allure, charm, decoy, bait.

adj attractive, attracting, enticing, seductive, alluring; have pull, magnetic, gravitational.

312 rotation *n* revolution, gyration, circulation, roll; spinning, pirouette, convolution; whir, whirl, eddy, vortex, whirlpool, maelstrom; cyclone, tornado.

v rotate, turn, spin, revolve, wheel, whirl, twirl, spin around; pivot, swivel, circle around.

adj rotating, rotary, gyratory, revolving.

313 evolution *n* evolvement, unfolding, development.

v evolve, unfold, unfurl, unroll, unwind, develop.

adj evolutionary, evolutional.

314 [motion to and fro] **oscillation** *n* vibration, pulsation, undulation; pulse, beat, (*informal*) vibes, ripple, wave; alternation, coming and going, ebb and flow, ups and downs, flux and reflux; fluctuation, vacillation, irresolution.

v oscillate, vibrate, vacillate, swing, fluctuate, vary; undulate, wave; pulsate, beat, throb, ripple; reel, quake, quiver, quaver, shake; roll, toss, pitch; flounder, stagger, totter.

adj oscillating; undulatory; pulsating.

adv to and fro, up and down, back and forth, seesaw, zigzag, in and out, from side to side.

315 [irregular motion] **agitation** *n* stir, ripple, tremor, shake, jog, jolt, jar, jerk, shock, quiver, quaver, twitter, flicker, flutter; disquiet, perturbation, commotion, turbulence, turmoil, tumult, hubbub, bustle, fuss, ado, racket, fits; spasm, throe, throb, palpitation, convulsion, fit; disturbance, disorder, restlessness, hypertension; ferment, fermentation, ebullition, effervescence, hurly-burly; tempest, storm, groundswell, whirlpool, vortex; whirlwind, tornado, cyclone, twister.

v be agitated, shake, tremble, quiver, quaver, quake, shiver, twitter, writhe, toss, shuffle, tumble, stagger, bob, reel, sway; waggle, wriggle, dance, prance, stumble, shamble, flounder, totter, teeter, flounce, flop; throb, pulsate, beat, palpitate, go pit-a-pat; flutter, flicker, bicker, bustle; ferment, effervesce, foam, boil, bubble, simmer; agitate, shake, convulse, toss, tumble, bandy, flap, whisk, jerk, hitch, jolt, joggle, jostle, buffet, hustle, disturb, stir, shake up, churn, jounce, wallop, whip.

adj agitated, shaking, pulsating, tremulous, convulsive, jerky, shaky, throbbing.

adv by fits and starts; in convulsions, in fits.

Class III
Words Relating to Matter
I. Matter in General

316 materiality *n* corporeality, substantiality, flesh and blood, physicality; matter, body, substance, brute matter, physical elements, material; object, article, thing, materials.

science of matter: physics, natural philosophy, physical science, materialism.

materialist, physicist.

v materialize, embody, body in.

adj material, bodily, corporeal, physical, somatic; sensible, tangible, palpable, touchable, substantial, unspiritual, materialistic.

317 immateriality *n* incorporeality, insubstantiality, spirituality, ineffability.

adj immaterial, incorporeal, unsubstantial, intangible, ineffable, untouchable, bodiless, unreal, unearthly, spiritual, psychical, otherworldly.

318 world *n* creation, nature, universe, solar system, galaxy, globe, earth, wide world, sphere, macrocosm; heavens, firmament, vault, celestial spaces, space, sky; heavenly bodies, planets, asteroids, comets, meteors, constellations.

adj worldly, mundane, terrestrial, earthly, sublunary; cosmic, celestial, heavenly, astral, solar, lunar.

adv in all creation, on the face of the earth, under the sun, here below.

319 gravity *n* gravitation, weight, heaviness, pull, pressure, load, burden.

v gravitate, weigh, pull, press, encumber, load, be heavy.

adj weighty, heavy, heavy as lead, ponderous, lumpish, cumbersome, burdensome, cumbrous, massive, unwieldy, like a ton of bricks.

320 levity *n* lightness, buoyancy, volatility; ferment, leaven, yeast.

v be light, float, swim, waft; lighten, leaven.

adj light, subtle, airy, weightless, ethereal, volatile, buoyant, feathery.

II. Inorganic Matter

321 density *n* solidity, solidness, impenetrability, impermeability; condensation, solidification, consolidation, concretion, coagulation, petrification, hardening, crystallization, thickening; solid body, mass, block, knot, lump, conglomerate.

v be dense; solidify, condense,

consolidate, coagulate, congeal, set, cohere, crystallize, petrify, harden; condense, compress, thicken.

adj dense, solid, compact, close, thick, substantial, massive; impenetrable, impermeable, coherent, cohesive; indivisible, indissoluble, insoluble.

322 thinness *n* rarity, tenuity; rarefaction, expansion, dilation, inflation.

v thin, rarefy, expand, dilate, inflate.

adj thin, rare, fine, tenuous, compressible, flimsy, slight, light; unsubstantial.

323 hardness *n* rigidity, firmness, inflexibility, temper; induration, petrification, ossification, crystallization.

v harden, stiffen, cement, petrify, temper, ossify.

adj hard, solid, firm, inflexible, rigid, resistant, adamantine, impenetrable, strong, hard as a rock, hard as nails, tough.

324 softness *n* pliability, flexibility, pliancy, malleability, ductility, tractility, plasticity, flaccidity, elasticity; mollification, softening.

v soften, mollify, mash, knead, temper, bend, yield, give, relent, relax.

adj soft, tender, supple, pliant, pliable, flexible, limber, plastic, ductile, tractile, tractable, plastic, malleable, moldable, impressible, elastic; flabby, limp, flimsy, flaccid, doughy, mushy, squishy, waxy, soft as butter.

325 elasticity *n* springiness, spring, resilience, resiliency, give.

v be elastic, spring, give, bend, stretch; spring back, recoil.

adj elastic, tensile, springy, resilient, buoyant, rubbery.

326 inelasticity *n* want of elasticity, flaccidity, limpness, softness, mushiness.

adj inelastic, flaccid, limp.

327 tenacity *n* toughness, strength, cohesiveness, cohesion; stubbornness, obstinacy, grit.

adj tenacious, cohesive, tough, strong, resistant, gristly, stringy, gummy, adhesive, sticky, viscous, glutinous; stubborn, obstinate.

328 brittleness *n* fragility, frailty, breakability.

v be brittle; break, crack, snap, split, shiver, splinter, crumble, burst, fly, fly to pieces, shatter, give way.

adj brittle, fragile, breakable, frangible, delicate, frail, splintery, crisp.

329 structure *n* organization, constitution, anatomy, frame, framework, mold, form, architecture, construction. texture: tissue, grain, web, surface; coarseness; fineness.

adj structural, organizational, anatomical, anatomic, architectural textural: fine, delicate, subtle, gossamery, filmy; coarse, homespun, rough, woolly.

330 granularity *n* pulverulence, sandiness, graininess, friability; powder, dust, sand, grit, grain, particle, crumb, fine powder.

reduction to powder; pulverization, granulation, disintegration, abrasion, attenuation, filing.

tools for pulverization: mill, grater, rasp, file, mortar and pestle, grinder, grindstone.

v grind, pulverize, granulate, grate, scrape, file, abrade, rasp, pound, beat, crush, crumble, disintegrate.

adj granular, powdery, mealy, floury, branny, dusty, sandy, arenose, gritty, crumbly.

331 friction *n* attrition, rubbing, abrasion, elbow-grease.

v rub, scratch, scrape, scrub, fray, rasp, curry, scour, polish, rub out, erase, grind.

332 [absence or prevention of friction] **lubrication** *n* anointment, oiling, greasing, coating, lathering.

v lubricate, oil, grease, lather; anoint.

333 fluidity *n* liquidity, liquefaction, solubility, fluency.

v be fluid, flow, run, pour, stream; liquefy.

adj fluid, liquid, watery, serous, sappy, juicy, soluble; fluent, unstable.

334 gaseity *n* gaseousness, vaporousness, volatility.

adj gaseous, vaporous, airy, etheric, voluble, evaporable; flatulent, windy.

335 liquefaction *n* liquefying, deliquescence, melting, thawing, solubleness, dissolution.

v liquefy, melt, thaw, dissolve.

adj deliquescent, soluble, dissolvable, solvent.

336 vaporization *n* atomization, steaming, boiling, distillation, gasification, evaporation.

v vaporize, atomize, distill, evaporate, gasify, boil, steam.

adj vapory, vaporous, volatile, evaporable, gaseous.

337 water *n* liquid, serum, lymph, fluid, aqua.

v add water, water, wet, moisten,

dip, immerse, submerge, plunge, douse, dunk, drown, soak, steep, wash, sprinkle, splash, souse, drench; dilute; deluge, inundate.

adj watery, aqueous, liquid, fluid, wet, moist, humid, soggy, sodden, rheumy, hydrous, juicy, lush, succulent; waterish, adulterated, transparent, thin, weak, tasteless, insipid, vapid, flat, feeble, dull.

338 air *n* atmosphere, stratosphere, the open, open air, blue sky; sky; weather, climate, clime; ventilation, current, breath of air, wind, breeze.

v air, ventilate, fan, aerate, freshen, refresh, cool.

adj airy, open, exposed, breezy, windy; flatulent; effervescent; atmospheric, aerial, ethereal, aeriform.

adv in the open air, out in the open, out of doors, in the wide open spaces, under the stars.

339 moisture *n* dampness, humidity, dankness, dew, wetness, condensation; perspiration.

v moisten, sponge, damp, bedew, wet, soak, saturate, sodden, sop, drench; perspire.

adj moist, damp, watery, humid, dank, dewy, muggy, juicy, wet; soggy, mushy, marshy, muddy.

340 dryness *n* drought, aridity; dessication, drainage, evaporation.

v dry, dry up, soak up, sponge, swab, wipe; drain, parch, evaporate.

adj dry, arid, parched, juiceless, sapless, dry as a bone.

341 ocean *n* sea, main, deep, brine, salt water, waters, high seas, waves, billows, great waters, tides.

adj oceanic, marine, maritime, sea-going, oceanographic.

342 land *n* earth, ground, dry land, mother earth, *terra firma;* continent, inlands, interior, shore, coast, terrain, dirt, soil, rock, chalk; real estate, lands, grounds, acres, acreage.

v land, alight, arrive, disembark, come ashore, go ashore, tie up, set foot on dry land.

adj earthy, terrestrial, earthly, alluvial, landed, territorial, continental.

adv ashore, on land, on dry land.

343 gulf, lake *n* gulf, bay, inlet, estuary, bayou, arm, fjord, firth, lagoon, cove, mouth, natural harbor, sound, straits.

lake, loch, lough, mere, tarn, basin, reservoir, lagoon, pond, pool.

344 plain *n* plateau, champaign, grassland, pasture, pasturage, meadow, flat, moor, heath, tundra, prairie, lowland, steppe, field, desert, basin, fields, grounds.

345 marsh *n* swamp, morass, moss, fen, bog, quagmire, slough, wash, mud.

adj marshy, swampy, boggy, quaggy, soft, muddy, sloppy, squashy.

346 island *n* isle, islet, atoll, reef, ait, key, bar, holm, ridge, eyot, archipelago.

adj insular, sea-girt.

347 [fluid in motion] **stream** *n* stream, etc. (of water) 348; (of air) 249. *v* flow, etc., 348; blow, etc., 349.

348 [water in motion] **river** *n* running water, jet, spurt, squirt, spout, splash, rush, gush, torrent; fall, cascade, inundation, deluge; rain, rainfall, storm; trickle, drizzle, shower; stream, course, flux, flow, flowing, current, tide, race; spring, rill, rivulet, stream, river, tributary; rapids, flood, whirlpool, maelstrom, vortex, eddy; wave, billow, surge, swell, ripple, surf, breaker, white caps, rough seas, rolling seas, choppy seas; irrigation, pump, hose.

v flow, run, gush, pour, spout, roll, jet, well issue; drop, drip, dribble, drizzle, trickle, stream, overflow, inundate, deluge, flow over, splash, swash; gurgle, murmur, babble, bubble, sputter, spurt, regurgitate; ooze, flow out, squeeze; rain, rain hard, rain cats and dogs, rain in torrents, rain in buckets; rain into, open into, drain into; pour, pour out, shower down, irrigate, drench, spill.

adj fluent, tidal, streamy, showery, rainy, trickly, drizzly, bubbly.

349 [air in motion] **wind** *n* draft, air, breath of air, puff, whiff, zephyr, drift, blow; fresh wind, stiff breeze, keen blast, trade wind, gust, blast, breeze, squall, gale, storm, tempest, hurricane, whirlwind, tornado, twister, cyclone, monsoon.

v blow, waft, blow hard, blow great guns, stream, gust, blast, storm; respire, breathe, pant, puff, gasp, wheeze, cough; fan, ventilate, inflate, pump, blow up.

adj windy, drafty, breezy, stormy, tempestuous, cyclonic.

350 [channel for the passage of water] **conduit** *n* channel, duct, aqueduct, canal, trough, gutter, dike, main, gully, moat, ditch, drain, sewer, culvert, sough, siphon, pipe, tube, hose, funnel, tunnel, artery, spout, floodgate, watergate, sluice, lock, valve.

351 [channel for the passage of air] **air-pipe** *n* tube, shaft, flue, chimney, funnel, vent, hole, windpipe, duct.

352 semiliquidity *n* viscosity, adhesiveness, stickiness, glutinosity, pastiness.

v thicken, mash, squash, churn, beat up, blend.

adj semiliquid, semifluid; milky, muddy, creamy, slushy, starchy, gummy, gluey, sticky, slimy, oozy, thick, succulent, viscous, viscid, glutinous, adhesive, clammy.

353 [mixture of air and water] **bubble. cloud** *n* bubble, foam, froth, head, lather, suds, spray, surf, yeast; effervescence, fermentation, bubbling, boiling, gurgling, foaming.

cloud, vapor, fog, mist, haze, steam; nebula, nebulosity, cloudiness, opacity, dimness.

v bubble, boil, foam, froth, gurgle, lather, effervesce, ferment, fizzle.

cloud, fog, mist, steam, shadow, darken, cast over, steam up.

adj bubbly, foamy, frothy; effervescent.

cloudy, foggy, misty, hazy, steamy.

354 pulpiness *n* pulp, paste, dough, curd; fleshiness, fattiness, sponginess.

v pulp, mash, squeeze, juice, squash.

adj pulpy, pasty, doughy, fleshy, meaty, fatty.

355 unctuousness *n* unctuosity, oiliness, greasiness, lubricity; lubrication, ointment, grease, oil, anointment.

v oil, grease, lubricate.

adj unctuous, oily, greasy, oleaginous, slippery, slimy, slick.

356 oil *n* fat, butter, cream, grease, tallow, suet, lard, dripping, blubber; soap, wax; petroleum, gasoline, kerosene, propane, naphtha; vegetable oil, salad oil, olive oil, linseed oil; ointment, unguent, liniment, salve, balm.

356a resin *n* rosin, gum, wax, amber, ambergris, bitumen, pitch, tar, asphalt; varnish, lacquer, shellac, mastic, sealing wax, putty.

v resin, rosin; varnish, shellac, lacquer, overlay.

adj resinous, gummy, waxy.

III. Organic Matter

357 animate matter *n* nature, natural world, animated nature, living beings, organisms, organic remains, animal life, plant life, fauna, flora; protoplasm, cell.

science of living beings: biology, natural history, zoology, botany, anatomy, physiology, organic chemistry.

naturalist, biologist, zoologist, botanist.

adj animate, organic.

358 inanimate matter *n* mineral world, mineral kingdom, inorganic matter, brute matter.

science of the mineral kingdom: mineralogy, geology, metallurgy.

adj inanimate, inorganic, mineral.

359 life *n* existence, being; animation, vigor, vivacity, vitality, energy, vital spark, vital flame, lifeblood, spirit, soul; respiration, breath, breath of life; nourishment, nutriment, staff of life.

v be alive, live, breathe, respire, exist, subsist; be born, come into the world, see the light; quicken, revive, come to; give birth to, bring to life, vitalize; vivify, reanimate; keep alive, *(informal)* keep going, *(informal)* hang in there.

adj alive, live, vigorous, vivacious, vital, energetic, lively, alive and kicking, active.

360 death *n* decease, demise, expiration, passing, dissolution, departure, release, rest, quietus, fall; end, cessation, loss of life, extinction, dying, mortality, doom, finale, stop; last breath, final gasp, death rattle, death agonies, hand of death, dying day, *rigor mortis;* decay, fatality, natural causes, death blow.

v die, decease, pass away, pass on, perish, expire, depart, dissolve; cease, end, vanish, disappear; fail, subside, fade, sink, fall, decline, wither, decay; be taken, yield, give in, breathe one's last, end one's days, end this life, be no more, drop off, pop off, drop dead, drop down dead, break one's neck, give up the ghost, shuffle off the mortal coil, go the way of all flesh, turn to dust, *(informal)* kick the bucket, *(informal)* go out like a light, *(informal)* croak.

adj dead, lifeless, extinct, defunct, late, gone, no more, dead and gone, dead as a door nail; deadly, fatal, lethal.

361 [destruction of life; violent death] **killing** *n* murder, homicide, assassination, slaughter, bloodshed, carnage, butchery, massacre, holocaust; suffocation, strangulation, garrote, hanging, electrocution, gassing, drawing and quartering; suicide, regicide, parricide, matricide, fratricide, infanticide; death blow, finishing stroke, *coup de grace,* execution; suicide; slaughtering, hunting, coursing, shooting, fishing; butcher, slayer, murderer, executioner, assassin, cutthroat, thug, guerilla, saboteur, garroter.

v kill, put to death, murder,

slaughter, butcher, massacre, execute, behead, decapitate, guillotine, dispatch, (informal) waste; (informal) wipe out, strangle, garrote, hang, throttle, choke, stifle, suffocate, smother, asphyxiate, drown, gas, electrocute, stab, bayonet, cut, cut to pieces, cut to ribbons, mutilate, run through, put to the sword, shoot, gun down, do away with, (informal) blow away; hunt, spear; cut off, nip in the bud, cut down, give no quarter, decimate; commit suicide, destroy oneself, blow one's brains out, put an end to oneself.

adj murderous, homicidal, bloodthirsty, bloody, gory; mortal, fatal, lethal, deadly, deathly; suicidal.

362 corpse n body, remains, carcass, corse, cadaver, empty vessel, bones, skeleton, relics, mortal remains, mortal coil, clay, dust, ashes, earth, carrion, fodder, food for worms, shade, ghost.

adj corpselike, cadaverous.

363 interment n burial, sepulture, entombment, inhumation; cremation; funeral, funeral rites, obsequies, wake; knell, death bell, dirge, elegy; shroud, winding sheet, grave clothes; coffin, shell, sarcophagous, urn, pall, bier, catafalque, hearse; grave, pit, sepulchre, tomb, vault, crypt, catacomb, mausoleum, cemetery, burial ground, mortuary, graveyard, charnel house, morgue; monument, gravestone, tombstone, headstone, *memento mori*; exhumation, disinterment, autopsy, post mortem examination.

v inter, bury, lay in the grave, lay to rest, lay in the ground, consign to the grave, entomb; lay out, mummify, embalm; cremate; exhume, disinter, unearth.

adj burial, funereal, funeral, mortuary, sepulchral, cinerary.

364 animality n corporality, animal life, living being, flesh, flesh and blood; physique, strength, vigor, vitality.

adj animalistic, bodily, corporeal, fleshly.

365 vegetation n vegetable life, growth, plant life.

adj vegetative; rank, dense, lush, fecund.

366 animal n animal kingdom, brute creation, fauna; beast, brute, creature, living thing, creeping thing, dumb animal; mammal, quadruped, bird, reptile, fish, crustacean, shellfish, mollusk, worm, insect; flocks and herds, wild animals, domestic animals, livestock, game, beasts of the field, fowls of the air.

adj animal, animalistic, zoological.

367 vegetable n vegetable kingdom, flora, plant life, flowerage, herbage, shrubbery, foliage, leafage, leaves, foliation, verdure, greens; tree, shrub, bush, creeper, herb, fruit, grass.

v vegetate, germinate, shoot, sprout, shoot up, grow, swell, spring up, develop, increase, flourish, blossom, bloom.

adj vegetable, vegetal, vegetative, leguminous, herbal, herbaceous, botanic, verdant.

368 [science of animals] **zoology** n morphology, zoography, embryology, anatomy; comparative anatomy, animal physiology, comparative physiology, anthropology, ornithology, icthyology, paleontology, entomology.

adj zoological.

369 [science of plants] **botany** n phytology, vegetable physiology, dendrology; flora, botanic garden.

adj botanical herbal, horticultural.

370 [management of animals] **ranching** n breeding, raising; taming, domestication; veterinary science.

v ranch, raise, breed; tame, domesticate, train, housebreak; cage, bridle, restrain.

adj bred; tame, domestic, domesticated, housebroken.

371 [management of plants] **agriculture** n farming, cultivation, husbandry, tillage; agronomy, agrobiology, agrology, agronomics; gardening, horticulture, floriculture, landscaping, arboriculture; forestry.

v cultivate, till, till the soil, work the land, farm, garden, sow, seed, plant; reap, mow, cut; plow, plough, harrow, rake, weed, hoe, lop; garden, landscape.

adj agricultural, agrarian; arable, fertile.

372 mankind n human race, man, woman, humankind, human species, humanity, mortality, people, human being, person, personage, individual, creature, fellow creature, fellow man, mortal, body, soul, somebody, someone, one, party, head, hand, heart.

people, persons, folk, public, society, community, group, general public, society of men, civilization, commonwealth, commonweal, body politic, human community, population, millions, multitudes.

adj human, mortal, personal, individual; social, national, civic, public; cosmopolitan, humanitarian.

373 man n make, manhood, masculinity, he him; gentleman, sir, mister,

Mr., master, swain, fellow, chap, boy.
male animal: cock, drake, gander,
dog, boar, stag, hart, buck, stallion,
tomcat, billygoat, ram, bull, ox;
gelding, steer.

adj male, masculine, manly.

374 woman *n* female, womanhood,
femininity, she, her; lady, gentlewoman, madam, madame, miss, *(informal)* ma'am, Ms., Mrs., matron, girl.

female animal: hen, bitch, sow, doe,
roe, mare, nannygoat, ewe, cow.

adj female, feminine, womanly.

375 sensibility *n* sensation, sensitiveness, feeling, responsiveness, impressibility; sensation, impression, touch;
consciousness.

v be sensible, be sensitive to, feel,
touch, perceive; render sensible, sharpen, cultivate, stir, excite, sensitize;
cause sensation, impress, excite an
impression, stir.

adj sensitive, sensible, sensuous;
perceptive, sentient, responsive, susceptible, conscious, aware, alive, acute,
sharp, keen, vivid, lively.

adv to the quick.

376 insensibility *n* lack of feeling,
obtuseness, paralysis, numbness, anesthesia; insusceptibility, unresponsiveness, unconsciousness.

v be insensible; render insensible,
blunt, pall, numb, benumb, paralyze,
deaden, freeze, anesthetize; cloy, stuff,
satiate, drown; stupefy, stun.

adj insensible, senseless, unsusceptible, unresponsive, insensitive,
numb, hard, dead; dull, dense, thick,
obtuse, unperceptive; anesthetic, paralytic.

377 pleasure *n* bodily pleasure, sensuality, sensuousness, physical gratification, sex, sexuality, sensual delight,
ecstasy, orgasm, climax; titillation,
teasing; comfort, ease, relish, delight,
joy, luxury, luxuriousness, pleasure,
lap of luxury.

v feel pleasure, receive pleasure,
enjoy, relish, revel in, bask in, swim
in, luxuriate, feast on, wallow in, gloat
over, *(informal)* dig, *(informal)* get off
on, *(informal)* be turned on, *(informal)*
get into; give pleasure, *(informal)* turn
on, thrill, excite.

adj pleasurable, sensual, sensuous,
sexual, voluptuous, luxurious, ecstatic,
orgasmic, climactic; agreeable, comfortable, cordial, delightful, joyful;
palatable, sweet, tasty; fragrant; melodious, lovely.

adv in comfort, in ecstasy, on a
bed of roses.

378 pain *n* suffering, dolor, ache,

aching, smart, shoot, shooting, twinge,
twitch, gripe, grip, hurt, cut, sore,
soreness, tenderness, discomfort, malaise, disease; spasm, cramp, crick,
stitch, convulsion, throe, throb, pang;
torment, torture, rack, anguish, agony.

v feel pain, suffer, undergo pain,
ache, smart, bleed, tingle, shoot,
twinge, twitch, writhe, wince, hurt;
inflict pain, hurt, chafe, sting, bite,
gnaw, gripe, pinch, tweak, grate, gall,
fret, prick, pierce, wring, convulse;
torment, torture, wrack, agonize.

adj painful, dolorous, sore, tender,
raw, uncomfortable; convulsive, torturous.

379 touch *n* contact, feeling, tactility,
palpability, impact, feel, sensation;
manipulation, handling, rubbing, massaging, fondling, fingering, kneading,
stroking, brushing, grazing over.

v touch, feel, handle, finger, fondle,
thumb, paw, grab, rub, massage,
knead, stroke, brush, manipulate, run
the fingers over, graze over.

adj tactual, tactile, palpable.

380 sensations of touch *n* itching,
tickling, titillation, scratching, pricking, stinging.

v itch, tingle, creep, thrill, prick,
scratch, sting.

adj itching; ticklish, scratchy,
itchy.

381 numbness *n* physical insensibility, lack of feeling, deadness.

v benumb, anesthetize, deaden,
dull, drug.

adj numb, dull, benumbed, insensible, unfeeling, frozen, drugged, dead,
deadened, dulled.

382 heat *n* warmth, caloricity, caloric, temperature; glow, flush, warmth, intensity, ardor, passion, fever,
fervor, zeal; fire, spark, flame, blaze.

v be hot, glow, flush, sweat,
swelter, smoke, stew, simmer, seethe,
boil, burn, broil, blaze, flame; smolder,
parch, fume, pant; heat, warm, thaw,
defrost; stimulate, stir, animate, a-
rouse.

adj hot, warm, mild, genial, tepid,
lukewarm, unfrozen; heated, torrid,
sultry, burning, fiery; sunny, tropical,
suffocating, stifling, sweltering, oppressive, reeking, baking; fiery, incandescent, ebullient, glowing, smoking,
blazing, on fire, afire, in flames, aflame,
ablaze; ardent, fervent, fervid, angry,
furious, vehement, intense, excited,
excitable, irascible, animated, violent,
passionate.

383 cold *n* coldness, iciness, frigidity,
chilliness, coolness.

v be cold, shiver, quake, shake,

tremble, shudder, quiver; chill, freeze, refrigerate.

adj cold, chilly, chill, cool, frigid, gelid, frozen, freezing, bitter, bitter cold, numbing, nipping, cutting, shivering, bleak, raw, frost-bitten, icy, glacial, frosty, wintry, hibernal, arctic, polar; impassionate, unemotional, apathetic, unresponsive, unsympathetic, stoical, unfeeling, indifferent, cold-blooded, heartless, imperturbable; polite, formal, reserved, hostile; deliberate, depressing, dispiriting, disheartening.

adv coldly, bitterly.

384 calefaction *n* heating, melting, fusion, liquefaction, combustion; cauterization; calcination; incineration, cremation; carbonization.

v heat, warm, chafe; fire, set fire to, set on fire, kindle, light, ignite, rekindle; melt, thaw, fuse, liquefy; burn, inflame, roast, broil, toast, cook, fry, grill, singe, parch, bake, scorch; brand, cauterize, sear, burn in; boil, digest, stew, sauté, cook, scald, parboil, simmer; take fire, catch fire.

adj heated, warmed, fired, burnt, scorched; molten; flammable, combustible, volcanic.

385 refrigeration *n* cooling, congelation, glaciation, icing; solidification, hardening.

v refrigerate, keep cold, chill, ice, congeal, freeze; cool, fan, refresh; benumb, starve, pinch, nip, cut, pierce, bite; quench, put out, stamp out, extinguish.

adj cooled, frozen, chilled; incombustible, inflammable, fireproof.

386 furnace *n* oven, stove, range; hearth, heater, kiln, oil burner, space heater, blast furnace, forge, fire place, fiery furnace.

387 refrigerator *n* ice box, fridge, ice chest, frigidaire, cold storage, freezer, ice house.

388 fuel *n* firing, combustible; coal, hard coal, anthracite, bituminous coal, soft coal, carbon, coke, charcoal; wood, firewood, kindling, brushwood, log, cinder, ember, ash; turf, peat, fuel oil, fossil fuel, petroleum, gasoline, kerosene; gas, natural gas, propane; electricity; nuclear power; solar energy; waterpower; windpower.

v fuel, feed, stoke, fire; power.

adj carbonaceous; combustible, flammable, burnable.

389 thermometer *n* thermometograph, thermoscope, thermostat, telethermometer, pyrometer, calorimeter, glass, mercury.

390 taste *n* flavor, savor, sensation, gusto, relish; smack, smatch, tang, aftertaste; morsel, bit, sip.

v taste, flavor, savor, smatch, smack; tickle the palate, tickle the tastebuds; smack the lips.

adj tasty, savory, flavory, flavorful, flavored; palatable, digestible, *(informal)* edible.

391 tastelessness *n* insipidity, blandness, flatness, unsavoriness.

v be tasteless.

adj tasteless, insipid, bland, flat, weak, mild, vapid, wishy-washy, *(informal)* plastic, pasty.

392 pungency *n* piquancy, poignancy, tang, bite, nip, sharpness, acridity, bitterness, hotness, sourness, unsavoriness.

v be pungent; make pungent, season, spice, salt, pepper, pickle, brine, devil, smoke, curry.

adj pungent, strong, full-flavored, seasoned, highly seasoned; spiced; sharp, biting, nippy, acrid, bitter, sour, stinging, spicy, salty, peppery, piquant, hot; unsavory.

393 condiment *n* seasoning, flavoring, sauce, spice, relish; salt, pepper.

v season.

394 savoriness *n* flavor, flavorfulness, taste, tastiness, relish, piquancy, zest, tang, delectability, palatability.

v be savory, tickle the palate, taste good, taste great; savor, enjoy, appreciate, relish, like, taste.

adj savory, good, tasty, palatable, nice, dainty, delectable, flavorful, appetizing, delicate, delicious, exquisite, rich, luscious, full-flavored, pungent, ambrosial.

395 unsavoriness *n* tastelessness, flavorlessness, blandness; acridness, sourness.

v be unsavory, be unpalatable, taste bad, sicken, disgust, pall, nauseate, turn the stomach, make one sick.

adj unsavory, tasteless, flavorless, bland, flat; bad tasting, ill-flavored, acrid, bitter, sour, unpalatable, inedible, offensive, repulsive, nasty, vile, sickening, nauseous, loathsome, unpleasant, awful.

396 sweetness *n* sugariness, saccharinity, syrupiness, stickiness.

v sweeten, sugar, candy.

adj sweet, sugary, syrupy, honeyed, saccharine, candied, sticky, gooey, luscious, lush, cloying; sweetened.

397 sourness *n* acridity, tartness,

sharpness, vinegariness, acerbity, acidity.

v sour, acidify, acerbate, curdle, acidulate, ferment, spoil.

adj sour, acid, bitter, tart, sharp, vinegary, acidulous, astringent, acerbic, acrid; fermented, rancid, bad, spoiled, turned, curdled, gone bad; styptic, hard, rough.

398 odor *n* smell, scent; effluvium; exhalation, emanation; fume, essence, redolence.

v have an odor, smell, smell of, give out a smell; smell, scent, sniff, snuff, inhale.

adj odorous, odoriferous, smelly, strong smelling, redolent, pungent.

399 inodorousness *n* absence of smell, odorlessness.

v be inodorous, not smell, have no odor, be odorless.

adj odorless, scentless, unsmelling.

400 fragrance *n* aroma, redolence, perfume, sweet smell, sweet scent, smell.

v be fragrant, smell sweet, have a perfume, scent, perfume.

adj fragrant, aromatic, redolent, spicy, scented, perfumed, sweet scented, sweet smelling, odoriferous, odorific.

401 fetor *n* bad smell, bad odor, foul smell, offensive smell, stink, stench, fume, foulness, fetidness, rancidity, rankness, fustiness, mustiness.

v have a bad smell, smell bad, smell rotten, smell, stink, reek.

adj fetid, strong smelling, bad, strong, fulsome, offensive, rank, rancid, noisome, mephitic, miasmic, musty, fusty, foul, rotten, putrid, reeking, stinking, stinky, suffocating, nauseating, nauseous, *(informal)* gross.

402 sound *n* noise, tone, pitch, sound vibrations, strain, sonority, sonorousness, twang, intonation, cadence; audibility, resonance, voice.

science of sound: acoustics, phonology, phonetics, electronic sound reproduction.

v sound, make a noise; give out sound, emit sound; resound, echo.

adj sounding, sonorous, resonant, audible, distinct.

403 silence *n* stillness, quiet, peace, hush, lull, quiescence, dead silence; muteness, speechlessness, taciturnity.

v silence, still, hush, stifle, muffle, stop, muzzle, gag; be silent, hold one's tongue, shut up, keep quiet, be still.

adj silent, quiet, still, calm, noiseless, soundless, hushed, quiescent; mute, speechless, taciturn; solemn, soft, deathlike, awful, silent as the grave.

adv silently.

404 loudness *n* loud noise, power, resonance, thunderousness, roaring, vociferousness, clamorousness; din, clang, clangor, clamor, noise, roar, uproar, hubbub, boom, racket, outcry; blast, peal, swell, flourish of trumpets, boom; thunder, explosion.

v be loud, peal, swell, clang, boom, thunder, fulminate, roar, resound, bellow, scream, holler, shout; ring in the ears, pierce the ears, split the eardrums, stun, deafen; shake, awake.

adj loud, noisy, vociferous, resounding, clamorous, deafening, stentorian, boisterous, tumultuous, sonorous, deep, full, powerful, thundering, ear-splitting, piercing, uproarious, obstreperous, shrill, sharp.

adv loudly, noisily, at the top of one's voice, at the top of one's lungs, aloud.

405 faintness *n* faint sound, whisper, breath, undertone, murmur, hum; inaudibility; hoarseness.

v whisper, breathe, murmur, hum, mutter, speak softly, speak in low tones.

adj faint, whispered, indistinct, dim, inaudible, barely audible, low, stifled, muffled, murmured, muted; gentle, soft, languid, floating, flowing; hoarse, husky.

406 [sudden and violent sounds] **snap** *n* rap, thud, burst, explosion, detonation, discharge, firing, salvo, pop, bang, blast.

v rap, snap, tap, knock, click, clash, crack, crackle, crash, beat.

407 [repeated and protracted sounds] **roll** *n* drumming, tapping, rumbling, grumbling; dingdong, whirring, droning; ratatat, rubadub, pitapat; quaver, quiver, clutter, racket; peal of bells; reverberation.

v roll, drum, rumble, grumble, rattle, clatter, patter, clack; hum, trill, shake; chime, peal, toll; tick, beat.

408 resonance *n* ring, ringing, chime, clang, clangor, boom, roll, roar, rumble, thunder, vibrato, timbre, twang, vibration, reverberation, tintinnabulation, booming, quaver, dingdong, echoing, sonorousness.

v resound, reverberate, re-echo; ring, jingle, chink, clink; gurgle, echo, ring in the ear.

adj resonant, resounding, reverberant, reverberating; deep-toned, deep-sounding.

408a nonresonance *n* dead sound, thud, thump, muffled drums, cracked bell; damper, mute, muffler.

v sound dead, thud, thump; muffle, dampen, mute.

adj nonresonant, dampened, muted, muffled, deadened; dead.

409 [hissing sounds] **sibilation** *n* hissing, wheezing, buzzing, zipping, whooshing; high note.

v hiss, buzz, whiz, wheeze, whoosh, zip, rustle, whistle, fizzle; squash, sneeze.

adj sibilant; hissing, wheezy.

410 [harsh sounds] **stridency** *n* discord, dissonance, harshness, raucousness, atonality, clashing, grinding, grating, rasping, sharpness, creaking, shrillness.

v creak, grate, jar, jangle, clank, clink, grind, grate; scream, yelp.

adj strident, sharp, high, acute, shrill, atonal, unharmonious, unmusical, dissonant, discordant, cacophonous; piercing, ear-piercing, cracked; creaking, harsh, coarse, hoarse, rough, gruff, grating, jarring, guttural, squawking, acute, scratching, croaking, rasping, sour, clashing.

411 cry *n* shout, scream, yell, shriek, roar, howl, wail; exclamation, outcry, clamor, vociferation; hubbub, hullabaloo, chorus, hue and cry; entreaty, appeal, solicitation, plea, plaint, prayer, crying, weeping, wailing, sobbing, lament, whimper, whimpering, tears, moaning.

v cry, roar, shout, bawl, brawl, hoop, whoop, yell, bellow, howl, scream, screech, shriek, squeak, squeal, whine, whimper, wail, weep, sob, moan, lament; cheer, hoot; grumble, groan, complain; vociferate, raise one's voice, sing out, cry out, yell out, exclaim, holler, shout at the top of one's lungs.

adj crying, clamorous; vociferous; solicitous; stentorian.

412 [animal sounds] **ululation** *n* howling, crying, belling, screeching, singing, growling, purring.

v cry, roar, bellow, bark, yelp, yap, growl, snarl, howl, bay, grunt, snort, neigh, bray, mew, purr, caterwaul, bleat, low, moo, squeak, oink, baa, crow, croak, screech, caw, coo, gobble, quack, cackle, gaggle, chuck, cluck, clack, chirp, chirrup, twitter, cuckoo, hum, buzz, hiss, blatter.

413 melody, concord *n* melodiousness, tunefulness, sweet sounds, mellifluence, musicalness, euphony; timbre, tone color, pitch; tune, song, aria, theme, measure, plainsong, canticle, strain, lay.

harmony, harmoniousness; rhythm, meter; symphony, euphony, consonance, attunement, modulation, syncopation; counterpoint, polyphony; concordance, pleasing combination.

v harmonize, chime, symphonize, blend; tune, accord.

adj melodious, musical, tuneful, melodic, lyrical, euphonious, singing, ringing, sweet-sounding, euphonic, mellifluous, dulcet, mellow, clear, sweet, rich, soft, silvery, agreeable, pleasing.

concordant, harmonious, agreeing, symphonious, suiting, congenial, blending, synchronized, consistent, in rapport, in unison, consonant, conjoined, symmetrical, proportionate, consonant, compatible.

414 discord *n* dissonance, atonality; harshness; racket, noise, inharmoniousness.

v be discordant; jar, grate.

adj discordant, dissonant, atonal, harsh; out of tune, tuneless, unmelodious, inharmonious, unmusical; jarring, grating, cacophonous; screeching.

415 music *n* sweet sounds, pleasing sounds, harmonious sounds, melody, song, tune, strain, air, harmony; classical music, popular music, folk music, jazz, electronic music; orchestral music, instrumental music, symphonic music, chamber music; ragtime, reggae, swing, bebop, bop, barrelhouse, rock; pop music, vocal music, choral music, solo, duet, duo, sonata, trio, quartet, quintet, sextet, septet, octet.

v make music, perform; compose.

adj musical, lyrical; instrumental, orchestral, symphonic, vocal, choral, operatic.

416 musician [performance of music] *n* artist, performer, concert artist, player, soloist, instrumentalist, vocalist, accompanist, singer, minstrel; symphony orchestra, orchestra, chamber orchestra, band, rock and roll band, group, combo, ensemble, chamber group, quartet, trio; chorus, choir, vocal group.

v make music, play, perform, strike up, concertize, execute, accompany, present the music, solo, improvise, play the notes; sing, croon, warble, vocalize, spin a melody.

adj musical, instrumental, vocal, choral, operatic; lyrical, harmonious, brilliant, sharp, incisive.

417 musical instruments *n* orchestra, band, brass band, marching band,

military band, ensemble, group; strings, plucked instruments, bowed instruments, hammered instruments; woodwinds, winds, tubed instruments, reed instruments, brass instruments; percussion; synthesizer.

418 hearing *n* audition, auscultation, listening, perception, audibility, ear; regarding, attending, heeding.

hearer, auditor, listener; eavesdropper.

v hear, listen, attend, lend an ear, bend an ear, *(informal)* tune in, give a hearing to, give audience to, prick up one's ears, be all ears; overhear, eavesdrop; heed, regard.

adj hearing, auditory, auricular.

419 deafness *n* hardness of hearing, inaudibility.

v be deaf, not hear; turn a deaf ear to, plug up one's ears; deafen, stun, split the eardrums.

adj deaf, stone-deaf, hard of hearing; deafened, stunned; unheeding, inattentive.

420 light *n* ray, beam, stream, gleam, streak; sunbeam, moonbeam, aurora, dawn, sunrise, day-break, day, daylight, light of day, sunshine, broad daylight, glow, glint, glimmering; sun, moon; flush, halo, glory, aureole; spark, scintilla, scintillation, flash, blaze, coruscation; flame, lightening, flare; luster, sheen, shimmer, reflection, refraction; brightness, brilliancy, splendor, effulgence, radiance, illumination, radiation; luminosity, lucidity.

science of light: optics, photography, radioactivity.

v shine, glow, glitter, glisten, gleam, beam, flare, flare up, glare, flash, glimmer, shimmer, flicker, sparkle, scintillate, coruscate, flash, blaze; light, reflect, dazzle, bedazzle, daze, radiate; lighten, enlighten, light, irradiate, shed light upon, cast light upon, illuminate, illumine, kindle, fire.

adj luminous, lucent; light, bright, vivid, splendid, resplendent, lustrous, shiny, radiant; sheeny, glossy, glassy, sunny, burnished; cloudless, clear, unclouded; effulgent, blazing, ablaze, phosphorescent, aglow; iridescent.

421 darkness *n* blackness; obscurity, doom, murkiness, murk; duskiness, dusk, dimness; night, midnight, dead of night; shade, shadow, umbra, penumbra; obscuration, adumbration, extinction, eclipse, total eclipse.

v be dark; darken, obscure, shade, dim, shadow, overcast, cloud, becloud; extinguish, put out, blow out, snuff out.

adj dark, obscure, black, pitch black, nocturnal, overcast, cloudy, darkened; dingy, lurid, murky, gloomy, oppressive; shadowy, shady, umbrageous.

422 dimness *n* duskiness, shadowiness, gloominess, cloudiness, mist, mistiness, haze, haziness, fogginess, paleness, shade, nebulosity, gray, grayness.

v be dim, grow dim, darken, obscure, adumbrate, becloud, cloud, shadow, shade, eclipse, cloud over; blur, dull, fade, pale; glimmer, twinkle, flutter, flicker, waver.

adj dim, dull, dingy, lackluster, darkish, darkened, gray, dark, faint, pale, cloudy, misty, murky, overcast, nebulous, shadowy, umbrageous, blurry, hazy, opaque, foggy, bleary, gloomy, lurid, leaden.

423 [source of light] **luminary** *n* natural light, sun, moon, stars, flame, fire, spark, phosphorescence; artificial light, lamp, gas lamp, oil lamp, kerosene lamp, electric light, lantern, torch, candle, taper, light bulb.

v light, illuminate.

adj self-luminous; phosphorescent, radiant.

424 shade *n* cover, awning, umbrella, parasol, sunshade; screen, curtain, shutter, blind, gauze, veil, mantle, mask, sunglasses, *(informal)* shades; cloud, mist, fog, shadow.

v shade, veil, cover, screen, curtain, veil, draw a curtain, pull the shade, cast a shadow.

adj shady, shadowy, cloudy.

425 transparency *n* transparence, transluscence, diaphanousness, clearness, lucidity, limpidity, thinness, sheerness, gauziness, flimsiness.

v be transparent, transmit light.

adj transparent, pellucid, lucid, diaphanous, translucent, limpid, clear, crystalline, see-through, sheer, gauzy, flimsy.

426 opacity *n* opaqueness, darkness, cloudiness, filminess, haziness, mistiness, nontransparency.

v be opaque, obstruct the passage of light.

adj opaque, impervious to light, impenetrable to light, dim, filmy, thick, smoky, misty, smoggy, shady, murky, cloudy, hazy, obscure, clouded, foggy, unclear, frosted, nontransparent, nontranslucent.

427 semitransparency *n* opalescence, milkiness, pearliness; film, mist.

v let in partial light.

adj semitransparent, semipellucid, semiopaque, opalescent, pearly, nacreous, milky.

428 color *n* hue, tint, tinge, dye, complexion, shade, tincture, cast, coloration, tone, key; primary color, secondary color, complementary color; coloring; spectrum, prism, spectroscope; pigment, paint, dye, wash, stain.

v color, dye, tinge, stain, tint, paint, wash; illuminate, emblazon.

adj colored, dyed, tinted; prismatic, chromatic; bright, vivid, intense, deep, rich, gorgeous; fresh, unfaded; gaudy, florid, garish, showy, flashy, glaring; mellow, harmonious, pearly, sweet, delicate, tender, refined; dull, gray.

429 [absence of color] **colorlessness** *n* neutral tint, black and white, chiaroscuro, monochrome; etiolation, pallor, paleness, discoloration.

v lose color, fade, turn pale, become colorless, pale; deprive of color, bleach, wash out, blanch, tarnish, etiolate, tone down, whiten.

adj uncolored, colorless, hueless, pale, pallid, faint, dull, dun, wan, sallow, dingy, ashy, gray, ashen, lackluster; discolored; light-colored, fair blond, white.

430 whiteness *n* milkiness, frostiness, silveriness, pearliness; etiolation, albification, decoloration, colorlessness; albinism.

v whiten, bleach, blanch, etiolate, whitewash.

adj white, snowy, frosted, snow-white, milk-white, milky, chalky, pearly, ivory, silver, silvery, opaline, whitish, albinistic, etiolated, bleached, blanched, fair, light, wan, pallid, pale, lackluster, colorless, anemic, sallow, faint.

431 blackness *n* darkness, swarthiness, lividness; ink, ebony, coal, charcoal, pitch; obscurity.

v black, blacken, darken; blot, smutch, smut, smirch.

adj black, sable, somber, livid, dark, inky, ebony, pitchy, swarthy, sooty, dingy, dusky, murky; jet-black, pitch-black, black as coal, coal-black, kohl-black, black as night.

432 gray *n* grayness, neutral tint, silver, salt and pepper, dove color.

adj gray, iron-gray, silver, silvery, silverish, grayish, dun, drab, ashy, ashen, dove-colored, dapple-gray; grizzly, grizzled, hoary.

433 brown *n* brownness, beige, khaki.

adj brown, bay, dapple, auburn, nutbrown, chocolate, chestnut, cinnamon, russet, tawny, tan, brunette, mahogany, khaki, beige, ochre, sepia, hazel, brownish, coffee, cocoa, rust, roan, sorrel.

434 red *n* redness; blush, color.

v redden, blush, flush, get red in the face, turn color.

adj red, reddish, scarlet, crimson, blood red, bloody, cherry-colored, vermilion, carmine, maroon, pink, hot pink, rosy, ruby, salmon, wine-colored; red-faced, blushing, embarrassed, red as beet, red as a lobster, flushed, burning, fuming, flaming, inflamed; ruddy, glowing, blooming, warm, hot.

435 green *n* greenness, verdure, blue and yellow.

adj green, greenish, verdant, olive, pea-green, emerald, apple, Kelly green, blue-green, aquamarine, sea-green; grassy, verdurous; fresh, new, recent, young, innocent, naive, raw, unseasoned, immature, inexperienced, ignorant; sickly, wan, pale, livid-jealous, envious.

436 yellow *n* yellowness, jaundice.

v yellow, age, turn color, dry up.

adj yellow, yellowish, gold, golden, ocher, lemon, citrine, saffron, aureate, creamy, straw-colored, flaxen, blond, tawny, sallow; sordid, cheap; cowardly, *(informal)* chicken, craven, lily-livered, contemptible, despicable, mean, cringing, groveling; jaundiced.

437 purple *n* blue and red.

adj purple, purplish, lavender, lilac, magenta, orchid, violet, plum-colored, mauve.

438 blue *n* blueness.

adj blue, bluish, azure, marine blue, navy, aquamarine, greenish blue, sapphire, turquoise, cobalt, baby blue; depressed, down in the dumps, *(informal)* in the pits, *(informal)* down, low.

439 orange *n* red and yellow; flame.

adj orange, orangy, orangish, brass, copper, apricot, tangerine, gold, flame-colored.

440 variegation *n* striation, spottiness, streakiness, iridescence, play of colors.

v variegate, diversify, streak, stripe, checker, speckle, bespeckle, fleck, dapple; dot, striate, tattoo, inlay; embroider, quilt.

adj variegated, multi-colored, many-colored, kaleidoscopic; irides-

cent, prismatic, opaline, nacreous, pearly; pied, piebald, mottled; dappled, salt and pepper, marbled, flecked, speckled, spotty, studded, freckled, flecky, spotted, diversified; striped, veined, lined, striated, streaked, brindled, banded, checked, checkered, plaid, mosaic, inlaid.

441 vision *n* sight, optics, eyesight; view, look, glance, ken, glimpse, peep, peek, gaze, stare, leer; contemplation, regard, survey; point of view, outlook, viewpoint, perspective, standpoint; perspicacity, discernment, perception, penetration.

v see, behold, discern, perceive, have in sight, descry, sight, make out, discover, distinguish, recognize, spy, espy, catch a glimpse of, command a view of, witness; envision, contemplate; look, view, eye, survey, scan, inspect, run the eye over, glance around; observe, watch, watch for, peep, peer, peek, pry, take a peep, leer, ogle, glare.

adj visual, ocular, optic; clear-sighted, eagle-eyed, discerning; visionary, farsighted.

adv on sight, at first sight, at a glance

442 blindness *n* sightlessness; cataract; ignorance.

v be blind, not see; grope in the dark; blind, hoodwink, dazzle; screen, hide, mask.

adj blind, eyeless, sightless, unseeing, dark, purblind, stone-blind; dimsighted, undiscerning, ignorant.

adv blindly, blindfold, darkly.

443 [imperfect vision] **dimsightedness** *n* nearsightedness, farsightedness, purblindness, presbyopia, myopia, astigmatism, color blindness, cataract, ophthalmia; squint, cross-eye, strabismus, lazy eye, cockeye, swivel eye, goggle eyes.

fallacies of vision: refraction, distortion, illusion, mirage, phantasm, vision, specter, apparition, ghost; mirror, lens.

v be dimsighted, see double, wink, blink, squint, look askance, screw up the eyes.

adj dimsighted, purblind, myopic, astigmatic, nearsighted, farsighted, colorblind; blear-eyed, goggle-eyed, cockeyed, crosseyed.

444 spectator *n* beholder, observer, looker-on, onlooker, witness, eyewitness, bystander, passerby; sightseer, audience, crowd; spy, sentinel.

v witness, behold, look on.

445 optical instruments *n* lens, magnifying glass, microscope; spectacles, monocle, eyeglasses, glasses, contact lens, goggles, pince-nez; telescope, lorgnette, binoculars, spyglass, opera glasses; mirror, looking glass, reflector; prism, kaleidoscope, stereoscope.

446 visibility *n* perceptibility, discernibleness, distinctness, clearness, clarity, perceivability, conspicuousness, definition, sharp outline; appearance, manifestation.

v be visible, appear, open to the view, present itself, show itself, reveal itself, peep up, show up, turn up, start up, pop up, crop up; glimmer, loom; burst forth, burst upon the view, come into sight, come into view, come forth, come forward, attract attention.

adj visible, perceptible, discernible, perceivable, apparent, obvious, manifest, plain, clear, distinct, definite, well-defined, outlined, well-marked; recognizable, palpable, glaring, conspicuous, in full view, in full sight, in front of one's nose, under one's nose, before one's eyes.

447 invisibility *n* indistinctness, imperceptibility, invisibleness, indefiniteness; mystery, obscurity, delitescence, haziness, cloudiness; concealment; latency.

v be invisible; be hidden; escape notice; render invisible, conceal, hide.

adj invisible, imperceptible; not in sight, out of sight, out of view, unseen; inconspicuous, covert; dim, faint, mysterious, dark, obscure, confused, indistinct, indistinguishable, shadowy, indefinite, undefined, unmarked, blurry, blurred, unfocused, out of focus, misty, veiled; concealed, hidden.

448 appearance *n* phenomenon, sight, show, scene, view; prospect, vista, perspective, lookout, outlook, bird's-eye view, scenery, landscape, picture, tableau; display, exposure; pageant, spectacle; aspect, phase, seeming, shape, form, manifestation, guise, look, complexion, color, image, mien, air, cast, carriage, comportment, demeanor; presence; feature, trait, lines, outline, contour, face, countenance, physiognomy, visage, profile, outsides.

v appear, be visible, seem, look, show, present; figure, cut a figure; present to the view.

adj apparent, seeming, ostensible.

adv apparently, to all appearance, ostensibly, seemingly, on the face of it, at first sight, to the eye.

449 disappearance *n* evanescence, eclipse; departure, exit; loss.

v disappear, vanish, dissolve, melt,

melt away, fade, pass, pass out, go, depart, leave no trace, be gone.

adj disappearing, evanescent; departed, left; missing, lost, vanished.

Class IV

Intellectual Faculties

I. Formation of Ideas

450 intellect *n* rationality, mind, understanding, reason, faculties, judgment, sense, common sense, wits, brains, (*informal*) smarts; brain, head, pate, (*informal*) noodle, skull, (*informal*) upstairs.

v intellectualize, reason, understand, realize, ruminate; note, notice, mark, be aware of, take cognizance of.

adj intellectual, mental, cerebral, rational, sensical, commonsensical.

450a absence of intellect *n* want of intellect; inanity, imbecility, brutishness, brute instinct.

adj. unintellectual, unintelligent, unrational, nonrational, empty-headed.

451 thought *n* abstraction, concept, conception, opinion, judgment, belief, idea, notion, tenet, conviction, speculation, consideration, contemplation; meditation, pondering, reflection, musing, cogitation, thinking; intention, design, purpose, intent; anticipation, expectation; consideration, attention, care, regard; trifle, mote.

v think, cogitate, meditate, reflect, muse, ponder, ruminate, contemplate; consider, regard, suppose, look upon, judge, esteem, deem, count, account; bear in mind, recollect, recall, remember; intend, mean, design, purpose; believe, suppose; anticipate, expect.

adj thoughtful, contemplative, meditative, reflective, pensive, deliberate; lost in thought, absorbed, engrossed in; careful, heedful, mindful, regardful, considerate, attentive; discreet, prudent, wary, cautious, circumspect.

452 absence of thought *n* incogitancy, vacancy of mind, thoughtlessness, fatuity, vacuity, emptiness; inattention.

v not think, make the mind a blank, (*informal*) turn off the brain, (*informal*) tune out.

adj vacant, unoccupied, empty; unthinking; inattentive, absent, (*informal*) turned off, (*informal*) tuned out; thoughtless, inconsiderate, unmindful, unheedful, imprudent; unreflective.

453 idea *n* thought, conception, theory, notion; observation, impression, apprehension, perception, brainstorm, brainchild, fancy, (*informal*) flash; opinion, view, belief, sentiment, judgment, supposition; plan, object, objective, aim.

adj ideational.

454 topic *n* subject, theme, thesis, subject-matter, food for thought; business, affair, argument.

adj topical, thematic.

adv under consideration, in question.

455 curiosity *n* interest, inquisitiveness, inquiring mind, thirst for knowledge; spying, prying, meddlesomeness.

spy, eavesdropper, gossip.

v be curious, take an interest in, stare, gape, spy, pry.

adj curious, inquisitive, inquiring, prying, spying, peeping, meddlesome, interested.

456 incuriosity *n* lack of interest, incuriousness, indifference, unconcern.

v have no curiosity, take no interest in.

adj incurious, uninquisitive, uninquiring, uninterested, indifferent, impassive, bored, apathetic.

457 attention *n* attending to, attentiveness, intentiveness, care, consideration, observation, heed, regard, mindfulness, notice, watchfulness, alertness; study, scrutiny; civility, courtesy, respect, politeness.

v be attentive, attend, observe, look, see, notice, remark, regard, pay attention, heed; examine, study, scrutinize.

adj attentive, observant, mindful, heedful, thoughtful, alive, alert, awake, on the watch, wary, circumspectful, watchful, careful; polite, courteous, respectful, deferential.

458 inattention *n* inattentiveness, inconsideration, heedlessness, unmindfulness, disregard, unconcern.

v be inattentive, overlook, disregard, pay no attention to, gloss over.

adj inattentive, unobservant, unmindful, unheeding, thoughtless, blind to, deaf to, napping, asleep, lost.

459 care *n* heed, caution, prudence, pains, anxiety, regard, attention, vigilance, carefulness, solicitude, circumspection, alertness, watchfulness, wakefulness; accuracy, exactness.

v be careful, take care.

adj careful, cautious, circumspect, watchful, vigilant, guarded, wary,

prudent, tactful; painstaking, meticulous, discerning, exact, thorough, concerned, scrupulous, particular, finical, conscientious, attentive, heedful, thoughtful.

460 neglect *n* disregard, dereliction, negligence, remissness, carelessness, failure, omission, default, inattention, heedlessness, recklessness.

v neglect, disregard, ignore, slight, overlook, omit, be remiss, be negligent.

adj neglectful, disregardful, remiss, careless, negligent, unmindful, inattentive, indifferent, heedless, inconsiderate, thoughtless, imprudent; unwary, unguarded; neglecting, neglected, unheeded, uncared for, unobserved, unnoticed, unattended to.

461 inquiry *n* investigation, examination, study, scrutiny, exploration, research, search, pursuit; inquiring, questioning, interrogation; query, question.

inquirer, investigator, inquisitor, inspector.

v inquire, ask, question, interrogate, query, investigate, examine, seek, search, look for, study, consider.

adj inquiring, inquisitive, curious, scrutinizing, questioning, exploring; inquisitorial, exploratory, interrogative.

462 answer *n* reply, response, retort, rejoinder; discovery, solution; rationale.

v answer, reply, respond, rebut, retort, rejoin; explain, interpret, discover, solve; satisfy, set at rest, atone for.

adj responsive; answerable, discoverable, soluble.

463 experiment *n* test, trial, examination, proof, assay, procedure; experimentation, research, investigation, analysis.

experimenter, analyzer, adventurer.

v experiment, try, test, examine, analyze, prove, assay, essay.

adj experimental, probative, analytic.

464 comparison *n* collation, association, relating, likening, correlation, comparative relation, setting side by side, juxtaposition.

v compare, collate, confront, place side by side, pit one against another, juxtapose, relate, correlate.

adj comparative, metaphorical, compared with; comparable.

465 discrimination *n* distinction, differentiation, diagnosis; appreciation,

estimation, discernment, critique, judgment; nicety, refinement, taste.

v discriminate, distinguish, set apart, differentiate.

adj discriminating, critical, distinguishing, discriminative, discriminatory, choosy, picky; discerning, perceptive; tasteful, refined.

465a indiscrimination *n* indistinction, indistinctness, lack of discernment.

v be indiscriminate, not discriminate, confound, confuse.

adj indiscriminate, miscellaneous, undiscriminating.

466 measurement *n* survey, valuation, appraisement, assessment, estimate, estimation, reckoning, gauging; measure, standard, rule, gauge, scale.

v measure, survey, assess, rate, value, appraise, estimate.

adj measurable.

467 [on one side] **evidence** *n* facts, indication, sign, signal; ground, grounds, proof, testimony; information, deposition, affidavit, exhibit, citation, reference, confirmation, corroboration.

v be evident, evince, show, tell, cite, signal, indicate, imply, argue, bespeak; give evidence, testify, depose, witness.

adj evident, evidential, indicative, inferential, referential, corroborative, confirmatory.

468 counter-evidence *n* disproof, refutation, rebuttal, conflicting evidence, negation.

v rebut, refute, check, weaken, contravene, contradict, deny.

adj countervailing, contradictory, conflicting, unsupportive, uncorroborative.

469 qualification *n* modification, limitation, mitigation, narrowing, restriction, coloring, allowance, consideration, extenuation, extenuating circumstances, condition, proviso, exception.

v qualify, modify, limit, mitigate, restrain, narrow, restrict, color, allow, allow for, make allowance for, consider, extenuate, except, make an exception, take into account, take into consideration.

adj qualified, qualifying, provided, conditional, extenuating, mitigating, admitting, supposing, with the proviso, provided that.

470 possibility *n* feasibility, practicality, likelihood, potentiality; contingency, chance.

v be possible, stand a chance, admit of, (*informal*) could be.

adj possible, imaginable, conceivable, credible, feasible, practical, performable, achievable, within reach, within the bounds of possibility, potential.

adv possibly, perhaps, perchance, peradventure, maybe.

471 impossibility *n* impracticality, unfeasibility, hopelessness.

v be impossible, have no chance.

adj impossible, not possible, inconceivable, incredible, unimaginable, unreasonable, unfeasible, impractical, unobtainable, unperformable, unachievable, beyond the bounds of reason, absurd, (*informal*) fat chance, (*informal*) no way.

472 probability *n* likelihood, likeliness, plausibility, tendency, prospect, good chance, reasonable chance, expectation.

v be probable, point to, tend, imply, bid fair.

adj probable, likely, plausible, reasonable, presumable, well-founded, hopeful.

adv probably, in all probability, in all likelihood, most likely, presumably.

473 improbability *n* unlikelihood, bare possibility, implausibility, doubtfulness, questionableness.

v be improbable, not have much of a chance.

adj improbable, unlikely, implausible, doubtful, questionable, beyond all reasonable expectation.

474 certainty *n* fact, truth; infallibility, reliability, unquestionableness, inevitability, certitude, assurance, confidence, conviction.

v be certain, stand to reason, render certain, clinch, make sure; know.

adj certain, confident, sure, assured, convinced, satisfied, indubitable, indisputable, unquestionable, undeniable, incontestable, unimpeachable, irrefutable, unquestioned, incontrovertible, absolute, positive, plain, patent, obvious, clear; sure, inevitable, infallible, unfailing; fixed, agreed upon, settled, prescribed, determined, determinate, constant, stated, given; definite, particular, special, especial; reliable, trustworthy, dependable, trusty.

adv certainly, for certain, no doubt, doubtless, undoubtedly, (*informal*) sure enough.

475 uncertainty *n* insecurity, instability, unreliability, fallibility, danger; incertitude, doubt, doubtfulness, ambiguity, vagueness, questionableness, dubiousness; haziness, fogginess, obscurity; undependability, changeableness, variability, capriciousness, irregularity, fitfulness, chanciness.

v be uncertain, hesitate, flounder, waver; render uncertain, pose, puzzle, perplex, confuse, confound, bewilder; doubt, question.

adj uncertain, insecure, precarious, unsure, doubtful, unpredictable, problematical, unstable, unreliable, unsafe, fallible, perilous, dangerous; unassured, undecided, indeterminate, undetermined, unfixed, unsettled, indefinite, ambiguous, questionable, dubious; doubtful, vague, indistinct; undependable, changeable, variable, capricious, unsteady, irregular, fitful, desultory, chance, (*informal*) chancy.

476 reasoning *n* ratiocination, rationalism, dialectics; discussion, comment, argumentation, debate, disputation.

logic, induction, deduction, chain of thought, analysis, synthesis, syllogistic reasoning.

argument, case, proposition, terms, premises, postulate, data; inference, *argumentum ad hominem, paralipsis, a priori, a posteriori, reductio ad absurdum,* enthymeme, dilemma, on the horns of a dilemma.

reasoner, logician, dialectician, disputant, wrangler, arguer, debater, polemicist, casuist, rationalist.

arguments, reasons, pros and cons.

v to reason, discuss, argue, debate, dispute, wrangle; deduce, induce, infer, analyze, synthesize, postulate, propose, contend, demonstrate.

adj reasoning, rationalistic, dialectical, dialectic, argumentative, disputatious; logical, inductive, deductive, analytical, synthetic, syllogistic, inferential; demonstrable.

477 [the absence of reasoning] **intuition.**
[false reasoning] **sophistry** *n* intuition, instinct, hunch, presentiment; insight, discernment, inspiration.

casuistry, jesuitry, perversion, equivocation, evasion, chicanery, quiddity, speciousness, (*informal*) bull, (*informal*) malarkey, bunk; false statement; fallacy, sophism.

sophist.

v intuit; reason falsely, pervert, quibble, equivocate, evade, mislead, gloss over, cavil, refine, subtilize, misrepresent, fence, beg the question.

adj intuitive, instinctive, instinctual, sophistical, equivocal, evasive

specious, fallacious, illogical, unsound, false, incorrect, untenable; inconsequential, weak, feeble, poor, flimsy, vague, nonsensical, absurd, foolish; frivolous, pettifogging, trifling, quibbling, nit-picking, subtle, over-refined.

adv intuitively, by intuition; illogically.

478 demonstration *n* proof, conclusiveness, example, verification, explanation.

v demonstrate, prove, establish, verify; evince, show, explain.

adj demonstrative, demonstrable, probative, conclusive, convincing; demonstrated, proven, proved, shown.

479 confutation *n* refutation, answer, disproof, invalidation, exposure.

v confute, refute, disprove, expose the error, overturn, invalidate.

adj confutable, refutable.

480 judgment *n* verdict, decree, decision, determination, conclusion, result, upshot, deduction, inference, assessment, opinion, estimate, criticism, critique; understanding, discrimination, discernment, perspicacity, sagacity, wisdom, intelligence, prudence, brains, taste, penetration, discretion, common sense.

judge, assessor, reviewer, critic, commentator; connoisseur.

v judge, estimate, consider, regard, esteem, appreciate, appraise, reckon, value; decide, determine, conclude, form an opinion, pass judgment; criticize, rate, rank; try, pass sentence upon, rule.

adj judicious, judicial, judgmental, determinate, conclusive; critical, discriminating, penetrating, perspicacious.

480a discovery *n* detection, determination, disclosure, trove, find.

v discover, learn of, ascertain, unearth, uncover, determine, ferret out, flush out, dig up; find out, detect, espy, descry, discern, see, notice, hit upon, stumble onto.

481 misjudgment *n* miscalculation, miscomputation, misconception, misinterpretation, misapprehension.

v misjudge, misconjecture, misconceive, misunderstand, misconstrue, misinterpret; overestimate, underestimate.

adj misjudging, ill-judging, wrongheaded, (*informal*) off base, wrong, in error.

482 overestimation *n* exaggeration, overvaluation, optimism; miscalculation.

v overestimate, overrate, overprize, overpraise, exaggerate, magnify, attach too much importance to, set too high a value on; miscalculate.

adj overestimated, overrated, inflated, pompous, pretentious.

483 underestimation *n* undervaluation, depreciation, detraction; modesty, self-depreciation; pessimism.

v underestimate, undervalue, underrate, depreciate, disparage, detract, slight, minimize, make light of, make little of, disregard.

adj underestimating, depreciating, depreciative, deprecatory; underestimated, depreciated, unvalued, unprized; modest, pessimistic.

484 belief *n* opinion, view, tenet, doctrine, dogma, creed; certainty, conviction, assurance, confidence, persuasion, believing, trust, reliance; credence, credit, acceptance, faith, assent.

v believe, credit, give credence to, accept, have faith in, give assent, accept; know, see, realize, assume, presume; think, opine, hold, conceive, consider; rely on, put one's trust on, have confidence in.

adj certain, sure, assured, positive, cocksure, satisfied, confident, convinced, secure; believing, trusting, confiding, credulous; believed, accredited, trusted, accepted; believable, credible, trustworthy.

485 disbelief, doubt *n* disbelief, incredulity; dissent, change of mind, retraction.

uncertainty, irresolution, hesitation, hesitancy, vacillation, misgiving, suspense; scruple, qualm, mistrust, distrust, suspicion, skepticism.

unbeliever, nonbeliever; skeptic.

v disbelieve, discredit, dissent, doubt, distrust, mistrust, suspect, have qualms; hesitate, waver, demur.

adj unbelieving, incredulous, doubtful, disputable, questionable, suspicious; uncertain, unsure; doubting, hesitating, hesitant, wavering, irresolute, dubious, skeptical.

486 credulity *n* credulousness, gullibility, infatuation, superstition, self-deception, self-delusion.

gull, dupe, (*informal*) sucker.

v be credulous, swallow.

adj credulous, believing, trusting, unsuspecting, gullible; simple, silly, childish, stupid; infatuated, superstitious.

487 incredulity *n* incredulousness, caution, wariness, suspicion, doubt, skepticism, disbelief.

nonbeliever, skeptic, heretic.

v be incredulous, distrust, doubt, suspect.

adj incredulous, cautious, wary; suspicious, dubious, doubtful, skeptical, unbelieving.

488 assent *n* acknowledgment, agreement, concurrence, acquiescence, consent, allowance, approval, concord, accord, approbation.

v assent, acquiesce, accede, concur, agree, fall in, acknowledge, admit, yield, allow; own, avow, confess.

adj assenting, agreeing, concurring, consenting, of one accord, of the same mind; agreed, acquiescent.

489 dissent *n* difference, discordance, dissension, disagreement, dissatisfaction; opposition, protest; nonconformity, separation.

dissenter, protester, rebel, radical, dissident, nonconformist.

v dissent, differ, disagree, protest, contradict; repudiate.

adj dissenting, negative; dissident, contradictory, disagreeing, opposing; nonconformist.

490 knowledge *n* enlightenment, erudition, wisdom, science, letters, information, learning, scholarship, lore; understanding, discernment, perception, apprehension, comprehension, judgment.

v know, be aware of; understand, discern, perceive, realize, fathom, apprehend, comprehend, (*informal*) dig; (*informal*) be hip; learn, discover.

adj knowing, aware of, cognizant of, acquainted with, privy to; discerning, perceptive, (*informal*) sharp, shrewd; knowledgeable, educated, enlightened, erudite, wise, instructed, learned, well-educated, bookish, well-read; known, recognized, received.

491 ignorance *n* illiteracy, unenlightenment, unawareness, unlearnedness, unacquaintance, unconsciousness, inexperience, darkness, blindness, incomprehension, simplicity, stupidity.

v be ignorant, know nothing, have no idea, be blind to.

adj ignorant, illiterate, unlettered, uneducated, uninstructed, untaught, untutored, uninformed, unenlightened, nescient; shallow, superficial; stupid, dumb, thick, dull.

492 scholar *n* savant, wise man, sage, academician, thinker, intellectual, bibliomaniac, bookworm, pedant; student, pupil, disciple, learner.

493 ignoramus *n* illiterate,

know-nothing, blockhead, numskull, dullard, simpleton, dunce, ass, fool, bonehead, duffer, dolt, turkey, twerp, idiot, imbecile, cretin, moron, dimwit, (*informal*) jerk.

494 truth *n* fact, reality, verity, veracity; accuracy, precision, exactness.

v be true, be the case, have a true ring.

adj true, factual, actual, real, authentic, genuine, veracious, truthful, veritable; pure, natural; accurate, exact, faithful, correct, precise; agreeing; right, proper; legitimate, rightful; to the point, (*informal*) right on, (*informal*) where it's at, (*informal*) on target.

495 error *n* fallacy, misconception, misapprehension, misunderstanding, misinterpretation, misjudgment; aberration, inexactness, laxity; mistake, fault, blunder, slip, oversight, flaw, stumble, bungle; delusion, false impression.

v err, be in error, mistake, blunder, slip, go astray, trip up; misconceive, misapprehend, misunderstand, misinterpret, miscalculate, misjudge.

adj erroneous, in error, fallacious, mistaken, incorrect, inaccurate, false, wrong, untrue, (*informal*) off base, (*informal*) off the mark.

496 maxim *n* proverb, aphorism, dictum, saying, adage, apothegm, motto, epigram, *mot juste*, truism, words of wisdom, axiom.

adj proverbial, aphoristic, axiomatic, truistic, (*informal*) corny, trite.

adv as they say, as the saying goes.

497 absurdity *n* nonsense, imbecility, foolishness, silliness, inanity, stupidity; farce, rhapsody, farrago, blunder, bathos; inconsistency, paradox, *non sequitur*, jargon, extravagance, exaggeration.

v be absurd, talk nonsense, play the fool.

adj absurd, nonsensical, ridiculous, silly, preposterous, foolish, inane, asinine, stupid, senseless, unreasonable, irrational, incongruous, self-contradictory, paradoxical; farcical, rhapsodic, bathetic, extravagant, exaggerated, bombastic, fantastic, meaningless.

498 intelligence, wisdom *n* intelligence, intellect, mind, capacity, understanding, discernment, reason, acumen, aptitude, penetration, brains, (*informal*) smarts; knowledge, news, information, tidings.

discretion, reasonableness, judg-

ment, discernment, insight, sense, common sense, sagacity, insight, understanding, prudence; knowledge, information, learning, sapience, erudition, enlightenment.

v be intelligent; understand, discern, reason; be wise, discriminate.

adj intelligent, understanding, intellectual, quick, bright; astute, clever, sharp, alert, bright, apt, discerning, canny, shrewd, nimble, penetrating, piercing, on the ball.

wise, discerning, judicious, sage, sapient, sensible, sound, penetrating, sagacious, intelligent, perspicacious, profound, rational, prudent, cautious, politic, reasonable, thoughtful, reflective; learned, educated, erudite, schooled.

499 imbecility, folly n imbecility, want of intelligence, incompetence, incapacity, vacancy, dull understanding, meanness, simplicity, shallowness, stolidity, hebetude, puerility, fatuity, silliness, foolishness, driveling, stupidity, idiocy.

frivolity, irrationality, trifling, ineptitude, silliness, eccentricity, extravagance; rashness.

v be imbecilic,

be foolish, trifle, drivel, dote, ramble.

adj imbecile, imbecilic, idiotic, fatuous, driveling; vacant, mindless, witless, brainless, weak-headed, addlebrained, muddle-headed, dull-witted, feeble-minded, half-witted, dull, shallow, stolid, dim-witted, thick-skulled; shallow, weak, wanting, soft, sappy, stupid, obtuse, blunt, stolid, doltish, thick as a brick, asinine; childish, childlike, infantile, puerile, simple.

foolish, silly, senseless, irrational, insensate, nonsensical, inept, frivolous, trifling; eccentric, crazed, rash, thoughtless, giddy, obstinate, bigoted, narrow-minded; foolish, unwise, injudicious, improper, unreasonable, ridiculous, stupid, asinine; ill-conceived, ill-advised, ill-judged, inexpedient, extravagant, frivolous, trivial, useless.

500 sage n wise man, master mind, thinker, philosopher, oracle, luminary, man of learning, expert, authority.

501 fool n simpleton, dolt, dunce, blockhead, nincompoop, ninny, numskull, ignoramus, booby, sap, dunderhead, dunderpate, idiot, natural, oaf, lout, loon, dullard; jester, buffoon, droll, zany, harlequin, clown; imbecile, moron, idiot, cretin.

502 sanity n soundness, mental balance, rationality, reason, sense, clear-headedness, lucidity, coherence, normality, sobriety, (informal) good head.

v be sane, (informal) have one's act together.

adj sane, rational, reasonable, sensible, clearheaded, level-headed, logical, sober, lucid, self-possessed, (informal) together.

503 insanity n disorder, imbalance, derangement, dementia, lunacy, madness, craziness, aberration; frenzy, raving, incoherence, delirium, delusion; (informal) oddity, eccentricity, twist, mania.

v be insane, become insane, lose one's senses, go mad, rave, rant, (informal) lose it.

adj insane, deranged, demented, lunatic, crazed, crazy, maniacal, mad, touched, cracked, unhinged, unsettled, daft, frenzied, possessed, delirious, far gone, wild, flighty, distracted, frantic, mad as a hatter, (informal) crackers, (informal) zonkers, (informal) nuts, (informal) zonko, (informal) weird, (informal) bananas, (informal) kaput.

504 madman n lunatic, maniac, bedlamite, raver, (informal) nut, (informal) weirdo, (informal) crazy; dreamer, romantic, rhapsodist, enthusiast, visionary, seer, fanatic.

505 memory n retention, retentiveness, remembrance, recollection, reminiscence, retrospect; recognition; reminder, hint, suggestion, keepsake, souvenir, memento, token, memorial.

v remember, recall, recollect, call up, call to mind, bring to mind, think back upon, haunt one's thoughts, (informal) flash on; remind, suggest, hint, prompt, summon up, reminisce; retain, keep in mind, bear in mind, memorize, engrave in the mind, learn by heart; keep the memory alive.

adj reminiscent (of), mindful (of); fresh, alive, vivid; unforgotten, enduring, indelible, memorable, never to be forgotten, unforgettable, stirring, eventful.

506 oblivion n forgetfulness, short memory, slippery memory, untrustworthy memory, obliteration of the past, amnesia.

v forget, be forgetful, have a short memory, lose sight of, sink into oblivion; unlearn, efface from the memory, think no more of, consign to oblivion, banish from one's thoughts.

adj oblivious, forgetful, heedless, deaf to the past, insensible; out of mind, unremembered, forgotten, past recollection, buried, sunk into oblivion.

507 expectation *n* expectancy, anticipation, prospect, reckoning, calculation; suspense, waiting; hope, trust, assurance, confidence, reliance, presumption.

v expect, look for, look out for, look forward to, anticipate, await, hope for, wait for, foresee, prepare for, count on, rely on; predict, prognosticate, forecast.

adj expectant, watchful, vigilant, open-eyed, on tenterhooks, on one's toes, ready, in readiness, prepared, (*informal*) all set for; foreseen, long expected, prospective, in view, in sight, on the horizon, impending.

adv expectantly, on the watch, on edge, with bated breath.

508 nonexpectation *n* unforeseen occurrence, surprise, shock, blow, wonder, bolt out of the blue, astonishment; miscalculation, false expectation.

v not expect, be taken by surprise, catch unawares; burst upon, come out of nowhere, drop from the clouds; surprise, startle, stun, stagger, throw off one's guard, astonish.

adj nonexpectant, surprised, unwarned, unaware, off one's guard; unanticipated, unexpected, unlooked for, unforeseen; unheard of, startling; sudden.

adv unexpectedly, abruptly, suddenly, without warning.

509 [failure of expectation] **disappointment** *n* failure, defeat, frustration, unfulfillment, blighted hope, vain expectation, disillusion, (*informal*) come-down.

v be disappointed; disappoint, dash one's hopes, dash one's expectations, balk, jilt, tantalize; dumfound, disillusion, let down.

adj disappointed; disgruntled, disconcerted, aghast.

510 foresight *n* prudence, forethought, prevision, anticipation, precaution; forecast; prescience, fore-knowledge, prospect.

v foresee; look forward to, look ahead, look beyond; look into the future; see one's future, catch the lay of the land; anticipate, expect, assume, surmise, predict, forewarn.

adj anticipatory, prescient; far-sighted, prudent, provident; prospective, expectant.

511 prediction *n* prophecy, forecast, augury, prognostication, foretoken, portent, divination, soothsaying, presage.

v predict, foretel!, prophesy, foresee, forecast, presage, augur, prognosticate, foretoken, portend, divine.

adj prophetic, oracular, portentous, premonitory.

512 omen *n* portent, foreboding, augury, sign, harbinger; sign of the times, symbol, warning.

513 oracle *n* prophet, prophetess, seer, soothsayer, augur, fortune-teller, witch, sibyl, necromancer, sorcerer, clairvoyant, interpreter.

514 supposition *n* assumption, presumption, condition, hypothesis, theory, postulate, proposition, thesis, theorem; conjecture, suggestion, guess, guesswork, suspicion, inkling, speculation.

v suppose, conjecture, surmise, suspect, guess, divine; theorize, speculate, presume, presuppose, assume, predicate; believe, take for granted; propound, put forth, propose, advance, hazard a suggestion, suggest.

adj assumed, given; conjectural, hypothetical, presumptive, theoretical, speculative, suggestive.

515 imagination *n* imaginativeness, fancy, invention, inspiration, creativity, originality, fiction, vision, fantasy, illusion, ideality, castles in the air, dreaming, dream, golden dreams; mental image, conception, idea, notion, thought, conceit, fancy, whim, figment, romance, vision, dream, chimera, shadow, illusion, phantasm, supposition, delusion; verve, vivacity, liveliness, animation.

v imagine, fancy, conceive, dream, idealize; create, originate, think up, devise, invent, coin, fabricate.

adj imaginative, fanciful, original, inventive, creative, visionary, ideal, unreal, illusory, unsubstantial, dreamy, dreamlike, romantic, fantastic, fabulous, chimerical, fantastical; vivacious, lively, animated; imaginable, conceivable, possible, believable; imagined.

II. Communication of Ideas

516 [idea to be conveyed] **meaning** *n* tenor, spirit, gist, trend, idea, purport, significance, signification, sense, import, denotation, conotation, interpretation; intent, intention, aim, object, purpose, design.

thing signified: matter, subject matter, substance, gist, argument.

v mean, signify, denote, conote, express, import, purport; convey, imply, indicate, point to, allude to, touch on, drive at, involve; declare,

affirm, state; intend, aim, design, purpose.

adj meaning; meaningful, pointed, poignant, significant, expressive.

517 meaninglessness *n* unmeaningness, absence of meaning, senselessness, emptiness, empty words, rhetoric, platitude, nonsense, jargon, gibberish, jabber, rant, bombast, (*informal*) hot air; inanity, rigmarole, absurdity, ambiguity.

v mean nothing, jabber, rant, say nothing.

adj meaningless, senseless, nonsensical, inexpressive, vague, trivial, insignificant.

518 intelligibility *n* comprehensibility, clarity, clearness, lucidity, coherence, explicitness, persicuity, precision, plain-speaking.

v be intelligible; render intelligible, clear up, simplify, elucidate, explain; understand, comprehend, take in, catch on, grasp, follow, master.

adj intelligible, understandable, comprehensible, clear, clear as day, lucid, luminous, transparent; plain, distinct, pointed, clear-cut, obvious, explicit, precise; graphic, illustrative, expressive.

519 unintelligibility *n* incomprehensibility, vagueness, obscurity, ambiguity, uncertainty, confusion.

v be unintelligible; render unintelligible, conceal, darken, confuse, perplex, mystify, bewilder.

adj unintelligible, incomprehensible, indecipherable, unfathomable, inexplicable, inscrutable, insoluble, impenetrable; puzzling, enigmatic, obscure, muddy, dim, nebulous, mysterious, (*informal*) strange, (*informal*) weird; inexpressible, incommunicable, ineffable, unutterable.

520 equivocalness *n* ambiguity, uncertainty, questionableness, dubiousness, indeterminateness; double-meaning, word-play, double entendre, pun, play on words, conundrum, riddle, quibble; equivocation, duplicity, prevarication, white lie.

v be equivocal; have two meanings; equivocate, prevaricate.

adj equivocal, ambiguous, uncertain, doubtful, questionable, dubious, indeterminate; duplicitous, enigmatic, double-edged, deceptive, misleading.

521 figure of speech *n* phrase, expression, euphemism, manner of speaking, colloquialism, idiom, image; metaphor, simile, imagery, poetic device, poetics, figures of beauty.

v employ figures of speech; image, speak prettily.

adj figurative, idiomatic, colloquial, colorful, imagistic, poetic, expressive, allusive.

522 interpretation *n* definition, explanation, explication, elucidation, translation; exegesis, exposition, comment, commentary, gloss; solution, answer, meaning.

v interpret, define, explain, explicate, elucidate, translate, shed light on, cast light on, decipher, decode, unravel, disentangle, gloss, annotate, expound, comment upon; construe, understand.

adj explanatory, expository, exegetical, interpretative, interpretive; interpretable, explicable, intelligible.

adv in explanation, that is to say, namely.

523 misinterpretation *n* misapprehension, misconception, misunderstanding, misreading, misconstruction, mistake; misrepresentation, perversion, exaggeration, false coloration, falsification, travesty.

v misinterpret, misapprehend, misconceive, misunderstand, misread, misconstrue, misapply, mistake; misrepresent, pervert, misstate, garble, falsify, distort, travesty, stretch the meaning, twist the meaning.

524 interpreter *n* translator, explainer, expounder, expositor, commentator, annotator, guide, critic; spokesman, speaker, representative.

525 manifestation *n* indication, expression, exposition, demonstration, showing, display, exhibition, declaration; materialization; openness, candor.

v make manifest, show, display, reveal, disclose, open, exhibit, evince, evidence, demonstrate, declare, express, make known; appear, be plain, come to light, materialize; indicate, point out.

adj manifest, evident, obvious, apparent, plain, clear, distinct, patent, open, palpable, visible, unmistakable, conspicuous, explicit; unreserved, downright, frank, plain spoken; barefaced, bold; manifested.

adv manifestly, openly, plainly, above board, in broad daylight, in plain sight.

526 latency *n* dormancy, latentness, quiescence, obscurity, darkness, hidden meaning, obscure meaning, undercurrent, suggestion, concealment; potentiality.

v be latent, lurk, smolder, under-lie.

adj latent, dormant; lurking, secret, cryptic, veiled, hidden; potential; implied, implicit; allusive.

527 information *n* enlightenment, knowledge, news, data, facts, circumstances, situations, intelligence, advice; communication, notification, announcement, record; hint, suggestion, innuendo, inkling, whisper, insinuation.

informant, authority, intelligencer, reporter; informer, eavesdropper, detective, newsmonger; messenger.

guide, guidebook, handbook, manual, map, chart.

v inform, tell, acquaint with, impart to, make acquainted with, apprize, advise, enlighten; communicate, make known, express, mention, let fall, intimate, hint, insinuate, allude to, suggest; announce, report, give an account, disclose; know, learn, find out, get the scent of.

adj informed, communicated, reported, advised, apprized of, acquainted with, enlightened, published, (*informal*) filled in; declarative, expository, communicative.

528 concealment *n* hiding, secretion, ensconcing, sheltering, covering, burying, screening; keeping secret, secrecy, hiding, disguising, veiling, camouflaging, obscuring, dissembling, obfuscation, evasiveness; reticence, reserve, reservation, suppression, silence, secretiveness.

v conceal, hide, secrete, cover, put away, ensconce, bury, screen, shelter, keep out of sight, stow away; keep secret, hide, disguise, veil, cloak, mask, camouflage, obscure, obfuscate, dissemble, be evasive.

adj concealed, hidden, secret, private, privy, confidential, in secret, close, undercover, in hiding, in disguise, covert, mysterious; furtive, stealthy, surreptitious, secretive, evasive, clandestine; reserved, reticent, suppressed, uncommunicative.

adv secretly, in secret, in private, behind closed doors, on the sly; confidentially; stealthily.

529 disclosure *n* revelation, divulgence, exposition, exposure; exposé, uncovering, muckraking; acknowledgment, avowal, confession.

v disclose, discover, uncover, lay open, expose, bring to light, unmask; reveal, make known, divulge, show, tell, unveil, unmask, communicate; let slip, let drop, betray, blurt out;

acknowledge, allow, concede, grant admit, own up, confess.

adj disclosed, revealed.

530 [means of concealment] **ambush** *n* ambuscade, lurking place, trap, snare, pitfall; hiding place, secret place, recess, hole, cubbyhole; screen, cover, shade, blinker, veil, curtain, cloak, cloud; mask, visor, disguise, masquerade.

v ambush, lie in wait for, set a trap for.

531 publication *n* issuance, distribution; announcement, proclamation, promulgation, propagation, pronouncement, declaration, disclosure, divulgence, advertisement, publicity; edition.

v publish, issue, distribute, print; make public, make known, announce, proclaim, promulgate, propagate, circulate, spread, disseminate, declare, disclose, divulge, advertise, publicize, get into print.

adj published; current, public, in circulation, in print, in black and white.

532 news *n* information, intelligence, tidings, report, rumor, scuttlebutt, hearsay, gossip, (*informal*) the word; newsstory, headlines, copy.

reporter, newsmonger, talebearer gossip, tattler, informer.

v transpire, make news, make headlines; be rumored.

adj in the news, in the headlines, current, in circulation, in print.

533 secret *n* mystery; problem, question, difficulty, a confidence; unintelligibility.

adj secret, hidden, concealed, unrevealed, unknown, mysterious; reticent, secretive; private.

534 messenger *n* envoy, emissary, representative, intermediary, go-between, delegate, courier, runner, errand boy; intelligencer, reporter, newsmonger, spokesman, informant; forerunner, harbinger, herald, precursor.

535 affirmation *n* statement, profession, pronouncement, deposition, assertion, declaration; confirmation, ratification, endorsement; swearing, oath, affidavit; emphasis, dogmatism.

v affirm, state, assert, aver, avow, maintain, declare, swear, asseverate, depose, testify, say, pronounce; establish, confirm, ratify, approve, endorse, assent, acknowledge; swear, emphasize.

adj affirmative, declaratory, de-

clarative, positive, assertive, emphatic, dogmatic; confirmative, corroborative, affirming, acquiescent.

536 negation. denial *n* nullification, invalidation.

disputation, confutation, contradiction, qualification; repudiation, rejection, abjuration, disavowal, disclaimer, recantation, retraction, rebuttal.

v negate, nullify, cancel, invalidate.

deny, dispute, controvert, contravene, oppose, gainsay, contradict, rebut; reject, renounce, abjure, disclaim, disavow; recant, revoke; refuse, repudiate, disown.

adj contradictory; negative.

537 teaching *n* instruction, education, pedagogy, pedagogics, edification, tutelage, tutorship; guidance, direction, preparation, schooling, learning, discipline; lesson, lecture, disquisition, discourse, explanation, harangue, homily, sermon, lore; doctrine, dogma, tenet, principle, rule, maxim, article of faith, creed, credo, belief, opinion.

v teach, instruct, edify, educate, inform, enlighten, prepare, discipline, train, drill, tutor, prime, coach, guide, direct, school, indoctrinate, inculcate, infuse, instill, imbue; expound, interpret, lecture, discourse, hold forth, sermonize, moralize.

adj educational, scholastic, academic, pedagogic, pedagogical, didactic; edifying, instructive.

538 misteaching *n* misinformation, misdirection, misguidance, perversion, sophistry, error.

v misteach, misinform, misinstruct, misdirect, misguide, pervert, mislead, misrepresent, confuse, bewilder, lie.

539 learning *n* acquisition of knowledge, acquirements, attainment, mental cultivation, scholarship, erudition, study, inquiry, questioning, search, pursuit of knowledge.

apprenticeship, tutelage, matriculation.

v learn, acquire, gain knowledge, memorize, master, study, grind, cram, (*informal*) book, read, peruse, pore over, wade through, ingest, burn the midnight oil, (*informal*) pull an all-nighter.

adj studious, industrious; scholarly, scholastic, well-read, learned, erudite.

540 teacher *n* instructor, tutor, lecturer, professor, don, master, schoolmaster, guide, counselor, adviser, mentor; preacher, missionary, propagandist.

541 learner *n* scholar, student, pupil, apprentice, novice, neophyte, beginner; disciple, acolyte, follower.

542 school *n* academy, educational institution, college, university, institute, seminary, place of learning.

schoolbook, textbook, text, primer, grammar, reader, workbook.

adj scholastic, academic, collegiate.

543 veracity *n* truthfulness, frankness, truth, sincerity, candor, honesty, probity, fidelity, accuracy.

v speak the truth, (*informal*) level with, (*informal*) be straight with.

adj veracious, true, truthful, sincere, honest, honorable, candid, frank, open, straightforward, honest, scrupulous, punctilious, trustworthy.

544 falsehood *n* falsification, lie, fib, untruth, distortion, deception, misrepresentation, fabrication, fiction, sham; untruthfulness, lying, prevarication, duplicity, double dealing, deceitfulness, equivocation, dissembling, cunning, guile, insincerity, dishonesty, inaccuracy.

v lie, fib, falsify, prevaricate, misrepresent, deceive, (*informal*) come on to, doctor, feign, pretend, play false, dissemble, counterfeit, fabricate.

adj false, untrue, wrong, mistaken, incorrect, erroneous; untruthful, lying, mendacious, dishonest, deceitful, treacherous, faithless, insincere, hypocritical, disingenuous, unfaithful, cunning, perfidious, two-faced, recreant; deceptive, misleading, fallacious, spurious, fraudulent, bogus, phony, sham, counterfeit.

545 deception *n* deceiving, guiling, falseness, untruthfulness; artifice, sham, cheat, imposture, deceit, treachery, subterfuge, stratagem, ruse, hoax, fraud, trick, wile, snare, trap, illusion, delusion.

v deceive, mislead, lead astray, take in, delude, cheat, cozen, dupe, gull, fool, bamboozle, hoodwink, (*informal*) con, trick, double-cross, defraud, outwit; entrap, ensnare, betray.

adj deceptive, misleading, delusive, illusory, fallacious, specious, untrue, false, deceitful; tricky, cunning, insidious.

546 untruth *n* falsehood, fib, lie, fiction, story, tale, tall tale, fabrication, fable, forgery, invention.

v make believe, pretend, feign, sham, fib, lie.

adj untrue, false, trumped up, unfounded, invented, fictitious, fabulous.

547 dupe *n* gull, pigeon, laughingstock, greenhorn, fool, sucker, puppet, (*informal*) nebbish.

v be deceived, be the dupe of, fall into a trap, go for the bait, bite, swallow.

adj credulous, gullible, unsuspecting, trusting.

548 deceiver *n* dissembler, hypocrite, sophist, liar, (*informal*) fast talker, storyteller, (*informal*) faker, (*informal*) phony, fraud, (*informal*) four-flusher, (*informal*) shyster, confidence man, con man, cheat, swindler, imposter, pretender, humbug, adventurer, adventuress, serpent, snake in the grass.

549 exaggeration *n* overstatement, hyperbole, extravagance, coloring, coloration, embroidery; yarn, tale, (*informal*) shaggy dog story, (*informal*) fish story; tempest in a teacup, much ado about nothing, puffery, rant.

v exaggerate, magnify, amplify, expand, overestimate, overstate; heighten, color, embroider, puff up, fill out.

adj exaggerated, overwrought, bombastic, magniloquent, hyperbolic, fabulous, extravagant, preposterous.

550 [means of communication] **indication** *n* symbolism, semiology; sign, symbol, index, indicator, pointer, note, token, symptom; type, mark, figure, emblem, insigne, cipher, device, representation; signal, beacon, alarm; feature, trait, characteristic, peculiarity, quality, earmark, cast; gesture, gesticulation, motion, cue, hint, clue, scent.

v indicate, denote, betoken, designate, signify, represent, stand for, typify, symbolize; note, mark, stamp; label, ticket; make a sign, signalize, signal, gesture, gesticulate; sign, seal, attest, underline, underscore, call attention to.

adj indicative, indicatory; connotative, denotative, typical, representative, symbolic, symbolical, characteristic, significant, emblematic.

551 record *n* trace, vestige, relic, remains; monument, achievement; account, chronicles, annals, history, note, register, memorandum, document, diary, log, journal, ledger.

v record, set down, place in the record, chronicle, enter, register, enter, list, enroll; commemorate, celebrate.

552 [suppression of sign] **obliteration** *n* erasure, cancelation, deletion, blot, effacement, extinction.

v obliterate, efface, expunge, erase, cancel, delete, blot out, rub out, strike out, wipe out, leave no trace.

adj obliterated, erased, blotted out; unrecorded.

553 recorder *n* notary, clerk, registrar, register, secretary, scribe, bookkeeper; annalist, historian, historiographer, chronicler, biographer, journalist, antiquarian, memorialist.

554 representation *n* depiction, imitation, illustration, delineation, expression, imagery, portraiture, figuration.

v represent, delineate, depict, portray, picture, figure, describe, trace, copy, illustrate, symbolize; personate, personify, play, mimic.

adj representative, imitative, illustrative, figurative, symbolic, descriptive.

555 misrepresentation *n* distortion, exaggeration, misfiguration, falsification, bad likeness, caricature.

v misrepresent, distort, overdraw, exaggerate, falsify, caricature, daub.

556 painting *n* fine art, picture, depiction, representation, pictorialization, delineation, design, drawing, likeness, copy, imitation, fake, image.

art gallery, picture gallery, studio.

v paint, design, limn, draw, sketch, pencil, color; depict, represent.

adj pictorial, picturesque.

557 sculpture *n* carving, modeling, statuary; ceramics, potting.

statue, statuette, bust; cast, mold.

v sculpt, fashion, cast, mold, model, chisel, carve, cut, shape, form, figure, hew.

558 engraving *n* etching, chiseling, incising, plate engraving, photoengraving.

v engrave, grave, carve, incise, chisel, hatch, etch, stipple, print.

559 artist *n* painter, drawer, sketcher, designer, draftsman, cartoonist, caricaturist, sculptor, engraver.

560 language *n* speech, phraseology, style, expression, diction, jargon, dialect, terminology, vernacular, lingo, tongue.

literature, letters, belles lettres, humanities, classics, dead language.

linguist.

v express, say, express by words.

adj lingual, linguistic; dialectic, vernacular, current, colloquial, slangy, polyglot, literary.

561 letter *n* character, hieroglyph, symbol, alphabet, consonant, vowel.

syllable, monosyllable, dissyllable, polysyllable.

spelling, orthography; phonetics; cipher, code; monogram, anagram.

v spell.

adj literal; alphabetical; syllabic; phonetic.

562 word *n* term, symbol, name, part of speech.

dictionary, vocabulary, lexicon, index, thesaurus, glossary.

etymology, derivation, philology, terminology, lexicography.

adj literal, verbal.

563 neology *n* neologism, new-fangled expression, (*informal*) hip expression, barbarism, corruption.

neologist, word coiner.

v coin words.

adj neologic, neological; colloquial, slang, (*informal*) hip, cant, barbarous.

564 nomenclature *n* naming; name, appellation, designation, epithet, nickname, (*informal*) moniker, (*informal*) handle, label, title, head, heading; style, proper name, surname, namesake.

v name, call, term, designate, denominate, style, entitle, dub, christen, baptize, nickname, characterize, specify, label.

adj titular, nominal.

565 misnomer *n* misnaming, malapropism; sobriquet, nickname, assumed name, alias, pen name, stage name, pseudonym, nom de plume, nom de guerre.

v misname, miscall, misterm; take an assumed name.

adj misnamed; soi-disant, self-styled; so-called.

566 phrase *n* expression, set phrase, turn of speech, idiom, tag phrase, figure of speech, euphemism, motto; phraseology.

v phrase, express, put into words, find the right words, arrange in words, voice, vocalize.

567 grammar *n* rules of language, usage, forms, style, formal features, constructions, parts of speech; accidence, syntax, inflection, case, declension, conjugation; grammar book, primer, rulebook.

grammarian.

adj grammatical, syntactic, syntactical.

568 solecism *n* ungrammatical usage, bad grammar, faulty grammar, error, slip, inconsistency, impropriety.

v solecize.

adj ungrammatical, incorrect, inaccurate, faulty, inconsistent, improper.

569 style *n* diction, phraseology, wording; composition, mode of expression, choice of words, command of language, mode, manner, method, approach; kind, form, appearance, character, touch, characteristic, mark, signature, imprint, (*informal*) name.

v style, compose, express by words; write.

adj stylistic; characteristic; expressive.

570 perspicuity *n* clearness, clarity, lucidity, plainness, plain-speaking, distinctness, explicitness, exactness, intelligibility.

adj perspicuous, pellucid, clear, lucid, intelligible, plain, distinct, explicit, exact, definite, unequivocal.

571 obscurity *n* unintelligibility, involution, confusion, indistinctness, indefiniteness, ambiguity, vagueness, inexactness, impenetrability.

adj obscure, involved, confused, unintelligible, impenetrable, indefinite, vague, inexact, hidden, dark.

572 conciseness *n* brevity, summary, abridgment, terseness, pithiness, compression, tightness.

v be concise, condense, abridge, abstract, compress, tighten; come to the point.

adj concise, brief, compendious, short, terse, laconic, pithy, trenchant, succinct, compact, tight.

adv concisely, briefly, summarily, in short.

573 diffuseness *n* long-windedness, verbosity, wordiness, verbiage, looseness, exuberance, redundancy, profuseness, richness.

v be diffuse, enlarge, amplify, expand, inflate; meander, digress, ramble, run on and on.

adj diffuse, profuse, wordy, verbose, copious, exuberant; lengthy, long-winded, protracted, prolix, diffusive, roundabout; digressive, discursive, loose.

574 vigor *n* power, force, boldness, spirit, verve, heart, ardor, enthusiasm, raciness, glow, fire, warmth; loftiness, elevation, gravity, sublimity; eloquence, strong language.

adj vigorous, nervous, powerful, forcible, forceful, trenchant, biting, incisive, impressive; spirited, lively, glowing, sparkling, racy, bold, pungent, pithy; lofty, elevated, sublime, grand, weighty; eloquent, vehement, impassioned, passionate.

575 feebleness *n* weakness, enervation, frailty, faintness.

adj feeble, tame, weak, meager, vapid, insipid; trashy, poor, dull, dry, languid; prosy, prosaic, slight; careless, loose, slip-shod, wishy-washy, sloppy, slovenly; puerile, childish.

576 plainness *n* simplicity, homeliness, restraint, severity.

v speak plainly, speak directly, come straight to the point, be straightforward, not beat around the bush.

adj plain, simple, homely, homey, unadorned, unvarnished, neat, homespun; severe, chaste, pure.

adv in plain terms, in plain English; point-blank.

577 ornament *n* floridness, ornateness, elegance, grandiloquence, magniloquence, rhetorical flourish, declamation, rhetoric, flourish, fancy talk, (*informal*) big words; pretention, inflation, bombast, fustian, rant, fine writing, fine speaking.

v ornament, overcharge, talk big, talk fancy.

adj ornate, ornamented, beautified, florid, rich, flowery, fancy; euphuistic, euphemistic; sonorous, high sounding, inflated, swelling, turgid, pompous, pedantic, stilted, high-flown, sententious, rhetorical, declamatory, grandiose, grandiloquent, magniloquent, bombastic, flashy.

578 elegance *n* taste, good taste, propriety, correctness; lucidity, purity, grace, ease; gracefulness, euphony, gentility, cultivation, polish, refinement.

purist, classicist.

adj elegant, polished, classic, classical, fine, tasteful, proper, correct; chaste, pure, graceful, easy, readable, fluent, flowing, unaffected, natural, mellifluous, euphonious, felicitous, neat, well put.

579 inelegance *n* tastelessness, vulgarity, impropriety; bad diction, awkwardness, stiffness, turgidity, abruptness; barbarism, solecism, slang, mannerism, affectation, formality.

adj inelegant, graceless, ungraceful, harsh, abrupt, dry, stiff, cramped, formal, forced, labored, awkward, ponderous, turgid; artificial, mannered, affected, euphuistic; tasteless, barbarous, uncouth, rude, crude, vulgar.

580 voice *n* vocality, intonation, articulation, enunciation, distinctness, clearness, delivery; accent, accentuation, emphasis, stress; utterance, vocalization.

v voice, speak, utter; articulate, enunciate, vocalize, intone, pronounce, accent, accentuate, deliver.

adj vocal, oral; articulate, distinct, euphonious, melodious.

581 muteness *n* dumbness, silence, speechlessness; aphasia.

v be mute, be silent, be dumb; silence, muzzle, muffle, suppress, smother, gag, strike dumb, dumfound.

adj mute, silent, dumb, mum, tongue-tied; voiceless, speechless.

582 speech *n* talk, parlance, locution, conversation, parley, communication, prattle; talk, oration, address, discourse, lecture, recitation, sermon, harangue, tirade; oratory, eloquence, rhetoric, declamation.

speaker, spokesman, mouthpiece, orator, rhetorician.

v speak, utter, talk, voice, converse, communicate, pronounce, say, articulate; declaim, harangue, stump, spout, rant, lecture, sermonize, discourse, expatiate, soliloquize, address.

adj oral; talkative, conversational; declamatory.

583 [imperfect speech] **inarticulateness** *n* stammering, hesitation, muttering, mumbling, stuttering; reticence, taciturnity; speech impediment, aphasia.

v be inarticulate, stammer, hesitate, mutter, mumble, slur one's words, garble, sputter, hem and haw, whisper, croak, crack.

adj inarticulate, tongue-tied, speechless, voiceless, hesitant, reticent, taciturn.

584 loquacity *n* loquaciousness, volubility, talkativeness, verbosity, garrulity, volubility; chatter, jabber, prattle, twaddle.

talker, chatterer, chatterbox, babbler, ranter.

v be loquacious, talk a mile a minute, pour forth, prate, chatter, babble, gab, run off at the mouth, jabber, jaw, gush.

adj loquacious, voluble, talkative, verbose, wordy, garrulous, chatty, chattering, glib, fluent, effusive.

585 taciturnity *n* silence, muteness, reserve, reticence, uncommunicativeness.

v be silent, keep silence, keep quiet, hold one's tongue, say nothing.

adj taciturn, silent, mute, mum, reserved, reticent, guarded, uncommunicative, close-mouthed, quiet.

586 public address *n* allocution, speech, formal speech, address, invocation.

v speak to, address; invoke, hail, salute; lecture, pronounce.

587 response *n.* See answer 462.

588 conversation *n* interlocution, colloquy, confabulation, talk, (*informal*) rap, discourse, verbal interchange, dialog, oral communication; chat, chit, chit-chat, small talk, table talk, idle talk, prattle, gossip; conference, parley, interview, audience, *tête-à-tête*, council, congress; palaver, debate, discussion.

v converse, confabulate, talk together, hold a conversation, carry on a conversation, engage in a discussion; bandy words, chat, chit-chat, gossip, tattle, prate; discourse with, confer with; talk it over, (*informal*) rap, (*informal*) chew the fat.

adj conversational, conversable; chatty, gossipy.

589 soliloquy *n* monolog, apostrophe, aside.

v soliloquize, talk to oneself, think out loud, apostrophize.

590 writing *n* chirography, penmanship, calligraphy, hand, script, longhand, shorthand, stenography; handwriting, signature, mark, hand; manuscript, MS., document, script, writ, author's copy, copy, original; composition, authorship, work, opus, book, volume, tome, publication, article, poetry, verse, literature.

writer, author, scribe, scrivener, clerk, copyist, secretary.

v write, pen, copy, transcribe; print, scribble, scrawl, scratch; compose, draw out, write down, set down, put pen to paper, take up the pen, take pen in hand.

adj written, in writing, in black and white.

591 printing *n* lettering, typography; type; composition, print, letterpress, text, matter; copy, impression, proof.

printer, compositor, reader, proofreader, copyeditor.

v print, compose; go to press, publish, bring out, issue.

adj typographical, printed.

592 correspondence *n* letter, epistle, missive, note, post card; communication, dispatch, bulletin, circular.

v correspond, communicate, write to, send a letter.

adj epistolary; in touch with, in communication with.

593 book *n* booklet; writing, work, volume, tome, opus, tract, treatise, brochure, handbook; novel, story; script, libretto; publication.

writer, author, essayist, editor; bookseller, publisher; librarian, bibliophile, bookworm.

594 description *n* narration, account, recounting, telling, recital, relation, statement, report, record; delineation, portrayal, characterization, representation, depiction, sketch, vignette.

v describe, set forth, narrate, account, recount, recite, rehearse, tell, relate, detail; picture, delineate, portray, characterize, limn, represent, depict.

595 dissertation *n* treatise, essay, thesis, theme, tract, discourse, disquisition, investigation, study, discussion, exposition; commentary, critique, criticism, review, article, commentator, critic, essayist, reviewer.

v discuss a subject, treat, examine, comment, criticize, explain.

596 compendium *n* abstract, précis, epitome, analysis, digest, compendium, brief, abridgment, abbreviation, condensation, summary; draft, note, synopsis, outline, syllabus, contents, prospectus; compilation, collection, album, anthology; extracts, cuttings, fragments, pieces; list, inventory, survey.

v abridge, abstract, précis, epitomize, summarize; abbreviate, shorten, condense, compress; compile, collect, note; list, inventory, survey.

adj compendious, synoptic, analytic, analytical.

597 poetry *n* poetics; verse, poesy, versification, rhyming, rhymes, making verses, metrics; doggerel.

poet, laureate, bard, troubadour, minstrel, versifier, rhymer, sonneteer, rhapsodist, poetaster.

v poeticize, sing, versify, rhyme, make verses, compose.

adj poetic, poetical, rhythmic, metrical, lyrical, tuneful, musical; beautiful, lovely, tender, sensitive.

598 prose *n* writing, fiction, imaginative writing, narrative prose.

v write prose.

adj prosy, unpoetic, rhymeless; prosaic, dull, flat, matter-of-fact, unimaginative, commonplace, humdrum, pedestrian, trite, hackneyed, mediocre, stock, ordinary; fictional.

599 the drama *n* the stage, the theater; theatricals, dramaturgy, playwriting; play, drama, stage-play, opera.

performance, acting, representation, impersonation, stage business, actor, actress, player, performer, thespian.

theater, playhouse, operahouse, amphitheater.

dramatist, playwriter, playwright.

v dramatize, act, play, perform, personate, act a part, put on the stage, enact.

adj dramatic, theatrical, histrionic, stagy.

Class V
Voluntary Powers
I. Individual Volition

600 will n volition, free will, freedom; choice, wish, desire, pleasure, disposition, inclination; intent, purpose, option; determination, resolution, resoluteness, decision, forcefulness; force of will, will power, self-control.

v will, see fit, think fit, decide, decree, determine, direct, command, bid.

adj willful, voluntary, volitional, intentional; free, optional, discretionary; autocratic, obdurate, adamant.

adv willfully, voluntarily, at will; of one's own accord, intentionally, deliberately.

601 necessity n obligation, compulsion, subjection; fate, destiny, fatality; inevitability, inevitableness, unavoidability, unavoidableness, irresistibility; requirement, requisite, demand; instinct, impulse.

v be obligated, be obliged, be fated; necessitate, compel, subject; require.

adj necessary, essential, requisite, needful; inevitable, unavoidable, ineluctable, irresistible, inexorable; compulsory; involuntary, instinctive, automatic, blind, mechanical.

adv necessarily, of necessity, willy nilly.

602 willingness n disposition, inclination, leaning, propensity, frame of mind, liking, humor, mood, vein, bent, penchant, aptitude; geniality, cordiality, good will; alacrity, readiness, eagerness, enthusiasm; assent, compliance, agreement.

v be willing, incline, lean to, mind, hold to, cling to; desire; acquiesce, assent, comply; find one's way to, give it a shot, (informal) take a swing at, (informal) lay into.

adj willing, fain, favorable, content, well disposed; ready, earnest, eager, desirous; genial, cordial.

adv willingly, freely, with pleasure, with all one's heart, graciously.

603 unwillingness n indisposition, disinclination, reluctance, dislike; aversion, indifference, slowness, lack of readiness, obstinacy; scrupulousness, hesitation, qualm, shrinking, holding back, recoil; averseness, dissent, refusal.

v be unwilling, dislike; demur, hesitate, shrink from, swerve, recoil; dissent, refuse.

adj unwilling, loath, reluctant, averse; laggard, backward, slow, slack, indifferent; scrupulous, hesitant.

adv unwillingly, grudgingly, against one's will, under protest.

604 resolution n determination, will, decision, strength of mind, resolve, firmness, energy, manliness, vigor, resoluteness; pluck, zeal, devotion; self-control, self-command, self-possession, self-reliance, self-restraint, self-denial; tenacity, perseverance, obstinacy, (informal) gumption.

v be resolute, resolve, will, determine, decide, make a resolution, conclude, fix, bring to a crisis, take a decisive step; stand firm, insist upon, make a point of, not give an inch.

adj resolute, firm, steadfast, resolved, purposeful, fixed, inflexible, bold, game, indomitable, relentless, tenacious, gritty, stern, irrevocable, obstinate.

adv resolutely, in earnest, earnestly, manfully.

604a perseverance n persistence, tenacity, resolution, doggedness, determination, steadfastness, indefatigability, pluck, stamina, backbone.

v persevere, persist, continue, keep on, last, stick it out, hang in there.

adj persevering, constant, steady, steadfast, persistent, tenacious, resolute, dogged, indefatigable, indomitable, staunch, true, game, (informal) tough.

605 irresolution n indecision, indetermination, instability, uncertainty; hesitation, hesitancy, vacillation, oscillation, changeableness, fluctuation, fickleness, weakness, frailty, timidity, cowardice.

v be irresolute, dawdle, dilly-dally, shilly-shally, hesitate, falter, waver, vacillate, change, fluctuate, blow hot and cold.

adj irresolute, indecisive, indeterminate, unstable, uncertain; hesitant, changeable, capricious, fickle, frail, feeble, weak, timid, (informal) soft, cowardly.

606 obstinacy n doggedness, persistence, pertinacity, resolution, intractability, firmness, immovability, inflexibility, obduracy, willfulness, perver-

sity, stubborness, mulishness; uncontrollability, wildness.

fixed idea, *idée fixe*, fanaticism, zealotry, infatuation, monomania; bigotry, intolerance, dogmatism.

bigot, dogmatist, zealot, fanatic.

v be obstinate, persist, die hard, fight, stick to an idea.

adj obstinate, dogged, persistent, pertinacious, resolute, intractable, firm, refractory, headstrong, willful, inflexible, immovable, perverse, stubborn, mulish, pig-headed; wayward, unruly, incorrigible, uncontrollable, wild; fanatic, zealous, monomaniacal; intolerant, dogmatic, arbitrary.

607 recantation *n* tergiversation, renunciation, abjuration, retraction, defection, apostasy, disavowal, revocation, reversal.

turncoat, apostate, renegade, deserter.

v recant, change one's mind, abjure, retract, renounce, disavow, revoke, defect, change sides.

adj changeful, irresolute, slippery, timeserving.

608 caprice *n* fancy, humor, whim, quirk, freak, fad, vagary, prank.

v be capricious.

adj capricious, erratic, eccentric, fitful, inconsistent, fanciful, whimsical, crotchety, freakish, wayward, wanton; contrary, captious, unreasonable, arbitrary, fickle; frivolous.

609 choice *n* selection, decision, pick, choosing, election, option, alternative, preference, predilection, desire.

v choose, select, elect, make a choice, prefer, pick, cull, decide.

adj optional, discretional, preferential.

609a neutrality. absence of choice *n* neutrality, indifference; indecision, irresolution.

no choice, first come first served.

v be neutral, have no preference, waive, abstain.

take what's offered.

adj neutral, indifferent; indecisive, irresolute.

610 rejection *n* refusal, repudiation, renunciation; exclusion, elimination.

v reject, refuse, repudiate, decline, deny, rebuff, repel, renounce; discard, throw away, exclude, eliminate; jettison.

611 predetermination *n* premeditation, predeliberation, foregone conclusion; resolve, intention; fate, predestination, destiny.

v predetermine, predestine, premeditate, resolve beforehand, calculate.

adj aforethought; foregone.

adv advisedly, deliberately, intentionally.

612 impulse *n* sudden thought, flash, spurt, inspiration, improvisation.

v improvise, extemporize; flash on, hit on, come up with, pull out of a hat, pull out of the air; say what comes to mind.

adj impulsive, impromptu, spontaneous; extemporaneous.

adv extempore, extemporaneously; impromptu, offhand, impulsively.

613 habit *n* addiction, disposition, tendency, bent, wont; custom, prescription, practice, way, usage, wont, manner; prevalence, observance; conventionalism, conventionality, mode, fashion, vogue, conformity; rule, precedent, routine, rut, groove.

v habituate, inure, harden, season; accustom, familiarize; acclimate, accommodate; cling to, adhere to, acquire a habit, fall into a rut; be habitual, come into use, become a habit, take root.

adj habitual, customary, prescriptive, usual, general, ordinary, common, frequent, everyday, familiar, trite, commonplace, conventional, regular, set, stock, fixed, permanent; prevalent, current, fashionable; addictive.

adv habitually, as usual, as things go, as the world goes; as a rule, for the most part, generally.

614 disuse *n* desuetude, disusage, lack of practice.

v be unaccustomed, break a habit; disuse.

adj unaccustomed; unusual, original.

615 motive *n* reason, ground, principle, mainspring, purpose, cause, occasion, influence, impulse, instigation, spur, stimulus, incitement, incentive, inducement, consideration, temptation, motivation; intention, ulterior motive.

v motivate, induce, move, inspire, put up to, prompt, stimulate, spur, excite, arouse, rouse, incite, instigate; influence, sway, incline, dispose, lead, persuade, prevail upon, enlist, engage, invite, court, tempt, charm.

adj suasive, persuasive, seductive, attractive, provocative.

615a absence of motive *n* caprice, chance, absence of design.

v have no motive.

adj capricious, without rhyme or reason.

adv capriciously.

616 dissuasion *n* expostulation, remonstrance, deprecation, discouragement, damper, restraint, curb, check.

v dissuade, cry out against, remonstrate, expostulate, warn, disincline, indispose, shake, discourage, dishearten, disenchant; deter, hold back, restrain, repel, turn aside, wean from, damp, cool, chill, blunt.

adj dissuasive.

617 [ostensible motive, ground, or reason] **plea** *n* pretext, allegation, excuse; pretense, shallow excuse, lame excuse, makeshift.

v plead, allege, excuse, make a pretext of, pretend.

adj ostensible, alleged.

adv ostensibly, under the pretense of.

618 good *n* benefit, interest, service, behalf, advantage, improvement, gain, boot, profit, harvest; boon, blessing, good luck, prize, good fortune, windfall, godsend; prosperity, happiness, goodness.

v benefit, serve, profit, advantage.

adj commendable; useful, good, beneficial, advantageous.

619 evil *n* ill, harm, hurt, mischief, nuisance; damage, loss; disadvantage, drawback; disaster, accident, casualty, mishap, misfortune; calamity, catastrophe, tragedy, ruin, destruction, adversity; mental suffering, pain, anguish; outrage, wrong, injury, foul play.

v be in trouble; harm, hurt, injure, ruin, destroy, torture.

adj evil, hurtful, injurious, harmful; disastrous, catastrophic, cataclysmic, tragic, ruinous.

620 intention *n* intent, purpose, project, undertaking, design, ambition, contemplation, view, proposal, meaning; object, aim, end, destination, mark, point, goal, target, prey, quarry, game; decision, determination, resolve, resolution, settled purpose.

v intend, mean, design, purpose, propose, contemplate, plan, expect, mediate, calculate, project, aim for, aim at, aspire at.

adj intentional, advised, express, determinate, bound for, bent upon, in view, in prospect.

adv intentionally, advisedly, wittingly, knowingly, purposely, on purpose, by design, pointedly; deliberately.

621 [absence of design] **chance** *n* destiny, lot, fate, luck, good luck, turn, (*informal*) break, (*informal*) jinx, fortune; speculation, venture, stake, shot in the dark, fluke; wager, gambling, betting.

gambler, gamester, adventurer.

v chance, chance it, tempt fate, speculate, risk, venture, hazard, stake, wager, bet, place a bet, gamble, play for.

adj unintentional, accidental, random; fortuitous, lucky; speculative, venturesome.

adv unintentionally, unwittingly.

622 pursuit *n* pursuance, enterprise, undertaking, business, adventure, essay, quest, search.

v pursue, prosecute, follow, do, engage in, undertake, endeavor, seek, aim at, fish for, press on, go after, chase.

adj in quest of, in pursuit of.

623 avoidance *n* evasion, flight, escape, retreat, recoil, departure; abstention, abstinence, forbearance, inaction.

avoider, shirker, quitter, truant; fugitive, refugee, runaway, deserter.

v avoid, shun, steer clear of, keep clear of, evade, elude, shirk, fly from, turn away from; abstain, refrain, eschew, leave alone, not get involved; shrink, hold back, retire, recoil, flinch, blink, shy, dodge, beat a retreat, turn tail, run for one's life, head for the hills, take flight, beat it out; desert, sneak off, shuffle off, slink away, steal away, slip, sneak, bolt, abscond.

adj elusive, evasive, escapist, fugitive.

624 relinquishment *n* surrender, resignation, yielding, waiver, waiving, abdication, leaving, desertion, withdrawal, secession, abandonment, renunciation.

v relinquish, surrender, give up, resign, yield, cede, waive, forswear, forgo, abdicate, leave, forsake, desert, renounce, quit, abandon, let go, resign, (*informal*) throw in the towel, call it quits, (*informal*) hang it up.

625 business *n* occupation, trade, craft, profession, calling, employment, vocation, pursuit; affair, matter, concern, transaction, undertaking; function, duty, office, position, part, role, capacity.

v employ oneself, undertake, turn one's hand to; be at work on, be engaged in, be occupied with.

adj businesslike; workaday, professional, official, functional; busy.

626 plan *n* scheme, plot, stratagem,

policy, procedure, project, formula, method, system, organization, design, contrivance, device; drawing, sketch, draft, map, chart, diagram, representation; intrigue, cabal, conspiracy.

planner, designer, organizer, schemer, strategist, intriguer.

v plan, arrange, frame, scheme, plot, design, devise, contrive, invent, concoct, hatch; project, forecast; systematize, organize, cast, recast, lay groundwork.

adj procedural, formulaic, methodological, systematic, organizational; conspiratorial; strategic.

627 [path] **method** *n* road, procedure, way, means, manner, fashion, technique, process, course, route, track, beat, tack; door, gateway, channel, passage, avenue, means of access, approach.

adv how, in what way, in what manner; by what mode; one way or another, after this fashion.

628 mid-course *n* middle way, middle course, mean, golden mean; compromise, (*informal*) six of one and half a dozen of another, half measures, neutrality.

v steer a middle course, go straight; compromise, go half way, make a compromise.

adj moderate, midway; neutral, impartial.

629 circuit *n* roundabout way, digression, detour, loop, winding.

v go round about, make a circuit, detour, wind around, circle around; deviate, digress.

adj circuitous, indirect, roundabout; zigzag.

adv in a roundabout way, by an indirect course, indirectly.

630 requirement *n* requisite, requisition, need, necessity, wants, claim, demand, prerequisite; mandate, order, command, directive, injunction, charge, claim, precept.

v require, need, call for, have occasion for, necessitate, obligate; demand, request, need, order, enjoin, direct, ask.

adj requisite, necessary, essential, indispensable, needful; urgent, exigent, instant, crying.

adv of necessity.

631 instrumentality *n* mediation, intervention, medium, intermedium, vehicle, hand; aid; subservience.

go-between, intermediary, minister.

v mediate, minister, intervene; be instrumental, aid.

adj instrumental, useful, serviceable; intermediary, intermediate.

adv through, by, whereby, thereby, by the agency of, by dint of, by means of.

632 means *n* resources, wherewithal, way, ways and means, know how, ability; agency, method, approach; capital, provisions.

v have the means, find the means, possess the means.

adj instrumental.

adv by means of; herewith, therewith; wherewithal.

633 instrument *n* tool, implement, utensil, machinery, equipment.

adj instrumental; mechanical.

634 substitute *n* deputy, alternate, understudy, stand-in, proxy, (*informal*) sub, replacement.

v to substitute for, sub.

635 materials *n* raw materials, resources, stuff, stock, staples, supplies.

636 store *n* stock, fund, mine, supply, reserve, reservoir, (*informal*) stash; accumulation, hoard, storing, storage.

v store, put aside, lay away; store up, put up, hoard away, accumulate, amass, garner; reserve, husband, (*informal*) stash, hold back.

adj in store, in reserve, spare.

637 provision *n* supply, grist, resources, store, provender, stock, food; catering, providing, purveying, purveyance, supplying.

v make provision, provide, lay in, lay in a stock, lay in a store; supply, furnish, purvey, provision, cater, stock, store, replenish.

638 waste *n* consumption, expenditure, dissipation, diminution, decline, emaciation, exhaustion, loss, destruction, decay, impairment; misuse, prodigality, wasting; ruin, devastation, spoliation, desolation.

v waste, consume, spend, throw out, expend, squander, misuse, misspend, dissipate; destroy, wear away, erode, eat away, reduce, wear down, exhaust, enfeeble, wear out.

adj wasteful, prodigal, spendthrift; destructive; wasted, gone to waste.

639 sufficiency *n* adequacy, enough, competence.

v be sufficient, suffice, do, just do, satisfy; have enough.

adj sufficient, enough, adequate, ample, up to the mark, competent, commensurate, satisfactory.

adv sufficiently, amply.

640 insufficiency *n* inadequacy, incompetence, incompleteness, deficiency, imperfection, shortcoming; paucity, scarcity, dearth; dole, pittance; emptiness, poorness, depletion, flaccidity.

v be insufficient, not suffice, not do, fall short of, (*informal*) not cut it; want, lack, need, require, be in want.

adj insufficient, inadequate, too little, not enough, incomplete, deficient, imperfect, wanting, short, scarce, meager, poor, thin, sparse, scant; incompetent, perfunctory.

641 redundance *n* superfluity, superabundance, too much, too many, exuberance, profuseness, profusion, plenty, repletion, plethora, congestion, surfeit, overdose, overflow; excess, surplus; repetition, verbosity.

v superabound, overabound, swarm, overflow, run over, run riot, overrun, overdose, overload, overdo, overwhelm; supersaturate, gorge, glut, load, drench, inundate, deluge, flood; choke, cloy, suffocate, pile on, lay on thick, lavish.

adj redundant, exuberant, inordinate, superabundant, excessive, overmuch, replete, profuse, lavish; exorbitant, extravagant, overweening, (*informal*) much; superfluous, unnecessary, needless, over and above, spare, duplicate; repetitious, verbose.

adv over and above, over much, out of proportion, beyond bounds, over one's head.

642 importance *n* consequence, substance, weight, moment, prominence, consideration, significance, import, concern, emphasis, interest, momentousness, weightiness; gravity, seriousness, solemnity; pressure, urgency, stress.

v be important, deserve consideration, be worthy of notice, merit attention; attach importance, ascribe importance, value, care for, set store by; import, signify, matter, boot, carry weight; accentuate, emphasize, lay stress on; mark, underline, underscore.

adj important, consequential, weighty, momentous, prominent, considerable, significant, notable, salient; grave, serious, earnest, grand, solemn, impressive, commanding, imposing; urgent, pressing, critical, crucial, paramount, essential, vital, prime, primary, principal, all-important, capital, foremost, of vital importance; superior, considerable; significant, telling, trenchant, emphatic.

643 unimportance *n* insignificance, immateriality, triviality, paltriness,

indifference, nothing, trifling; trumpery, trash, rubbish, frippery, chaff bauble, trifle.

v be unimportant, not matter, matter little, signify little; make light of.

adj unimportant, of little account, of small importance, immaterial, unessential, nonessential, inconsequential, insignificant, inconsiderable, so-so; commonplace, ordinary, uneventful, mere, common; trifling, trivial, slight, slender, light, flimsy, shallow; frivolous, petty, niggling, piddling; poor, paltry, pitiful, sorry, mean, meager, shabby, beggarly, worthless, cheap, tawdry, trashy, gimmicky; unworthy of consideration, unworthy of notice; useless, of no account.

644 utility *n* usefulness, efficacy, helpfulness, service, use, stead, avail, help, aid; applicability, value, worth, productiveness.

v be useful, avail, serve, perform, help, aid, benefit; act a part, discharge a function, stand one in good stead.

adj useful, serviceable, functional, advantageous, valuable, productive, profitable, helpful, effectual, effective, efficacious, beneficial, salutary; applicable, available, practical, practicable, workable.

645 inutility *n* uselessness, inefficacy, ineptitude, inaptitude, inadequacy, inefficiency, unfruitfulness, futility, worthlessness, hopelessness.

v be useless, be of no help.

adj useless, unavailing, futile, inutile, fruitless, vain, ineffectual, profitless, bootless, valueless, worthless, hopeless; unserviceable, unusable, inoperative.

646 expedience *n* expediency, fitness, utility, suitability, profitability, advisability, propriety, appropriateness, desirability; opportunism, pragmatism, realism.

v be expedient, suit, befit, suit the occasion.

adj expedient, advantageous, opportune, fit, suitable, convenient, profitable, worthwhile, advisable, meet, proper, becoming, appropriate, desirable.

647 inexpedience *n* inexpediency, impropriety, unfitness, unsuitability, inappropriateness, undesirability; inconvenience, impracticality.

v be inexpedient, be inconvenient, hinder.

adj inexpedient, inopportune, unfit, unsuitable, disadvantageous, discommodious, unadvisable, unseemly, improper, unworkable, impractical,

inconvenient, unprofitable, useless, worthless.

648 [good qualities] **goodness** *n* virtue, excellence, merit, value, worth; perfection, eminence, superiority, masterpiece, *chef d'oeuvre*, prime, flower, cream, elite, pick, pick of the litter, salt of the earth, *(informal)* A-1, *(informal)* tops, second to none; gem, jewel, treasure, one in a million; beneficence.

v be good, excel, transcend, stand the test, pass muster, challenge comparison, vie, emulate, rival, *(informal)* dwarf the competition; be beneficial, do good, profit, benefit, improve, be the making of, do a world of good, produce a good effect, do a good turn.

adj good, excellent, better, superior, above par, fine, genuine, true; best, choice, select, rare, invaluable, priceless, inestimable, superlative, perfect, inimitable, first-rate, first-class, very best, crack, prime, tip-top, capital, *(informal)* tops; beneficial, valuable, advantageous, profitable, edifying, salutary, serviceable; favorable, propitious.

649 [bad qualities] **badness** *n* harmfulness, hurtfulness, virulence, painfulness, abomination, pestilence, guilt, depravity, vice, evil, malignity, malevolence; bane, plague, evil star, ill wind, bad omen, *(informal)* jinx, *(informal)* whammy; snake in the grass, skeleton in the closet, *(informal)* ghosts, *(informal)* demons; ill-treatment, annoyance, molestation, abuse, oppression, persecution, outrage, misusage, injury, damage.

v hurt, harm, injure, damage, pain; wrong, aggrieve, oppress, persecute, trample upon, tread upon, walk over, overburden, weigh down, run down; victimize, maltreat, molest, abuse, illuse, bruise, scratch, maul, smite, do violence, do harm, stab, pierce.

adj hurtful, harmful, baleful, injurious, deleterious, detrimental, noxious, pernicious, mischievous; oppressive, burdensome, onerous, malign, malevolent; virulent, venomous, corrosive, poisonous, deadly, destructive; bad, ill, dreadful, horrid, horrible, dire, rank, foul, rotten, as low as one can go, *(informal)* the pits; evil, wrong, reprehensible, hateful, abominable, detestable, execrable, damnable, infernal, diabolical; vile, base, villainous, cruel, mean, low; deplorable, wretched, sad, grievous, lamentable, pitiable, pitiful, woeful, painful.

650 **perfection** *n* ideal, summit, paragon, model, standard, pattern, mirror; impeccability, faultlessness, excellence; masterpiece, master stroke; transcendence, superiority.

v perfect, bring to perfection, ripen, mature, complete, finish; be perfect, transcend.

adj perfect, faultless, immaculate, spotless, unblemished, impeccable, exquisite, consummate; in perfect condition, sound, intact; best, model, standard, inimitable, beyond all praise.

651 **imperfection** *n* deficiency, inadequacy, insufficiency, immaturity; fault, defect, weak point, weak spot, flaw, taint, blemish, weakness, shortcoming, drawback.

v be imperfect, have a defect, not pass muster, fall short.

adj imperfect, deficient, inadequate, insufficient, immature, defective, faulty, unsound, out of order, out of tune, warped, lame, frail, weak, crude, incomplete, below par, found wanting; indifferent, middling, ordinary, mediocre, average, so-so, tolerable, fair, passable, decent, not bad, bearable, better than nothing; inferior, secondary, second-rate, poor substitute.

652 **cleanness** *n* purity, purification, purgation, cleanliness; ablution, lavation; neatness, tidiness, orderliness; cathartic, purgative, laxative; detergent, disinfectant.

v clean, cleanse, purify, purge, expurgate, clarify, refine; wash, launder, scour, scrub, disinfect, fumigate, deodorize, ventilate; rout out, clear out, sweep out, make a clean sweep of, start fresh; neaten, tidy up, order, put things in order.

adj clean, pure, immaculate, spotless, stainless, unsullied, sweet; neat, spruce, tidy, trim, kempt.

653 **uncleanness** *n* impurity, defilement, contamination, taint; decay, putrefaction, corruption, mold, mildew, rot, dry rot; squalor, slovenliness, filth, dirt, smut, grime, mud, mire, muck, quagmire, slime.

v be unclean, rot, putrefy, fester, rankle, reek, stink, mold, go bad; dirty, soil, tarnish, spot, smear, blot, blur, smudge, smirch; besmear, befoul, splash, stain, sully, pollute, defile, debase, contaminate, taint, corrupt.

adj unclean, dirty, filthy, grimy, soiled; dusty, smutty, sooty, slimy; slovenly, untidy, sluttish, dowdy, unkempt, unscoured, squalid; nasty, coarse, foul, impure, offensive, abominable, beastly, reeky, fetid; moldy, musty, moth-eaten, bad, gone bad, rancid, rotten, corrupt, putrid, carious, fecal; gory, bloody; gross.

654 health *n* soundness, well-being, vigor, good health, bloom, color, vitality, robust health.

v be in health, be healthy, bloom, flourish, feel fine, feel good.

adj healthy, healthful, in health, well, sound, hearty, hale, strong, hardy, robust, vigorous, fit as a fiddle, in top shape, chipper, *(informal)* all together.

655 disease *n* illness, sickness, ill health, ailment, infirmity, indisposition, complaint, disorder, malady; delicacy, delicate condition, decline, deterioration, decay.

v ail, suffer, be affected with, droop, flag, languish, sicken, pine, gasp, waste away, fail; take sick, take ill, come down with, contract a disease, catch a bug.

adj ill, sick, indisposed, not well, unwell, in poor health, in bad health, ailing, poorly, laid up, bed-ridden, out of sorts, under the weather, *(informal)* in bad shape; sickly, infirm, unsound, unhealthy, *(informal)* falling apart, weak, lame, decrepit; diseased, morbid, mangy, corrupt, contaminated, leprous.

656 salubrity *n* healthiness, healthfulness, wholesomeness.

v be salubrious, be good for, agree with.

adj salubrious, healthy, healthful, salutary, wholesome, sanitary, bracing, invigorating, benign, nutritious, tonic, hygienic.

657 insalubrity *n* unhealthiness, unsoundness.

v be unhealthy, not be good for, disagree with.

adj insalubrious, unhealthy, unwholesome, noxious, noisome, deleterious, pestilential, bad, harmful, virulent, venomous, poisonous, septic, toxic, deadly.

658 improvement *n* amelioration, amendment, emendation, correction, revision, reformation, restoration, repair, betterment, gain, advancement, elevation, increase, refinement, elaboration; acculturation, cultivation, civilization.

reformer, radical.

v improve, mend, amend, get better; ameliorate, better, amend, emend, correct, right, rectify, revise, reform, restore, repair; advance, progress, ascend, increase, fructify, ripen, mature; refine, enrich, elaborate; promote, cultivate, foster, enhance.

adj better, better off, all for the better; emendatory, corrective, refor-mative, restorative, improving, progressive, improved.

659 deterioration *n* debasement, recession, retrogradation, degeneracy, degeneration, degradation, deprivation, depravity, retrogression; detriment, damage, loss, injury, impairment, contamination, spoilage, corruption, adulteration; decline, declension, senility, decrepitude; decadence, decay, dilapidation, falling off, wear and tear, erosion, corrosion, rottenness, blight, atrophy, collapse.

v deteriorate, degenerate, fall off, wane, ebb, decline, droop, go down, go downhill, sink, go to seed, go to waste, lapse, break down, crack, shrivel, fade, wither, molder, rot, rankle, decay, go bad, rust, crumble, shake, totter, perish, die; taint, infect, contaminate, poison, canker, corrupt, pollute, vitiate, debase, degrade, adulterate; injure, impair, damage, harm, hurt, spoil, mar, despoil, dilapidate, waste, ravage; wound, maim, cripple, scotch, mangle, mutilate, disfigure, blemish, deface, warp; blight, rot, corrode, erode, wear away, wear out, sap, mine, undermine, shake the foundations of, break up, destroy, decimate.

adj deteriorated, unimproved, injured, degenerate, imperfect; battered, weathered, weather-beaten, all the worse for wear, stale, dilapidated, faded, shabby, threadbare, worn, far gone, *(informal)* had it; decayed, moth-eaten, worm-eaten, mildewed, rusty, moldy, seedy, time-worn, wasted, crumbling, moldering, rotten, blighted, tainted; decrepit, broken down, worn-out, used up, out of commission, in a bad way, past cure, past hope, *(informal)* long gone.

660 restoration *n* reestablishment, replacement, reinstatement, renewal, rehabilitation, reconstruction, reproduction, rebuilding, renovation, revival; refreshment, resuscitation, revivification; renaissance, renascence, new birth, regeneration, reconversion; redress, retrieval, reclamation, recovery, resumption; repair, reparation, restitution, relief, deliverance, rectification, cure, healing; redemption.

v restore, recover, rally, revive, come round, pull through, get well, get over; reestablish, replace, rehabilitate, reinstate; reconstruct, rebuild, reproduce, reorganize, reconstitute, renew, renovate; redeem, reclaim, recover, retrieve, rescue, deliver; redress, recure; cure, heal, remedy, doctor, bring round; resuscitate, revive, reanimate, revivify, reinvigorate, refresh; recoup, make good, square,

set to rights, correct, put in order; repair, retouch, patch up, fix.

adj restorative, recuperative, curative, remedial; restorable, remediable, retrievable, curable; restored, convalescent, renascent, reborn.

661 relapse *n* lapse, falling back, retrogradation, deterioration, backsliding.

v relapse, lapse, fall back, slip back, sink back, suffer a relapse, fall again.

adj retrograde.

662 remedy *n* help, redress, solution, answer, panacea; cure, relief, medicine, treatment, restorative, specific, medication, ointment, balm; antidote, corrective, antitoxin, counteractive.

doctor, physician, surgeon.

v remedy, cure, heal, set right, put right, doctor, nurse, restore, recondition, repair, redress; counteract, remove, correct, right, solve.

adj remedial, restorative, corrective, palliative; medicinal, therapeutic, curative; soluble.

663 bane *n* curse, evil, plague, scourge, pain, nuisance, thorn in the side, pain in the neck; poison, virus, venom; fungus, mildew, dry rot, canker, cancer; sting, fang, thorn, bramble, briar, nettle.

adj baneful, bad, sinister, pernicious, evil, baleful, poisonous, venomous, ruinous, unwholesome, harmful, deadly.

664 safety *n* security, surety, impregnability, invulnerability; safeguard, safety valve, precaution, custody, safe keeping, preservation, protection.

protector, guardian, warden, preserver, custodian, watchdog, sentinel, scout.

v be safe; protect, take care of, care for, preserve, cover, screen, shelter, shroud, guard, defend, secure, house, garrison; watch, patrol, look out, take precautions.

adj safe, secure, snug, warm, sure, sound, on the safe side, out of danger; dependable, trustworthy, sure, reliable; cautious, wary, careful; defensible, tenable, invulnerable, impregnable, unassailable, safe and sound.

665 danger *n* hazard, insecurity, instability, precariousness, slipperiness, risk, peril, jeopardy, liability, exposure; injury, evil; warning, alarm, apprehension.

v be in danger, run into trouble, lay oneself open to, hang by a thread, totter; endanger, expose to danger,

imperil, jeopardize, adventure, venture, risk, hazard, threaten.

adj dangerous, hazardous, risky, perilous, precarious, unsafe, insecure, unstable, untrustworthy, unsteady, shaky, slippery, ominous, fearful, explosive, fraught with danger; defenseless, vulnerable, open, liable.

666 refuge *n* sanctuary, retreat, asylum, hiding place, stronghold, fortress, shelter, cover; anchor, mainstay, support, check, last resort, safeguard.

v seek refuge, take refuge, find refuge, take shelter, find safety.

667 pitfall *n* snare, trap, snag, ambush, snake in the grass, wolf in sheep's clothing, menace, complication, danger; slippery ground, weak foundation, rocks, reefs, sunken rocks, sand, quicksand, breakers, shoals, shallows, precipice, maelstrom.

668 warning *n* caution, notice, premonition, prediction, admonition, advice, lesson; alarm, omen, sign, signal, augury, portent, presage.

sentinel, sentry, watch, watchman, watchdog, patrol, scout, spy.

v warn, caution, admonish, forewarn; give notice, notify, appraise, inform; menace, threaten, portend.

adj premonitory, cautionary, advisory; ominous, portentous.

669 [indication of danger] **alarm** *n* alarum, alarm bell, tocsin, distress signal, siren, danger signal, hue and cry, SOS, cry, scream.

v alarm, sound the alarm, warn, cry out.

670 preservation *n* safekeeping, conservation; guarding, safeguard, shelter, protection, defense; maintenance, support, sustenance, continuance, retention, salvation.

v preserve, keep, conserve; guard, safeguard, shelter, shield, protect, defend, rescue; keep up, maintain, continue, support, uphold, sustain; retain; store, husband; cure, pickle, bottle, can.

adj preserved, unimpaired, uninjured, unhurt, safe, sound, intact; conservative, preservative.

671 escape *n* flight, evasion, loophole, retreat; reprieve, release, liberation; narrow escape, close call, near miss.

v escape, flee, abscond, fly, steal away, run away, *(informal)* take off, *(informal)* split; shun, fly, elude, evade, avoid.

adj stolen away, fled, *(informal)* cut out.

672 deliverance *n* extrication, disentanglement, rescue, reprieve, respite; liberation, release, emancipation, freedom; redemption, salvation.

v deliver, extricate, disentangle, rescue, reprieve, save, redeem; set free, liberate, release, emancipate, free; come to the rescue.

673 preparation *n* provision, plan, arrangement, anticipation, precaution, forecast, rehearsal; groundwork, homework, foundation, scaffolding; training, education, dissemination; readiness, ripeness, maturity.

v prepare, get ready, make ready, prime, arrange, make preparations, plan, devise, anticipate, lay the foundations, provide, order; mature, ripen, mellow, season, nurture; equip, arm, fit out, furnish; train, teach, prepare for, rehearse, make provision for, take steps, provide against.

adj prepatory, precautionary, provident, preparative, preparatory; provisional, preliminary; prepared, ready, available, all ready, handy; ripe, mature, mellow.

674 nonpreparation *n* unpreparedness, unreadiness; improvidence.

v be unprepared; extemporize, improvise.

adj unprepared, incomplete, premature, rudimental, embryonic, immature, unripe, raw, green, coarse, crude, rough, unhewn, untaught, fallow, unready; out of order, nonfunctional, *(informal)* on the fritz, in disrepair, *(informal)* out of whack; shiftless, improvident, thoughtless, careless, slack, remiss, happy-go-lucky.

675 essay *n* trial, endeavor, effort, attempt, struggle, venture, adventure, speculation, experiment.

v essay, try, experiment; endeavor, strive, tempt, attempt, venture, adventure, speculate, tempt fortune, *(informal)* give it a go, *(informal)* take a shot at.

adj experimental, tentative, probationary; venturesome, adventurous, speculative.

adv experimentally, on trial.

676 undertaking *n* task, job, venture, engagement, compact, contract, enterprise; pilgrimage, quest.

v undertake, engage in, embark on, launch into, plunge into, volunteer; engage, promise, contract, take upon onself, devote onself to, determine, take up, take in hand; tackle, set about, fall to, begin, broach.

677 use *n* employ, exercise, application, appliance; disposal; consumption; agency, usefulness; benefit, recourse, resort, avail; utilization, utility, service, wear; usage.

v use, make use of, employ, put to use, put into operation, apply, set in motion, set to work; ply, work, wield, handle, manipulate; exert, exercise, practice, avail oneself of, profit by; resort to, have recourse to, recur to, take up, try; utilize, bring into play, press into service; use up, consume, expend, tax, task, wear.

adj useful, instrumental, utilitarian, subservient, employable, applicable, beneficial.

678 disuse *n* forbearance, abstinence; relinquishment, abandonment; desuetude.

v not use, do without, dispense with, let alone, forbear, abstain, spare, waive, neglect; keep back, reserve; disuse, lay up, shelve, set aside, put aside, leave off, have done with; supersede, discard, throw aside, relinquish, dismantle.

adj not in use, unemployed, unapplied; disused, unused, done with.

679 misuse *n* misusage, misemployment, misapplication, misappropriation; abuse, profanation, prostitution, desecration; waste.

v misuse, misemploy, misapply, misappropriate; abuse, profane, prostitute, desecrate; waste, squander, destroy; overwork, overtask, overtax.

680 action *n* movement, work, labor, performance, moving, working, performing, operation; deed, act, feat, exploit; conduct, behavior, procedure, execution; energetic activity, exercise, exertion, energy, effort; affair, encounter, meeting, engagement, conflict, combat, fight, battle.

actor, doer, worker.

v act, do, perform, execute, achieve, transact, enact; commit, perpetrate, inflict; exercise, prosecute, carry on, work, function, labor, operate, exert energy, be active; behave, conduct oneself, comport oneself; play, feign, fake, imitate.

· *adj* in action, in operation, operative.

681 inaction *n* passivity, inactivity, idleness, slothfulness; waiting, mulling around, killing time; rest, repose.

v not act, not do, be inactive, abstain from doing, do nothing, let alone, let things take their course; stand aloof, refrain, pause, wait, bide one's time, cool one's heels, waste time, lie idle.

adj inactive, passive, idle, slothful; out of work.

682 activity *n* movement, hustle, bustle, stir, fuss, flurry, action, business; industry, assiduity, assiduousness, laboriousness, drudgery; diligence, perseverance, vigilance, wakefulness, restlessness, fidgetiness; briskness, liveliness, animation, life, vivacity, spirit, dash, energy; eagerness, zeal, ardor, vigor, abandon, exertion; earnestness, intentness, devotion.

v be active, busy oneself in, stir about, rouse oneself, speed, hasten, bustle, fuss, (*informal*) raise a ruckus; push, push ahead, (*informal*) step on it, (*informal*) move it, make progress; toil, plod, persist, persevere, hustle, (*informal*) hustle it, (*informal*) push; look sharp, keep moving, seize the opportunity, *carpe diem*, lose no time, dash off, make haste; have a hand in, trouble oneself about.

adj active, brisk, lively, busy as a bee, vivacious, alive, frisky; quick, prompt, ready, alert, spry, sharp, smart, awake, wide awake, eager, zealous; industrious, assiduous, diligent, vigilant; businesslike; restless, fussy, fidgety, busy.

683 inactivity *n* inaction, inertness, lull, quiescence; idleness, remissness, sloth, indolence, dawdling, laziness, dullness, languor, sluggishness, torpor, stupor, lethargy; procrastination.

idler, drone, dawdler, moper, lounger, loafer, sluggard, laggard, slumberer.

v be inactive, do nothing, dawdle, lag, hang back, slouch, loll, lounge, loaf, loiter, take it easy; fritter away time, idle, piddle, putter, dabble, dally, dilly-dally; languish, flag, relax; kill time, waste time.

adj inactive, motionless; indolent, lazy, slothful, idle, remiss, slack, inert, torpid, sluggish, languid, supine, heavy, dull, listless; laggard, slow, rusty, lackadaisical, irresolute; drowsy, lethargic, soporific, dreamy, dreamy-eyed.

684 haste *n* urgency, need, hurry, flurry, bustle, spurt, rush, dash, scramble, bustle, ado, precipitancy, precipitation; swiftness, celerity, alacrity, quickness, rapidity, dispatch, speed, expedition, promptitude, timeliness, promptness.

v haste, hasten, make haste, hurry, dash, push on, press on, press forward, scurry, bustle, scramble, rush, accelerate, urge, expedite, quicken, speed, precipitate, dispatch.

adj hasty, speedy, quick, hurried, swift, rapid, fast, fleet, brisk; precipi-

tate, rash, foolhardy, reckless, indiscreet, thoughtless, headlong; testy, touchy, irascible, petulant, waspish, fretful, fiery, excitable, irritable, peevish.

685 leisure *n* spare time, free time, convenience, liberty, pause, stay, halt, lull, breather, (*informal*) letup, breathing spell, break, (*informal*) time out; interlude, vacation, holiday.

v have leisure, take one's time; rest, relax, repose.

adj leisure, spare, free; leisurely, slow, deliberate, quiet, calm, restful, peaceful, languid, easy, gradual.

686 exertion *n* effort, action, activity, endeavor, struggle, attempt, strain, trial, stress; labor, work, toil, travail; trouble, pain; energy.

v exert, exert oneself, labor, work, toil, sweat, drudge, strive, strain; work hard, rough it, buckle to, take pains, concentrate, spare no effort.

adj laborious, wearisome, burdensome, (*informal*) tough, (*informal*) rough, strenuous, herculean, Sisyphean.

687 repose *n* rest, sleep, slumber; relaxation, breathing spell; halt, pause, respite, cessation; day of rest, Sabbath; holiday, vacation, recess.

v repose, rest; relax, unbend, slacken, catch one's breath, get one's wind, take a breather, pause; recline, lie down, go to bed, take a nap, go to sleep; take a holiday, go on vacation, shut up shop.

adj reposing, resting.

adv at rest.

688 fatigue *n* weariness, lassitude, tiredness, exhaustion, faintness; ennui, boredom, tedium, languor, yawning, drowsiness.

v be fatigued, yawn, droop, sink, flag, (*informal*) give out; gasp, pant, puff, blow, drop, swoon, faint; fatigue, tire, weary, exhaust, wear out; tax, task, strain; bore, tire, irritate, annoy.

adj fatigued, weary, drowsy, haggard, faint, exhausted, spent, tired, tired to death, worn out, (*informal*) gone; breathless.

689 refreshment *n* recovery of strength, restoration, revival, repair, relief.

v refresh, brace, strengthen, reinvigorate, revive, stimulate, freshen, cheer, enliven, reanimate; restore, repair, renew.

adj refreshing, restoring.

690 agent *n* doer, actor, performer, perpetrator, operator; practitioner, executioner, executor, executrix, min-

ister, representative, deputy, servant, worker; participant, party to.

691 workshop *n* laboratory, factory, mill, mint, forge, studio; hive, beehive, seat of activity.

692 conduct *n* behavior, demeanor, action, actions, deportment, bearing, carriage, mien, manners; process, ways, practice, procedure, method; policy, tactics, strategy, plan; direction, management, execution, guidance, leadership, administration.

v conduct, behave, deport, act, bear; transact, execute, dispatch, discharge, proceed with, enact; direct, manage, carry on, supervise, regulate, administer, guide, lead.

adj procedural, practical, methodical, tactical, strategical, businesslike; directive, managerial, administrative, executive.

693 direction *n* guidance, advice, regulation, conduct, management, disposition, supervision, auspices, steerage, stewardship, ministration, administration, control, leadership, government, rule, command; order, command, instruction.

v direct, guide, advise, regulate, conduct, manage, control, dispose, supervise, overlook, steer, steward, pilot, minister, administer, legislate, lead, rule, govern, have charge of, command; order, instruct, prescribe.

adj directing, guiding, supervisory, managing, administering.

694 director *n* manager, governor, controller, superintendent, supervisor, overseer, inspector, foreman, surveyor, taskmaster, master, leader, boss; adviser, guide, pilot, captain, helmsman, driver; head, chief, principal, president, minister, official, functionary.

695 advice *n* counsel, opinion, recommendation, guidance, suggestion, persuasion, urging, exhortation; instruction, charge, injunction; admonition, warning, caution.

adviser, council, counselor, mentor.

v advise, give counsel to, suggest, recommend, prescribe, advocate, exhort, persuade; enjoin, enforce, charge, instruct; admonish, caution, warn; take counsel, confer, deliberate, discuss, consult, refer to; give counsel, offer counsel.

adj advisory, suggestive, persuasive, suasive; admonitory.

696 council *n* committee, court, chamber, cabinet, board, board of directors, advisory board, staff, syndicate,

chapter; assembly, caucus, conclave, meeting, conference, session.

697 precept *n* direction, instruction, charge, prescript, prescription; golden rule, maxim, canon, law, code, act, statute, regulation, formula, form, technicality, rubric; order, command.

698 skill *n* skillfulness, dexterity, adroitness, expertness, proficiency, competence, facility, knack, mastery; accomplishment, acquirement, attainment, ability, craft; knowledge, wisdom, *savoir faire*, tact, wit, sagacity, discretion, finesse, craftiness, cunning, management; cleverness, ingenuity, capacity, talent, talents, faculty, endowment, *forte*, turn, gift, genius; intelligence, sharpness, readiness, invention, inventiveness, aptness, aptitude, proclivity, capacity for, genius for, felicity, capability, qualification.

v be skillful, excel in, be master of, have a knack for; take advantage of.

adj skillful, dextrous, adroit, adept, expert, apt, handy, quick, deft, proficient, masterly, crack, first-rate, conversant; skilled, experienced, practiced, competent, efficient, qualified, capable, fit, fit for, trained, prepared, finished; clever, able, ingenious, felicitous, inventive; shrewd, sharp, smart, intelligent, cunning, tactful, discreet, wise, knowledgeable.

adv skillfully, artistically, with consummate skill.

699 unskillfulness *n* want of skill, incompetence, inability, inexpertness, maladroitness, ineptitude, clumsiness, awkwardness, carelessness, bumbling, bungling; indiscretion.

v be unskillful, blunder, bungle, boggle, fumble, botch, stumble.

adj unskillful, unskilled, inexpert, incompetent, unable, inapt, bungling, inept, maladroit, awkward, clumsy, gawky; unfit, ill-qualified, unhandy, not conversant; raw, rusty, out of practice.

700 expert *n* specialist, authority, master, professional, connoisseur, veteran, old hand, old soldier; genius, mastermind, wizard, prodigy, *(informal)* pro.

701 bungler *n* blunderer, blunderhead, fumbler, duffer, clown, *(informal)* turkey, butter-fingers, greenhorn, amateur, rookie, novice, *(informal)* Sunday driver, *(informal)* armchair quarterback.

702 cunning *n* craftiness, skillfulness, shrewdness, artfulness, wiliness, subtlety, finesse, artifice, device, stratagem, intrigue, craft, guile, chicanery, du-

plicity, subterfuge, deceit, deceitfulness, slyness, deception; ability, skill, adroitness, expertness.

v be cunning, maneuver, contrive, manipulate, intrigue, finesse, surprise.

adj crafty, shrewd, artful, wily, subtle, tricky, foxy, politic, insidious, stealthy, Machiavellian, deceitful, duplicitous, sly, deceptive; canny, astute; ingenious, clever, skillful, sharp.

703 artlessness *n* simplicity, innocence, naivete, unworldliness, inexperience, inexposure, plainness, plain speaking, sincerity, honesty, openness, candor, matter of factness, bluntness.

v be artless, speak one's mind, come to the point, pull no punches.

adj artless, natural, simple, innocent, naive, childlike, unsuspicious, unworldly, unartificial, plain; sincere, frank, open, candid, honest, ingenuous, guileless, straightforward, aboveboard, point-blank, plain spoken, outspoken, blunt, direct, matter of fact.

adv in plain English, in simple words, without mincing words.

704 difficulty *n* dilemma, predicament, quandary, fix, exigency, emergency, crisis, trouble, problem, scrape, entanglement, strait, pass, pinch; reluctance, unwillingness, obstinacy, stubbornness; demur, objection, obstacle; labor, task, hard task, herculean task.

v be difficult, pose, perplex, bother, nonplus, hinder; encumber, embarrass, entangle.

adj difficult, hard, arduous, troublesome, irksome, laborious, formidable; awkward, unwieldy, unmanageable; fastidious, particular, stubborn, intractable, perverse; obscure, complex, intricate, delicate, uncertain, ticklish, critical; unfeasible, impractical, impossible, hopeless; austere, rigid.

705 facility *n* ease, easiness, capability, feasibility, practicability; flexibility, pliancy, smoothness, child's play.

v be easy, run smoothly, work well; facilitate, smooth, ease, lighten, free, clear, disencumber, disentangle, extricate, unravel.

adj easy, facile; feasible, practicable, within reach, accessible; manageable, tractable, pliant, smooth.

adv easily, readily, smoothly.

706 hindrance *n* impediment, deterrent, hitch, encumbrance, obstruction, check, stricture, restraint, hobble, obstacle, stumbling block; interruption, interference; impeding, stopping, stoppage, preventing.

v hinder, interrupt, check, impede, retard, encumber, delay, hamper, obstruct, trammel, cramp, handicap; block, thwart, frustrate, disconcert, prevent.

adj obstructive, intrusive; onerous, burdensome, cumbersome, obtrusive.

707 aid *n* help, support, succor, assistance, service, furtherance; relief, rescue, charity; assistant, helper, supporter, servant; patronage, championship, advocacy, favor, interest.

v aid, support, help, succor, assist, serve, abet, back, second; spell, relieve, rescue; sustain, uphold, prop, hold up, bolster; promote, facilitate, ease, advocate; be of help, give help, give assistance, oblige, accommodate, humor, encourage.

adj aiding, auxiliary, helpful, supportive; charitable; friendly, amicable, well-disposed, neighborly.

708 opposition *n* antagonism, hostility, resistance, counteraction; competition, enemy, foe, adversary, antagonist; opposing, resisting, combating.

v oppose, resist, combat, withstand, thwart, confront, contravene, interfere; hinder, obstruct, prevent, check; contradict, gainsay, deny, refuse, dissent.

adj adverse, antagonistic, contrary, at variance, at odds, anti, at issue, in opposition; unfavorable, unfriendly, hostile, inimical, resistant.

adv against, versus, counter to, in conflict with, at cross purposes; in spite, in defiance.

709 cooperation *n* concert, concurrence, agreement, concord, togetherness, harmony, unanimity; complicity, collusion, participation, combination, union, team-work; association, partnership, alliance, pool, coalition, confederation, fusion, fellowship, fraternity; unanimity, partisanship, spirit, party spirit, *esprit de corps.*

v cooperate, concur, combine, unite, pool, share, band together, pull together; act in concert, join forces, fraternize; conspire, be in league with; side with, go along with, join hands with, throw in one's lot with, rally round; participate, have a hand in.

adj cooperating, cooperative, participatory; in league, party to.

adv cooperatively, unanimously, shoulder to shoulder.

710 opponent *n* adversary, antagonist, competitor, rival, opposition; enemy, foe.

711 auxiliary *n* helper, aid, ally,

assistant, confederate, collaborator, colleague, associate, partner, mate, friend.

712 party *n* group, gathering, assembly, assemblage, company, crew, band; clan, family, fellowship, community; body, faction, side, circle, clique, set, gang, claque, coterie, combination, ring, league, alliance, association.

v unite, join, band together, cooperate, assemble.

adj clannish, cliquish, communal, familial, fraternal.

713 discord *n* dissidence, dissonance, disagreement, clash, shock; variance, difference, dissension, misunderstanding, cross-purposes, odds, division, split, rupture, disruption, breach, schism, feud, conflict, struggle, argument, contention, quarrel, dispute, tiff, squabble, altercation, words; strife, outbreak.

v be discordant, disagree, clash, jar, conflict, differ, dissent, fall out, quarrel, dispute, squabble, wrangle, bicker, have words with; split, break, disunite, feud.

adj discordant, dissident, dissonant; divisive, disruptive; contentious, argumentative, quarrelsome, disputatious, fractious; at variance, at cross purposes.

714 concord *n* accord, harmony, sympathy, agreement, union, unison, unity, peace; amity, friendship, alliance, *detente*, understanding, togetherness, conciliation.

v agree, accord, harmonize with, fraternize, understand one another, concur, pull together; side with, sympathize with.

adj concordant, congenial, in accord; harmonious, sympathetic, friendly, fraternal, conciliatory.

adv with one voice, unanimously, in concert with.

715 defiance *n* daring, courage, courageousness, bravery, boldness; assertiveness, aggressiveness; antagonism, insubordination, recalcitrance, rebelliousness, insolence, resistance.

v defy, challenge, resist, dare, brave, flout, scorn, despise.

adj defiant, daring, courageous, brave, bold; resistant, insolent, rebellious, recalcitrant, contumacious, insubordinate, antagonistic.

adv in the face of, under one's very nose.

716 attack *n* onslaught, assault, offense, battery, onset, charge, encounter, aggression, incursion, invasion, sally, sortie, raid, foray; criticism, blame, censure, abuse.

assailant, aggressor, invader, attacker.

v assail, assault, molest, threaten, storm, charge, set upon, invade, bombard, beset, besiege, lay siege, storm; criticize, impugn, blame, censure, abuse; declare war, begin hostilities.

adj aggressive, offensive; critical, abusive.

adv on the offensive.

717 defense *n* guard, garrison, fortification, shield, shelter, screen, preservation, protection, guardianship, safeguard, security; justification, pleading, vindication.

v defend, guard, fortify, shield, shelter, screen, preserve, protect, keep safe, guard against, watch over, safeguard, secure; parry, repel, put to flight; uphold, maintain, justify, vindicate.

adj defensive, protective.

718 retaliation *n* reprisal, requital, retort, counterstroke, counterattack, retribution, reciprocation, reciprocity, recrimination, revenge, vengeance, reaction.

v retaliate, requite, retort, counterattack, revenge, repay, return, avenge.

adj retaliatory, vengeful, revengeful, retributive, reciprocal, reactive.

adv in retaliation.

719 resistance *n* opposition, withstanding, front, stand, oppugnance, reluctance, repulsion; interference, friction; insurrection, insurgence, rebellion.

v resist, withstand, stand up, stand; confront, oppose, grapple with, rise up, revolt, rebel, repel, repulse.

adj resistant, refractory, recalcitrant, repulsive, repellent; stubborn, indomitable, obstinate.

720 contention *n* struggling, struggle, strife, discord, dissention, quarrel, disagreement, squabble, feud; rupture, break, falling out; opposition, belligerency, combat, conflict, competition, rivalry, contest; disagreement, dissension, debate, wrangle, altercation, dispute, argument, controversy.

v contend, struggle, strive, fight, battle, combat, vie, compete, rival; debate, dispute, argue, wrangle; assert, maintain, claim.

adj contentious, combative, belligerent, bellicose, warlike, quarrelsome, pugnacious; competitive.

721 peace *n* treaty, truce, accord,

amity, harmony, concord; calm, quiet, tranquillity, peacefulness, calmness; order, security.

v be at peace; keep the peace; make peace.

adj peaceful, tranquil, placid, serene, calm, complacent; mellow, halcyon, pacific; peaceable, amicable, friendly, amiable, mild, gentle.

722 warfare n fighting, hostilities, war, combat, battle, ordeal; tactics, strategy, generalship.

v war, make war, wage war, fight, give fight, battle, do battle, combat, contend, cross swords.

adj warlike, contentious, belligerent, combative, bellicose, martial, military, militant.

adv to arms.

723 pacification n conciliation, reconciliation, accommodation, arrangement, adjustment, compromise; amnesty, peace offering, truce, armistice, suspension of hostilities.

v pacify, reconcile, propitiate, placate, conciliate, accommodate, appease, make peace; quiet, calm, tranquilize, assuage, still, smooth, moderate, ameliorate, mollify, meliorate, soothe, bury the hatchet.

adj pacific, conciliatory.

724 mediation n negotiation, arbitration, parley; intervention, intercession, interposition.

mediator, arbiter, arbitrator, peacemaker, go-between, negotiator, moderator, diplomat.

v mediate, intercede, intervene, interpose, interfere; step in, negotiate, arbitrate.

adj mediatory.

725 submission n nonresistance, obedience, compliance, acquiescence, yielding, submissiveness, pliancy; surrender, cessation, capitulation; resignation, passivity, docility.

v succumb, submit, yield, bend, acquiesce, resign, agree, obey, comply, bow, surrender, capitulate.

adj submissive, obedient, compliant, acquiescent, passive, docile, tame, humble.

726 combatant n fighter, contestant, disputant, battler, litigant, contender, competitor, militarist, soldier, warrior, polemic, candidate; antagonist, foe, enemy, opponent, rival, adversary, assailant, opposition, assailer, assailant, assaulter, opposer, opponent.

727 arms n weapons, weaponry, armaments, armor, ammunition, munitions, deadly weapons.

v arm, outfit, ready for battle, prepare for battle.

728 arena n battleground, battlefield, field of battle, theater, ring, lists; playhouse, amphitheater, stage, boards; Colosseum, gymnasium, playing field.

729 completion n culmination, finish, conclusion, close, termination, end, finale; upshot, result; final touch, crowning touch; consummation, accomplishment, achievement, fulfillment; performance, execution; perfection, thoroughness.

v complete, finish, end, conclude, close, terminate, finalize; consummate, perfect, accomplish, do, fulfill, achieve, effect, execute, enact, dispatch, discharge.

adj whole, entire, full, intact, unbroken, one, perfect; done, consummate, perfect, thorough, through-and-through.

adv completely, thoroughly; perfectly.

730 noncompletion n incompleteness, nonfulfillment, nonperformance; neglect, shortcoming.

v not complete, leave unfinished, leave undone; neglect, let alone, let slip; fall short of.

adj. incomplete, unfinished, sketchy.

731 success n progress, advance; hit, stroke, trump card; good fortune, good luck, luck, break; prosperity, achievement, fulfillment, accomplishment; ascendancy, mastery, conquest, victory, triumph; proficiency, skill, mastery.

v succeed, attain an end, secure an objective; progress, advance; accomplish, achieve, effect, complete; prosper, find fulfillment, fulfill oneself; master, conquer, triumph, surmount, overcome.

adj successful, prosperous, well-to-do; victorious, triumphant; masterful, proficient.

adv successfully, with flying colors, in triumph.

732 failure n unsuccessfulness, miscarriage, abortion, failing; neglect, omission, dereliction, non-performance; deficiency, insufficiency, defectiveness; blunder, mistake, fault, slip, mishap, scrape, mess, fiasco, breakdown; decline, decay, deterioration, loss; bankruptcy, insolvency, bust, dud.

v fail, come short, fall short, disappoint, miss the mark, miscarry, abort, blunder, botch, make a mess of, (informal) blow it, founder, flounder, sink, go amiss, go wrong, go hard with; fall

off, dwindle, decline, fade, weaken, wane, give out, cease; desert, forsake.

adj unsuccessful, abortive, stillborn, fruitless, bootless, ineffectual, inefficient, insufficient, useless; lost, undone, bankrupt; wide of the mark, erroneous; frustrated, thwarted, foiled, defeated; defective, faulty.

adv unsuccessfully, in vain, to little purpose.

733 trophy *n* medal, prize, palm, laurel, honor, accolade, decoration, reward, recognition, triumph, celebration.

734 prosperity *n* well-being, success, fortune, wealth, affluence.

v prosper, thrive, flourish, rise, make one's way, flower, grow, blossom, bloom, fructify, succeed, (*informal*) make it.

adj prosperous, successful, wealthy, rich, well-to-do, well-off; favorable, propitious, fortunate, lucky, auspicious, golden, bright.

735 adversity *n* calamity, distress, catastrophe, crisis, disaster, failure; bad luck, hard times, misfortune, (*informal*) downers, (*informal*) bummers, trouble, hardship, pressure, affliction, wretchedness.

v go downhill, go to the dogs, decay, sink, decline, come to grief, (*informal*) hit the pits, fall on evil days.

adj adverse, unfavorable, unlucky, unfortunate; calamitous, disastrous, critical, dire, catastrophic; unprosperous, hapless, in a bad way, under a cloud, in adverse circumstances, down in the mouth.

adv adversely; if worst comes to worst.

736 mediocrity *n* average capacity, ordinariness, commonplaceness, insignificance, passableness, tolerableness, indifference, inferiority, paltriness, triviality; moderation, golden mean.

v jog on, get along.

adj mediocre, average, normal, ordinary, commonplace, run-of-the-mill, insignificant, tolerable, unimportant, indifferent, inferior, poor, slight, paltry; moderate, reasonable, temperate, respectable.

II. Intersocial Volition

737 authority *n* control, influence, jurisdiction, command, rule, sway, power, dominion, supremacy; expert, adjudicator, arbiter, judge, sovereign, ruler; warrant, justification, permit, permission, sanction, liberty, authorization.

v authorize, empower, commission, allow, permit, sanction, approve; warrant, justify, legalize, support, back; rule, sway, control, administer, govern.

adj authoritative, peremptory, magisterial, imperative, dogmatic, masterful; executive, administrative, sovereign, regnant, supreme, dominant, paramount, predominant, preponderant, influential, official, decisive, valid, absolute.

738 [absence of authority] **laxity** *n* laxness, looseness, slackness, lenience, toleration, relaxation, loosening, licence, freedom.

v be lax, tolerate, relax, give a free rein.

adj lax, loose, slack, remiss, lenient, negligent, careless, weak.

739 severity *n* seriousness, gravity, sternness, harshness, austerity, rigidity, rigorousness, strictness, stringency, relentlessness, abruptness, curtness; arbitrariness, absolutism, despotism, dictatorship, autocracy, tyranny, oppression; strength, force, brute force, coercion.

tyrant, disciplinarian, despot, taskmaster, oppressor, inquisitor.

v be severe, tyrannize, domineer, dominate, bully, inflict, wreak, be hard on, ill-treat, maltreat, oppress, trample on, crush, coerce.

adj severe, serious, grave, stern, harsh, austere, rigid, stiff, dour, rigorous, strict, strait-laced, stringent, relentless, hard, inexorable, abrupt, peremptory, curt, short; arbitrary, absolute, despotic, dictatorial, autocratic, tyrannical, oppressive, coercive, inquisitorial, ruthless, cruel, malevolent, arrogant.

adv severely, with a high hand, with a heavy hand.

740 lenience *n* leniency, tolerance, toleration, moderation, mildness, gentleness, favor, indulgence, forbearance, quarter, compassion, clemency, mercy.

v be lenient, tolerate, bear with, favor, indulge, allow.

adj lenient, tolerant, mild, easy, easy-going, gentle, tender, indulgent, compassionate, sympathetic, merciful.

741 command *n* order, ordinance, direction, bidding, injunction, charge, mandate, behest, ukase, commandment, requisition, requirement, instruction, dictum, act, fiat; demand, exaction, claim, request; control, mastery, disposal, rule, sway, power, domination.

v command, order, direct, bid, demand, charge, instruct, enjoin, require, impose; decree, enact, ordain, dictate, prescribe, appoint; claim, lay claim to.

adj commanding, authoritative.

742 disobedience *n* noncompliance, nonobservance, insubordination, contumacy, infraction, infringement, defiance, unruliness, rebelliousness, obstinacy, stubbornness, resistance, mutinousness, mutiny, rebellion.

insurgent, mutineer, rebel, revolutionary, rioter, traitor, *(informal)* radical.

v disobey, transgress, violate, disregard, defy, infringe, shirk, resist, mutiny, rebel, revolt.

adj disobedient, insubordinate, contumacious, defiant, refractory, unruly, fractious, rebellious, mutinous, obstinate, stubborn, unsubmissive, uncompliant, recalcitrant, insurgent, riotous.

743 obedience *n* observance, compliance, docility, tractability, deference, respect, duty, subservience, submissiveness, obsequiousness; allegiance, loyalty, fealty, homage, devotion.

v obey, comply, submit, follow, attend to, serve.

adj obedient, submissive, compliant, tractable, docile, deferential, respectful, dutiful, loyal, subservient.

adv obediently, in compliance with, in obedience to.

744 compulsion *n* coercion, constraint, duress, enforcement, conscription, force; impulse, necessity.

v compel, force, make, drive, coerce, constrain, enforce, impel, require, necessitate, oblige, motivate; subdue, subject, bend, bow, overpower.

adj compelling, compulsory, coercive, forcible, constraining; obligatory, necessary, unavoidable, inescapable, ineluctable, irresistible, inexorable.

adv by force, forcibly, on compulsion.

745 master *n* lord, commander, commandant, chief, head, leader, director, ruler, boss, authority.

746 servant *n* subject, retainer, follower, henchman, domestic, menial, help, helper, employee, worker, laborer.

v serve, function, answer, assist, help, aid, provide, cater, satisfy; wait on, attend.

747 [insignia of authority] **scepter** *n*

regalia, staff, symbol, emblem, flag, badge; title.

748 freedom *n* liberty, independence, autonomy, noninterference; immunity, franchisement, franchise, privilege, latitude, scope; ease, facility; frankness, openness; familiarity, license, looseness, laxity.

v be free, have scope, do as one likes, do what one wants; free, liberate, permit, allow, set free.

adj free, independent, at large, loose, scot free; unconstrained, unconfined, unchecked, unhindered, unobstructed, unbound, uncontrolled, ungoverned, unchained, unfettered, unshackled, uncurbed, unbridled, unmuzzled; unrestricted, unlimited, unconditional; absolute; discretionary; wanton, rampant, irrepressible, unvanquished; immune, exempt, freed; autonomous.

adv freely.

749 subjection *n* dependence, subordination, thrall, thralldom, subjugation, bondage, serfdom, slavery, servitude, enslavement; service, employ, tutelage, constraint, yoke, submission, obedience.

v be subject, be at the mercy of, depend upon, fall prey to, play second fiddle to, serve, submit; subject, subjugate, master, tame, tread down, weigh down, enslave, enthral, rule.

adj subject, dependent, subordinate; under control, in harness.

750 liberation *n* disengagement, release, enlargement, emancipation, enfranchisement, deliverance, extrication, discharge, dismissal, acquittal, absolution.

v liberate, set free, free, disengage, release, emancipate, enfranchise, deliver, extricate, discharge, dismiss, unfetter, disenthrall, set loose, loose, let out, acquit, absolve.

adj liberated, freed.

751 restraint *n* restriction, circumscription, limitation, control, confinement, curb, check, suppression, constraint, repression.

v restrain, check, keep down, repress, curb, bridle, suppress, compel, hold, keep, constrain; restrict, circumscribe, confine, hinder.

adj restrained, constrained, restrictive, suppressive, repressive; imprisoned, pent up, under restraint.

752 prison *n* jail, gaol, cage, coop, pen, penitentiary, jailhouse, cell, block, dungeon, lock-up, stir, irons, *(informal)* calaboose, *(informal)* hoosegow, *(informal)* the joint, *(informal)* the big house.

753 keeper *n* custodian, guard *(informal)* screw, jailer, gaoler, warder, escort, body-guard; protector, guardian, governor, governess, teacher, tutor, nurse.

754 prisoner *n* captive, convict, con, jailbird.

v be imprisoned, stand convicted.

adj in prison, in custody, in chains, under wraps, in stir.

755 [vicarious authority] **commission** *n* delegation, consignment, assignment, deputation, legation, mission, embassy, agency, special committee; errand, charge, permit; appointment, nomination, charter.

v commission, delegate, consign, assign, charge, entrust, authorize; appoint, name, nominate, ordain; install, induct, invest, employ, empower.

756 abrogation *n* abolition, cancelation, annulment, repeal, retraction, revocation, remission, recision, nullification, invalidation.

v abrogate, abolish, cancel, annul, repeal, retract, revoke, rescind, nullify, void, invalidate.

adj null and void.

757 resignation *n* abjuration, renunciation, abdication, abandonment, desertion, relinquishment, retirement.

v resign, quit, give up, abjure, renounce, forgo, disclaim, abrogate, abandon, desert, relinquish, retire.

758 consignee *n* trustee, nominee, committee, delegation, delegate, commission; functionary, agent, representative, messenger.

759 deputy *n* substitute, proxy, delegate, representative, surrogate, alternate, second, assistant.

v stand for, represent, answer for.

760 permission *n* authorization, warrant, sanction, liberty, license, enfranchisement, franchise, leave, permit, liberty, freedom, allowance, consent, concession, tolerance, sufferance, indulgence, favor.

v permit, allow, let, tolerate, bear with, agree to, suffer, concede, accord, favor, humor, indulge; grant, empower, franchise, charter, confer, license, authorize, warrant, sanction.

adj permitted, permissive, indulgent, libertarian, tolerant; permissible, allowable, legal, legalized, lawful, legitimate.

761 prohibition *n* interdiction, injunction, prevention, embargo, ban, restriction, disallowance.

v prohibit, forbid, interdict, veto, disallow, bar, restrict, limit; prevent, hinder, preclude, obstruct.

adj prohibitive, proscriptive, restrictive; preventive.

762 consent *n* assent, acquiescence, acceptance, acknowledgment, permission, compliance, concurrence, agreement, approval; accord, concord, consensus, settlement, ratification, confirmation.

v consent, assent, agree, concur, permit, allow, let, yield, grant, comply, accede, acquiesce.

adj compliant, agreeable, amenable.

763 offer *n* proposal, proposition, overture, tender, bid; offering, gift.

v offer, present, proffer, tender; propose, give, move, put forward, advance, invite, hold out, make a motion; hawk, merchandise, offer for sale.

adj for sale, in the open market.

764 refusal *n* rejection, spurning, denial, rebuff, repulse, repudiation; abnegation, protest, renunciation, disclaimer.

v refuse, decline, reject, spurn, turn down, deny, rebuff, repulse, repudiate; resist, repel, repudiate, renounce, disclaim, rescind, revoke.

adj noncompliant, dissident, recalcitrant, reluctant.

765 request *n* claim, demand, application, appeal, solicitation, petition, suit, entreaty, supplication, prayer.

v request, ask, ask for, beg, sue, petition, entreat, supplicate, solicit, beseech, plead, implore, require, demand, importune, clamor for.

adj importunate, clamorous, solicitous.

766 [negative request] **deprecation** *n* expostulation, intercession, mediation, protest, disapproval, remonstrance.

v deprecate, protest, expostulate, enter a protest, disapprove, remonstrate.

adj deprecatory, expostulatory, remonstrative; unsought.

767 petitioner *n* claimant, aspirant, postulant, seeker, solicitor, suitor, applicant, suppliant, supplicant; competitor, bidder; beggar, mendicant, panhandler, *(informal)* bum, *(informal)* streetwalker.

768 promise *n* undertaking, word, covenant, commitment, pledge, assurance, profession, vow, oath, guarantee, warranty, obligation, contract.

v promise, undertake, engage,

enter into, bind oneself, commit oneself, pledge, agree, assure, warrant, guarantee, covenant, swear, give one's word; secure, give security, underwrite.

adj promissory, upon one's oath, on one's honor; promised, pledged, committed, bound, sworn.

769 compact *n* covenant, pact, contract, treaty, agreement, negotiation, bargain, arrangement, *(informal)* deal.

v contract, negotiate, bargain, stipulate, make terms; agree, engage, promise; complete, settle, confirm, subscribe, endorse.

adj compactual, contractual, promissory.

770 conditions *n* terms, articles, clauses, provisions, provisos, stipulations, promises, obligations, covenants.

v condition, stipulate, insist upon, contract, provide, bind, tie, oblige.

adj conditional, provisional.

adv conditionally, provisionally, on condition.

771 security *n* guarantee, warranty, bond, tie, pledge, promise, contract; mortgage, lien, pawn; stake, deposit, collateral, *(informal)* IOU, *(informal)* mark, promissory note; deed, bill of sale, receipt, certificate, title; sponsorship, surety, bail.

v give security, post bail, pawn, mortgage; guarantee, warrant, assure, promise; accept, endorse, underwrite, sponsor, stand for.

772 observance *n* performance, compliance, obedience, execution, discharge, acquittance, fulfillment, satisfaction; adhesion, acknowledgment, fidelity, faithfulness.

v observe, comply with, respect, abide by, acknowledge, adhere to, be faithful to, obey, act up to; meet, fulfill; carry out, execute, perform, satisfy, discharge.

adj observant, compliant, faithful, obedient, true, honorable; punctilious, scrupulous, as good as one's word.

adv faithfully.

773 nonobservance *n* evasion, failure, omission, noncompliance, neglect, negligence, laxity, laxness, carelessness, irresponsibility, disobedience; infringement, infraction, violation, transgression.

v fail, neglect, evade, omit, elude, ignore, disregard, discard, set at naught; infringe, transgress, violate, break.

adj nonobservant, lax, loose, disdainful, evasive, elusive, negligent, irresponsible, disobedient.

774 compromise *n* adjustment, negotiation, concession; compensation.

v compromise, bend, give and take, split the differences, come to an agreement, opt for the mean, adjust, arrange, settle.

775 acquisition *n* procurement, appropriation, gain, attainment, purchase, gift, find; profit, earnings, wages, winnings, income, proceeds, produce, crop, harvest, benefit.

v acquire, appropriate, gain, win, earn, attain, gather, collect; take over, take possession of, procure, secure, obtain, get, come into, receive, get hold of; profit, turn to profit.

adj profitable, advantageous, gainful, remunerative.

776 loss *n* damage, injury, privation, lapse, forfeiture, deprivation.

v lose, incur a loss, miss, mislay, let slip, forfeit; waste, get rid of.

adj lost, bereft, minus, deprived of, cut off, rid of; long lost, irretrievable.

777 possession *n* ownership, occupancy, holding, proprietorship, tenure, tenancy, control, custody; belonging.

v possess, own, have, hold, occupy, control, command, have to oneself, have in hand, belong to.

adj possessing, possessed of, in possession of, master of, in hand, at one's disposal; possessive, custodial.

777a exemption *n* exception, immunity, impunity, release.

v exempt, excuse, release; not have, be without.

adj exempt from, immune from, devoid of, without.

778 [joint possession] **participation** *n* partnership, co-ownership, joint tenancy, common holding, communion, community of possessions; communism, socialism, collectivism; cooperation.

participant, sharer, partner, copartner, shareholder; communist, socialist.

v participate, partake, share, share in, go halves, split up, divide, have in common, own in common.

adj participatory, joint, common, collective, communal, communist, communistic, socialist, socialistic.

779 possessor *n* holder, occupant, tenant, lessee; proprietor, proprietress, master, mistress, owner.

780 property *n* possession, possessions, goods, effects, chattels, estate, belongings, assets, means, resources, land, real estate, acreage; ownership,

right; attribute, quality, characteristic, feature.

781 retention *n* keeping, holding, detention, custody, preservation, maintenance.

v retain, keep, hold, hold fast, secure, withhold, preserve, detain, reserve, maintain.

adj retentive.

782 relinquishment *n* renunciation, surrender, resignation, yielding, waiver, abdication, desertion, abandonment, quitting.

v relinquish, renounce, surrender, give up, resign, yield, cede, waive, forswear, forgo, abdicate, leave, forsake, desert, quit, abandon, let go, discard, cast off, dismiss, divest oneself.

adj cast off, done away with, left, forsworn, given up, left behind.

783 transfer *n* sale, lease, release, exchange, interchange; transference, transmission, changing hands.

v transfer, convey, assign, grant, consign, make over, hand over, pass, transmit, change, exchange, interchange, change hands; devolve, succeed.

adj transferable, conveyable, transmissive, exchangeable.

784 giving *n* bestowal, presentation, concession, delivery, consignment, dispensation, endowment, investiture, award; charity, almsgiving, liberality, generosity, philanthropy; gift, donation, present, boon, favor, grant, offering; allowance, contribution, donation, bequest, legacy; alms, largesse, bounty, help, gratuity; bribe, bait.

giver, granter, donor.

v give, bestow, confer, grant, accord, award, assign, entrust, consign; invest, allow, settle upon, donate, bequeath, leave; furnish, supply, help; afford, spare, favor with, lavish; deliver, hand, pass, turn over, present, give away, dispense, dispose of, give out, deal out, dole out, mete out, fork out; pay, render, impart.

adj charitable, beneficent, tributary, liberal, generous, philanthropic.

785 receiving *n* acquisition, reception, acceptance, admission, recipient, receiver, legatee, grantee, donee, beneficiary, pensioner.

v receive, take, acquire, admit, take in, accept; come into, fall to one, accrue.

adj receiving; received.

786 apportionment *n* allotment, consignment, assignment, allocation, distribution, dispensation, division, partition; portion, lot, share, measure, dose, dole, ration, ratio, proportion, quota, allowance.

v apportion, divide, distribute, dispense, allot, share, mete, portion out, parcel out, dole out, deal, carve, administer; partition, assign, appropriate, appoint.

adj distributive; respective.

787 lending *n* loan, advance, accommodation, mortgage, investment.

v lend, loan, advance, accommodate, lend on security, pawn; let, lease.

788 borrowing *n* pledging, pawning; appropriating, stealing, theft.

v borrow, pledge, pawn, borrow money; hire, rent, lease; appropriate, use, steal from, imitate.

789 taking *n* appropriation, capture, apprehension, seizure, abduction, dispossession, deprivation, expropriation, divestment, confiscation, eviction; extortion, theft; reprisal, recovery.

v take, catch, hook, nab, bag, pocket, receive, accept; reap, cull, pluck, gather; appropriate, assume, possess oneself of, help oneself to, commandeer, make free with; take away, abduct, steal, seize, snatch, snap up, capture, get hold of, take from, take away from, dispossess, expropriate, oust, eject, divest, confiscate, usurp, strip, fleece; retake, resume, recover.

adj predatory, rapacious, parasitic, greedy, ravenous.

790 restitution *n* return, restoration, reinvestment, rehabilitation, reparation, atonement, compensation, recovery.

v return, restore, give back, render, give up, let go; recoup, reimburse, compensate, reinvest, remit, rehabilitate, repair, make good, settle up; recover, get back, redeem, take back again.

adj compensatory, redemptive, recouperative.

791 stealing *n* theft, thievery, robbery, swindling, fraud, appropriation.

v steal, take, thieve, rob, pilfer, purloin, (informal) swipe, filch, embezzle, swindle, appropriate, fleece, defraud, (informal) rip off, (informal) screw.

adj thievish, light-fingered, piratical, predatory.

792 thief *n* robber, pilferer, filcher, rifler, crook, (informal) rip-off artist,

cheat; burglar, house-breaker, second-story man, safecracker.

793 booty *n* spoils, plunder, prize, loot, catch, pickings, stolen goods, *(informal)* haul.

794 barter *n* exchange, trade, traffic, commerce, business, bargain; dealing, transaction, negotiation.

v barter, trade, exchange, traffic, bargain, swap, buy and sell, give and take, deal, haggle, negotiate, drive a bargain, transact.

adj commercial, mercantile; interchangeable, in trade, for sale, marketable.

795 purchase *n* buying, purchasing, acquisition; bargain, buy.

buyer, purchaser, shopper, customer, client, patron, clientele.

v purchase, buy, acquire, get, obtain, procure; shop, market, go shopping.

796 sale *n* selling, vendition, commerce, mercantilism, transaction, exchange, auction, trade.

seller, vendor, merchant.

v sell, trade, barter, vend, exchange, deal in, dispose, merchandise, hawk.

adj salable, marketable, vendible, for sale.

797 merchant *n* trader, dealer, seller, salesman, saleswoman, tradesman, shopkeeper, retailer, hawker, huckster, peddler, broker.

798 merchandise *n* goods, wares, commodity, articles, stock, produce, product, staple commodity, store, cargo.

v merchandise, sell.

799 market *n* mart, marketplace, fair, bazaar, business district, mall, shopping center, store, department store, establishment, place of business, office.

800 money *n* finance, accounts, funds, assets, wealth, supplies, ways and means, wherewithal, capital, almighty dollar, cash, currency, hard cash, *(informal)* bucks, change, small change, *(informal)* green, greenbacks; sum, amount, balance.

adj monetary, pecuniary, financial, fiscal.

801 treasurer *n* bursar, banker, purser, receiver, steward, trustee, accountant, paymaster, cashier, teller, financier.

802 treasury *n* bank, exchequer, strongbox, stronghold, coffer, chest, depository, purse, moneybag, safe, vault, cash box, cash register, till; securities, stocks, bonds, notes.

803 wealth *n* riches, fortune, opulence, affluence, easy circumstance, *(informal)* silver spoon, independence, competence, sufficiency, solvency; provision, livelihood, maintenance, means, resources, substance; income, capital, money.

v be wealthy, be rich.

adj wealthy, rich, affluent, well-off, well-to-do, comfortable.

804 poverty *n* indigence, penury, pauperism, destitution, want, need, neediness, lack, privation, distress, difficulties, straits, bad straits.

v be poor, want, lack, starve, live from hand to mouth, go to the dogs.

adj poor, indigent, destitute, poverty-stricken, needy, penniless, broke, *(informal)* bust, hard up, insolvent, seedy, beggarly.

805 credit *n* trust, score, tally, account, *(informal)* tab, bill.

creditor, lender, usurer.

v credit, accredit, entrust, keep an account with.

806 debt *n* obligation, liability, debit, score, duty, due.

debtor, borrower.

adj liable, answerable for, in debt; unpaid, in arrear.

807 payment *n* discharge, settlement, clearance, liquidation, satisfaction, reckoning, arrangment; acknowledgment, release, receipt, voucher; installment, remittance.

v pay, settle, liquidate, discharge, quit, acquit oneself of, reckon up, satisfy, compensate, reimburse, remunerate, recompense, make payment, square accounts, balance accounts, pay in full.

adj out of debt, solvent; straight, clear.

808 nonpayment *n* default, protest, repudiation; insolvency, bankruptcy, failure.

v not pay, default, fail, stop payment; run up bills.

adj in debt.

809 expenditure *n* outlay, expenses, disbursement, payment, costs, fees.

v expend, spend, pay out, disburse, *(informal)* fork out, lay out.

810 receipt *n* value received, acknowledgment of payment.

v receive, take, get, bring in.

adj profitable, remunerative.

811 accounts n money matters, finance, budget, bill, score, reckoning, account; statement, ledger, inventory, register, book, books, sheet; balance.

accountant, auditor, bookkeeper, financier.

v keep accounts, enter, post, book, credit, debit, balance.

812 price n amount, cost, expense, charge, figure, demand, damage, fare, hire, wages; worth, rate, value, valuation, appraisal; market price, quotation; bill, invoice.

v price, set a price, fix a price, appraise, assess, charge, demand, ask, require, exact; fetch sell for, bring in, yield, accord.

813 discount n abatement, reduction depreciation, allowance, qualification, rebate, sale.

v discount, put on sale, reduce, take off, allow, deduct, abate, rebate.

814 dearness n expensiveness, costliness, high price; overcharge, extravagance, exorbitance.

v be expensive, cost a lot; overcharge, bleed, fleece, extort.

adj dear, expensive, costly, precious; extravagant, exorbitant, unreasonable; priceless.

815 cheapness n low price, depreciation, bargain, value, (informal) steal, (informal) great buy.

v be cheap, cost little.

adj cheap, moderate, reasonable, inexpensive, dirt cheap.

816 liberality n generosity, munificence, bounty, bounteousness, hospitality, charity.

v be liberal, spend freely, give, spare no expense.

adj liberal, free, generous, bountiful, hospitable, munificent, beneficient, princely, charitable.

817 economy n frugality, thrift, thriftiness, saving, care, husbandry, retrenchment, parsimony.

v economize, save, retrench, husband.

adj economical, frugal, careful, thrifty, chary, parsimonious.

818 prodigality n unthriftiness, waste, wastefulness, profusion, profuseness, extravagance, profligacy, lavishness, squandering.

prodigal, spendthrift, squanderer.

v be prodigal, squander, lavish, misspend, waste, dissipate, fritter one's money.

adj prodigal, profuse, unthrifty, improvident, wasteful, profligate, extravagant, lavish.

819 parsimony n stinginess, illiberality, avarice, rapidity, rapacity, venality, cupidity, selfishness.

miser, niggard, churl, skinflint, codger, scrimp, (informal) tightwad, usurer, Scrooge.

v be parsimonious, grudge, begrudge, stint, pinch, hold back, withhold, starve, famish.

adj parsimonious, penurious, stingy, cheap, miserly, mean, pennywise, niggardly, tight, ungenerous, churlish, mercenary, venal, covetous, usurious, avaricious, greedy, rapacious, selfish.

Class VI

Words relating to the Sentient and Moral Powers

I. Affections in General

820 affections n character, qualities, disposition, nature, spirit, temper, temperament, idiosyncracy, habit, bent, bias, predisposition, proclivity, propensity, humor, mood, sympathy; soul, heart, inner man, essence; passion, driving spirit, ruling passion.

adj affected, characterized, formed, cast, molded, tempered, predisposed, prone, inclined, imbued; inborn, ingrained, deep-rooted.

adv at heart.

821 feeling n consciousness, impression; emotion, passion, sentiment, sensibility; sympathy, empathy; fervor, ardor, zeal, warmth, tenderness, sensitivity, sentimentality, susceptibility, pity; sentiment, opinion.

v feel, receive an impression respond to.

adj feeling, emotional, sensitive, tender; sympathetic; emotional, impassioned, passionate, fervent, tender, sensitive; heart-felt, thrilling, rapturous, soul-stirring; moved, touched affected.

adv heart and soul, from the bottom of one's heart.

822 sensibility n responsiveness, sensitiveness, awareness, susceptibility, impressibility, tenderness, sentimentality, sentimentalism; excitability; appreciation, understanding, moral sensibility.

v be sensitive, have a soft spot in one's heart.

adj sensitive, impressionable, susceptible, tender, warm-hearted, sentimental; excitable; aware, understanding, appreciative.

823 insensibility n insensitiveness

impassivity, apathy, coldness, callousness; imperturbable; dullness, boorishness.

v be insensitive, not care, be unaffected, have no interest in.

adj insensitive, unconscious, unaware; inattentive, indifferent, lukewarm; apathetic, impassive, unimpressionable; cold-blooded, cold-hearted, unmoved, unaffected, callous, thick-skinned, uncaring.

adv in cold blood.

824 excitation *n* excitation of feeling; mental excitation; galvanism, stimulation, provocation, inspiration; infection; animation, agitation, perturbation; fascination, intoxication, ravishment; irritation, anger, passion, thrill.

v excite, affect, touch, move, impress, interest, animate, inspire, infect, awake; evoke, provoke; stir up, wake up, light up; rouse, arouse, stir, fire, kindle, inflame; stimulate, quicken, sharpen, whet, wet the appetite, fan the fire, raise to a fervor; absorb, rivet, intoxicate, fascinate, enrapture; agitate, perturb, ruffle, fluster, disturb, startle, shock, stagger, astound, electrify, galvanize; irritate.

adj excited, excitable, wrought up, overwrought, upset, hysterical, hot, red-hot, flushed, feverish, boiling, ebullient, seething, fuming, raging, raving, frantic, mad, distracted, beside oneself; exciting, warm, glowing, fervid, soul-stirring, thrilling, overwhelming, overpowering, sensational.

825 [excess of sensitiveness] **excitability** *n* impetuosity, vehemence, boisterousness, impatience, intolerance, irritability, restlessness, agitation; passion, excitement, fever, tumult, ebullition, tempest, fit, paroxysm, explosion, outburst, agony; violence, rage, fury, furor, desperation, madness, distraction, delirium, frenzy, hysterics.

v be impatient, lose patience, fuss, fidget; lose one's temper, flare up, burn, boil over, foam, fume, rage, rant, run wild, go mad, go into hysterics.

adj excitable, high-strung, nervous, irritable, impatient, intolerant; feverish, hysterical, delirious, mad; hurried, restless, fidgety, fussy; vehement, violent, wild, furious, fierce, fiery, hotheaded; overzealous, enthusiastic, impassioned, fanatical; rabid, clamorous, turbulent, tumultuous, boisterous; impulsive, impetuous, passionate, uncontrolled, uncontrollable, ungovernable, irrepressible, volcanic.

826 inexcitability *n* imperturbability, even temper, dispassion, patience, impassivity; coolness, calmness, composure, placidity, serenity, quietude; self-possession, self-restraint, stoicism; resignation, submission, sufferance, endurance, forbearance, fortitude, moderation, restraint.

v bear, endure, tolerate, suffer, put up with, reconcile oneself to, resign oneself to, brook, swallow, make the best of, stomach; compose, appease, propitiate, repress, calm down, cool down.

adj inexcitable, imperturbable, unsusceptible, dispassionate, enduring, stoical, staid, sober, sedate; easygoing, peaceful, placid, calm, cool; composed, collected, unruffled, content, resigned, subdued.

II. Personal Affections

827 pleasure *n* happiness, gladness, delectation, enjoyment, delight, joy, glee, cheer, cheerfulness, well-being, satisfaction, gratification, comfort, ease; felicity, bliss, enchantment, transport, rapture, ravishment, ecstasy, luxury, sensuality, voluptuousness.

v be pleased, joy, enjoy oneself, have one's head in the clouds, fall into raptures; be pleased with, derive pleasure from, take pleasure in, (*informal*) get into, delight in, rejoice in, indulge in, luxuriate in, relish, love, enjoy, like, (*informal*) dig, take a fancy to, take a shine to.

adj happy, blissful, joyful, gladsome, cheerful; comfortable, at ease, content; ecstatic.

adv happily, with pleasure.

828 pain *n* suffering, distress, torture, misery, dolor, anguish, agony, torment, throe, pang, ache, smart, twinge, stitch; displeasure, dissatisfaction, discomfort, discomposure, disquiet, malaise, inquietude, uneasiness, vexation, discontent, dejection, weariness; annoyance, irritation, worry, affliction, bore, bother, mortification, plague; care, solicitude, trouble, trial, ordeal, burden, load, fret; prostration, desolation, despair.

v suffer, afflict, torture, torment, distress, despair; hurt, harm, injure, trouble, grieve, disquiet, discomfort, discompose, worry, irritate, vex, mortify, plague.

adj uncomfortable, uneasy, weary; unhappy, infelicitous, poor, wretched, miserable, woebegone, careworn, cheerless, sorry, sorrowful, stricken, in tears, in despair.

829 pleasurableness *n* pleasantness, agreeableness, delectability, delight, congeniality; sprightliness, cheer, cheerfulness, liveliness; attraction, attractiveness, charm, fascination, enchant-

ment, witchery, seduction, winning ways, amenity, amiability; loveliness, beauty, brightness; goodness.

v be pleasurable, afford pleasure, offer pleasure, please, charm, delight, gladden, cheer; attract, invite, allure, stimulate, interest, captivate, fascinate, enchant, entrance, enrapture, bewitch, ravish, enravish, transport; agree with, satisfy, gratify; slake, satiate, quench; regale, refresh, treat, amuse.

adj pleasurable, pleasant, agreeable, enjoyable, delightful, congenial, amiable; comfortable, cordial, genial, gladsome, sweet, delectable, nice, dainty, delicate, delicious, luscious, luxurious, voluptuous, sensual; attractive, lovely, beautiful, seductive, rapturous, ecstatic, beatific, heavenly; fair, sunny, bright; gay, sprightly, merry, cheery, cheerful, lively, vivacious.

830 painfulness *n* trouble, care, trial, affliction, blow, burden, curse, mishap, misfortune, adversity; annoyance, nuisance, grievance, bore, bother, vexation, mortification; wound, sore, sore subject, thorn in the side, skeleton in the closet; sorry sight, heavy news, bad news; affront, insult, offense.

v pain, hurt, wound, sadden, displease, annoy, trouble, disturb, cross, perplex, irk, vex, mortify, worry, plague, bother, pester, harass, badger, bait, heckle, irritate, anger, persecute, provoke; harrow, torment, torture; affront, insult, give offense, offend, maltreat, mistreat; sicken, disgust, revolt, nauseate, repel, shock, horrify, appal.

adj painful, hurtful, dolorous; unpleasant, disagreeable, unpalatable, bitter, distasteful; unwelcome, undesirable, obnoxious; dismal, dreary, melancholy, grievous, piteous, woeful, rueful, mournful, deplorable, pitiable, lamentable, pathetic; invidious, vexatious, troublesome, irksome, wearisome, worrisome; intolerable, insufferable, unsupportable, unbearable, unendurable, grim, dreadful, fearful, frightful, dire, odious, hateful, repulsive, repellant, abhorrent, horrid, horrible, offensive, nauseous, loathsome, vile, hideous; sore, severe, grave, hard, harsh, cruel; ruinous, disastrous, calamitous, tragic; burdensome, onerous, oppressive, cumbersome.

adv painfully.

831 content *n* contentment, complacency, satisfaction, ease, serenity, comfort; conciliation, resignation.

v gratify, satisfy, set at ease, comfort, appease, conciliate, reconcile.

adj contented, complacent, satisfied, sanguine, comfortable; assenting, acceding, resigned, willing, agreeable.

adv to one's heart's content.

832 discontent *n* discontentment, dissatisfaction, uneasiness, disquietude, restlessness, displeasure.

v be discontented, repine, regret, fret, chafe, grumble; dissatisfy, disappoint, disconcert.

adj discontented, dissatisfied, displeased, uneasy, restless, dejected, malcontent, regretful, down in the dumps.

833 regret *n* sorrow, lamentation, grief; remorse, penitence, contrition, repentance.

v regret, deplore, lament, feel sorry about, grieve at, bemoan, bewail, rue, mourn for, repent.

adj regretful, sorry, lamentable, rueful; penitent, contrite.

834 relief *n* deliverance, alleviation, ease, assuagement, mitigation, comfort, solace, consolation; help, assistance, aid.

v relieve, ease, alleviate, assuage, mitigate, allay, comfort, soothe, lessen, abate, diminish; cheer, comfort, console; aid, help, assist, succor, refresh, remedy, support.

adj soothing, consoling, assuaging, comforting, palliative, curative.

835 aggravation *n* worsening, heightening, intensification, exaggeration; (*informal*) annoyance, irritation, vexation.

v aggravate, worsen, intensify, heighten, increase, make serious, make grave.

adj worse, intensified, irritated.

adv from bad to worse, out of the frying pan and into the fire.

836 cheerfulness *n* geniality, high spirits, liveliness, vivacity, joviality, jocularity, mirth, merriment, exhilaration.

v cheer, gladden, enliven, inspirit, delight, rejoice, exhilarate, animate, encourage; shout, applaud, acclaim, salute.

adj cheery, gay, blithe, happy, lively, spirited, sprightly, joyful, joyous, mirthful, buoyant, sparkling, vivacious, gleeful, sunny, jolly; pleasant, bright, gay, winsome, gladdening, cheery, cheering, inspiring, animating, hearty, robust.

adv cheerfully.

837 dejection *n* depression, heaviness, heavy heart, melancholy, sadness, dumps, doldrums, despondency, gloom, weariness, disgust, despair, hopelessness.

v be dejected, lose heart, frown, mope, droop, despond, brood over, sink, despair.

adj unhappy, depressed, dispirited, disheartened, discouraged, despondent, (*informal*) down, downhearted, sad, melancholy, lugubrious, heartsick, dismal, gloomy, miserable, desolate; pessimistic, cynical.

adv with a long face, with tears in one's eyes.

838 rejoicing *n* exaltation, triumph, jubilation, reveling, merrymaking, celebration, paean; smile, smirk, grin, giggle, titter, laughter, guffaw, shout, peal of laughter.

v rejoice, congratulate oneself, clap one's hands, dance, skip, sing, hurrah, cry for joy, leap with joy, exalt, triumph; smile, smirk, grin, giggle, titter, chuckle, cackle, laugh, crow, burst out, shout, split, roar, shake one's sides, split one's sides.

adj jubilant, exultant, triumphant, flushed, (*informal*) high, elated, laughing, convulsed with laughter.

839 lamentation *n* lament, howl, wail, wailing, complaint, moan, moaning, groan, sob, sigh; dirge, elegy, monody, threnody.

v lament, bewail, bemoan, deplore, grieve, scream, sob, cry, weep, mourn over, sorrow over.

adj lamenting, in mourning, sorrowful, mournful, lamentable, tearful, plaintive.

840 amusement *n* enjoyment, entertainment, recreation, diversion, relaxation, pastime, pleasure, playing, festivity.

v amuse, entertain, cheer, divert, enliven, interest; amuse oneself, play, sport, make merry.

adj amusing, entertaining, diverting, relaxing, pleasant, witty, jovial, jolly, playful.

841 weariness *n* ennui, lassitude, fatigue, exhaustion, boredom; tedium, monotony, dullness.

v weary, tire, fatigue, bore, exhaust.

adj wearisome, tiresome, boring, tedious, irksome, monotonous, humdrum, dull, prosaic, trying; weary, drowsy, exhausted, tired, wearied, fatigued; uninterested, impatient, dissatisfied.

842 wit *n* drollery, facetiousness, pleasantry, repartee, cleverness, humor, fun; understanding, intelligence, sagacity, wisdom, intellect, mind, sense.

v joke, jest, banter, pun.

adj witty, quick, quick-witted, nimble, sharp, clever, facetious, whimsical, pleasant, humorous, playful, sparkling, scintillating; intelligent, sagacious, wise, perceptive, insightful.

843 dullness *n* heaviness, flatness, stupidity, obtuseness, lack of originality, banality.

v be dull, blunt, deaden, benumb.

adj dull, uninteresting, unimaginative, dry, prosaic, matter-of-fact, commonplace, boring, tedious, dreary, vapid; stupid, stolid, slow, flat.

844 humorist *n* wit, wag, comedian, comedienne, joker, jester, wisecracker, epigrammatist, punster, buffoon, clown, fool, satirist, lampooner, cutup, funnyman.

845 beauty *n* loveliness, pulchritude, elegance, grace, gracefulness, comeliness, seemliness, fairness, attractiveness, brilliance, radiance, splendor, gorgeousness, magnificence, sublimity.

v beautify.

adj beautiful, handsome, comely, seemly, attractive, lovely, pretty, fair, fine, elegant, beauteous, graceful, pulchritudinous, brilliant, radiant, gorgeous, magnificent; artistic, aesthetic, picturesque.

846 ugliness *n* homeliness, inelegance, unsightliness, distortion, disfigurement, deformity, frightfulness.

v deface, disfigure, distort.

adj ugly, displeasing, hard-featured, unlovely, unsightly, unseemly, homely; hideous, gruesome, repulsive, offensive, revolting, terrible, base, vile, squalid, gross, monstrous, heinous; disagreeable, unpleasant, objectionable.

847 ornament *n* ornamentation, adornment, decoration, embellishment, frills, finery.

v ornament, embellish, adorn, decorate, beautify.

adj ornamental, decorative; ornamented, ornate, embellished, beautified.

848 blemish *n* disfigurement, deformity, defect, flaw, fault, taint, blot, spot, speck.

v stain, sully, spot, taint, tarnish, injur, mar, damage, deface, impair.

adj disfigured, injured, imperfect, discolored, freckled, pitted.

849 simplicity *n* plainness, homeliness; clarity, chasteness, restraint, severity, lack of adornment, lack of affectation.

v simplify, uncomplicate, clarify, strip to essentials, get back to basics.

adj simple, plain, homely, natural, unadorned, unaffected, unembellished, neat, unassuming, unpretentious; chaste, severe; clear, straightforward, lucid.

850 [good taste] **taste** *n* good taste, delicacy, refinement, polish, elegance, grace, discrimination, culture, cultivation.

v show taste, appreciate, judge, criticize, discriminate.

adj tasteful, in good taste, decorous, attractive, cultivated, cultured, refined, discriminative, polished felicitous, appropriate, suitable, apt, becoming, pleasing.

adv tastefully, elegantly.

851 [bad taste] **vulgarity** *n* bad taste, barbarism, coarseness, lack of decorum, ill-breeding, boorishness; gaudiness, tawdriness, finery, frippery, tinsel.

v be vulgar; vulgarize.

adj vulgar, in bad taste, unrefined, boorish, common, coarse, ill-bred, ill-mannered, ignoble, mean, plebeian, crude, rude, shabby; gaudy, tawdry, flashy, garish, crass, showy, (*informal*) tacky.

852 **fashion** *n* custom, style, vogue, mode, rage, craze; conventionality, conformity; society, polite society, beau monde; manners, breeding, air, demeanor, savoir-faire, gentility, decorum, propriety, etiquette.

v be fashionable, be the rage; fashion, adapt, suit, fit, adjust; make, shape, frame, form, mold.

adj fashionable, in vogue, à la mode, all the rage; modish, stylish, conventional, customary; well-bred, well-mannered, civil, polite, courteous, polished, refined, genteel, decorous.

853 **ridiculousness** *n* outrageousness, silliness, absurdity.

v be ridiculous, make a fool of oneself, play the fool.

adj absurd, preposterous, extravagant, asinine, laughable, nonsensical, silly, funny, ludicrous, droll, comical, farcical, outlandish, outrageous, fantastic.

854 **fop** *n* fine gentleman, dandy, (*informal*) dude, coxcomb, beau, man about town, prig, jackanapes.

855 **affectation** *n* affectedness, pretense, pretention, airs, mannerisms, unnaturalness, display, show, sham, feigning, simulation, foppery.

v affect, act a part, put on airs, pretend, assume, feign, counterfeit, simulate, pose, attitudinize.

adj affected, pretentious, ostentatious, feigned, artificial, stilted, mannered, stagey, theatrical, modish, unnatural.

856 **ridicule** *n* derision, scoffing, mockery, gibes, jeers, taunts, raillery; satire, burlesque, sneer, banter, wit, irony.

v ridicule, deride, banter, chaff, twit, mock, taunt, make fun of, sneer at, burlesque, satirize, rail at, lampoon, jeer at, scoff at, (*informal*) put down.

adj derisory, derisive, sarcastic, ironic, ironical, burlesque, mocking.

857 [object and cause of ridicule] **laughing-stock** *n* butt, game, fair game, fool, dupe, original, oddity, queer fish, square, straight, buffoon.

858 **hope** *n* confidence, trust, reliance, faith, assurance; expectation, expectancy, anticipation, aspiration, longing, desire, dream, wish.

v hope, trust, rely on, lean on, have faith in; hope for, expect, presume, anticipate; long for, desire.

adj hopeful, expectant, sanguine, optimistic, confident; probable, promising, propitious, reassuring, encouraging, cheering, inspiriting.

859 **hopelessness** *n* despair, desperation, despondency, dejection, pessimism.

v despair, give up hope, despond.

adj hopeless, despairing, desperate, despondent, forlorn, disconsolate; irremediable, remediless, unremedial, incurable.

860 **fear** *n* apprehension, consternation, dismay, alarm, trepidation, dread, terror, fright, horror, panic; anxiety, solicitude, suspicion, misgiving, concern; awe, reverence, veneration.

v fear, be afraid of, apprehend, distrust, dread; revere, venerate, reverence.

adj fearful, afraid, apprehensive, dismayed, alarmed, frightened, terrified, horrified, aghast, terror-stricken, horror-stricken, panic-stricken; anxious, concerned, solicitous, suspicious; fearful, awesome, awe-inspiring; awful, dreadful, terrible.

861 **courage** *n* fearlessness, dauntlessness, intrepidity, guts, fortitude, pluck, spirit, nerve, heroism, daring, audacity, bravery, mettle, valor, hardihood, bravado, gallantry.

v dare, venture, look danger in the face, take heart, take the bull by the horns.

adj courageous, fearless, dauntless, intrepid, (*informal*) gutsy, spirited,

stout-hearted, resolute, bold, heroic, daring, audacious, brave, valorous, enterprising, adventurous, gallant.

862 cowardice *n* fear, poltroonery, dastardliness, faint-heartedness, yellow streak, dread, timidity, baseness, abject fear.

coward, poltroon, craven, sneak, lily-liver, (*informal*) chicken.

v be cowardly, cower, skulk, quail, hide.

adj cowardly, fearful, craven, dastardly, pusillanimous, recreant, timid, timorous, faint-hearted, lily-livered, chicken-hearted, fearful, afraid, scared, spineless, (*informal*) chicken.

863 rashness *n* haste, impetuosity, recklessness, impulsiveness, heedlessness, thoughtlessness, imprudence, indiscretion, audacity, carelessness, foolhardiness.

v be rash, plunge.

adj rash, hasty, impetuous, reckless, headlong, precipitate, impulsive, thoughtless, heedless, imprudent, indiscreet, careless, unwary, foolhardy, presumptuous, audacious.

864 caution *n* prudence, discretion, circumspection, heed, care, wariness, heedfulness, vigilance, forethought; warning, admonition, advice, injunction, counsel.

v be cautious, take care; warn, admonish, advise, counsel.

adj cautious, prudent, heedful, careful, watchful, discreet, wary, vigilant, alert, provident, chary, circumspect, guarded.

865 desire *n* longing, fancy, craving, yearning, wish, want, need, hunger, appetite, thirst; request, wish, ambition, aspiration; love, passion, lust.

v desire, wish for, long for, crave, want, wish, covet, fancy; ask, request, solicit; lust for.

adj desirous, desiring, craving, wishful, hungry, thirsty, covetous, fervent, ardent, lustful.

866 indifference *n* unconcern, listlessness, apathy, insensibility, coolness, insensitiveness, inattention.

v be indifferent, take no interest in, have no heart for, spurn, disdain.

adj indifferent, unconcerned, listless, apathetic, cool, cold, lukewarm, insensitive, inattentive.

867 dislike *n* disinclination, disrelish, distaste, disgust, repugnance, antipathy, antagonism, aversion, hatred, horror, loathing.

v dislike, disrelish, be averse to, be disinclined, be reluctant, have no taste for; disgust, repel, nauseate, hate, loathe.

adj disliking, disinclined, averse, loath; dislikable, distasteful, disagreeable, offensive, repulsive, repugnant, repellent, abhorrent, nauseating, disgusting, loathsome.

868 fastidiousness *n* nicety; hypercriticism; discernment, discrimination, judiciousness, keenness, perspicacity.

v be fastidious, split hairs.

adj fastidious, nice, dainty, delicate; hard to please, finicky, hypercritical, fussy, querulous, meticulous, exacting, scrupulous, proper, priggish, prim; discerning, discriminative, judicious, keen, sharp, perspicacious, sagacious.

869 satiety *n* repletion, saturation, glut, surfeit; disgust, weariness.

v sate, satiate, saturate, cloy, glut, stuff, gorge, surfeit; gall, disgust, bore, tire, weary.

adj satiated, glutted, stuffed, gorged, surfeited; disgusted, bored, tired, weary.

870 wonder *n* surprise, marvel, astonishment, stupefaction, amazement, awe, admiration, bewilderment, puzzlement.

v wonder, think, speculate, conjecture, meditate, ponder, question; marvel, admire, be surprised, start, stare, startle, astonish, amaze, astound, stagger, stupefy, bewilder, dumfound.

adj marvelous, wonderful, extraordinary, remarkable, awesome, startling, wondrous, miraculous, astonishing, amazing, astounding, unique, curious, strange, odd, peculiar; astonished, surprised, aghast, agog, startled, breathless, awe-struck, spell-bound, lost in wonder, amazed, fascinated, bewildered.

871 expectance *n* expectancy, expectation.

v expect, foresee, assume, not be surprised, make nothing of.

adj expecting, expectant, relied on, expected, figured on, foreseen.

872 prodigy *n* phenomenon, wonder, marvel, miracle; freak, monstrosity, spectacle, curiosity; genius, intellectual giant, wizard, mastermind, expert, sage, child genius, wunderkind.

873 repute *n* estimation, reputation, account, regard, report; name, standing, distinction, credit, respect, respectability, dignity, greatness, eminence, honor, renown.

v consider, esteem, account, hold,

regard, deem, reckon; be held in high repute, be distinguished.

adj reputed, regarded, accounted; reputable, respected, respectable, esteemed, celebrated, distinguished, dignified, honored, renowned, eminent.

874 disrepute *n* disgrace, dishonor, disfavor, discredit, ill repute, low repute, bad name, shame, degradation, obloquy, debasement, ignominy, infamy, stain, spot, blot, tarnish, taint.

v disgrace oneself, have a bad name, shame, disgrace, dishonor, tarnish, stain, taint, blot.

adj disreputable, base, low, unsavory, shady, unworthy, disgraced, vile, ignominious, dishonorable, opprobrious, shameful, disgraceful, infamous, tainted, tarnished.

875 nobility *n* distinction, eminence, stateliness, majesty, grandeur, dignity, loftiness, profundity, highmindedness; rank, condition, high birth, gentility quality, royalty, aristocracy, lord, lady

v be noble; ennoble.

adj noble, exalted, honorable, dignified, imposing, stately; titled, aristocratic, patrician, high-born.

876 commonalty *n* the common people, the lower classes, commoners, multitude, proletariat, populace, rank and file, bourgeoisie, general public, citizenry, peasantry, crowd, herd, rabble.

adj common, mean, low, base, ignoble, vulgar, homely, plebeian, proletarian, low-born, obscure, rustic, boorish, uncivilized.

877 title *n* honor, name, designation, decoration.

adj titled.

878 pride *n* self-respect, self-assurance, self-esteem, conceit, vanity, egotism, arrogance, vainglory, self-importance; insolence, haughtiness, superciliousness, presumption.

v be proud, presume, swagger, give oneself airs.

adj proud, high-minded, dignified, stately, noble, imposing, honorable, creditable; self-assured, self-satisfied, contented, egotistical, vain, conceited, arrogant, haughty, smug, overbearing, over-confident, snobbish, supercilious, presumptuous.

879 humility *n* modesty, humbleness, meekness, lowliness, submissiveness.

v lower, abase, debase, degrade, humiliate, mortify, shame, subdue, crush, break.

adj humble, low, lowly, unassuming, plain, common, poor meek, modest, submissive, unpretentious· respectful, polite, courteous.

adv with downcast eyes, on bended knee.

880 vanity *n* pride, conceit, self-esteem, self-complacency, egotism, self-admiration, self-love, self-glorification; hollowness, emptiness, sham, triviality.

v be vain, have too high an opinion of oneself, inflate, puff up.

adj vain, conceited, egotistical, self-complacent, proud, vainglorious, arrogant, overweening, inflated; useless, hollow, trifling, trivial.

881 modesty *n* humility, diffidence, timidity, bashfulness; moderation, decency, propriety, simplicity, chastity, prudery, prudishness.

v be modest, retire, give way to, stay in the background.

adj modest, humble, diffident, timid, timorous, bashful, sheepish, shy; moderate, humble, unpretentious, decent, becoming, proper, inextravagant, unostentatious, retiring, unassuming, unobtrusive; demure, prudish, chaste, pure, virtuous.

adv modestly, humbly, quietly, privately, without ceremony.

882 ostentation *n* pretention, pretentiousness, semblance, show, showiness, pretense, display, pageantry, pomp, pompousness, flourish, splendor.

v show off, parade, display, exhibit, blazon forth, emblazon, flaunt.

adj ostentatious, pretentious, showy, flashy, grand, pompous, garish, gaudy, flaunting, high-sounding, sumptuous, theatrical, dramatic, solemn, majestic, ceremonious, punctilious over-blown.

adv with a flourish.

883 celebration *n* ceremony, ceremonial, commemoration, solemnization, observance, memorialization, festival, festivity.

v celebrate, commemorate, observe, keep; proclaim, announce; praise, extol, laud, glorify, honor, applaud, commend; solemnize, ritualize.

adj celebrational, commemorative, honorific, commendatory; celebrated, famous, renowned, illustrious, eminent, famed.

adv in honor of, in commemoration of, in celebration of.

884 boasting *n* bragging, swaggering, braggadocio, bravado.

boaster, braggart, blusterer, (*informal*) windbag.

v exaggerate, brag, vaunt, swagger, crow, strut, talk big.

adj boasting, boastful, pretentious, vainglorious, elated, exultant, jubilant, triumphant.

885 [undue assumption of superiority] **insolence** *n* boldness, rudeness, disrespect, impertinence, impudence, haughtiness, arrogance, audacity, abusiveness, contemptuousness.

v be insolent, swagger, assume, presume, take liberties, ride roughshod over.

adj insolent, bold, rude, disrespectful, impertinent, impudent, brazen, brassy, haughty, arrogant, audacious, presumptuous, overbearing, abusive, contemptuous, insulting.

886 servility *n* submissiveness, obsequiousness, abasement, slavishness, cringing, fawning, meanness, baseness, groveling, sycophancy, slavery.

toady, sycophant, boot-licker, (*informal*) apple-polisher, (*informal*) brown-noser.

v be servile, cringe, bow, stoop, kneel, toady, fawn, lick the boots of; sneak, crawl, crouch, cower.

adj servile, obsequious, slavish, cringing, fawning, sycophantic, groveling, sniveling, mealy-mouthed, abject, base, mean.

887 blusterer *n* swaggerer, braggart, boaster, windbag, bully, ruffian, rowdy, redneck.

III. Sympathetic Affections

888 friendship *n* amity, friendliness, harmony, concord, fellow-feeling, sympathy, good will, affection; companionship, comradeship, fellowship, fraternity, intimacy.

v be friendly, have an acquaintance with, keep company with, know, sympathize with, befriend, make friends with.

adj friendly, kind, kindly, amiable, neighborly, brotherly, cordial, genial, well-disposed, benevolent, kind-hearted, affectionate; helpful, advantageous, propitious; acquainted, familiar, intimate.

adv amicably, with open arms.

889 enmity *n* unfriendliness, dislike, discord, ill will, antagonism, animosity, hostility, malevolence, hatred.

v be at odds with.

adj inimical, unfriendly, alienated, estranged, hostile.

890 friend *n* companion, acquaintance, crony, chum, pal, mate, fellow, bosom buddy, intimate, confidant; well-wisher, patron, supporter, backer, advocate, partisan, defender, sympathizer; ally, associate.

891 enemy *n* foe, adversary, opponent, antagonist, attacker.

892 sociality *n* sociableness, gregariousness, social interaction, social intercourse, comradeship, camaraderie, companionship, cordiality, good fellowship, conviviality.

v be sociable, consort with, fraternize, welcome.

adj sociable, gregarious, social, warm, genial, cordial, friendly, convivial, amicable, clubbish, chummy, neighborly, hospitable.

893 seclusion, exclusion *n* privacy, retirement, withdrawal, solitude, sequestration, retreat, isolation, hiding, secrecy, elimination, prohibition, exception, omission, preclusion, rejection, ejection, expulsion, banishment, ostracism, exile.

recluse, hermit, cenobite, outcast, castaway, pariah, wastrel, foundling.

v seclude oneself, retire, withdraw, retreat, sequester, isolate, hide; exclude, eliminate, prohibit, reject, eject, expel.

adj secluded, retired, withdrawn, sequestered, private, isolated, solitary, excluded, eliminated, prohibited, omitted, precluded, rejected, ejected, repulsed, banished, ostracized, exiled.

894 courtesy *n* civility, sociability, politeness, good manners, good behavior, affability, gentility, graciousness, courtliness, respect.

v be courteous, behave well.

adj courteous, civil, polite, well-mannered, well-bred, gentlemanly, gallant, urbane, debonair, affable, gracious, courtly, respectful, obliging.

895 discourtesy *n* disrespect, ill-breeding, bad manners, tactlessness, rudeness, impudence, vulgarity.

v be discourteous.

adj discourteous, ill-bred, ill-mannered, ill-behaved, ungentlemanly, uncivil, impolite, ungracious, vulgar, crude, disrespectful, rude.

896 congratulations *n* felicitation, compliment, salute, salutation.

v congratulate, offer congratulations, salute.

adj congratulatory; complimentary.

897 love *n* affection, liking, regard, friendliness, kindness, kindliness, tenderness, fondness, devotion, warmth,

attachment, yearning, passion, rapture, adoration, idolatry.

lover, admirer, suitor, adorer, wooer; beau, sweetheart, flame, love, truelove, paramour, boyfriend, girlfriend, ladylove, idol, darling, angel, beloved.

v love, like, be fond of, have affection for, be enamored of, be in love with, cherish, adore, revere, adulate, idolize.

adj loving, smitten, affectionate, tender, fond, attached, enamored, devoted, amorous, passionate, adoring; lovable, adorable, winning, enchanting, bewitching.

898 hate *n* dislike, aversion, animosity, hatred, antipathy, detestation, loathing, abhorrence, odium, horror, repugnance.

v hate, dislike, detest, abhor, loathe, despise, execrate, abominate.

adj hateful, detestable, odious, abominable, loathsome, abhorrent, repugnant, invidious, obnoxious, offensive, disgusting, nauseating, revolting, vile, repulsive; hating, averse from, set against, bitter, spiteful, malicious.

899 favorite *n* pet, minion, idol, jewel, spoiled child, apple of one's eye, man after one's own heart; love, dear, darling, honey, sweetheart.

900 resentment *n* displeasure, pique, umbrage, animosity, bitterness, envy, jealousy, anger, wrath, indignation.

v resent, take offense, bristle over, chafe, fume, frown, pout, snarl, gnash, growl, scowl, glower, grouch, bear a grudge.

adj resentful, offended, bitter, worked up, angry, wrathful, irate, indignant; envious, jealous.

901 irascibility *n* irritability, excitability, sensitivity.

v be irascible, quick to fly off the handle, have a temper.

adj irascible, testy, short-tempered, hot-tempered, quick-tempered, touchy, temperamental, irritable, snappish, petulant, overly sensitive, choleric.

901a sullenness *n* moodiness, moroseness, churlishness, sluggishness.

v be sullen, frown, scowl, sulk, pout.

adj silent, reserved, sulky, morose, moody, ill-humored, sour, vexatious, bad-tempered, surly, cross, grumpy, peevish, perverse; gloomy, dismal, cheerless, overcast, somber, mournful, dark; slow, sluggish, dull, stagnant.

902 [expression of affection or love]

endearment *n* embrace, caress, hug, kiss, blandishment, dalliance, love token.

v endear, embrace, caress, blandish, flirt, dally.

adj endearing.

903 marriage *n* wedding, nuptials, matrimony, wedlock; union, alliance, association, confederation.

married man, married woman, husband, wife, spouse, mate, partner, consort, better half, (*informal*) old man, (*informal*) old lady.

v marry, tie the knot, take to the altar, wive, couple.

adj married, wed, united.

904 celibacy *n* sexual abstinence; bachelorhood.

celibate, unmarried man, bachelor, unmarried woman, spinster, old maid, virgin, maiden; priest.

adj celibate, unmarried.

905 divorce *n* marital separation, legal separation; separation, disunion, isolation.

v divorce, (*informal*) split up, separate, isolate.

adj divorced, separated, (*informal*) split up.

906 benevolence *n* kindness, kindliness, humanity, tenderness, kindheartedness, unselfishness, generosity, liberality, charity, philanthropy, altruism.

good Samaritan, sympathizer, altruist.

v wish well, take an interest in, treat well, comfort, benefit, assist, aid.

adj benevolent, kind, kindly, well-disposed, kind-hearted, humane, tender, tender-hearted, unselfish, generous, liberal, benevolent, obliging, charitable, philanthropic, altruistic.

907 malevolence *n* ill will, enmity, rancor, resentment, malice, maliciousness, spite, spitefulness, grudge, hate, hatred, venom.

v bear ill will.

adj malevolent, malicious, resentful, spiteful, begrudging, hateful, venomous, vicious, hostile, ill-natured, evil-minded, rancorous.

908 malediction *n* curse, swear, imprecation, denunciation, cursing, damning, damnation, execration; slander.

v curse, swear, imprecate, denounce, damn, execrate; slander.

909 threat *n* menace, danger, indication, portent, foreboding, prognostication; intimidation.

v threaten, menace, endanger, indicate, presage, impend, portend, augur,

forebode, foreshadow, prognosticate; frighten, denounce. intimidate, cow, badger.

adj threatening, menacing, endangering, impending, auguring, foreshadowing, foreboding, ominous, inauspicious, sinister, frightening, intimidating.

910 philanthropy *n* humaneness, compassion, humanitarianism, benevolence, helpfulness, munificence, public spirit, charity.

philanthropist, humanitarian, patriot.

adj philanthropic, humanitarian, benevolent, munificent, altruistic, public spirited, civic minded, charitable.

911 misanthropy *n* hatred of mankind, incivism.

misanthrope, man-hater; misogynist, woman-hater.

adj misanthropic, antisocial, uncivil.

912 benefactor *n* succorer, patron, supporter, contributor, friend.

913 evildoer *n* wrongdoer, troublemaker, subversive, oppressor, destroyer.

914 pity *n* sympathy, compassion, commiseration, condolence, mercy.

v pity, commiserate, feel sorry for, be sorry for, sympathize with, feel for.

adj pitying, compassionate, sympathetic, touched, moved, affected, feeling.

914a pitilessness *n* cruelty, meanness, ruthlessness, hard-heartedness.

v have no pity for.

adj pitiless, merciless, cruel, mean, unmerciful, ruthless, implacable, relentless, inexorable, hard-hearted, stony.

915 condolence *n* lamentation, sympathy, consolation.

v condole with, console, sympathize, lament.

916 gratitude *n* thanks, thankfulness, appreciation, indebtedness.

v be grateful, thank, appreciate.

adj grateful, appreciative, thankful, obliged, beholding, indebted, in one's debt.

917 ingratitude *n* thanklessness, unthankfulness.

ingrate.

v be ungrateful.

adj ungrateful, unthankful, un mindful, thankless.

918 forgiveness *n* pardon, excuse, indulgence, remission, reprieve, amnesty, grace, absolution.

v forgive, pardon, excuse, absolve, reprieve, acquit.

adj forgiving.

919 revenge *n* vengeance, retaliation, requital, reprisal, retribution, vindictiveness, vengefulness.

avenger, vindicator, nemesis.

v revenge, avenge, retaliate, requite, vindicate.

adj revengeful, vengeful, vindictive, spiteful, malevolent, resentful, malicious, malignant, unforgiving, implacable.

920 jealousy *n* envy, resentment; suspicion; watchfulness, vigilance.

v be jealous.

adj jealous, envious, resentful; suspicious; solicitous, watchful, vigilant.

921 envy *n* jealousy, enviousness, grudge, covetousness.

v envy, covet, begrudge, resent.

adj envious, covetous, jealous, begrudging.

IV. Moral Affections

922 right *n* virtue, justice, fairness, integrity, equity, equitableness, uprightness, rectitude, morality, morals, goodness, honor, lawfulness; accuracy, truth.

v be right; do right.

adj right, just, good, equitable, moral, fair, upright, honest, lawful; correct, proper, suitable, fit; correct, true, accurate; genuine, legitimate, rightful.

adv righteously, rightfully, lawfully, rightly, justly, fairly, equitably.

923 wrong *n* evil, wickedness, misdeed, sin, vice, immorality, iniquity, inequity, injustice, unlawfulness.

v wrong, injure, harm, maltreat, abuse, oppress, cheat, defraud, dishonor.

adj wrong, bad, evil, wicked, sinful, immoral, iniquitous, reprehensible, unjust, crooked, dishonest; erroneous, inaccurate, incorrect, false, untrue, mistaken; improper, unappropriate, unfit; awry, amiss, out of order.

adv wrongly, wickedly, sinfully.

924 claim *n* due, right, privilege, prerogative, prescription, demand, sanction, warrant, license.

claimant, appellant.

v claim, deserve, have the right, be entitled.

adj claiming, having a right to,

privileged, prescribed, sanctioned, allowed, licensed, authorized, due.

925 [absence of right] **unrightfulness** *n* impropriety, illegitimacy, presumption.

usurper, pretender.

v be unentitled.

adj unrightful, having no right to, unentitled, unauthorized, unwarranted, illegitimate, not licensed.

926 duty *n* obligation, function, responsibility, onus, burden, business; conscience, moral imperative, sense of duty; homage, respect, reverence.

v do one's duty, behoove, become, befit, beseem; observe, perform, fulfill, discharge.

adj obligatory, binding, imperative, incumbent, under obligation, obliged, bound, tied, duty bound; dutiful, respectful, docile, submissive, deferential, reverential, obedient.

927 dereliction of duty *n* nonobservance, nonperformance, neglect, failure, carelessness, fault, infraction, violation, transgression.

v neglect, slight, fail, violate.

adj undutiful, negligent, careless, at fault, failing, in violation.

927a exemption *n* immunity, impunity, privilege, freedom, exception, excuse, dispensation.

v exempt, excuse, release, acquit, discharge, free.

adj exempt, immune, privileged, freed, excepted, excused, unbound.

928 respect *n* esteem, deference, regard, consideration, estimation, veneration, reverence, homage, honor, admiration, approbation, approval, affection, feeling; respects, regards, duty; regard, consideration, attention, devotion.

v honor, revere, reverence, esteem, venerate, regard, consider, defer to, admire, adulate, adore, love; regard, heed, attend, notice, consider.

adj respectful, courteous, polite, well-mannered, well-bred, civil, deferential; respected, estimable, venerable, admirable; respecting, heeding, considering, regarding, attending.

929 disrespect *n* discourtesy, impoliteness, rudeness, crudeness, incivility, impudence, impertinence, irreverence, derision.

v hold in disrespect, be disrespectful, insult, deride, scoff, mock, sneer, jeer, deride, ridicule, scorn.

adj disrespectful, discourteous, impolite, rude, crude, uncivil, impudent, impertinent, irreverent, insulting, derisive, scornful.

930 contempt *n* scorn, disdain, derision, contumely; dishonor, disgrace, shame.

v feel contempt for, contemn, scorn, disdain, deride, despise.

adj contemptible, despicable, mean, low, miserable, abject, base, vile; contemptuous, scornful, disdainful, derisive; dishonorable, disgraceful, shameful.

931 approbation *n* approval, sanction, esteem, admiration, commendation.

v approbate, approve, esteem, value, honor, admire, appreciate, sanction, endorse, commend, praise.

adj commendatory, complimentary, laudatory; approved, praised, in high esteem, in favour; praiseworthy, commendable, good, meritorious, estimable, creditable.

932 disapprobation *n* disapproval, dislike, disesteem, odium, disparagement, deprecation, denunciation, censure.

v disapprove, dislike, object to, frown upon, censure, blame, reproach, reprove, admonish, berate.

adj disapproving, disparaging, reproachful, defamatory, denunciatory, condemnatory.

933 flattery *n* adulation, charming, lip-service, (*informal*) brown-nosing, fawning, flunkeyism, sycophancy.

v flatter, curry favor, slobber over, (*informal*) lay it on thick, wheedle, fawn, court, (*informal*) brown-nose, pander to, overpraise.

adj flattering, adulatory, honeymouthed, smooth-tongued, servile, sycophantic.

934 detraction *n* detracting, disparagement, belittling, defamation, vilification, calumny, abuse, slander, aspersion, deprecation.

v detract, run down, criticize, decry, disparage, blacken, belittle, depreciate, cast aspersions, defame, malign, abuse, slander, vilify.

adj detracting, disparaging, belittling, derogatory, depreciating, calumnious, abusive, slanderous, vilifying, scurrilous.

935 flatterer *n* adulator, toady, flunkey, (*informal*) apple-polisher, fawner, sycophant, (*informal*) brown-noser, bootlicker, opportunist, courtier.

936 detractor *n* reprover, critic, carper, slanderer, (*informal*) hatchet man,

backbiter, defamer, castigator, satirist, cynic, reviler.

937 vindication n exoneration, exculpation, acquittal; justification, warrant, support, defense.

apologist, vindicator, defender.

v vindicate, exonerate, acquit, clear; uphold, justify, maintain, defend, support.

adj vindicating, vindicated, exonerated, exonerating, exculpatory, acquitted; justified, warranted, supported.

938 accusation n arraignment, indictment, charge, incrimination, impeachment; accusal, blaming, inculpation, charging, imputation.

accuser, prosecutor, plaintiff; relator, informer; appellant.

v charge; arraign, indict, charge, incriminate, impeach; blame, inculpate, charge, involve, point to, impute.

adj accused, accusing, accusatory, accusative, incriminatory, imputative.

939 probity n honesty, uprightness, virtue, rectitude, integrity.

v be honorable.

adj honest, honorable, virtuous, upright, scrupulous, high-principled.

940 improbity n dishonesty, wickedness, immorality, evil.

v be dishonest, play false.

adj dishonest, dishonorable, unscrupulous, immoral, wicked, evil.

941 knave n rogue, rascal, blackguard, sneak, villain, scoundrel.

942 disinterestedness n impartiality, fairness, lack of bias, unselfishness, generosity, liberality.

v be disinterested.

adj disinterested, unbiased, unprejudiced, unselfish, impartial, fair, generous, liberal.

943 selfishness n self-interest, self-seeking, self-love, egoism, egotism, solipsism, illiberality, parsimony, stinginess, meanness.

v be selfish, cultivate one's own garden, look after oneself, feather one's own nest.

adj selfish, self-centered, self-indulgent, self-interested, self-seeking, egotistical, solipsistic, illiberal, parsimonious, stingy, cheap, mean.

944 virtue n virtuousness, goodness, uprightness, morality, ethics, probity, rectitude, integrity; excellence, merit, quality, asset; innocence, chastity, purity.

v be virtuous, have the virtue of.

adj virtuous, right, upright, moral, righteous, good, chaste, pure.

945 vice n fault, sin, depravity, iniquity, immorality, wickedness; blemish, blot, imperfection, defect.

v sin, err, transgress, trespass.

adj vicious, immoral, depraved, profligate, wicked, sinful, sinning, corrupt, bad, iniquitous; reprehensible, blameworthy, censurable, wrong, improper; spiteful, malignant, malicious, malevolent; faulty, defective; ill-tempered, bad-tempered, refractory.

946 innocence n purity, virtue, virtuousness, faultlessness, spotlessness; guiltlessness, blamelessness; uprightness, honesty; naïveté, simplicity, artlessness, guilelessness, ingenuousness.

v be innocent.

adj innocent, pure, untainted, sinless, virtuous, virginal, blameless, faultless, impeccable, spotless, immaculate; guiltless, blameless; upright, honest, forthright; naïve, simple, unsophisticated, artless, guileless, ingenuous.

947 guilt n guiltiness, culpability, criminality; sinfulness.

v be guilty.

adj guilty, culpable, to blame, in fault.

948 good man n model, paragon, hero, soldier, saint, salt of the earth, (informal) ace.

949 bad man n wrong-doer, evildoer, sinner, scoundrel, miscreant, villain, wretch, monster, devil, demon, scum of the earth.

950 penitence n contrition, atonement, compunction, repentance, remorse, regret.

penitent, prodigal son.

v be penitent, repent, rue, regret.

adj penitent, sorry, contrite, repenting; repentant, atoning, amending, remorseful, regretful; penitential.

951 impenitence n irrepentance, obduracy, hardness of heart.

v be impenitent, show no remorse.

adj impenitent, uncontrite, not sorry, obdurate, unrepentant, remorseless; unrepenting, unrepented, unatoned; irreclaimable.

952 atonement n satisfaction, reparation, compensation, amends, quittance; redemption, expiation, reclamation, conciliation, propitiation.

v atone, atone for; give satisfac-

tion, satisfy, make amends; expiate, propitiate, reclaim, redeem, repair, absolve, purge, shrive, do penance, repent.

adj atoning, propitiating, propitiatory, redemptive, expiating, expiatory.

953 temperance *n* moderation, self-restraint, self-control, continence; sobriety, even-temperedness, calmness, coolness, detachment, dispassion.

vegetarian; teetotaler; abstainer.

v be temperate, abstain, forbear, restrain.

adj temperate, moderate, self-controlled, self-restrained, frugal, sparing; sober, calm, cool, detached, dispassionate.

954 intemperance *n* excess, exorbitance, inordinateness, extravagance; indulgence, high living, self-indulgence, epicurism, epicureanism, sybaritism; inabstinence, alcoholism.

v be intemperate, indulge, wallow in.

adj intemperate, excessive, exorbitant, inordinate, extravagant; indulgent, self-indulgent, epicurean.

954a sensualist *n* sybarite, voluptuary, pleasure-seeker, epicure, epicurean, libertine, hedonist.

955 asceticism *n* puritanism, austerity, abstemiousness, self-abnegation, self-denial, total abstinence, self-motification.

ascetic, anchorite, puritan, martyr; hermit, recluse.

v abstain, deny oneself, fast, starve.

adj ascetic, puritanical, austere, abstemious, rigorous, rigid, stern, severe, harsh, strict, self-denying, self-mortifying.

956 fasting *n* day of fasting; going hungry, starving oneself, starvation.

v fast, starve, famish.

adj fasting, starving, unfed; starved, half-starved, hungry.

957 gluttony *n* greed, greediness, voracity; epicurism, gormandizing, gulosity, crapulence, over-eating, (*informal*) piggishness.

glutton, epicure, cormorant, hog, (*informal*) pig.

v be gluttonous, hog; overeat, gorge, stuff oneself, make a pig of oneself, guzzle, bolt, devour engorge, gobble up.

adj gluttonous, greedy, voracious; epicurean, gormandizing, crapulent, swinish, (*informal*) piggish.

958 sobriety *n* abstinence teetotalism.

teetotaler, abstainer.

v be sober, abstain, take the pledge.

adj sober, unintoxicated, on the wagon, (*informal*) straight, (*informal*) dry, dry as a bone.

959 drunkenness *n* intemperance, drinking, inebriety, insobriety, intoxication, alcoholism.

drunkard, sot, tippler, drinker, inebriate, dipsomaniac, alcoholic, (*informal*) boozer, (*informal*) lush, (*informal*) juicer.

v be drunk, drink, imbibe, booze, guzzle, swill, soak, sot, lush, drink like a fish, hit the bottle.

adj drunk, drunken, sotted, intoxicated, inebriated, tipsy, tight, (*informal*) potted, (*informal*) stewed, (*informal*) stewed to the gills, dead drunk, (*informal*) plowed, (*informal*) plastered, (*informal*) tanked, (*informal*) wasted, (*informal*) juiced, (*informal*) blown away, (*informal*) high, (*informal*) flying, (*informal*) feeling no pain.

960 purity *n* cleanness; decency, decorum, delicacy; continence, chastity, innocence, modesty, virtue, virginity; simplicity, genuineness, faultlessness, perfection; guiltlessness, honesty, uprightness.

virgin, vestal virgin.

v be pure.

adj pure, decent, delicate; innocent, continent, chaste, viginal, modest, virtuous, undefiled, unsullied, unstained, untainted, uncorrupted, clean, spotless, immaculate; simple, genuine, faultless, perfect; honest, upright; unmixed, unadulterated, uncontaminated.

961 impurity *n* indecency, indelicacy; incontinence, immodesty, lewdness, concupiscence, prurience, lechery; grossness, obscenity, ribaldry, smut, bawdry; uncleanness, adulteration, contamination, defilement; fault, flaw, imperfection; guilt, sin, sinfulness.

v be impure.

adj impure, indecent, indelicate; incontinent, immodest, unchaste, concupiscent, lewd, prurient, lecherous; gross, obscene, ribald, dirty, smutty, bawdy; unclean, sullied, defiled, contaminated, adulterated, tainted, stained, corrupted, jaded; faulty, flawed, imperfect; guilty, sinning, sinful, wicked.

962 libertine *n* rake, roué, debauchee, lecher, sensualist, voluptuary, profligate, seducer, deceiver. courtesan, prostitute, strumpet, harlot, whore, street-walker, trollop, hussy, bitch, slut, minx.

963 legality n legitimacy, legitimateness, lawfulness; duty, obligation.

law, code, constitution, charter, statute, regulation, decree, order.

v legalize; legislate, enact, ordain, decree, codify, formulate, pass a law.

adj legal, legitimate, authorized, licit, lawful, legalized, legislated; constitutional.

964 illegality n illegitimacy, unlawfulness, illicitness, lawlessness.

v be illegal, offend against the law, violate the law.

adj illegal, unlawful, illegitimate, illicit, contraband, unconstitutional, unchartered, unwarranted, unauthorized, unlicensed, proscribed, prohibited, outlawed, criminal; lawless, arbitrary, despotic, unanswerable, unaccountable.

965 [executive] **jurisdiction** n judicature, authority, power, right, control; territory, range, magistracy.

v judge, sit in judgment; administer.

adj jurisdictive, judicial, administrative; inquisitorial.

966 tribunal n court, courtroom, board, bench, court of law, court of justice, bar of justice, judgment seat, dock, forum, witness-chair.

967 judge n justice, judiciary, magistrate, judicator, adjudicator, jurist, juror; moderator, arbiter, arbitrator, umpire, referee.

v judge, adjudge, determine, hear a cause, try a case, pass sentence.

adj judicial, judicious, juridical, legal, juristic, judicatory, jurisdictive.

968 lawyer n attorney, attorney-at-law, counselor, barrister, solicitor, pleader, counsel, advocate, counselor-at-law, legal adviser; prosecutor, prosecuting attorney, district attorney, public prosecutor, attorney general.

bar, legal profession.

v practice law, be called to the bar, plead, read the law.

adj learned in the law.

969 lawsuit n suit, action, cause, dispute, contention; case, debate, litigation, legal proceedings, legal action, legal process, trial, debate, pleadings, argument, argumentation, disputation, prosecution; writ, summons, subpoena, affidavit, suitor; party to a suit, litigant, verdict, decision; precedent.

v go to the law, sue, file a claim, bring to trial, put on trial, serve, serve with a writ, cite, arraign, prosecute, bring an action against, indict, impeach, attach, summon.

adj litigious.

970 acquittal n clearance, exculpation, exoneration, absolution, discharge, pardon; impunity, immunity.

v acquit, exculpate, exonerate, clear, absolve, pardon; discharge, release, liberate, set free.

adj acquitted, cleared, exculpated, exonerated; discharged, released, set free.

971 condemnation n conviction, guilty verdict, proscription.

v condemn, convict, find guilty, damn, doom, proscribe; stand condemned.

adj condemned, condemnatory, convicted.

972 punishment n sentence, judgment, penalty, retribution, discipline, chastisement, castigation, reproof, correction.

v punish, inflict punishment, correct, discipline, penalize, reprove, castigate, chasten, administer correction, scold, berate, jail, incarcerate, execute, torture, banish, flog, whip, lash, scourge.

adj punishing, punitive, castigatory, penalized, penalizing; punished, castigated.

973 reward n recompense, prize, desert, compensation, pay, remuneration, requital, merit; bounty, premium, bonus; reparation, redress; retribution, reckoning, amends.

v reward, recompense, requite, compensate, pay, remunerate.

adj rewarding, remunerative, compensatory, retributive, reparatory; rewarded.

974 penalty n punishment, retribution, pain, pains, penance; fine, forfeit, damages, sequestration, incarceration, confiscation.

v penalize, punish; fine, confiscate, sequester; penalized, punished.

975 scourge n punishment, flogging; affliction, calamity, plague, bane, pest, nuisance; whip, lash, strap, throng, rod, cane, stick; prison, house of correction.

gaoler, jailer, executioner, hangman.

976 deity n divinity, god, godhead, omnipotence, providence, lord, the almighty, supreme being, first cause, prime mover, author, creator, the infinite, the eternal, the all-powerful, the all-merciful, omnipresence.

adj divine, godly, almighty, holy, hallowed, sacred, heavenly, celestial, sacrosanct; superhuman, supernatural, spiritual, ghostly, unearthly.

977 angel *n* glorified spirit, beneficent spirit, ministering spirit, heavenly spirit, winged being, seraph, cherub, archangel, helper, spirit, guardian; (*informal*) friend, patron, protector, guardian angel, love.

adj angelic, seraphic, cherubic, spiritual, ethereal; pure, good, righteous, ideal, beautiful; (*informal*) adorable, entrancing, transporting, rapturous, lovely, enrapturing.

978 devil *n* Satan, Lucifer, Beelzebub; tempter, evil one, evil spirit, serpent, prince of darkness, demon, evil incarnate.

diabolism, satanism.

adj devilish, satanic, diabolic, infernal, hellish.

979 fabulous spirit *n* god, goddess, fairy, fay, sylph, faun, nymph, nereid, dryad, sea-maid, oread, naiad, mermaid, kelpie, nixie, sprite, pixie, elf.

adj fabulous, mythological, imaginary, sylphic.

980 demon *n* demonology; devil, fiend, evil spirit, incubus, monster, succubus, succuba, fury, harpy, ghoul, vampire, ogre, gnome, imp, kobold, dwarf, urchin, troll, sprite, bad fairy, leprechaun; ghost, specter, apparition, spirit, shade, shadow, vision, hobgoblin, wraith, spook, banshee, siren, satyr.

adj demonic, supernatural, weird, uncanny, unearthly, spectral, ghostly, ghostlike, elfin, fiendish, impish, haunted.

981 heaven *n* kingdom of heaven, kingdom of god, heavenly kingdom, paradise, nirvana; celestial bliss, glory.

adj heavenly, celestial, supernal, unearthly, paradisaic, paradisical, beatific, elysian, blissful, beautiful, divine, blessed, beatified, glorified.

982 hell *n* Gehenna, inferno, Hades, Erebus, pandemonium, abyss, limbo; [*informal*] torment, torture, pain, agony, suffering.

adj hellish, infernal, stygian, satanic, diabolic, devilish; [*informal*] painful, agonizing, excruciating, horrifying, unendurable.

983 theology *n* theosophy, divinity, hagiography, theologics, theism, monotheism, religion, religious persuasion, dogma, creed, credo, doctrine, tenet, articles of faith.

theologian, theologue, divine.

adj theological, religious, theosophical, hagiological.

983a orthodoxy *n* soundness; strictness, faithfulness, adherence, observance; truth, true faith, religious truth.

adj orthodox, sound, strict, faithful, catholic, doctrinal, authoritative, official, traditional; scriptural, divine, Christian; conventional, established, approved, prescriptive, prevailing, customary.

984 heterodoxy *n* unorthodoxy, nonconformity, iconoclasm, doubt, skepticism, recusancy, dissent, misbelief, error, heresy, schism, apostasy.

pagan, heathen, dissenter, nonconformist, skeptic, heretic, atheist.

adj heterodox, nonconformist, nonconforming, iconoclastic, doubting, skeptical, unscriptural, unorthodox, uncanonical, recusant, dissenting, misbelieving, heretical, schismatic.

985 revelation *n* disclosure, discovery, expression, declaration, expression, utterance, publication, admission, convession, acknowledgment; enlightenment, proclamation, announcement; Christian Revelation. Scriptures, Word of God.

adj revelatory; instructive; confessional.

986 religious writings *n* Scriptures, *Bible*, Old Testament, New Testament, The Vedas, Upanishads, Bhagavad Gita, Koran, Alcoran, Avesta.

987 piety *n* godliness, devoutness, devotion, humility, veneration, sanctity, grace, holiness; reverence, regard, respect.

believer, devotee, pietist, righteous man.

v be pious, have faith; believe, revere, venerate, sanctify, consecrate.

adj pious, devout, godly, reverent, religious, holy, sacred, pietistic, saintly; devoted, humble, reverential.

988 impiety *n* irreverence, irreligion, scoffing, profaneness, profanity, blasphemy, desecration, sacrilege, sin, sinfulness; hypocrisy, cant, sanctimony, sanctimoniousness.

sinner, scoffer, blasphemer, sacrilegist, hypocrite.

v be impious, scoff, swear, profane, blaspheme, desecrate, revile, commit sacrilege.

989 irreligion *n* ungodliness, laxity, impiety, indifference, apathy, skepticism, doubt, disbelief, incredulity, agnosticism, freethinking, atheism, infidelity.

skeptic, doubter, nonbeliever, agnostic, cynic, freethinker, atheist, infidel, heathen.

v be irreligious, doubt, disbelieve, lack faith, question.

adj irreligious, godless, ungodly, unholy, unhallowed, undevout; skeptical, doubting, unbelieving, indifferent, apathetic, incredulous, freethinking, agnostic, atheistic, faithless; worldly, earthly, unspiritual.

990 worship *n* reverence, homage, adoration, honor; regard, idolizing, idolatry, deification; prayer, supplication, petition; service, celebration, rites.

worshiper, congregation, suppliant, communicant, celebrant.

v worship, adore, adulate, idolize, deify, love, like; pray, kneel, bow, fall on one's knees; invoke, supplicate, offer prayers, petition; praise, bless, laud, glorify, magnify, sing praises.

adj worshiping, revering, adoring, honoring; worshipful, reverential, honorific, celebrational.

991 idolatry *n* idolism, idolatrousness, idolization, fetishism, idol-worship, deification, demonology; blind adoration, extravagant love, fervor, ardency, enchantment, hero worship.

idol, image, icon, symbol, statue, false god, pagan deity.

v idolize, worship idols, idolatrize, worship, glorify, put on a pedestal, canonize, deify, apotheosize; dote upon, treasure, prize.

adj idolatrous, idol-worshiping, pagan, fetishistic; adoring, impassioned, lovesick.

992 sorcery *n* occultism, magic, witchery, enchantment, witchcraft, spell, necromancy, divination, charm, conjuration, bewitchery, spiritualism.

v practice sorcery, conjure, charm, enchant, bewitch, divine, entrance, mesmerize, cast a spell, call up spirits, raise spirits.

adj magic, magical, bewitching, enchanting, charming, incantory, weird, cabalistic, talismanic; charmed, bewitched, enchanted.

993 spell *n* charm, incantation, exorcism, voodoo, trance, rapture, suggestion, jinx, hocus-pocus, mumbo-jumbo, abracadabra.

994 sorcerer *n* magician, conjuror, necromancer, wizard, witch, exorcist, charmer, medicine man, shaman, medium, clairvoyant, mesmerist, soothsayer, guru.

995 churchdom *n* church, ministry, priesthood, sisterhood, prelacy, hierarchy.

v call, ordain, consecrate, bestow, elect.

adj ecclesiastical, clerical, priestly, pastoral, ministerial, hierarchical.

996 clergy *n* clerical, ministry, priesthood, the cloth, clergyman, divine, ecclesiastic, churchman, pastor, shepherd, minister, preacher, parson, father, reverend, priest, rabbi.

v receive the call, take orders.

adj clerical; ordained.

997 laity *n* fold, flock, congregation, assembly, brethren, people; layman, parishioner.

v secularize.

adj lay, laical, secular, civil, temporal.

998 rite *n* ceremony, observance, function, service, procedure, form, usage.

v perform a rite.

adj ritualistic, ceremonial.

999 canonicals *n* religious garments, vestments, robe, gown, surplice.

1000 temple *n* place of worship, house of god, cathedral, church, chapel, meetinghouse, synagogue, tabernacle, mosque, shrine, pantheon; monastery, priory, abbey, friary, convent, nunnery, cloister; parsonage, rectory, vicarage.

adj churchly, cloistered, monastic.

Index

A

A.M. *n* 125
abandon *n* 682; *v* 293, 624, 757, 782
abandonment *n* 624, 678, 757, 782
abase *v* 308, 879
abasement *n* 308, 886
abate *v* 36, 174, 287, 813, 834
abatement *n* 36, 813
abbreviate *v* 38, 201, 596
abbreviated *adj* 201
abbreviation *n* 38, 201, 596
abdicate *v* 624, 782
abdication *n* 624, 757, 782
abduct *v* 789
abduction *n* 789
aberrant *adj* 83, 279
aberration *n* 20a, 83, 279, 291, 495, 503
abet *v* 707
abeyance *n* 142
abhor *v* 898
abhorrence *n* 898
abhorrent *adj* 830, 867, 898
abide *v* 1, 110, 141, 143, 186
abide by *v* 772
abiding *adj* 110, 141, 150
ability *n* 79, 157, 632, 698, 702
abject *adj* 207, 886, 930
abject fear *n* 862
abjuration *n* 536, 607, 757
abjure *v* 536, 607, 757
ablaze *adj* 382, 420
able *adj* 157, 698
able-bodied *adj* 159
ablution *n* 652
abnegation *n* 764
abnormal *adj* 83
abnormality *n* 83
abode *n* 189
abolish *v* 756
abolition *n* 756
abominable *adj* 649, 653, 898
abominate *v* 898
abomination *n* 649
aboriculture *n* 371

aboriginal *adj* 124
abort *v* 732
abortion *n* 732
abortive *adj* 732
about *adv* 9, 32, 227
aboutface *adv* 283
above all *adv* 33
aboveboard *adj* 246, 703; *adv* 525
above par *adj* 648
abracadabra *n* 993
abrade *v* 330
abrasion *n* 331, 330
abreast *adv* 236
abridge *v* 36, 201, 572, 596
abridged *adj* 201
abridgment *n* 36, 201, 572, 596
abrogate *v* 756, 757
abrogation *n* 756
abrupt *adj* 113, 173, 217, 579, 739
abruptly *adv* 508
abruptness *n* 113, 579, 739
abscond *v* 623, 671
absence *n* 187
absence of choice *n* 609a
absence of design *n* 615a
absence of influence *n* 175a
absence of intellect *n* 450a
absence of meaning *n* 517
absence of motive *n* 615a
absence of smell *n* 399
absence of thought *n* 452
absence of time *n* 107
absent *v* 293; *adj* 187, 452
absenteeism *n* 187
absent oneself *v* 187
absolute *adj* 1, 31, 52, 104, 474, 737, 739, 748
absolutely *adv* 31
absolution *n* 750, 918, 970
absolutism *n* 739
absolve *v* 750, 918, 952, 970
absorb *v* 48, 296, 824
absorbed *adj* 451
absorption *n* 296

abstain *v* 623, 678, 953, 955, 958, 609a
abstainer *n* 953, 958
abstain from doing *v* 681
abstemious *adj* 955
abstemiousness *n* 955
abstention *n* 623
abstinence *n* 623, 678, 958
abstract *n* 596; *v* 78, 572, 596; *adj* 2, 4
abstraction *n* 451
absurd *adj* 47, 471, 477, 497, 853
absurdity *n* 497
absurdity *n* 517, 853
abundance *n* 31, 102
abundant *adj* 31
abundantly *adv* 31
abuse *n* 649, 679, 716, 934; *v* 649, 679, 716, 923, 934
abusive *adj* 716, 885, 934
abusiveness *n* 885
abutment *n* 199
abut on *v* 199
abysmal *adj* 208
abyss *n* 180, 198, 208, 982
academic *adj* 537, 542
academician *n* 492
academy *n* 542
accede *v* 488, 762
acceding *adj* 831
accelerate *v* 132, 173, 274, 684
acceleration *n* 274
accent *n* 580; *v* 580
accentuate *v* 580, 642
accentuation *n* 580
accept *v* 76, 82, 484, 771, 785, 789
acceptance *n* 484, 762, 785
acceptance into *n* 76
accepted *adj* 484
access *n* 197, 286
accessible *adj* 260, 705
accession *n* 37
accessory *n* 39, 88; *adj* 37, 88
accidence *n* 567
accident *n* 156, 619
accidental *adj* 6, 156, 621
acclaim *v* 836
acclimate *v* 613
acclivitous *adj* 305

acclivity n 217, 305
accolade n 733
accommodate v 23, 613, 707, 723, 787
accommodate oneself to v 82
accommodation n 723, 787
accompaniment n 88
accompaniment n 39
accompanist n 416
accompany v 88, 120, 416
accompanying adj 88
accomplish v 52, 161, 729, 731
accomplishment n 698, 729, 731
accord n 23, 178, 488, 714, 721, 762; v 23, 413, 714, 760, 784, 812
accordance n 16, 23, 178
accordant adj 23
accordingly adv 8
accord with v 16
account n 551, 594, 805, 811, 873; v 451, 594, 873
accountable adj 177
accountant n 801, 811
accounted adj 873
account for v 155
accounting for n 155
accounts n 811
accounts n 800
accouterments n 225
accredit v 805
accredited adj 484
accretion n 35
accrue v 37, 785
acculturation n 658
accumulate v 37, 72, 636
accumulation n 72, 636
accuracy n 459, 494, 543, 922
accurate adj 246, 494, 922
accusal n 938
accusation n 938
accusative adj 938
accusatory adj 938
accused adj 938
accuser n 938
accusing adj 938
accustom v 613
ace n 948
acerbate v 397
acerbic adj 397
acerbity n 397
ache n 378, 828; v 378
achievable adj 470
achieve v 161, 680, 729, 731

achievement n 161, 551, 729, 731
aching n 378
acid adj 397
acidify v 397
acidity n 397
acidulate v 397
acidulous adj 397
acknowledge v 488, 529, 535, 762
acknowledgment n 488, 529, 762, 772, 807, 985
acknowledgment of payment n 810
acme n 206, 210
acolyte n 541
acoustics n 402
acquaintance n 890
acquainted adj 888
acquainted with adj 490, 527
acquaint with v 527
acquiesce v 488, 602, 725, 762
acquiescence n 488, 725, 762
acquiescent adj 488, 535, 725
acquire v 539, 775, 785, 795
acquire a habit v 613
acquirement n 698
acquirements n 539
acquisition n 775
acquisition n 785, 795
acquisition of knowledge n 539
acquit v 750, 918, 927a, 937, 970
acquit oneself of v 807
acquittal n 970
acquittal n 750, 937
acquittance n 772
acquitted adj 937, 970
acreage n 342, 780
acres n 342
acrid adj 392, 395, 397
acridity n 392, 397
acridness n 395
act n 680, 697, 741; v 170, 599, 680, 692
act a part v 599, 644, 855
act in concert v 709
acting n 599
action n 680
action n 264, 682, 686, 692, 969
actions n 692
activate v 175
active adj 171, 359, 682
activity n 682
activity n 171, 264, 686
actor n 599, 680, 690
actress n 599

actual adj 1, 118, 494
actuality n 1
actually adv 1
act up to v 772
acumen n 498
acute adj 171, 173, 253, 375, 410, 410
acute angle n 244
acutely adv 31
acuteness n 173, 253
adage n 496
adamant adj 600
adamantine adj 323
adapt v 23, 852
adaptability n 149
adaptable adj 82, 149
adapt to v 82
add v 37, 85
addendum n 37, 39
addiction n 613
addictive adj 613
addition n 37
addition n 35, 39
additional adj 35, 37, 39
addle-brained adj 499
address n 189, 582, 586; v 582, 586
add to v 35
add up v 37, 85
add up to v 50
add water v 337
adept adj 698
adequacy n 639
adequate adj 157, 639
adhere v 46, 199
adherence n 46, 983a
adhere to v 613, 772
adhering adj 46
adhesion n 46, 772
adhesive adj 46, 327, 352
adhesiveness n 46, 352
adieu n 293
ad infinitum adv 104
adjacent adj 197
adjoin v 197, 199
adjoining adj 197
adjourn v 133
adjournment n 133
adjudge v 967
adjudicator n 737, 967
adjunct n 39
adjunct n 37, 88
adjust v 23, 27, 58, 774, 852
adjustable adj 149
adjustment n 723, 774
administer n 965; v 692, 693, 737, 786, 965
administer correction v 972
administering adj 693
administration n 692, 693
administrative adj

692, 737, 965
admirable *adj* 928
admiration *n* 870, 928, 931
admire *v* 870, 928, 931
admirer *n* 897
admission *n* 76, 296, 785, 985
admit *v* 54, 76, 296, 488, 529, 785
admit of *v* 470
admittance *n* 296
admitting *adj* 469
admixture *n* 41
admonish *v* 668, 695, 864, 932
admonition *n* 668, 695, 864
admonitory *adj* 695
ado *n* 315, 684
adolescence *n* 131
adolescent *adj* 131
adorable *adj* 897, 977
adoration *n* 897, 990
adore *v* 897, 928, 990
adorer *n* 897
adoring *adj* 897, 990, 991
adorn *v* 847
adornment *n* 847
adrift *adj* 10, 44, 73; *adv* 44
adroit *adj* 698
adroitness *n* 698, 702
adulate *v* 897, 928, 990
adulation *n* 933
adulator *n* 935
adulatory *adj* 933
adult *adj* 131
adulterate *v* 41, 659
adulterated *adj* 337, 961
adulteration *n* 41, 659, 961
adulthood *n* 131
adumbrate *v* 422
adumbration *n* 421
advance *n* 282, 286, 731, 787; *v* 35, 109, 282, 307, 514, 658, 731, 763, 787
advanced *adj* 128, 282
advanced age *n* 128
advanced guard *n* 234
advancement *n* 282, 658
advancing *adj* 282
advantage *n* 33, 618; *v* 618
advantageous *adj* 618, 644, 646, 648, 775, 888
advent *n* 121, 286, 292
adventitious *adj* 6, 8, 156
adventure *n* 151, 622, 675; *v* 665, 675

adventurer *n* 463, 548, 621
adventuress *n* 548
adventur'ous *adj* 675, 861
adversary *n* 708, 710, 726, 891
adverse *adj* 708, 735
adversely *adv* 735
adversity *n* 735
adversity *n* 619, 830
advertise *v* 531
advertisement *n* 531
advice *n* 695
advice *n* 527, 668, 693, 864
advisability *n* 646
advisable *adj* 646
advise *v* 527, 693, 695, 864
advised *adj* 527, 620
advisedly *adv* 611, 620
adviser *n* 540, 694, 695
advisory *adj* 668, 695
advisory board *n* 696
advocacy *n* 707
advocate *n* 890, 968; *v* 695, 707
aerate *v* 338
aerial *adj* 267, 338
aeriform *adj* 338
aeronautical *n* 267
aeronautics *n* 267
aesthetic *adj* 845
afar *adj* 196; *adv* 196
affability *n* 894
affable *adj* 894
affair *n* 151, 454, 625, 680
affairs *n* 151
affect *v* 9, 175, 176, 824, 855
affectation *n* 855
affectation *n* 579
affected *adj* 579, 820, 821, 855, 914
affectedness *n* 855
affection *n* 888, 897, 928
affectionate *adj* 888, 897
affections *n* 820
affidavit *n* 467, 535, 969
affiliated *adj* 9, 11
affiliation *n* 11
affinity *n* 9, 17, 216, 288
affirm *v* 516, 535
affirmation *n* 535
affirmative *adj* 535
affirming *adj* 535
affix *n* 39; *v* 37, 43
afflict *v* 828
affliction *n* 735, 828, 830, 975
affluence *n* 734, 803

affluent *adj* 803
afford *v* 784
afford pleasure *v* 829
affront *n* 830; *v* 830
afire *adj* 382
aflame *adj* 382
afloat *adj* 1, 267
aforementioned *adj* 116
aforethought *adj* 611
afraid *adj* 860, 862
afresh *adv* 104, 123
aft *adv* 235
after *adj* 117; *adv* 63, 117, 235, 281
aftermath *n* 65
afternoon *n* 126
afterpiece *n* 65
aftertaste *n* 390
after the flood *adv* 59
after this fashion *adv* 627
afterthought *n* 65
afterwards *adv* 117
again *adv* 104
again and again *adv* 104
against *adv* 708; *prep* 179
against one's will *adv* 603
against the grain *adv* 256
age *n* 128
age *n* 106, 108, 124; *v* 124, 435
aged *adj* 124, 128, 130
agency *n* 170
agency *n* 632, 677, 755
agent *n* 690
agent *n* 153, 758
agglomerate *v* 46
aggrandize *v* 35, 194
aggrandizement *n* 35, 37, 194
aggravate *v* 173, 835
aggravation *n* 835
aggregate *n* 50, 72; *v* 50
aggregation *n* 46, 72
aggression *n* 716
aggressive *adj* 716
aggressiveness *n* 715
aggressor *n* 716
aggrieve *v* 649
aghast *adj* 509, 860, 870
agile *adj* 274
agitate *v* 315, 824
agitated *adj* 149, 315
agitation *n* 315
agitation *n* 59, 149, 171, 173, 824, 825
aglow *adj* 420
agnostic *adj* 989
agnosticism *n* 989

ago *adv* 122
agog *adj* 870
agonize *v* 378
agonizing *adj* 982
agony *n* 378, 825, 828, 982
agrarian *adj* 371
agree *v* 23, 82, 178, 488, 714, 725, 762, 768, 769
agreeable *adj* 23, 82, 377, 413, 762, 829, 831
agreeableness *n* 829
agreed *adj* 488
agreed upon *adj* 474
agreeing *adj* 23, 413, 488, 494
agreement *n* 23
agreement *n* 16, 17, 82, 178, 242, 488, 602, 709, 714, 762, 769
agree to *v* 760
agree with *v* 656, 829
agricultural *adj* 371
agriculture *n* 371
agrobiology *n* 371
agrology *n* 371
agronomics *n* 371
agronomy *n* 371
ahead *adv* 234, 280, 282, 303
aid *n* 707
aid *n* 631, 644, 711, 834; *v* 215, 631, 644, 707, 746, 834, 906
aiding *adj* 707
ail *v* 655
ailing *adj* 655
ailment *n* 655
aim *n* 278, 453, 516, 620; *v* 278, 516
aim at *v* 278, 620, 622
aim for *v* 620
air *n* 338
air *n* 349, 415, 448, 852; *v* 338
aircraft *n* 273
airing *n* 266
airman *n* 269
air-pipe *n* 351
airplane *n* 273
airs *n* 855
airtight *adj* 261
air travel *n* 267
airy *adj* 4, 320, 334, 338
ait *n* 346
ajar *adj* 260
akimbo *adj* 244
akin *adj* 11
akin to *adj* 17
alacrity *n* 132, 274, 602, 684
à la mode *adj* 852
alarm *n* 669
alarm *n* 550, 665, 668,

860; *v* 669
alarm bell *n* 669
alarmed *adj* 860
alarum *n* 669
albeit *adv* 30
abification *n* 430
albinism *n* 430
albinistic *adj* 430
album *n* 596
alchemy *n* 144
alcoholic *n* 959
alcoholism *n* 954, 959
Alcoran *n* 986
alert *adj* 457, 498, 682, 864
alertness *n* 457, 459
algebra *n* 85
algebraic *adj* 85
alias *n* 565
alien *adj* 10, 57
alienated *adj* 889
alight *v* 265, 292, 306, 342
aligned *adj* 216
alignment *n* 278
alike *adj* 17
alive *adj* 359, 375, 457, 505, 682
alive and kicking *adj* 359
all *adv* 50
allay *v* 834
all but *adv* 32
all day long *adv* 110
allegation *n* 617
allege *v* 617
alleged *adj* 617
allegiance *n* 743
all-embracing *adj* 76
all-encompassing *adj* 78
alleviate *v* 174, 834
alleviation *n* 834
all for the better *adj* 658
alliance *n* 9, 11, 178, 709, 712, 714, 903
allied *adj* 9, 11, 216
allied to *adj* 17
allied with *adj* 178
all-important *adj* 642
all in all *adv* 50
all-inclusive *adj* 78
all manner of kinds *adj* 81
allocation *n* 786
allocution *n* 586
all of a sudden *adv* 113
all one *adj* 27
allot *v* 51, 60, 786
allotment *n* 60, 786
all over *adv* 180
allow *v* 469, 488, 529, 737, 740, 748, 760, 762, 784, 813
allowable *adj* 760
allowance *n* 469, 488,

760, 784, 786, 813
allowed *adj* 924
allow for *v* 469
alloy *n* 41, 48
all-purpose *adj* 148
all ready *adj* 673
all set for *adj* 507
all the livelong day *adv* 110
all the rage *adj* 852
all the time *adv* 106
all the worse for wear *adj* 659
allude to *v* 516, 527
allure *v* 288, 829
alluring *adj* 288
allusive *adj* 521, 526
alluvial *adj* 342
ally *n* 711, 890; *v* 174
almanac *n* 114
almighty *adj* 157, 976
almighty dollar *n* 800
almost *adv* 32
alms *n* 784
almsgiving *n* 784
aloft *n* 267
alone *adj* 87
alongside *adv* 236
a long way off *adv* 196
a long while back *adv* 122
along with *adv* 37, 88
aloud *adv* 404
alphabet *n* 561
alphabetical *adj* 561
already *adv* 116, 122
also *adv* 37
alter *v* 15, 140
alteration *n* 20a, 140
altercation *n* 713, 720
altered *adj* 15, 20a
alter ego *n* 17
alternate *adj* 634, 759; *v* 12, 20a, 70, 138, 147, 149 *adj* 12, 70, 138
alternately *adv* 138
alternation *n* 138, 145, 149, 314
alternative *n* 147, 609
alter one's course *v* 279
although *adv* 30, 179
altitude *n* 206
altogether *adv* 50, 52
altruism *n* 906
altruist *n* 906
altruistic *adj* 906, 910
always *adv* 16, 112
amalgam *n* 41, 48
amalgamate *v* 41, 48
amalgamation *n* 41, 48
amass *v* 50, 72, 636
amateur *n* 701
amaze *v* 870
amazed *adj* 870
amazement *n* 870

amazing adj 870
amazingly adv 31
amber n 356a
ambergris n 356a
ambiguity n 475, 517, 519, 520, 571
ambiguous adj 475, 520
ambition n 620, 865
amble v 275
ambrosial adj 394
ambuscade n 530
ambush n 530
ambush n 667; v 530
ameliorate v 658, 723
amelioration n 658
amenable adj 762
amend v 658
amending adj 950
amendment n 658
amends n 30, 952, 973
amenity n 829
amiability n 829
amiable adj 721, 829, 888
amicable adj 707, 721, 892
amicably adv 888
amid adv 41, 228
amidst adv 41
amiss adj 923
amity n 714, 721, 888
ammunition n 727
amnesia n 506
amnesty n 723, 918
among adv 41, 228
amongst adv 41, 228
amorous adj 897
amorphism n 241
amorphous adj 241
amount n 25, 26, 800, 812
amount to v 50
amphitheater n 599, 728
ample adj 31, 180, 192, 202, 639
amplification n 194
amplify v 194, 549, 573
amplitude n 102, 192, 202
amplitudinous adj 192
amply adv 31, 639
amputate v 38
amputation n 38
amuse v 829, 840
amusement n 840
amuse oneself v 840
amusing adj 840
anachronism n 115
anachronism n 135
anachronistic adj 115
anagram n 561
analogous adj 12, 17, 216
analogy n 9, 17, 216
analysis n 49, 60, 463,

476, 596
analytic adj 85, 463, 596
analytical adj 476, 596
analyze v 49, 463, 476
analyzer n 463
anarchic adj 59
anarchism n 59
anarchy n 59
anatomic adj 329
anatomical adj 329
anatomy n 329, 357, 368
ancestral adj 166
ancestry n 122, 166
anchor n 666
anchorage n 184
anchorite n 955
ancient adj 124
ancient times n 122
and adv 37
and everywhere adv 186
and so forth adv 37
anemic adj 430
anesthesia n 376
anesthetic adj 376
anesthetize v 376, 381
anew adv 104, 123
angel n 977
angel n 164, 897
angelic adj 977
anger n 824, 900; v 830
angle n 244; v 244
angry adj 382, 900
anguish n 378, 619, 828
angular adj 244
angularity n 244
anility n 128
animal n 366
animal adj 366
animalistic adj 364, 366
animality n 364
animal kingdom n 366
animal life n 357, 364
animal physiology n 368
animate v 382, 824, 836; adj 357
animated adj 171, 382, 515
animated nature n 357
animate matter n 357
animating adj 836
animation n 359, 515, 682, 824
animosity n 889, 898, 900
ankle-deep adj 209
annalist n 553
annal(s) n 114
annals n 551
annex n 39; v 37
annexation n 37, 43

annihilate v 2
annihilation n 2, 162
annotate v 522
annotator n 524
announce v 527, 531, 883
announcement n 527, 531, 985
annoy v 688, 830
annoyance n 649, 828, 830, 835
annul v 756
annulment n 756
anoint v 332
anointment n 332, 355
anomalous adj 59, 83
anomaly n 59, 83
anon adv 132
another adj 15
another time n 119
answer n 462
answer n 479, 522, 662; v 462, 746
answerable adj 177, 462
answerable for adj 806
answer for v 759
antagonism n 14, 24, 179, 708, 715, 867, 889
antagonist n 708, 710, 726, 891
antagonistic adj 14, 24, 179, 708, 715
antagonize v 14, 179
antecedence n 116
antecedence n 62
antecedent n 64, 116; adj 62, 116
antedate v 115, 116
antediluvian adj 124
antemeridian n 125
anterior adj 62, 116, 234
anteriority n 116
anthology n 596
anthracite n 388
anthropology n 368
anti adj 708
anticipate v 115, 121, 132, 451, 507, 510, 673, 858
anticipation n 121, 132, 451, 507, 510, 673, 858
anticipatory adj 132, 510
antidote n 662
antipathy n 14, 289, 867, 898
antipodal adj 237
antipodean adj 14
antipodes n 14
antiquarian n 553
antiquarianism n 124
antiquated adj 124
antique adj 124

antiquity n 122, 124
antisocial adj 911
antithesis n 14, 218, 237
antithetical adj 14, 237
antitoxin n 662
anxiety n 459, 860
anxious adj 860
any adj 25
apace adv 274
apart adj 44, 87; adv 44
apathetic adj 383, 456, 823, 866, 989
apathy n 823, 866, 989
ape v 19
aperture n 260
apex n 8, 67, 210
aphasia n 581, 583
aphorism n 496
aphoristic adj 496
apiece adv 79
aping n 19
apologist n 937
apostasy n 607, 984
apostate n 607
a posteriori n 476
apostrophe n 589
apostrophize v 589
apothegm n 496
apotheosize v 991
appal v 830
apparel n 225; v 225
apparent adj 446, 448, 525
apparently adv 448
apparition n 4, 443, 980
appeal n 411, 765
appear v 446, 448, 525
appearance n 448
appearance n 220, 240, 446, 569
appease v 174, 723, 826, 831
appellant n 924, 938
appellation n 564
append v 37
appendage n 39, 65
appendix n 39
appertain to v 9, 56
appetite n 865
appetizing adj 394
applaud v 836, 883
apple adj 435
apple of one's eye n 899
apple-polisher n 886, 935
appliance n 677
applicability n 644
applicable adj 644, 677
applicant n 767
application n 677, 765
apply v 677
appoint v 741, 755, 786
appointment n 755
apportion v 44, 51, 60,

73, 786
apportionment n 786
apportionment n 60, 73
apposite adj 23
apposition n 23, 199
appraisal n 812
appraise v 466, 480, 668, 812
appraisement n 466
appreciate v 394, 480, 850, 916, 931
appreciation n 465, 822, 916
appreciative adj 822, 916
apprehend v 490, 860
apprehension n 453, 490, 665, 789, 860
apprehensive adj 860
apprentice n 541
apprenticeship n 539
apprize v 527
apprized of adj 527
approach n 286
approach n 197, 569, 627, 632; v 121, 152, 286
approaching adj 286
approbate v 931
approbation n 931
approbation n 488, 928
appropriate v 775, 786, 788, 789, 791; adj 79, 134, 646, 850
appropriateness n 646
appropriating n 788
appropriation n 775, 789, 791
approval n 488, 762, 928, 931
approve v 535, 737, 931
approved adj 931, 983a
approximate v 17, 197; adj 17, 197, 286
approximation n 9, 17, 19, 286
apricot adj 439
a priori n 476
apt adj 23, 498, 698, 850
aptitude n 176, 498, 602, 698
aptness n 176, 698
aqua n 337
aquamarine adj 435, 438
aquatics n 267
aqueduct n 350
aqueous adj 337
arable adj 371
arbiter n 724, 737, 967
arbitrariness n 739
arbitrary adj 83, 606,

608, 739, 964
arbitrate v 174, 724
arbitration n 724
arbitrator n 724, 967
arc n 245
arcade n 245
arced adj 245
arch n 245, 250; v 245; adj 31
archaic adj 124
archaism n 124
archangel n 977
arched adj 245, 250
archetype n 22
archipelago n 346
architect n 164
architecture n 161, 329
arch over v 245
arctic adj 383
ardency n 991
ardent adj 382, 865
ardor n 382, 574, 682, 821
arduous adj 704
area n 181
arena n 728
arenose adj 330
areola n 247
argue v 24, 467, 476, 720
arguer n 476
argument n 454, 476, 516, 713, 720, 969
argumentation n 476, 969
argumentative adj 476, 713
arguments n 476
argumentum ad hominem n 476
aria n 413
arid adj 169, 340
aridity n 340
arise v 151, 305
aristocracy n 875
aristocratic adj 875
arithmetic n 85
arithmetical adj 85
arithmetic operations n 85
arm n 343; v 157, 673, 727
armaments n 727
armistice n 723
armlet n 247
armor n 727
arms n 727
army n 72
aroma n 400
aromatic adj 400
around adv 227
arouse v 175, 382, 615, 824
arraign v 938, 969
arraignment n 938
arrange v 58, 60, 626, 673, 774

arranged *adj* 60
arrange in a series *v* 69
arrange in words *v* 566
arrangement *n* 60
arrangement *n* 58, 673, 723, 769
arrangment *n* 807
array *n* 58, 102; *v* 60, 225
arrest *v* 142
arrival *n* 292
arrive *v* 151, 265, 292, 342
arrogance *n* 878, 885
arrogant *adj* 739, 878, 885, 880
artery *n* 350
artful *adj* 702
artfulness *n* 702
art gallery *n* 556
article *n* 3, 316, 590, 595
article of faith *n* 537
articles *n* 770, 798
articles of faith *n* 983
articulate *v* 580, 582; *adj* 580
articulation *n* 43, 580
artifice *n* 545, 702
artificial *adj* 579, 855
artificial light *n* 423
artist *n* 559
artist *n* 416
artistic *adj* 845
artistically *adv* 698
artless *adj* 703, 946
artlessness *n* 703
artlessness *n* 946
as a consequence *adv* 154
as a matter of course *adv* 82
as a rule *adv* 613
ascend *v* 35, 305, 658
ascendancy *n* 33, 157, 175, 731
ascendant *adj* 305
ascending *adj* 217
ascension *n* 305
ascent *n* 305
ascent *n* 35, 217
ascertain *v* 480a
ascetic *n* 955; *adj* 955
asceticism *n* 955
as chance will have it *adv* 156
ascribe importance *v* 642
ascribe to *v* 155
ascription *n* 155
as good as one's word *adj* 772
ash *n* 388
ashen *adj* 429, 432
ashes *n* 362
ashore *adv* 342

ashy *adj* 429, 432
aside *n* 589
as if *adv* 17
as if it were *adv* 17
asinine *adj* 497, 499, 853
as it happens *adv* 151
as it were *adv* 17
ask *v* 461, 630, 765, 812, 865
askance *adv* 217
askew *adj* 217, 243; *adv* 217
ask for *v* 765
asleep *adj* 458
as low as one can go *adj* 649
as matters stand *adv* 8
aspect *n* 183, 220 448
aspects *n* 5
asperity *n* 256
aspersion *n* 934
asphalt *n* 356a
asphyxiate *v* 361
aspirant *n* 767
aspiration *n* 858, 865
aspire at *v* 620
asquint *adj* 217
as regards *adv* 9
ass *n* 493
assail *v* 716
assailant *n* 716, 726
assailer *n* 726
assassin *n* 165, 361
assassination *n* 361
assault *n* 716; *v* 716
assaulter *n* 726
assay *n* 463; *v* 463
assemblage *n* 72
assemblage *n* 43, 102, 712
assemble *v* 50, 72, 72, 712
assembled *adj* 72
assembly *n* 43, 72, 696, 712, 997
assent *n* 488
assent *n* 23, 82, 178, 484, 602, 762; *v* 82, 488, 535, 602, 762
assenting *adj* 488, 831
assert *v* 535, 720
assertion *n* 535
assertive *adj* 535
assertiveness *n* 715
assess *v* 466, 812
assessment *n* 466, 480
assessor *n* 480
asset *n* 944
assets *n* 780, 800
asseverate *v* 535
assiduity *n* 682
assiduous *adj* 682
assiduousness *n* 682
assign *v* 60, 755, 783, 784, 786
assignment *n* 155, 755,

assign to *v* 155
assimilate *v* 16, 144
assimilation *n* 144
assist *v* 707, 746, 834, 906
assistance *n* 707, 834
assistant *n* 707, 711, 759
associate *n* 88, 711, 890; *v* 9, 41, 43, 72, 216
associated *adj* 9
associated with *adj* 88
associate with *v* 88
association *n* 9, 72, 88, 464, 709, 712, 903
assortment *n* 60, 72
assuage *v* 174, 723, 834
assuagement *n* 174, 834
assuaging *adj* 834
assume *v* 484, 510, 514, 789, 855, 871, 885
assumed *adj* 514
assumed name *n* 565
assumption *n* 514
assurance *n* 474, 484, 507, 768, 858
assure *v* 768, 771
assured *adj* 474, 484
asteroids *n* 318
as the saying goes *adv* 496
as the world goes *adv* 613
as they say *adv* 496
as things go *adv* 151, 613
astigmatic *adj* 443
astigmatism *n* 443
astonish *v* 508, 870
astonished *adj* 870
astonishing *adj* 870
astonishingly *adv* 31
astonishment *n* 508, 870
astound *v* 824, 870
astounding *adj* 870
astral *adj* 318
astray *adv* 279
astringent *adj* 195, 397
astronaut *n* 269
astute *adj* 498, 702
asunder *adj* 44; *adv* 44
as usual *adv* 613
as well as *adv* 37
asylum *n* 666
asymmetrical *adj* 241
asymmetry *n* 241, 243
at a different time *adv* 119
at a distance *adj* 196
at a glance *adv* 441
at all events *adv* 30
at all times *adv* 136

at a low ebb adj 308
at an angle adv 217
at any rate adv 30
at a snail's pace adv 275
at a standstill adj 265
at bottom adv 5
at cross purposes adj 713; adv 59, 708
at ease adj 827
at fault adj 927
at first sight adv 441, 448
at full gallop adv 274
at full speed adv 274
at half speed adv 275
at hand adj 152, 197
at heart adv 82b
atheism n 989
atheist n 984, 989
atheistic adj 989
athletic adj 159
at intervals adv 70
at issue adj 708
at its height adv 33
at large adj 748
atlas n 86
at last adv 67, 133
at length adv 133, 200
atmosphere n 338
atmospheric adj 338
at no time adv 107
at odds adj 708
atoll n 346
atom n 32, 180a
atomization n 336
atomize v 336
atonal adj 410, 414
atonality n 410, 414
at once adv 132
atone v 30, 952
atone for v 462, 952
atonement n 952
atonement n 790, 950
at one's disposal adj 777
at one's fingertips adv 197
at one's leisure adv 133
at one with adj 178
atoning adj 950, 952
at present adv 118
at random adv 156
at regular intervals adv 58
at rest adj 265; adv 687
atrophy n 195, 659
at short notice adv 132
at sight adv 132
at some other time adv 119
at some time or other adv 119
attach v 37, 43, 969
attached adj 897

attach importance v 642
attachment n 37, 39, 43, 88, 897
attach too much importance to v 482
attack n 716
attacker n 716, 891
attain v 292, 775
attain an end v 731
attain majority v 131
attainment n 292, 539, 698, 775
attempt n 675, 686; v 675
attend v 186, 281, 418, 457, 746, 928
attendance n 186
attendant n 88; adj 88
attending n 418; adj 186, 928
attending to n 457
attend regularly v 136
attend to v 743
attention n 457
attention n 451, 459, 928
attentive adj 451, 457, 459
attentiveness n 457
attenuate v 195
attenuation n 195, 330
attest v 550
at that instant adv 119
at that time adv 119
at the eleventh hour adv 133
at the heels adv 235
at the least adv 32
at the present time adv 118
at the same time adv 30, 120
at the top of one's lungs adv 404
at the top of one's voice adv 404
at this moment adv 118
at this time adv 118
at times adv 136
attire n 225
attitude n 8, 183, 240
attitudinize v 855
attorney n 968
attorney-at-law n 968
attorney general n 968
attract v 288, 829
attract attention v 446
attracting adj 288
attraction n 288
attraction n 829
attractive adj 288, 615, 829, 845, 850
attractiveness n 288, 829, 845
attributable adj 155

attribute n 780
attributed adj 155
attribute to v 155
attribution n 155
attrition n 331
attunement n 413
at variance adj 24, 708, 713
at will adv 600
at work adj 170
auburn adj 433
auction n 796
audacious adj 861, 863, 885
audacity n 861, 863, 885
audibility n 402, 418
audible adj 402
audience n 444, 588
audition n 418
auditor n 418, 811
auditory adj 418
auger n 262
augment v 35, 37
augmentation n 35, 39, 194
augur n 513; v 511, 909
auguring adj 909
augury n 511, 512, 668
au naturel adj 226
aureate adj 435
aureole n 420
auricular adj 418
aurora n 420
auscultation n 418
auspices n 175, 693
auspicious adj 134, 734
austere adj 704, 739, 955
austerity n 739, 955
authentic adj 494
author n 153, 164, 590, 593, 976
authoritative adj 175, 737, 741, 983a
authority n 737
authority n 157, 175, 500, 527, 700, 745, 965
authorization n 737, 760
authorize v 157, 737, 755, 760
authorized adj 924, 963
author's copy n 590
authorship n 161, 590
autocracy n 739
autocratic adj 600, 739
automatic adj 601
automobile n 272
autonomous adj 748
autonomy n 748
autopsy n 363
autumn n 126
auxiliary n 711

auxiliary *adj* 37, 707
avail *n* 644, 677; *v* 644
available *adj* 260, 644, 673
avail oneself of *v* 677
avarice *n* 819
avaricious *adj* 819
avenge *v* 718, 919
avenger *n* 919
avenue *n* 302, 627
aver *v* 535
average *n* 29; *adj* 29, 651, 736
average capacity *n* 736
averse *adj* 289, 603, 867
averse from *adj* 898
averseness *n* 603
aversion *n* 289, 603, 867, 898
Avesta *n* 986
aviate *v* 267
aviation *n* 267
aviational *adj* 267
aviator *n* 269
aviatrix *n* 269
avoid *v* 287, 623, 671
avoidance *n* 623
avoider *n* 623
avow *v* 488, 535
avowal *n* 529
await *v* 121, 152, 507
awake *v* 404, 824; *adj* 457, 682
award *n* 784; *v* 784
aware *adj* 375, 822
awareness *n* 822
aware of *adj* 490
away *adj* 187, 196; *adv* 196
awe *n* 860, 870
a wee bit *adv* 32
awe-inspiring *adj* 860
awesome *adj* 860, 870
awe-struck *adj* 870
awful *adj* 395, 403, 860
awhile *adv* 111
awkward *adj* 579, 699, 704
awkwardness *n* 579, 699
awl *n* 262
awning *n* 223, 424
awry *adj* 217, 243, 923
ax *v* 44
axiom *n* 496
axiomatic *adj* 496
axis *n* 153, 222

B

baa *v* 412
babble *v* 348, 584
babbler *n* 584
babe *n* 129
babe in arms *n* 129
baby *n* 129

baby blue *adj* 438
babyish *adj* 129
bachelor *n* 904
bachelorhood *n* 904
back *n* 235; *v* 707, 737; *adj* 235
back and forth *adv* 314
backbiter *n* 936
backbone *n* 5, 221, 604a
back down *v* 283
backer *n* 164, 890
backfire *n* 277
backfiring *adj* 277
background *n* 196, 235
backlash *n* 145, 277
back out *v* 283
backside *n* 235
backsliding *n* 283, 661
backward *adj* 133, 603; *adv* 133
backwards *adv* 283
backwater *n* 283
bad *adj* 34, 397, 401, 649, 653, 657, 663, 923, 945
bad diction *n* 579
bad fairy *n* 980
badge *n* 747
badger *v* 830, 909
bad grammar *n* 568
bad likeness *n* 555
bad luck *n* 735
bad man *n* 949
bad manners *n* 895
bad name *n* 874
badness *n* 649
bad news *n* 830
bad odor *n* 401
bad omen *n* 649
bad smell *n* 401
bad straits *n* 804
bad taste *n* 851
bad tasting *adj* 395
bad-tempered *adj* 901a, 945
bad timing *n* 135
bag *v* 789
bail *n* 771
bait *n* 784; *v* 288, 830
bake *v* 384
baker's dozen *n* 98
baking *adj* 382
balance *n* 27, 29, 40, 150, 242, 800, 811; *v* 27, 30, 811
balance accounts *v* 807
balanced *adj* 27, 150, 242
balance out *v* 30, 179
bale *n* 190
baleful *adj* 649, 663
balk *v* 509
ball *n* 249
ballast *n* 30
balloon *n* 273

ball-shaped *adj* 249
balm *n* 356, 662
balustrade *n* 232
bamboozle *v* 545
ban *n* 761
banal *adj* 209
banality *n* 209, 843
bananas *adj* 503
band *n* 72, 247, 416, 417, 712
bandage *n* 223, 263
banded *adj* 440
band together *v* 709, 712
bandy *v* 148, 315
bandy words *v* 588
bane *n* 663
bane *n* 165, 649, 975
baneful *adj* 663
bang *n* 406; *v* 276
bang into *v* 276
banish *v* 55, 185, 297, 972
banished *adj* 893
banish from one's thoughts *v* 506
banishment *n* 185, 297, 893
bank *n* 217, 802
banker *n* 801
bankrupt *adj* 732
bankruptcy *n* 732, 808
banshee *n* 980
banter *n* 856; *v* 842, 856
baptize *v* 564
bar *n* 215, 346, 968; *v* 55, 261, 761
barb *n* 253; *v* 253
barbarism *n* 563, 579, 851
barbarous *adj* 241, 563, 579
barbed *adj* 253
bard *n* 597
bare *v* 226, 260; *adj* 226
barefaced *adj* 525
barely *adv* 32
barely audible *adj* 405
bareness *n* 226
bare possibility *n* 473
barf *v* 297
bargain *n* 769, 794, 795, 815; *v* 769, 794
barge *n* 271, 273
bark *n* 223; *v* 412
bar of justice *n* 966
barrel *n* 249
barrelhouse *n* 415
barren *adj* 158, 169
barrenness *n* 158, 169
barricade *n* 232
barrier *n* 232, 261
barrister *n* 968
barter *n* 794
barter *n* 148; *v* 148,

base

794, 796
base n 211
base n 208, 215; v 215; adj 34, 207, 211, 649, 846, 874, 876, 886, 930
based on adj 19, 211
baseless adj 2, 4
baseness n 862, 886
bashful adj 881
bashfulness n 881
basic adj 5, 42, 211
basics n 66
basin n 252, 343, 344
basis n 211, 215
bask in v 377
batch n 25, 72
bathetic adj 497
bathos n 497
batter v 162, 276
battered adj 659
battery n 716
battle n 680, 722; v 720, 722
battlefield n 728
battleground n 728
battler n 726
battle with words v 148
bauble n 643
bawdry n 961
bawdy adj 961
bawl v 411
bay n 343; v 412; adj 433
bayonet n 262; v 361
bayou n 343
bazaar n 799
be v 1
be absent v 187
be absurd v 497
beacon n 550
be active v 680, 682
be affected with v 655
be afraid of v 860
be agitated v 315
beak n 250
be alive v 359
be all ears v 418
beam n 420; v 420
be an example v 22
bear v 215, 270, 692, 826
bearable adj 651
bear a grudge v 900
bear a resemblance v 17
bearer n 271
bear fruit v 161
bear ill will v 907
bearing n 9, 278, 692
bearings n 183
bear in mind v 451, 505
bear no resemblance v 18
bear off v 279

be artless v 703
bear upon v 9
bear with v 740, 760
beast n 366
beastly adj 653
beast of burden n 271
beasts of the field n 366
beat n 104, 138, 314, 627; v 138, 276, 314, 315, 330, 406, 407
beat a retreat v 623
beat back v 289
beatific adj 829, 981
beatified adj 981
beat it out v 623
be at odds with v 889
be at peace v 721
be attendant on v 281
be attentive v 457
be at the mercy of v 749
beat time v 114
beat up v 352
be at work on v 625
beau n 897, 854
beau monde n 852
beauteous adj 845
beautified adj 577, 847
beautiful adj 242, 597, 829, 845, 977, 981
beautify v 845, 847
beauty n 845
beauty n 242, 829
be averse to v 867
be aware of v 450, 490
be beforehand v 132
be behind v 235
be beneficial v 648
be blind v 442
be blind to v 491
be blunt v 254
bebop n 415
be born v 359
be bound for v 278
be brittle v 328
be broad v 202
be called to the bar v 968
becalm v 265
be capricious v 608
be careful v 459
because adv 153, 155
be cautious v 864
be central v 222
be certain v 474
be cheap v 815
be cheek to cheek v 236
becloud v 421, 422
be cold v 383
become v 144, 926
become a habit v 613
become colorless v 429
become insane v 503
become large v 192

become little v 193
become old v 124
become small v 195
becoming adj 646, 850, 881
be composed of v 54
be concise v 572
be contiguous v 199
be contrary v 14
be converted into v 144
be courteous v 894
be cowardly v 862
be credulous v 486
be cunning v 702
be curious v 455
be curved v 245
bed n 204
be dark v 421
bedazzle v 420
be deaf v 419
be deceived v 547
be degrees adv 26
be dejected v 837
be dense v 321
bedew v 339
be difficult v 704
be diffuse v 573
be dim v 422
be dimsighted v 443
be disappointed v 509
be discontented v 832
be discordant v 414, 713
be discourteous v 895
be dishonest v 940
be disinclined v 867
be disinterested v 942
be disrespectful v 929
be distant v 196
be distinguished v 873
bedlamite n 504
bed-ridden adj 655
be drunk v 959
bedtime n 126
be due to v 154
be dull v 843
be dumb v 581
be early v 132
be easy v 705
beehive n 691
be elastic v 325
bee line n 246
Beelzebub n 978
be enamored of v 897
be engaged in v 625
be entitled v 924
be equivocal v 520
be evasive v 528
be evident v 467
be expedient v 646
be expeditious v 134
be expensive v 814
be exterior v 220
be extraneous v 57
be faithful to v 772
befall v 151

be fashionable v 852
be fastidious v 868
be fated v 601
be fatigued v 688
be firm v 150

befit v 23, 646, 926
be fluid v 333
be fond of v 897
be foolish v 499
before adj 62; adv 62, 116, 234, 280
beforehand adv 116, 132
before long adv 132
before now adv 122
before one's eyes adj 446
be forgetful v 506
befoul v 653
be fragrant v 400
be free v 748
befriend v 888
be friendly v 888
beg v 765
be general v 78
beget v 161
beggar n 767
beggarly adj 643, 804
begin v 66, 676
begin at the beginning v 66
begin hostilities v 716
beginner n 541
beginning n 66
be gluttonous v 957
be gone v 449
be good v 648
be good for v 656
be grateful v 916
be great v 31
begrudge v 819, 921
begrudging adj 907, 921
beg the question v 277, 477
be guilty v 947
be habitual v 613
behalf n 618
be haphazard v 139
be hard on v 739
behave v 680, 692
behave well v 894
behavior n 680, 692
behead v 361
be healthy v 654
be heavy v 319
be held in high repute v 873
behemoth n 192
behest n 741
be hidden v 447
behind adv 63, 235, 281
behind closed doors adv 528
behind time adv 133
be hip v 490

behold v 441, 444
beholder n 444
beholding adj 916
be honorable v 939
behoove v 926
be horizontal v 213
be hot v 382
be identical v 13
beige n 433; adj 433
be ignorant v 491
be illegal v 964
be ill timed v 135
be imbecilic v 499
be impatient v 825
be impenitent v 951
be imperfect v 651
be impious v 988
be important v 642
be impossible v 471
be impotent v 158
be imprisoned v 754
be improbable v 473
be impure v 961
be inactive v 172, 265, 681, 683
be inarticulate v 583
be in a state v 7
be inattentive v 458
be incomplete v 53
be inconvenient v 647
be incredulous v 487
be in danger v 665
be indifferent v 866
be indiscriminate v 465a
be in error v 495
be inert v 172
be inexpedient v 647
be inferior v 34
be infinite v 104
be influential v 175
be infrequent v 137
be in front v 234
being n 1, 3, 359
be in health v 654
be inherent v 5
be in league with v 709
be in love with v 897
be innocent v 946
be inodorous v 399
be insane v 503
be insensible v 376
be insensitive v 823
be inside v 221
be insolent v 885
be instantaneous v 113
be instrumental v 631
be insufficient v 640
be intelligent v 498
be intelligible v 518
be intemperate v 954
be interior v 221
be intrinsic v 5
be in trouble v 619
be inverted v 218
be invisible v 447

be in want v 640
be irascible v 901
be irregular v 139
be irreligious v 989
be irresolute v 605
be jealous v 920
be large v 192
be late v 133
belated adj 133
be latent v 526
be lax v 738
belch out v 297
be left v 40
be left over v 40
be lenient v 740
be liable v 177
be liberal v 816
belief n 484
belief n 451, 453, 537
believable adj 484, 515
believe v 451, 484, 514, 987
believed adj 484
believer n 987
believing n 484; adj 484, 486
be light v 320
be little v 193, 934
belittling n 934; adj 934
belles lettres n 560
bellicose adj 720, 722
bellied adj 250
belligerency n 720
belligerent adj 720, 722
belling n 412
bellow v 404, 411, 412
bellwether n 64
belly n 221
be located v 183
be long v 200
belonging n 777
belongings n 780
belonging to adj 9
belong to v 9, 56, 777
be loquacious v 584
be loud v 404
beloved n 897
be low v 207; adv 207
below par adj 651
belowstairs adv 207
belt n 247, 276
be made up of v 54
be master of v 698
bemoan v 833, 839
be modest v 881
be mute v 581
be narrow v 203
bench n 966
bend n 217, 244, 245; v 217, 244, 245, 278, 279, 311, 324, 325, 725, 744, 774
bend an ear v 418
bending n 245

bend over v 308
bend to v 176
be near v 197
beneath adv 207
benefactor n 912
beneficence n 648
beneficent adj 784
beneficent spirit n 977
beneficial adj 618, 644, 648, 677
beneficiary n 785
beneficient adj 816
benefit n 618, 677, 775; v 618, 644, 648, 906
be negligent v 460
be neutral v 609a
benevolence n 906
benevolence n 910
benevolent adj 888, 906, 906, 910
benign adj 656
be noble v 875
be no more v 360
bent n 176, 602, 613, 820; adj 244
bents n 5
bent upon adj 620
benumb v 376, 381, 385, 843
benumbed adj 381
be numerous v 102
be obligated v 601
be obliged v 601
be oblique v 217
be obstinate v 606
be occupied with v 625
be odorless v 399
be of help v 707
be of no help v 645
be old v 124
be one's fortune v 151
be one's lot v 151
be on the side v 236
be opaque v 426
be opportune v 134
be opposite v 237
be owing to v 154
be parsimonious v 819
be part of v 56
be penitent v 950
be perfect v 650
be pious v 987
be plain v 525
be pleased v 827
be pleased with v 827
be pleasurable v 829
be poor v 804
be possible v 470
be powerful v 157
be present v 186
be probable v 472
be prodigal v 818
be proud v 878
be pungent v 392
be pure v 960
bequeath v 784

bequest n 784
be rare v 137
be rash v 863
berate v 932, 972
bereft adj 776
be regular v 82
be related to v 11
be reluctant v 867
be remiss v 460
be resolute v 604
be rich v 803
be ridiculous v 853
be right v 922
be rumored v 532
be safe v 664
be salubrious v 656
be sane v 502
be savory v 394
beseech v 765
beseem v 926
be selfish v 943
be sensible v 375
be sensitive v 822
be sensitive to v 375
be servile v 886
beset v 716
be severe v 739
be sharp v 253
be short v 20 i
beside adv 83, 236
be side by side v 236
beside oneself adj 824
besides adv 37
beside the mark adj 10
besiege v 716
be silent v 403, 581, 585
be similar v 17
be situated v 183
be skillful v 698
be small v 32
besmear v 653
be sober v 958
be sociable v 892
be sorry for v 914
bespeak v 132, 467
be specific v 79
bespeckle v 440
best adj 648, 650
be still v 265, 403
bestow v 784, 995
bestowal n 784
be straight v 246
be straightforward v 576
be straight with v 543
bestride v 206
be subject v 749
be subsequent to v 117
be sufficient v 639
be suitable v 134
be sullen v 901a
be superior v 33
be surprised v 870
bet v 621
be taken v 360
be taken by surprise v

508
be tasteless v 391
be temperate v 953
be that as may adv 30
be the case v 494
be the dupe of v 547
be the effect of v 154
be the making of v 648
be the rage v 852
be thick v 202
be thin v 203
betimes adv 132
betoken v 550
be transient v 111
be transparent v 425
betray v 529, 545
be true v 494
be true for everyone v 78
better v 658; adj 648, 658
better half n 903
betterment n 658
better off adj 658
better than nothing adj 651
betting n 621
between adv 228
betwixt adv 228
betwixt and between adv 228
be unaccustomed v 614
be unaffected v 823
be uncertain v 475
be unclean v 653
be unconformable v 83
be unentitled v 925
be unequal v 28
be ungrateful v 917
be unhealthy v 657
be uniform v 16
be unimportant v 643
be unintelligible v 519
be universal v 78
be unlike v 18
be unnecessary v 57
be unpalatable v 395
be unprepared v 674
be unproductive v 169
be unsavory v 395
be unskillful v 699
be unwilling v 603
be useful v 644
be useless v 645
be vain v 880
beverage n 298
be vertical v 212
be violent v 173
be virtuous v 944
be visible v 446, 448
be vulgar v 851
bevy n 72
bewail v 833, 839
be weak v 160

be wealthy v 803
bewilder v 475, 519, 538, 870
bewildered adj 870
bewilderment n 870
be willing v 602
be wise v 498
bewitch v 829, 992
bewitched adj 992
bewitchery n 992
bewitching adj 897, 992
be without v 777a
be worthy of notice v 642
beyond adv 33
beyond all bounds adv 31
beyond all praise adj 650
beyond all reasonable expectation adj 473
beyond bounds adv 641
beyond compare adj 33; adv 31
beyond measure adv 31
beyond one's depth adv 208
beyond the bounds of reason adj 471
beyond the mark adv 303
Bhagavad Gita n 986
bias n 176, 820; v 175, 217
Bible n 986
bibliomaniac n 492
bibliophile n 593
bicker v 315, 713
bicycle n 272
bid n 763; v 600, 741
bidder n 767
bidding n 741
bide v 133, 141
bide one's time v 681
bid fair v 472
bier n 363
biformity n 89
bifurcate v 91, 244; adj 244
bifurcated adj 91
bifurcation n 91, 244
big adj 31, 192
bigot n 606
bigoted n 499
bigotry n 606
big words n 577
bike n 272
biker n 268
biking n 266
bill n 805, 811, 812
bill of sale n 771
billow n 348
billows n 341

billygoat n 373
binary adj 89
bind v 9, 43, 45, 770
binding adj 926
bind oneself v 768
binoculars n 445
binomial adj 89
biographer n 553
biologist n 357
biology n 357
bipartite adj 91
bird n 366
bird's-eye view n 448
birds of a feather n 17
birth n 66
bisect v 91
bisected adj 91
bisection n 91
bisection n 68
bit n 32, 51, 390
bit by bit adv 26, 51, 275
bitch n 374, 962
bite n 392; v 298, 378, 385, 547
bite into v 298
biting adj 171, 392, 574
bitter adj 383, 392, 395, 397, 830, 898, 900
bitter cold adj 383
bitterly adv 31, 383
bitterness n 392, 900
bitumen n 356a
bituminous coal n 388
bivouac v 184
bizarre adj 83
black v 431; adj 421, 431
black and white n 429
black as coal adj 431
black as night adj 431
blackball v 55
blacken v 431, 934
blackguard n 941
blackness n 431
blackness n 421
blame n 716; v 716, 932, 938
blameless adj 946
blamelessness n 946
blameworthy adj 945
blaming n 938
blanch v 429, 430
blanched adj 430
bland adj 174, 391, 395
blandish v 902
blandishment n 902
blandness n 391, 395
blank n 2, 4; adj 2, 4
blanket n 223
blaspheme v 988
blasphemer n 988
blasphemy n 988
blast n 173, 349, 404, 406; v 349

blast furnace n 386
blatter v 412
blaze n 382, 420; v 382, 420
blazing adj 382, 420
blazon forth v 882
bleach v 429, 430
bleached adj 430
bleak adj 383
blear-eyed adj 443
bleary adj 422
bleat v 412
bleed v 378, 814
bleeding n 299
blemish n 848
blemish n 651, 945; v 659
blend n 48; v 41, 41, 48, 352, 413
blending n 48, 413
bless v 990
blessed adj 981
blessing n 618
blight n 659; v 659
blighted adj 659
blighted hope n 509
blimp n 273
blind n 424; v 442; adj 442, 601
blind adoration n 991
blindfold adv 442
blindly adv 442
blindness n 442
blindness n 491
blind to adj 458
blink v 443, 623
blinker n 530
bliss n 827
blissful adj 827, 981
blister n 250
blithe adj 836
bloated adj 194, 250
block n 192, 321, 752; v 706
blockade n 261; v 261
blockhead n 493, 501
block up v 261
blond adj 429, 435
blood n 11
blood red adj 434
blood relation n 11
bloodshed n 361
bloodthirsty adj 361
bloody adj 361, 434, 653
bloom n 654; v 161, 367, 654, 734
blooming adj 161, 434
blossom v 161, 367, 734
blot n 552, 848, 874, 945; v 431, 653, 874
blot out v 552
blotted out adj 552
blow n 276, 349, 508, 830; v 347, 349, 688
blow great guns v 349

blow hard v 349
blow hot and cold v 605
blown away adj 959
blow one's brains out v 361
blow one's chance v 135
blow out v 421
blow over v 122
blow-up n 173; v 173, 194, 349
blubber n 356
blue n 438
blue adj 438
blue and red n 437
blue and yellow n 435
blue-green adj 435
blueness n 438
blue sky n 338
bluff adj 173
bluish adj 438
blunder n 495, 497, 732; v 495, 699, 732
blunderer n 701
blunderhead n 701
blunt n 376, 616, 843; adj 172, 246, 254, 499, 703
bluntness n 254
bluntness n 703
blur v 422, 653
blurred adj 447
blurry adj 422, 447
blurt out v 529
blush n 434; v 434
blushing adj 434
bluster v 173
blusterer n 887
blusterer n 884
blustering adj 173
boar n 373
board n 204, 298, 696, 966
boarder n 188
board of directors n 696
boards n 728
boaster n 884, 887
boastful adj 884
boasting n 884
boasting adj 884
boat n 273
boating n 267
boat ride n 267
bob v 309, 315
bodiless adj 4, 317
bodiliness n 3
bodily adj 3, 316, 364
bodily pleasure n 377
body n 3, 50, 72, 202, 316, 362, 372, 712
body-guard n 753
body in v 316
body politic n 372
bog n 345
boggle v 699

boggy adj 345
bogus adj 544
bohemian n 268
boil n 250; v 173, 315, 336, 353, 382, 384
boiling n 336, 353; adj 824
boil over v 173, 825
boisterous adj 173, 404, 825
boisterousness n 173, 825
bold adj 525, 574, 604, 715, 861, 885
boldness n 574, 715, 885
bolster v 215, 707
bolt n 43, 261, 274, 298, 623, 957
bolt out of the blue n 508
bolt upright adj 212
bombard v 716
bombast n 517, 577
bombastic adj 497, 549, 577
bond n 9, 45, 771; v 45
bondage n 749
bonds n 802
bonehead n 493
bones n 362
bonus n 973
booby n 501
book n 593
book n 590, 811; v 539 811
bookish adj 490
bookkeeper n 553, 811
booklet n 593
books n 811
bookseller n 593
bookworm n 492, 593
boom n 215, 404, 408; v 404
boomerang n 145, 277; v 277
booming n 408
boon n 618, 784
boorish adj 851, 876
boorishness n 823, 851
boot n 618; v 642
bootless adj 158, 645, 732
bootlicker n 886, 935
booty n 793
booze v 959
boozer n 959
bop n 415
border n 231, 232, 233; v 199, 231
bordering adj 197
border upon v 197
bore n 828, 830; v 260, 688, 841, 869
bored adj 456, 869
boredom n 688, 841
borer n 262

boring adj 275, 841, 843
borrow v 788
borrower n 806
borrowing n 788
borrow money v 788
bosom n 208
bosom buddy n 890
boss n 694, 745
bossed adj 250
botanic adj 367
botanical adj 369
botanic garden n 369
botanist n 357
botany n 369
botany n 357
botch v 699, 732
both adj 89
bother n 828, 830; v 704, 830
bottle v 670
bottom n 208, 211; adj 211
bottomless adj 208
bottomless pit n 208
bough n 51
bounce n 159
bound n 309; v 229, 233, 274, 309; adj 768, 926
boundary n 232, 233
boundary line n 233
bound for adj 278, 620
boundless adj 104, 180
boundlessness n 105
bounds n 233
bounteousness n 816
bountiful adj 816
bounty n 784, 816, 973
bourgeois adj 29
bourgeoisie n 876
bout n 138
bow n 245, 308; v 245, 308, 725, 744, 886, 990
bowed adj 245, 250
bowed instruments n 417
bowels n 221
boxcar n 272
boy n 129, 373
boyfriend n 897
boyhood n 127
boyish adj 129
brace n 89, 215; v 159, 215, 689
bracelet n 247
bracing adj 656
bracket n 45, 215; v 43, 89
brag v 884
braggadocio n 884
braggart n 884, 887
bragging n 884
braid v 219
brain n 450

brainchild *n* 453
brainless *adj* 499
brains *n* 450, 480, 498
brainstorm *n* 453
brake *v* 275
bramble *n* 663
branch *n* 51
branching *n* 291
branch off *v* 291
brand *v* 384
brand-new *adj* 123
branny *adj* 330
brass *adj* 439
brass band *n* 417
brass instruments *n* 417
brassy *adj* 885
bravado *n* 861, 884
brave *v* 715; *adj* 715, 861
bravery *n* 715, 861
brawl *v* 411
brawny *adj* 192
bray *v* 412
brazen *adj* 885
breach *n* 44, 198, 260, 713
breadth *n* 202
breadth *n* 202
break *n* 44, 53, 70, 106, 140, 142, 198, 621, 685, 720, 731; *v* 44, 51, 70, 328, 713, 773, 879
breakability *n* 328
breakable *adj* 328
break a habit *v* 614
break bread *v* 298
breakdown *n* 162, 732; *v* 304, 659
breaker *n* 348
breakers *n* 667
breakfast *v* 298
break ground *v* 66
break in *v* 294
breaking down *n* 49
breaking up *n* 162
break in upon *v* 70, 135
break of day *n* 125
break off *v* 142
break one's neck *v* 360
break out *v* 66
break the ground *v* 116
breakup *n* 67, 146; *v* 44, 73, 162, 659
breast *n* 250
breath *n* 359, 405
breathe *v* 1, 349, 359, 405
breathe new life into *v* 163
breathe one's last *v* 360
breather *n* 70; *n* 685

breathing space *n* 180
breathing spell *n* 685, 687
breathless *adj* 688, 870
breath of air *n* 338, 349
breath of life *n* 359
bred *adj* 370
breed *n* 75, 167; *v* 161, 370
breeding *n* 370, 852
breeze *n* 338, 349
breezy *adj* 338, 349
brethren *n* 997
brevity *n* 201, 572
brewing *adj* 152
briar *n* 663
bribe *n* 784
bridge *n* 45; *v* 45
bridge over *v* 43
bridle *v* 370, 751
brief *n* 596; *adj* 111, 201, 572
briefly *adv* 111, 572
brig *n* 273
brigantine *n* 273
bright *adj* 420, 428, 498, 734, 829, 836
brightness *n* 420, 829
brilliance *n* 845
brilliancy *n* 420
brilliant *adj* 416, 845
brim *n* 231
brimful *adj* 52
brimming *adj* 52
brindled *adj* 440
brine *n* 341; *v* 392
bring *v* 270
bring about *v* 153
bring an action against *v* 969
bring back to life *v* 163
bring forth *v* 161
bring in *v* 296, 810, 812
bring into *v* 144
bring into focus *v* 222
bring into play *v* 677
bring into relation with *v* 9
bring low *v* 308
bring out *v* 74, 591
bring round *v* 660
bring to a crisis *v* 604
bring to a focus *v* 74
bring to an end *v* 67
bring to a point *v* 74
bring to a standstill *v* 142
bring to bear upon *v* 170
bring together *v* 72
bring to life *v* 359
bring to light *v* 529
bring to mind *v* 505
bring to pass *v* 153
bring to perfection *v* 650
bring to trial *v* 969

bring up *v* 161, 235
bring up the rear *v* 235
brink *n* 231
brisk *adj* 111, 274, 682, 684
briskness *n* 682
bristle over *v* 900
bristling *adj* 253
bristly *adj* 256
brittle *adj* 328
brittleness *n* 328
broach *v* 153, 676
broad *adj* 78, 202
broadcast *adj* 73
broad daylight *n* 420
broadside *n* 236; *adv* 236
brochure *n* 593
broil *v* 382, 384
broke *adj* 804
broken *adj* 70
broken down *adj* 659
broker *n* 797
brood *n* 167
brood over *v* 837
brook *v* 826
brother *n* 27
brotherhood *n* 11, 17, 72
brotherly *adj* 888
brown *n* 433
brown *adj* 433
brownish *adj* 433
brownness *n* 433
brown-nose *v* 933
brown-noser *n* 886, 935
brown-nosing *n* 933
browse *v* 264
bruise *v* 649
brunette *adj* 433
brunt *n* 66
brush *v* 379
brush aside *v* 297
brushing *n* 379
brushwood *n* 388
brusque *adj* 173
brutal *adj* 173
brutality *n* 173
brute *n* 366
brute creation *n* 366
brute force *n* 739
brute instinct *n* 450a
brute matter *n* 316, 358
brutishness *n* 450a
bubble *n* 353
bubble *n* 353; *v* 315, 348, 353
bubbling *n* 353
bubbly *adj* 348, 353
buck *n* 309, 373
buckle *n* 243, 248; *v* 43, 243
buckle to *v* 686
bud *n* 66; *v* 161, 194, 300

budding

budding adj 127
budge v 264
budget n 811
buff v 255
buffet v 276, 315
buffoon n 501, 844, 857
buggy n 272
build n 240; v 161, 235, 240
building n 161
built on adj 211
bulb n 249
bulbous adj 250
bulge n 250; v 250
bulk n 31, 50, 202
bulk containers n 191
bulky adj 192, 202
bull n 373, 477
bulletin n 592
bully n 887; v 739
bum v 266
bum around v 266
bumbling n 699
bumming around n 266
bump n 250, 276
bump against v 276
bunch n 250
bunchy adj 250
bungle n 495; v 699
bungler n 701
bungling n 699; adj 699
bunk n 477
buoyancy n 320
buoyant adj 320, 325, 836
burden n 190, 319, 828, 830, 926
burdensome adj 319, 649, 686, 706, 830
burglar n 792
burial n 363; adj 363
burial ground n 363
buried adj 208, 506
buried in adj 229
burlesque n 21, 856; v 856; adj 856
burn v 382, 384, 825
burnable adj 388
burn in v 384
burning adj 382, 434
burnish v 255
burnished adj 420
burnt adj 384
burn the midnight oil v 539
burp out v 297
burrow v 184
bursar n 801
burst n 113, 406; v 44, 173, 328
burst forth v 66, 194, 446
burst in v 294
burst out v 838

burst upon v 508
burst upon the view v 446
bury v 229, 363, 528
burying n 528
bury the hatchet v 723
bush n 367
bushy adj 256
business n 625
business n 454, 622, 682, 794, 926
business district n 799
businesslike adj 58, 625, 682, 692
bust n 557, 732
bustle n 171, 315, 682, 684; v 315, 682, 684
bustling adj 151
busy adj 151, 625, 682
busy as a bee adj 682
busy oneself in v 682
but adv 30
butcher n 361; v 361
butchery n 361
butt n 857; v 276
butt against v 276
butter n 356
butter-fingers n 701
butt in v 135
buttocks n 235
button n 250; v 43
button up v 261
buttress n 215
buy n 795; v 795
buy and sell v 794
buyer n 795
buying n 795
buzz v 409, 412
buzzing n 409
by adv 631
by accident adv 156
by and by adv 132
by an indirect course adv 629
by chance adv 156
by design adv 620
by dint of adv 631; prep 157
by fits and starts adv 70, 139, 315
by force adv 159, 173, 744
bygone adj 122
by installments adv 51
by intuition adv 477
by means of adv 170, 631, 632
by no means adv 32
by rule adv 82
bystander n 444
by storm adv 173
by the agency of adv 631
by the by adv 10, 134
by the way adv 10, 134
by turns adv 138
by virtue of prep 157

C

cabal n 626
cabalistic adj 992
cabinet n 696
cackle v 412, 838
cacophonous adj 410, 414
cadaver n 362
cadaverous adj 362
cadence n 402
caesura n 70, 198
cage n 752; v 370
calamitous adj 735, 830
calamity n 619, 735, 975
calcination n 384
calculable adj 85
calculate v 85, 611, 620
calculation n 85, 507
calculus n 85
calefaction n 384
calendar n 86, 114
caliber n 26
call v 564, 995
call attention to v 550
call for v 630
calligraphy n 590
calling n 625
call it quits v 67, 624
callous adj 823
callousness n 823
callow adj 127
call to mind v 505
call up v 505
call up spirits v 992
calm n 174, 265, 721; v 174, 723; adj 174, 265, 403, 685, 721, 826, 953
calm down v 826
calmness n 174, 265, 721, 826, 953
caloric n 382
caloricity n 382
calorimeter n 389
calumnious adj 934
calumny n 934
camaraderie n 892
camouflage v 528
camouflaging n 528
can v 670
canal n 350
cancel v 536, 552, 756
cancelation n 552, 756
cancel out v 179
cancer n 663
candid adj 246, 543, 703
candidate n 726
candied adj 396
candle n 423
candor n 525, 543, 703
candy v 396
cane n 975
canker n 663; v 659

cankerworm *n* 165
canny *adj* 498, 702
canon *n* 697
canonicals *n* 999
canonize *v* 991
canopy *n* 223
cant *n* 988; *adj* 563
canticle *n* 413
cap *n* 261, 263; *v* 33, 206
capability *n* 157, 175, 698, 705
capable *adj* 157, 698
capacious *adj* 180, 192
capacity *n* 157, 159, 180, 192, 498, 625, 698
capacity for *n* 698
cape *n* 250
caper *n* 309; *v* 309
capillary *adj* 205
capital *n* 632, 800, 803; *adj* 210, 642, 648
capitulate *v* 725
capitulation *n* 725
caprice *n* 608
caprice *n* 615a
capricious *adj* 139, 149, 475, 605, 608, 615a
capriciously *adv* 139, 615a
capriciousness *n* 139, 149, 475
capsule *n* 273
captain *n* 269, 694
captious *adj* 608
captivate *v* 829
captive *n* 754
capture *n* 789; *v* 789
car *n* 272
caravan *n* 266
carbon *n* 21, 90, 388
carbonaceous *adj* 388
carbonization *n* 384
carcass *n* 362
cardinal points *n* 278
care *n* 459
care *n* 451, 457, 817, 828, 830, 864
careen *v* 217
care for *v* 642, 664
careful *adj* 451, 457, 459, 664, 817, 864
carefulness *n* 459
careless *adj* 460, 575, 674, 738, 863, 927
carelessness *n* 460, 699, 773, 863, 927
caress *n* 902; *v* 902
careworn *adj* 828
cargo *n* 190, 798
caricature *n* 21, 555; *v* 19, 555
caricaturist *n* 559
carious *adj* 653

carmine *adj* 434
carnage *n* 361
carpe diem *v* 134, 682
carper *n* 936
carriage *n* 271, 272, 448, 692
carrier *n* 271
carrion *n* 362
carry *v* 215, 270
carry on *v* 143, 680, 692
carry on a conversation *v* 588
carry out *v* 772
carry weight *v* 175, 642
cart *n* 272
cartoonist *n* 559
carve *v* 44, 240, 557, 558, 786
carving *n* 557
cascade *n* 348
case *n* 7, 232, 476, 567, 969; *v* 223
case in point *n* 82
cash *n* 800
cash box *n* 802
cashier *n* 801
cash register *n* 802
cast *n* 21, 75, 176, 240, 428, 448, 550, 557; *v* 73, 240, 284, 557, 626; *adj* 820
cast a shadow *v* 424
cast a spell *v* 992
cast aspersions *v* 934
castaway *n* 893
cast down *v* 308
cast forth *v* 73
castigate *v* 972
castigated *adj* 972
castigation *n* 972
castigator *n* 936
castigatory *adj* 972
castles in the air *n* 515
cast light on *v* 522
cast light upon *v* 420
cast off *v* 297, 782; *adj* 782
cast over *v* 353
casualty *n* 619
casuist *n* 476
casuistry *n* 477
cataclysm *n* 162
cataclysmic *adj* 619
catacomb *n* 363
catafalque *n* 363
catalog *n* 86; *v* 60
catalyst *n* 153
cataract *n* 442, 443
catastrophe *n* 619, 735
catastrophic *adj* 619, 735
catch *n* 793; *v* 789
catch a bug *v* 655
catch a glimpse of *v* 441

catch fire *v* 384
catch on *v* 518
catch one's breath *v* 687
catch the lay of the land *v* 510
catch unawares *v* 508
category *n* 75
cater *v* 637, 746
catering *n* 637
caterwaul *v* 412
cathartic *n* 652
cathedral *n* 1000
catholic *adj* 78, 983a
catholicity *n* 78
cattle car *n* 272
caucus *n* 696
causal *adj* 153, 156
causality *n* 153
causation *n* 153, 170
cause *n* 153
cause *n* 66, 615, 969; *v* 153, 161
caused by *adj* 154
cause sensation *v* 375
cauterization *n* 384
cauterize *v* 384
caution *n* 864
caution *n* 459, 487, 668, 695; *v* 668, 695
cautionary *adj* 668
cautious *adj* 451, 459, 487, 498, 664, 864
cavalcade *n* 266
cave *n* 189, 221, 252
cave in *v* 304
cavern *n* 252
cavernous *adj* 252
cavil *v* 477
cavity *n* 252
caw *v* 412
cease *v* 142, 265, 360, 732
ceaseless *adj* 112
ceaselessness *n* 112
cede *v* 624, 782
ceiling *n* 223
celebrant *n* 990
celebrate *v* 551, 883
celebrated *adj* 873, 883
celebration *n* 883
celebration *n* 733, 838, 990
celebrational *adj* 883, 990
celerity *n* 274, 684
celestial *adj* 318, 976, 981
celestial bliss *n* 981
celestial spaces *n* 318
celibacy *n* 904
celibate *n* 904; *adj* 904
cell *n* 189, 357, 752
cement *v* 46, 48, 323
cemetery *n* 363
cenobite *n* 893
censurable *adj* 945

censure n 716, 932; v 716, 932
census n 85
centenary n 98
center n 29, 68, 74, 221, 222; v 290
center of gravity n 222
center on v 74
central adj 68, 222
centrality n 222
centralization n 48, 222
centralize v 48, 222
centrally adv 222
central part n 208
centrifugal adj 291
century n 98, 108
ceramics n 557
cerebral adj 450
ceremonial n 883; adj 240, 998
ceremonious adj 240, 882
ceremony n 240, 883, 998
certain adj 79, 246, 474, 484
certainly adv 474
certainty n 474
certainty n 484
certificate n 771
certitude n 474
cessation n 142
cessation n 261, 265, 360, 687, 725
chafe v 378, 384, 832, 900
chaff n 643; v 856
chain n 69; v 43
chain of thought n 476
chaise n 272
chalk n 342
chalky adj 430
challenge v 715
challenge comparison v 648
chamber n 696
chamber group n 416
chamber music n 415
chamber orchestra n 416
champaign n 344
championship n 707
chance n 156, 621
chance n 152, 470, 615a; v 151, 156, 621; adj 475
chance it v 621
chanciness n 475
chancy adj 156, 475
change n 140
change n 20a, 144, 147, 800; v 15, 20a, 140, 146, 147, 605, 783
changeable adj 140, 144, 149, 475, 605
changeableness n 149

changeableness n 111, 140, 475, 605
changed adj 15, 20a, 140
change direction v 279
changeful adj 607
change hands v 783
changelessness n 150
change of mind n 485
change one's mind v 607
changeover n 144
change sides v 607
changing hands n 783
channel n 260, 302, 350, 627; v 259
chaos n 59, 162, 241
chaotic adj 59, 241
chap n 373
chapel n 1000
chapter n 696
character n 5, 7, 561, 569, 820
characteristic n 79, 550, 569, 780; adj 5, 15, 79, 550, 569
characterization n 594
characterize v 564, 594
characterized adj 820
charcoal n 388, 431
charge n 630, 695, 697, 716, 741, 755, 812, 938; v 52, 190, 695, 716, 741, 755, 812, 938, 938, 938
charging n 938
charitable adj 707, 784, 816, 906, 910
charity n 707, 784, 816, 906, 910
charm n 829, 992, 993; v 288, 615, 829, 992
charmed adj 992
charmer n 994
charming adj 933; adj 992
charnel house n 363
chart n 183, 527, 626
charter n 755, 963; v 760
chary adj 817, 864
chase v 622
chase away v 289
chasm n 208, 260
chaste adj 242, 576, 578, 849, 881, 944, 960
chasten v 972
chasteness n 849
chastisement n 972
chastity n 881, 944, 960
chat n 588; v 588
chattels n 780
chatter n 584; v 584
chatterbox n 584
chatterer n 584

chattering adj 584
chatty adj 584, 588
cheap adj 435, 643, 815, 819, 943
cheapness n 815
cheat n 545, 548, 792; v 545, 923
check n 179, 616, 666, 706, 751; v 179, 233, 275, 468, 706, 708, 751
checked adj 440
checker v 440
checkered adj 440
checklist n 86
cheek n 236
cheek by jowl adv 236
cheer n 827, 829; v 411, 689, 829, 834, 836, 840
cheerful adj 827, 829
cheerfully adv 836
cheerfulness n 836
cheerfulness n 827, 829
cheering adj 836, 858
cheerless adj 828, 901a
cheery adj 829, 836, 836
chemistry n 144
cherish v 897
cherry-colored adj 434
cherub n 129, 977
cherubic adj 977
chest n 802
chestnut adj 433
chew v 298
chewing n 298
chew the fat v 588
chiaroscuro n 429
chicanery n 477, 702
chick n 129
chicken n 862; adj 862
chicken-hearted adj 862
chief n 694, 745
chiefly adv 31
child n 129, 167
childbirth n 163
child genius n 872
childhood n 127
childish adj 129, 486, 499, 575
childlike adj 499, 703
children n 167
child's play n 705
chill v 383, 385, 616; adj 383
chilled adj 385
chilliness n 383
chilly adj 383
chime n 408; v 407, 413
chimera n 515
chimerical adj 515
chimney n 351
chink n 198; v 408

chip n 32; v 44, 195
chip off the old block n 17, 167
chipper adj 654
chirography n 590
chirp v 412
chirrup v 412
chisel v 240, 557, 558
chiseling n 558
chit n 588
chit-chat n 588; v 588
chock-full adj 52
chocolate adj 433
choice n 609
choice n 600; adj 648
choice of words n 569
choir n 416
choke v 261, 361, 641
choleric adj 901
chomp v 298
choose v 609
choosing n 609
choosy adj 465
chop v 44
choppy seas n 348
chop up v 201
choral adj 415, 416
choral music n 415
chorus n 411, 416
christen v 564
Christian adj 983a
Christian Revelation n 985
chromatic adj 428
chronicle n 114; v 114, 551
chronicler n 553
chronicles n 551
chronological adj 114
chronological error n 115
chronology n 114
chronometer n 114
chronometry n 114
chubby adj 194
chuck v 284, 412
chuckle v 838
chug v 298
chum n 890
chummy adj 892
church n 995, 1000
churchdom n 995
churchman n 996
churl n 819
churlish adj 819
churlishness n 901a
churn v 315, 352
cilia n 205
cinder n 388
cinerary adj 363
cinnamon adj 433
cipher n 84, 550, 561
circle n 181, 247, 712; v 227, 247, 311
circle around v 312, 629

circling n 311; adj 248
circuit n 629
circuit n 181, 230, 247, 279, 311; v 311
circuitous adj 279, 311, 629
circuitously adv 279
circular n 592; adj 245, 247, 249, 311
circularity n 247
circularity n 311
circular motion n 311
circulate v 531
circulation n 311, 312
circumference n 230
circumjacent adj 227
circumnavigate v 311
circumnavigation n 311
circumscribe v 76, 195, 221, 229, 232, 233, 751
circumscribed adj 229
circumscription n 229
circumscription n 751
circumspect adj 451, 459, 864
circumspectful adj 457
circumspection n 459, 864
circumstance n 8
circumstance n 151
circumstances n 7, 527
circumstantial adj 8
circumvention n 311
citation n 467
cite v 467, 969
citizen n 188
citizenry n 876
civic adj 372
civil adj 852, 894, 928, 997
civility n 457, 894
civilization n 372, 658
clack v 407, 412
clad adj 225
claim n 924
claim n 630, 741, 765; v 720, 741, 924
claimant n 767, 924
claiming adj 924
claim relationship with v 11
clairvoyant n 513, 994
clamber v 305
clammy adj 352
clamor n 404, 411
clamor for v 765
clamorous adj 404, 411, 765, 825
clamorousness n 404
clamp v 43
clan n 72, 75, 712
clandestine adj 528

clang n 404, 408; v 404
clangor n 404, 408
clank v 410
clannish adj 712
clap one's hands v 838
claque n 712
clarify v 74, 652, 849
clarity n 446, 518, 570, 849
clash n 276, 713; v 24, 179, 406, 713
clashing n 179, 410; adj 24, 410
clasp v 43, 46
class n 75
class n 51, 58
classic adj 242, 578
classical adj 242, 578
classical music n 415
classicist n 578
classics n 560
classification n 60
classify v 60
clatter v 407
clauses n 770
clay n 362
clean v 42, 652; adj 652, 960
cleanliness n 652
cleanness n 652
cleanness n 960
clean out v 297
cleanse v 652
clean sweep n 146
clear v 705, 937, 970; adj 42, 413, 420, 425, 446, 474, 518, 525, 570, 807, 849
clearance n 807, 970
clear as day adj 518
clear-cut adj 518
cleared adj 970
clearheaded adj 502
clearheadedness n 502
clearness n 425, 446, 518, 570, 580
clear out v 297, 652
clear-sighted adj 441
clear stage n 134
clear up v 518
cleave v 44, 46, 91, 259
cleft n 198, 260; adj 91
clemency n 740
clergy n 996
clergyman n 996
clerical n 996; adj 995, 996
clerk n 553, 590
clever adj 498, 698, 702, 842
cleverness n 698, 842
click v 406
client n 795
clientele n 795
cliff n 212, 306
climactic adj 8, 377
climate n 181, 338

climax *n* 8, 67, 210, 377; *v* 210
climb *v* 305
climb upward *v* 305
clime *n* 181, 338
clinch *v* 43, 474
cling *v* 46
cling to *v* 602, 613
clink *v* 408, 410
clip back *v* 201
clique *n* 712
cliquish *adj* 712
cloak *n* 530; *v* 528
clock *n* 114
clockwork *n* 80
clod *n* 192
clogging *n* 261
close *n* 67, 729; *v* 67, 261, 729; *adj* 17, 43, 186, 197, 199, 203, 321, 528
close at hand *adj* 121
close by *adj* 152
close call *n* 671
closed *adj* 261
closely packed *adj* 72
close-mouthed *adj* 585
closeness *n* 186, 197, 203
close of the day *n* 126
close quarters *n* 197
close to *adv* 197
close upon *adv* 117, 197
close up shop *v* 142
closure *n* 261
clothe *v* 225
clothed *adj* 223, 225
clothes *n* 225
clothing *n* 223, 225
cloud *n* 353
cloud *n* 353, 424, 530; *v* 353, 421, 422
clouded *adj* 426
cloudiness *n* 353, 422, 426, 447
cloudless *adj* 420
cloud over *v* 422
cloudy *adj* 353, 421, 422, 424, 426
cloven *adj* 91
clown *n* 501, 701, 844
cloy *v* 376, 641, 869
cloying *adj* 396
club *n* 74
clubbish *adj* 892
cluck *v* 412
clue *n* 550
clump *n* 72, 250
clumsiness *n* 699
clumsy *adj* 699
cluster *n* 72; *v* 72
clutter *n* 407
coach *n* 272; *v* 537
coagulate *v* 321
coagulation *n* 321
coal *n* 388, 431

coal-black *adj* 431
coalesce *v* 13, 48
coalescence *n* 48
coalescent *adj* 13
coalition *n* 709
coarse *adj* 241, 256, 329, 410, 653, 674, 851
coarseness *n* 329, 851
coast *n* 231, 342; *v* 267
coat *n* 204; *v* 204, 224
coating *n* 223, 224, 332
cobalt *adj* 438
cock *n* 373
cockcrow *n* 125
cockeye *n* 443
cockeyed *adj* 443
cocksure *adj* 484
cocoa *adj* 433
code *n* 561, 697, 963
codger *n* 819
codify *v* 963
coequal *adj* 27
coerce *v* 739, 744
coercion *n* 739, 744
coercive *adj* 739, 744
coeval *adj* 120
coexist *v* 120, 199
coexistence *n* 88, 120
coexisting *adj* 120
coexist with *v* 88
coextension *n* 216
coextensive *adj* 216
coffee *adj* 433
coffer *n* 802
coffin *n* 363
cogency *n* 157
cogitate *v* 451
cogitation *n* 451
cognizant of *adj* 490
cohere *v* 46, 321
coherence *n* 46
coherence *n* 502, 518
coherent *adj* 321
cohesion *n* 46, 327
cohesive *adj* 46, 321, 327
cohesiveness *n* 46, 327
coil *n* 248, 311; *v* 245, 248
coiled *adj* 248
coin *v* 515
coincide *v* 13, 199
coincidence *n* 120
coincident *adj* 13, 120
coinciding *adj* 13
coin words *v* 563
coke *n* 388
cold *n* 383
cold *adj* 383, 866
cold-blooded *adj* 383, 823
cold-hearted *adj* 823
coldly *adv* 383
coldness *n* 383, 823
cold storage *n* 387
collaborate *v* 178

collaboration *n* 178
collaborative *adj* 178
collaborator *n* 711
collapse *n* 158, 195, 659; *v* 158, 195, 304
collar *n* 247
collate *v* 464
collateral *n* 771; *adj* 6, 216
collation *n* 464
colleague *n* 711
collect *v* 72, 596, 775
collected *adj* 826
collection *n* 72, 102, 596
collective *adj* 78, 778
collectively *adv* 50
collectivism *n* 778
college *n* 542
collegiate *adj* 542
collide with *v* 276
collision *n* 179, 276
colloquial *adj* 521, 560, 563
colloquialism *n* 521
colloquy *n* 588
collusion *n* 709
colonize *v* 184
color *n* 428
color *n* 434, 448, 654; *v* 428, 469, 549, 556
coloration *n* 428, 549
colorblind *adj* 443
color blindness *n* 443
colored *adj* 428
colorful *adj* 521
coloring *n* 428, 469, 549
colorless *adj* 429, 430
colorlessness *n* 429
colorlessness *n* 430
colossal *adj* 192, 206
Colosseum *n* 728
column *n* 69, 266
combat *n* 173, 680, 720, 722; *v* 708, 720, 722
combatant *n* 726
combating *n* 708
combative *adj* 173, 720, 722
combination *n* 48
combination *n* 41, 54, 709, 712
combine *v* 41, 48, 87, 178, 709
combined *adj* 48
combo *n* 416
combustible *n* 388; *adj* 384, 388
combustion *n* 384
come about *v* 151
come after *v* 63, 117
come ashore *v* 342
come before *v* 62, 116, 280
come between *v* 228

come close to v 197
comedian n 844
comedienne n 844
come-down n 509; v 306
come down with v 655
come first v 33, 62, 280
come forth v 446
come forward v 446
come from v 154
come in v 294
come in its turn v 138
come in sequence v 281
come into v 775, 785
come into play v 170
come into sight v 446
come into the world v 359
come into use v 613
come into view v 446
comeliness n 242, 845
comely adj 845
come near v 121
come of age v 131
come on v 121, 152
come on to v 544
come out of v 295
come out of nowhere v 508
come round v 151, 660
come round again v 138
come short v 732
come short of v 34, 304
come straight to the point v 576
come to v 50, 292, 359
come to a close v 67
come to an agreement v 774
come together v 72, 290
come to grief v 735
come to light v 525
come to nothing v 169, 304
come to pass v 151
come to rest v 184
come to the front v 234
come to the point v 79, 572, 703
come to the rescue v 672
comets n 318
come up short v 304
come up to v 27
come up with v 612
comfort n 377, 827, 831, 834; v 831, 834, 834, 906
comfortable adj 23, 377, 803, 827, 829, 831
comforting adj 834
comical adj 853

coming n 292; adj 121, 152
coming after n 63, 281
coming and going n 314
coming before n 62
coming beforehand n 280
coming together n 290
command n 741
command n 157, 630, 693, 697, 737; v 157, 206, 600, 693, 741, 777
commandant n 745
commandeer v 789
commander n 269, 745
commanding adj 642, 741
commandment n 741
command of language n 569
commemorate v 551, 883
commemoration n 883
commemorative adj 883
commence v 66
commencement n 66
commend v 883, 931
commendable adj 618, 931
commendation n 931
commendatory adj 883, 931
commensurate adj 23, 639
comment n 476, 522; v 595
commentary n 522, 595
commentator n 480, 524, 595
comment upon v 522
commerce n 794, 796
commercial adj 794
commingle v 41
commiserate v 914
commiseration n 914
commission n 755
commission n 758; v 737, 755
commit v 680
commitment n 768
commit oneself v 768
commit sacrilege v 988
commit suicide v 361
committed adj 768
committee n 696, 758
commodity n 798
common adj 34, 78, 82, 613, 643, 778, 851, 876, 879

commonalty n 876
commonalty n 34
commoners n 876
common holding n 778
common law n 124
commonly adv 136
commonness n 34
commonplace adj 29, 34, 598, 613, 643, 736, 843
commonplaceness n 736
common run n 78
common sense n 450, 480, 498
commonsensical adj 450
commonweal n 372
commonwealth n 372
commotion n 315
communal adj 712, 778
communicant n 990
communicate v 527, 529, 582, 592
communicated adj 527
communication n 43, 527, 582, 592
communicative adj 527
communion n 778
communism n 778
communist n 778; adj 778
communistic adj 778
community n 188, 372, 712
community of possessions n 778
commutation n 147, 148
commute v 147, 148
compact n 769
compact n 202, 676; v 201; adj 43, 195, 201, 202, 321, 572
compactness n 195
compactual adj 769
companion n 890
companion piece n 237
companionship n 888, 892
company n 72, 88, 186, 712
comparable adj 464
comparative adj 26, 464
comparative anatomy n 368
comparative physiology n 368
comparative relation n 464
compare v 216, 464

compared with adj 464
comparison n 464
comparison n 9, 216
compartment n 51
compass n 26; v 227
compassion n 740,
910, 914
compassionate adj
740, 914
compatible adj 23, 413
compel v 157, 601,
744, 751
compelling adj 744
compendious adj 76,
201, 572, 596
compendium n 596
compendium n 195,
596
compensate v 30, 179,
790, 807, 973
compensating adj 30
compensation n 30
compensation n 774,
790, 952, 973
compensatory adj 30,
790, 973
compete v 720
competence n 157,
639, 698, 803
competency n 157
competent adj 157,
639, 698
competition n 720
competitition n 708
competitive adj 720
competitor n 710, 726,
767
compilation n 54, 72,
596
compile v 72, 596
complacency n 831
complacent adj 721,
831
complain v 411
complaint n 655, 839
complement n 39, 88,
237
complementary adj
12, 237
complementary color
n 428
complete v 52, 67, 142,
292, 650, 729, 731,
769; adj 31, 50, 52
completely adv 31, 50,
52, 729
completeness n 52
completeness n 50
completion n 729
completion n 142, 261
complex adj 59, 248,
704
complexion n 7, 428,
448
compliance n 82, 602,

725, 743, 762, 772
compliant adj 82, 725,
743, 762, 772
complicate v 61
complicated adj 59,
248
complication n 59, 667
complications n 154
complicity n 709
compliment n 896
complimentary adj
896, 931
comply v 82, 602, 725,
743, 762
comply with v 772
component n 56
component n 51
component part n 56
comportment n 448
comport oneself v 680
compose v 54, 161,
174, 415, 569, 590,
591, 597, 826
composed adj 826
composite n 48; adj 41
composition n 54
composition n 48, 569,
590, 591
compositor n 591
composure n 174, 826
compound n 48, 232; v
41
comprehend v 54, 76,
490, 518
comprehensibility n
518
comprehensible adj
518
comprehension n 76,
490
comprehensive adj 56,
76, 78, 192
compress v 195, 201,
321, 572, 596
compressed adj 201
compressible adj 322
compression n 195,
572
comprise v 76
compromise n 774
compromise n 29, 30,
68, 628, 723; v 628,
774
compulsion n 744
compulsion n 601
compulsory adj 601,
744
compunction n 950
computable adj 85
computation n 85
compute v 85
comradeship n 888,
892
con n 754; v 545
concatenation n 43
concave adj 252

concavity n 252
concavity n 308
conceal v 223, 447,
519, 528
concealed adj 447,
528, 533
concealment n 528
concealment n 447,
526
concede v 529, 760
conceit n 515, 878, 880
conceited adj 878, 880
conceivable adj 470,
515
conceive v 66, 168,
484, 515
concentrate v 72, 222,
290, 686
concentric adj 222
concept n 451
conception n 451, 453,
515
conceptual adj 2
concern n 9, 625, 642,
860; v 9
concerned adj 459, 860
concerning adv 9
concert n 178, 709
concert artist n 416
concertize v 416
concession n 760, 774,
784
concilatory adj 723
conciliate v 723, 831
conciliation n 714,
723, 831, 952
conciliatory adj 714
concise adj 201, 572
concisely adv 572
conciseness n 572
conciseness n 201
conclave n 72, 696
conclude v 67, 480,
604, 729
concluded adj 67
concluding adj 67
conclusion n 65, 67,
154, 480, 729
conclusive adj 67, 478,
480
conclusiveness n 478
concoct v 626
concomitance n 120
concomitant n 88; adj
88, 120
concomitants n 154
concord n 413, 714
concord n 23, 413, 488,
709, 721, 762, 888
concordance n 413
concordant adj 413,
714
concourse n 72, 290
concrete adj 3
concretion n 321
concupiscence n 961
concupiscent adj 961

concur *v* 120, 178, 290, 488, 709, 714, 762
concurrence *n* 178
concurrence *n* 23, 120, 290, 488, 709, 762
concurrent *adj* 120, 178, 290
concurrently *adv* 120
concurring *adj* 488
condemn *v* 971
condemnation *n* 971
condemnatory *adj* 932, 971
condemned *adj* 971
condensation *n* 195, 201, 321, 339, 596
condense *v* 195, 201, 321, 572, 596
condensed *adj* 201
condiment *n* 393
condition *n* 7, 8, 469, 514, 875; *v* 770
conditional *adj* 8, 469, 770
conditionally *adv* 8, 770
conditions *n* 770
condolence *n* 915
condolence *n* 914
condole with *v* 915
conduce *v* 176, 178
conduce to *v* 153
conducive *adj* 176
conduct *n* 692
conduct *n* 680, 693; *v* 270, 692, 693
conduct oneself *v* 680
conductor *n* 271
conduct to *v* 278
conduit *n* 350
conduit *n* 302
confabulate *v* 588
confabulation *n* 588
confederate *n* 711
confederation *n* 709, 903
confer *v* 695, 760, 784
conference *n* 588, 696
confer power *v* 157
confer with *v* 588
confess *v* 488, 529
confession *n* 529, 985
confessional *adj* 985
confidant *n* 890
confidence *n* 474, 484, 507, 533, 858
confidence man *n* 548
confident *adj* 474, 484, 858
confidential *adj* 221, 528
confidentially *adv* 528
confiding *adj* 484
configuration *n* 240
confine *n* 233; *v* 195,

229, 233, 751
confined *adj* 203, 229
confinement *n* 229, 751
confirm *v* 535, 769
confirmation *n* 467, 535, 762
confirmative *adj* 535
confirmatory *adj* 467
confiscate *v* 789, 974
confiscation *n* 789, 974
conflict *n* 24, 680, 713, 720; *v* 713
conflicting *adj* 14, 24, 179, 468
conflicting evidence *n* 468
conflict with *v* 179
confluence *n* 43, 290
confluent *adj* 290, 413
conflux *n* 72, 290
conform *v* 82
conformable to rule *adj* 82
conformity *n* 82
conformity *n* 16, 23, 80, 240, 613, 852
conform to *v* 16, 82
confound *v* 61, 465a, 475
confront *v* 234, 464, 708, 719
confuse *v* 41, 59, 61, 185, 465a, 475, 519, 538
confused *adj* 59, 447, 571
confusion *n* 59, 519, 571
confutable *adj* 479
confutation *n* 479
confutation *n* 536
confute *v* 479
congeal *v* 321, 385
congelation *n* 385
congenial *adj* 23, 413, 714, 829
congeniality *n* 829
congenital *adj* 5
congestion *n* 641
conglomerate *n* 72, 321
conglomeration *n* 41, 46, 72
congratulate *v* 896
congratulate oneself *v* 838
congratulations *n* 896
congratulatory *adj* 896
congregate *v* 72
congregation *n* 72, 990, 997
congress *n* 72, 290, 588
congruity *n* 23
congruous *adj* 23

conical *adj* 253
conjectural *adj* 514
conjecture *n* 514; *v* 514, 870
conjoin *v* 41, 45
conjoined *adj* 413
conjugation *n* 567
conjunction *n* 8, 43
conjuration *n* 992
conjure *v* 992
conjuror *n* 994
con man *n* 548
connect *v* 9, 43, 45, 216
connected *adj* 9, 11
connection *n* 9, 11, 43, 45, 46
connective *n* 45
connoisseur *n* 480, 700
connotative *adj* 550
connotation *n* 516
conote *v* 516
conquer *v* 731
conquest *n* 731
consanguineous *adj* 11
consanguinity *n* 11
conscience *n* 926
conscientious *adj* 246, 459
conscious *adj* 375
consciousness *n* 375, 821
conscription *n* 744
consecrate *v* 987, 995
consecutive *adj* 63, 69
consecutively *adv* 69
consecutiveness *n* 69
consensus *n* 762
consent *n* 762
consent *n* 23, 178, 488, 760; *v* 762
consenting *adj* 488
consequence *n* 62, 63, 65, 154, 642
consequent *adj* 63
consequential *adj* 642
consequently *adv* 154
conservation *n* 141, 670
conservative *adj* 670
conserve *v* 670
consider *v* 451, 461, 469, 480, 484, 873, 928
considerable *adj* 31, 192, 642
considerate *adj* 451
consideration *n* 451, 457, 469, 615, 642, 928
considering *adj* 928
consign *v* 270, 755, 783, 784
consignee *n* 758
consignment *n* 755, 784, 786
consign to oblivion *v* 506

consign to the grave v
363
consistency n 16, 23
consistent adj 16, 23,
413
consistent with adv 82
consist in v 1
consist of v 54
consolation n 834, 915
console v 834, 915
consolidate v 46, 48,
321
consolidation n 46,
321
consoling adj 834
consonance n 413
consonant n 561; adj
23, 413
consort n 903; v 41
consort with v 88, 892
conspicuous adj 446,
525
conspicuousness n 446
conspiracy n 626
conspiratorial adj 626
conspire v 178, 709
constancy n 16, 80,
112, 141, 150
constant adj 16, 69, 80,
110, 136, 138, 141,
150, 474, 604a
constant flow n 69
constantly adv 112,
136
constellations n 318
consternation n 860
constipation n 261
constituent n 51, 56
constitute v 54, 56, 161
constituting adj 54
constitution n 5, 7, 54,
329, 963
constitutional n 266;
adj 963
constrain v 744, 751
constrained adj 751
constraining adj 744
constraint n 744, 749,
751
constrict v 195
construct v 161, 240
construction n 5, 161,
240, 329
constructions n 567
constructive adj 161
construe v 522
consult v 695
consume v 638, 677
consummate v 67,
729; adj 31, 52, 67,
650, 729
consummately adv 31
consummation n 67,
729
consumption n 162,
638, 677

contact n 199, 379
contact lens n 445
contain v 54, 76
container n 191
contaminate v 653,
659
contaminated adj 655,
961
contamination n 653,
659, 961
contemn v 930
contemplate v 441,
451, 620
contemplation n 441,
451, 620
contemplative adj 451
contemporaneous adj
120
contemporaneousness
n 120
contemporary adj 120
contempt n 930
contemptible adj 435,
930
contemptuous adj 885,
930
contemptuousness n
885
contend v 476, 720,
722
contender n 726
content n 831
content adj 602, 826,
827
contented adj 831, 878
contention n 720
contention n 713, 969
contentious adj 713,
720, 722
contentment n 831
contents n 190
contents n 56, 221, 596
contest n 720
contestant n 726
contiguity n 199
contiguity n 197
contiguous adj 199
contiguousness n 199
continence n 953, 960
continent n 342; adj
960
continental adj 342
contingency n 151,
156, 470
contingent adj 8, 177
continual adj 136, 138
continually adv 136
continuance n 143
continuance n 110,
117, 200, 670
continuation n 63, 65,
143
continue v 1, 106, 110,
136, 143, 604a, 670
continuing adj 143
continuity n 69

continuity n 16, 58,
143, 150
continuous adj 69,
112, 143
continuously adv 69,
112
continuousness n 69
contort v 243, 248
contortion n 243
contour n 230, 448
contraband adj 964
contract n 676, 768,
769, 771; v 36, 195,
676, 769, 770
contract a disease v
655
contracted adj 195
contracting adj 195
contraction n 195
contraction n 36, 261
contractual adj 769
contradict v 14, 468,
489, 536, 708
contradiction n 14,
218, 536
contradictory adj 14,
468, 489, 536
contraposition n 218,
237
contrariety n 14
contrariety n 15, 179,
218
contrary adj 14, 179,
608, 708
contrast n 14, 15; v 15
contrasted adj 14
contrast with v 14
contravene v 14, 468,
536, 708
contribute v 153, 176,
178
contribution n 784
contributor n 912
contrite adj 833, 950
contrition n 833, 950
contrivance n 626
contrive v 161, 626,
702
control n 157, 175,
693, 737, 741, 751,
777, 965; v 157, 175,
693, 737, 777
controller n 694
controversy n 720
controvert v 536
contumacious adj 715,
742
contumacy n 742
contumely n 930
conundrum n 520
convalescent adj 660
convene v 72
convenience n 685
convenient adj 646
convention n 72, 80,
240

conventional *adj* 80, 82, 240, 246, 613, 852, 983a
conventionalism *n* 613
conventionality *n* 82, 613, 852
converge *v* 197, 290
convergence *n* 290
convergent *adj* 290
conversable *adj* 588
conversant *adj* 698
conversation *n* 588
conversation *n* 582
conversational *adj* 582, 588
converse *v* 582, 588; *adj* 14, 237
conversion *n* 144
conversion *n* 140, 218
convert *v* 140
convertibility *n* 13
convertible *adj* 144, 149
convert into *v* 144
convex *adj* 250
convexity *n* 250
convey *v* 270, 516, 783
conveyable *adj* 783
conveyance *n* 272
conveyor *n* 271
convict *n* 754; *v* 971
convicted *adj* 971
conviction *n* 451, 474, 484, 971
convinced *adj* 474, 484
convincing *adj* 478
convivial *adj* 892
conviviality *n* 892
convoluted *adj* 59, 248
convolution *n* 248
convolution *n* 59, 312
convoy *v* 88
convulse *v* 61, 173, 315, 378
convulsed with laughter *adj* 838
convulsion *n* 59, 146, 173, 315, 378
convulsive *adj* 173, 315, 378
coo *v* 412
cook *v* 384, 384
cool *v* 338, 385, 616; *adj* 174, 383, 826, 866, 953
cool down *v* 826
cooled *adj* 385
cooling *n* 385
coolness *n* 383, 826, 866, 953
cool one's heels *v* 681
coop *n* 752
cooperate *v* 178, 709, 712
cooperating *adj* 709
cooperation *n* 709
cooperation *n* 23, 178,

778
cooperative *adj* 178, 709
cooperatively *adv* 709
coordinate *v* 60
co-ownership *n* 778
co-partner *n* 778
copious *adj* 168, 573
copper *adj* 439
copula *n* 45
copy *n* 21
copy *n* 13, 19, 22, 90, 532, 556, 590, 591; *v* 19, 554, 590
copyeditor *n* 591
copying *n* 19
copyist *n* 590
cord *n* 247
cordial *adj* 377, 602, 829, 888, 892
cordiality *n* 602, 892
core *n* 5, 68, 208, 222
cork *n* 263; *v* 261
corkscrew *n* 248, 262, 311
cork up *v* 261
cormorant *n* 957
corner *n* 244
cornered *adj* 244
corny *adj* 496
corollary *n* 39
corona *n* 247
coronet *n* 247
corporal *adj* 3
corporality *n* 3, 364
corporate *adj* 43
corporeal *adj* 3, 316, 364
corporeality *n* 316
corpse *n* 362
corpselike *adj* 362
corpulence *n* 192
corpulent *adj* 192, 194
corral *n* 232
correct *v* 246, 658, 660, 662, 972; *adj* 246, 494, 578, 922, 922
correction *n* 658, 972
corrective *n* 662; *adj* 658, 662
correctness *n* 578
correlate *v* 12, 464
correlation *n* 12
correlation *n* 9, 464
correlative *adj* 12, 216
correspond *v* 12, 23, 592
correspondence *n* 592
correspondence *n* 12, 13, 17, 23, 216
correspondent *adj* 23
corresponding *adj* 12, 17, 216
correspond to *v* 216
corroboration *n* 467

corroborative *adj* 467, 535
corrode *v* 659
corrosion *n* 659
corrosive *adj* 649
corrugate *v* 258
corrugation *n* 256
corrupt *v* 653, 659; *adj* 653, 655, 945
corrupted *adj* 961
corruption *n* 49, 563, 653, 659
corse *n* 362
cortege *n* 266
coruscate *v* 420
coruscation *n* 420
cosmic *adj* 318
cosmonaut *n* 269
cosmopolitan *adj* 372
cost *n* 812
cost a lot *v* 814
costliness *n* 814
cost little *v* 815
costly *adj* 814
costs *n* 809
costume *n* 225
cote *n* 232
coterie *n* 712
cough *v* 349
could be *v* 470
council *n* 696
council *n* 72, 588, 695
counsel *n* 695, 864, 968; *v* 864
counselor *n* 540, 695, 968
counselor-at-law *n* 968
count *v* 85, 451
count among *v* 76
countenance *n* 448
counter *adj* 14
counteract *v* 30, 179, 662
counteracting *adj* 179
counteraction *n* 179
counteraction *n* 708
counteractive *n* 662
counterattack *n* 718; *v* 718
counterbalance *n* 27; *v* 30
counterblast *n* 179
counter-evidence *n* 468
counterfeit *n* 21; *v* 19, 544, 855; *adj* 19, 544
countering *adj* 237
counter maneuver *n* 179
counterpart *n* 17, 21, 237
counterpoint *n* 413
counterpoise *n* 30; *v* 30, 179
counterrevolution *n* 146

counterstroke n 718
counter to adv 708
countervail v 30
countervailing adj 468
countless adj 104
count on v 507
country n 181, 189
county n 181
coup n 146
coup de grace n 361
coup d'état n 146
couple n 89, 100; v 43, 89, 903
coupled adj 89
coupled with adj 88
couple with v 88
coupling n 43
courage n 861
courage n 715
courageous adj 715, 861
courageousness n 715
courier n 271, 534
course n 109
course n 58, 106, 264, 278, 348, 627
course of time n 109
coursing n 361
court n 696, 966; v 615, 933
courteous adj 457, 852, 879, 894, 928
courtesan n 962
courtesy n 894
courtesy n 457
courtier n 935
courtliness n 894
courtly adj 894
court of justice n 966
court of law n 966
courtroom n 966
cove n 343
covenant n 768, 769; v 768
covenants n 770
cover n 223, 263, 424, 530, 666; v 30, 204, 223, 224, 225, 424, 528, 664
covered adj 223
covering n 223
covering n 220, 225, 528
coverlet n 223
cover over v 223
covert adj 447, 528
covet v 865, 921
covetous adj 819, 865, 921
covetousness n 921
cow n 374; v 909
coward n 862
cowardice n 862
cowardice n 172, 605
cowardly adj 435, 605, 862
cower v 862, 886

coxcomb n 854
cozen v 545
crack n 44, 70, 113, 198, 259; v 44, 328, 406, 583, 659; adj 648, 698
cracked adj 410, 503
cracked bell n 408a
crackers adj 503
crackle v 406
crack of doom n 121
cradle n 66, 127
craft n 625, 698, 702
craftiness n 698, 702
craftsmanship n 161
crafty adj 702
craggy adj 253, 256
cram v 194, 539
crammed adj 52
cramp n 378; v 158, 160, 195, 706
cramped adj 579
cranny n 198
crapulence n 957
crapulent adj 957
crash n 276; v 406
crashpad n 189
crass adj 851
crater n 208, 252
crave v 865
craven n 862; adj 435, 862
craving n 276, 865; adj 865
crawl v 109, 275, 886
craze n 852
crazed adj 499, 503
craziness n 503
crazy n 504; adj 503
creak v 410
creaking n 410; adj 410
cream n 356, 648
creamy adj 352, 435
crease n 258; v 258
create v 153, 515
creation n 161, 318
creative adj 153, 161, 515
creativity n 168, 515
creator n 153, 164, 976
creature n 3, 366, 372
credence n 484
credible adj 470, 484
credit n 805
credit n 484, 873; v 484, 805, 811
creditable adj 878, 931
credo n 537, 983
credulity n 486
credulous adj 484, 486, 547
credulousness n 486
creed n 484, 537, 983
creep v 109, 275, 380
creeper n 367
creeping thing n 366

cremate v 363
cremation n 363, 384
crescent n 245; adj 245
crescent-shaped adj 245
cretin n 493, 501
crevice n 198
crew n 72, 269, 712
crick n 378
criminal adj 964
criminality n 947
crimson adj 434
cringe v 886
cringing n 886; adj 435, 886
crinkle v 256, 258
cripple v 158, 659
crippled adj 158
crisis n 8, 134, 151, 704, 735
crisp adj 328
criss-cross v 219
critic n 480, 524, 595, 936
critical adj 8, 465, 480, 642, 704, 716, 735
criticism n 480, 595, 716
criticize v 480, 595, 716, 850, 934
critique n 465, 480, 595
croak v 412, 583
croaking adj 410
crony n 890
crook n 244, 245, 792; v 217, 245, 279
crooked adj 217, 243, 244, 279, 923
crookedness n 243
croon v 416
crop n 154, 775; v 201
crop up v 151, 446
cross n 41; v 41, 179, 219, 302, 830; adj 41, 901a
crossed adj 219
cross-eye n 443
crosseyed adj 443
cross-fire n 148
crossing n 219
crossing adj 219
cross-purposes n 713
crossroad n 219
cross swords v 722
crotch n 244
crotchety adj 608
crouch v 207, 886
crouched adj 207
crow v 412, 838, 884
crowd n 72, 102, 444, 876; v 72, 102, 197
crowded adj 72, 102
crown n 247; v 210
crowning adj 33, 67
crowning point n 210
crowning touch n 729

crucial *adj* 642
crude *adj* 53, 579, 651, 674, 851, 895, 929
crudeness *n* 929
cruel *adj* 649, 739, 830, 914a
cruelly *adv* 31
cruelty *n* 914a
cruise *n* 267; *v* 267
cruiser *n* 273
crumb *n* 32, 330
crumble *v* 49, 160, 162, 328, 330, 659
crumbling *adj* 124, 659
crumbly *adj* 330
crumbs *n* 40
crumple *n* 256, 258
crumple up *v* 195
crunch *v* 298
crush *n* 72; *v* 162, 195, 330, 739, 879
crush out *v* 162
crust *n* 223
crustacean *n* 366
crutch *n* 215
cry *n* 411
cry *n* 669; *v* 411, 412, 839
cry for joy *v* 838
crying *n* 411, 412; *adj* 411, 630
cry out *v* 411, 669
cry out against *v* 616
crypt *n* 363
cryptic *adj* 526
crystalline *adj* 425
crystallization *n* 321, 323
crystallize *v* 321
cubbyhole *n* 530
cube *v* 93
cuckoo *v* 412
cue *n* 550
cull *v* 609, 789
culminate *v* 210
culmination *n* 65, 206, 210, 261, 729
culpability *n* 947
culpable *adj* 947
cultivate *v* 371, 375, 658
cultivated *adj* 850
cultivate one's own garden *v* 943
cultivation *n* 371, 578, 658, 850
culture *n* 850
cultured *adj* 850
culvert *n* 350
cumbersome *adj* 319, 706, 830
cumbrous *adj* 319
cunning *n* 702
cunning *n* 544, 698; *adj* 544, 545, 698
cup *n* 252

cupidity *n* 819
cupola *n* 250
cupped *adj* 252
curable *adj* 660
curative *adj* 660, 662, 834
curb *n* 179, 616, 751; *v* 174, 179, 275, 751
curd *n* 354
curdle *v* 397
curdled *adj* 397
cure *n* 660, 662; *v* 660, 662, 670
curfew *n* 126
curiosity *n* 455
curiosity *n* 872
curious *adj* 455, 461, 870
curiously *adv* 31
curl *n* 245, 248; *v* 245, 248, 258
currency *n* 800
current *n* 338, 348; *adj* 1, 78, 118, 151, 531, 532, 560, 613
curry *v* 331, 392
curry favor *v* 933
curse *n* 663, 830, 908; *v* 908
cursing *n* 908
cursory *adj* 209
curt *adj* 201, 739
curtail *v* 38
curtailed *adj* 201
curtailment *n* 38, 201
curtain *n* 424, 530; *v* 424
curtness *n* 739
curtsy *n* 308; *v* 308
curvature *n* 245
curve *n* 217, 245, 245; *v* 245, 279
curved *adj* 245
custodial *adj* 777
custodian *n* 664, 753
custody *n* 664, 777, 781
custom *n* 80, 124, 613, 852
customarily *adv* 136
customariness *n* 82
customary *adj* 80, 82, 124, 136, 613, 852, 983a
customer *n* 795
cut *n* 44, 70, 198, 240, 257, 259, 276, 378; *v* 44, 240, 257, 259, 361, 371, 385, 557
cut across *v* 302
cut adrift *v* 44, 297
cut a figure *v* 448
cut away *v* 38
cutback *n* 38; *v* 38, 201; *adj* 201
cut down *v* 195, 361
cut in two *v* 91

cut off *v* 38, 44, 361; *adj* 776
cut open *v* 260
cut out *v* 293
cut short *v* 142, 201
cutter *n* 273
cutthroat *n* 361
cutting *adj* 253, 383
cutting edge *n* 253
cuttings *n* 596
cut to pieces *v* 361
cut to ribbons *v* 361
cutup *n* 844; *v* 44
cycle *n* 138, 247
cyclic *adj* 138
cyclical *adj* 138
cyclically *adv* 138
cycling *n* 266
cyclist *n* 268
cyclone *n* 312, 315, 349
cyclonic *adj* 349
cylinder *n* 249
cylindrical *adj* 249
cylindricality *n* 249
cynic *n* 165, 936, 989

D

dab *n* 32, 276; *v* 276
dabble *v* 683
dad *n* 166
dado *n* 211
daft *adj* 503
daily *adv* 136
dainty *adj* 394, 829, 868
dale *n* 252
dalliance *n* 902
dally *v* 683, 902
damage *n* 619, 649, 659, 776, 812; *v* 649, 659, 848
damages *n* 974
damn *v* 908, 971
damnable *adj* 649
damnation *n* 908
damning *n* 908
damp *n* 339, 616; *adj* 339
dampen *v* 408a
dampened *adj* 408a
damper *n* 408a, 616
dampness *n* 339
dam up *v* 261
dance *n* 309; *v* 309, 315, 838
dance all night *v* 309
dandy *n* 854
danger *n* 665
danger *n* 475, 667, 909
dangerous *adj* 475, 665
danger signal *n* 669
dangle *v* 214
dangler *n* 281
dangling *adj* 214
dank *adj* 339

dankness n 339
dapple v 440; adj 433
dappled adj 440
dapple-gray adj 432
dare v 715, 861
daring n 715, 861; adj 715, 861
dark adj 421, 422, 431, 442, 447, 571, 901a
darken v 353, 421, 422, 431, 519
darkened adj 421, 422
darkish adj 422
darkly adv 442
darkness n 421
darkness n 426, 431, 491, 526
darling n 897, 899
dart v 274
dash n 32, 41, 274, 310, 682, 684; v 41, 274, 276, 310, 684
dash off v 274, 682
dash one's expectations v 509
dash one's hopes v 509
dastardliness n 862
dastardly adj 862
data n 476, 527
date n 106; v 114
daub v 555
daughter n 167
dauntless adj 861
dauntlessness n 861
dawdle v 133, 275, 605, 683
dawdler n 683
dawdling n 683
dawn n 125, 420; v 116
day n 420
day after day adv 136
daybreak n 125, 420
daylight n 420
day of fasting n 956
day of judgment n 121
day of rest n 687
days gone by n 122
days of old n 122
days of yore n 122
daze v 420
dazzle v 420, 442
de n 220, 234
dead adj 172, 360, 376, 381, 408a
dead and gone adj 360
dead as a door nail adj 360
dead drunk adj 959
deaden v 376, 381, 843
deadened adj 381, 408a
dead heat n 27
dead language n 560
deadly adj 162, 360, 361, 649, 657, 663

deadly weapons n 727
deadness n 381
dead of night n 126, 421
dead silence n 403
dead sound n 408a
deaf adj 419
deafen v 404, 419
deafened adj 419
deafening adj 404
deafness n 419
deaf to adj 458
deaf to the past adj 506
deal v 786, 794
dealer n 797
deal in v 796
dealing n 794
deal out v 73, 784
dear n 899; adj 814
dearness n 814
dearth n 640
death n 360
death n 67, 142
death agonies n 360
death bell n 363
death blow n 67, 360, 361
deathlike adj 403
deathly adj 361
death rattle n 360
debark v 292
debarkation n 292
debase v 308, 653, 659, 879
debased adj 207
debasement n 207, 308, 659, 874
debate n 476, 588, 720, 969; v 476, 720
debater n 476
debauchee n 962
debilitate v 160
debility n 158, 160
debit n 177, 806; v 811
debonair adj 894
debt n 806
debt n 177
debtor n 806
decade n 98, 108
decadence n 659
decapitate v 361
decay n 49, 124, 360, 638, 653, 655, 659, 732; v 36, 49, 195, 360, 659, 735
decayed adj 124, 160, 659
decease n 360; v 360
deceit n 545, 702
deceitful adj 544, 545, 702
deceitfulness n 544, 702
deceive v 544, 545
deceiver n 548
deceiver n 962

deceiving n 545
decency n 881, 960
decent adj 246, 651, 881, 960
deception n 545
deception n 21, 544, 702
deceptive adj 520, 544, 545, 702
decide v 153, 480, 600, 604, 609
decided adj 31, 67
decidedly adv 31
decimal adj 84
decimate v 361, 659
decipher v 522
decision n 480, 600, 604, 609, 620, 969
decisive adj 737
deck out v 225
declaim v 582
declamation n 577, 582
declamatory adj 577, 582
declaration n 525, 531, 535, 985
declarative adj 527, 535
declaratory adj 535
declare v 516, 525, 531, 535
declare war v 716
declension n 306, 567, 659
declination n 306
decline n 36, 124, 217, 306, 638, 655, 659, 732; v 36, 160, 217, 306, 360, 610, 659, 732, 735, 764; adj 128
declining adj 217
declining years n 128
declivitous adj 217, 306
declivity n 217, 306
decode v 522
decoloration n 430
decompose v 49
decomposed adj 49
decomposition n 49
decorate v 847
decoration n 733, 847, 877
decorative adj 847
decorous adj 850, 852
decorum n 852, 960
decoy v 288
decrease n 36
decrease n 38, 195, 283; v 36, 38, 193, 195
decreased adj 36
decreasing adj 36
decree n 480, 963; v

600, 741, 963
decrement n 40a
decrepit adj 124, 158, 160, 655, 659
decrepitude n 128, 158, 160, 659
decry v 934
deduce v 476
deduct v 38, 813
deductible adj 38
deduction n 38
deduction n 40a, 65, 476, 480
deductive adj 476
deed n 680, 771
deem v 451, 873
deep n 341; adj 208, 404, 428
deepen v 35, 208
deepness n 208
deep-rooted adj 820
deep-seated adj 208, 221
deep-sounding adj 408
deep-toned adj 408
deface v 241, 659, 846, 848
defacement n 241
defalcation n 304
defamation n 934
defamatory adj 932
defame v 934
defamer n 936
default n 304, 460, 808; v 808
defeat n 509
defeated adj 732
defect n 40a, 53, 651, 848, 945; v 607
defection n 607
defective adj 53, 651, 732, 945
defectiveness n 732
defend v 664, 670, 717, 937
defender n 890, 937
defense n 717
defense n 670, 937
defenseless adj 665
defensible adj 664
defensive adj 717
defer v 133
deference n 743, 928
deferential adj 457, 743, 926, 928
defer to v 928
defiance n 715
defiance n 742
defiant adj 715, 742
deficiency n 28, 34, 53, 304, 640, 651, 732
deficient adj 28, 34, 53, 304, 640, 651
deficit n 53
defile v 653
defiled adj 961

defilement n 653, 961
define v 233, 522
definite adj 79, 233, 246, 446, 474, 570
definition n 446, 522
definitive adj 67
deflect v 245, 279
deflection n 245, 291
deform v 241, 243
deformed adj 243
deformity n 241, 243, 846, 848
defraud v 545, 791, 923
defrost v 382
deft adj 698
defunct adj 2, 360
defy v 715, 742
degeneracy n 659
degenerate v 659; adj 659
degeneration n 659
degradation n 308, 659, 874
degrade v 308, 659, 879
degraded adj 207
degree n 26
degree n 58, 71
deification n 990, 991
deify v 990, 991
deity n 976
dejected adj 832
dejection n 837
dejection n 828, 859
delay n 133; v 133, 142, 706
delayed adj 133
delectability n 394, 829
delectable adj 394, 829
delectation n 827
delegate n 534, 758, 759; v 270, 755
delegation n 755, 758
delete v 552
deleterious adj 649, 657
deletion n 552
deliberate v 695; adj 174, 275, 383, 451, 685
deliberately adv 133, 600, 611, 620
deliberateness n 174, 275
delicacy n 160, 655, 850, 960
delicate adj 160, 203, 328, 329, 394, 428, 704, 829, 868 960
delicate condition n 655
delicious adj 394, 829
delight n 377, 827, 829; v 829, 836
delightful adj 377, 829

delight in v 827
delineate v 554, 594
delineation n 554, 556, 594
deliquescence n 335
deliquescent adj 335
delirious adj 503, 825
delirium n 503, 825
delitescence n 447
deliver v 270, 580, 660, 672, 750, 784
deliverance n 672
deliverance n 660, 750, 834
delivery n 580, 784
dell n 252
delude v 545
deluge n 72, 348; v 337, 348, 641
delusion n 495, 503, 515, 545
delusive adj 545
delve v 252
demand n 601, 630, 741, 765, 812, 924; v 630, 741, 765, 812
demeanor n 448, 692, 852
demented adj 503
dementia n 503
demi- adj 91
demi-lune adj 245
demise n 360
demolish v 162
demolition n 162
demon n 980
demon n 949, 978
demonic adj 980
demonology n 980, 991
demonstrable adj 476, 478
demonstrate v 476, 478, 525
demonstrated adj 478
demonstration n 478
demonstration n 525
demonstrative adj 478
demur n 704; v 485, 603
demure adj 881
den n 189
dendrology n 369
denial n 536
denial n 764
denominate v 564
denotation n 516
denotative adj 550
denote v 516, 550
denounce v 908, 909
dénouement n 65, 67
dense adj 72, 202, 275, 321, 365, 376
denseness n 202
density n 321
density n 202

dent n 252, 257
dented adj 252
denunciation n 908, 932
denunciatory adj 932
deny v 468, 536, 610, 708, 764
deny oneself v 955
deodorize v 652
depart v 66, 185, 293, 302, 360, 449
departed adj 2, 449
department n 51, 75
department store n 799
depart this life v 360
departure n 293
departure n 287, 360, 449, 623
departure from n 279
depend v 214
dependable adj 474, 664
dependence n 749
dependent adj 214, 749
depend upon v 154, 749
depict v 554, 556, 594
depiction n 554, 556, 594
deplane v 292
depletion n 640
deplorable adj 649, 830
deplore v 833, 839
deport v 270, 692
deportation n 270
deportment n 692
depose v 467, 535
deposit n 771
deposition n 467, 535
depository n 191, 802
depraved adj 945
depravity n 649, 659, 945
deprecate v 766
deprecation n 766
deprecation n 616, 932, 934
deprecatory adj 483, 766
depreciate v 36, 483, 934
depreciated adj 483
depreciating adj 483, 934
depreciation n 36, 483, 813, 815
depreciative adj 483
depress v 207, 252, 308
depressed adj 207, 308, 438, 837
depressing adj 383
depression n 308
depression n 207, 208, 252, 837

deprivation n 659, 776, 789
deprived of adj 776
deprive of v 38
deprive of color v 429
depth n 208
deputation n 755
deputy n 759
deputy n 634, 690
derange v 59, 61, 185
deranged adj 59, 503
derangement n 61
derangement n 59, 185, 503
dereliction n 460, 732
dereliction of duty n 927
deride v 856, 929, 930
derision n 856, 929, 930
derisive adj 856, 929, 930
derisory adj 856
derivable from adj 154
derivation n 154, 155, 562
derivative adj 154
derived from adj 154
derive from v 155
derive pleasure from v 827
derogatory adj 934
descend v 217, 306, 310
descendant n 167
descending n 306; adj 217, 306
descent n 306
descent n 153
describe v 554, 594
description n 594
descriptive adj 554
descry v 441, 480a
desecrate v 679, 988
desecration n 679, 988
desert n 180, 344, 973; v 623, 624, 732, 757, 782
deserter n 607, 623
desertion n 624, 757, 782
deserve v 924
deserve consideration v 642
design n 22, 451, 516, 556, 620, 626; v 451, 516, 556, 620, 626
designate v 79, 550, 564
designation n 564, 877
designer n 559; 626
desirability n 646
desirable adj 646
desire n 865
desire n 600, 609, 858; v 602, 858, 865

desiring adj 865
desirous adj 602, 865
desist v 67, 142, 265
desolate v 162; adj 837
desolation n 162, 638, 828
despair n 828, 837, 859; v 828, 837, 859
despairing adj 859
desparation n 859
desperate adj 173, 859
desperately adv 31
desperation n 825
despicable adj 435, 930
despise v 715, 898, 930
despoil v 659
despond v 837, 859
despondency n 837, 859
despondent adj 837, 859
despot n 739
despotic adj 739, 964
despotism n 739
dessication n 340
destination n 67, 620
destine v 152
destined adj 152
destiny n 121, 152, 601, 611, 621
destitute adj 804
destitution n 804
destroy v 2, 162, 619, 638, 659, 679
destroyed adj 162
destroyer n 165
destroyer n 913
destroy oneself v 361
destruction n 162
destruction n 146, 173, 619, 638
destructive adj 162, 638, 649
desuetude n 614, 678
desultory adj 59, 70, 279, 475
detach v 44, 47
detached adj 10, 47, 953
detachment n 44, 291, 953
detail v 79, 594
details n 32, 79
detain v 781
detect v 480a
detection n 480a
detective n 527
detention n 781
deter v 616
detergent n 652
deteriorate v 36, 195, 659
deteriorated adj 659
deterioration n 659
deterioration n 36,

283, 655, 661, 732
determinate *adj* 474, 480, 620
determination *n* 150, 278, 480, 600, 604, 620, 480a, 604a
determine *v* 79, 153, 278, 480, 600, 604, 676, 967, 480a
determined *adj* 474
deterrent *n* 706
detest *v* 898
detestable *adj* 649, 898
detestation *n* 898
detonate *v* 173
detonation *n* 406
detour *n* 245, 279, 629; *v* 629
detract *v* 483, 934
detracting *n* 934; *adj* 934
detraction *n* 934
detraction *n* 483
detractor *n* 936
detrain *v* 292
detriment *n* 659
detrimental *adj* 649
deuce *n* 89
devastate *v* 162
devastation *n* 162, 638
develop *v* 153, 161, 194, 282, 313, 367
developing *adj* 127
development *n* 35, 144, 154, 161, 194, 282, 313
developmental *adj* 35
deviant *adj* 15
deviate *v* 20a, 140, 245, 279, 291, 629
deviating *adj* 15, 279
deviation *n* 279
deviation *n* 20a, 140, 245, 291
device *n* 550, 626, 702
devil *n* 978
devil *n* 949, 980; *v* 392
devilish *adj* 978, 982
devise *v* 515, 626, 673
devoid *adj* 187
devoid of *adj* 777a
devolve *v* 783
devoted *adj* 897, 987
devotee *n* 987
devote onself to *v* 676
devotion *n* 604, 682, 743, 897, 928, 987
devour *v* 162, 298, 957
devout *adj* 987
devoutness *n* 987
dew *n* 339
dewy *adj* 339
dexterity *n* 698
dextral *adj* 238
dextrous *adj* 698
diabolic *adj* 978, 982

diabolical *adj* 649
diabolism *n* 978
diagnosis *n* 465
diagonal *adj* 217
diagram *n* 626
dialect *n* 560
dialectic *adj* 476, 560
dialectical *adj* 476
dialectician *n* 476
dialectics *n* 476
dialog *n* 588
diameter *n* 202
diametrically opposite *adj* 237
diaphanous *adj* 425
diaphanousness *n* 425
diaphragm *n* 68
diary *n* 114, 551
dichotomy *n* 91
dictate *v* 741
dictatorial *adj* 739
dictatorship *n* 739
diction *n* 560, 569
dictionary *n* 86
dictum *n* 496, 741
didactic *adj* 537
die *n* 22; *v* 2, 67, 142, 360, 659
die hard *v* 606
die out *v* 2, 142
differ *v* 15, 489, 713
difference *n* 15
difference *n* 18, 24, 28, 291, 489, 713
different *adj* 15, 18
differentiate *v* 18, 79, 465
differentiation *n* 465
different time *n* 119
differ from *v* 14, 18
difficult *adj* 704
difficulties *n* 804
difficulty *n* 704
difficulty *n* 177, 533
diffidence *n* 881
diffident *adj* 881
diffuse *v* 73; *adj* 73, 573
diffused *adj* 186
diffuseness *n* 573
diffusion *n* 73, 186
diffusive *adj* 73, 573
dig *v* 208, 252, 259, 490, 827
digest *n* 596; *v* 384
digestible *adj* 299, 390
dig in *v* 298
digit *n* 84
dignified *adj* 873, 875, 878
dignity *n* 873, 875
digress *v* 279, 573, 629
digression *n* 279, 629
digressive *adj* 279, 573
dig to daylight *v* 260
dig up *v* 480a

dike *n* 198, 259, 350
dilapidate *v* 659
dilapidated *adj* 659
dilapidation *n* 162, 659
dilate *v* 35, 194, 322
dilation *n* 322
dilatory *adj* 133
dilemma *n* 476, 704
diligence *n* 682
diligent *adj* 682
dilly-dally *v* 133, 605, 683
dilly-dallying *n* 133
dilute *v* 160, 203, 337
diluted *adj* 203
dim *v* 421; *adj* 405, 422, 426, 447, 519
dimensions *n* 31, 192
diminish *v* 36, 38, 103, 174, 195, 834
diminished *adj* 34, 103
diminution *n* 36, 195, 638
diminution of number *n* 103
diminutive *adj* 32, 193
diminutiveness *n* 32, 193
dimness *n* 422
dimness *n* 353, 421
dimple *n* 252
dim-sighted *adj* 442, 443
dimsightedness *n* 443
dimwit *n* 493
dimwitted *adj* 254, 499
din *n* 404
dine *v* 298
dingdong *n* 407, 408
dingy *adj* 421, 422, 429, 431
dining *n* 298
dint *n* 252
dip *n* 217, 252, 300, 306, 308, 310; *v* 300, 310, 337
diplomat *n* 724
dipsomaniac *n* 959
dire *adj* 649, 735, 830
direct *v* 175, 278, 537, 600, 630, 692, 693, 741; *adj* 246, 278, 703
directing *adj* 693
direction *n* 278, 693
direction *n* 183, 537, 692, 697, 741
directive *n* 630; *adj* 692
direct line *n* 246
directly *adv* 132, 278
directness *n* 246
director *n* 694
director *n* 745
directory *n* 86
dirge *n* 363, 839

dirigible n 273
dirt n 342, 653
dirt cheap adj 815
dirty v 653; adj 653, 961
disability n 158
disable v 158
disabled adj 158
disadvantage n 619
disadvantageous adj 647
disagree v 24, 291, 489, 713
disagreeable adj 24, 830, 846, 867
disagreeing adj 24, 489
disagreement n 24
disagreement n 10, 15, 47, 489, 713, 720
disagree with v 657
disallow v 761
disallowance n 761
disappear v 2, 4, 360, 449
disappearance n 449
disappearing adj 449
disappoint v 509, 732, 832
disappointed adj 509
disappointment n 509
disapprobation n 932
disapproval n 766, 932
disapprove v 766, 932
disapproving adj 932
disarm v 158
disarrange v 61
disarray n 59, 61
disaster n 619, 735
disastrous adj 619, 735, 830
disavow n 536; v 607
disavowal n 536, 607
disband v 44, 73
disbelief n 485
disbelief n 485, 487, 989
disbelieve v 485, 989
disburse v 809
disbursement n 809
discard v 297, 610, 678, 773, 782
discern v 441, 480a, 490, 498
discernible adj 446
discernibleness n 446
discerning adj 441, 459, 465, 490, 498, 868
discernment n 441, 465, 477, 480, 490, 498, 868
discharge n 284, 295, 297, 299, 406, 750, 772, 807, 970; v 284, 295, 297, 692, 729, 750, 772, 807, 926, 927a, 970

discharge a function v 644
discharged adj 970
disciple n 492, 541
disciplinarian n 739
discipline n 58, 537, 972; v 537, 972
disclaim n 536; v 757, 764
disclaimer n 536, 764
disclose v 525, 527, 529, 531
disclosed adj 529
disclosure n 529
disclosure n 480a, 531, 985
discoloration n 429
discolored adj 429, 848
discomfort n 378, 828; v 828
discommodious adj 647
discompose v 61, 828
discomposure n 61, 828
disconcert v 61, 706, 832
disconcerted adj 509
disconnect v 44, 70
disconnected adj 10, 70
disconnectedness n 70
disconnection n 10, 44, 47
disconsolate adj 859
discontent n 832
discontent n 828
discontented adj 832
discontentment n 832
discontinuance n 142
discontinuation n 142
discontinue v 44, 70, 142, 265
discontinuity n 70
discontinuity n 44, 53
discontinuous adj 44, 70
discord n 414, 713
discord n 24, 59, 410, 720, 889
discordance n 489
discordant adj 24, 410, 414, 713
discount n 813
discount n 40a; v 813
discourage v 616
discouraged adj 837
discouragement n 616
discourse n 537, 582, 588, 595; v 537, 582
discourse with v 588
discourteous adj 895, 929
discourtesy n 895
discourtesy n 929
discover v 441, 462, 480a, 490, 529

discoverable adj 462
discovery n 480a
discovery n 462, 985
discredit n 874; v 485
discreet adj 451, 698, 864
discrepancy n 15, 24
discretion n 480, 498, 698, 864
discretional adj 609
discretionary adj 600, 748
discriminate v 15, 465, 498, 850
discriminating adj 465, 480
discrimination n 465
discrimination n 15, 480, 850, 868
discriminative adj 15, 465, 850, 868
discriminatory adj 465
discursive adj 279, 573
discuss v 476, 695
discuss a subject v 595
discussion n 476, 588, 595
disdain n 930; v 866, 930
disdainful adj 773, 930
disease n 655
disease n 378
diseased adj 655
disembark v 292, 342
disembarkation n 292
disenchant v 616
disencumber v 705
disengage v 44, 750
disengagement n 44, 750
disentangle v 42, 44, 60, 522, 672, 705
disentanglement n 672
disenthrall v 750
disestablish v 185
disesteem n 932
disfavor n 874
disfigure v 241, 243, 659, 846
disfigured adj 848
disfigurement n 241, 243, 846, 848
disgrace n 874, 930; v 874
disgraced adj 874
disgraceful adj 874, 930
disgrace oneself v 874
disgruntled adj 509
disguise n 530; v 528
disguising n 528
disgust n 837, 867, 869; v 289, 395, 830, 867, 869
disgusted adj 869
disgusting adj 867, 898
dishabille n 226

dishearten v616
disheartened adj837
disheartening adj383
disheveled adj73
dishonest adj544, 923, 940
dishonesty n544, 940
dishonor n874, 930; v 874, 923
dishonorable adj874, 930, 940
disillusion n509; v 509
disinclination n603, 867
disincline v616
disinclined adj867
disinfect v652
disinfectant n652
disingenuous adj544
disintegrate v330
disintegration n330
disinter v363
disinterested adj942
disinterestedness n 942
disinterment n363
disjoin v44, 47, 51
disjoined adj44
disjunction n44
disjunction n10, 47, 49, 70
disjunctive adj44
dislikable adj867
dislike n867
dislike n289, 603, 889, 898, 932; v603, 867, 898, 932
disliking adj867
dislocate v44, 61
dislocation n44, 61, 185
dislodge v185, 297
dislodgment n297
dismal adj830, 837, 901a
dismantle v162, 678
dismay n860
dismayed adj860
dismemberment n44
dismiss v750, 782
· dismissal n750
dismount v292, 306
disobedience n742
disobedience n773
disobedient adj742, 773
disobey v742
disorder n59
disorder n61, 173, 241, 315, 503, 655; v 59, 61, 185
disordered adj241
disorderly adj59, 173
disorganization n61
disorganize v61, 162
disorganized adj59

disown v536
disparage v483, 934
disparagement n932, 934
disparaging adj932, 934
disparate adj18, 24, 28
disparity n15, 18, 24, 28, 291
dispassion n826, 953
dispassionate adj826, 953
dispatch n592, 684; v 361, 684, 692, 729
dispel v73, 162
dispensation n784, 786, 927a
dispense v73, 784, 786
dispense with v678
disperse v44, 49, 73, 291
dispersed adj73
dispersion n73
dispersion n44, 186
dispirited adj837
dispiriting adj383
displace v61, 185, 270
displaced adj185
displacement n185
displacement n140
display n448, 525, 855, 882; v525, 882
displease v289, 830
displeased adj832
displeasing adj846
displeasure n828, 832, 900
disposal n60, 677, 741
dispose v60, 176, 615, 693, 796
dispose of v784
disposition n58, 60, 176, 600, 602, 613, 693, 820
dispossess v789
dispossession n789
disproof n468, 479
disproportion n24
disproportionate adj 24
disprove v479
disputable adj485
disputant n476, 726
disputation n476, 536, 969
disputatious adj476, 713
dispute n536, 713, 720, 969; v24, 476, 713, 720
disputing adj24
disqualify v158
disquiet n149, 315, 828; v828
disquietude n149, 832
disquisition n537, 595

disregard n458, 460; v 458, 460, 483, 742, 773
disregardful adj460
disregard of time n115
disrelish n867; v867
disreputable adj874
disrepute n874
disrespect n929
disrespect n885, 895
disrespectful adj885, 895, 929
disrobe v226
disrobed adj226
disruption n162, 713
disruptive adj713
dissatisfaction n489, 828, 832
dissatisfied adj832, 841
dissatisfy v832
dissect v44, 49
dissection n49
dissemble v528, 544
dissembler n548
dissembling n528, 544
disseminate v73, 531
dissemination n73, 673
dissension n24, 489, 713, 720
dissent n489
dissent n485, 603, 984; v291, 485, 489, 603, 708, 713
dissenter n489, 984
dissenting adj24, 489, 984
dissention n720
dissertation n595
dissever v44
dissidence n24, 713
dissident n489; adj 489, 713, 764
dissimilar adj18
dissimilarity n18
dissimilarity n15, 28
dissimilitude n18
dissipate v162, 638, 818
dissipation n73, 638
dissociate v44
dissociation n10, 44
dissolution n49, 162, 335, 360
dissolvable adj335
dissolve v2, 4, 49, 162, 335, 360, 449
dissonance n24, 410, 414, 713
dissonant adj24, 410, 414, 713
dissuade v616
dissuasion n616
dissuasive adj616
dissyllable n561

distance n 196
distance n 198, 200, 235
distanced adj 10
distant adj 196
distaste n 867
distasteful adj 830, 867
distend v 194
distention n 194
distill v 336
distillation n 336
distinct adj 402, 446, 518, 525, 570, 580
distinction n 15, 31, 465, 873, 875
distinctive adj 15
distinctive feature n 79
distinctness n 446, 570, 580
distinguish v 15, 441, 465
distinguished adj 206, 873
distinguishing adj 465
distort v 217, 243, 523, 555, 846
distorted adj 243
distortion n 243
distortion n 443, 544, 555, 846
distracted adj 503, 824
distraction n 825
distress n 735, 804, 828; v 828
distress signal n 669
distribute v 60, 73, 531, 786
distribution n 60, 73, 531, 786
distributive adj 786
district attorney n 968
distrust n 485; v 485, 487, 860
disturb v 61, 185, 315, 824, 830
disturbance n 59, 61, 315
disunion n 24, 44, 59, 905
disunite v 44, 713
disusage n 614
disuse n 614, 678
disuse v 614, 678
disused adj 678
ditch n 198, 259, 350
ditto n 21; adv 104
dive n 208, 310; v 310
diverge v 20a, 291
divergence n 291
divergence n 15, 18, 24, 73, 279
divergency n 20a
divergent adj 15, 24, 291
divers adj 15
diverse adj 15, 81

diversified adj 15, 16a, 18, 20a, 81, 440
diversify v 15, 18, 140, 440
diversion n 140, 279, 840
diversity n 15, 16a, 18, 81
divert v 279, 840
diverting adj 840
divest v 226, 789
divestment n 789
divest oneself v 782
divide v 44, 44, 51, 60, 73, 85, 91, 291, 778, 786
divided adj 51
divide into four parts v 97
divide into three parts v 94
divide in two v 91
divination n 511, 992
divine n 996; v 511, 514, 992; adj 976, 981, 983a
divinity n 976, 983
division n 44, 51, 60, 73, 75, 198, 291, 713, 786
divisive adj 713
divorce n 905
divorce n 44; v 44, 905
divorced adj 905
divulge v 529, 531
divulgence n 529, 531
do v 161, 170, 622, 639, 680, 729
do a good turn v 648
do as one likes v 748
do away with v 162, 297, 361
do a world of good v 648
do battle v 722
docile adj 725, 743, 926
docility n 725, 743
dock n 966
doctor n 662; v 544, 660, 662
doctrinal adj 983a
doctrine n 484, 537, 983
document n 551
dodge v 264, 279, 623
doe n 374
doer n 680, 690
doff v 226
dog n 373
dogged adj 150, 604a, 606
doggedness n 150, 604a, 606
doggerel n 597
dogma n 484, 537, 983

dogmatic adj 535, 606, 737
dogmatism n 535, 606
dogmatist n 606
do good v 648
do harm v 649
doing adj 151
doings n 151
doldrums n 837
dole n 32, 640, 786
dole out v 60, 73, 784, 786
dolor n 378, 828
dolorous adj 378, 830
dolt n 493, 501
doltish adj 499
domain n 75, 181
dome n 250
domestic n 746; adj 188, 221, 370
domestic animals n 366
domesticate v 184, 370
domesticated adj 370
domestication n 370
domicile n 189
dominance n 175
dominant adj 175, 737
dominate v 175, 739
domination n 741
domineer v 739
dominion n 157, 737
don n 540
donate v 784
donation n 784
done adj 729
done away with adj 782
donee n 785
done with adj 678
donor n 784
do nothing v 169, 681, 683
doom n 152, 360, 421; v 152, 971
doomsday n 121
do one's duty v 926
door n 231, 232, 260, 627
doorway n 232, 260
do over v 104
do penance v 952
do right v 922
dormancy n 526
dormant adj 172, 265, 526
dose n 25, 786
dot n 32; v 440
dote v 499
dote upon v 991
double n 17, 90, 147; v 90, 258; adj 90, 147
double-cross v 545
doubled adj 90
double dealing n 544
double-edged adj 520

double entendre *n* 520
double-meaning *n* 520
doubleness *n* 89
doubling *n* 90
doubt *n* 485
doubt *n* 475, 487, 984, 989; *v* 475, 485, 487, 989
doubter *n* 989
doubtful *adj* 473, 475, 485, 487, 520
doubtfulness *n* 473, 475
doubting *adj* 485, 984, 989
doubtless *adv* 474
dough *n* 354
doughy *adj* 324, 354
dour *adj* 739
douse *v* 310, 337
dove color *n* 432
dove-colored *adj* 432
dovetail *v* 23, 219
do violence *v* 649
dowdy *adj* 653
do what one wants *v* 748
do without *v* 678
down *v* 298; *adj* 837; *adv* 207
downfall *n* 162, 306
downhearted *adj* 837
downhill *n* 217; *adj* 217
down in the dumps *adj* 438, 832
down in the mouth *adj* 735
downright *adj* 525; *adv* 31
downstairs *adv* 207
downward *adv* 207
downy *adj* 255, 256
dozen *n* 98
drab *adj* 432
draft *n* 208, 349, 596, 626
draftsman *n* 559
drafty *adj* 349
drag *n* 285; *v* 109, 275, 285, 288, 307
drag on *v* 110
drag out *v* 110, 133
drag up *v* 307
drain *n* 295, 350; *v* 295, 297, 340
drainage *n* 295, 340
drain into *v* 348
drake *n* 373
drama *n* 599
dramatic *adj* 599, 882
dramatist *n* 599
dramatize *v* 599
dramaturgy *n* 599
drape *v* 225

drapery *n* 225
draught *n* 298
draw *n* 27; *v* 153, 230, 285, 288, 301, 556
draw a curtain *v* 424
draw aside *v* 279
drawback *n* 177, 619, 651
drawer *n* 559
draw forth *v* 301
draw in *v* 195
drawing *n* 285, 556, 626
drawing and quartering *n* 361
drawl *v* 275
drawn *adj* 27
draw near *v* 121, 286
drawn game *n* 27
draw out *v* 110, 133, 200, 301, 590
draw to a close *v* 67
draw together *v* 72
dread *n* 860, 862; *v* 860
dreadful *adj* 649, 830, 860
dreadfully *adv* 31
dream *n* 4, 515, 515, 858; *v* 515
dreamer *n* 504
dreaming *n* 515
dreamlike *adj* 515
dreamy *adj* 4, 515, 683
dreamy-eyed *adj* 683
dreary *adj* 16, 830, 843
dredge *v* 307
dregs *n* 40
drench *v* 337, 339, 348, 641
dress *n* 225
dress *v* 225
dressed *adj* 225
dribble *v* 295, 348
drift *n* 176, 278, 349; *v* 176, 264, 267, 279, 287
drift away *v* 287
drill *n* 262; *v* 260, 537
drink *n* 298; *v* 298, 959
drinkable *adj* 299
drinker *n* 959
drinking *n* 296, 298, 959
drink like a fish *v* 959
drink one's fill *v* 298
drink up *v* 298
drip *v* 295, 348
dripping *n* 356
drive *n* 266, 284; *v* 276, 284, 744
drive a bargain *v* 794
drive at *v* 516
drive away *v* 289
drive in *v* 300
drivel *n* 499
driveling *n* 499; *adj* 499

driver *n* 268, 694
driving *n* 266
driving spirit *n* 820
drizzle *n* 32, 348; *v* 348
drizzly *adj* 348
droll *n* 501; *adj* 853
drollery *n* 842
drone *n* 683
droning *n* 407
droop *v* 306, 655, 659, 688, 837
drooping *adj* 160
drop *n* 32, 306; *v* 158, 160, 306, 310, 348, 688
drop by drop *adv* 26
drop dead *v* 360
drop down *v* 306
drop down dead *v* 360
drop from the clouds *v* 508
drop in the ocean *n* 32
droplet *n* 32
drop off *v* 283, 360
drop out *v* 283
dropsical *adj* 194
dropsy *n* 194
drought *n* 340
droves *n* 102
drown *v* 337, 361, 376
drowsiness *n* 688
drowsy *adj* 683, 688, 841
drudge *v* 686
drudgery *n* 682
drug *v* 381
drugged *adj* 381
drum *n* 249; *v* 407
drumming *n* 407
drunk *adj* 959
drunkard *n* 959
drunken *adj* 959
drunkenness *n* 959
dry *v* 340; *adj* 340, 575, 579, 843, 958
dryad *n* 979
dry as a bone *adj* 340, 958
dry land *n* 342
dryness *n* 340
dry rot *n* 653, 663
dry up *v* 340, 435
dual *adj* 89
dualism *n* 89
duality *n* 89
dub *v* 564
dubious *adj* 475, 485, 487, 520
dubiousness *n* 475, 520
ducking *n* 310
duct *n* 350, 351
ductile *adj* 324
ductility *n* 324
dud *n* 732
dude *n* 854
due *n* 806, 924; *adj* 924

duet n 415
due to adj 154, 155
duffer n 493, 701
dulcet adj 413
dull v 254, 381, 422;
   adj 160, 172, 254,
   275, 337, 376, 381,
   422, 428, 429, 491,
   499, 575, 598, 683,
   841, 843, 901a
dullard n 493, 501
dulled adj 381
dullness n 843
dullness n 172, 254,
   683, 823, 841
dull understanding n
   499
dull-witted adj 499
dumb adj 491, 581
dumb animal n 366
dumbness n 581
dumfound v 509, 581,
   870
dumps n 837
dumpy adj 193, 201,
   202
dun adj 429, 432
dunce n 493, 501
dunderhead n 501
dunderpate n 501
dungeon n 752
dunk v 310, 337
dunking n 310
duo n 415
dupe n 547
dupe n 486, 857; v 545
duplex adj 89
duplexity n 89
duplicate n 13, 21, 90;
   v 19, 90, 104; adj 19,
   90, 641
duplicated adj 90
duplication n 90
duplication n 19, 104
duplicitous adj 520,
   702
duplicity n 520, 544,
   702
durability n 110
durability n 112, 141,
   150
durable adj 106, 110,
   141, 150
duration n 106, 200
duress n 744
during adv 106
dusk n 126, 421
duskiness n 421, 422
dusky adj 431
dust n 330, 362
dusty adj 330, 653
dutiful adj 743, 926
duty n 926
duty n 625, 743, 806,
   928, 963
duty bound adj 926

dwarf n 980; adj 193
dwarfish adj 193
dwell v 186, 188, 265
dweller n 188
dwelling n 189
dwindle v 36, 195, 732
dwindling n 36
dye n 428; v 428
dyed adj 428
dying n 360
dying day n 360
dynamic adj 171

E

each adv 79
each to each adv 79
each to his own adv 79
eager adj 602, 682
eagerness n 602, 682
eagle-eyed adj 441
ear n 418
earlier adv 116
earliness n 132
early adj 132; adv 121,
   132
earmark n 550
earn v 775
earnest adj 602, 642
earnestly adv 604
earnestness n 682
earnings n 775
ear-piercing adj 410
earshot n 197
ear-splitting adj 404
earth n 318, 342, 362
earthly adj 318, 342,
   989
earthy adj 342
ease n 377, 578, 705,
   748, 827, 831, 834; v
   705, 707, 834
easily adv 705
easiness n 705
easy adj 275, 578, 685,
   705, 740
easy circumstance n
   803
easy going adj 174,
   740, 826
eat v 298
eatable adj 299
eat away v 638
eating n 298
eating n 296
eavesdrop v 418
eavesdropper n 418,
   455, 527
ebb n 36; v 36, 195,
   283, 287, 659
ebb and flow n 314
ebbing n 36
ebon adj 431
ebony n 431
ebullience n 171
ebullient adj 171, 382,
   824

ebullition n 171, 173,
   315, 825
eccentric adj 83, 499,
   608
eccentricity n 83, 499,
   503
ecclesiastic n 996
ecclesiastical adj 995
echo n 21, 104; v 104,
   277, 402, 408
echoing n 408
eclipse n 421, 449; v
   33, 422
economical adj 817
economize v 817
economy n 817
economy n 58
ecstasy n 377, 827
ecstatic adj 377, 827,
   829
ecumenical adj 78
eddy n 312, 348
edge n 231
edge n 233; v 231
edgewise adv 217
edging n 231
edible adj 299
edification n 537
edify v 537
edifying adj 537, 648
edition n 531
editor n 593, 805
educate v 537
educated adj 490, 498
education n 537, 673
educational adj 537
educational
   institution n 542
eel n 248
efface v 552
efface from the
   memory v 506
effacement n 552
effect n 154
effect n 65; v 153, 729,
   731
effective adj 157, 175,
   644
effects n 780
effectual adj 170, 644
effervesce v 173, 315,
   353
effervescence n 171,
   173, 315, 353
effervescent adj 338,
   353
efficacious adj 157,
   170, 644
efficacy n 157, 644
efficient adj 157, 170,
   698
effigy n 21
effluence n 295
effluvium n 398
effort n 675, 680, 686

effulgence *n* 420
effulgent *adj* 420
effusion *n* 295, 297, 299
effusive *adj* 584
egalitarian *adj* 29, 78
egg *n* 153
egg-shaped *adj* 247, 249
ego *n* 5
egoism *n* 943
egotism *n* 878, 880, 943
egotistical *adj* 878, 880, 943
egregiously *adv* 31
egress *n* 295
egress *n* 302
eight *n* 98
eject *v* 185, 297, 789, 893
ejected *adj* 893
ejection *n* 297
ejection *n* 185, 301, 893
eke out *v* 110
elaborate *v* 658
elaboration *n* 658
elapse *v* 109
elapsed *adj* 122
elastic *adj* 277, 324, 325
elasticity *n* 325
elasticity *n* 159, 277, 324
elated *adj* 838, 884
elbow *n* 244
elbow-grease *n* 331
elbowroom *n* 180
elder *n* 130; *adj* 128
elderly *adj* 124, 128
eldership *n* 128
eldest *adj* 128
elect *v* 609, 995
election *n* 609
electricity *n* 388
electric light *n* 423
electrify *v* 824
electrocute *v* 361
electrocution *n* 361
electronic music *n* 415
electronic sound reproduction *n* 402
elegance *n* 578
elegance *n* 577, 845, 850
elegant *adj* 578, 845
elegantly *adv* 850
elegy *n* 363, 839
element *n* 51, 56, 153, 211
elemental *adj* 42, 211
elementary *adj* 42
elements *n* 66
elephant *n* 192
elevate *v* 206, 235, 307

elevated *adj* 206, 307, 574
elevation *n* 307
elevation *n* 206, 574, 658
eleven *n* 98
elf *n* 979
elfin *adj* 980
elicit *v* 153, 301
eliminate *v* 38, 42, 55, 103, 297, 299, 301, 610, 893
eliminated *adj* 893
elimination *n* 42, 55, 103, 297, 299, 301, 610, 893
elite *n* 648
ellipse *n* 247
elliptic *adj* 247
elliptical *adj* 247
elongate *v* 200
elongation *n* 196, 200
eloquence *n* 574, 582
eloquent *adj* 574
elsewhere *adv* 187
elucidate *v* 74, 518, 522
elucidation *n* 522
elude *v* 623, 671, 773
elusive *adj* 623, 773
elysian *adj* 981
emaciated *adj* 203
emaciation *n* 638
emanate *v* 295, 299
emanate from *v* 154
emanation *n* 295, 299, 398
emancipate *v* 672, 750
emancipation *n* 195, 672, 750
emasculate *v* 158
emasculated *adj* 158
embalm *v* 363
embargo *n* 761
embark *v* 66, 267, 293
embarkation *n* 293
embark on *v* 676
embarrass *v* 704
embarrassed *adj* 434
embassy *n* 755
embed *v* 221
embedded *adj* 221, 229
embellish *v* 847
embellished *adj* 847
embellishment *n* 847
ember *n* 388
embezzle *v* 791
emblazon *v* 428, 882
emblem *n* 550, 747
emblematic *adj* 550
embody *v* 50, 54, 76, 82, 316
embosomed *adj* 229
emboss *v* 250
embrace *n* 902; *v* 54, 76, 902
embroider *v* 440, 549

embroidery *n* 549
embroil *v* 61
embryo *n* 153
embryology *n* 368
embryonic *adj* 66, 153, 674
emend *v* 658
emendation *n* 658
emendatory *adj* 658
emerald *adj* 435
emerge *v* 295
emergence *n* 295
emergency *n* 8, 151, 704
emigrant *n* 268
eminence *n* 31, 33, 206, 648, 873, 875
eminent *adj* 206, 873, 883
eminently *adv* 33
emissary *n* 534
emission *n* 297
emit sound *v* 402
emotion *n* 821
emotional *adj* 821
empathy *n* 821
emphasis *n* 535, 580, 642
emphasize *v* 535, 642
emphatic *adj* 535, 642
emphatically *adv* 31
employ *n* 677, 749; *v* 677, 755
employable *adj* 677
employee *n* 746
employ figures of speech *v* 521
employment *n* 625
employ oneself *v* 625
empower *v* 157, 737, 755, 760
emptiness *n* 2, 187, 209, 452, 517, 640, 880
empty *v* 185, 297; *adj* 2, 4, 187, 209, 298, 452
empty-headed *adj* 450a
empty vessel *n* 362
empty words *n* 517
emulate *v* 19, 648
enact *v* 599, 680, 692, 729, 741, 963
enamored *adj* 897
encamp *v* 184
encampment *n* 184
encase *v* 223
enchant *v* 829, 992
enchanted *adj* 992
enchanting *adj* 897, 992
enchantment *n* 827, 829, 991, 992
encircle *v* 76, 220, 227, 247

enclose v 227, 232
enclosure n 232
enclosure n 229
encompass v 76, 227
encore adv 104
encounter n 276, 680, 716; v 151
encourage v 707, 836
encouraging adj 858
encroach v 303
encroachment n 303
encumber v 319, 704, 706
encumbrance n 706
end n 67
end n 65, 142, 152, 154, 360, 620, 729; v 67, 142, 360, 729
endanger v 665, 909
endangering adj 909
endear v 902
endearing adj 902
endearment n 902
endeavor n 675, 686; v 622, 675
ended adj 67
endemic adj 79
endless adj 102, 104, 112
endlessness n 105, 112
end of the day n 126
end one's days v 360
endorse v 535, 769, 771, 931
endorsement n 535
endow v 157
endowment n 698, 784
end result n 161
end to end adj 199
endurance n 112, 141, 150, 826
endure v 1, 106, 110, 112, 141, 151, 826
enduring adj 110, 141, 150, 505, 826
endwise adv 212
enemy n 891
enemy n 708, 710, 726
energetic adj 157, 171, 359
energetic activity n 680
energize v 171
energized adj 171
energy n 171
energy n 157, 159, 173, 359, 604, 680, 682, 686
enervate v 158, 160
enervation n 575
enfeeble v 160, 638
enfold v 229
enforce v 695, 744
enforcement n 744
enfranchise v 750
enfranchisement n

750, 760
engage v 132, 288, 615, 676, 768, 769
engage in v 622, 676
engage in a discussion v 588
engagement n 676, 680
engender v 161
engorge v 957
engrave v 259, 558
engrave in the mind v 505
engraver n 559
engraving n 558
engrossed in adj 451
enhance v 307, 658
enigmatic adj 519, 520
enjoin v 630, 695, 741
enjoy v 377, 394, 827
enjoyable adj 829
enjoyment n 827, 840
enjoy oneself v 827
enlarge v 31, 35, 35, 194, 573
enlargement n 35, 37, 194, 750
enlighten v 420, 527, 537
enlightened adj 490, 527
enlightenment n 490, 498, 527, 985
enlist v 615
enliven v 689, 836, 840
enmity n 889
enmity n 907
ennervation n 160
ennoble v 875
ennui n 688, 841
enormity n 102, 192
enormous adj 31, 192
enormously adv 31
enormousness n 31, 192
enough n 639; adj 639; adv 31
enplane v 293
enrapture v 824, 829
enrapturing adj 977
enravish v 829
enrich v 658
enroll v 551
ensconce v 528
ensconced adj 184
ensconcing n 528
ensemble n 416, 417
enslave v 749
enslavement n 749
ensnare v 545
ensue v 63, 151
ensuing adj 117
entangle v 43, 61, 219, 704
entangled adj 59
entanglement n 59, 219, 704
enter v 294, 551, 811

enter a protest v 766
enter into v 56, 768
enterprise n 622, 676
enterprising adj 861
entertain v 840
entertaining adj 840
entertainment n 840
enthral v 749
enthusiasm n 574, 602
enthusiast n 504
enthusiastic adj 825
enthymeme n 476
enticing adj 288
entire adj 50, 52, 729
entirely adv 31, 50
entirety n 50, 52
entitle v 564
entity n 1
entomb v 363
entombment n 363
entomology n 368
entrain v 293
entrance n 294; v 829, 992
entrancing adj 977
entrap v 545
entreat v 765
entreaty n 411, 765
entrée n 296
entrust v 755, 784, 805
entry n 294, 296
entwine v 43, 248
enumerate v 85
enumeration n 85
enunciate v 580
enunciation n 580
envelope n 232
envious adj 435, 900, 920, 921
enviousness n 921
environ v 227
environment n 227
environs n 227
envision v 441
envoy n 534
envy n 921
envy n 900, 920; v 921
eon n 108
ephemeral adj 111
ephemerality n 111
epicure n 954a, 957
epicurean n 954a; adj 954, 957
epicureanism n 954
epicurism n 954, 957
epigram n 496
epigrammatist n 844
epilog n 65
episode n 39, 70, 151
episodic adj 228
epistle n 592
epistolary adj 592
epithet n 564
epitome n 193, 596
epitomize v 201, 596
epoch n 106, 108
equal v 27; v 27; adj

13, 27, 30, 216, 242
equality n 27
equality n 13
equalization n 30
equalize v 27, 30
equally adv 27
equal to adj 157
equate v 216
equation n 30, 216
equator n 68
equestrian n 268
equidistance n 68
equidistant adj 68
equilibrium n 27, 150
equip v 225, 673
equipment n 225, 633
equipoise n 27
equitable adj 246, 922
equitableness n 922
equitably adv 922
equity n 922
equivalence n 27
equivalent n 27, 30,
147; adj 12, 13, 27,
30, 216
equivocal adj 477, 520
equivocalness n 520
equivocate v 477, 520
equivocation n 477,
520, 544
era n 106, 108
eradicate v 103, 162,
301
eradication n 301
erase v 162, 331, 552
erased adj 552
erasure n 552
ere adv 116
Erebus n 982
erect v 161, 235, 307;
adj 212, 246
erection n 161, 307
erectness n 212
ere now adv 122
ergo adv 155
erode v 638, 659
erosion n 659
err v 495, 945
errand n 755
errand boy n 534
errant adj 279
erratic adj 149, 279,
608
erroneous adj 4, 495,
544, 732, 923
error n 495
error n 538, 568, 984
erudite adj 490, 498,
539
erudition n 490, 498,
539
eruption n 173, 295
escape n 671
escape n 623; v 295,
671
escape notice v 447
escapist adj 623

eschew v 623
escort n 753; v 88
esoteric adj 83
especial adj 79, 474
especially adv 33, 79
esprit de corps n 709
espy v 441, 480a
essay n 675
essay n 595, 622; v
463, 675
essayist n 593, 595
essence n 5, 398, 820
essential adj 5, 31, 66,
601, 630, 642
essentiality n 5
essentially adv 31
establish v 62, 150,
161, 184, 478, 535
established adj 150,
983a
establishment n 161,
184, 799
establish roots v 184,
265
estate n 780
esteem n 928, 931; v
451, 480, 873, 928,
931
esteemed adj 873
estimable adj 928, 931
estimate v 466, 480; v
466, 480
estimation n 465, 466,
873, 928
estranged adj 889
estuary n 343
etc. adv 37
etch v 259, 558
etching n 558
eternal adj 104, 112
eternalize v 112
eternity n 112
ethereal adj 4, 320,
338, 977
etheric adj 334
ethical adj 246
ethics n 944
etiolate v 429, 430
etiolated adj 430
etiolation n 429, 430
etiquette n 852
etymology n 562
euphemism n 521, 566
euphemistic adj 577
euphonic adj 413
euphonious adj 413,
578, 580
euphony n 413, 578
euphuistic adj 577, 579
evacuate v 293, 297,
299
evacuation n 295, 297,
299
evade v 477, 623, 671,
773
evanescence n 111,
449

evanescent adj 111,
449
evaporable adj 334,
336
evaporate v 4, 111,
336, 340
evaporation n 336, 340
evasion n 477, 623,
671, 773
evasive adj 477, 528,
623, 773
evasiveness n 528
eve n 126
even v 16; adj 16, 27,
174, 213, 242, 246,
251, 255
evening n 126
evening n 126
even keel n 27
evenness n 16, 27, 242,
251
even off v 251
even out v 30
even so adv 30
event n 8, 151
even temper n 826
even-temperedness n
953
eventful adj 151, 505
even the score v 27
eventide n 126
eventual adj 121
eventuality n 121, 151
eventually adv 121,
151, 152
eventuate v 151
ever adv 16, 112
everlasting adj 112,
141
everlastingness n 112
evermore adv 112
ever so little adv 32
ever so long adv 110
ever so much adv 31
everyday adj 613; adv
136
every inch adv 52
every once in a while
adv 136
every other adj 138
every which way adv
227
every whit adv 52
evict v 297
eviction n 297, 789
evidence n 467
evidence v 525
evident adj 467, 525
evidential adj 467
evil n 619
evil n 649, 663, 665,
923, 940; adj 619,
649, 663, 923, 940
evildoer n 913
evil-doer n 949
evil incarnate n 978
evil-minded adj 907

evil one n 978
evil spirit n 978, 980
evil star n 649
evince v 467, 478, 525
evoke v 153, 824
evolution n 313
evolution n 161
evolutional adj 313
evolutionary adj 313
evolve v 301, 313
evolved from adj 154
evolvement n 313
ewe n 374
exacerbate v 173
exacerbation n 173
exact v 812; adj 17, 21, 459, 494, 570
exacting adj 868
exaction n 741
exactness n 13, 80, 459, 494, 570
exaggerate v 194, 482, 549, 555, 884
exaggerated adj 194, 497, 549
exaggeration n 549
exaggeration n 482, 497, 523, 555, 835
exalt v 35, 307, 838
exaltation n 307, 838
exalted adj 206, 875
examination n 461, 463
examine v 457, 461, 463, 595
example n 22, 82, 478
exasperate v 173
exasperation n 173
excavate v 208, 252
excavation n 252
exceed v 33, 303
exceeding adj 33
exceedingly adv 31
excel v 33, 648
excel in v 698
excellence n 33, 648, 650, 944
excellent adj 33, 648
except v 469; adv 38, 83
excepted adj 927a
excepting adv 38
exception n 55, 83, 469, 777a, 893, 927a
exceptional adj 20, 79, 83
excess n 40, 641, 954
excessive adj 31, 641, 954
excessively adv 31
exchange n 12, 147, 148, 783, 794, 796; v 12, 147, 148, 783, 794, 796
exchangeable adj 783
exchequer n 802

excise v 38
excitability n 825
excitability n 173, 822, 901
excitable adj 382, 684, 822, 824, 825
excitation n 824
excitation of feeling n 824
excite v 171, 173, 375, 377, 615, 824
excite an impression v 375
excited adj 173, 382, 824
excitement n 825
exciting adj 824
exclaim v 411
exclamation n 411
exclude v 55, 610, 893
excluded adj 57, 893
exclusion n 5, 77, 893
exclusion n 610
exclusive adj 55, 79
exclusive of adv 38
excrete v 299
excretion n 299
excruciating adj 982
exculpate v 970
exculpated adj 970
exculpation n 937, 970
exculpatory adj 937
excursion n 226, 302, 311
excursionist n 268
excuse n 617, 918, 927a; v 617, 777a, 918, 927a
excused adj 927a
execrable adj 649
execrate v 898, 908
execration n 908
execute v 361, 416, 680, 692, 729, 772, 972
execution n 361, 680, 692, 729, 772
executioner n 165, 361, 690; 975
executive adj 692, 737
executor n 690
executrix n 690
exegesis n 522
exegetical adj 522
exemplar n 22
exemplary adj 82
exemplification n 82
exempt v 777a, 927a; adj 748, 927a
exempt from adj 777a
exemption n 777a, 927a
exercise n 170, 677, 680; v 677, 680
exert v 171, 677, 686
exert energy v 680

exert force v 288
exertion n 686
exertion n 171, 680, 682
exert oneself v 686
exhalation n 299, 398
exhale v 299
exhaust v 158, 638, 688, 841
exhausted adj 2, 158, 688, 841
exhaustion n 158, 638, 688, 841
exhaustive adj 52
exhibit n 467; v 525, 882
exhibition n 525
exhilarate v 836
exhilaration n 836
exhort v 695
exhortation n 695
exhumation n 363
exhume v 363
exigency n 8, 704
exigent adj 630
exiguity n 203
exile n 55, 185, 297, 893; v 55, 185, 297
exiled adj 893
exist v 1, 359
existence n 1
existence n 1, 359
existent adj 1
existing adj 118
exit n 293, 295, 449
exodus n 293
exonerate v 937, 970
exonerated adj 937, 970
exonerating adj 937
exoneration n 937, 970
exorbitance n 814, 954
exorbitant adj 31, 641, 814, 954
exorbitantly adv 31
exorcism n 993
exorcist n 994
exotic adj 10, 83
expand v 31, 35, 192, 194, 202, 322, 549, 573
expanded adj 194
expanse n 105, 180, 192
expansion n 194
expansion n 35, 180, 322
expansive adj 180, 194, 202
expatiate v 582
expect v 121, 451, 507, 510, 620, 858, 871
expectance n 871
expectancy n 507, 858, 871
expectant adj 507, 510, 858, 871

expectantly adv 507
expectation n 507
expectation n 121, 451, 472, 858, 871
expectations n 152
expected adj 871
expecting adj 871
expedience n 646
expediency n 646
expedient n 147; adj 646
expedite v 132, 684
expedition n 132, 266, 684
expeditious adj 132, 274
expel v 185, 284, 297, 893
expend v 638, 677, 809
expenditure n 809
expenditure n 638
expense n 812
expenses n 809
expensive adj 814
expensiveness n 814
experience v 151
experienced adj 698
experiment n 463
experiment n 675; v 463, 675
experimental adj 463, 675
experimentally adv 675
experimentation n 463
experimenter n 463
experiment with v 140
expert n 700
expert v 500, 737, 872; adj 698
expertness n 698, 702
expiate v 952
expiating adj 952
expiation n 952
expiatory adj 952
expiration n 67, 360
expire v 67, 109, 360
expired adj 122
explain v 462, 478, 518, 522, 595
explainer n 524
explanation n 155, 478, 522, 537
explanatory adj 522
explicable adj 522
explicate v 522
explication n 522
explicit adj 518, 525, 570
explicitness n 518, 570
explode v 173
exploit n 680
exploration n 461
exploratory adj 461
exploring adj 461

explosion n 173, 404, 406, 825
explosive adj 173, 665
exposé n 529; v 226, 260, 529
exposed adj 177, 226, 260, 338
expose oneself to v 177
expose the error v 479
expose to danger v 665
exposition n 522, 525, 529, 595
expositor n 524
expository adj 522, 527
expostulate v 616, 766
expostulation n 616, 766
expostulatory adj 766
exposure n 448, 479, 529, 665
expound v 522, 537
expounder n 524
express v 516, 525, 527, 560, 566; adj 620
express by words v 560, 569
expression n 521, 525, 554, 560, 566, 985, 985
expressive adj 516, 518, 521, 569
expropriate v 789
expropriation n 789
expulsion n 185, 297, 893
expunge v 162, 552
expurgate v 652
exquisite adj 394, 650
exquisitely adv 31
extant adj 1
extemporaneous adj 612
extemporaneously adv 612
extempore adv 612
extemporize v 612, 674
extend v 35, 194, 200
extended adj 200, 202
extend to v 196, 200
extension n 35, 65, 180, 194
extensive adj 31, 76, 180
extensively adv 180
extent n 26, 106, 180, 200, 202, 233
extenuate v 469
extenuating adj 469
extenuating circumstances n 469
extenuation n 469
exterior n 220; adj 220
exteriority n 220

exterminate v 162
extermination n 301
external adj 6, 57, 220
externality n 57
externally adv 220
externals n 6
extinct adj 2, 122, 162, 360
extinction n 2, 162, 360, 421, 552
extinguish v 162, 385, 421
extirpate v 301
extirpation n 301
extol v 883
extort v 814
extortion n 789
extra adj 37
extract v 301
extraction n 301
extracts n 596
extradite v 270
extradition n 270
extraneous adj 6, 10, 57, 220
extraneousness n 57
extraneousness n 6
extraordinary adj 31, 83, 870
extravagance n 497, 499, 549, 814, 818, 954
extravagant adj 31, 497, 499, 549, 641, 814, 818, 853, 954
extravagant love n 991
extravagantly adv 31
extreme n 67; adj 31
extremely adv 31
extremity n 67
extricate v 301, 672, 705, 750
extrication n 301, 672, 750
extrinsic adj 6, 57, 220
extrinsicality n 6
extrinsicality n 57
extrinsically adv 6
exuberance n 573, 641
exuberant adj 573, 641
exude v 295
exultant adj 838, 884
eye n 247; v 441
eye for an eye n 30
eyeglasses n 445
eyeless adj 442
eyesight n 441
eyewitness n 444
eyot n 346

F

fable n 546
fabric n 7
fabricate v 161, 515, 544
fabrication n 161, 544, 546

fabulous adj 2, 515,
546, 549, 979
fabulous spirit n 979
façade n 220, 234
face n 220, 234, 448; v
223, 224, 234
facet n 220
facetious adj 842
facetiousness n 842
face to face adv 237
facile adj 705
facilitate v 705, 707
facility n 705
facility n 157, 698, 748
facing n 223; adj 237
facsimile n 13, 21, 90
fact n 1, 151, 474, 494
faction n 712
factious adj 24
factory n 691
facts n 467, 527
factual adj 494
faculties n 450
faculty n 698
fad n 608
faddish adj 123
faddishness n 123
fade v 4, 111, 124, 160,
287, 360, 422, 429,
449, 659, 732
faded adj 659
fail v 160, 304, 360,
655, 732, 773, 808,
927
failing n 732; adj 53,
128, 927
failure n 732
failure n 304, 460, 509,
735, 773, 808, 927
fain adj 602
faint v 158, 688; adj 32,
160, 203, 405, 422,
429, 430, 447, 688
faint-hearted adj 862
faint-heartedness n
862
faintly adv 32
faintness n 405
faintness n 575, 688
faint sound n 405
fair n 799; adj 174,
246, 429, 430, 651,
829, 845, 922, 942
fair game n 857
fairly adv 922
fairness n 174, 845,
922, 942
fairy n 979
faith n 484, 858
faithful adj 17, 21, 494,
772, 983a
faithfully adv 772
faithfulness n 772,
983a
faithless adj 544, 989

fake n 556; v 680; adj
19
fake god n 991
faker n 548
fall n 126, 162, 217,
283, 306, 348, 360; v
162, 306, 310, 360
fallacious adj 4, 477,
495, 544, 545
fallacy n 4, 477, 495
fall again v 661
fall away v 195
fall back v 145, 283,
287, 661
fall behind v 281, 283
fallibility n 475
fallible adj 475
fall in v 488
falling n 306; adj 217
falling back n 145, 287,
661
falling-off n 36, 659
falling out n 720
falling short n 304
fall into a rut v 613
fall into a trap v 547
fall into raptures v 827
fall off v 36, 659, 732
fall on evil days v 735
fall on one's knees v
990
fall out v 151, 713
fallow adj 674
fall prey to v 749
fall short v 304, 651,
732
fall short of v 28, 34,
53, 640, 730
fall through v 304
fall to v 151, 298, 676
fall to one v 785
fall to one's lot v 156
fall to pieces v 162
fall under v 76
false adj 19, 477, 495,
544, 545, 546, 923
false coloration n 523
false expectation n 508
false god n 991
falsehood n 544
falsehood n 546
false impression n 495
falseness n 545
false statement n 477
falsification n 523,
544, 555
falsify v 523, 544, 555
falter v 605
famed adj 883
familial adj 11, 166,
712
familiar adj 613, 888
familiarity n 748
familiarize v 613
family n 11, 75, 166,
167, 712

family likeness n 17
famish v 819, 956
famous adj 883
famously adv 31
fan v 338, 349, 385
fanatic n 504, 606; adj
606
fanatical adj 825
fanaticism n 606
fanciful adj 149, 515,
608
fancy n 453, 515, 608,
865; v 515, 865; adj
577
fancy talk n 577
fang n 663
fantastic adj 83, 497,
515, 853
fantastical adj 515
fantasy n 515
fan the fire v 173, 824
far adj 196
far and wide adv 180
far away adj 196; adv
196
farce n 497
farcical adj 497, 853
far cry to n 196
fare n 298, 812
farewell n 293
farfetched adj 10
far gone adj 503, 659
farm v 371
farming n 371
farness n 196
far off adj 196; adv 196
farrago n 41, 497
farsighted adj 441,
443, 510
farsightedness n 443
fascinate v 288, 824,
829
fascinated adj 870
fascination n 824, 829
fashion n 852
fashion n 7, 123, 613,
627; v 240, 557, 852
fashionable adj 123,
613, 852
fashionableness n 123
fast n 955, 956; adj 43,
150, 274, 684; adv
43
fast as a bullet adj 274
fasten v 43, 45, 150
fastidious adj 704, 868
fastidiousness n 868
fasting n 956
fasting adj 956
fast talker n 548
fat n 356; adj 192, 194
fatal adj 162, 360, 361
fatality n 360, 601
fat chance adj 471
fate n 121, 156, 601,
611, 621

father n 166, 996
fatherhood n 166
fatherland n 189
fathership n 166
fathom v 490
fathomless adj 208
fatigue n 688
fatigue n 841; v 688, 841
fatigued adj 688, 841
fatten v 194, 298
fattiness n 354
fatty adj 354
fatuity n 452, 499
fatuous adj 499
faucet n 263
fault n 70, 495, 651, 732, 848, 927, 945, 961
faultless adj 50, 650, 946, 960
faultlessness n 650, 946, 960
faulty adj 568, 651, 732, 945, 961
faulty grammar n 568
faun n 979
fauna n 357, 366
favor n 707, 740, 760, 784; v 740, 760
favorable adj 134, 602, 648, 734
favorite n 899
favor with v 784
fawn v 886, 933
fawner n 935
fawning n 886, 933; adj 886
fay n 979
fealty n 743
fear n 860
fear n 862; v 860
fearful adj 665, 830, 860, 862
fearfully adv 31
fearless adj 861
fearlessness n 861
feasibility n 470, 705
feasible adj 470, 705
feast on v 298, 377
feat n 680
feather one's own nest v 943
feathery adj 320
feature n 56, 79, 448, 550, 780
features n 5
fecal adj 653
fecund adj 168, 365
fecundity n 168
feeble adj 32, 158, 160, 203, 337, 477, 575, 605
feeble-minded adj 499
feebleness n 575
feebleness n 158

feed v 298, 388
feel n 379; v 375, 379, 821
feel contempt for v 930
feel fine v 654
feel for v 914
feel good v 654
feeling n 821
feeling n 375, 379, 928; adj 821, 914
feeling no pain adj 959
feel pain v 378
feel pleasure v 377
feel sorry about v 833
feel sorry for v 914
fees n 809
feign v 544, 546, 680, 855
feigned adj 855
feigning n 855
felicitation n 896
felicitous adj 23, 578, 698, 850
felicity n 698, 827
fell v 162, 213, 308
fellow n 17, 27, 88, 373, 890; adj 88
fellow creature n 372
fellow-feeling n 888
fellow man n 372
fellowship n 709, 712, 888
female n 374; adj 374
female animal n 374
feminine adj 374
femininity n 374
fen n 345
fence n 232; v 277, 477
fence in v 229
ferment n 59, 171, 173, 315, 320; v 173, 315, 353, 397
fermentation n 171, 315, 353
fermented adj 397
ferocious adj 173
ferocity n 173
ferret out v 480a
fertile adj 168, 371
fertility n 168
fertilize v 168
fervent adj 382, 821, 865
fervid adj 382, 824
fervor n 382, 821, 991
fester v 653
festival n 883
festivity n 840, 883
fetch v 270, 812
fetid adj 401, 653
fetidness n 401
fetishism n 991
fetishistic adj 991
fetor n 401
fetter v 43

feud n 713, 720; v 713
fever n 382, 825
feverish adj 824, 825
few n 100; adj 32, 103, 137
few and far between adj 103
fewness n 103
fewness n 32
fiasco n 732
fiat n 741
fib n 544, 546; v 544, 546
fiber n 205
fibrous adj 205
fickle adj 149, 605, 608
fickleness n 605
fiction n 515, 544, 546, 598
fictional adj 598
fictitious adj 546
fidelity n 543, 772
fidget v 825
fidgetiness n 149, 682
fidgety adj 149, 682, 825
field n 344
field of battle n 728
fields n 344
fiend n 980
fiendish adj 980
fierce adj 173, 825
fiery adj 382, 684, 825
fiery furnace n 386
fifty n 98
fifty-fifty chance n 156
fifty-fifty split n 91
fight n 680; v 606, 720, 722
fighter n 726
fighting n 173, 722
figment n 515
figuration n 554
figurative adj 521, 554
figure n 84, 550, 812; v 240, 448, 554, 557
figured on adj 871
figure of speech n 521
figure of speech n 566
figures of beauty n 521
filament n 205
filch v 791
filcher n 792
file n 69, 86, 266, 330; v 38, 60, 69, 195, 255, 330
file a claim v 969
filial adj 167
filiation n 11
filigree n 219
filing n 330
fill v 52, 186, 190, **224**
filled in adj 527
fill in v 52
filling n 224
fill out v 194, 549

fill up v 52, 261
fill up the time v 106
film n 204, 427
filminess n 426
filmy adj 204, 329, 426
filth n 653
filthy adj 653
final adj 67
finale n 65, 67, 360, 729
final gasp n 360
finality n 67
finalize v 729
finally adv 67, 151
final stage n 67
final touch n 729
finance n 800, 811
financial adj 800
financier n 801, 811
find n 480a, 775; v 151
find fulfillment v 731
find guilty v 971
find oneself v 186
find one's way to v 602
find out v 480a, 527
find refuge v 666
find safety v 666
find the means v 632
find the right words v 566
find vent v 295
fine n 974; v 974; adj 32, 203, 322, 329, 578, 648, 845
fine art n 556
fine gentleman n 854
fineness n 329
fine powder n 330
finery n 847, 851
fine speaking n 577
finesse n 698, 702; v 702
fine writing n 577
finger v 379
fingering n 379
finical adj 459
finicky adj 868
finish n 65, 67, 142, 242, 729; v 52, 67, 142, 650, 729
finished adj 242, 698
finishing stroke n 361
fire n 171, 382, 423, 574; v 384, 388, 420, 824
fired adj 384
fire off v 284
fire place n 386
fireproof adj 385
firewood n 388
firing n 388, 406
firm adj 43, 150, 323, 604, 606
firmament n 318
firmly adv 43
firmness n 150, 323,

604, 606
first adj 66; adv 66
first and foremost adv 66
first blush n 125
first cause n 153, 976
first-class adj 648
first come first served n 607, 609a
first move n 66
first rank n 234
first-rate adj 33, 648, 698
first step n 66
firth n 343
fiscal adj 800
fish n 366
fish for v 622
fishing n 361
fish story n 549
fish up v 307
fissure n 44, 198, 260
fit n 7, 173, 315, 825; v 23, 852; adj 646, 698, 922
fit as a fiddle adj 654
fit for adj 698
fitful adj 70, 139, 149, 475, 608
fitfully adv 139
fitfulness n 139, 475
fitness n 646
fit out v 225, 673
fits n 315
five, etc. n 98
five n 98
fivefold division n 99
fix n 704; v 43, 60, 150, 184, 604, 660
fix a price v 812
fixed adj 5, 141, 150, 240, 265, 474, 604, 613
fixed idea n 606
fixedness n 150
fixity n 150, 265
fix the time v 114
fizzle v 353, 409
fjord n 343
flabby adj 324
flaccid adj 160, 324, 326
flaccidity n 160, 324, 326, 640
flag n 747; v 160, 275, 655, 683, 688
flaky adj 204
flame n 382, 420, 423, 439, 897; v 382, 897
flame-colored adj 439
flaming adj 434
flammable adj 384, 388
flank n 236; v 236
flanked adj 236

flanking adj 236
flap n 214; v 214, 315
flare n 420; v 173, 420
flare up v 420, 825
flash n 113, 420, 453, 612; v 113, 420
flash on v 505; v 612
flashy adj 428, 577, 851, 882
flat n 344; adj 172, 207, 213, 251, 337, 391, 395, 598, 843
flat as a pancake adj 251
flatlands n 207
flatness n 251
flatness n 207, 213, 391, 843
flatten v 213, 251, 255
flatter v 933
flatterer n 935
flattering adj 933
flattery n 933
flatulent adj 334, 338
flaunt v 882
flaunting adj 882
flavor n 390, 394; v 390
flavored adj 390
flavorful adj 390, 394
flavorfulness n 394
flavoring n 393
flavorless adj 395
flavorlessness n 395
flavory adj 390
flaw n 70, 198, 495, 651, 848, 961
flawed adj 961
flaxen adj 435
fleck v 440
flecked adj 440
flecky adj 440
fled adj 671
flee v 671
fleece n 223; v 789, 791, 814
fleet n 273; adj 274, 684
fleeting adj 111
flesh n 364
flesh and blood n 3, 316, 364
fleshiness n 354
fleshly adj 364
fleshy adj 354
flexibility n 324, 705
flexible adj 324
flexure n 245
flicker n 315; v 315, 420, 422
flickering adj 139
flier n 269
flier n 269
flight n 267, 274, 287, 293, 623, 671
flighty adj 149, 503

flimsiness n 4, 209, 425
flimsy adj 160, 209, 322, 324, 425, 477, 643
flinch v 623
fling n 284; v 284
flip out v 173
flipside n 235
flirt v 902
flit v 109, 111, 264, 266, 274
flitting adj 111, 266
float v 267, 320
floating adj 405
flock n 72, 997; v 72
flocks and herds n 366
flog v 972
flogging n 975
flood n 72, 121, 348; v 641
flood gate n 233, 350
floor n 204; v 213
flop v 315
flora n 357, 367, 369
floriculture n 371
florid adj 428, 577
floridness n 577
flounce v 309, 315
flounder v 149, 314, 315, 475, 732
flourish n 577, 882; v 367, 654, 734
flourish of trumpets n 404
floury adj 330
flout v 715
flow n 264, 348; v 109, 214, 264, 333, 347, 348
flower n 648; v 161, 734
flowerage n 367
flowering n 161
flowery adj 577
flow from v 154
flow in v 294
flowing n 348; adj 405, 578
flow into v 348
flow out v 295, 348
flow out of v 295
flow over v 348
fluctuate v 149, 314, 605
fluctuating adj 149
fluctuation n 149, 314, 605
flue n 351
fluency n 333
fluent adj 333, 348, 578, 584
fluffy adj 256
fluid n 337; adj 333, 337
fluidity n 333
fluke n 156, 621

flukey adj 156
flunkey n 935
flunkeyism n 933
flurry n 682, 684
flush n 382, 420; v 382, 434
flushed adj 434, 824, 838
flush out v 480a
fluster v 824
flute v 259
fluted adj 259
flutter n 315; v 315, 422
flux n 109, 144, 264, 348
flux and reflux n 314
fly v 109, 111, 267, 287, 328, 671
fly back v 277
fly from v 623
flying n 274, 267; adj 111, 267, 959
fly over v 267
fly to pieces v 328
foam n 353; v 173, 315, 353, 825
foaming n 353
foamy adj 353
focal adj 222
focus n 74
focus v 74
focus on v 222
fodder n 362
foe n 708, 710, 726, 891
fog n 353, 424
fogginess n 422, 475
foggy adj 422, 426, 353
foil n 14
foiled adj 732
fold n 258
fold n 232, 997; v 258
folded adj 258
foliage n 367
foliation n 367
folk n 372
folk music n 415
follow v 19, 63, 281 518, 622, 743
follow after v 117
follower n 117, 541 746
follow in a line v 69
following n 63, 117, 281; adj 63, 117, 281
follow in the steps of v 281
follow in the wake of v 281
follow the rules v 82
folly n 499
fond adj 897
fondle v 379
fondling n 379
fondness n 897

font n 153
food n 298, 637
food for thought n 454
food for worms n 362
fool n 501
fool n 493, 547, 844, 857; v 545
foolhardiness n 863
foolhardy adj 684, 863
foolish adj 477, 497, 499
foolishness n 497, 499
foot n 211
footing n 8, 71, 183, 215
fop n 854
foppery n 855
for adv 155
for a long time adv 110
for a time adv 111
foray n 716
forbear v 678, 953
forbearance n 623, 678, 740, 826
forbears n 122
forbid v 761
force n 157, 159, 170, 171, 173, 574, 739, 744; v 157, 744
forced adj 10, 579
forceful adj 157, 159, 171, 574
forcefulness n 600
force of will n 600
for certain adv 474
forcible adj 171, 574, 744
forcibly adv 744
ford v 302
fore adj 234
forebode v 909
foreboding n 512, 909; adj 909
forecast n 510, 511, 673; v 507, 511, 626
forefather n 130
forefront n 234
foregoing adj 62, 116, 122
foregone adj 611
foregone conclusion n 611
foreground n 234
foreign adj 10, 57, 220
foreign body n 57
foreign parts n 196
foreign substance n 57
fore-knowledge n 510
foreman n 694
foremost adj 33, 66, 234, 642
forenoon n 125
foreordain v 152
forerun v 62, 116, 280
forerunner n 64, 116, 534

foresee v 121, 507, 510, 511, 871
foreseen adj 507, 871
foreshadow v 909
foreshadowing adj 909
foresight n 510
forestall v 132
forestry n 371
foretell v 511
forethought n 510, 864
foretoken n 511; v 511
forever adv 16, 112
forewarn v 510, 668
foreword n 64
forfeit n 974; v 776
forfeiture n 776
for form's sake adv 82
forge n 386, 691
forge ahead v 282
forgery n 19, 21, 546
forget v 506
forgetful adj 506
forgetfulness n 506
forgive v 918
forgiveness n 918
forgiving adj 918
forgo v 624, 757, 782
for good adv 106, 141
for good and all adv 141
forgotten adj 122, 506
fork n 244; v 91, 244, 291
forked adj 244
for keeps adv 106
forking v 91, 291
fork out v 784
forlorn adj 859
form n 240
form n 7, 21, 54, 80, 329, 448, 569, 697, 998; v 54, 56, 60, 144, 161, 240, 557, 852
formal adj 80, 82, 240, 242, 383, 579
formal features n 567
formality n 240, 579
formal speech n 586
form an opinion v 480
formation n 161, 240
formative adj 127, 153, 161
formative years n 127
form a whole v 50
formed adj 820
former adj 62, 116, 122
formerly adv 122
former times n 122
formidable adj 704
form into a sphere v 249
formless adj 241
formlessness n 241
form part of v 56
forms n 567

formula n 80, 240, 626, 697
formulaic adj 80, 626
formulate v 963
forsake v 624, 732, 782
for sale adj 763, 794, 796
forswear v 624, 782
forsworn adj 782
forte n 698
forth adv 282
forthcoming adj 152
for the moment adv 111
for the most part adv 613
for the sake of conformity adv 82
for the time being adv 106
forthright adj 246, 946
forthwith adv 132
fortification n 717
fortify v 159, 717
fortitude n 826, 861
fortress n 666
fortuitous adj 134, 156, 621
fortunate adj 134, 734
fortune n 152, 156, 621, 734, 803
fortune-teller n 513
forum n 966
forward adj 234; adv 282
fossil fuel n 388
foster v 658
foul adj 401, 649, 653
foulness n 401
foul play n 619
foul smell n 401
found v 153, 215
foundation n 153, 211, 215, 673
founded on adj 211
founder n 164; v 732
foundling n 893
found wanting adj 651
fount n 153
fountain n 153
four n 95; adj 95, 96
four-flusher n 548
fourfold adj 95, 96
fourfold division n 97
fourth adj 96
fourthly adv 96
fourth part n 97
four times adv 96
fowls of the air n 366
foxy adj 702
fracas n 59
fraction n 100a
fraction n 32, 51, 84
fractional adj 51, 84
fractional part n 100a
fractious adj 713, 742

fracture n 44, 70
fragile adj 160, 203, 328
fragility n 160, 328
fragment n 32, 51
fragmentary adj 51
fragments n 596
fragrance n 400
fragrant adj 377, 400
frail adj 158, 160, 203, 328, 605, 651
frailty n 158, 160, 328, 575, 605
frame n 7, 231, 240, 329; v 161, 626, 852
frame of mind n 602
framework n 329
franchise n 748, 760; v 760
franchisement n 748
frangible adj 328
frank adj 246, 525, 543, 703
frankness n 543, 748
frantic adj 173, 503, 824
fraternal adj 712, 714
fraternity n 11, 709, 888
fraternize v 709, 714, 892
fratricide n 361
fraud n 545, 548, 791
fraudulent adj 544
fraught adj 52
fraught with danger adj 665
fray v 331
freak n 156; v 608, 872
freaked adj 173
freakish adj 608
freckled adj 440, 848
free v 672, 705, 748, 750, 927a; adj 44, 600, 685, 748, 816
freed adj 748, 750, 927a
freedom n 748
freedom n 600, 672, 738, 760, 927a
freely adv 602, 748
free space n 180
free spirit n 268
free swinging n 214
freethinker n 989
freethinking n 989; adj 989
free time n 685
free will n 600
freeze v 376, 383, 385
freezer n 387
freezing adj 383
freight n 190
freighter n 271, 273
frenzied adj 173, 503
frenzy n 503, 825

frequency *n* 136
frequent *adj* 104, 136, 613
frequently *adv* 136
fresh *adj* 123, 428, 435, 505
freshen *v* 338, 689
freshness *n* 123
fresh wind *n* 349
fret *n* 828; *v* 378, 832
fretful *adj* 684
fretwork *n* 219
friability *n* 330
friction *n* 331
friction *n* 179, 719
fridge *n* 387
friend *n* 890
friend *n* 711, 912, 977
friendliness *n* 888, 897
friendly *adj* 707, 714, 721, 888, 892
friendship *n* 888
friendship *n* 714
fright *n* 860
frighten *v* 909
frightened *adj* 860
frightening *adj* 909
frightful *adj* 830
frightfully *adv* 31
frightfulness *n* 846
frigid *adj* 158, 383
frigidaire *n* 387
frigidity *n* 383
frills *n* 847
fringe *n* 231
frippery *n* 643, 851
frisk *n* 309; *v* 309
frisky *adj* 309, 682
fritter away time *v* 683
fritter one's money *v* 818
frivolity *n* 4, 209, 499
frivolous *adj* 4, 477, 499, 608, 643
frizz *v* 248
frizzle *v* 248, 258
from all points of the compass *adv* 180
from bad to worse *adv* 835
from beginning to end *adv* 52
from first to last *adv* 52
from head to foot *adv* 52
from pole to pole *adv* 180
from side to side *adv* 314
from the beginning *adv* 66
from the bottom of one's heart *adv* 821
from the four corners of the world *adv* 180

from this time *adv* 121
from time to time *adv* 136
from top to bottom *adv* 52
front *n* 234
front *n* 719; *v* 234; *adj* 234
frontage *n* 234
frontal *adj* 234
frontier *n* 233
fronting *adj* 237
frontispiece *n* 64, 234
front rank *n* 234
frost-bitten *adj* 383
frosted *adj* 426, 430
frostiness *n* 430
frosty *adj* 383
froth *n* 353; *v* 353
frothy *adj* 353
frown *v* 837, 900, 901a
frown upon *v* 932
frozen *adj* 381, 383, 385
fructification *n* 161
fructify *v* 168, 658, 734
frugal *adj* 817, 953
frugality *n* 817
fruit *n* 154, 367
fruitful *adj* 168
fruitfulness *n* 168
fruition *n* 161
fruitless *adj* 158, 645, 732
frustrate *v* 706
frustrated *adj* 732
frustration *n* 509
fry *v* 384
fuel *n* 388
fuel *v* 388
fuel oil *n* 388
fugitive *n* 268, 623; *adj* 623
fulfill *v* 52, 161, 168, 729, 772, 926
fulfilled *adj* 52
fulfillment *n* 161, 729, 731, 772
fulfill oneself *v* 731
full *adj* 31, 50, 52, 52, 404, 729
full-blown *adj* 194
full circle *n* 311
full-flavored *adj* 392, 394
full grown *adj* 131, 192, 194
fullness *n* 31, 52, 131
full of incident *adj* 151
full turn *n* 311
fully *adv* 31, 52
fulminate *v* 404
fulsome *adj* 401
fumble *v* 61, 699
fumbler *n* 701

fume *n* 398, 401; *v* 173, 382, 825, 900
fumigate *v* 652
fuming *adj* 434, 824
fun *n* 842
function *n* 170, 625, 926, 998; *v* 680, 746
functional *adj* 625, 644
functionary *n* 694, 758
fund *n* 636
fundamental *adj* 5, 211, 215
fundamentally *adv* 31
fundamental part *n* 211
funds *n* 800
funeral *n* 363; *adj* 363
funeral rites *n* 363
funereal *adj* 363
fungus *n* 663
funish *v* 784
funnel *n* 350, 351
funny *adj* 853
funnyman *n* 844
fur *n* 223
furcation *n* 291
furious *adj* 173, 382, 825
furiously *adv* 31
furnace *n* 386
furnish *v* 637, 673
furor *n* 825
furrow *n* 259
furrow *v* 259
furrowed *adj* 259
further *adv* 37
furtherance *n* 707
furthermore *adv* 37
furtive *adj* 528
fury *n* 173, 825, 980
fuse *v* 43, 48, 384
fusion *n* 48, 384, 709
fuss *n* 315, 682; *v* 682, 825
fussy *adj* 682, 825, 868
fustian *n* 577
fustiness *n* 401
fusty *adj* 401
futile *adj* 158, 645
futility *n* 645
future *n* 117, 152; *adj* 121
future events *n* 152
futurism *n* 123

G

gab *v* 584
gad about *v* 266
gadding *adj* 266
gadding about *n* 266
gag *v* 403, 581
gaggle *v* 412
gain *n* 618, 658, 775; *v* 775
gainful *adj* 775
gain ground *v* 282

gain knowledge v 539
gain on v 286
gainsay v 536, 708
gait n 264
galaxy n 318
gale n 349
gall v 378, 869
gallant adj 861, 894
gallantry n 861
gallimaufry n 41
gallop v 111
galvanism n 824
galvanize v 824
gamble n 156; v 621
gambler n 621
gambling n 156, 621
game n 366, 620, 857;
   adj 604, 604a
gamester n 621
gaming n 156
gander n 373
gang n 72, 712
gaol n 752
gaoler n 753
gap n 70, 196, 198, 260
gape v 198, 260, 455
gaping adj 208, 260
garb n 225; v 225
garble v 523, 583
garden v 371, 371
gardening n 371
garish adj 428, 851,
   882
garland n 247
garner v 636
garrison n 717; v 664
garrote n 361; v 361
garroter n 361
garrulity n 584
garrulous adj 584
gas n 388; v 361
gaseity n 334
gaseous adj 334, 336
gaseousness n 334
gash n 198
gasification n 336
gasify v 336
gas lamp n 423
gasoline n 356, 388
gasp v 349, 655, 688
gassing n 361
gate n 232, 260
gateway n 232, 260,
   627
gather v 72, 258, 775,
   789
gathering n 72, 712
gathering place n 74
gather together v 290
gaudiness n 851
gaudy adj 428, 851,
   882
gauge n 466
gauging n 466
gaunt adj 203
gauze n 424

gauziness n 425
gauzy adj 425
gawky adj 699
gay adj 829, 836
gaze n 441
gazette n 86
gear n 225
Gehenna n 982
gelding n 373
gelid adj 383
gem n 648
genealogy n 69, 166
general adj 78, 613
generality n 78
generalization n 78
generalize v 78
generally adv 613
general public n 372,
   876
generalship n 722
generate v 161, 168
generation n 11, 108,
   161, 163
generative adj 153,
   161, 168
generator n 164
generic adj 78
generosity n 784, 816,
   906, 942
generous adj 784, 816,
   906, 942
genesis n 66, 153, 161
genial adj 382, 602,
   829, 888, 892
geniality n 602, 836
genius n 698, 700, 872
genius for n 698
genteel adj 852
gentility n 578, 852,
   875, 894
gentle adj 174, 275,
   405, 721, 740
gentleman n 373
gentlemanly adj 894
gentleness n 174, 740
gentlewoman n 374
genuflect v 308
genuflection n 308
genuine adj 494, 648,
   922, 960
genuineness n 960
genus n 75
geography n 183
geology n 358
germ n 66, 153
germinate v 194, 367
gestation n 161
gesticulate v 550
gesticulation n 550
gesture n 550; v 550
get v 775, 795, 810
get a footing v 184
get a head start v 132
get along v 282, 736
get back v 790
get back to basics v

849
get better v 658
get between v 228
get closer to v 286
get close to v 286
get down v 306
get down to
   particulars v 79
get going v 66, 276,
   284
get hold of v 775, 789
get into v 827
get into print v 531
get on v 282
get one's wind v 687
get over v 660
get ready v 673
get red in the face v
   434
get rid of v 297, 776
get the scent of v 527
get through v 67
get to v 292
get to the heart of v
   222
get under way v 293
get up v 305
get well v 654
ghost n 362, 980; 443
ghostlike adj 980
ghostly adj 976, 980
ghoul n 980
giant n 192
gibberish n 517
gibes n 856
giddy adj 499
gift n 698, 763, 775,
   784
gigantic adj 31, 159,
   192, 206
giggle n 838; v 838
gimmicky adj 643
gird v 43, 227
girdle n 232, 247
girl n 129, 374
girlfriend n 897
girlhood n 127
girlish adj 129
gist n 5, 516
give n 325; v 324, 325,
   763, 784, 816
give a free rein v 738
give a hearing to v 418
give an account v 527
give and take v 148,
   774, 794
give a new turn to v
   140
give assent v 484
give a start to v 276
give assistance v 707
give audience to v 418
give away v 784
give back v 790
give birth to v 163, 359
give counsel v 695

give counsel to v 695
give credence to 484
give energy v 171
give entrance to v 296
give evidence v 467
give fight v 722
give help v 707
give in v 82, 360
give it a shot v 602
given adj 474, 514
give no quarter v 361
give notice v 668
given time n 134
given up adj 782
give offense v 830
give oneself airs v 878
give one's word v 768
give out v 732, 784
give out a smell v 398
give out sound v 402
give pleasure v 377
giver n 784
give rise to v 153
give satisfaction v 952
give security v 768, 771
give up v 624, 757, 782, 790
give up hope v 859
give up the ghost v 360
give way v 160, 328
give way to v 881
giving n 784
glacial adj 383
glaciation n 385
gladden v 829, 836
gladdening adj 836
glade n 252
gladness n 827
gladsome adj 827, 829
glance n 441
glance around v 441
glare v 420, 441
glaring adj 428, 446
glaringly adv 31
glass n 389
glasses n 445
glassy adj 255, 420
glaze v 255
gleam n 420; v 420
glee n 827
gleeful adj 836
glen n 252
glib adj 584
glide v 264, 267
glider n 273
gliding n 267
glimmer v 420, 422, 446
glimmering n 420
glimpse n 441
glint n 420
glisten v 420
glitter v 420
gloat over v 377
globe n 249, 318

globe-trotter n 268
globular adj 249
globularity n 249
globule n 249
gloom n 837
gloominess n 422
gloomy adj 421, 422, 837, 901a
glorified adj 981
glorified spirit n 977
glorify v 883, 990, 991
glory n 420, 981
gloss n 255, 522; v 522
glossary n 562
gloss over v 458, 477
glossy adj 255, 420
glow n 382, 420, 574; v 382
glower v 900
glowing adj 382, 434, 574, 824
glue v 46
gluey adj 352
glut n 869; v 641, 869
glutinosity n 352
glutinous adj 327, 352
glutted adj 869
glutton n 957
gluttonous adj 957
gluttony n 957
gnarled adj 256
gnash v 900
gnaw v 298, 378
gnome n 980
go v 264, 293, 302, 449
go about v 218
go adrift v 279
go after v 117, 281, 622
goal n 67, 620
go along with v 709
go amiss v 732
go around v 247, 311
go ashore v 342
go astray v 279, 495
go away v 293, 302
go back v 287
go back to v 104
go bad v 653, 659
gobble v 412
gobble up v 957
go before v 116, 280
go beserk v 173
go-between n 534, 631, 724
go beyond v 303
go boating v 267
go by v 109
go by the rules v 82
god n 976, 979
goddess n 979
godhead n 976
godless adj 989
godliness n 987
godly adj 976, 987
go down v 306, 659
go downhill v 659, 735

godsend n 618
go forth v 293
go for the bait v 547
goggle-eyed adj 443
goggle eyes n 443
goggles n 445
go half way v 628
go halves v 91; v 778
go hand in hand with v 178
go hard with v 732
going n 264
going back n 145
going hungry n 956
going on adj 53, 151
go into hysterics v 825
gold adj 435, 439
golden adj 435, 734
golden dreams n 515
golden mean n 29, 628, 736
golden opportunity n 134
golden rule n 697
golden years n 128
go mad v 503, 825
gone adj 2, 122, 360
gone bad adj 397, 653
gone by adj 122, 124
gone to waste adj 638
good n 618
good adj 52, 394, 618, 648, 922, 931, 944, 977
good behavior n 894
goodbye n 293
good chance n 472
good fellowship n 892
good fortune n 618, 731
good head n 502
good health n 654
good luck n 618, 621, 731
goodly adj 31
good man n 948
good manners n 894
goodness n 648
goodness n 618, 829, 922, 944
goods n 780, 798
good samaritan n 906
good taste n 578, 850
good will n 602, 888
gooey adj 396
go off v 173
go on v 106, 143
go on forever v 104, 112
go on vacation v 687
go out v 142
go over v 218
go over again v 104
go over the same ground v 104
go pit-a-pat v 315

gore *v* 260
gorge *n* 198; *v* 641, 869, 957
gorged *adj* 869
gorgeous *adj* 428, 845
gorgeousness *n* 845
gormandizing *n* 957; *adj* 957
go round about *v* 629
gory *adj* 361, 653
go shopping *v* 795
go side by side *v* 120
gossamer *n* 205
gossamery *adj* 329
gossip *n* 455, 532, 588; *v* 588
gossipy *adj* 588
go straight *v* 246, 628
go the way of all flesh *v* 360
go through *v* 151, 302
go to *v* 278
go to bed *v* 687
go to press *v* 591
go to seed *v* 659
go to sleep *v* 687
go to the dogs *v* 162, 735, 804
go to the law *v* 969
go to waste *v* 659
go to wrack and ruin *v* 162
gouge *n* 262; *v* 252
go up *v* 305
govern *v* 693, 737
governess *n* 753
government *n* 693
governor *n* 694, 753
go wild *v* 173
gown *n* 999
go wrong *v* 732
grab *v* 379
grace *n* 242, 578, 845, 850, 918, 987
graceful *adj* 578, 845
gracefulness *n* 242, 578, 845
graceless *adj* 579
gracious *adj* 894
graciously *adv* 602
graciousness *n* 894
gradation *n* 26, 58, 69
grade *n* 26, 58, 71, 217, 305, 306
grade crossing *n* 219
gradual *adj* 26, 69, 275, 685
gradually *adv* 26, 69, 275
graduate *v* 60, 69
graduation *n* 60
graft *v* 184, 300
grain *n* 5, 256, 329, 330
graininess *n* 330
grammar *n* 567
grammar *n* 542

grammar book *n* 567
grammarian *n* 567
grammatical *adj* 567
grand *adj* 574, 642, 882
grandchildren *n* 167
grandeur *n* 875
grandfather *n* 130, 166
grandiloquence *n* 577
grandiloquent *adj* 577
grandiose *adj* 577
grandmother *n* 130, 166
grandsire *n* 130, 166
grant *n* 784; *v* 529, 760, 762, 783, 784
grantee *n* 785
granter *n* 784
granular *adj* 330
granularity *n* 330
granulate *v* 330
granulation *n* 330
granule *n* 32
graphic *adj* 518
grapple with *v* 719
grasp *v* 518
grass *n* 367
grassland *n* 344
grassy *adj* 435
grate *v* 330, 378, 410, 414
grateful *adj* 916
grater *n* 330
gratification *n* 827
gratify *v* 829, 831
grating *n* 219, 410; *adj* 410, 414
gratitude *n* 916
gratuity *n* 784
grave *n* 363; *v* 558; *adj* 642, 739, 830
grave clothes *n* 363
gravestone *n* 363
graveyard *n* 363
gravitate *v* 306, 319
gravitate toward *v* 176
gravitation *n* 319
gravitational *adj* 288
gravity *n* 319
gravity *n* 288, 574, 642, 739
gray *n* 432
gray *n* 422; *adj* 128, 422, 428, 429, 432
graybeard *n* 130
gray hairs *n* 128
grayish *adj* 432
grayness *n* 422, 432
graze *v* 199
graze over *v* 379
grazing over *n* 379
grease *n* 355, 356; *v* 255, 332, 355
greasiness *n* 355
greasing *n* 332
greasy *adj* 355
great *adj* 31, 192

greaten *v* 35
greater *adj* 33
greatest *adj* 33
greatly *adv* 31
greatness *n* 31
greatness *n* 33, 192, 873
great waters *n* 341
greed *n* 957
greediness *n* 957
greedy *adj* 789, 819, 957
green *n* 435
green *adj* 123, 127, 435, 674
greenbacks *n* 800
greenhorn *n* 547, 701
greenish *adj* 435
greenish blue *adj* 438
greenness *n* 123, 435
greens *n* 367
gregarious *adj* 892
gregariousness *n* 892
gridiron *n* 219
grief *n* 833
grievance *n* 830
grieve *v* 828, 839
grieve at *v* 833
grievous *adj* 649, 830
grievously *adv* 31
grill *v* 384
grille *n* 219
grim *adj* 830
grimace *v* 243
grime *n* 653
grimy *adj* 653
grin *n* 838; *v* 838
grind *v* 195, 253, 330, 331, 410, 539
grinder *n* 330
grinding *n* 410
grindstone *n* 330
grip *n* 378
gripe *n* 378; *v* 378
grist *n* 637
gristly *adj* 327
grit *n* 327, 330
gritty *adj* 330, 604
grizzled *adj* 432
grizzly *adj* 432
groan *n* 839; *v* 411
groove *n* 259, 613; *v* 259
grope in the dark *v* 442
gross *adj* 653, 846, 961
grossness *n* 961
grouch *v* 900
ground *n* 181, 211, 215, 342, 467, 615; *v* 215
grounded on *adj* 211
groundless *adj* 4
grounds *n* 342, 344, 467
groundswell *n* 315
groundwork *n* 60, 64,

153, 211, 673
group n 72, 372, 416,
417, 712; v 60, 72
groupings n 60
grove n 252
grovel v 207, 275
groveling n 886; adj
207, 435, 886
grow v 35, 144, 194,
282, 367, 734
grow dim v 422
grow from v 154
growing adj 35
grow into v 144
growl v 412, 900
growling n 412
grown up adj 131
growth n 35, 144, 161,
194, 250, 282, 365
grow up v 131
grudge n 907, 921; v
819
grudgingly adv 603
gruesome adj 846
gruff adj 254, 410
grumble v 407, 411,
832
grumbling n 407
grumpy adj 901a
grunt v 412
guarantee n 768, 771;
v 768, 771
guard n 717, 753; v
664, 670, 717
guard against v 717
guarded adj 459, 585,
864
guardian n 664, 753,
977
guardian angel n 977
guardianship n 717
guarding n 670
guerilla n 361
guess n 514; v 514
guesswork n 514
guffaw n 838
guidance n 537, 692,
693, 695
guide n 524, 527, 540,
694; v 537, 692, 693
guidebook n 527
guiding adj 693
guile n 544, 702
guileless adj 703, 946
guilelessness n 946
guiling n 545
guillotine v 361
guilt n 947
guilt n 649, 961
guiltiness n 947
guiltless adj 946
guiltlessness n 946,
960
guilty adj 947, 961
guilty verdict n 971

guise n 448
gulf n 343
gulf n 198, 343
gull n 486, 547; v 545
gulley n 259
gullibility n 486
gullible adj 486, 547
gully n 350
gulosity n 957
gulp v 298
gulp down v 298
gum n 356a
gummy adj 327, 352,
356a
gun down v 361
gunshot n 197
gurgle v 348, 353, 408
gurgling n 353
guru n 994
gush n 295, 348; v 295,
348, 584
gush out v 295
gust n 349; v 349
gusto n 390
gut v 162
guts n 221, 861
gutsy adj 861
gutter n 259, 350
guttural adj 410
guzzle v 957, 959
gymnasium n 728
gypsy n 268
gyration n 312

H

habit n 613
habit n 5, 820
habitat n 189
habitation n 189
habitation n 189
habitual adj 82, 104,
136, 613
habitually adv 136,
613
habituate v 613
hack v 44
hackneyed adj 598
hack up v 201
Hades n 982
haggard adj 203, 688
haggle v 794
hagiography n 983
hagiological adj 983
hail v 586
hair n 205
hair's breadth n 197
hairy adj 256
halcyon adj 721
hale adj 654
half a dozen n 98
half a hundred n 98
half and half adj 27, 41
half measures n 628
half-moon n 245
half-starved adj 956
halfway adj 68; adv 68

half-witted adj 499
hallowed adj 976
halo n 420
halt n 142, 685, 687; v
142, 160, 265, 275
halve v 91
halved adj 91
halving n 91
hammer v 104
hammered
instruments n 417
hamper v 706
hamstring v 158
hand n 236, 372, 590,
590, 631; v 784
handbook n 527, 593
handful n 25, 32
handicap v 706
hand in hand adv 88
handle n 564; v 379,
677
handling n 379
hand of death n 360
hand over v 270, 783
hands n 269
handsome adj 845
handwriting n 590
handy adj 197, 673,
698
hang v 214, 361
hang a turn v 140
hang back v 683
hang by a thread v 665
hanging n 361; adj 214
hanging down n 214
hang in there v 604a
hang it up v 624
hangman n 975
hang over v 152
hang together v 46,
178
hap n 156; v 156
haphazard adj 139,
156
haphazardness n 139
hapless adj 735
happen v 1, 151
happening n 8, 151;
adj 151
happily adv 827
happiness n 618, 827
happy adj 23, 134, 827,
836
happy-go-lucky adj
674
harangue n 537, 582; v
582
harass v 830
harbinger n 64, 512,
534
hard adj 159, 323, 376,
397, 704, 739, 830
hard and fast law n 80
hard as a rock adj 323
hard as nails adj 323
hard by adv 197

hard cash *n* 800
hard coal *n* 388
harden *v* 48, 159, 321, 323, 613
hardening *n* 321, 385
hard-featured *adj* 846
hard-hearted *adj* 914a
hard-heartedness *n* 914a
hardihood *n* 861
hardiness *n* 159
hardly *adv* 32, 137
hardly ever *adv* 137
hardness *n* 323
hardness of hearing *n* 419
hardness of heart *n* 951
hard of hearing *adj* 419
hardship *n* 735
hard task *n* 704
hard times *n* 735
hard to please *adj* 868
hard up *adj* 804
hardy *adj* 159, 654
harlequin *n* 501
harlot *n* 962
harm *n* 619; *v* 619, 649, 659, 828, 923
harmful *adj* 619, 649, 657, 663
harmfulness *n* 649
harmless *adj* 158
harmonious *adj* 23, 242, 413, 416, 428, 714
harmoniousness *n* 413
harmonious sounds *n* 415
harmonize *v* 23, 82, 413
harmonize with *v* 714
harmony *n* 23, 58, 242, 413, 415, 709, 714, 721, 888
harness *v* 43, 225
harping *n* 104; *adj* 104
harp on *v* 104
harpy *n* 980
harrow *v* 371, 830
harsh *adj* 410, 414, 579, 739, 830, 955
harshness *n* 410, 414, 739
hart *n* 373
harvest *n* 154, 618, 775
harvest time *n* 126
hash *n* 59
haste *n* 684
haste *n* 132, 863; *v* 274, 684
hasten *v* 132, 274, 310, 682, 684
hastily *adv* 132
hasty *adj* 684, 863

hatch *n* 260; *v* 161, 558, 626
hatchet man *n* 936
hate *n* 898
hate *n* 907; *v* 867, 898
hateful *adj* 649, 830, 898, 907
hating *adj* 898
hatred *n* 867, 889, 898, 907
hatred of mankind *n* 911
haughtiness *n* 878, 885
haughty *adj* 878, 885
haul *n* 190; *v* 190, 285
hauling *n* 285
haunt *n* 74, 189
haunted *adj* 980
haunt one's thoughts *v* 505
have *v* 777
have a bad name *v* 874
have a bad smell *v* 401
have a defect *v* 651
have affection for *v* 897
have a hand in *v* 153, 682, 709
have a knack for *v* 698
have an acquaintance with *v* 888
have an odor *v* 398
have a perfume *v* 400
have a say *v* 175
have a short memory *v* 506
have a soft spot in one's heart *v* 822
have a temper *v* 901
have a true ring *v* 494
have charge of *v* 693
have confidence in *v* 484
have done with *v* 678
have enough *v* 639
have faith *v* 987
have faith in *v* 484, 858
have free play *v* 170
have had its day *v* 124
have in common *v* 778
have in hand *v* 777
have input *v* 175
have in sight *v* 441
have in store for *v* 152
have its seat in *v* 183
have leisure *v* 685
have no bearing upon *v* 10
have no chance *v* 471
have no connection with *v* 10
have no curiosity *v* 456
have no heart for *v* 866
have no idea *v* 491
have no interest in *v* 823

have no limits *v* 104
have no motive *v* 615a
have no odor *v* 399
have no pity for *v* 914a
have no preference *v* 609a
have no relation to *v* 10
have no taste for *v* 867
have nothing to do with *v* 10
have occasion for *v* 630
have one's act together *v* 502
have one's head in the clouds *v* 827
have precedence *v* 62
have priority *v* 280
have pull *adj* 288
have qualms *v* 485
have recourse to *v* 677
have scope *v* 748
have seen its day *v* 124
have the advantage *v* 28
have the lead *v* 208
have the means *v* 632
have the right *v* 924
have the virtue of *v* 944
have to do with *v* 9
have too high an opinion of oneself *v* 889
have to oneself *v* 777
have two meanings *v* 520
have words with *v* 713
having a right to *adj* 924
having no right to *adj* 925
havoc *n* 162
hawk *v* 763, 796
hawker *n* 797
hazard *n* 156, 665; *v* 621, 665
hazard a suggestion *v* 514
hazardous *adj* 665
haze *n* 353, 422
hazel *adj* 433
haziness *n* 422, 426, 447, 475
hazy *adj* 353, 422, 426
head *n* 66, 353, 372, 450, 564, 694, 745; *v* 62, 66, 280; *adj* 210
head for the hills *v* 623
heading *n* 64, 66, 75, 280, 564
headland *n* 250
headlines *n* 532
headlong *adj* 684, 863

head of the column *n* 234
headquarters *n* 74
heads or tails *n* 156
headstone *n* 363
headstrong *adj* 606
headway *n* 282
heal *v* 660, 662
healing *n* 660
health *n* 654
health *n* 159
healthful *adj* 654, 656
healthfulness *n* 656
healthiness *n* 656
healthy *adj* 654, 656
heap *n* 31, 72, 192
hear *v* 418
hear a cause *v* 967
hearer *n* 418
hearing *n* 418
hearing *adj* 418
hearsay *n* 532
hearse *n* 363
heart *n* 5, 68, 208, 221, 222, 372, 574, 820
heart and soul *adv* 821
heart-felt *adj* 821
hearth *n* 386
heartless *adj* 383
heartsick *adj* 837
hearty *adj* 654, 836
heat *n* 382
heat *v* 382, 384
heated *adj* 382, 384
heater *n* 386
heath *n* 344
heathen *n* 984, 989
heating *n* 384
heave *v* 276, 284, 307
heaven *n* 981
heavenly *adj* 318, 829, 976, 981
heavenly bodies *n* 318
heavenly kingdom *n* 981
heavenly spirit *n* 977
heavens *n* 180, 318
heaviness *n* 202, 319, 837, 843
heavy *n* 202; *adj* 172, 194, 319, 683
heavy as lead *adj* 319
heavy heart *n* 837
heavy news *n* 830
hebetude *n* 499
heckle *v* 830
hedge *n* 232
hedge in *v* 229
hedonist *n* 954a
heed *n* 457, 459, 864; *v* 418, 457, 928
heedful *adj* 451, 457, 459, 864
heedfulness *n* 864
heeding *n* 418; *adj* 928
heedless *adj* 460, 506, 863

heedlessness *n* 458, 460, 863
heel *n* 211; *v* 279
he him *n* 373
height *n* 206
height *n* 26, 125, 210, 307
heighten *v* 35, 206, 307, 549, 835
heightening *n* 835
heinous *adj* 846
heir *n* 167
heirs *n* 121, 167
helicopter *n* 273
hell *n* 982
hellish *adj* 978, 982
helmsman *n* 269, 694
help *n* 644, 662, 707, 746, 784, 834; *v* 215, 644, 707, 746, 784, 834
helper *n* 707, 711, 746, 977
helpful *adj* 644, 707, 888
helpfulness *n* 644, 910
helpless *adj* 158
helplessness *n* 158
help onself to *v* 789
helter skelter *adv* 59
hem *n* 231; *v* 43, 231, 258
hem and haw *v* 149, 583
hemi- *adj* 91
hem in *v* 227
hemisphere *n* 181
hemorrhage *n* 299
hen *n* 374
hence *adv* 155
henceforth *adv* 121
henchman *n* 746
her *n* 374
herald *n* 64, 534; *v* 116, 280
herb *n* 367
herbaceous *adj* 367
herbage *n* 367
herbal *adj* 367, 369
Herculean *adj* 159
herculean *adj* 686
herculean task *n* 704
herd *n* 876; *v* 72
here *adv* 186
hereabouts *adv* 183
hereafter *n* 121, 152; *adv* 121
here and there *adv* 182, 183
here below *adv* 318
hereditary *adj* 5, 154
heredity *n* 167
heresy *n* 984
heretic *n* 487, 984
heretical *adj* 984

heretofore *adv* 122
herewith *adv* 88, 632
heritage *n* 11, 121, 122
hermetically sealed *adj* 261
hermit *n* 893, 955
hero *n* 948
heroic *adj* 861
heroism *n* 861
hero worship *n* 991
hesitancy *n* 485, 605
hesitant *adj* 485, 583, 603, 605
hesitate *v* 475, 485, 583, 603, 605
hesitating *adj* 485
hesitation *n* 485, 583, 603, 605
heterodox *adj* 984
heterodoxy *n* 984
heterogeneity *n* 10, 16a, 291
heterogeneous *adj* 10, 15, 41, 81
hew *v* 44, 240, 557
hiatus *n* 198
hiburnal *adj* 383
hidden *adj* 447, 526, 528, 533, 571
hidden meaning *n* 526
hide *n* 223; *v* 442, 447, 528, 862, 893
hideous *adj* 830, 846
hiding *n* 528, 893
hiding place *n* 189, 530, 666
hie *v* 264, 274
hierarchical *adj* 995
hierarchy *n* 995
hieroglyph *n* 561
high *adj* 206, 410, 838, 959
high birth *n* 875
high-born *adj* 875
high caliber *n* 33
higher *adj* 33
highest *adj* 210
high-flown *adj* 577
high living *n* 954
highly seasoned *adj* 392
high-minded *adj* 878
highmindedness *n* 875
high note *n* 409
high price *n* 814
high-principled *adj* 939
high relief *n* 250
high seas *n* 341
high sounding *adj* 577, 882
high spirits *n* 836
high-strung *adj* 825
high time *n* 134
hike *n* 266
hill *n* 217, 250, 305,

306
hinder v 179, 233, 261, 275, 647, 704, 706, 708, 751, 761
hindmost adj 235
hindquarters n 235
hindrance n 706
hindrance n 177, 179
hinge n 43, 153
hinge upon v 154
hint n 505, 527, 550; v 505, 527
hinterland n 235
hip adj 563
hire n 812; v 788
hirsute adj 256
hiss v 409, 412
hissing n 409; adj 409
historian n 553
historiographer n 553
history n 122, 551
histrionic adj 599
hit n 276
hitch n 706; v 43, 315
hither adv 278
hitherto adv 122
hit on v 612
hit the bottle v 959
hit the road v 264, 266
hit upon v 480a
hive n 189, 691
hoard n 636
hoard away v 636
hoarse adj 405, 410
hoarseness n 405
hoary adj 124, 432
hoax n 545
hobble n 706; v 275
hobgoblin n 980
hobo n 268
hocus-pocus n 993
hodgepodge n 59
hoe v 371
hog n 957; v 957
hoist v 307
hold n 215; v 46, 54, 142, 151, 215, 265, 484, 751, 777, 781, 873
hold a conversation v 588
hold a course for v 278
hold back v 616, 623, 636, 819
holder n 191, 779
hold fast v 781
hold forth v 537
hold in disrespect v 929
holding n 777, 781
holding back n 603
hold on v 143
hold one's tongue v 403, 585
hold out v 763
hold to v 602

hold up v 143, 215, 235, 707
hole n 182, 189, 260, 351, 530
hole puncher n 262
holiday n 685, 687
holiness n 987
holler v 404, 411
hollow n 208, 252; v 208, 252; adj 4, 252, 880
hollowed out adj 252
hollowness n 4, 880
hollows n 221
holm n 346
holocaust n 361
holy adj 976, 987
homage n 743, 926, 928, 990
home n 189; adj 221
homeless adj 185
homeliness n 576, 846, 849
homely adj 576, 846, 849, 876
homespun adj 329, 576
homestead n 189
homework n 673
homey adj 576
homicidal adj 361
homicide n 361
homily n 537
homogeneity n 9, 16, 42
homogeneous adj 16, 42
honest adj 246, 543, 703, 922, 939, 946, 960
honesty n 543, 703, 939, 946, 960
honey n 899
honeyed adj 396
honey-mouthed adj 933
honor n 733, 873, 877, 922, 928, 990; v 883, 928, 931
honorable adj 246, 543, 772, 875, 878, 939
honored adj 873
honorific adj 883, 990
honoring adj 990
hoodwink v 442, 545
hook n 245; v 43, 789
hooked adj 244, 245
hoop n 247; v 411
hoot v 411
hop n 309; v 309
hope n 858
hope n 507; v 858
hope for v 507, 858
hopeful adj 472, 858
hopeless adj 645, 704, 859
hopelessness n 859

hopelessness n 471, 645, 837
horde n 72
horizon n 196, 213
horizontal adj 213, 251, 308
horizontality n 213
horizontally adv 213
horrible adj 649, 830
horribly adv 31
horrid adj 649, 830
horrified adj 860
horrify v 830
horrifying adj 982
horror n 860, 867, 898
horror-stricken adj 860
horseback riding n 266
horseman n 268
horsemanship n 266
horse-shoe n 245
horsewoman n 268
horticultural adj 369
horticulture n 371
hose n 348, 350
hospitable adj 816, 892
hospitality n 816
host n 72, 102
hostile adj 14, 24, 383, 708, 889, 907
hostilities n 173, 722
hostility n 708, 889
hot adj 382, 392, 434, 824
hot air n 517
hotchpotch n 41
hotheaded adj 825
hotness n 392
hot pink adj 434
hot-tempered adj 901
hourly adv 136
house v 184, 664
housebreak v 370
house-breaker n 792
housebroken adj 370
house of correction n 975
house of god n 1000
housing n 189
hover v 152, 206, 305
hover about v 264
hover around v 264
how adv 627
howbeit adv 30
however adv 30
howl n 411, 839; v 411, 412
howling n 412
hub n 222
hubbub n 315, 404, 411
huckster n 797
huddle v 72
hue n 428
hue and cry n 411, 669
hueless adj 429
hug n 902; v 46

huge *adj* 31, 192, 206
hugeness *n* 192
hulky *adj* 192
hullabaloo *n* 411
hum *n* 405; *v* 405, 407, 412
human *adj* 372
human being *n* 372
human community *n* 372
humane *adj* 906
humaneness *n* 910
humanitarian *n* 910; *adj* 372, 910
humanitarianism *n* 910
humanities *n* 560
humanity *n* 372, 906
humankind *n* 372
human race *n* 372
human species *n* 372
humble *adj* 34, 725, 879, 881, 987
humbleness *n* 879
humbly *adv* 881
humbug *n* 548
humdrum *adj* 275, 598, 841
humid *adj* 337, 339
humidity *n* 339
humiliate *v* 879
humility *n* 879
humility *n* 881, 987
hummocky *adj* 250
humor *n* 5, 176, 602, 608, 820, 842; *v* 707, 760
humorist *n* 844
humorous *adj* 842
hump *n* 250
hunch *n* 250, 477
hundred *n* 98
hunger *n* 865
hungry *adj* 865, 956
hunt *v* 361
hunting *n* 361
hurdle *v* 309
hurl *v* 284
hurly-burly *n* 315
hurrah *v* 838
hurricane *n* 349
hurried *adj* 684, 825
hurry *n* 684; *v* 132, 274, 310, 684
hurt *n* 378, 619; *v* 378, 619, 649, 659, 828, 830
hurtful *adj* 619, 649, 830
hurtfulness *n* 649
hurtle *v* 276, 309
hurtle over *v* 310
husband *n* 903; *v* 636, 670, 817
husbandry *n* 371, 817

hush *n* 403; *v* 174, 265, 403
hushed *adj* 403
husky *adj* 405
hussy *n* 962
hustle *n* 682; *v* 276, 315, 682
hybrid *n* 41; *adj* 41
hydrous *adj* 337
hygienic *adj* 656
hyperbola *n* 245
hyperbole *n* 549
hyperbolic *adj* 549
hypercritical *adj* 868
hypercriticism *n* 868
hypertension *n* 315
hypocrisy *n* 988
hypocrite *n* 548, 988
hypocritical *adj* 544
hypothesis *n* 514
hypothetical *adj* 514
hysterical *adj* 173, 824, 825

I

ice *v* 385
ice box *n* 387
ice chest *n* 387
ice house *n* 387
iciness *n* 383
icing *n* 385
icon *n* 991
iconoclasm *n* 984
iconoclast *n* 165
iconoclastic *adj* 984
icthyology *n* 368
icy *adj* 383
idea *n* 453
idea *n* 451, 515, 516
ideal *n* 650; *adj* 2, 515, 977
ideality *n* 515
idealize *v* 515
ideational *adj* 453
idée fixe *n* 606
identical *adj* 13, 17
identically *adv* 13
identity *n* 13
identity *n* 17, 27
idiocy *n* 499
idiom *n* 521, 566
idiomatic *adj* 79, 521
idiosyncracy *n* 820
idiosyncrasies *n* 5
idiosyncrasy *n* 79, 83, 176
idiosyncratic *adj* 5
idiot *n* 493, 501, 501
idiotic *adj* 499
idle *v* 683; *adj* 681, 683
idleness *n* 681, 683
idler *n* 683
idle talk *n* 588
idol *n* 897, 899, 991
idolatrize *v* 991
idolatrous *adj* 991

idolatrousness *n* 991
idolatry *n* 991
idolatry *n* 897, 990
idolism *n* 991
idolization *n* 991
idolize *v* 897, 990, 991
idolizing *n* 990
idol-worship *n* 991
idol-worshiping *adj* 991
if *adv* 8
iffy *adj* 156
if it so happen *adv* 8
if so *adv* 8
if worst comes to worst *adv* 735
ignite *v* 384
ignoble *adj* 207, 851, 876
ignominious *adj* 874
ignominy *n* 874
ignoramus *n* 493
ignoramus *n* 501
ignorance *n* 491
ignorance *n* 442
ignorant *adj* 435, 442, 491
ignore *v* 460, 773
ill *n* 619; *adj* 649, 655
ill-advised *adj* 499
ill-behaved *adj* 895
ill-bred *adj* 851, 895
ill-breeding *n* 851, 895
ill-conceived *adj* 499
illegal *adj* 964
illegality *n* 964
illegitimacy *n* 925, 964
illegitimate *adj* 925, 964
ill-fashioned *adj* 243
ill-flavored *adj* 395
ill health *n* 655
ill-humored *adj* 901a
illiberal *adj* 32, 943
illiberality *n* 819, 943
illicit *adj* 964
illicitness *n* 964
illiteracy *n* 491
illiterate *n* 493; *adj* 491
ill-judged *adj* 499
ill-judging *adj* 481
ill-made *adj* 243
ill-mannered *adj* 851, 895
ill-natured *adj* 907
illness *n* 655
illogical *adj* 47, 477
illogically *adv* 477
ill-proportioned *adj* 243
ill-qualified *adj* 699
ill repute *n* 874
ill-tempered *adj* 945
ill-timed *adj* 135
ill-treat *v* 739
ill-treatment *n* 649

illuminate v 420, 423, 428

illumination n 420

illumine v 420

ill-use v 649

illusion n 4, 443, 515, 545

illusory adj 4, 515, 545

illustrate v 82, 554

illustration n 82, 554

illustrative adj 82, 518, 554

illustrious adj 883

ill will n 889, 907

ill wind n 649

image n 17, 21, 448, 521, 556, 991; v 521

imagery n 521, 554

imaginable adj 470, 515

imaginary adj 4, 979

imagination n 515

imaginative adj 2, 515

imaginativeness n 515

imaginative writing n 598

imagine v 515

imagined adj 515

imagistic adj 521

imbalance n 15, 28, 503

imbalanced adj 28

imbecile n 493, 501; adj 499

imbecilic adj 499

imbecility n 499

imbecility n 450a, 497, 499

imbibe v 296, 959

imbibition n 298

imbue v 41, 300, 537

imbued adj 820

imitate v 19, 680, 788

imitation n 19

imitation n 21, 554, 556; adj 19

imitative adj 17, 19, 554

immaculate adj 650, 652, 946, 960

immaterial adj 4, 317, 643

immateriality n 317

immateriality n 643

immature adj 53, 123, 127, 435, 651, 674

immaturity n 53, 123, 651

immeasurability n 105

immeasurably adv 31

immediate adj 132

immediately adv 113, 132

immemorial adj 124

immense adj 31, 104, 192

immensity n 31, 192

immerse v 300, 310, 337

immersed in adj 229

immersion n 300, 310

immigrant n 268

immigrate v 266

immigration n 266

imminent adj 152, 286

immobile adj 172

immobility n 141, 150, 172, 265

immobilize v 265

immoderately adv 31

immodest adj 961

immodesty n 961

immoral adj 923, 940, 945

immorality n 923, 940, 945

immortal adj 112

immortalize v 112

immovability n 141, 150, 606

immovable adj 150, 606

immune adj 748, 927a

immune from adj 777a

immunity n 748, 777a, 927a, 970

immutability n 141, 150

immutable adj 110, 150

imp n 980

impact n 276, 379

impair v 659, 848

impairment n 638, 659

impale v 260

impart v 784

impartial adj 246, 628, 942

impartiality n 942

impart to v 527

impassable adj 261

impasse n 151

impassionate adj 383

impassioned adj 574, 821, 825, 991

impassive adj 456, 823

impassivity n 823, 826

impatience n 825

impatient adj 825, 841

impeach v 938, 969

impeachment n 938

impeccability n 650

impeccable adj 650, 946

impede v 179, 275, 706

impediment n 177, 706

impeding n 706

impel v 175, 264, 276, 284, 744

impend v 121, 152, 909

impending adj 121, 152, 286, 507, 909

impenetrability n 321, 571

impenetrable adj 261, 321, 323, 519, 571

impenetrable to light adj 426

impenitence n 951

impenitent adj 951

imperative adj 737, 926

imperceptibility n 447

imperceptible adj 193, 447

imperceptibly adv 32

imperfect adj 34, 53, 304, 640, 651, 659, 848, 961

imperfection n 651

imperfection n 28, 34, 53, 304, 640, 945, 961

imperfectly adv 32

imperil v 665

imperishable adj 112

impermanence n 111

impermanent adj 111

impermeability n 321

impermeable adj 261, 321

impersonate v 19

impersonation n 19, 599

impertinence n 885, 929

impertinent adj 885, 929

imperturbability n 826

imperturbable n 823; adj 383, 826

impervious adj 261

impervious to light adj 426

impetuosity n 173, 825, 863

impetuous adj 173, 825, 863

impetus n 276, 284

impiety n 988

impiety n 989

impish adj 980

implacable adj 914a, 919

implant v 300

implantation n 300

implanted adj 5

implausibility n 473

implausible adj 473

implement n 633

implicit adj 526

implied adj 526

implore v 765

implosion n 276

imply v 467, 472, 516

impolite adj 895, 929

impoliteness n 929

import n 516, 642; v

296, 516, 642
importance n 642
importance n 31, 62, 175
important adj 31, 33, 175, 642
importation n 296, 300
importunate adj 765
importune v 765
impose v 741
imposing adj 642, 875, 878
impossibility n 471
impossible adj 471, 704
imposter n 548
imposture n 545
impotence n 158
impotence n 160, 169, 175a
impotent adj 158, 160, 175a
impractical adj 471, 647, 704
impracticality n 471, 647
imprecate v 908
imprecation n 908
impregnability n 664
impregnable adj 159, 664
impregnate v 168, 300
impress v 175, 375, 824
impressibility n 375, 822
impressible adj 324
impression n 375, 453, 591, 821
impressionable adj 822
impressive adj 574, 642
imprint n 569
imprison v 229
imprisoned adj 229, 751
improbability n 473
improbable adj 473
improbity n 940
impromptu adj 612; adv 612
improper adj 499, 568, 647, 923, 945
improper time n 135
impropriety n 568, 579, 647, 925
improve v 282, 648, 658
improved adj 658
improvement n 658
improvement n 282, 618
improvidence n 674
improvident adj 674, 818
improving adj 658

improvisation n 612
improvise v 416, 612, 674
imprudence n 863
imprudent adj 452, 460, 863
impudence n 885, 895, 929
impudent adj 885, 929
impugn v 716
impulse n 276, 612
impulse n 284, 601, 615, 744
impulsion n 284
impulsive adj 149, 612, 825, 863
impulsively adv 612
impulsiveness n 863
impunity n 777a, 927a, 970
impure adj 653, 961
impurity n 961
impurity n 653
imputation n 155, 938
imputative adj 938
impute v 938
impute to v 155
in a bad way adj 659, 735
in abeyance adv 172
inability n 158, 699
in a body adv 50
inabstinence n 954
inaccessible adj 196
in accord adj 714
in accordance with adj 23; adv 82
inaccuracy n 544
inaccurate adj 495, 568, 923
in a column adv 69
inaction n 681
inaction n 623, 683; adj 170, 680
inactive adj 172, 265, 681, 683
inactivity n 683
inactivity n 172, 681
in addition adv 37
inadequacy n 28, 34, 640, 645, 651
inadequate adj 28, 158, 540. 651
inadmissible adj 55
in advance adv 62, 234, 280
in adverse circumstances adj 735
in a fair way to adj 176
in a great measure adv 31
in a jiffy adv 113
in a line adj 69
in all aspects adv 52
in all creation adv 318

in all likelihood adv 472
in all probability adv 472
in a moment adv 113
in and out adv 248, 314
inane adj 497
inanimate adj 358
inanimate matter n 358
inanity n 4, 450a, 497, 517
in anticipation adv 132
inapplicable adj 10
inappreciable adj 32
inappropriateness n 647
inapt adj 699
inaptitude n 645
in a roundabout way adv 629
in arrear adj 806
inarticulate adj 583
inarticulateness n 583
inattention n 458
inattention n 452, 460, 866
inattentive adj 419, 452, 458, 460, 823, 866
inattentiveness n 458
inaudibility n 405, 419
inaudible adj 405
inaugural adj 66
inaugurate v 66
inauguration n 66
inauspicious adj 135, 909
in bad health adj 655
in bad taste adj 851
inbeing n 5
in black and white adj 531, 590
inborn adj 5, 221, 820
inbound adj 294
inbred adj 5
in broad daylight adv 525
incalculable adj 104
incalculably adv 31
incandescent adj 382
incantation n 993
incantory adj 992
incapability n 158
incapable adj 158
incapacitate v 158
incapacitated adj 158
incapacity n 158, 499
incarcerate v 972
incarceration n 974
incase v 229; adv 8
in celebration of adv 883
incendiary adj 162

incentive *n* 615
incertitude *n* 475
incessant *adj* 104, 112, 136
incessantly *adv* 136
inch *v* 275
in chains *adj* 754
inch by inch *adv* 26, 275
incident *n* 151
incidental *adj* 6, 8, 10, 177
incidentally *adv* 10
incineration *n* 384
incipient *adj* 66
in circulation *adj* 531, 532
incise *v* 259, 558
incising *n* 558
incision *n* 44, 259
incisive *adj* 171, 416, 574
incite *v* 173, 175, 615
incitement *n* 615
incivility *n* 929
incivism *n* 911
inclination *n* 176, 217, 278, 288, 306, 600, 602
incline *n* 217; *v* 176, 217, 278, 602, 615
inclined *adj* 217, 820
inclose *v* 76, 221, 227, 229
include *v* 54, 76
including *adj* 76
inclusion *n* 76
inclusion *n* 54
inclusive *adj* 56, 76
incogitancy *n* 452
incoherence *n* 47
incoherence *n* 503
in cold blood *adv* 823
incombustible *adj* 385
income *n* 775, 803
in comfort *adv* 377
incoming *adj* 294
in commemoration of *adv* 883
incommunicable *adj* 519
in communication with *adj* 592
in company with *adv* 88
incomparable *adj* 33
incomparably *adv* 31
incompatible *adj* 24
incompetence *n* 158, 499, 640, 699
incompetent *adj* 158, 640, 699
incomplete *adj* 53, 304, 640, 651, 674, 730
incompletely *adv* 53
incompleteness *n* 53

incompleteness *n* 304, 640, 730
in compliance with *adv* 743
incomprehensibility *n* 519
incomprehensible *adj* 104, 519
incomprehension *n* 491
inconceivable *adj* 471
in concert with *adj* 178; *adv* 714
in conflict with *adv* 708
in conformity with *adv* 82
incongruity *n* 24, 47, 83
incongruous *adj* 24, 47, 83, 497
in conjunction with *adv* 37, 43
in connection with *adv* 9
inconsequence *n* 10
inconsequential *adj* 32, 477, 643
inconsequentiality *n* 32
inconsiderable *adj* 32, 643
inconsiderate *adj* 452, 460
inconsideration *n* 458
inconsistency *n* 15, 16a, 47, 83, 497, 568
inconsistent *adj* 14, 16a, 47, 83, 568, 608
inconsistent with *adj* 24
inconspicuous *adj* 447
inconstancy *n* 149
inconstant *adj* 149
in contact *adj* 199
incontestable *adj* 159, 474
incontinence *n* 961
incontinent *adj* 961
incontrovertible *adj* 474
inconvenience *n* 647
inconvenient *adj* 647
in convulsions *adv* 315
incorporate *v* 48, 76
incorporating *adj* 76
incorporation *n* 48, 54, 76
incorporeal *adj* 4, 317
incorporeality *n* 317
incorrect *adj* 477, 495, 544, 568, 923
incorrigible *adj* 606
in course of time *adv* 121
increase *n* 35
increase *n* 37, 194, 282,

658; *v* 31, 35, 37, 194, 282, 367, 658, 835
increasing *adj* 35
incredible *adj* 471
incredibly *adv* 31
incredulity *n* 487
incredulity *n* 485, 989
incredulous *adj* 485, 487, 989
incredulousness *n* 487
increment *n* 35, 37, 39, 194
incremental *adj* 35
incriminate *v* 938
incrimination *n* 938
incriminatory *adj* 938
incrust *v* 224
incubus *n* 980
inculcate *v* 537
inculpate *v* 938
inculpation *n* 938
incumbent *adj* 926
incur *v* 177
incurable *adj* 5, 859
incur a loss *v* 776
incuriosity *n* 456
incurious *adj* 456
incuriousness *n* 456
incursion *n* 294, 716
incurvature *n* 245
incurved *adj* 252
in custody *adj* 754
in danger of *adj* 177
in debt *adj* 806, 808
indebted *adj* 916
indebtedness *n* 177, 916
indecency *n* 961
indecent *adj* 961
indecipherable *adj* 519
indecision *n* 149, 605, 609a
indecisive *adj* 149, 605, 609a
indecisiveness *n* 172
indeed *adv* 31
indefatigability *n* 604a
indefatigable *adj* 604a
in defiance of *adv* 708
indefinite *adj* 447, 475, 571
indefinitely *adv* 31
indefiniteness *n* 447, 571
indelible *adj* 505
indelicacy *n* 961
indelicate *adj* 961
indemnification *n* 30
indemnify *v* 30
indemnity *n* 30
indent *v* 257
indentation *n* 252, 257
indented *adj* 252
independence *n* 10, 748, 803

independent *adj* 10, 748

in despair *adj* 828

in detail *adv* 51, 79

indeterminate *adj* 156, 475, 520, 605

indeterminateness *n* 520

indetermination *n* 605

index *n* 86, 550; *v* 60, 562

indicate *v* 467, 516, 525, 550, 909

indication *n* 550

indication *n* 467, 525, 909

indicative *adj* 467, 550

indicator *n* 550

indicatory *adj* 550

indict *v* 938, 969

indictment *n* 938

indifference *n* 866

indifference *n* 456, 603, 609a, 643, 736, 989

indifferent *adj* 34, 383, 456, 460, 603, 609a, 651, 736, 823, 866, 989

indigence *n* 804

indigenous *adj* 5, 188

indigent *adj* 804

indignant *adj* 900

indignation *n* 900

indirect *adj* 279, 629

indirectly *adv* 629

indiscreet *adj* 684, 863

indiscretion *n* 699, 863

indiscriminate *adj* 41, 59, 81, 465a

indiscrimination *n* 465a

in disguise *adj* 528

indispensable *adj* 630

indispose *v* 616

indisposed *adj* 655

indisposition *n* 603, 655

indisputable *adj* 474

in disrepair *adj* 674

indissoluble *adj* 43, 50, 321

indistinct *adj* 405, 447, 475

indistinction *n* 465a

indistinctness *n* 447, 465a, 571

indistinguishable *adj* 13, 447

individual *n* 372; *adj* 79, 87, 372

individuality *n* 79, 83, 87

individualize *v* 79

indivisibility *n* 50

indivisible *adj* 50, 321

indoctrinate *v* 537

indolence *n* 172, 275, 683

indolent *adj* 275, 683

indomitable *adj* 159, 604, 604a, 719

indoors *adv* 221

in dribs and drabs *adv* 51

in drips and snatches *adv* 51

indubitable *adj* 474

induce *v* 153, 161, 175, 476, 615

inducement *n* 615

induct *v* 296, 755

induction *n* 296, 476

inductive *adj* 476

in due course *adv* 109

in due season *adv* 109

in due time *adv* 106, 109, 134

indulge *v* 740, 760, 954

indulge in *v* 827

indulgence *n* 740, 760, 918, 954

indulgent *adj* 740, 760, 954

induration *n* 323

industrious *adj* 539, 682

industry *n* 682

in earnest *adv* 604

inebriate *n* 959

inebriated *adj* 959

inebriety *n* 959

in ecstasy *adv* 377

inedible *adj* 395

ineffability *n* 317

ineffable *adj* 2, 317, 519

in effect *adv* 5

ineffective *adj* 158

ineffectual *adj* 158, 645, 732

inefficacy *n* 158, 645

inefficiency *n* 158, 645

inefficient *adj* 158, 732

inelastic *adj* 326

inelasticity *n* 326

inelegance *n* 579

inelegance *n* 846

inelegant *adj* 579

ineluctable *adj* 601, 744

inept *adj* 158, 499, 699

ineptitude *n* 158, 499, 645, 699

inequality *n* 28

inequality *n* 15, 24

inequity *n* 15, 24, 923

ineradicable *adj* 5

in error *adj* 481, 495

inert *adj* 172, 683

inertia *n* 172

inertness *n* 172

inertness *n* 683

inescapable *adj* 246, 744

inestimable *adj* 648

in every respect *adv* 52

inevitability *n* 474, 601

inevitable *adj* 474, 601

inevitableness *n* 601

inexact *adj* 571

inexactness *n* 495, 571

in exchange *adv* 148

inexcitability *n* 826

inexcitability *n* 172

inexcitable *adj* 826

inexhaustibility *n* 105

inexhaustible *adj* 104

inexistence *n* 2

inexistent *adj* 2

inexorable *adj* 601, 739, 744, 914a

inexpedience *n* 647

inexpediency *n* 647

inexpedient *adj* 499, 647

inexpensive *adj* 815

inexperience *n* 491, 703

inexperienced *adj* 435

inexpert *adj* 699

inexpertness *n* 699

in explanation *adv* 522

inexplicable *adj* 519

inexposure *n* 703

inexpressible *adj* 519

inexpressive *adj* 517

inextension *n* 180a

inextinguishable *adj* 159

inextravagant *adj* 881

inextricable *adj* 46

in fact *adv* 1

infallibility *n* 474

infallible *adj* 474

infamous *adj* 874

infamy *n* 874

infancy *n* 127

infant *n* 129

infant *n* 129

infanticide *n* 361

infantile *adj* 129, 499

infantlike *adj* 129

infatuated *adj* 486

infatuation *n* 486, 606

in fault *adj* 947

in favour *adj* 931

infect *v* 659, 824

infection *n* 824

infelicitous *adj* 828

infer *v* 476

inference *n* 65, 476, 480

inferential *adj* 467, 476

inferior *adj* 28, 34, 651, 736

inferiority *n* 34

inferiority *n* 28, 736

infernal *adj* 649, 978, 982

inferno *n* 982

infertile *adj* 169

infertility *n* 169

infidel *n* 989

infidelity *n* 989

infiltrate *v* 41, 294

infiltration *n* 41, 294, 302

infinite *adj* 31, 102, 104, 180

infinitely *adv* 31, 104

infiniteness *n* 105

infinitesimal *adj* 32, 193

infinitude *n* 105

infinity *n* 105

infinity *n* 112, 180

infirm *adj* 158, 160, 655

infirmity *n* 158, 160, 655

in fits *adv* 315

inflame *v* 171, 173, 384, 824

inflamed *adj* 434

in flames *adj* 382

inflammable *adj* 385

inflate *v* 194, 322, 349, 573, 880

inflated *adj* 482, 577, 880

inflation *n* 322, 577

inflect *v* 245

inflection *n* 567

inflexibility *n* 141, 246, 323, 606

inflexible *adj* 323, 604, 606

inflict *v* 680, 739

inflict pain *v* 378

inflict punishment *v* 972

in flight *adj* 267

influence *n* 175

influence *n* 153, 170, 615, 737; *v* 62, 153, 170, 176, 615

influential *adj* 157, 175, 176, 737

influx *n* 294

in force *adj* 170

inform *v* 527, 537, 668

informality *n* 83

informant *n* 527, 534

information *n* 527

information *n* 467, 490, 498, 532

informed *adj* 527

informer *n* 527, 532, 938

infraction *n* 83, 303, 742, 773, 927

infrequency *n* 137

infrequency *n* 103

infrequent *adj* 103, 137

infrequently *adv* 137

infringe *v* 303, 742, 773

infringement *n* 303

infringement *n* 83, 742, 773

in front *adv* 234, 280

in front of one's nose *adj* 446

in full sight *adj* 446

in full view *adj* 446

infuriate *v* 173

infuse *v* 41, 300, 537

infusion *n* 41, 300

ingathering *n* 72

ingenious *adj* 698, 702

ingenuity *n* 698

ingenuous *adj* 703, 946

ingenuousness *n* 946

ingest *v* 296, 539

ingestion *n* 296, 298

in good taste *adj* 850

in good time *adv* 152

ingraft *v* 300

ingrained *adj* 5, 221, 820

ingrate *n* 917

ingratitude *n* 917

ingredient *n* 51, 56, 211

ingress *n* 294

ingress *n* 302

inhabit *v* 184, 186, 188, 189

inhabitant *n* 188

inhabiting *adj* 186

inhale *v* 398

in hand *adj* 777

inharmonious *adj* 24, 414

inharmoniousness *n* 414

in harmony with *adj* 23

in harness *adj* 749

in health *adj* 654

inherence *n* 5

inherent *adj* 5, 221

inherited *adj* 5

in hiding *adj* 528

in high esteem *adj* 931

in honor of *adv* 883

inhumation *n* 363

inimical *adj* 708, 889

inimitable *adj* 20, 33, 648, 650

iniquitous *adj* 923, 945

iniquity *n* 923, 945

initial *adj* 66

initiate *v* 66, 296

initiation *n* 66, 296

initiative *n* 66

in its infancy *adv* 66

in its own sweet time *adv* 152

in its turn *adv* 58

inject *v* 300

injection *n* 296, 300

injudicious *adj* 499

injunction *n* 630, 695, 741, 761, 864

injur *v* 848

injure *v* 619, 649, 659, 828, 923

injured *adj* 659, 848

injurious *adj* 619, 649

injury *n* 173, 619, 649, 659, 665, 776

injustice *n* 173, 923

ink *n* 431

in keeping with *adj* 23; *adv* 82

inkling *n* 514, 527

inky *adj* 431

inlaid *adj* 221, 440

inlands *n* 342

inlay *v* 440

in league *adj* 709

inlet *n* 260, 343

in lieu of *adv* 147

inmate *n* 188

in moderation *adv* 174

inmost *adj* 221

in motion *adj* 264

in mourning *adj* 839

innate *adj* 5, 221

inner *adj* 221

inner coating *n* 224

inner man *n* 820

innermost *adj* 221

innermost recesses *n* 221

inner part *n* 221

innocence *n* 946

innocence *n* 703, 944, 960

innocent *adj* 435, 703, 946, 960

in no respect *adv* 32

in no time *adv* 113

innovate *v* 140

innovation *n* 20a, 123, 140

innovative *adj* 140

innuendo *n* 527

in obedience to *adv* 743

inoculate *v* 300

inoculation *n* 300

inodorousness *n* 399

in one's birthday suit *adj* 226

in one's debt *adj* 916

in operation *adj* 170, 680

inoperative *adj* 158, 645

inopportune *adj* 135, 647

inopportuneness *n* 135

in opposition *adj* 708

in order adj 58; adv 58
inordinate adj 31, 641, 954
inordinately adv 31
inordinateness n 954
inorganic adj 358
inorganic matter n 358
in part adv 32, 51
in particular adv 79
in perfect condition adj 650
in place of adv 147
in plain English adv 576, 703
in plain sight adv 525
in plain terms adv 576
in play adj 170
in poor health adj 655
in possession of adj 777
in preparation adj 53
in presence of adv 186
in print adj 531, 532
in prison adj 754
in private adv 528
in progress adj 53
in prospect adj 121, 152, 620
in proximity adj 186
in pursuit of adj 622
input n 175
in question adv 454
in quest of adj 622
inquietude n 828
inquire v 461
inquirer n 461
inquiring n 461; adj 455, 461
inquiring mind n 455
inquiry n 461
inquiry n 539
inquisitive adj 455, 461
inquisitiveness n 455
inquisitor n 461, 739
inquisitorial adj 461, 739, 965
in rapport adj 413
in readiness adj 507
in reality adv 1
in relief adj 250
in reserve adj 636
in retaliation adv 718
inroad n 294
in rotation adv 138
insalubrious adj 657
insalubrity n 657
insane adj 173, 503
insanity n 503
inscrutable adj 519
in secret adj 528; adv 528
insect n 366
insecure adj 475, 665
insecurity n 475, 665
insensate adj 499

insensibility n 376, 823
insensibility n 866
insensible adj 376, 381, 506
insensitive adj 376, 823, 866
insensitiveness n 823, 866
inseparability n 46
inseparable adj 43, 46
insert v 221, 228, 300
insertion n 300
insertion n 37, 228, 294, 296
in short adv 572
inside n 221; adj 221
inside out adj 218
insidious adj 545, 702
insight n 477, 498; adj 507
insightful adj 842
insigne n 550
insignificance n 32, 643, 736
insignificant adj 4, 32, 517, 643, 736
in simple words adv 703
insincere adj 544
insincerity n 544
insinuate v 527
insinuate oneself v 294
insinuation n 228, 294, 300, 527
insipid adj 337, 391, 575
insipidity n 391
insist upon v 604, 770
in snatches adv 70
insobriety n 959
insolence n 885
insolence n 715, 878
insolent adj 715, 885
insoluble adj 321, 519
insolvency n 732, 808
insolvent adj 804
in some degree adv 26
in some place adv 182
inspect v 441
inspector n 694; 461
inspiration n 477, 515, 612, 824
inspire v 615, 824
inspiring adj 836
inspirit v 836
inspiriting adj 858
in spite adv 708
in spite of prep 179
instability n 149, 475, 605, 665
install v 184, 755
installation n 184
installment n 807
instance n 82
instant n 113; adj 113, 118, 630

instantaneous adj 111, 113, 132
instantaneously adv 113, 132
instantaneousness n 113
instead adv 147
instigate v 615
instigation n 170, 615
instill v 41, 300, 537
instinct n 477, 601
instinctive adj 5, 477, 601
instinctual adj 5, 477
in stir adj 754
institute n 542; v 153, 161
in store adj 152, 636
instruct v 537, 693, 695, 741
instructed adj 490
instruction n 537, 693, 695, 697, 741
instructive adj 537, 985
instructor n 540
instrument n 633
instrument adj 415
instrumental adj 176, 416, 631, 632, 633, 677
instrumentalist n 416
instrumentality n 631
instrumentality n 170
instrumental music n 415
insubordinate adj 715, 742
insubordination n 715, 742
insubstantiality n 2, 317
in succession adv 69
in such and such a place adv 183
in such wise adv 8
insufferable adj 830
insufficiency n 640
insufficiency n 53, 304, 651, 732
insufficient adj 28, 32, 304, 640, 651, 732
insufficiently adv 32
insular adj 10, 44, 87, 346
insularity n 44
insulate v 44, 87
insulation n 44
insult n 830; v 830, 929
insulting adj 885, 929
insurgence n 719
insurgent n 742; adj 742
insurrection n 719
insusceptibility n 376
in suspense adv 172

intact adj 50, 52, 141, 650, 670, 729
intactness n 52
intaglio n 22
intangible adj 2, 4, 317
in tears adj 828
integer n 84
integral adj 50
integral part n 56
integrate v 50
integrity n 50, 922, 939, 944
intellect n 450
intellect n 498, 842
intellectual n 492; adj 450, 498
intellectual giant n 872
intellectualize v 450
intelligence n 498
intelligence n 480, 498, 527, 532, 698, 842
intelligencer n 527, 534
intelligent adj 498, 698, 842
intelligibility n 518
intelligibility n 570
intelligible adj 518, 522, 570
intemperance n 954
intemperance n 959
intemperate adj 954
intend v 451, 516, 620
intense adj 51, 171, 382, 428
intensely adv 31
intensification n 835
intensified adj 835
intensify v 35, 171, 835
intensity n 26, 31, 171, 173, 382
intent n 451, 516, 600, 620
intention n 620
intention n 278, 451, 516, 611, 615
intentional adj 600, 620
intentionally adv 600, 611, 620
intentiveness n 457
intentness n 682
inter v 363
interact v 12
intercalation n 228
intercede v 724
intercession n 724, 766
interchange n 148
interchange n 12, 219, 783; v 12, 147, 148, 783
interchangeability n 148
interchangeable adj 12, 148, 794
intercourse n 148

interdepend v 12
interdependence n 12
interdict v 761
interdiction n 761
interest n 455, 618, 642, 707; v 288, 824, 829, 840
interested adj 455
interfere v 228, 708, 724
interference n 179, 228, 706, 719
interfere with v 179
interim n 106, 198
interior n 221, 342; adj 221
interiority n 221
interjacence n 228
interjacent adj 228
interject v 228
interjection n 228
interlace v 41, 43, 219
interlaced adj 219
interlard v 41
interlarding n 41
interlineation n 228
interlink v 219
interlocation n 228
interlocution n 588
interlude n 106, 198, 685
intermediary n 534, 631; adj 631
intermediate adj 29, 68, 631
intermedium n 631
interment n 363
interminable adj 104, 112, 200
intermission n 70, 106
intermittence n 138
intermittent adj 70, 138
intermittently adv 138
intern v 221
internal adj 5, 221
internally adv 221
interpenetrate v 228
interpenetration n 228
interpolate v 41, 228
interpolation n 41, 228, 300
interpose v 70, 228, 724
interposition n 37, 228, 724
interpret v 462, 522, 537
interpretable adj 522
interpretation n 522
interpretation n 155, 516
interpretative adj 522
interpreter n 524
interpreter n 513
interpretive adj 522

interregnum n 106, 142, 198
interrogate v 461
interrogation n 461
interrogative adj 461
interrupt v 70, 142, 198, 706
interrupted adj 70
interruption n 61, 70, 142, 198, 706
intersect v 219
intersection n 219
interspace n 198, 221
intersperse v 228
interspersion n 228
interstice n 198
intertwine v 41, 43, 219
intertwined adj 219
interval n 198
interval n 53, 70, 106, 196
intervene v 70, 198, 228, 631, 724
intervening adj 228
intervention n 228, 631, 724
interview n 588
interweave v 41, 43, 219
in the altogether adj 226
in the background adv 235
in the blood adj 5
in the bud adv 66
in the buff adj 226
in the cards adj 152
in the course of adv 106
in the course of things adv 151
in the event of adv 8
in the face of adv 715
in the first place adv 66
in the foreground adv 234
in the fourth place adv 96
in the genes adj 5
in the headlines adj 532
in the interim adv 106
in the lead adv 234
in the long run adv 29, 152
in the main adv 50
in the matter of adv 9
in the meantime adv 106
in the middle adv 68
in the midst of adv 41
in the news adj 532
in the nick of time adv

in the open air adv 338
in the open market adj
763
in the rear adv 235,
281
in the same category
adj 9
in the thick of adv 228
in the third place adv
93
in the vanguard adv
280
in the wide open
spaces adv 338
in the wind adj 152
intimacy n 888
intimate n 890; v 527;
adj 197, 221, 888
intimately adv 43
in time adv 109, 152
intimidate v 909
intimidating adj 909
intimidation n 909
intolerable adj 830
intolerance n 606, 825
intolerant adj 606, 825
intonation n 402, 580
intone v 580
in top shape adj 654
in touch with adj 592
in tow adj 285
intoxicate v 824
intoxicated adj 959
intoxication n 824, 959
intractability n 606
intractable adj 606,
704
in trade adj 794
intrepid adj 861
intrepidity n 861
intricate adj 248, 704
intrigue n 626, 702; v
702
intriguer 626
intrinsic adj 5, 221
intrinsicality n 5
intrinsically adv 5
in triumph adv 731
introduce v 62, 228,
280, 296, 300
introduction n 64, 66,
296, 300
introductory adj 62,
64, 66, 116
intrude v 135, 228, 294
intrusion n 57, 135,
228, 294
intrusive adj 228, 706
intuit v 477
intuition n 477
intuition n 477
intuitive adj 477
intuitively adv 477
in turn adv 58, 138

intwine v 219
in two shakes (of a
lamb's tail) adv 113
inundate v 337, 348,
641
inundation n 348
in unison adj 413
inure v 613
inutile adj 645
inutility n 645
invade v 294, 716
invader n 716
in vain adv 732
invalidate v 158, 479,
536, 756
invalidation n 479,·
536, 756
invaluable adj 648
invariability n 16, 141
invariable adj 5, 16,
110, 141, 150
invariably adv 16, 82
in various places adv
182
invasion n 294, 716
invent v 515, 626
invented adj 546
invention n 515, 546,
698
inventive adj 515, 698
inventiveness n 168,
698
inventor n 164
inventory n 86, 596,
811; v 596
inverse n 237; adj 218,
237
inversely adv 218
inversion n 218
inversion n 14, 140,
145
invert v 14, 61, 218
inverted adj 59, 218
invest v 157, 755, 784
invested adj 225
investigate v 461
investigation n 461,
463, 595
investigator n 461
investiture n 784
investment n 787
inveterate adj 124
invidious adj 830, 898
in view adj 507, 620
invigorate v 159, 171
invigorating adj 171,
656
invigoration n 159
invincible adj 159
inviolate adj 141
in violation adj 927
invisibility n 447
invisible adj 193, 447
invisibleness n 447
invite v 288, 615, 763,
829

invocation n 586
in vogue adj 852
invoice n 812
invoke v 72, 586, 990
involuntary adj 601
involution n 248, 571
involve v 516, 938
involved adj 59, 248,
571
invulnerability n 664
invulnerable adj 664
inward adj 221; adv
221
in what manner adv
627
in what way adv 627
in writing adj 590
iota n 32
irascibility n 901
irascible adj 382, 684,
901
irate adj 900
iridescence n 440
iridescent adj 420, 440
irk v 830
irksome adj 704, 830,
841
iron v 255
iron-gray adj 432
ironic adj 856
ironical adj 856
irons n 752
irony n 856
irradiate v 420
irrational adj 497, 499
irrationality n 499
irreclaimable adj 951
irreconcilability n 10
irreconcilable adj 24
irrecoverable adj 122
irrefutable adj 246,
474
irregular adj 16a, 59,
70, 81, 83, 139, 243,
256, 475
irregularity n 139
irregularity n 16a, 59,
83, 256, 475
irregularly adv 59, 139
irrelation n 10
irrelevancy n 175a
irrelevant adj 10
irreligion n 989
irreligion n 988
irreligious adj 989
irremediable adj 859
irrepentance n 951
irrepressible adj 173,
748, 825
irresistibility n 601
irresistible adj 159,
601, 744
irresolute adj 149, 485,
605, 607, 609a, 683
irresolution n 605

irresolution n 149, 172, 314, 485, 609a
irrespective adj 10
irresponsibility n 773
irresponsible adj 773
irretrievable adj 776
irreverence n 929, 988
irreverent adj 929
irrevocable adj 604
irrigate v 348
irrigation n 348
irritability n 825, 901
irritable adj 684, 825, 901
irritate v 173, 289, 688, 824, 828, 830
irritated adj 835
irritation n 824, 828, 835
irruption n 294
island n 346
isle n 346
islet n 346
isolate v 44, 79, 87, 893, 905
isolated adj 10, 44, 87, 893
isolation n 44, 893, 905
issuance n 531
issue n 154, 167, 295; v 73, 151, 295, 531, 591
issue from v 154
issues n 151
itch v 380
itching n 380; adj 380
itchy adj 380
items n 79
iterate v 104
iteration n 90, 104, 136
iterative adj 104
itinerant n 268; adj 266

J

jabber n 517, 584; v 517, 584
jackanapes n 854
jaded adj 961
jag v 257
jagged adj 244
jail n 752; v 972
jailbird n 754
jailer n 753; 975
jailhouse n 752
jangle v 410
jar n 315; v 24, 410, 414, 713
jargon n 497, 517, 560
jarring adj 410, 414
jaundice n 435, 436
jaundiced adj 435
jaunt n 266
jaw v 584
jazz n 415
jealous adj 435, 900,
920, 921
jealousy n 920
jealousy n 900, 921
jeapardize v 665
jeer v 929
jeer at v 856
jeers n 856
jeopardy n 665
jerk n 285, 315, 493; v 285, 315
jerky adj 315
jest v 842
jester n 501, 844
jesuitry n 477
jet n 273, 348; v 267, 348
jet-black adj 431
jet-setter n 268
jetting adj 267
jettison v 610
jetty n 250
jewel n 648, 899
jibe v 23
jilt v 509
jingle v 408
jinx n 621; n 993
job n 676
jocularity n 836
jog n 315; v 276
joggle v 315
jog on v 736
join v 37, 41, 43, 45, 72, 87, 88, 199, 290, 712
joined adj 43
join forces v 709
join hands with v 709
joining n 37, 43, 290
joint n 43; adj 43, 88, 178, 778
jointly adv 43
joint tenancy n 778
joke v 842
joker n 844
jolly adj 836, 840
jolt n 315; v 276, 315
jostle v 179, 276, 315
jot n 32
jounce v 315
journal n 114, 551
journalist n 553
journey n 266
journey n 302; v 266
journeyer n 268
journeying adj 266
jovial adj 840
joviality n 836
jowl n 236
joy n 377, 827; v 827
joyful adj 377, 827, 836
joyous adj 836
jubilant adj 838, 884
jubilation n 838
judge n 967
judge n 480, 737, 965; v 451, 480, 850, 965,
967

judgment n 480
judgment n 450, 451, 453, 465, 490, 498, 972
judgmental adj 480
judgment seat n 966
judicator n 965, 967
judicatory adj 967
judicature n 965
judicial adj 480, 965, 967
judiciary n 967
judicious adj 174, 480, 498, 868, 967
judiciousness n 174, 868
juice v 354
juiced adj 959
juiceless adj 340
juicer n 959
juicy adj 333, 337, 339
jumble n 41, 59; v 41, 59, 61
jumbo jet n 273
jump n 305, 309; v 309, 310
junction n 43
junction n 41, 45, 48
juncture n 8, 43, 134
jungle n 59
junior adj 127
juridical adj 967
jurisdiction n 965
jurisdiction n 737
jurisdictive adj 965, 967
jurist n 967
juristic adj 967
juror n 967
just adj 246, 922
just as adv 17
just do v 639
justice n 922, 967
justification n 717, 737, 937
justified adj 937
justify v 717, 737, 937
just in time adv 134
justly adv 922
just now adv 123
jut out v 250
juvenile adj 127
juvenility n 123, 127
juxtapose v 464

K

kaleidoscope n 445
kaleidoscopic adj 440
kaput adj 503
karma n 152
keen adj 171, 253, 375, 868
keen blast n 349
keenness n 868
keep n 298; v 141, 143, 670, 751, 781, 883

keep accounts v 811
keep alive v 359
keep an account with
  v 805
keep apart v 44
keep away v 187
keep back v 678
keep clear of v 623
keep cold v 385
keep company with v
  888
keep down v 751
keeper n 753
keep going v 143
keep hold v 150
keeping n 781
keeping out n 55
keeping secret n 528
keep in mind v 505
keep moving v 264,
  682
keep on v 136, 143,
  604a
keep on one's toes v
  264
keep out v 55
keep out of sight v 528
keep pace with v 27,
  120, 178
keep quiet v 265, 403,
  585
keep safe v 717
keepsake n 505
keep secret v 528
keep silence v 585
keep the memory alive
  v 505
keep the peace v 721
keep up v 141, 143,
  670
Kelly green adj 435
kelpie n 979
kempt adj 652
ken n 441
kernel n 68, 222
kerosene n 356, 388
kerosene lamp n 423
ketch n 273
key n 346, 428
keyhole n 260
khaki n 433; adj 433
kick n 276
kick up a row v 173
kid n 129
kill v 361
killer n 165
killing n 361
killing time n 681
kill time v 106, 683
kiln n 386
kind n 75, 569; adj 888,
  906
kind-hearted adj 888,
  906
kindheartedness n 906
kindle v 153, 171, 173,

384, 420, 824
kindliness n 897, 906
kindling n 388
kindly adj 888, 906
kindness n 897, 906
kindred n 11; adj 11
kinfolk n 11
kingdom of god n 981
kingdom of heaven n
  981
kinsman n 11
kiss n 902
kith and kin n 11
knack n 698
knave n 941
knead v 324, 379
kneading n 379
knee n 244
knee-deep adj 209
kneel n 308, 886, 990
knell n 363
knife n 262
knife edge n 253
knit v 43, 259
knob n 249, 250
knock n 276; v 276,
  406
knock down v 213
knot n 219, 321; v 219
knotted adj 59, 256
know v 474, 484, 490,
  527, 888
know how n 632
knowing adj 490
knowingly adv 620
knowledge v 490
knowledge n 498, 527,
  698
knowledgeable adj
  490, 698
known adj 490
know no bounds v 104
know-nothing n 493; v
  491
knuckle n 244
kobold n 980
kohl-black adj 431
Koran n 986

L

label n 564; v 550, 564
labor n 680, 686, 704;
  v 680, 686
laboratory n 691
labored adj 579
laborer n 746
laborious adj 686, 704
laboriousness n 682
labyrinth n 59, 248
labyrinthine adj 248
lace n 219; v 43
lack n 804; v 34, 53,
  304, 640, 804
lackadaisical adj 683
lack faith v 989
lacking adj 53, 187,
  304

lackluster adj 422, 429
  430
lack of adornment n
  849
lack of affectation n
  849
lack of bias n 942
lack of connection n
  10
lack of decorum n 851
lack of discernment n
  465a
lack of feeling n 376,
  381
lack of interest n 456
lack of originality n
  843
lack of practice n 614
lack of readiness n 603
lack of uniformity n
  16a
laconic adj 572
lacquer n 356a; v 356a
lad n 129
lade v 190
lading n 190
ladle v 270
lady n 374, 875
ladylove n 897
lag n 275, 281, 683
laggard n 683; adj 603,
  683
lagoon n 343
laical adj 997
laid low adj 160
laid up adj 655
laim v 158
lair n 189
laity n 997
lake n 343
lake n 343
lamb n 129
lame adj 53, 160, 651,
  655
lame excuse n 617
lament n 411, 839; v
  411, 833, 839, 915
lamentable adj 649,
  830, 833, 839
lamentably adv 31
lamentation n 839
lamentation n 833, 915
lamenting adj 839
lamp n 423
lampoon v 856
lampooner n 844
lance v 260
lancet n 262
land n 342
land n 780; v 292, 342
landed adj 342
landing n 292
lands n 342
landscape n 448; v 371
landscaping n 371
language n 560

languid *adj* 160, 172, 275, 405, 575, 683, 685
languish *v* 36, 160, 655, 683
languor *n* 160, 172, 275, 683, 688
lankness *n* 203
lanky *adj* 200, 203
lantern *n* 423
lap *n* 221, 311
lap of luxury *n* 377
lapse *n* 661, 776; *v* 109, 122, 144, 659, 661
lapsed *adj* 122
lard *n* 356
large *adj* 31, 192, 202
largeness *n* 192
larger *adj* 194
largesse *n* 784
lash *n* 975; *v* 43, 173, 972
lass *n* 129
lassitude *n* 688, 841
last *v* 1, 106, 110, 141, 604a; *adj* 67, 122
last breath *n* 360
last forever *v* 112
lasting *adj* 106, 110, 141, 150
lastingness *n* 110
last resort *n* 666
last stage *n* 67
last word *n* 67
late *adj* 122, 123, 133, 275, 360; *adv* 133
lately *adv* 122, 123
latency *n* 526
latency *n* 172, 447
lateness *n* 133
latent *adj* 172, 526
latentness *n* 526
later *adj* 117; *adv* 117
lateral *adj* 236
laterality *n* 236
laterally *adv* 236
lather *n* 353; *v* 332, 353
lathering *n* 332
latitude *n* 180, 181, 202, 748
latitude and longitude *n* 183
latter *adj* 122
lattice *n* 219
laud *v* 883, 990
laudatory *adj* 931
laugh *v* 838
laughable *adj* 853
laughing *adj* 838
laughing-stock *n* 857
laughingstock *n* 547
laughter *n* 838
launch *n* 273; *v* 66, 284
launch into *v* 676
launder *v* 652

laureate *n* 597
laurel *n* 733
lavation *n* 652
lavender *adj* 437
lavish *v* 641, 784, 818; *adj* 641, 818
lavishness *n* 818
law *n* 80, 697, 963
lawful *adj* 246, 760, 922, 963
lawfully *adv* 922
lawfulness *n* 922, 963
lawless *adj* 964
lawlessness *n* 964
lawsuit *n* 969
lawyer *n* 968
lax *adj* 47, 738, 773
laxative *n* 652
laxity *n* 738
laxity *n* 47, 495, 748, 773, 989
laxness *n* 738, 773
lay *n* 413; *v* 184; *adj* 997
lay aside *v* 55
lay away *v* 636
lay bare *v* 260
lay claim to *v* 741
layer *n* 204
layer *v* 204
layered *adj* 204
lay groundwork *v* 626
lay in *v* 637
lay in a stock *v* 637
lay in a store *v* 637
lay in the grave *v* 363
lay in the ground *v* 363
lay it on thick *v* 933
layman *n* 997
lay oneself open to *v* 177, 665
lay on thick *v* 641
lay open *v* 226, 260, 529
lay out *v* 363, 809
lay over *v* 133
lay siege *v* 716
lay stress on *v* 642
lay the foundations *v* 673
lay the groundwork *v* 60
lay to rest *v* 363
lay up *v* 678
lay waste *v* 162
laziness *n* 683
lazy *adj* 275, 683
lazy eye *n* 443
lead *n* 234; *v* 116, 176, 615, 692, 693
lead astray *v* 545
leaden *adj* 422
leader *n* 64, 694, 745
leadership *n* 692, 693
leading *n* 280; *adj* 66
lead the way *v* 62, 66,

280
leaf *n* 204
leafage *n* 367
league *n* 712
leak *n* 198; *v* 295
leakage *n* 295
lean *v* 176, 217; *adj* 203
leaning *n* 176, 217, 602; *adj* 176
leanness *n* 203
lean on *v* 858
lean to *v* 602
leap *n* 309
leap *n* 305, 310; *v* 309, 310
leaping *adj* 309
leap with joy *v* 838
learn *v* 490, 527, 539
learn by heart *v* 505
learned *adj* 490, 498, 539
learned in the law *adj* 968
learner *n* 541
learner *n* 492
learning *n* 539
learning *n* 490, 498, 537
learn of *v* 480a
lease *n* 783; *v* 787, 788
leash *v* 43
leave *n* 760; *v* 44, 185, 293, 302, 624, 782, 784
leave alone *v* 623
leaven *n* 320; *v* 320
leave no trace *v* 449, 552
leave off *v* 142, 678
leave out *v* 55
leaves *n* 367
leave-taking *n* 287, 293
leave undone *v* 730
leave unfinished *v* 730
leaving *n* 624
leavings *n* 40
lecher *n* 962
lecherous *adj* 961
lechery *n* 961
lecture *n* 537, 582; *v* 537, 582, 586
lecturer *n* 540
ledge *n* 215, 250
ledger *n* 86, 551, 811
lee *n* 236
leer *n* 441; *v* 441
lee side *n* 236
leeway *n* 180
left *n* 239
left *adj* 40, 449, 782
left behind *adj* 782
left hand *n* 239
left-handed *adj* 239

leftover n 40; adj 40
left side n 239
legacy n 784
legal adj 760, 963, 967
legal action n 969
legal adviser n 968
legality n 963
legalize v 737, 963
legalized adj 760, 963
legal proceedings n 969
legal process n 969
legal profession n 968
legal separation n 905
legatee n 785
legation n 755
legislate v 693, 963
legislated adj 963
legitimacy n 963
legitimate adj 494, 760, 922, 963
legitimateness n 963
leguminous adj 367
leisure n 685
leisure adj 685
leisureliness n 275
leisurely adj 275, 685; adv 133, 275
lemon adj 435
lend v 787
lend an ear v 418
lender n 805
lending n 787
lend on security v 787
length n 200
lengthen v 110, 133, 200
lengthened adj 200
lengthiness n 200
lengthwise adv 200
lengthy adj 200, 573
lenience n 740
lenience n 174, 738
leniency n 740
lenient adj 174, 738, 740
lenity n 174
lens n 443, 445
leprechaun n 980
leprous adj 655
less adj 34; adv 34, 38
lessee n 779
lessen v 36, 174, 195, 834
lessening n 36, 195
lesser adj 34
lesson n 537, 668
let v 760, 762, 787
let alone v 678, 681, 730
let down v 308, 509
let drop v 308, 529
let fall v 308, 527
let fly v 284
let go v 624, 782, 790
lethal adj 162, 360, 361

lethargic adj 683
lethargy n 683
let in partial light v 427
let out v 750
let slip v 529, 730, 776
letter n 561
letter n 592
letter carrier n 271
lettering n 591
letterpress n 591
letters n 490, 560
let the opportunity slip by v 135
let things take their course v 681
levee n 72
level n 26, 27, 213, 251; v 16, 27, 162, 213, 251, 255, 308; adj 16, 27, 207, 213, 251, 255
level at v 278
level-headed adj 502
level with v 543
leverage n 175
leviathan n 192
levity n 320
lewd adj 961
lewdness n 961
lexicography n 562
lexicon n 562
liability n 177
liability n 665, 806
liable adj 176, 177, 665, 806
liar n 548
liberal adj 784, 816, 906, 942
liberality n 816
liberality n 784, 906, 942
liberate v 44, 672, 748, 750, 970
liberated adj 750
liberation n 750
liberation n 671, 672
libertarian adj 760
libertine n 962
libertine n 954a
liberty n 685, 737, 748, 760, 760
librarian n 593
libretto n 593
licence n 738
license n 748, 760, 924; v 760
licensed adj 924
licit adj 246, 963
lick the boots of v 886
lid n 223, 261, 263
lie n 544, 546; v 183, 213, 538, 544, 546
lie around v 220
lie down v 213, 687

lie flat v 207, 213
lie idle v 681
lie in v 1
lie in wait for v 530
lie low v 207
lien n 771
lie still v 265
life n 359
life n 151, 171, 682
lifeblood n 5, 359
life-giving adj 168
lifeless adj 172, 360
lifelessness n 172
lifelike adj 17, 21
lifetime n 108
lift n 307; v 235, 307
lift up v 235, 307
light n 420
light n 7; v 292, 384, 420, 423; adj 320, 322, 420, 430, 643
light bulb n 423
light-colored adj 429
lighten v 320, 420, 705
lightening n 420
light-fingered adj 791
light-footed adj 274
lightness n 320
light of day n 420
light on v 156
light up v 824
like v 394, 827, 897, 990; adj 17, 216
like a shot adv 113
like a ton of bricks adj 319
likelihood n 470, 472
likeliness n 472
likely adj 176, 177, 472
likeness n 17, 21, 216, 556
likening n 464
like two peas in a pod n 17
likewise adv 37
liking n 602, 897
lilac adj 437
lily-liver n 862
lily-livered adj 435, 862
limb n 51
limber adj 324
limbo n 982
limit n 233
limit n 67, 71; v 195, 229, 233, 469, 761
limitation n 229, 469, 751
limited adj 103, 203, 233
limitless adj 104, 180
limitlessness n 105
limn v 556, 594
limp adj 160, 275; adj 53, 158, 160, 324, 326
limpid adj 425

limpidity *n* 425
limpness *n* 326
line *n* 69, 278; *v* 224
lineage *n* 11, 69, 122, 166
lineal *adj* 166, 200
linear *adj* 69, 200, 246
lined *adj* 224, 440
line of march *n* 278
liner *n* 273
lines *n* 230, 448
linger *v* 133, 275
lingering *adj* 110
lingo *n* 560
lingual *adj* 560
linguist *n* 560
linguistic *adj* 560
liniment *n* 356
lining *n* 224
link *n* 45
link *n* 9, 43; *v* 9, 43, 45, 219
linkage *n* 43
link up *v* 43, 219
linseed oil *n* 356
lip *n* 231
lip-service *n* 933
liquefaction *n* 335
liquefaction *n* 333, 384
liquefy *v* 333, 335, 384
liquefying *n* 335
liquid *n* 337; *adj* 333, 337
liquidate *v* 807
liquidation *n* 807
liquid containers *n* 191
liquidity *n* 333
list *n* 86
list *n* 217, 596; *v* 551, 596
listen *v* 418
listener *n* 418
listening *n* 418
listing *n* 86
listless *adj* 683, 866
listlessness *n* 866
lists *n* 728
literal *adj* 561, 562
literally *adv* 19
literary *adj* 560
literature *n* 560, 590
litigant *n* 726, 969
litigation *n* 969
litigious *adj* 969
litter *n* 167; *v* 61
little *adj* 32, 193
little by little *adv* 26, 275
littleness *n* 193
littleness *n* 32, 201
little one *n* 129
live *n* 374; *v* 1, 141, 186, 188, 359; *adj* 359
live from hand to

mouth *v* 804
livelihood *n* 803
liveliness *n* 515, 682, 829, 836
lively *adj* 309, 359, 375, 515, 574, 682, 829, 836
live off *v* 298
live on *v* 298
livery *n* 225
livestock *n* 366
live through *v* 151
livid *adj* 431, 435
lividness *n* 431
living being *n* 364
living beings *n* 357
living thing *n* 366
load *n* 190, 319, 828; *v* 52, 190, 319, 641
loaf *v* 683
loafer *n* 683
loan *n* 787; *v* 787
loath *adj* 603, 867
loathe *v* 867, 898
loathing *n* 867, 898
loathsome *adj* 395, 830, 867, 898
local *adj* 183
locale *n* 182, 183
locality *n* 182, 183
locate *v* 183, 184
located *adj* 183, 184
locate oneself *v* 184
location *n* 184
location *n* 183
loch *n* 343
lock *n* 350; *v* 43
lock-up *n* 752
locomotion *n* 264
locomotive *n* 271
locution *n* 582
lodge *v* 184, 186
lodger *n* 188
lodging *n* 189
loft *v* 235
loftiness *n* 206, 574, 875
lofty *adj* 206, 574
log *n* 114, 388, 551
logic *n* 23, 476
logical *adj* 23, 476, 502
logician *n* 476
loiter *v* 133, 275, 683
loitering *n* 133
loll *v* 683
lone *adj* 87
long *adj* 200; *adv* 110
long ago *adv* 110, 122
long dozen *n* 98
longevity *n* 110, 128
long expected *adj* 507
long for *v* 858, 865
longhand *n* 590
longing *n* 858, 865
longitude *n* 200
longitudinal *adj* 200

longitudinally *adv* 200
long lost *adj* 776
long shot *n* 137
longstanding *adj* 110
long-winded *adj* 573
long-windedness *n* 573
look *n* 441, 448; *v* 441, 448, 457
look after oneself *v* 943
look ahead *v* 510
look askance *v* 443
look beyond *v* 510
look danger in the face *v* 861
looker-on *n* 444
look for *v* 461, 507
look forward *v* 121
look forward to *v* 507, 510
looking back *adj* 122
looking glass *n* 445
look into the future *v* 510
look like *v* 17
look on *v* 186, 444
lookout *n* 448
look out for *v* 507
look sharp *v* 682
look upon *v* 451
loom *v* 152, 446
looming *adj* 152
loon *n* 501
loop *n* 245, 247, 629
loophole *n* 671
loose *v* 44, 750; *adj* 44, 47, 279, 573, 575, 738, 748, 773
loosen *v* 47
looseness *n* 47, 573, 738, 748
loosening *n* 47, 738
loot *n* 793
lop *v* 371
loquacious *adj* 584
loquaciousness *n* 584
loquacity *n* 584
lord *n* 745, 875, 976
lore *n* 490, 537
lorgnette *n* 445
lose *v* 776
lose an opportunity *v* 135·
lose color *v* 429
lose ground *v* 283
lose heart *v* 837
lose it *v* 503
lose no time *v* 682
lose one's senses *v* 503
lose one's temper *v* 825
lose patience *v* 825
lose sight of *v* 506
loss *n* 776
loss *n* 40a, 449, 619, 638, 659, 732

443

make a resolution

loss of life n 360
lost adj 2, 449, 458,
732, 776
lost in thought adj 451
lost in wonder adj 870
lot n 25, 152, 621, 786
lottery n 156
loud adj 404
loudly adv 404
loudness n 404
loud noise n 404
lough n 343
lounge v 683
lounger n 683
lout n 501
lovable adj 897
love n 897
love n 865, 897, 899,
977; v 827, 928, 990
loveliness n 829, 845
lovely adj 242, 377,
597, 829, 845, 977
lover n 897
lovesick adj 991
love token n 902
loving adj 897
low v 412; adj 32, 207,
405, 438, 649, 874,
876, 879, 930
low-born adj 876
lower v 307, 308, 879;
adj 34
lowering n 308
lowland n 344
lowlands n 207
lowliness n 879
lowly adj 207, 879
low-lying adj 207
lowness n 207
low price n 815
low quality n 34
low relief n 250
low repute n 874
loyal adj 743
loyalty n 743
lubricate v 255, 332,
355
lubrication n 332
lubrication n 255, 355
lubricity n 255, 355
lucent adj 420
lucid adj 425, 502, 518,
570, 849
lucidity n 420, 425,
502, 518, 570, 578
Lucifer n 978
luck n 152, 156, 621,
731
lucky adj 134, 621, 734
ludicrous adj 853
lug v 285
lugubrious adj 837
lukewarm adj 382,
823, 866
lull n 142, 265, 403,
683, 685; v 174, 265

lull to sleep v 265
lumber v 275
luminary n 423
luminary n 500
luminosity n 420
luminous adj 420, 518
lump n 50, 51, 72, 192,
321
lumpish adj 192, 319
lump together v 72
lunacy n 503
lunar adj 245, 318
lunatic n 504; adj 503
lunch v 298
lunge n 276
lurch n 306; v 306
lure v 288
lurid adj 421, 422
lurk v 526
lurking adj 526
lurking place n 530
luscious adj 394, 396,
829
lush n 959; v 959; adj
337, 365, 396
lust n 865
luster n 420
lust for v 865
lustful adj 865
lustihood n 159
lustrous adj 420
luxuriate v 377
luxuriate in v 827
luxurious adj 377, 829
luxuriousness n 377
luxury n 377, 827
lying n 544; adj 544
lying down n 213
lymph n 337

M

ma n 166
ma'am n 374
Machiavellian adj 702
machinery n 633
macrocosm n 318
mad adj 173, 503, 824,
825
madam n 374
madame n 374
mad as a hatter adj 503
madden v 173
madman n 504
madness n 503, 825
maelstrom n 312, 348,
667
magenta adj 437
magic n 992; adj 992
magical adj 992
magician n 994
magisterial adj 737
magistracy n 965
magistrate n 967
magnetic adj 288
magnetism n 288
magnetize v 288
magnificence n 845

magnificent adj 192,
845
magnify v 35, 194, 482,
549, 990
magnifying glass n 445
magniloquence n 577
magniloquent adj 549,
577
magnitude n 25, 31,
192
mahogany adj 433
maiden n 129, 904; adj
66
maim v 158, 659
main n 341, 350
mainly adv 31
mainspring n 153, 615
mainstay n 666
maintain v 141, 143,
170, 215, 535, 670,
717, 720, 781, 937
maintain course v 143
maintenance n 141,
143, 170, 670, 781,
803
majestic adj 882
majesty n 875
major adj 33
majority n 33, 100, 131
make n 240; v 54, 56,
144, 161, 744, 852
make a choice v 609
make a circuit v 629
make a clean sweep of
v 652
make a complete
circle v 311
make a compromise v
628
make acquainted with
v 527
make a fool of oneself
v 853
make a fresh start v 66
make a generalization
v 78
make allowance for v
469
make amends v 30,
952
make a mess of v 732
make a motion v 763
make an addition to v
37
make an end of v 67
make an exception v
469
make a noise v 402
make a pig of oneself v
957
make a place for v 184
make a point of v 604
make a pretext of v
617
make a resolution v
604

make a sign v 550
make a U-turn v 311
make believe v 546
make faces v 243
make for v 278
make free with v 789
make friends with v 888
make fun of v 856
make good v 660, 790
make grave v 835
make haste v 132, 682, 684
make headlines v 532
make headway v 282
make known v 525, 527, 529, 531
make light of v 483, 643
make little of v 483
make loose v 47
make manifest v 525
make merry v 840
make music v 415, 416
make news v 532
make nothing of v 871
make obeisance v 308
make one sick v 395
make one's way v 734
make out v 441
make over v 783
make payment v 807
make peace v 721, 723
make preparations v 673
make productive v 168
make progress v 282, 682
make provision v 637
make provision for v 673
make public v 531
make pungent v 392
maker n 164
make ready v 673
make sail v 267
make serious v 835
makeshift n 147, 617
make solid v 150
make strides v 282
make sure v 150, 474
make terms v 769
make the best of v 826
make the mind a blank v 452
make time v 132
make-up n 54
make up for v 30
make use of v 677
make verses v 597
make war v 722
making verses n 597
maladroit adj 699
maladroitness n 699
malady n 655
malaise n 378, 828

malapropism n 565
malarkey n 477
malcontent adj 832
male n 373; adj 373
male animal n 373, 374
malediction n 908
malevolence n 907
malevolence n 649, 889
malevolent adj 649, 739, 907, 919, 945
malformation n 243
malformed adj 243
malice n 907
malicious adj 898, 907, 919, 945
maliciousness n 907
malign v 934; adj 649
malignant adj 919, 945
malignity n 649
mall n 799
malleability n 149, 324
malleable adj 82, 149, 324
maltreat v 649, 739, 830, 923
mamma n 166
mammal n 366
mammoth n 192; adj 31
man n 373
man n 372
man about town n 854
man after one's own heart n 899
manage v 58, 692, 693
manageable adj 705
management n 692, 693, 698
manager n 694
managerial adj 692
managing adj 693
mandate n 630, 741
maneuver v 702
manfully adv 604
mangle v 659
mangy adj 655
man-hater n 911
manhood n 131, 373
mania n 503
maniac n 504
maniacal adj 503
manifest adj 446, 525
manifestation n 525
manifestation n 446, 448
manifested adj 525
manifestly adv 525
manifold adj 15, 81, 102
manipulate v 379, 677, 702
manipulation n 379
mankind n 372
mankind n 372

manliness n 604
manly adj 131, 373
manner n 569, 613, 627
mannered adj 579, 855
mannerism n 79, 83, 579
mannerisms n 855
manner of speaking n 521
manners n 692, 852
man of learning n 500
mantle n 424
manual n 527
manufacture n 161; v 161
manuscript n 590
many adj 100, 102
many-colored adj 440
many-sided adj 81
map n 183, 527, 626
mar v 659, 848
marble n 249
marbled adj 440
march n 266
marches n 233
marching band n 417
march of time n 109
mare n 374
margin n 231
marine adj 341
marine blue adj 438
mariner n 269
mariner n 269
marital separation n 905
maritime adj 267, 341
mark n 26, 71, 550, 569, 590, 620; v 450, 550, 642
marked adj 79
market n 799
market v 795
marketable adj 794, 796
marketplace n 799
market price n 812
mark the time v 114
mark time v 114, 265
maroon adj 434
marquee n 223
marriage n 903
marriage n 43
marriageable adj 131
married adj 903
married man n 903
married woman n 903
marrow n 5, 221
marry v 43, 48, 903
marsh n 345
marshal v 60
marshy adj 339, 345
mart n 799
martial adj 722
martyr n 955
marvel n 870, 872; v

870
marvelous *adj* 31, 870
marvelously *adv* 31
masculine *adj* 373
masculinity *n* 373
mash *v* 324, 352, 354
mask *n* 223, 424, 530·
v 442, 528
masquerade *n* 530
mass *n* 25, 31, 50, 72,
102, 192, 321
massacre *n* 361; *v* 361
massage *v* 379
massaging *n* 379
massive *adj* 192, 319,
321
massy *adj* 192
master *n* 745
master *n* 129, 540, 694,
700, 779; *v* 518, 539,
731, 749
masterful *adj* 731, 737
masterly *adj* 698
master mind *n* 500,
700, 872
master of *adj* 777
masterpiece *n* 648, 650
master stroke *n* 650
mastery *n* 698, 731,
741
mastic *n* 356a
masticate *v* 298
mastication *n* 298
mat *n* 219; *v* 219
match *n* 17, 27; *v* 17,
23, 27
matchless *adj* 33
mate *n* 17, 27, 711,
890, 903; *v* 89
material *n* 316; *adj* 3,
316
material existence *n* 3
materialism *n* 316
materialist *n* 316
materialistic *adj* 3, 316
materiality *n* 316
materiality *n* 3
materialization *n* 525
materialize *v* 316, 525
materials *n* 635
materials *n* 316
maternal *adj* 166
maternity *n* 11, 166
mates *n* 269
matins *n* 125
matriarch *n* 130
matriarchal *adj* 166
matricide *n* 361
matriculation *n* 539
matrimony *n* 903
matrix *n* 22
matted *adj* 219
matter *n* 3, 316, 516,
591, 625; *v* 642
matter little *v* 643
matter of fact *n* 1; *adj*

598, 703, 843
matter of factness *n*
703
matters *n* 151
matting *n* 219
mature *v* 144, 650, 658,
673; *adj* 673
mature years *n* 128
maturity *n* 124, 128,
131, 673
maul *v* 649
mausoleum *n* 363
mauve *adj* 437
maxim *n* 496
maxim *n* 537, 697
maximum *n* 210
maybe *adv* 470
maze *n* 248
mazy *adj* 248
meadow *n* 344
meager *adj* 32, 53, 103,
203, 575, 640, 643
meagerness *n* 203
mealy *adj* 330
mealy-mouthed *adj*
886
mean *n* 29
mean *n* 68, 628; *v* 451,
516, 620; *adj* 29, 32,
34, 68, 207, 435, 643,
649, 819, 851, 876,
886, 914a, 930, 943
meander *v* 248, 264,
266, 279, 573
meandering *n* 248
meaning *n* 516
meaning *n* 522, 620;
adj 516
meaningful *adj* 516
meaningless *adj* 497,
517
meaninglessness *n* 517
meanness *n* 32, 34,
499, 886, 914a, 943
mean nothing *v* 517
means *n* 632
means *n* 627, 780, 803
means of access *n* 627
meantime *adv* 106
meanwhile *adv* 106
measurable *adj* 466
measure *n* 25, 26, 174,
413, 466, 786; *v* 106,
466
measured *adj* 174
measure for measure *n*
30
measureless *adj* 104
measurement *n* 466
measurement *n* 25
measure time *v* 114
meaty *adj* 354
mechanical *adj* 601,
633
medal *n* 733
meddlesome *adj* 455

meddlesomeness *n* 455
medial *adj* 68
median *n* 29; *adj* 68
mediate *v* 620, 631,
724
mediation *n* 724
mediation *n* 631, 766
mediator *n* 724
mediatory *adj* 724
medication *n* 662
medicinal *adj* 662
medicine *n* 662
medicine man *n* 994
mediocre *adj* 28, 29,
34, 598, 651, 736
mediocrity *n* 736
mediocrity *n* 28, 34
meditate *v* 451, 870
meditation *n* 451
meditative *adj* 451
medium *n* 29, 631, 994
medley *n* 41
meek *adj* 879
meekness *n* 879
meet *v* 23, 72, 199, 290,
772; *adj* 646
meeting *n* 43, 72, 199,
290, 680, 696
meetinghouse *n* 1000
meet up with *v* 151
meet with *v* 151
melancholy *n* 837; *adj*
830, 837
mélange *n* 41
melee *n* 59
meliorate *v* 174, 723
mellifluence *n* 413
mellifluous *adj* 413,
578
mellow *v* 144, 673; *adj*
128, 413, 428, 673,
721
melodic *adj* 413
melodious *adj* 377,
413, 580
melodiousness *n* 413
melody *n* 413
melody *n* 415
melt *v* 111, 144, 335,
384, 449
melt away *v* 4, 449
melting *n* 335, 384
member *n* 51, 56
membrane *n* 204
membranous *adj* 204
memento *n* 505
memento mori n 363
memorable *adj* 505
memorandum *n* 551
memorial *n* 505
memorialist *n* 553
memorialization *n* 883
memorize *v* 505, 539
memory *n* 505
memory *n* 122
menace *n* 667, 909; *v*

668, 909
menacing *adj* 909
menagerie *n* 72
mend *v* 658
mendacious *adj* 544
mendicant *n* 767
menial *n* 746
mental *adj* 450
mental balance *n* 502
mental cultivation *n* 539
mental excitation *n* 824
mental image *n* 515
mental suffering *n* 619
mention *v* 527
mentor *n* 540, 695
mephitic *adj* 401
mercantile *adj* 794
mercantilism *n* 796
mercenary *adj* 819
merchandise *n* 798
merchandise *v* 763, 796, 798
merchant *n* 797
merchant *n* 796
merchant ship *n* 273
merciful *adj* 740
merciless *adj* 914a
mercurial *adj* 149, 264
mercury *n* 389
mercy *n* 740, 914
mere *n* 343; *adj* 643
merely *adv* 32
merge *v* 48, 300
merge in *v* 56
merge into *v* 144
meridian *n* 125, 181
merit *n* 648, 944, 973
merit attention *v* 642
meritorious *adj* 931
mermaid *n* 979
merriment *n* 836
merry *adj* 829
merrymaking *n* 838
mesh *n* 219
mesmerist *n* 994
mesmerize *v* 992
mess *n* 59, 61, 162, 732
messenger *n* 534
messenger *n* 271, 527, 758
mess up *v* 59
messy *adj* 59
metallurgy *n* 358
metamorphose *v* 140
metamorphosis *n* 140
metaphor *n* 521
metaphorical *adj* 464
mete *v* 786
meteors *n* 318
mete out *v* 784
meter *n* 413
method *n* 627
method *n* 58, 60, 569, 626, 632, 692

methodical *adj* 58, 60, 692
methodically *adv* 58
methodological *adj* 626
methodology *n* 58
meticulous *adj* 459, 868
metrical *adj* 597
metrics *n* 597
mettle *n* 861
mew *v* 412
miasmic *adj* 401
microcosm *n* 193
microscope *n* 445
microscopic *adj* 32, 193
mid *adj* 68
mid-course *n* 628
midcourse *n* 68
midday *n* 125
middle *n* 68
middle *n* 29, 208, 222; *adj* 29, 68, 222; *adv* 222
middle class *adj* 29
middle course *n* 628
middle ground *n* 68, 174
middlemost *adj* 222
middle of the road *n* 174
middle way *n* 628
middling *adj* 32, 651
midmost *adj* 68
midnight *n* 126
midnight *n* 421
mid-point *n* 29, 68
midriff *n* 68
midst *n* 68, 208, 222; *adv* 222
midsummer 125
midway *adj* 628; *adv* 68
mien *n* 448, 692
might *n* 31, 157, 159, 173
mightily *adv* 31
mighty *adj* 31, 157, 159, 192, 192
migrate *v* 266
migration *n* 266
migratory *adj* 266
mild *adj* 174, 382, 391, 721, 740
mildew *n* 653, 663
mildewed *adj* 659
mildness *n* 174, 740
militant *adj* 722
militarist *n* 726
military *adj* 722
military band *n* 417
milkiness *n* 427, 430
milk-white *adj* 430
milky *adj* 352, 427, 430
mill *n* 330, 691

millennium *n* 108, 121
millions *n* 372
mimic *v* 19, 554
mimicry *n* 19
mince *v* 275
mince steps *v* 275
mind *n* 450, 498, 842; *v* 602
mindblower *n* 137
mindful *adj* 451, 457
mindfulness *n* 457
mindful (of) *adj* 505
mindless *adj* 499
mine *n* 636; *v* 252, 260, 659
mineral *adj* 358
mineral kingdom *n* 358
mineralogy *n* 358
mineral world *n* 358
mingle *v* 41
mingling *n* 41
miniature *adj* 32, 193
minimize *v* 483
minion *n* 899
minister *n* 631, 690, 694, 996; *v* 631, 693
ministerial *adj* 995
ministering spirit *n* 977
ministration *n* 693
ministry *n* 995, 996
minor *n* 129; *adj* 32, 34
minority *n* 34, 127
minstrel *n* 416, 597
mint *n* 22, 691
minus *adj* 776; *adv* 38, 187
minuscule *adj* 32
minute *adj* 32, 193
minutiae *n* 32
minx *n* 962
miracle *n* 872
miraculous *adj* 870
mirage 443
mire *n* 653
mirror *n* 445, 650; *v* 19; 443
mirth *n* 836
mirthful *adj* 836
misanthrope *n* 165
misanthropic *adj* 911
misanthropy *n* 911
misapplication *n* 679
misapply *v* 523, 679
misapprehend *v* 495, 523
misapprehension *n* 481, 495, 523
misappropriate *v* 679
misappropriation *n* 679
misbelief *n* 984
misbelieving *adj* 984
miscalculate *v* 482,

495

miscalculation n 481, 482, 508

miscall v 565

miscarriage n 732

miscarry v 732

miscellaneous adj 15, 41, 465a

miscellaneousness n 78

miscellany n 41, 72, 78

mischief n 619

mischievous adj 649

miscomputation n 481

misconceive v 481, 495, 523

misconception n 481, 495, 523

misconjecture v 481

misconstruction n 523

misconstrue v 481, 523

miscreant n 949

misdate n 115; v 115

misdated adj 115

misdeed n 923

misdirect v 538

misdirection n 538

misemploy v 679

misemployment n 679

miser n 819

miserable adj 828, 837, 930

miserably adv 31, 32

miserly adj 819

misery n 828

misfiguration n 555

misfortune n 619, 735, 830

misgiving n 485, 860

misguidance n 538

misguide v 538

mishap n 619, 732, 830

misinform v 538

misinformation n 538

misinstruct v 538

misinterpret v 481, 495, 523

misinterpretation n 523

misinterpretation n 481, 495

misjudge v 481, 495

misjudging adj 481

misjudgment n 481

misjudgment n 495

mislay v 61, 776

mislead v 477, 538, 545

misleading adj 520, 544, 545

mismatch n 24; v 15

mismatched adj 24

misname v 565

misnamed adj 565

misnaming n 565

misnomer n 565

misogynist n 911

misplace v 61, 185

misplaced adj 115, 185

misplacement n 115, 185

misproportion n 241, 243

misread v 523

misreading n 523

misrepresent v 277, 477, 523, 538, 544, 555

misrepresentation n 555

misrepresentation n 523, 544

miss n 129, 374; v 776

misshape v 243

misshapen adj 241, 243

missing adj 187, 449

missing link n 53

mission n 755

missionary n 540

missive n 592

misspend v 638, 818

misstate v 523

miss the mark v 732

mist n 353, 422, 424, 427; v 353

mistake n 495, 523, 732; v 495, 523

mistaken adj 495, 544, 923

misteach v 538

misteaching n 538

mister n 373

misterm v 565

mistime v 135

mistimed adj 135

mistiness n 422, 426

mistreat v 830

mistress n 779

mistrust n 485; v 485

misty adj 353, 422, 426, 447

misunderstand v 481, 495, 523

misunderstanding n 495, 523, 713

misusage n 649, 679

misuse n 679

misuse n 638; v 638, 679

mite n 32

mitigate v 174, 469, 834

mitigating adj 469

mitigation n 174, 469, 834

mix n 41, 48; v 41, 48, 61

mixed adj 41

mixture n 41

mixture n 48

moan n 839; v 411

moaning n 411, 839

moat n 259, 350

mob n 72, 102

mobile adj 149, 264

mobility n 149, 264

mobilization n 264

mobilize v 264

mock v 19, 856, 929· adj 17, 19

mockery n 856

mocking n 19; adj 856

mode n 7, 569, 613, 852

model n 21, 22, 80, 240, 650, 948; v 144, 240, 557; adj 650

modeled after adj 19

modeled on adj 19

modeling n 557

model oneself on v 19

mode of expression n 569

moderate v 174, 275, 723; adj 174, 275, 628, 736, 815, 881, 953

moderately adv 174

moderation n 174

moderation n 275, 736, 740, 826, 881, 953

moderator n 724, 967

modern adj 123

modernism n 123

modernity n 123

modernize v 123

modest adj 483, 879, 881, 960

modestly adv 881

modesty n 881

modesty n 483, 879, 960

modicum n 32

modification n 20a, 140, 469

modified adj 15, 20a

modify v 15, 20a, 140, 469

modish adj 852, 855

modulate v 140

modulation n 140, 413

module n 22, 273

moist adj 337, 339

moisten v 337, 339

moisture n 339

mold n 7, 21, 22, 240, 329, 557, 653; v 144, 240, 557, 653, 852

moldable adj 324

molded adj 820

molder v 659

moldering adj 659

moldy adj 653, 659

molecule n 32

molest v 649, 716

molestation n 649

mollification n 324

mollify v 174, 324, 723

mollusk n 366

molten *adj* 384
mom *n* 166
moment *n* 113, 642
momentary *adj* 111, 113
momentous *adj* 642
momentousness *n* 642
monetary *adj* 800
money *n* 800
money *n* 803
moneybag *n* 802
money matters *n* 811
mongrel *n* 41; *adj* 41
moniker *n* 564
monochrome *n* 429
monocle *n* 445
monody *n* 839
monogram *n* 561
monolog *n* 589
monomania *n* 606
monomaniacal *adj* 606
monosyllable *n* 561
monotheism *n* 983
monotonous *adj* 16, 27, 104, 841
monotony *n* 16, 27, 104, 841
monsoon *n* 349
monster *n* 192, 949, 980
monstrosity *n* 192, 243, 872
monstrous *adj* 31, 192, 846
monstrously *adv* 31
monument *n* 363, 551
moo *v* 412
mood *n* 7, 176, 602, 820
moodiness *n* 901a
moods *n* 5
moody *adj* 901a
moon *n* 420, 423
moonbeam *n* 420
moor *n* 344; *v* 43
moored *adj* 184, 186
mooring *n* 184
mope *v* 837
moper *n* 683
moral *adj* 922, 944
moral imperative *n* 926
morality *n* 922, 944
moralize *v* 537
morals *n* 922
moral sensibility *n* 822
morass *n* 345
moratorium *n* 133
morbid *adj* 655
more *adv* 33, 37
more or less *adj* 25
moreover *adv* 37
more than one *adj* 100
morgue *n* 363
morn *n* 125

morning *n* 125
morning *n* 125
morningtide *n* 125
moron *n* 493, 501
morose *adj* 901a
moroseness *n* 901a
morphology *n* 368
morrow *n* 121
morsel *n* 32, 390
mortal *n* 372; *adj* 111, 361, 372
mortal coil *n* 362
mortality *n* 111, 360, 372
mortal remains *n* 362
mortar and pestle *n* 330
mortgage *n* 771, 787; *v* 771
mortification *n* 828, 830
mortify *v* 828, 830, 879
mortuary *n* 363; *adj* 363
mosaic *adj* 81, 440
moss *n* 345
most *adv* 31
most likely *adv* 472
mote *n* 32, 451
moth-eaten *adj* 653, 659
mother *n* 166, 192
mother earth *n* 342
motherhood *n* 166
motherland *n* 189
motion *n* 264
motion *n* 550
motionless *adj* 172, 265, 683
motivate *v* 615, 744
motivation *n* 615
motive *n* 615
motive power *n* 264
mot juste *n* 496
motley *adj* 16a, 41, 81
motorboat *n* 273
motorcar *n* 272
motorcycle *n* 272
motoring *n* 266
motorscooter *n* 272
mottled *adj* 440
motto *n* 496, 566
mound *n* 192
mount *v* 206, 305
mountain *n* 192, 250
mourn for *v* 833
mournful *adj* 830, 839, 901a
mourn over *v* 839
mouth *n* 231, 343
mouthful *n* 25, 32
mouthpiece *n* 582
movable *adj* 264, 270
movableness *n* 264
move *n* 264, 270; *v* 175, 264, 266, 270,

302, 615, 763, 824
move away from *v* 287
move back *v* 287
moved *adj* 821, 914
movement *n* 264, 680, 682
move off *v* 293
move out *v* 293
move quickly *v* 274
mover *n* 164
move slowly *v* 275
move to the center *v* 29
move towards *v* 286
moving *n* 266, 680; *adj* 264
mow *v* 371
Mr. *n* 373
Ms. *n* 374
much *adj* 641; *adv* 31
much ado about nothing *n* 549
much the same *adj* 17, 27
muck *n* 653
muckraking *n* 529
mud *n* 345, 653
muddle *n* 59; *v* 61
muddle-headed *adj* 499
muddy *adj* 339, 345, 352, 519
muffle *v* 403, 408a, 590
muffled *adj* 405, 408a
muffled drums *n* 408a
muffler *n* 408a
muggy *adj* 339
mulish *adj* 606
mulishness *n* 606
mulling around *n* 681
multi-colored *adj* 440
multifarious *adj* 16a, 81
multifold *adj* 81
multiformity *n* 81
multiple *adj* 102
multiplication *n* 168
multiplicity *n* 102
multiply *v* 35, 85, 102, 163, 168
multiply by four *v* 96
multiplying by four *n* 96
multi-purpose *adj* 148
multitude *n* 102
multitude *n* 31, 72, 100, 876
multitudes *n* 372
multitudinous *n* 102; *adj* 102
mum *n* 166; *adj* 581, 585
mumble *v* 583
mumbling *n* 583
mumbo-jumbo *n* 993

mummify v 363
mummy n 166
munch v 298
mundane adj 318
munificence n 816, 910
munificent adj 816, 910
munitions n 727
murder n 361; v 361
murderer n 361
murderous adj 361
murk n 421
murkiness n 421
murky adj 421, 422, 426, 431
murmur n 405; v 348, 405
murmured adj 405
muscular adj 159
muse v 451
mushiness n 326
mushy adj 324, 339
music n 415
musical adj 413, 415, 416, 597
musical instruments n 417
musicalness n 413
musician n 416
musing n 451
muster n 72; v 72, 85
mustiness n 401
musty adj 401, 653
mutability n 149
mutable adj 149
mutation n 140
mute n 408a; v 408a; adj 403, 581, 585
muted adj 405, 408a
muteness n 581
muteness n 403, 585
mutilate v 38, 241, 361, 659
mutilation n 38, 241
mutineer n 742
mutinous adj 742
mutinousness n 742
mutiny n 146, 742; v 742
mutter v 405, 583
muttering n 583
mutual adj 12, 148
mutuality n 12
muzzle v 158, 403, 581
myopia n 443
myopic adj 443
mysterious adj 208, 447, 519, 528, 533
mystery n 447, 533
mystify v 519

N

nab v 789
nacreous adj 427, 440

nadir n 211
naiad n 979
naive adj 435, 703, 946
naivete n 703, 946
naked adj 226
nakedness n 226
name n 13, 562, 564, 569, 873, 877; v 564, 755
namely adv 522
namesake n 564
naming n 564
nannygoat n 374
nap n 256
naphtha n 356
napping adj 458
narrate v 594
narration n 594
narrative prose n 598
narrow v 195, 203, 469; adj 32, 203
narrow escape n 671
narrowing n 469
narrow-minded adj 32, 499
narrow-mindedness n 32
narrowness n 203
narrowness n 203
nascent adj 66
nasty adj 395, 653
natal adj 66
nation n 188
national adj 372
native n 188; adj 188
nativity n 66
natural n 501; adj 82, 494, 578, 703, 849
natural causes n 360
natural gas n 388
natural harbor n 343
natural history n 357
naturalist n 357
natural light n 423
natural philosophy n 316
natural world n 357
nature n 5, 80, 176, 318, 357, 820
naught n 4, 101
nauseate v 395, 830, 867
nauseating adj 401, 867, 898
nauseous adj 395, 401, 830
nautical adj 267
naval adj 267
navel n 222
navigable adj 267
navigate v 267
navigation n 267
navigator n 269
navy n 273; adj 438
near v 286; adj 17, 121, 152, 186, 197, 199;

adv 197
nearly adv 32
near miss n 671
nearness n 197
nearness n 9, 186, 286
near side n 239
nearsighted adj 443
nearsightedness n 443
near the mark adv 32
neat adj 58, 576, 578, 652, 849
neaten v 652
neatness n 652
nebbish n 547
nebula n 353
nebulosity n 353, 422
nebulous adj 422, 519
necessarily adv 154, 601
necessary adj 601, 630, 744
necessitate v 601, 630, 744
necessity n 601
necessity n 630, 744
neck and neck race n 27
necklace n 247
necromancer n 513, 994
necromancy n 992
need n 630, 684, 804, 865; v 630, 640
needful adj 601, 630
neediness n 804
needle n 253, 262
needless adj 641
needy adj 804
negate v 536
negation n 536
negation n 468
negative n 22; adj 14, 84, 489, 536
neglect n 460
neglect n 730, 732, 773, 927; v 53, 460, 678, 730, 773, 927
neglected adj 460
neglectful adj 460
neglecting adj 460
negligence n 460, 773
negligent adj 460, 738, 773, 927
negotiate v 724, 769, 794
negotiation n 724, 769, 774, 794
negotiator n 724
neigh v 412
neighbor v 197
neighborhood n 197, 227
neighboring adj 197
neighborly adj 707, 888, 892
nemesis n 919

neologic *adj* 563
neological *adj* 563
neologism *n* 563
neologist *n* 563
neology *n* 563
neophyte *n* 541
nereid *n* 979
nerve *n* 159, 861; *v* 159
nervous *adj* 574, 825
nescient *adj* 491
ness *n* 250
nest *n* 189
nestle *v* 186
net *n* 219; *v* 219
nethermost *adj* 211
netting *n* 219
nettle *n* 663
network *n* 219
neutral *adj* 29, 609a,
628
neutrality *n* 609a
neutrality *n* 29, 609a,
628
neutralization *n* 179
neutralize *v* 30, 179
neutral tint *n* 429, 432
never *adv* 107
never-ending *adj* 104,
112
nevermore *adv* 107
nevertheless *adv* 30
never to be forgotten
adj 505
new *adj* 18, 123, 146,
435
new birth *n* 660
newborn *adj* 129
newfangled *adj* 83,
123, 140
new-fangled
expression *n* 563
newfangledness *n* 123
newly *adv* 123
newness *n* 123
news *n* 532
news *n* 498, 527
newsmonger *n* 527,
532, 534
newsstory *n* 532
New Testament *n* 986
next *adj* 63; *adv* 117
next generation *n* 127
next world *n* 152
nibble *v* 298
nice *adj* 394, 829, 868
nice distinction *n* 15
nicety *n* 465, 868
niche *n* 182, 221, 244
nick *n* 257; *v* 257
nickname *n* 564, 565;
v 564
nick of time *n* 134
niggard *n* 819
niggardly *adj* 819
niggling *adj* 643
nigh *adj* 197; *adv* 197
night *n* 421

nightfall *n* 126
nihilist *n* 165
nil *n* 4
nimble *adj* 274, 498,
842
nincompoop *n* 501
nine *n* 98
ninny *n* 501
nip *n* 392; *v* 385
nip in the bud *v* 361
nipping *adj* 383
nipple *n* 250
nippy *adj* 392
nirvana *n* 981
nit-picking *adj* 477
nixie *n* 979
nobility *n* 875
nobility *n* 33
noble *adj* 31, 875, 878
nobody *n* 101
no choice *n* 609a
nocturnal *adj* 421
node *n* 250
no doubt *adv* 474
nodular *adj* 250
nodulation *n* 256
nodule *n* 250
noise *n* 402, 404, **414**
noiseless *adj* 403
noisily *adv* 404
noisome *adj* 401, 657
noisy *adj* 404
nomad *n* 268
nomadic *adj* 264, 266
nomadism *n* 266
nom de guerre *n* 565
nom de plume *n* 565
nomenclature *n* 564
nominal *adj* 564
nominate *v* 755
nomination *n* 755
nominee *n* 758
no more *adj* 360
no more than *adv* 32
nonadhesion *n* 47
nonadhesive *adj* 47
nonappearance *n* 187
nonattendance *n* 187
nonbeliever *n* 485,
487, 989
noncohesive *adj* 47
noncompletion *n* 730
noncompletion *n* 53,
304
noncompliance *n* 742,
773
noncompliant *adj* 764
nonconforming *adj*
984
nonconformist *n* 489,
984; *adj* 489, 984
nonconformity *n* 16a,
24, 79, 83, 489, 984
none *n* 101
nonentity *n* 2
nonessential *adj* 57,
643

nonetheless *adv* 30
nonexistence *n* 2
nonexistent *adj* 2, 187
nonexpectant *adj* 508
nonexpectation *n* 508
nonextension *n* 180a
nonfulfillment *n* 730
nonfunctional *adj* 674
nonimitation *n* 20
noninterference *n* 748
nonlinear *adj* 245
nonobservance *n* 773
nonobservance *n* 83,
742, 927
nonobservant *adj* 773
nonpayment *n* 808
nonperformance *n*
730, 732, 927
nonplus *v* 704
nonpreparation *n* 674
nonrational *adj* 450a
non-relation *n* 10
nonresidence *n* 187
nonresistance *n* 725
nonresonance *n* 408a
nonresonant *adj* 408a
nonsense *n* 497, 517
nonsensical *adj* 477,
497, 499, 517, 853
non sequitur *n* 497
nontranslucent *adj*
426
nontransparency *n*
426
nontransparent *adj*
426
noodle *n* 450
nook *n* 182, 221, 244
noon *n* 125
noon *n* 125
noonday *n* 125
noontide *n* 125
noontime *n* 125
normal *adj* 5, 29, 82,
736
normalcy *n* 80
normality *n* 502
normal state *n* 80
nose *n* 250
not a bit *adv* 32
notable *adj* 31, 642
notably *adv* 31
not act *v* 681
not a jot *adv* 32
notary *n* 553
not at all *adv* 32
not a whit *adv* 32
not bad *adj* 651
not beat around the
bush *v* 576
not be good for *v* 657
not be surprised *v* 871
not care *v* 823
notch *n* 257
notch *n* 244; *v* 257

notched *adj* 257
not come up to *v* 28, 34
not come up to snuff *v* 28
not complete *v* 730
not conversant *adj* 699
not curved *adj* 246
not cut it *v* 640
not discriminate *v* 465a
not do *v* 640, 681
not enough *adj* 640
notes *n* 802
noteworthy *adj* 31
not exist *v* 2
not expect *v* 508
not germane *adj* 57
not get involved *v* 623
not give an inch *v* 604
not have *v* 777a
not have much of a chance *v* 473
not hear *v* 419
not here *adj* 187
nothing *n* 4, 101, 643
nothingness *n* 2, 4
notice *n* 457, 668; *v* 450, 457, 480a, 928
notification *n* 527
notify *v* 668
no time *n* 107
not in *adj* 187
not included in *adj* 55
not in sight *adj* 447
not in the least *adv* 32
not in use *adj* 678
notion *n* 451, 453, 515
not licensed *adj* 925
not many *adj* 103
not matter *v* 643
not often *adv* 137
not pass muster *v* 34, 651
not pay *v* 808
not pertinent *adj* 10
not possible *adj* 471
not present *adj* 187, 187
not quite *adv* 32
not reach *v* 304
not see *v* 442
not smell *v* 399
not sorry *adj* 951
not straight *adj* 243
not suffice *v* 640
not the same *adj* 15
not think *v* 452
not true *adj* 243
not use *v* 678
not well *adj* 655
not with it *adj* 246
notwithstanding *adv* 30

nourishment *n* 298, 359
novel *n* 593; *adj* 18, 123
novelty *n* 18, 123
novice *n* 541, 701
now *adv* 118
nowadays *adv* 118
now and then *adv* 136
no way *adj* 471
noway *adv* 32
nowhere *adv* 187
nowise *adv* 32
now or never *adv* 134
noxious *adj* 649, 657
nozzle *n* 250
nuance *n* 15
nub *n* 68, 222
nubile *adj* 131
nuclear power *n* 388
nucleus *n* 68, 153, 222
nude *adj* 226
nudity *n* 226
nuisance *n* 619, 663, 830, 975
null and void *adj* 756
nullification *n* 536, 756
nullify *v* 2, 30, 179, 536, 756
nullity *n* 4
numb *v* 376; *adj* 376, 381
number *n* 84
number *v* 85
number among *v* 76
numbering *n* 85
numberless *adj* 104
numbers *n* 102
numbing *adj* 383
numbness *n* 381
numbness *n* 376
numerable *adj* 85
numeral *n* 84; *adj* 84, 85
numeration *n* 85
numerical *adj* 85
numerous *adj* 100, 102
numskull *n* 493, 501
nuptials *n* 903
nurse *n* 753; *v* 662
nursery *n* 127
nursling *n* 129
nurture *v* 235, 673
nutriment *n* 298, 359
nutrition *n* 298
nutritious *adj* 299, 656
nutritive *adj* 299
nuts *adj* 503
nutshell *n* 32

O

oaf *n* 501
oath *n* 535, 768

obduracy *n* 606, 951
obdurate *adj* 600, 951
obedience *n* 743
obedience *n* 725, 749, 772
obedient *adj* 725, 743, 772, 926
obediently *adv* 743
obeisance *n* 308
obese *adj* 192, 194
obesity *n* 192
obey *v* 725, 743, 772
obey the rules *v* 82
obfuscate *v* 528
obfuscation *n* 528
object *n* 3, 316, 453, 516, 620
objection *n* 704
objectionable *adj* 846
objective *n* 453; *adj* 6
object to *v* 932
obligate *v* 630
obligation *n* 177, 601, 768, 806, 926, 963
obligations *n* 770
obligatory *adj* 744, 926
oblige *v* 707, 744, 770
obliged *adj* 177, 916, 926
obliging *adj* 894, 906
oblique *adj* 217
obliquely *adv* 217
obliquity *n* 217
obliquity *n* 243
obliterate *v* 2, 552
obliterated *adj* 552
obliteration *n* 552
obliteration *n* 2
obliteration of the past *n* 506
oblivion *n* 506
oblivious *adj* 506
obloquy *n* 874
obnoxious *adj* 830, 898
obscene *adj* 961
obscenity *n* 961
obscuration *n* 421
obscure *v* 421, 422, 528; *adj* 208, 421, 426, 447, 519, 571, 704, 876
obscure meaning *n* 526
obscuring *n* 528
obscurity *n* 571
obscurity *n* 208, 421, 431, 447, 475, 519, 526
obsequies *n* 363
obsequious *adj* 886
obsequiousness *n* 743, 886
observance *n* 772
observance *n* 82, 613, 743, 883, 983a, 998

observant adj 457, 772
observation n 453, 457
observe v 441, 457, 772, 883, 926
observer n 444
obsolete adj 122, 124
obstacle n 177, 704, 706
obstinacy n 606
obstinacy n 141, 150, 327, 603, 604, 704, 742
obstinate adj 150, 327, 499, 604, 606, 719, 742
obstreperous adj 173, 404
obstruct v 261, 275, 706, 708, 761
obstruction n 261, 706
obstructive adj 706
obstruct the passage of light v 426
obtain v 775, 795
obtrude v 228
obtrusive adj 706
obtuse adj 254, 376, 499
obtuse angle n 244
obtuseness n 254, 376, 843
obverse adj 218
obvious adj 446, 474, 518, 525
occasion n 8, 134, 615; v 153
occasional adj 103, 137
occasionally adv 136
occultism n 992
occupancy n 186, 777
occupant n 188, 779
occupation n 186, 625
occupy v 186, 777
occupying adj 186
occur v 1, 151
occurrence n 151
ocean n 341
ocean-going adj 267
oceanic adj 341
oceanographic adj 341
ocher n 435
ochre adj 433
octet n 415
ocular adj 441
odd adj 40, 83, 87, 870
oddity n 83, 503, 857
odds n 28, 156, 713
odds and ends n 40
odious adj 830, 898
odium n 898, 932
odor n 398
odoriferous adj 398, 400
odorific adj 400
odorless adj 399

odorlessness n 399
odorous adj 398
oeuvre n 161
of age adj 131
of a piece adj 16, 17
of every description adj 81
off adj 187
off and on adv 138
off base adj 10, 481, 495
offend v 289, 830
offend against the law v 964
offended adj 900
offense n 716, 830
offensive adj 395, 401, 653, 716, 830, 846, 867, 898
offensive smell n 401
offer n 763
offer v 763
offer congratulations v 896
offer counsel v 695
offer for sale v 763
offering n 763, 784
offer pleasure v 829
offer prayers v 990
offhand adv 132, 612
office n 170, 625, 799
official n 694; adj 625, 737, 983a
offing n 196
off one's guard adj 508
off-set n 30; v 30, 179
offshoot n 39, 51, 65, 154
offside n 238
offspring n 154, 167
off the mark adj 495
of late adv 122, 123
of little account adj 643
of long standing adj 124
of necessity adv 601, 630
of no account adj 643
of old adv 122
of one accord adj 488
of one mind adj 178
of one's own accord adv 600
of other times adj 124
of small importance adj 643
oft adv 136
often adv 104, 136
oftentimes adv 136
of the same mind adj 488
oft-repeated adj 136
of various kinds adj 16a
of vital importance adj

642
of yore adv 122
ogle v 441
ogre n 980
oil n 356
oil n 355; v 255, 332, 355
oil burner n 386
oiliness n 355
oiling n 332
oil lamp n 423
oily adj 255, 355
oink v 412
ointment n 355, 356, 662
old adj 124, 128, 130
old age n 124, 128
older adj 128
old-fashioned adj 124
old hand n 700
old lady n 166, 903
old maid n 904
old man n 130, 166, 903
oldness n 124
old soldier n 700
Old Testament n 986
old woman n 130
oleaginous adj 355
olive adj 435
olive oil n 356
omen n 512
omen n 668
ominous adj 665, 668, 909
omission n 53, 55, 460, 732, 773, 893
omit v 55, 460, 773
omitted adj 893
omnipotence n 157, 976
omnipotent adj 104, 157
omnipresence n 186, 976
omnipresent adj 186
on adv 125, 282
on a bed of roses adv 377
on account of adv 155
on a large scale adv 31
on a level with adj 27
on a line with adv 278
on all sides adv 227
on a moment's notice adv 113
on an equal footing with adj 27
on a par with adj 27
on bended knee adv 879
once and for all adv 67
once more adv 90, 104
on compulsion adv 744
on condition adv 770

on dry land adv 342
one n 372; adj 13, 52, 87, 729
one and the same adj 27
one by one adv 44
on edge adv 507
one in a million n 648
on end adv 212
oneness n 87
one of a kind adj 20
onerous adj 649, 706, 830
oneself n 13
one's own n 11
one's own flesh and blood n 11
one step at a time adv 275
on every side adv 227
one way or another adv 627
on fire adj 382
on foot adj 170
ongoing adj 53
on land adv 342
onlooker n 444
only adv 32
only just adv 32
only so far adv 233
on no account adv 32
on no occasion adv 107
on one's back adv 213
on one's honor adj 768
on one side adv 217, 236
on one's own time adv 133
on one's toes adj 507
on purpose adv 620
onset n 66, 716
on sight adv 441
onslaught n 716
on target adj 494
on tenterhooks adj 507
on that occasion adv 119
on the average adv 29
on the ball adj 498
on the brink of adv 121
on the dot adv 132
on the eve of adv 121
on the face of it adv 448
on the face of the earth adv 180, 318
on the go adv 264
on the horizon adj 152, 507
on the horns of a dilemma n 476
on the instant adv 132
on the march adv 264
on the move adv 264

on the offensive adv 716
on the other hand adv 30
on the point of adv 121
on the road adj 264, 266
on the road to adv 278
on the safe side adj 664
on the sly adv 528
on the spot adv 132, 134
on the spur of the moment adv 113, 132, 134
on the wagon adj 958
on the wane adj 36
on the watch adj 457; adv 507
on the whole adv 50
on time adj 132; adv 132
ontology n 1
on trial adv 675
onus n 926
onward adv 282
ooze v 295, 348
oozing n 295
oozy adj 352
opacity n 426
opacity n 353
opalescence n 427
opalescent adj 427
opaline adj 430, 440
opaque adj 422, 426
opaqueness n 426
ope v 260
open v 66, 194, 198, 260, 525; adj 177, 260, 338, 525, 543, 665, 703
open air n 338
open-eyed adj 507
open field n 134
opening n 260
opening n 66, 198, 260
open into v 348
openly adv 525
openness n 525, 703, 748
open space(s) n 180
open to the view v 446
opera n 599
opera glasses n 445
operahouse n 599
operate v 161, 170, 680
operatic adj 415, 416
operation n 170, 680
operative adj 170, 680
operator n 690
ophthalmia n 443
opine 484
opinion n 451, 453, 480, 484, 537, 695, 821
opponent n 710

opponent n 726, 891
opportune adj 134, 646
opportunely adv 134
opportuneness n 134
opportunism n 646
opportunist n 935
opportunity n 134
oppose v 14, 179, 237, 536, 708, 719
opposed adj 14
opposer n 726
opposing n 708; adj 14, 237, 489
opposite n 237; adj 14, 218, 237
oppositeness n 14
opposite poles n 237
opposite side n 237
opposition n 237, 708
opposition n 14, 24, 218, 489, 710, 719, 720, 726
opposition n 179
oppress v 649, 739, 923
oppression n 649, 739
oppressive adj 382, 421, 649, 739, 830
oppressor n 739, 913
opprobrious adj 874
oppugnance n 719
opt for the mean v 774
optic adj 441
optical instruments n 445
optics n 420, 441
optimism n 482
optimistic adj 858
option n 600, 609
optional adj 600, 609
opulence n 803
opus n 590, 593
oracle n 513
oracle n 500
oracular adj 511
oral adj 580, 582
oral communication n 588
orange n 439
orange adj 439
orangish adj 439
orangy adj 439
oration n 582
orator n 582
oratory n 582
orb n 181, 247
orbit n 247
orchestra n 416, 417
orchestral adj 415
orchestral music n 415
orchid adj 437
ordain v 741, 755, 963, 995
ordained adj 996
ordeal n 722, 828
order n 58

order *n* 63, 75, 242, 630, 693, 697, 721, 741, 963; *v* 58, 630, 652, 673, 693, 741
ordered *adj* 60, 242
ordering *n* 60
orderliness *n* 58, 652
orderly *adj* 58, 60
order of succession *n* 63
ordinance *n* 741
ordinariness *n* 736
ordinary *adj* 82, 598, 613, 643, 651, 736
ordinary condition *n* 80
oread *n* 979
organic *adj* 357
organic chemistry *n* 357
organic remains *n* 357
organisms *n* 357
organization *n* 60, 161, 329, 626
organizational *adj* 329, 626
organize *v* 60, 161, 626
organized *adj* 58
organizer *n* 626
orgasm *n* 173, 377
orgasmic *adj* 173, 377
orifice *n* 260
origin *n* 66, 153
original *n* 22, 590, 857; *adj* 20, 79, 83, 153, 515, 614
originality *n* 18, 20, 83, 123, 168, 515
originate *v* 66, 153, 515
originate from *v* 154
originate in *v* 154
origination *n* 153
originator *n* 164
ornament *n* 577, 847
ornament *v* 577, 847
ornamental *adj* 847
ornamentation *n* 847
ornamented *adj* 577, 847
ornate *adj* 577, 847
ornateness *n* 577
ornithology *n* 368
orthodox *adj* 82, 983a
orthodoxy *n* 983a
orthography *n* 561
oscillate *v* 149, 314
oscillating *adj* 149, 314
oscillation *n* 314
oscillation *n* 138, 149, 605
ossification *n* 323
ossify *v* 323
ostensible *adj* 448, 617
ostensibly *adv* 448, 617

ostentation *n* 882
ostentatious *adj* 855, 882
ostracism *n* 893
ostracized *adj* 893
other *adj* 15
other side of the coin *n* 235
other time *n* 119
otherworldly *adj* 317
oust *v* 297, 789
out *adj* 187; *adv* 220
out and out *adv* 52
outbound *adj* 295
outbreak *n* 66, 173, 295, 713
outburst *n* 173, 295, 825
outcast *n* 893
outcome *n* 63, 65, 154
outcry *n* 404, 411
outdated *adj* 124
outdo *v* 33, 303
outer *adj* 220
outer edges *n* 233
outer space *n* 180
outfit *n* 225; *v* 225, 727
outflank *v* 236
outgoing *adj* 295
outgrow *v* 194
outgrowth *n* 65, 154
outing *n* 266
out in the open *adv* 338
outlandish *adj* 10, 83, 853
outlast *v* 110
outlawed *adj* 964
outlay *n* 809
outlet *n* 260
outline *n* 230
outline *n* 240, 448, 596; *v* 230
outlined *adj* 446
outlive *v* 110, 141
outlook *n* 441, 448
outlying *adj* 196, 220
outmoded *adj* 124
outnumber *v* 102
out of all proportion *adv* 31
out of commission *adj* 659
out of danger *adj* 664
out of date *adj* 124
out of debt *adj* 807
out of doors *adv* 338
out-of-fashion *adj* 124
out of focus *adj* 447
out of its element *adj* 185
out of joint *adj* 24
out of mind *adj* 506
out of one's depth *adv* 208

out of order *adj* 59, 651, 674, 923
out of place *adj* 59, 115, 185
out of practice *adj* 699
out of proportion *adj* 241; *adv* 641
out of shape *adj* 243
out of sight *adj* 447
out of sorts *adj* 655
out of step *adj* 24
out-of-style *adj* 124
out of the frying pan and into the fire *adv* 835
out-of-the-way *adj* 10, 196
out of tune *adj* 24, 414, 651
out of view *adj* 447
out of work *adj* 681
outpost *n* 196
outpouring *n* 295
outrage *n* 173, 619, 649
outrageous *adj* 31, 853
outrageousness *n* 853
outrank *v* 33
outride *v* 303
outrigger *n* 215
outright *adv* 52
outrival *v* 33
outrun *v* 303
outset *n* 66, 293
outside *n* 220; *adj* 220
outsides *n* 448
outside time *n* 107
outskirts *n* 196, 227
outspoken *adj* 703
outspread *adj* 202
outstretched *adj* 200, 202
outstrip *v* 33, 303
outward *adj* 220, 295
outwards *adv* 220
outweigh *v* 33, 175
outwit *v* 545
oval *n* 247; *adj* 247
oven *n* 386
over *adj* 40, 67; *adv* 33, 122, 220, 237
overabound *v* 641
over again *adv* 90, 104
over against *adv* 237
over and above *adj* 641; *adv* 33, 37, 641
over and done with *adv* 67
over and over *adv* 104
overbearing *adj* 878, 885
over-blown *adj* 882
overburden *v* 649
overcast *v* 421; *adj* 421, 422, 901a
overcharge *n* 814; *v* 577, 814

overcome v 731
over-confident adj 878
overdo v 641
overdose n 641; v 641
overdraw v 555
overdue adj 115, 133
overeat v 957
over-eating n 957
overestimate v 481, 482, 549
overestimated adj 482
overestimation n 482
overflow n 641; v 348, 641
overgrown adj 192, 194
overhang v 206
overhanging adj 206
overhear v 418
overlay v 223, 356a
overload v 641
overlook v 458, 460, 693
overlying adj 206
overly sensitive adj 901
overmatch v 28
overmuch adj 641; adv 641
over one's head adv 208, 641
overpower v 744
overpowering adj 824
overpraise v 482, 933
overprize v 482
overrate v 482
overrated adj 482
overreach v 303
over-refined adj 477
override v 175
overripe adj 128
overrun v 194, 303, 641
overseer n 694
overshoot v 303
oversight n 495
oversimplification n 78
overspread v 223
overstate v 549
overstatement n 549
overstep v 303
overtask v 679
overtax v 679
over the way adv 237
overthrow n 146, 162, 308; v 162, 308
overture n 763
overturn n 146, 218, 308; v 162, 218, 308, 479
overvaluation n 482
overweening adj 641, 880
overwhelm v 641
overwhelming adj 824

overwork v 679
overwrought adj 549, 824
overzealous adj 825
ovoid adj 249
owing to adj 154, 155
own v 488, 777
owner n 779
ownership n 777, 780
own in common v 778
own up v 529

P

P.M. n 126
pace n 264; v 106
pacific adj 174, 721, 723
pacification n 723
pacification n 174
pacify v 174, 723
pack n 72
pack it up v 293
pact n 23, 769
pad n 189; v 194, 224
padding n 224, 263
paddle v 267
paddock n 232
paean n 838
pagan n 984; adj 991
pagan deity n 991
pageant n 448
pageantry n 882
pain n 378, 828
pain n 619, 663, 686, 974, 982; v 649, 830
painful adj 378, 649, 830, 982
painfully adv 31, 830
painfulness n 830
painfulness n 649
pain in the neck n 663
pains n 459, 974
painstaking adj 459
paint n 428; v 428, 556
painter n 559
painting n 556
pair n 17, 89; v 89
pair off v 89
pal n 890
palatability n 394
palatable adj 377, 390, 394
palaver n 588
pale n 232, 233; v 422, 429; adj 422, 429, 430, 435
paleness n 422, 429
paleontology n 368
paling n 232
pall n 363; v 376, 395
palliative adj 174, 662, 834
pallid adj 429, 430
pallor n 429
palm n 733
palmer n 268

palpability n 379
palpable adj 3, 316, 379, 446, 525
palpitate v 315
palpitation n 315
palsied adj 160
paltriness n 32, 643. 736
paltry adj 32, 34, 643, 736
panacea n 662
pandemonium n 59, 982
pander to v 933
pang n 378, 828
panhandler n 767
panic n 860
panic-stricken adj 860
pant v 349, 382, 688
pap n 250
papa n 166
paper n 223
par n 27
parabola n 245
parade v 882
paradigm n 22
paradisaic adj 981
paradise n 981
paradisical adj 981
paradox n 497
paradoxical adj 497
paragon n 650, 948
paralipsis n 476
parallel n 17; v 9, 17, 19, 216; adj 17, 216, 242
parallelism n 216
parallelism n 13, 17, 23, 242
paralysis n 158, 376
paralytic adj 158, 376
paralyze v 158, 376
paralyzed adj 158
paramount adj 33, 642, 737
paramour n 897
paraphrase n 19, 21
parasitic adj 789
parasol n 223, 424
parboil v 384
parcel out v 60, 786
parch v 340, 382, 384
parched adj 340
pardon n 918, 970; v 918, 970
pare v 38, 195, 204
pared back adj 103
pare down v 38, 201
parentage n 166
parentage n 11
parental adj 166
parenthesis n 70
parenthetical adj 10, 228
parenthetically adv 10, 228

pariah *n* 893
parishioner *n* 997
parity *n* 27
parlance *n* 582
parley *n* 582, 588, 724
parody *n* 19, 21; *v* 19
paroxysm *n* 173, 825
parricide *n* 361
parry *v* 717
parsimonious *adj* 817, 819, 943
parsimony *n* 819
parsimony *n* 817, 943
parson *n* 996
part *n* 51
part *n* 56, 100a, 625; *v* 44, 51, 291
partake *v* 778
part company *v* 44
partial *adj* 28
partially *adv* 32, 51
participant *n* 690, 778
participate *v* 56, 709, 778
participation *n* 778
participation *n* 709
participatory *adj* 709, 778
particle *n* 32, 330
particular *n* 151; *adj* 79, 459, 474, 704
particularity *n* 79
particularize *v* 79
particularly *adv* 31, 33
particulars *n* 79
parting *n* 44
partisan *n* 890
partisanship *n* 709
partition *n* 786; *v* 51, 786
partly *adv* 51
partner *n* 711, 778, 903
partnership *n* 88, 178, 709, 778
part of speech *n* 562
parts of speech *n* 567
party *n* 712
party *n* 72, 372
party spirit *n* 709
party to *n* 690; *adj* 709
party to a suit *n* 969
pass *n* 7, 8, 151, 704; *v* 33, 109, 122, 264, 270, 302, 449, 783, 784
passable *adj* 651
passableness *n* 736
passably *adv* 32
passage *n* 302
passage *n* 144, 260, 267, 270, 627
pass a law *v* 963
pass away *v* 2, 67, 111, 122, 142, 360
pass by *v* 109
passed away *adj* 122

passenger *n* 268
passerby *n* 444
passing *n* 360; *adj* 111
passing time *n* 109
pass into *v* 144
passion *n* 173, 382, 820, 821, 824, 825, 865, 897
passionate *adj* 382, 574, 821, 825, 897
passive *adj* 172, 681, 725
passiveness *n* 172
passivity *n* 172, 681, 725
pass judgment *v* 480
pass muster *v* 648
pass off *v* 151
pass on *v* 360
pass out *v* 449
pass out of *v* 295
pass over *v* 55
pass sentence *v* 967
pass sentence upon *v* 480
pass through *v* 302
pass time *v* 106
past *adj* 122
past cure *adj* 659
paste *n* 354; *v* 46
past hope *adj* 659
pastiche *n* 41
pastime *n* 840
pastiness *n* 352
pastor *n* 996
pastoral *adj* 995
past recollection *adj* 506
past time *n* 122
pasturage *n* 344
pasture *n* 344
pasty *adj* 354, 391
pat *n* 276; *v* 276; *adj* 23
patch up *v* 660
patchwork *n* 41; *adj* 16a
pate *n* 450
patent *adj* 474, 525
paternal *adj* 166
paternity *n* 11, 166
path *n* 260, 278, 302
pathetic *adj* 830
pathless *adj* 261
patience *n* 826
patriarch *n* 130
patriarchal *adj* 166
patrician *adj* 875
patriot *n* 910
patrol *v* 664, 668
patron *n* 795, 890, 912, 977
patronage *n* 175, 707
patronize *v* 136
patter *v* 407
pattern *n* 22, 240, 650
pattern after *v* 19

paucity *n* 32, 103, 640
pauperism *n* 804
pause *n* 70, 142, 198, 265, 685, 687; *v* 70, 142, 265, 681, 687
paw *v* 379
pawn *n* 771; *v* 771, 787, 788
pawning *n* 788
pay *n* 973; *v* 784, 807, 973
pay attention *v* 457
pay in full *v* 807
paymaster *n* 801
payment *n* 807
payment *n* 809
pay no attention to *v* 458
pay out *v* 809
pea *n* 249
peace *n* 721
peace *n* 265, 403, 714
peaceable *adj* 721
peaceful *adj* 174, 265, 685, 721, 826
peacefulness *n* 174, 721
peacemaker *n* 724
peace offering *n* 723
pea-green *adj* 435
peak *n* 206, 210
peaked *adj* 253
peal *n* 404; *v* 404, 407
peal of bells *n* 407
peal of laughter *n* 838
pearliness *n* 427, 430
pearly *adj* 427, 428, 430, 440
pear-shaped *adj* 249
peasantry *n* 876
peat *n* 388
peck at *v* 298
peculiar *adj* 5, 79, 83, 870
peculiarities *n* 5
peculiarity *n* 83, 550
peculiarly *adv* 31, 33
pecuniary *adj* 800
pedagogic *adj* 537
pedagogical *adj* 537
pedagogics *n* 537
pedagogy *n* 537
pedant *n* 492
pedantic *adj* 577
peddler *n* 797
pedestal *n* 211
pedestrian *n* 268; *adj* 598
pedigree *n* 69
peek *n* 441; *v* 441
peel *n* 204, 223; *v* 204, 226
peep *n* 441; *v* 441
peephole *n* 260
peeping *adj* 455
peep of day *n* 125

peep up v 446
peer n 27; v 441
peevish adj 684, 901a
peg n 250
pellet n 249
pellucid adj 425, 570
pelt v 276
pen n 232, 752; v 590
penalize v 972, 974
penalized v 974; adj 972
penalizing adj 972
penalty n 974
penalty n 972
penance n 974
penchant n 177, 602
pencil v 556
pendant n 214
pendent adj 214
pendulous adj 214
pendulum n 214
penetrate v 294, 302
penetrating adj 480, 498
penetration n 294, 302, 441, 480, 498
penitence n 950
penitence n 833
penitent n 950; adj 833, 950
penitential adj 950
penitentiary n 752
penmanship n 590
pen name n 565
penniless adj 804
pennywise adj 819
pensioner n 785
pensive adj 451
pent up adj 751
penumbra n 421
penurious adj 819
penury n 804
people n 188, 372, 997; v 102
people the world v 163
pep n 171
pepper n 393; v 392
peppery adj 392
peradventure adv 470
perambulate v 264
perambulation n 266
perceivability n 446
perceivable adj 446
perceive v 375, 441, 490
perceptibility n 446
perceptible adj 446
perception n 418, 441, 453, 490
perceptive adj 375, 465, 490, 842
perch n 189; v 184, 186
perchance adv 156, 470

percolation n 295
percussion n 417
perdition n 162
peregrination n 266
peremptory adj 737, 739
perennial adj 69
perfect v 650, 729; adj 31, 52, 104, 648, 650, 729, 960
perfection n 650
perfection n 52, 648, 729, 960
perfectly adv 729
perfidious adj 544
perforate v 260
perforated adj 260
perforation n 260
perforator n 262
perform v 161, 170, 415, 416, 599, 644, 680, 772, 926
performable adj 470
performance n 161, 599, 680, 729, 772
perform a rite v 998
performer n 416, 599, 690
performing n 680
perfume n 400; v 400
perfumed adj 400
perfunctory adj 53, 640
perhaps adv 470
peril n 665
perilous adj 475, 665
perimeter n 230
period n 108
period n 71, 106, 138, 198, 200
periodic adj 70, 138
periodical adj 138
periodically adv 138
periodicity n 138
peripatetic adj 266
periphery n 230
perish v 2, 162, 360, 659
perishable adj 111
permanence n 141
permanence n 16, 110, 150
permanent adj 106, 110, 141, 150, 613
permanently adv 141
permeable adj 260
permeate v 186, 228, 302
permeation n 186, 228, 302
permissible adj 760
permission n 760
permission n 737, 762
permissive adj 760
permit n 737, 755, 760; v 737, 748, 760, 762

permitted adj 760
permutation n 140, 148
pernicious adj 649, 663
perpendicular adj 212, 246
perpendicularity n 212
perpetrate v 680
perpetrator n 690
perpetual adj 104, 110, 112, 136, 143, 150
perpetually adv 112, 136
perpetuate v 112, 143
perpetuation n 143
perpetuity n 112
perpetuity n 105
perplex v 475, 519, 704, 830
perplexed adj 59
perplexity n 59
persecute v 649, 830
persecution n 649
perseverance n 604a
perseverance n 143, 150, 604, 682
persevere v 604a, 682
persevering adj 604a
persicuity n 518
persist v 106, 110, 141, 143, 604a, 606, 682
persistence n 110, 141, 143, 604a, 606
persistent adj 141, 143, 604a, 606
person n 3, 372
personage n 372
personal adj 5, 79, 372
personality n 5, 13, 79
personate v 19, 554, 599
personify v 554
personnel n 56
persons n 372
perspective n 183, 441, 448
perspicacious adj 480, 498, 868
perspicacity n 441, 480, 868
perspicuity n 570
perspicuous adj 570
perspiration n 299, 339
perspire v 299, 339
persuade v 175, 615, 695
persuasion n 175, 484, 695
persuasive adj 615, 695
pertain to v 9
pertinacious adj 150, 606

pertinacity n 150, 606
pertinent adj 23
perturb v 61, 824
perturbation n 61, 315, 824
peruse v 539
pervade v 186
pervasion n 186
pervasive adj 186
pervasiveness n 186
perverse adj 606, 704, 901a
perversion n 477, 523, 538
perversity n 606
pervert v 477, 523, 538
pessimism n 483, 859
pessimist n 165
pessimistic adj 483, 837
pest n 975
pester v 830
pestilence n 649
pestilential adj 657
pet n 899
petite adj 32
petition n 765, 990; v 765, 990
petitioner n 767
petrification n 321, 323
petrify v 321, 323
petroleum n 356, 388
pettifogging adj 477
pettiness n 32
petty adj 32, 643
petulant adj 684, 901
phantasm n 443, 515
phantom n 4
phase n 7, 8, 71, 448
phenomenon n 151, 448, 872
philanthropic adj 784, 906, 910
philanthropist n 910
philanthropy n 910
philanthropy n 784, 906
philology n 562
philosopher n 500
phonetic adj 561
phonetics n 402, 561
phonology n 402
phony n 548; adj 19, 544
phosphorescence n 423
phosphorescent adj 420, 423
photoengraving n 558
photography n 420
phrase n 566
phrase n 521; v 566
phraseology n 560, 566, 569

physical adj 3, 173, 316
physical elements n 316
physical gratification n 377
physical insensibility n 381
physicality n 316
physical science n 316
physician n 662
physicist n 316
physics n 316
physiognomy n 448
physiology n 357
physique n 364
phytology n 369
pick n 609, 648; v 609
picket v 43
pickings n 793
pickle n 7; v 392, 670
pick of the litter n 648
pickup n 274
picky adj 465
pictorial adj 556
pictorialization n 556
picture n 448, 556; v 554, 594
picture gallery n 556
picturesque adj 556, 845
piddle v 683
piddling adj 643
piebald adj 440
piece n 51
piecemeal adv 51
pieces n 596
piece together v 43
pied adj 440
pierce v 260, 378, 385, 649
piercer n 262
pierce the ears v 404
piercing adj 404, 410, 498
pietist n 987
pietistic adj 987
piety n 987
pig n 957
pigeon n 547
pigeonhole n 182
piggish adj 957
piggishness n 957
pig-headed adj 606
pigment n 428
pigmy adj 193
pile n 72, 256
pile on v 641
pile up v 37
pilfer v 791
pilferer n 792
pilgrim n 268
pilgrimage n 266, 676
pill n 249
pilot n 269, 694; v 693

pimple n 250
pin n 253, 262, 263; v 43, 45
pince-nez n 445
pinch n 8, 704; v 195, 378, 385, 819
pinched adj 203
pinch hit v 147
pine v 655
pinhole n 260
pink adj 434
pinnacle n 206, 210
pioneer n 64
pious adj 987
pipe n 350
piquancy n 392, 394
piquant adj 392
pique n 900
piratical adj 791
pirouette n 312
pit n 208, 252, 363
pitapat n 407
pitch n 26, 210, 356a, 402, 413, 431; v 284, 306, 314
pitch black adj 421, 431
pitchy adj 431
piteous adj 830
piteously adv 31
pitfall n 667
pitfall n 530
pith n 5, 221
pithiness n 572
pithy adj 572, 574
pitiable adj 649, 830
pitiful adj 643, 649
pitiless adj 914a
pitilessness n 914a
pit one against another v 464
pittance n 640
pitted adj 848
pity n 914
pity n 821; v 914
pitying adj 914
pivot n 43, 153, 222; v 312
pivotal adj 222
pixie n 979
placate v 723
place n 182
place n 8, 58, 71, 183, 184; v 60, 184
place a bet v 621
place before v 62
placed adj 184
place in the record v 551
place of business n 799
place of departure n 293
place of learning n 542
place of worship n 1000
place side by side v 464

place together v 72
placid adj 721, 826
placidity n 826
plagiarism n 19
plague n 649, 663, 828, 975; v 828, 830
plaid adj 440
plain n 344
plain adj 16, 246, 446, 474, 518, 525, 570, 576, 703, 849, 879
plainly adv 525
plainness n 576
plainness n 570, 703, 849
plainsong n 413
plain-speaking n 518, 570, 703
plain spoken adj 525, 703
plaint n 411
plaintiff n 938
plaintive adj 839
plait n 219, 258; v 219, 258
plan n 626
plan n 60, 453, 673, 692; v 60, 620, 626, 673
plane n 213, 251; v 255, 267, 273; adj 213, 251
planets n 318
planning n 60
plant v 184, 300, 371
plant life n 357, 365, 367
plastered adj 959
plastic adj 324
plasticity n 324
plat v 219
plate n 22, 251; v 204
plateau n 344
plate engraving n 558
platitude n 517
platter n 204, 251
plausibility n 472
plausible adj 472
play n 170, 175, 180, 599; v 170, 416, 554, 599, 680, 840
played out adj 67
player n 416, 599
play false v 544, 940
play for v 621
playful adj 840, 842
playhouse n 599, 728
playing n 840
playing field n 728
play of colors n 440
play on words n 520
play second fiddle to v 749
play the fool v 497, 853
play the notes v 416

play truant v 187
play with v 140
playwright n 599
playwriter n 599
playwriting n 599
plea n 617
plea n 411
plead v 617, 765, 968
pleader n 968
pleading n 717
pleadings n 969
pleasant adj 829, 836, 840, 842
pleasantness n 829
pleasantry n 842
please v 829
pleasing adj 413, 850
pleasing combination n 413
pleasing sounds n 415
pleasurable adj 377, 829
pleasurableness n 829
pleasure n 377
pleasure n 827
pleasure n 377, 600, 840
pleasure-seeker n 954a
pleat n 258; v 258
plebeian adj 851, 876
pledge n 177, 768, 771; v 768, 788
pledged adj 768
pledging n 788
plenty n 641
plethora n 641
pliability n 324
pliable adj 324
pliancy n 324, 705, 725
pliant adj 324, 705
plight n 7, 8
plod v 275, 682
plot n 626; v 626
plough v 371
plow v 259, 371
plowed adj 959
pluck n 150, 604, 604a, 861; v 789
plucked instruments r 417
pluck out v 301
plug n 261, 263; v 261
plugging n 261
plug up one's ears v 419
plumb adj 212
plum-colored adj 437
plump adj 192
plumpness n 192
plunder n 793
plunge n 310
plunge n 300; v 208, 300, 310, 337, 863
plunge into v 676
plural adj 100
plurality n 100

plus adv 37
ply n 258; v 677
pock n 250
pocket v 789
poesy n 597
poet n 597
poetaster n 597
poetic adj 521, 597
poetical adj 597
poetic device n 521
poeticize v 597
poetics n 521, 597
poetry n 597
poetry n 590
poignancy n 392
poignant adj 516
point n 8, 26, 32, 71, 180a, 182, 253, 620; v 253, 278
point-blank adj 703; adv 278, 576
pointed adj 201, 253, 516, 518
pointedly adv 31, 620
pointedness n 253
pointer n 550
point of departure n 293
point of view n 441
point out v 525
points of the compass n 278
point to v 155, 472, 516, 938
point toward v 278
poison v 659, 663
poisonous adj 649, 657, 663
polar adj 210, 383
polarity n 89, 179, 218, 237
pole n 222
polemic n 726
polemicist n 476
poles apart adv 237
policy n 626, 692
polish n 255, 578, 850; v 255, 331
polished adj 255, 578, 850, 852
polite adj 383, 457, 852, 879, 894, 928
politeness n 457, 894
polite society n 852
politic adj 498, 702
poll n 85; v 85
pollute v 653, 659
poltroon n 862
poltroonery n 862
polyglot adj 560
polyp n 250
polyphony n 413
polysyllable n 561
pommel n 249
pomp n 882
pompous adj 482, 577,

882
pompousness n 882
pond n 343
ponder v 451, 870
pondering n 451
ponderous adj 319, 579
pool n 343, 709; v 709
poor adj 34, 477, 575, 640, 643, 736, 804, 828, 879
poorer adj 34
poorly adj 655
poorly timed adj 135
poorness n 34, 640
poor substitute adj 651
pop n 166, 406
pop music n 415
pop off v 360
populace n 72, 876
popular music n 415
populate v 102
population n 188, 372
populous adj 72, 102
pop up v 446
porch n 231, 260
pore over v 539
porous adj 260
port n 239
portable adj 270
portal n 231, 260
portend v 511, 668, 909
portent n 511, 512, 668, 909
portentous adj 511, 668
porter n 271; 532
portion n 51, 100a, 786
portion out v 786
portly adj 192
portrait n 21
portraiture n 554
portray v 554, 594
portrayal n 594
pose n 183; v 475, 704, 855
position n 8, 71, 183, 625
positive adj 1, 31, 84, 246, 474, 484, 535
possess v 777
possessed adj 503
possessed of adj 777
possessing adj 777
possession n 777
possession n 780
possessions n 780
possessive adj 777
possess oneself of v 789
possessor n 779
possess the means v 632
possibility n 470
possibility n 2, 156

possible adj 2, 177, 470, 515
possibly adv 470
post n 183; v 184, 274, 811
post bail v 771
post card n 592
postdate v 115
posterior n 235; adj 117, 235
posteriority n 117
posteriority n 63
posterity n 167
posterity n 121
posthaste adv 274
posthumous adj 117
postman n 271
post meridian n 126
post mortem examination n 363
postpone v 133
postponement n 133
postscript n 65
postulant n 767
postulate n 476, 514; v 476
posture n 8, 183, 240
potable adj 298
pot-bellied adj 194
potency n 157, 159
potent adj 157, 159, 171, 175
potential n 2; adj 2, 470, 526
potentiality n 470, 526
potion n 298
potpourri n 41
potted adj 959
potting n 557
pound n 232; v 330
pour v 333, 348
pour forth v 584
pour in v 294
pour out v 295, 348
pour out of v 295
pout v 900, 901a
poverty n 804
poverty-stricken adj 804
powder n 330
powdery adj 330
power n 157
power n 159, 171, 175, 404, 574, 737, 741, 965; v 388
powerful adj 157, 159, 171, 175, 404, 574
powerfully adv 31, 157
powerless adj 158, 160
powerlessness n 158, 175a
practicability n 705
practicable adj 644, 705
practical adj 170, 470, 644, 692

practicality n 470
practically adv 5
practice n 613, 692; v 677
practiced adj 698
practice law v 968
practice sorcery v 992
practitioner n 690
pragmatism n 646
prairie n 344
praise v 883, 931, 990
praised adj 931
praiseworthy adj 931
prance v 315
prank n 608
prate v 584, 588
prattle n 582, 584, 588
pray v 990
prayer n 411, 765, 990
preacher n 540, 996
preamble n 64
precarious adj 111, 475, 665
precariousness n 665
precaution n 510, 664, 673
precautionary adj 673
precede v 62, 116, 280
precedence n 62, 280
precedence n 116
precedent n 22, 64, 80, 613, 969; adj 62
preceding adj 62, 116
precept n 697
precept n 630
precincts n 227
precious adj 31, 814
precipice n 212, 306, 667
precipitancy n 684
precipitate v 684; adj 132, 684, 863
precipitately adv 132
precipitation n 132, 684
precipitous adj 217, 306
précis n 596; v 596
precise adj 494, 518
precision n 80, 494, 518
preclude v 761
precluded adj 893
preclusion n 893
precocious adj 132
precocity n 132
precursor n 64
precursor n 62, 116, 280, 534
precursory adj 64, 116
predatory adj 789, 791
predecessor n 64, 116
predeliberation n 611
predestination n 611
predestine v 152, 611

predetermination *n* 611

predetermine *v* 611

predicament *n* 8, 183, 704

predicate *v* 514

predict *v* 507, 510, 511

prediction *n* 511

prediction *n* 668

predilection *n* 177, 609

predisposed *adj* 820

predisposition *n* 176, 820

predominance *n* 33, 175

predominant *adj* 175, 737

predominate *v* 33, 175

pre-eminence *n* 33, 206

pre-eminent *adj* 33, 206

pre-eminently *adv* 31 33

pre-engage *v* 132

pre-existence *n* 116

pre-existent *adj* 116

preface *n* 64; *v* 62

prefatory *adj* 62, 64

prefer *v* 609

preference *n* 62, 609

preferential *adj* 609

prefix *n* 64; *v* 62

prehistoric *adj* 124

prelacy *n* 995

preliminary *adj* 62, 64, 673

prelude *n* 64, 66

premature *adj* 132, 135, 674

prematurely *adv* 132

prematurity *n* 132

premeditate *v* 611

premeditation *n* 611

premises *n* 476

premium *n* 973

premonition *n* 668

premonitory *adj* 511 668

preordain *v* 152

preparation *n* 673

preparation *n* 60, 64, 537

preparative *adj* 673

preparatory *adj* 62, 673

prepare *v* 60, 537, 673

prepared *adj* 507, 673, 698

prepare for *v* 507, 673

prepare for battle *v* 727

prepatory *adj* 673

preponderance *n* 33. 175

preponderant *adj* 737

preposterous *adj* 497, 549, 853

preposterously *adv* 31

prepubescence *n* 131

prerequisite *n* 630

prerogative *n* 924

presage *n* 511, 668; *v* 116, 511, 909

presbyopia *n* 443

prescience *n* 510

prescient *adj* 510

prescribe *v* 693, 695, 741

prescribed *adj* 474, 924

prescript *n* 697

prescription *n* 613, 697, 924

prescriptive *adj* 124, 613, 983a

presence *n* 186

presence *n* 1, 448

present *n* 784; *v* 448, 763, 784; *adj* 118, 186

presentation *n* 784

present events *n* 151

presentiment *n* 477

present itself *v* 446

presently *adv* 132

present the music *v* 416

present time *n* 118

present to the view *v* 448

preservation *n* 670

preservation *n* 141, 664, 717, 781

preservative *adj* 670

preserve *v* 141, 143, 664, 670, 717, 781

preserved *adj* 670

preserver *n* 664

president *n* 694

press *n* 72; *v* 255, 319

press forward *v* 684

press in *v* 300

pressing *adj* 642

press into service *v* 677

press on *v* 622, 684

press onward *v* 282

pressure *n* 175, 319, 642, 735

presto *adv* 113

presumable *adj* 472

presumably *adv* 472

presume *v* 484, 514, 858, 878, 885

presumption *n* 507, 514, 878, 925

presumptive *adj* 514

presumptuous *adj* 863, 878, 885

presuppose *v* 514

pretend *v* 544, 546, 617, 855

pretender *n* 548, 925

pretense *n* 617, 855, 882

pretention *n* 577, 855, 882

pretentious *adj* 482, 855, 882, 884

pretentiousness *n* 882

pretext *n* 617

pretty *adj* 845; *adv* 31

pretty well *adv* 31, 32

prevail *v* 33, 78, 175

prevailing *adj* 78, 983a

prevail upon *v* 615

prevalence *n* 33, 78, 175, 613

prevalent *adj* 1, 78, 175, 613

prevaricate *v* 520, 544

prevarication *n* 520, 544

prevent *v* 706, 708, 761

preventing *n* 706

prevention *n* 761

preventive *adj* 761

previous *adj* 116

previously *adv* 116

prevision *n* 510

prey *n* 620

price *n* 812

price *v* 812

priceless *adj* 33, 648, 814

prick *n* 253; *v* 260, 378, 380

pricking *n* 380

prickle *n* 253

prickly *adj* 253, 256

prick up one's ears *v* 418

pride *n* 878

pride *n* 880

priest *n* 904, 996

priesthood *n* 995, 996

priestly *adj* 995

prig *n* 854

priggish *adj* 868

prim *adj* 868

primal *adj* 66, 153

primary *adj* 153, 642

primary color *n* 428

prime *n* 125, 648; *v* 537, 673; *adj* 84, 642, 648

prime mover *n* 153, 976

prime of day *n* 125

primer *n* 542, 567

primeval *adj* 124

primitive *adj* 124

primordial *adj* 124

princely *adj* 816

prince of darkness *n* 978

principal *n* 694; *adj* 642

principally *adv* 33
principle *n* 5, 80, 153, 211, 537, 615
print *n* 591; *v* 531, 558, 590, 591
printed *adj* 591
printer *n* 591
printing *n* 591
prior *adj* 62, 116
priority *n* 62, 116, 280
prior to *adv* 116
prism *n* 428, 445
prismatic *adj* 428, 440
prison *n* 752
prison *n* 975
prisoner *n* 754
pristine *adj* 122
privacy *n* 893
private *adj* 79, 221, 528, 533, 893
privately *adv* 881
privation *n* 776, 804
privilege *n* 748, 924, 927a
privileged *adj* 924, 927a
privy *adj* 528
privy to *adj* 490
prize *n* 618, 733, 793, 973; *v* 991
probability *n* 472
probability *n* 156
probable *adj* 472, 858
probably *adv* 472
probationary *adj* 675
probative *adj* 463, 478
probe *n* 262
probity *n* 939
probity *n* 543, 944
problem *n* 533, 704
problematical *adj* 59, 475
procedural *adj* 80, 626, 692
procedure *n* 80, 463, 626, 627, 680, 692, 998
proceed *v* 109, 282, 302
proceed from *v* 154
proceeding *n* 151, 282; *adj* 53
proceeds *n* 775
proceed with *v* 692
process *n* 627, 692
procession *n* 69, 266
proclaim *v* 531, 883
proclamation *n* 531, 985
proclivity *n* 176, 698, 820
procrastinate *v* 133
procrastination *n* 133, 683
procreate *v* 161, 168
procreation *n* 161, 168

procreative *adj* 168
procreator *n* 166
procure *v* 775, 795
procurement *n* 775
prod *v* 276
prodigal *n* 818; *adj* 638, 818
prodigality *n* 818
prodigality *n* 638
prodigal son *n* 950
prodigious *adj* 31
prodigy *n* 872
prodigy *n* 700
produce *n* 775, 798; *v* 153, 161, 168
produce a good effect *v* 648
produce nothing *v* 169
producer *n* 164
producer *n* 153
product *n* 84, 154, 161, 798
production *n* 161
production *n* 153
productive *adj* 153, 161, 168, 644
productiveness *n* 168
productiveness *n* 644
productivity *n* 168
proem *n* 64
profanation *n* 679
profane *v* 679, 988
profaneness *n* 988
profanity *n* 988
profession *n* 535, 625, 768
professional *n* 700; *adj* 625
professor *n* 540
proffer *v* 763
proficiency *n* 698, 731
proficient *adj* 698, 731
profile *n* 230, 236, 448; *v* 230
profit *n* 618, 775; *v* 618, 648, 775
profitability *n* 646
profitable *adj* 644, 646, 648, 775, 810
profit by *v* 677
profitless *adj* 645
profligacy *n* 818
profligate *n* 962; *adj* 818, 945
profound *adj* 31, 208, 498
profundity *n* 208, 875
profuse *adj* 102, 573, 641, 818
profuseness *n* 573, 641, 818
profusion *n* 102, 641, 818
progenitor *n* 166
progeny *n* 167
prognosticate *v* 507,

511, 909
prognostication *n* 511, 909
progress *n* 144, 264, 282, 731; *v* 282, 658, 731
progression *n* 282
progression *n* 58, 69
progressive *adj* 69, 282, 658
prohibit *v* 761, 893
prohibited *adj* 893, 964
prohibition *n* 761
prohibition *n* 55, 893
prohibitive *adj* 761
project *n* 620, 626; *v* 250, 284, 620, 626
projection *n* 250, 284
proletarian *adj* 876
proletariat *n* 876
prolific *adj* 161, 168
prolix *adj* 573
prolog *n* 64
prolong *v* 35, 110, 133, 143, 200
prolongation *n* 110, 133, 143
prolonged *adj* 110
promenade *n* 266
prominence *n* 206, 250, 307, 642
prominent *adj* 206, 250, 642
prominently *adv* 31, 33
promiscuous *adj* 41
promise *n* 768
promise *n* 771; *v* 676, 768, 769, 771
promised *adj* 768
promises *n* 770
promising *adj* 858
promissory *adj* 768, 769
promissory note *n* 771
promontory *n* 250
promote *v* 176, 658, 707
prompt *v* 505, 615; *adj* 132, 682
promptitude *n* 132, 684
promptness *n* 684
promulgate *v* 531
promulgation *n* 531
prone *adj* 207, 213, 820
proneness *n* 176, 207, 213
pronounce *v* 535, 580, 582, 586
pronouncement *n* 531, 535
proof *n* 463, 467, 478, 591
proofreader *n* 591

prop n 215; v 707
propagandist n 540
propagate v 161, 531
propagation n 168, 531
propane n 356, 388
propel v 264, 284
propensity n 176, 177, 602, 820
proper adj 79, 494, 578, 646, 868, 881, 922
proper name n 564
proper time n 134
property n 780
prophecy n 511
prophesy v 511
prophet n 513
prophetess n 513
prophetic adj 511
propinquity n 197
propitiate v 723, 826, 952
propitiating adj 952
propitiation n 952
propitiatory adj 952
propitious adj 134, 648, 734, 858, 888
proportion n 9, 242, 786
proportionate adj 413
proportions n 180, 192
proposal n 620, 763
propose v 476, 514, 620, 763
proposition n 476, 514, 763
propound v 514
proprietor n 779
proprietorship n 777
proprietress n 779
propriety n 578, 646, 852, 881
propulsion n 284
propulsion n 276
propulsive adj 284
propulsive force n 284
prop up v 215
prosaic adj 575, 598, 841, 843
pros and cons n 476
proscenium n 234
proscribe v 971
proscribed adj 964
proscription n 971
proscriptive adj 761
prose n 598
prosecute v 622, 680, 969
prosecuting attorney n 968
prosecution n 969
prosecutor n 938, 968
prospect n 121, 448, 472, 507, 510
prospective adj 507, 510

prospectively adv 121
prospects n 152
prospectus n 596
prosper v 731, 734
prosperity n 734
prosperity n 618. 731
prosperous adj 731, 734
prostitute n 962; v 679
prostitution n 679
prostrate v 213, 308; adj 207, 213, 308
prostration n 158, 207, 213, 308, 828
prosy adj 575, 598
protect v 664, 670, 717
protected adj 223
protection n 175, 664, 670, 717
protective adj 717
protector n 664, 753, 977
protest n 489, 764, 766, 808; v 489, 766
protester n 489
protoplasm n 357
prototype n 22
prototype n 80
protract v 110, 133, 200
protracted adj 110, 200, 573
protraction n 110, 133, 143
protrude v 250
protrusion n 250
protuberance n 250
protuberant adj 250
proud adj 878, 880
prove v 151, 463, 478
proved adj 478
proven adj 478
provender n 298, 637
proverb n 496
proverbial adj 496
provide v 637, 673, 746, 770
provide against v 673
provided adj 469; adv 8
provided that adj 469
providence n 976
provident adj 510, 673, 864
providential adj 134
providing n 637
province n 75, 181
provincial adj 181, 246
provision n 637
provision n 673, 803; v 637
provisional adj 8, 111, 673, 770
provisionally adv 8, 770
provisions n 298, 632, 770

proviso n 469
provisos n 770
provocation n 824
provocative adj 615
provoke v 153, 824, 830
prowl v 266
proximate adj 63, 197
proximation n 197
proximity n 186, 197, 199
proxy n 634, 759
prudence n 459, 480, 498, 510, 864
prudent adj 451, 459, 498, 510, 864
prudery n 881
prudish adj 881
prudishness n 881
prune v 38, 201
prurience n 961
prurient adj 961
pry v 441, 455
prying n 455; adj 455
pseudo adj 17
pseudonym n 565
psychical adj 317
puberty n 127, 131
pubescence n 131
pubescent adj 131
public n 372; adj 260, 372, 531
public address n 586
publication n 531
publication n 161, 590, 593, 985
publicity n 531
publicize v 531
public prosecutor n 968
public spirit n 910
public spirited adj 910
publish v 531, 591
published adj 527, 531
publisher n 593
pucker n 258; v 258, 259
puerile adj 129, 499, 575
puerility n 499
puff n 349; v 349, 688
puffery n 549
puffiness n 194
puff up v 194, 549, 880
pugnacious adj 720
puissance n 157
puissant adj 159
puke v 297
pulchritude n 845
pulchritudinous adj 845
pull n 288, 319; v 267, 285, 288, 301, 319
pull an all-nighter v 539
pulling n 285, 301

pull no punches

pull no punches v 703
pull out v 301
pull out of a hat v 612
pull out of the air v 612
pull the shade v 424
pull through v 660
pull together v 178, 709, 714
pull to pieces v 162
pull up v 142, 301
pulp n 354; v 354
pulpiness n 354
pulpy adj 354
pulsate v 138, 314, 315
pulsating adj 314, 315
pulsation n 138, 314
pulse n 138, 314
pulverization n 330
pulverize v 330
pulverulence n 330
pump n 348; v 349
pun v 520; v 842
punch n 22, 276; v 276
puncher n 262
punctilious adj 543, 772, 882
punctual adj 132, 138
punctuality n 132, 138
punctually adv 132
puncture v 260
pungency n 392
pungent adj 392, 394, 398, 574
punish v 972, 974
punished v 974; adj 972
punishing adj 972
punishment n 972
punishment n 974, 975
punitive adj 972
punster n 844
punt v 267
puny adj 193
pupil n 492, 541
puppet n 547
purblind adj 442, 443
purblindness n 443
purchase n 795
purchase n 775; v 795
purchaser n 795
purchasing n 795
pure adj 42, 494, 576, 578, 652, 881, 944, 946, 960, 977
purely adv 32
purgation n 652
purgative n 652
purge v 297, 652, 952
purification n 42, 652
purify v 42, 652
purist n 578
puritan n 955
puritanical adj 955
puritanism n 955
purity n 960

purity n 42, 578, 652, 944, 946
purlieus n 227
purloin v 791
purple n 437
purple adj 437
purplish adj 437
purport v 516; v 516
purpose n 451, 516, 600, 615, 620; v 451, 516, 620
purposeful adj 604
purposely adv 620
purr v 412
purring n 412
purse n 802
purser n 801
pursuance n 622
pursue v 143, 286, 281, 622
pursuit n 622
pursuit n 461, 625
pursuit of knowledge n 539
purvey v 637
purveyance n 637
purveying n 637
push n 276, 284; v 276, 284, 682
push ahead v 682
push aside v 297
push away v 297
push back v 289
push on v 684
pusillanimous adj 862
pustule n 250
put v 184
put about v 311
put an end to v 67
put an end to oneself v 361
put aside v 55, 636, 678
put away v 528
put down v 856
put forth v 514
put forward v 763
put in v 300
put in motion v 284
put in order v 660
put in the place of v 147
put into operation v 677
put into shape v 60
put into words v 566
put off v 133, 226
put on airs v 855
put on a pedestal v 991
put one's trust on v 484
put on sale v 813
put on the brakes v 275
put on the stage v 599
put on trial v 969
put out v 385, 421
put out of order v 59

put out to sea v 293
put pen to paper v 590
putrefaction n 49, 653
putrefy v 653
putrid adj 401, 653
put right v 246, 662
put straight v 246
putter v 683
put things in order v 652
put to death v 361
put to flight v 717
put together v 43
put to sea v 267
put to the sword v 361
put to use v 677
putty n 356a
put up v 161, 235, 636
put up to v 615
put up with v 151, 826
puzzle v 475
puzzlement n 870
puzzling adj 519

Q

quack v 412
quadrilateral adj 95
quadripartite adj 97
quadripartition n 97
quadrisection n 97
quadruped n 366
quadruple adj 96
quadruplicate v 96
quadruplication n 96
quadrupling n 96
quaff v 298
quaggy adj 345
quagmire n 345, 653
quail v 862
quaint adj 83
quake v 314, 315, 383
qualification n 469
qualification n 140, 536, 698, 813
qualified adj 469, 698
qualify v 140, 174, 469
qualifying adj 469
qualities n 820
quality n 5, 33, 176, 550, 780, 875, 944
qualm n 485, 603
quandary n 704
quantitative adj 25
quantity n 25
quantity n 31, 72, 102
quarrel n 713, 720; v 24, 713
quarrelsome adj 713, 720
quarry n 620
quarter n 95, 97, 181, 236, 740; v 97, 184
quartered adj 97
quartering n 97
quarter of a hundred n 98
quarters n 189

quartet n 95, 415, 416
quasi adv 17
quaternity n 95
quaver n 315, 407, 408; v 314, 315
queer adj 83
queer fish n 857
quell v 265
quench v 385, 829
querulous adj 868
query n 461; v 461
quest n 622, 676
quester n 268
question n 461, 533; v 461, 475, 870, 989
questionable adj 473, 475, 485, 520
questionableness n 473, 475, 520
questioning n 461, 539; adj 461
quibble n 520; v 477
quibbling adj 477
quick adj 111, 274, 498, 682, 684, 698, 842
quick as lightning adj 274
quicken v 132, 170, 173, 274, 359, 684, 824
quickly adv 132
quickness n 132, 274, 684
quicksand n 667
quick-tempered adj 901
quick to fly off the handle v 901
quick-witted adj 842
quiddity n 477
quid pro quo n 30
quiescence n 150, 172, 265, 403, 526, 683
quiescent adj 172, 265, 403
quiet n 174, 403, 721; v 174, 723; adj 174, 403, 585, 685
quietly adv 881
quietude n 265, 826
quietus n 360
quilt n 223; v 440
quinquepartite adj 99
quinquesection n 99
quintessence n 5
quintet n 415
quirk n 83, 608
quit v 293, 624, 757, 782, 807
quite adv 52
quits n 27; adj 27
quittance n 952
quitter n 623
quitting n 782
quiver n 315, 407; v 277, 314, 315, 383

quota n 786

R

rabbi n 996
rabble n 876
rabid adj 825
race n 11, 75, 188, 274, 348; v 274
raciness n 574
rack n 378
racket n 315, 404, 407, 414
racy adj 574
radial adj 291
radiance n 420, 845
radiant adj 291, 420, 423, 845
radiate v 291, 420
radiation n 73, 291, 420
radical n 489, 658, 742; adj 52
radioactivity n 420
rage n 825, 852; v 173, 825
raging adj 173, 824
ragtime n 415
raid n 716
rail n 232
rail at v 856
railing n 232
raillery n 856
raiment n 225
rain n 348; v 348
rain cats and dogs v 348
rainfall n 348
rain hard v 348
rain in buckets v 348
rain in torrents v 348
rainy adj 348
raise v 35, 161, 235, 250, 307, 370
raised adj 250
raise one's voice v 411
raise spirits v 992
raise to a fervor v 824
raise up v 206
raising n 307, 370
rake n 962; v 371
rake out v 301
rally v 660
rallying point n 74
rally round v 709
ram n 373
ramble v 266, 279, 499, 573
rambler n 268
rambling adj 47, 266, 279
ramification n 51, 291
ramify v 291
ram in v 300
rammer n 263
rampage v 173
rampant adj 173, 175, 307, 748

ramrod n 263
ramshackle adj 124
ranch v 370
ranching n 370
rancid adj 397, 401, 653
rancidity n 401
rancor n 907
rancorous adj 907
random adj 156, 621
range n 26, 69, 180, 196, 200, 278, 386, 965; v 60, 196, 266
rank n 26, 58, 69, 71, 875; v 58, 60, 480; adj 365, 401, 649
rank and file n 876
rankle v 653, 659
rankness n 401
rant n 517, 549, 577; v 503, 517, 582, 825
ranter n 584
rap n 276, 406, 588; v 276, 406, 588
rapacious adj 789, 819
rapacity n 819
rapid adj 274, 684
rapidity n 274, 684, 819
rapids n 348
rapture n 827, 897, 993
rapturous adj 821, 829, 977
rare adj 20, 83, 103, 137, 322, 648
rarefaction n 322
rarefy v 322
rarely adv 137
rare occurrence n 137
rarity n 137, 322
rascal n 941
rash n 72; adj 499, 684, 863
rashness n 863
rashness n 499
rasp n 330; v 330, 331
rasping n 410; adj 410
rafatat n 407
rate n 26, 264, 812; v 466, 480
rather adv 32
ratification n 535, 762
ratify v 535
ratio n 9, 26, 786
ratiocination n 476
ration n 786
rational adj 450, 498, 502
rationale n 155, 462
rationalism n 476
rationalist n 476
rationalistic adj 476
rationality n 450, 502
rations n 298
rattle v 407
raucousness n 410
ravage v 162, 659

ravager n 165
rave v 503
ravel v 219
raveled adj 59
raveling n 59
ravenous adj 789
raver n 504
ravine n 198, 259
raving n 503; adj 173, 824
ravish v 829
ravishment n 824, 827
raw adj 378, 383, 435, 674, 699
raw materials n 635
ray n 420
raze v 162
razor edge n 253
razor sharp adj 253
reach n 26, 196, 200; v 27, 270
reach a point v 292
reaching n 292
reach to v 196, 200
react v 179, 277, 287
reaction n 145, 179, 276, 277, 287, 718
reactionary adj 179, 277
reactive adj 718
read v 539
readable adj 578
reader n 542, 591
readily adv 705
readiness n 132, 602, 673, 698
read the law v 968
ready adj 507, 602, 673, 682
ready for battle v 727
real adj 1, 494
real estate n 342, 780
realism n 646
reality n 1, 494
realize v 450, 484, 490
realm n 181
reanimate v 163, 359, 660, 689
reanimation n 163
reap v 371, 789
reappear v 104
reappearance n 104, 163
reappearing adj 163
rear n 235
rear n 235; v 161, 235, 307; adj 235
rearguard n 235
rear rank n 235
rearward adv 235
reason n 450, 498, 502, 615; v 450, 498
reasonable adj 174, 472, 498, 502, 736, 815
reasonable chance n

472
reasonableness n 174; 498
reasoner n 476
reason falsely v 477
reasoning n 476
reasoning adj 476
reasons n 476
reason why n 155
reassuring adj 858
rebate n 813; v 813
rebel n 165, 489; v 146, 719, 742
rebellion n 146, 719, 742
rebellious adj 146, 715, 742
rebelliousness n 715, 742
reborn adj 660
rebound n 145, 277; v 145, 277
rebuff n 277, 289, 764; v 289, 610, 764
rebuild v 660
rebuilding n 660
rebut v 462, 468, 536
rebuttal n 468, 536
recalcitrance n 715
recalcitrant adj 715, 719, 742, 764
recall v 451, 505
recant v 536, 607
recantation n 607
recantation n 536
recapitulate v 104
recapitulation n 104
recast v 140, 146, 626
recede v 283, 287
receipt n 810
receipt n 771, 807
receive v 76, 296, 775, 785, 789, 810
receive an impression v 821
received adj 490, 785
receive pleasure v 377
receiver n 191, 785, 801
receive the call v 996
receiving n 785
receiving adj 785
recent adj 122, 123, 435
recentness n 123
receptacle n 191
reception n 296
reception n 76, 292, 785
recess n 198, 244, 530, 687
recesses n 221
recession n 287
recession n 283, 659
recipient n 785
reciprocal adj 12, 148,

718
reciprocally adv 12
reciprocate v 12, 148
reciprocation n 12, 148, 718
reciprocity n 12, 148, 718
recision n 756
*recital n 594
recitation n 582
recite v 85, 594
reckless adj 684, 863
recklessness n 460, 863
reckon v 85, 480, 873
reckoning n 85, 466, 507, 807, 811, 973
reckon up v 807
reclaim v 660, 952
reclamation n 660, 952
reclination n 213
recline v 213, 687
recluse n 893, 955
recognition n 505, 733
recognizable adj 446
recognize v 441
recognized adj 490
recoil n 277
recoil n 145, 283, 287, 603, 623; v 145, 179, 277, 287, 325, 603, 623
recollect v 451, 505
recollection n 505
recommend v 695
recommendation n 695
recompense n 973; v 30, 807, 973
reconcilable adj 23
reconcile v 723, 831
reconcile oneself to v 826
reconciliation n 723
recondition v 662
reconstitute v 660
reconstruct v 660
reconstruction n 660
reconversion n 660
record n 551
record n 86, 527, 594; v 60, 551
recorder n 53
recount v 594
recounting n 594
recoup v 660, 790
recouperative adj 790
recourse n 677
recover v 660, 789, 790
recovery n 660, 789, 790
recovery of strength n 689
recreant adj 544, 862
recreation n 840
recrimination n 718

rectification n 660
rectify v 246, 658
rectilinear adj 246
rectitude n 922, 939, 944
recumbency n 213
recuperative adj 660
recur v 104, 136, 138
recure v 660
recurrence n 104, 136
recurrent adj 70, 104, 138
recurring adj 104, 136, 138
recur to v 677
recurve v 245
recusancy n 984
recusant adj 984
red n 434
red adj 434
red and yellow n 439
red as a lobster adj 434
red as beet adj 434
redden v 434
reddish adj 434
redeem v 30, 147, 660, 672, 790, 952
redemption n 660, 672, 952
redemptive adj 790, 952
redesign v 140
red-faced adj 434
red-hot adj 824
redneck n 887
redness n 434
redolence n 398, 400
redolent adj 398, 400
redouble v 35, 90
redress n 660, 662, 973; v 660, 662
reduce v 38, 103, 195, 201, 308, 638, 813
reduced adj 34, 103, 201
reduce to v 144
reduce to a square v 95
reducible adj 38
reductio ad absurdum n 476
reduction n 36, 103, 144, 195, 201, 813
reduction to power n 330
redundance n 641
redundance n 104
redundancy n 573
redundant adj 104, 641
reduplicate v 90
reduplication n 90
re-echo v 408
reed instruments n 417
reef n 346
reefs n 667
reek v 401, 653
reeking adj 382, 401

reeky adj 653
reel v 314, 315
reestablish v 660
reestablishment n 660
refashion v 163
referable adj 155
referable to adj 9
referee n 967; v 174
reference n 9, 467
reference to n 155
referential adj 467
refer to v 9, 155, 695
refine v 477, 652, 658
refined adj 428, 465, 850, 852
refinement n 465, 578, 658, 850
reflect v 19, 420, 451
reflection n 420, 451
reflective adj 451, 498
reflector n 445
reflex n 145, 276, 277; adj 283
reflexion n 21
refluent adj 283
reflux n 283
reform v 144, 658
reformation n 658
reformative adj 658
reformer n 658
refraction n 279, 291, 420; 443
refractory adj 606, 719, 742, 945
refrain n 623, 681
refresh v 159, 338, 385, 660, 689, 829, 834
refreshing adj 689
refreshment n 689
refreshment n 159, 660
refrigerate v 383, 385
refrigeration n 385
refrigerator n 387
refuge n 666
refugee n 268, 623
refusal n 764
refusal n 603, 610
refuse n 40; v 536, 603, 610, 708, 764
refutable adj 479
refutation n 468, 479
refute v 468, 479
regale v 829
regalia n 747
regard n 441, 451, 457, 459, 873, 897, 928, 987, 990; v 9, 418, 451, 457, 480, 873, 928
regarded adj 873
regardful adj 451
regarding v 418; adj 928
regards n 928
regenerate v 163
regeneration n 163, 660

regenerative adj 163
reggae n 415
regicide n 361
regiment n 72
regimentals n 225
region n 181
regional adj 181
register n 86, 114, 551, 553, 811; v 60, 114, 551
registrar n 553
regnant adj 737
regress n 287; v 145, 283, 287
regression n 283
regression n 287
regressive adj 283
regret n 833
regret v 950; v 832, 833, 950
regretful adj 832, 833, 950
regular adj 16, 58, 60, 80, 138, 240, 242, 613
regular as clockwork adj 138
regularity n 138
regularity n 16, 58, 80, 138 242
regularly adv 138
regulate v 58, 60, 174, 692, 693
regulation n 80
regulation n 693, 697, 963
regurgitate v 297, 348
regurgitation n 297
rehabilitate v 660, 790
rehabilitation n 660, 790
rehash v 104
rehearsal n 673
rehearse v 104, 594, 673
reign n 175
reimburse v 790, 807
reinforce v 37, 159
reinforcement n 39
reinstate v 660
reinstatement n 660
reinvest v 790
reinvestment n 790
reinvigorate v 660, 689
reiterate v 104, 136
reiteration n 104, 136
reject v 55, 297, 536, 610, 764, 893
rejected adj 893
rejection n 610
rejection n 55, 297, 536, 764, 893
rejoice v 836, 838
rejoice in v 827
rejoicing n 838
rejoin v 72, 462

rejoinder n 462
rekindle v 384
relapse n 661
relapse v 145, 287, 661
relate v 12, 216, 464, 594
related adj 9, 11
relate to v 9
relating n 464
relating to adj 9
relation n 9
relation n 11, 594
relationship n 9, 11
relative n 11; adj 9
relative to adj 9
relator n 938
relax v 47, 160, 275, 324, 683, 685, 687, 738
relaxation n 47, 160, 174, 687, 738, 840
relaxed adj 47, 160, 174
relaxing adj 840
release n 360, 671, 672, 750, 777a, 783, 807; v 672, 750, 777a, 927a, 970
released adj 970
relegate v 55, 270
relegation n 270
relent v 324
relentless adj 604, 739, 914a
relentlessness n 739
relevant adj 9
reliability n 150, 474
reliable adj 150, 246, 474, 664
reliance n 484, 507, 858
relic n 40, 124, 551
relics n 362
relied on adj 871
relief n 834
relief n 250, 660, 662, 689, 707
relieve v 707, 834
religion n 983
religious adj 983, 987
religious garments n 999
religious persuasion n 983
religious truth n 983a
religious writings n 986
relinquish v 624, 678, 757, 782
relinquishment n 624, 782
relinquishment n 678, 757
relish n 377, 390, 393, 394; v 377, 394, 827
relocate v 184
reluctance n 603, 704,

719
reluctant adj 603, 764
rely on v 484, 507, 858
remain v 1, 40, 106, 110, 141, 186, 265
remainder n 40
remaining adj 40
remains n 40, 362, 551
remake v 144
remark v 457
remarkable adj 31, 870
remarkably adv 31
remediable adj 660
remedial adj 660, 662
remediless adj 859
remedy n 662
remedy n 660, 662, 834
remember v 451, 505
remembrance n 505
remind v 505
reminder n 505
reminisce v 505
reminiscence n 505
reminiscent (of) adj 505
remiss adj 460, 674, 683, 738
remission n 756, 918
remissness n 460, 683
remit v 790
remittance n 807
remnant n 40
remodel v 140, 144, 146
remonstrance n 616, 766
remonstrate v 616, 766
remonstrative adj 766
remorse n 833, 950
remorseful adj 950
remorseless adj 951
remote adj 10, 196
remote cause n 153
remoteness n 196
remote past n 122
removable adj 38
removal n 38, 185, 270, 287, 293, 301
remove n 196; v 2, 38, 185, 270, 301, 662
removed adj 196
remunerate v 30, 807, 973
remuneration n 973
remunerative adj 775, 810, 973
renaissance n 660
renascence n 660
renascent adj 163, 660
rend v 44
render v 144, 784, 790
render blunt v 254
render certain v 474
render concave v 252
render curved v 245
render few v 103

render general v 78
render horizontal v 213
render insensible v 376
render intelligible v 518
render invisible v 447
render oblique v 217
render powerless v 158
render sensible v 375
render straight v 246
render uncertain v 475
render unintelligible v 519
render violent v 173
rendezvous n 74
renegade n 607
renew v 90, 123, 163, 660, 689
renewal n 90, 163, 660
renounce v 536, 607, 610, 624, 757, 764, 782
renovate v 123, 163, 660
renovated adj 123
renovation n 123, 163, 660
renown n 31, 873
renowned adj 873, 883
rent n 44, 198, 260; v 788
renunciation n 607, 610, 624, 757, 764, 782
reorganize v 144, 660
repair n 658, 660, 689; v 658, 660, 662, 689, 790, 952
reparation n 30, 660, 790, 952, 973
reparatory adj 973
repartee n 842
repay v 718
repeal n 756; v 756
repeat v 90, 104, 136
repeated adj 104
repeatedly adv 104, 136
repel v 289, 610, 616, 717, 719, 764, 830, 867
repellant adj 830
repellent adj 289, 719, 867
repelling adj 289
repent v 833, 950, 952
repentance n 833, 950
repentant adj 950
repenting adj 950
repercussion n 145
repetition n 104
repetition n 17, 90, 136, 143, 641

repetitious adj 104, 641

repetitive adj 104

repine v 832

replace v 63, 147, 660

replacement n 147, 634, 660

replenish v 52, 637

replete adj 52, 641

repletion n 641, 869

replica n 13, 19, 21

reply n 462; v 462

report n 532, 594, 873; v 527

reported adj 527

reporter n 527, 532, 534

repose n 687

repose n 265, 681; v 265, 685, 687

reposing adj 687

repository n 191

reprehensible adj 649, 923, 945

represent v 147, 550, 554, 556, 594, 759

representation n 554

representation n 17, 19, 21, 550, 556, 594, 599, 626

representative n 147, 524, 534, 690, 758, 759; adj 17, 550, 554

representing adj 17

repress v 179, 751, 826

repression n 179, 751

repressive adj 751

reprieve n 133, 671, 672, 918; v 672, 918

reprint n 21

reprisal n 148, 718, 789, 919

reproach v 932

reproachful adj 932

reproduce v 19, 104, 163, 168, 660

reproduction n 163

reproduction n 13, 19, 21, 104, 660

reproductive adj 163

reproof n 972

reprove v 932, 972

reprover n 936

reptile n 366

repudiate v 55, 489, 536, 610, 764

repudiation n 55, 536, 610, 764, 808

repugnance n 867, 898

repugnant adj 867, 898

repulse n 145, 277, 289, 764; v 289, 719, 764

repulsed adj 893

repulsion n 289

repulsion n 719

repulsive adj 289, 395, 719, 830, 846, 867, 898

reputable adj 246, 873

reputation n 873

repute n 873

reputed adj 873

request n 765

request n 741, 865; v 630, 765, 865

require v 601, 630, 640, 741, 744, 765, 812

requirement n 630

requirement n 601, 741

requisite n 601, 630; adj 601, 630

requisition n 630, 741

requital n 30, 148, 718, 919, 973

requite v 148, 718, 919, 973

rescind v 44, 756, 764

rescue n 672, 707; v 660, 670, 672, 707

research n 461, 463

resemblance n 13, 17, 216

resemble v 17, 197

resembling adj 17

resent v 900, 921

resentful adj 900, 907, 919, 920

resentment n 900

resentment n 907, 920

reservation n 528

reserve n 528, 585, 636; v 636, 678, 781

reserved adj 383, 528, 585, 901a

reservoir n 191, 343, 636

reside v 188

residence n 189

resident n 188; adj 186

residual adj 40

residue n 40

residuum n 40

resign v 624, 725, 757, 782

resignation n 757

resignation n 624, 725, 782, 826, 831

resigned adj 826, 831

resign oneself to v 826

resilience n 325

resiliency n 325

resilient adj 325

resin n 356a

resin v 356a

resinous adj 356a

resist v 179, 708, 715, 719, 742, 764

resistance n 719

resistance n 179, 708,

715, 742

resistant adj 323, 327, 708, 715, 719

resisting n 708

resolute adj 150, 604, 604a, 606, 861

resolutely adv 604

resoluteness n 150, 600, 604

resolution n 604

resolution n 144, 150, 600, 604a, 606, 620

resolve n 604, 611, 620; v 604

resolve beforehand v 611

resolved adj 604

resolve into v 144

resolve into its elements v 49

resonance n 408

resonance n 277, 402, 404

resonant adj 402, 408

resort n 677

resort to v 677

resound v 402, 404, 408

resounding adj 404, 408

resources n 632, 635, 637, 780, 803

respect n 928

respect n 457, 743, 873, 894, 926, 987; v 772

respectability n 873

respectable adj 736, 873

respected adj 873, 928

respectful adj 457, 743, 879, 894, 926, 928

respecting adj 928

respective adj 79, 786

respectively adv 79

respects n 928

respiration n 359

respire v 349, 359

respite n 106, 133, 142, 198, 672, 687

resplendent adj 420

respond v 277, 462

respond to v 821

response n 587

response n 179, 276, 277, 462

responsibility n 177, 926

responsible adj 177

responsive adj 375, 462

responsiveness n 375, 822

rest n 265

rest n 40, 70, 142, 211,

360, 681, 687; v 70,
142, 265, 685, 687
restate v 104
restatement n 104
restful adj 265, 685
resting adj 687
restitution n 790
restitution n 660
restless adj 149, 264,
682. 825. 832
restlessness n 149, 264,
315, 682, 825, 832
restorable adj 660
restoration n 660
restoration n 123, 145,
163, 658, 689, 790
restorative n 662; adj
163, 658, 660, 662
restore v 123, 145, 159,
163, 658, 660, 662,
689, 790
restored adj 123, 660
restore equilibrium v
27
restoring adj 689
restrain v 179, 195,
229, 233, 370, 469,
616, 751, 953
restrained adj 229, 751
restraint n 751
restraint n 55, 179,
229, 576, 616, 706,
826, 849
restrict v 233, 469, 751,
761
restricted adj 203
restriction n 469, 751,
761
restrictive adj 751, 761
restructure v 140
result n 63, 65, 480,
729
result from v 154
resulting adj 117
resulting from adj 154
resume v 104, 789
resumption n 660
resurgent adj 163
resurrect v 163
resurrection n 163
resuscitate v 163, 660
resuscitation n 163,
660
retailer n 797
retain v 150, 505, 670,
781
retainer n 746
retake v 789
retaliate v 148, 718,
919
retaliation n 718
retaliation n 30, 148,
919
retaliatory adj 718
retard v 133, 275, 706
retardation n 133

retch v 297

retention n 781
retention n 505, 670
retentive adj 781
retentiveness n 505
reticence n 528, 583,
585
reticent adj 528, 533,
583, 585
reticulated adj 260
reticulation n 219
retinue n 69
retire v 283, 287, 293,
623, 757, 881, 893
retired adj 893
retirement n 283, 287,
757, 893
retiring adj 881
retort n 148, 462, 718;
v 148, 462, 718
retouch v 660
retract v 607, 756
retraction n 485, 536,
607, 756
retreat n 74, 189, 283,
287, 623, 666, 671,
893; v 145, 283, 893
retrench v 38, 201, 817
retrenchment n 38,
201, 817
retribution n 718, 919,
972, 973, 974
retributive adj 718,
973
retrievable adj 660
retrieval n 660
retrieve v 660
retroactive adj 122
retrogradation n 145,
659, 661
retrograde adj 283, 661
retrogression n 145,
283, 659
retrogressive adj 283
retrospect n 505
retrospection n 122,
145
retrospective adj 122
retrospectively adv
122
return n 145, 283, 287,
790; v 104, 138, 145,
283, 718, 790
returning n 145
return to v 104
reunion n 43, 72
revamp v 140
reveal v 260, 525, 529
revealed adj 529
reveal itself v 446
revelation n 985
revelation n 529
revelatory adj 985
revel in v 377
reveling n 838

revenge n 919
revenge v 718; v 718,
919
revengeful adj 718,
919
reverberant adj 104,
408
reverberate v 277, 408
reverberating adj 104,
408
reverberation n 104,
277, 407, 408
revere v 860, 897, 928,
987
reverence n 860, 926,
928, 987, 990; v 860,
928
reverend n 996
reverent adj 987
reverential adj 926,
987, 990
revering adj 990
reversal n 14, 140, 218,
287, 607
reverse n 235, 237; v
145, 218; adj 14,
218, 237
reversion n 145
reversion n 218
revert v 14, 104, 145,
283, 287
reverting n 145
review n 595
reviewer n 480, 595
revile v 988
reviler n 936
revise v 658
revision n 658
revival n 163, 660, 689
revive v 163, 359, 660,
689
revivification n 163,
660
revivify v 159, 163, 660
revocation n 607, 756
revoke v 536, 607, 756,
764
revolt n 146; v 146,
289, 719, 742, 830
revolting adj 846, 898
revolution n 146
revolution n 138, 140,
218, 312
revolutionary adj 146,
742
revolutionize v 146
revolve v 138, 312
revolving adj 312
revulsion n 145, 146,
218, 277
reward n 973
reward n 733; v 973
rewarded adj 973
rewarding adj 973
rhapsodic adj 497
rhapsodist n 504, 597

rhapsody n 497

rhetoric n 517, 577, 582

rhetorical adj 577

rhetorical flourish n 577

rhetorician n 582

rheumy adj 337

rhyme v 597

rhymeless adj 598

rhymer n 597

rhymes n 597

rhyme with v 17

rhyming n 597

rhythm n 104, 138, 413

rhythm n 413

rhythmic adj 104, 138, 597

rhythmical adj 138

rib n 215

ribald adj 961

ribaldry n 961

ribbed adj 259

rich adj 394, 413, 428, 577, 734, 803

riches n 803

richly adv 31

richness n 573

rickety adj 160

ricochet n 145, 277; v 277

riddle n 520; v 260

ride n 226

rider n 39, 268

ride roughshod over v 885

ride the waves v 267

ridge n 250, 346

ridicule n 856

ridicule v 856, 929

ridiculous adj 497, 499

ridiculousness n 853

rid of adj 776

rife adj 78, 175

rifler n 792

rift n 44, 198, 260

rig n 272

rigging n 225

right n 238, 922

right n 780, 924, 965; v 246, 658, 662; adj 494, 922, 944

right ahead adv 234

right and left adv 180, 227

right angle n 244

righteous adj 944, 977

righteously adv 922

righteous man n 987

rightful adj 494, 922

rightfully adv 922

right hand n 238

right-handed adj 238

rightly adv 922

right now n 118

right on adj 494

right side n 238

rigid adj 82, 150, 240, 323, 704, 739, 955

rigidity n 141, 323, 739

rigmarole n 517

rigor mortis n 360

rigorous adj 739, 955

rigorousness n 739

rig out v 225

rill n 348

rim n 231

rimple n 258; v 258

rind n 223

ring n 247, 408, 712, 728; v 408

ringing n 408; adj 413

ring in the ear v 408

ring in the ears v 404

riot n 59, 173; v 173

rioter n 742

riotous adj 59, 173, 742

ripe adj 128, 673

ripe age n 128

ripen v 144, 650, 658, 673

ripeness n 124, 131, 673

ripen into v 144

ripe old age n 128

rip open v 260

rip out v 301

ripple n 258, 314, 315, 348; v 258, 314

rise n 35, 217, 282, 305; v 35, 146, 305, 734

rise above v 31

rise from v 154

rise up v 146, 206, 719

rising n 146, 305; adj 217, 305

rising ground n 217

risk n 665; v 621, 665

risky adj 665

rite n 998

rites n 990

ritualistic adj 998

ritualize v 883

rival n 710, 726; v 648, 720

rivalry n 720

rive v 44

river n 348

river n 348

rivet v 43, 824

rivulet n 348

road n 278, 302, 627

road to ruin n 162

roam v 266

roan adj 433

roar n 404, 408, 411; v 173, 404, 411, 412, 838

roaring n 404

roast v 384

rob v 791

robber n 792

robbery n 791

robe n 999; v 225

robust adj 159, 654, 836

robust health n 654

rock n 342, 415

rock and roll band n 416

rocks n 667

rod n 215, 975

roe n 374

rogue n 941

role n 625

roll n 407

roll n 86, 248, 249, 312, 408; v 248, 255, 264, 314, 348, 407

roll call n 85

roller n 249

rolling pin n 249

rolling seas n 348

roll into a ball v 249

roll on v 264

romance n 515

romantic n 504; adj 515

romp v 173

roof n 223

rookie n 701

room n 180

roomy adj 180

roost n 189; v 186

root n 153; v 184

rooted adj 124, 184

root out v 301

ropy adj 205

rosin n 356a; v 356a

rosy adj 434

rot n 49, 653; v 49, 653, 659

rotary adj 312

rotate v 312

rotating adj 312

rotation n 312

rotation n 138, 145

rotten adj 160, 401, 649, 653, 659

rottenness n 659

rotund adj 249

rotundity n 249

rotundity n 247

roué n 962

rough adj 16a, 173, 241, 254, 256, 329, 397, 410, 674

roughen v 256

rough-hewn adj 256

rough it v 686

roughness n 256

roughness n 254

rough seas n 348

rough up v 256

round n 69, 138; v 245, 247, 249; adj 247, 249, 254

roundabout adj 279, 311, 573, 629; adv 279

roundabout way n 629

round and round adv 138, 248

rounded adj 245, 247, 254

rounded inward adj 252

roundness n 247, 249

round number n 84

round the edge v 254

rouse v 175, 615, 824

rouse oneself v 682

rousing adj 171

route n 302, 627

routine n 16, 58, 80, 138, 613; adj 16, 138

rout out v 652

rove v 266, 279

rover n 268

roving n 266; adj 266

row n 59, 69; v 267

rowdy n 887

royalty n 875

rpm n 138

rub v 255, 331, 379

rubadub n 407

rubbery adj 325

rubbing n 331, 379

rubbish n 643

rub out v 331, 552

rubric n 697

ruby adj 434

ruckus n 59

ruddy adj 434

rude adj 173, 241, 579, 851, 885, 895, 929

rudeness n 885, 895, 929

rudimental adj 66, 674

rudiments n 66

rue v 833, 950

rueful adj 830, 833

ruffian n 887

ruffle n 258; v 59, 256, 258, 824

rugged adj 241, 256

ruin n 162, 619, 638; v 162, 619

ruinous adj 162, 619, 663, 830

ruins n 40

rule n 80, 157, 175, 240, 466, 537, 613, 693, 737, 741; v 157, 480, 693, 737, 749

rulebook n 567

ruler n 737, 745

rules of language n 567

ruling passion n 820

rumble n 408; v 59, 407

rumbling n 407

ruminate v 450, 451

rumor n 532

rump n 235

rumple v 256, 258

rumpus n 59

run n 264; v 109, 264, 274, 333, 348

run abreast v 27

run against v 276

run amuck v 173

runaway n 623

run away v 287, 671

run counter to v 179

run down v 649, 934; adj 124

run for one's life v 623

run headlong v 173

run into v 276

run into trouble v 665

run its course v 67, 109, 122

runner n 271, 534

running water n 348

run off at the mouth v 584

run of the mill adj 29, 736

run on and on v 573

run out v 67

run over v 641

run parallel v 178

run riot v 173, 641

run smoothly v 705

run the eye over v 441

run the fingers over v 379

run the risk of v 177

run through v 186, 361

run up against v 179

run up bills v 808

run wild v 173, 825

rupture n 44, 713, 720; v 44

ruse n 545

rush n 72, 274, 310, 348, 684; v 173, 274, 310, 684

russet adj 433

rust v 659; adj 433

rustic adj 876

rustle v 409

rusty adj 659, 683, 699

rut n 259, 613

ruthless adj 739, 914a

S

Sabbath n 687

sable adj 431

saboteur n 361

saccharine adj 396

saccharinity n 396

sacred adj 976, 987

sacrilege n 988

sacrilegist n 988

sacrosanct adj 976

sad adj 649, 837

sadden v 830

sadly adv 31

sadness n 837

safe n 802; adj 664, 670

safe and sound adj 664

safecracker n 792

safeguard n 664, 666, 670, 717; v 670, 717

safekeeping n 664, 670

safety n 664

safety valve n 664

saffron adj 435

sag v 245

sagacious adj 498, 842, 868

sagacity n 480, 498, 698, 842

sage n 500

sage n 492, 872; adj 498

sail n 267; v 267

sailboat n 273

sailing n 267; adj 267

sailor n 269

saint n 948

saintly adj 987

salable adj 796

salad oil n 356

sale n 796

sale n 783, 813

salesman n 797

saleswoman n 797

salient adj 250, 642

sallow adj 429, 430, 435

sally n 716; v 293

salmon adj 434

salt n 393; v 392

salt and pepper n 432; adj 440

salt of the earth n 648, 948

salt water n 341

salty adj 392

salubrious adj 656

salubrity n 656

salutary adj 644, 648, 656

salutation n 896

salute n 896; v 586, 836, 896

salvation n 670, 672

salve n 356

salvo n 406

sameness n 13, 16, 17, 104

sample n 82

sanctify v 987

sanctimoniousness n 988

sanctimony n 988

sanction n 737, 760, 924, 931; v 737, 760, 931

sanctioned adj 924

sanctity n 987

sanctuary n 666

sand n 330, 667; v 255

sand bar n 209

sanded adj 255

sandiness *n* 330
sandpaper *v* 255
sandy *adj* 330
sane *adj* 246, 502
sanguine *adj* 831, 858
sanitary *adj* 656
sanity *n* 502
sans *adv* 187
sap *n* 5, 501; *v* 162, 659
sapience *n* 498
sapient *adj* 498
sapless *adj* 340
sapphire *adj* 438
sappy *adj* 333, 499
sarcastic *adj* 856
sarcophagous *n* 363
sash *n* 247
Satan *n* 978
satanic *adj* 978, 982
satanism *n* 978
sate *v* 869
satiate *v* 376, 829, 869
satiated *adj* 869
satiety *n* 869
satire *n* 856
satirist *n* 844, 936
satirize *v* 856
satisfaction *n* 772, 807, 827, 831, 952
satisfactory *adj* 639
satisfied *adj* 474, 484, 831
satisfy *v* 462, 639, 746, 772, 807, 829, 831, 952
saturate *v* 52, 339, 869
saturated *adj* 52
saturation *n* 869
satyr *n* 980
sauce *n* 393
saunter *n* 266; *v* 266, 275
sauté *v* 384
savage *adj* 173
savant *n* 492
save *v* 672, 817; *adv* 38, 83
saving *n* 817
savoir faire n 698; *n* 852
savor *n* 390; *v* 390, 394
savoriness *n* 394
savory *adj* 390, 394
saw *n* 257; *v* 44
say *n* 175; *v* 535, 560, 582
saying *n* 496
say nothing *v* 517, 585
say what comes to mind *v* 612
scabrous *adj* 256
scaffolding *n* 673
scald *v* 384
scale *n* 69, 71, 204, 466; *v* 305
scale the heights *v* 305

scallop *n* 257; *v* 257
scalpel *n* 262
scaly *adj* 204
scamper *v* 274
scan *v* 441
scant *adj* 32, 137, 640
scantiness *n* 103, 203
scanty *adj* 32, 103
scarce *adj* 32, 103, 137, 640
scarcely *adv* 32, 137
scarcity *n* 32, 103, 640
scared *adj* 862
scarify *v* 257
scarlet *adj* 434
scatter *v* 61, 73, 291
scattered *adj* 73
scene *n* 448
scenery *n* 448
scent *n* 398, 550; *v* 398, 400
scented *adj* 400
scentless *adj* 399
scepter *n* 747
schedule *n* 86
scheme *n* 626; *v* 626
schemer *n* 626
schism *n* 713, 984
schismatic *adj* 984
scholar *n* 492
scholar *n* 541
scholarly *adj* 539
scholarship *n* 490, 539
scholastic *adj* 537, 539, 542
school *n* 542
school *v* 537
schoolbook *n* 542
schoolboy *n* 129
schooled *adj* 498
schoolgirl *n* 129
schooling *n* 537
schoolmaster *n* 540
schooner *n* 273
science *n* 490
science of existence *n* 1
science of light *n* 420
science of living beings *n* 357
science of matter *n* 316
science of sound *n* 402
science of the mineral kingdom *n* 358
scintilla *n* 32, 420
scintillate *v* 420
scintillating *adj* 842
scintillation *n* 420
scion *n* 167
scoff *v* 929, 988
scoff at *v* 856
scoffer *n* 988
scoffing *n* 856, 988
scold *v* 972
scoop *n* 262; *v* 252
scoop out *v* 252
scope *n* 26, 180, 748

scorch *v* 384
scorched *adj* 384
score *n* 98, 259, 805, 806, 811; *v* 259
scores *n* 102
scorn *n* 930; *v* 715, 929, 930
scornful *adj* 929, 930
scotch *v* 659
scot free *adj* 748
scoundrel *n* 941, 949
scour *v* 331, 652
scourge *n* 975
scourge *v* 663, 972
scour the country *v* 266
scout *n* 664, 668
scowl *v* 900, 901a
scraggly *adj* 256
scramble *n* 59, 684; *v* 684
scrap *n* 32
scrape *n* 704, 732; *v* 38, 195, 255, 330, 331
scratch *n* 257, 259; *v* 257, 331, 380, 590, 649
scratching *n* 380; *adj* 410
scratchy *adj* 380
scrawl *v* 590
scrawny *adj* 203
scream *n* 411, 669; *v* 404, 410, 411, 839
screech *v* 411, 412
screeching *n* 412; *adj* 414
screen *n* 223, 424, 530, 717; *v* 424, 442, 528, 664, 717
screening *n* 528
screw *n* 243; *v* 43, 243
screw up the eyes *v* 443
scribble *v* 590
scribe *n* 553, 590
scrimp *v* 819
script *n* 590, 593
scriptural *adj* 983a
Scriptures *n* 985, 986
scrivener *n* 590
Scrooge *n* 819
scrub *v* 331, 652
scruple *n* 485
scrupulous *adj* 246, 459, 543, 603, 772, 868, 939
scrupulousness *n* 603
scrutinize *v* 457
scrutinizing *adj* 461
scrutiny *n* 457, 461
scull *v* 267
sculpt *v* 557
sculptor *n* 559
sculpture *n* 557

scum of the earth *n* 949

scurrilous *adj* 934

scurry *v* 684

scuttle *v* 162

scuttlebutt *n* 532

sea *n* 341

sea dog *n* 269

seafaring *adj* 267

seafaring man *n* 269

sea-girt *adj* 346

seagoing *adj* 267, 341

sea-green *adj* 435

seal *n* 22; *v* 261, 550

sealing *n* 261

sealing wax *n* 356a

seam *n* 43; *v* 259

sea-maid *n* 979

seaman *n* 269

sear *v* 384

search *n* 461, 539, 622; *v* 461

season *n* 106, 106; *v* 41, 392, 393, 613, 673

seasonable *adj* 134

seasoned *adj* 392

seasoning *n* 41, 393

seat *v* 184

seat of activity *n* 691

secession *n* 624

seclude *v* 55, 87

secluded *adj* 893

seclude oneself *v* 893

seclusion *n* 893

seclusion *n* 55

second *n* 113, 759; *v* 707; *adj* 90

secondary *adj* 32, 34, 651

secondary color *n* 428

second hand *adj* 19

second-rate *adj* 34, 651

second-story man *n* 792

second thoughts *n* 65

second to none *n* 648

secrecy *n* 528, 893

secret *n* 533

secret *adj* 221, 526, 528, 533

secretary *n* 553, 590

secrete *v* 299, 528

secretion *n* 299, 528

secretive *adj* 528, 533

secretiveness *n* 528

secretly *adv* 528

secret place *n* 530

sect *n* 75

section *n* 51, 75

sectional *adj* 51

secular *adj* 997

secularize *v* 997

secure *v* 43, 132, 664, 717, 768, 775, 781; *adj* 43, 150, 484, 664

secure an objective *v* 731

securities *n* 802

security *n* 771

security *n* 664, 717, 721

sedate *adj* 826

seducer *n* 962

seduction *n* 829

seductive *adj* 288, 615, 829

see *v* 441, 457, 480a; 484

seed *n* 32, 153; *v* 371

see double *v* 443

seedy *adj* 160, 659, 804

see fit *v* 600

seeing that *adv* 8

seek *v* 461, 622

seeker *n* 268, 767

seek refuge *v* 666

seem *v* 448

seeming *n* 448; *adj* 448

seemingly *adv* 448

seemliness *n* 845

seemly *adj* 845

see one's future *v* 510

seer *n* 130, 504, 513

seesaw *adv* 314

seethe *v* 382

see the light *v* 359

seething *adj* 824

see-through *adj* 425

segment *n* 51, 100a

segregate *v* 44, 55

segregated *adj* 47

segregation *n* 44, 55

seize *v* 789

seize the day *v* 134

seize the opportunity *v* 134, 682

seize the time *v* 134

seizure *n* 789

seldom *adv* 137

select *v* 609; *adj* 648

selection *n* 609

self *n* 13; *adj* 13

self-abnegation *n* 955

self-admiration *n* 880

self-assurance *n* 878

self-assured *adj* 878

self-centered *adj* 943

self-command *n* 604

self-complacency *n* 880

self-complacent *adj* 880

self-contradictory *adj* 497

self-control *n* 600, 604, 953

self-controlled *adj* 953

self-deception *n* 486

self-delusion *n* 486

self-denial *n* 604, 955

self-denying *adj* 955

self-depreciation *n* 483

self-esteem *n* 878, 880

self-glorification *n* 880

self-importance *n* 878

self-indulgence *n* 954

self-indulgent *adj* 943, 954

self-interest *n* 943

self-interested *adj* 943

selfish *adj* 32, 819, 943

selfishness *n* 943

selfishness *n* 32, 819

self-love *n* 880, 943

self-luminous *adj* 423

self-mortifying *adj* 955

self-motification *n* 955

self-possessed *adj* 502

self-possession *n* 604, 826

self-reliance *n* 604

self-respect *n* 878

self-restrained *adj* 953

self-restraint *n* 604, 826, 953

selfsame *adj* 13

self-satisfied *adj* 878

self-seeking *n* 943; *adj* 943

self-styled *adj* 565

sell *v* 796, 798

seller *n* 796, 797

sell for *v* 812

selling *n* 796

semblance *n* 17, 19, 21, 216, 882

semi- *adj* 91

semi-circular *adj* 245

semifluid *adj* 352

semiliquid *adj* 352

semiliquidity *n* 352

seminary *n* 542

semiology *n* 550

semiopaque *adj* 427

semipellucid *adj* 427

semitransparency *n* 427

semitransparent *adj* 427

send *v* 270

send a letter *v* 592

send off *v* 284

senile *adj* 124, 128, 158

senility *n* 124, 128, 158, 160, 659

seniority *n* 128

sensation *n* 375, 379, 390

sensational *adj* 824

sensations of touch *n* 380

sense *n* 450, 498, 502, 516, 842

senseless *adj* 376, 497, 499, 517

senselessness *n* 517

sense of duty *n* 926

sensibility n 375, 822
sensibility n 821
sensible adj 316, 375, 498, 502
sensical adj 450
sensitive adj 375, 597, 821, 822
sensitiveness n 375, 822
sensitivity n 821, 901
sensitize v 375
sensual adj 377, 829
sensual delight n 377
sensualist n 954a
sensualist n 962
sensuality n 377, 827
sensuous adj 375, 377
sensuousness n 377
sentence n 972
sententious adj 577
sentient adj 375
sentiment n 453, 821
sentimental adj 822
sentimentalism n 822
sentimentality n 821, 822
sentinel n 444, 664, 668
sentry n 668
separate v 44, 55, 291, 905; adj 44
separated adj 905
separately adv 44
separateness n 44
separation n 44, 55, 198, 291, 489, 905
sepia adj 433
septet n 415
septic adj 657
sepulchral adj 363
sepulchre n 363
sepulture n 363
sequel n 65
sequel n 39, 63, 117, 281
sequence n 63, 281
sequence n 58, 117, 281
sequential adj 63, 281
sequester v 893, 974
sequestered adj 893
sequestration n 893, 974
seraph n 977
seraphic adj 977
serene adj 265, 721
serenity n 265, 826, 831
serfdom n 749
serial adj 69, 138
serially adv 138
series n 58, 63, 69
serious adj 642, 739
seriousness n 642, 739
sermon n 537, 582
sermonize v 537, 582

serous adj 333
serpent n 248, 548, 978
serpentine adj 248
serrated adj 244, 257
serum n 337
servant n 746
servant n 690, 707
serve v 618, 644, 707, 743, 746, 749, 969
serve with a writ v 969
service n 618, 644, 677, 707, 749, 990, 998
serviceable adj 631, 644, 648
servile adj 886, 933
servility n 886
servitude n 749
session n 696
set n 7, 240, 278, 712; v 150, 184, 306, 321; adj 43, 240, 613
set about v 676
set against adj 898
set an example v 22
set apart v 44, 465
set a price v 812
set aside v 55, 185, 678
set at ease v 831
set at naught v 773
set a trap for v 530
set at rest v 462
set down v 551, 590
set fire to v 384
set foot on dry land v 342
set forth v 293, 594
set forward v 293
set free v 44, 672, 748, 750, 970; adj 970
set going v 276
set in motion v 66, 284, 677
set in one's ways adj 5
set loose v 750
setoff n 30
set one's sights on v 278
set on fire v 384
set out v 60, 66, 293
set phrase n 566
set right v 662
set sail v 293
set store by v 642
set the fashion v 62
setting side by side n 464
settle v 60, 150, 184, 265, 306, 769, 774, 807
settled adj 67, 184, 474
settle down v 184, 265
settled purpose n 620
settlement n 23, 184, 762, 807
settle up v 790
settle upon v 784

set too high a value on v 482
set to rights v 660
set to work v 677
set up v 153, 161, 307
set upon v 716
seven n 98
sever v 44, 291
several n 100; adj 100, 102
severally adv 44, 79
severance n 44, 291
severe adj 242, 576, 739, 830, 849, 955
severely adv 31, 739
severity n 739
severity n 173, 576, 849
sew v 43
sewer n 350
sex n 377
sextet n 415
sexual adj 377
sexual abstinence n 904
sexual failure n 158
sexuality n 377
shabby adj 34, 643, 659, 851
shade n 424
shade n 15, 26, 223, 362, 421, 422, 428, 530, 980; v 421, 422, 424
shading off adj 26
shadow n 4, 21, 281, 421, 424, 515, 980; v 281, 353, 421, 422
shadowiness n 422
shadowy adj 4, 421, 422, 424, 447
shady adj 421, 424, 426, 874
shaft n 208, 351
shaggy adj 256
shaggy dog story n 549
shake n 315; v 160, 314, 315, 383, 404, 407, 616, 659
shake one's sides v 838
shake the foundations of v 659
shake up v 315
shaking adj 315
shaky adj 160, 315, 665
shallow n 209; adj 209, 491, 499, 643
shallow excuse n 617
shallowness n 209
shallowness n 499
shallows n 667
sham n 544, 545, 855, 880; v 546; adj 544
shaman n 994
shamble v 275, 315

shame *n* 874, 930; *v* 874, 879

shameful *adj* 874, 930

shape *n* 448; *v* 240, 557, 852

shapeless *adj* 241

shapelessness *n* 241

shapeliness *n* 242

shapely *adj* 242

share *n* 786; *v* 709, 778, 786

shareholder *n* 778

share in *v* 56, 778

sharer *n* 778

sharp *adj* 171, 173, 217, 253, 375, 392, 397, 404, 410, 416; *adj* 490, 498, 682, 698, 702, 842, 868

sharp edged *adj* 253

sharpen *v* 171, 173, 253, 375, 824

sharpness *n* 253

sharpness *n* 392, 397, 410, 698

sharp outline *n* 446

shatter *v* 44, 158, 162, 328

shattered *adj* 160

shave *v* 195, 201, 204, 255

she *n* 374

shear *v* 195, 201

sheathe *v* 225

shed *n* 223; *v* 73

shed light on *v* 522

shed light upon *v* 420

sheen *n* 420

sheeny *adj* 420

sheepish *adj* 881

sheer *adj* 52, 425

sheerness *n* 425

sheet *n* 204, 223, 811

shelf *n* 215

shell *n* 363

shellac *n* 356a; *v* 356a

shellfish *n* 366

shelter *n* 666, 670, 717; *v* 528, 664, 670, 717

sheltering *n* 528

shelve *v* 133, 678

shepherd *n* 996

shield *n* 223, 717; *v* 670, 717

shift *n* 140, 147, 270; *v* 140, 144, 264, 270, 279

shifting *n* 144; *adj* 264

shiftless *adj* 674

shilly-shally *v* 133, 605

shimmer *n* 420; *v* 420

shine *v* 420

shiny *adj* 255, 420

ship *n* 273

ship *n* 271; *v* 190

shipment *n* 190

ship out *v* 293

shipping *n* 267

shipshape *adj* 58

shirk *v* 623, 742

shirker *n* 623

shiver *n* 315, 328, 383

shivering *adj* 383

shoal *n* 209

shoals *n* 667

shock *n* 276, 315, 508, 713; *v* 824, 830

shockingly *adv* 31

shoot *n* 378; *v* 194, 274, 284, 361, 367, 378

shoot ahead of *v* 303

shooting *n* 361, 378

shoot up *v* 250, 367

shop *v* 795

shopkeeper *n* 797

shopper *n* 795

shopping center *n* 799

shore *n* 231, 342

shore up *v* 215

short *adj* 28, 53, 201, 572, 640, 739

shortcoming *n* 304

shortcoming *n* 28, 34, 53, 640, 651, 730

short distance *n* 197

shorten *v* 36, 38, 201, 596

shortened *adj* 201

shortening *n* 36, 38, 201

shorthand *n* 590

short-lived *adj* 111

shortly *adv* 132

short memory *n* 506

shortness *n* 201

short of *adj* 53; *adv* 32, 34, 38

short-tempered *adj* 901

shot *n* 284

shot in the dark *n* 621

shoulder *n* 236; *v* 215, 276

shoulder to shoulder *adv* 709

shout *n* 411, 838; *v* 404, 411, 836, 838

shout at the top of one's lungs *v* 411

shove *n* 276; *v* 276, 284

shove in *v* 300

shovel *v* 270

shove off *v* 267, 293

show *n* 448, 855, 882; *v* 448, 467, 478, 525, 529

shower *n* 348

shower down *v* 348

showery *adj* 348

showiness *n* 882

showing *n* 525

show itself *v* 446

shown *adj* 478

show no remorse *v* 951

show off *v* 882

show taste *v* 850

show up *v* 446

showy *adj* 428, 851, 882

shred *n* 32

shrewd *adj* 490, 498, 698, 702

shrewdness *n* 702

shriek *n* 411; *v* 411

shrill *adj* 203, 404, 410

shrillness *n* 410

shrink *v* 36, 195, 283, 287, 623

shrink from *v* 603

shrinking *n* 36, 195, 603

shrive *v* 952

shrivel *v* 195, 659

shroud *n* 363; *v* 664

shrub *n* 367

shrubbery *n* 367

shrunk *adj* 195

shrunken *adj* 195

shudder *v* 383

shuffle *v* 149, 275, 315

shuffle off *v* 623

shuffle off the mortal coil *v* 360

shun *v* 623, 671

shunt *v* 279

shut *v* 261; *adj* 261

shutout *n* 101; *v* 55

shutter *n* 424

shutting up *n* 261

shut up *v* 261, 403

shut up shop *v* 687

shy *v* 283, 623; *adj* 881

shyster *n* 548

sibilant *adj* 409

sibilation *n* 409

sibyl *n* 513

sick *adj* 655

sicken *v* 289, 395, 655, 830

sickening *adj* 395

sickly *adj* 160, 435, 655

sickness *n* 655

side *n* 236

side *n* 712

side by side *adv* 88, 236

side effects *n* 154

sidelong *adj* 236; *adv* 217, 236

sideways *adv* 217, 236

side with *v* 709, 714

sidle *v* 217, 236

sift *v* 42, 60

sifting *n* 42

sigh *n* 839

sight *n* 441, 448; *v* 441

sightless *adj* 442
sightlessness *n* 442
sightseer *n* 268, 444
sign *n* 467, 512, 550, 668; *v* 550
signal *n* 467, 550, 668; *v* 467, 550
signalize *v* 550
signally *adv* 31
signature *n* 569, 590
significance *n* 516, 642
significant *adj* 516, 550, 642
signification *n* 516
signify *v* 516, 550, 642
signify little *v* 643
sign of the times *n* 512
silence *n* 403
silence *n* 265, 528, 581, 585; *v* 403, 581
silent *adj* 265, 403, 581, 585, 901a
silent as the grave *adj* 403
silently *adv* 403
silken *adj* 255
silky *adj* 255
silliness *n* 497, 499, 853
silly *adj* 486, 497, 499, 853
silouette *n* 230
silver *n* 432; *adj* 430, 432
silveriness *n* 430
silverish *adj* 432
silvery *adj* 413, 430, 432
similar *adj* 17, 21, 216
similarity *n* 17
similarity *n* 9, 13, 27
simile *n* 17, 521
similitude *n* 17, 21
simmer *v* 315, 382, 384
simple *adj* 42, 486, 499, 576, 703, 849, 946, 960
simpleness *n* 42
simpleton *n* 493, 501
simplicity *n* 849
simplicity *n* 491, 499, 576, 703, 881, 946, 960
simplification *n* 78
simplify *v* 42, 78, 518, 849
simply *adv* 32
simulate *v* 19, 855
simulating *adj* 17
simulation *n* 19, 855
simultaneity *n* 120
simultaneous *adj* 120
simultaneously *adv* 120
simultaneousness *n* 120

sin *n* 923, 945, 961, 988; *v* 945
since *adv* 8, 117, 155
sincere *adj* 543, 703
sincerity *n* 543, 703
since the occasion presents itself *adv* 134
sinewy *adj* 159
sinful *adj* 923, 945, 961
sinfully *adv* 923
sinfulness *n* 947, 961, 988
sing *v* 416, 597, 838
singe *v* 384
singer *n* 416
singing *n* 412; *adj* 413
single *adj* 42, 87
singlehanded *adj* 87
singleness *n* 87
single out *v* 79
singly *adv* 87
sing out *v* 411
sing praises *v* 990
singular *adj* 79, 83, 87
singularity *n* 79, 87
singularly *adv* 31
sinister *adj* 663, 909
sinistral *adj* 239
sink *v* 162, 210, 306, 308, 360, 659, 688, 732, 735, 837
sink back *v* 661
sinking *n* 306
sink into oblivion *v* 506
sinless *adj* 946
sinner *n* 949, 988
sinning *adj* 945, 961
sinuosity *n* 248
sip *n* 298, 390
siphon *n* 350
sir *n* 373
sire *n* 166
siren *n* 669, 980
sisterhood *n* 11, 72, 995
Sisyphean *adj* 686
site *n* 183
sit in judgment *v* 965
situate *v* 183, 184
situated *adj* 183
situation *n* 183
situation *n* 7, 8, 151, 182, 184
situations *n* 527
six *n* 98
six of one and half a dozen of another *n* 628; *adj* 27
sizable *adj* 192
size *n* 192
size *n* 25, 31, 200
skeletal *adj* 203
skeleton *n* 40, 362
skeleton in the closet *n*

649, 830
skeptic *n* 485, 487, 984, 989
skeptical *adj* 485, 487, 984, 989
skepticism *n* 485, 487, 984, 989
sketch *n* 594, 626; *v* 230, 556
sketcher *n* 559
sketchy *adj* 53, 730
skill *n* 698
skill *n* 79, 702, 731
skilled *adj* 698
skillful *adj* 698, 702
skillfully *adv* 698
skillfulness *n* 698, 702
skin *n* 220, 223
skin-deep *adj* 209
skinflint *n* 819
skinniness *n* 203
skinny *adj* 203
skip *n* 198; *v* 309, 838
skipper *n* 269
skirt *n* 231; *v* 231, 236
skirting *n* 231; *adj* 236
skulk *v* 862
skull *n* 450
sky *n* 318, 338
skyscraping *adj* 206
slab *n* 204, 251
slack *adj* 47, 160, 172, 275, 603, 674, 683, 738
slacken *v* 47, 275, 687
slackness *n* 275, 738
slake *v* 174, 829
slam *n* 276; *v* 276
slander *n* 908, 934; *v* 908, 934
slanderer *n* 936
slanderous *adj* 934
slang *n* 579; *adj* 563
slangy *adj* 560
slant *n* 217; *v* 217
slantwise *adv* 217
slap *n* 276; *v* 276
slash *v* 44
slaughter *n* 361; *v* 361
slaughtering *n* 361
slavery *n* 749, 886
slavish *adj* 886
slavishness *n* 886
slayer *n* 361
sleek *v* 255; *adj* 255
sleep *n* 687
sleeping *adj* 172, 265
sleeping car *n* 272
slender *adj* 32, 203, 643
slenderize *v* 203
slenderness *n* 32, 203
slice *n* 204; *v* 44, 204
slick *adj* 355
slide *v* 109, 264, 306
slight *v* 460, 483, 927;

adj 4, 32, 209, 322, 575, 643, 736
slightly adv 32
slightness n 4, 32, 203
slim v 203; adj 203
slime n 653
slimness n 203
slimy adj 352, 355, 653
sling v 284
slink away v 623
slip n 32, 306, 495, 568, 732; v 109, 306, 495, 623
slip back v 661
slipperiness n 665
slippery adj 255, 355, 607, 665
slippery ground n 667
slippery memory n 506
slip-shod adj 575
slit n 44, 198, 259, 260; v 44
sliver n 32
slobber over v 933
sloop n 273
slope n 217, 306; v 217
sloping adj 217, 306
sloppy adj 345, 575
slot n 260
sloth n 133, 172, 275, 683
slothful adj 681, 683
slothfulness n 681
slouch v 207, 217, 275, 683
slough n 345
slovenliness n 653
slovenly adj 59, 575, 653
slow v 275, 420; adj 133, 172, 275, 603, 683, 685, 843, 901a
slowly adv 133, 275
slowness n 275
slowness n 133, 603
sluggard n 683
sluggish adj 172, 275, 683, 901a
sluggishness n 275, 683, 901a
sluice n 350
slumber n 687
slumberer n 683
slump v 306
slur one's words v 583
slushy adj 352
slut n 962
sluttish adj 653
sly adj 702
slyness n 702
smack n 32, 276, 390; v 390
smack the lips v 390
small adj 32, 193

small change n 800
smallness n 32
smallness n 193
small number n 103
small quantity n 32, 103
small talk n 588
smart n 378, 828; v 378; adj 682, 698
smarts n 450, 498
smash v 162
smatch n 390; v 390
smear v 653
smell n 398, 400; v 398, 401
smell bad v 401
smell of v 398
smell rotten v 401
smell sweet v 400
smelly adj 398
smile n 838; v 838
smirch n 431, 653
smirk n 838; v 838
smite v 649
smitten adj 897
smoggy adj 426
smoke v 382, 392
smoking adj 382
smoky adj 426
smolder v 382, 526
smoldering adj 172
smooth v 16, 174, 255, 705, 723; adj 174, 213, 251, 255, 705
smoothly adv 705
smoothness n 255
smoothness n 251, 705
smooth-tongued adj 933
smother v 361, 581
smudge v 653
smug adj 878
smut n 653, 961; v 431
smutch v 431
smutty adj 653, 961
snag n 667
snaggy adj 253
snake n 248
snake in the grass n 548, 649, 667
snaky adj 248
snap n 406
snap n 277· v 44, 328, 406
snap back v 277
snappish adj 901
snap up v 789
snare n 530, 545, 667
snarl v 412, 900
snatch n 32; v 789
sneak n 941; v 275, 623, 862, 886
sneak off v 623
sneer n 856; v 929
sneer at v 856
sneeze v 409

sniff v 398
snip v 44
snippet n 32
sniveling adj 886
snobbish adj 878
snort v 412
snout n 250
snow-white adj 430
snowy adj 430
snuff v 398
snuff out v 421
snug adj 261, 664
soak v 337, 339, 959
soak up v 340
soap n 356
soar v 31, 206, 267, 303, 305
sob n 839; v 411, 839
sobbing n 411
sober v 174; adj 174, 246, 502, 826, 953, 958
sobriety n 958
sobriety n 502, 953
sobriquet n 565
so-called adj 565
sociability n 894
sociable adj 892
sociableness n 892
social adj 372, 892
social interaction n 892
social intercourse n 892
socialism n 778
socialist n 778; adj 778
socialistic adj 778
sociality n 892
society n 188, 372, 852
society of men n 372
sodden v 339; adj 337
soft adj 255, 324, 345, 403, 405, 413, 499
soft as butter adj 324
soft coal n 388
soften v 174, 324
softening n 324
softness n 324
softness n 160, 326
soggy adj 337, 339
soi-disant adj 565
soil n 181, 342; v 653
soiled adj 653
sojourn v 186
solace n 834
solar adj 318
solar energy n 388
solar system n 180, 318
solder v 43, 46
soldier n 726, 948
sole n 211; adj 87
solecism n 568
solecism n 579
solecize v 568
solemn adj 403, 642, 882

solemnity n 642
solemnization n 883
solemnize v 883
solicit v 765, 865
solicitation n 411, 765
solicitor n 767, 968
solicitous adj 411, 765, 860, 920
solicitude n 459, 828, 860
solid adj 16, 52, 150, 202, 321, 323
solidarity n 52
solid body n 321
solidification n 321, 385
solidify v 46, 48, 321
solidity n 150, 321
solidness n 321
soliloquize v 582, 589
soliloquy n 589
solipsism n 943
solipsistic adj 943
solitary adj 87, 893
solitude n 893
solo n 415; adj 87; v 416
soloist n 416
solubility n 333
soluble adj 333, 335, 462, 662
solubleness n 335
solution n 462, 522, 662
solve v 462, 662
solvency n 803
solvent adj 335, 807
somatic adj 316
somber adj 431, 901a
some adj 25, 100; adv 32
somebody n 372
someone n 372
somersault n 218
something like adj 17
some time ago adv 122
sometimes adv 136
somewhere adv 182
somewhere about adv 32
son n 167
sonata n 415
song n 413, 415
sonneteer n 597
sonority n 402
sonorous adj 402, 404, 577
sonorousness n 402, 408
soon adv 111, 121, 132
sooner or later adv 121
soothe v 723, 834
soothing adj 834
soothsayer n 513, 994
soothsaying n 511

sooty adj 431, 653
sop v 339
sophism n 477
sophist n 477, 548
sophistical adj 477
sophistry n 477
sophistry n 538
soporific adj 683
sorcerer n 994
sorcerer n 513
sorcery n 992
sordid adj 32, 207, 435
sordidness n 32
sore n 378, 830; adj 378, 830
sorely adv 31
soreness n 378
sore subject n 830
sorority n 11
sorrel adj 433
sorrow n 833
sorrowful adj 828, 839
sorrow over v 839
sorry adj 643, 828, 833, 950
sorry sight n 830
sort n 75; v 60
sortie n 716
sorting n 60
SOS n 669
so-so adj 32, 643, 651
sot n 959; v 959
so to speak adv 17
sotted adj 959
sough n 350
soul n 5, 359, 372, 820
soul-stirring adj 821, 824
sound n 402
sound n 343; v 208, 402; adj 50, 150, 246, 498, 650, 654, 664, 670, 983a
sound dead v 408a
sounding adj 402
soundings n 208
soundless adj 208, 403
soundness n 150, 502, 654, 983a
sound the alarm v 669
sound vibrations n 402
soupçon n 32
sour v 397; adj 392, 395, 397, 410, 901a
source n 66, 153
sourness n 397
sourness n 392, 395
souse v 310, 337
souvenir n 505
sovereign n 737; adj 737
sovereignty n 157
sow v 374; v 73, 371
sow the seeds of v 153
space n 180
space n 106, 198, 318

space heater n 386
spaceman n 269
spaceship n 273
space station n 273
spacious adj 180, 192
span n 106, 180, 196, 200; v 43, 45
spare v 678, 784; adj 40, 636, 641, 685
spare no effort v 686
spare no expense v 816
spare time n 685
sparing adj 953
spark n 382, 420, 423
sparkle v 420
sparkling adj 574, 836, 842
sparse adj 32, 73, 103, 640
sparseness n 32, 103
spasm n 146, 173, 315, 378
spasmodic adj 70, 139, 173
speak v 580, 582
speak directly v 576
speaker n 524, 582
speaking of adv 134
speak in low tones v 405
speak one's mind v 703
speak plainly v 576
speak prettily v 521
speak softly v 405
speak the truth v 543
speak to v 586
spear n 262; v 260, 36
special n 79; adj 20, 79, 474
special committee n 755
specialist n 700
speciality n 79
specialize v 79
specially adv 79
specialty n 79
species n 75
specific n 662; adj 79
specify v 79, 564
specimen n 82
specious adj 477, 545
speciousness n 477
speck n 32, 848
speckle v 440
speckled adj 440
spectacle n 448, 872
spectacles n 445
spectator n 444
specter n 980; 443
spectral adj 2, 4, 980
spectroscope n 428
spectrum n 428
speculate v 155, 514, 621, 675, 870

speculation *n* 156, 451, 514, 621, 675
speculative *adj* 514, 621, 675
speech *n* 582
speech *n* 560, 586
speech impediment *n* 583
speechless *adj* 403, 581, 583
speechlessness *n* 403, 590
speed *n* 264, 274, 684; *v* 274, 682, 684
speedily *adv* 132
speediness *n* 132
speed up *v* 274
speedy *adj* 274, 684
spell *n* 993
spell *n* 106, 198, 992; *v* 561, 707
spell-bound *adj* 870
spelling *n* 561
spend *v* 638, 809
spend freely *v* 816
spendthrift *adj* 638, 818
spend time *v* 106
spent *adj* 158, 160, 688
spew *v* 297
sphere *n* 26, 181, 249, 318; *v* 249
spherical *adj* 249
sphericity *n* 249
spheroid *n* 249
spice *n* 41, 393; *v* 392
spiced *adj* 392
spick and span *adj* 123
spicy *adj* 392, 400
spigot *n* 263
spike *n* 253, 263; *v* 260
spiked *adj* 253
spiky *adj* 253
spill *v* 348
spin *n* 266; *v* 312
spin a melody *v* 416
spin around *v* 312
spindly *adj* 203
spine *n* 253
spineless *adj* 862
spinelessness *n* 172
spinning *n* 312
spin out *v* 200
spinster *n* 904
spiny *adj* 253
spiral *n* 248, 311; *adj* 248
spirit *n* 5, 171, 359, 516, 574, 682, 709, 820, 861, 977, 980
spirited *adj* 171, 574, 836, 861
spiritual *adj* 2, 317, 976, 977
spiritualism *n* 992
spirituality *n* 317

spit *v* 260
spite *n* 907
spiteful *adj* 898, 907, 919, 945
spitefulness *n* 907
splash *n* 348; *v* 337, 348, 653
splendid *adj* 420
splendor *n* 420, 845, 882
splice *v* 43, 219
splint *n* 215
splinter *n* 32; *v* 44, 328
splintery *adj* 328
split *n* 44, 713; *v* 44, 91, 293, 328, 713, 838
split down the middle *v* 91
split hairs *v* 868
split one's sides *v* 838
split the difference *v* 29
split the differences *v* 774
split the eardrums *v* 404, 419
split up *v* 778, 905; *adj* 51, 905
spoil *v* 397, 659
spoilage *n* 659
spoilation *n* 638
spoiled *adj* 397
spoiled child *n* 899
spoiler *n* 165
spoils *n* 793
spokesman *n* 524, 534, 582
sponge *v* 339, 340
sponginess *n* 354
sponsor *v* 771
sponsorship *n* 771
spontaneous *adj* 612
spook *n* 980
spoonful *n* 25, 32
sporadic *adj* 103, 137, 139
sport *v* 840
spot *n* 182, 848, 874; *v* 653, 848
spotless *adj* 650, 652, 946, 960
spotlessness *n* 946
spotted *adj* 440
spottiness *n* 440
spotty *adj* 440
spouse *n* 903
spout *n* 348, 350; *v* 295, 348, 582
sprawl *v* 200, 213, 306
spray *n* 353
spread *n* 180, 291; *v* 73, 194, 291, 531; *adj* 73
spreading *n* 73, 194
spread out *v* 35, 194

spread the sails *v* 267
spread to *v* 196
sprightliness *n* 829
sprightly *adj* 829, 836
spring *n* 153, 159, 309, 325, 348; *v* 274, 309, 325
spring back *v* 277, 325
spring from *v* 154
springiness *n* 325
springtime *n* 125
spring up *v* 367
springy *adj* 309, 325
sprinkle *v* 73, 337
sprinkling *n* 32, 41
sprite *n* 979, 980
sprout *n* 35, 194, 367
spruce *adj* 652
spry *adj* 682
spun-out *adj* 110
spur *n* 250, 253, 615; *v* 615
spurious *adj* 544
spurn *v* 764, 866
spurning *n* 764
spurt *n* 274, 348, 612, 684; *v* 348
sputter *n* 348, 583
spy *n* 444, 455; *v* 441, 455
spyglass *n* 445
spying *n* 455; *adj* 455
squabble *n* 713, 720; *v* 713
squad *n* 72
squadron *n* 72
squalid *adj* 653, 846
squall *n* 349
squalor *n* 653
squander *v* 162, 638, 679, 818
squanderer *n* 818
squandering *n* 818
square *n* 857; *v* 30, 95, 660; *adj* 246
square accounts *v* 807
square one *n* 66
square-rigger *n* 273
square with *v* 23
squash *v* 162, 195, 352, 354, 409
squashy *adj* 345
squat *v* 184; *adj* 193, 201, 202, 207
squawking *adj* 410
squeak *v* 411, 412
squeal *v* 411
squeeze *v* 195, 348, 354
squeeze out *v* 301
squeezing *n* 195, 301
squelch *v* 162
squint *n* 443; *v* 443
squirt *n* 348
squishy *adj* 324
stab *v* 260, 361, 649

stability n 150
stability n 16, 110, 141
stabilization n 150
stabilize v 150
stable adj 110, 141, 150, 265
staff n 215, 696, 747
staff of life n 359
stag n 373
stage n 26, 71, 106, 204, 728
stage business n 599
stage name n 565
stage-play n 599
stagey adj 855
stagger v 275, 314, 315, 508, 824, 870
stagnant adj 265, 901a
stagnate v 265
stagnation n 265
stagy adj 599
staid adj 826
stain n 428, 874; v 428, 653, 848, 874
stained adj 961
stainless adj 652
stake n 621, 771; v 621
stale adj 124, 659
stalk n 215
stall v 133
stallion n 373
stalwart adj 192
stamina n 159, 604a
stammer v 583
stammering n 583
stamp n 7, 22; v 240, 550
stamp out v 162, 385
stand n 71, 211, 719; v 106, 110, 141, 719
stand a chance v 177, 470
stand aloof v 681
standard n 22, 26, 80, 466, 650; adj 29, 82, 650
standardization n 16
standardize v 58
stand as an example v 82
stand as opposites v 237
stand at the head v 66
stand by v 186
stand condemned v 971
stand convicted v 754
stand erect v 212
stand fast v 141, 265
stand firm v 150, 265, 604
stand for v 147, 550, 759, 771
stand immobile v 265
stand-in n 634
stand in front v 234

standing n 8, 26, 71, 110, 183, 873
stand next to v 197
stand one in good stead v 644
stand out v 250
standpoint n 183, 441
stand still v 265
stand straight and tall v 212
stand the test v 648
stand to reason v 474
stand up v 719
stand upright v 212
stand up straight v 212
staple commodity n 798
staples n 635
starboard n 238
starchy adj 352
stare n 441; v 455, 870
stark adj 31
stark-naked adj 226
stars n 423
start n 66, 293; v 66, 151, 276, 284, 293, 309, 870
start again v 66
start fresh v 652
starting point n 66, 293
startle v 508, 824, 870
startled adj 870
startling adj 508, 870
start over v 66
start up v 250, 446
starvation n 956
starve v 385, 804, 819, 955, 956
starved adj 956
starving adj 956
starving oneself n 956
stash n 636; v 636
state n 7
state n 188; v 516, 535
stated adj 474
stateliness n 875
stately adj 875, 878
statement n 535, 594, 811
station n 26, 71, 183; v 184
stationary adj 265
statistical adj 85
statistics n 85
statuary n 557
statue n 557, 963, 991
statuette n 557
stature n 206
status n 7, 8, 71
statute n 697; 963
staunch adj 150, 604a
stave in v 252
stay n 133, 215, 685; v 1, 133. 141, 142, 186, 265

stay away v 187
stay in the background v 881
stay together v 46
stead n 644
steadfast adj 150, 604, 604a
steadfastness n 150, 604a
steadiness n 138, 150
steady adj 80, 138, 150, 604a
steal v 275, 789, 791
steal a march on v 132
steal away v 623, 671
steal from v 788
stealing n 791
stealing n 788
stealthily adv 528
stealthy adj 528, 702
steam n 353; v 267, 336, 353
steamer n 273
steaming n 336
steam press v 255
steam up v 353
steamy adj 353
steel v 159
steep v 337; adj 217, 306
steepness n 217
steer n 373; v 693
steerage n 693
steer a middle course v 628
steer clear of v 279, 623
steer for v 278
steersman n 269
stench n 401
stencil n 21
stenography n 590
stentorian adj 404, 411
step n 71, 264
step by step adv 26, 58, 69, 275
step in v 724
steppe n 344
stereoscope n 445
sterile adj 158, 169
sterility n 169
stern adj 604, 739, 955
sternness n 739
stew v 382, 384
steward n 801; v 693
stewardship n 693
stewed adj 959
stewed to the gills adj 959
stick n 215, 975; v 46, 260
stick fast v 150, 265
stick in v 300
stickiness n 46, 352, 396
stick it out v 604a

stick out *v* 250
stick to *v* 143
stick to an idea *v* 606
stick up *v* 250
sticky *adj* 46, 327, 352, 396
stiff *adj* 240, 579, 739
stiff breeze *n* 349
stiffen *v* 323
stiffness *n* 246, 579
stifle *v* 361, 403
stifled *adj* 405
stifling *adj* 382
stiletto *n* 262
still *v* 174, 403, 723; *adj* 174, 265, 403; *adv* 30
still-born *adj* 732
stillness *n* 265, 403
stilted *adj* 307, 577, 855
stilts *n* 215
stimulate *v* 171, 173, 382, 615, 689, 824, 829
stimulating *adj* 171
stimulation *n* 824
stimulus *n* 615
sting *v* 378, 380, 663
stinginess *n* 819, 943
stinging *n* 380; *adj* 392
stingy *adj* 819, 943
stink *n* 401; *v* 401, 653
stinking *adj* 401
stinky *adj* 401
stint *v* 819
stipple *v* 558
stipulate *v* 769, 770
stipulations *n* 770
stir *n* 264, 315, 682, 752; *v* 264, 315, 375, 382, 824
stir about *v* 682
stirring *adj* 151, 505
stir up *v* 173, 824
stitch *n* 43, 378, 828; *v* 43
stock *n* 11, 25, 635, 636, 637, 798; *v* 637; *adj* 598, 613
stocks *n* 802
stock-still *adj* 265
stockyard *n* 232
stoical *adj* 383, 826
stoicism *n* 826
stoke *v* 388
stolen away *adj* 671
stolen goods *n* 793
stolid *adj* 499, 843
stolidity *n* 499
stomach *v* 826
stone-blind *adj* 442
stone-deaf *adj* 419
stone's throw *n* 197
stony *adj* 914a
stoop *v* 217, 306, 886

stop *n* 133, 142, 360; *v* 67, 70, 142, 261, 265, 403
stopcock *n* 263
stopgap *n* 147
stoppage *n* 142, 261, 706
stop payment *v* 808
stopper *n* 263
stopper *n* 261
stopping *n* 142, 263, 706
stop short *v* 142, 265
stop up *v* 261
stopwatch *n* 114
storage *n* 636
storage areas *n* 191
store *n* 636
store *n* 31, 637, 798, 799; *v* 72, 636, 637, 670
store up *v* 636
storing *n* 636
storm *n* 173, 315, 348, 349; *v* 173, 349, 716
stormy *adj* 173, 349
story *n* 204, 546, 593
storyteller *n* 548
stout *adj* 159, 192
stout-hearted *adj* 861
stoutness *n* 159
stove *n* 386
stow away *v* 528
strabismus *n* 443
straggle *v* 279
straggler *n* 268
straggling *adj* 59
straight *n* 857; *adj* 212, 246, 278, 807, 958; *adv* 132, 278
straighten *v* 246
straighten out *v* 60
straightforward *adj* 543, 703, 849; *adv* 278
straight line *n* 246
straightness *n* 246
straightway *adv* 132
strain *n* 402, 413, 415, 686; *v* 42, 686, 688
strait *n* 704
strait-laced *adj* 739
straitness *n* 203
straits *n* 343, 804
strand *n* 205, 205
strange *adj* 10, 83, 519, 870
strangely *adv* 31
strangle *v* 158, 361
strangulation *n* 361
strap *n* 975; *v* 43
strapper *n* 192
strapping *adj* 159
stratagem *n* 545, 626, 702
strategic *adj* 626

strategical *adj* 692
strategist *626*
strategy *n* 692, 722
stratified *adj* 204
stratosphere *n* 338
stratum *n* 204, 213
straw-colored *adj* 435
stray *v* 279; *adj* 73, 279
streak *n* 259, 420; *v* 440
streaked *adj* 440
streakiness *n* 440
stream *n* 347
stream *n* 264, 347, 348, 420; *v* 72, 264, 333, 348, 349
streamy *adj* 348
street-walker *n* 962
strength *n* 159
strength *n* 25, 26, 31, 157, 171, 327, 364, 739
strengthen *v* 157, 159, 171, 689
strengthening *n* 159
strength of mind *n* 604
strenuous *adj* 686
stress *n* 580, 642, 686
stretch *n* 180; *v* 194, 200, 325
stretch out *v* 200
stretch the meaning *v* 523
stretch to *v* 196, 200
strew *v* 73
strewn *adj* 73
striate *v* 440; *adj* 440
striated *adj* 259
striation *n* 440
stricken *adj* 828
strict *adj* 82, 739, 955, 983a
strictness *n* 739, 983a
stricture *n* 706
stride *n* 264
stride forward *v* 282
stridency *n* 410
strident *adj* 410
strife *n* 713, 720
strike *v* 170, 276
strike a balance *v* 27
strike dumb *v* 581
strike out *v* 552
strike up *v* 416
strike while the iron is hot *v* 134
strikingly *adv* 31
string *n* 69; *v* 43
stringency *n* 739
stringent *adj* 739
strings *n* 417
string together *v* 69
stringy *adj* 200, 205, 327
strip *v* 226, 789
stripe *v* 440

striped adj 440
stripling n 129
strip to essentials v 849
strive v 675, 686, 720
stroke n 276, 731; v 379
stroking n 379
stroll n 266; v 264
strong adj 31, 150, 157, 159, 171, 323, 327, 392, 401, 654
strongbox n 802
stronghold n 666, 802
strong language n 574
strongly adv 159
strong smelling adj 398, 401
strop v 253
structural adj 329
structure n 329
structure n 7
struggle n 675, 686, 713, 720; v 720
struggling n 720
strumpet n 962
strut v 884
stubble n 40
stubborn adj 150, 327, 606, 704, 719, 742
stubbornness n 150, 327, 606, 704, 742
stubby adj 201
stud n 250
studded adj 253, 440
student n 492, 541
studio n 556, 691
studious adj 539
study n 457, 461, 539, 595; v 457, 461, 539
stuff n 3, 635; v 190, 194, 224, 376, 869
stuffed adj 869
stuff in v 300
stuffing n 190, 224, 263
stuff oneself v 957
stuff up v 261
stumble n 495; v 306, 315, 699
stumble on v 156
stumble onto v 480a
stumbling block n 706
stump n 40; v 582
stumpy adj 201
stun v 376, 404, 419, 508
stunned adj 419
stunted adj 193, 195. 201
stupefaction n 870
stupefy v 376, 870
stupendous adj 31, 192
stupendously adv 31
stupid adj 275, 486, 491, 497, 499, 843

stupidity n 491, 497, 499, 843
stupor n 683
sturdy adj 150, 159
stuttering n 583
stygian adj 982
style n 569
style n 7, 560, 564, 567, 852; v 564, 569
stylish adj 123, 852
stylishness n 123
stylistic adj 569
styptic adj 397
suasive adj 615, 695
sub n 634; v 147, 634
subdivide v 44
subdivision n 44, 51, 75, 100a
subdue v 744, 879
subdued adj 826
subject n 454, 746; v 601, 744, 749; adj 177, 749
subjection n 749
subjection n 34, 601
subjective adj 5
subject-matter n 454, 516
subjoin v 37
subjugate v 749
subjugation n 749
sublimation n 307
sublime adj 206, 574
sublimity n 206, 574, 845
sublunary adj 318
submerge v 310, 337
submerged adj 208
submersion n 208, 300, 310
submicroscopic adj 193
submission n 725
submission n 749, 826
submissive adj 725, 743, 879, 926
submissiveness n 725, 743, 879, 886
submit v 725, 743, 749
subordinate adj 34, 749
subordination n 34, 749
subpar adv 34
subpoena n 969
subscribe v 769
subsequence n 117
subsequent adj 63, 117
subsequently adv 63, 117
subservience n 631, 743
subservient adj 176, 677, 743
subside v 36, 287, 360

subsidiary adj 176
subsist v 1, 141, 359
subsistence n 1, 298
subsoil n 221
substance n 3, 25, 221, 316, 516, 642, 803
substanceless adj 209
substantial adj 1, 3, 316, 321
substantiality n 3
substantiality n 316
substantially adv 5
substantive adj 1, 3
substitute n 634
substitute n 147, 759; v 147
substitute for v 147
substitution n 147
substratum n 204, 221
substructure n 211
subterfuge n 545, 702
subtilize v 477
subtle adj 320, 329, 477, 702
subtlety n 15, 702
subtract v 36, 38, 85
subtracted adj 38
subtracting adj 38
subtraction n 36, 38
suburbs n 227
subversion n 14, 146, 162, 218
subversive n 913; adj 162
subvert v 162, 218
succeed v 63, 117, 731, 734, 783
succeeding adj 63, 117
success n 731
success n 734
successful adj 731, 734
successfully adv 731
succession n 63, 69, 117
successive adj 69, 117
successor n 117
succinct adj 572
succor n 707; v 707, 834
succorer n 912
succuba n 980
succubus n 980
succulent adj 337, 352
succumb v 725
sucker n 486, 547
sucking n 296
suction n 296
sudden adj 111, 113, 132, 508
sudden impulse n 276
suddenly adv 113, 132, 508
suddenness n 111, 113, 132
sudden thought n 612

suds n 353
sue v 765, 969
suet n 356
suffer v 378, 655, 760, 826, 828
sufferance n 760, 826
suffer a relapse v 661
suffering n 378, 828, 982
suffice v 639
sufficiency n 639
sufficiency n 31, 803
sufficient adj 31, 639
sufficiently adv 639
suffix n 39, 65
suffocate v 361, 641
suffocating adj 382, 401
suffocation n 361
suffuse v 41
suffusion n 41
sugar v 396
sugariness n 396
sugary adj 396
suggest v 505, 514, 527, 695
suggestion n 505, 514, 526, 527, 695, 993
suggestive adj 514, 695
suicidal adj 361
suicide n 361, 361
suit n 225, 765, 969; v 23, 646, 852
suitability n 134, 646
suitable adj 134, 646, 850, 922
suitable time n 134
suite n 69
suiting adj 413
suitor n 767, 897, 969
suit the occasion v 134, 646
sulk v 901a
sulky adj 901a
sullenness n 901a
sullied adj 961
sully v 653, 848
sultry adj 382
sum n 50, 84, 800; v 37, 85
summarily adv 132, 572
summarize v 596
summary n 572, 596
summer n 125
summertime n 125
summit n 210
summit n 206, 650
summon v 969
summons n 969
summon up v 505
sumptuous adj 882
sun n 420, 423
sunbeam n 420
sundown n 126
sundry adj 102

sunglasses n 424
sunk adj 208
sunken adj 252
sunken rocks n 667
sunk into oblivion adj 506
sunny adj 382, 420, 829, 836
sunrise n 125, 420
sunset n 126
sunshade n 223, 424
sunshine n 420
sunup n 125
sup v 298
superabound v 641
superabundance n 641
superabundant adj 641
superannuation n 124, 128
supercilious adj 878
superciliousness n 878
superficial adj 209, 220, 491
superficiality n 209
superficies n 220
superfluity n 40, 641
superfluous adj 40, 57, 641
superfluousness n 57
superhuman adj 976
superimpose v 223
superintendent n 694
superior adj 33, 642, 648
superiority n 33
superiority n 28, 62, 648, 650
superlative adj 33, 648
superlatively adv 31, 33
supernal adj 210, 981
supernatural adj 976, 980
supersaturate v 641
supersede v 147, 678
superstition n 486
superstitious adj 486
supervise v 692, 693
supervision n 693
supervisor n 694
supervisory adj 693
supination n 213
supine adj 207, 213, 683
supping n 298
supplant v 147
supplanting n 147
supple adj 324
supplement n 37, 39, 65; v 37
supplemental adj 37
supplementary adj 37
suppliant n 767, 990
supplicant n 767
supplicate v 765, 990
supplication n 765,

990
supplies n 635, 800
supply n 636, 637; v 637, 784
supplying n 637
support n 215
support n 153, 666, 670, 707, 937; v 170, 215, 670, 707, 737, 834, 937
supported adj 215, 937
supporter n 215, 707, 890, 912
supporting adj 215
supportive adj 707
suppose v 451, 514
supposing adj 469
supposition n 514
supposition n 453, 515
suppress v 581, 751
suppressed adj 528
suppression n 162, 528, 751
suppressive adj 751
supremacy n 33, 737
supreme adj 31, 33, 210, 737
supreme being n 976
supremely adv 31, 33
sure adj 246, 474, 484, 664
sure enough adv 474
surety n 664, 771
surf n 348, 353
surface n 220, 329
surfeit n 641, 869; v 869
surfeited adj 869
surge n 348; v 72
surgeon n 662
surly adj 901a
surmise v 510, 514
surmount v 206, 303, 305, 731
surname n 564
surpass v 33, 303
surpassingly adv 33
surplice n 999
surplus n 40, 641
surprise n 137, 508, 870; v 508, 702
surprised adj 508, 870
surprisingly adv 31
surrender n 624, 725, 782; v 624, 725, 782
surreptitious adj 528
surrogate n 759
surround v 227, 229
surrounding adj 227
surroundings n 7, 227
survey n 441, 466, 596; v 441, 466, 596
surveyor n 694
survival n 110
survive v 1, 40, 110,

surviving adj 40
susceptibility n 176, 177, 821, 822
susceptible adj 375, 822
suspect v 485, 487, 514
suspend v 133, 142, 214
suspended adj 214
suspense n 485, 507
suspension n 214
suspension n 133, 142
suspension of hostilities n 723
suspicion n 485, 487, 514, 860, 920
suspicious adj 485, 487, 860, 920
sustain v 143, 159, 170, 215, 670, 707
sustenance n 298, 670
swab v 340
swaddle v 225
swagger v 878, 884, 885
swaggerer n 887
swaggering n 884
swain n 373
swallow v 298, 486, 547, 826
swamp n 345; v 162
swampy adj 345
swap n 148; v 148, 794
swarm n 72; v 72, 102, 641
swarming adj 72
swarm with v 102
swarthiness n 431
swarthy adj 431
swash v 348
swathe v 225
sway n 157, 175, 737, 741; v 175, 217, 315, 615, 737
swear n 908; v 535, 768, 908, 988
swearing n 535
sweat n 299; v 299, 382, 686
sweep n 180, 245; v 245, 274
sweep along v 264
sweep away v 162
sweeping adj 52, 76
sweep out v 652
sweet adj 377, 396, 413, 428, 652, 829
sweeten v 396
sweetened adj 396
sweetheart n 897, 899
sweetness n 396
sweet scent n 400
sweet scented adj 400
sweet smell n 400
sweet smelling adj 400

sweet-sounding adj 413
sweet sounds n 413, 415
swell n 348, 404; v 194, 367, 404
swelling n 194, 250; adj 250, 577
swell up v 250
swelter v 382
sweltering adj 382
swerve v 140, 279, 291, 603
swerving n 279
swift adj 274, 684
swiftly adv 274
swiftness n 111, 274, 684
swill v 959
swim v 320
swim in v 377
swindle v 791
swindler n 548
swindling n 791
swing n 180, 415; v 214, 314
swinging adj 214
swinish adj 957
swivel v 312
swivel eye n 443
swollen adj 194, 250
swoon v 158, 688
swoop down v 306
sworn adj 768
sybarite n 954a
sybaritism n 954
sycophancy n 886, 933
sycophant n 886, 935
sycophantic adj 886, 933
syllabic adj 561
syllable n 561
syllabus n 596
syllogistic adj 476
syllogistic reasoning n 476
sylph n 979
sylphic adj 979
symbol n 84, 512, 550, 561, 562, 747, 991
symbolic adj 550, 554
symbolical adj 550
symbolism n 550
symbolize v 550, 554
symmetrical adj 27, 58, 242, 413
symmetry n 242
symmetry n 27, 58
sympathetic adj 714, 740, 821, 914
sympathize v 915
sympathizer n 890, 906
sympathize with v 714, 888, 914
sympathy n 714, 820, 821, 888, 914, 915

symphonic adj 415
symphonic music n 415
symphonious adj 413
symphonize v 413
symphony n 413
symphony orchestra n 416
symptom n 550
synagogue n 1000
synchronism n 120
synchronize v 120
synchronized adj 413
syncopation n 413
syndicate n 696
synonymous adj 27
synopsis n 596
synoptic adj 596
syntactic adj 567
syntactical adj 567
syntax n 567
synthesis n 48, 54, 476
synthesize v 476
synthesizer n 417
synthetic adj 476
syrupiness n 396
syrupy adj 396
system n 58, 626
systematic adj 58, 60, 626
systematically adv 58
systematization n 60

T

table n 86, 251; v 133
tableau n 448
tablet n 204, 251
table talk n 588
tabula rasa n 2
tabulate v 60, 69
taciturn adj 403, 583, 585
taciturnity n 585
taciturnity n 403, 583
tack n 278, 627; v 140
tackle v 676
tack on v 37
tacky adj 851
tact n 698
tactful adj 459, 698
tactical adj 692
tactics n 692, 722
tactile adj 379
tactility n 379
tactlessness n 895
tactual adj 379
tag n 65
tag phrase n 566
tail n 214
taint n 651, 653, 848, 874; v 653, 659, 848, 874
tainted adj 659, 874, 961
take v 785, 789, 791, 810
take a breather v 70,

687
take account v 85
take a decisive step v 604
take advantage of v 698
take a fancy to v 827
take after v 17, 19
take a holiday v 687
take aim v 278
take a nap v 687
take an assumed name v 565
take an interest in v 455, 906
take apart v 162
take a peep v 441
take a shine to v 827
take a trip v 266
take a turn v 140
take away v 2, 38, 789
take away from v 789
take back again v 790
take care v 459, 864
take care of v 664
take cognizance of v 450
take counsel v 695
take down v 308
take effect v 170
take fire v 384
take flight v 623
take for granted v 514
take from v 38, 789
take heart v 861
take hold v 46
take ill v 655
take in v 54, 518, 545, 785
take in hand v 676
take into account v 469
take into consideration v 469
take in tow v 285
take it easy v 683
take its course v 151
take liberties v 885
take no interest in v 456, 866
take no note of time v 115
take oar v 267
take off v 19, 226, 267, 293, 813
take offense v 900
take off like a shot v 274
take off the point v 254
take one's chances v 156
take one's leave v 293
take one's time v 685
take orders v 996
take out v 301
take over v 775
take pains v 686

take pen in hand v 590
take place v 1, 151, 151
take pleasure in v 827
take possession of v 775
take precautions v 664
take precedence v 33, 62, 280
take refuge v 666
take root v 184, 613
take shelter v 666
take sick v 655
take soundings v 208
take steps v 673
take the average v 29
take the bull by the horns v 861
take the first step v 66
take the initiative v 66
take the lead v 66, 280
take the place of v 147
take the pledge v 958
take time v 133
take to the altar v 903
take to the skies v 267
take up v 307, 676, 677
take up one's abode v 189
take upon oneself v 676
take up quarters v 184
take up the pen v 590
take what's offered v 607
take wing v 266, 267
taking n 789
taking nourishment n 298
tale n 546, 549
talebearer n 532
talent n 79, 698
talents n 698
talismanic adj 992
talk n 582, 588; v 582
talk a mile a minute v 584
talkative adj 582, 584
talkativeness n 584
talk big v 577, 884
talker n 584
talk fancy v 577
talk it over v 588
talk nonsense v 497
talk together v 588
talk to oneself v 589
tall adj 200, 206
tallness n 206
tallow n 356
tall tale n 546
tally n 86, 805; v 23, 85
tallying n 85
tame v 174, 370, 749; adj 172, 370, 575, 725
taming n 370
tamper with v 140
tan adj 433
tang n 390, 392, 394

tangerine adj 439
tangibility n 3
tangible adj 3, 316
tangle v 61, 219
tangled adj 59
tanked adj 959
tanker n 273
tantalize v 509
tantamount adj 27
tap n 263, 276; v 260, 276, 406
taper n 423; v 203
tapering adj 253
taper to a point v 253
tapping n 407
tar n 356a
tardiness n 133, 275
tardy adj 133, 275
target n 620
tarn n 343
tarnish n 874; v 429, 653, 848, 874
tarnished adj 874
tarpaulin n 223
tarry v 110, 133
tarrying n 133
tart adj 397
tartness n 397
task n 676, 704; v 677, 688
taskmaster n 694, 739
taste n 390, 850
taste n 394, 465, 480, 578; v 298, 390, 394
taste bad v 395
tasteful adj 465, 578, 850
tastefully adv 850
taste good v 394
taste great v 394
tasteless adj 337, 391, 395, 579
tastelessness n 391
tastelessness n 395, 579
tastiness n 394
tasty adj 377, 390, 394
tattle v 588
tattler n 532
tattoo v 440
taunt v 856
taunts n 856
taut adj 43
tautological adj 104
tautology n 104
tawdriness n 851
tawdry adj 643, 851
tawny adj 433, 435
tax v 677, 688
teach v 537, 673
teacher n 540
teacher n 753
teaching n 537
team-work n 709
tear v 44, 173, 274
tearful adj 839
tear out v 301

tears *n* 411
tear to pieces *v* 44
tear up *v* 162
teasing *n* 377
teat *n* 250
technicality *n* 697
technique *n* 627
tedious *adj* 275, 841, 843
tedium *n* 688, 841
teem *v* 168
teeming *adj* 72, 102, 168
teem with *v* 102
teenage *adj* 131
teenage years *n* 131
teeter *v* 160, 275, 315
teetering *adj* 160
teetotaler *n* 953, 958
teetotalism *n* 958
telescope *n* 445
telethermometer *n* 389
tell *v* 85, 467, 527, 529, 594
teller *n* 801
telling *n* 594; *adj* 642
temper *n* 5, 7, 323, 820; *v* 174, 323, 324
temperament *n* 5, 176, 820
temperamental *adj* 901
temperance *n* 953
temperance *n* 174
temperate *adj* 174, 736, 953
temperateness *n* 174
temperature *n* 382
tempered *adj* 820
tempest *n* 173, 315, 349, 825
tempest in a teacup *n* 549
tempestuous *adj* 349
temple *n* 1000
temporal *adj* 111, 997
temporarily *adv* 111
temporary *adj* 111
tempt *v* 615, 675
temptation *n* 615
tempter *n* 978
tempt fate *v* 621
tempt fortune *v* 675
ten *n* 98
tenable *adj* 664
tenacious *adj* 46, 150, 327, 604, 604a
tenacity *n* 327
tenacity *n* 150, 604, 604a
tenancy *n* 777
tenant *n* 188, 779; *v* 186
tend *v* 176, 278, 472
tendencies *n* 5
tendency *n* 176

tendency *n* 177, 278, 472, 613
tender *n* 763; *v* 763; *adj* 324, 378, 428, 597, 740 821, 822, 897, 906
tender age *n* 127
tender-hearted *adj* 906
tenderness *n* 378, 821, 822, 897, 906
tender years *n* 127
tending *adj* 176
tendril *n* 205, 248
tend toward *v* 278
tenet *n* 451, 484, 537, 983
tenor *n* 7, 26, 278, 516
tensile *adj* 325
tension *n* 159
tent *n* 223
tentative *adj* 675
tenuity *n* 322
tenuous *adj* 322
tenure *n* 777
tepid *adj* 382
tergiversation *n* 607
term *n* 71
term *n* 106, 108, 198, 200, 233, 562; *v* 564
terminal *adj* 67, 233
terminate *v* 67, 142, 729
termination *n* 67, 142, 233, 261, 729
terminology *n* 560, 562
terminus *n* 233
terms *n* 476, 770
terrain *n* 342
terrestrial *adj* 318, 342
terrible *adj* 846, 860
terribly *adv* 31
terrified *adj* 860
territorial *adj* 181, 342
territory *n* 181, 965
terror *n* 860
terror-stricken *adj* 860
terse *adj* 572
terseness *n* 572
tertiary *adj* 92
test *n* 463; *v* 463
testify *v* 467, 535
testimony *n* 467
testy *adj* 684, 901
tête-à-tête *n* 588
tether *v* 43
tetrad *n* 95
text *n* 22, 542, 591
textbook *n* 542
texture *n* 256, 329
textured *adj* 256
thank *v* 916
thankful *adj* 916
thankfulness *n* 916
thankless *adj* 917

thanklessness *n* 917
thanks *n* 916
that being the case *adv* 8
thatch *n* 223
that is to say *adv* 522
thaw *v* 335, 382, 384
thawing *n* 335
the all-merciful *n* 976
the all-powerful *n* 976
the almighty *n* 976
theater *n* 599, 728
theatrical *adj* 599, 855, 882
theatricals *n* 599
the cloth *n* 996
the common people *n* 876
the converse *n* 14
the drama *n* 599
the eternal *n* 976
theft *n* 788, 789, 791
the future *n* 121
the infinite *n* 976
the inverse *n* 14
theism *n* 983
the latest thing *n* 123
the lead *n* 62, 280
the like *n* 17
the lower classes *n* 876
thematic *adj* 454
theme *n* 413, 454, 595
then *adv* 119
thence *adv* 155
theologian *n* 983
theological *adj* 983
theologics *n* 983
theologue *n* 983
theology *n* 983
the open *n* 338
the opposite *n* 14
theorem *n* 514
theoretical *adj* 514
theorize *v* 155, 514
theory *n* 155, 453, 514
theosophical *adj* 983
theosophy *n* 983
the past *n* 122
the present day *n* 118
the present juncture *n* 118
therapeutic *adj* 662
there *adv* 186
thereabouts *adv* 32, 183
thereafter *adv* 117
thereby *adv* 631
therefore *adv* 155
thereupon *adv* 117
the reverse *n* 14
therewith *adv* 88, 632
thermometer *n* 389
thermometograph *n* 389
thermoscope *n* 389
thermostat *n* 389

the same adj 13
thesaurus n 86; 562
thesis n 454, 514, 595
thespian n 599
the stage n 599
the theater n 599
the time being n 118
the times n 118, 151
The Vedas n 986
the void n 180
the whole time adv 106
the word n 532
the world n 151
thick n 202; adj 102, 321, 352, 376, 426, 491
thick as a brick adj 499
thicken v 202, 321, 352
thickening n 321
thickness n 202
thickness n 202
thickset n 202
thick-skinned adj 823
thick-skulled adj 499
thief n 792
thieve v 791
thievery n 791
thievish adj 791
thimbleful n 32
thin v 38, 103, 203, 322; adj 4, 32, 203, 322, 337, 640
thing n 3, 316
thing mixed n 41
thing of the past n 124
things n 151
thing signified n 516
think v 451, 870; 484
think back upon v 505
thinker n 492, 500
think fit v 600
thinking n 451
think no more of v 506
think out loud v 589
think up v 66, 515
thinness n 203, 322
thinness n 4, 32, 203, 425
thin out v 38
third n 94; adj 93
thirdly adv 93
third part n 94
thirst n 865
thirst for knowledge n 455
thirsty adj 865
thirteen n 98
thistly adj 253
thither adv 278
thorn n 253, 663
thorn in the side n 663, 830
thorny adj 253
thorough adj 52, 459, 729

thoroughfare n 302
thoroughgoing adj 52
thoroughly adv 52, 729
thoroughness n 52, 729
though adv 30
thought n 451
thought n 453, 515
thoughtful adj 451, 457, 459, 498
thoughtless adj 452, 458, 460, 499, 674, 684, 863
thoughtlessness n 452, 863
thousand n 98
thrall n 749
thralldom n 749
thread n 205; v 69, 302
threadbare adj 659
threadlike adj 203, 205
threat n 909
threaten v 121, 152, 665, 668, 716, 909
threatening adj 909
three n 92; adj 92
threefold adj 92, 93
threefold division n 94
three times adv 93
threnody n 839
threshold n 231
thrice adv 93
thrift n 817
thriftiness n 817
thrifty adj 817
thrill n 151, 824; v 377, 380
thrilling adj 821, 824
thrive v 734
throb n 315, 378; v 314, 315
throbbing adj 315
throe n 146, 173, 315, 378, 828
throng n 72, 102, 975; v 72
throttle v 158, 261, 361
through adv 631
through-and-through adj 729
throughout adv 52, 106
through the agency of adv 170
throw n 284; v 284
throw aside v 678
throw away v 610
throw in v 228
throw in one's lot with v 709
throw in the towel v 624
throw off one's guard v 508

throw of the dice n 156
throw open v 260
throw out v 55, 297, 638
throw out of gear v 61
throw out of whack v 61
throw up v 297
thrust n 276, 284; v 276
thrust in v 300
thud n 406, 408a; v 408a
thug n 361
thumb v 379
thump n 276, 408a; v 276, 408a
thumper n 192
thumping adj 192
thunder n 404, 408; v 173, 404
thundering adj 192, 404
thunderousness n 404
thus adv 8
thus far adv 233
thus far and no further adv 233
thwack n 276; v 276
thwart v 706, 708
thwarted adj 732
tick v 407
ticket v 550
tickle the palate v 390, 394
tickle the tastebuds v 390
tickling n 380
ticklish adj 380, 704
tidal adj 348
tide n 348
tides n 341
tidiness n 652
tidings n 498, 532
tidy adj 58, 652
tidy up v 652
tie n 9, 11, 27, 45, 771; v 9, 43, 45, 770
tied adj 926
tier n 69, 204
tiered adj 204
ties of blood n 11
tie the hands v 158
tie the knot v 903
tie up v 342
tie up in knots v 158
tiff n 713
tight adj 43, 46; adj 261, 572, 819, 959
tighten v 572
tightness n 572
till n 802; v 371; adv 106
tillage n 371
till the soil v 371
tilt n 217, 306; v 217,

244, 306
tilted *adj* 217
tilt over *v* 218
tilt up *v* 307
timber *n* 413
timbre *n* 408
time *n* 106
time *n* 108; *v* 106
time-honored *adj* 124
time immemorial *n* 122
timeless *adj* 112
timelessness *n* 112
timeliness *n* 134, 684
timely *adj* 106, 132, 134
timeout *n* 106
timepiece *n* 114
timeserving *adj* 607
timetable *n* 114
time to come *n* 121
timeworn *adj* 124, 659
timid *adj* 605, 862, 881
timidity *n* 605, 862, 881
timorous *adj* 862, 881
tincture *n* 41, 428; *v* 41
tinge *n* 32, 41, 428; *v* 41, 428
tingle *v* 378, 380
tininess *n* 32, 193
tinsel *n* 851
tint *n* 26, 428; *v* 428
tinted *adj* 428
tintinnabulation *n* 408
tiny *adj* 32, 193
tippler *n* 959
tipsy *adj* 959
tiptop *adj* 210, 648
tirade *n* 582
tire *v* 688, 841, 869
tired *adj* 688, 841, 869
tiredness *n* 688
tired to death *adj* 688
tiresome *adj* 841
tissue *n* 329
tit for tat *n* 30
titillation *n* 377, 380
title *n* 877
title *n* 564, 747, 771
titled *adj* 875, 877
title page *n* 66
titter *n* 838; *v* 838
titular *adj* 564
to a certain degree *adv* 32
toady *n* 886, 935; *v* 886
to a large extent *adv* 31
to all appearance *adv* 448
to all intents and purposes *adv* 27, 52
to and fro *adv* 314
to arms *adv* 722
to a small extent *adv* 32

toast *v* 384
to blame *adj* 947
to boot *adv* 37
to come *adj* 121, 152
to crown all *adv* 33
tocsin *n* 669
toddler *n* 129
together *adj* 46, 502; *adv* 120
togetherness *n* 709, 714
together with *adv* 37, 88
togs *n* 225
toil *n* 686; *v* 682, 686
token *n* 505, 550
tolerable *adj* 32, 651, 736
tolerableness *n* 736
tolerance *n* 740, 760
tolerant *adj* 740, 760
tolerate *v* 738, 740, 760, 826
toleration *n* 738, 740
to little purpose *adv* 732
toll *v* 407
tomb *n* 363
tombstone *n* 363
tomcat *n* 373
tome *n* 590, 593
tomorrow *n* 121, 152; *adv* 121
tone *n* 7, 26, 159, 402, 428
tone color *n* 413
tone down *v* 429
tongue *n* 560
tongue-tied *adj* 581, 583
tonic *adj* 656
tonnage *n* 192
too *adv* 37
tool *n* 633
too late *adv* 133
too little *adj* 640
tools for pulverization *n* 330
too many *n* 641
too much *n* 641
to one's heart's content *adv* 831
too soon *adv* 132
tooth *n* 257
toothed *adj* 257
top *n* 206, 210, 223, 261; *v* 33, 210; *adj* 210
topic *n* 454
topical *adj* 183, 454
topmost *adj* 210
topographical *adj* 183
topography *n* 183
topple *v* 28, 162, 306
topsy-turvy *adj* 59, 218

torch *n* 423
to reason *v* 476
torment *n* 378, 828; *v* 378, 828, 830
tornado *n* 312, 315, 349
torpid *adj* 172, 683
torpor *n* 172, 683
torrent *n* 348
torrid *adj* 382
tortuous *adj* 248
torture *n* 378, 828, 982; *v* 378, 619, 828, 830, 972
torturous *adj* 378
to some degree *adv* 32
to some extent *adv* 26
toss *n* 284; *v* 284, 314, 315
tossup *n* 156
to substitute for *v* 634
tot *n* 129
total *n* 50, 84; *v* 37; *adj* 31, 50
total abstinence *n* 955
total destruction *n* 2
total eclipse *n* 421
totality *n* 50, 52
totally *adv* 31, 50, 52
to the eye *adv* 448
to the four winds *adv* 180
to the letter *adv* 19
to the minute *adv* 132
to the point *adj* 494
to the quick *adv* 375
totter *v* 160, 275, 314, 315, 659, 665
tottering *adj* 160
touch *n* 379
touch *n* 41, 375, 569; *v* 9, 197, 199, 375, 379, 824
touchable *adj* 316
touched *adj* 503, 821, 914
touching *n* 199; *adj* 199
touch on *v* 516
touchstone *n* 211
touchy *adj* 684, 901
tough *adj* 46, 323, 327
toughness *n* 327
tour *n* 266, 302; *v* 266
tourist *n* 268
tourniquet *n* 263
tow *v* 285
towage *n* 285
toward *adv* 278
tower *v* 31, 206, 305
towering *adj* 31, 192, 206
towing *n* 285
townsman *n* 188
toxic *adj* 657

trace n 551; v 230, 554
tracery n 219
trace to v 155
track n 627
tract n 181, 593, 595
tractability n 743
tractable adj 324, 705, 743
tractile adj 285, 324
tractility n 324
traction n 285
trade n 148, 625, 794, 796; v 148, 794, 796
trader n 797
tradesman n 797
trade wind n 349
tradition n 124
traditional adj 124, 983a
traffic n 794; v 794
tragedy n 619
tragic adj 619, 830
trail n 65; v 214, 275, 285, 286, 281
train n 65, 69, 214, 235, 271, 272, 281; v 285, 370, 537, 673
trained adj 698
training n 673
traipse v 275
trait n 448, 550
traitor n 742
trammel v 706
tramp n 268
trample on v 739
trample out v 162
trample upon v 649
trance n 993
tranquil adj 174, 265, 721
tranquilization n 174
tranquilize v 265, 723
tranquillity n 265, 721
transact v 680, 692, 794
transaction n 151, 625, 794, 796
transcend v 31, 33, 303, 648, 650
transcendence n 33, 650
transcendent adj 33
transcribe v 590
transcript n 21
transcription n 21
transfer n 783
transfer n 21, 270; v 185, 270, 783
transferable adj 270, 783
transference n 270
transference n 140, 783
transfiguration n 140
transfigure v 140
transform v 140

transformable adj 140, 149
transformation n 140, 144
transfuse v 41
transfusion n 41
transgress v 303, 742, 773, 945
transgression n 303, 773, 927
transience n 111
transient adj 111, 264
transit n 144, 270
transition n 144, 270
transitional adj 264
transitoriness n 111
transitory adj 111
translate v 522
translation n 522
translator n 524
translucent adj 425
transluscence n 425
transmissible adj 270
transmission n 270, 302, 783
transmissive adj 783
transmit v 270, 783
transmit light v 425
transmittable adj 270
transmutable adj 144
transmutation n 140, 144
transmute v 140
transparence n 425
transparency n 425
transparent adj 337, 425, 518
transpire v 532
transplant v 270
transplantation n 270
transport n 270, 827; v 270, 829
transportable adj 270
transportation n 272
transporter n 271
transporting adj 977
transposal n 218
transpose v 148, 185, 218, 270
transposition n 140, 148, 185, 218, 270
transverse adj 217, 219
trap n 530, 545, 667
trappings n 225
trash n 643
trashy adj 209, 575, 643
travail n 686
travel n 266; v 266
traveler n 268
traveling n 266; adj 264, 266
traverse v 266, 302
travesty n 21, 523; v 19, 523
trawler n 273

treacherous adj 544
treachery n 545
tread n 264
tread down v 749
tread upon v 649
treasure n 648; v 991
treasurer n 801
treasury n 802
treat v 595, 829
treatise n 593, 595
treatment n 662
treat well v 906
treaty n 23, 721, 769
treble v 93; adj 93
trebly adv 93
tree n 367
trellis n 219
tremble v 149, 160, 315, 383
tremendously adv 31
tremor n 315
tremulous adj 149, 315
trench n 259
trenchant adj 171, 253, 572, 574, 642
trend n 176, 278, 516
trendiness n 123
trendy adj 123
trepidation n 860
trespass n 303; v 303, 945
trestle n 215
triad n 92
trial n 463, 675, 686, 828, 830, 969
triality n 92
tribe n 72, 75
tribunal n 966
tributary n 348; adj 784
trice n 113
trick n 545; v 545
trickle n 348; v 295, 348
trickly adj 348
tricky adj 545, 702
trifle n 32, 451, 643; v 499
trifling n 499, 643; adj 4, 32, 477, 499, 643, 880
triform adj 92
trill v 407
trim n 231, 240; v 27, 231; adj 652
trimming n 231
trinity n 92
trio n 92, 415, 416
trip n 266, 302, 306; v 306, 309
tripartition n 94
triple v 93; adj 93
triplet n 92
triplicate adj 93
triplication n 93
triplicity n 93

tripling n 93
triply adv 93
trip the light fantastic toe v 309
trip up v 495
trisect v 94
trisection n 94
trite adj 496, 598, 613
triumph n 731, 733, 838; v 731, 838
triumphant adj 731, 838, 884
trivial adj 32, 209, 499, 517, 643, 880
triviality n 32, 209, 643, 736, 880
troll n 980
trollop n 962
troop n 72
trophy n 733
tropical adj 382
troubadour n 597
trouble n 59, 686, 704, 735, 828, 830; v 61, 828, 830
troublemaker n 913
trouble oneself about v 682
troublesome adj 59, 704, 830
trough n 252, 259, 350
trove n 480a
truant n 623
truce n 142, 721, 723
truck n 271, 272; v 264
trudge v 275
true adj 1, 17, 246, 246, 494, 543, 648, 772, 922, 604
true faith n 983a
truelove n 897
true to life adj 17
truism n 496
truistic adj 496
truly adv 31
trump card n 731
trumped up adj 546
trumpery n 643
truncate v 201, 241
truncation n 241
trunk n 50
truss n 215
trust n 484, 507, 805, 858; v 858
trusted adj 484
trustee n 758, 801
trusting adj 484, 486, 547
trustworthy adj 474, 484, 543, 664
trusty adj 474
truth n 494
truth n 1, 474, 543, 922, 983a
truthful adj 494, 543

truthfulness n 543
try v 463, 480, 675, 677
try a case v 967
trying adj 841
tube n 350, 351
tubed instruments n 417
tuck n 258; v 258
tuck in v 300
tug n 285; v 285
tugboat n 273
tumble n 306; v 162, 306, 315
tumid adj 194
tumult n 59, 315, 825
tumultuous adj 59, 173, 404, 825
tundra n 344
tune n 413, 415; v 413
tuned out adj 452
tuneful adj 413, 597
tunefulness n 413
tuneless adj 414
tune out v 452
tunnel n 350; v 252, 260
turbulence n 173, 315
turbulent adj 59, 173, 825
turf n 388
turgid adj 194, 577, 579
turgidity n 579
turkey n 493
turmoil n 59, 173, 315
turn n 7, 134, 138, 140, 176, 245, 311, 621, 698; v 49, 140, 245, 248, 279, 311, 312
turn about v 218
turn a circle v 311
turn a deaf ear to v 419
turn and turn about adv 148
turn around v 311
turn aside v 140, 279, 616
turn away v 297
turn away from v 623
turn back v 145, 283
turncoat n 607
turn color v 434, 435
turn down v 764
turned adj 397
turned off adj 452
turning n 311
turning point n 8, 67, 134, 145, 153, 210, 233
turn into v 144
turn off the brain v 452
turn of speech n 566
turn of the tide n 145, 218
turn one's hand to v 625

turn on the juice v 274
turn out v 151, 297
turn over v 218, 270, 784
turn pale v 429
turn tail v 623
turn the scale v 28
turn the stomach v 395
turn the tide v 28, 145
turn to dust v 360
turn to profit v 775
turn topsy-turvy v 61, 218
turn up v 151, 156, 446
turn upside down v 14, 61
turquoise adj 438
tutelage n 537, 539, 749
tutor n 540, 753; v 537
tutorship n 537
twaddle n 584
twain adj 89
twang n 402, 408
tweak v 378
twelve n 98
twenty n 98
twenty-five n 98
twerp n 493
twice adv 90
twilight n 126
twin n 17; adj 17, 88, 89, 90
twine v 219, 248
twine round v 227
twinge n 378, 828; v 378
twinkle v 113, 422
twinkling n 113
twins n 89
twirl n 248; v 248, 311, 312
twist n 243, 248, 503; v 43, 219, 243, 248, 279, 311
twisted adj 248
twister n 315, 349
twist the meaning v 523
twit v 856
twitch n 378; v 378
twitter n 315; v 315, 412
two n 89; adj 89
two-faced adj 544
twofold division n 91
two or more n 100
two-sided adj 89
type n 5, 17, 22, 75, 550, 591; v 240
typical adj 82, 550
typify v 550
typographical adj 591
typography n 591
tyrannical adj 739
tyrannize v 739

tyrant *n* 739

U

ubiquity *n* 186
ubiquitous *adj* 186
ugliness *n* 846
ugliness *n* 243
ugly *adj* 846
ukase *n* 741
ulterior *adj* 121
ulterior motive *n* 615
ultimate *adj* 67
ultimately *adv* 117, 121, 133
ululation *n* 412
umbra *n* 421
umbrage *n* 900
umbrageous *adj* 421, 422
umbrella *n* 223, 424
umpire *n* 967; *v* 174
unable *adj* 158, 699
unaccompanied *adj* 87
unaccountable *adj* 964
unaccustomed *adj* 614
unachievable *adj* 471
unacquaintance *n* 491
unadorned *adj* 576, 849
unadulterated *adj* 42, 960
unadvisable *adj* 647
unaffected *adj* 578, 823, 849
unallied *adj* 10
unalterability *n* 141
unalterable *adj* 150
unanimity *n* 23, 709
unanimously *adv* 709, 714
unanswerable *adj* 964
unanticipated *adj* 508
unapplied *adj* 678
unapproachable *adj* 196
unappropriate *adj* 923
unartificial *adj* 703
unassailable *adj* 664
unassuming *adj* 849, 879, 881
unassured *adj* 475
unatoned *adj* 951
unattached *adj* 44
unattended *adj* 87
unattended to *adj* 460
unauthorized *adj* 925, 964
unavailing *adj* 645
unavoidability *n* 601
unavoidable *adj* 601, 744
unavoidableness *n* 601
unaware *adj* 508, 823
unawareness *n* 491
unbearable *adj* 830
unbegotten *adj* 2

unbeliever *n* 485
unbelieving *adj* 485, 487, 989
unbend *v* 246, 687
unbent *adj* 246
unbiased *adj* 942
unblemished *adj* 650
unborn *adj* 2
unbound *adj* 748, 927a
unbridled *adj* 748
unbroken *adj* 50, 69, 729
uncanny *adj* 980
uncanonical *adj* 984
uncared for *adj* 460
uncaring *adj* 823
unceasing *adj* 104, 112
uncertain *adj* 139, 475, 485, 520, 605, 704
uncertainty *n* 475
uncertainty *n* 111, 139, 485, 519, 520. 605
unchained *adj* 748
unchangeable *adj* 5, 150
unchangeableness *n* 150
unchanged *adj* 16, 141
unchanging *adj* 16, 141, 150
unchartered *adj* 964
unchaste *adj* 961
unchecked *adj* 748
uncivil *adj* 895, 911, 929
uncivilized *adj* 876
unclad *adj* 226
unclean *adj* 653, 961
uncleanness *n* 653
uncleanness *n* 961
unclear *adj* 426
unclose *v* 260
unclosed *adj* 260
unclouded *adj* 420
uncolored *adj* 429
uncomfortable *adj* 378, 828
uncommon *adj* 83, 137
uncommonly *adv* 31
uncommunicative *adj* 528, 585
uncommunicativeness *n* 585
uncompleted *adj* 53
uncompliant *adj* 742
uncomplicate *v* 849
uncompromising *adj* 82
unconceived *adj* 2
unconcern *n* 456, 458, 866
unconcerned *adj* 866
unconditional *adj* 52, 748
unconfined *adj* 748
unconformable *adj* 83

unconformity *n* 83
uncongenial *adj* 24
unconnected *adj* 10, 44, 70
unconquerable *adj* 159
unconscious *adj* 823
unconsciousness *n* 376, 491
unconsolidated *adj* 47
unconstitutional *adj* 964
unconstrained *adj* 748
uncontaminated *adj* 960
uncontrite *adj* 951
uncontrollability *n* 606
uncontrollable *adj* 173, 606, 825
uncontrolled *adj* 748, 825
unconventional *adj* 83
unconventionality *n* 83
uncopied *adj* 20
uncorroborative *adj* 468
uncorrupted *adj* 960
uncouth *adj* 579
uncover *v* 226, 260, 480a, 529
uncovered *adj* 260
uncovering *n* 529
uncreated *adj* 2
unctuosity *n* 355
unctuous *adj* 355
unctuousness *n* 355
uncurbed *adj* 748
uncurl *v* 246
uncurved *adj* 246
uncustomary *adj* 83
undated *adj* 115
undecided *adj* 475
undefiled *adj* 960
undefined *adj* 447
undeniable *adj* 474
undependability *n* 475
undependable *adj* 475
under *adv* 34, 207
under a cloud *adj* 735
underage *adj* 127
under consideration *adv* 454
under control *adj* 749
undercover *adj* 528
undercurrent *n* 526
undercut *v* 179
underdeveloped *adj* 193
underestimate *v* 481, 483
underestimated *adj* 483
underestimating *adj* 483
underestimation *n* 483

underfoot *adv* 207
undergo *v* 151
undergo pain *v* 378
underground *adv* 207
underlie *v* 207, 526
underline *v* 550, 642
undermine *v* 179, 659
undermost *adj* 211
underneath *adv* 207
under obligation *adj* 926
under one's nose *adj* 446
under one's very nose *adv* 715
under protest *adv* 603
underrate *v* 483
under restraint *adj* 751
underscore *v* 550, 642
undersized *adj* 193
understand *v* 450, 490, 498, 518, 522
understandable *adj* 518
understanding *n* 23, 450, 480, 490, 498, 714, 822, 842; *adj* 498, 822
understand one another *v* 714
understructure *n* 211
understudy *n* 634
undertake *v* 622, 625, 676, 768
undertaking *n* 676
undertaking *n* 620, 622, 625, 768
under the circumstances *adv* 8
under the conditions *adv* 8
under the head of *adv* 9
under the pretense of *adv* 617
under the stars *adv* 338
under the sun *adv* 180, 318
under the weather *adj* 655
undertone *n* 405
undervaluation *n* 483
undervalue *v* 483
under way *adv* 264
under wraps *adj* 754
underwrite *v* 768, 771
undesirability *n* 647
undesirable *adj* 830
undetermined *adj* 475
undeviating *adj* 278
undevout *adj* 989
undiminished *adj* 50
undirected *adj* 279
undiscerning *adj* 442
undiscriminating *adj*

465a
undisturbed *adj* 265
undiversified *adj* 16
undivided *adj* 50, 52
undo *v* 145, 162, 179
undone *adj* 732
undoubtedly *adv* 474
undraped *adj* 226
undress *n* 226
undress *v* 226
undressed *adj* 226
undulate *v* 248, 314
undulating *adj* 248
undulation *n* 248, 314
undulatory *adj* 314
undutiful *adj* 927
unearth *v* 363, 480a
unearthly *adj* 317, 976, 980, 981
uneasiness *n* 828, 832
uneasy *adj* 828, 832
uneducated *adj* 491
unembellished *adj* 849
unemotional *adj* 383
unemployed *adj* 678
unendurable *adj* 830, 982
unenlightened *adj* 491
unenlightenment *n* 491
unentitled *adj* 925
unequal *adj* 15, 28
unequaled *adj* 18, 33
unequivocal *adj* 31, 246, 570
unequivocally *adv* 31
unessential *adj* 643
unestablished *adj* 185
uneven *adj* 16a, 28, 243, 256
unevenness *n* 16a, 28
uneventful *adj* 643
unexciting *adj* 174
unexpected *adj* 132, 508
unexpectedly *adv* 132, 508
unfaded *adj* 428
unfading *adj* 112
unfailing *adj* 474
unfaithful *adj* 544
unfashioned *adj* 241
unfathomable *adj* 208, 519
unfathomable space *n* 208
unfathomed *adj* 208
unfavorable *adj* 135, 708, 735
unfeasibility *n* 471
unfeasible *adj* 471, 704
unfed *adj* 956
unfeeling *adj* 381, 383
unfetter *v* 750
unfettered *adj* 748
unfinished *adj* 53, 730

unfit *adj* 158, 647, 699, 923
unfitness *n* 647
unfitted *adj* 158
unfixed *adj* 149, 475
unfocused *adj* 447
unfold *v* 246, 313
unfolding *n* 313
unforeseen *adj* 508
unforeseen occurrence *n* 508
unforgettable *adj* 505
unforgiving *adj* 919
unfriendly *adj* 708, 889
unfrozen *adj* 382
unfruitful *adj* 169
unfruitfulness *n* 169, 645
unfulfillment *n* 509
unfurl *v* 313
ungenerous *adj* 32, 819
ungentlemanly *adj* 895
ungodliness *n* 989
ungodly *adj* 989
ungovernable *adj* 173, 825
ungoverned *adj* 748
ungraceful *adj* 579
ungracious *adj* 895
ungrammatical *adj* 568
ungrammatical usage *n* 568
ungrateful *adj* 917
ungrounded *adj* 4
unguarded *adj* 460
unguent *n* 356
unhallowed *adj* 989
unhandy *adj* 699
unhappy *adj* 828, 837
unharmonious *adj* 410
unhealthiness *n* 657
unhealthy *adj* 655, 657
unheard of *adj* 137, 508
unheeded *adj* 460
unheedful *adj* 452
unheeding *adj* 419, 458
unhewn *adj* 674
unhindered *adj* 748
unhinge *v* 61
unhinged *adj* 173, 503
unhip *adj* 246
unholy *adj* 989
unhoused *adj* 185
unhurried *adj* 275
unhurt *adj* 670
unification *n* 48, 87
unified *adj* 46, 48
uniform *v* 225; *adj* 16,

42, 58, 80, 242
uniformity n 16
uniformity n 17, 23,
   58, 80, 87, 150, 242
uniformly adv 16, 82
uniforms n 225
unimaginable adj 471
unimaginative adj 598,
   843
unimitated adj 20
unimpaired adj 50, 670
unimpeachable adj
   474
unimportance n 643
unimportance n 32,
   175a
unimportant adj 32,
   34, 643, 736
unimpressionable adj
   823
unimproved adj 659
uninfluential adj 175a
uninformed adj 491
uninjured adj 670
uninquiring adj 456
uninquisitive adj 456
uninstructed adj 491
unintellectual adj 450a
unintelligent adj 450a
unintelligibility n 519
unintelligibility n 533,
   571
unintelligible adj 519,
   571
unintentional adj 621
unintentionally adv
   621
uninterested adj 456,
   841
uninteresting adj 843
uninterrupted adj 69,
   112, 143
unintoxicated adj 958
union n 23, 43, 46, 48,
   178, 709, 714, 903
unique adj 18, 20, 79,
   83, 87, 870
uniqueness n 18, 20,
   123
unison n 87, 714
unite v 41, 43, 48, 72,
   87, 178, 290, 709,
   712
united adj 46, 903
uniting n 37
unity n 87
unity n 13, 23, 50, 52,
   714
universal adj 78
universality n 78
universalize v 78
universe n 180, 318
university n 542
unjust adj 923
unkempt adj 653

unknown n 233; adj
   533
unlawful adj 964
unlawfulness n 923,
   964
unlearn v 506
unlearnedness n 491
unless adv 8, 83
unlettered adj 491
unlicensed adj 964
unlike adj 15, 18
unlikelihood n 473
unlikely adj 473
unlikeness n 18
unlimited adj 31, 104,
   180, 748
unlimited space n 180
unload v 185
unlooked for adj 508
unlovely adj 846
unlucky adj 135, 735
unmake v 145
unman v 158
unmanageable adj 704
unmarked adj 447
unmarried adj 904
unmarried man n 904
unmarried woman n
   904
unmask v 529, 529
unmatched adj 15, 18,
   20
unmeaningness n 517
unmelodious adj 414
unmerciful adj 914a
unmindful adj 452,
   458, 460, 917
unmindfulness n 458
unmistakable adj 525
unmitigated adj 52
unmixed adj 42, 960
unmoved adj 265, 823
unmoving adj 172
unmusical adj 410, 414
unmuzzled adj 748
unnatural adj 83, 855
unnaturalness n 855
unnecessary adj 641
unnerve v 158, 160
unnerved adj 160
unnoticed adj 460
unobservant adj 458
unobserved adj 460
unobstructed adj 748
unobtainable adj 471
unobtrusive adj 881
unoccupied adj 452
unopened adj 261
unorthodox adj 984
unorthodoxy n 984
unostentatious adj 881
unpaid adj 806
unpalatable adj 395,
   830
unparalleled adj 20, 33
unperceptive adj 376

unperformable adj 471
unpersuasive adj 175a
unpierced adj 261
unplaced adj 185
unpleasant adj 395,
   830, 846
unpoetic adj 598
unpointed adj 254
unpolished adj 256
unprecedented adj 18,
   137
unpredictability n 139
unpredictable adj 139,
   475
unprejudiced adj 942
unprepared adj 674
unpreparedness n 674
unpretentious adj 849,
   879, 881
unprized adj 483
unproductive adj 169
unproductiveness n
   169
unprofitable adj 169,
   647
unprofitableness n 169
unpropitious adj 135
unprosperous adj 735
unpunctual adj 133,
   135
unqualified adj 52, 158
unquestionable adj
   474
unquestionableness n
   474
unquestioned adj 474
unquiet adj 264
unrational adj 450a
unravel v 60, 246, 522,
   705
unreadiness n 674
unready adj 674
unreal adj 2, 317, 515
unreasonable adj 471,
   497, 499, 608, 814
unrecorded adj 552
unrefined adj 851
unreflective adj 452
unrelated adj 10
unreliability n 475
unreliable adj 149, 475
unremedial adj 859
unremembered adj
   506
unrepentant adj 951
unrepented adj 951
unrepenting adj 951
unreserved adj 525
unresponsive adj 376,
   383
unresponsiveness n
   376
unrest n 149, 264
unrestricted adj 748
unrevealed adj 533
unrightful adj 925

unrightfulness n 925
unripe adj 123, 674
unrivaled adj 33
unroll v 313
unruffled adj 174, 265, 826
unruliness n 742
unruly adj 606, 742
unsafe adj 475, 665
unsavoriness n 395
unsavoriness n 391, 392
unsavory adj 392, 395, 874
unscoured adj 653
unscriptural adj 984
unscrupulous adj 940
unseasonable adj 135
unseasonableness n 135
unseasoned adj 435
unseeing adj 442
unseemly adj 647, 846
unseen adj 447
unselfish adj 906, 942
unselfishness n 906, 942
unserviceable adj 645
unsettle v 61, 185
unsettled adj 149, 185, 475, 503
unshackled adj 748
unshaped adj 241
unshapely adj 241
unsharpened adj 254
unsightliness n 846
unsightly adj 846
unskilled adj 699
unskillful adj 699
unskillfulness n 699
unsmelling adj 399
unsmooth adj 256
unsophisticated adj 946
unsought adj 766
unsound adj 203, 477, 651, 655
unsoundness n 657
unspiritual adj 316, 989
unstable adj 149, 333, 475, 605, 665
unstained adj 960
unsteady adj 149, 475, 665
unstrung adj 160
unsubmissive adj 742
unsubstantial adj 2, 4, 203, 317, 322, 515
unsubstantiality n 4
unsuccessful adj 732
unsuccessfully adv 732
unsuccessfulness n 732
unsuitability n 647

unsuitable adj 135, 647
unsuitable time n 135
unsuited adj 135
unsullied adj 652, 960
unsupportable adj 830
unsupportive adj 468
unsure adj 475, 485
unsurpassed adj 31, 33
unsusceptible adj 376, 826
unsuspecting adj 486, 547
unsuspicious adj 703
unswerving adj 278
unsymmetrical adj 243
unsympathetic adj 383
unsystematic adj 59
untainted adj 946, 960
untaught adj 491, 674
untenable adj 4, 477
untested adj 123
unthankful adj 917
unthankfulness n 917
unthinking adj 452
unthriftiness n 818
unthrifty adj 818
untidiness n 59
untidy adj 59, 653
until adv 106
untimeliness n 135
untimely adj 135
untouchable adj 317
untoward adj 135
untried adj 123
untrue adj 495, 544, 545, 546, 923
untrustworthy adj 665
untrustworthy memory n 506
untruth n 546
untruth n 544
untruthful adj 544
untruthfulness n 544, 545
untutored adj 491
unusable adj 645
unused adj 40, 678
unusual adj 83, 137, 614
unusually adv 31
unutterable adj 519
unvalued adj 483
unvanquished adj 748
unvaried adj 16
unvarnished adj 576
unvarying adj 16, 143, 150
unveil v 529
unventilated adj 261
unvulnerable adj 112
unwarned adj 508
unwarranted adj 925, 964
unwary adj 460, 863
unwavering adj 150
unwelcome adj 830

unwell adj 655
unwholesome adj 657, 663
unwieldy adj 192, 319, 704
unwilling adj 603
unwillingly adv 603
unwillingness n 603
unwillingness n 704
unwind v 313
unwise adj 499
unwittingly adv 621
unworkable adj 647
unworldliness n 703
unworldly adj 703
unworthy adj 874
unworthy of consideration adj 643
unworthy of notice adj 643
up and down adv 314
Upanishads n 986
upgrowth n 305
upheaval n 307
uphill adj 217
uphold v 143, 670, 707, 717, 937
uplift v 307
upon one's oath adj 768
uppermost adj 210
upraise v 307
uprear v 307
upright adj 212, 246, 922, 939, 944, 946, 960
uprightness n 922, 939, 944, 946, 960
uprising n 146
uproar n 59, 173, 404
uproarious adj 404
uproot v 301
ups and downs n 314
upset n 308; v 162, 218, 308; adj 824
upshot n 154, 480, 729
upside down adj 218
upstairs n 450
up to adj 157; adv 106
up to a point adv 26
up-to-date adj 123
up to the mark adj 27, 639
up to this time adv 122
upturn v 218
upwards of adj 100
urbane adj 894
urchin n 980
urge v 173, 276, 684
urgency n 642, 684
urgent adj 630, 642
urging n 695
urinate v 299
urination n 299
urn n 363

usage n 567, 613, 677, 998
use n 677
use n 644; v 677, 788
used up adj 158, 659
useful adj 176, 618, 631, 644, 677
usefulness n 644, 677
useless adj 169, 499, 643, 645, 647, 732, 880
uselessness n 645
use the occasion v 134
use up v 677
usher v 296
usher in v 62, 66, 280
usual adj 82, 613
usurer n 805, 819
usurious adj 819
usurp v 789
usurper n 925
utensil n 633
utilitarian adj 677
utility n 644
utility n 646, 677
utilization n 677
utilize v 677
utmost adj 33
utter v 580, 582; adj 31
utterance n 580, 985
utterly adv 52
uttermost adj 31

V

vacancy n 187, 209, 499
vacancy of mind n 452
vacant adj 4, 187, 209, 452, 499
vacate v 185, 293
vacation n 685, 687
vacationer n 268
vacillate v 149, 314, 605
vacillating adj 149
vacillation n 149, 314, 485, 605
vacuity n 187, 452
vacuous adj 4, 187, 209
vacuum n 187
vagabond n 268
vagabondism n 266
vagary n 608
vagrant n 268; adj 266
vague adj 475, 477, 517, 571
vagueness n 475, 519, 571
vain adj 158, 645, 878, 880
vain expectation n 509
vainglorious adj 884, 880
vainglory n 878
vale n 252
valediction n 293
valid adj 737

validity n 157
valley n 252, 259
valor n 861
valorous adj 861
valuable adj 644, 648
valuation n 466, 812
value n 644, 648, 812, 815; v 466, 480, 642, 931
valueless adj 645
value received n 810
valve n 263, 350
vampire n 980
van n 280
vanguard n 234, 280
vanish v 4, 111, 360, 449
vanished adj 449
vanishing point n 193
vanity n 880
vanity n 878
vantage ground n 175
vapid adj 337, 391, 575, 843
vapor n 353
vaporization n 336
vaporize v 336
vaporous adj 334, 336
vaporousness n 334
vapory adj 336
variability n 475
variable adj 140, 149, 475
variance n 15, 24, 291, 713
variant adj 15
variation n 20a
variation n 15, 83, 140
varied adj 15, 16a, 20a
variegate v 440
variegated adj 41, 440
variegation n 440
variety n 75, 81
various adj 15, 102
varnish n 223, 356a; v 356a
vary v 15, 18, 20a, 140, 149, 291, 314
vast adj 31, 104, 180, 192
vastness n 31, 105
vault n 245, 309, 318, 363, 802; v 309
vaulted adj 245
vaunt v 884
veer v 140, 279
vegetable n 367
vegetable adj 367
vegetable kingdom n 367
vegetable life n 365
vegetable oil n 356
vegetable physiology n 369
vegetal adj 367
vegetarian n 953
vegetate v 367

vegetation n 365
vegetative adj 365, 367
vehemence n 173, 825
vehement adj 173, 382, 574, 825
vehicle n 272
vehicle n 271, 631
veil n 424, 530; v 424, 528
veiled adj 447, 526
veiling n 528
vein n 176, 205, 602
veined adj 440
velocity n 274
velocity n 264
velvety adj 255, 256
venal adj 211, 819
venality n 819
vend v 796
vendible adj 796
vendition n 796
vendor n 796
veneer n 223; v 204, 223
venerable adj 124, 128, 928
venerate v 860, 928, 987
veneration n 860, 928, 987
vengeance n 718, 919
vengeful adj 718, 919
vengefulness n 919
venom n 663, 907
venomous adj 649, 657, 663, 907
vent n 260, 351
ventilate v 338, 349, 652
ventilation n 338
venture n 621, 675, 676; v 621, 665, 675, 861
venturesome adj 621, 675
veracious adj 494, 543
veracity n 543
veracity n 494
verbal adj 562
verbal interchange n 588
verbiage n 573
verbose adj 573, 584, 641
verbosity n 573, 584, 641
verdant adj 367, 435
verdict n 480, 969
verdure n 367, 435
verdurous adj 435
verge n 231, 233; v 176, 278
verification n 478
verify v 478
veritable adj 494
verity n 494

vermilion adj 434
vernacular n 560; adj 560
versatile adj 149
versatility n 149
verse n 590, 597
versification n 597
versifier n 597
versify v 597
versus adv 708
vertex n 210
vertical adj 212, 246
verticality n 212
vertically adv 212
verve n 159, 515, 574
very adv 31
very best adj 648
very much adv 31
vespers n 126
vessel n 191, 273
vestal virgin n 960
vestige n 551
vestments n 999
veteran n 130
veteran n 700
veterinary science n 370
veto v 761
vex v 828, 830
vexation n 828, 830, 835
vexatious adj 830, 901a
vibes n 314
vibrate v 314
vibration n 138, 314, 408
vibrato n 408
vice n 945
vice n 649, 923
vice versa adv 148
vicinity n 186, 197
vicious adj 907, 945
vicissitude n 111, 149
victimize v 649
victorious adj 731
victory n 731
vie v 648, 720
view n 441, 448, 453, 484, 620; v 441
viewpoint n 441
vigilance n 459, 682, 864, 920
vigilant adj 459, 507, 682, 864, 920
viginal adj 960
vignette n 594
vigor n 574
vigor n 157, 159, 171, 359, 364, 604, 654, 682
vigorous adj 159, 171, 359, 574, 654
vile adj 207, 211, 395, 649, 830, 846, 874, 898, 930
vilification n 934

vilify v 934
vilifying adj 934
villager n 188
villain n 941, 949
villainous adj 649
vinculum n 45
vindicate v 717, 919, 937
vindicated adj 937
vindicating adj 937
vindication n 937
vindication n 717
vindicator n 919, 937
vindictive adj 919
vindictiveness n 919
vinegariness n 397
vinegary adj 397
vintage adj 124
violate v 742, 773, 927
violate the law v 964
violation n 773, 927
violation of custom n 83
violence n 173
violence n 825
violent adj 59, 173, 382, 825
violently adv 31, 173
violet adj 437
virgin n 904, 960; adj 66, 123
virginal adj 123, 946
virginity n 960
virility n 159
virtually adv 5
virtue n 944
virtue n 648, 922, 939, 946, 960
virtuous adj 881, 939, 944, 946, 960
virtuousness n 944, 946
virulence n 649
virulent adj 649, 657
virus n 663
visage n 448
viscid adj 352
viscosity n 352
viscous adj 327, 352
visibility n 446
visible adj 446, 525
vision n 441
vision n 443, 515, 980
visionary n 504; adj 2, 4, 441, 515
visit often v 136
visor n 530
vista n 448
visual adj 441
vital adj 359, 642
vital flame n 359
vitality n 159, 359, 364, 654
vitalize v 359
vital spark n 359
vitiate v 659
vivacious adj 359, 515,

682, 829, 836
vivacity n 359, 515, 682, 836
vivid adj 171, 375, 420, 428, 505
vivify v 159, 359
vocabulary 562
vocal adj 415, 416, 580
vocal group n 416
vocalist n 416
vocality n 580
vocalization n 580
vocalize v 416, 566, 580
vocal music n 415
vocation n 625
vociferate v 411
vociferation n 411
vociferous adj 404, 411
vociferousness n 404
vogue n 613, 852
voice n 580
voice n 402; v 566, 580, 582
voiceless adj 581, 583
void n 2, 4, 187; v 2, 297, 756; adj 2, 187
volatile adj 149, 320, 336
volatility n 149, 320, 334
volcanic adj 173, 384, 825
volition n 600
volitional adj 600
volubility n 584
voluble adj 334, 584
volume n 25, 31, 102, 192, 590, 593
voluminous adj 192
voluntarily adv 600
voluntary adj 600
volunteer v 676
voluptuary n 954a, 962
voluptuous adj 377, 829
voluptuousness n 827
vomit v 297
voodoo n 993
voracious adj 957
voracity n 957
vortex n 312, 315, 348
voucher n 807
vow n 768
vowel n 561
voyage n 267, 302
voyager n 268
V-shaped adj 244
vulgar adj 579, 851, 876, 895
vulgarity n 851
vulgarity n 579, 895
vulgarize v 851
vulnerability n 177

W

wad v 224

wadding n 224, 263
waddle v 275
wade through v 539
waft v 320, 349
wag n 844
wager n 621; v 621
wages n 775, 812
wage war v 722
waggle v 315
wagon n 272
waif n 268
wail n 411, 839; v 411
wailing n 411, 839
wait v 133, 265, 681
wait for v 507
waiting n 507, 681
wait on v 88, 746
waive v 624, 678, 782,
609a
waiver n 624, 782
waiving n 624
wake n 65, 235, 363
wakefulness n 459, 682
wake up v 824
walk n 266; v 264
walker n 268
walk over v 649
wall n 212, 232
wall in v 229
wallop v 315
wallow n 207
wallow in v 377, 954
wan adj 429, 430, 435
wander v 266, 264, 279
wanderer n 268
wane n 36; v 36, 195,
287, 659, 732
waning adj 128, 195
want n 804, 865; v 34,
304, 640, 804, 865
wanting adj 53, 187,
499, 640
want of elasticity n
326
want of intellect n
450a
want of intelligence n
499
want of skill n 699
wanton adj 83, 149,
608, 748
wants n 630
war n 722; v 722
warble v 416
ward n 862
warden n 664
warder n 753
wardrobe n 225
wares n 798
warfare n 722
warfare n 173
wariness n 487, 864
warlike adj 720, 722
warm v 382, 384; adj
382, 434, 664, 824,
892

warmed adj 384
warm-hearted adj 822
warmth n 382, 382,
574, 821, 897
warn v 616, 668, 669,
695, 864
warning n 668
warning n 512, 665,
695, 864
warp n 243, 279; v 140,
217, 243, 279, 659
warped adj 651
warrant n 737, 760,
924, 937; v 737, 760,
768, 771
warranted adj 937
warranty n 768, 771
warrior n 726
wary adj 451, 457, 459,
487, 664, 864
wash n 345, 428; v 337,
428, 652
wash out v 429
waspish adj 684
waste n 638
waste n 162, 180, 679,
818; v 162, 195, 638,
659, 679, 818
waste an occasion v
135
waste away v 655
wasted adj 124, 160,
203, 638, 659, 959
wasteful adj 638, 818
wastefulness n 169,
818
waster n 165; v 776
waste time v 106, 135,
681, 683
wasting n 638
wastrel n 893
watch n 114; v 441,
664, 668
watchdog n 664, 668
watch for v 441
watchful adj 457, 459,
507, 864, 920
watchfulness n 457,
459, 920
watchman n 668
watch over v 717
water n 337
water v 337
water down v 160, 203
watergate n 350
waterish adj 203, 337
waterpower n 388
waters n 341
watershed n 210
watertight adj 261
watery adj 203, 333,
337, 339
wave n 248, 314, 348; v
248, 314
waver v 149, 422, 475,
485, 605

wavering adj 485
waves n 341
wavy adj 248
wax n 356, 356a; v 255
waxy adj 324, 356a
way n 260, 302, 302,
613, 627, 632
wayfarer n 268
wayfaring n 266; adj
266
ways n 692
ways and means n 632,
800
wayward adj 149, 606,
608
weak adj 32, 158, 160,
175a, 203, 337, 391,
477, 499, 575, 605,
651, 655, 738
weaken v 158, 160,
468, 732
weak foundation n 667
weak-headed adj 499
weakness n 160
weakness n 158, 575,
605, 651
weak point n 651
weak spot n 651
wealth n 803
wealth n 734, 800
wealthy adj 734, 803
wean from v 616
weaponry n 727
weapons n 727
wear n 677; v 677
wear and tear n 659
wear away v 142, 638,
659
wear down v 638
wearied adj 841
weariness n 841
weariness n 688, 828,
837, 869
wearisome adj 686,
830, 841
wear out v 638, 659,
688
weary v 688, 841, 869;
adj 688, 828, 841,
869
weather n 338
weather-beaten adj
659
weathered adj 659
weave v 219
weaved adj 219
web n 219, 329
wed v 43; adj 903
wedding n 903
wedlock n 43, 903
wee adj 193
weed v 103, 371
weeding n 103
weed out v 55, 301
weep v 411, 839

weeping n 411
weigh v 319
weigh down v 649, 749
weight n 175, 319, 642
weightiness n 642
weightless adj 320
weighty adj 175, 319, 574, 642
weird adj 503, 519, 980, 992
weirdo n 504
welcome n 292; v 892
welcoming n 292
weld v 43, 46
well n 153, 208; adj 654
well-being n 654, 734, 827
well-bred adj 852, 894, 928
well-defined adj 446
well disposed adj 602, 707, 888, 906
well-educated adj 490
well enough adv 32
well founded adj 1, 472
well grounded adj 1
well issue v 348
well-mannered adj 852, 894, 928
well-marked adj 446
well nigh adv 32
well-off adj 734, 803
well-organized adj 58
well put adj 578
well-read adj 490, 539
well-regulated adj 58
well set adj 242
well-timed adj 134
well-to-do adj 731, 734, 803
well-wisher n 890
wet v 337, 339; adj 337, 339
wetness n 339
wet the appetite v 824
whack n 276; v 276
wheedle v 933
wheel n 247; v 311, 312
wheel about v 218
wheels n 272
wheeze n 349, 409
wheezing n 409
wheezy adj 409
when adv 119
whenever adv 119
whensoever adv 119
whereabouts n 183
whereby adv 631
where it's at adj 494
wherewithal n 632, 800; adv 632
whet v 253, 824

whiff n 349
while adv 106
while away the time v 106
while on the subject adv 134
whilst adv 106
whim n 515, 608
whimper n 411; v 411
whimpering n 411
whimsical adj 83, 608, 842
whine v 411
whip n 975; v 315, 972
whip into a frenzy v 173
whip up v 173
whir n 312
whirl n 312; v 312
whirlpool n 312, 315, 348
whirlwind n 315, 349
whirring n 407
whisk v 274, 311, 315
whisper n 405, 527; v 405, 583
whispered adj 405
whistle v 409
white adj 429, 430
white caps n 348
white lie n 520
whiten v 429, 430
whiteness n 430
whitewash v 430
whither adv 278
whitish adj 430
whittle v 253
whiz v 409
whole n 50
whole adj 50, 52, 729
wholeness n 52
whole number n 84
wholesale adj 31; adv 50
wholesome adj 656
wholesomeness n 656
wholly adv 31, 50, 52
whoop v 411
whoosh v 409
whooshing n 409
whopper n 192
whopping adj 192
whore n 962
wicked adj 923, 940, 945, 961
wickedly adv 923
wickedness n 923, 940, 945
wicker n 219
wide adj 202
wide apart adj 15
wide awake adj 682
widely adv 31
widen v 194, 202
wide of the mark adj 732; adv 279

wide-open adj 260
widespread adj 31, 73, 78, 180, 194
wide world n 180, 318
width n 202
wield v 677
wife n 903
wild n 180; adj 173, 503, 606, 825
wild animals n 366
wilderness n 59, 180
wildness n 606
wile n 545
wiliness n 702
will n 600
will n 150, 604; v 600, 604
willful adj 150, 600, 606
willfully adv 600
willfulness n 606
willing adj 602, 831
willingly adv 602
willingness n 602
will power n 600
willy nilly adv 601
wilt v 306
wily adj 702
win v 775
wince v 378
wind n 349
wind n 338; v 248, 279
wind around v 629
windbag n 884, 887
windfall n 618
winding n 245, 248, 629; adj 248
winding sheet n 363
windpipe n 351
windpower n 388
winds n 417
windup n 261
windy adj 334, 338, 349
wine-colored adj 434
winged being n 977
wink v 443
winning adj 897
winnings n 775
winning ways n 829
winnow v 42, 55
winsome adj 836
winter n 126
wintry adj 383
wipe v 340
wiped out adj 162
wipe off the face of the earth v 2
wipe out v 162, 552
wire n 205
wiry adj 205
wisdom n 498
wisdom n 480, 490, 698, 842
wise adj 490, 498, 698,

wisecracker n 844
wise man n 492, 500
wish n 600, 858, 865, 865; v 865
wish for v 865
wishful adj 865
wish well v 906
wishy-washy adj 175a, 391, 575
wit n 842
wit n 698, 844, 856
witch n 513, 994
witchcraft n 992
witchery n 829, 992
witching hour n 126
with adv 37, 41, 88
with a flourish adv 882
with a heavy hand adv 739
with a high hand adv 739
with all one's heart adv 602
with a long face adv 837
with a vengeance adv 31
with bated breath adv 507
with consummate skill adv 698
with downcast eyes adv 879
withdraw v 38, 283, 287, 293, 893
withdrawal n 38, 283, 287, 624, 893
withdrawn adj 893
wither v 195, 360, 659
withered adj 160
with flying colors adv 731
withhold v 781, 819
within adv 221
withindoors adv 221
within reach adj 470, 705; adv 197
within reason adv 174
within the bounds of possibility adj 470
with one voice adv 714
with open arms adv 888
without adj 777a; adv 38, 187, 227
without ceremony adv 881
without exception adv 16
without foundation adj 4
without mincing words adv 703
without rhyme or reason adj 615a

without warning adv 508
with pleasure adv 602, 827
with reference to adj 9; adv 9
with regard to adv 9
with relation to adv 9
with respect to adv 9
withstand v 179, 708, 719
withstanding n 719
with tears in one's eyes adv 837
with the exception of adv 38
with the proviso adj 469
witless adj 499
witness n 444; v 441, 444, 467
witness-chair n 966
wits n 450
wittingly adv 620
witty adj 840, 842
wive v 903
wizard n 700, 872, 994
wizen v 195
wizened adj 128, 195
wobble v 275
woebegone adj 828
woeful adj 649, 830
woefully adv 31
wolf v 298
wolf in sheep's clothing n 667
woman n 374
woman n 372
woman-hater n 911
womanhood n 131, 374
womanly adj 131, 374
womb n 208, 221
wonder n 870
wonder n 508, 872; v 870
wonderful adj 870
wonderfully adv 31
wondrous adj 870
wont n 613, 613
wood n 388
woodwinds n 417
wooer n 897
woolly adj 256, 329
word n 562
word n 768
word coiner n 563
word for word adv 19
wordiness n 573
wording n 569
Word of God n 985
word-play n 520
words n 713
words of wisdom n 496
wordy adj 573, 584

work n 170, 590, 593, 680, 686; v 170, 677, 680, 686
workable adj 644
workaday adj 625
workbook n 542
worked up adj 900
worker n 680, 690, 746
work hard v 686
work in v 228
working n 170, 680
working toward adj 176
workmanship n 161
works n 161
workshop n 691
work the land v 371
work well v 705
world n 318
worldly adj 318, 989
worldwide adj 78, 180
worm n 248, 366
worm-eaten adj 659
worm one's way v 275
worn adj 160, 659
worn out adj 158, 659, 688
worrisome adj 830
worry n 828; v 828, 830
worse adj 835
worsen v 835
worsening n 835
worship n 990
worship v 990, 991
worshipful adj 990
worship idols v 991
worshiper n 990
worshiping adj 990
worth n 644, 648, 812
worthiness n 33
worthless adj 643, 645, 647
worthlessness n 645
worthwhile adj 646
worthy adj 246
wound n 830; v 659, 830
woven adj 219
wrack n 162; v 378
wraith n 980
wrangle v 720; v 476, 713, 720
wrangler n 476
wrap v 223, 225
wrapped adj 223
wrapper n 232
wrapping n 191
wrappings n 223
wrap up v 67, 225
wrath n 900
wrathful adj 900
wreak v 739
wreath n 247
wreathe v 219
wreck n 162; v 162
wrecker n 165

wrench *n* 301; *v* 44, 285, 301

wrest *v* 243
wretch *n* 949
wretched *adj* 649, 828
wretchedly *adv* 32
wretchedness *n* 735
wriggle *v* 315
wring *v* 248, 378
wring from *v* 301
wrinkle *n* 258; *v* 248, 258, 259

wrinkled *adj* 128
writ *n* 590, 969
write *v* 569, 590
write down *v* 590
write prose *v* 598
writer *n* 590, 593
write to *v* 592
writhe *v* 243, 315, 378
writing *n* 590
writing *n* 593, 598
written *adj* 590
wrong *n* 923
wrong *n* 173, 619; *v* 649, 923; *adj* 481, 495, 544, 649, 923, 945

wrongdoer *n* 913, 949
wrongheaded *adj* 481
wrongly *adv* 923
wrong side out *adj* 218
wrought up *adj* 824

Y

yacht *n* 273
yachting *n* 267
yank *n* 285; *v* 285
yap *v* 412
yard *n* 232
yarn *n* 549
yawl *n* 273
yawn *v* 260, 688
yawning *n* 688; *adj* 208, 260
year *n* 106, 108
year after year *adv* 104
yearning *n* 276, 865, 897
years *n* 128
years ago *adv* 122
yeast *n* 320, 353
yell *n* 411; *v* 411
yell out *v* 411
yellow *v* 435; *adj* 435
yellow *n* 436
yellowish *adj* 435
yellow streak *n* 862
yelp *v* 410, 412
yesterday *n* 122
yesteryear *n* 122
yet *adv* 30, 106, 116, 122
yield *v* 82, 324, 360, 488, 624, 725, 762, 782, 812
yielding *n* 624, 725, 782

yoke *n* 749; *v* 43, 89
yon *adj* 196
yonder *adj* 196
young *adj* 123, 127, 129, 435
younger *adj* 127
youngster *n* 129
young years *n* 127
youth *n* 127
youth *n* 123, 129

Z

zany *n* 501
zeal *n* 171, 382, 604, 682, 821
zealot *n* 606
zealotry *n* 606
zealous *adj* 171, 606, 682
zenith *n* 206, 210
zephyr *n* 349
zero *n* 101
zero *n* 4
zest *n* 394
zigzag *n* 279; *adj* 279, 629; *adv* 314
zip *n* 101; *v* 409
zipping *n* 409
zone *n* 181, 204, 247
zonkers *adj* 503
zonko *adj* 503
zoography *n* 368
zoological *adj* 366, 368
zoologist 357
zoology *n* 368
zoology *n* 357

FOR GIFT GIVING

WEDDING
ANNIVERSARY SYMBOLS

	TRADITIONAL	MODERN
1st	paper	clocks
2nd	cotton	china
3rd	leather	crystal, glass
4th	books	electrical appliances
5th	wood	silverware
6th	sugar, candy	wood
7th	wool, copper	desk sets
8th	bronze, pottery	linens, laces
9th	pottery, willow	leather
10th	tin, aluminum	diamond jewelry
11th	steel	fashion jewelry
12th	silk, linen	pearls, colored gems
13th	lace	textiles, furs
14th	ivory	gold jewelry
15th	crystal	watches
20th	china	platinum
25th	silver	silver
30th	pearl	diamond
35th	coral	jade
40th	ruby	ruby
45th	sapphire	sapphire
50th	gold	gold
55th	emerald	emerald
60th	diamond	diamond
75th	diamond	diamond

BIRTHSTONES

January	Garnet
February	Amethyst
March	Bloodstone or Aquamarine
April	Diamond
May	Emerald
June	Pearl or Alexandrite
July	Ruby
August	Sardonyx or Peridot
September	Sapphire
October	Opal or Tourmaline
November	Topaz
December	Turquoise or Zircon

WEIGHTS AND MEASURES

CUBIC MEASURE

1,728 cubic inches	1 cubic foot
27 cubic feet	1 cubic yard
128 cubic feet	1 cord (wood)
40 cubic feet	1 ton (shipping)
2,150.42 cubic inches	1 standard bushel
231 cubic inches	1 U.S. standard gallon
1 cubic foot	about 4/5 of a bushel

DRY MEASURE

2 pints	1 quart
8 quarts	1 peck
4 pecks	1 bushel

LIQUID MEASURE

4 gills	1 pint
2 pints	1 quart
4 quarts	1 gallon
31½ gallons	1 barrel

IMPERIAL LIQUID MEASURE

1 U.S. gallon	0.833 Imperial gallon
1 U.S. gallon	3.785 liters
1 Imperial gallon	1.201 U.S. gallons
1 Imperial gallon	4.546 liters
1 liter	0.264 U.S. gallon
1 liter	0.220 Imperial gallon

LONG MEASURE

12 inches	1 foot
3 feet	1 yard
5½ yards	1 rod
40 rods	1 furlong
8 furlongs	1 sta. mile
3 miles	1 league

MARINER'S MEASURE

6 feet	1 fathom
120 fathoms	1 cable length
7½ cable lengths	1 mile
5,280 feet	1 staute mile
6,080.2 feet	1 nautical mile

SQUARE MILE

144 square inches	1 square foot
9 square feet	1 square yard
30¼ square yards	1 square rod
40 square rods	1 rood
4 roods	1 acre
640 acres	1 square mile

AVOIRDUPOIS WEIGHT

27-11/32 grains	1 dram
16 drams	1 ounce
16 ounces	1 pound
25 pounds	1 quarter
4 quarters	1 cwt
2,000 pounts	1 short ton
2,240 pounds	1 long ton

TROY WEIGHT

24 grains	1 pwt
20 pwt	1 ounce
12 ounces	1 pound

Used for weighing gold, silver and jewels

METRIC EQUIVALENTS
Linear Measure

1 centimeter		0.3937 inches
1 inch		2.54 centimeters
1 decimeter	3.937 inch	0.328 foot
1 foot		3.048 decimeters
1 meter	39.37 inches	1.0936 yards
1 yard		0.9144 meter
1 dekameter		1.9684 rods
1 rod		0.5029 dekameter
1 kilometer		0.621 mile
1 mile		1.609 kilometers

Square Measure

1 square centimeter	0.1550 square inches
1 square inch	6.452 square centimeters
1 square decimeter	0.1076 square foot
1 square foot	9.2903 square decimeters
1 square meter	1.196 square yards
1 square yard	0.8361 square meter
1 acre	160 square rods
1 square rod	0.00625 acre
1 hectare	2.47 acres
1 acre	0.4047 hectare
1 square kilometer	0.386 square mile
1 square mile	2.59 square kilometers

Weights

1 gram	0.03527 ounce
1 ounce	28.35 grams
1 kilogram	2.2046 pounds
1 pound	0.4536 kilogram

1 metric ton	0.98421 English ton
1 English ton	1.016 metric tons

Measure of Volume

1 cubic centimeter	0.061 cubic inch
1 cubic inch	16.39 cubic centimeters
1 cubic decimeter	0.0353 cubic foot
1 cubic foot	28.317 cubic decimeters
1 cubic meter	1.308 cubic yards
1 cubic yard	0.7646 cubic meter
1 stere	0.2759 cord
1 cord	3.624 steres
1 liter	0.908 dry quart... 1.0567 liquid quarts
1 quart dry	1.101 liters
1 quart liquid	0.9463 liter
1 dekaliter	2.6417 gallons... 1.135 pecks
1 gallon	0.3785 dekaliter
1 peck	0.881 dekaliter
1 hektoliter	2.8375 bushels
1 bushel	0.3524 hektoliter

APPROXIMATE METRIC EQUIVALENTS

1 decimeter	4 inches
1 liter	1.06 quarts liquid... 0.9 quart dry
1 meter	1.1 yards
1 kilometer	⅝ of a mile
1 hektoliter	2⅝ bushels
1 hectare	2½ acres
1 kilogram	2⅕ pounds
1 stere, or cubic meter	¼ of a cord
1 metric ton	2,204.6 pounds

States and Territories of the United States with their Post Office Abbreviations and Capitals

Alabama (AL)	Montgomery
Alaska (AK)	Juneau
Arizona (AZ)	Phoenix
Arkansas (AR)	Little Rock
California (CA)	Sacramento
Colorado (CO)	Denver
Connecticut (CT)	Hartford
Delaware (DE)	Dover
District of Columbia (DC)	

Florida (FL) . . . . Tallahassee
Georgia (GA) . . . . Atlanta
Hawaii (HI) . . . . Honolulu
Idaho (ID) . . . . Boise
Illinois (IL) . . . . Springfield
Indiana (IN) . . . . Indianapolis
Iowa (IA) . . . . Des Moines
Kansas (KS) . . . . Topeka
Kentucky (KY) . . . . Frankfort
Louisiana (LA) . . . . Baton Rouge
Maine (ME) . . . . Augusta
Maryland (MD) . . . . Annapolis
Massachusetts (MA) . . . . Boston
Michigan (MI) . . . . Lansing
Minnesota (MN) . . . . St. Paul
Mississippi (MS) . . . . Jackson
Missouri (MO) . . . . Jefferson City
Montana (MT) . . . . Helena
Nebraska (NE) . . . . Lincoln
Nevada (NV) . . . . Carson City
New Hampshire (NH) . . . . Concord
New Jersey (NJ) . . . . Trenton
New Mexico (NM) . . . . Santa Fe
New York (NY) . . . . Albany
North Carolina (NC) . . . . Raleigh
North Dakota (ND) . . . . Bismarck
Ohio (OH) . . . . Columbus
Oklahoma (OK) . . . . Oklahoma City
Oregon (OR) . . . . Salem
Pennsylvania (PA) . . . . Harrisburg
Rhode Island (RI) . . . . Providence
South Carolina (SC) . . . . Columbia
South Dakota (SD) . . . . Pierre
Tennessee (TN) . . . . Nashville
Texas (TX) . . . . Austin
Utah (UT) . . . . Salt Lake City
Vermont (VT) . . . . Montpelier
Virginia (VA) . . . . Richmond
Washington (WA) . . . . Olympia
West Virginia (WV) . . . . Charleston
Wisconsin (WI) . . . . Madison
Wyoming (WY) . . . . Cheyenne

American Samoa (AS) . . . . . Pago Pago
Guam (GU) . . . . Agaña
Puerto Rico (PR) . . . . San Juan
Virgin Islands (VI) . . . . Charlotte Amalie